The Ashgate Encyclopedia of Literary and Cinematic Monsters

For William, the most wonderful monster of all

The Ashgate Encyclopedia of Literary and Cinematic Monsters

JEFFREY ANDREW WEINSTOCK
Central Michigan University, USA

ASHGATE

Published by
Ashgate Publishing Limited
Wey Court East
Union Road
Farnham
Surrey, GU9 7PT
England

Ashgate Publishing Company
110 Cherry Street
Suite 3-1
Burlington VT, 05401-3818
USA

www.ashgate.com

British Library Cataloguing in Publication Data
A catalogue record for this book is available from the British Library

Library of Congress Cataloging-in-Publication Data
Weinstock, Jeffrey Andrew.
The Ashgate encyclopedia of literary and cinematic monsters / by Jeffrey Andrew Weinstock.
pages cm
Includes bibliographical references and index.
ISBN 978-1-4094-2562-5 (hardback) – ISBN 978-1-4094-2563-2 (ebook) –
ISBN 978-1-4724-0060-4 (epub) 1. Monsters in literature–Encyclopedias. 2. Monsters in motion pictures–Encyclopedias. I. Title.

PN56.M55W45 2013
809'933703–dc23

2012047426

ISBN 9781409425625 (hbk)
ISBN 9781409425632 (ebk – PDF)
ISBN 9781472400604 (ebk – ePUB)

Printed in the United Kingdom by Henry Ling Limited
at the Dorset Press, Dorchester, DT1 1HD

Contents

Acknowledgments

This monstrous project could not have been completed without the help and support of many people. I would like to thank Anthony Magistrale for having suggested me to Ashgate as editor, and the team at Ashgate, especially Dymphna Evans, for all their work in assembling the text. Maria Kioussis served ably as editorial assistant and Timothy Hutchings helped coordinate the wonderful original illustrations. The list of inclusions was developed with suggestions from the participants on the listserv for the International Association for the Fantastic in the Arts—a discussion list that has often been a valuable source of information for me. In addition, the subject area experts were particularly important in making recommendations. I therefore would like to acknowledge the hard work of Paul Acker, Emily Alder, Debbie Felton, R. Keller Kimbrough, Filippo del Lucchese, Muireann Maguire, Jess Martin, Barry Murnane, Karin Myhre, Gretchen Papazian, Amy Ransom, Cristina Santos, Lavanya Vemsani, and Stephenie Young. I would also like to thank all the contributors to this volume, either for their patience in watching it develop over the course of several years or for "stepping into the breach" late in the game to fill important gaps. The English department at Central Michigan University has provided a supportive and congenial environment for my work. Most crucially, I am thankful to my parents, Alan and Madeline Weinstock, my wife, Astrid, and my son, William—who arrived during the early stages of this project—for their unflagging love and encouragement.

List of Illustrations

List of Entries

Introduction: Monsters are the Most Interesting People

Jeffrey Andrew Weinstock

> In my business you meet so many interesting people ... but the most interesting ones are the monsters.
>
> *Bugs Bunny, "Water, Water Every Hare"*

There's no arguing with Bugs on this point.

In both the classic "Water, Water Every Hare" (1952) and the earlier episode of Warner Bros' *Loony Tunes*, "Hair-Raising Hare" (1946), that it reprises, Bugs Bunny finds himself pursued by a large hairy red monster through the gloomy Gothic castle of a mad scientist who wants Bugs's brain to animate his robotic Frankenstein's monster. In typical Bugs fashion, the irreverent rabbit turns the tables on his would-be assailant by role-playing a flamboyant hairdresser in the 1952 episode (an equally flamboyant manicurist in the 1946 version) and engaging his confused conscripted client with a monologue about just how interesting monsters are. Although the sweet talk here is a ruse designed to mollify the tennis-shoed monstrosity as Bugs dresses his hair with dynamite in place of curlers, the generalization nevertheless holds true: monsters are always interesting—if not usually people. In their various forms, monsters have invariably fascinated and held humanity's imagination in their red hairy grip since the dawn of recorded history.

The word "monster" derives from the Latin *monstrum*, which is related to the verbs *monstrare* (to show or reveal) and *monere* (to warn or portend). The monster is thus at root, as Stephen Asma observes, a type of omen (13) that indicates something unsettling or threatening about the universe we inhabit. Its appearance may be interpreted as a form of divine judgment revealing the will of God or the gods (Beal 7); its hideous and threatening form may embody the consequences of vice, warning others against following a similar path; or as a freak or accident of nature, it may reveal not the will of the gods but rather the absence of a divine plan governing creation, as well as the limitations of human knowledge.

Monsters in short are inevitably the most interesting—and, one should add, threatening—of "people" because they are ontological puzzles that demand solutions. They are things that should not be, but nevertheless are—and their existence therefore raises vexing questions about humanity's understanding of and place in the universe. In this way, they are symptoms of deeper, more profound distress. In works of horror, according to philosopher Noël Carroll, the monster is "an extraordinary character in our ordinary world" (16)—that is, the monster is a threatening disturbance of the natural order that fills the other characters in the narrative, as well as the audience members whose affective responses parallel those of the characters (17), with fear and disgust.

The "unnaturalness" of the monster inheres in its violation of established conceptual categories. As anthropologist Mary Douglas argues, hybrids and other manifestations of categorical confusion that upset human systems of classification are threatening abominations, and a quick glance at any bestiary (medieval or modern) confirms that monsters are always to some extent such categorical violations. Zombies, ghosts, vampires, and other "undead" creatures, for example, upset the distinction between living and dead, while the Bronze Horseman of Russian myth, the doll Chucky of the "Child's Play" series of films, robots, Stephen King's killer car Christine, detached body parts that move on their own, and other unexpectedly volitional objects upset the distinction between animate and inanimate; griffins, manticores, and cockatrices each combine aspects of different animals, while lamias, donestres, harpies, satyrs, werewolves, gorgons, and so on are human–animal hybrids. In some cases, monstrosity is associated with size or attributes well outside of the normal range of variation for a species. The kraken is an excessively large squid while a giant is an excessively large human; Cerberus has three heads, while Cyclopes have one eye, and so forth.

Monsters thus pose a dual threat. There is of course the immediate danger to life and limb presented by the prospect of ending up as a snack for a sea monster, dragon, ogre, troll, or blob. Beyond this, however, there is the epistemological threat of confronting that which should not be. Timothy Beal, drawing on theologian and religious scholar Rudolf Otto's description of religious experience as an encounter with the *mysterium tremendum*—the overwhelming dread, mystery, and awe of the spiritual realm—casts the confrontation with the monster in similar terms: "Whether demonized or deified or something in between, monsters bring on a limit experience, an experience of being on the edge of certainty and security, drawn toward and repulsed by a *monstrum tremendum*. The monstrous is an embodiment of overwhelming and chaotic excess, a too-muchness that brings on a vertigo-like sense of fear and desire: standing on the threshold of an unfathomable abyss" (195). The monster undoes our understanding of the way things are and violates our sense of how they are supposed to be.

From a more secular perspective, Sigmund Freud's concept of the uncanny suggests a similarly vertiginous limit experience associated with the encounter with the monster. The unsettling affective sense of the uncanny is triggered, according to Freud, by a variety of experiences in which one's understanding of how the world works is called into question. When one mistakes an automaton for a living person, for example, or confuses her reflection for another person, one momentarily experiences the *frisson* of the uncanny, a brief undoing of the world. Of particular note to Freud in his discussion are instances in which old, superstitious beliefs in an animistic world populated by magical spirits and monsters, and filled with sorcery seem confirmed. "Many people experience the feeling [of the uncanny] in the highest degree in relation to death and dead bodies, to the return of the dead, and to spirits and ghosts," observes Freud. More generally, "an uncanny effect is often and easily produced when the distinction between imagination and reality is effaced, as when something that we have hitherto regarded as imaginary appears before us in reality ..." When the monster appears, rationalist frameworks for organizing experience are undone. The monster therefore threatens both our physical and our psychological wellbeing.

That monsters invariably upset and therefore call into question the boundaries of existing conceptual categories tells us something else essential about them: that what is or is not considered monstrous depends on and is defined against prevailing conceptions of the human and of normalcy. The monster's body is thus, as Jeffrey Jerome Cohen observes, always "pure culture" (4)—the embodiment of the fears, tabooed desires, and overall zeitgeist of a particular time and place. "Monsters are metaphors of our own anxiety," asserts Richard Kearney, who adds in a pithy formulation that, "*Without them we know not what we are. With them we are not what we know*" (117). The human is defined against the monster (and vice versa). The monster tells us what we hope or imagine we are not, as well as what we fear deep down we are or may become.

We are intimately familiar with monsters, therefore, because they are our own. Monsters are not finally absolutely other—foreign and unknowable. They are, rather, human creations, whether real world entities swept up in the net of conceptual categorization or conjurations of the fertile imaginations of authors and filmmakers. Monsters are always inevitably the disowned and disavowed children of the human mind. For Kearney, the monster is that part of ourselves that we repudiate by projecting outward (4)—what theorist Julia Kristeva refers to as the "abject." Mr Hyde in Robert Louis Stevenson's famous novella is everything Dr Jekyll abjures—he is the selfish, appetitive part, the Freudian Id, the ungovernable monster within that dispenses with the social contract in the single-minded pursuit of his own desires. He is, as N. Scott Poole says of monsters in general, "a beast of excess" (xiv), a primal force of chaos whose existence undermines humanistic pretensions to completeness and self-knowledge.

In the same way that Mr Hyde is Dr Jekyll's dark reflection, monsters in general are our own, repellant and fascinating in equal measure—for it must be acknowledged that, however horrific and disgusting they may be, we love our monsters anyway (and perhaps precisely because they are horrific and disgusting, they engage our sympathies. Their outsiderdom magnifies human anxieties about belonging). The entertainment that human beings derive from contemplating monsters presents us with another problem: if monsters are scary and being scared is unpleasant, then why do we so enjoy our monsters? To a certain extent, as Carroll suggests, this may reflect basic human curiosity and the power of narrative to engage human interest. The conventional monster within a story presents a problem to the characters. The reader, listener, or viewer becomes involved in the tale and follows along, waiting to discover how the problem of the monster is solved. Curiosity in this model is opposed to disgust. If one gets too scared or grossed out, one halts the narrative by leaving the theater, turning off the TV, putting the book down (or in the freezer), and so on. If curiosity wins out, the story is finished—and often the resolution expunges the monstrous threat and the *status quo ante* is more or less restored.

This theory of horror certainly makes sense but only goes so far in explaining the human fascination with monsters; notably, it does not fully engage with the dual polarity of the monster—both the dread and the desire it provokes. Although the threatening monster instructs us in how *not* to act and where *not* to go, it simultaneously dangles before us tabooed possibilities—all the more tempting for being forbidden. According to Cohen, "The same creatures who terrify and interdict can evoke potent escapist fantasies; the linking of monstrosity with the forbidden makes the monster all the more appealing as a temporary egress from constraint" (17). Mr Hyde is a monster and a threat to society because he acts outside human laws, both written (the legal code) and unwritten (good taste, "proper" behavior). He is nevertheless dangerously attractive for the same reason—he pursues his desires free of inhibition and social obligation or constraint.

This freedom of the monster from the necessity of conforming to social expectations may in fact go a long way toward explaining the contemporary rehabilitation of many traditional monsters. The modern allure of vampires and, to a lesser extent, zombies, demons, werewolves, and other conventional monsters reflects both the twenty-first-century Western suspicion of centralized power (governmental, patriarchal, religious, and so on) and its emphasis instead on multiculturalism, "tolerance," and the unfettered expression of individuality. In narratives such as the "Twilight" and "Shrek" film franchises, the true monster is not the vampire or the ogre, but rather the conservative forces of society itself with their insistence that proper subjects conform to established rules of decorum and behavior. Increasingly, it seems that modern readers and audiences envy the freedom and power of the monster, without feeling the burden of shame associated with transgressing societal mores and expectations.

That our monsters keep changing—or that the same monsters look, act, and function differently in different historical contexts—demonstrates the extent to which our understanding of them is always dependent upon time, place, and worldview. In Asma's "unnatural history" of monsters, he speculates that in the ancient world, a world "relatively unexplored and so much larger than it is now" (32), it would have seemed quite reasonable to populate mysterious far-off places with monstrous races and creatures—as does Pliny the Elder in his first-century CE *Natural History*. Gods and monsters in the ancient polytheistic world, notes Asma, "existed in a counteracting, dualistic relationship" (63), with humans caught in the middle.

With the rise of monotheism during the Middle Ages, in contrast, monsters needed to be reconciled with the divine plan of an omnipotent God. As Asma explains, the existence of monsters became intertwined with the larger question of the existence of evil itself. Why do bad things happen to good people? And why would a benevolent deity create evil monsters? One answer is that monsters were recast as "God's lackeys" (Asma 63). They serve a divine purpose, even if that plan is obscured from human vision. They also function as examples of God's might and as cautionary tales of the dangers of defying God.

And whereas the ancients were inclined to interpret monstrous births and the traces or appearances of monsters as omens or signs, the modern era increasingly has sought to dispel superstition and to substitute rational explanations for what had been conceived of as monstrous. Starting with the Renaissance, abnormal births and other monsters of the natural world "came under the new umbrella of a mechanistic worldview, and spiritual monsters (e.g., demons and devils) were sent packing" (Asma 149). Developments in embryology, genetics, archeology, paleontology, and other "materialist" approaches to teratology (the study of monsters) offered rational explanations for the existence of birth defects, bizarre animals, and remnants of monsters such as dinosaur bones. As Asma notes, in the era of Darwin, the concept of monstrosity was drained of its association with evil (164).

In our present moment—although we still meet with plenty of vampires, mummies, zombies, ghosts, and other traditional monsters—the link between appearance and monstrosity has in large measure been severed and our monsters instead have become invisible to the naked eye. As I argue elsewhere, ubiquitous narratives of psychopaths and terrorists who live among us and could be anyone, of corporations and government agencies governed by greed as they infiltrate our lives, of deadly viruses that invade and infect the body, and of an anthropomorphized Mother Nature that responds to human despoilment of the environment in dramatic and deadly ways, all express a deep-seated anxiety about the limitations of vision and elicit a type of free-floating paranoia most evident in conspiracy theories (Weinstock 276).

In these ways, although monsters are a perennial focus of human interest, the significance of any given monster is always time-bound and culturally specific. Beyond this, however, when we bear in mind that the monster limns the human, this indicates that changes in our monsters then signal that our understanding of ourselves and of what it means to be human have shifted as well. The monsters we create reflect an inverted image of ourselves. As the ironic title of the BBC/Syfy Network program *Being Human*—about a cohabitating ghost, vampire, and werewolf—suggests, by studying monsters in all their overdetermined complexity (see Halberstam), we implicitly study what it means to be human as well.

HOW TO USE THIS VOLUME

This encyclopedia in and of itself is a sort of Frankenstein's monster, an assemblage of pieces and parts cobbled together and sent out into the world. Starting from a catalog of well over 1,000 possible inclusions, the list was whittled down to the approximately 200 entries now included. Limited by space, the volume is as a consequence far from being an exhaustive bestiary or compendium of all the monsters in human history worldwide (such a project would be ambitious indeed and would extend to an entire series of volumes such as this). This project instead has sought to attend to the most common and significant monsters found primarily in the literature, cinema, and popular culture of English-speaking regions.

In many cases, determining whether to include or exclude a given creature was relatively easy—ubiquitous monsters such as vampires, dragons, werewolves, and zombies, as well as many monsters of the classical world and the Middle Ages, of course are included here. Decisions about more obscure beasties were made in consultation with a team of subject area experts who provided recommendations related both to period and geographic region. Particularly as concerns modern monsters, the determination as to whether to allot a creature its own entry, to include discussion of it as part of a larger, more generic entry (such as those devoted to extraterrestrials, psychopaths, and demons), or to exclude mention of it had a great deal to do with the editors' and contributors' sense of the significance of the monster in question. These kinds of decisions are endlessly debatable and I trust the reader will understand—if not entirely agree with—the decisions, for example, to give Freddy Krueger, Pinhead, and the vampire Lestat their own entries, while subsuming many other contemporary horror movie nasties and vampires into the more generic categories. In a handful of cases in which an individual author includes many monsters—Dante, Lovecraft, J.K. Rowling, Jonathan Swift, and Tolkien—the entries are grouped under the authors' names.

Considered as embodiments of human fears and longings, all monsters can be considered as types of metaphors. For the purpose of this project, however, to be included, an entity was required in some way to exceed or violate the laws of nature as we know them. This definition tended to exclude human beings, however evil they may have been. Hitler and Pol Pot were indisputably monstrous in their actions and intentions, but are not found within the pages of this volume. The Countess Bathory, however, is included—not because her crimes were any more monstrous, but rather because she has been shaped by literary and cinematic traditions as a species of "actual" vampire.

Cross-listing is indicated within the body of individual entries by bold-faced type on the first occasion a cross-listed monster is mentioned. When titles of movies are introduced, the name of the director and the year of release will be indicated parenthetically, if not previously introduced within the body of the discussion. Following each entry is a list of references and suggested reading. Included here is bibliographic information for any works quoted directly by the entry, as well as other works of particular interest vis-à-vis the focus of the entry. Translations are presumed to be the author's own, unless otherwise indicated.

The focus on literature and cinema, rather than folklore, is what distinguishes this volume from other related projects. While many of the individual entries may gesture toward the folkloric roots of particular monsters or use this background to introduce the beastie in question, entries then trace the manifestations of the creature in the written literary and cinematic traditions, in some cases extending from Homer or ancient Greek drama all the way to contemporary movie blockbusters and video games. The entries thus illustrate both continuity and change—the ways in which monsters, both ancient and modern, appear and reappear in different contexts. Taken together, what the entries convey is the fertility of the monstrous imagination—that is, the ways in which human beings have populated this world (and others) with all manner of strange and fascinating beings that reflect our own anxieties and desires. Nowhere is the power of human creativity more evident than in the wealth of monstrous creatures we have invented to entertain and instruct ourselves. Monsters truly are the most interesting of people!

REFERENCES AND SUGGESTED READING

Asma, Stephen T. *On Monsters: An Unnatural History of Our Worst Fears*. Oxford: Oxford University Press, 2009.

Beal, Timothy K. *Religion and Its Monsters*. New York: Routledge, 2002.

Carroll, Noël. *The Philosophy of Horror or Paradoxes of the Heart*. New York: Routledge, 1990.

Cohen, Jeffrey Jerome. "Monster Culture (Seven Theses)." In *Monster Theory: Reading Culture*, edited by Jeffrey Jerome Cohen, 3–25. Minneapolis: University of Minnesota Press, 1996.

Douglas, Mary. *Purity and Danger: An Analysis of the Concepts of Pollution and Taboo*. London: Routledge, 1966.

Freud, Sigmund. "The Uncanny." 1919. <http://www-rohan.sdsu.edu/~amtower/uncanny.html>.

Halberstam, Judith. *Skin Shows: Gothic Horror and the Technology of Monsters*. Durham, NC: Duke University Press, 1995.

Kearney, Richard. *Strangers, Gods and Monsters: Interpreting Otherness*. New York: Routledge, 2002.

Kristeva, Julia. *The Powers of Horror: An Essay on Abjection*. Translated by Leon S. Roudiez. New York: Columbia University Press, 1982.

Newitz, Annalee. *Pretend We're Dead: Capitalist Monsters in American Pop Culture*. Durham, NC: Duke University Press, 2006.

Poole, W. Scott. *Monsters in America: Our Historical Obsession with the Hideous and the Haunting*. Waco, TX: Baylor University Press, 2011.

Weinstock, Jeffrey Andrew. "Invisible Monsters: Vision, Horror, and Contemporary Culture." In *The Ashgate Research Companion to Monsters and the Monstrous*, edited by Asa Simon Mittman and Peter J. Dendle, 275–89. Farnham, UK: Ashgate, 2012.

A–Z: The Monsters

ABBADON—*see* Demon

ABBOT, LEON—*see* Demon

ACROMANTULA—*see* Harry Potter, Monsters in

AEREUM—*see* Demon

ALICHINO—*see* Demon

ANDHAKA—*see* Demon

ANGEL

Fig. 1 ***Angel*** **by Anki King**

Western theology and folklore conceive of angels as God's messengers, beings of pure spirit who may appear in human form, often with wings, to interact with humans. According to Judaism, Christianity, and Islam, angels are to carry out the will of God and be extensions of that will on Earth. The three faiths also agree that the essential nature of angels is good. Still, religious and secular literature, as well as film, abounds in angels who are portrayed as evil or monstrous through their own actions, or who are perceived as such by fearful human beings.

Early Jewish and Christian texts often refer to fallen angels who tempt humans to evil. Much folklore about fallen angels, as well as a great deal of their literary and filmic portrayal, stems from a brief passage from the Book of Genesis (6:4) that refers to the "sons of God" (King James) or "sons of heaven" (New American)—often though not always interpreted as angels—who, through relations with human women, beget a race of half-angel **giants**, called the Nephilim. Because of the story's place in Genesis, right before the story of Noah's Ark, the wickedness of the Nephilim has sometimes been interpreted, especially in popular religious belief, as a cause of the Biblical flood. The Genesis account is interpreted and expanded upon in the non-Biblical First Book of Enoch (c. 167 BCE), which refers to the Watchers, 200 angels who come down from Heaven with the task of spying on human beings. Disobeying God, the Watchers, led by the angels Shemjaza and Azazel, also teach people secret and potentially dangerous lore, including weaponry, the application of make-up (for women), and the arts of prophecy and magic. The narrative of the Watchers' interaction with humanity is also treated in the pseudoepigraphical Book of Jubilees (c. 100 BCE), and Enoch is referenced in the New Testament Epistle of Jude, in which we are warned (as in Enoch) that eternal chains await the angels who rebelled against God. A related story also appears in Islam: the Koran (see **Koran, Monsters in The**) discusses the angels Harut and Marut whom God sent to test people by showing them how to do magic, leading those who failed the test into damnation. While the Koran makes clear that Harut and Marut are doing the divine will, in the Persian epic poem *Masnavi-y*

Ma-navi (c. 1258), the Sufi mystic Rumi portrays Harut and Marut as prideful angels who succumb to human temptations and commit evil acts. This view is controversial among many adherents of Islam.

Fallen angels—angels punished for desiring to be like God—are discussed throughout the New Testament, especially in their capacity as followers of Satan (see **Devil, The**). Many Christian commentators perceived Old Testament support for their understanding of the fall of Satan and his angels in a line from the Book of Isaiah: "How art thou fallen from heaven, O Lucifer, son of the morning!" (King James, 14:12). While explicitly directed at the King of Babylon, many Christians interpreted the passage as referring metaphorically to Satan. In the Gospel of Luke, Satan is described as falling from Heaven like lightning and the Book of Revelation describes a "war in Heaven" (12:7) in which the good angels, led by the Archangel Michael, defeat Satan and his angelic followers, casting them down to Earth. Both the Gospel of Matthew and the Epistle of Peter refer to the punishments waiting for the rebellious fallen angels. In the Second Epistle to the Corinthians, the Apostle Paul also reminds readers that Satan's angels can disguise themselves as righteous beings in their attempts to lead humans astray.

Fallen angels are central to the works of early and medieval Christian writers, especially Saint Augustine of Hippo (354–430), the medieval scholastic writers Saint Anselm of Canterbury (1033–1109) and Saint Thomas Aquinas (1224–74), and the Franciscan theologian Saint Bonaventure (1217–74). While maintaining the belief (shared by Jews and Muslims) that angels generally have no free will, the Christian writers believed in one exception to this idea—that the angels chose to rebel through a single instance of free will and that their choice and subsequent fall were irrevocable. These writers also believed that in their fall, the rebellious angels lost their beauty and the perfection of their wisdom, and became **demons**. In his *Summa Theologica* (1273), Aquinas asserts: "The fallen angels that beset man on earth, carry with them their own dark and punishing atmosphere, and wherever they are they endure the pains of hell" (64:4).

Obedient (non-fallen) angels may also be portrayed as monstrous, or as having a terrifying appearance. In the Book of Ezekiel, the angels who appear before that prophet are beings of fire with four faces and multiple wings. In various religious texts, angels may appear monstrous when punishing sinners or enemies of the righteous. In the Second Book of Samuel, God stops his angel from laying waste to Jerusalem, while the Second Book of Kings describes an "angel of the Lord" (19:35) who slays 185,000 Assyrian invaders of Israel. The Book of Revelations (9:11) refers to Abaddon or Apollyon, the "angel of the bottomless pit" (King James) or "the angel of the abyss" (New American), who lets loose a plague of grotesque locusts to punish the ungodly. In the Koran, angels are described as pitilessly and precisely carrying out Allah's commands of punishment on sinners, and we are told that 19 angels guard Hell.

In the New Testament, the Angel of the Lord is often called the "destroyer" (see 1 Corinthians 10:10) and has sometimes been confused or equated with the Angel of Death. Many Jewish texts—both Talmudic texts, which collect and comment on Jewish law and belief, and the Midrash, which comment on the Bible—also discuss the angel turned demon Sammael or Samael, sometimes equated with the Angel of Death and sometimes with Satan. The Koran depicts the Angel of Death as kindly to the righteous dead but as a monster to those who die in sin. The Koran refers to this angel only as the Malak al-Maut (literally "angel of death"). Traditional commentary has given him the name Izra'il or Azra'il—sometimes Azrael or Azriel—a version of which is used in many tales in the literary collection known as *One Thousand and One Nights* (see **Arabian Nights, Monsters In**), which dates back to at least the ninth century CE, as well as in Rumi's *Masnavi*. Azrael (Azriel) as the name of the Angel of Death also appears in some Jewish Midrashic texts.

Monstrous angels appear throughout literature and film, often inspired by religious books and treatises. In his *Inferno* (c. 1308–21), the Italian poet Dante Alleghieri follows Augustine and Aquinas concerning fallen angels, equating them with demons and referring to the loss of their angelic beauty. Dante's fallen angels guard the City of Dis, in which the lowest circles of Hell are found. The idea of angels tempting humans to wickedness recurs in Christopher Marlowe's *Doctor Faustus* (1604) in which a good angel and an evil angel fight to influence Dr Faustus, as Lucifer offers him a deal for his soul. The so-called war in Heaven between the rebellious and obedient angels has also been the inspiration for many literary works. In John Milton's epic poem *Paradise Lost* (1667), fallen angels retain the function of tempters and leaders astray, their equation with demons made clear by the fact that many carry the names of Old Testament demons or pre-Biblical gods. Aside from Lucifer, Milton's poem features **Moloch**, Bellial, Mammon, and Beelzebub arguing about the best way to poison human character.

Milton's work may be the first to portray the fallen angels sympathetically—especially Lucifer, whom Milton says was the highest and most beautiful of all God's angels. Milton's portrayal is alluded to and expanded upon in numerous later works, most particularly Philip Pullman's "His Dark Materials" trilogy of novels (1995–2000), a reimagining of *Paradise Lost* in which the rebel angels are seen as heroes. These include Balthamos and Baruch, who protect the heroine of the series, Lyra Belacqua, and help her father—not coincidentally called Lord Asriel—establish a Republic of Heaven. In Pullman's work, the evil angels are those who represent Christianity, here called the Magisterium. These include the Magisterium's weakened senile leader, called the Authority, and his powerful second-in-command, Metatron, an angel known in the Babylonian Talmud (c. 600 BCE) as second in power only to God. Metatron also shows up as God's officious representative in Terry Pratchett and Neil Gaiman's novel *Good Omens* (1990), insisting that the Apocalypse is inevitable: "Things *have* to happen like this. All the choices have been made" (364). Stephen Brust's 1984 novel *To Reign in Hell* provides another sympathetic portrait of the angels who rebel against God, while Memnoch, the fallen angel in Anne Rice's *Memnoch the Devil* (1995), is cast out of Heaven for his sympathy for (and sexual relations with) humans. Neil Gaiman's "Sandman" series of graphic novels (1989–94) also includes numerous fallen angels, both sympathetic and unsympathetic, while British author Storm Constantine's novel *Burying the Shadow* (1992) deals with fallen angel vampires. In *The Master and Margarita*, novelist Mikhail Bulgakov's 1930s satire of Soviet Russia, the companions of the disguised Satan, Professor Woland, include angelically named Azazello and Abadonna.

Many modern books and films are influenced by earlier stories of the Watchers and Nephilim. These include contemporary novels about angels falling in love with humans. Becca Fitzpatrick's *Hush Hush* (2009) and its sequels detail the romance of a male fallen angel and a female human with Nephilim blood, while also recalling the theme of the war between good and evil angels. In "The Mortal Instruments" (2007–09) and "The Infernal Devices" (2010–11), two series of novels by Cassandra Clare, the

Nephilim appear as the Shadowhunters and are tasked with fighting and killing demons. Danielle Trussoni's novel *Angelology* (2010) tells a story of the Nephilim, described as "beautiful iridescent monsters" (85), and their infiltration into and corruption of all aspects of human society.

Literary and cinematic depictions of the Angel of Death include George Gordon Lord Byron's poem "The Destruction of Sennecharib" (1813) in which the poet describes the Angel of the Lord from First Kings as the Angel of Death with wings outspread, breathing into the faces of the Assyrians. Sometimes the Angel of Death is portrayed as a sympathetic and merciful figure: in *Hellboy II: The Golden Army* (Guillermo del Toro, 2008), the angel brings a mortally wounded Hellboy back to life. Andrew, the Angel of Death character in the television series *Touched by an Angel* (created by John Masius, 1994–2003) is also portrayed in a positive light, as are Sammael and Samiel, the two handsome black-clad angels of death who appear in episodes of the television series *Millennium* (created by Chris Carter, 1996–99).

In many modern films and books, angels who are conventionally seen as "good" may behave monstrously, often out of pride or impatience with human frailty. Some recent films give us an evil version of the Archangel Gabriel, revered in Christianity for announcing the birth of Jesus to Mary. In the film *Constantine* (Francis Lawrence, 2005), Gabriel envies human beings, God's favorites, and seeks to punish them by bringing Hell to Earth. In *The Prophecy* (Gregory Widen, 1995), Gabriel tries to steal a human soul as a means to overthrow Heaven. The film *Legion* (Scott Charles Stewart, 2009) shows Gabriel leading hosts of angels to destroy sinful humankind, this time at God's behest. *Gabriel* (Shane Abbess) is also a 2007 Australian film in which the angel resumes his position as hero with the Archangel Michael—traditionally humanity's defender—as rebel. The television series *Supernatural* (created by Eric Kripke, 2005–present) included a story arc in which angels and demons move ruthlessly towards the Apocalypse, at the expense of human survival. While the series portrays some angel characters such as Gabriel and Castiel as by turns destructive and sympathetic, the callous and often murderous behavior of the traditionally righteous Michael and Raphael prompts series hero Dean Winchester (Jensen Ackles) to declare that "angels are dicks." In Neil Gaiman's *Neverwhere*, which appeared as both a television mini-series (Dewi Humphreys, 1996) and a novel (1996), the deceptively beautiful Angel Islington (for whom the London tube station is named) orchestrates a brutal murder. A character remarks of him: "When angels go bad … they go worse than anyone. Remember, Lucifer used to be an angel" (303). In Michael Moorcock's novel, *The War Amongst the Angels* (1998), the war must be averted by humans.

Literature also gives us more ambiguous characters, those who seem monstrous at first but who may be angels in disguise. In Gabriel Garcia Marquez's "A Very Old Man with Enormous Wings" (1955), the title character becomes both a sideshow attraction and the subject of theological debate. It is never clear whether the old man is an angel or a **freak**, though his arrival coincides with the healing of a sick child. David Almond's novel *Skellig* (1998) concerns a young man who finds a strange, weakened creature in his garage—who turns out to have both wings and healing powers. John Travolta's *Michael* (Nora Ephron, 1996) concerns a vacationing angel who drinks and carries on with women. The angel Gibreel, the Islamic form of the name Gabriel, is central to Salman Rushdie's novel *The Satanic Verses* (1988), in which plane crash survivor Gibreel Farishta believes himself to be reincarnated as an angel. This belief, attributed possibly to schizophrenia, may cause him to commit murder and other bad acts. Also, in a dream sequence from the book, a supposed vision of the angel Gibreel prompts a young woman to lead her fellow villagers to drown in the Arabian Sea. In Tony Kushner's play *Angels in America: A Gay Fantasia on National Themes* (1993), the HIV positive character Prior Walter metaphorically wrestles with an angel as Jacob did in the Bible. Like many writers and filmmakers, Rushdie and Kushner employ scriptural themes to remind their audience of the potential monstrousness of angels.

Regina Hansen

References and Suggested Reading

Fowkes, Kate. *Giving Up the Ghost: Spirits, Ghosts, and Angels in Mainstream Comedy Films.* Michigan: Wayne State University Press, 1998.

Gaiman, Neil. *Neverwhere.* New York: Harper Perennial, 2003. Reprint. 1996.

Gaiman, Neil and Terry Pratchett. *Good Omens.* New York: Workman Publishing. 1990.

Giorgievski, Sandra. *Face to Face with Angels: Images in Medieval Art and in Film.* Jefferson, NC: McFarland and Company, 2010.

Reed, Annette Yoshiko. *Fallen Angels and the History of Judaism and Christianity.* Cambridge, UK: Cambridge University Press, 2005.

Sullivan, Kevin P. *Wrestling with Angels: A Study of the Relationship between Angels and Humans in Ancient Jewish Literature and the New Testament.* Leiden, Netherlands: Brill, 2004.

Trussoni, Danielle. *Angelology.* New York: Penguin Books, 2010.

ANIMALS, MONSTROUS

Animals become monstrous as their relationship or proximity to human beings is brought into focus, sometimes because of the animal's lack of humanity, but even at times because the animals represent amplifications of "human" characteristics. The metaphorical relation to being human is often a site where the literal boundary between human and animal is transgressed through scientific or metaphysical means. In either case, "animal" becomes a way to understand what "human" means and often what humans fear. Addressed here are categories of monstrous animals that demonstrate the imaginative extension of human fears of the natural world and questions about the nature of humanity itself.

Swarming Insects, Flocking Birds, and Herding Small Animals

One category of monstrous animals features creatures that become threatening simply as a consequence of overwhelming numbers. Large populations of animals acting or moving simultaneously, whether swarming, flocking, or herding, present an obvious danger. The natural swarming behavior of locusts, for example, happens as a youthful phase of grasshopper development. In both the Bible (see **Bible, Monsters In The**) and the Koran (see **Koran, Monsters In The**), however, this swarming is interpreted as a curse or a plague.

One of the earlier short horror stories to feature large numbers of insects swarming is E.F. Benson's 1912 short story "Caterpillars." The seething mass of caterpillars seen by the central character is arguably a phantasm standing in for the cancer of two other guests in the villa, but the vividness of the image of a bed completely covered in caterpillars is horrifying and links the animals with disease. Carl Stephenson's classic 1938 *Esquire* short story, "Leiningen Versus the Ants," presents an obstinate American plantation owner in Brazil fighting a swarm of army ants eating everything in its path. Human presence and ingenuity fail to stop the threat until the central character endangers his own life to burn the ants, along with his crops and everything else around. While one perspective might characterize the threat as nature on the rampage, Leiningen himself refers to the destructive swarm, in keeping with Biblical precedent, as an act of God. The story was adapted for Byron Haskin's 1954 film *The Naked Jungle*, starring Charlton Heston, in which human sexual passion is paralleled with rampaging nature. Another take on the natural insect as monstrous threat is raised in the 1971 pseudo-documentary, *The Hellstrom Chronicle* (Ed Spiegel and Walon Green). This production features a fictional scientist's theory that the reproductive capacity and adaptability of insects will allow them eventually to hold dominion over the Earth. A more obviously fictional treatment of insect activity exhibiting collective aggression is Saul Bass's 1974 film *Phase IV*, which hypothesizes a contest between humans and insects as an evolutionary event.

Perhaps the most popular example of animal monstrosity due to large numbers is Alfred Hitchcock's *The Birds* (1963). Adapted from the 1952 novella by Daphne du Maurier, the movie stars large flocks of birds that begin to attack humans without any apparent cause. Neither ecological revenge nor act of God is offered as a rationale for the attacks, leading interested viewers (and psychoanalytic critics like Slavoj Žižek—see *Looking Awry*) to speculate on other, more poetic interpretations for the violent behavior. More recently, *Birdemic: Shock and Terror* (2008), an independent horror film written, directed, and produced by James Nguyen, revisited the idea of attacks by flocks of birds, though with a less generous critical reception. Its reputation for being particularly poorly made has earned it a place at midnight screenings in both the US and the UK.

The fear and anxiety produced by the monstrousness attributed to animals combines human primal fears of physical harm with threats that have a more mythic or poetic origin. Snakes are a threat that combine myth and danger. In mythic terms, they are cursed by God to crawl the earth on their bellies, sometimes as serpents in general, sometimes as Satan (see **Devil, The**) in specific. The origin of the board game *Chutes and Ladders* was originally an Indian game called *Snakes and Ladders*. This mythology ties to ophidophobia, the abnormal fear of snakes. Robert E. Howard's *Conan The Barbarian* stories from the 1930s frequently featured snakes as threats, and the 1982 film of the same name (John Milius) combined a suggestion of Conan's anxiety related to snakes with the spread of a snake cult. We see a demonstration of this in the Indiana Jones (Harrison Ford) character in *Raiders of the Lost Ark* (Steven Spielberg, 1981). The fear is combined with claustrophobia and aviophobia (fear of flying) in the thriller *Snakes On a Plane* (David R. Ellis, 2006). The fear of snakes is also one among the many fears that afflicts the lead character of the TV program *Monk* (2002–09), played by actor Tony Shalhoub.

Similar threats are connected to spiders, which have a complex mythological history, sometimes portrayed as spinners of fate, other times as clever tricksters lying in wait. Typical of the threat is the idea of using a tarantula to commit murder in the 1959 film version of *Hound of the Baskervilles* (Terence Fisher). In *Kingdom of the Spiders* (John Cardos, 1977), people are overrun by migrating hordes of tarantulas, and in *Arachnophobia* (Frank Marshall, 1990), the threat of an aggressive foreign species of South American spiders reaches the US (see below for a further discussion of giant spider threats). One of the more memorable scenes from J.K. Rowling's *Harry Potter and the Chamber of Secrets* (1998) and its cinematic adaptation by Chris Columbus in 2002 features Harry and Ron Weasley fleeing from an ocean of spiders—the offspring of the "Acromantula" Aragog (an enormous, sentient spider; see **Harry Potter, Monsters In**).

Narratives like *The Birds* leave viewers to speculate on the cause of the threatening behavior. Other narratives offer ecological causes. Conspiracies of species are responsible for attacks and deaths in films including George McCowan's *Frogs* (1972) and William Girdler's *Day of the Animals* (1977). In these tales, humans are attacked in response to some destructive force in the environment. Although these are not supernatural tales per se, the suggestion of a conscious reaction that identifies and retaliates against human environmental degradation connotes a fantastic ability on the part of the animals. In a variation on this theme, Irwin Allen's *The Swarm* (1978) suggests that aggressive "African" bees mate with gentler American bees, resulting in dangerous swarms. (The racist implications of "natural hybridization" here are far from subtle.) Films such as these offer cautionary tales concerning the consequences of tampering with the environment. The idea of such a threat is satirized in the documentary *Cane Toads: An Unnatural History*, Mark Lewis's 1988 documentary film that uses horror and monster motifs throughout.

A contrast to the films mentioned above, in which the animals represented lack conscious intent, can be found in Michael Wadleigh's *Wolfen* (1981), based on the 1978 novel by Whitley Strieber. *Wolfen* tells the story of a secret species that looks like wolves, but possesses sentience. The wolfen kill several prominent people in an effort to prevent the gentrification and destruction of their environment—a dilapidated area of the Bronx that serves as their feeding ground. When the wolfen corner the lead character, detective Dewey Wilson (Albert Finney), he destroys the architectural model of the building project, indicating that he will help stop the gentrification of their hunting grounds. The wolfen then allow him to live. The film cleverly juxtaposes **werewolves** with Native American **shapeshifters**; it is a false lead, but it increases suspense in the film.

Narratives also exist of swarms acting under conscious human control. In Dario Argento's *Phenomena* (1985), a young woman demonstrates the ability to will a swarm of flies to kill a man who is threatening her. The novel *Ratman's Notebooks* (1969) by Stephen Gilbert features an unnamed narrator who trains a large number of rats to kill for him. He eventually abandons the rats, but they find him later and turn on him. This novel was adapted into *Willard* (Daniel Mann, 1971), followed by the sequel *Ben* (Phil Karlson, 1972). *Willard* was remade in 2003 by Glen Morgan, shifting the emphasis from the difficulties of adjusting to the world of adults and work to an emphasis on the eponymous central character (played here by Crispin Glover) and his desire for control.

Other monstrous animal tales have been constructed out of domesticated or assistance animals who turn on their owners. Poe's 1843 tale "The Black Cat" features a man whose attempts to hide his evil deeds are undone by a cat. The film *The Uncanny* (Denis Heroux, 1977) presents a trilogy of tales of pet cats exacting revenge on deserving owners or their relatives. Stephen King's 1981 novel *Cujo* (made into a film in 1983 by Lewis Teague) has a St Bernard attacking its owners after contracting rabies from a bat. In the 1988 film *Monkey Shines* (George Romero), a helper monkey injected with human brain tissue acts out the violent desires of his quadriplegic owner. These tales are related to the ecological animal monster stories, since they are premised on the danger that animals—even trusted ones—can represent.

Water Animals

Sea serpents and **sea monsters** appear in the Bible (see **Leviathan**), in Norse mythology (Jörmungandr), in ancient Greek legend (Ketos), in Phoenecian myth (the Hippocamp), and in the folklore and fiction of cultures across the world. Indeed, monstrous threats from beneath the surface of lakes, rivers, or oceans are a source of fear across the history of storytelling. These stories play on the fear of entering the water and on the anxieties about what lies beneath the surface. The monstrous possibilities of biology and evolution are a regular component of the interpretation of deep-sea images of odd animal life forms. Some water monsters threaten by virtue of size and some due to number; others unsettle as a result of "unnatural hybridity," unexpected cleverness, or simple malevolence. While attention to large sizes or group behaviors might align them with other categories, the fear these monsters evoke is directly connected to an environment inhospitable to human life.

Among the most threatening of sea creatures are of course sharks. Combining unusually large size with unnatural malevolence is the shark in *Jaws*—the successful 1974 novel by Peter Benchley that was turned into an enormously popular film by Steven Spielberg in 1975. *Jaws* tells the story of a series of shark attacks on a small New England seaside town and the ensuing battle with the culpable shark. It was based in part on a series of attacks that took place in New Jersey in 1916. The success of *Jaws* led to the production of a number of other films echoing the large, vicious sea creature storyline. Sequels to the film were released in 1978 (*Jaws 2*, Jeannot Szwarc), 1983 (*Jaws 3 in 3-D*, Joe Alves), and 1987 (*Jaws: The Revenge*, Joseph Sargent). Reflecting the iconic status of the films and developing from the Universal Studios Hollywood backlot tour, a *Jaws* ride was introduced to the Universal Studios Theme Park in Florida in 1990. Capitalizing on the success of *Jaws*, Rene Cardona directed *Tintorera* about a large tiger shark terrorizing the Mexican coast and Michael Anderson directed *Orca, The Killer Whale* (both in 1977). The trend continued in 1999 with both *Deep Blue Sea* (Renny Harlin) and the made-for-TV *Shark Attack* (Bob Misiorowski), both of which featured malicious giant sharks that are at least partially the product of out-of-control scientific experiments. Merging the shark attack scenario with the "lost world" theme are the series of narratives starring prehistoric megalodons—Steve Alten's 1997 novel *Meg* begat the films *Megalodon* (Pat Corbitt) and *Shark Attack 3: Megalodon* (David Worth), both in 2002 (see **Dinosaur**).

While even single sharks can be intimidating due to size and temperament, the voracious piranha, in contrast, has acquired its monstrous reputation in popular culture through numbers. Stories of these fish hunting in schools connect them to horrific narratives of swarming insects and flocking birds. Much of this is not supported through scientific observation, with studies finding that they gather more out of fear than to hunt; nevertheless, the possibility of schooling piranha tearing through meat appears, for example, in the James Bond film *You Only Live Twice* (Lewis Gilbert, 1967). The project that most directly monsterized the piranha, however, was the Joe Dante film, *Piranha* (1978)—a horror parody that intentionally drew from *Jaws*. It was followed in 1981 by *Piranha II: The Spawning*—a James Cameron-directed sequel that played the horror straight. When the original film was remade in 1995 by Scott P. Levy, producer Roger Corman, who had also produced the 1978 film, removed the humor, but kept the basic plot and even several of the special effects shots. The tongue-in-cheek attitude then returned in the 2010 remake, *Piranha 3D* (Alexandre Aja), and its 2012 sequel *Piranha 3DD* (John Gulager), which supplements the humor with extreme amounts of gore.

The notion of monsters lurking in the depths formed the premise for the short-lived science fiction TV series *Surface* that aired on NBC from 2005 to 2006 and presented a gargantuan reptile-like undersea creature. Although the series was taken off the air before completing its story arc, it incorporated the suggestion that the creature was the product of human technological intervention and biotechnology.

Gargantuan Animals

While small creatures in great numbers acting aggressively can be threatening, so too are gigantic variants of existing creatures. Even the most benign creature can become threatening when expanded to gigantic proportions. And when the creature is already dangerous to begin with—ape, shark, alligator, poisonous spider, or snake, and so on—it becomes monstrous indeed. In some narratives, the monstrous giant animal is a part of the magical universe presented; in others, it is an anomaly or "freak of nature"; in still others, giant animals are the direct result of human tampering with the environment.

In fantasy series such as the worlds created by J.K. Rowling and J.R.R. Tolkien, giant creatures come with the territory. While the giant spider Aragog in the "Harry Potter" series mentioned above is hideous but not a direct threat to the protagonists, the giant spider Shelob in Tolkien's 1954 *Lord of the Rings: The Two Towers* certainly is (see **Tolkien, Monsters In**). In Peter Jackson's 2003 film *Lord of the Rings: Return of the King*, the giant spider threat combines spider physiology with invented elements, like a stinger as a source of venom rather than fangs. Giant birds have featured prominently in mythology including rocs, the Persian simurgh, and the garuda of Hindu myth (see **Birds, Giant**). Sometimes these mythic birds function as transportation, sometimes they are mythic antagonists of serpents and snakes. Their presence as gargantuan threats in films includes *The Giant Claw* (Fred F. Sears, 1957), in which a giant bird materializes out of an antimatter galaxy; *The Vulture* (Lawrence Huntington, 1967), in which the giant bird actually turns out to be a half-scientist/half-bird; and the made-for-TV *Roadkill* (Johannes Roberts, 2011), in which a group of friends are hunted down by a "Simuroc," a giant bird of prey created via a gypsy curse.

In some cases, giant-sized animal monstrosities are natural anomalies rather than the product of magic or scientific hubris. The snakes in 1981's *Venom* (Piers Haggard) and in *Anaconda* (Luis Llosa, 1997) are larger than usual but occur in nature, as does the giant mother snake in the film *Copperhead* (Todor Chapkanov, 2008), set during the nineteenth-century US Civil War.

The most common monstrous giant animals in Western fiction and film are ones that are the byproducts of the irresponsible use of science. Of particular note is science fiction author H.G. Wells's 1904 novel, *The Food of the Gods and How It Came to Earth*. This narrative tells the story of two scientists who invent "Herakleophorbia IV," a food that causes animals to grow to massive sizes. Setting a pattern that has often been repeated, the material gets out of control and is consumed by pigs, wasps, rats, and eventually by babies and children. The human test subjects become political problems, social pariahs, and are eventually put to work; they are even occasionally killed by military force. The scene of the military firing on an enormous human child is quite moving. This novel, in which human invention produces enormous insects, was inspirational for many of the 1950s "giant bug" films, but *Food of the Gods* wasn't itself adapted into a film until 1976 (Bert I. Gordon). In the film version, the "food" is discovered rather than scientifically engineered, and the monster rats, wasps, and worms result in a variant of the "nature strikes back" plot, echoing some of the swarming animal films.

Human technological hubris took center stage in a series of films in the 1950s that feature gigantic animals created by science that outstrips human control. Most famous is arguably Gordon Douglas's *Them*! (1954). In the film, accidental exposure to atomic radiation creates giant ants. Eventually, the mutual efforts of scientists and the military are able to destroy the colonies of ants, but the conclusion of the film suggests that entering the atomic age opened a door onto a new world of unpredictable and dangerous possibilities. Easily predictable, however, was that the success of *Them!* would spawn a whole subgenre of related films. Scientifically altered food that makes animals big and dangerous is the plot device for grasshoppers in *Beginning of the End* (Bert I. Gordon, 1957), for a tarantula in *Tarantula* (Jack Arnold, 1957), and even taming-resistant shrews in Ray Kellogg's *The Killer Shrews* (1959). In *The Black Scorpion* (Edward Ludwig, 1957), it is not scientific hubris but volcanic activity that releases giant scorpions, who then threaten Mexico City. Volcanic activity is also the culprit in *The Deadly Mantis* (Nathan Juran, 1957), unleashing a giant prehistoric praying mantis. And in *Earth Vs. The Spider* (Bert I. Gordon, 1958) and *The Giant Gila Monster* (Ray Kellogg, 1959), no real explanation is ever offered for the giant menaces. The giant animal idea reached a new level of sublime absurdity with the 1972 film *Night of the Lepus* (William F. Claxton), in which rabbits produced through genetic alteration reach large sizes and (unfortunately) become carnivorous. The film features slow motion footage of giant rabbits rampaging through notably artificial miniature sets. In Ellory Elkayem's 2002 comedy, *Eight-Legged Freaks*, toxic waste enlarges and monsterizes spiders.

The idea of relative scale between humans and animals can also work on fears when natural animals retain their size, but humans become smaller through different means; this is the case in the battles with the spider and the house cat in *The Incredible Shrinking Man* (Jack Arnold, 1957) that happen when the lead character is exposed to a mysterious cloud and proceeds to shrink. This motif was frequently used in the TV series *Land of the Giants* (1968–70), where arrival on a gigantic alternative "Earth" included evading giant cats and dogs. And the film *Honey, I Shrunk the Kids* (Joe Johnston, 1989) includes shrunken kids suffering an attack from what to them is a giant scorpion.

"Lost World" Animals

A variant on the monstrous giant animal theme is found in what has come to be known as "Lost World" literature and film. The idea is most directly connected to the 1912 Arthur Conan Doyle novel *The Lost World*. Influenced by both the imperial exploration of so-called lost civilizations and the imagination inspired by the paleontological findings, "lost world" stories developed over the course of the nineteenth century, with roots in fantasy literature going back into the eighteenth.

From "Lost World" origins, **dinosaurs** appear as a significant part of the gigantic monstrous animals genre and have had wide representation in a variety of media. Prehistoric civilization stories have two different variations. The first includes the anachronistic use of dinosaurs or other giant animal monsters in the world of early homo sapiens, such as the comic strips *Alley Oop* (begun in 1932 by American cartoonist V.T. Hamlin), and *B.C.* (started in 1958 by American cartoonist Johnny Hart); the films *One Million B.C.* (Hal Roach, together with Hal Roach, Jr, 1940), its 1966 Hammer Films remake *One Million Years B.C.* (Don Chaffey), the Roger Corman 1958 film *Teenage Cave Man*, and the slapstick comedy *Caveman* (Carl Gottlieb, 1981); and TV series including *The Flintstones* (1960–66) and *It's About Time* (1966–67). Both humor and horror are drawn from the juxtaposition of dinosaurs and humans.

A second variation attempts to construct the world of prehistoric animals based on archeological and historical evidence. Early versions of this design can be found in a series of novels by J.H. Rosny aîné (Joseph Henri Honoré Boex) written between 1892 and 1930 (*Vamireh* [1892], *Eyrimah* [1893], *Nomai* [1897], *La Guerre du Feu* (translated as *Quest for Fire*, 1909], *Le Félin Géant* [1918], and *Helgvor du Fleuve Bleu* [1930]). More recent non-fantasy prehistoric novels include the "Earth's children" series by Jean M. Auel, which began in 1980 with *Clan of the Cave Bear*, and the "First North Americans" series begun in 1990 by Kathleen and W. Michael Gear. Films reflecting this subgenre include *Quest for Fire* (Jean-Jacques Annaud, 1981), *Clan of the Cave Bear* (Michael Chapman, 1986), and *10,000 B.C.* (Roland Emmerich, 2008). The animals represented in these works include threatening species that co-existed with early human ancestors, like mammoths, saber-toothed tigers, woolly *rhinoceroses*, and species of wolf/dogs and horses.

Monstrous Apes

It is impossible to discuss the threat of monstrous giant animals without having in mind arguably the most famous of all: the giant ape, **King Kong**. Any discussion of Kong, however, leads naturally into another subclass of monstrous animal narratives: those dealing with apes in general. For example, similarities between humans and their evolutionary relatives—the so-called higher apes—are central to Edgar Allan Poe's "Murders in the Rue Morgue" (1841) (often credited as the first detective or ratiocination story) in which the murderer turns out to be an orangutan afraid of punishment rather than a human afraid of getting caught. Kong, however, offers one of the strongest and most compelling icons of the relationship between animal and human.

This story originated in a nightmare reported by writer Merian C. Cooper, who also co-directed the original 1933 film with Ernest B. Schoedsack. The story has been produced multiple times, including the 1976 version directed by John Guillermin and the 2005 version directed by Peter Jackson. The various versions play with many dimensions of the relationship between animal and human, simultaneously evoking fear of the monstrous and sympathy for emotions we recognize. Figuring the monstrous are the exotic and dangerous jungle setting, the "uncivilized" tribe that worships Kong, and the sacrificial rituals that emphasize the God-like power of the creature. In the original 1933 film, the size of the creature changed frequently throughout the film, ranging anywhere from 18 feet to 60 feet, but was orchestrated in a way that audiences generally did not find problematic. These changes, however, offer a hint of what is so significant about Kong: like his size, his relative level of monstrousness and the pathos he evokes fluctuate throughout the film.

The power of Kong's character lies in the anthropomorphic display of emotions and actions. His attraction to Ann Darrow (famously played by Fay Wray in the 1933 version) defies species logic, but plays up the human side; lust becomes love, kidnapping becomes dedication, and the efforts of men to subdue the bestial becomes cruelty to the animal and insensitivity to the emotions of the creature. Kong appears to be the last of his kind, eliciting sympathy for his isolation and loneliness, which is emphasized in the 2005 remake. These same characteristics appear in generically similar films using the same themes, such as Schoedsack's 1949 *Mighty Joe Young* (remade by Ron Underwood in 1998), John Lemont's *Konga* (1961), and a variety of spin-offs that range from live action, to animation, to graphic novel and comic appearances.

Special attention also needs to be paid to the phenomenon of *Planet of the Apes* (Franklin J. Schaffner, 1968) and its impact on popular culture. The basic plot finds astronauts from the near future awakening from hibernation to crash land on a planet where the dominant form of life turns out to be apes—who appear to have evolved to the point of being essentially like humans. The leader of the earthmen (played by Charlton Heston) resists and eventually escapes from his ape captors, only to discover that he is not on another planet, but the Earth far in the future. The complexities of the plots of subsequent films (in the first cycle of five films produced between 1968 and 1973) reinforce the allegorical value of the contrast between intelligent apes and intelligent humans, and their struggle for power and dominance.

The first *Planet of the Apes* film drew directly from author Pierre Boulle's 1963 novel, *Planet of the Apes* (*La Planète des singes*), which itself might have been influenced by Aldous Huxley's 1948 experimental novel, *Ape and Essence*. In each of these narratives, the difference between animal and human is inverted and then erased. The remake of *Planet of the Apes* by Tim Burton in 2001 focuses more on the competitive relationship between the apes and humans, while the 2011 *Rise of the Planet of the Apes*, directed by Rupert Wyatt, suggests that a more critical appraisal of "scientific progress" might be the best way to understand the relationship between ape and human.

Hybrids and Produced Monstrous Animals

As is discussed above, much of the history of animal threats arises as a result of direct human intervention. In addition to *Food of the Gods*, another of Wells's novels, *The Island of Dr Moreau* (1896), offers controversial (and bitingly sarcastic) thinking about the idea of animals whose monstrousness arises as a result of trying to make them more human: Moreau performs surgical experiments that attempt to turn animals into beings that are human–animal hybrids. As a result of his acts of creation, Moreau establishes himself as a God to the beast-men and creates a litany of rules that the hybrids must ritualistically repeat that discourages actions that are more animal than human, like walking on all fours, or getting down on all fours to drink water, or eating live rabbits as prey. The surgical experiments cause extreme amounts of pain in the animals. Eventually Moreau is killed by one of his creations. The novel plays with the idea of the bestial possibilities inherent in all humans.

Cinematic adaptations of *The Island of Dr Moreau* variously highlight or obscure different themes. The 1933 Erle C. Kenton adaptation, *Island of Lost Souls*, is considered a classic of early horror cinema and features Charles Laughton as Moreau and Bela Lugosi as the leader of the beast-men. The film plays with the idea of sexual bestiality through the addition of "The Panther Woman" (Kathleen Burke, who was only credited as "The Panther Woman" on the posters). At the end, the beast-men exact their revenge on Moreau using the same surgical tools he had used in their painful transformations. Additional adaptations appeared in 1959, 1977, and 1996—this latest one notable for replacing the surgical procedures in Wells's novel and the 1933 film with drugs and shock therapy to keep the hybrids from returning to their animal state. The means of creating hybrids changes as the culture uses different tools for defining what it means to be human.

In addition to surgical animal hybrids, contemporary narrative often depicts industrial excesses and scientific experimentation in the name of "progress" as catalysts for ecological and biological disaster, unintentionally creating hybrids that end up threatening humanity. In John Frankenheimer's *Prophesy* (1979), for example, a mercury-like mutagen used as fungicide by the logging industry causes mutations in frogs, salmon, raccoon, and eventually in a mother bear and her two cubs, who become hideous monstrosities as a result of industrial pollution. Jonathan King's 2007 New Zealand horror comedy *Black Sheep* features a farmer who conducts genetic experiments that turn sheep into carnivores that infect the humans they bite, turning them in turn into sheep-human hybrids. Genetically altered dogs figure in *Man's Best Friend* (John Lafia, 1993) and *Rottweiler* (Brian Yuzna, 2004). Genetically altered killer wasps figure in Susan Collins's *Hunger Games* novels (2008, 2009, and 2010). The Syfy Channel has produced several films with genetically engineered beasties at their centers, including *Sharktopus* (Mike MacLean, 2010) and *Mega Python Vs. Gatoroid* (Mary Lambert, 2011)—the latter featuring genetically altered alligators.

Cryptozoological Animals

Literally translated as the study of hidden animals, cryptozoology refers to the search for and study of animals—**cryptids**—whose existence is supposed by some but has not been proven. This premise is a cousin to the "lost world" stories, as particularly exemplified in ***Creature from the Black Lagoon*** (Jack Arnold, 1954) and its sequels. This "gill-man" represents a missing link in the evolutionary chain, whose existence is unknown because of the obscure location where the Creature survives. A fascinating variation on the cryptid theme is offered in the 1970 film *Skullduggery* (Gordon Douglas) in which a tribe of "missing link" creatures is discovered by an expedition in New Guinea. The animal-human boundary is tested when one of the creatures is impregnated by a scientist, and again when one of the creatures commits a murder.

Fiction and films that focus on these animals use hoaxes and conspiracies as story elements to rationalize the lack of scientific evidence. Most prominent in this group are the films that tell stories about sasquatch (AKA **bigfoot**) and the **Loch Ness monster**. Many recent incarnations for these cryptid animals are being presented in a "what if ...?" reality TV series. *Lost Tapes*, which began airing on Animal Planet in early 2009, depicts "found footage" of human encounters with cryptids. The program combines the conspiratorial nature of "hidden animals" with the "found footage" motif made popular in horror films such as Daniel Myrick and Eduardo Sánchez's *The Blair Witch Project* (1999; see **Blair Witch**) and Matt Reeves's *Cloverfield* (2008; see **Sea Monsters**). Since these productions are drawing from the tradition of "strange but true" stories, following Charles Fort's *Book of the Damned* (1919), Frank Edwards's *Stranger Than Science* (1959), and the *Ripley's Believe It Or Not!* newspaper panel series, the narratives of animals presented occupy a space between science and faith—which has often been the uncanny contact zone depicted in narratives of monstrous animals in general.

Ralph Beliveau

References and Suggested Reading

Cartmell, Deborah, I.Q. Hunter, Heidi Kaye, and Imelda Whelehan, eds. *Alien Identities: Exploring Differences in Film and Fiction*. London: Pluto Press, 1999.

Day, John. *God's Conflict with the Dragon and the Sea: Echoes of a Canaanite Myth in the Old Testament*. Cambridge: Cambridge University Press, 1985.

Dendle, Peter. "Cryptozoology in the Medieval and Modern Worlds." *Folklore* 117, no. 2 (August 2006): 190–206.

Frayling, Christopher. *Mad, Bad, and Dangerous? The Scientist and the Cinema*. London: Reaktion Books, 2005.

Hand, Richard J., and Jay McRoy, eds. *Monstrous Adaptations: Generic and Thematic Mutations in Horror Film*. New York: Manchester University Press, 2007.

Hendershot, Cyndy. *I Was A Cold War Monster: Horror Films, Eroticism, and the Cold War Imagination*. Bowling Green, OH: Bowling Green State University Popular Press, 2001.

Jancovich, Mark. *Rational Fears: American Horror in the 1950s*. New York: Manchester University Press, 1996.

Muir, John Kenneth. *Horror Films of the 1970s*. 2 vols. Jefferson, NC: McFarland, 2007.

——. *Horror Films of the 1980s*. Jefferson, NC: McFarland, 2007.

Murgatroyd, Paul. *Mythical Monsters in Classical Literature*. London: Duckworth, 2007.

Urbanski, Heather. *Plagues, Apocalypses, and Bug-eyed Monsters: How Speculative Fiction Shows Us Our Nightmares*. Jefferson, NC: McFarland, 2007.

Weaver, Tom. *A Sci-fi Swarm and Horror Horde: Interviews with 62 Filmmakers*. Jefferson, NC: McFarland, 2010.

Žižek, Slavoj. *Looking Awry: An Introduction to Jacques Lacan Through Popular Culture*. Cambridge: MIT Press, 1992.

ANQA—*see* Birds, Giant

ANTAEUS— *see* Dante, Monsters In

APPOLLYON—*see* Bible, Monsters In

AQUATICUM—*see* Demon

ARABIAN NIGHTS, MONSTERS IN THE

The *Thousand and One Nights* (Arabic: *Alf layla wa-layla*), better known in English as *The Arabian Nights' Entertainments* or, in short, *The (Arabian) Nights*, is a widely known and highly influential collection of tales, originally of Near Eastern origin. The collection has a characteristic frame-tale that serves to integrate all ensuing narratives: King Shahriyar is so disappointed by the apparent infidelity of the female sex that he has vowed to marry a different woman every night and to kill her in the morning. Shahrazad, the vizier's clever daughter, decides to reform him and diverts him at night by telling stories. Using the technical device of "cliff-hanger," she breaks off her narrative at a critical point and thus arouses the ruler's curiosity for the sequel, so that he lets her live on. After a thousand nights of storytelling, the ruler is finally cured of his cruel habit and they live happily ever after.

Besides the frame-tale and a core corpus of tales at the beginning, *The Arabian Nights* is not so much a work with a clearly defined content, but rather a phenomenon whose presently known shape has developed over many centuries. Its origins go back to a pre-Islamic Persian prototype, now lost, that was translated to Arabic in the first centuries of the Islamic period (seventh to ninth centuries). Most of the collection's presently known tales were added at various later stages. The oldest preserved manuscript dates from the fifteenth century. It is fragmentary, containing less than a third of the expected 1,001 nights. *The Arabian Nights* were "discovered" by French scholar Antoine Galland (1646–1715). Galland translated the fifteenth-century Arabic manuscript to French, publishing the translation's first volume in 1704. He then "completed" the work by adding tales from a variety of other sources, such as those derived from the oral performance of talented Syrian Christian storyteller Hanna Diyab (born around 1690). In particular, those tales that are most famous in Western tradition, such as "Aladdin, or the Magic Lamp" and "Ali Baba and the Forty Thieves," originate from Hanna's storytelling. Galland also integrated into *The Arabian Nights* the originally independent collection of tales narrated by Sindbad "the sailor"—actually a seafaring merchant.

The collection's two major editions, known as Bulaq I (1835) and Calcutta II (1839–42), served as the basis of new translations prepared directly from the Arabic, such as those by Edward William Lane (1839) and Richard Burton (1885–88). Both of these translators responded to the spirit of their days—Lane by excessive "ethnographic" annotation, Burton by an obsessive focus on sexual matters. The collection's most recent, scholarly English translation was prepared by Malcolm C. Lyons (2008). Particularly as of the nineteenth century, *The Arabian Nights* enjoyed great success beyond its numerous literary versions and adaptations, as demonstrated by its inspirational power for drama, music, painting, architecture, and, later, film and popular culture.

Deriving from Indian, Persian, and Arabic tradition, the tales of *The Arabian Nights* draw on a large variety of popular beliefs concerning supernatural creatures, **demons**, and monsters that interact with human beings. The most widespread of these, such as **Div**, **Genie**, **Ghoul**, Ifrit (see **Djinn/Genie**), and Roc (see **Birds, Giant**), are treated in separate entries in this encyclopedia.

Various monsters make a particularly prominent appearance in the adventures of Sindbad. These tales derive from sailors' yarns such as those documented by Iranian captain Buzurg ibn Shahriyar of Ramhormoz, who compiled his *Book of the Wonders of India* in the tenth century. During his first voyage, Sindbad's company rests on a small island that they later discover to be a huge fish. The Roc—a gigantic bird—appears in the second and fifth voyages. On the third voyage, Sindbad and his companions are imprisoned by a cannibal monster reminiscent of the **Cyclops** Polyphemus in Homer's eighth-century BCE *Odyssey* (9, 106–545). When the monster threatens to devour them one after the other, they use a red-hot spit to blind him and manage to escape. The fourth voyage brings them to the island of the cannibal magians (that is, Iranian Zoroastrians) who fatten and slaughter his companions as food for their ruler. This adventure is similar to the one Odysseus experiences with the sorceress **Circe** (*Odyssey* 10, 229–347). On the fourth voyage, Sindbad himself is shipwrecked on an island inhabited by an apparently feeble old man. When Sindbad, in compassion, takes the old man on his back or shoulders to help him move around, the monster wraps his legs around his body and forces Sindbad to carry him. Only by making him drunk does Sindbad manage to rid himself of this monstrous burden. Similar monsters are also mentioned in the story of Sayf ibn Dhi Yazan contained in the nineteenth-century Reinhardt manuscript of *The Arabian Nights*. On his seventh and last voyage, Sindbad is in the company of the flying bird-men. When he praises God in fascination, the demonic nature of these creatures is revealed by a streak of lightning that almost kills them. Monstrous snakes of tremendous size are mentioned in the third and seventh voyages (see **Animals, Monstrous**).

Specifics of particular monsters are given rarely. Probably the most famous of all monsters in *The Arabian Nights* is the huge **demon** that Salomon had imprisoned in a small bottle. When later found by a fisherman, the demon at first threatens to kill his saviour out of wrath for having been imprisoned for so long. But then the fisherman dupes him into returning back into the bottle and only releases him again when the demon promises to act kindly. In the modern world, this "demon from the bottle" has gained a proverbial status implying a supernatural power that is hard or even impossible to constrain once it has been released.

From the tale "The Merchant and the jinni," readers learn that an ifrit can be killed by as little as a carelessly discarded date stone. The "Story of King Yunan and Duban the sage" includes a short tale in which a prince meets a female ghoul that first appears as a young woman, then changes into a hideous cannibalistic monster. The tales of "Aladdin, or the Magic Lamp" and "Ma'ruf the cobbler" mention genies that are bound to a magic ring with whose help they can be summoned. The story of Sayf al-muluk informs readers about the specifics of a demon's external soul that is here preserved within the body of a sparrow that itself is hidden in a series of boxes, caskets, and chests, and finally in an alabaster coffer that is submerged in the sea. In order to vanquish the demon, the hero must first kill the sparrow containing its soul. The adventure with the bird-men in Sindbad's seventh voyage documents that demonic creatures shun true belief. In the story of Sayf ibn Dhi Yazan, when mortally wounded by the hero, the cannibal monster asks to be given a final blow. The hero, however, is wise enough not to strike the monster twice, since the second blow resuscitates.

Besides carnivorous **sea monsters** mentioned in passing in tales such as "The Shipwrecked Woman," humanoid sea-creatures that communicate and even mate with humans appear in the stories "Julnar of the sea and her son, Badr Basim," and "'Abd Allah of the land and 'Abd Allah of the sea." In the latter tale, the particularly interesting sea monster Dandan makes its appearance. The vicious Dandan is so huge that on land it could easily swallow a camel or an elephant. An ointment prepared from this creature's liver allows the humanoid creatures living in the sea to move around and breathe under water. Even though the Dandan is huge and dangerous to all creatures living in the sea, it is killed when it either eats human flesh, such as that of a drowned corpse, or when it hears a human voice.

Supernatural creatures encountered by the protagonists of *The Arabian Nights* tales are usually taken as a natural given, without questioning their existence. Though constituting a feature of folk and fairy tales, this attitude is, above all, an element of the traditional Islamic belief system. According to this belief system, God is omnipotent and capable of permitting the existence of the strangest and most unfathomable beings. Beyond the boundaries of popular narrative, this belief is celebrated in a whole genre of learned literature known as *'Aja'ib al-makhluqat*, whose most prominent work was compiled by thirteenth-century author Zakariya ibn Muhammad al-Qazwini.

Ulrich Marzolph

References and Suggested Reading

Buzurg ibn Shahriyar, Captain, of Ramhormuz. *The Book of the Wonders of India: Mainland, Sea and Islands*. Edited and translated by G.S.P. Freeman Grenville. London and The Hague: East-West Publications, 1981.

Gerhardt, Mia. *The Art of Storytelling: A Literary Study of the Thousand and One Nights*. Leiden: Brill, 1963.

Irwin, Robert. *The Arabian Nights: A Companion*. London: Allen Lane, 1994.

Lyons, Malcolm S. *The Arabian Nights: Tales of 1001 Nights*. 3 vols. Translated by Ursula Lyons. London: Penguin, 2008.

Marzolph, Ulrich, and Richard van Leeuwen. *The Arabian Nights Encyclopedia*. 2 vols. Santa Barbara: ABC-Clio, 2004.

Pinault, David. *Story-Telling Techniques in the Arabian Nights*. Leiden: Brill, 1992.

Qazwini, Zakariya ibn Muhammad al-. *Die Wunder des Himmels und der Erde*. Translated by A. Giese. Lenningen: Erdmann, 2004.

ARAGOG—*see* Animals, Monstrous; Harry Potter, Monsters In

ASTAROTH—*see* Demon

ASURA—*see* Demon

ATE—*see* Demon

AZAZEL—*see* Bible, Monsters In The; Devil, The

AZAZELLO—*see* Demon

BAAL—*see* Demon

BABA YAGA—*see* Witch/Wizard

BACCHAE—*see* Maenad

BADB—*see* Banshee

BAKA—*see* Mahābhārata, Monsters In

BAKENEKO—*see* Shapeshifter

BALROG—*see* Tolkien, Monsters In

BAN NIGHECHAIN—*see* Banshee

BANSHEE

The banshee is a supernatural creature of the Celtic British Isles (Ireland, Scotland, and the Isle of Man) whose name comes from the Irish *bean sídhe* (woman of the mound/Otherworld). Her wild and grief-stricken wailing (or keening) foretells, but usually does not cause, the death of an individual. She can often be heard at twilight, midnight, or dawn beneath the windows of the soon-to-be-deceased's home or along the trail of his or her funeral procession, and occasionally by a stream, grave mound, or other natural feature. Literature often features the banshee as a sorrowful old woman with bloodshot eyes and white hair, wearing a gray or green dress, and weeping at impending death, although at times she is a more sinister being who delights in or even causes death. Some traditions believe that the banshee is the spirit of a woman who died while giving birth or of a murdered pregnant woman; and Patricia Lysaght describes how the banshee is often thought to be the deceased ancestor of a family of noble Irish descent and is therefore an "attendant spirit" whose lamentation is an extension of the family's sorrow and grief (53–6). The banshee is sometimes known as the young and beautiful but terrifying *badb* (or *badhbh*) or the *bean chaointe* (keening woman), and is associated with other female spirits, such as the Scotch-Gaelic *ban nighechain* (washerwoman), the Scottish *glaistig*, and the Welsh *cyhiraeth*.

The banshee's origins lie in the *Tuatha Dé Danann* (People of the Goddess Dana), a mythical race of prehistoric Ireland. These pre-Christian deities cohabitated with humans and included the banshee-like goddess, the Mórrígan (Phantom Queen), who incited conflict, directed the course of battle, and appeared to those who were about to die on the battlefield. This war spirit appears in the famous Irish epic *Táin Bó Cuailnge* (*The Cattle Raid of Cooley*), which is extant in manuscripts from the twelfth to the fourteenth centuries. In this narrative of country-wide warfare and destruction, the Mórrígan first appears in the shape of a raven "ravenous / among corpses of men," and pushes the combatants into further warfare and seeks "affliction and outcry / and war everlasting ... death of sons / death of kinsmen / death death!" (Kinsella 98). She is able to cast spells and take many forms in the epic, including a beautiful young woman, an eel, a gray she-wolf, a red cow, and an old hag.

As James MacKillop describes, through centuries of myth and legend, the realm of the *Tuatha Dé Danann* became indistinguishable from the Irish Otherworld or *sídhe*, the **fairy** realm that parallels mortal human existence. The mythical Otherworld and the real world remain connected through the other meaning of the word *sídhe*, the cairns and burial mounds that dot the Irish landscape. The banshees of modern literature have a strong connection to Celtic fairy culture, but are more often comforting familial spirits than harrowing war goddesses. The Welsh antiquarian Thomas Pennant's travelogue, *A Tour in Scotland* (1769), mentions the banshee as a peculiar belief of the Scottish peasantry, and the Scottish novelist and poet Sir Walter Scott mentions the banshee in his poems *The Lady of the Lake* (1810) and *Mackrimmon's Lament* (1818), as his proud highland characters acknowledge that their ensuing battles with opposing clans will bring about their inevitable deaths. Scott further opines on the banshee in *Letters on Demonology and Witchcraft* (1829) in which he describes the Irish banshee as a household fairy who announces death's approach and the Scottish banshee as a spirit that protects children, wards off battle, and may even intervene in the chess and card games of the clan's chieftain. The English journalist Walter Thornbury also encountered fairy belief in his travels, and his *Cross Country* (1861) includes a description of Dunluce Castle on the Antrim coast in Northern Ireland and the banshee who is believed to haunt the castle and its rocky promontory.

The banshee figures prominently in nineteenth-century Ireland in folklore collections, such as T. Crofton Croker's *Fairy Legends and Traditions of the South of Ireland* (1824), and in poetry. J.L. Forrest's poem "The Banshee" tells the story of a young woman who learns that the love of her life has died overseas by the banshee's shrill wail: "From the depths of the grave, from the darkness of hell. / The Phantom comes forth with her death-breathing spell; / For the gleam of her dark eye, the hiss of her breath, / But herald the coming of sorrow and death!" (Hayes, vol. 2, 153). Forrest's poem "The Banshee's Song" includes a harrowing declaration by the spirit herself that ends with a lamenting Irish refrain: "Hark to my tidings of gloom and of sorrow! / Go, weep tears of blood, for—*Och! d'eag an chorra!*" (Alas! The beloved has died!) (Hayes, vol. 2, 154). John Todhunter uses the banshee to craft a political message in his poem "The Banshee" (1888), which envisions the country of Ireland as a desolate old woman who plays a mournful harp and keens for all of her exiled and dead children.

During the Irish Literary Revival, the cultural and literary flourishing that lasted from about 1890 to 1922, the banshee remained a favorite subject for Irish authors. The Revival grew out of nineteenth-century antiquarian work and was championed by folklorists, dramatists, and poets like W.B. Yeats and Lady Augusta Gregory. Yeats published a collection of folklore titled *Fairy and Folk Tales of the Irish Peasantry* (1888) that included stories of the banshee, and such mythical tales directly influenced Yeats's own poetry and drama. Irish cultural belief surges through the literature of the period, such as Dora Sigerson Shorter's poem "The Banshee" (1899), which describes how the speaker sees a banshee keening at her neighbor's door and knows that her neighbor or her husband is doomed to die, and Alice Furlong's poem "The Warnings" (1905), which describes the otherworldly sensation of a speaker who hears the banshee's keen and realizes that it is calling her own name.

The figure of the banshee continues to populate literary culture in the twentieth and twenty-first centuries, such as British author Terry Pratchett's comedy/fantasy series "Discworld." Pratchett's *Reaper Man* (1991) includes the humorous and awkward banshee Mr Ixolite, who has a speech impediment and prefers to notify those who are about to die with a short note instead of the traditional keen. The banshee also makes an appearance in J.K. Rowling's *Harry Potter and the Prisoner of Azkaban* (1999) when Professor Remus Lupin exposes his students to a creature known as a boggart that changes its appearance into whatever the viewer fears most. For Seamus Finnigan, an Irish classmate and friend of Potter, the boggart takes the shape of a howling banshee (see **Harry Potter, Monsters In**). This character is also popular in American fantasy literature, most notably Ray Bradbury's autobiographical short story "Banshee" (first published in 1984) in which the narrator travels to Ireland to meet his friend, but also encounters a spectral being: "She stood leaning against a tree, dressed in a long, moon-colored dress over which she wore a hip-length heavy woolen shawl that had a life of its own, rippling and winging out and hovering with the weather ... She had a face of snow, cut from that white cool marble that makes the finest Irish women; a long swan neck, a generous if quivering mouth, and eyes soft and luminous green" (142). Banshee characters appear elsewhere in American fantasy, such as R.A. Salvatore's *Dark Elf Trilogy* and Rachel Vincent's young adult *Soul Screamer* series, as well as in comic books. For example, an Irish **mutant** named Banshee first appears in Marvel's *Uncanny X-Men #28* (1967), and his special power is a sonic scream that shatters solid objects, renders his opponents unconscious, and can even propel him off the ground and through the air.

The Marvel superhero Banshee appears in the film *X-Men: First Class* (Matthew Vaughn, 2011) as a young superhero in training, but the cinematic banshee is more often a howling monster that wreaks havoc in horror films, such as *Cry of the Banshee* (Gordon Hessler, 1970) and *Banshee* (Michael Elkin, 2010). The most memorable cinematic depiction occurs in *Darby O'Gill and the Little People* (Robert Stevenson, 1958). In the film, O'Gill interacts with **leprechauns**, meets a howling banshee dressed in an ethereal green cloak and, at the film's climax, enters an otherworldly death coach driven by a headless fairy until the king of the leprechauns saves his life and guarantees a happy ending.

Justin T. Noetzel

References and Suggested Reading

Bradbury, Ray. *Bradbury Stories.* New York: HarperCollins, 2003.

Hayes, Edward, ed. *The Ballads of Ireland.* 2 vols. London: A. Fullerton, 1855.

Kinsella, Thomas, ed. *The Tain: Translated from the Irish Epic Tain Bo Cuailnge.* Oxford: Oxford University Press, 1969.

Lysaght, Patricia. *The Banshee: The Irish Death Messenger.* 2nd edn. Boulder: Roberts Rinehart Publishers, 1997.

MacKillop, James. *A Dictionary of Celtic Mythology.* Oxford: Oxford University Press, 1998.

BARBARICCIA—*see* Demon

BARROW-WIGHT—*see* Tolkien, Monsters In

BARUCH—*see* Angel

BASILISK

The basilisk is an ordinary-sized snake, sometimes called the "prince of snakes" (Latin *regulus*), characterized as a monster primarily by its power to kill by sight. According to Pliny the Elder, a Roman encyclopedist writing c. 77 CE, the basilisk "does not move its body forward in manifold coils like other snakes but advancing with its middle raised high." Its arch-enemy, somewhat surprisingly, is the weasel: "They throw the basilisks into weasels' holes, which are easily known by the foulness of the ground, and the weasels kill them by their stench and die themselves at the same time, and nature's battle is accomplished" (*Naturalis Historia* 3.57–9). Pliny's account is slightly modified by Isidore (c. 560–636), who writes in his *Etymologies* that the basilisk "kills a human if it looks at one. Indeed no flying bird may pass unharmed by the basilisk's face, but however distant it may be it is burnt up and devoured by this animal's mouth. However, the basilisk may be overcome by weasels" (255).

In Literature

The classical and late antique traditions seen in Pliny and Isidore were appropriated by later Christian writings. In the Latin Bible, the word *basiliscus* is sometimes used as an alternative name for a snake. The best-known passage is Psalm 90:13: "Thou shall go upon the asp and the basilisk; the lion and the dragon shall you tread under your feet." The lines were interpreted as referring to Christ, who was thus often depicted in Christian art as treading upon some combination of these four beasts. Isaiah 11:8, also associated with the Messiah, has "And the sucking child shall play on the hole of the asp: and the weaned child shall thrust his hand into the den of the basilisk." In a few lives of Christian holy men, the basilisk sometimes takes the place of the dragon as an adversary. The anonymous *Liber Pontificalis* claims that, during the reign of Pope Leo IV (847–55 CE), "in some noisome and hidden caverns arose a serpent of dire sort called *basilisk* in Greek and *regulus* in Latin; by its breath and glance it speedily overwhelmed all who went into those caves" (118). The creature is put to flight by Pope Leo's tearful prayers.

The basilisk is sometimes called a **cockatrice** in Middle English; Psalm 90, in a version of the Wyclif Bible (c. 1400), has the words "adder and cockatrice" in place of "asp and basilisk." The word cockatrice descends from Latin *calcatrix*, but the English word was misinterpreted as being related to cock (rooster), and so both the cockatrix and basilisk were sometimes depicted as being part-serpent, part-rooster in illustrated bestiaries and also in coats-of-arms.

The basilisk lives on in English writers, mainly in the form of brief allusions to a creature who kills by sight. Chaucer in the *Canterbury Tales* (c. 1400) has his Parson claim that envious looks slay a sinner just as the basilisk-cock slays people by the "venom of its sight." Polixenes in Shakespeare's *The Winter's Tale* (c. 1610) remarks: "Make me not sighted like the Basilisque. I have look'd on thousands, who have sped the better by my regard, but kill'd none so" (I.ii.508–10). Romantic poet Percy Bysshe Shelley in his "Ode to Naples" (1820) writes, "Be thou like the imperial Basilisk / Killing thy foe with unapparent wounds!" (83–4).

A few English poets have alluded to the Biblical passages involving basilisks. Alexander Pope in his sacred eclogue "The Messiah" (1712) writes of the Christ child, drawing on Isaiah 11:8: "The smiling infant in his hand shall take / The crested basilisk and speckled snake" (181–2). In his poem "In the Wilderness" (1918), Robert Graves writes of Christ in the desert: "Basilisk, cockatrice, / Flocked to his homilies, / With mail of dread device, / With monstrous barbed slings, / With eager dragon-eyes" (13–17). **[PA]**

In Film

Likely the first attempt to portray the basilisk on screen is *The Basilisk* (Cecil M. Hepworth), a British silent film from 1914 in which the creature endows a mystic with the power to mesmerize and control the heroine, in his effort to steal her love and have her murder her fiancée. The man is saved by the timely intervention of the creature, who revolts and kills the mystic. The creature represents the access to power allowed through human frailty, greed, and jealousy, and the destruction that follows.

More familiar to modern audiences, the basilisk is featured in the second installment of the "Harry Potter" series (see **Harry Potter, Monsters in**), *Harry Potter and the Chamber of Secrets* (Chris Columbus, 2002). The basilisk provides the central conflict in the film; it is computer-generated, with a snaky body and menacing reptilian head. Its gaze causes death, following traditional notions, but not by turning to stone. Several characters escape death by viewing the basilisk through various semi-transparent films, and the monster's poison provides significant plot points through the rest of the series.

In the SyFy Channel's original television movie, *Basilisk: The Serpent King* (Stephen Furst, 2006), the titular creature is re-awakened by an archeologist and wreaks havoc in a museum and university. The basilisk is again computer-generated and features a crocodilian head and snaky body, with several protuberances resembling undersized centipede legs. Its gaze can turn its victims to stone. According to the movie, it was a creature from the ancient Middle East that was subdued by the Eye of **Medusa**, a golden staff containing a crystal having the same nature as the eyes of the basilisk. Drawing upon established monster-in-the-city formulas, such as **King Kong** and **Godzilla**, *Basilisk* follows the creature as it devours several characters, defeats military attempts to subdue it, and navigates quickly through the sewer-like urban infrastructure. In an unlikely conclusion, it is frozen in the cooling tanks of a nuclear power station.

Paul Acker and Thomas Rowland

References and Suggested Reading

Chaucer, Geoffrey. *The Riverside Chaucer. Edited by Larry D. Benson*. 3rd edn. Boston: Houghton Mifflin, 1987.

Davis, Raymond, trans. *The Lives of the Ninth-Century Popes (Liber Pontificalis)*. Liverpool: Liverpool University Press, 1995.

Graves, Robert. *Fairies and Fusiliers*. New York: Knopf, 1918. Google Books. Online.

Isidore. *The Etymologies of Isidore of Seville*. Translated by Stephen A. Barney. Cambridge: Cambridge University Press, 2006.

Pliny the Elder. *Natural History*. Translated by H. Rackham. Cambridge: Harvard University Press, 1938.

Pope, Alexander. *Poetical Works*. Edited by Herbert Davis. Oxford: Oxford University Press, 1966.

Shelley, Percy Bysshe. *Poetical Works*. Edited by Neville Rogers. Oxford: Oxford University Press, 1975.

BATEMAN, PATRICK—*see* Psychopath

BATES, NORMAN

The character Norman Bates first appeared as the protagonist of Robert Bloch's novel *Psycho* (1959) and was played by Anthony Perkins in Alfred Hitchcock's *Psycho* (1960), a close adaptation of the novel. Bloch, influenced by the story of serial killer Ed Gein who lived just 40 miles from Bloch's Wisconsin home, wrote a novel "in which a seemingly normal and ordinary rural resident led a dual life as a psychotic murderer" (Bloch, *Once* 228; see **Psychopath**). Bloch based his story on the situation rather than on the individual, though he eventually discovered that Bates and Gein had a lot in common.

The novel and the film both explain that Bates's psychological problems started in early childhood, when he was dominated by his demanding mother. After his father died, the young Bates became so pathologically attached to his mother that, when she planned to remarry, he went insane, killed her and her lover with strychnine, and was promptly committed to a mental institution. Bates developed dissociative identity disorder, with three distinct personalities: *Norman*, the boy who needed his mother and hated anyone who came between him and her; *Norma*, the mother, arising from Bates's guilt over committing matricide; and *Normal*, the adult Norman Bates who lived a seemingly commonplace life, concealing the existence of the other personalities. Apparently rehabilitated, the adult Bates was discharged from the hospital and returned to run the family motel. But he stole Mother's body from her grave and preserved it, and Mother's personality took over Bates in times of crisis—as when Marion Crane (Mary in the novel) arrived at the motel. Bates was attracted to her, but jealous Mother killed her. Bates, dressed up as Mother, also killed Arbogast, a detective looking for Marion. Bates was finally caught just before killing Marion's sister Lila who, with Marion's fiancé Sam, had come looking for Arbogast. At the end of both the novel and the film, Bates is back in the asylum and Mother's personality has taken over.

The movie's plot hewed quite closely to that of the novel, with the exception of Bates's character. In the novel he is in his forties, balding, fat, and an alcoholic, with interests in psychology, the occult, and metaphysics. He also collects pornography, a hobby only alluded to in the movie. Hitchcock, however, wanted a main character audiences could sympathize with more easily. He envisioned the "trim, handsome, and likeable young Anthony Perkins" as Norman (Smith 15). With the physical changes in Norman, screenwriter Joseph Stefano also omitted Bates's drinking problem and any overt mention of his potentially alienating reading material.

In both novel and movie form *Psycho* was so popular that Bloch and Hollywood produced sequels, though they did not overlap in plot at all. Norman Bates appears in Bloch's *Psycho II* (1982). Film sequels about Bates's character include *Psycho II* (Richard Franklin, 1983), *Psycho III* directed by Anthony Perkins (1986), and the television movie *Psycho IV: The Beginning* (Mick Garris, 1990). Also, Gus Van Sant produced and directed a much-reviled 1998 shot-for-shot remake of the original *Psycho*.

More than Bloch's novel, Hitchcock's movie had a huge influence on pop culture. Anthony Perkins became inseparably associated with Norman Bates, eventually satirizing his own portrayal by appearing as Bates in a 1976 *Saturday Night Live* sketch ("The Norman Bates School of Motel Management," #1.16) and in a 1990 commercial for General Mills' Oatmeal Raisin Crisp cereal ("Look, Mother, I'm eating my oatmeal!"). Bates, the model for "an entire race of cinematic psychos" (Schechter xi), ranks number two (behind **Hannibal Lecter**) on the American Film Institute's list of "100 Villains." Musical tributes to Bates include the 1980s punk band Norman Bates and the Showerheads; Landscape's 1981 single "My Name Is Norman Bates"; The Burning of Rome's 2008 single "Norman Bates"; and Eminem and 50 Cent's 2009 collaboration "Norman Bates Motel." A Norman Bates action figure, dressed as Mother and holding a kitchen knife, is available from McFarlane Toys' Movie Maniacs series. Bates Mansion sold separately.

D. Felton

References and Suggested Reading

Bloch, Robert. *Once Around the Bloch: An Unauthorized Autobiography.* New York: Tor, 1993.

——. *Three Complete Novels: Psycho, Psycho II, Psycho House.* New York and Avenel, NJ: Wings Books, 1993.

Briggs, Scott D. "The Keys to the Bates Motel: Robert Bloch's *Psycho* Trilogy." In *The Man Who Collected Psychos: Critical Essays on Robert Bloch*, edited by Benjamin Szumskyj, 102–20. Jefferson, NC and London: McFarland & Company, Inc., 2009.

Janicker, Rebecca. "'Better the House Than an Asylum': Gothic Strategies in Robert Bloch's *Psycho*." In *The Man Who Collected Psychos: Critical Essays on Robert Bloch*, edited by Benjamin Szumskyj, 121–33. Jefferson, NC and London: McFarland & Company, Inc., 2009.

Punter, David. "Robert Bloch's *Psycho*: Some Pathological Contexts." In *American Horror Fiction From Brockden Brown to Stephen King.* New York: St. Martin's Press, 1990.

Rebello, Stephen. *Alfred Hitchcock and the Making of* Psycho. New York: St. Martin's Griffin, 1990.

Schechter, Harold. *Deviant: The Shocking True Story of the Original "Psycho."* New York: Pocket Books, 1989.

Smith, Joseph W., III. *The Psycho File: A Comprehensive Guide to Hitchcock's Classic Shocker.* Jefferson, NC and London: McFarland & Company, Inc., 2009.

BATHORY, COUNTESS

Erzsébet (Elizabeth) Bathory (1560–1614), also known as the "Blood Countess," was a Hungarian noblewoman alleged to have murdered over 650 young female virgins. An interweaving of historical fact and fictional invention characterizes her monstrosity, which is linked not only to serial murder, but to her suspected lesbianism, marital infidelities, and to accusations of vampirism (see **Vampire**) and witchcraft (see **Witch/ Wizard**). Among the gruesome legends attached to her is that she bathed in the blood of her victims to retain her youth.

The Countess was the child of aristocratic inbreeding during a time of warfare, when torture and violence were everyday occurrences. During her lifetime she witnessed the struggle between Reformation and Counter-Reformation forces, as well as the Turkish wars for the conquest of Europe (the same wars that kept her husband away from her for years at a time). A child of privilege, Elizabeth was able to indulge in the luxuries and sexual and intellectual freedoms that her social rank allowed her.

Valentine Penrose, in *The Bloody Countess: Atrocities of Erzsébet Bathory* (2000), relates the Countess's sexual and murderous perversions to psychopathic madness, education in witchcraft, and/

or her alleged epilepsy, said to have been caused by the inbreeding typical of the Hungarian upper class to which her family belonged. In Andrei Codrescu's *The Blood Countess* (1995), he notes that she received a traditional education under the auspices of both a Protestant minister and a Catholic monk in her childhood, as well as instruction in the art of witchcraft, magic, and **devil** worship.

The number of young virgins she is claimed to have murdered ranges from 50 to 650. The legend surrounding her asserts that she experienced both psychological and sexual gratification in her killings: not only would the torturing of her victims alleviate her "epileptic" seizures and attacks of melancholy (and anger), but they would also replenish the youthfulness of her skin. Penrose, as well as Alejandra Pizarnik in her 1968 short story "La condesa sangrienta" ("The Bloody Countess"), claim that Elizabeth first noticed the power of virginal blood when she scratched a servant for having tugged her hair too hard while brushing it. It is then that she noticed that the spot on her hand where the young girl's blood had fallen seemed to plump up and become youthful. Penrose extrapolates from the trial transcripts that the Countess, however, did not simply kill her victims but employed methods of torture that evolved over time, from simply biting and piercing servants who did not do their tasks properly to more intricate and elaborate methods of extracting personal pleasure from inflicting pain and ultimately death on her victims. Some of the techniques she used to arouse pain (and pleasure), in addition to branding, piercing, biting, and the severing of body parts, are alleged to have included the Iron Maiden (an iron cage in the shape of a woman embedded with precious stones that would close upon its victim, piercing her with its daggers located in the interior of the cage); "death by water," in which victims would be taken outside in the middle of winter, stripped naked, and frozen to death by having water poured over them; and a cage lined with sharp blades that would be pulled up to the ceiling, piercing the victim's flesh as it swayed. Even forced cannibalism has been numbered among her alleged crimes.

Although her noble class provided her with more freedom than women of lower social standing, the Countess was not beyond reproach. Prior to the rumors of lesbianism and other "unnatural" sexual tendencies, Elizabeth had already established a questionable reputation. At the age of eleven, she had an affair with a peasant villager and gave birth to a daughter from this encounter (Howard and Smith 33). Elizabeth's family hid her pregnancy and, following the birth of the child, quickly gave it away (see Julie Delpy's *The Countess*, 2009). She was married at the age of 15 but engaged in numerous extramarital affairs during her husband's prolonged absences while waging war against the Turks. Presumably, one such affair led to her eloping "with a young man rumored to be a vampire" (Howard and Smith 33), but her defection was short-lived and she hastily returned to her position at the castle.

Although frequently figured in literature and film as a vampire, the Bloody Countess's vampiric qualities are not attributed to having ingested the blood of her victims, but rather to the use of virginal blood in potions and blood baths. Although also mentioned in the fictional works of Codrescu and Pizarnik, as well as Gia Bathory in *The Trouble with Pears* (2006), more historically reliable information is provided by Penrose documenting that Elizabeth was instructed by witches that bathing in the blood of a young virgin girl would help preserve her beauty and youth. As time began to show itself in her appearance, however, despite these baths in virginal blood, Elizabeth was advised by her witches that she must bathe in blood similar to her own: the noble blood of young ladies. Penrose describes that Elizabeth, with the aid of her witches, was able to secure young noble ladies to come to her castles under the premise that they would be receiving special training in good manners and languages. Although rumors had been widespread for some time concerning the mysterious disappearance of pretty young girls while in the service of the Countess Bathory, it was only when the young ladies of noble lineage began to vanish that a formal investigation was begun.

Penrose, Codrescu, and Gia Bathory question the validity of the investigation due to the influence that Elizabeth's nobility and social status allowed her. It is also important to note that Hungary's King Matthias (1557–1619) himself owed a great deal of money to the Bathory-Nadazdy family and if Elizabeth were to have been formally charged by the King's court, the family riches would have automatically passed on to the reigning monarch. In order to prevent this, Count Gyorgy Thurzo, her cousin, led a raid on her home on New Year's Eve 1610, and formally arrested her on 2 January 1611 on various charges. The Countess was tried and found guilty of torture, murder, witchcraft, and bathing in human blood, and was condemned to live out the remainder of her life walled in one of her rooms in her castle at Cahtice. She died on 21 August 1614.

Given the scandal surrounding the Countess's life, it is not surprising that she has been represented numerous times in literature and film. Robert McNally, in *Dracula was a Woman: In Search of the Blood Countess of Transylvania* (1983), delves into both the political and historical context to the Countess's story, while the films *Daughters of Darkness* (Harry Kümel, 1971) and *Eternal* (Wilhelm Liebenberg and Federico Sanchez, 2004) provide lurid narratives of Elizabeth's sexual proclivities. Both of these films place Elizabeth into contemporary settings and represent the Countess as a traditional vampire who seduces rather than attacks her prey—in each, the lesbian eroticism of the vampiric bite is emphasized.

In her 2006 novella, Gia Bathory describes the Countess as "the most notorious female serial killer in world history" (11). In this text, Elizabeth views killing her victims as merciful, since they would have starved or been raped anyway; but, most importantly, she has no regret for her actions. Although Penrose, in his text, points to Elizabeth's madness as a contributing factor to her actions, films such as Peter Sasdy's *Countess Dracula* (1971) and Delpy's *The Countess* depict the Countess not as a vampire figure but as a living woman whose obsession with blood as a source of youth is due to her sexual relationship with a younger man. A commonality in the majority of these depictions is the Countess's disconnection from those of lower social standing and her rationalization that she is only expediting their inevitable deaths. Jorge Grau portrays the Countess within her historical context in his film *Ceremonia de sangre* (Ritual of Blood, 1974) and highlights the involvement of her witches in her blood-draining rituals.

Cristina Santos

References and Suggested Reading

Bathory Al Babel, Gia. *The Trouble with Pears: An Intimate Portrait of Erzsebet Bathory.* Bloomington, IN: Authorhouse, 2006.

Cavallaro, Dani. *The Gothic Vision: Three Centuries of Horror, Terror, and Fear.* New York: Continuum, 2002.

Craft, Kimberly L. *Infamous Lady: The True Story of Countess Erzsébet Báthory.* Charleston, SC: CreateSpace, 2009.

Howard, Amanda, and Martin Smith. *River of Blood: Serial Killers and their Victims*. Boca Raton, FL: Universal Publishers, 2004.

Penrose, Valentine. *The Bloody Countess: Atrocities of Erzsébet Bathory*. Translated by Alexander Trocchi. London: Creation Books, 2000.

Santos, Cristina. "Vampire, Witch, Serial Killer or All of the Above? The Bloody Countess Elizabeth Bathory." In *Monstrous Deviations in Literature and the Arts*, edited by Cristina Santos and Adriana Spahr, 177–92. Oxford: Interdisciplinary Press, 2010.

BATLHAMOS—*see* Angel

BEAST, (BEAUTY AND THE)

The Beast has long haunted folkloric, literary, and cinematic traditions. He, or she in gender role reversals, has represented human beings' animal and magical alter egos in stories that reach across widely distributed cultures and time periods. The version most familiar to Western audiences is "Beauty and the Beast" (1756) by Madame Le Prince de Beaumont, who published an abbreviated version of Madame Gabrielle-Suzanne de Villeneuve's elaborate 1740 salon fairy tale. (Both are available in fine translations by Jack Zipes.) Although the focus of this entry is on later versions influenced by these two French writers, it is important to realize that basic elements of the tale date back to the "Eros and Psyche" tale included by Apuleius in his second century CE Latin novel *Metamorphoses* (or *The Golden Ass*) and even earlier Sanskrit texts. The fact that variants of "Beauty and the Beast" (classified as ATU 425C by folklorists) have persisted in oral traditions from Europe, Asia, Africa, and the Americas, and have then transitioned into contemporary versions by writers and filmmakers, suggests how deeply the tale reflects core human experience. The cast of primary characters, in spite of shifting details, usually features a father, daughter, and supernatural suitor. The plot involves a journey for all three: the father into old age, the daughter into maturity, and the Beast from outsider to accepted acclaimed status.

In Beaumont's "Beauty and the Beast," a merchant with three daughters loses his fortune and moves to a country cottage. Hearing of his ship's safe return, he sets off to reclaim its cargo, whereupon the older girls clamor for rich gifts but the youngest, called Beauty for her looks and good heart, requests only a rose. After a fruitless journey, the merchant gets lost in a forest, discovers a magic palace, and picks a rose from the garden. An angry Beast appears, demanding the merchant's life or marriage to one of his daughters. Beauty insists on sacrificing herself but becomes, instead, mistress of the palace and grows to respect the Beast. In spite of her developing affection, however, she misses her ailing father and requests leave to visit him. Once home, she is diverted by her two sisters from returning to the palace until nearly too late. She misses the Beast, arrives to find him almost dead with grief, and declares her love, thereby transforming him into a prince who makes her his bride.

Since the late eighteenth century, the tale has become an iconic fantasy of transformation in genres that include opera, ballet, children's books, adult novels, poetry, film, video, graphic novels, and recent popular culture formats such as FanFiction, YouTube, and electronic games. Beauty is overtly the story's star and the focus of persistent critical attention. The Beast, however, is generally the most riveting character in terms of literary and artistic imagination, with his final human counterpart dull by contrast. An exception is Angela Carter's brilliant "Courtship of Mr Lyon" (1979) in which the transformed

Beast, Mr Lyon, is "a man with an unkempt mane of hair and, how strange, a broken nose, such as the noses of retired boxers, that gave him a distant, heroic resemblance to the handsomest of all beasts" (133). In her even more unusual version, "The Tiger's Bride" (1979), Carter has the Beast retaining his animal form, with Beauty transformed to join him. Ingeniously, Tanith Lee's science fiction tale "Beauty" (1983) also leaves the alien Beast untransformed; it is the heroine's task to accustom herself to his terrible beauty. Indeed, authors have increasingly subverted the traditional ending. Of Robin McKinley's two young adult novels that feature the Beast, *Beauty* (1978) and *Rose Daughter* (1997), the first transforms the Beast but the second leaves him in his original form, nonetheless beloved by Beauty as they prepare to marry. Donna Jo Napoli's fantasy, *Beast* (2000), is set in ancient Persia and narrated by the Beast himself, named Orasmyn, after the Beast in Charles Lamb's 1811 poem "Beauty and the Beast." An eerie graphic novel, Marian Churchland's *Beast* (2009), has one of the most mysterious endings, in which a sixteenth-century Beast seems to lure a beautiful modern-day sculptress into a timeless hideaway of artistry.

While literary nineteenth-century fairy tales cast the Beast variously as a boar, bear, walrus, elephant, or monster, twentieth-century images were dominated by Beasts with a leonine visage, including Jean Cocteau's classic film *La Belle et la bête* (1946), Marianna and Mercer Mayer's illustrious 1978 picture book, Shelley Duvall's Faerie Tale Theater live-action adaptation for television (Roger Vadim, 1982), and Disney's famous animation (Gary Trousdale and Kirk Wise, 1991). Cocteau's Beast most clearly projects the symbolic split between animal and human, with the actor Jean Marais doubling as both a human suitor (Avenant) and the Beast, in a persona requiring four hours of make-up per shooting (Cocteau 56). The teenage blockbuster *Beastly* (Daniel Barnz, 2011) updates the Beast as a high school student disfigured—because of his cruelty—by scars and tattoos, making an obvious association between inner and outer values.

Modern Beasts are often bewitched by a **fairy/witch** figure, either for vengeance or in retribution for their inhumane behavior, and are then redeemed by a woman's love and loyalty. Scholars including Bruno Bettelheim, Jack Zipes, Marina Warner, Maria Tatar, Jacques Barchilon, Betsy Hearne, Jerry Griswold, and Ruth Bottigheimer have different approaches to interpreting the story, depending on their disciplines and theoretical orientations—Freudian, Jungian, socio-cultural, historical, structuralist, and/or feminist. Issues of sexuality and gender dominate these discussions. On the one hand, Beauty saves two relatively passive males, her father and a fierce-looking but vulnerable Beast, making her a hero figure not through violence or cunning, but through patience and perception. The Beast, on the other hand, "uses none of the traditional male accoutrements of power and daring; what he does is set a good table and wait. In fact, he shows traditionally female attributes of delicate respect for Beauty's feelings, nurturance, comfort, gentleness, and patience, all of which he has learned through humbling experience. He has learned the hard way that life without undeceived affection is rather a thorny paradise, even fenced with roses" (Hearne 133). Susan Jeffords, discussing masculinity in Disney's film compared with various popular male protagonists in 1980s cinema, argues that the film "offered the reasons for men's aggressive behaviors and suggested that they should not only be forgiven but helped along toward revealing their 'true' inner selves"—despite the fact that they have created the stereotype (172). June Cummins's analysis underscores the polarized feminine and masculine identities in Disney's version, pointing out that "many of the characteristics that make the Beast ugly are exaggerations of normal male traits: his size, his hairiness, his gruffness, and his strength" (26). Jerry Griswold suggests that "there is in Disney's movie a special link between hostility towards the Beast and hostility toward homosexuals" (243).

The Beast has lurked in various literary guises—Christine Butterworth-McDermott draws parallels between the Beast and Rochester in Charlotte Brontë's *Jane Eyre* (1847)—and there are romances between Beauty and Beast figures that end tragically with the Beast untransformed, from ***King Kong*** (Merian C. Cooper and Ernest B. Schoedsack, 1933; Peter Jackson, 2005) to *Edward Scissorhands* (Tim Burton, 1990), not to mention rampant **vampire** and **werewolf** romances in both fiction and film. Award-winning contemporary novels such as *The Tiger's Wife* by Téa Obreht (2011) continue—through conscious or unconscious reflections of Beauty and the Beast—to revisit and explore what it means to be both human and animal, even as humanity becomes increasingly alienated from nature.

Betsy Hearne

References and Suggested Reading

Butterworth-McDermott, Christine. "Grains of Truth in the Wildest Fable: 'Beauty and the Beast' Retold as Jane Eyre." In *Twice-Told Children's Tales: The Influence of Childhood Reading on Writers for Adults,* edited by Betty Greenway. New York: Routledge, 2005.

Carter, Angela. "The Courtship of Mr Lyon"; and "The Tiger's Bride." In *The Bloody Chamber.* London: Gollancz Press, 1979.

Cocteau, Jean. *Beauty and the Beast: Diary of a Film.* New York: Dover, 1972.

Cummins, June. "Romancing the Plot: The Real Beast of Disney's Beauty and the Beast." *Children's Literature Association Quarterly* 20, no. 1 (Spring 1995): 22–8.

Griswold, Jerry. *The Meanings of Beauty and the Beast: A Handbook.* Peterborough, Ontario: Broadview Press, 2004.

Hearne, Betsy, ed. *Beauties and Beasts: The Oryx Multicultural Folktale Series.* Phoenix, AZ: Oryx Press, 1993.

———. *Beauty and the Beast: Visions and Revisions of an Old Tale.* Chicago: University of Chicago Press, 1989.

Jeffords, Susan. "The Curse of Masculinity: Disney's Beauty and the Beast." In *From Mouse to Mermaid: The Politics of Film, Gender, and Culture,* edited by Elizabeth Bell, Lynda Haas, and Laura Sells. Bloomington, IN: Indiana University Press.

Tatar, Maria. "Beauties and Beasts: From Blind Obedience to Love at First Sight." In *Off With Their Heads: Fairy Tales and the Culture of Childhood.* Princeton, NJ: Princeton University Press, 1992.

Warner, Marina. "Reluctant Brides: Beauty and the Beast 1"; *and* "Go, Be a Beast: Beauty and the Beast II." In *From the Beast to the Blonde: On Fairy Tales and Their Tellers.* New York: Farrar, Straus, and Giroux, 1994.

Zipes, Jack. *Beauties, Beasts, and Enchantment: Classic French Fairy Tales.* New York: Penguin Meridian, 1991.

BEELZEBUB—*see* Angel; Devil, The

BEETLE—*see* Mutant and Freak

BEGEMOT—*see* Demon

BEHEMOTH

It is in the Biblical address by the voice from the whirlwind to Job that the plural Hebrew noun translated as "behemoth," meaning "beasts" or "animals," is first given its mythic meaning. In Job 40:15–24,

Behemoth is introduced as a monstrous beast without a rival, full of strength and power. It is described as having limbs as strong as copper and bones like iron, and can only be laid to rest by the sword of God, his maker. Within the dialogues in the Book of Job, this description functions to demonstrate to Job the futility of questioning God, who alone has created these beings and who alone can contend with them.

According to Jewish tradition, both **Leviathan** and Behemoth were created on the fifth day but were soon separated and sent to different domains (4 Esdras 6:49–52; 1 Enoch 60:8–90). All efforts definitively to associate Behemoth with an existing creature—for example, a hippopotamus, elephant, or crocodile—have failed; however, some Creationists believe that the Behemoth is identical to a **dinosaur** that became extinct after the great flood.

In Western civilization, this mythic monster has been utilized in two different yet connected roles. In his 1668 treatise *Behemoth*, which can be seen as the follow-up to his *Leviathan*, Thomas Hobbes uses the figure of Behemoth to indicate the effect of governmental blunders such as those he saw during the English Civil War. In a similar vein, the German political scientist Franz Leopold Neumann, in his *Behemoth: The Structure and Practice of National Socialism 1933–1944* (first published 1942; revised 1944), equated Behemoth with German national socialism for its lawlessness and inhumanity.

In modern popular culture, Behemoth plays the role of a devastating, inimical monster. For example, in the 1959 British-American science fiction movie directed by Douglas Hickox and Eugène Lourié, *The Giant Behemoth*, Behemoth is depicted as a dinosaur. In the Marvel Comics series *Tales to Astonish* (1966), Behemoth appears as an undersea monster and defender of the civilization of Atlantis. Behemoth is also the name of a Polish death metal band.

Bob Becking

References and Suggested Reading

Batto, Bernhard F. "Behemoth." In *Dictionary of Deities and Demons in the Bible: Second Extensively Revised Edition*, edited by Karel van der Toorn, Bob Becking, and Pieter W. van der Horst, 165–9. Leiden, Grand Rapids, and Cambridge, UK: Eerdmands and Brill,1999.

Beal, Timothy K. *Religion and its Monsters*. New York and London: Routledge, 2001.

Mills, Charles Wright. "Neumann and Behemoth the Best of German Tradition." In *Power, Politics and People*, 170–78. New York: Oxford University Press, 1967.

Neumann, Franz Leopold. *Behemoth: The Structure and Practice of National Socialism 1933–1944*. 2nd edn. New York: Oxford University Press, 1944.

BELLIAL—*see* Angel; Devil, The

BELL WITCH, THE

"The Bell Witch" was the name given to a series of unexplained events that occurred in and around the home of the Bell family of Robertson County, Tennessee, from 1817 to 1821. It is one of the best-documented cases of allegedly paranormal phenomena and, at least initially, resembled a **poltergeist** manifestation. The Bell family themselves occasionally referred to the cause of the disturbances as a "**Witch**," but more frequently used the term "Spirit," believing that a **demon**ic entity from the spirit world was behind the events. The unsolved mystery of the Bell Witch haunting has contributed to the story's retaining a high level of popularity even 200 years after the disturbances ceased.

The many accounts of the Bell Witch phenomena—none of them contemporary

Fig. 2 ***Bell Witch*** **by Riley Swift**

with the disturbances—agree on the sequence of events. The first unsettling occurrence was Mr John Bell's encounter with a strange animal on his farm; he shot at it, but it disappeared. Some time later the family began to experience nocturnal disturbances, being awakened by a variety of rapping and scratching sounds of unknown origin. Soon, various members of the Bell family reported having their bedclothes torn off while they were trying to sleep, and had their hair violently pulled and felt their cheeks slapped by an unseen force. Mr Bell and his daughter Elizabeth (Betsy) were targets of the most frequent and physically violent attention of the force, which was, however, very gentle toward Mrs Bell (Lucy). Eventually the force manifested as a disembodied voice and called itself "Old Kate Batts' witch." Kate Batts was an eccentric but kind-hearted neighbor to the Bell family. They did not believe the Spirit's statement, and although some in the county did, no harm came to Kate Batts because of it—other than that the Spirit was thereafter addressed and referred to as "Kate."

As rumors of the mysterious occurrences spread, the Bell house became crowded with neighbors and other visitors who came both to comfort the family and to witness the strange events for themselves. The Spirit grew increasingly loquacious and enjoyed showing off, confounding everyone with its intimate knowledge of their lives and of faraway events. It would also sing, curse, and babble. The Bell family considered moving, but were convinced that the entity would follow them everywhere, as it threatened to do. Yet "Kate" showed unusual compassion toward Mrs Bell when she became ill. The Spirit seemed sorrowful, and sang comfortingly to her. In one noteworthy incident, "Kate" caused grapes and hazelnuts to appear out of thin air for Mrs Bell to eat.

The culmination of the disturbance was the illness and death of John Bell, whom the Spirit had never ceased to harass verbally and physically for over three years. Mr Bell was afflicted with facial seizures and swellings of his tongue that became increasingly severe. In December of 1820 he fell into a coma and died the next day; "Kate" claimed to have poisoned him. The Spirit continued to visit the family until spring of 1821, promising to return in seven years, which it did, according to various accounts, though its visit in 1828 lasted only two weeks. The cause of the apparently supernatural events was never discovered.

The original texts related most directly to the Bell Witch case, and which were largely responsible for perpetuating the legend, include the short manuscript *Our Family Trouble* by John Bell's son Richard Williams

Bell (1811–57), who was six years old when the disturbances began. Although Richard Bell was an eyewitness to the events, he did not record his journalistic memoir until 1846, noting: "The importance of a diary at that time did not occur to anyone" (Moretti 20–21). M.V. Ingram's *An Authenticated History of the Famous Bell Witch* (1894) attempted to "record events of historical fact" (Moretti 129) and included Richard Bell's manuscript; Ingram's narrative is generally considered the most important literary source for the Bell Witch haunting. Descendant Charles Bailey Bell, great-grandson of John Bell, published *The Bell Witch: A Mysterious Spirit* in 1934, partially in response to the frequent inquiries he received about his ancestors' experiences.

Several modern retellings of the Bell Witch story have incorporated the psychoanalytical explanation that Betsy Bell had been sexually abused by her father and had somehow created the entity "Kate" to defend herself. Examples include *The Bell Witch: An American Haunting* by Brent Monahan (1997) and *All That Lives: A Novel of the Bell Witch* by Melissa Sanders-Self (2002), both fictionalized versions of the legend. Barbara Michaels's fictional *Other Worlds* (1999) has Harry Houdini retell the Bell Witch legend to a group of friends, who then theorize as to what might actually have been the cause of the disturbances. Their theories, which reflect historical attempts at explanation, include fraud on the part of the Bell children, the possibility of Betsy Bell's having multiple personalities, and the sexual abuse theory. Alternatively, *The Bell Witch Haunting* (1999) and *The Bell Witch: The Full Account* (2000), both by Pat Fitzhugh, present the available evidence on the case without speculation.

The Bell Witch Haunting (Ric White, 2004), based on Ingram's account of the case, is generally considered the cinematic version most true to the story. Other film adaptations include the direct-to-video release *Bell Witch: The Movie* (Shane Marr, 2007) and the widely panned *An American Haunting* (Courtney Solomon, 2006, based on Monahan's novel). An interesting musical take on the legend comes courtesy of Mercyful Fate, a Danish heavy metal band, who included a song titled "The Bell Witch" on their 1993 album *In the Shadows* and then released *The Bell Witch EP* in 1994. The lyrics, based on the legend, describe the attacks on Betsy and John Bell.

D. Felton

References and Suggested Reading

Fitzhugh, Pat. *The Bell Witch: The Full Account.* Nashville: Armand Press, 2000.

Michaels, Barbara. *Other Worlds.* New York: HarperCollins, 1999.

Moretti, Nick, ed. *The Bell Witch Anthology: The Essential Texts of America's Most Famous Ghost Story.* Charleston, SC: BookSurge Publishing, 2008.

BELOVED—*see* Demon

BENNU—*see* Phoenix

BESERKER—*see* Robot

BHASMASURA—*see* Demon

BIBLE, MONSTERS IN THE

The monster's terrifying and abnormal shape typically gives physical form to its wickedness and evil, and within the context of the Old and New Testaments, monsters function as warnings, omens, or demonstrations of the consequences of transgressing cultural and religious boundaries. In general, monsters in the Bible threaten humans at the command of God who has created evil and integrated it into His greater, mysterious plan.

Beasts

Accounts of monsters in the Bible do exist but have in part been greatly contested, as some of these creatures might actually have been born out of translation errors. If one compares the different translations of the Bible—for instance, the King James Version (KJV) and the New International Version (NIV)—the variability of translations becomes clear: where the NIV translates Deuteronomy 33:17 as describing the horn of a wild ox, the KJV relates the horns to be like those of unicorns. Similar controversy exists around the concept of the presence of **vampires** in the Bible: scholars tend to find translating these blood suckers as "leeches" or similar insects to make more sense than making them out to be **demons** or vampires. Proverbs 30:15, which deals with avarice and ambition, and tends to be translated as "leech," is such an instance. The sayings in Proverbs often feature insects, which is why the translators favor this line of reasoning. In addition, references to monsters in the Bible frequently function as metaphors. For example, the "flying serpent" in Isaiah (14:29, 30:6) is intended as a political metaphor for a new leader instead of the actual **cockatrice**. Creatures such as the **phoenix**, which has been interpreted into Job 29:18 ("I shall die in my nest, and I shall multiply my days as the sand"), have been taken as representatives of expectations of a long life. Nevertheless, the KJV features a number of unambiguously monstrous creatures.

The most widely known mythical creature in the Bible is the **Dragon**, with its most prominent description in Revelation (13:1–2, 17:3; also Deuteronomy 32:33). With its seven heads and ten horns, the beast is also reminiscent of the **hydra** in Greek mythology. The Beast, the Dragon, and the Serpent are each signifiers of the Antichrist, yet should not simply be equated with this figure. In fact, the Book of Revelation speaks of several Beasts (the Dragon and the two Beasts are mentioned in Rev. 9:12–13, 16:13, and 20:10). This beastly imagery is mostly interpreted as a reference to contemporary dangers by the author of Revelation—namely the imperially sanctioned religious persecution of Christians under Nero (37–68 CE) and Domitian (51–96 CE). With its fiery appearance and aggressive behavior, the dragon represents the powers of chaos. According to the Book of Revelation, the Dragon and his army will participate in the ultimate battle of good versus evil on Earth, a scenario that has been portrayed in many installments of popular fiction—although oftentimes in a secularized fashion: for example, Rob Bowman's *Reign of Fire* (2002) is set in a world overrun by fierce dragons, yet does not base this plot on a Biblical framework.

The beasts detailed in the Book of Revelation are also described in the Book of Daniel, in which the prophet foretells the rising of four frightening beasts from the sea. Here, too, the monsters are often interpreted as representations of empires instead of literal beings. There is a lioness with the wings of an eagle (Babylon); a bear with three rows of teeth in its mouth (Median Empire); a four-winged, four-headed leopard (Persian Empire); and the beast with iron teeth and ten horns—including one horn that has eyes and a mouth of its own—that leads them into war (Greek and Macedonian Empire). These monsters are warnings of insurgency and obedience, or life without the Abrahamic God, and have widely influenced literature and popular culture. John Bunyan's monster Apollyon in the Christian allegory *The Pilgrim's Progress from This World to That Which Is to Come* (1678) is an amalgamation of these monsters. Although never placed in a religious context, H.P. Lovecraft's array of cosmos-threatening monsters (the

Old Ones; see **Lovecraft, Monsters In**) proves very Biblical upon closer inspection, suggesting a combination of the monsters of the Apocalypse and the chaos monsters **Leviathan** and **Behemoth**.

Leviathan, the "dragon that is in the sea" (Isaiah 27:1), is a mythical monster with a distinguished role in the fight between good and evil. It is one of the chaos monsters that inhabit the sea, along with Rahab, Tannin, Tehom/**Tiamat**, and Yam. An exhaustive description of Leviathan can be found in the Book of Job (41:1–34). This tightly scaled creature breathes smoke, spews fire, and brings sorrow and terror. Psalm 104:26 praises God for having created all things, including the sea and Leviathan to live in it. Leviathan is sometimes referred to as a type of **sea monster**, and is mentioned together with the term dragon in Isaiah 27:1 (KJV), though it has not been conclusively established whether "dragon" is merely another term describing Leviathan. At the end of time, according to Isaiah 27:1, Leviathan will be slain by God himself. The role of this monster as inhabitant of the sea with the intention to destroy the earth has been constant up into modern times. The "combat myth," with Leviathan as "a threatening but vanquished enemy" (Van der Toorn et al. 957), has been transported into numerous works in the field of politics, such as Thomas Hobbes's social contract theory of the same name (1651).

In contrast to Leviathan's apocalyptic destiny, Rahab is described in the Old Testament (Psalm 89:10, 87:4; Isaiah 51:9, 30:1; Job 9:13, 26:12) as one of the forces in the battle between Yahweh and chaos before Heaven and Earth were created (with the exception of the mentions in Isaiah 30:1 and Psalm 87:4, which serve as a reference to Egypt, according to Karel van der Toorn et al.)

Whereas the word Behemoth today is used to describe something overly large and powerful, it also originates in the Book of Job (40:15–24), immediately following the description of Leviathan. Like Leviathan, Behemoth is so powerful that man cannot control him—only God can tame and defeat these beasts. Living on land and feeding on grass, Behemoth has tough skin, is enormous in size, and has obscure supernatural characteristics; it is "the 'Beast' par excellence" (Van der Toorn et al. 315). Modern scholars are uncertain about the categorization of this creature and three interpretations exist: some identify it with a naturally occurring animal such as the elephant or the hippopotamus; some contend that there was no Behemoth (saying that Job fabricated it as a symbol of chaotic forces threatening God); and some characterize it as a mythic figure in the same vein as Leviathan.

Although Behemoth's exact function and character remain ambiguous, it nevertheless has found its way into literature and popular culture. It makes an appearance in John Milton's *Paradise Lost* (1667) in the description of the creation of living creatures, and is also the name of Thomas Hobbes's 1682 book accompanying *Leviathan*. In his novel *The Master and Margarita* (1967), Russian writer Mikhail Bulgakov named the character of a talking cat after this giant creature. Both Marvel and DC Comics feature characters named Behemoth, as does the popular *Final Fantasy* media franchise. The Marvel and DC characters are highly secularized installments, borrowing the name Behemoth in order to point out a character's enormous size and super-human characteristics; DC Comics' Behemoth is part of a supervillain group named "The Hybrid," which appeared in *The New Teen Titans*. Marvel's Behemoth, a character appearing in *Tales to Astonish*, re-appropriates the Biblical characteristics. Here, this sea-dwelling monster was not created by God but rather by a race of aquatic beings, the Atlanteans, as a means of defense. Several films have adopted this creature as well, such as *The Giant Behemoth* (Douglas Hickox, 1959), which depicts the monster as a **dinosaur**-type, reminiscent of later **Godzilla** films.

Giants

Monstrous in shape due to their abnormal size, the Nephilim are the Bible's **giants**. Two accounts of this race of demigods can be found: Numbers 13:33 and Genesis 6:4. They are the progeny of the sons of God and the daughters of men—that is, the products of divine–human intermarriages that would also render humans immortal. This upsetting of boundaries provoked God's fury, bringing about the Flood, which destroyed the Nephilim and finally weakened humans with mortality. The Nephilim have been incorporated into popular culture as fallen angels, such as in the horror film *The Devil's Tomb* (Jason Connery, 2009) or as "shadowhunters" in the young adult saga, "The Mortal Instruments" (2007–present) by Cassandra Clare, in which they are referred to as a human–divine cross-breed. A permutation of the Nephilim has also been featured in the mystery television series, *The X-Files* (Season 5, episode 17, "All Souls," directed by Allen Coulter).

Another enigmatic set of characters is that of Gog and Magog. Here too a definitive interpretation has not been established and these figures have been construed both as persons and geographical locations (Gog may originate in the Hebrew version of the name of Gyges of Lydia [seventh century BCE]; Magog has been interpreted as another name for Babylon). A modification of Gog and Magog is mentioned in combination with giants in Geoffrey of Monmouth's twelfth-century *De gestis Britonum* (*The History of the Kings of Britain*), where he describes a fierce giant by the name of Gogmagog who inhabited Cornwall. Due to their mention in an apocalyptic context in Ezekiel 38–39 and Revelation 20:7–9, Gog and Magog are usually considered supernatural, eschatological enemies of God and representatives of darkness. They are prophesied to invade Jerusalem with their army, only to be defeated by the Messiah. Gog and Magog were identified with the Romans in early Christian times, and later with the Antichrist himself. They have been characterized as contemporary enemies throughout the centuries, such as Hitler and Napoleon, and identified with the state of Russia by Fundamentalist Christians (see, for example, the *Scofield Reference Bible* and the 1835 *Gesenius Thesaurus*) as Van der Toorn et al. explain. Gog and Magog have thus been used in popular culture as representatives of evil and destruction or as heralds of the end. In 1954, for instance, the science fiction film *Gog* (Herbert L. Strock), which revolves around machines developing a life of their own, introduced two **robots** named Gog and Magog. Magog is also a supervillain in the DC comic *Kingdom Come*.

Angels and Demons

Other creatures and entities in the Bible, such as the Cherubim, the angelic creatures with four faces that are often compared in appearance and function to the **Sphinx** (see **angels**), or demons (such as the goat demons or **satyrs**), cannot be easily categorized as monsters.

Although demons are capable of taking on any appearance they wish, they are often described as hideous and monstrous; nevertheless, their roles and functions in the Biblical framework often place them beyond the mere role of a monster. Azazel, for instance, is only mentioned once in the Old Testament (Leviticus 16:8–10) and three times in Jewish scripture, and can be interpreted as a desert demon or the name of an elimination rite involving sending a scapegoat into the desert (depending on the translation, Leviticus 16:8–10 either speaks of a goat being chosen for Azazel or as a scapegoat to be sent into the desert). Yet perhaps because of this ambiguity, Azazel has taken on a life of his own and become a monster that permeates popular culture. He appears as a comic book character (the father of the *X-Men* character Nightcrawler), one of the rulers of Hell in Neil Gaiman's *The Sandman: Season of Mists* (1992), a two-centimeter tall demon in a series of Isaac Asimov short stories that have been published in a collection called *Azazel*, a character in the video game *Tekken*, and a demon in a multitude of popular media including the movie *Fallen* (Gregory Hoblit, 1998) and the television show *Supernatural* (2005–present). While the original meanings and intentions of these Biblical creatures are never entirely clear due to the differing translations alone, their adaptation in popular culture is equally diverse. Monsters of Biblical heritage have long found their way into secularized versions, where the original religious framework is re-appropriated to become more of a special effect or mannerism than a religious tale cautioning humans to beware of the supernatural.

Jana Toppe

References and Suggested Reading

Asma, Stephen T. *On Monsters: An Unnatural History of Our Worst Fears*. Oxford: Oxford University Press, 2009.

Beal, Timothy. *Religion and its Monsters*. New York: Routledge, 2001.

Metzger, Bruce M., and Michael D. Coogan, eds. *The Oxford Guide to People and Places of the Bible*. Oxford: Oxford University Press, 2004.

Van der Toorn, Karel, Bob Becking, and Pieter W. van der Horst, eds. *Dictionary of Deities and Demons in the Bible (DDD)*. New York: E.J. Brill, 1995.

BIGFOOT

Fig. 3 ***Bigfoot* by Scott Ogden**

Called sasquatch, bigfoot, yeti, and other names, the general figure of a large ape-like man or man-like ape has perennially stoked the human imagination and evoked awe, fear, and sometimes sympathy. These creatures, on the borderline between humankind and animals, provoke both a fascination with and fear of our bestial nature. Especially after the 1960s, they also represent nature in a positive, pro-ecological way, and human beings often became the monster instead.

Origins and History

In the ancient Mesopotamian *Epic of Gilgamesh*, which dates to approximately

2000 BCE, Gilgamesh's friend Enkidu is a hairy wild man; in the Old Testament, Esau, Jacob's brother, is furry (Genesis 25:25). In his *Natural History*, Pliny the Elder, a Roman of the first century CE, describes creatures in India that look human but are furry and cannot speak; five centuries earlier, in *The Histories*, Herodotus placed the hairy race in Libya. Medieval European myth called the figure the "wodewose" (spelling varies), from the Old English words for "woods" and "living being"; *Sir Gawain and the Green Knight*, from the late fourteenth century, refers to "wodwos." The male wodwos were hairy except for their hands, feet, and upper faces; the lower faces and breasts of the females were also bare. Located in exotic foreign lands or the unreachable depths of the woods, these creatures were often known as cannibals. Sometimes they could command animals and even call up storms. Yet they were seen as natural creatures, not supernatural. Carl Linnaeus, the eighteenth-century founder of modern biological taxonomy, in *Systemae Naturae*, published in 1735, even proposed the category of *Homo ferus*, the wild man.

By the nineteenth century, science left little room for a species of furry hominids, but the figure's popularity continued. P.T. Barnum (1810–91) exploited people's awe and fear with various exhibits. In 1846, he presented London with an ape-man from "the wilds of California," played by an actor in a fur suit who ate raw meat. Barnum called his second such exhibit "What-Is-It," which became the name for these man-beasts in carnival sideshows. Although many recognized the What-Is-It as an African-American actor in a costume, that did not reduce its appeal. Edgar Rice Burroughs's *Tarzan the Ape Man*, published in *All-Story Magazine* in 1912, also shows the attraction of both intelligent apes and men gone back to the wild.

One possibly scientific claim arose out of the exploration of the Himalayas by Europeans. According to Myra Shackley, lore in Tibet, Bhutan, and Nepal included at least three types of hairy humanoids, recognized as physical creatures but also having supernatural powers. Some European mountaineers dismissed footprints and sightings, attributing them to bears or apes, but others acknowledged a new species. The term "Abominable Snowman" resulted when Lt Col Charles Howard-Bury (1881–1963) mistranslated "*metoh*," "man-bear," as "filthy." The term spread but was replaced by the more accurate "yeti," used by indigenous people for the creatures.

In the late 1920s and early 1930s, North America read about its own wild humanoid, named sasquatch by John W. Burns ("Introducing B.C.'s Hairy Giants," *Maclean's*, 1 April 1929, 61–2), based on stories from his students on the Chehalis Indian Reservation in British Columbia. Again, the stories joined the natural with the fantastic and were quite diverse; Burns combined and streamlined the stories to tell of one hidden species. At first taken as a joke, the story spread and attracted sasquatch seekers, as well as reports of current sightings. In 1958, a California logger, Jerry Crew, connected some thefts and disturbances at the work site to unnaturally large footprints, and people began to write about Big Foot (two words). Later that year in the *Humbolt Times*, columnist Andrew Genzoli made national news out of Bigfoot (one word). Many suspected the 16-inch tracks were a hoax, yet thousands wrote to the newspaper about their own sightings. Long after What-Is-It, the hirsute wild man had come back home to California. The creature has been sighted across Canada and the US, including in Arizona, Pennsylvania, Montana, and Oregon; sometimes it has local names, such as the skunk ape in Florida. It has become a fixture of popular culture, appearing in advertising for products from beef jerky to cameras, in video games and as remote-control **robot** dolls, and even as the mascot for the 2010 Winter Olympics in Vancouver.

Films and Television

Both documentaries and fictional movies about the yeti, sasquatch, and bigfoot abound. The division is sometimes obscured, with some "factual" films now acknowledged as hoaxes, such as *The Legend of Bigfoot* by Ivan Marks (1976), and fictional films that examine (often poking fun at) actual bigfoot fans, such as *They Call Him Sasquatch* (David H. Venghaus, Jr, 2003). This ambiguity characterizes *The Legend of Boggy Creek*, independently directed and produced by Charles B. Pierce in 1972, concerning the Fouke Monster, a hairy and foul-smelling ape-man in Arkansas. Like *The **Blair Witch** Project* (Daniel Myrick and Eduardo Sánchez, 1999), the movie is a mockumentary, ostensibly depicting people seeking the truth about the monster, but actually a horror film in which, for instance, a kitten is scared to death by it. After the success of *Boggy Creek*, the furry hominid became a staple of horror films.

Two films about the yeti that precede *Boggy Creek* show these films' wide range of quality. *Man Beast*, a 1956 film set in the Himalayas (Jerry Warren), is padded with stock footage and tells a sensationalistic story of miscegenation and violence. Val Guest's 1957 film, *The Abominable Snowman of the Himalayas*, from Hammer Films, benefits from a script by British science-fiction author and playwright Nigel Kneale (1922–2006).

Films about furry wild men fall into three broad categories: pure horror, in which the creature is a threat to be destroyed; sympathetic films, in which the real monsters are the human beings who want to kill or trap the creature; and enigmatic films, in which the violence of the creature may be merely defensive or may not. Examples of the first category include *Snowbeast* (Herb Wallerstein, 1977), in which a white-furred man-beast terrorizes a Colorado ski resort; *Yeti: Curse of the Snow Demon*, a 2008 TV movie directed by Paul Ziller in which plane-crash survivors in the Himalayas face both the monster and a decision whether to eat the crash victims or starve; *Suburban Sasquatch*, an extremely low-budget film from 2004 (Dave Wascavage); *Abominable*, made for TV in 2006 (Ryan Schifrin); the bloody and humorless *Blood Beast of Monster Mountain* (Massey Cramer, 1976); and *Bigfoot at Holler Creek Canyon* (John Poague, 2005). *Teenagers Battle the Thing* (Dave Flocker), a 1976 expanded video release of *Curse of Bigfoot* (1972), associated the creature with Native Americans in an unusually negative way: a horrible bigfoot mummy protecting a Native-American burial ground must be destroyed by fire.

A change in public attitudes towards this creature shows in the contrast between the first *Boggy Creek*, a pure horror film, and its 1977 sequel, *Return to Boggy Creek* (Tom Moore), in which the creature rescues a woman lost in the woods. The most famous movie sympathetic to bigfoot is *Harry and the Hendersons* (William Dear), a 1987 film starring John Lithgow about a family that befriends the eponymous hairy Harry. These hunted hominids are also aided by humans in other films, often a child: the young girl in Bob Keen's 1995 TV movie *To Catch a Yeti*, starring Meat Loaf; the eleven-year-old boy rescued from a grizzly bear by a sasquatch in *Bigfoot: The Unforgettable Encounter* (Corey Michael Eubanks, 1995); the lost children helped by a bigfoot couple in Disney's 1987 made-for-TV *Bigfoot* (Danny Huston); and the teenager in *Cry Wilderness* (Jay Schlossberg-Cohen, 1987) who shares a Coca Cola with an ape-man. Two films by Art Comancho, *Little Bigfoot* (1997) and *Little Bigfoot 2: The Journey Home* (1997), create sympathy for young sasquatches. In *The Revenge of Bigfoot* (Harry Thomason,

1979, AKA *Rufus J. Pickle and the Indian*), set in Texas, the creature keeps a bigot from driving a Native American off his land.

One of the more ambiguous films, *The Snow Creature* (W. Lee Wilder, 1954) depicts a yeti who first steals the wife of a botanist, but then is taken captive, evoking our sympathy; when it escapes in Los Angeles, however, it appears to be a pure threat. Its passage into the USA is delayed by a debate over whether it is human or a zoo animal. In *Clawed* (AKA *The Unknown*, Karl Kozak, 2005), the creature's violence is probably defensive; the film also contains two elements common in sympathetic bigfoot films: the appalling, drunken rednecks who hunt it and a heroic Native American character (often played by a European American) who understands it due to tribal lore. In *Sasquatch Hunters* (Fred Tepper, 2005), the species may just be defending its burial grounds, but it probably is inherently hostile. *Stomp! Shout! Scream!* (Jay Edwards, 2005), an homage to and parody of 1950s teen movies, treats the Skunk Ape as a monster but also eulogizes it as the embodiment of nature's force.

Whether because the culture associates sexuality with our animal side or because sex and violence often go together in films, some films depict this creature as libidinously desirous of humans, including the soft-core pornographic *Search for the Beast* (R.G. Arledge, 1997). *Ape Canyon* (Jon Olsen, 2002), named for a real place in the Pacific Northwest, depicts a dangerous love triangle of a truck-stop waitress, the lustful bigfoot she falls in love with, and her jealous husband. This association is taken to the meta-level in *Among Us* (Jon McBride and John Polonia, 2004), featuring a maker of bad movies who began with a sasquatch porno film.

Television series usually treat the creature sympathetically, such as *Harry and the Hendersons*, a half-hour show based on the movie that aired from 1991 through 1993, and *Bigfoot and Wildboy*, a half-hour show from 1977–78 about a young boy raised in the forest by a sasquatch. Surprisingly, *The X-Files* had no actual sasquatch episode, although Mulder (David Duchovny) is shown watching real-life popular footage of bigfoot. "Skin and Bones," one episode of NBC's 2009 series *Fear Itself*, produced in Canada, features the **windigo**, a semi-human cannibal creature from Algonquin legend (Larry Fessenden); as in many sasquatch and bigfoot films, a Native American character understands and explains the menace.

Comic Books

Compared to the many cheap and badly done films, the hairy man-creature has done well in comic books and graphic novels. An early sympathetic treatment of the yeti appears in *Tintin in Tibet*, drawn and written by Belgian cartoonist Hergé (1958), while a recent one appears in *The Gawaii* (2009), a graphic novel by Sean Patrick O'Reilly, also made into a 3-D computer app, in which a young sasquatch, Tanu, is orphaned when his mother is shot and must face the "fearsome creature": humans. *The Big Bigfoot Book* (1996), from Mojo Press, features a wide range of stories, some outright horror and others humorous, with presentations of the creature as a mysterious nature spirit, a beleaguered lab animal, a tired and jaded celebrity, and the nemesis of Theodore Roosevelt. Robert Crumb's "Whiteman Meets Bigfoot," in the 1971 underground comic *Home Grown Funnies*, depicts a female "yetti" as a freely sexual creature who lives "happily ever after" with the now-liberated Whiteman.

Both knowledgeable and inventive, *Proof*—an Image comic written by Alex Grecian and drawn by Riley Rossmo, begun in 2007—features a bigfoot named John Prufrock who appears mostly human and works for a secret government organization that protects him and other cryptozoological creatures (see **Cryptid**). The comic also features Mi-Chen Po, a yeti, and explores Proof's ancestry, which it connects to the real nineteenth-century sideshow Hairy Lady, Julia Pastrana (1834–60), revealed here as a bigfoot.

Fiction

Though less than films, some novels about the sasquatch straddle the line between fiction and non-fiction. For instance, in *Clan of Cain: The Genesis of Bigfoot* (2001), Shane Lester uses fiction to present the theory that bigfoot is actually the Biblical Cain, cursed for fratricide with immortality and a beastly appearance; this view, based in a meeting with the creature in Tennessee in 1835 by David Patten, is an obscure Mormon belief, often tied to the curse of Ham against all African-Americans. *The Great Sasquatch Controversy* by Joe H. Beelart (1999) includes both a novel—in which a genuine bigfoot corpse is the object of competitive bidding by museums, the tabloid press, Native Americans, loggers, a secret government organization, and cryptozoologists—and non-fiction articles by Ray Crowe, director of the Western Bigfoot Society. Lisa A. Shiel writes both non-fiction, including *Backyard Bigfoot: The True Story of Stick Signs, UFOs, and the Sasquatch* (2006), and *The Hunt for Bigfoot* (2011), a novel featuring a community of the creatures in the Michigan woods, protected by an ancient race with advanced technology. Also, authors developing the new genre called cryptofiction, such as Douglas Tanner, Lee Murphy, and Tabitca Cope, all have novels concerning hairy hominids (see **Cryptid**).

Much of the fiction about the furry man-beast is genre horror. Anthony Giangregorio's 2011 novel *Clan of the Bigfoot* is set in the Adirondack National Forest; in the introduction he identifies bigfoot as a common monster in film, but one offering "a fresh and powerful new sub-genre" for horror fiction (1). He also edited *Tales of Bigfoot* and has a short story in *Bigfoot Tales*, edited by Mark Christopher—all three books from specialty-press horror publishers in 2011. Some of the short stories are horror and some humor; the creature is sometimes seen as sympathetic but always as monstrous and intimidating. Eric S. Brown's *Bigfoot War* (2010) pits a group of the creatures against the small town of Babble Creek, North Carolina, including a protagonist whose entire family was killed 15 years before by the hairy—and strong, intelligent, and violent—hominids. The series continues with *Dead in the Woods* and *Food Chain* (both 2011). Clint Romag's "Sasquatch Encounter" novels—*The Unleashing* (2006), *The Ape Cave Horror* (2007), and *The Fury of Sasquatch* (2009)—depict the creatures as violently threatening, yet living in groups and possessing human emotions.

Dark Woods, by Jay C Kumar (2004), more thriller than horror, concerns a hunter who has wounded a violent bigfoot and goes back to end its pain; the descriptions of the forest and hunting are lush, and some scenes present the bigfoot's point of view. Another thriller, *Esua*, by Phillip Kerr (1998), features a search for the yeti, here seen as an evolutionary missing link, and the search's conflict with international politics; the inhospitable Himalayan climate adds complications. In Richard Hoyt's *Bigfoot* (1995), private detective John Denson and his partner Willie Prettybird encounter a murder mystery while helping a Russian scientist search for sasquatch near Mount St Helens. *Sasquatch* by Roland Smith (1999) is a young-adult mystery/suspense novel in which young Dylan accompanies his father on a bigfoot-tracking expedition.

Some fiction uses the figure of the hairy man-beast to examine what it means to be human and to critique modern industrialized society, either seriously or humorously. Lynn David Hebert's 2001 story *Bigfoot Autumn*, set in the Green Mountains of Vermont, features a society of the creatures beset by humans and recruiting a human advisor to help them. The protagonist of Paul Doyle's 1992 story, *Nokia, Bride of Bigfoot*, seeking peace in the forests of the Pacific Northwest, discovers both bigfoot and a more authentic existence for herself. In sharp contrast to the generic Native Americans in too many films, *Monkey Dreams*, a prize-winning 2002 novel by Eden Robinson, accurately and evocatively presents life in the Haisla community of Kitamaat, British Columbia; this coming-of-age story blends the natural and supernatural worlds, including visions of bigfoot.

Donations to Clarity, a 2011 novel by Noah Baird, and *Bigfoot Dreams*, from Francine Prose in 1998, both take a satirical approach. In the former, three slackers want to make money guiding fake bigfoot tours, but the one in the Chewbacca costume is kidnapped by a lovesick real bigfoot. *Bigfoot Dreams*, called "ur-chicklit" by one reviewer, accompanies Vera, a tabloid writer, in her search for meaning that seems as elusive as bigfoot. Our culture is also lampooned in three odd and humorous illustrated books by Graham Roumieu: *In Me Own Word: The Autobiography of Bigfoot* (2003), *Me Write Book: The Bigfoot Memoir* (2005), and *Bigfoot: I Not Dead* (2008). The protagonist goes from a murderous savage to a celebrity, then to post-celebrity life, making money as a spirit guide or on TV game shows.

Bernadette Bosky

References and Suggested Reading

Alley, J. Robert. *Raincoast Sasquatch: The Bigfoot/Sasquatch Records of Southeast Alaska, Coastal British Columbia and Northwest Washington from Puget Sound to Yakutat*. Surrey, BC: Hancock House Publishers Ltd, 2003.

Bigfoot Encounters. "Bigfoot-Sasquatch Legends: Native American and First Nation Canadian Legends, Folklore and Stories." Accessed 21 June 2012. <http://www.bigfootencounters.com/legends.htm>.

Buhs, Joshua Blu. *Bigfoot: The Life and Times of a Legend*. Chicago: University of Chicago Press, 2009.

Forth, Gregory. *Images of the Wildman in Southeast Asia: An Anthropological Perspective*. New York and Oxford: Routledge, 2008.

Giangregorio, Anthony. *Clan of the Bigfoot*. N.p.: Living Dead Press, 2011.

Oregon Bigfoot Library, The. Accessed 21 June 2012. <http://www.oregonbigfoot.com/books.php>.

Paghat the Ratgirl. *"Horror of Sasquatch: Cinematic Bigfoots."* Accessed 21 June 2012. <http://www.weirdwildrealm.com/f-sasquatch.html>.

Shackley, Myra. *Still Living? Yeti, Sasquatch, and the Neanderthal Enigma*. New York: Thames & Hudson, 1983.

BIRDS, GIANT

Legendary birds of a gigantic size make their appearance in the literature and oral tradition of many cultures and include the Indian Garuda, the Persian Simorgh, and the Arabic Anqa (*al-'anqâ'*) and Roc (*al-rukhkh*).

The Indian Garuda is imagined as a gigantic winged creature with a human body and an eagle's head. In Hindu mythology, it serves as the mount of the God Vishnu. The Garuda is mentioned in the ancient Indian epic *Mahabharata* and unspecified monstrous birds "of the race of Garuda" make an appearance in later folkloric sources. The *Kathasaritsagara* (Ocean of the Streams of Stories) compiled by Somadeva in the latter half of the eleventh century CE has several stories in which these birds appear. For instance, in the "Story of Udayana, King of

Vatsa," Mrigâvatî was taking a bath in a tank filled with a liquid that looked like blood, when the bird "suddenly pounced upon her and carried her off, thinking she was raw flesh" (98). In the "Story of Rûpinikâ," the Brahman Lohanjangha is trapped in an elephant's carcass that is carried away by the bird; when the bird "tore open the elephant's hide with its claws and, seeing that there was a man inside it, fled away" (142). While the texts do not specify the birds' characteristics, they are clearly of gigantic size, and the motif of the Garuda carrying a large and heavy load links it with other giant birds.

The Simorgh belongs to ancient Iranian tradition. It is prominently mentioned in the Persian national epic, Ferdowsi's *Shahnameh* (The Book of Kings), compiled around the turn of the first millennium CE Here it saves the infant Zal, the son of Sam, who had been abandoned in the wilderness because, although his face was extremely beautiful, his hair was completely white. At first, the bird takes Zal to her nest in the Alborz mountains of northern Iran to feed him to her chicks. But then she pities him and raises him until he grows up. In the numerous images illustrating this story in Persian manuscript tradition, the Simorgh is usually depicted with colorful plumage and a long tail. The Simorgh's feathers possess special benevolent qualities that link them to the qualities of the Vârengana bird mentioned in the *Zend-Avesta*, the sacred scripture of Zoroastrianism: "If a man holds a bone of that strong bird, or a feather of that strong bird, no one can smite or turn to flight that fortunate man. The feather of that bird of birds brings him help; it brings unto him the homage of men, it maintains in him his glory" (Darmesteter, 241). In the *Shahname*, Zal calls the Simorgh for help by burning her feather; when the Simorgh appears, she advises Zal how to heal his wife after their son Rostam has been cut from her belly; as a last step, he should strike her body with the Simorgh's feather "since its shadow is auspicious" (105). In a similar manner, Rostam is healed after being mortally wounded by Esfandiyar (410).

The Anqa, a bird of ancient Arabic tradition, is regarded as equivalent to the **phoenix**. It is mentioned in various works of Arabic literature, such as al-Qazwini's thirteenth-century *Book of the Wonders of Creation* or al-Damiri's fifteenth-century encyclopedia, *Hayat al-hayawan* (The Life of Animals). An early narrative about the Anqa is contained in al-Tha'labi's eleventh-century *The Lives of the Prophets*. The author here tells a tale in which the bird challenges Solomon by claiming that the former can circumvent the fate of two newborn babies that are predestined to come together. The bird is described with the following words: "She was as large as a camel, but her face was human, and her hands were human, and her breasts were the breasts of a woman, and her fingers likewise" (498). After challenging Solomon's insight into the future, the bird takes the girl to a mountain "high in the sky, in the midst of an island far within the sea. On the island was a tree, so tall that no bird could reach its branches except by the most arduous flight. It had more than a thousand mighty branches—each one like the greatest of all the trees on earth—with many leaves" (498). There, the Anqa builds a nest and raises the girl. When the girl has grown up, the boy who is predestined to meet her happens to come to the island. Noticing her up on the tree, but not knowing how to get there, he hides inside the belly of a dead horse that the girl has the bird lift up to the nest. Once the bird has left, the two youngsters join, as had been predicted, and Solomon's prophecy is fulfilled. Like other gigantic birds, the Anqa is able to transport large loads and traverse large distances to otherwise inaccessible places. The motif mentioned here of hiding oneself inside the carcass or hide of an animal in order to be transported by the gigantic bird to a place that would otherwise be unreachable becomes a stock motif of later narrative lore linked with other gigantic birds, in particular the Roc.

While in popular tradition combining characteristics of the aforementioned legendary birds, the Roc to some extent relates to a physically existing species of gigantic birds, the Aepyornis maximus or "elephant birds" of the islands south of Madagascar, which have been extinct since the seventeenth century. In his travelogue, the Venetian merchant Marco Polo (1254–1324) compares the Roc to the European Gryphon (see **Griffin**). Quoting the accounts of eye-witnesses, Polo speaks of a bird whose shape was that of an eagle of enormous size, "so big in fact that its wings covered an extent of 30 paces, and its quills were 12 paces long, and thick in proportion. And it is so strong that it will seize an elephant in its talons and carry him high into the air, and drop him so that he is smashed to pieces; having so killed him the bird gryphon swoops down on him and eats him at leisure" (412). Similar accounts are contained in various works of medieval Arabic literature. The Iranian captain Buzurg ibn Shahriyar of Ramhormoz, who compiled his collection of sailors' yarns, *The Book of the Wonders of India*, in the tenth century, quotes tales of a bird so large that it could seize an elephant (tale number 127); the feather veins of this bird could be used for containing water like a pottery vessel (tale number 34); and shipwrecked merchants would attach themselves to the bird's feet so that it could carry them away from the island where they were stranded (tale number 8).

The Roc makes its best-known appearance in the tales of Sindbad the seafaring merchant in the *Arabian Nights* (see **Arabian Nights, Monsters In The**). During his second journey, Sindbad finds the bird's huge egg. He escapes from the island by binding himself to the bird's leg, and is transported to a mountain next to a valley filled with diamonds. He remembers the practice of the local people of depositing a bloody animal carcass that the bird would carry to the valley, where the diamonds would stick to the carcass and could later be collected. The bird is so enormous that Sindbad later learns of it preying upon a rhinoceros. On his fifth journey, Sindbad's companions destroy a Roc's egg. When the returning parents witness the damage, they sink the company's ship by throwing large boulders, and only Sindbad is saved. "'Abd al-Rahman the Maghribi and the rukh" tells a similar tale, while adding the motif that whoever eats from the meat of a Roc will regain his youth and the gray hair in his beard will turn black again. The motif of a man hiding inside a carcass so as to be carried by the bird onto an otherwise inaccessible mountain is again mentioned in the *Arabian Nights*' tale of Hasan of Basra.

In film, a double-headed Roc features spectacularly in the 1958 fantasy movie *The Seventh Voyage of Sinbad*, conceptualized, animated, and produced by Ray Harryhausen. Drawing on motifs from Sindbad's second and fifth voyages, the shipwrecked party reaches the Roc's nest just as a giant hatchling emerges from the egg. When some of the men kill the bird to eat it, the infuriated parents return and attack them. A fantastic Roc that is much removed from its original model features in the 2003 animated film *Sinbad: Legend of the Seven Seas*. Here, the Roc, by the order of Eris, the Greek Goddess of Chaos, sends temperatures freezing; only after Sinbad has killed the bird can the party continue.

Ulrich Marzolph

References and Suggested Reading

Bies, Werner. "Phönix." In *Enzyklopädie des Märchens*, 1021–35. Vol. 10. Berlin and New York: De Gruyter, 2002. col.s.

Buzurg ibn Shahriyar, Captain, of Ramhormuz. *The Book of the Wonders of India: Mainland, Sea and Islands*. Translated by G.S.P. Freeman-Grenville. London and The Hague: East-West Publications, 1981.

Chauvin, Victor. *Bibliographie des ouvrages arabes ou relatifs aux arabes publiés dans L'Europe chrétienne de 1810 à 1885*. Vol. 7. Liège: H. Vaillant Carmanne, 1903.

Darmesteter, James, trans. *The Zend-Avesta*. Vol. 2. Oxford: Clarendon Press, 1883.

De Gubernatis, Angelo. *Zoological Mythology or the Legends of Animals*. Vol. 2. London: Trübner & Co., 1872.

Ferdowsi, Abolqasem. *Shahnameh: The Persian Book of Kings*. Translated by Dick Davis. New York: Viking, 2006.

Lyons, Malcolm S., and Ursula Lyons, trans. *The Arabian Nights: Tales of 1001 Nights*. 3 vols. London: Penguin, 2008.

Marzolph, Ulrich. "al-Rukhkh." In *Encyclopedia of Islam*, 595. Vol. 8. Leiden: Brill, 1994.

Polo, Marco, and Rustichello of Pisa. *The Travels of Marco Polo*. Edited by Henri Yule and Henri Cordier. Vol. 2. 1920. Reprint, New York: Dover, 1993.

Somadeva. *The Ocean of Story, Being C.H. Tawney's Translation of Somdeva's Kathâ Sarit Sâgara*. Edited by Norman M. Penzer. Vol. 1. 2nd edn. 1923. Reprint, Delhi: Motilal Banarsidass, 1968.

Tha'labî, Abû Ishâq Ahmad Ibn Muhammad Ibn Ibrâhîm al-. *"Arâ'is al-majâlis fî qisas al-anbiyâ"* or *"Lives of the Prophets."* Translated by William M. Brinner. Leiden: Brill, 2002.

BLACK RIDER—*see* Tolkien, Monsters In

BLAIR WITCH

The Blair **Witch** is the subject of the 1999 horror film *The Blair Witch Project* (directed by Daniel Myrick and Eduardo Sánchez), its companion website, a simulated documentary also directed by Myrick and Sánchez (*Curse of the Blair Witch*), a sequel released in 2000 (*Book of Shadows: Blair Witch 2*, directed by Joe Berlinger), and a host of derivative works. A character purpose-built for the film by its makers, the Blair Witch occurs as both an amalgam of folkloric traditions and an index of the persuasive force of well-wrought folklore.

According to legends recounted in those materials released in 1999, the Blair Witch is the specter of Elly Kedward, convicted of witchcraft in February 1785 and left to die from exposure by the citizens of Blair Township. Credited with the disappearance of her young accusers and a number of additional children during the following winter, Kedward ostensibly haunts the Black Hills Forest near Burkittsville, Maryland (a town founded on the site of the abandoned Blair) and may manifest in response to intrusions. The same materials suggest that the Blair Witch appears as an old woman covered in coarse equine hair, although accounts also indicate that she may take other unearthly forms. While no photographs or video recordings of the witch exist in the milieu of the film, folklore implies that she floats above the ground and may be credited with several paranormal capabilities: the power of suggestion, the capacity to entrance and possibly possess her prey, the ability to cause spatial disorientation, the ability to imitate the voices of her victims, the capacity to travel and transport objects through solid matter, and the ability to materialize in order to menace or harm her quarry. Small cairns and totems consisting of sticks lashed together symbolize the presence or passage of the otherwise unseen witch. *The Blair Witch Project* itself, offered as footage discovered during an anthropological dig in the forest, may also be taken as confirmation of the existence of the witch.

Some difficulty attends discussion of *The Blair Witch Project*, as the film and its supplements call into question the existence of their own antagonist. The film is, in effect, a fabrication presented as an accumulation of facts that might still be understood as fiction. The filmmakers, Daniel Myrick and Eduardo Sánchez, participate in the tradition of found footage, offering the film as a reconstruction of events spanning 20–28 October 1994, when three students from Montgomery College (Heather Donahue, Joshua Leonard, and Michael Williams) entered the woods to shoot a documentary about the witch. The first days of filming describe forays into Burkittsville and the fringes of the Black Hills Forest, but the trio becomes lost on the third day and increasingly disoriented thereafter. Leonard eventually disappears, Donahue and Williams set out to find him, and their search culminates in the discovery of an abandoned house, where the footage ends in a manner that recalls an earlier description of the methods of Rustin Parr, a hermit who murdered several children in 1940–41 at the behest of an "old lady ghost." The camera carried by Williams inexplicably drops to the floor of the cellar, and the camera carried by Donahue falls to the ground as well—after she is apparently waylaid by an unseen assailant—and fixes on Williams, who is standing alone in the corner. The ambiguous conclusion, as supported by the dubious folklore recounted by the residents of Burkittsville and the uncertain discoveries made by the students, offers only circumstantial support for the substantiality of the witch.

The Blair Witch Project website, a pioneering promotional supplement that enriches the mythology of the film, supplies contextual information that substantiates reports of the disappearance and thereby implies the existence of the witch: a detailed timeline that spans over 200 years, documents and newspaper clippings chronicling her infamous history, pictures of the film canisters and audiotape cases left behind by the students, and the like. All of this corroborating evidence, however, is fabricated. A simulated documentary, *Curse of the Blair Witch*, further develops the illusion of authenticity. It includes interviews with a Burkittsville historian, the professor who authorized Donahue's thesis proposal, and a folklorist who considers the events of 1994 to be nothing more than a hoax. Most of the personalities featured, however, are actors portraying characters, and the directors are none other than the creators of *The Blair Witch Project* itself. *Book of Shadows*, the sequel to the film, makes similarly double-edged claims. It purports to be "a fictionalized re-enactment of events" that followed the release of the original and self-reflexively refers to the cultural fascination with its authenticity. The narrative describes the uncanny tribulations that beset a tour group during and after a visit to the site of Rustin Parr's cabin, and while it hints at the involvement of the witch (four members of the party, inspired by suggestive hallucinations that recall mythological particulars from *The Blair Witch Project*, commit murder, and the fifth appears to be possessed by the witch herself), *Book of Shadows* only deepens the associated folklore cursorily and supports claims to legitimacy perfunctorily.

Admissions by the filmmakers—and the survival of Donahue, Leonard, and Williams, all recognized as actors under their real names and credited with further film and television work—belies the central conceit of *The Blair Witch Project*. Nevertheless, despite definitive evidence of the falsity of the film, claims to authenticity (and corresponding refutations) persist. The deft manipulation of folkloric devices and expectations in the depiction of the witch effectively improves on the truth.

William H. Wandless

References and Suggested Reading

Higley, Sarah L., and Jeffrey Andrew Weinstock, eds. *The Nothing That Is: Millennial Cinema and the Blair Witch Controversies*. Detroit: Wayne State University Press, 2004.

BLAST-ENDED SKREWT—*see* Harry Potter, Monsters In

BLEMMYAE—*see* Mutant and Freak; Races, Monstrous

BLOB, THE

The Blob, a low-budget independent 1958 American sci-fi/horror film directed by Irvin Yeaworth, tells the story of a gelatinous alien life form that arrives on Earth in a meteor and invades a small town (see **Extraterrestrial**). The movie, though not a critical hit, resonated with its target audience of teenagers, becoming a cult favorite. Its lasting appeal has been attributed partly to its small-town atmosphere, partly to its savvy use of teenagers as the heroes, but mainly to its unique monster.

Teenager Steve Andrews (a not-yet-famous Steve McQueen) and his girlfriend Jane Martin (Aneta Corseaut) see a shooting star. An old man finds the meteorite and breaks it open, whereupon a small glob of transparent goo emerges and envelops the old man's hand. Steve and Jane bring the old man to the local doctor's office but the goo spreads and consumes the old man, the nurse, and the doctor. As it digests the humans, the creature grows larger and turns blood red. Steve alerts the authorities, but with typical 1950s adult mistrust of teenagers, they dismiss his concern. Meanwhile, the Blob kills several locals before Steve and Jane find it in a grocery store. When they barricade themselves in the walk-in refrigerator, the creature begins to squeeze under the door but inexplicably retreats. While Steve again tries to warn the police, the Blob, in the movie's most famous scene, enters the local movie theater and oozes through the projection booth into the seating area. The mob of screaming people racing from the theater finally convinces the town of the danger, but in the chaos several people, including Steve and Jane, become trapped in the nearby diner. The Blob, now immense, engulfs the diner but Steve, realizing that the creature withdraws from cold, advises the police (via payphone) to freeze it, which they do. In the final scene, a military jet transports the Blob to the North Pole, but the movie's "The End" morphs into a question mark, suggesting that the Blob may return.

The Blob, which became a sleeper hit, introduced an entirely different type of creature to a 1950s audience accustomed to humanoid aliens, **robots**, and radiation-mutated insects (see **Animals, Monstrous**). Jack H. Harris, the film's producer, reportedly said of his project: "There's got to be a new and unique type of monster, one that's never been done before" (Shank 14). The movie's initial title was *The Molten Meteor*; the working screenplay title became *The Molten Monster*, but the production was also variously called *The Night of the Creeping Dread* and *The Glob That Girdled the Globe*. During filming, Harris suggested *The Blob*, though the shooting script refers to the creature only as "the mass" and no one in the movie ever actually calls it "the Blob" (Murdico 19).

The Blob, created by the special effects team at the movie's production company, Valley Forge Films, was made from two gallons of liquid silicone dyed red. Because silicone flows slowly, time-lapse photography sped up the creature's movements (Shank 59). Nearly all shots featuring the Blob were done in miniature: the silicone was easier to control in small amounts and the tiny sets made the Blob seem increasingly huge. Occasionally a modified weather balloon covered with a layer of the liquid silicone stood in for the creature, allowing the Blob to appear as though it were pulsing with life.

Part of what makes the creature so effective, besides its amorphous appearance, is the lack of specific information about its origins and motivation. The movie never explains where the creature came from or why it feeds on humans. The Blob has no personality—no human traits whatsoever; "it is merely a mass of unexplained protoplasm driven to ingest living creatures, and does so in a very simple fashion: it merely absorbs them into its own body" (Warren 119). The creeping red menace has sometimes been interpreted as an allegory of communism (Murdico 29), but no proof exists that the screenwriter or director intended such a reading.

The Blob has had a lasting impact on popular culture. Its title song, "Beware of the Blob," co-written by Burt Bacharach, was a major hit, spending three weeks on Billboard's Top 40. In the 1972 movie sequel *Beware! The Blob* (also called *Son of the Blob*, directed by Larry Hagman), a scientist brings home a piece of the original Blob from the Arctic, only to have his wife accidentally thaw it. The 1988 remake *The Blob* (directed by Chuck Russell) explains the Blob as a government weapons project but otherwise adheres closely to the original's narrative. *The Blob*'s popularity also resulted in various parodies including *The Stuff* (1985), featuring an amorphous substance taking over human bodies; a scene in *Ghostbusters II* (1989), in which supernatural slime squeezes through a ventilator; *Blobermouth* (1991), which re-dubbed the original film with comic dialogue; and *The Simpsons* "Treehouse of Horror XVII" episode "Married to the Blob" (2006), in which Homer eats alien goo and turns into a ravenous blob.

Additionally, many television shows and movies have paid homage to *The Blob* with verbal or visual references. An episode of *M*A*S*H* anachronistically mentions the film (#2.1, 1974). Seinfeld (#2.1, 1991) and *Red Dwarf* (#4.1, 1991), among others, also reference *The Blob*. Scenes from *The Blob* appear in the background of *Grease* (1978) and *Alien Trespass* (2009). "The Blob" has been an answer on various game shows, and several video games feature intentionally Blob-like obstacles. The amorphous creature also influenced "B.O.B.," the blue blob in *Monsters vs. Aliens* (Rob Letterman and Conrad Vernon, 2009), and Marvel Comics' super-villain "The Blob," whose pliable skin and formidable girth render him nearly invulnerable. But the most enduring legacy of *The Blob* is the annual "BlobFest," held at the Colonial Theater in Phoenixville, PA, where much of the original movie was shot. Although the BlobFest includes movie screenings and costume contests, the highlight of the festival is the re-enactment of the scene in which the audience runs screaming from the theater.

D. Felton

References and Suggested Reading

Murdico, Suzanne J. *Meet the Blob (Famous Movie Monsters)*. New York: The Rosen Publishing Group, Inc., 2005.

Shank, Wes. *From Silicone to the Silver Screen: Memoirs of The Blob* (1958). 2nd edn. Bryn Mawr, PA: Wes Shank, 2009.

Viera, Mark A. *Hollywood Horror from Gothic to Cosmic*. New York: Harry N. Abrams, Incorporated, 2003.

Warren, Bill. *Keep Watching the Skies! American Science Fiction Movies of the Fifties, The 21st Century Edition*. Jefferson, NC and London: McFarland & Company, Inc., 2010.

BODY PARTS

Bodily deformity and disfigurement are basic themes in depictions of monsters, and the disconnection of the body from itself is a fitting variation. Monstrous body parts are found in the theme of body divided, in the horror of decapitation, dismemberment and amputation, in disgust at invasion of the body by the body parts of others, and in the terror at loss of control over one's own body.

Dismemberment and the Magic of the Body

Heads and limbs can be severed, but the power of the head and body remain even in dismemberment. Despite being decapitated, the **gorgon Medusa**'s head retains its power to petrify those who look upon it. In Perseus's hands, the monster's head becomes a weapon used to defeat foes both human and monstrous. Also in Greek myth, Orpheus's head continues singing after it is decapitated; in the medieval Welsh *Mabinogion*, Bran the Blessed's head holds talismanic power; in the medieval Norse *Poetic Edda* and *The Völsunga Saga*, the god Mimir's head is resurrected as a source of wisdom by Odin; in Hindu myth, Shiva enshrines the leonine head of the monster Kirtimukha as guardian of thresholds; and the Malaysian spirit called the Penanggalan is the head of a woman that detaches from her body at night, trailing entrails to suck the blood of babies and pregnant women (see **Ghost**).

Other monsters simply fight on after decapitation. The **hydra** grows new heads to replace those lost in battle. Magic allows the Green Knight of the late fourteenth-century *Sir Gawain and the Green Knight* to survive decapitation, and headless ghosts and spirits like the Irish dullahan menace travelers. The **Headless Horseman** of Washington Irving's (1820) "The Legend of Sleepy Hollow" plays on this tradition, embodying it in particular in film adaptations like Disney's animated rendering (Clyde Geronimi and Jack Kinney, 1949) and Tim Burton's *Sleepy Hollow* (1999), which depict the horseman as a genuine ghost.

Film treatments of the severed head with independent thought and often malicious

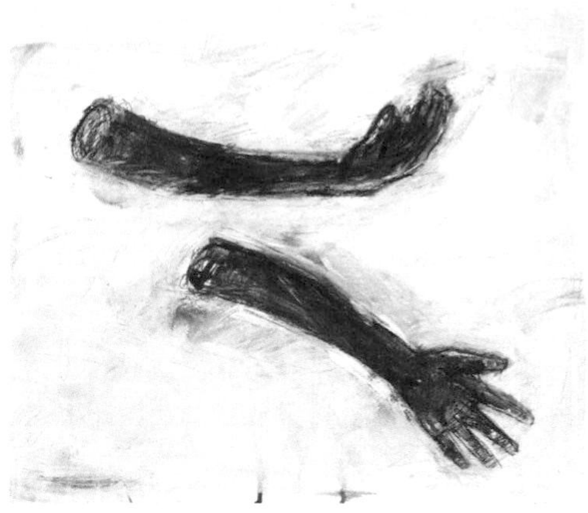

Fig. 4 ***Arms* by Anki King**

will include Joseph Green's *The Brain that Wouldn't Die* (1962), a tale of a scientist who keeps the head of his former lover alive as he searches for a woman to kill and use as a replacement body. In Freddie Francis's *The Skull* (1965), adapted from Robert Bloch's "The Skull of the Marquis De Sade" (1965), the skull of the Marquis De Sade drives men to madness and murder. Stuart Gordon's cult horror film, *Re-Animator* (1985), inspired by H.P. Lovecraft's 1922 "Herbert West—Reanimator" serialized short story, uses the separated head and body of Herbert West's rival Dr Carl Hill for gory and comedic effect (see **Lovecraft, Monsters In**). Lovecraft's writings included other, more effective, uses of body parts, of which his 1930 "Whisperer in Darkness" is a particularly striking example. The tale includes the puppet-like animation of a man's face and hands by a race of interstellar beings (the "Mi-Go," or "Fungi from Yuggoth"). The same tale includes disembodied brains held in storage capsules for travel through space, a Lovecraftian version of the "brain in a jar" convention.

Other dismembered body parts contain power as well. Medieval Europeans made the collection of body parts, in the form of saints' relics, an ordinary if gruesome part of everyday life. The hand of glory, a candle made from the real hand of an executed murderer, also had a place in medieval and early modern magical tradition. Freud did not overlook the severed part in his 1919 discussion of the uncanny, including severed limbs, heads, and hands among his examples of anxieties and fears that are revealed—and often suppressed—when the familiar is made alien. In the case of severed limbs, the sense of the uncanny is further associated in Freud's view with fear of castration and, by extension, of emasculation. In fiction, W.W. Jacobs's "The Monkey's Paw" (1902) includes a wish-granting artifact that turns wishes to monstrous ends. W.F. Harvey's "The Beast with Five Fingers" (1919) presents an unusually commonsensical response to a killer dismembered hand, as Eustace Borslover and his secretary Saunders hunt the thing in a rather matter-of-fact way. Robert Florey's 1946 film adaptation borrows the story's title, but differs substantially in its plot. Herbert L. Strocks's *The Crawling Hand* (1963) follows in this tradition, as does Oliver Stone's *The Hand* (1981), in which a comic book artist's hand is lost in an accident and goes on a killing spree (this film is based on the novel *The Lizard's Tail* [1979], by Marc Brandel). Sam Raimi's *Evil Dead II: Dead by Dawn* (1987) depicts the iconic battle of the protagonist Ash (Bruce Campbell) with his hand, which he severs, destroys, and replaces with a chainsaw. Rodman Flender's *Idle Hands* (1999) is another example. A dismembered hand named "Thing" serves as a kind of pet in the *Addams Family* TV series (originally 1964–66) and films.

It is now commonplace for dismembered parts of **zombies** to continue to menace their victims, a convention used early in Dan O'Bannon's *Return of the Living Dead* (1985) to establish that the zombies of the film were more difficult to destroy than those of George A. Romero's seminal *Night of the Living Dead* (1968). After decapitation, the body of the first zombie introduced in O'Bannon's film continues to run amok. Even after complete dismemberment, its limbs remain animated, grasping at the living. Monsters or antagonists who can detach body parts for evil purposes can also be found in TV series such as the *X-Files*, *Buffy: The Vampire Slayer*, and *Angel*.

Foreign and Traitorous Bodies

The bad transplant is an enduring trope of body horror, speaking to the disgust and alienation of having a piece of another's body transplanted into one's own. Since Robert Wiene's 1924 film *Orlacs Hände* (*The Hands of Orlac*), based on Maurice Renard's 1921 novel *Les Mains d'Orlac*, the bad transplant has been a recurring theme in horror films. *The Hands of Orlac* presents the tale of a concert pianist who loses his hands in an accident. His replacement hands, transplanted from the hands of a murderer, appear to take on a murderous will of their own. The theme has been picked up by a number of sources since, including Karl Freund's *Mad Love* (1935), Edmond T. Gréville's *The Hands of Orlac* (1960) remake, Newt Arnold's *The Hands of a Stranger* (1962), and Eric Red's *Body Parts* (1991). In each of these films, evil is located not in the mind of the killer but in the body itself, and is transferred to the new host. The invasiveness of the transplant goes beyond the physical, carrying a moral taint as well. These tales echo a real neurological disorder known as "alien hand syndrome," in which the sufferer feels that his or her hands act independently, of their own volition.

The hand is not the only monstrous transplant in film. Hong Kong directors Danny Pang Fat and Oxide Pang Chun's 2002 film *The Eye* presents the case of an eye transplant that gives the recipient the ability to see ghosts. Michael Apted's *Blink* (1994) offers a more indirect case, wherein the killer is a former admirer of the organ donor, rather than the donor herself. David Cronenberg has returned multiple times to bodily horrors, transplants, infection, and sexuality, including the parasitic transplants of *Shivers* (1975); the phallic, vampiric appendage that develops from a skin graft in *Rabid* (1977); the deformities and mutations of *The Brood* (1979), *The Fly* (1986), and *Dead Ringers* (1988); and the techno-organic horrors of *Videodrome* (1983) and *eXistenZ* (1999). As a comic take on the premise of the monstrous transplant, Homer Simpson, in the "Hell Toupée" segment of 1998's "Treehouse of Horror IX" (season 10, episode 4), develops murderous tendencies following a hair transplant from executed criminal Snake.

Finally, the sex organs have also been treated as direct, rather than simply metaphorical, monsters in horror films and marginalia. In Mitchell Lichtenstein's independent film, *Teeth* (2009), it is a toothed vagina that is monstrous, used for self-defense and revenge. Adam Fields's 2008 horror comedy *One-Eyed Monster* has an alien force possessing the penis of porn star Ron Jeremy. The severed phallus as monster was anticipated in the stage show and concert videos of the band GWAR—in particular *Phallus in Wonderland* (1992), featuring the monstrous penis of the band's lead singer, referred to as the "Cuttlefish of Cthulhu."

Richard W. Forest

References and Suggested Reading

Badley, Linda. *Film, Horror, and the Body Fantastic*. Westport: Greenwood Press, 1995.

Beard, William. *The Artist as Monster: The Cinema of David Cronenberg*. Toronto: University of Toronto Press, 2006.

Croker, Thomas Crofton. *Fairy Legends and Traditions of the South of Ireland*. London: John Murray, 1834.

Freud, Sigmund. *The Uncanny [1919]. Translated by David McClintock*. New York: Penguin Books, 2003.

Goldberg, Ruth. "Of Mad Love, Alien Hands and the Film under your Skin: Some Further Meditations on the Horror of Identity." *Kinoeye: New Perspectives on European Film 2, no. 4* (2002). <http://www.kinoeye.org/02/04/goldberg04.php>.

Lalond, Frank. "A Hand Full of Horrors: Maurice Tourneur's La Main du diable (The Devil's Hand, 1942)." *Kinoeye: New Perspectives on European Film 2, no. 4* (2002). <http://www.kinoeye.org/02/04/lafond04.php>.

Olney, Ian. "The Problem Body Politic, or 'These Hands Have a Mind All Their Own!': Figuring Disability in the Horror Film Adaptations of Renard's Les mains d'Orlac." *Literature/Film Quarterly* 34, no. 4 (2006): 294–302.

Siddique, Sophie. "Haunting Visions of the Sundelbolong: Vampire Ghosts and the Indonesian National Imaginary." In *Axes to Grind: Re-Imagining the Horrific in Visual Media and Culture*, edited by H. Wu. Special issue of *Spectator* 22, no. 2 (2002): 24–33.

BOGGART—*see* Banshee; Brownie; Goblin; Harry Potter, Monsters In; Shapeshifter

BOGGLE—*see* Goblin

BOTO—*see* Mermaid/Merman

BOWSER—*see* Video Games, Monsters In

BRAN THE BLESSED—*see* Giant

THE BRONZE HORSEMAN

The Bronze Horseman (literally, the "copper" horseman or *mednyi vsadnik*) is a supernatural character in the narrative poem of the same title by the Russian poet Aleksandr Pushkin (1799–1837). Written in

1833, a censored version of the poem was published in 1837; the full version only appeared in 1948. The poem is based on the statue of the same name, a monument opened in 1782 in St Petersburg to honor Tsar Peter the Great (1672–1725), who was known for forcibly introducing Western customs, science, and mores to Russian culture. The Bronze Horseman sits astride a rearing horse, treading a snake under its hooves. The sculpture was commissioned by the Empress Catherine the Great (1729–96) and executed by the French sculptor Étienne Maurice Falconet (1716–91). On the pedestal, the famously massive "Thunder Rock," the words "Petro prima Catharina secunda" ("Catherine the second to Peter the first) are carved in both Latin and Russian to stress Catherine's continuation of Peter's imperial achievements. The combination of Peter's iconoclastic resonance in Russian culture and his statue's imposing presence in the center of Peter's city has cast a long shadow over the Russian imagination, most famously expressed in Pushkin's poem and in the novel *Petersburg* (1913, revised version 1922) by the Symbolist author Andrei Bely.

Pushkin's poem centers on an actual event, the flood that inundated St Petersburg on 7 November 1824. The poem's protagonist, Yevgenii, a lowly clerk, has escaped drowning by perching astride a stone lion on the façade of a mansion near the Bronze Horseman. However, as the bridges linking different parts of the city have been swept away, he is unable to reach Parasha, his fiancée. The next morning he discovers that Parasha's district was devastated by the flood; her house has been washed away and both she and her mother are missing, presumably drowned. Yevgenii loses his sanity; he leaves his job, dresses in rags, and drifts through the city like a **ghost**. Late one night, passing the Bronze Horseman, Yevgenii recollects the tragedy. With a surge of uncharacteristic arrogance, he shakes his fist at the sculpture of Peter, whom he blames for the tragedy since it was Peter's decision to build the city on a flood plain. His puny rebellion changes to horror as Yevgenii imagines that the statue stirs in response to his challenge. When he flees, he hears the Bronze Horseman galloping after him. Whether the Bronze Horseman's ride is an hallucination or a supernatural phenomenon, Yevgenii's rebellion is thoroughly crushed; eventually his corpse is found on the threshold of an old hut, presumably Parasha's.

Pushkin's poem established the Bronze Horseman as a symbolic representation of Tsar Peter, the city of St Petersburg, and the uncanny reach of autocracy over the lives of ordinary people. In subsequent literature and criticism, the Horseman simultaneously represents creation and destruction, reflecting Peter's ambiguous historical legacy and the perils of St Petersburg, a city said to have been built on the corpses of forced laborers.

Aleksandr Blok depicted the Bronze Horseman in his poem "Peter" (1904, published 1907), dedicated to his friend Yevgenii Ivanov. In 1907, Ivanov wrote the essay "Horseman," which connected both the Horseman and St Petersburg with the Biblical Apocalypse. Blok's poem represents the snake carved by Falconet as the snake from the Apocalypse. The Bronze Horseman may be perceived both as one of the riders from the Book of Revelation and as the city's guardian.

Valerii Briusov depicts the statue in his poem "To the Bronze Horseman" (1906), following the First Russian Revolution of 1905. Briusov sees the monument as a representation of eternity, indifferent to battles and slaughter as it was to Yevgenii's curses. Yet the Bronze Horseman, eternally galloping on its pedestal, is the only living character in the supernatural city created by Peter. Innokentii Annenskii's poem "Petersburg" (1910) highlights the Horseman's inability to kill the snake. The doomed city is portrayed as a tragic, irredeemable error.

The most important representation of the Bronze Horseman in Russian literature after Pushkin is by Andrei Bely (the pen-name of Boris Bugaev) in his novel *Petersburg*. The plot unfolds in St Petersburg during the First Russian Revolution at the beginning of October 1905. Bely blames Peter the Great for Russia's loss of national character and the consequent destructive split between Western and Eastern influences. Peter appears in the novel as a series of doubles (**dvoiniks**; see also **Doppelganger**), one of whom is the Bronze Horseman, whose copper (not bronze) essence and green color are emphasized in the Russian original. Bely's novel pits the Horseman against two young men, both linked to anti-government terrorism, Nikolai Ableukhov and Aleksandr Dudkin. The former, like Pushkin's Yevgenii, flees from the pursuing statue; the latter is visited by it in his room. During this encounter, Dudkin hallucinates that the Horseman is melting, pouring molten metal into the young man's body. The revolutionary and the Tsar become one being, linking autocracy and terror in a disastrous unity. Dudkin loses his mind, kills the provocateur Lippanchenko, and stands astride his dead body, thus parodying Falconet's monument. Bely argues for the circularity of history: Peter the Great is the father-figure who destroys his terrorist-sons when they challenge him.

In her *Poem without a Hero* (1940–62), the poet Anna Akhmatova refers to the Bronze Horseman first as the thudding of unseen hooves (Part 1, Chapter 4, line 9). Later, in the epilogue, written in 1942 after her escape from the siege of Leningrad (as St Petersburg was called between 1924 and 1991), she explicitly describes her escape from the pursuing Horseman. This apocalyptic vision is directly related to her experience of war.

The émigré poet Josef Brodsky, in his essay *A Guide to a Renamed City* (1979), compares Falconet's monument to Lenin riding on an armored car in front of the Finnish railway station in Leningrad. Lenin's introduction of the "dictatorship of the proletariat" supposedly reversed the historical oppression of the "little man" by rulers (as enacted in the Horseman's pursuit of Yevgenii); but Brodsky's poem shows both Lenin and the Horseman to be equally heartless arbiters of others' fates.

The Bronze Horseman has galloped through Russian literature, spreading terror and riding down its victims, presaging revolution and war, from Pushkin to the present day. Falconet's sculpture continues to stand on the Neva embankment in St Petersburg.

Larisa Fialkova

References and Suggested Reading

Elsworth, J.D. "Petersburg." In *Andrey Bely: A Critical Study of the Novels*. Cambridge: Cambridge University Press, 1983.

Jakobson, Roman. *Puškin and his Sculptural Myth*. Translated and edited by John Burbank. The Hague and Paris: Mouton, 1975.

Nepomnyashchy, Catharine Theimer. "The Poet, History and the Supernatural: A Note on Puŝkin's "The Poet" and The Bronze Horseman." In *The Supernatural in Slavic and Baltic Literature: Essays in Honor of Victor Terras*, edited by Amy Mandelker and Roberta Reeder. Columbus: Slavica Publishers, 1988.

Rosenshield, Gary. "The Bronze Horseman and The Double: The Depoeticization of the Myth of Petersburg in the Young Dostoevskii." *Slavic Review* 55, no. 2 (1996): 399–428.

BROWNIE

The brownie is a type of **fairy** from Scotland and the North of England that bears kinship with hobgoblins, **pixies**, and silkies. Their folkloric origin is uncertain, although, according to some writers, they are related to Irish fairies, and therefore Gaelic in origin. Ronald McDonald Douglas suggests that, in spite of his English name, "[the brownie] is maybe of Gaelic or Cymric origin" (118). With other kinds of Northern European fairies, brownies share their humanoid appearance and diminutive size and, like the Scandinavian **trolls**, they are notable for their disheveled appearance. As William Henderson explains, brownies are akin to other fairy creatures from Britain and Europe. Brownies are dismissed by the offer of clothes and are grateful if they are given a bowl of cream, and so are the Devonshire Pixies and the Dutch Kaboutermannekin or Redcap; Silky, a female sort of brownie, would appear to travelers at night and bewilder them by her sudden apparition; like the brownie, she would also tidy houses at night, and would disappear forever if her work was not needed. Padfoot, "about the size of a small donkey, black, with shaggy hair and large eyes like saucers" (237) would also follow travelers in Yorkshire. Other fairy folks with similar qualities to brownies include Killmoulis, who haunts Scottish mills; the Wag-at-the-wa', who looks after kitchens in the Scottish Borders region; and Habetrot, who is in charge of the spinning wheel (211–43).

Although their unattractive aspect may elicit fear in human beings, brownies frequently display exceptional good nature and loyalty. Brownies are associated with the domestic sphere of the family home, where they hide during the day and only come out to perform chores and help with any unfinished business at night. Their behavior in the human world is similar, as Lamont Brown suggests, to the role they perform in the world of fairies: "It was the Brownies and **Elves** who undertook the work in Elfame [fairyland], said the believers, and from time to time they work for mortals" (68). Evans-Wentz confirms the presence of a similar belief in Ireland, as he records a description of the services performed by such fairies: "I knew of people ... who would milk in the fields about here and spill milk on the ground for the *good people*; and pots of potatoes would be put out for the *good people* at night" (34). Because of their domesticity and the propitiatory rituals attached to the belief in brownies, William Gunnyon compares them to the *Lares Familiares*, the domestic gods of ancient Rome, and emphasizes the brownie's distinctively pagan origin "by his ineradicable aversion to the Bible" (333), an aspect also confirmed by Sir Walter Scott in *Letters on Demonology and Witchcraft* (1830) (283).

Brownies do not accept payment for the services they provide, but are grateful if they are given some food or drink for the work done. When the master of the house wants to discharge the brownie, he can give him clothes. Brownies will disappear immediately when offered hoods or similar garments: significantly, J.K. Rowling follows this tradition in her treatment of house-elves in her "Harry Potter" series (books published from 1997 to 2007; see **Harry Potter, Monsters In**). In *Letters on Demonology and Witchcraft*, Scott also records that brownies are automatically discharged by the master when they are offered clothes or food, in a similar fashion to Robin Goodfellow (282), which John Milton refers to in *L'Allegro* (1645; lines 105–114): like the brownie, this "drudging **Goblin** swet[s] / To earn his creame-bowle duly set" (105–106). Gunnyon supports this point, claiming that "[i]f offered reward, especially in the shape of food, he [the Brownie] withdrew from the house in displeasure, and never appeared again. The offer of clothes also seems to have been offensive to him" (333).

Brownies are notable for their strong—if, at times, ambiguous—sense of morality: although they may work hard to support the household to which they are attached, they are also capable of revenge against those who have offended them in some way. R.M. Douglas stresses the difference between the "highly moral" brownie and the "wanton creed of Elfhame [Fairyland]," writing: "woe betide the plough-lad or the dairy-maid whose conduct is not utterly circumspect, and woe betide, too, the amorous house keeper who sets her cap at the Brownie's farmer-master. The day will not be far distant when she will be looking for another place" (119). Because of the unique moral code to which they respond, brownies may establish complex relationships with their human counterparts. What stories about brownies frequently unveil is a moral message that often revolves around a strong sense of duty and mutual loyalty. When the brownie's loyalty is not appreciated or reciprocated, the brownie will either abandon the household or seek revenge to punish those who did not behave accordingly. For this, and their frightful appearance, brownies may be regarded, in popular tradition, with a mixture of respect and suspicion.

James Hogg's novella *The Brownie of Bodsbeck* (1818) uses the superstitious fear of brownies to produce a narrative about the importance of tolerance and mutual understanding. Set in 1685, at the time of the persecutions suffered by the Covenanters, a Scottish Presbyterian sect, the story is structured around two sources of mysteries. To begin with, when food disappears from Walter of Chapelhope's farm, people fear it may be the Brownie of Bodsbeck, one of "a great hantle [handful]," Walter's wife claims. "[T]hey say they're ha'f deils ha'f fock" (6). In the meantime, Katherine, their daughter, seems to have secret meetings at night, and the village people suspect her of holding a relationship with the Brownie of Bodsbeck, or to be a **witch**. As the plot unfolds, the mysteries are gradually solved, leading to a rational, rather than supernatural, explanation of events: Walter has been giving the food to the Covenanters, who have been hiding for fear of persecution by Graham of Claverhouse and his troops. In the meantime, while Walter is arrested and taken to court in Edinburgh, his wife invites the curate to spend the night with Katherine, in the hope that she may be exorcised of her fatal attraction to the Brownie of Bodsbeck. Katherine is then rescued from the curate's attempt to assault her by the so-called Brownie, who turns out to be John Brown, the leader of the Covenanters. The story foreshadows a theme close to Hogg's better known work, *The Private Memoirs and Confessions of a Justified Sinner* (1824): a warning against the excesses of religious fanaticism and dogmatism.

In Hogg's "The Brownie of the Black Haggs" (1828), a popular tale originally published in *Blackwood's* as part of the "Shepherd's Calendar" series, the eponymous brownie is a much less benevolent creature, displaying a vengeful and manipulative nature. As in *The Brownie of Bodsbeck*, religious intolerance is a pervasive theme in "The Brownie of the Black Haggs," which centers around the evil Lady Wheelhope: any male servant known to hold religious views is given "up to the military and ... shot," and "several girls that were regular in their devotions ... [were] supposed to have got rid of by poison" (242). In spite of her cruelty, the Lady finds a particular servant who resists her authority and whose small stature and strange appearance is strongly evocative of that of a brownie: Merodach has "the form of a boy, but the features of one a hundred years old," and his eyes bear "a strong resemblance to the eyes of a well-known species of monkey" (244). The truth about Merodach's peculiar appearance and supernatural nature remain undisclosed throughout the story.

His behavior is equally unsettling, leading some to believe that he may be a brownie: "Some thought he was a mongrel, between a Jew and an ape, some a wizard, some a kelpie, or a fairy, but most of all, that he was really and truly a Brownie" (250). Like the brownies of folk tradition, Merodach displays an overtly pagan attitude towards religion and cannot stand the sight of the Bible, although this does not help him ingratiate himself to Lady Wheelhope who, for no apparent reason, hates him from the very beginning. Significantly, however, all of her attempts at killing him backfire, causing instead the death of people dear to the Lady, including her own son. The modality of Merodach's departure also follows traditional accounts of the brownie, as it is understood that he does not accept any payment. The end of the story, however, signals a departure from traditional accounts in that the Lady, affected by a perverse longing for the missing brownie, ends up following him, as if possessed "by an irresistible charm" and is ultimately "tormented ... to death" by this unfulfilled desire (254).

Hogg's rendition of the traditional brownie in "The Brownie of the Black Haggs" denotes demonic qualities that, while clearly indebted to popular lore, also share the ambiguous duality of modern villains and anti-heroes of Gothic fiction, including the couplings of Mary Shelley's eponymous scientist and unnamed creature in *Frankenstein* (1818) (see **Frankenstein's Monster**) and Robert Louis Stevenson's Dr Jekyll and Mr Hyde in *Strange Case of Dr Jekyll and Mr Hyde* (1886; see **Hyde, Edward**). With such archetypal Gothic **demons**, brownies, and Merodach in particular, share the human conflict between rigid morality on one hand and brutal sadism on the other. Commenting on Hogg's development of the brownie's sado-masochistic appeal in "The Brownie of the Black Haggs," Douglas Gifford has advanced the hypothesis that the character may have also influenced Emily Brontë's treatment of Heathcliff in *Wuthering Heights* (1847). Like the brownie, Heathcliff's uncouth appearance and inscrutable behavior denote an ambiguous blend of human and supernatural features; moreover, when his initial loyalty is betrayed, his existence is primarily driven by the passion of revenge.

As Charlotte Brontë's diary confirms, the Brontë siblings would have been familiar with *Blackwood's* and Hogg's fiction, which may have inspired the deployment of the brownie motif in their writing. Brownies and other similar fairies appear as early as *Tales of the Islanders* (1829–30), part of Charlotte and Branwell Brontë's juvenilia. In this semi-autobiographical piece, the children saw themselves as the small protective "Genii" of their "Islanders." In particular, in "The Glasstown Saga" section of *Tales of the Islanders*, Branwell's own genius, Little King, is explicitly compared to a brownie: "His constant disposition to all kinds of mischief was well known and he was considered by every member of the house at Strathfieldsaye not excepting the duke himself more as an evil brownie than a legitimate fairy" (Alexander, vol. 1, 202). According to Emily Brontë's biographer, Winifred Gérin (1901–81), the Brontë children's deployment of the brownie as source semi-autobiographical characterization owed much to their reading of James Hogg's traditional tales in *Blackwood's* in 1828, including "The Brownie of the Black Haggs" (16). The brownie's proverbial generosity also features marginally in Charlotte Brontë's *Villette* (1853). In chapter XXIX of the novel's second volume, "Monsieur's Fète," Lucy Snowe learns that her friend Emanuel has been secretly helping her with her work, like a brownie, at night time: "I saw the Brownie's work in exercises left overnight full of faults, and found next morning carefully corrected: I profited by his capricious goodwill in loans full welcome and refreshing" (351). Significantly, though his nocturnal assistance is clearly welcome, the notion of the brownie's "capriciousness" seeps into the description of Emanuel's concealed behavior.

A popular example of the brownie's loyalty is the traditional story of the brownie of Fearnden, which inspired both the eponymous poem (1850) by Alexander Laing and the tale by Elizabeth Grierson (1908). In both cases, the plot revolves around the brownie of Fearnden who, although known to be helpful and good-natured, nevertheless scares everybody due to the irrational superstition attached to his unconventional appearance. Nobody dares to make any contact with him except for the farmer's wife. When the wife's health is in danger (in the poem she is in labor), nobody dares to cross the glen in the darkness, for fear of meeting the brownie. It is, however, the brownie himself who rides to the nurse's house and takes her to the wife's sickbed, thus saving her life. In contrast to human selfish behavior, the brownie's helpfulness points to a selfless attitude toward those in need, interrogating, in turn, the moral foundations of the human category. In Grierson's tale, this is made clear when the nurse, who is unknowingly riding a horse behind the brownie, claims: "I warrant that ye are a true man, for the care you have taken of a poor old woman" (41).

Since the nineteenth century, brownies have continued to inspire stories about loyalty and mutual assistance, particularly in writing for children and young adults. The helpfulness of brownies features prominently in Juliana Horatia Ewing's eponymous novella, *The Brownies* (1871). The frame narrative opens with a recently widowed doctor and the rector's children, who are the audience of "the story of the brownies" (13). The doctor's tale is set in a northern county of England and revolves around a widowed tailor, Thomas Trout, his elderly mother and two children, Tommy and Johnnie. The tailor's old mother laments the brownie's departure from their household, noting that "[t]he maids caught sight of him one night ... and his coat was so ragged, that they got a new suit, and a linen shirt for him, and laid them by the bread and milk bowl" (26). The story's pedagogical subtext emerges when the Old Owl, a magical character, appears in a dream to Tommy to claim that "all children are Brownies" (34). The moral of the story seems clear: brownies are role models of helpfulness, and, in this case, children are called on to assist their parents in household chores. This is reinforced by the Old Owl's warning about the brownies' ability to misbehave: "When they are idle and mischievous, they are called Boggarts, and are a curse to the house they live in" (36).

In the Noddy series, Enid Blyton introduces a character called "Big-Ears," a brownie who lives in a toad-stool house just outside Toytown. In *The Book of Brownies* (1926), Blyton follows the adventures of a mischievous trio of brownies—Hop, Skip, and Jump—who dwell in Crab-apple Cottage. The story revolves around the brownies' attempt to get to the party thrown by the King of Fairyland under false pretences, disguised as Twirly-Wirly, the Great Conjuror from the Land of Tiddlywinks, and his two helpers. In J.K. Rowling's "Harry Potter" series, the superstition attached to brownies emerges in her references to the house-elves who, like the traditional brownies, are loyal helpers to their masters, who can send them away with a gift of clothing. In appearance, too, Rowling's house-elves resemble brownies, being small in size, with a larger head and ears. Among other supernatural beings, Rowling also uses the Scottish boggarts which, in a similar fashion to brownies, are household fairies, though Rowling twists the tradition, which associates boggarts with house-elves, to create more sinister creatures whose shapes change to match their victim's worst fear. Warrior-like brownies play a crucial role in the fantasy film *Willow* (1988). Directed by George Lucas, this is the story of the eponymous hero, Willow of the Nelwyn **dwarf**-like people (Warwick Davis), and his successful quest to rescue a human baby (Elora Danan) from the wrath of evil Queen Bavmorda (Jean Marsh). Following the prophecy that a baby born with a distinctive birthmark would signal the end of her power, the Queen's attempts to find and kill the baby are wrecked by Willow, who fights her troops accompanied by another human, Madmartigan (Val Kilmer), and two brownies. In the film, brownies, who are only a couple of inches in height and armed with bows and arrows, make their first appearance after they have succeeded in kidnapping the baby from Madmartigan. Their good intentions, however, become clear once it is unveiled that they work for the Brownie fairy queen of the forest, Cherlindrea (Maria Holvoe).

Boggarts and brownies have more recently appeared as two of a kind in Tony DiTerlizzi and Holly Black's "The Spiderwick Chronicles" (2003–2008), which follow the adventures of twins Jared and Simon Grace and their sister Mallory, after their move into the Spiderwick Estate. In the first book of the series, *The Field Guide* (2003), while visiting the house library, Jared discovers books on folklore, such as *A Historie of Scottish Dwarves, A Compendium of Brownie Visitations from Around the World*, and *Anatomy of Insects and Other Flying Creatures* (31). He also finds Arthur Spiderwick's *Field Guide to the Fantastical World Around You* (50), where he reads that, "brownies are these helpful guys, but then if you make them mad, they go crazy. They start doing all these bad things and you can't stop them. They become boggarts" (59). Later, in the same library, Jared and Simon meet Thimbletack, "a little man about the size of a pencil" (91), and note that, "[h]is eyes were as black as beetles, his nose was large and red, and he looked very like the illustration from the Guide" (91). The brownie Thimbletack shares the boys' adventures throughout the series.

In line with their folkloric origins, in their recent incarnations, brownies would appear to have retained their strong—if at times capricious—morality, embodying, simultaneously, extreme loyalty and vindictive behavior. Although their strange appearance may initially look frightful, their helpfulness can be crucial for the positive resolution of challenges faced by humans.

Monica Germanà

References and Suggested Reading

Alexander, Christine, ed. *An Edition of The Early Writings of Charlotte Bronte*. 3 vols. Oxford: Blackwell, 1987.

Blyton, Enid. *The Book of Brownies*. London: George Newnes, 1926.

Brontë, Charlotte. *Villette*. 1853. Reprint, Harmondsworth: Penguin, 1994.

Brown, R.L. *Scottish Superstitions*. Edinburgh: Chambers, 1990.

DiTerlizzi, Tony, and Holly Black. *The Spiderwick Chronicles: The Completely Fanatical Edition*. London and New York: Simon and Schuster, 2009.

Douglas, Ronald M. *The Scots Book*. 1953. Reprint, London: Bracken Books, 1995.

Evans-Wentz, Walter Yeeling. *The Fairy-Faith in Celtic Countries*. London: Henry Frowde, 1911.

Ewing, Juliana H. *The Brownies and Other Tales*. 1871. Reprint, London: George Bell and Sons, 1886.

Gérin, Winifred. *Emily Brontë*. London: Oxford University Press, 1971.

Gifford, Douglas. *James Hogg*. Edinburgh: The Ramsay Press, 1976.

Grierson, Elizabeth. "The Brownie of Fern-den." In *Scottish Folk and Fairy Tales*, edited by Gordon Jarvie. 1908. Reprint, London: Penguin, 1992.

Gunnyon, William. *Illustrations of Scottish History, Life and Superstition from Song and Ballad*. Edinburgh: Menzies and Co., 1877.

Henderson, William. *Notes on the Folk-lore of the Northern Counties of England and the Border*. London: Longman, Green and Co., 1886.

Hogg, James. *The Brownie of Bodsbeck*. Edited by Douglas S. Mack. 1818. Reprint, Edinburgh: Scottish Academic Press, 1976.

——. *The Shepherd's Calendar*. Edited by Douglas S. Mack. 1828. Reprint, Edinburgh: Edinburgh University Press, 1995.

Laing, Alexander. *Wayside Flowers: Being Poems and Songs by Alexander Laing*. Edited by George Gilfillan. 1846. Reprint, Glasgow: Blackie, 1857.

Scott, Walter. *Letters on Demonology and Witchcraft*. Edited by Raymond Lamont Brown. 1830. Reprint, Wakefield: S.R. Publishers Limited, 1968.

BUNYIP

Bunyips are a type of monster prevalent in Australian folklore that developed from the mythology of Aboriginal Australians. They are distinct from **yowies** because of their strong association with water and are often described as lurking around or living in creeks, billabongs, and rivers. "Bunyip" also entered the Australian vernacular as a synonym for imposter, fake, or sham.

Descriptions of the bunyip vary considerably in the written record and illustrations. It is large, but is also capable of hiding under stones in a riverbed; it has been compared both to a calf and a platypus; other attributions have included fins, hooves, a tail, shaggy hair, and scales. The distinguishing features of the bunyip therefore are not unique physical traits, but rather that it is non-humanoid, inhabits an aquatic environment, and possesses a generally antagonistic attitude towards humans.

There was sufficient cultural saturation of the idea of the bunyip by the nineteenth century that the word was used to highlight Australian origins, even when the text did not include the monster itself. *The Australian Bunyips*, a play from 1857, does not actually include the monster (Holden 132); the Gawler Humbug Society (a society formed in the South Australian town of Gawler in 1861 for the purpose of lampooning the South Australian Parliament) in 1863 named their new monthly newsletter *The Bunyip*; and on 27 October 1858, an extravagant political parody titled *The Bunyip* focused on a circus that turns its tightrope performer into a bunyip in order to attract a new audience (Holden 133). Eugéne McNeil's autobiography, *A Bunyip Close Behind Me: Recollections of the Nineties*, published in 1972, makes only passing reference to a bunyip in an otherwise conventional recounting of Australian life at the end of the nineteenth century.

The bunyip features significantly in Australian fiction from the mid-nineteenth century, especially children's fiction, such as William Howitt's *Boys' Adventures in the Wilds of Australia* (1855). These earlier narratives portray the bunyip as either a monster to be feared or as a con, but bunyips were soon subsumed into Australian fairytales and rehabilitated. *Mr Bunyip*, a children's book published in 1871, is a good illustration of this transition, as it features a bunyip protagonist who is a monster, but one with a gentle demeanor who "[imparts] moral lessons to a young colonial girl" (Holden 159). Thomas Knox's *The Boy Travellers in Australasia* was published in New York and thereby assisted in introducing bunyips to the United States in 1889, and Australian authors continued to produce children's literature featuring bunyips, such as *Steve Brown's Bunyip and Other Stories* by John Arthur Barry in 1893 and Ethyl Pedley's *Dot and the Kangaroo* in 1899, in which the titular Dot pretends to be a bunyip to save her friend, the Kangaroo, from hunters.

During the twentieth century, bunyips remained prominent in children's stories, especially the boy's adventure sub-genre. Robert P. Macdonald's "The Bunyip," published by *Australian Boys' Annual* in 1911, "The Haunt of the Bunyip" by L.B. Thoburn-Clarke in *The Empire Annual for Australian Boys*, published in 1920, and Reid Whitly's 1927 "The Baleful Bunyip" in boy's annual *Chums* are good examples of the popularity of the native monster stories with boys. Toward the end of the century, bunyips appear in the picture books of Michael Salmon and Jenny Wagner. *The Monster who Ate Canberra* was published in 1972 and was the first appearance of Salmon's Alexander Bunyip. The character became so popular that he featured in theater for children, radio shows, and a television show populated by puppets. Wagner's 1973 *The Bunyip of Berkeley's Creek* follows the adventures of a bunyip trying to find out what a bunyip really is. The popularity of bunyips in children's picture books has continued and examples include: *Koala and the Bunyip* by Esta De Fossard, Neil McLeod, and Lynn Twelftree (1982); *The Bunyip in the Billycan* by Mavis Scott (1991); *Spot the Bunyip* by Michael Salmon (1992); *Mitch and the Littlest Bunyip* by William Garrett (1993); *The Bunyip of Haig Park* by Kathleen McConnell (1997); *The Bilby and the Bunyip: An Easter Tale* by Irena Sibley (1998); *What Is a Bunyip* by Nette Hilton (1999); *Emily and the Big Bad Bunyip* by Jackie French (2008); and *Rosie and the Bunyip* by Meredith Costain (2008). Patricia Wrightson's 1977 children's book, *The Ice Is Coming*, revitalized the more menacing aspects of the monster by making bunyips a tangible threat to the protagonists, and bunyips even feature in a science fiction collection edited by Van Ikin, *Australian Science Fiction* (1982).

By the late 1970s and 1980s, successful children's books featuring bunyips began to be adapted into films. *Dot and the Kangaroo* (1899) was made into an animated film in 1977 (Yoram Gross) featuring particularly wicked bunyips singing a haunting song, and was followed up with a series of eight sequels. *The Phantom Treehouse* (Paul Williams, 1984) features more benign bunyips, as does *The Steam-driven Adventures of Riverboat Bill* (Paul Williams, 1986). Children's plays have also continued to draw on these mythical monsters, as in Peter Mapleson's *Bill the Bunyip* (1998). The 2011 play *I, Bunyip* (Scott Wright) demonstrates the increasing intersection between indigenous narratives and mainstream children's culture. This play was written in consultation with Aboriginal communities, and aims to present traditional stories to children in an engaging way.

Twentieth-century theatrical productions also occasionally drew on bunyips for their subject matter. In 1916, an extremely successful pantomime titled *The Bunyip* opened in Sydney; Ray Mathew's *We Find the Bunyip* was staged by the Pioneer Hall in 1955; and *The Bunyip and the Satellite* was first performed in 1957 by the National Theatre of Australia. The incorporation of bunyips into children's entertainment was also reflected in the 1959 children's play, *Mumba Jumba and the Bunyip* (Peter O'Shaughnessy and Barry Humphries).

While the bunyip has played a major role in children's literature, the monster can be found in twentieth-century adult satire and humor as well, such as in "Twitchy the Bunyip on Cadaghi Ridge" by David Myers

(*Cornucopia Country: Satiric Tales*, 1991). Poetry regarding bunyips largely moved from the adult realm to that of children, as demonstrated by collections such as Mark Svendsen's *The Bunyip and the Night* (1994) and "The Bathroom Bunyip" in *Poems in My Language* by Colin Thiele (1989), but adult and humor collections still surface from time to time, including "The Ballad of the Blue Lake Bunyip" by Graham Jenkin (1991) and Frank L. Owens's three poems in *A Slice of Margaret* (1993). The bunyip maintains the power to menace in John Streeter Manifold's poem "The Bunyip and the Whistling Kettle" (first published in 1946 in *Meanjin Papers* vol. 5, no.4) that uses the bunyip as a metaphor for the dangers of the Australian bush.

The popularization of authentic indigenous narratives and dreaming stories about the bunyip from the mid-twentieth century contrast with the appropriation of Aboriginal mythology into white literary production, children's literature, and folklore. Anthropologists investigating and preserving the culture of indigenous Australians had been recording myths about bunyips and similar creatures from as early as 1824, and authors such as Catherine Langloh-Parker (1856–1940) and W. Ramsay Smith (1859–1937) had published popular collections. Publications by indigenous Australians about Aboriginal myths, such as Kath Walker's "The Bunyip" in *My People* (1970) and her *Stradbroke Dreamtime* (1972), as well as Kevin Gilbert's "Nooni's Bunyip Story" in his 1978 book *People Are Legends: Aboriginal Poems*, increased starting in the 1970s. Jean A. Ellis's *From the Dreamtime: Australian Aboriginal Legends* (1991) includes the short story "Beware of the Bunyip!" and *Gadi Mirrabooka: Australian Aboriginal Tales from the Dreaming*, by Pauline E. Macleod, June E. Barker, Francis Firebrace, and Helen F. McKay, includes "The Little Koala and the Bunyip" and "The Bunyip in the Forest." Overall, bunyips in Australian literature and film have evolved from indigenous oral legends, to frightening folktales, into a children's fairytale.

A.C. Blackmore

References and Suggested Reading

Barrett, Charles. *The Bunyip and Other Mythical Monsters and Legends*. Melbourne: Reed & Harris, 1946.

Holden, Robert. *Bunyips: Australia's Folklore of Fear*. Canberra: National Library of Australia, 2001.

Parker, K. Langloh. *Woggheeguy: Australian Aboriginal Legends*. Adelaide: F.W. Preece & Sons, 1930.

Wignell, Edel. *A Boggle of Bunyips*. Sydney: Hodder & Stoughton, 1989.

BURIEL—*see* Demon

CALIBAN

In William Shakespeare's *The Tempest* (1610–11), Caliban is Prospero's slave and an original dweller of the island that the former Duke of Milan and his daughter Miranda have occupied after being exiled. Prospero initially endeavors to educate Caliban, but enslaves him after he attempts to rape Miranda. After Prospero uses his magic to cause the shipwreck of his usurpers on the island, Caliban tries to involve the characters Stephano and Trinculo in a grotesque attempt to overthrow the master. Following Miranda and Ferdinando's marriage, Caliban is abandoned on the island when all the other characters, now reconciled, board the ship to return to Milan.

Although every character in the play has his or her own complexity, Caliban seems to epitomize a number of theoretical kernels that make him one of the most discussed characters in the whole Shakespearian repertoire. He is the originary and legitimate owner of the land that was left to him by his mother Sycorax, a Scythian **witch** whose name derives from the Greek *korax* (crow; see Orgel 19–20). Scythia is a region traditionally associated with primitive magic, as well as cannibalism and threatening barbarism. Sycorax's character is derived from Medea, daughter of King Aeëtes of Colchis and niece of **Circe** in Greek mythology. Shakespeare reworks in particular the material of book 7 of Ovid's first century CE *Metamorphoses*. Sycorax does not seem to have left her magic powers to Caliban. Or, as Francis Yates suggests, her black magic was inferior and completely tamed by Prospero's white magic, which represents Francis Bacon's (1561–1626) idea of the dominion and superiority of modern science over magic and old superstition.

Caliban's barbaric and evil origin, then, make him a semi-human creature—earthly, inferior, and prone to evil. Caliban also arguably anticipates the early modern English proletariat. As Prospero himself confesses to Miranda: "We cannot miss him: he does make our fire, / Fetch in our wood and serves in offices / That profit us" (I.ii.370–73). Heir to the Biblical curse of Joshua against the Gibeonites (Joshua 9:21), Caliban represents the new slaves, waged or unwaged, of the rising agrarian and merchant capitalism—the people that, between British, African, and the New World's coasts, were building the new system of production (see Rediker and Linebaugh; and Federici).

Caliban's very humanity is questioned in *The Tempest*. He is called "mooncalf" and, like the Man in the Moon, he is represented with a bundle of wood on the shoulders, both by Shakespeare and by William Hogarth, faithful interpreter of the play's moral tensions in *Scene from Shakespeare's The Tempest* (c. 1735). To Caliban's moral deformity, Shakespeare adds physical deformity as well, hyperbolically and ironically staged in the encounter of Caliban with Stephano and Trinculo on the beach in Act 2, Scene 2.

To Prospero, Caliban is the rebel slave, justly subdued not for his physical or moral inferiority, but for having betrayed Prospero's trust. Initially, theirs was a relation of exchange. Prospero taught Caliban his own language, "and how / To name the bigger light, and how the less, / That burn by day and night" (I.ii.399–401). Caliban reciprocated with filial affection, showing him "the fresh springs, brine-pits, barren place and fertile" (I.ii.403). Yet the moral elevation of Caliban was doomed to fail, as shown when he tried to rape Miranda.

Caliban is therefore subdued and enslaved, and the relationship with Prospero becomes conflictual and rich with implications. Caliban claims his violence ("O ho, O ho! Would't had been / done! / Thou didst prevent me – I had peopled else / This isle with Calibans" [I.ii.501–503]) and his rebellion is an attempt to recover the island that he has lost. The Good Savage becomes the monstrous barbarian who does not hesitate voluntarily to subjugate himself to the new masters, Stephano and Trinculo, in order to break Prospero's yoke.

This opposition between the savage, potentially open to the reception of Western values and therefore "Good," and the barbarian who embodies irreconciliable conflict, violence, and destruction, was already widespread in early modern culture. In his *Essays* (1580), translated into English in 1603 by John Florio, Montaigne had developed his skeptical and modern vision of cannibals in chapter 30 of Book 1. Here, Montaigne suggests an open and tolerant attitude toward the "barbarian," which is particularly salient after the "discovery" of the New World. After the Valladolid Debate (1550), when the opinions of Bartolomé de las Casas and Juan Ginés de Sepúlveda clashed concerning the treatment of natives of the New World, this attitude declined.

An especially influential opinion on the opposition between a noble and Western principle and an ignoble and barbarian principle was developed by Edmund Spenser. In the sixth book of the *Faerie Queene* (1596), written in honour of Queen Elizabeth I, Spenser opposed the character of Calidore or Courtesie to the Blatant Beast. Reworking the influential Renaissance model of Baldassarre Castiglione's *The Book of the Courtier* (1528), Shakespeare's Prospero parallels Calidore, while Caliban parallels the Blatant Beast. Furthermore, Spenser had maintained the necessity of a complete destruction of the language and customs of the natives in his *A View of the Present State of Ireland* (1596, published in the seventeenth century), in which he tried to prove that, like Caliban, the Irish descend from barbarian Scythian stock.

The metaphysical tensions embodied by the vile Caliban facing the noble Prospero are developed in Robert Browning's drama *Caliban Upon Setebos* (1864). Browning allows Caliban to express his opinion on why Setebos—the fictional god worshipped by Sycorax—created the world. In the soliloquy, narrated in the third person, the barbarian Caliban reflects on the barbarian god he believes in, on the natural order, and on theodicy. In his 1878 drama *Caliban*, Ernest Renan imagines a continuation for *The Tempest*. Caliban is the protagonist of a popular uprising that unexpectedly puts him on the throne of Milan. Renan rails against populism and the ignorance of the people. He depicts Caliban as a rude usurper who, pushed by the violence of the mob, finds himself in charge and is immediately corrupted by power.

It is only after World War II, in the wake of the decolonization movement, that Caliban is revisited as a symbol of resistance of indigenous peoples against the Western usurpers. In his 1956 work, *Prospero and Caliban: The Psychology of Colonization*, Octave Mannoni is among the first to rework Caliban from a postcolonial perspective. Mannoni focuses on the psychological dimension of colonialism, using the base of his own experience in French Madagascar. He offers an interpretation of colonialism completely based on psychology, developing the idea of an "inferiority complex" and a "dependence complex," which he sees as constitutive features of the Malagasy culture. Although respecting Mannoni, Frantz Fanon, in 1968's *Black Skin, White Masks*, provided a harsh crititique of his work. Fanon criticizes in particular the essentialism of Mannoni's view. It is not possible, Fanon maintains, to speak about a pure "Malagasy culture" outside of the struggle with the "culture" of the colonizing West. The Malagasy has been reformulated by the Western colonial enterprise and he exists by now only in and through the clash with the European. Insofar as it is the racist who creates the inferior, in Fanon's view Mannoni has forced the Malagasy between the devil of inferiority and the deep blue sea of dependence.

The poet of blackness (*négritude*), Aimé Cesaire from the Antilles was also very critical of the psychoanalytic interpretation of Mannoni and rewrote *The Tempest* in 1960, offering an important role to Caliban. In Cesaire's postcolonial *A Tempest*, the triumph of humanity, that is to say, a new and non-alienated humanism, is not teleologically inscribed within the development of the productive forces. Liberation is rather the result of a struggle, as well as of a subjective effort against the impostures of Prospero's Western rationality. To the violence of the colonizer, a just and active violence must be opposed.

The Uruguayan José Enrique Rodò, in his essay *Ariel* of 1900, had opposed the "Calibanesque" brutality of the United

States' intervention in the Cuban War with the pure spirit of South America, which he had identified with Ariel. In his essay of 1971, the Cuban Roberto Fernández Retamar reverses this idea, stressing that, although brutal, Caliban is the true "symbol" of the oppressed as well as the noble tradition of revolt. He opposes the revolutionary tradition of the Incan Túpac Amaru (1545–72) and François-Dominique Toussaint Louverture (c. 1743–1803), of Fidel Castro (b. 1926), and Che Guevara (1928–67), to Ariel's voluntary servitude to the imperialist Prospero.

Cinematic representation of Caliban owes much to prior theatrical interpretations of the character, such as Sir Francis Robert Benson's (1891), Herbert Beerbohm Tree's (1904), and Giorgio Strehler's (1978) who, in a stage production for the *Piccolo Teatro* of Milan, follows Roberto Fernández Retamar's interpretation by representing Caliban as an earthly element, hissing and crawling, but sincerely aspiring to freedom and opposing the illusory freedom of the "aerial" Ariel, faithful servant of his master. In his 1979 *The Tempest*, the iconoclast Derek Jarman offers a free interpretation of the Shakespearian masterpiece in which he introduces a vigorous homoerotic reading of Caliban, thanks to a wonderful performance by Jack Birkett. In a memorable scene, provocatively shabby, Jarman shows Sycorax breastfeeding a grown-up Caliban. Peter Greenaway's *Prospero's Books* (1991) is more conventional and relies largely on special effects. Caliban's performance of an elaborate dance and pantomime is explicitly influenced by Herbert Beerbohm Tree's 1904 stage interpretation. A remarkable interpretation is also given by Djimon Hounsou in Julie Taymor's *The Tempest* (2010), in which Caliban's master has become Prospera, a witch.

Filippo Del Lucchese

References and Suggested Reading

Bloom, Harold, ed. *Caliban*. New York and Philadelphia: Chelsea House Publications, 1992.

Cesaire, Aimé. *A Tempest*. New York: Theatre Communications Group, 1992.

——. *Discourse on Colonialism*. New York: Monthly Review Press, 2001.

Colás, Santiago. "Caliban." In *Encyclopedia of Latin American and Caribbean Literature, 1900–2003*, edited by Daniel Balderston and Mike Gonzalez, 100–101. London and New York: Routledge, 2004.

Fanon, Frantz. *Black Skin, White Masks*. New York: Grove Press, 1968.

Federici, Silvia. *Caliban and the Witch: Women, the Body and Primitive Accumulation*. New York: Autonomedia, 2004.

Griffiths, Trevor R. "'The Island Is Mine': Caliban and Colonialism." *Yearbook of English Studies* 13 (1983): 159–80.

Joseph, Margaret P. *Caliban in Exile: The Outsider in Caribbean Fiction*. New York and London: Greenwood Press, 1992.

Mannoni, Octave. *Prospero and Caliban: The Psychology of Colonization*. London: Methuen & Co., 1956.

Orgel, Steven. *Introduction to The Tempest, by William Shakespeare*. Oxford: Oxford University Press, 1987.

Rediker, Marcus, and Peter Linebaugh. *The Many-Headed Hydra: Sailors, Slaves, Commoners, and the Hidden History of the Revolutionary Atlantic*. Boston: Beacon Press, 2000.

Renan, Ernst. "Caliban." In *Oeuvres Complètes, vol. III*, 375–435. Paris: Calmann-Lévy, 1949.

Retamar, Roberto F. *Caliban and Other Essays*. Minneapolis: University of Minnesota Press, 1989.

Simon, Robin. "Hogarth's Shakespeare." *Apollo 109* (March 1979): 216–19.

Vaughan, Alden T. *Shakespeare's Caliban: A Cultural History*. Cambridge: Cambridge University Press, 1993.

Yates, Frances. *Shakespeare's Last Plays: A New Approach*. London: Routledge and Kegan Paul, 1975.

CARMILLA

Carmilla is the eponymous **vampire** antagonist of Irish author Joseph Sheridan Le Fanu's 1872 Gothic novella. Next to Bram Stoker's **Dracula**—a story which *Carmilla* precedes by 25 years—Carmilla is arguably the most significant vampire in English-language literature and has given rise to an entire subgenre of the vampire tale: the lesbian vampire. Like *Dracula*, *Carmilla* has been adapted for film numerous times and Carmilla remains a significant vampiric point of reference in contemporary popular culture.

Le Fanu's story was first published in the short-lived British magazine *Dark Blue* for graduates of Oxford University and was then included in the author's collection of stories, *In a Glass Darkly*, which was also published in 1872. The story is presented as part of the casebook of the fictional Dr Martin Hesselius, whose willingness to investigate supernatural matters makes him literature's first occult detective. The story is told through the voice of a young woman named Laura, who relates her strange experiences living with her father, a wealthy English widower, in Styria (a southeastern part of Austria). She reports that when she was six years old, she had a vision of a beautiful visitor in her bedchamber and felt that she had been bitten on the chest, although no bite marks were found.

The story proper begins twelve years later when a carriage accident near Laura's home introduces a mysterious stranger: Carmilla, a girl who appears to be about Laura's age. The lonely and isolated Laura is thrilled by this chance event and an additional element of mystery is introduced in that both recognize each other from the "dream" they inexplicably shared when Laura was younger. Carmilla appears injured and, because Carmilla's mother claims her journey is urgent, Laura and her father agree to care for Carmilla until her mother's return.

Laura and Carmilla form a strong bond, but Carmilla occasionally manifests strange behavior, such as scolding Laura for singing a Christian hymn in the wake of a passing funeral procession, sleeping all day, and apparently sleepwalking at night. On other occasions, Carmilla makes unsettling and seemingly romantic advances toward Laura. Throughout, Carmilla steadfastly refuses to divulge any information about herself or her background. The plot thickens more when a restored portrait of one of Laura's ancestors, "Mircalla, Countess Karnstein" resembles Carmilla, right down to the mole on her neck.

Laura begins to experience nightmares featuring a monstrous cat-like beast that bites her on the chest, assumes female form, and disappears. Of greater concern is that Laura's health begins to fail rapidly. The physician consulted speaks privately with her father, leaving directions that under no circumstances should Laura be left alone. Laura and her father subsequently set off for the ruined village of Karnstein, encountering en route a family friend, General Spielsdorf, whose own niece of approximately Laura's age died under mysterious circumstances just prior to a planned visit. The General recounts what turns out to be a very familiar story: he and his niece met a beautiful young woman named Millarca and her mother at a costume ball. The mother convinced the General to look after Millarca, with whom his niece was quite taken, while she attended to an urgent matter. His niece's health failed and, after a consultation with a priestly doctor, the General concluded that a vampire was at work. He hid in his niece's closet at night and observed a cat-like creature bite her. Emerging from his hiding place, he watched the creature take the form of Millarca and disappear through a locked door.

The trio arrive at Karnstein and, while Laura's father seeks the tomb of Mircalla Karnstein, Carmilla appears and the General, recognizing her as Millarca, attacks her with an axe and she flees. The General then explains to Laura that Carmilla and Millarca are one and the same, and that both names are anagrams of their real identity: the vampire Countess Mircalla Karnstein. The party is then joined by Baron Vordenberg, an authority on vampires and a descendant of the hero who cleared the area of vampires long ago. They locate the tomb of Mircalla and an Imperial Commission is summoned to exhume and destroy the body of the vampire.

Although the lesbian element in *Carmilla*, in keeping with the time period in which Le Fanu was writing, is relatively subdued, nevertheless it has ironically been extraordinarily fertile in spawning vampiric female offspring with lesbian inclinations. Danish director Carl Dreyer was inspired by *Carmilla*, and more generally by the five stories of the fantastic that constitute *In a Glass Darkly*, for his surreal *Vampyr* (1932). A more faithful adaptation—and one that draws out the implications of the lesbian theme—is French director Roger Vadim's *Et mourir de plaisir* (translated into English as *Blood and Roses*, 1960), a film considered by many aficionados to be among the high points of the vampire film genre. The British Hammer Film Productions released a trio of films, referred to as "The Karnstein Trilogy," that are all related to the vampires of the Karnstein family. The first, *The Vampire Lovers*, directed by Roy Ward Baker and starring Ingrid Pitt as Carmilla (1970), is a fairly faithful adaptation of Le Fanu's tale. The two films that followed, *Lust for a Vampire* (Jimmy Sangster, 1971) and *Twins of Evil* (John Hough, 1971), have far less to do with the original story, but further develop the theme of the lesbian vampire by introducing hungry and buxom female vampires with predilections for beautiful (and generally scantily clad) young women. Also based on *Carmilla* is the 1972 Spanish horror film, *The Blood Spattered Bride*, written and directed by Vicente Aranda, which has achieved cult status for its mix of gore and lesbian themes. More recently, Carmilla is the central protagonist in Phil Claydon's 2009 British comedy film, *Lesbian Vampire Killers*.

Carmilla has also continued her undead existence in arenas of popular culture beyond film. Kyle Marffin's 1999 novel *Carmilla: The Return* follows Carmilla into 1990s Michigan. She has inspired comics, including a six-issue mini-series by Aircel Comics in 1991. Heavy metal and goth bands have credited Le Fanu's novella for inspiration, including Cradle of Filth on their 1996 release *Dusk ... and her Embrace* and the darkwave musical duo Oneiroid Psychosis, whose eerie 1999 release *Garden of Remembrance* features tracks titled "Mircalla" and "Carmilla." A female vampire named Carmilla is a character in several of the *Castlevania* series of video games; and in the second season of the HBO series *True Blood* (2009), characters visit a hotel in Dallas built for vampires called "Hotel Carmilla" that provides dark rooms and room service in the form of human "snacks."

Jeffrey Andrew Weinstock

References and Suggested Reading

Geary, Robert F. "Carmilla and the Gothic Legacy: Victorian Transformations of Supernatural Horror." In *The Blood is the Life: Vampires in Literature*, edited by Leonard G. Heldreth and Mary Pharr, 19–29. Bowling Green, OH: Popular, 1999.

Major, Adrienne Antrim. "Other Love: Le Fanu's Carmilla as Lesbian Gothic." In *Horrifying*

Sex: Essays on Sexual Difference in Gothic Literature, edited by Ruth Bienstock Anolik, 151–66. Jefferson, NC: McFarland, 2007.

Senf, Carol A. "Women and Power in 'Carmilla'." *Gothic* 2 (1987): 25–33.

Veeder, William. "'Carmilla': The Arts of Repression." *Texas Studies in Literature and Language* 22 (1980): 197–223.

Weinstock, Jeffrey Andrew. *The Vampire Film: Undead Cinema*. New York: Columbia University Press, 2012.

CENOBITES

The Cenobites are a group of **demons** originating in Clive Barker's *The Hellbound Heart* (1986), in which they are referred to as the Order of the Gash, and its filmic adaptation *Hellraiser* (Clive Barker, 1987). They specialize in inflicting pain in the name of pleasure and experience, and the most famous of their ranks is **Pinhead**. They are summoned by opening an ornate puzzle box, referred to as "Lemarchand's Configuration" in the novella and the "Lament Configuration" in the films that followed. In *The Hellbound Heart*, the Cenobites appear as a collective of heavily mutilated and scarified figures who possess a dark glamour. Barker's descriptions suggest more explicitly sexual imagery than those depicted in *Hellraiser*. The Cenobites' look is based on extreme expressions of the fetish scene from the 1970s and 1980s, a sartorial code that incorporates their own ruined bodies into the leather, metal, and PVC in which they are clad.

Within the film series the Cenobites are portrayed principally as Pinhead's minions, such as the eyeless Chatterer—reminiscent of H.R. Giger's designs for Ridley Scott's *Alien* (1979)—bloated Butterball, and otherworldly Female Cenobite, all three of which appear in the first two films. Pinhead and the Cenobites provide continuity across the series, as the stories become increasingly stand-alone in nature. In *Hellbound: Hellraiser II* (Tony Randel, 1988), we learn that they were once human, before the dark god of Hell, **Leviathan**, repurposed them as agents of its will. Indeed, Dr Channard (Kenneth Cranham) is eager to enter Hell and become converted into a demon, which he does later in the film. The Channard Cenobite is characterized by excess: controlled directly by Leviathan, which is connected to him by a biomechanical tube, he has tentacular appendages that spring from his palms and sprout surgical blades with which he kills Pinhead and his three followers as they attempt to rebel. In *Hellraiser III: Hell on Earth* (Anthony Hickox, 1992), Pinhead's demonic essence is freed to wreak havoc, creating some pseudo-Cenobites from his human victims. In *Hellraiser: Bloodline* (Kevin Yagher and Joe Chappelle, 1996), a demon that precedes the Cenobites, Angelique (Valentina Vargas), is introduced, hinting that the order of Leviathan has not always held sway over Hell. Later in the film she is revealed as a Cenobite, suggesting that she too has been reconfigured. The last four films in the series released to date reduce the role of the lesser Cenobites to silent killers and sinister figures that foreshadow death.

Alongside the films, an official series of comics ran from 1989 to 1993 that frequently focused on Cenobites other than Pinhead as principal antagonists and even protagonists. In fiction, Paul Kane and Marie O'Regan edited an anthology of short stories based on *The Hellbound Heart* mythology, *Hellbound Hearts* (2009), featuring many new Cenobites.

David McWilliam

References and Suggested Reading

Brown, Michael, ed. *Pandemonium: Further Explorations into the Worlds of Clive Barker*. New York, NY: Eclipse Books, 1991.

Kane, Paul. *The Hellraiser Films and their Legacy*. Jefferson, NC: McFarland, 2006.

CENTAUR

Fig. 5 *Centaur* by Richard Ellis

The half-human, half-horse Centaurs, creatures from ancient Greek mythology, traditionally represent man's divided nature: they have a capacity for intelligence and wisdom but retain the aggressive, untamed instincts of animals, thus embodying the best and worst of human potential (Harris and Platzner 308). Early Greek art depicted Centaurs as men with equine hindquarters, but by the fifth century BCE Greek vase paintings regularly showed Centaurs as human down to the waist only. Centaurs were predominantly male; female Centaurs, called Centaurides, do not appear in classical literature until the first century CE.

The earliest mythological accounts, such as those of Homer and Hesiod (eighth to seventh centuries BCE) describe the Centaurs as simply a race of "uncivilized" humans inhabiting the forested mountain terrain of Thessaly in northern Greece. The Greek poet Pindar (c. 518–438 BCE) was the first to describe the Centaurs as a human–horse hybrid, also giving what became their principal origin myth: the Centaurs were the offspring of Centaurus (the son of the Thessalian king Ixion and the cloud nymph Nephele) and a herd of mares roaming the foothills of Mt Pelion in Thessaly. These creatures resembled their mother below the waist but their father above it (*Pythian Ode* ii.40–49). In variants of the origin myth from the first century CE and later, the Centaurs are the offspring of Ixion and Nephele themselves (for example, Diodorus Siculus 4.69.4). Ancient accounts agree that the Centaurs were a savage race who were particularly violent when drunk; even the mere odor of wine caused them to stampede in an uncontrollable rage.

In a separate Greek origin story for the Centaur race, Palaiphatos (fourth century BCE) narrates that Ixion, looking to rid Thessaly of herds of wild cattle, offered a substantial reward for anyone who could accomplish the task. A group of archers from a village called Nephele answered the call, coming over on horseback and shooting down the cattle. Thus, the tale arose that Ixion was the father by Nephele of a race of beings called the Centauroi, "goaders of bulls," who were a mixture of man and horse (Scobie 142). This story, particularly its etymology, remained unconvincing even to the Greeks, who continued to look for more plausible explanations for the purported existence of this mythical creature. Current theory favors the explanation that the ancient Greek concept of the Centaur as a horse–human composite arose from the first reactions of the inhabitants of Greece to nomadic, horse-riding invaders (Scobie 144–5), a concept not far from Palaiphatos's theory.

Whatever their origins, the main stories about Centaurs reflect the inherent contradictions of the creatures' hybrid nature. The Thessalian Centaurs are best known for their battle with the Lapiths, a race of Thessalian men, in a conflict generally referred to as the *Centauromachy* ("Battle of the Centaurs"). Ancient sources agree that the conflict arose when Pirithous, a Lapith king (son of Ixion), invited the Centaurs, as relatives, to his wedding: they became drunk on the wine and grew violent, assaulting the bride and the rest of the Lapith women. This resulted in a bloody battle that ended with the Lapiths driving the Centaurs out of Thessaly. The Centauromachy, which to the Greeks represented the struggle between civilization (Greek) and barbarian (Other), was depicted in many ancient Greek works of art, including a pediment on the temple of Zeus at Olympia and on the Parthenon metopes. The Centauromachy was used similarly in later European art to depict the triumph of civilization over savagery, as, for example, in works by Michelangelo (1492) and Piero di Cosimo (1515).

Not all Centaurs were wild and brutal, however; two Centaurs were notable exceptions. Both had unusual lineage. Chiron, renowned for his wisdom, appears in the earliest Greek literature. He was the son of the Titan Cronus and the sea nymph Philyra and was thus immortal. Although not a member of the Thessalian Centaur tribe, he lived on Mt Pelion until the Lapiths expelled all Centaurs from the country. During his time on Mt Pelion, Chiron became tutor to some of the most accomplished Greek heroes, such as Jason and Achilles. The Centaur taught them various subjects including music, astronomy, and archery; he also taught medicine to Asclepius, who subsequently became god of healing. Later Greek and Roman literature tells of the death of Chiron: Although immortal, he was suffering terribly after being struck accidentally by one of Hercules's poison arrows, so Zeus pitied him and transformed him into the constellation Sagittarius (or possibly Centaurus; Ovid, *Fasti* v. 379ff).

The other exceptional Centaur was Pholus, son of the woodland god Silenus and a tree nymph. Pholus was connected with a tribe of Peloponnesian Centaurs in southern Greece who may have originated with the exiled Thessalian race. When Hercules was hunting the Erymanthian Boar (his fourth Labor), the hospitable Pholus received the hero into his cave as a guest. But when Hercules asked for wine, Pholus hesitated, afraid that the scent would draw the other Centaurs. Hercules opened the flask anyway and the maddened Centaurs attacked. Hercules killed many of them and drove the rest away, but Pholus himself died as well, accidentally poisoned by one of Hercules's arrows. Some ancient authors say it is Pholus, not Chiron, who became the constellation Centaurus. In a few versions of this myth, Chiron is present as well, and it is during this skirmish that he accidentally receives his fateful wound.

Among the Peloponnesian Centaurs driven away by Hercules was Nessus, whose next encounter with the hero was ultimately fatal to both of them. Nessus had taken up a job as a ferryman on a river in Aetolia, near the gulf of Corinth. In a story very popular in antiquity, Hercules and his new bride Deianeira encounter Nessus when they need to cross this river. Nessus takes Deianeira across first but then tries to rape her. At her screams, Hercules shoots Nessus with one of his poison arrows. The dying Centaur persuades the naïve Deianeira to use some of his blood as a love charm should Hercules's affections ever wander, which they do; Deianeira smears the Centaur's blood on a tunic that she sends to Hercules as a gift, not realizing the blood is poisoned. The hero, in agony as the blood infects his system, throws himself on a burning pyre.

In addition to the Thessalian and Peloponnesian Centaurs, two other Centaur tribes appear in Greek myth, specifically in the work of Nonnus, the fifth-century CE Greek author of an epic poem about the god Dionysus. Nonnus describes a race of bull-horned Centaurs native to the island of Cyprus who were the offspring of Zeus and Gaia, the Earth, and were thus unrelated to the other Centaur tribes. These Cyprian

Centaurs joined with Dionysus in his battle against the Indians, as did another race of Centaurs, whom Nonnus named the Lamian Centaurs, who were originally woodland spirits with human form, offspring of the river Lamos, but were changed to animal form by Zeus's wife Hera, angry that they had helped protect Dionysus, Zeus's illegitimate son (*Dionysiaca* 14).

Nonnus's work may have been influenced by his increasing interest in Christianity, and in fact because of their association with man's uncivilized instincts, Centaurs became incorporated into early Christian culture as representatives of man's baser nature, of the uncontrollable passions that could lead him into sin. Athanasius of Alexandria's fourth-century CE biography *Life of Anthony* tells how St Anthony, on a journey in the desert to find St Paul, meets two **demons** in the forms of a Centaur and a **satyr** who represent temptations of the flesh. Later Christian iconography continued to use Centaurs to depict demons aiming fiery arrows at the ungodly in an attempt to stimulate man's animal nature and "rouse his passions to commit acts of lewd indecency" (Matthews and Matthews 114). Dante placed the Centaurs, including Chiron and Nessus, in the Seventh Circle of *The Inferno*, where they guard the passage and torment the sinners (see **Dante, Monsters In**).

The duality of the Centaur has persisted into the modern era. Centaurs either represent the libidinous aspect of man's nature or, being modeled after Chiron, they represent learning and wisdom. For example, C.S. Lewis's "Narnia" books consistently depict Centaurs as wise prophets, loyal followers, and brave warriors. Like Chiron, they are skilled in various branches of learning such as astronomy and medicine. John Updike, in *The Centaur* (1963), expands and updates the story of Chiron to the twentieth century. In J.K. Rowling's "Harry Potter" series—and the movies based on it—the Centaurs, though living insularly in the Forbidden Forest, are renowned for their skills in archery, healing, and particularly divination (see **Harry Potter, Monsters In**). Rick Riordan's "Percy Jackson & The Olympians" series features Chiron as the head instructor at Camp Half-Blood, whereas other Centaurs in this series are members of the "Party Ponies" who, as their name suggests, party hearty, but who are also loyal allies when the occasion demands.

Marcin Konrad Kaleta

References and Suggested Reading

Harris, Stephen L., and Gloria Platzner. *Classical Mythology: Images and Insights*. 4th edn. New York: McGraw-Hill, 2004.

Matthews, John, and Caitlin Matthews. *The Element Encyclopedia of Magical Creatures.* London: Sterling, 2004.

Murgatroyd, Paul. *Mythical Monsters in Classical Literature*. London: Duckworth, 2007.

Scobie, Alex. "The Origins of 'Centaurs'." *Folklore* 89, no. 2 (1978): 142–7.

CERBERUS

In classical mythology, the monstrous multi-headed dog Cerberus guarded the entrance to Hades, the Land of the Dead. His function was to keep the souls of the dead in and to keep the living out, though he apparently failed regularly at the latter, given the number of mortals who managed to infiltrate the Underworld. Cerberus is not the protagonist of any myths but features prominently in the story of Heracles, making cameo appearances in the quests of other heroes including Orpheus, Aeneas, and Psyche. Cerberus remained the traditional guardian of Hades throughout literature and art of the medieval and Renaissance periods, and the character of a monstrous canine guardian is still popular in various media today.

The Homeric epics of the eighth century BCE mention a "hound of Hades" but do not name the creature or provide a physical description (*Iliad* 8.368, *Odyssey* 11.623). The poet Hesiod (c. 700 BCE), however, provides many details, naming Cerberus as the offspring of the monsters Echidna and **Typhoeus** and thus as a sibling of monsters such as the **Hydra** and the **Chimera**. Hesiod describes Cerberus as a 50-headed dog who eats raw flesh and stands guard before the palace of Hades (*Theogony*, 311–12,769–70). The creature fawns on anyone entering Hades, wagging his tail and laying back his ears, but devours anyone who tries to leave (770–73). The Greek poet Pindar (sixth century BCE) gave the creature no fewer than 100 heads (frag. 249b), creating a minor tradition followed by the first-century BCE Roman poet Horace (*Ode* 2.13.34) and the *Apocolocyntosis*, a first-century CE satirical work that also describes the creature as black and shaggy haired (13.3). Most writers, though, were content to give Cerberus only three heads, along with a number of snake's heads jutting from his back. Greek vase paintings of the sixth and fifth centuries BCE reflect such descriptions, and many of these paintings even limit the dog to two heads.

The most well-known myth to feature Cerberus is that of Heracles (Hercules, to the Romans). The Greek hero, famous for his strength, was assigned twelve horrendous tasks to atone for killing his wife and children in a fit of madness. The twelfth and worst task, which represents the conquering of death itself, was to fetch Cerberus from Hades. In relating this story, pseudo-Apollodorus tells us that Cerberus had three canine heads, a snake for a tail, and snakes on his back, and that when Heracles asked Hades for Cerberus, the god told him that he might take the animal as long as he mastered him without the use of any weapons. So Heracles flung his arms around the creature's head and managed to carry the dog back to Eurystheus, his cousin, who had assigned the Labors. Having proven himself, Heracles returned the creature to Hades (*Bibliotheca* 2.5.12).

Whereas Heracles had to overcome Cerberus by sheer strength, other heroes found less risky but equally effective methods of controlling the guard dog. The legendary musician Orpheus, for example, traveling to the Underworld in the hope of bringing back his wife Eurydice, charmed the beast with his song. The Roman poet Virgil describes how, when Orpheus played his music, Cerberus simply stood quietly at his post with his three mouths open (*Georgics* IV 483, first century BCE). The poet Ovid, Virgil's younger contemporary, has Orpheus explain to Hades that, unlike Heracles, he has come not to fetch the dog, but Eurydice (*Metamorphoses* 10.21–2). Ovid also describes Cerberus as having a **Medusa**-like effect, due to his snaky appendages: a man who saw the triple-headed dog was so terrified that he turned to stone (*Metamorphoses* 65–6). The hero Aeneas, guided to Hades by the Cumaean Sibyl (a prophetess), was able to pass by Cerberus only because the Sibyl tossed to the "gigantic, triple-jawed, snaky-necked" dog a honey-flavored lump of flour laced with soporific herbs. The ravenous creature, after greedily gulping the treat down all three of his throats, promptly fell asleep, its huge length stretched along the cavern floor (Virgil, *Aeneid* 417–25).

The heroine Psyche, in a story told by the Roman author Apuleius (second century CE), used a similar tactic to pass in and out of Dis (Hades). Psyche was assigned a series of dangerous tasks by the goddess Venus, who was envious of Psyche's beauty and furious that her own son Cupid had fallen in love with the mortal girl. Psyche, despite frequently receiving excellent advice from various helpers as to how to complete her tasks, had a tendency to despair, and upon being ordered by Venus to go to the Underworld, the miserable girl ascended a tower with the intent of throwing herself to her death. But the Tower spoke to Psyche, explaining how she could reach Dis safely. In addition to providing directions, the Tower instructed Psyche to bring with her two barley cakes, explaining: "On the very threshold of Dis stands an incredibly huge and dreadful dog, with three heads yoked on one neck. He barks furiously at the dead with his thundering throats, although he cannot actually hurt them" (*Metamorphoses* 6.19). The hound can harm the living, however, and the Tower tells Psyche to distract the creature by offering him a barley cake. She does so, giving him one cake on her way into Dis and the other on her way out, thus passing through safely.

Another dangerous aspect of Cerberus, mentioned by Ovid, concerns the dog's saliva. The poet adds an etiological detail to Hercules's twelfth Labor, explaining the origin of the poisonous plant aconite (more commonly known as monkshood or wolfsbane). As Hercules was dragging Cerberus up from the Underworld (here using chains instead of his bare hands), the daylight proved agonizing to a creature used to living in darkness. Enraged and confused, the monster dog "filled the air with howls from all three throats at once and spattered the green fields with white spittle," which mixed with the soil; the resulting plant was poisonous (*Metamorphoses* 7.414–15). The sorceress Medea (see **Witch/Wizard**), aiming to kill her stepson Theseus before he supplanted her in his father's attentions, unsuccessfully tried to poison the young man with a potion brewed from aconite, a plant that "originated from the teeth of the Echidnean dog" (*Metamorphoses* 7.408–9).

Although Cerberus was traditionally known as the guardian dog of Hades and became associated with the Christian Hell, particularly in relation to the myth of Orpheus, the dog's first major appearance in literature after classical antiquity did not come until the *Inferno*, the first part of Dante Alighieri's fourteenth-century epic poem *The Divine Comedy* (see **Dante, Monsters In**). Dante employs Cerberus as the guardian of the Third Circle of Hell (Canto VI), where he watches over the souls of those damned for the sin of Gluttony. This version of Cerberus "howls rabidly with triple throats / ... His eyes are crimson red, his beard greasy and dark / his belly huge, and his hands clawed" (14–17). Dante apparently visualized Cerberus as a half-human monster: "The beard (line 15) suggests that at least one of his three heads is human, and many illuminated manuscripts so represent him" (Ciardi 69). In a move intentionally recalling the Sibyl's approach, the Roman poet Virgil—Dante's guide through the Inferno—throws clods of dirt down the three heads of Cerberus and the monster, momentarily pausing from his frenzy to choke down his food, allows the visitors to pass.

Cerberus clearly provided the inspiration for the facetiously named Fluffy, the monstrous, three-headed, drooling, foul-breathed dog guarding the trapdoor leading to the underground chambers at Hogwarts in J.K. Rowling's *Harry Potter and the Sorcerer's Stone* (1997). As in the story of Orpheus, music lulls the creature to sleep. In Chapter 18 of Rick Riordan's *The Lightning Thief* (2005), Cerberus plays his traditional role as guardian of the Underworld, but here, though his terrifying howling is audible for miles, he is nearly invisible to the living. In this case, the character Annabeth, friend to protagonist Percy Jackson, distracts the dog by engaging it in a game of fetch with a large rubber ball. Cerberus's role in cinema has been surprisingly negligible; aside from his part as the antagonist in the direct-to-video Sci Fi Channel *Cerberus: The Guardian of Hell* (John Terlesky, 2005), his only other major film appearance was in the movie adaptation of *Harry Potter and the Sorcerer's Stone* (Chris Columbus, 2001), in the guise of Fluffy. Cerberus has been adopted in various other modern media, including as a character in video games and as an emblem in Mamoru Oshii's multimedia *Kerberos Saga*. He has also appeared, again as the three-headed guardian of the Underworld, as a character in various Marvel Comics.

D. Felton

References and Suggested Reading

Ciardi, John, trans. *The Inferno: Dante's Immortal Drama of a Journey Through Hell*. New York: Penguin Books, 1982.

Smith, R. Scott, and Stephen M. Trzaskoma, trans. *Apollodorus' Library and Hyginus' Fabulae: Two Handbooks of Greek Mythology*. Indianapolis: Hackett Publishing, 2007.

CERIDWEN—*see* Shapeshifter

CHILDREN, MONSTROUS

Monsters tend to be defined by some physical or mental divergence from the established order. In keeping with this principle, monstrous children deviate from the familiar contemporary characterization of the child as innocent, helpless, and harmless. How this inversion of expectations is represented in literary and cinematic narratives, however, varies substantially and attention to images of the monstrous child in popular culture reveals the deep imbrication of the literary and cinematic genres.

The Prehistory of the Monstrous Child

While the argument can readily be made that the contemporary notion of the child as young and innocent must be in place before the notion of the monstrous or evil child can arise, the literary tradition does possess more than a few children seemingly "born bad"—often as a consequence of unsanctioned or illicit liaisons or complications during pregnancy. In these instances, the monstrous offspring serve as embodied metaphors for the consequences of disobeying established codes of conduct. For example, the ancient myth of **Lilith** from the Babylonian *Talmud* holds that the former wife of Adam, upon expulsion from the Garden of Eden for her refusal to be subservient to him, mated with the Archangel Samael (see **Angel**) and literally gave birth to **demons**. Or consider the "Monk Calf" of Philip Melanchton and Martin Luther. Discussed in a pamphlet that the two published in 1523 entitled *The Papal Ass of Rome and The Monk Calf of Fryberg*, the Monk Calf was a disfigured beast "born with a large flap of skin on its back and a bald spot on its head, deformities resembling the cowl and tonsure of a monk" (Crawford 28). As one might expect of two Protestant reformers, the object of critique of the Monk Calf happens to be the Catholic Church. Related and less obscure is Shakespeare's calvaluna **Caliban**. In *The Tempest* (1610–11), the character Stephano refers to Caliban—the offspring of the **witch** Sycorax—as a "mooncalf," which literally refers to the abortive fetus of a cow or other farm animal but came to signify any monstrous or grotesque thing. Despite kind treatment by Prospero (see **Witch/Wizard**), he attempts to rape Prospero's daughter Miranda, suggesting that he is by nature bad. The fifteenth-century tale of Sir Gowther presents another example of an evil or monstrous child. Gowther as an infant literally drains his wet nurse of all her milk and remains a terror for much of his life.

Despite these examples, the idea of the "evil" child seems to be a relatively contemporary invention. The most obvious explanation for this is that the concepts of childhood and of the "innocent child" are a relatively modern (and controversial) phenomenon. While Jean-Jacques Rousseau is most often credited with painting the concept with broad strokes in *Émile* (1762) and elsewhere (see Brown), equally implicated are texts published during the Industrial Revolution. The novels of Charles Dickens (1812–70) and others describe monstrous working conditions in factories prior to the establishment of child labor laws. The children exploited are generally portrayed as innocent victims deprived of their childhoods. The emergence of the concept of the innocent child then allows for divergence from this model, resulting in a new breed of vexed creature: the monstrous child.

A reasonable starting point for discussing modern instances of monstrous children can be found in Henry James's *The Turn of the Screw* (1898), with its haunting portrayal of young Miles's likely encounter with and subsequent destruction by **ghosts** that transform him into a boy seemingly with two separate personalities, one sweet and the other corrupted. James's tale, told from the perspective of the governess, is notoriously ambiguous; one reading of the text, however—which has been adapted multiple times for cinema, including the 1961 version, *The Innocents*, by Jack Clayton—supports that, having been corrupted by the debased servants Peter Quint and Miss Jessel who continue to direct him and his sister Flora from beyond the grave, Miles prevaricates and steals.

The King of Monstrous Children

The concept of the monstrous child, essentially invented in the nineteenth century, has held great appeal for film, which readily adapted novels focusing on the topic including William Golding's *Lord of the Flies* (1954), William March's *The Bad Seed* (1954), and David Selzer's treatment of the Antichrist in *The Omen* (1976). The contemporary master of the monstrous concept, however, is undoubtedly Stephen King (1947–).

Starting with the publication of *Carrie* in 1973, works by King that portray or focus on a monstrous child include *Salem's Lot* (1975), *The Shining* (1977), "Children of the Corn" (1977), *Firestarter* (1980), *Pet Sematary* (1983), "The Body" (1982), *It* (1985), *The Girl Who Loved Tom Gordon* (2004), and *Cell* (2006)—all of which have been adapted to film or are presently under development for adaptation. In *Carrie*, the eponymous protagonist (as portrayed in the film by Sissy Spacek) is a cloistered, bookish loner who discovers that she has telekinetic abilities after reaching menarche. Problematically for the residents of the high school who cruelly torture her, their toying with her emotions leads Carrie to burn them alive after they dump pig's blood on her following a rigged election for Prom Queen. It is worth noting that only a few people actually laugh at the blood-soaked Carrie; most have been shocked into silence by the actions of a select few who the movie seems to identify as the real monsters. Nevertheless, fire cleanses all things, and Carrie's telekinetic abilities take command of the situation, slaughtering faculty and causing an inferno that engulfs everyone trapped within the school's gym. Not unlike Gage Creed from King's later work *Pet Sematary*, Carrie's victimization precipitates her transformation into a monster.

Less sympathetic are monstrous children in other King works. The children of "Children of the Corn" are little more than a religious cult who slaughter the adults of a small rural town when the crops fail and repeat the process when adults stray through the town; *Firestarter*'s protagonist, Charlie (Drew Barrymore in the 1984 film by Mark L. Lester) revisits the psychic conceit of *Carrie* through her pyrokinetic abilities, as does Danny in *The Shining*. *The Shining* actually approaches the idea of extrasensory perception from a variety of angles; Danny (played by Danny Lloyd in the 1980 Stanley Kubrick adaptation) possesses both telepathy and an ominous imaginary friend named Tony who warns him that the Overlook Hotel, a facility his family has been paid to care for over the winter, could be trouble as it was built on Indian burial grounds. In the Kubrick adaptation, Danny is haunted by an ominous pair of ghostly twin girls (Lisa and Louise Burns) who, not unlike the other ghosts haunting the Overlook, wish Danny's father (Jack Nicholson) to murder his wife and child and join their coterie.

Pet Sematary (adapted for film by Mary Lambert in 1989) might be the King narrative that toys most horrifically with the concepts of childhood innocence and monstrosity. When Louis Creed (Dale Midkiff) purchases a home for his family too close to a road on which truckers regularly speed by, the viewer senses it is only a matter of time before some tragedy occurs. Sure enough, his young son Gage is promptly run down. That there happens to be a pet cemetery nearby with resurrective powers comes with the movie's title; that Creed would place his son within it even after being warned that the resurrection would go poorly by local old-timer Jud Crandall (Fred Gwynne) goes without saying. Grief, in this situation, outweighs common sense, and the Creed boy becomes a soulless monster that first murders Jud while playing a perversely homicidal game of hide and seek, before slaughtering his own mother (Denise Crosby). The compounded horror of the situation then becomes apparent: Louis Creed not only loses his son, but violating the natural order of life has resulted in his undead child murdering his wife.

The Devil's Children

King, although central to the monstrous child canon, is in good company. While there were explorations of this concept prior to the 1970s (most notably director Mervyn LeRoy's 1956 *The Bad Seed*), the late 1960s and 1970s were a fertile time for the exploration of evil children, starting with 1968's *Rosemary's Baby*. Within the film, directed by Roman Polanski and based on the 1967 Ira Levin novel, Rosemary (Mia Farrow) dreams that she has conceived a child through demonic impregnation; the scratches and claw marks on her body, however, seem to prove otherwise. Her husband, Guy (John Cassavettes) informs her that in fact he had sexual relations with her while she slept the night prior. Rosemary becomes pregnant and undergoes an unusual transformation that leaves her losing weight, craving raw meats, and becoming increasingly sickly in appearance. Eventually, it is revealed to her that her dream was real and her child is the son of Satan himself. According to W. Scott Poole, Polanski's film in the era of the "women's lib" movement offers a "satanic send-up of religious conservatism's efforts to control women's bodies, particularly their role in reproduction" (176).

Christian apocalyptic or otherwise religious treatments of monstrous children became increasingly popular in the 1970s, which saw the rise of *The Omen*'s Damien (Richard Donner, 1976), Robert Wise's *Audrey Rose*, and Alfred Sole's *Alice, Sweet Alice* (both 1977). The latter two films deal respectively with childhood reincarnation and a young girl accused of murdering her sister after her first communion. *The Omen*, however, with its plot set not merely in the violation of a variety of Christian taboos, but in the idea that the Beast of the Apocalypse arrives swaddled in the guise of an otherwise adorable child named Damien (Harvey Stephens), is the ground-breaker. Within the film, Robert Thorn (Gregory Peck) and wife Kathy (Lee Remick) lose their child shortly after its birth in Rome, but a local priest persuades Thorn, unbeknownst to his wife, to swap their dead child with one whose mother died in childbirth. Strange events seem to follow young Damien as he grows, including the suicide of his original nanny (Holly Palance) who hangs herself, claiming that she is doing it for the five-year-old. As the movie progresses, Damien provokes behavior or responds in such a way as to establish his devilish nature: he cannot stand the idea of approaching a church for a wedding, animals at a local zoo become deathly afraid of his mere presence, and so on. After a series of extraordinary and unsettling circumstances, Robert Thorn concludes that his son is likely the Antichrist and attempts to kill the boy, only to be gunned down by police who tend to find infanticide under any circumstances objectionable.

No discussion of the interplay between the monstrous child and its parents would be complete without mentioning the most widely known entry into the sub-genre, William Peter Blatty's *The Exorcist*. Published in 1971 and adapted for film by William Friedkin in 1973, the book and movie were lauded by both the public and critics, with the movie garnering ten Academy Award nominations and winning the Oscar for Best Adapted Screenplay. The story seems permanently etched into the popular zeitgeist of the monstrous child for its construction of a young girl (Regan MacNeil, played by Linda Blair) possessed by a demon who exhibits curious behavior, such as speaking in tongues, levitation, and impossible revolutions of her head. Ultimately, the purging of the demon from Regan's body takes the lives of two priests: the elder Father Merrin (Max von Sydow) by heart attack and Father Karras (Jason Miller) by altruistic sacrifice as he invites the demon into his body before committing suicide.

While not specifically identified as demonic, one of the most terrifying representations of a monstrous child occurs in the 1953 short story "It's a Good Life" by Jerome Bixby, famously adapted in 1961 as an episode of the *Twilight Zone* (Season 3, episode 8; directed by James Sheldon). Within this episode, six-year-old Anthony Fremont (Bill Mumy) possesses god-like powers and must be carefully placated by his family and the townspeople who walk on tenterhooks around him to avoid a horrible fate.

The Monstrous Child Built For Film

Recent efforts in the monstrous children category have tended to eschew the corruption of innocence plot entirely and instead present their antagonists as simply born bad. **Jason Voorhees** in the "Friday the 13th" series, **Michael Myers** in the "Halloween" series, Henry (Macaulay Culkin) in *The Good Son* (Joseph Ruben, 1993), Samara (Deveigh Chase) in *The Ring* (Gore Verbinski, 2003), Esther (Isabelle Fuhrman) in *The Orphan* (Jaume Collet-Serra, 2009), and the **mutant** Dren (Delphine Chaneac) in *Splice* (Vincenzo Natali, 2009), among many, many others, represent manifestations of children rendered as incredibly one-dimensional monsters who exist primarily to threaten and terrify others with their bloody shenanigans and poorly constructed (or endlessly repetitive in the case of the series monsters) motivations.

The monstrous child of the horror story and film traditions, it is worth noting, finds its comic parallel in children whose monstrosity is applauded by their counter-normative families. Pugsly and Wednesday in *The Addams Family* iterations and Eddie (and perhaps Marilyn) in *The Munsters* are monstrous children by conventional standards, but their difference generally serves—in keeping with the series in general—to foreground the bland, tepid nature of those who conform to social expectations.

Joseph Michael Sommers

References and Suggested Reading

Balmain, Colette. "The Enemy Within: The Child as Terrorist in the Contemporary American Horror Film." In *Monsters and the Monstrous: Myths and Metaphors of Enduring Evil*, edited by Niall Scott. Netherlands: Rodopi. 2007.

Bontly, Thomas J. "Henry James's 'General Vision of Evil' in the Turn of the Screw." *SEL: Studies in English Literature, 1500–1900* 9, no. 4 (1969): 721–35.

Brown, Marilyn R., ed. *Picturing Childhood: Constructions of Childhood Between Rousseau and Freud*. Aldershot: Ashgate, 2002.

Crawford, Julie. *Marvelous Protestantism: Monstrous Births in Post-Reformation England*. Baltimore: Johns Hopkins University Press.

Jackson, Chuck. "Little, Violent, White: The Bad Seed and the Matter of Children." *Journal of Popular Film and Television* 28, no. 2 (2000): 64–72.

Petley, Julian. "The Monstrous Child." In *The Body's Perilous Pleasures: Dangerous Desires and Contemporary Culture*, edited by Michele Aaron, 87–107. Edinburgh, Scotland: Edinburgh University Press, 1999.

Poole, W. Scott. *Monsters in America: Our Historical Obsession with the Hideous and the Haunting*. Waco: Baylor University Press, 2012.

Tuveson, Ernest. "The Turn of the Screw: A Palimpsest." *SEL: Studies in English Literature, 1500–1900* 12, no. 4 (1972): 783–800.

Ziolkowski, Josef. *Evil Children in Religion, Literature, and Art*. New York: St. Martin's Press, 2001.

CHILDREN'S LITERATURE, MONSTERS IN

The monsters in texts for children are the same as monsters in any other sort of text. There are the conventional kinds and types (mythic, supernatural, hybrid, technological; **basilisk**, **djinn**, **ghost**, **vampire**, **windigo**); there are individual, invented monsters who inhabit their specific text (*Five Children and It*'s Psammead [1902], *Through the Looking Glass*'s **Jabberwock** [1871], *Monsters, Inc.*'s Mike Wazowski [Pete Docter, 2001], the Pokémon franchise's Pikachu [1996–present], the "Twilight" series' Edward Cullen [2005–2008], and so on); and they exhibit the same sorts of characteristics and behaviors one typically expects of monsters (oversized, misshapen, hairy/hairless/scaly; menacing, "of the night," cannibalistic). Nonetheless, the monsters in texts for children demand focused attention, in no small part because such texts emerge out of and exist only in relation to adults' historically and culturally variable notions of "the child."

Ideologies of the Monster in Texts for Children

The oldest texts for children with monsters are those that emerge from the traditional oral stories of various cultures around the world. Likewise, contemporary oral stories, in the form of playground gossip, camp tales, and what folklorist Jan Harold Brunvald (b. 1933) has termed "Urban Legend," offer some of the most recent monsters of children's literature. In *The Gruesome Guide to World Monsters*, Judy Sierra identifies two general roles that monsters play in these sometimes ancient, sometimes very current stories: to protect children (by scaring them away from certain places such as bodies of water, caves, and abandoned buildings) and to instruct children in the rules of their culture—

those who fall victim to monsters are, more often than not, those who foolishly and/or intentionally violate those rules. Of course, folk stories—be they "traditional" or "contemporary"—are not only for children; their monsters act as a caution to all as they express the "fears and desires of the people who invented them" (Sierra 64).

The more distinctive, more exclusively child audience-oriented monsters have come into being only fairly recently. Once infant mortality rates declined, and people had less need for "monsters" to embody the dangers of childhood, monsters, rather than being a threat to the child, became associated with the child and childhood—or rather, the child and childhood became likened to the monster and, sometimes, became the monster itself. In her study of monsters, *No Go the Bogeyman*, scholar and mythographer Marina Warner explains the phenomenon, arguing that the modern child's "affinity with monsters [grew] with the stresses modern childhood [put on] parents" (14). This relationship between the idea of the child and the idea of the monster, perhaps most pointedly embodied in contemporary picture books such as Maurice Sendak's *Where the Wild Things Are* (1963; see **Wild Things**), Jane Yolan and Mark Teague's *How Do Dinosaurs Say Goodnight?* (2000; see **Dinosaur**), and Sara Weeks's *If I Were a Lion* (2007), reflects and embodies, according to Warner, the "threatening quality of child-rearing and the conflicts between parents and children" (15). In other words, the child-as-monster situates the child in the position of "other," much as the monster is used in a variety of types of texts to explore cultural anxieties about race, gender, and/or physical and mental ability.

Beyond replicating the fears of the adults who create texts for children, the monsters of children's literature have also become the child's best friend, alter ego, and inner self. Here, the monster functions more as a psychological tool for the imagined child, offering the child ways to externalize and interact with his/her own needs and feelings. Notably, these monsters seem to lack the quality of monstrousness that typically characterizes the monster. As marker of this variety, these monsters are often given personal names rather than simply being a type (for example, Moominpappa, Moominmamma, and Moomintroll of the Finnish "Moomin" series [1945–present: nine books, five picture books, comic strips, several television series, and a number of films], Elmo of the American children's television program *Sesame Street* [1966–]; Bunnicula, the vampire bunny from James Howe's "Bunnicula" series [1979–2006]; Skellig from David Almond's 1998 *Skellig*; the many-eyed, **dragon**-esque cherubim, Proginoskes, from Madeleine L'Engle's 1973 *A Wind in the Door*, and so on). Of note, in one of the more recent turns, children's texts offer stories told from the monster's point of view (for example, Jon Stone and Mike Smollin's *The Monster at the End of This Book* [1971], Mo Willems's *Leonardo the Terrible Monster* [2005], Barbara Jean Hicks and Sue Hendra's *Monsters Don't Eat Broccoli* [2009], Pete Docter's *Monsters, Inc.* [2001]), perhaps interceding in the child-as-monster "othering" by generating understanding of the monster's position.

A Chronology of the Monsters in Texts for Children—Early Manifestations

In Western culture, the first "modern" monsters for children appeared with the first fantasy texts written for children—specifically, Charles Kingsley's 1862–63 serialized novel *The Water-Babies, A Fairy Tale for a Land Baby*, and Lewis Carroll's 1865 *Alice's Adventures in Wonderland*. Although John Newbery's 1744 *Little Pretty*

Pocket-book had introduced the idea that books for children could entertain as well as instruct, religious feelings and the Rationalist Moralists' notions of the child inspired by the work of John Locke (1632–1704) and Jean-Jacques Rousseau (1712–78) continued to discourage fantastical stories for children until Kingsley's Christian allegory *Water-Babies* breached the barrier. Kingsley's monsters are more **fairy**, creature, and talking animal (see **Animals, Monstrous**) than true monsters, but the book's idea that people cannot assume that just because they have not seen something (like a human soul or a water baby) it does not exist diminished the objections to fantasy in texts for children. Along with talking animals, animate objects (see **Objects, Animate**), and curious and hybrid creatures, Carroll's *Alice's Adventures in Wonderland* (1865), *Through the Looking-Glass, and What Alice Found There* (1871), and *The Hunting of the Snark* (1874) added a number of proper monsters to children's literature, including the **Jabberwock**, the Bandersnatch, and the Snark. Perhaps, though, the Alice books create the monster most cogently, as scholars such as Marina Warner suggest, in Alice herself. She grows big and small; she is unidentifiable ("Who are *you*?" the caterpillar asks several times); and she is even accused (by the pigeon) of being a monster. This is not, however, to say that Carroll's books accuse the child of monstrousness; instead, his stories highlight the monstrous difficulty that the inexperienced person has with finding the logic in the rules of society.

Carroll's friend and contemporary, George MacDonald (1824–1905), along with one of fantasy's greatest early innovators, E. Nesbit (1858–1924), quickly expanded the monster conventions in children's literature. The **goblins** of MacDonald's 1872 children's fantasy *The Princess and the Goblins* follow the earlier fairytale tradition of monsters threatening the child, but the book also introduces the monster as a kind of comic relief character, especially in the figure of the goblin queen who is quite silly about her shoes. E. Nesbit's cranky, wily Psammead, who initially appears in *Five Children and It*, may be the first truly developed figure to embody the creature/monster divide that characterizes many of the monsters in contemporary children's literature. Further, her deployment of classical monsters from Greek, Egyptian, and Mesopotamian mythologies in *The Phoenix and the Carpet* (1904) and *The Story of the Amulet* (1906) established a model for relocating such monsters into more-or-less contemporary settings and then exploring the consequences. Susan Cooper (b. 1935) used the technique quite effectively as she invoked Arthurian mythologies in her award-winning "The Dark is Rising" series (1965–77), while it has found greater purchase and popularity in the twenty-first century in Rick Riordan's 2005–2009 "Percy Jackson" series (Greek mythologies) and 2010–present "Kane Chronicles" (Egyptian mythologies), as well as in Jonathan Stroud's extraordinary "Bartimaeus" books (Mesopotamian mythologies), 2003–10.

In American literature, Washington Irving's **Headless Horseman** (from Irving's 1819–20 serially published *The Sketch Book of Geoffrey Crayon, Gentleman*) may offer itself as a kind of monster that has been appropriated into children's literature. Much like Jonathan Swift's *Gulliver's Travels* (1726; see **Swift, Jonathan, Monsters In**) and its monsters, "The Headless Horseman" was not initially thought of as a text for children; instead, it was part of Irving's efforts to establish a kind of American folk literature tradition in the post-Revolutionary period. Nathaniel Hawthorne, however, did write his 1852 *A Wonder-book for Girls and Boys* and its 1853 sequel, *Tanglewood Tales for Boys and Girls*, explicitly for children. These collections offer rewritten Greek myths with all of their monsters intact (that is to say, **Gorgons**, **Chimera**, the **Minotaur**).

Nonetheless, monsters do not really find their place in American children's literature until the publication of L. Frank Baum and W.W. Denslow's *The Wonderful Wizard of Oz* in 1900. Like Carroll's, MacDonald's, and Nesbit's creatures, Baum and Denslow's monsters are not particularly monstrous. With the exception of the Kalidahs (monstrous beasts with bodies like bears and heads like tigers), the Beast costume that Oz wears when the Woodman enters the great Throne Room for the first time, and a lion-eating, spider-like creature who appears late in the book, the animated objects (such as the scarecrow and china figures), talking animals (such as the lion and field mice), the **cyborg** (the tin man), and even the hybrids and odd creatures (such as the flying monkeys and the Quadlings) lack actual menace. Indeed, in his introduction to the story, Baum directly lays out his intention to create a "modernized fairy tale, in which the wonderment and joy are retained and the heart-aches and nightmares are left out" (4). Denslow's illustrations follow suit, as the menace of even potentially scary characters is minimized through goofy facial expressions, friendly smiles, ridiculous hairstyles, and/or placement of the images in relation to the text. In contrast to Victor Fleming's 1939 film version, *The Wizard of Oz*, in fact, the only true monsters in *The Wonderful Wizard of Oz* are the people: those like the **witches** of the East, West, and North who enslave others, as well as the **Wizard** himself who, while having good intentions, lies and deceives. In other words, Baum and Denslow, perhaps like Carroll, deploy monstrousness in relation to behavior rather than figure.

A Chronology of the Monsters in Texts for Children—Contemporary Manifestations

As Western texts for children (and later "young adults") came into their own over the course of the twentieth century, developing both as a form and in relationship to various media technologies, the monsters proliferated, especially post-World War II when the publishing of children's books expanded exponentially. Heffalumps and Woozles come by way of A.A. Milne's *Winnie-the-Pooh* (1926) and *The House at Pooh Corner* (1928). J.R.R. Tolkien offers a rather large set of monsters in *The Hobbit* (1937), including but not only man-eating **trolls**; giant spiders; the evil, **werewolf**-like Wargs; Gollum; and Beorn, the man-**ogre**-bear **shapeshifter** (see **Tolkien, Monsters In**). Dr Seuss (Theodor Seuss Geisel) also created a number of monsters for children's literature, including the monstrously behaved Grinch, Sylvester McMonkey McBean, Oncer-ler, and Yooks and Zooks of, respectively, *How the Grinch Stole Christmas!* (1957), *The Sneeches* (1961), *The Lorax* (1971), and *The Butter Battle Book* (1984), as well as his more simply fuzzy, misshapen, and/or mischievous monster-like creatures including Thing One and Thing Two of *The Cat in the Hat* (1957), Sam and his grumpy friend in *Green Eggs and Ham* (1960), and the various Yeps, Nooth Grushes, and Yottles of *There's a Wocket in My Pocket* (1974).

In the 1961 original fairytale and now classic of children's literature, *The Phantom Tollbooth*, Norton Juster created Tock (the hybrid dog-clock), the Humbug and Spelling Bee (enemy, talking insects), the Dodecahedron (a creature with twelve faces), the Lethargarians (extremely lazy, tiny creatures), the Everpresent Wordsnatcher (a bird-like creature that steals the words right out of your mouth), the Terrible

Trivium (a **demon** who wastes time with useless jobs), the Gelatinous **Giant** (an extremely fearful being who tries to hide by blending in with his surroundings), along with a host of other monsters—some of which help and some of which hinder the main character Milo's journey through "The Lands Beyond." Maurice Sendak crafted perhaps the most well-known monsters of American children's literature, the Wild Things, in 1963. Renowned British author of books for children Roald Dahl created the shapeshifting, cannibalistic, **extraterrestrial** Vermicious Knids in *Charlie and the Great Glass Elevator* (1972), sequel to his *Charlie and the Chocolate Factory* (1964). This is perhaps the only actual monster in Dahl's cannon, which may be surprising given Dahl's work's reputation for the fantastical, grotesque, and gruesome. His books and stories dwell instead on the monstrous behavior of people (child abuse, selfishness, classism, spoiled children having temper tantrums, and so on); even texts such as *James and the Giant Peach* (1961) with its giant insects, and *The BFG* (1982) with its cannibalistic giants, only use such "monsters" to highlight the true horror of people.

Most recently, writers and illustrators such as Quentin Blake (b. 1932), Ellen Blance (b. 1931), Sandra Boynton (b. 1953), Bruce Coville (b. 1950), Ed Emberley (b. 1931), Mercer Mayer (b. 1943), Neil Gaiman (b. 1960), Terry Pratchett (b. 1948), J.K. Rowling (b. 1965), Alvin Schwartz (1927–92), Judy Sierra (b. 1945), Shaun Tan (b. 1974), and Mo Willems (b. 1968) stand as some of the best-known makers of monsters and monster stories in contemporary children's literature. Likewise, in response to both publishing trends in children's literature and popular interest in monsters, a number of monster encyclopedias have been produced for children, including Judy Sierra's above-mentioned *The Gruesome Guide to World Monsters* (2005), James Otis Thatch's *A Child's Guide to Common Household Monsters* (2007); Ernest Drake, Dugald Steer, et al.'s *Monsterology* (2008); and *Encyclopedia Mythologica* (2011) by the much-acclaimed pop-up book writer/artist team of Matthew Reinhart and Robert Sabuda.

Expanding "Children's Literature": Monsters in "Young Adult Literature"

In addition, along with shifting notions of "the child," the partitioning and expansion of the children's publishing industry since the 1970s has created other monsters and types of monsters for young adult literature (children 12+, 15+, and 17+). Unlike the "cute monsters" of books for younger children and the sense of reassurance and security these monsters often generate, the monsters of young adult literature tend to offer more menace, horror, and/or engage with the dramas and anxieties of contemporary adolescence. The various genetically manipulated "Muttations" of Suzanne Collins's post-apocalyptic "Hunger Games" trilogy (2008–11) terrorize the main characters (see **Mutant and Freak**), while in the award-winning "Chaos Walking" trilogy (2008–10), Patrick Ness's alien Spackles appear to have released a biological weapon against the humans who have come to settle their planet. At the other end of the spectrum, books such as M.T. Anderson's *Thirsty* (1997), Annette Curtis Klause's *Blood and Chocolate* (1997), and Stephenie Meyer's "Twilight" series (2005–2008) feature vampires and werewolves exploring their identities and romantic possibilities as they try to find their place in the world.

Young adult fictions also offer an exceptional set of people with monstrous—or seemingly monstrous—behavior: adults who use or hurt children (Nancy Farmer's *The House of the Scorpion* [2002]); adolescents who are emotionally and/or physically cruel to one another (Laura Halse Anderson's *Speak* [2000]; Lauren Oliver's *Before I Fall* [2010]); and/or socio-cultural circumstances that damage children (Walter Dean Myer's *Monster* [1999]; G. Neri and Randy Duburke's *Yummy: The Last Days of a Southside Shorty* [2010]). Conventional comic books and the growing set of young adult graphic novels offer a wide range of monsters as well.

Beyond Print: Monsters in Children's TV, Film, and Video Games

The monsters of children's and young adult literature proliferate in other media as well. Indeed, as suggested by the references to film and television above, some of the most recognized monsters for children and teens have appeared in film, television, and/or video games. The Muppets of the long-running American Public Broadcasting Service program *Sesame Street*, including Cookie, Grover, Elmo, and Zoey, stand as some of the earliest "cute" TV monsters and perhaps paved the way for a myriad of other children's television monsters, including *Seven Little Monsters* (2000–2003), the creatures of *Foster's Home for Imaginary Friends* (2004–2009), and *Robot and Monster* (2012–), as well as films like *Monsters, Inc.*, *Monster House* (Gil Kenan, 2006), and *Monsters versus Aliens* (Rob Letterman and Conrad Vernon, 2009). The animated program *Scooby-Doo*'s not-really-monsters ("those meddling kids!") generated a way of creating and diffusing menace that may have opened the path for the scary-but-not creatures in films like *ET: The Extraterrestrial* (Steven Spielberg, 1982), *Gremlins* (Joe Dante, 1984), *Shrek* (Andrew Adamson and Vicky Jenson, 2001), *Wallace and Gromit: The Curse of the Were-Rabbit* (Nick Park and Steve Box, 2005), *How to Train Your Dragon* (DreamWorks, 2010), and *Frankenweenie* (Tim Burton, 1984; expanded and re-released, 2012). Meanwhile, US "Saturday Morning Cartoons" offer a set of monsters—both "cute" and scary, gentle and ill-intentioned—ranging from superheroes (for example, the Hulk, the Thing), nemeses of the superheroes (for example, werewolves, yeti, **Dracula**), **robots** (for example, Transformers), and anthropomorphized objects (for example, trucks, tools, airplanes) to **ghosts** (for example, Casper) and the just plain goofy (for example, the Schmoo).

In addition to showcasing numerous examples of cute, best friend, alter ego, transforming, sympathetic, not-really-scary monsters, film in particular offers a set of quite scary monsters to children's culture, including the Fireys of Jim Henson's *Labyrinth* (1986), the Skeksis of Jim Henson and Frank Oz's *The Dark Crystal* (1982), and the Sea Witch/polyp-creature, Ursula, from Disney's *The Little Mermaid* (1989). Monster movies geared towards teens/young adults likewise trend toward the scary, although some, perhaps drawing on the tendency towards irony that characterizes a lot of young adult fiction in print, capitalize on the silly (for example, *An American Werewolf in London* [John Landis, 1981] or *Teen Wolf* [Rod Daniel, 1985]).

Beyond film and television, children-oriented video games such as *Pokémon*, *Skylanders*, and *Monster Lab* offer the experience of tending, training, and/or making monsters, while teen games such as *Quake* and *Doom* offer the experience of being hunted by and/or tracking and killing monsters (see **Video Games, Monsters In**). The iOS game *Monsterology*, based on Ernest Drake, Dugald Steer, et al.'s book of the same name, offers multiplayer gaming via collecting, trading, and battling with monsters, while the online adventure game *Wizard 101* features a world filled with dragons, trolls, and various monstrous creatures. In their book *Millennial Monsters*

(2006), Anne Allison and Gary Cross offer a broader survey of the monster "beyond print," as they survey one of the most recent movements monsters have made in and through children's "literature"—namely, their explosion out of Japanese monster culture via film, televisions, video games, toys, and transmedia conglomerates, creating and expanding into, perhaps, one of the first global children's "literatures."

Gretchen Papazian

References and Suggested Reading

Allison, Anne, and Gary Cross. *Millennial Monsters: Japanese Toys and the Global Imagination*. Berkeley: University of California Press, 2006.

Drake, Ernest, Dugald Steer, et al. *Monsterology: The Complete Book of Monstrous Beasts*. Cambridge, MA: Candlewick, 2008.

Reinhart, Matthew, and Robert Sabuda. *Encyclopedia Mythologica: Dragons and Monsters Pop-Up*. Cambridge, MA: Candlewick, 2011.

Sierra, Judy. *The Gruesome Guide to World Monsters*. Illustrated by Henrik Drescher. Cambridge, MA: Candlewick Press, 2005.

Thatch, James Otis. *A Child's Guide to Common Household Monsters*. Illustrated by David Udovic. Honesdale, PA: Front Street Press, 2007.

Warner, Marina. *No Go the Bogeyman: Scaring, Lulling, and Making Mock*. New York: Farrar, Straus, and Giroux, 1998.

CHIMERA

Originating in Greek mythology, the Chimera is a female fire-breathing hybrid monster typically composed of a lion, a goat, and a snake. According to the ancient Greek poet Hesiod (c. 700 BCE), its parents were the monsters **Typhoeus** and Echidna (Echidna in Greek mythology is a half-woman, half-snake sometimes known as the "mother of all monsters"); its siblings included **Cerberus** and the **Hydra**. Ancient authors agree that the Chimera was slain by the Corinthian hero Bellerophon, riding on the winged **Pegasus**. The etymological origin of the name "Chimera" is uncertain, but the Greek word *chimaira* means "she-goat" and the monster may simply have been named after its goat parts.

In ancient Greek literature, descriptions of the Chimera's physical composition vary greatly. In the eighth century BCE, the poet Homer wrote that the Chimera was comprised of three parts: a lion's front, a goat's middle, and a snake's tail (*Iliad*, 6.180–181). Hesiod agreed, but added that the Chimera also had three heads, those of a lion, a goat, and a snake (*Theogony*, 321–2). Both Homer and Hesiod say that the creature breathed fire, a tradition accepted by later classical authors such as the second century CE Pseudo-Apollodorus (*Bibliotheca*, 2.3.1), who specified that the Chimera breathed fire from its goat head. Hesiod does not say whether all three heads grew from one neck, and in ancient art the creature typically had a lion's head growing on its main neck, with the goat's head growing out of its back and a serpent as a tail. Some Greek and Etruscan Chimeras, however, have not only the goat head but also the forelegs of a goat erupting from the lion's back. The varying shapes of the Chimera eventually coalesced into a canonical monster with a lion's head and body, a goat's head protruding from its back, and a snake as a tail, though deviations persist to today. A famous representation of the canonical Chimera is the *Chimera of Arezzo*, a fifth-century BCE Etruscan bronze, which influenced Renaissance and subsequent literary and artistic depictions of the Chimera's body.

As for the upbringing of the Chimera, sources agree that Amisodares, the king of Caria in Asia Minor, raised the Chimera to cause destruction, and when Bellerophon finally arrived, the Chimera was devastating the countryside of neighboring Lycia. Bellerophon had been at the court of King Proetus of Tiryns, where the king's wife Stheneboea attempted to seduce the young man. When he rejected her advances, she accused him of rape. Therefore, Proetus asked his father-in-law Iobates, king of Lycia, to kill Bellerophon. Assuming Bellerophon would die in the attempt, Iobates sent him to slay the Chimera. Riding on Pegasus, the hero killed the Chimera either with arrows (Pseudo-Apollodorus, *Bibliotheca*, 2.3.2) or, as told by the twelfth-century Byzantine scholar Tzetzes, by breaking off the lead point from his spear in the Chimera's mouth; the lead then melted in the monster's fiery breath, suffocating it (*On Lycophron*, 17). According to medieval traditions, it was the Greek hero Perseus, not Bellerophon, who rode Pegasus and killed the Chimera. After death, the Chimera inhabited the Underworld with other monsters such as **Gorgons** and **Harpies** (Virgil, *Aeneid*, 6.288–9).

It seems unlikely that anyone in antiquity believed such a creature as the Chimera could really have existed. Philosophers, in particular, were highly skeptical. In Plato's *Phaedrus* (c. 370 BCE), for example, Socrates lists the Chimera, along with **Centaurs** and Gorgons, as inconceivable and portentous creatures, saying that their existence is unlikely but could perhaps be rationalized (229d). The philosopher-poet Lucretius, in his first-century BCE *On the Nature of Things*, mentions the Chimera twice, both in contexts of disbelief. While explaining his theory of atoms, he proves that certain ways of combining atoms are not possible since otherwise composite monstrosities such as the Chimera would inhabit the Earth (2.700–706). He also notes the illogicality of the Chimera's breathing fire when it consists of the very flesh and blood that fire destroys (5.901–906). Cicero, in his *On the Nature of Gods* (45 BCE), asks whether anyone still believes in the Chimera, arguing for the reality of what exists in nature instead of what humans have invented in their minds (2.2). Plutarch, in his late first-century CE *Moralia*, reasons that the Chimera is simply a mythological interpretation of a pirate ship with a lion on the prow, a goat on the sail, and a snake on the stern (247F–248A). Pliny the Elder, in his first-century CE *Natural History*, records the belief that Chimera is an eternally burning volcano in Lycia (5.100). The first-century CE Greek historian and geographer Strabo believed that Chimera was the name of a ravine in Lycia, though different from Pliny's volcano (*Geographica*, 14.3.5). Isidore of Seville, a seventh-century CE encyclopedist, held that the Chimera was a mountain in Cilicia (the southern coastal region of Asia Minor) populated by lions, goats, and snakes, on fire in certain spots, and that Bellerophon made it habitable, hence, he "killed Chimera" (*Etymologiae*, 11.3.36). Given these attempts at rationalization, the word "Chimera" came to mean simply an unreal creature of the imagination.

Always female in the myths, the Chimera was also a point of comparison for women; for example, the Greek comedian Anaxilas (fourth-century BCE) claimed that female courtesans were more evil than the Chimera or any other female monster (fragment 22). This misogynistic use of the Chimera continued into the late Middle Ages: in the *Malleus Maleficarum* (*The Witches' Hammer*, 1486), a treatise on how to recognize and combat witchcraft, women are compared to the Chimera in its three animal forms: beautiful to see (lion), poisonous to the touch (snake), and deadly to keep (goat).

As a common noun, the word "Chimera" can simply signify a terrifying monster or, more loosely, anything composed of two or more parts, though the tendency is to reflect the canonical three elements of the Chimera.

Currently, many hybrid creatures are referred to as Chimeras since they are composed of two or more elements. In paleontology, Chimeras are **dinosaurs** reconstructed from more than one genus. A famous example is the "Brontosaurus," which in 1879 was identified as a new sauropod genus, but in 1978 was discovered not to be a distinct genus at all: it was an Apatosaurus outfitted with the skull of a Camarasaurus. Similarly, geneticists use "Chimera" to refer to an animal with two or more genetically distinct populations of cells coming from more than one zygote. Chimerism occurs naturally in many species, though it was demonstrated in the lab most dramatically in 1984 with a goat-sheep Chimera called a "geep," formed by combining genetic material from both goats and sheep. The Chimera is scientifically distinct from a hybrid, which would result from goat-sheep mating.

The genetic understanding of Chimeras appears in literature and film, as in Stephen Gallagher's 1982 book *Chimera*, made into a four-part mini-series directed by Lawrence Gordon Clark in 1991, and later released in America as the film *Monkey Boy*. Gallagher's plot involves a journalist who, investigating a murder in a clinic, discovers that the lab has genetically engineered a human-monkey hybrid named Chad who has escaped. Similarly, Vincenzo Natali's *Splice* (2009) features Dren (Delphine Chanéac), described as the first human-animal Chimera. Dren can take on the characteristics of each of the animals as she chooses, for example, by sprouting wings or changing gender. Both films play on fears that contemporary science could create such monstrosities as a real-life Chimera.

The canonical Chimera, too, occasionally appears in literature. In Rick Riordan's *The Lightning Thief* (2005), protagonist Percy Jackson meets a woman and a chihuahua who are soon revealed to be Echidna and the Chimera. The Chimera poisons Percy atop the Gateway Arch in St. Louis, but the young hero escapes. More frequently, the Chimera is evoked figuratively rather than literally, as in John Barth's 1972 postmodern novel *Chimera*, comprised of three separate novellas, "Dunyazadiad," "Perseid," and "Bellerophoniad." The "Dunyazadiad" describes the Arabian Nights' story of Scheherazade (see **Arabian Nights, Monsters In The**) from the viewpoint of her younger sister Dunyazade, while in the "Perseid" and "Bellerophoniad," Perseus and Bellerophon narrate their myths from their now middle-aged perspectives. The novel connects all three through a complicated narrative structure. Barth both writes about the Chimera in the "Bellerophoniad" while creating a Chimera of his own—the novel itself.

Films and television shows have tended to employ Chimeras more loosely. Zelgadis Greywords in *Slayers*, a Japanese anime, is transformed into a Chimera that is part human, part **Golem**, and part **demon**. In another anime, *Fullmetal Alchemist* (from the manga series of the same name), Chimeras are creatures synthesized by mixing two different beings together through alchemy. In John Woo's *Mission Impossible II* (2000), Ethan Hunt (Tom Cruise) must recover a **virus** "Chimera" and its antidote "Bellerophon," created by a Russian biochemist. Many video games, such as the *Final Fantasy* and *World of Warcraft* series, have featured Chimeras. The Chimera's illusory nature persists from antiquity to these modern usages.

Craig Jendza

References and Suggested Reading

Bompiani, Ginevra. "The Chimera Herself." In *Fragments for a History of the Human Body: Part One*, edited by Michel Feher, Ramona Naddaff, and Nadia Tazi, 364–409. New York: Zone Books, 1989.

Gantz, Timothy. *Early Greek Myth: A Guide to Literary and Artistic Sources*. Baltimore: The Johns Hopkins University Press, 1993.

CHRISTINE

Christine is the title of a 1983 novel by Stephen King, a 1983 film by John Carpenter, and the monstrous automobile in both that destroys her enemies and miraculously regenerates.

King is well known for demonstrating that tools, machines, or appliances are sentient and that they hunger for human blood (see **Objects, Animate**). *Christine* provides the most fully developed of these monstrous machines, but King experimented with the ambivalent relationship with machines in several short stories. "The Mangler," first published in *Cavalier* in December of 1972 and anthologized in King's collection *Night Shift* (1978), is one of King's first experiments with a **demon**-possessed machine. A direct ancestor of *Christine*, "Trucks" (*Cavalier*, June 1973 and *Night Shift*) also reveals that machines work independently of their human owners and operators.

King began *Christine* during the summer of 1978 as a story about a teenage boy whose car's odometer runs backward while he grows younger. As King wrote, however, the story gained a life of its own and became a novel about America's possession by the automobile. Dennis Guilder narrates much of the novel about his childhood friend, a loser named Arnie Cunningham, who buys a broken-down 1958 Plymouth Fury named Christine from an old man, Roland LeBay. The name Fury reinforces the anger of the car's original owner and echoes the Greek goddesses of vengeance. The story takes on sinister overtones when several characters suspect Christine of miraculous powers to kill people and restore herself. Christine (or LeBay) possesses Arnie and destroys the people around Arnie and finally Arnie himself.

Christine explores the dark side of the 1950s. Not only does King begin each chapter with quotations from poems or songs that feature automobiles, but he describes the decade as "the dark ditty-bop days ... when all the oil millionaires were from Texas and the Yankee dollar was kicking the shit out of the Japanese yen instead of the other way around" (155). Often nostalgically imagined in 1970s films and TV shows such as *American Graffiti* (George Lucas, 1973) and the television program *Happy Days* that ran from 1974 until 1984 (in which the main character, Richie Cunningham, and his friends congregate at "Arnold's," the local soda shop), 1950s values were being criticized in 1978, the year in which *Christine* is set. Four years later, Dennis, grown up and a teacher, reflects on adolescent problems and examines a period when America's love affair with technological products, especially her gas-guzzling muscle cars, had soured, and concludes with a loss of innocence and the fear that Christine may return.

Carpenter began shooting within days of the book's publication and released the film within a year. Less nuanced than the novel, the film eliminates multiple plot lines and suggests that the car was evil from the moment it rolled off the assembly line. Dissatisfied with Carpenter's presentation, King wrote and directed his own version of the monstrous machine in *Maximum Overdrive* (1986), inspired by and loosely based on "Trucks."

Carol Senf

References and Suggested Reading

King, Stephen. "The Mangler." In *Night Shift*, 74–92. New York: Doubleday, 1978.

——. *Maximum Overdrive*. New York: De Laurentis, 1986.

——. "Trucks." In *Night Shift*, 127–42. New York: Doubleday, 1978.

Magistrale, Tony. *Hollywood's Stephen King*. New York: Palgrave Macmillan, 2003.

Winter, Douglas E. *Stephen King: The Art of Darkness*. New York: New American Library, 1984.

CHUCKY

Depending upon the viewer's perspective, Chucky is either the primary antagonist or the anti-hero of the five *Child's Play* horror films, beginning in 1988 with *Child's Play*, directed by Tom Holland, and presumably ending with 2004's *Seed of Chucky*, directed by Don Mancini. Chucky itself is no more than a child's animatronic doll from the films' "Good Guys" collection. Granted, over the course of the movies, the doll becomes something more akin to a homicidal, malevolent talking Elmo bearing an increasingly familiar resemblance to a patchwork man or diminutive **Frankenstein's monster**.

The plot of the original *Child's Play* holds that serial killer and, by remarkable coincidence, voodoo practitioner, Charles Lee "Chucky" Ray (played, and later voiced, by Brad Dourif) was fatally wounded after a shoot-out with the police. Fortunately, being a voodoo practitioner cornered in a toy store before dying, Ray is able to transfer his soul into the body of the nearest Good Guys doll. The doll lands in the hands of a young and unsuspecting Andy Barclay (Alex Vincent) and Ray, now the soul-infused "Chucky" doll, must try to transfer his soul from the doll into Andy. Ray's "little" problem, as he learns while torturing his former voodoo instructor, is that by transferring his soul into the body of a plastic doll, he, through a remarkably contrived yet largely unexplained manner, is *becoming* the doll. Or, rather, the doll is becoming fully human (to the extent that a piece of plastic can). Thus, Ray becomes obsessed with transferring his soul into the body of Andy in an effort to become a normal human, in what amounts to a sort of devilishly parodic slant on Carlo Collodi's *Pinocchio* story (1883).

Eventually, Chucky is dispatched when he is shot through the heart—ironically, the thing that has magically become all-too-human already. As with most contemporary monster feature films, however, with great sequel comes great rejuvenation of the monster through absurd means. Though the body of the original Chucky doll is destroyed in the first film, its remains are retained by the Play Pals, Inc. corporation for analysis where, as one might suspect, the doll is reconstructed and reconstituted with the soul of Ray, who resumes his search for Andy and the voodoo ceremony that will grant him a human body. As one would expect, Ray continues to fail throughout the series and becomes destroyed in increasingly gruesome ways: for example, before being melted to death in *Child's Play 2* (John Lafia, 1990), Chucky is thrown into a conveyor assembly where he has multiple body parts sewn to his increasingly hybridic human–doll body before turning to goo. Fortunately for the series, an element of the Chucky flesh falls into the hot plastic of a new Good Guys doll, enabling a third *Child's Play* film (Jack Bender, 1991) in which Ray is sliced into pieces by an industrial strength fan.

Ray's somewhat gruesome quest for a human body is the driving trope of the series until the final two installments, whereupon the classic slasher motif of the prior movies becomes amalgamated with a greater emphasis on dark humor and self-referential parody. Along those lines, the *Child's Play* name is discarded in lieu of titles emphasizing Chucky: 1998's *Bride of Chucky*, directed by Ronny Yu, and the final film, *Seed of Chucky*, directed by Don Mancini. In the fourth installment of the series, Chucky is reassembled by a former lover named Tiffany (Jennifer Tilly). Alive again, Chucky takes his reincarnation in stride by murdering Tilly's character and transferring her soul into a female version of a similar model of doll. While their relationship is something less than ordinary, they do take time between murdering people to consummate their affection for each other in what amounts to sex between toys. In fact, the two *do* possess the ability to sleep with each other as the penultimate Chucky movie ends with Tiffany giving birth to Glen(da). Being the offspring of plastic toys, a running joke in the movie harkens back to the debate over the Ken Doll's sexuality. The voice of their doll progeny, however, is provided by male actor Billy Boyd. The final movie in the franchise becomes an exercise in self-reflexivity and an examination of the family life of Chucky. In it, Ray finally embraces his life as Chucky and decides to stay that way. As one might expect, this means he is, again, killed and, as one might expect, the seeds of a sixth movie are left at the end of the fifth.

As ridiculous as the films and the character of Chucky might be considered, the movies, particularly the third, may have played a role in the brutal 1993 murder of a young child named James Bulger in England. Connections were made by British tabloids between the third movie and the two children who committed the murder of Bulger, who cited the movie as an inspiration. While both the police and the *Child's Play* filmmakers have denied the accusations made by the British tabloids, there have been further acts of violence (though not fatal) directly attributed to the Chucky character since the 1993 murder (Bracchi).

Joseph Michael Sommers

References and Suggested Reading

Bracchi, Paul. "The police were sure James Bulger's ten-year-old killers were simply wicked. But should their parents have been in the dock?" The Mail Online, 13 March 2010. <http://www.dailymail.co.uk/news/article-1257614/The-police-sure-James-Bulgers-year-old-killers-simply-wicked-But-parents-dock.html#ixzz1KCU1keDO>.

Halberstam, Judith. "Bride of Chucky and the Horror of Heteronormativity." *Film International* 3 (2005): 32–41.

Holland, Patricia. "Living for Libido; or Child's Play IV—The Imagery of Childhood and the Call for Censorship." In *Ill Effects: The Media/Violence Debate*, edited by Martin Baker and Julian Petley, 78–86. New York: Routledge, 2001.

CHUPACABRA

The word "chupacabra" literally means "goat-sucker" in Spanish and this monster is often described as the "**Bigfoot** of Latino Culture." The name derives from the creature's habit of attacking livestock, especially goats, making several holes in the body of its prey, gruesomely sucking the blood (and sometimes the organs) from the animals, and then leaving a trail of blood and half-eaten carcasses in its wake. Although the location of the first sightings of this elusive creature is disputed, Michael Newton in *Hidden Animals* notes that the first sighting was reported in the 1970s in Puerto Rico and the victim, Juan Muñiz, described how he was attacked by a "horrible creature with feathers," known locally as the "Moca **vampire**" (128). This account was followed by subsequent reports from other regions of South America including Mexico and Chile, and then sightings spread to locations as diverse as Florida, Maine, and the desert southwest in the United States, and then to the rest of the world (Newton 127).

Some have speculated that the Chupacabra is **extraterrestrial** in origin, the product of a failed genetic experiment (see **Mutant and Freak**), or even a descendant of **dinosaurs** that has "escaped detection for centuries in the nearly impenetrable jungle of the El Yunque rain forest" in Puerto Rico (Corrales, *Chupacabra Diaries* 4). Descriptions of the elusive Chupacabra vary as widely as theories concerning its origins and the geographic locations in which it has appeared (see Corrales, *Chupacabra Diaries* 13–17; Newton 130–31). In Benjamin Radford's *Tracking the Chupacabra*, the author describes the creature as resembling a wild dog or a coyote, leading many to believe that it is indeed nothing more than that. Radford also notes that witnesses often say that the monster is hairless—resembling a larger and more grotesque version of the 3,000-year-old Mexican hairless dog, the Xoloitzcuintle, known as the "xolo." Descriptions taken by Corrales from "eye-witnesses" in Puerto Rico, in contrast, compare it to a kangaroo-like animal that stands on its hind legs and hops; it can be anywhere from three feet to twenty feet in height and gives off a smell of sulfur as a "defense mechanism" (*Chupacabras and Other Mysteries* 121). One of the most chilling descriptions that Corrales reports is of a creature that is similar to a large reptile with a dog face and eyes that supposedly glow in the dark and have the power to makes its victim nauseous. Its skin is greenish or grayish in hue and it possesses large, sharp teeth, a forked tongue, and an exposed spinal column running down its back. It makes a hissing sound when it is scared or alarmed and leaves behind the stench of rotten eggs.

Radford asserts that the terrifying Chupacabra has captivated the contemporary imagination as a consequence of "Chupacabra panic." Since the latest wave of reported sightings starting in 1995 in Puerto Rico, the dread of its vampire-like attacks has been continually reinforced by everything from the fear instilled by Hollywood movies that feature that blood-sucking creature, to superstition and groupthink, to a number of sightings throughout different parts of the Americas and Europe (Corrales, *Chupacabra Diaries* 11).

The Chupacabra has been absorbed fully into popular culture, especially in the horror genre, children's stories, and films. Two children's books by Mexican-American author Rudolfo Anaya that focus on the Chupacabra are *The Curse of the Chupacabra* (2006) and its sequel *ChupaCabra and the Roswell UFO* (2008). The latter focuses on the adventures of a university professor from California who finds that her interest in folklore has gone beyond academic boundaries when she follows the path of the mysterious Chupacabra to Roswell, New Mexico. Although the Chupacabra tends to be missing from classic or canonical works of literature, it has found its way into an array of recent pulp publications including: *Border Crossing (Twelve Terrifying Tales for 2011)* by Shana Hammaker, which follows the story of a gun smuggler who works on the border of San Diego, California and Sinaloa, Mexico; *Dance of the Chupacabras: The Tome Trilogy of Trilogies* (2009) by Lori R. Lopez; and the mystery novel *Lucy Cruz and the Chupacabra Killings* (2011), which is part of a series by Steven Torres. Torres's young adult story focuses on Lucy, a young photojournalist who, while searching for a Chupacabra as part of an assignment, instead witnesses a murder. Clifton C. Phillips has also published a children's picture book entitled *Chupacabra, You Don't Scare Me!* (1998), which was written after the Los Angeles-based teacher discovered that this was one of the things that most frightened his predominately Hispanic student population. He wrote this book about an orphanage in Puerto Rico to dispel the fears about the Chupacabra of those who read it.

Chupacabra-like creatures appear in a number of recent films including the

1995 Roger Donaldson science fiction thriller, *Species*. *The Guns of Chupacabra* (1997) is a monster film with a martial arts twist directed by Donald G. Jackson. This film features a lead character that is an alien that comes to earth to battle the Chupacabra. Many other B horror movies have been produced with the Chupacabra as their focus, including Brennon Jones's *Chupacabra: The Island of Terror* (1997) and Bob Scott's *Adventures Beyond: Chupacabra* (2000). The Chupacabra is also highlighted in *Scooby-Doo and the Monster of Mexico* (2003) in which the gang comes up against the ferocious monster during the Day of the Dead in Mexico.

Stephenie Young

References and Suggested Reading

Anaya, Rudolfo. *The Curse of the Chupacabra*. Albuquerque: University of New Mexico Press, 2006.

Corrales, Scott. *The Chupacabra Diaries: An Unofficial Chronicle of Puerto Rico's Paranormal Predator*. Derrick City, PA: Samizdat Press, 1996.

——. *Chupacabras and Other Mysteries*. Murfreesboro, TN: Greenleaf Publications, 1997.

Newton, Michael. *Hidden Animals: A Field Guide to Batsquatch, Chupacabra, and Other Elusive Creatures*. Santa Barbara, CA: Greenwood Press, 2009.

Radford, Benjamin. *Tracking the Chupacabra: The Vampire Beast in Fact, Fiction and Folklore*. Albuquerque: University of New Mexico Press, 2011.

CIRCE

A major character in Greek mythology, Circe is an enchanting seductress, dangerous sorceress, and impressive pharmacologist (see **Witch/Wizard**). She is best known for turning men—and the occasional woman—into animals; in Homer's *Odyssey* (c. eighth century BCE), her first appearance in Western literature, she transforms Odysseus's companions into swine. Daughter of the sun god Helios and the Oceanid Perse, her home is the mythical island of Aeaea, in the far east. Homer calls her a "dread goddess" in honor of her prophetic powers; she has "luscious locks" that bolster her erotic appeal and she exhibits an "extensive knowledge of drugs" (*Odyssey* 10.136; 276).

Although Circe eventually becomes a benign host and helper-figure to the hero Odysseus, their relationship starts unpromisingly. When Odysseus and his crew land on her island, he sends a group of men, led by Eurylochus, to explore the unfamiliar territory. They discover a dwelling surrounded by wolves and lions that, to their surprise, fawn at the approaching visitors. They hear sweet singing and enter the home. Eurylochus, however, sensing danger, hangs back, reporting to Odysseus what happened next. Welcoming at first, Circe serves the men food and drink into which she has mixed potent drugs; when the men finish their meals, she taps each with her wand to complete the spell, changing them into swine. Hearing this story, Odysseus sets out to rescue his men.

The god Hermes intercepts Odysseus, giving him an antidote to Circe's potion: *moly*, a white flower with a black root, which inures Odysseus to the effects of Circe's *pharmaka* (drugs), to her great astonishment. Realizing he is Odysseus, who was prophesied to visit her, the goddess turns his swine-companions back into men by rubbing them with an ointment that restores their human form. But after a year of pleasant life on Aeaea, Odysseus's crew grows restless; they encourage him to turn his thoughts homeward. Circe cooperates, instructing Odysseus to visit the famous blind prophet Tiresias in the Underworld, who will prophesy about Odysseus's future, including the hero's death. Circe also tells Odysseus how to navigate the twin dangers of **Scylla** and **Charybdis**, as well as the **sirens**.

Prophecy, erotic trysts, and magic are similarly at the core of the later Greek and Roman literary reception of Circe. For example, in Apollonius's epic *Argonautica* (third century BCE), Jason and his Argonauts stop by Aeaea on their way back from stealing the Golden Fleece. Circe, sensing the blood pollution that they bring with them from the murder of Medea's brother, performs ritual purification. But she also prophesies that Medea will not long escape her father's fury (4.741). The Roman poet Ovid (43 BCE–17/18 CE) reveals a sadistic side of Circe in his tale of her unreciprocated love for Glaucus, a fisherman-turned-sea god who himself fancies Scylla, at this time a beautiful maiden. Jealous, Circe pours poisons into Scylla's favorite bathing pool, turning her into the monstrous dog-limbed creature later encountered by Odysseus (*Metamorphoses* 13.900–14.74); this poisoned bath is the subject of John William Waterhouse's well-known painting, *Circe Invidiosa* (1892). Similar is the fate of Picus, whom Circe transforms into a woodpecker after he rejects her amorous advances (*Metamorphoses* 14.320–434). Striking a more comic note, Plutarch's *Gryllus* (second century CE) presents a humorous dialogue between Odysseus and one of Circe's enchanted pigs, named Gryllus ("Grunter"). This pig-man makes the rhetorically compelling case that animals have many more natural virtues than humans, and he resists Odysseus's efforts to "rescue" him.

Circe's mythical offspring include Telegonus, her son by Odysseus. In the *Telegony* (of uncertain date, but most likely sixth century BCE), a lost Greek epic, he travels to Ithaca in search of his father but, failing to recognize Odysseus, accidentally kills him. Full of remorse, he takes Odysseus's corpse, along with Odysseus's wife Penelope and their son Telemachus, to his mother, who makes all of them immortal. Telemachus ultimately marries Circe, and Telegonus marries Penelope.

Post-classical adaptations of Circe adhere closely to her ancient prototype. Arcasia, who turns men into animals in Book II of Spencer's *Faerie Queene* (1590), is modeled on Circe, as is the character named Circe who helps the protagonist, Macon "Milkman" Dead III, discover his origins in Toni Morrison's *Song of Solomon* (1977). In Nathaniel Hawthorne's *Tanglewood Tales* (1853), the smell of roasting pork draws men into Circe's Palace, where they themselves assume their true hog form after they have "sat at dinner a prodigiously long while ... and behaved like pigs in a sty" (112). Carol Ann Duffy performs yet a further twist on the "men are pigs" theme by drawing out the cannibalistic undertones of Hawthorne's tale in her poem "Circe" (1999), written from Circe's first-person perspective. The poem evolves into an elaborate recipe, including the tip that "well-cleaned pig's ears should be blanched, singed, tossed in a pot, boiled, kept hot, scraped, served, garnished with thyme" (47). The message of female empowerment echoes even more clearly when Circe urges the reader: "Look at the simmering lug, at that ear, did it listen, ever, to you ...?" (47). Less cannibalistic but no less unsettling is Bella Cohen's brothel, the update of Circe's Palace in the 15th episode of James Joyce's *Ulysses* (1922). In a more comic vein, Circe runs a "spa" in Rick Riordan's *The Sea of Monsters* (2006), where she turns main character Percy Jackson into a guinea pig.

Present in other media as well, the enchantress has been a favorite with the Pre-Raphaelite painters, and of John Waterhouse in particular. Circe is also the subject of a modern ballet, "Circe" (1963), choreographed by Martha Graham. Circe is Wonder Woman's nemesis in the DC Comics, and an inspiration behind the Sersi character in the Marvel Universe. Despite originally being integral to Odysseus's story, Circe has recently been integrated into the story of Hercules, having a cameo in the 1983 Italian *Hercules* film (Luigi Cozzi), as well as various television adaptations of the Hercules story.

Melissa Mueller

References and Suggested Reading

Duffy, Carol Ann. "Circe." In *The World's Wife*. London: Picador, 1999.

Hawthorne, Nathaniel. *Tanglewood Tales: A Wonder Book for Girls and Boys*. London: Frederick Warne and Co., 1853. Reprint, London: Electric Book Co., 2001. E-book.

Lattimore, Richmond, trans. *The Odyssey of Homer*. New York: Harper Perennial Modern Classics, 2007.

CITRARATHA—*see* Mahābhārata, Monsters In

CLURICAUNE—*see* Leprechaun

COCKATRICE

The cockatrice is a monstrous creature with the body and tail of a serpent and the head, legs, and wings of a cock. This snake-like hybrid creature was said to hatch from a cock's egg that had been incubated by a serpent or a toad. It was extremely venomous and its glance was lethal; however, it could be killed by a weasel. Seeing its own reflection would also do it in. The cockatrice was sometimes identified with the **basilisk**, another monster with bird and reptilian features that hatched from an egg. Aspects of the cockatrice were also confused with descriptions of the Nile crocodile. In heraldry, it is a hybrid monster with the head, wings, and feet of a cock and a serpent's tail that frequently ends in a second serpentine head linking it to the *amphisbaena*, a snake with a head at each end. In alchemical literature, it had features in common with the salamander, which could survive in fire, the reptilian winged **dragon**, and the mysterious *ourobourus*, another serpent-like creature that swallowed its own tail and constantly renewed itself. In this context, the cockatrice became a symbol for the transmutation of metals in the alchemical process itself.

The monstrous cockatrice therefore has a complex heritage that combines beliefs about snakes and crocodiles as well as some of the natural enemies of these creatures, such as the weasel and the ichneumon (sometimes identified as a type of rat or mongoose). The history of this fabulous creature begins with the Greek physician and poet Nicander (second century BCE) whose poem on the nature of venomous animals, *Theriaca*, describes a small, hissing, extremely poisonous snake that he calls a basilisk. A combination of beliefs about North African snakes like the hooded cobra and the spitting viper may lie behind this description. The *Natural History* of Pliny the Elder (23–79 CE) also contains a description of the basilisk (Book 8, 33). Pliny says that a glance from this animal is lethal, its breath destroys vegetation, it has crown-like markings on its head, and moves with its forepart upright. It is even dangerous in death since its venom can travel up a spear shaft and kill both man and horse. Its only enemy is the weasel. Pliny's description was repeated and expanded by subsequent authors. In the seventh century, Isidore of Seville's *Etymologies* (Book 12, 4:6–9) described the basilisk as the king (*regulus*) of snakes because of its extremely poisonous nature. Alexander Neckham (c. 1180) adds that the basilisk is hatched from a cock's egg incubated by a toad. This unnatural parentage from the seemingly infertile cock's egg adds an additional unnatural element to the already dangerous behavior of both basilisk and cockatrice. The appearance of the basilisk was also influenced by ancient Egyptian imagery. A hieroglyph depicting a cobra with its hood raised ready to strike was associated with the royal power of the Egyptian pharaohs. Such hieroglyphs and their significance informed early descriptions and also influenced illustrations that found their way into medieval bestiaries.

Pliny's description of another beast, the crocodile (Book 8, 37–8), also contributed to the creation of the cockatrice. According to him, a little bird enters the crocodile's mouth in order to clean its teeth while it is asleep. A creature called the ichneumon, however, can also enter the mouth of a sleeping crocodile and kill it by tearing its stomach open. Descriptions of the basilisk are included in medieval bestiaries, but some bestiaries also have dramatic illustrations of a water-dwelling *hydrus*, a mythical water-snake, being ripped apart by a creature that emerges through its stomach or side. Elements from all these descriptions were absorbed into the natural history of the cockatrice and emerged as a separate animal in twelfth-century French sources identifying the crocodile as *cockatris*. In the medieval compendium of knowledge, *Li Livres dou Trésor* (c. 1263) by Brunetto Latini, the author employs the term *cocatris* specifically in the context of Pliny's remarks about the crocodile and its enemies. The cockatrice surfaces again in fourteenth-century English sources. In the Wyclif Bible (1382), for example, "kokatrice" is used to translate *basiliscus*, while John of Trevisa (1342–1402) equated *cocatrice* with Latin *basiliscus in his fourteenth-century English translation of* Bartholomew Anglicus's work, *On the Properties of Things* (*De Proprietatibus Rerum*, Book 18). In the seventeenth century, Sir Thomas Browne in *Pseudodoxia Epidemica* (*Vulgar Errors*, Book III, vii; 1658) attempted to resolve this complex mixture of creatures by distinguishing the real serpent, the basilisk, from the mythical cockatrice.

As the deadly king of serpents, the cockatrice was associated with sin and the **devil**, especially the serpent in the Garden of Eden. In heraldry, however, its potency, upright posture, and crown-like markings suggested kingly power or the immortality of fame. English alchemical works such as George Ripley's *The Compound of Alchymie* (1477) and Thomas Vaughan's *Lumen de lumine* (1651) identified the cockatrice with the basilisk. The alchemical cockatrice, as noted above, developed qualities associated with the salamander's alleged resistance to fire and the tail-devouring *ourobouros*, and it became associated with the resolution of opposites as expressed by the alchemical process. Alchemical manuscripts stressed the nature rather than the appearance of the cockatrice and, in this context, it became a symbol for transformation and transmutation, specifically the death and rebirth imagery so often used to characterize the alchemical process.

Elizabethan poetry and drama frequently used the cockatrice symbol, sometimes as a synonym for a creature like the basilisk, sometimes as a more abstract image of tension and resolution. Both William Shakespeare in *Romeo and Juliet* (1595; III.4.54) and Edmund Spenser in a love sonnet "Amoretti 49" (1599) use the cockatrice to invoke the power of a deadly glance. In the poem "Sinne's round" (1633), George Herbert applies the alchemical meaning of cockatrice as a symbol of renewal to the dialectic of sin and penitence, and John Donne uses the idea that a cockatrice could be killed by seeing its own reflection to characterize a suspicious father in one of his *Elegies*, "The Perfume" (1633).

The cockatrice is not common among British dragon stories, but one allegedly hatched from a duck egg and terrorized the village of Wherwell in Hampshire (England). It was finally killed by a brave man who lowered a mirror into its lair. The tale is associated with medieval Wherwell Abbey, and the local museum houses a weathervane from the village church in the shape of a cockatrice. Edward Topsell, in *The History of Serpents* (1608), cites an old wives' tale about a man who wore crystal armor and destroyed many cockatrices by making them see their own reflections.

The cockatrice is still found in twentieth-century fantasy stories such as Edith Nesbit's "Kind Little Edmund or the Cave and the Cockatrice" from *The Book of Dragons* (1900), in which the main character rescues a dying cockatrice who advises the boy on how to defeat a dragon. A cockatrice is one of the many perils encountered by the young hero in John Masefield's fantasy novel, *A Box of Delights* (1935). Walter Wangerin Jr's fantasy *The Book of the Dun Cow* (1978) makes use of the complex monster lore connecting serpents, basilisks and the cockatrice. The latter is the evil reflection of the good cockerel Chanticleer. His serpentine half associated him with the forces of evil and he attempts to invade Chanticleer's kingdom at the head of an army of basilisks. The cockatrice is a popular monster in role-playing games such as *Dungeons & Dragons* (see **Dungeons & Dragons, Monsters In**) and *Final Fantasy* (see **Video Games, Monsters In**).

The lore surrounding the cockatrice evokes human revulsion to reptilian coldness, poison, parasitic invasion, and slimy death. The changing attitudes toward the cockatrice reveal the ways in which we conceptualize these fears and how we externalize them. Although unnamed, monstrous creatures that embody such widespread fear of reptiles, parasitic invasion of the body, and painful death by poison exist in contemporary horror films and fiction. The dystopian future depicted in Margaret Atwood's *Orynx and Crake* (2005), for example, is full of bio-engineered animals (see **Animals, Monstrous**; **Mutant and Freak**), many of which combine threatening and unpleasant features. The modern monster that seems to encapsulate the mixed heritage of the cockatrice best, however, is one of the most successful science fiction beasties—the terrifying creature of the *Alien* films (see **Extraterrestrial**). This creature, with its reptile-like appearance, corrosive body fluid, preternatural speed, seemingly unstoppable nature, and worst of all, parasitic larvae that burst out of the human body, echoes characteristics found in earlier sources and has given the cockatrice new life.

Juliette Wood

References and Suggested Reading

Alexander, R. McN. "The Evolution of the Basilisk." *Greece & Rome*, 2nd ser., 10, no. 2 (1963): 170–81.

Breiner, Laurence A. "The Career of the Cockatrice." *Isis* 70, no. 1 (1979): 30–47.

Robin, P. Ansell. "The Cockatrice and the 'New English Dictionary.'" In *Animal Lore in English Literature*. London: John Murray, 1932.

Simpson, Jacqueline. *British Dragons*. 1980. Reprint, London: Wordsworth and The Folklore Society, 2001.

COLLINS, BARNABAS

Barnabas Collins is the central **vampire** protagonist of the American Gothic television soap opera, *Dark Shadows*. Barnabas is the head of the aristocratic Collins family, which resides at their ancestral New England home of Collinwood. Raised from a long period of deep sleep by the estate's groundskeeper, Barnabas masquerades as a distant English cousin to the American Collins family and soon inserts himself into the daily affairs of the household. Barnabas entered the narrative in the first season of the original series in 1966, after several episodes that explored other supernatural occurrences at Collinwood and in the neighboring town of Collinsport. Barnabas, as played by Jonathan Frid in the original series, soon "proved so popular that he became the show's central protagonist" (Benshoff 18).

The original *Dark Shadows* program was created by Dan Curtis and ran from 1966 to 1971. Even after the series was cancelled, it fittingly had a considerable afterlife. There were two one-off films: *House of Dark Shadows* (Dan Curtis, 1970) and *Night of Dark Shadows* (Dan Curtis, 1971). While *House of Dark Shadows* retained a good deal of the series' original cast, including Jonathan Frid as Barnabas, the second film focused attention away from Barnabas and onto other supernatural characters. Alongside the original series, there was also a series of 32 *Dark Shadows* books published between 1966 and 1970, the majority of which focus their attention on Barnabas, creating a more elaborate backstory and further parallel adventures. The *Dark Shadows* television series was revived in 1991 for one season as an evening soap opera, with actor Ben Cross as Barnabas. The revival series focused from the outset on Barnabas.

Initially positioned as a monster, Barnabas's popularity (particularly with female viewers) dictated that he be endowed with a greater range of dramatic possibilities. The show's overwrought and complex storylines then regularly placed Barnabas in situations taken from a range of classic Gothic works. The characterization of Barnabas as sympathetic, but nonetheless dark, distant, and brooding, arguably paved the way for a host of sympathetic and seductive vampire heroes in literature and on television. Barnabas is very much the antecedent of both Spike (James Marsters) and Angel (David Boreanaz) of Joss Whedon's *Buffy the Vampire Slayer* and *Angel*, as well as the more recent Bill Compton (Stephen Moyer) of *True Blood*.

Frequently depicted as searching for a lost romantic companion, or expressing regret over his vampire status, Barnabas enacts many aspects of Bram Stoker's *Dracula* figure as played by Gary Oldman in Francis Ford Coppola's 1992 film adaptation, as well as the desirable aspects of the Gothic villain popularized by works such as Daphne Du Maurier's *Rebecca* (1938), and the cycle of Gothic women's films of the 1940s, such as Alfred Hitchcock's *Rebecca* (1940) and *Suspicion* (1941), in which unwary and innocent heroines are often simultaneously drawn to and repelled by mysterious male lovers. *Dark Shadows* continues to have an active fan community and much fandom centers on the figure of Barnabas. Director Tim Burton's film adaptation of *Dark Shadows*, starring Johnny Depp as Barnabas, was released in 2012.

S. Artt

References and Suggested Reading

Benshoff, Harry. *Dark Shadows* (Television Milestones). Detroit, MI: Wayne State University Press: 2011.

Wheatley, Helen. *Gothic Television*. Manchester: Manchester University Press, 2006.

CRAWLY—*see* Demon

CREATURE FROM THE BLACK LAGOON, THE

The Creature from the Black Lagoon (or "Gill-man," as he is sometimes referred to) is an amphibious humanoid who makes his first appearances in three 1950s Saturday matinee creature feature films from Universal Studios: *Creature from the Black Lagoon* (Jack Arnold, 1954), *Revenge of the Creature* (Jack Arnold, 1955), and *The Creature Walks Among Us* (John Sherwood, 1956). The Creature made a lasting impression, threatening screaming women on screen, and audiences as well, through the first two films' pioneering use of 3-D. The Creature, a relic of another time—the Devonian age, as explained in the first film—lives quietly in a lagoon in the upper reaches of the Amazon until scientific expeditions repeatedly disturb him as they try to study or capture him. Played in the first film by the 6 feet 5 inches Ben Chapman, the Creature presents an imposing figure with his well-developed pectorals and abdominals, webbed and clawed hands and feet, full lips, large intense eyes, and gills on the sides of his head. Although there is no visual evidence, the Creature is apparently male and heterosexual, as he spends most of the first two films watching and abducting the leading ladies.

The first two Creature films were directed by Jack Arnold. Arnold was basically a B movie director, but his effective use of lighting and beautiful underwater sequences, such as the shots of the Creature (Ricou Browning in the water) mirroring the swimming strokes of the heroine, Kay Lawrence (Julia Adams), earned the Creature a lasting place in US popular culture. Moreover, the iconic image of the Creature coming out of the primordial waters of his home or carrying away bathing suit-clad damsels to his hidden grotto are some of the most enduring in science fiction film.

The plot of the first film is fairly simple. A geology expedition led by Dr Maia (Antonio Moreno) in the Amazon uncovers a strange fossil: a webbed hand. When he takes his find to the nearby marine institute, we meet the rest of the central characters, Ichthyologist Dr David Reed (Richard Carlson), Kay Lawrence, and their boss Dr Mark Williams (Richard Denning). The newly established group decides to go back to the dig site to find the rest of the fossil. After days finding nothing, David suggests that it might have been washed downstream. Once they arrive at the titular lagoon, they make a stunning discovery: there is a live specimen. When they try to capture the Creature, the film becomes about more than studying an "evolutionary dead end"; it becomes a tale about gender, sexuality, and race as the Creature, David, and Mark all vie for Kay's affection, with fatal results.

In *Revenge of the Creature* (shot in 3-D but screened in standard format), the sequel to *Creature from the Black Lagoon*, an expedition returns to the Amazon and successfully brings the Creature (here played by Tom Hennesy on land and Ricou Browning in the water) back alive to the United States for study. Again there is a cadre of males all interested in the one female, Helen Dobson (Lori Nelson). Not long after arriving at Florida's Oceanarium, the Creature escapes, killing one of his rivals, and begins terrorizing the Florida coastline in his pursuit of Helen. As the film progresses, the Creature's on-screen appearances coincide with Dr Clete Ferguson's (John Agar) growing desire for Helen; the connection between the two is made stronger through the film's editing, which often cross-cuts from romantic scenes of Clete and Helen together to the Creature observing them. Sequences such as this serve to link Clete's desire for Helen to the primitive, uncontrollable passion of the Creature.

The third entry in the Creature series, *The Creature Walks Among Us*, directed by John Sherwood, arguably lacks the artistic and cinematic grace of Arnold's films and presents a different sort of Creature (Don Megowan on land, Ricou Browning again in the water). Picking up where *Revenge* ends, the Creature, again believed dead, is actually alive and roaming the Everglades. The Gill-man is quickly captured, but things go terribly awry and he is set on fire. As Dr Bill Barton (Jeff Morrow), the team's leader, and Dr Tom Morgan (Rex Reason) attempt to save him, they discover that he has a primitive set of lungs that he must now use—making him the Gill-man no more. They also notice that the Creature's outside scales have been burned away, and dark, human-like skin exists underneath; his webbed hands and feet are now practically human. His face has also changed; he now has deep-set human eyes glinting beneath a pronounced furrowed brow. His nose is flat and wide and his lips large and exaggerated; even his upper body is bulked up in a provocatively racialized manner.

Moreover, Sherwood's Creature not only transforms from evolutionary dead end to missing link, but also from a threat to white womanhood and masculinity to the "noble savage." Instead of spending his time pursuing Barton's beautiful blonde wife Marcia (Leigh Snowden), the Creature spends his time trying to return to the water and protecting the weak, especially Marcia, from the real monster of the film—Barton. The Creature's "honorable" actions and connection to nature align him with the stereotype of the noble savage and, like the noble savage, he cannot live in the modern world. However, thanks to modern science, he also cannot return to the sanctuary of his black lagoon. The film ends with the Creature at the sea cliffs; he looks longingly at the water and shuffles toward it and, presumably, his death.

Scholars largely ignore Sherwood's film and focus on those directed by Arnold. Cyndy Hendershot, for instance, notes that, "these two films create complicated metaphorical links between the Bomb, sexuality and gender, and paranoia" (91). She also notes how the representation of the Creature "creates sf metaphors which intertwine eroticism and the Bomb" (100). For Mark Jancovich, the *Creature from the Black Lagoon* and *Revenge of the Creature* are about sexuality, gender, and race. He writes: "The creature is not only associated with the oppression of women, but also the tyranny of WASP culture over other ethnic and racial groups, particularly through the film's concern with colonization" (184). Certainly, the Creature of Arnold's films is the dark alien Other that threatens white masculinity, white womanhood, and the "American way of life."

Beyond the three Universal films, the Creature has made an array of popular culture appearances, from Uncle Gilbert (Richard Hale) in the television comedy *The Munsters* (1964–66), to Gillman (Tom Woodruff, Jr) in Fred Dekker's 1987 film *The Monster Squad*. The Cartoon Network program *Robot Chicken* in fact foregrounded the usually implicit racial subtext of the Creature narratives in the 9 September 2007 episode, "Shoe," in which the Creature explains that he prefers to be called the "Creature from the African-American Lagoon." The character Abraham "Abe" Sapien in the *Hellboy* comic book series created by Mike Mignola and the film adaptations is clearly based on the Creature, as is the Creature-like denizen of Halloweentown in Henry Selick's *The Nightmare Before Christmas* (1993). A short-lived musical called *Creature from the Black Lagoon: The Musical* debuted at the Universal Studios Hollywood theme park in July of 2009.

Susan A. George

References and Suggested Reading

Hendershot, Cyndy. *Paranoia, the Bomb, and 1950s Science Fiction Films.* Bowling Green: Bowling Green University Popular Press, 1999.

Jancovich, Mark. *Rational Fears: American Horror in the 1950s.* Manchester: Manchester University Press, 1996.

CREEPER—*see* Video Games, Monsters in

CRYPTID

"Cryptids" are organisms (plant, animal, or fungi) whose existence is suspected by some but not yet proven to the scientific community; the term comes from "cryptozoology," the study of hidden or mysterious animals, and was coined by John E. Wall in a 1983 letter to the International Society of Cryptozoology newsletter. Cryptids can be a part of ordinary zoology, including specimens that redefine a species (such as spotted lions, blue tigers, giant squid, and pigmy hippopotamuses), new species that are first heard of as legends, and animals thought to be extinct. The coelacanth, a lobe-limbed fish considered extinct until one was caught in 1938 off the coast of South Africa, is a poster child for scientific cryptozoology; gorillas, the Congo peacock, giant pandas, and the okapi, a striped relative of the giraffe, were all cryptids before definitive proof of their existence was established.

Many cryptids, however, such as **sea monsters** and giant hominids (see **Bigfoot**) may never be incontrovertibly documented. These excite the public imagination and engender the same emotions as any purely fictional monster. Some cryptids purportedly exhibit supernatural abilities; the study of these creatures is often called "Fortean zoology"—named after Charles Fort (1874–1932), whose books catalog inexplicable phenomena—to distinguish it from scientific cryptozoology. The Center for Fortean Zoology was founded in 1992 by Jonathan Downes (1959–). Creatures that appear to read and project thoughts, such as some sasquatches, or cause radiation-like symptoms in people, such as the mothman (see below), are considered Fortean animals.

Cryptids also include animals that appear without logical explanation where they are not naturally found, as well as unusually large animals. For instance, ABCs—"alien big cats" or "alien black cats" ("alien" meaning not extraterrestrial but non-native)—appear in real-life reports and in fiction, including a boys' adventure novel from 1921, Warren H. Miller's *Black Panther of the Navajo*. And the 30-foot-long crocodile in the 2000 horror video *Blood Surf* (James D.R. Hickox) probably qualifies as a cryptid, because the record size is 22 feet, so it may be a new species. To be a cryptid, however, the animal must be a product of nature, not deliberate or accidental scientific meddling. Thus, Steve Miner's 1999 *Lake Placid* is a cryptid film, as the crocodile inexplicably survives and even grows huge in Maine, but David Flores's 2007 made-for-TV *Lake Placid 2* is not, because that alligator is fed government-banned meat with hormones that affect its size.

Although Fortean animals may be considered cryptids, outright supernatural creatures are excluded. Thus, although the **phoenix**, merpeople (see **Mermaid/ Merman**), and **basilisk** in J.K. Rowling's "Harry Potter" books (1997–2011) are sometimes called "cryptids," including in fan fiction, they do not fit the term any more than **vampires** do (see **Harry Potter, Monsters In**). Finally, although a story featuring a **dinosaur** in the present is cryptofiction, this is not true if the dinosaur is found on another world or if human beings travel back in time. Some stories—such as *The Monster that Challenged the World* (Arnold Laven, 1957) concerning ancient mollusks attacking California—are borderline: the mollusks are liberated by an earthquake, rather than having survived as an ongoing species, but they represent a genuine, living, non-supernatural species that survives on its own.

In certain cases, a reader or viewer may not know if a cryptid is involved until the very end of the work. For instance, in "The

Flying Death," a story by Samuel Hopkins Adams from around 1905, the suspect is a pteronadon believed to have somehow survived and killed a man near Montauk Point, New York; however, the murderer was human and the creature a hoax to mislead the investigator. Also, as fits creatures that may or may not exist, some of the writing and films about cryptids straddle the line between fiction and reportage. Many creatures discussed here and elsewhere, including the mothman, the **Loch Ness monster**, and sasquatch, are the subject of pure documentaries/non-fiction or films/fiction, but also of mockumentaries (fictional films presented as fact), films or written reports that are purportedly real but turn out to be hoaxes, and fictional films or texts based—with various degrees of artistic license—on reported events.

Classic Cryptids

Most of the cryptids of antiquity have long ago been proven impossible, such as the salamander that lived in fire, or explained in terms of existing species, such as some reports of unicorns being traced to sightings of the rhinoceros. Thus, medieval or classical Greek or Roman creatures in American fiction and films are generally treated as supernatural, including unicorns and a **harpy** in *The Last Unicorn* (novel by Peter S. Beagle, 1968; animated film by Jules Bass and Arthur Rankin, Jr, 1982); the poisonous **cockatrice** and **basilisk** in Dungeons & Dragons (see **Dungeons & Dragons, Monsters In**) and various video games; or the **dragon**, **Chimera**, and others in the 2005–2007 TV series from Disney, *Jake Long: American Dragon*.

One exception is the mermaid, which is sometimes presented as a supernatural creature and sometimes as a crypto-zoological specimen. Besides the TV show *Sanctuary* (see below), the film *Splash* (Ron Howard, 1984) depicts the mermaid (played by actress Daryl Hannah) as a physical being, with its own ear-piercing language, housing and habitat requirements, and ability to learn our language through mimicry of TV. In a deleted scene on the DVD, the mermaid's assumption of human form is shown to be supernatural, but in the movie itself, it stands as a characteristic of the species. *Pirates of the Caribbean: On Stranger Tides* (Rob Marshall, 2011) features a race of mermaids, which also have the singing voice and deadly inclinations of the ancient Greek **sirens**; they may be supernatural or they may be cryptids.

Another classical beast sometimes treated as a cryptid in American fiction and film is the sea monster. Snake-like sea serpents are more likely interpreted as supernatural, although Cecil the seasick sea serpent, in the animated TV series *The Beany and Cecil Show* by Bob Clampett (1962), seems more like a cryptid. Four-legged sea monsters, however, are often explained as a survival of a prehistoric species, an explanation many genuine cryptozoologists propose for various animals. In *The Beast from 20,000 Fathoms*, a 1953 film directed by Eugéne Laurié, an atomic bomb set off in the Arctic awakens a rhedosaurus (a fictional type of dinosaur) that attacks New York City; the movie is based on Ray Bradbury's 1951 short story, "The Fog Horn," about a dinosaur surviving in the modern era. The 1959 film *The Giant Behemoth* (Douglas Hickox and Eugéne Laurié), originally about an amorphous cloud of radiation, was changed at the distributor's request to concern another surviving dinosaur. The eponymous creature in *The Crater Lake Monster* (William R. Stromberg, 1977) is a surviving plesiosaur that appears in Oregon.

The Circus of Dr Lao, a novel by Charles G. Finney (1935), features many classical monsters and treats all of them as cryptids, caught in the wild and needing to be fed and tended to like any other circus animal. For instance, the **sphinx** sheds in captivity, and the snakes on the **medusa**'s head must be fed independently of her and of each other. The circus also features a **satyr**, the chick of a giant roc (see **Birds, Giant**), a sea serpent, a mermaid, a Chimera, and a unicorn. Even the **werewolf** is depicted as a member of an exotic species, not the victim of a curse. The novel also describes a new kind of cryptid, the hound of the hedges, a canine made entirely of plants. This quirky and lyrical novel was adapted as *7 Faces of Dr Lao*, a 1964 film directed by George Pal, from a script by Charles Beaumont. In the movie, the sea serpent was known when young as the Loch Ness monster, and an ambiguous figure in the novel, which some circus goers think is a bear and others think is a human being, is explicitly presented as a yeti (see **Bigfoot**).

Current Cryptids

Dinosaurs and Other Survivals

Dinosaurs surviving into the modern era are among the most common and popular cryptozoological subjects in American film and fiction. For example, Wardon Allan Curtis's "The Monster from Lake LaMetrie" (1889) concerns a 28-foot-long elasmosaurus; *Pterodactyl*, a 2005 made-for-TV movie (Mark L. Lester) features not only the titular creature but also a tyrannosaurus, discovered on the Turkish/Armenian border. Sometimes the dinosaurs are horrifying, as in *It's Alive!*, a 1969 film directed by Larry Buchanan, in which an insane farmer tries to feed a lost pair of newlyweds to an 80-foot-tall dinosaur he found and keeps in a cave. In other cases, the dinosaurs may be charming, as in the "Prehysteria" trilogy—*Prehysteria!* (Charles and Albert Band, 1993), *Prehysteria! 2* (Albert Band, 1994), and *Prehysteria! 3* (David DeCoteau, 1995)—which features five miniature dinosaurs that hatch from eggs found in a temple in South America. In *Baby: Secret of the Lost Legend*, a 1985 film directed by Bill L. Norton, an American couple finds a baby brontosaurus (now known as an apatasaurus) in the Republic of Congo; the film links the creature to the African legend of mokélé-mbembé, a huge creature that some cryptozoologists believe may be an actual surviving dinosaur.

While those stories and films depict dinosaurs brought into our human civilizations, many works concern the discovery of a land in which many prehistoric species survive. The two major novels in this subgenre are Sir Arthur Conan Doyle's *The Lost World*—a British novel from 1912, adapted in American films including *Lost Continent* (Sam Newfield, 1951)—and *The Land That Time Forgot*, by Edgar Rice Burroughs, originally published as a series in *Blue Book Magazine* in 1918. Adaptations of the latter appeared in 1975 (Kevin Connor) and 2009 (C. Thomas Howell). Of course, dinosaurs survive in the same isolated environment that protects the title character in both the 1933 and 2005 films ***King Kong*** (respectively, co-directed by Merian C. Cooper and Ernest B. Schoedsack, directed by Peter Jackson). Dinosaurs also live in a warm volcanic crater within the Antarctic in the extremely low-budget film *The Land Unknown* (Virgil W. Vogel, 1957), on an island off Australia in *Two Lost Worlds* (Norman Dawn, 1950), and in a place called the Forbidden Valley in the southwestern USA in *The Valley of Gwangi* (AKA *The Lost Valley*, *The Valley Time Forgot*, and other titles), a 1969 film directed by Jim O'Connolly.

One favorite prehistoric species is an extinct, giant ancestor of modern sharks, *Carcharpodon megalodon*. In fact, Steve Alten has written an entire series of novels concerning these huge cryptids and their adversary, Navy-diver-turned-paleontologist Jonas Taylor: *Meg: A Novel of Deep Terror* (1997), *The Trench* (1999), *Meg:*

Primal Waters (2004), *Meg: Hell's Aquarium* (2009), and *Meg: Origins* (2011). *Megalodon Lives*, a 2011 Kindle book by Flash Rex, features a mother and baby megalodon. Finally, in the spirit of **Godzilla** and his various adversaries, this monster appears in the 2009 film *Mega Shark vs. Giant Octopus* (Jack Perez) and the 2010 film *Mega Shark vs. the Crocosaurus* (Christopher Ray).

Other stories of cryptozoological appearances of prehistoric creatures in the modern world include a live mammoth in the Yukon in Jack London's story "A Relic of the Plioscene" (1904), and vicious trilobites in the 2005 novel by Kenneth Gass, *Trilobites!*

The Kraken

The **kraken** is one cryptid now known to exist: what the Bishop of Bergen called one of the largest sea monsters in the world in his study *The Natural History of Norway* in 1723 is actually the giant squid, finally scientifically proven in the 1870s. Even now, no zoologists know exactly how large the squids can grow; one 65-foot specimen was found on a New Zealand beach in 1880, but scars on sperm whales may suggest squid 150 feet long. For fictional representations of the kraken, see the separate entry in this encyclopedia.

The Jersey Devil

Unlike most cryptozoological animals, the Jersey devil has a supernatural origin: the legend, from 1735 or earlier, concerns a woman in Leeds Point, in the Pine Barrens of New Jersey, who swore that her next child would be a devil, which it was. In one version of the story recounted by Grace-Ellen McCrann on the New Jersey Historical Society's website, she was tired of having children, and cursed the 13th as it was born. The resultant monster has a horse's head, cloven hoofs, bat wings, and a serpent tail. The interest of cryptozoology comes from sightings, starting in 1909, of unidentifiable cloven hoofprints in the snow across eastern Pennsylvania and southern New Jersey. Finally the creature itself was seen and, in one account, driven off with water from a fire hose. People have seen the devil or its footprints as recently as 1993.

Two works of fiction invoke the Jersey devil but provide different explanations for the events. "The Barrens," by F. Paul Wilson (1990), depicts the life and lore of the Pine Barrens, but the Jersey devil is merely folklore; the story, inspired by the fiction of American horror author H.P. Lovecraft (see **Lovecraft, Monsters In**), actually concerns the lights sometimes seen in the area, which in the story are consciousness-altering pan-dimensional intelligences. Harper William's *The Thing in the Woods*, a 1927 novel that H.P. Lovecraft mentions as an influence, also features the Jersey devil as mere folklore; the murders in the story are by a human being with atavistic tendencies.

On film and TV, the Jersey devil is more of a straightforward monster. "The Jersey Devil," a 1993 episode of *The X-Files* (season 1, episode 5; Joe Napolitano), features a race of hairy hominids, perhaps prehistoric relicts, that do attack and eat human beings. It was filmed on the west coast and only marginally tied to the New Jersey events. The movie *Thirteenth Child* (Thomas Ashley and Steven Stockage, direct-to-video, 2002) was filmed in the correct area and is closer to the legend, but many viewers say that the plot does not make sense. The origin of the titular character is supernatural, but the creature is basically cryptozoological—its DNA is an unprecedented combination of goat, bat, and other species. In *Carny* (Sheldon Wilson, made-for-TV, 2009), a local captures a Jersey devil, which looks somewhat like a cross between a pig and a dragon; it goes on exhibition at a carnival and then escapes and kills people to drink their blood.

The Mothman

The mothman is a large, humanoid flying creature with glowing red eyes that has fluttered between non-fiction and fiction. It first became public in *The Mothman Prophecies*, a 1976 non-fiction book by John A. Keel concerning sightings in 1966–67 in Point Pleasant, West Virginia. In 1997, an episode of the fictional TV show *The X-Files*, "Detour," featured the creature; and a 2002 movie, *The Mothman Prophecies* (Mark Pellington), presented some of the incidents Keel reports but changed aspects of the plot and characterization. *Perverted Communion*, a 2010 novel by Steve Ressel featuring the mothman, also includes some facts, but the author adds major fictional elements to explain the mystery. *Mothman*, a made-for-TV movie from 2010 (Sheldon Wilson), changes the story significantly, adding the illogical characteristics that the mothman rips out eyes but cannot fight a person who cannot see it; the movie, however, includes scenes set at the real annual mothman festival held in Point Pleasant. Returning to the original non-fiction approach, *The Eyes of the Mothman* is a full-length documentary from 2011 (Matthew J. Pellowski).

The Hodag

The hodag proves that any cryptid, no matter how obscure or clearly fake, can establish itself in American fiction and film. The creature was a hoax by Eugene Shepherd, a resident of Rhinelander, Wisconsin, who announced the discovery in 1893; he even exhibited it at the Oenida County Fair, but when the Smithsonian Institution called to investigate, Shepherd confessed. It was seven feet long, lizard-like with spines along its back but furry, with horns growing from its forehead and tail, huge tusks, and green eyes; it was said to smell bad. Even after exposure, the hodag legend grew, including the datum that it only ate white bulldogs. It became the town's unofficial mascot, and Rhinelander holds an annual Hodag Country Festival of folk music.

Two children's storybooks and one young-adult novel feature the hodag, all sympathetically. *Tales from the Trees* (2006) and its sequel *A Monster Misunderstanding* (2007), by Jill Kuczmarski, are rhyming read-along books; in the second, the hodag and the white bulldog become friends. *The Terrible Hodag*, written by Caroline Arnold and illustrated by John Sanford (2006), keeps the physical appearance of the monster but shows that he is a peaceful creature and friend to the local loggers.

However risible the hodag may seem, Trent Hergenrader's short story "The Hodag" (in *Best Horror of the Year 1*, editor Ellen Datlow, 2009) makes it a thing of real horror: a bloody encounter with it haunts the protagonist over the decades. The hodag also appears as a monster in the card-based role-playing game Arcana.

Cryptofiction

In 1998, Craig Heinselman, publisher of the newsletter *Crypto*, coined the term "cryptofiction," replacing clumsier terms including "cryptozoological-themed fiction," and in 2007 two major articles explored this possible "new genre": one by Eric Penz, author of the 2005 novel *Cryptid: The Lost Legacy of Lewis & Clark*, and one by Matt Billie, a writer of non-fiction cryptozoology. Penz cites earlier examples such as *King Kong* and Sir Arthur Conan Doyle's *The Lost World* (each popular in many versions), but argues that we need stories of exploration and discovery more than ever today, now that the globe is mapped and the mystery mostly gone. Billie further defines the genre, distinguishing it from "monster thrillers" in that the writers of cryptofiction must make the existence of their creatures biologically plausible. Because cryptids often survive in exotic locales and encounters with them put people into extreme situations, Billie argues, they fit well with the thriller genre; he also discusses traits of good and bad cryptofiction.

Several books, many in ongoing series, already represent this twenty-first-century genre. Penz's *Cryptids*, often praised in reviews, combines a story about cryptids with crypto-history, fiction about events that could have happened in the past but did not. Often, as in some novels by Tim Powers (1952–), the events are supernatural; in Penz's novel, portions of the explorers' journals—genuinely lost to history—describe a secret search for a giant hominid species that survived from prehistory. Dallas Tanner's "Cryptids" trilogy—*Shadow of the Thunderbird* (2002), *Track of the Bigfoot* (2003), and *Wake of the Lake Monster* (2004)—are thrillers featuring Ian McQuade, an unemployed museum curator recruited by the Chimaera Foundation to identify cryptids. Lee Murphy, himself a cryptobiologist, writes adventure novels featuring cryptobiologist George Kodiak. In *Where Legends Roam* (2000), Kodiak is manipulated by a billionaire into a search for sasquatch; in *Naitaka* (2002), he goes to British Colombia's Lake Okanagan in search of a huge aquatic creature; and in *Heretofore: Unknown* (2007), Kodiak is asked by the police in Louisiana to investigate an aggressive, fur-coated animal that may be the Honey Island Swamp Monster.

Although many cryptofiction series follow the conventions of the adventure or thriller genre, some are based on other templates. In Roland Smith's young-adult fiction, 13-year-old Marty and Grace O'Hara join their uncle (revealed as Grace's father) in finding cryptids. *Cryptid Hunters* (2004) describes an encounter in the Congo with a surviving dinosaur, known locally as mokélé-mbembé; in *Tentacles* (2009), the protagonists go to New Zealand in search of a giant squid. Tabitha Cope adapts the mystery genre in both *Dark Ness*, a 2011 eBook and 2012 paperback that depicts an attack on a local laird in Loch Ness, complete with a loch-dwelling monster, and *Dark Wear*, an eBook from later in 2011, featuring an ABC (alien big/black cat).

Cryptofiction even has its own publishers. CFZ Press, the publishing arm for the Center for Fortean Zoology, in addition to non-fiction, published *While the Cat's Away* (2005), a novel by zoologist Chris Moiser featuring mystery big cats in the English countryside, including the famous Beast of Exmoor. Coachwhip Publications has issued a number of collections of short fiction about plant and animal cryptids, written by older, often well-known British and American authors. For instance, *Flora Curiosa: Cryptobotany, Mysterious Fungi, Sentient Trees, and Deadly Plants in Fantasy and Science Fiction* (2008) includes Nathaniel Hawthorne's "Rappacini's Daughter," a story from 1844 about a woman raised in a garden of deadly plants, and an 1894 story with a self-explanatory title, "The Flowering of the Strange Orchid," by H.G. Wells. Other collections feature stories about strange insects (*Invertebrata Enigmatica*, 2008), dinosaur survivals into the modern era (*Sauria Monstra*, 2009), and sea serpents, giant cephalopods, and others (*Cetus Insolitus*, 2008).

Cryptofiction on TV and Film

Television was years ahead of print fiction as regards cryptofiction. Like cryptofiction novels, TV shows featuring cryptids demonstrate the compatibility of the creatures with genre conventions of adventure/thriller shows, mystery shows, and young-adult adventure. The episodic nature of TV shows also lends itself to individual shows about different types of cryptids, often woven into an ongoing plot.

The forerunner of cryptofiction TV was *The X-Files*, a Fox series created by Chris Carter that ran from 1993 through 2002. Although the continuing plot and first episodes concerned UFOs, the protagonists, FBI agents Fox Mulder (David Duchovny) and Dana Scully (Gillian Anderson), also encountered established cryptids such as the Jersey devil (see above) and the **Chupacabra**, as well as unknown semi-human, animal, and other species. The 1994 episode "Darkness Falls" (season 1, episode 20; Joe Napolitano) features green-glowing mites that wrap their prey in cocoons and desiccate them; the flukeman in 1994's "The Host" (season 2, episode 2; Daniel Sackheim) is a parasitic humanoid living in the sewers; and in 1999's "Field Trip" (season 6, episode 21; Kim Manners), a sentient fungus grows in the caves under North Carolina. The 1996 episode "Quagmire" (season 3, episode 22; Kim Manners) demonstrates how the series played with the question of the reality of such creatures: Mulder believes that a surviving aquatic dinosaur is responsible for murders around a lake, but a large alligator is actually responsible; however, when no witnesses are present, viewers see an elasmosaur emerge from the lake. Many of the cryptids on *The X-Files* are benign, and others are harmful only because of their biological needs; true malevolence and deviousness is a human characteristic, especially seen in the ongoing plot about government conspiracies concerning alien visitors (see **Extraterrestrial**).

An even more cryptid-heavy series, *Sanctuary*, debuted in 2008 and was in its fourth season in 2011. Damian Kindler created this Canadian series shown on the SyFy network, featuring an organization that captures what they call "abnormals" and protects people from the creatures and the creatures from people. The protagonists include Dr Helen Magnus (Amanda Tapping), an immortal human being born in England in 1850; her daughter (Emilie Ullerup), trained from childhood to fight; a nerd who does technology and who is secretly a werewolf (Ryan Robbins); and a forensic psychologist whom Magnus rescued when a creature killed his mother (Robin Dunne). As on *The X-Files*, many of the "abnormals" are basically humans with extraordinary abilities, such as a child from Chernobyl with a long clawed appendage growing from his abdomen. The series does, however, feature animals from actual cryptozoology, including the creature behind Quetzlcoatl, the Aztec god depicted as a feathered serpent, as well as a lizard-man, mermaid, flying man, and bigfoot—the last of which is on the Sanctuary staff.

Sanctuary also features new cryptids, such as the coleanthropus, a cross between an insect and reptile that is a **parasite** of human beings; the macri, a supposedly extinct spider that also needs a human host to survive; the nubbins, cute creatures whose prolific reproduction is reminiscent of the tribbles in *Star Trek* and whose pheromones have an aphrodisiac effect on the Sanctuary staff; a marine creature named Big Bertha, with the power to shift the Earth's tectonic plates; and a telepathic creature from the Himalayas. One episode concerns the vampire squid, a genuine species, but on the show it is both highly intelligent and hundreds of times the size of the actual cephalopod. As in *The X-Files*, the creatures may be dangerous, but only humans (some of them abnormals because of their extra-human abilities) actually enjoy doing harm.

Although special effects have become inexpensive enough for live-action TV shows to feature credible renderings of impossible creatures, more exotic-looking cryptids are a natural for animated shows. *Extreme Ghostbusters*, an animated show from 1997 through 1999, featured Egon Spengler, a character developed in the 1984 movie *Ghostbusters*, directed by Ivan Reitman and written by Dan Ackroyd and Harold Ramis. In this series, Spengler leads a team of his students against **ghosts** and other supernatural entities, but also against legendary cryptids such as the Jersey devil and a bird-like **dragon** called the Hraesvelg in Norse mythology, as well as new cryptids such as an insect that can shape-shift into a human appearance.

The Secret Saturdays, an animated series created by Canadian cartoonist Jay Stephens for the Cartoon Network, debuted in 2008 and was put on hiatus in 2010. The show concerns a family of cryptozoologists who keep the creatures' existence secret, to protect people from panic and the unusual animals from people. The art style is influenced by comic-book artist Alex Toth (1928–2006) and 1960s Hanna-Barbara animated adventure series such as *Jonny Quest* (1964–65) and *The Herculoids* (1967–69). The Saturdays—parents Solomon "Doc" Saturday and Drew Saturday, and eleven-year-old Zak Saturday—are aided by cryptids such as Fiskerton, a seven-foot-tall furry humanoid "gorilla-cat" that provides Scooby-Doo-like comic relief, and Zon, from an ostensibly extinct pterosaur species in the Amazon rainforest. The family lives in a secret base and is part of an international group called The Secret Scientists, but the plot also includes magical talismans and Zak's own psychic power over cryptids. Creatures encountered in individual episodes include the Hibagon, a Japanese creature similar to bigfoot; the Amarok, a gigantic wolf from Inuit mythology; the Alkali Lake monster from Nebraska; the Owlman, a British equivalent of the humanoid flying mothman (see above); a South African giant snake called the Groot Slang; the Garuda, a huge bird in both Hindu and Buddhist lore (see **Birds, Giant**); and many bigfoot-like humanoids including Momo (the Missouri Monster) and the Honey Island Swamp Monster.

While films have been discussed throughout this entry, one series of American films in particular deserves mention because of the cryptozoological rigor with which the species of monsters is developed. *Tremors*, a 1990 film directed by Ron Underwood, introduces a gigantic worm-like animal that is sensitive to motion and reaches up from under the ground for its prey, including human beings. These graboids have prehensile tongues and go through a smaller, two-legged stage, known as shriekers. The protagonists, residents of the poor ex-mining town of Perfection, Nevada, deduce the nature of the cryptids and fight them with explosives and other techniques suitable to a gargantuan but non-supernatural animal. In *Tremors 2: Aftershocks* (S.S. Wilson, 1996), the protagonists are paid by an oil company to exterminate the creatures from its drilling fields, and *Tremors 3: Back to Perfection* (Brent Maddock, direct-to-video, 2001) depicts another infestation in their town. As the title indicates, *Tremors 4: The Legend Begins* (S.S. Wilson, direct-to-video, 2004) depicts an early confrontation with the graboids in 1889. A short-lived 2003 TV series, *Tremors*, was created by Brent Maddock, Nancy Roberts, and S.S. Wilson; it begins after the events of *Tremors 3*.

Cryptofiction in Comic Books

Proof, from Image Comics, is the story of an organization dedicated to finding and protecting cryptids; written by Alex Grecian and drawn by Riley Rossmo, the works began in the anthology comic *Negative Burn* in 2006, and the comic's first issue was released in 2007. The title refers to

John Prufrock, known as Proof, who looks like an unusually tall human being but actually is a cultured bigfoot who shaves and wears suits. His colleagues include Ginger Brown, a young female ex-FBI agent, and Elvis Aaron Chesnut, a small-town sheriff when he was recruited. They work for The Lodge, a sanctuary run by elderly, wise, and mysterious Leander Wight. One adversary is Colonel Werner Dachshund, who likes to kill cryptids and serve them to friends at lavish dinners.

Inhabitants of The Lodge include outright supernatural creatures such as a **Golem**, but are primarily cryptids such as the Chupacabra, condor-like huge avians called thunderbirds, and even a living jackalope—in our world less a cryptid than a taxidermy-created hoax made by putting antelope horns on a stuffed jackrabbit. **Fairies** are treated as a cryptozoological species, rather than as supernatural beings, but are called the Cottingley Faeries, in reference to a twentieth-century hoax famous for deceiving Sir Arthur Conan Doyle (1859–1930). Also, dodos and passenger pigeons are not extinct, but survive on the grounds of The Lodge. The comic weaves various story arcs into one narrative, marked by strong characterization, especially of Proof, who is torn between identifying with humans and categorizing himself with the other animals at The Lodge.

The jackalope briefly had its own comic books: *Junior Jackalope*, from Nevada City Publishing Company in 1982 through 1983, and *Tales of the Jackalope*, from Blackthorne Comics in 1986 through 1987, both by R.L. Crabb. One issue of *Tales of the Jackalope* informs the reader that jackalopes are friends with bigfoot and shows the two skipping down a hillside together.

Charles Berlin, whose blog calls him "the cryptoonist," writes and draws the exploits of Professor Wexler, world explorer, as he encounters lost civilizations, cryptozoological animals, and other exotic and legendary phenomena. A collection of the single-panel comics and short narratives, *Professor Wexler, World Explorer: The Wacky Adventures of the World's Greatest Explorer*, was published by Adventures Unlimited Press in 2005. The protagonist combines aspects of pulp-hero Doc Savage, and George Lucas (1944–) and Stephen Spielberg's (1946) Indiana Jones character, and the stories include parodies of pulp era and nineteenth-century adventure narrative conventions.

Finally, *Cryptozoo Crew* (2005) is a humorous young-adult graphic novel featuring a cryptozoologist named Tork Darwyn, his wife Tara, and creatures such as a man-eating plant (see **Plants, Monstrous**), the yeti, the mothman, and a giant squid.

Bernadette Bosky

References and Suggested Reading

Arnold, Neil. *Monster! The A–Z of Zooform Phenomena*. North Devon, UK: CFZ, 2007.

Billie, Matt. "Notes on Cryptozoological Fiction." Matt's Sci/Tech Blog. 24 October 2007. <http://mattbille.blogspot.com/2007/10/notes-on-cryptozoological-fiction.html>.

The Center for Fortean Zoology. <http://www.cfz.org.uk/>.

Cohen, Daniel. *The Encyclopedia of Monsters*. New York: Hippocrene Books, 1989.

——. *The Greatest Monsters in the World*. New York: Simon Pulse, 1977.

Coleman, Loren, and Jerome Clark. *Cryptozoology A–Z*. New York: Touchstone, 1999.

"Cryptofiction." StrangeArk.com. <http://www.strangeark.com/czfiction.html> (links to whole texts).

Landis, John. *Monsters in the Movies: 100 Years of Cinematic Nightmares*. London: DK Adult, 2011.

McCrann, Grace-Ellen. "Legend of the New Jersey Devil." *New Jersey Historical Society, 26 October 2000*. <http://www.jerseyhistory.org/legend_jerseydevil.html>.

Purcell, Rosamond Wolff. *Special Cases: Natural Anomalies and Historical Monsters*. San Francisco: Chronicle Books, 1997.

Zell-Ravenheart, Oberon. *A Wizard's Bestiary: A Menagerie of Myth, Magic, and Mystery*. New Jersey: New Page Books, 2007.

CTHULHU—*see* Lovecraft, Monsters In

CÚ CHULAINN—*see* Shapeshifter

CYBERDEMON—*see* Video Games, Monsters In

CYBORG

Manfred Clynes and Nathan S. Kline first coined the term "cyborg," short for "cybernetic organism," in 1960 to encapsulate their idea of future space explorers: "For the exogenously extended organizational complex functioning as an integrated homeostatic system unconsciously, we propose the term 'Cyborg.' The Cyborg deliberately incorporates exogenous components extending the self-regulatory control function of the organism in order to adapt it to new environments" (27). Thus, external technology can adapt biological organisms to environments in which the organism cannot exist alone. Cyborgs are hybrids of biology and technology. More specifically, a cyborg is a person whose interaction with or experience of the world is mediated by technology. Since its inception, the concept of a cyborg has become more comprehensive through the further technologization of daily life and a growing number of diversified fictional depictions across media. Besides the monstrous physical appearance of many cyborgs, their monstrosity also derives from a perceived threat to humanity by technology through its transformation, control, or infiltration.

Early Examples of Cyborgs

The earliest example of a cyborg in literature is arguably **Frankenstein's monster** in Mary Shelley's *Frankenstein* (1818). Victor Frankenstein creates by surgically reassembling dead human tissues, which are then electrochemically reanimated. The creature's life is made possible by the techno-scientific advances of the early nineteenth century, and he has enhanced abilities such as greater speed, strength, and hardiness in extreme climates. Other early cyborg stories emphasize technological alterations to the body and brain, such as the clockwork replacement brain of Baron Savitch in Edward Page Mitchell's "The Ablest Man in the World" (1879) or the bodily regulating, dimension-shifting mechanism implanted in the head of the titular, oddly behaving character of E.V. Odle's *The Clockwork Man* (1923). Some cyborg narratives focus on brains in mechanical bodies, including Edmond Hamilton's "The Comet Doom" (1928), and others focus on monstrous brains preserved in vats, such as Curt Siodmak's *Donovan's Brain* (1942).

Human Augmentation and Transformation

Augmentation stories focus on the enhancement needs of accident victims, of those with disabilities, of those adapting to harsh environments, or of those inhabiting an increasingly digital world. The fusion of technology to the human body is meant to serve some purpose. Beginning with the twentieth-century cyberpunk movement (though there are earlier exceptions that inspired the cyberpunks, some of which are explored below), the emphasis of these stories shifts towards transformation of the human via technology into the "posthuman," a new category that embraces human–technology hybridity that is often synonymous with the cyborg.

Cordwainer Smith's "Scanners Live in Vain" (1950), Anne McCaffrey's *The Ship Who Sang* (1969), and Frederik Pohl's *Man Plus* (1976) are each about cyborgs adapted to life in outer space. Smith's Habermen and Scanners have their central nervous system, save vision, disconnected from their brains, so that they can endure the painful experience of space travel. Unlike other stories, these cyborgs lose rather than enhance their natural abilities. McCaffrey's Helva is a "shell person," or a physically disabled person encased in a permanent shell and adapted as the "brain" of a "brainship." Pohl's Roger Torraway receives an artificial body with wings, artificial eyes, and specifically suited support systems for his new life on Mars.

Martin Caidin's *Cyborg* (1972), adapted into the successful television series *The Six Million Dollar Man* (1974–78) and which inspired *The Bionic Woman* (1976–78), is about Steve Austin, a military test pilot whose body is enhanced with robotic prostheses called bionics after a tragic crash. Austin struggles to come to terms with his new superhuman abilities and his isolated existence.

The physically disfigured P. Burke in James Tiptree, Jr's "The Girl Who Was Plugged In" (1973) receives cybernetic implants from a corporation, which enable her to remotely control a brainless body named Delphi for the purposes of promoting goods on reality television. P. Burke inhabits Delphi's body remotely—like a "waldo," itself a term referenced in the story and originally coined by Robert A. Heinlein in his 1942 short story of the same name to describe what is now known as a remote manipulator—from a claustrophobic closet where her naked body is connected to computers via permanently implanted wires. Ultimately, Burke's cyborg relationship to Delphi is revealed to be a veneer over techno-scientific monstrosity. Paul, Delphi's lover, considers P. Burke hideous, but Joe, her technician, loves her as a great cybernetic system.

William Gibson's influential cyberpunk novel *Neuromancer* (1984) contains a number of cyborg characters. Of these, Case uses a "cyberspace deck" to enter the computer network matrix and experience the "consensual hallucination" of cyberspace, a term coined by the author (51). Through technology, Case seeks to "escape the prison of his own flesh" (6). His counterpart, Molly, is a "razor girl," with surgically implanted "mirrorshade" lenses with data displays over her real eyes, enhanced musculature and reflexes, and retractable razor blades under her fingernails.

Bruce Sterling's *Schismatrix Plus* (1996) collects his Shaper/Mechanist stories. Shapers employ "soft" technologies such as surgery, genetic manipulation, and psychological training methods to transform themselves. Mechanists, on the other hand, favor "hard" or technological augmentation to adapt their bodies for life and work in deep space. Of the Mechanists, the prominent image is that of the "Lobster," or a sealed, self-contained support system. In their respective ways, the Shapers and the Mechanists eschew the trappings of humanism. Other notable posthuman cyborgs can also be found in Kathleen Ann Goonan's *Queen City Jazz* (1994), Paul Di Filippo's *Ribofunk* (1996), and Paolo Bacigalupi's *The Windup Girl* (2009).

Technological Influence Over the Human

The power relationship in human-technology hybridity is often skewed in literary and cinematic narrative as a warning against technological mastery over the human. One such example is the widely anthologized overcoming-disability-with-technology narrative, "No Woman Born"

(1944) by C.L. Moore. Deirdre, a famous singer-dancer, reboots her career after a lithe robotic body replaces her organic one following a disfiguring fire. Deirdre's body appears under her control, but there are questions about what influence the technology and its limitations will have on her lingering humanity.

Another example is the film *RoboCop* (Paul Verhoeven, 1987). Following police officer Alex Murphy's (Peter Weller) death in the line of duty, OCP, the company contracted by Detroit to privatize the police force, takes possession of his body, and installs his brain and face into an armored anthropomorphic robot body called RoboCop. OCP's robot body enforces certain directives on RoboCop, but he eventually overrides this programming and reasserts his human identity.

George Lucas explores the transformative and controlling nature of technology on humans (and aliens) in the original *Star Wars* trilogy (1977–83) and the prequels (1999–2005). Notable examples include Lobot (John Hollis) from *The Empire Strikes Back* (1980), who is controlled by a computer implant that wraps around the sides and back of his head, and General Grievous (voiced by Matthew Wood) from *Revenge of the Sith* (2005), who is an alien dependent upon his robotic exoskeleton and life support system. However, the most recognized cyborgs in the films are Luke Skywalker (Mark Hamill) and, to a greater extent, Anakin Skywalker/Darth Vader (Hayden Christensen as Anakin, Darth Vader voiced by James Earl Jones and performed by David Prowse). Luke receives a surgically implanted, authentic looking right hand after his unfortunate lightsaber duel with his father in *The Empire Strikes Back*. In the case of Darth Vader, Anakin assumes his new identity when he turns to the dark side of the Force. However, he transforms into his better-known appearance after his fateful duel in *Revenge of the Sith* with his mentor Obi-Wan Kenobi (Ewan McGregor), which ends in his multiple dismemberments and body-wide burns. He receives robotic limbs and custom-built, pitch black armor, accented with displays and controls, that protects his body and provides necessary life support functions, including breathing maintenance. Vader's iconic helmet has hard, angular lines and large, unmoving lenses, and it conjures images of death: a skull, a gas mask, and a German *Stahlhelm*, or steel helmet. Obi-Wan (Alec Guinness), in *Return of the Jedi* (1983), says of the cyborg Darth Vader that: "He's more machine now than man. His mind is twisted and evil."

The *Star Trek: The Next Generation* television series (1987–94) prominently features the cyborg character Lt Cmd. Geordi La Forge (LeVar Burton), whose vision is enabled by technology. The series also features the cyborg race known as the Borg as a significant threat to humanity. Portrayed as ashen and deathly gray, with numerous devices and hoses penetrating their bodies, the Borg use external technological augmentation coupled with nanotechnological support systems. Their purpose is to assimilate, often violently, other cultures and technologies into their own (compare with the "Exterminate!" mantra of the cyborg Daleks in the *Doctor Who* television series [1969–89, 1996, 2005–present]). Assimilation subjects the individual to identity erasure and control by the Borg collective hive mind. The Emmy Award-winning two-part episode, "The Best of Both Worlds" (18 June 1990 and 24 September 1990), in which Captain Jean Luc Picard (Patrick Stewart) is assimilated into and eventually freed from the Borg, epitomizes their menace to individuals as well as societies.

In *The Matrix* (Andy and Lana Wachowski, 1999), autonomous machines revolt and make humans a source of electrical power. In order to maintain control, the machines create artificially gestated human cyborgs, each with various support tubing and a round metal implant on the base of the skull that facilitates the direct connection of the human brain to the virtual world known as the Matrix. The sleeping human batteries live out their simulated waking lives there. A human resistance force utilizes these interfaces to challenge machine rule.

Building on the ideas in his earlier film *Videodrome* (1983), David Cronenberg presents a disturbing vision of cyborgs and gaming technologies in *eXistenZ* (1999). The game technologies in this film simultaneously challenge bodily boundaries and reality boundaries. Fleshy "game pods" connect to a person's implanted "bioport" via a twisted, sinewy "umbycord." Once connected to the game, a person cannot distinguish where reality ends and the virtual begins. The game pods can become "infected" and "diseased," with dire results for players.

Subversive Infiltrations

In a number of significant works, autonomous technologies fuse with artificially created biological elements in order to infiltrate human society without detection. Philip K. Dick (1928–82) developed a number of cyborg characters in his fictions, including Hoppy Harrington, the egomaniacal phocomelus without arms or legs, gifted with telekinetic powers and a robotic wheelchair in *Dr Bloodmoney* (1965), and Palmer Eldritch, the drug-peddling space explorer with an artificial limb, steel teeth, and electronic eyes in *The Three Stigmata of Palmer Eldritch* (1965). However, Dick's "androids" from *Do Androids Dream of Electric Sheep?* (1968) are a widely discussed example of technology subverting humanity. The Nexus-6 androids, or "andys," are fabricated techno-biological beings that are nearly indistinguishable from humans, but they can be detected through the specialized, yet imperfect, "Voight-Kampff empathy test" or a postmortem bone marrow examination. They feel compelled to return to Earth after shucking the bonds of slavery on the outer planets, but their discovery on Earth results in an instant death sentence meted out by bounty hunters. Ridley Scott directed the film adaptation of Dick's novel as *Blade Runner* (1982). In the movie, the androids, or "replicants," are equally difficult to distinguish from humans. Both works question authenticity, particularly of the human, and they also demonstrate that systems, rather than technological artifacts, can turn humans into unfeeling cyborgs or androids (to use Dick's term).

The re-imagined *Battlestar Galactica* television series (2004–2009) also features this kind of biologically based cyborg that masquerades as human. The human-created Cylon robot race develops twelve humanoid models that seem biologically human, but are actually artificially created. Representing different races, ages, and sexes, the twelve humanoid Cylons have enhanced strength, computer-interfacing capability, and the capacity to "download" their consciousness into a new body. Each model has many copies. Due to their disturbing indistinguishability from authentic humans, the humanoid Cylons infiltrate the human societies of the Twelve Colonies in preparation for their nearly successful genocide of humanity. Human characters on the program often call humanoid Cylons "skinjobs" or "toasters."

Arnold Schwarzenegger's T-800 cyborg characters in *The Terminator* (James Cameron, 1984), *Terminator 2: Judgment Day* (James Cameron, 1991), and *Terminator 3: Rise of the Machines* (Jonathan Mostow, 2003) are artificially intelligent endoskeletal robots equipped with a biological exterior of flesh and skin that mimics human appearance. More recently, *Terminator:*

The Sarah Connor Chronicles (2008–2009) features actress Summer Glau as the female Terminator Cameron Phillips.

Cyborg Politics

Some consider the cyborg as threatening and monstrous, while others see it as emancipatory and beautiful. The increasing integration of technology, especially computer and communication technologies, into our everyday lives has led to radical re-evaluations by some scholars, including Donna J. Haraway (b. 1944) and N. Katherine Hayles (b. 1943), to theorize the political potential and promise of the cyborg. Philosophers Gilles Deleuze (1925–95) and Félix Guattari (b. 1930) theorize on the implication of human–technology assemblages, and Bruce Mazlish (b. 1923) argues that humans have co-evolved with technology, which effectively makes us all cyborgs.

Jason W. Ellis

References and Suggested Reading

Bacigalupi, Paolo. *The Windup Girl*. San Francisco: Night Shade Books, 2009.

Caidin, Martin. *Cyborg*. New York: Warner Books Library, 1972.

Clynes, Manfred, and Nathan S. Kline. "Cyborgs and Space." *Astronautics* (September 1960): 26–7, 74–5.

Deleuze, Gilles, and Félix Guattari. *A Thousand Plateaus: Capitalism and Schizophrenia*. Translated by Brian Massumi. Minneapolis: University of Minnesota Press, 1987.

Dick, Philip K. *Do Androids Dream of Electric Sheep?* Garden City, NY: Doubleday, 1968.

——. *Dr Bloodmoney, or How We Learned to Get Along After the Bomb*. New York: Ace, 1965.

——. *The Three Stigmata of Palmer Eldritch*. Garden City, NY: Doubleday, 1965.

Di Filippo, Paul. *Ribofunk*. New York: Four Walls Eight Windows, 1996.

Gibson, William. *Neuromancer*. New York: Ace, 1984.

Goonan, Kathleen Ann. *Queen City Jazz*. New York: Tor, 1994.

Gray, Chris Hables, ed. *The Cyborg Handbook*. New York: Routledge, 1995.

Hamilton, Edmond. "The Comet Doom" [1928]. In *The Metal Giants and Others: The Collected Edmond Hamilton*, Volume One, 349–92. Royal Oak, MI: Haffner, 2009.

Haraway, Donna J. *Simians, Cyborgs, and Women: The Reinvention of Nature*. New York: Routledge, 1991.

Hayles, N. Katherine. *How We Became Posthuman: Virtual Bodies in Cybernetics, Literature, and Informatics*. Chicago: University of Chicago Press, 1999.

Mazlish, Bruce. *The Fourth Discontinuity: The Co-Evolution of Humans and Machines*. New Haven: Yale University Press, 1993.

McCaffrey, Anne. *The Ship Who Sang*. New York: Walker, 1969.

Mitchell, Edward Page. "The Ablest Man in the World" [1879]. In *The Crystal Man*, edited by Sam Moskowitz. Garden City, NY: Doubleday, 1973.

Moore, C.L. "No Woman Born" [1944]. In *The Best of C.L. Moore*. New York: Doubleday, 1975.

Odle, E.V. *The Clockwork Man*. London: William Heinemann, 1923.

Pohl, Frederik. *Man Plus*. New York: Random House, 1976.

Shelley, Mary. *Frankenstein; Or, the Modern Prometheus* [1818]. Reprint, New York: Norton, 1995.

Siodmak, Curt. *Donovan's Brain*. New York: Knopf, 1943.

Smith, Cordwainer. "Scanners Live in Vain" [1950]. In *The Best of Cordwainer Smith*, 1–39. New York: Ballentine, 1975.

Sterling, Bruce. *Schismatrix Plus*. New York: Ace, 1996.

Telotte, J.P. *Replications: A Robotic History of the Science Fiction Film*. Urbana: University of Illinois Press, 1995.
Tiptree, James, Jr. "The Girl Who Was Plugged In" [1973]. In *Her Smoke Rose Up Forever*, 43–78. San Francisco: Tachyon, 2004.

CYCLOPS

According to ancient Greek myth, there were three separate tribes of the mythical, one-eyed **giants** known as Cyclops, or Cyclopes: the Ouranian Cyclopes, offspring of Gaea and Ouranos; the mason-Cyclopes, workers in Hephaestus's forge, located in the vicinity of Mt Etna on Sicily; and the shepherd-like Cyclopes, neighbors of the island-dwelling Polyphemus, a son of Poseidon. Although each of these Cyclopean tribes boasts a separate mythology, they are as one with regard to their unique anatomy: a single round eye in the middle of their foreheads, which the Greek poet Hesiod posits as the source of their name in his eighth-century BCE *Theogony* (143–45). In Greek, Cyclops means "circle-eye."

The Ouranian Cyclopes play a vital role in helping Zeus defeat the Titans in the generational conflict known as the Titanomachy: they fashion for Zeus his signature thunderbolts and lightning (*Theogony* 141). But when Zeus uses one of these thunderbolts to kill Apollo's son Asclepius, Apollo retaliates by killing the Cyclopes. As related in the *Bibliotheca* of Pseudo-Apollodorus (c. first century BCE), Asclepius was an extraordinarily talented healer, but Zeus deemed his use of the medical arts to rehabilitate the dead an intolerable violation of the sacred boundary between gods and mortals (1.2.2; 3.10.4).

The mason-Cyclopes appear in *Hymn* 3 of the third-century BCE Hellenistic poet Callimachus, where they work in Hephaestus's forge. First-century CE naturalist Pliny the Elder reported that, according to Aristotle, the Cyclopes invented towers (*Natural History* 7.80), and a century later Pausanias, a travel writer, noted in *Description of Greece* the traditional belief that the walls of Mycenae, including the Lion Gate, "are the works of the Cyclopes, who made the wall at Tiryns for Proetus" (2.16.5). Because they were credited with building such impressively large prehistoric monuments and walls at these ancient city sites, even today these edifices are called "Cyclopean masonry."

For later eras, including our own, it is the Homeric Cyclopes that would achieve canonical status, undergoing numerous adaptations and reinventions. Best known for playing "host" to Odysseus in the ninth book of Homer's *Odyssey* (c. eighth century BCE), the Cyclops Polyphemus devours several of Odysseus's men before being tricked and blinded by the hero. In the *Odyssey*, the Cyclops' savagery is marked by his rejection of Olympian religion and his appetite for man-flesh. The *Odyssey* describes Cyclopean society through a series of absences: they have no ships and no commerce; no city (*polis*), laws, customs, or religious practices. An appeal to the justice of Zeus thus falls flat with Polyphemus, who revels in his freedom to eat Odysseus's companions without fear of retribution. The violent encounter between giant and hero shapes up as a somberly inverted recasting of the important Greek social ritual of "guest-friendship." A host usually welcomes his guest, who has come from afar, feeding and entertaining him. But the Cyclops feasts on rather than with his guests.

Odysseus relies on his wits to defeat the Cyclops, first by withholding his true name—proclaiming himself to be "Nobody"—and later by getting his enemy drunk and blinding him with a wooden stake (a popular scene in Greek vase paintings of the seventh and sixth centuries BCE). When Polyphemus's fellow Cyclopes ask him why he cries out in pain, they are, ironically, reassured by his response that "Nobody" has injured him. Odysseus and his companions then slip out undetected from the Cyclops' cave, clinging to the fleecy bellies of the giant's sheep. All would have ended well if only Odysseus had resisted the temptation to reveal his true name to the Cyclops, thereby claiming credit for the heroic act of blinding. Once he knows his enemy's name, Polyphemus prays to his father, Poseidon, to avenge his injury by delaying Odysseus's homecoming as long as possible. Thanks to Poseidon's curse, Odysseus must wander for many more years, only returning home to Ithaca 20 years after he had originally set sail for Troy. In this regard, the encounter between man and monster offers a cautionary tale about the terrible costs of hubris. Odysseus pays for his boast with the lives of his companions and through unparalleled personal suffering.

Ancient Greek and Roman poets appropriated Homer's Cyclops story for their own ends. In Euripides's play *Cyclops* (fifth century BCE), for example, Polyphemus has found religion—the religion of his own gluttony. Superficially more cultured than his Homeric counterpart, his sophisticated bantering makes his cannibalism that much harder to swallow. The pastoral poet Theocritus (third century BCE) showcases a youthfully romantic Polyphemus expurgating his intense crush on the sea nymph Galataea through poetry (*Idyll* 11). The romantic longings of the bucolic Polyphemus also form the basis of first-century CE Roman poet Ovid's tale about Acis and Galataea (*Metamorphoses* 13.738–88). Ovid presents a love triangle with Polyphemus cast as the jealous rival to Acis for Galataea's affections. She chooses Acis, but the frustrated Cyclops kills him with a boulder. Ovid's story in turn inspired several musical works, including Jean-Baptiste Lully's opera *Acis et Galatée* (1686); Antonio de Lieteres's 1708 lyric-dramatic zarzuela *Acis y Galatea*; and Georg Friedrich Handel's pastoral opera *Acis and Galatea* (1718). Jean Cras's opera *Polyphème* (1922), whose script was based on French poet Alain Samain's play of the same name, also draws its inspiration from the pastoral Polyphemus.

It is a cannibalistic rather than a pastoral Polyphemus, however, that Virgil's readers encounter in the first-century BCE *Aeneid* (3.568–683). Recently blinded by Odysseus, the Cyclops narrowly misses hitting Aeneas's ship with the projectile he hurls at it. A forgotten member of Odysseus's original crew, rescued by Aeneas, offers a first-hand account of what happened inside the cave; Aeneas and his men sail away, escaping harm.

Like Virgil, modern reception tends to focus on the monstrosity of the Cyclops, with some notable exceptions. For instance, in Jonathan Swift's 1726 satire *Gulliver's Travels* (Part II, chapters 1–2), Gulliver is initially startled and repelled by the Brobdingnagian giants who, in contradistinction to Polyphemus, turn out to be relatively benign hosts (see **Swift, Jonathan, Monsters In**). In the 1960s, in the Marvel Comic Universe, Cyclops is a member of the X-Men, a humanity-saving team of **mutants**; his special power is the ability to emit a powerful blast of energy from his eyes. The protective visor he wears gives him a one-eyed Cyclopean appearance. Also less barbaric is Mike Wazowski (voiced by Billy Crystal), a green monster with a single huge eye in Pixar's *Monsters, Inc.* (Peter Docter, 2001). Mike is a joke-cracking sidekick to tall, purple, furry monster James "Sully" Sullivan (voiced by John Goodman).

In modern literature, Polyphemus resurfaces in the character of the xenophobic and anti-Semitic "Citizen" who heckles protagonist Leopold Bloom in Episode 12 of James Joyce's *Ulysses* (1922). The encounter is set in Barney Kiernan's pub, which in its dark and claustrophobic ambience is reminiscent of the Cyclops' cave. The "Citizen" throws a tin of biscuits at Leopold as he leaves, but misses. In Thomas Wolfe's short story, "Polyphemus" (1935), a one-eyed Spaniard (the only name given to the protagonist) sails uncharted seas with his ragged crew, "their greedy little minds, obsessed then as now by the European's greedy myth about America" (22). A cipher for Christopher Columbus, the Spaniard plants the Spanish flag proudly in the sand when he steps ashore, only to find that the Indian village is completely void of gold. But what they miss, in their one-eyed myopia, is the gold in the land itself.

Turning to more fantastical fiction, we meet several Cyclopean figures in Rick Riordan's young-adult series "Percy Jackson and the Olympians." *The Sea of Monsters* (2006), second of the five books, is particularly Cyclops-centered: Polyphemus captures Percy's **satyr**-friend Grover. To free him, Percy relies on the help of his recently rediscovered half-brother Tyson, who is also a Cyclops. Tyson, who reappears in later books of the series, has one eye, immense physical strength, and is skilled with metals.

Film adaptations of the *Odyssey* provide another venue for appreciating the Cyclops' transition to the big screen, as in the 1955 film *Ulysses* (Mario Camerini) and the 1997 television mini-series *The Odyssey* (Andrei Konchalovsky). Also noteworthy is *The 7th Voyage of Sinbad* (Nathan H. Juran, 1958). The film features two different Cyclopes, the first attacking Sinbad and his crew at the start, and the second appearing at the close of the film, where it falls prey to a **dragon**.

In a less literal-minded adaptation, John Goodman plays Daniel "Big Dan" Teague in *O Brother, Where Art Thou?* (Joel and Ethan Coen, 2000). A Bible salesman by day, "Big Dan" is blind in one eye and a leading member of the Ku Klux Klan by night. And, in what may be a unique case of gender-bending myth-making, given that female Cyclopes are not attested in classical sources, the animated television series *Futurama* (1999–2003; revived in 2008) features the character of Leela, voiced by Katey Sagal, whose single eye is her only recognizable Cyclopean trait.

Melissa Mueller

References and Suggested Reading

Gantz, Timothy. *Early Greek Myth: A Guide to Literary and Artistic Sources.* Vol. 1. Baltimore: The Johns Hopkins University Press, 1993.

Lattimore, Richmond, trans. *The Odyssey of Homer*. New York: Harper Perennial Modern Classics, 2007.

Wolfe, Thomas. "Polyphemus." *The North American Review* 240 (1935): 20–26.

CYHIRAETH—*see* Banshee

CYNOCEPHALI—*see* Donestre; Races, Monstrous

DAITHYA—*see* Demon

DAMNED THING, THE

The Damned Thing is the eponymous invisible monster that, assuming it exists at all, may have been responsible for tearing the character Hugh Morgan to shreds in American author Ambrose Bierce's 1893 short story.

The story focuses on a coroner's inquest into the death of Morgan. A young man named William Harker, who was witness to Morgan's death, is called to testify and, reading from his journal, recounts an experience of being attacked by an invisible creature—referred to by Morgan as "that Damned Thing" (286)—while out hunting with Morgan. They first witnessed the foliage move as the creature approached,

Morgan shot at what appeared to be empty air, and then Morgan was attacked, although Harker "saw nothing but [Morgan] and then not always distinctly" (288). The other men present at the inquest dismiss Harker's testimony, call into question his sanity, and conclude that "the remains come to their death at the hands of a mountain lion, but some of us thinks, all the same, they had fits" (292).

Following this account, details of Morgan's diary—withheld by the coroner—are introduced that seem to substantiate Harker's story. The entries document Morgan's growing suspicion that an invisible creature is plaguing him, as well as his speculations on its nature. Rather than entertaining a supernatural explanation, the diary entries instead propose that, in the same way that there are sounds too high or too low for the human ear to perceive, there may be colors beyond the range of human perception. "And, God help me!" concludes the narrative, "the Damned Thing is of such a color!" (296).

Bierce was evidently influenced in the composition of the tale by two other stories: Fitz-James O'Brien's 1859 "What Was It? A Mystery" and Guy de Maupassant's 1887 "**The Horla**." In the former, a resident of a boarding house with the reputation of being haunted is attacked in the night and subdues an invisible creature whose likeness is revealed by a plaster of Paris cast. In the latter, the narrator is repeatedly tormented in his home while he sleeps by an invisible creature. Each story seems to reject the supposition that the creature is supernatural in origin and instead attempts to compare it to glass and other natural phenomena. Both stories, together with Bierce's "The Damned Thing," foreground the limitations of human senses and emphasize that human knowledge of the world is therefore dangerously incomplete. Bierce was also drawing upon late nineteenth-century theories of vision (see Smajić).

While narratives involving invisible magical creatures and magical artifacts that confer invisibility stretch from the cap of invisibility used by Perseus in some versions of the Greek myth of the slaying of **Medusa** and the Ring of Gyges, described by Plato in Book 2 of his first-century BCE *Republic* (2.359a–2.360d) to the cloak of invisibility used by Harry Potter in J.K. Rowling's *Harry Potter and the Sorcerer's Stone* (1997) and its sequels, the achievement of "The Damned Thing," along with "What Was It? A Mystery" and "The Horla," was to contemplate the prospect of invisibility from a scientific perspective. In this, the stories are more accurately described as science fiction than fantasy.

Bierce's "The Damned Thing" was adapted for television and appeared as the first episode in the second season of the Showtime cable network's series, "Masters of Horror" (2006). In this version—written by horror master Richard Matheson and directed by Tobe Hooper—an unseen force terrorizes a Texas town. More generally, "The Damned Thing," along with "What Was It? A Mystery" and "The Horla," have inspired numerous narratives concerning invisibility, the over-reliance of human beings on the faculty of sight, and the corresponding vulnerability of those deprived of this sense. Among such narratives must be numbered H.G. Wells's *The Invisible Man* (1897) and its many adaptations, H.P. Lovecraft's "The Colour Out of Space" (1927; see **Lovecraft, Monsters In**), and contemporary narratives about invisible assailants such as the films *Predator* (John McTiernan, 1987) and *Pitch Black* (David Twohy, 2000).

Jeffrey Andrew Weinstock.

References and Suggested Reading

Bierce, Ambrose. "The Damned Thing." In *Can Such Things Be?*, 280–96. Freeport, NY: Books for Libraries Press, 1971.

Smajić, Srdjan. *Ghost-Seers, Detectives, and Spiritualists: Theories of Vision in Victorian Literature and Science.* Cambridge: Cambridge University Press, 2010.

Stark, Cruce. "The Color of 'the Damned Thing': The Occult as the Suprasensational." In *The Haunted Dusk: American Supernatural Fiction, 1820–1920*, edited by Howard Kerr, John W. Crowley, and Charles L. Crow, 211–27. Athens: University of Georgia Press, 1983.

DANAVA—*see* Demon

DANDAN—*see* Arabian Nights, Monsters In The

DANTE, MONSTERS IN

Dante Alighieri (c. 1265–1321) is best known for writing an epic trilogy, *The Divine Comedy*, of which the first section, the *Inferno* (1317), contains a series of fantastic monsters drawn from Old and New Testament passages as well as the literature of classical Greece and Rome. The *Inferno*, or *Hell*, consists of a series of tableaux in which the condemned souls of sinners are shown being punished for eternity in ways that mirror the nature of their sins. The monsters act in some instances as guardians of certain zones or as boatmen who ferry the souls to the site of their ultimate torture, and in other instances they act as the torturers. The monsters also suffer according to the nature of their own sinful acts, and are chosen to add a further resonance with the sins being punished and the suitable punishment.

Biblical Monsters

In Canto 1, Dante the pilgrim, in a dream vision, is chased by three symbolic beasts in a dark wood, forcing him to descend into the Underworld. These are the leopard (Canto 1, line 32), symbolizing worldly pleasure, the lion (1.44), symbolizing ambition, and the she-wolf, symbolizing avarice. The Biblical source for the three is Jeremiah 5:6—"Wherefore a lion out of the forest shall slay them, and a wolf of the evenings shall spoil them, a leopard shall watch over their cities: every one that goeth out thence shall be torn in pieces: because their transgressions are many, and their backslidings are increased" (King James Version).

Demons do the legwork of Hell and can be divided into those seeming to come from classical sources and those drawn from the ranks of the **angels** that sided with Satan (see **Devil, The**) in his rebellion against God. Fallen angels attempt, unsuccessfully, to keep Dante and his guide, the poet Virgil, from entering the City of Dis within the Inferno (Canto 8.82–117). Later, when Guido da Montefeltro tells Dante of his sin of fraudulence being absolved by the pope, but of his dying unrepentant of this sin, he relates how St Francis came to take his soul to heaven, but "one of the Black Cherubim" claimed his soul for the Inferno instead because of this lack of repentance (27.146).

Giants stand buried up to their waists on the outer rim of the lowest pit, in almost impenetrable gloom (Canto 31). Their source in the Bible is Genesis 6:4, which states, "There were giants in the earth in those days" (King James) or "The Nephilim were on the earth in those days" (English Standard Version). Of these, Nimrod, associated with building the Tower of Babel and thus guilty both of pride, for attempting physically to reach God, and of consequently causing mankind to speak a multiplicity of languages, shouts an incomprehensible phrase at Dante and Virgil. Although there seems to be no Biblical tradition identifying Nimrod as a giant, he came to be so identified subsequently in folklore. Drawn from the classical tradition, Ephialtes is a giant who had fought in the war of the **Titans** against Zeus/Jupiter; he is chained to the Earth for this reason. Antaeus, another giant from the classical tradition, is unfettered because he had not taken part in the war of the Titans against the gods of Olympus. Because Antaeus is not half buried in the Earth or chained, he carries Virgil and Dante to the lowest circle of the Inferno (31.131–144).

Satan is at the deepest point in the Inferno, with all his body below mid-breast stuck in the frozen Lake Cocytus (Canto 34). He has three faces on his head, one red, one yellow, and one black, and the constant tears from his six eyes are what fill the lake. He has bat's wings that, because he is trying to escape, are constantly cooling the waters of Cocytus, thus keeping it frozen. He is an immense giant and in his three mouths he chews the worst human traitors: Judas Iscariot is in his central mouth, with Judas's head inside, while Brutus and Cassius, the chief assassins of Julius Caesar, are in the mouths on either side, with their heads outside—a slightly less hideous punishment than that of Judas, because the latter betrayed God Himself in the form of His Son, Jesus Christ. This is, of course, what Satan himself had done eons before, as the most powerful of the angels whose sin of Pride separated him from God.

Classical Monsters

Minos, the judge of the souls of the dead in Canto 5, "grins horribly" and has a tail that he wraps around the soul of each sinner; the number of times the tail wraps around him or her is the level to which Minos has assigned him (5.4–12). Minos was the son of Zeus and Europa, and was the ruler of Crete; he was so esteemed in the ancient world that he was one of the three judges in the classical Hades.

The guardian of the third circle, **Cerberus**, is a dog with three heads and throats that barks like thunder at the damned. He has red eyes and a greasy black beard. He rips, flays, and mangles the gluttons with his claws (6.13–18). Although he had often been depicted with differing numbers of heads, Cerberus was considered the guard-dog of the Underworld from quite early in classical antiquity, but figured as such particularly in Virgil's first-century BCE *Aeneid*, a major source of material for Dante's depiction of the Underworld.

The **Furies**, or Erinyes, are a trio of female spirits from ancient Greek myth that hounded someone who had committed a crime against blood ties, as when Orestes killed his mother Clytemnestra. In Canto 9, they have the arms and faces of women, are clothed in green **hydras**, have serpents and vipers for hair, and claws with which they rend their breasts (9.38–51). Their names are Megaera, Alecto, and Tisiphone. They represent the bad conscience, or reminder, of having done ill. They call upon the **Medusa** (9.52–54) to come and turn Dante to stone. The **Gorgon** Medusa is not described by Dante, as to look on her countenance in ancient Greek lore was to be turned to stone; Virgil covers Dante's eyes so that he will not be forced to remain in the Inferno for eternity (9.55–60). Medusa represents the heart of stone, or obduracy, that prevents sinners from humbling themselves to ask for grace.

The **Minotaur**, although not described by Dante, was the offspring of Pasiphaë, the wife of Minos, and a bull that Poseidon had made appear on the shore of Crete to punish Minos for neglecting his worship of the sea god. Pasiphaë lusted for the bull and had Daedalus build her an artificial cow in which she hid, enticing the miraculous bull to mount it/her. She conceived a child with a human body and a bull's head, the Minotaur, which Minos imprisoned in a labyrinth that he also had Daedalus design. Each year, Minos would demand a tribute of live young men and women to let loose in the labyrinth, where the Minotaur would kill and eat them. In the Inferno, the Minotaur guards the circle of the violent, and is himself so consumed with bestial wrath that he charges off without a clear direction when dismissed by Virgil (12.12–27).

Centaurs, the classical composite beings with the torso, arms, and head of men and the legs and body of horses, are used in Dante's Inferno to keep those guilty of violence against others inside a river of boiling blood in the seventh circle; they patrol the shore of that river with bows and arrows or javelins, with which they shoot any of the damned who should leave the river (12.55–56). The centaurs were generally known for violence, as at the wedding of the Lapiths, where a drunken centaur tried to rape the bride and started a general melee. Virgil seeks out Chiron, traditionally considered the wisest of the centaurs, to ask him where Dante should go next; Chiron assigns the centaur Nessus as a guide. Nessus in Greek myth stole Hercules's wife Deianeira and, when Hercules fatally wounded Nessus with a poisoned arrow, got his posthumous revenge by telling Deianeira to dip a cloth in his blood and give the shirt made from it to Hercules to give him strength. This she did, but the poisoned blood of the centaur kills the hero. Nessus is in this part of the Inferno because of this act of violent revenge (12.67–69). Nessus carries Virgil and Dante on his back to the ford, pointing out various of the violent sinners on the way, then carries them across to the seventh circle (12.100–139). Cacus, encountered later on, is called a centaur by Dante (25.16–24); he is not, however, grouped with the other centaurs, such as Chiron and Nessus, in the circle of the violent and instead punishes thieves in the eighth circle because he was also guilty of stealing a herd of cattle belonging to Geryon, for which he was killed by Hercules. He is additionally described by Dante as having many snakes on his haunches and a fire-breathing **dragon** on his back. In William Blake's illustration (1826), the dragon head hovers over the human one.

The seventh circle is where those who are violent against themselves are punished. There, Dante and Virgil encounter the **harpies**, which have human necks and faces but bodies of raptors, and perch on the trees into which the suicides have been transformed, eating their leaves, befouling them, and wailing (13.13–15). Dante's source is Virgil's *Aeneid* 3.212ff., where the Harpies ruin the Trojans' meal and predict misery for the future travels of Aeaneas and his men.

Geryon is emblematic of fraud, having a just man's face, beyond which he has two paws, is "hairy to the armpits," and possesses the body of a serpent painted with circles of many colors, and with a poisonous scorpion-like tip to his tail (17.10–27). Geryon was a king of Spain in Greek myth, defeated by Hercules, but Dante's description comes from the Book of Revelation 9:7–10, where locusts are given human faces and have tails with stingers like those of scorpions. Geryon lets Virgil and Dante ride on his back as he slowly spirals downward from the seventh infernal level to the eighth, or from the circle of the fraudulent to that of the traitors.

Demons in the eighth circle are for the most part not described except in relation to the torture they mete out to the damned souls wherever they are assigned. In Canto 21, they use prongs. Ten demons in Canto 22 are named and in some instances given brief descriptions: Ciriatto has tusks like those of a hog, while Cagnazzo has a snout. The demons walk along a chasm filled with pitch, and skewer or slash at any exposed parts of the souls of those who were fraudulent in Church affairs.

In a richly described metamorphosis reminiscent of Ovid's gradual descriptions of transformations in his first century CE *Metamorphoses*, serpents (not named and not associated with the creature who tempted Eve, but rather described as having six legs), come up on five noble Florentines described as thieves in Canto 25 and merge with them, transforming them into serpents or lizards—Dante here states that Ovid's poetic treatment of the transformation of Cadmus is nothing compared to what he, Dante, in fact saw in the eighth circle of the Inferno.

Influences and Afterlife

Dante's *Inferno* has supplied the popular Western imagination with many of its conceptions of the nature of Hell. In particular, the monsters have been depicted in elaborate series of illustrations by artists including William Blake (1757–1827), Gustave Doré (1832–83), and the Surrealist painter Salvador Dalí (1904–89). In film, Francesco Bertolini's *Dante's Inferno* (*L'Inferno*) (1911) was the first major cinematic expression of Dante's Underworld and, consequently, of its monsters. The primitive state of special effects at that time limited their visual expression: Minos is a naked obese man with an immense snake-like tail; Plutus is a horned devil with dark-stained skin who, through special effects, is much larger than Dante and Virgil—as is Satan, whose central face is shown with a squirming human body in it, and whose other two faces are suggested by the legs of the bodies they are chewing sticking out on either side. Monsters are much better realized in the 2010 video game *Dante's Inferno*, which reimagines Dante as a Knight Templar who must fight his way through Hell to save his love, Beatrice. The computer technology allows for the monsters to be suitably massive, but the correspondence between earthly sin and infernal punishment is lacking.

Don Riggs

References and Suggested Reading

Alighieri, Dante. *The Divine Comedy. Translated by John Aitken Carlyle, Thomas Okey, and Philip Henry Wicksteed.* New York: Vintage, 1950.

Austin, H.D. "Dante's Veltri." *Italica* 24, no. 1 (March 1947): 14–19.

Hunt, Patrick. "Dante's Monsters in the Inferno: Reimagining Classical to Christian Judgment." *Philolog.* Stanford University, April 2010. <http://traumwerk.stanford.edu/philolog/2010/04/dantes_monsters_in_the_inferno.html>.

Iannucci, Amilcare A., ed. *Dante, Cinema, and Television.* Toronto: University of Toronto Press, 2004.

DEATH, PERSONIFIED

Human unease with mortality has led us to personify Death as a character that interacts with us in terrifying, comedic, and even romantic ways. While myth and religion have depicted **angels** and gods associated with dying or passing from the mortal realm, Death itself also takes many forms, from a skeletal reaper to a beautiful woman to a well-dressed businessman.

In Greek mythology and the literature based on it, the personification of Death is Thanatos, a figure separate from Hades, the god of death who rules over the land that bears his name. In Homer's *Illiad* (c. eighth century BCE), a gentle-winged Thanatos appears with his brother Hypnos (Sleep) to remove the body of the Trojan warrior Sarpedon from the battlefield. The child of Nix (Night), Thanatos is also mentioned in Hesiod's *Theogony* (c. 700 BCE), a history of the Greek gods. In Euripides's *Alcestis* (438

BCE), the Greek hero Herakles (Hercules) wrestles and defeats Thanatos. In Virgil's Latin epic *Aeneid* (30–19 BCE), Death guards the entrance to the underworld, along with his siblings Care, Pain, and Sickness.

Personifications of Death, as distinct from angels who bring death, are also common in the Bible. In Jeremiah 9:21, Death is portrayed as an intruder: "For death has come into our windows, and is entered into our palaces." The Second Book of Samuel refers to the "snares of death" (22:6), while Psalm 116:3 also sees Death as one who traps us in "chords" (New American) or "sorrows" (King James). Most influentially, in the Book of Revelation 6:8, Death rides a "pale" (King James) or "pale green" (New American) horse to usher in the Apocalypse alongside Famine, War, and Pestilence.

Personifications of mortality were particularly popular in the Middle Ages as a reaction to the bubonic plague, also called the Black Death. Death, or *Mort*, appears as an allegorical figure in *Le Roman de la Rose* (c. 1230–70) by Guillaume de Lorris and Jean de Meun, as well as in the morality play *Everyman* (c. fifteenth century). In "The Pardoner's Tale," from Geoffrey Chaucer's late fourteenth-century *Canterbury Tales*, Death is a thief who carries a spear. Perhaps the best-known depiction of Death to come from this period is that of a skeletal figure carrying a scythe or sickle and robed in black. The image may come from representations of the Greek god Chronos, or from Revelation 14:15–20 in which angels are shown reaping the souls of the dead.

Although the term "Grim Reaper" does not seem to have appeared until the nineteenth century, medieval visual art makes many allusions to the concept. The motif known as the *Danse Macabre*—from numerous series of paintings and woodcuts found on the walls of churches and cemeteries throughout Europe—features a skeletal, often scythe-wielding Death leading a procession of dancers. They come from all walks of life to show that dying makes everyone equal. The images are accompanied by poems describing each dancer's ultimate fate.

The personification of Death has remained common in European and American literature, retaining and sometimes combining characteristics from earlier sources. Book 2 of John Milton's *Paradise Lost* (1674) portrays Death "brandishing his fatal Dart" (78:10) and making even "Hell trembl[e] at his hideous Name" (78:12). In Robert Burns's "Death and Doctor Hornbook" (1785), a skeletal Death is shown carrying both a scythe and a dart. Sir Walter Scott's narrative poem *Marmion* (1808) describes Death as having "claimed his prey" (Canto 1). Many poems illustrate the speaker's defiance toward Death, as in John Donne's "Death Be Not Proud" (1633), or at least impertinence, as in e.e. cummings's "Portrait" or "buffalo bill's" (1920): "how do you like your blueeyed boy / Mister Death" (10–11). In "Adonais: An Elegy on the Death of John Keats" (1821), Percy Bysshe Shelley depicts Death as one who "laughs at our despair" but also as "kingly"; and in Edna St Vincent Millay's pacifist poem, "Conscientious Objector" (1934), the poet portrays Death as a horseman whom she will not assist: "And he may mount by himself / I will not give him a leg up" (9–10).

Death's egalitarian nature, as seen in the theme of the *Danse Macabre*, recurs in Edgar Allan Poe's short story, "The Masque of the Red Death" (1842), in which nobles gather in an abbey to wait out a plague. The titular character comes disguised as a masquerade party guest, robed, with a face like "a stiffened corpse" (272). Roger Corman's 1964 film of the same name expands upon the story. Eugene Ionesco's play *Jeux de Massacre* (1971) has Death roaming a pestilence-stricken medieval village in the form of a hooded monk. In Charles Dickens's novella

A Christmas Carol (1843)—and its many retellings in film and on television—the dark-robed Ghost of Christmas Yet to Come is often associated with Death.

Other literary works explicitly make use of the image of Death from the Book of Revelation, as can be seen in the title of Piers Anthony's novel *On a Pale Horse* (1983). The book portrays Death not as a being in itself but rather as a role or "office" performed by a human being. Neil Gaiman and Terry Pratchett's novel *Good Omens* (1990) satirizes apocalyptic writing and includes the character of the horseman Death. Death is also important in Pratchett's "Discworld" series of novels and is depicted as a giant, black-hooded **skeleton** with a scythe, recalling the figure that has come to be known iconically as the "Grim Reaper." He also has a pale horse named Binky. In Discworld, Death has become sympathetic to humanity, raising an adopted daughter and standing in for the Hogfather (the Discworld version of Santa Claus). Another sympathetic Death narrates Markus Zusak's Holocaust novel, *The Book Thief* (2005). There is even a rabbit Death figure, the Black Rabbit of Inle, depicted in Richard Adams's 1972 novel *Watership Down* and its 1978 film adaption (Martin Rosen).

Death as a Woman

Many writers have seen Death as female. As early as 1224, in "The Canticle of the Sun," Francis of Assisi addresses and glorifies "Sister Bodily Death," while the Italian poet Petrarch's "The Triumph of Death" (1348) depicts her as a kindly old woman. In France, Pierre de Ronsard's "Hymn of Death" (1555) gives us Death as goddess. In Samuel Taylor Coleridge's "The Rime of the Ancient Mariner" (1798), Death appears in two guises: male Death playing dice with the pale female "Night-mare Life-in-Death" sometimes identified as a **vampire** (188–194). Charles Baudelaire's poem "Danse Macabre" (1857) portrays Death as a skeletal "coquette" (4) at a ball. The seductress Madame LaMort appears in the 1891 play of the same name by Rachilde (Marguerite Eymery). In the fifth of the "Duino Elegies" (1922) by German poet Rainer Maria Rilke, Madame Lamort is a hat maker, and in Algernon Blackwood's story "The Dance of Death" (1927), she appears as Issidy, a beautiful girl in a green dress. In Dante Gabriel Rossetti's series of sonnets, "The House of Life" (1870), the Pre-Raphaelite poet sees Death as both "an infant child" ("Newborn Death – I," 1) and a "veiled woman" ("Death in Love," 9), while in Maurice Maeterlinck's play, *The Death of Tintangiles* (1909), Death is described as a queen. In Neil Gaiman's "Sandman" series of comics, she is a charming and beautiful young goth. In the novel *One Hundred Years of Solitude* (1967), Gabriel Garcia Marquez personifies Death as a woman with long hair. The character Saint Death from Mexican folk religion is the subject of a 2007 documentary, *La Santa Muerte* (Eva Aridjis), and is portrayed as an evil seductress in evangelical filmmaker Paco Del Toro's film, also called *La Santa Muerte* and released in the same year.

Death Personified on Television and in Film

The personification of death is common in film and television, very often recalling the visual characteristics of the Grim Reaper. In Ingmar Bergman's *The Seventh Seal* (1957), Death plays chess with a medieval knight during a plague; the film later enacts a version of the *Danse Macabre*. Woody Allen's 1975 film *Love and Death* satirizes the latter image, while in *Bill and Ted's Bogus Journey* (Peter Hewitt, 1991), the heroes play a variety of games including Twister with Death. In the television series *Scrubs*, the lead character has a vision of Death beating him at Connect Four ("My Old Lady," 16 October 2001). The 1993 film *The Last Action Hero* (John McTiernan) finds Bergman's Death wandering the streets of Manhattan. In Monty Python's *The Meaning of Life* (Terry Jones, 1983) the Grim Reaper visits a dinner party but cannot get anyone to stop talking long enough to be reaped. Death also appears as the Grim Reaper in two films by Python's Terry Gilliam, *The Adventures of Baron Munschausen* (1988) and *The Brothers Grimm* (2005).

Death as a comedic figure is common on television. John Waters plays a recurring character called the Groom Reaper in *'Til Death Do Us*—true stories of marriages that end in murder. On the series *Married with Children*, an episode entitled "Take My Wife Please" (24 October 1993) gives us Maggie Bundy as Death. Death also shows up as a recurring character on the animated program *Family Guy*, with Peter Griffin standing in for Death in the episode "Death is a Bitch" (21 March 2000). Matt Groening's *The Simpsons* portrays Homer taking over Death's duties in "Treehouse of Horror XIV" (2 November 2002). *South Park* gives us a Grim Reaper who can be distracted from his duties by television ("Death," 17 September 1997). *The Grim Adventures of Billy and Mandy* follows the adventures of two children who are best friends with the Grim Reaper. Death appears as a gutter salesman in "Grim Reaper Gutters," the 19 November 2006 episode of *Aqua Unit Patrol Squad 1*.

In several films and television series, Death is also portrayed as sympathetic to humans. In *Monkeybone* (Henry Selick, 2001), Whoopie Goldberg's Death shows mercy on a comatose cartoonist. There have been numerous filmic variations on the theme of Death falling in love, starting with the 1934 movie *Death Takes a Holiday* (Mitchell Leisen), from the play by Alberto Casella, first produced in Italy in 1924. The film was made into a 1971 television movie, directed by Robert Butler, and was reimagined in 1989 as *Meet Joe Black* (Martin Brest, 1998). Two episodes of Rod Serling's *The Twilight Zone* series portray Death as a friend to humans: in "Nothing in the Dark" (5 January 1962), a fearful old woman encounters Death as a pleasant young Robert Redford, and in "One for the Angels" (9 October 1959), a salesman tricks a benevolent Death into letting him take the place of a young girl.

Tricking Death, a staple of folklore, is central to *On Borrowed Time* (Harold S. Bucquet, 1939), in which a grandfather holds Death's envoy captive in a tree. Based on Lawrence Edward Watkins's 1937 novel and a 1938 play by Paul Osborn, *On Borrowed Time* was also remade for television in 1957. In "The Soldier and Death" (15 May 1988), an episode of Jim Henson's *The Storyteller* (1988), a soldier captures Death in a sack. Death is not so easily tricked in all films: in *Black Orpheus* (Marcel Camus, 1959), Death pursues and catches a beautiful woman hiding among carnival goers in Rio. Death also wins out in many modern horror films, including *Final Destination* (James Wong, 2000) and its sequels in which Death, portrayed by movement and shadow, stalks the teenaged survivors of mass catastrophes. A related film, *Soultaker* (Michael Rissi, 1990), features teenagers fleeing a reaper-like character called "The Man," and is famous as an episode of *Mystery Science Theater 3000* (11 April 1999). J.K. Rowling's 2007 novel, *Harry Potter and the Deathly Hallows*, also gives us a Death who does not like to be cheated in "The Tale of Three Brothers," a story within the novel, also retold in the film *Harry Potter and the Deathly Hallows, Part 1* (David Yates, 2010; see **Harry Potter, Monsters In**).

Many other works, mostly film and television, also feature characters portrayed not as Death himself but as his representatives. In *Mulberry*, the British television series, the titular character is Death's son and an apprentice Grim Reaper, while in *Dead Like Me*, a young Seattle woman becomes one of multiple Grim Reapers after dying in a freak accident. In *Reaper*, a young man is forced to work for the **Devil**, collecting souls that have escaped from Hell. Characters called "Reapers" also appear in the television series *Supernatural* as servants of Death who appear in advance of catastrophes and can be controlled by magic. Death himself is introduced as a character in the "Two Minutes to Midnight" episode of *Supernatural* (6 May 2010). A version of the horseman from Revelation 6:8, this Death also owns a scythe, enjoys pizza, and might be more powerful than God, suggesting that the attributes of Death introduced in ancient, Biblical, and medieval works will continue to be interpreted in new ways.

Regina Hansen

References and Suggested Reading

Brodman, Barbara. *The Mexican Cult of Death in Myth, Art and Literature*. Bloomington, IN: iUniverse, 2011.

Gertsman, Elina. *The Dance of Death in the Middle Ages: Image, Text, Performance*. Turnhout, Belgium: Brepols Publishers, 2010.

Guthke, Karl. *The Gender of Death: A Cultural History in Art and Literature*. Cambridge, UK: Cambridge University Press, 1999.

Poe, Edgar Allan. "The Masque of the Red Death." *Complete Tales and Poems* [1842]. Reprint, New York: Vintage Books, 1975. 269–73.

DEMENTOR—*see* Harry Potter, Monsters In

DEMON

In the Western Christian tradition, demons embody pure evil: they include the **imp**s who assailed medieval saints, such as the English St Guthlac (673–714) in his Fenland hermitage; the **gargoyle**s who capered through religious mystery plays; and the smooth-tongued Mephistophelean charlatans (see **Mephistopheles**) of the early modern period who inveigle priests and scholars into moral corruption and apostasy. Yet even in medieval times, this Manichaean supernaturalism was being undermined by persistent subtexts of carnival and parody; John Milton's charismatic, if not sympathetic, fiends in *Paradise Lost* (1667) sprang a crack in the demonic façade of absolute evil that would be widened by writers of the Romantic era. While even today we remain fascinated by the stench of the pit—as cult films such as William Friedkin's *The Exorcist* (1973) or Richard Donner's *The Omen* (1976) and their sequels and imitations make clear—the modern demon has become a complex and even attractive figure. Since the nineteenth century, European and American prose has created demons who exemplify all-too-human pride, vulnerability, and passion; to the nineteenth-century realist Fyodor Dostoyevsky (1821–81), demons signified intellectual futility and the moral nullity of atheism; to the *fin de siècle* Symbolists, following Charles Baudelaire (1821–67), they represented aesthetic freedom and ethical autonomy. The demon remains a conflicted figure, often symbolizing modern man's painful self-recognition in a traumatically secularized world. The modern demon may even struggle with his own capacity for virtues and positive desires; like Johann Wolfgang von Goethe's (1749–1832) Mephistopheles, he wills evil, but accomplishes only good.

In global cultural mythology, demons are polyvalent entities. In South Asian culture, Sanskrit deities and demons are warring step-siblings, locked in endless cycles of conquest and concession. In Japan and China, strongly influenced by Buddhist mythology, not all demons are even evil—a panoply of animal and tree spirits, besides reanimated corpses and even discarded tools (see **Objects, Animate**), are capable of becoming demonic. The demons of Africa and the Caribbean reflect not only indigenous folklore but also both regions' angst against Western colonialism; while European demons are black as cinders, Afro-Caribbean demons are frequently pale-skinned, duplicitous tempters. As this survey of the demonic presence in world literature and culture amply demonstrates, demons are truly legion.

Muireann Maguire

Medieval Demons

The demons of medieval literature derive from Biblical tradition and Christian theology, and occur in genres as diverse as poetry, drama, romance, saints' lives, and even theological and scientific literature. In this tradition, the **Devil** and demons were good **angels** who fell from grace because they rebelled against God. They preyed upon mortals who were susceptible to demonic possession and torment because of their own fallen state, stemming from Original Sin. Early medieval literature (c. 500–1100) often grouped multiple demons together as a collective identity, and the Devil was thus interchangeable with a single demon or a host of demons. Early medieval literature tended to be preoccupied with manifestations of demonic forces and the cultural motifs that demons represented, while later medieval literature (c. 1100–1500) often sought to classify its demons, and this impulse reached its ontological and aesthetic peak in the celebrated literary and demonological texts of the fourteenth century.

Peter Dendle skillfully analyzes the collective identity of most Anglo-Saxon demons, and his extensive examples include the tenth-century Vercelli Homily 12, which utilizes the Old English plural "helle gæstes" (evil spirits) and "dioflum" (devils) alongside the singular "dioful" (devil). The most common appearance of demons in Anglo-Saxon literature was in saints' lives, such as Cynewulf's poem "Juliana" from the tenth-century *Exeter Book*, which depicts how the fourth-century martyr St Juliana meets the son or emissary of Satan in an underworld prison and describes this demon as "wrohtes wyrhtan" (worker of evil) and "fyrnsynna fruman" (author of old sins) (lines 346 and 347). This demon claims responsibility for all human suffering since the world began, including the Fall in Eden, and thus Cynewulf furthers the medieval understanding of a collective and interchangeable demonic identity.

Similar demons occur elsewhere in Anglo-Saxon literature, notably in the narratives of St Guthlac, who died in the early eighth century. The English monk Felix composed the Latin *Life of Guthlac* just after the saint's death to describe how Guthlac established a hermitage in Crowland in the fenlands of eastern England, where he was tormented by the indigenous demons. Felix portrays this host of demons as "inmundorum spirituum" (filthy spirits); the Old English poem "Guthlac A" (from the *Exeter Book*) further characterizes these enemies as "wraðe wræcmacgas" (wrathful outcasts) and "wærlogan" (oathbreakers) (lines 558 and 623). Felix also includes a physical description of the demons and their monstrous physiques, including their "yellow complexions, filthy beards, shaggy ears, wild foreheads, fierce eyes, foul mouths, horses' teeth, [and] throats vomiting flames" (Colgrave 103). These demons threaten Guthlac with their ever-increasing multitude, preferring to destroy the saint and the land rather than relinquish their geographic advantage. The saintly warrior (whom the poem repeatedly describes as being "ana" [alone]) defies this clamorous throng and eventually disperses the demons with his holy speech.

The most common demonic presence in later medieval literature also took the form of temptation. William Langland's fourteenth-century mystical text *Piers Plowman* is a series of visions that depict, among other things, humanity threatened by vice and demonic temptation, but the most elaborate imagery occurs in the story of Christ's passion and death in Vision 6. As Christ approaches Hell on Holy Saturday, charging in full armor, demons including Gobelyn, Ragamoffyn, and Astarot hold a frantic council to decide how they will defend their home. These three derive from Biblical tradition and enhance the plural identity and multi-vocal communication evidenced by many instances of the medieval demonic. Here, this parliament of demons foreshadows Langland's debate between Christ and Lucifer and the heroic resurrection on Easter Sunday.

In addition to narrating temptation, later medieval authors created demonological and philosophical literature that further illuminated the nature of the demonic. As Dyan Elliott argues, literature such as Caesarius of Heisterbach's thirteenth-century *Dialogue on Miracles* echoed earlier conceptions of the collective demonic, but also sought to clarify and classify specific demonic typology. For example, the *Dialogue* describes human susceptibility to demonic sexual harassment and nocturnal intercourse—men fell victim to a demon known as a **succubus**, while women were violated by the male **incubus**. The fourteenth-century peasant Ermine de Reims suffered nightly visitations by demons in the shape of serpents, toads, pigs, and even saints. These demons could fashion their corporeal bodies from wasted human seed, as described by the thirteenth-century theologian St Thomas Aquinas in his texts *On Evil* (1269–72) and *On the Power of God* (1259–68), because they (like angels) were merely composed of air. Aquinas's *Theological Compendium* (1265–73) furthered the conceptions of the incubus and succubus by describing how demons could change sex (as well as shape) in an effort to acquire human seed from a man, later implanting this seed in a woman in order to propagate their monstrous offspring.

Perhaps the most famous literary source on the nature of demons was Jakob Sprenger and Heinrich Krämer's *Malleus Maleficarum* (1486). This theological manual was primarily a guide to understanding, identifying, and prosecuting **witches**, and in early modern Europe it helped fuel the witch-hunting craze. Medieval demonology, such as the *Mystical Chronology* and *Stenographia* by the German churchman Johannes Trithemius (1462–1516), further attempted to classify demons according to the four elements. His dynasty of demons includes land-demons who inhabit the woodlands and caves, like Buriel, the light-shunning half-serpent half-woman who lives underground; the Aereum (air demons) such as Icosiel, who cause overcast skies and storms; the Igneum (fire-devils); and the Aquaticum (water demons) like Hydriel, who topple ships and drown humans. Such elemental demons appear in other literary works from the later Middle Ages, including Jean d'Arras's fourteenth-century romance *Song of Melusine*, which describes the succubus-like female water demon whose beautiful face distracts attention from her piscine tail.

The medieval world encountered the demonic face-to-face through manuscript art, such as the thirteenth-century *Harley Roll* (British Library, Harley MS Roll Y.6), which depicts flying demons dangling St Guthlac in the air over the gaping mouth of Hell. This visualization and many other haunting images from the fifteenth-century

Book of the Vine and Our Lord (Bodleian Library, Oxford, MS Douce 134) reveal the typical medieval artistic conception of the chaotic physicality of demons, with their horns, long or hooked noses, goat or bird legs, hooves or claws, tails, dragon wings, and other hideous features. The hooked noses and dark complexions in medieval demonic art are also evidence of a socially constructed image of the demonic, because, as Debra Higgs Strickland reveals, medieval Christian Europe defined itself as an ordered center enclosed by a monstrous periphery, populated by natural disasters, sickness, and different religions and races, especially Jews and Ethiopians (a collective term for several African peoples). Because of their respective facial features and skin color, these two groups were often described or depicted as demons in medieval literature, another example of cultural beliefs expressed through the demonic (see **Races, Monstrous**).

The later medieval world also used demonic visages for humorous entertainment. In dramas such as the "Fall of Man" from the fifteenth-century *York Mystery Plays*, the "stage demon" was a common buffoon character that represented vice and temptation on the medieval stage. In one example given by Jeffrey Burton Russell, the demon Tutivillus from the fifteenth-century morality play *Mankind* parodied religious life by collecting the sins of a monastery and the lines that careless monks left out of their prayers and manuscript writing. Other demons had humorous names ridiculing sin, such as "Schonspigel" (Pretty Mirror), who poked fun at the vanity of women. Medieval drama was a vernacular extension of the Latin liturgy that brought the stories of the Bible and the lives of the saints into the public domain, where everyone could marvel at the fantastic on-stage portrayal of demons and laugh at their oafishness. Dante Alighieri's fourteenth-century *Divine Comedy* includes a number of demons whose dysfunctionality is intended to evoke similar humor. In Canto 21 of Dante's *Inferno*, the poet and Virgil encounter many demons in the eighth circle of Hell, all constantly quarreling in demonic chaos and discord. The demon Alichino (Allurer) wields a hook and keeps the souls of the damned submerged in boiling pitch, assisted by a menagerie of ferociously named creatures, including Barbariccia (Malicious) and Draghignazzo (Fell-dragon). Malacoda (Evil Tail) attempts to apprehend Virgil and throw him into the pitch, but the poet claims that divine will protects the travelers and forces Malacoda and his quarrelsome brotherhood into submission (see **Dante, Monsters In**).

Justin T. Noetzel

References and Suggested Reading

Colgrave, Bertram, ed. *Felix's Life of Saint Guthlac*. Cambridge: Cambridge University Press, 1956.

Dendle, Peter. *Satan Unbound: The Devil in Old English Narrative Literature*. Toronto: University of Toronto Press, 2001.

Elliott, Dyan. *Fallen Bodies: Pollution, Sexuality, and Demonology in the Middle Ages*. Philadelphia: University of Pennsylvania Press, 1999.

Russell, Jeffrey Burton. *Lucifer: The Devil in the Middle Ages*. Ithaca: Cornell University Press, 1984.

Strickland, Debra Higgs. *Saracens, Demons, & Jews: Making Monsters in Medieval Art*. Princeton: Princeton University Press, 2003.

British and Irish Demons

Demons have figured prominently in the popular literature of the British Isles from the Middle Ages to the present day as evil spirits explicitly associated with Hell, or mysterious beings who exhibit sinister tendencies that suggest they are in league with the Devil. The earliest demons were hideous monsters that had to be overcome in order for good to triumph. In more recent literature, demons are portrayed as increasingly human-like, Romantic heroes (or anti-heroes) with very human emotions and motivations.

Among the earliest English literary works to feature demons were the Medieval Mystery or Miracle Plays, dramas that re-enacted Bible stories from Creation to Resurrection, and the Morality Plays, allegorical interludes that personified virtues and vices and man's struggle with good and evil, often represented by a good and bad angel respectively. Particularly popular between the thirteenth and sixteenth centuries, these dramas include *The Fall of Lucifer*, *The Creation and Fall of Angels*, *The Castle of Perseverance*, *Mary Magdalen*, *Nature*, and *Mankind*. While Lucifer features far more prominently in Miracle Plays than do lesser demons, the latter occupy a crucial role as a threat to or antithesis of human society, jeopardizing the spiritual wellbeing of individuals and consequently enforcing the need for spiritual discipline. These demons were bestial in appearance, a motley composition of animal parts. In the Morality Plays, they were often highly comical, disrupting the action through bumbling incompetence rather than devilish cunning.

Demons appeared even more frequently in English Renaissance literature, particularly in Elizabethan and Jacobean drama where they were an extremely popular device, serving as supernatural agents to complicate the human action. The most well-known of these stage demons is Mephistopheles in Christopher Marlowe's *Doctor Faustus* (c. 1590), the story of the ill-fated Wittenberg academic who sells his soul for unlimited knowledge and power, only to discover that Mephistopheles's abilities are severely restricted. Most stage demons from this period conform to the Mephistophelean model, tricking people into signing over their souls by making promises they are unable and unwilling to fulfill. When Renaissance demons did bestow magical powers, these usually only enhanced the natural ability and intellect of the human in question. A good example is Robert Greene's comedy *Friar Bacon and Friar Bungay* (c. 1590). Bacon, modeled on the medieval philosopher Roger Bacon, requires demonic assistance to create a brazen head that, when complete, will utter strange truths and lecture on philosophy, only to have his efforts to create artificial intelligence thwarted by his foolish servant Miles. Demonic magic thus works only in the presence of an initiated intellectual.

In other dramas of this period, particularly in plays about witchcraft, devils facilitate revenge, promising to inflict supernatural malice on unkind neighbors. Both Dekker, Ford, and Rowley's *The Witch of Edmonton* (1621) and Heywood and Brome's *The Late Lancashire Witches* (1634) dramatize contemporary witch trials; each play features devils in the form of animal familiars who suck the witches' blood and bear affectionate, domestic monikers such as Tom, Mawsy, and Puckling.

While the witches' familiars take animal form, other stage devils appear human, blurring the distinctions between the human and the demonic. Faustus demands that Mephistopheles adopt the semblance of a Franciscan friar, deeming this guise the most appropriate for a devil. In Ben Jonson's *The Devil Is An Ass* (1616), the demon Pug comes to London, possesses the corpse of a newly hanged criminal, and is consequently unable to implement any real evil on Earth because the humans he meets fail to recognize him as a devil. Jonson's play suggests that demons are much less capable of evil-doing than people. While Pug is absurdly incompetent, the charismatic, human-like Mephistopheles attracts the audience's sympathy by revealing the compelling back-story of his own fall. Such humane representations of the Devil foreshadow the still more sympathetic treatment of Lucifer (see **Devil, The**) in John Milton's *Paradise Lost* (1667), which casts Satan as a Romantic hero, a fallen angel beyond redemption. This trope is also used in William Blake's *The Marriage of Heaven and Hell* (1790).

Not all demons in Renaissance literature are male. Spenser's allegorical *Faerie Queene* (1590–96) features several female demons including Duessa, who serves the evil sorcerer Archimago. She seduces a knight with her beauty but is then revealed as a hideous old crone. Duessa's demonic accomplice Ate also appears as a beautiful young woman in order to lure a knight into moral corruption.

In post-Renaissance literature, demons and devils usually appeared human or near-human, enticing their unwitting victims to commit subtly insidious sins and revealing their demonic origins only when it is too late for repentance. They featured significantly in popular Gothic fiction of the late eighteenth century. Matthew Lewis's lurid novel *The Monk* (1796) chronicles the moral corruption of the devout monk Ambrosio. The demon **Matilda** seduces him, disguised as a novice whose face resembles the picture of the Madonna that Ambrosio worships. The demon thus exploits his intense piety in order to tempt him into sin. After revealing herself as a woman, and threatening suicide if he does not satisfy her desires, Matilda initiates Ambrosio into sexual depravity. She then helps Ambrosio to rape and murder another young woman, later revealed to be his sister. Only after Ambrosio has sold his soul to the Devil to escape the Inquisition does he realize that Matilda is a demon.

Other Gothic novels consider the possibility of demons residing within humans, most notably James Hogg's *The Private Memoirs and Confessions of a Justified Sinner* (1824) and Charles Robert Maturin's ***Melmoth the Wanderer*** (1820). Like *The Monk*, Hogg's deeply disconcerting *Confessions* features a protagonist punished for his arrogant self-righteousness. Set in early eighteenth-century Scotland against a backdrop of religious conflict and uncertainty, Hogg's novel challenges the Calvinist doctrine of predestination. The protagonist Robert Wringham, encouraged by his **doppelganger** demon Gil-Martin, murders his brother before committing a series of atrocious crimes in the belief that he is a "justified sinner" and that his actions on Earth cannot affect his pre-ordained salvation. Far from being a cloven-hoofed beast, Hogg's demon takes human form. He may even be Robert himself, for the book merges the idea of an external demonic agent with that of psychological disorder.

Maturin's *Melmoth the Wanderer* similarly conflates human and demon. The eponymous hero sells his soul in order to live for 150 years, but he can evade the agreement by finding someone to replace him. Much of the plot follows Melmoth's attempts to escape this satanic contract by attempting to pass it on to strangers. As in Hogg's *Confessions*, the demonic horror of *Melmoth* is primarily psychological, with few traces of the grotesque demons featured in earlier literature. By succumbing to temptation, Melmoth becomes an agent of Hell in his own right.

Robert Louis Stevenson's "The Bottle Imp" (1891) explores a similar concept, combining a Faustian motif with Polynesian myth. A bottle of hellish origins containing a mysterious imp brings wealth and power to its owner, but with devastating consequences. The bottle can only be passed on if bought for less than the purchase price, presenting a conundrum when the lowest unit of currency is reached. In Stevenson's *Markheim* (1884), a murderer debates the nature of good and evil with a stranger who claims to have been watching Markheim all his life. The stranger, possibly the Devil, convinces Markheim to confess the murder to the police. This demon thus acts as a benign agent, punishing human wrongdoing rather than luring people into transgression.

The Devil often appears in Scottish cautionary tales. In Robert Burns's *Tam o'Shanter* (1791), Auld Nick manifests as a beastly dog during the witches' Sabbath, which Tam witnesses in the Alloway Kirkyard after lingering too long at the pub. Walter Scott's *Redgauntlet* (1824) includes "Wandering Willie's Tale," in which Steenie Steenson is taken by a mysterious stranger to the ghost of his late landlord Redgauntlet to obtain a rent receipt. Steenie resists the Devil's temptations by refusing to eat, drink, or play music during the infernal revelry.

Female demons also feature in nineteenth-century literature, particularly **Lilith**, the apocryphal first wife of Adam who came to exemplify the Victorians' demonization of female sexuality. She is the subject of Robert Browning's poem "Adam, Lilith, and Eve" (1883), Dante Gabriel Rossetti's ballad *Eden Bower* (1869), and George MacDonald's 1895 novel, *Lilith*. In Rossetti's poem, Lilith is originally a serpent and begs to return to that form after her failed relationship with Adam. In MacDonald's novel, Lilith is a shape-shifting, witch-like figure who carries off babies born in her kingdom and prevents them growing up (see **Shapeshifter; Witch/Wizard**).

Also published in 1895 was Marie Corelli's enormously popular *The Sorrows of Satan*, one of the first modern bestsellers. Corelli's novel narrates the adventures of Geoffrey Tempest, a struggling author befriended by the eccentric aristocrat Prince Lucio Rimanez who helps him acquire wealth but not happiness. Lucio is revealed as the Devil and ultimately renounced by Tempest. As the title indicates, the Devil, in his doomed quest for personal salvation, is the main focus of the novel and of readers' sympathy.

Despite the twentieth-century trend towards secular subjects, British literature continued to manifest keen interest in the demonic—whether narrative, allegorical, or humorous. In Max Beerbohm's "Enoch Soames" (1916), a writer bargains with the Devil to spend an afternoon in the British Museum's Reading Room a century later to research his posthumous reputation. Disappointingly, he finds just one reference to Enoch Soames—as a third-rate poet. C.S. Lewis's *The Screwtape Letters* (1942) is an epistolary novel in which the demon Screwtape advises and admonishes his nephew Wormwood, instructing him on how to win the soul of a mortal man known simply as "the patient." Like *The Sorrows of Satan*, Lewis's book concerns the relationship between human and demonic tempters, although this story is written exclusively from the demon's viewpoint. John Banville's immensely complicated novel *Mefisto* (1986) re-examines the Faust legend, reconsidering human–demonic relations within an Irish context. Its protagonist, Gabriel Swan, is a mathematician obsessed with uncovering the numerical pattern of the entire universe. His faith in empirical knowledge is corrupted by the red-haired demon Felix, mysteriously linked with Gabriel's deceased twin brother. Felix's role resembles the Renaissance demons' promise to give scholars access to forbidden knowledge, and Gabriel's association with the mysterious demon forces him to reconsider chance, fate, and the ethics of scholarship.

In C.S. Lewis's *Chronicles of Narnia* (1950–56), demons play a vital role in a fictional world explicitly based on Christian theology. Evil is first introduced to Narnia by Digory, who accidentally admits the witch Jadis. In *The Lion, the Witch, and the Wardrobe* (1950), she rules Narnia and is served by various demonic minions including hags, boggles, incubi, **ogres**, and many others. Another Narnian demon personifying evil is Tash (in *The Horse and His Boy* [1954] and *The Last Battle* [1956]), the vengeful deity of neighboring Calormen. Part-human, part-bird, and emitting a corpse-like stench, Tash is the antithesis of the Narnian God, the lion Aslan.

Tolkien's *Lord of the Rings* (1954–55) contains a similarly complex ontology of good and evil, with numerous demonic characters including **goblins** and orcs, deformed creatures bred to serve evil. The Balrog, an ancient demon shrouded in fire and shadow, is defeated by Gandalf in the mines of Moria. The equally sinister Nazgûl, the Black Riders who pursue Frodo, were originally men, degraded by their allegiance to the evil sorcerer Sauron (see **Tolkien, Monsters In**).

Less somberly, Neil Gaiman and Terry Pratchett's popular novel, *Good Omens* (1990), parodies demonic literature with their demon Crawly, or Anthony J. Crowley. Crawly, who appears (nearly) human, is dispatched to guard the Antichrist. As he is particularly comfortable on Earth and has no wish to see it destroyed, Crawly enlists his angelic counterpart Aziraphale to thwart the impending Apocalypse, an unlikely alliance between Heaven and Hell.

Demons are now common characters in fantasy and children's literature, although their original Christian associations are either understated or left out altogether. Philip Pullman's "His Dark Materials" trilogy (1995–2000), a retelling of *Paradise Lost* in an alternative Oxford, introduces daemons. These animal-like creatures are external materializations of human souls, changing shape during childhood and assuming a fixed form at puberty. J.K. Rowling's "Harry Potter" series (1997–2007) removes the demonic from an explicitly Christian context with an array of uncompromisingly evil demonic characters. Harry Potter's malevolent nemesis Voldemort is a human who has become demonic, splitting his soul into seven parts for safekeeping and consequently destroying his humanity, defined by Rowling as his ability to love. While each side deploys supernatural beings against the other, the conflict remains essentially between human good and human evil: a psychological battle enhanced, but not governed, by supernatural agents (see **Harry Potter, Monsters In**). Eoin Colfer's popular "Artemis Fowl" series (2001–12) contains numerous demons including Qweffor, Qwan, No.1, and Leon Abbot. Jonathan Stroud's "Bartimaeus Trilogy" (2003–2005) is also populated by demonic creatures known as "djinnis," including the cynical eponymous character, summoned to serve the magician's apprentice Nathaniel (see **Djinn and Genie**).

Demons have been a key element of British cinematic horror, although films concerning the supernatural usually focus on the humans serving the Devil rather than on the Devil himself, and the demons are often little more than two-dimensional monsters controlled by evil humans. Demons flourished in the Hammer Horror films of the mid-twentieth century, most notably Terence Fisher's *The Devil Rides Out* (1968) and Peter Sykes's *To the Devil A Daughter* (1976), both based on novels by bestselling occult writer Dennis Wheatley (1897–1977). In the former, the skeptical Duc de Richleau investigates a satanic cult and witnesses the appearance of a real demon amid a ritual on Salisbury Plain. The latter presents a devil-worshipping cult intent on enabling the demon Astaroth to inhabit a young nun's body. Based on M.R. James's short story "Casting the Runes" (1911), Jacques Tourneur's 1957 film *Night of the Demon* also centers on a satanic cult. Its sinister leader, Dr Karswell (based on the

English Occultist Aleister Crowley [1875–1947]), sends a demon to kill enemies.

In other films, demons control humans. Piers Haggard's *The Blood on Satan's Claw* (1971) depicts a seventeenth-century English village plagued by supernatural occurrences after grotesque remains are uncovered in a field, apparently provoking the re-emergence of a powerful demon. The villagers develop amoral habits and bestial characteristics until the demon is destroyed. Clive Barker's 1987 *Hellraiser* features the "**Cenobites**," demonic creatures accessed from a magic puzzle box who send their victims to a sadomasochist dimension. The eponymous character of Richard Stanley's *Dust Devil* (1993) is a demon that haunts the desert disguised as a hitchhiker, preying on the humans he encounters.

The Faust myth is a continual preoccupation of British cinema. Notable adaptations include Stanley Donen's 1967 comedy *Bedazzled*, in which the protagonist exchanges his soul for seven wishes. In the same year, Richard Burton directed an adaptation of Marlowe's *Faustus*. Terry Gilliam's *The Imaginarium of Doctor Parnassus* (2009) also explores the Faustian theme, with the eponymous hero attempting to rescue his daughter from a bet with the devilish Mr Nick.

Bronwyn Johnston

References and Suggested Reading

Bloom, Clive. *Gothic Horror: A Guide for Students and Readers*. Basingstoke: Palgrave Macmillan, 2007.

Cox, John D. *The Devil and the Sacred in English Drama, 1350–1642*. Cambridge: Cambridge University Press, 2000.

Gray, William. *Fantasy, Myth and the Measure of Truth: Tales of Pullman, Lewis, Tolkien, MacDonald and Hoffmann*. Basingstoke: Palgrave Macmillan, 2009.

Vatter, Hannes. *The Devil in English Literature*. Bern: Francke, 1978.

North American Demons

The demons of North American literature and film emerge from the region's history and varied cultural composition, reflecting the myths and folk beliefs of the continent's indigenous peoples, as well as those of the numerous waves of settlers and immigrants up to the present day. Many alternative concepts of the demonic are represented in North American literature and film, including the idea of demons as servants of the Devil, as modern iterations of pagan gods, and as independent evil actors. Other supernatural beings, including **ghosts** and **extraterrestrials**, are sometimes described as demonic.

North American literary demons first appear in European accounts of the settlers' relationship with the land and its original inhabitants, and often represent Christian anxieties regarding the myths and practices of the native cultures. In *The Wonders of the Invisible World* (1693), Cotton Mather suggests that Satan has sent demons (sometimes called "devils" or "evil angels") specifically to tempt and persecute Christians in their efforts to sanctify the land and keep their covenant with God. *Wonders* describes the witch trials and advises readers on how to detect and deter witchcraft and spiritual possession by demons (see **Witch/Wizard**).

The literary tradition of the northeastern United States derives from these Puritan views of the demonic, while also interrogating them. In Charles Brockden Brown's *Wieland, or the Transformation: An American Tale* (1798), the hero, Theodore Wieland, claims to have heard voices (divine or demonic) ordering him to murder his family. This is revealed to be most likely the result of ventriloquism by a sinister stranger,

Carwin, although some ambiguity remains on this point. Nathaniel Hawthorne also questioned Puritan interpretations of the supernatural, and investigated the possibility of psychologically inspired demons. Thus, the eponymous protagonist of Hawthorne's story "Young Goodman Brown" (1835) meets his demonic double in the forest, and believes he sees his fellow villagers participating in a witches' Sabbath, an experience that forever poisons his marriage and relationship with his community. Hawthorne's conclusion hints that Brown may have dreamed everything.

The work of nineteenth-century American author Edgar Allan Poe tends not to include demons *per se*. Rather, Poe invests ordinary objects or animals with demonic attributes, in order to convey emotion and mood. This is exemplified by his short story "The Black Cat" (1843) in which a cat, its chest bearing a white mark shaped like a gallows, serves as a reminder of the narrator's subconscious guilt over a murder he has committed. Similarly, "The Raven" (1845) represents the narrator's heartbreak and despair in the figure of a bird whose "eyes have all the seeming of a demon's that is dreaming" (line 105). Other major works that employ demons and demonic activity to evoke a character's state of mind include Henry James's 1897 novella, *The Turn of the Screw*, in which a governess believes herself to be fighting for the souls of her young charges against two evil spirits haunting a stately home. While the novella can be seen as a **ghost** story—and its villains, Peter Quint and Miss Jessel, as ghosts—James called them "demon-spirits" and suggested a wider interpretation of their power and function: "[they] are not 'ghosts' at all, as we now know the ghost, but goblins, **elves**, imps, demons as loosely constructed as those of the old trials for witchcraft" (41).

The Turn of the Screw is one of many North American stories in which a ghost-like demon appears—or is believed by the protagonist to appear—in sites where violence has occurred. Shirley Jackson's *The Haunting of Hill House* (1959) portrays demonic activity of this sort, which may or may not be imagined or provoked by the emotionally scarred main character, Eleanor Vance. Jay Anson's *The Amityville Horror* (1977), supposedly based on actual events, explores similar demonic activity—specifically the demonic possession of a Long Island home that was the site of a multiple murder. *The Amityville Horror* was filmed in 1979 by Stuart Rosenberg and remade in 2005 by Andrew Douglas.

Variations on Cotton Mather's tempter demons appear throughout the American literary canon. In Ray Bradbury's *Something Wicked this Way Comes* (1962), the mysterious Messrs Coogar and Dark operate a traveling carnival offering patrons their hearts' desire, at a price. In Harlan Ellison's short story "The Whimper of Whipped Dogs" (1973), the demon antagonist is both in league with (and inspired by) human evil and a motivator of that evil. In Ellison's story, based on the 1964 Kitty Genovese murder case in New York, a malevolent force offers the central character the choice between easy evil and difficult integrity. In Isaac Bashevis Singer's "The Last Demon" (1963), like all his stories based in Jewish folklore, demonic power is undermined by human evil. There are "no more demons left," says the title character, calling himself the "last of the persuaders" (179). In Singer's "The Unseen" (1957) and "The Destruction of Kreshev" (1961), the temptation is often of a sexual nature. This theme recurs in Shirley Jackson's collection *The Lottery and Other Stories* (1949), in which a recurring character inspired by an anonymous Scots/English folk ballad is called alternately "James Harris" or "The Daemon Lover." James Harris appears by name or is alluded to in most of the stories.

In "The Daemon Lover" (1949), he is the mysterious, possibly imaginary Jaimie who seduces and abandons a lonely woman, driving her insane; in "The Tooth" (1949), he appears as the blue-suited Jim, who elopes with the story's protagonist, Clara. A more menacing demon lover is the cruel Arnold Friend, who combines seduction and terror to manipulate 15-year-old Connie Wyatt in Joyce Carol Oates's short story "Where Are You Going? Where Have You Been?" (1967).

Many American stories also feature a succubus, as in Eudora Welty's "The Purple Hat" (1941), in which a seductive woman bleeds money and willpower from a succession of gamblers, even after her apparent death. The demonic allure of femininity and pretended vulnerability is also seen in Mary E. Wilkins Freeman's short story "Luella Miller" (1902), in which the kindly residents of a Maine town fall prey to the energy-stealing charms of the seemingly helpless title character. Though clearly not a succubus, Rufus Johnson, a child character in Flannery O'Connor's short story "The Lame Shall Enter First" (1962), also appears to manipulate the well-intentioned. Rufus is fostered by a social worker who blames the boy's bad behavior on his past, but who later recognizes the child as a demon. Beloved, the title character of Toni Morrison's 1987 novel, is perceived as a succubus, among other negative identities: she drains health and vitality not only from men but also from the novel's female protagonist, Sethe. Beloved is also a revenant vengeful demon, representing the infant daughter that Sethe killed for fear of returning to slavery.

Like *Beloved* (based on African-American folklore and traditions), and Singer's stories (derived from Yiddish culture), many American demons originate in immigrant culture. When early European settlers carried their Christian perception of demons to the New World, the cultures they encountered already possessed concepts equivalent to the demonic, although the definition of a demon remains culturally relative. Several figures from Native American/First Nations folklore and myth are represented as demonic in modern novels from these cultures. In areas first settled by the French, such as eastern Canada and the Great Lakes region, literary demons developed at least partially from folk tradition based in Roman Catholicism rather than Puritanism, which often conflicted with indigenous beliefs. As early as 1636, the Jesuit priest Paul LeJeune was writing about the **Windigo** or Wendigo, a cannibal spirit from native Cree and Ojibwa (also known as Chippewa) culture. The Windigo appears in novels and poetry by the Minnesota-born Ojibwa author Louise Erdrich, including *Love Medicine* (1984) and *The Antelope's Wife* (1999). In Erdrich's *Tracks* (1989), Christian convert Pauline Puyat sees (or hallucinates) the Ojibwa lake-dwelling creature, Misshepeshu, as a demon. The Windigo also appears in Canadian fiction, including Metis author Joseph Boyden's novel *Three Day Road* (2005). Chinese-American author Maxine Hong Kingston's partially fictionalized memoir *The Woman Warrior* (1975) describes the *kuei*, a word Kingston translates as "ghost" but which can also mean demon, and which refers to a variety of personified malevolent forces (natural and supernatural) that assail the book's Chinese and Chinese-American characters.

Many infamous demons were appropriated from pre-classical cultures, such as in William Peter Blatty's *The Exorcist* (1971). Here Pazuzu, the demon possessing 12-year-old Regan McNeill, is based upon a Mesopotamian wind spirit. *The Exorcist* became a seminal 1973 horror film directed by William Friedkin, with two sequels and many imitations. Pazuzu appears by name in the film's two competing prequels, *Exorcist: The Beginning* (Renny

Harlin, 2004) and *Dominion: Prequel to the Exorcist* (Paul Schrader, 2005). The tradition of importing ancient Mesopotamian demons was comically exploited in *Ghostbusters* (Ivan Reitman, 1984) where the pseudo-Sumerian "Gozer the Destructor," helped by his minion Zuul, appears as a giant marshmallow man to destroy the world. An earlier borrowing is Dagon (based loosely on the Philistine God), used in H.P. Lovecraft's Cthulhu mythos (see **Lovecraft, Monsters In**). Lovecraft invented *The Necronomicon*, a fictional book empowered to summon demons, which has been borrowed as a narrative element by authors including August Derleth (1909–71), Stephen King (1947–), and Robert Bloch (1917–94), and in Sam Raimi's *Evil Dead* films (1981–92). Raimi's *Drag Me to Hell* (2009) also appropriates an ancient demon, in this case the **Lamia**, here summoned by a gypsy.

Cultural appropriation of demons features in several television series, including Dan Curtis's *Trilogy of Terror* (1975), in which a demon doll, supposedly a Zuni tribal fetish, terrorizes and finally possesses the heroine (see **Objects, Animate**). In the television series *Kolchak: The Night Stalker* (created by Jeffrey Grant Rice, 1974–75), reporter Carl Kolchak (Darren McGavin) encounters many supernatural demonic figures borrowed from non-European cultures, including the ancient Aztec god Nanautzin and the *rakshasas* from Hindu and Buddhist legend. Demons from Chinese mythology are integral to John Carpenter's 1986 cult film *Big Trouble in Little China*.

The demon as an ancient self-renewing force is a common North American theme. In Dan Simmons's *Summer of Night* (1992), set in fictional Elm Haven, Illinois, an ancient evil haunts the town and must be vanquished by five children. Ancient evil also re-emerges in F. Paul Wilson's *The Keep* (1981; filmed by Michael Mann in 1983), in which the demon Rasalom haunts a Romanian fortress, killing the Nazis that guard it. In Dean R. Koontz's *Darkfall* (1984), a New York detective battles demons that have opened the gate to Hell. Stephen King's 1986 novel *It* features a child-killing demon of extraterrestrial origin, frequently disguising itself as a clown named Pennywise, which terrorizes a small Maine town on a 27-year cycle. Like Jackson's James Harris, Stephen King created a recurring demonic character. Randall Flagg represents King's version of immortal evil, tempting and manipulating certain humans to commit evil while torturing and coercing others. He appears in many novels, including King's "Dark Tower" series (1982–2012), *The Eyes of the Dragon* (1987), and *The Stand* (1978, 1990). King also wrote a mini-series for television, *Storm of the Century* (1999), featuring the character André Linoge (Colm Feore), an anagram for Demon Legion, referring to the demon from the Gospel of Luke.

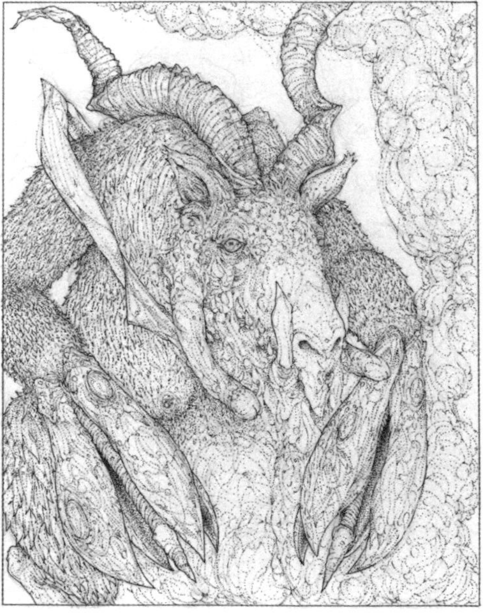

Fig. 6 ***Demon Azazel*** **by Sean McCarthy**

Both *The Stand* and *The Dark Tower* were made into a series of graphic novels. In turn, graphic novels have themselves inspired cinematic demons such as *Constantine* (2005), based on the *Hellblazer* cartoons, and Guillermo del Toro's semi-comedic "Hellboy" movies (2004–2008). Hellboy is a demon raised by humans to fight paranormal evil. In *Donny Darko* (Richard Kelly, 2001), a demonic giant rabbit (possibly a sustained hallucination) entices the film's title character (Jake Gyllenhaal) into committing a series of crimes. The original model for the comic demon could be the eponymous "Discomfited Demon" in Ambrose Bierce's 1870 short story, who flees after encountering a **ghoul** in a graveyard.

Many authors and filmmakers create entire taxonomies of demons, partially invented and partially derived from myth or theology. Canadian author Kelly Armstrong's "Women of the Otherworld" series (2001–10) features a hierarchy of demons and so-called half-demons, some responsible for creating chaos and others for maintaining order. Demon taxonomies abound in three cult television series of the 1990s and early 2000s: *Charmed* (1998–2006), which follows three benign witches known as the Charmed Ones as they fight against various evil demons; *Supernatural* (2005–present), in which the Winchester brothers encounter demons based on a mixture of folklore and scripture, including Azazel, Lilith, and the devious Crowley and Ruby; and the *Buffy* series. Joss Whedon's so-called Buffyverse, which includes both *Buffy the Vampire Slayer* (1997–2003) and *Angel* (1999–2004), and which has also inspired comic books, introduced viewers to a full bestiary of demons, mostly invented by Whedon. The demons of the Buffyverse vary greatly; not all are evil. The most famous include Anya Jenkins (played by Emma Caulfield), a former "vengeance demon" returned to mortal form; Lorne (Andy Hallett), a morally "neutral" recurring character who owns a nightclub for demons in *Angel*; Mayor Wilkins (Harry Groener), who reveals his demon form ("Olvikan") during Sunnydale high school's graduation; and Merl (Matthew James), a demon "snitch" who provides Angel with knowledge of the Underworld. Demons appear less frequently in Chris Carter's series *The X-Files*, although two episodes were dedicated to the theme: "Grotesque" (season 3) and "Daemonicus" (season 9). An episode of Carter's companion series *Millennium* (1996–99) features four demons who gather in a diner to discuss their successes in tempting humans to sin. This theme recalls Mather's Puritan concept of demons as tempters and represents a strain of North American demon narrative that embraces the concept of supernatural evil, of demons as potentially real forces acting in the world.

Three other recent American films also take seriously the possible existence of demons: in *The Last Exorcism* (Daniel Stam, 2010), a disillusioned evangelical preacher (ironically named Cotton Marcus, played by Patrick Fabian) takes part in a documentary intended to debunk the idea of demonic possession but, in a denouement that grotesquely recalls Hawthorne's "Young Goodman Brown," realizes that demons are real. The home movie scenario of the film *Paranormal Activity* (Oren Peli, 2007) and its 2010 sequel (Tod Williams) reinforces the possibility of the existence of demons in everyday life. In *The Rite* (Mikael Hafstrom, 2011), a skeptical young Catholic seminarian (Colin O'Donoghue) regains his faith by exorcizing the Biblical demon Baal from an older priest. Modern North American writers and directors thus vary their interpretation of the demonic from an emphasis on the comic and grotesque to an insistence that demons are active in human life. Their imagery of the demonic is filtered through theology, folklore, and sheer inspiration.

Regina Hansen

References and Suggested Reading

James, Henry. "Preface." In *The Turn of the Screw and The Aspern Papers, by Henry James*, 24–42. New York: Penguin Classics, 1986.

Singer, Isaac Bashevis. "The Last Demon." In *The Collected Stories of Isaac Bashevis Singer*, 179–87. New York: Farrar, Straus and Giroux, 1996.

Demons in European and Russian Literature

Since the medieval period, European demons have evolved from their folkloric and Biblical beginnings into a richly intertextual, intellectually complex pleiad of evil-doers. Distinct demonic tropes—such as the fallen angel, the demonic contract or Faustian bargain, the demon lover, and the repentant demon—have emerged in specific literary periods (Rudwin). In European literature, demons first separated themselves from religious and mythological discourse in the decades leading up to the Romantic period. Alain LeSage's widely imitated *The Limping Devil* (1707) uses the Devil primarily as a plot device to expedite the hero's miraculous observation of the goings-on inside a variety of dwellings. Jacques Cazotte's *The Amorous Devil* (1772), in which a devil takes female form to seduce a young man, introduces the literary demon as actively pursuant of human souls. In E.T.A. Hoffmann's *The Devil's Elixirs* (1815), the sanctity of the Church cannot protect the Capuchin hero, Medardus, from the fatal allure of voluptuous pleasure, worldly wealth, and temporal power, which draw him into a web of mistaken identities and murder. Demonic (auto)biographies became, and remain, a popular subgenre, with early exemplars including German writer Jean-Paul Richter's *Selection from the Papers of the Devil* (1787) and the French novelist and playwright Frederic Soulié's *The Devil's Memoirs* (1837–38).

A variation on the theme of the demonic pact (inevitably detrimental to the interests of the mortal party), made famous by the Faust legend, was introduced by Adelbert von Chamisso's *Peter Schlemihl's Wondrous Tale* (1814), in which the title character exchanges his shadow for infinite wealth. Schlemihl's riches are no compensation, however, when he is universally ostracized for his lack of a shadow. Honoré de Balzac's fascination with the theme of demonic pacts first emerged in his breakthrough novel *The Wild Ass's Skin* (1831), in which the hero obtains a cured skin that grants his every wish, but he squanders a portion of his life force with each wish; later, Balzac wrote a sequel to Charles Maturin's 1820 *Melmoth the Wanderer*. In Balzac's *Melmoth Reconciled* (1835), Melmoth returns to God after successfully passing on his satanic bargain to a cashier in dire financial straits (the bargain subsequently changes hands several more times before Satan [see **Devil, The**] claims the soul of the final possessor).

As aestheticized symbols of human evil, or as precursors of existentialist despair, demons feature extensively in the works of Symbolist and Decadent writers and poets, including Gerald de Nerval (1808–55), Alphonse Daudet (1840–97), Villiers de l'Isle-Adam (1838–89), Barbey d'Aureville (1808–89), and naturally Charles Baudelaire's *Fleurs du Mal* (1835). Joris-Karl Huysman's celebrated novels *À Rebours* (1884) and *Là-Bas* (1891), which describes a Black Mass, reflect the *fin de siècle* fascination with satanism. The Devil features briefly among other mythological characters in the final act of Henrik Ibsen's *Peer Gynt* (1867), where he considers and rejects the hero's soul; while Gustave Flaubert's novella *The Temptation of Saint Anthony* (1874) envisions Satan as a bat-like, horned monster that carries the hermit St Anthony into the heavens, to taunt him with a vision of infinity. The saint successfully resists this final challenge to his faith by shutting his eyes and silently invoking God. Anatole France's *The Revolt of the Angels* (1914) is a satire against the Catholic Church in which a group of rebel angels decamp from Heaven to Paris, attempting to replace God with Lucifer (who eventually refuses the honor). In Thomas Mann's *Doctor Faustus* (1947), the composer Adrian Leverkühn forges his own version of the Faustian contract by deliberately contracting syphilis in order to experience musical genius for 25 years; he hallucinates an encounter with a demon come to formalize the bargain.

Many of the demonic themes originating in Western sources—including the Faust legend, the Romantic demon, and the infernal grotesque—are recapitulated with new resonances in the context of Russian literature, where strict censorship made intellectual freedom especially fraught (and the archetype of the demon as a symbol of ethical and intellectual autonomy particularly appealing).

Russian Demons

As in Western Europe, the basic Russian conception of the demonic derives from both native folkloric devils, such as the *kikimora*, the *domovoi*, and the *leshchii*, overlaid by religious literature that caricatured and ridiculed Hell and its denizens (while emphasizing their power over sinners). Typical examples of the latter occur in saints' lives, chronicles, and the Orthodox ecclesiastical law codex or *Stoglav* (1551). In secular literature, the typically female *kikimora* and male *domovoi* are mischievous house spirits, often represented as a married couple; examples of each include the Ukrainian Orest Somov's short story "The Kikimora" (1829), and the writer and editor Osip Senkovskii's humorous "Notes of a Domovoi" (1835). The most famous literary reference to the *leshchii*, or forest demon, is Anton Chekhov's unsuccessful comedy *The Wood Demon* (1889), in which a nature-loving landowner is nicknamed "leshchii" by his friends.

The first important devil in Russian prose narrative appears in *The Tale of Savva Grudtsyn*, an anonymous narrative set during the Polish–Russian war of 1605–13. Here a demon, posing as a personable youth, tricks Savva, a merchant's son, into signing away his soul in exchange for the love of the woman he sinfully desires (his host's wife). Savva's new friend next estranges him from his family and sends him to fight the Poles, where Savva acquits himself honorably. But he fails to realize the gravity of his Faustian bargain, even after an invitation to pledge his obedience to his friend's "father," a king who dwells in a golden palace, served by winged fiends. Finally, suffering a serious illness, Savva realizes his companion's true, demonic shape. After the Russian Tsar and the Orthodox Church both intervene, Savva retracts his pledge to the Devil. His soul is saved and he enters a monastery.

Russian Romantic writers gave demons a central, although frequently grotesque or comic, role in literature. Aleksandr Pushkin (1799–1837) and Nikolai Gogol (1809–52) are the most significant writers shaping this trend, although other influential tales of this period include: Aleksandr Bestuzhev-Marlinskii's "The Terrible Fortune-Telling" (1831), in which a demonic stranger prophesies adultery and murder on New Year's Eve (and thus, unlike Savva Grudtsyn's demon, prevents their realization); and Mikhail Zagoskin's "Unexpected Guests" (1834), in which the demonic capering of uninvited diners makes their host realize his own venality and self-interest. Where Gogol's demons are typically ludic and grotesque, Pushkin's tend to be endowed with malignant Byronic charisma. Gogol's short story cycle *Evenings at a Farm in Dikanka* (1831–32) abounds in comic and sinister demons derived from Ukrainian and Polish folklore, most notably the wicked sorcerer in "A Terrible Vengeance," whose incestuous desire for his daughter transcends the grave (see **Witch/Wizard**). "Vii" (1835) describes the Ukrainian folk demon Vii, whose huge eyelids are so heavy that they have to be hauled up by imps. This terrifying creature rises in proto-Lovecraftian fashion through a church floor on the third night of a vigil held over a witch's corpse by a theology student, with fatal consequences for the latter. More subtly, Gogol's so-called "Petersburg Tales" create a vision of a demonically deceptive city, littered with spiritual traps for the unwary: "Nevskii Prospekt" (1835), named after the capital's main thoroughfare, speculates that the Devil himself lights the streetlamps in order to cast a false glow over everything. While Pushkin also recalled the Devil comically (as in his sacrilegious poem "The Gabrieliad" [1821], in which Satan pre-empts God by seducing the Virgin Mary) and in a folkloric context (as in the 1830 poem "The Devils," in which snowstorm-demons lead a carriage astray), his more serious work represents the Devil as a chastening, if not destructive, influence on human souls. The poem "The Demon" (1823) and the story "The Lonely Little House on Vasilevskii Island" (1829) cast the Devil as the destroyer of poetic inspiration and of true love, respectively; in the tale, a charismatic but evil stranger, Varfolomei, disrupts the lives of two innocent young people. Although Varfolomei's wicked intentions are defeated, both his victims soon die. Pushkin's Varfolomei inspired a long list of mostly eponymous, equally charismatic and mysterious demon-heroes, including Aleksandr Chaianov's "Venediktov" (1921), a precursor of Bulgakov's Woland.

The most famous Byronic demon-hero occurs in Mikhail Lermontov's widely influential narrative poem "The Demon" (1841), later evoked in the Symbolist artist Mikhail Vrubel's painting of a sorrowful *Seated Demon* (1890) amid craggy mountains. Although Lermontov began the poem in 1829, aged just 15, and continued revising it until the year he died, the setting was inspired by his military service in the Caucasus (now modern Dagestan). In the poem, a powerful but lonely demon becomes infatuated with a beautiful Georgian girl, Tamara. After bandits kill Tamara's bridegroom, the demon visits her convent retreat to declare his passion, offering her supreme power and supernatural glory in exchange for love. Although Tamara refuses to yield, the demon's fiery kiss kills her instantly. Tamara's soul is then borne off to Heaven by an angel, leaving the demon lonely and defiant as before.

Fedor Dostoevsky evoked devils both metaphorically (as in the title of his novel about a group of nihilists, *The Devils* [1872; sometimes translated less literally as *The Possessed*], which refers to the Biblical incident of the Gadarene swine) and literally, to convey mental illness or human evil. His last novel, *The Brothers Karamazov* (1881), contains instances of both. The uneducated and fanatical Father Ferapont (the antithesis of saintly Father Zosima, the hero's spiritual mentor) sees demons everywhere and kills them by stamping on them; he claims they hide in corners like spiders. A surprisingly banal devil, resembling a shabby gentleman, visits Ivan Karamazov for a companionable chat about the moral vacuity of Ivan's atheism; in this portrait of a down-at-heel demon, Dostoevsky "conclusively debunks the Romantic image of the devil as a beautiful rebel" (Connolly 227). The ultimate reduction of the Devil to pernicious banality is achieved in Fedor Sologub's 1905 novel *The Petty Demon*. Here, the sociopathic schoolteacher Peredonov is persecuted by a small, scuttling gray creature that he calls a *nedotykomka*: its constant presence irritates his grievances against society to a pitch of homicidal paranoia. Russian Symbolists and Decadents such as Zinaida Gippius ("Ivan Ivanovich and the Devil," 1906, and much poetry), Dmitri Merezhkovskii (the trilogy *Christ and Antichrist* [1895–1905]), and Leonid Andreev (*Satan's Diary*, 1919) revisited the image of Satan as a sub-Miltonic anti-hero in every major genre, including historical fiction, like Valerii Briusov's *The Fiery Angel* (1908). In this novel, a young German merchant becomes embroiled in the invocation of demons and satanic sabbaths against the background of the Inquisition and the rise of humanist study in early modern Europe. Briusov depicts Satan in the manner of a medieval woodcut, as a gigantic, hideous tyrant delighting in torture and sexual orgies.

The most significant literary demons in Russian twentieth-century literature are Professor Woland and his suite, depicted in Mikhail Bulgakov's satire on Soviet life, *The Master and Margarita* (finished in 1940, first published in 1966). Woland, a high-ranking demon reminiscent of Mephistopheles (his name is a moniker for this demon in Goethe's *Faust*), arrives in Stalin-era Moscow ostensibly to stage magic shows at the Variety Theatre. Instead, he takes over the theater director's apartment (after teleporting him to Yalta) and embarks on a spree of provocation and disorder: at his first and only magic show, he orders the impresario beheaded, distributes free money to the audience and free clothing to the women (which subsequently vanishes, leaving them naked), and allows his followers to play havoc with Moscow society. His visit culminates in a Satanic Ball attended by demons and lost souls temporarily released from Hell. His companion demons include the shape-shifting cat Begemot (an **oboroten**'), the enigmatic Abaddon, the ugly, red-headed Azazello, and Korov'ev (stage name, Fagot).

Korov'ev, sometimes posing as a former choirmaster and sometimes as Woland's interpreter, is modestly dressed and unassuming. He acts as Woland's manager and, during the Variety Theatre performance, as chief clown. According to the Hebrew Apocrypha, Azazel was a fallen angel who taught mortal women to beautify themselves; Azazello is therefore the demon who recruits Margarita (the Master's lover) as hostess for the Satanic Ball. He also brings her a miraculous rejuvenating cream, and later tricks both Margarita and the Master into drinking poison, to speed their resurrection into a new, peaceful existence. Abaddon, who appears only briefly, is described as a gaunt man in dark glasses who "sympathizes equally with both sides" (Bulgakov 259). All of these demons are former angels carrying out a prolonged penance for various grave sins. As Sokolov suggests (165), Woland's penance is to mediate divine justice, interceding on behalf of sinners against God's excessively literal-minded angels.

Muireann Maguire

References and Suggested Reading

Bulgakov, Mikhail. *The Master and Margarita*. Translated by Richard Pevear and Larissa Volokhonsky. London: Penguin, 1997.

Connolly, Julian W. *The Intimate Stranger: Meetings with the Devil in Nineteenth-Century Russian Literature*. New York: Peter Lang, 2001.

Davidson, Pamela, ed. *Russian Literature and its Demons*. New York: Berghahn, 2000.

Rudwin, Maximilian. *The Devil in Legend and Literature*. Chicago: The Open Court Company, 1931.

Sokolov, Boris. *Entsiklopediia Bulgakovskaia*. Moscow: Lokid-Mif, 1996.

Weiner, Adam. *By Authors Possessed: The Demonic Novel in Russia*. Evanston, IL: Northwestern University Press, 1998.

African and Caribbean Demons

The European concept of the demon is difficult to translate into the African and Caribbean contexts. Many beings change shape and tempt other characters in African and Caribbean literature and film, but they are rarely evil. Similarly, while numerous spirit and divine creatures inhabit animal, inanimate, or even human forms, they are rarely demonic in any Western sense of the word. Furthermore, any representation of demons in African and Caribbean literature must contend with the tendency of much European and American literature and film to demonize black characters and blackness. The paucity of demons in African and Caribbean film can thus be explained as a refusal to replicate Western stereotypes. Finally, the line between myth, folklore, oral literature, and literature and film is hotly contested. The exclusion of myth and folklore from literature may be associated with the colonial project to deny Africa and the Caribbean a pre-colonial history. Therefore, as authors of the last few centuries establish independent local literary traditions, many purposely blur artificial genre boundaries, creating hybrid genres like "oraliture."

Within this contested creative space, some entities roughly equivalent to the European demon can be found. These African and Caribbean demons are as culturally hybrid as the genres in which they occur. *Diablesse* is a French word meaning a female devil, but La Diablesse (also La Jablesse or *gouillabesse*) is a distinctively Caribbean demon, a mixed-race beauty marked by some physical abnormality. Many of the characters in Guadeloupian novelist Maryse Condé's *Who Slashed Célanire's Throat?* (2000) suspect the protagonist Célanire, who survives having her throat cut, to be a Diablesse. In St Lucian author Derek Walcott's play *Dream on Monkey Mountain* (1970), La Diablesse belongs to the Devil's army threatening Ti Jean and his brothers.

The soukougnan (also *soucougnan* or *Volant*) features frequently in Caribbean storytelling. The glossary that accompanies Condé's novel defines the soukougnan as a "blood-drinking sorcerer." The soukougnan is elsewhere described as a woman who sheds her skin by night and flies off to commit evil or destructive acts. In *Who Slashed Célanire's Throat?*, Célanire is often observed coming home in the early morning with a bloodstained mouth; she apparently kills the wife of her French lover while in soukougnan form. In Jamaica Kincaid's short story "In the Night" (1983), a soukougnan is just one of the many beings populating an Antiguan night: "The night-soil men can see a bird walking in the trees. It isn't a bird. It is a woman who has removed her skin and is on her way to drink the blood of her secret enemies" (6).

Known also as River Muma, Manman d'leau, Yemanja, la Sirène, and so on, Mami Wata is a mythico-religious, semi-demonic character prevalent throughout West Africa and the Caribbean. She lives in the water and may augur riches and success, but also death to those who disobey her, or who mistakenly follow her beautiful voice beneath the surface (never to emerge). Mami Wata's straight, silky hair and light skin link her with East Indians or Europeans. Her origins have been traced to the first encounters between Africans and Europeans in the fifteenth century when she became a syncretic icon, recoding various European and East Indian figures into Afro-Caribbean mythology and religion. Mami Wata features prominently in Martinican writer Patrick Chamoiseau's play *Water Mother Versus the Carabossa Fairy* (1982), in which she embodies Creole oral magic in a battle against white colonial witchcraft and writing. She reappears as Man L'Oubliée in Chamoiseau's novel *Biblical of the Last Gestures* (2002). Under the name Yemaya, she also appears as a main character in Nigerian author Helen Oyeyemi's novel *Opposite House* (2007), where she is the double or alter ego of Maja (see **Doppelganger**), a black Cuban immigrant to London struggling between cultures, religions, and countries. Mami Wata lurks figuratively within the mother in Kincaid's fictional *Autobiography of My Mother* (1996).

Ogun and Eshu are, like Yamanya, part of the Yoruba pantheon of West Africa, appearing also in Vodoun traditions in the Caribbean. They are demonic insofar as they represent dangerous, even evil, sides of divinity, or what can happen when an entity is imbued with both divine power and human fallibility. In Nigerian writer Wole Soyinka's long poem "Ogun Abibiman" (1976), Ogun is a powerful anti-colonial warrior who embodies the devastation and creative potential of war. In his novels *The Interpreters* (1964) and *Season of Anomy* (1973), Soyinka depicts the writer as an avatar of Ogun, preoccupied with the power of individual will, revolution, and the dangers of disillusionment and power-grabbing. The first Nigerian novelist, D.O. Fagunwa, named the protagonist of *The Forest of a Thousand Demons* (1938) Akara Ogun; but Fagunwa's Ogun fights against the demons he encounters in the forest.

Demons, named as such, feature as entities or ideas that plague characters in other African and Caribbean novels. Elizabeth, the protagonist of Botswanian novelist Bessie Head's *A Question of Power* (1974), struggles for her sanity and to escape a demonic husband. Kelvin Christopher James is of Trinidadian background, but his novel *A Fling with a Demon Lover* (1997) follows Sessela, an African-American woman travelling in Greece. Sessela's lover, Ciam, is preyed upon by Fifina, a **Lamia**. Demons also appear as black dogs that chase and sometimes kill those who stray too far from civilization, either literally or figuratively. In Mayotte Capécia's novel *I Am a Martinican Woman* (1948), the protagonist encounters a black dog demon as she walks through the woods to her father's house, although her innocence apparently protects her.

European fiction about African and Caribbean demons abounds, especially in the nineteenth century. And in the tradition of generic hybridization, Zimbabwean Daniel Mundishona's collection of short stories, *White Gods, Black Demons* (2009), explores not African demons but the demonization of Africans.

Keja Valens

References and Suggested Reading

Hurston, Zora Neale. *Tell My Horse: Voodoo and Life in Haiti and Jamaica*. New York: Harper Perennial Modern Classics, 2008.

Kincaid, Jamaica. "In the Night." In *At the Bottom of the River*, by Jamaica Kincaid, 6–12. New York: Plume, 1992.

Thomas, Greg. *The Sexual Demon of Colonial Power: Pan-African Embodiment and Erotic Schemes of Empire*. Bloomington: Indiana University Press, 2007.

Demons in South Asian Literature

Like their eternal arch-enemies, the gods, demons in Indian mythology are frequently anthropomorphized. There are various categories of demon: *rakshasa*, a generic term for demons, includes those types known by the Sanskrit terms *asura*, *danava*, and *daithya* in the classical literature of India. These terms are frequently (and incorrectly) used interchangeably. Hindu textual sources such as the Vedas, the Puranas, the *Mahabharata*, and the *Ramayana* provide extensive information on literary demons, which are classified by their physical features, each category displaying specific traits (see **Mahābhārata, Monsters In**). While all demons have the same father, each category is born from a different mother. The Puranas and epics are rich in demonic mythology, affording elaborate detail about the origins and lives of numerous demons. Kashyapa, an ancient sage and the forefather of humanity, also fathered both gods and demons: his wife Adithi gave birth to the *asuras*, his wife Dithi bore the *daithyas*, while with his wife Danu he fathered the *danavas*.

Demons in the Vedas (2000 BCE–600 BCE)

Vedic demons perpetrate actions ranging from the inconvenient to the dreadful; only the gods can intervene to control them. Their misdeeds, which affect gods as well as humans, vary from attacking women and children to destroying dwellings and resources. One of the most important demons in Vedic mythology is Vritra, who was vanquished by Indra (the King of the Gods). The name Vritra is derived from the Sanskrit root *vr*, which means to cover or encompass. Vritra is described as a serpent with power over lightning, mist, hail, and thunder, and the ability to dam water. By killing Vritra with his thunderbolt, Indra released the waters. Another important Vedic demon is the drought demon Kutsa, who was also killed by Indra: he takes the form of a horned **dragon**. A third major Vedic demon is Namuci, son of Trishiras (also slain by Indra), who obtained a special favor from Brahma: he could not be killed by any weapon during daytime or nighttime. Indra eventually killed Namuci by suffocating him with sea-foam at twilight. Besides these key figures, numerous other demons appear in the Vedas, including Sambara, Sushna, Pipru, Varcin, Kirata, Akuli, and Aru.

Demons in the Puranas (300 CE–1200 CE)

While Puranic demons derive their basic traits and source myths from the Vedic demons, the Puranas are enhanced by the addition of numerous demons. The Puranas describe in detail those demons destroyed by major Hindu deities. Among them is Andhaka, the son of Hiranyaksha, who received a boon from Vishnu that protected him from being killed. Thanks to this gift, the gods could not defeat him; they took refuge on Mount Mandara, at the bottom of the ocean. Andhaka built a fort nearby and attacked the gods, launching a prolonged war. Shiva came to the gods' defense, and became further incensed when Andhaka tried to seduce Parvathi, Shiva's consort. As soon as Shiva began winning the war for the gods, Andhaka tried to flee. Shiva then chased him, brandishing his trident. However, Andhaka surrendered immediately and successfully propitiated Shiva. Shiva forgave the demon and offered him a gift; Andhaka requested Shiva's grace both in this world and in the next. Shiva granted this wish and allowed him to inhabit a cave, which has ever since been consecrated to the worship of Shiva.

The demons Madhu and Kaitabha emerged from Vishnu's ear wax while he was reclining in an age-long yogic trance (a *kalpa*). They tormented Brahma, who prayed to the goddess Nidra for release. She woke Vishnu, who slew both demons immediately.

The demon Bhasmasura underwent grueling penances to please Shiva, who finally offered to grant him a wish. Bhasmasura asked to be allowed to kill people by placing his hand on their heads. Shiva granted this wish, but almost became Bhasmasura's first victim when the demon tried to test his new ability on the god. Vishnu then appeared in the form of a beautiful maiden, enticed the demon away from Shiva, and made him touch his own head with his hand, thus killing himself. Bhasmasura thus differs from other demons as he exemplifies the perils of excessive ambition. While other demons died heroic deaths in prolonged wars, Bhasmasura died due to his own folly.

Mahishasura is a demon with the head of a water buffalo (*Mahisha* means a male buffalo). His story is told most fully in the *Devibhagavatapurana* (dating to sometime between the sixth and fourteenth centuries CE). The son of a buffalo and the *apsarasa* (sky maiden) Rambha, Mahishasura could not be killed by any male being, which made him invincible in all three worlds. He began ruling these three worlds after ousting Indra. The gods then begged the goddess Shakti to intervene; she assumed the 18-armed form of Durga (the aggressive incarnation of Parvathi) and approached Mahishasura riding a lion. After refusing a marriage proposal from him, she warned him to withdraw to the Underworld. Mahishasura became enraged and tried to seduce the goddess by taking human form, but she killed him in the ensuing battle.

Ravana is a ten-headed demon killed by Vishnu in his avatar of Rama. Ravana had propitiated Shiva by praying to him with his ten heads. He had thus obtained the gift of invincibility: no god could kill him, nor would he die even if his heads were removed. Vishnu, however, was reborn in his human avatar (Rama), and killed the demon by first cutting off his heads and then shooting him in the stomach (the seat of his being) with an arrow.

Lavanya Vemsani

References and Suggested Reading

Kirfel, W. *Das Purana Pancalaksana*. Leiden: E.J. Brill, 1927.

Macdonell, Arthur Anthony. *Vedic Mythology* [1897]. Reprint, Varanasi: Indological Book House, 1963.

Pargiter, Frederick Eden. *The Puranic Texts of the Dynasties of the Kali Age* [1913]. Reprint, Delhi: Deep Publications, 1975.

Wilson, Horace Hayman. *Puranas: An Account of Their Contents and Nature*. Calcutta: Royal Asiatic Society, 1897.

Chinese Demons

Chinese demons are extremely diverse and many are closely associated with other types of beings, such as animal or plant spirits, deities, ghosts, and even living people. Major categories include the legendary antagonists of deified cultural heroes, animals and other spirits with special powers, minor members of the Taoist or Buddhist pantheon who may have committed transgressions against the rules of Heaven, and powers associated with the Underworld.

Both Chinese Buddhist and Taoist thought supported the notion that beings could transform repeatedly across the ordinarily stable boundaries of human, animal, and deity. These processes of spiritual transformation, whether beneficent or demonic, are commonly expressed through physical hybridity, including animal **chimeras**, shapeshifters, or monstrously large forms.

Both cultural heroes and gods, as well as the demons who challenge them, are depicted as inter-species hybrids. Thus, the flood monster Gong Gong may appear with the features of a ram, snake, or dragon. The novel *Investiture of the Gods*, a Ming era (1368 CE–1644 CE) account of the downfall of the Shang dynasty (sixteenth–eleventh centuries BCE) and the founding of the Zhou dynasty (1046 BCE–256 BCE), includes a vast pantheon of deities and rival demonic forces. Defeated fiends include Gong Gong, as well as numerous animal spirits such as the fox Da Ji and the nine-headed pheasant Hu Ximei.

Animal and other nature spirits, in addition to demonic shapeshifters, abound in early tales and vernacular language novels.

The central character in Wu Cheng'en's sixteenth-century novel *Journey to the West* is a magical monkey, Sun Wukong (see **Monkey King**). When accompanying a Buddhist monk on the long journey from the Chinese capital to India to collect scriptures, this monkey fights off assaults by a host of evil fiends including the white bone demon (see **Skeleton**), tree demons, and many others.

Sun Wukong, like many characters in similar story cycles, also travels to the Underworld. Narratives of the imperial period (221 BCE–1915 CE) include a highly articulated netherworld pantheon modeled on the Chinese administrative bureaucracy. Demons and gods from this complex of chthonic characters regularly appear in popular literature and performance genres. Prominent among such demons are Yama, the Lord of the Underworld, the ox- and horse-headed lictors (assistants to judges) who manage the courts of Hell, and the tall-hatted white and black *wuchang*, who function as envoys for the newly dead. In some contexts these *wuchang* emissaries are conflated with Wutong, a god of wealth, who is depicted in literature and folklore as a sexually rapacious and dangerous demon. Tales of Wutong possession (and subsequent exorcism) are included in Hong Mai's late twelfth-century *The Record of the Listener* and Pu Songling's late seventeenth-century *Strange Tales from a Chinese Studio*.

Similarly predatory are yaksa demons. Originally Hindu tree demons, in Buddhist mythology these beings are attendants to Vaisravana, the guardian of the north. One of the eight classes of supernatural beings mentioned in the *Lotus Sutra* (c.100 BCE–200 CE), yaksas appear on Earth (as well as in Hell) and can be portrayed as male or female. In one story from Duan Chengshi's ninth-century *Miscellaneous Morsels from Youyang*, a yaksa demon becomes a loving mate to a human girl, although she leaves him when she discovers his true form.

Jiangshi (literally "stiff corpse"), sometimes also called *tiaoshi* ("jumping corpse") are reanimated corpses that develop into a distinct type of demon, especially in eighteenth- and nineteenth-century horror tales. Today, they are found in Hong Kong cinema as well as popular television shows and video games. *Jiangshi* exhibit a characteristic jumping motion, with stiff legs and outstretched arms held in front of the body. Originally the term *jiangshi* referred to human remains left untended and unburied in the wild. According to popular belief, corpses could remain hidden in caves or coffins during the day and emerge at night to prey on domestic animals and humans. One purported source for the *jiangshi* legend is the practice of transporting those who had died far from home back to their own villages for burial. A corpse spirit (*shimo*) appears as a demonic adversary in Wu Cheng'en's novel *Journey to the West*; discussions of and stories about these demons are prevalent in two of the most celebrated Qing period (1644–1911) collections of strange tales, Yuan Mei's late eighteenth-century *Zibuyu* and Ji Yun's *Yuewei caotang biji* (1789–98).

Jiangshi are common in Hong Kong cinema from the 1980s, in particular Sammo Huang's film *Encounters of the Spooky Kind* (1980) and the *Mr Vampire* series (Ricky Lau, 1985–92). Reflecting Hong Kong cinema's enthusiasm for cultural hybridity, *jiangshi* take on some characteristics of Western **vampire**s. Shown with two protruding fangs in their upper mouth, the "hopping **zombie**s" in films are deadly killers who run amok and can only be controlled by traditional Chinese exorcists. In one film, Lam Ching-ying's *Vampire vs. Vampire* (1989), a European vampire is introduced that successfully resists traditional Chinese methods of expulsion.

Essential to all Chinese demons is the ability to transform their physical shape, so successfully that they cannot be distinguished from people, and their destructive effect on humans, or the human cultural order, and its defenders. Yet demons are closely aligned to both the divine and the mortal; humans may become gods, demons, or both.

Karin Elizabeth Myhre

References and Suggested Reading

De Groot, J.J.M. *The Religious System of China*. Taipei: Southern Materials Center, 1982.

Doré, Henri. *Researches into Chinese Superstitions*. Taipei: Ch'eng wen, 1966–67.

Kao, Karl S.Y. *Classical Chinese Tales of the Supernatural and Fantastic*. Bloomington: Indiana University Press, 1985.

Japanese Demons

Japanese demons emerged from multiple cultures—Japanese, Indian, and Chinese—and from the different religions and philosophies within them, including Shinto, Hinduism, Taoism, and Buddhism. They occur in Japanese literature from the oldest extant texts to the present. While ***oni*** is the term most consistently translated as demon in English, other spirit-creatures, such as shape-shifting animals and ***tengu***, often qualify as demons. Certain mythical beings in the *Kojiki* or *Record of Ancient Matters* (712 CE) and the *Chronicles of Japan* (720 CE)—especially Yomotsu-shikome (ugly women from the land of the dead), and the eight-headed, eight-tailed serpentine creature Yamata no Orochi, who consumes seven of an old couple's eight daughters—probably influenced many demons.

Informed by Buddhism, most Japanese demons cannot be understood in terms of good versus evil because no being is considered irrevocably evil or unable to become a buddha. Conversely, demons appropriated by Buddhism as protectors of Buddhist law never lose their demonic nature completely. Some demons can only be distinguished from unruly or raging *kami* (gods) because the former are not worshipped. Many may be former humans or beings who impersonate humans to deceive their victims.

Among the earliest demons are *mononoke*, invisible lethal spirits who cause illness and death, typically by possessing people, and who sometimes create natural disasters and epidemics. They are key forces in *The Tale of Genji* (c. 1011) and other classical works of the Heian period (794–1185). Contemporary *mononoke*, such as the forest spirits of the animated film *Princess Mononoke* (Hayao Miyazaki, 1997), differ from the earlier, intangible kind. Active in all periods of Japanese history, *mononoke* also include vengeful spirits of the dead—*onryō*, called *goryō* ("honorable spirits") when worshipped—who suffered unnatural deaths, and spirits of the living (*ikiryō*) who, fueled by anger or jealousy, roam outside the body. The most renowned *goryō* was Sugawara no Michizane (845–903), a high-ranking government official, scholar, and poet. In the thirteenth-century *Illustrated Legends of the Kitano Shrine*, Michizane is portrayed as a demonic thunder god. The spirit of Rokujō Lady in *Genji* is the most significant *ikiryō*.

Initially, *oni* were frequently insubstantial beings indistinguishable from early *mononoke*. By the mid to late Heian period, they were usually physically substantial but could become invisible at will. Most hunger for human flesh. They include the male and female warders of Buddhist hells (*gokusotsu*) in illustrated scrolls such as the twelfth-century *Scroll of Hells*. While some *gokusotsu* have equine or bovine heads, most are humanoid with three or more eyes, sharp teeth, large red or bluish-green bodies, wild hair, and, slightly later, horns. Developed from Hindu demons, *rasetsu* or *yasha* tend to impersonate women to destroy men. Additionally, jealous or resentful women often transform into *oni*. Depicted first as a woman longing for her lover and also as a deity, Uji Hashihime (Lady of the Bridge at Uji) is re-imagined as a demon in *The Tale of the Heike* (mid thirteenth century), the noh play *The Iron Crown*, and in some modern fiction. Demonic older women called *yamauba*, *yamanba*, or *onibaba* appear in the noh play *Yamanba*, the classic film *Onibaba* (Kaneto Shindō, 1964), and other works. Prototypes of these creatures can be found in certain collections of *setsuwa* (short, usually didactic tales, mostly but not exclusively Buddhist).

The saké-loving *oni* **Shuten Dōji** abducts and eats people, especially beautiful women. He and his cohort Ibaraki Dōji appear in many illustrated scrolls, such as the fourteenth-century *The Tale of Mt Ōe in Pictures and Words* and other art forms, as well as traditional theater such as puppet plays (*bunraku*). *Oni* also appear in early modern stories such as "The Kibitsu Cauldron" and "The Blue Hood" by Akinari Ueda (*Tales of Moonlight and Rain*, 1776). *Oni*-related themes recur in modern fiction by Ryūnosuke Akutagawa (1892–1927), Kenji Nakagami (1946–92), Kyoka Izumi (1873–1939), and Baku Yumemakura (1951–) among others. In film, *oni* are often used to address contemporary traumas. An episode of the film *Dreams* (Akira Kurozawa, 1990), "The Weeping Demon," presents Hell as a world devastated by nuclear bombs.

Many vengeful ghosts also act like demons. The demonic spirit of a murdered girl in *Ring* (Hideo Nakata, 1998) blurs the distinction between the two by killing indiscriminately through a cursed videotape. Another ghost-demon is the beautiful, long-haired Yuki-onna (Snow Woman), who murders travelers lost in snowstorms often by breathing on or kissing them; she may be the spirit of someone who perished in the snow.

The Night Procession of One Hundred Demons appears first in the Japanese literary genre, *setsuwa*, which consists of myth, legend, and folktale. In such tales, it is most often a haphazard parade or gathering. It features in picture scrolls, including Mitsunobu Tosa's sixteenth-century *Hyakki yagyō zu*, in which many demons are *tsukumogami*: discarded tools that, resenting their neglect, transform after many decades into demons (see **Objects, Animate**). The *Gazu Hyakki Yakō* ("The Illustrated Night Parade of One Hundred Demons," 1776) series by Sekien Toriyama catalogues Japanese monsters, including many demonic creatures. Other ukiyo-e woodblock print artists, including Hokusai (1760–1849), also created similar images.

Magical animals (see **Animals, Monstrous**) can behave demonically, and certain demons impersonate animals. Disguised as a lovely, intelligent courtesan, the nine-tailed fox Tamamo-no-Mae bewitches the Emperor in an attempt to murder him, as described in a Muromachi period (1333–1573) illustrated tale *otogizōshi* ("The Jewel Maiden"), bunraku, noh and kabuki plays, and other media. *Tengu* usually appear either as birds (often kites) or humanoids with bird-like features. In *setsuwa* tales, historical literature, various illustrated scrolls, and traditional theater, *tengu* often impersonate Buddhist mountain priests or are transformations of Buddhist monks or priests led astray by evil. They sometimes kidnap children. Typical modern *tengu* have red bodies with long noses instead of beaks.

In the Edo period, numerous previously feared demons often became tame, friendly or comical, including some *tengu*, who combined magical powers with helpful deeds, such as teaching humans martial arts, or suddenly pious *oni*. Yet malevolent Japanese demons have persisted despite this cultural shift, inspiring contemporary writers and filmmakers to create characters such as the morally complex witch Yubaba in *Spirited Away* (Hayao Miyazaki, 2001) or the lethal demonic ghosts in horror films such as *Ring* and *Ju-on: The Grudge* (Takashi Shimizu, 2003).

Michelle Osterfeld Li

References and Suggested Reading

Li, Michelle Osterfeld. *Ambiguous Bodies: Reading the Grotesque in Japanese Setsuwa Tales.* Stanford: Stanford University Press, 2009.

Reider, Noriko T. *Japanese Demon Lore: Oni, from Ancient Times to the Present*. Logan: Utah State University Press, 2010.

Shirane, Haruo, ed. *The Demon at Agi Bridge and Other Japanese Tales*. Translated by Burton Watson. New York: Columbia University Press, 2011.

DEVIL-BUG

Devil-Bug is a main character in American author George Lippard's 1844–45 novel *The Quaker City, or, The Monks of Monk Hall.* He is the depraved, monstrous doorman and enforcer of Monk Hall, a brothel and gambling den.

Lippard (1822–54) was a patriot devoted to a number of social causes, including women's and labor rights, economic justice for the socio-economically disadvantaged, and abolition. As a professional writer, he incorporated his patriotism and politics in several novels, including two histories of the American Revolution, a novel about corruption among New York City's upper classes, and a novel about poverty-created gangs in Philadelphia. Nowhere was Lippard more successful in combining his politics and fiction than in *Quaker City*. Lippard's combination of the Gothic form,

Fig. 7 "Fat reverend, you save souls; I tickles 'em! I'll tune you up, my pianey fortey! Ho! Ho!" by John Adastra

an imitation of Eugène Sue's *The Mysteries of Paris* (1842–43), and a fictionalization of the 1843 Singleton Mercer murder trial resulted in the best-selling American novel before *Uncle Tom's Cabin* (1852) and was influential enough to prompt the passing of an anti-seduction law by the New York State Assembly.

Quaker City has multiple plots and subplots, but they all revolve around the actions taking place in Monk Hall, built before the Revolution so that its owner could hold orgies in its three subterranean levels. The first major plot concerns Byrnewood Arlington visiting Monk Hall with his new friend Gus Lorrimer for the purpose of witnessing Lorrimer's seduction of a high society woman, only to discover that the woman is Arlington's sister, Mary. With the help of Devil-Bug, Lorrimer rapes Mary, who goes insane. Arlington pursues Lorrimer through the rest of the book, eventually catching and shooting him—for which he is acquitted by a jury. The second major plot is about the crimes of the swindler Colonel Fitz-Cowles and the attempted revenge of Mr Livingstone, whom the Colonel has cuckolded, and Luke Harvey, whose business has been ruined by Fitz-Cowles. The third major plot is about the supposedly immortal mesmerist Ravoni, who has founded a new cult in Philadelphia and has a harem of female followers serving him. His newest follower is the mysterious young woman Mabel, who it is eventually revealed is Devil-Bug's daughter. Devil-Bug kills Ravoni so that Mabel will not be made into his priestess and then kills himself. Luke Harvey then marries Mabel.

In the figure of Devil-Bug, Lippard created a modern, American version of the traditional Gothic hero-villain. A negative image of Victor Hugo's **Quasimodo**, Devil-Bug is haunted by the past, physically grotesque, and both licentious and sadistic. Lippard writes of him: "the same instinctive pleasure that other men, may feel in acts of benevolence, of compassion or love, warmed the breast of Devil Bug, when enjoyed in any deed, marked by especial *cruelty* ... he loved not so much to kill ... as to note the convulsive look of death" (91). Ultimately Lippard allows Devil-Bug to gain a limited absolution through death, just as the only redemption possible for the city in *Quaker City* is through the apocalypse of which Devil-Bug has a vision.

Quaker City was unique for its time for its combination of the Gothic mode with the social commentary/urban exposé novel. Lippard's intent was to write a muck-raking, American version of the "condition of England" novel that would scourge its readers for their own good. *Quaker City* could never live up to Lippard's high goals, but the novel succeeded as an attack on the corruption and hypocrisies of Philadelphia high society and on the economic and sexual predation of women and the working classes by the leisure classes. Leslie Fiedler, writing about *Quaker City* and the other "subpornographic novel[s] for males" (86), describes them as an "attempt to redeem the modern city for the imagination, to invent a myth of the City as moving and mysterious as the ancient myths of Sea and Forest" (86), and Lippard's version of the myth would prove to be long-lasting. Lippard's portrayal of the city as an unrelievedly negative space, a Bad Place similar to the haunted castles and ruins of Gothic novels, influenced later American urban exposé novels and the portrayal of cities in the dime novels of the 1860s and 1870s, and made *Quaker City* into an *ur*-text of urban fantasy. *Quaker City* further stands as a work of pornography that is repelled by carnality and views it with disgust and alarm.

Jess Nevins

References and Suggested Reading

Ehrlich, Heyward. "The 'Mysteries' of Philadelphia: Lippard's Quaker City and 'Urban' Gothic." *ESQ: A Journal of the American Renaissance* 18, no. 66 (Winter 1972): 50–65.

Fiedler, Leslie. "The Male Novel." *Partisan Review* 37, no. 1 (1970): 74–89.

Lippard, George. *The Quaker City: or, The Monks of Monk Hall, a Romance of Philadelphia Life.* Philadelphia: Leary, Stuart and Co., 1876.

Reynolds, David S. *Beneath the American Renaissance: The Subversive Imagination in the Age of Emerson and Melville.* New York: Knopf, 1988.

Ridgely, J.V. "George Lippard's The Quaker City: The World of the American Porno-Gothic." *Studies in the Literary Imagination* 7, no. 1 (Spring 1974): 77–94.

DEVIL, THE

The Devil is the author of evil, a multifarious figure who appears in myriad guises, goes by

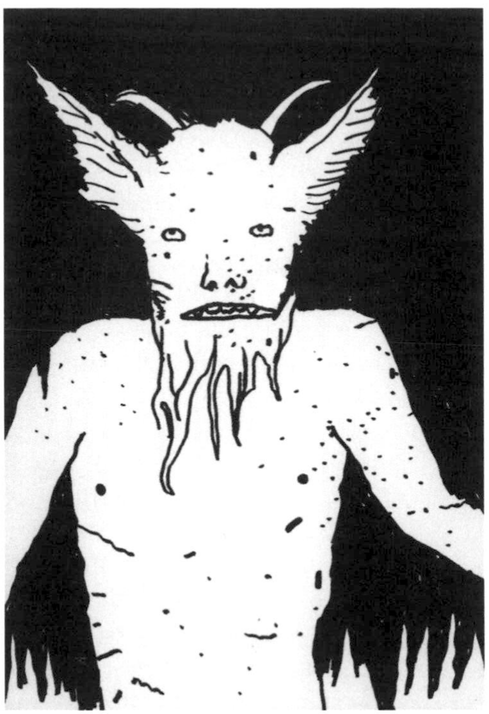

Fig. 8 ***Devil*** **by Christopher Mir**

innumerable names, and serves countless cultural functions in religious and secular traditions. As Jeffrey Burton Russell suggests in his multi-volume delineation of what the concept entails, the Devil writ large may be profitably understood as a first cause rather than a parochial or finite monstrous phenomenon: "The Devil is the personification of the principle of evil. Some religions have viewed him as a being independent of the good Lord, others as being created by him. Either way, the Devil is not a mere demon, a petty and limited spirit, but the sentient personification of the force of evil itself, willing and directing evil" (*Devil* 23). Nevertheless, literary and cinematic representations of the Devil tend to concentrate, crystallize, and localize the figure's malevolent potential. He (or in some rare cases, she) routinely appears as a deceiver, tempter, and adversary, one bent on bringing about the ruin of specific individuals, the spiritual fall of mankind, or the downfall of God himself.

Isolation and identification of the Devil proper in scripture, poetry, fiction, and film tends to involve some measure of speculation or approximation. In *Satan Unbound*, Peter Dendle offers a partial list of names historically attached to the figure—**Leviathan**, Rahab, Beelzebub, Azazel, Belial, Mastema, and Sammael among them (9)—and he indicates that a cluster of now-conventional associations drawn from the Bible only materialized over the course of several centuries: "By Anglo-Saxon times it was common to identify Lucifer (the morning-star from Isaiah 14:12ff) with Satan, and those with the devil, and all three with the serpent of Genesis and the dragon of Revelation" (10). Accordingly, to speak of *the* Devil rather than *a* devil requires circumspection. In the classic horror film *The Exorcist* (William Friedkin, 1973), for instance, a young girl possessed by some unearthly entity claims the Devil himself as her tenant; the framework of the narrative, however, makes insistent reference to Pazuzu, a Mesopotamian **demon**, complicating the business of attribution. In like fashion, the film *Fallen* (Gregory Hoblit, 1998) features a demon called Azazel, one of the appellations Dendle attaches to the Devil, yet in John Milton's *Paradise Lost* (1667), Azazel appears apart from Satan as the standard-bearer of the fallen angels (I.533–43). Perhaps the most influential literary type of the Devil, **Mephistopheles**, appears in Christopher Marlowe's *The Tragical History of Doctor Faustus* (1604) and both parts of Johann Wolfgang von Goethe's *Faust* (1808/1832), yet in Marlowe's play the character in question explicitly serves Lucifer, while Goethe's Mephisto is an amalgamation, "only one of whose components is the Christian Devil" (Russell, *Mephistopheles* 157; cf.

61). Diabolical energies run like current through a number of infernal figures, so it is also common to assign the Devil ultimate credit for the work of his underlings. The attempt to apply the designator "the Devil" in a precise, limited sense, especially in reference to a given literary or cinematic character, can thus involve awkward concessions to the pervasiveness and elusiveness of the underlying concept.

Efforts to describe the embodiment of the concept, the incarnation of the Devil himself, must contend with similar slipperiness. In the Biblical Book of Genesis, the Devil figures first as an ordinary serpent, the creature "more crafty than any other wild animal that the Lord God had made" (3:1), yet the Book of Revelation portrays "a huge red **dragon** with seven heads and ten horns" (12:3), and that dragon is then made cognate with "that ancient serpent, who is called the Devil and Satan, the deceiver of the whole world" (12:9). Landmark literary representations of the Devil venture comparably divergent depictions. In Dante Alighieri's *Inferno*, the first segment of his *Divine Comedy* (1321), Satan appears as a gigantic winged, three-faced beast trapped in a frozen lake in the ninth circle of Hell (34.28–51; see **Dante, Monsters In**); in *Paradise Lost*, the archfiend is equally enormous in stature, yet vestiges of his former glory are still discernible in his person, which bears the shape of a dimmed archangel scarred by God's thunder (1.587–604). The iconic, popular image of the Devil derived from folklore—a sinister humanoid with ruddy skin, cloven hooves, horns, barbed tail, and a pitchfork—is itself a piecemeal, contested composition, one probably cobbled together from Mesopotamian, Canaanite, Persian, Syrian, Egyptian, and Greek sources (Wray and Mobley 91–3). Christian encounters with Mediterranean, Celtic, Slavic, and Teutonic cultures expanded and complicated the collection of imagery and attributes associated with the Devil; a variety of pagan characteristics accordingly became attached to and detached from the essential concept of embodied iniquity as occasion required (Russell, *Lucifer* 62–9). Because the Devil is also held to be a peerless **shapeshifter**, capable of adapting to suit manifold temptations and deceptions, his influence is often implied rather than revealed (cf. Russell, *Devil* 254). Depictions of the Devil as a visible, tangible presence generally occur as situational representations, shapes tailored to serve particular contextual, narrative, and exemplary purposes.

Those purposes, too, are riddled with uncertainty and ambiguity. Although he may well be, as Russell argues, "the font and origin of all evil" (*Devil* 35), the Devil's operations are often mysterious and equivocal. In his two most prominent Biblical appearances, the Devil seemingly occurs as an instrument of God, a prosecuting agent in keeping with the Hebrew translation of *ha-satan*, or "the accuser." In the Book of Job, Satan is sent down to earth to test "a blameless and upright man who fears God and turns away from evil" (1:8); he visits destruction and affliction upon Job, attempting to demonstrate that his devotion depends on his prosperity, but the pious man remains steadfast in his faith. The Book of Matthew describes a more pivotal trial, as "Jesus was led by the Spirit out into the desert to be put to the test by the devil" (4:1); Jesus of course resists the three temptations proposed by the Devil and casts out his tormentor with an emphatic "Away with you, Satan!" (4:10). The Biblical Devil, while a formidable antagonist, reinforces what he ostensibly seeks to sabotage, thereby serving as an agent of God's will. The same principle holds true in a variety of theologically inflected texts and takes its most vivid form in *Paradise Lost*, in which Milton portrays the Devil's seduction of Eve and the consequent Fall of Man as a tortuous testament of divine design, a precursor to eventual salvation.

Milton's depiction of Satan, however, underscores the complexity of assigning the Devil a singular role. While he eventually suffers discipline proportioned to his crime—Satan entered the Garden of Eden as a serpent and thus becomes a serpent once more to conclude his role in the Fall, "punished in the shape he sinned, / According to his doom" (10.516–17)—the spiteful pawn in God's redemptive endgame also occurs as a proud, charismatic rebel against divine despotism. In the early books of *Paradise Lost*, he is cast as an epic hero, his admirable qualities and humane sensibilities rendering him more sympathetic than the cool and inscrutable God. The Romantic poets frequently emphasized the commendable attributes of the Devil, mitigating the monstrosity he embodies. From the perspective of William Blake, for example, "Milton's God is at least as evil as Milton's Satan" (Russell, *Mephistopheles* 180), and in *The Marriage of Heaven and Hell* (1790–93), Blake makes a case for complementing rigid divine order with unbridled satanic energies. George Gordon, Lord Byron, challenges the notion that the Devil must be the villain in the narrative of the Fall in "Cain: A Mystery" (1821); Percy Bysshe Shelley, in *Prometheus Unbound* and "On the Devil and Devils" (1821), details a figure at once fatally flawed and ardently progressive; and Mary Shelley, in her *Frankenstein* (1818), aligns her misunderstood monster with Satan rather than Adam in his attitude toward his creator (Russell, *Mephistopheles* 184–90; see **Frankenstein's Monster**). The Romantic vision of the righteous, if egoistic, rebel angel would be relatively short-lived, but traces of the impassioned, magnetic, self-divided Satan survive in more modern depictions of the ultimate adversary.

Russell argues that writers at the turn of the nineteenth century were largely responsible for dismantling the orthodox apprehension of the Devil: "Milton's is the last and greatest full-length portrait of the traditional role of lord of evil," he contends, and the understanding of evil as embodied by the Devil would "be worn down by rationalists and distorted by Romantics" (*Prince* 205). The same period, however, offered the Western tradition its most iconic formulation: Goethe's Mephistopheles in *Faust*. Goethe's variation on the devil concept is an idiosyncratic, hands-on operative attuned to popular folklore as well as Biblical tradition. As a literary figure, the reinvigorated Devil emerges as an urbane, mendacious monster, "partly a Christian Devil, partly an ironic commentator on society, partly a spokesman for secular, progressive humanism" (Russell, *Mephistopheles* 159). The narrative treatment of the now-familiar deal with the Devil has storied roots, and the formally Faustian bargain dates back to at least 1587. In Goethe's hands, however, the archetypical story of human trial and temptation is set more vividly in the secular sphere, with Mephistopheles winking at his own spiritual origin and the arc of the tale—which in many versions ends with the protagonist's deserved damnation—taking a redemptive turn that hinges on ethical reformation and diabolical miscalculation. *Faust*'s prologue echoes Job, with Mephistopheles in Heaven convincing the Lord to permit a trial of Faust, a troubled yet committed scholar dedicated to the pursuit of mysteries; a successful temptation follows, with Mephistopheles persuading his victim to give up the quest for understanding and to embrace instead the pleasures that the world affords. Despite this seeming success, which leads to a degenerate moral career and a decisive transgression,

Faust is nevertheless claimed by a chorus of angels at play's end. As a result of his ethical descent—a descent initiated and directed by the Devil—Faust earns wisdom, forgiveness, and salvation, and Mephistopheles, serio-comically distracted by what he calls the "stealthy-kittenishly lustful" ways of the chorus (299), is denied the prize of Faust's soul. Of special significance in Goethe's work are both the secular nature of the challenge and its equally earthly resolution: the trial of Faust emphasizes a proper attitude toward worldly things, and his final victory arises from a reflective selflessness rather than evidence of perfect piety. The secular emphasis advanced in Goethe's handling of the Faustian bargain effectively fortifies and diminishes the Devil, endowing the evil he embodies with verve, impishness, and wit, yet insisting that, in the sphere of human affairs, such evil may be overcome by mundane measures.

Following Goethe, what seems most important in modern narrative representations of the monstrosity of the Devil is a prominent anthropocentric tendency. Whether the Devil is suave or bestial, forthright or conniving, defeated or victorious, he tends to conduct his business in the mortal realm by material means to achieve worldly ambitions. While spiritual concerns do not vanish entirely, emphasis in narratives concerning the work of the Devil falls more squarely on responses to evil, decisions and actions that speak to the degeneracy or ennoblement of humankind. God is largely absent as an oppositional term, and the Devil's schemes seem modest in scope and contingent on human folly, iniquity, or altruism. In "The Devil and Tom Walker" (1824) by Washington Irving, for example, the satisfaction of a Faustian contract depends only dimly on a divine interest in earthly concerns; when Old Scratch (yet another name for the Devil) comes for Walker's soul, simple neglect—his failure to keep his Bible close at hand—results in the final forfeit. Similarly, the rescue of the soul of Jabez Stone, as depicted in Stephen Vincent Benét's "The Devil and Daniel Webster" (1937), has less to do with heavenly intercession than with the lofty rhetoric of the renowned American orator. The film *Angel Heart* (Alan Parker, 1987) involves an elaborate attempt by a musician, Johnny Favorite (Mickey Rourke), to break his contract with the Devil; a loss of memory incurred during the execution of his plan, however, eventually finds Favorite in the employ of the archfiend. In the thinly veiled form of Louis Cyphre (Robert De Niro), the Devil torments Favorite, toying with his amnesiac prey, plunging him more deeply into sin, restoring his memory, and finally claiming his prize. In the Stephen King novel *Needful Things* (1991) and its later film adaptation (Fraser Clark Heston, 1993), another surrogate for the Devil, Leland Gaunt (Max von Sydow), turns the citizens of Castle Rock toward evil—and against each other—merely by exchanging enchanted wares for sinister favors. The Devil at the center of Dante's Hell, the rebel angel who once warred against the Almighty, is much reduced in scale and scope.

Even the grandest plans of the Devil partake of this obsession with earthly things: not only does the Devil aim to corrupt the susceptible one by one, he also routinely seeks incarnation in the human realm. Landmark films such as *Rosemary's Baby* (Roman Polanski, 1968) and *The Omen* (Richard Donner, 1976) document the Devil's efforts—efforts abetted by both unwitting and ruthless humans—to give birth to evil in mortal form, and derivative works like *The Devil's Advocate* (Taylor Hackford, 1997) and *End of Days* (Peter Hyams, 1999) depict the exertions of a more monstrous, volatile Devil to father an heir. In the case of the former pair of films, the Devil succeeds as a result of misplaced human compassion; in the case of the latter, he fails as a result of heroic self-sacrifice. In *The Ninth Gate* (Roman Polanski, 1999), this secular emphasis takes on perhaps its most suggestive shape, as an unscrupulous dealer in rare books unravels the mystery of a text allegedly authored by Lucifer and thereby earns an audience with the Devil himself. If the Devil, as the ultimate author of evil, is a concept responsive to the vagaries of human experience, as Russell contends (*Satan* 222), then recent variations on that concept suggest a telling sense of identity, a resemblance of the creation to its creators.

William H. Wandless

References and Suggested Reading

Alighieri, Dante. *The Divine Comedy. New York:* Oxford University Press, 2008.

Dendle, Peter. *Satan Unbound: The Devil in Old English Narrative Literature*. Toronto: University of Toronto Press, 2001.

Goethe, Johann Wolfgang von. *Faust*. New York: Norton, 1976.

Milton, John. *Paradise Lost*. New York: Norton, 2005.

Oxford University Press. *The Complete Parallel Bible. New Revised Standard Version*. New York: Oxford University Press, 1993.

Russell, Jeffrey Burton. *The Devil: Perceptions of Evil from Antiquity to Primitive Christianity.* Ithaca, NY: Cornell University Press, 1977.

——. *Lucifer: The Devil in the Middle Ages.* Ithaca, NY: Cornell University Press, 1984.

——. *Mephistopheles: The Devil in the Modern World*. Ithaca, NY: Cornell University Press, 1986.

——. *The Prince of Darkness: Radical Evil and the Power of Good in History*. Ithaca, NY: Cornell University Press, 1988.

——. *Satan: The Early Christian Tradition.* Ithaca, NY: Cornell University Press, 1981.

Wray, T.J., and Gregory Mobley. *The Birth of Satan: Tracing the Devil's Biblical Roots*. New York: Palgrave Macmillan, 2005.

DIABLESSE, LA—*see* Demon

DINOSAUR

The generic term "dinosaur" was coined by the renowned Victorian paleontologist and anatomist Richard Owen in 1841, and originates from the Greek words for fearful or terrible and for lizard. It describes an extinct animal of the Mesozoic era, which was a period of geological time from 250 to 65 million years ago. Investigation into what dinosaurs were and how and when they lived only really took off in the Victorian period. As the nineteenth-century industrial revolution gathered speed, mining and other excavational pursuits, such as canal-building, uncovered abundant specimens of fossilized creatures from deep underground. For Victorians interested in the natural world, these ancient bones stimulated their imaginations, and writers conjured up terrifying images of ferocious and powerful beasts from millennia ago for the first time.

The most noteworthy example of how the dinosaur influenced popular culture in the mid-nineteenth century may be found in the Sydenham Crystal Palace park dinosaurs in London, designed by Richard Owen (1804–92) and sculpted by Benjamin Waterhouse Hawkins (1807–94). In 1854, these models were the first life-size prehistoric animals to be put on display, and they still survive today. The project to build these giant creatures was an ambitious one, but it sparked many creative interpretations of the dinosaur body. Though not paleontologically correct, the models represent the imaginative capabilities of some of the nineteenth century's most renowned naturalists. Following the erection of these giant monstrous beings, images of dinosaurs proliferated in various forms throughout Victorian culture on educational posters, in illustration books, and as miniature replicas of the life-sized models, which were put on sale from the 1850s onwards. It is owing to the significance of this early exhibition of the extinct monster that the dinosaur in Victorian fiction, and later twentieth-century film, became such a popular and marketable commodity.

Nineteenth-Century Fiction

Dinosaurs were pervasive in nineteenth-century fiction. From a brief mention of the megalosaurus in Charles Dickens's *Bleak House* (1853), to the plethoric underground dinosaurian world in Jules Verne's hollow earth story *Journey to the Centre of the Earth* (1864), the dinosaur held a firm place in the Victorian literary imagination. In some Victorian dinosaur narratives, such as Charles Kingsley's *Alton Locke* (1850) and John Mill's *The Fossil Spirit: A Boy's Dream of Geology* (1854), the narrator imagines himself as a dinosaur, traveling through time, experiencing the process of evolution for himself. In H.G. Wells's short story "A Vision of the Past," first published in the *Science Schools Journal* in 1887, the narrator dreams he has been transported into the deep past where he encounters giant three-eyed amphibians attending a lecture on their superiority and dominance over all other creatures. In response, the narrator mocks their arrogance and advises them to see beyond their transitory moment on earth. Rudyard Kipling's short story "A Matter of Fact" (1893) portrays a prehistoric sea serpent in its death throes. The journalists who witness this phenomenon cannot publish their story on their return to England because, though true, it is too far-fetched even for the sensationalized pages of the newspaper. In John Jacob Astor's science fiction fantasy novel *A Journey in Other Worlds: A Romance of the Future* (1894), space explorers discover dinosaurs on Jupiter. In this tale of otherworldly adventure, dinosaurs survive not on British or colonial soil, but on faraway planets yet to be explored by humans. In this story, prehistoric animals are alien creatures that belong to another place and time altogether.

Twentieth-Century Books, Television, and Film

In what Stephen Jay Gould termed "dinomania" in a 1993 *New York Review of Books* review essay, the twentieth century produced no shortage of films or books featuring dinosaurs in all their myriad shapes and sizes. The most popular and enduring dinosaur tale is Arthur Conan Doyle's *The Lost World* (1912), which has generated a number of film adaptations. In the novel, intrepid adventurers discover dinosaurs living on a South American plateau, far from human (white) civilization. But this was not Conan Doyle's only story to deal with the dinosaur trope. His lesser-known short story, *The Terror of the Blue John Gap* (1912), also explores the possibility that dinosaurs survive in the modern world, telling the tale of a man who finds a deep cave inhabited by a prehistoric monster. Building on Conan Doyle's dinosaur adventure stories, in the early twentieth century, Edgar Rice Burroughs's "Caspak" trilogy, *The Land that Time Forgot* (1918), *The People that Time Forgot* (1918), and *Out of Time's Abyss* (1918), featured many different varieties of dinosaurs, and involved exploration into unknown regions of the globe. The dinosaurs in these adventure narratives were often drawn from Burroughs's imagination and not from paleontological evidence. In 1975, Kevin Connor's film version of *The Land that Time Forgot* arrived on cinema screens, and two years later Connor's *The People that Time Forgot* was made into a film; however, despite plans to complete the trilogy in film, *Out of Time's Abyss* was never made. Film adaptations of Conan Doyle's *The Lost*

World have had huge success, with seven cinematic versions produced between 1925 and 2001.

The most successful of any cinematic adaptation of a dinosaur story is the sequel to Steven Spielberg's 1995 *Jurassic Park*, *Jurassic Park: The Lost World* (1997, also directed by Spielberg). Both of these films are adaptations of novels by author Michael Crichton (1942–2008); however, the plot of Crichton's *The Lost World* (1995), his sequel to *Jurassic Park* (1990), is itself an adaptation and follows a similar line to Conan Doyle's tale of the same name, except that the dinosaurs are recreated by genetic engineering rather than simply surviving over time. Another dinosaur story successfully adapted to film is Verne's *Journey to the Centre of the Earth*, which was used as the basis for film, television, radio, and theater many times throughout the latter half of the twentieth century—most successfully in the 2008 3D film of the same name, directed by Eric Brevig.

In the latter half of the twentieth century, dinosaurs began to appeal to children's sense of adventure. Following the post-Darwinian revolution in science, the dinosaur lost its main association with Gothic monstrosity and gained a more stable status as an animal understood and rationalized by science. Thus, children's fiction of the 1950s and 1960s often used dinosaurs as fun and interesting characters. These included American dino-stories such as Syd Hoff's magical adventure narrative *Danny and the Dinosaur* (1958), in which a young boy dreams that he has a friendly dinosaur as a companion on his trip through the city, and R. Faraday's *The Anytime Rings* (1963), which tells the tale of children being taken back to prehistoric times with their pet cynognathus. In 1992, the hugely popular Barney the Dinosaur aired on American televisions for the first time. Continuing the trend of using the dinosaur for the purposes of children's entertainment, this purple and green anthropomorphic tyrannosaurus rex jovially sang and danced his way into the hearts and minds of children across the globe. Interestingly, though, the dinosaur re-emerged as an amusing and ostensibly educational creature in children's entertainment at precisely the same time that Hollywood retained its Gothic elements for the adult market in films such as *Jurassic Park*.

In late twentieth-century literature and film for adults, dinosaurs became intelligent animals, as writers such as Crichton began to imagine how humans might recreate scenes from the past through scientific advancement rather than by wandering into unexplored spaces where dinosaurs lurk in the prehistoric undergrowth. With an increase in scientific knowledge of dinosaurs' physiological structure, habitat, and behavior, writers explored the possibility of bringing dinosaurs back to life after a 65 million-year period of extinction. This concept, which captured the imagination of writers and filmmakers throughout the twentieth century, still has resonance in the twenty-first century. Film writers, however, have recently returned to older ideas about discovering dinosaurs in their own environment in films such as ***King Kong*** (Peter Jackson, 2005) and *100 Million BC* (Griff Furst, 2008). In the former, dinosaurs inhabit the island where Kong is discovered and entrapped, while in the latter, time travel causes humans to stumble upon their primeval counterparts, enabling the dinosaur to invade the modern world. In both, the dinosaur is punished for daring to make its return. Nevertheless, since the 1950s and 1960s, the dinosaur has retained its appeal to children. In 2009, Carlos Saldanha and Michael Thurmeier's *Ice Age: Dawn of the Dinosaurs*, which presented the softer side of prehistoric animals in cartoon form, became the third highest grossing animated film of all time with $886.7 million worldwide.

A key secondary text for this topic is Allen A. Debus's *Dinosaurs in Fantastic Fiction: A Thematic Survey* (2006), which explores the genre of dinosaur film and fiction throughout the English-speaking world. This is an important source for those interested in the dinosaur trope. On the history of dinosaurs and paleontology, see Deborah Cadbury's *The Dinosaur Hunters: A True Story of Scientific Rivalry and the Discovery of the Prehistoric World* (2000) and Stephen Jay Gould's *Dinosaur in a Haystack: Reflections in Natural History* (1996).

Claire McKechnie

References and Suggested Reading

Freeman, Michael. *Victorians and the Prehistoric: Tracks to a Lost World*. New Haven, CT: Yale University Press, 2004.

O'Connor, Ralph. *The Earth on Show: Fossils and the Poetics of Popular Science, 1802–1856*. Chicago: University of Chicago Press, 2007.

Piggott, Jan. *Palace of the People: The Crystal Palace at Sydenham 1854–1936*. Madison: University of Wisconsin Press, 2004.

Rudwick, Martin. *Scenes from Deep Time: Early Pictorial Representations of the Prehistoric World*. Chicago: University of Chicago Press, 1992.

DIV

The div is a supernatural character of Iranian tradition. In the Persian literature of the Islamic period, he serves as the embodiment of evil, second only to the **dragon**. The concept of div apparently originates from a class of gods of the prehistoric Indo-Iranian period. While it is difficult to determine the various stages of the concept's historical development,

Fig. 9 The Div Akvan carries the sleeping Rostam away. From the 1858 edition of Ferdowsi's *Shahnameh*; illustration by Ostad Sattar. Copyright U. Marzolph.

at some stage the Avestan *daivas* appear to have been demonized. Though the existing evidence is inconsistent and ambiguous, daivas apparently were beings that, similar to humans, had been endowed with the freedom of choice but did not put this freedom to proper use. Their religion is false, and humanity's main weapon to defend itself against them is the proper observance of ritual. In later Zoroastrian ritual and theology, the concept of the *dew* is central—in Zoroastrian religious books, the dew serves as the stereotyped personification of every imaginable evil. This image is mirrored throughout the character's later appearance as div.

In the Persian literature of the Islamic period, particularly in the epics and popular romances that were compiled during the first half of the second millennium CE, divs are imagined as hideous creatures, sometimes black and furry, with long teeth, black lips, and claws on their hands. Some divs have several heads, while others have monstrous ears or gigantic teeth. They ride on hideous creatures like dragons and fight with gigantic clubs. The land of Mazandaran mentioned in the Persian national epic, Ferdowsi's *Shahnameh* (compiled around the turn of the first millennium CE), is a land of divs whose organization mirrors that of the human world, including a king and his armies, cities, fortresses, farms, herds, and so on. While the div became the ultimate representative of the evil forces hostile to humanity, the concept has also mingled with, and to a certain extent incorporated, additional features originally pertaining to similar **demon** characters of Arabic tradition, such as the **ghoul**, the jinn (see **Djinn and Genie**) or the ifrit.

In the Persian epics and in later Persian popular literature, the div is characterized by several peculiar traits. One curious characteristic is the div's tendency to do exactly the opposite of what he is asked to do. This is the reason why, in the *Shahname*, Rostam, when carried through the air by the div Akvan, asks to be thrown down to the Earth, since he is certain that Akvan will throw him into the sea instead. Another peculiarity is the fact that, when fighting a div, the hero must strike him only once, since a second blow will in fact restore the monster's forces. Consequently, when the div asks to be struck a second time, the informed hero would respond in a stereotypical wording: "My mother only bore me once, and so I will not strike again," in this manner delivering the div to final annihilation.

Though constituting the ultimate incarnation of evil harmful to the human existence, a div can enter into sexual union with a human being. Mostly, though not exclusively, imagined as male creatures, divs sometimes abduct human women to their underground abode, hoping they will eventually agree to marry them. In order to vanquish the div and free the maiden, the hero must destroy the monster's external soul that is usually hidden inside a small animal, such as a bird or a fish that in turn can only be found by superior knowledge about its complicated place of hiding. Since the div trusts the maiden, he reveals his soul's hiding place to her, and the maiden informs the hero who follows the procedure, kills the animal containing the div's external soul, and frees the maiden. The offspring of a div with a human woman is encountered in the nineteenth-century Persian popular narrative *Khosrou-e divzâd* (Khosrou, the div-born), in folklorist terms a version of the tale of the faithless sister. In this tale, a royal brother and his sister, who against the will of her father had not been killed immediately after birth, are driven away from their home. The brother ignores how his sister falls in love with a div. She becomes pregnant and gives birth to a son, Khosrou. Since his father is a demon, Khosrou possesses supernatural strength. He is, however, firmly committed to human ethical standards. Consequently, when his uncle has been mortally wounded by his mother's div lover, he saves his uncle from imminent death or even resuscitates him by procuring the water of life.

Divs make a prominent appearance in many of the popular romances of Persian tradition. In the romance about Princess Nush-Afarin that was probably compiled as early as the sixteenth century, one of three div brothers falls in love with the romance's eponymous princess, who is wooed by a number of human princes. With only his hand reaching down from within a cloud visible, he abducts his beloved. After he has been killed, his brothers seek revenge but are also annihilated. The mother of the divs is here portrayed as an evil sorceress (see

Witch/Wizard). The divs themselves are strong and possess superhuman qualities such as the ability to fly. Meanwhile, popular tradition has more or less turned the ancient evil character into the modern equivalent of the stupid **ogre** or **giant** of European folk tales.

The div's natural opponent, and sometimes his superior, is the pari, a character that equally goes back to ancient Iranian tradition. In the *Avesta*, the *pairika* is an evil being that is often associated with sorcerers and demons. The pairikas probably were a class of pre-Zoroastrian goddesses concerned with sexuality and closely connected with sexual festivals and ritual orgies. While the sexual connotation lingers on in the character's subsequent development, later texts also elaborate the pari's magic capacities. In the Middle Persian *Selections of Zatspram*, written about the end of the ninth century CE, the hero Srit fights with a pari in the shape of a dog. Every time he cuts the dog in half, the pari multiplies until the hero is finally overcome and killed by the large number of dogs.

In classical Persian literature of the early Islamic period (that is, roughly the tenth to fifteenth centuries), the pari is imagined as extremely beautiful, invisible, and capable of flying. Here, the pari often serves as a metaphor of spirituality. Paris make their appearance in the mythological part of the *Shahname*, fighting in the army of Gayomart and Hoshang against the Evil Spirit and his hosts. In the heroic part of the epic, the word is used almost exclusively in the sense of beautiful. The erotic attraction of the female pari, as well as her magic qualities, are further elaborated in the Persian prose epics such as *Samak-e 'ayyar* (thirteenth century) and *Romuz-e Hamze* (sixteenth century), as well as in the narrative texts used by professional storytellers. In these narratives, the pari to some extent merges with the concept of the swan-maiden, in particular when she disappears in the form of a dove or when the hero summons his pari helper by burning a bit of the pari's feather that he has kept for this purpose.

In Persian popular literature of the Islamic period, the pari is a non-human character living in a universe parallel to that of the human beings. The pari is endowed with immortality and magic powers, including the capacity of flying. Usually, but not necessarily, imagined as female, the pari is above all the acme of beauty. Considering her erotic appeal, nothing could be more desirable for a human man than to marry a pari, even though paris are also known for a certain obsessiveness, mercurial temperament, and jealousy. In contemporary Persian folk tales, the pari has matured into the acme of both physical and moral perfection, two qualities making her human husband ultimately inferior to her. The foreseeable outcome of this disparity is often her having to leave him, since he is incapable of understanding and accepting her rules.

While the pari in Persian folk narrative has turned into a benevolent character, she still bears traits of an ancient demonic character. Furthermore, she deserves mention as the stereotype counterpart of the div. She is not only morally superior to the div, but eventually subdues him physically, though paris and divs would not regularly engage in direct battle. Instead, the div would be vanquished by a human warrior who relies on the pari's support. Taking the interpretation of the two supernatural characters to greater lengths, one might regard them as the folkloric expression of the eternal dichotomy between the good and the evil that affects the world's fate, particularly, but not only, in ancient Iranian belief.

Ulrich Marzolph

References and Suggested Reading

Christensen, Arthur. *Essai sur la démonologie iranienne*. Copenhagen: Munksgaard, 1941.

Marzolph, Ulrich. "The Good, the Bad, and the Beautiful: The Survival of Ancient Iranian Ethical Concepts in Persian Popular Narratives of the Islamic Period." In *The Idea of Iran: Tradition and Innovation in Early Islamic Persia*, edited by Edmund Herzig, 16–29. London: I.B. Tauris, 2012.

Massé, Henri. *Croyances et coutumes persanes*. 2 vols. Paris: Maisonneuve, 1938.

Omidsalar, Mahmoud. "Div." In *Encyclopedia Iranica*, 428–31. Vol. 7. New York: Bibliotheca Persica Press, 2002.

———. "Peri (Pari)." In *Enzyklopädie des Märchens*, 734–46. Vol. 10. Berlin and New York: De Gruyter, 2002.

DJINN AND GENIE

In Islamic teachings and Middle Eastern folklore, djinns (or genies in Western culture) are powerful, intelligent, and complex beings made out of "the smokeless flame of fire" (Koran 15:27; see **Koran, Monsters In The**). Djinns have long played an important role in the folklore, literature, and arts of the Middle East, North Africa, South Asia, and Southeast Asia. While djinns were a part of pre-Islamic Arab mythology, their existence was affirmed and clarified by the Koran in the seventh century CE. Djinns are associated with shape-shifting (see **Shapeshifters**), trickery, magic, possession, obsession, and madness. Translated into French and English as genie/genii in the eighteenth century, djinns have been featured in Western texts since the Middle Ages under various names, taking on different cultural connotations and qualities in the process. In particular, as genies, they have become closely associated with the ability to grant or corrupt human wishes.

Lexicographers debate whether the word "djinn" itself comes from the Arabic word *id-j-tinan*, "to be hidden, concealed," or from the Latin *genius* meaning "spirit" (MacDonald). Strong and cunning djinn may be called *ifrit*/*afreet* or *marid*. The latter word is absent from the Koran and the word *ifrit* is used only as a qualifier, as in "an ifrit of the djinn," to imply a strong and willful djinn. In later literature, *ifrit* and *marid* came to be used interchangeably as nouns, implying a class of wicked and cunning djinns. In many Near Eastern and North African contexts, the word "djinn" is used interchangeably with *pari*/*peri* (**fairy**). Violent djinns who haunt deserted places and feast on human flesh, on the other hand, may be called *ghul* (**ghoul**), although the connection of these folkloric beings to Islamic theology is tenuous. The term *genie* was first used in 1704 by the French translator and populizer of *One Thousand and One Nights*, Antoine Galland (see **Arabian Nights, Monsters In The**); it soon migrated to other European languages.

Pre-Islamic Arab sources depict djinns as divine agents in a polytheistic world. According to the Koran, however, djinns were created to worship God just like humans and will be held accountable for their beliefs and actions like them (51:61). The phrase *ins wa djinn* (humans and djinn) occurs frequently in Islamic literature, pointing to the parallels between two creatures. Like humans, and unlike **angels**, djinns possess free will: they may belong to various religions, have their own laws and societies, and may be benign as well as evil. "Surat Al-Jinn," the 72nd chapter of the Koran, for example, depicts a band of djinns who become Muslim upon hearing the revelations of the Prophet Muhammad. In the Koran, djinns are also closely associated with the Prophet Solomon, for whom they performed miraculous deeds of heavy labor, constructing palaces, places of worship, and everyday objects, partially as a punishment for their vanity (34:2–23). Many Muslim scholars argue that Iblis or Sheytan, the **Devil** himself, was a powerful and rebellious djinn. According to the Koran, on the day of reckoning, God will gather all beings together and chastise djinn for having led many humans astray (6:128). The Koran also includes verses intended to protect humans from the ploys of evil djinn.

Djinns cross genres in classical Middle Eastern sources, appearing in folktales, theological and juridical documents, miniature paintings, and works of fiction, as well as non-fiction. The tenth-century political fable by the esoteric fraternity Ikhwan al-Safa, "The Case of the Animals versus Man Before the King of the Jinn," is a noteworthy example of an allegorical treatise featuring djinn (Goodman). Tales found in *One Thousand and One Nights* (*Kitab 'alf layla wa-layla*), known variously as *Arabian Nights* or *The Arabian Nights' Entertainment* in English sources, constitute some of the earliest and most famous fiction on djinns. In the framing story of the murderous Persian king and the young story-telling queen Scheherazade, the discovery of the king's adulterous wife is reinforced by his discovery of a powerful and malicious djinn who keeps his human wife locked up in a case with seven padlocks, but still cannot prevent her sexual escapades.

Djinns also appear in many of Scheherazade's tales, the sources for which include Chinese, Indian, Persian, Arabic, Egyptian, Greek, and Mesopotamian folklore. "The Fisherman and the Jinni," for example, recounts the tale of a fisherman who frees a powerful djinn (*ifrit*) locked up in a copper jar with the seal of Solomon on it. After tricking the angry djinn back into the jar and releasing him again on the condition that the djinn help him, the fisherman achieves riches and recognition. The trope of the djinn as helper is also repeated in the well-known story of "Aladdin, or the Magic Lamp" (not found in the earliest compilations), in which a ring and a lamp produce powerful djinns. In *One Thousand and One Nights*, many ifrits are found locked up in flasks marked with the seal of Solomon or in ruins; one emerges from the lavatory in "The Tale of Nur al-Din Ali and his Son." In "Adventures of Bulukiya," it is asserted that all evil djinns are the offspring of the Devil. In many tales, djinns transform humans and themselves into various creatures. Other tales depict sexual relations between humans and djinns; for example, "The Second Kalandar's Tale" features an ifrit named Jirjis bin Rajmus who spirits away a bride on her wedding night.

Even before the initial translation and publication of *One Thousand and One Nights* in France in the early eighteenth century, select Middle Eastern and South Asian folktales were reproduced in Europe. Early European travel and marvel literature contains stories of djinn-like creatures; the thirteenth-century German romance *Reinfried von Braunschweig*, for example, depicts a "devil" that emerges out of a bottle (Tuczay). Djinns are well represented in the Aarne-Thompson folktale classification system, which helps folklorists trace common folktale patterns; these include tales catalogued as "The Spirit in the Bottle" (AT 331) and "The Spirit in the Blue Light" (AT 562). Faustian literature depicting warped bargains with devils, as found in the Grimm's *Deutsche Sagen* (1816), were likely influenced by stories of djinns. The trope of genies granting wishes verbatim with disastrous consequences made its way into European literature from folktales and is reflected in stories such as "The Bottle Imp" (1893) by Robert Louis Stevenson.

In the West, djinn/genie took different connotations through the lenses of Orientalism, a way of "seeing" the East as ontologically and epistemologically different and inferior (see Said). In England, for example, the first English language edition, titled *Arabian Nights' Entertainment*, was published in 1706, not as a collection of ancient fairytales but as the truth about the contemporary Orient, with the claim on the cover that it provided "a better account of the customs, Manners and religion of the Eastern Nations ... than is to be met with in any author hitherto published." Rudyard Kipling's children's tale "How the Camel Got His Hump," published in *Just So Stories for Little Children* (1902), for example, builds upon Orientalist stereotypes of Middle Easterners as indolent and decadent beings living under authoritarian regimes, when a turbaned "Djinn in charge of All Deserts" punishes a lazy camel by giving him a hump that will allow him to work longer and eat less frequently.

In the United States, the publication of multiple versions of *Arabian Nights' Entertainment* in the 1790s and the young nation's conflicts with Algeria and the Barbary States led to a thirst for Orientalist tales featuring harems, sultans, and genies, which filled American periodicals of the eighteenth century (Isani). Edgar Allan Poe mocked this American vogue for Oriental **chimeras** and romances with the short story "The Thousand-and-Second Tale of Scheherazade" (1850), which imagines the sultan dismissing Scheherazade's tales of marvels and evil genii as "nonsense" and executing her. Similarly, in *The Adventures of Huckleberry Finn* (1884) by Mark Twain, Tom Sawyer, who has been influenced by Orientalist literature, tells Huck Finn that a Sunday school picnic they are observing is actually a caravan of "Spaniards and A-rabs" with camels and elephants. They test his theory by rubbing some old lamps and rings, but fail to produce any genies. Huck decides Tom's stories consist of lies, much like the Sunday school itself. Djinns have also been used as symbols in American literature. In his 1879 poem "The Khan's Devil," for example, Quaker poet John Greenleaf Whittier depicted alcoholism as a form of possession by an evil genie.

In the twentieth century, djinns/genies were also featured in films and on television, particularly in comedies, horror films, and cartoons. Orientalism is reflected in many European and North American films featuring djinns, including the highly influential 1940 technicolor fantasy adventure *The Thief of Baghdad* (Michael Powell, Ludwig Berger, and Tim Whelan), a remake of a 1924 silent film of the same name, directed by Raoul Walsh. In many movies and TV shows, the plot depicts wishes twisted by the genie, leading to unintended consequences, both comic and horrific. Silent films based on F. Anstey's 1900 comic novel called *The Brass Bottle* were released in 1914 (Sidney Morgan) and 1923 (Sidney Morgan) respectively. In the 1963 remake directed by Harry Keller, Burl Ives plays a genie that causes all sorts of humorous mischief for his modern owner. The film was influential in leading to the well-known TV situation comedy, *I Dream of Jeannie* (1965–70), featuring Barbara Eden as a 2,000-year-old blonde genie infatuated with her modern American "master," an astronaut named Tony Parker (Larry Hagman) whom she eventually marries. As in *The Brass Bottle*, Jeannie's powers often lead to complications because of her unfamiliarity with modern life.

The comedic modes of *The Brass Bottle* and *I Dream of Jeannie* heralded a softening of the role of the genie in Western popular culture, particularly in children's media. In the 1996 comedy *Kazaam* (Paul Michael Glaser), for example, basketball star Shaquille O'Neal plays a genie who helps a bullied boy by emerging out of a boom box. The children's TV show *Pee-wee's Playhouse* featured a friendly blue-faced genie named Jambi (John Paragon). Most famously, the successful 1992 Disney cartoon *Aladdin* (Ron Clements and John Musker) depicted a funny humanized blue genie, voiced by the famous comedian Robin Williams. The rags-to-riches story of "Aladdin and the Magic Lamp" particularly resonated with many American thinkers as a metaphor for redemptive capitalism, freedom to choose one's (heterosexual) marriage partner, and happy endings (Nance).

Djinns/genies, however, have also been represented in horror genres. The first *Twilight Zone* episode featuring a genie, "The Man in the Bottle" (1960), used the theme of wishes that lead to progressively worse results. In a later *Twilight Zone* episode titled "I Dream of Genie" (1963), on the other hand, a meek and careful protagonist avoids this fate by making a single, ironic wish: to become the stereotypical Oriental genie granting wishes to strangers who find him. In the 1987 cult film *The Outing*, a murderous djinn is released from an old lamp by intruders who break into the house of a woman of Arabic heritage. In *Wishmaster* (Robert Kurtzman, 1997) and its three sequels, a djinn released from an ancient jewel haunts his female rescuer. In *Long Time Dead* (Marcus Adams, 2002), a group of hard-partying college students inadvertently summon a djinn using a Ouija board. In Turkey, *Musallat* (The Haunting; 2007) claimed to be the first accurate depiction of djinns in a horror movie. The 2009 Hollywood movie *Red Sands* depicts a terrifying djinn haunting and murdering US soldiers stationed in a remote part of Afghanistan—in an apparent critique of US foreign policy. Many computer games and role-playing games also depict hostile as well as friendly djinns (Reichmuth and Werning).

Recent examples of djinns in world literature include fiction written by Western as well as non-Western and diasporic authors. Apart from fantasy fiction, such as "The Children of the Lamp" series (2004–) by P.B. Kerr, and horror novels such as *Jinn: A Novel* (2004) by Matthew B.J. Delaney, djinns are also featured in postmodern and magical realist texts. In his controversial *Satanic Verses* (1988), Salman Rushdie makes several passing references to djinns. A.S. Byatt's *The Djinn in the Nightingale's Eye* (1997) features a narratologist who is gifted with a glass bottle harboring a djinn during a trip to Istanbul, Turkey. Aware of the consequences of twisted wishes from her research, she takes her time deciding on her wishes, leading to tales within tales. Turkish author Elif Shafak's best-selling novel, *The Bastard of Istanbul* (2008), depicts not one but two djinns, one Muslim and good, the other pagan and evil, as characters and storytellers. In the twenty-first century, as djinns/genies continue to haunt literature, films, computer games, and the internet, taking them seriously is as important as ever. Djinns' shifting names, roles, and meanings reflect not only their volatile essence of fire but also the uncertainty of human beings' wishes and fates.

Perin E. Gurel

References and Suggested Reading

Aarne, Antti, and Stith Thompson. *The Types of the Folktale: A Classification and Bibliography.* Helsinki: The Finnish Academy of Science and Letters, 1961.

Anstey, F. *The Brass Bottle.* Charleston, SC: Bibliolife, 2010.

Arabian Nights Entertainments: Consisting of One Thousand and One stories, told by the Sultaness of the Indies to divert the Sultan from the Execution of a Bloody Vow ... London: Thomas Longman, 1736.

Brueder Grimm. *Deutsche Sagen.* Vienna: Gerlach, 1912.

Goodman, Lenn Evan, trans. *The Case of the Animals Versus Man before the King of the Jinn: A Tenth-century Ecological Fable of the Pure*

Brethren of Basra. Library of Classical Arabic Literature, vol. 3. Boston: Twayne, 1978.

Gurel, Perin. "Sing, O Djinn!: Memory, History, and Folklore in The Bastard of Istanbul." *The Journal of Turkish Literature* 6 (2009): 59–80.

Kipling, Rudyard. *Just So Stories for Little Children*. London: Macmillan, 1926.

MacDonald, D.B., trans. "Djinn." *In Encyclopaedia of Islam*, edited by P.J. Bearman, Th. Bianquis, C.E. Bosworth, E. van Donzel, and W.P. Heinrichs. 2nd edition. Brill Online, 2011.

Mukhtar Ali Isani. "The Oriental Tale in America through 1865: A Study in American Fiction." PhD dissertation, Princeton University, 1962.

Nance, Susan. *How the Arabian Nights Inspired the American Dream, 1790–1935*. Durham, NC: University of North Carolina Press, 2009.

Poe, Edgar Allan. "The Thousand-and-Second Tale of Scheherazade." *In Collected Tales and Poems [1850]*. Reprint, Hertfordshire, UK: Wordsworth, 2004. 369–82.

Reichmuth, Philipp, and Stefan Werning. "Pixel Pashas, Digital Djinns." *ISIM Review* 16 (2006): 46–7.

Said, Edward W. *Orientalism*. New York: Pantheon, 1978.

Stevenson, Robert Louis. "The Bottle Imp." *In Island Nights' Entertainments*. London: Random House, 1988.

Tuczay, Christa A. "Motifs in 'The Arabian Nights' and in Ancient and Medieval European Literature: A Comparison." *Folklore* 116, no. 3 (2005): 272–91.

Twain, Mark. *The Adventures of Huckleberry Finn*. Hauppauge, NY: Barron, 1999.

Yamanaka, Yuriko, and Tetsuo Nishio. *The Arabian Nights and Orientalism: Perspectives from East and West*. New York: I.B. Tauris, 2006.

DOMOVOI—*see* Demon

DONESTRE

Of all the monstrous races (see **Races, Monstrous**) of the Middle Ages, the Donestre are, in many ways, the most mysterious and intriguing. Old English sources describe these dangerous, deceitful creatures thus:

Fig. 10 A Donestre deceives, devours, and then weeps over the remains of an unwary traveller. © The British Library Board (British Library MS Cotton Tiberius B.V, fol. 83v, L col. (detail), c. 1000.)

> *Then there is an island in the Red Sea where there is a race of people we call Donestre, who have grown like soothsayers from the head to the navel, and the other part is human. And they know all human speech. When they see someone from a foreign country, they name him and his kinsmen with the names of acquaintances, and with lying words they beguile him and capture him, and after that eat him all up except for the head, and then sit and weep over the head.* (Orchard 179, 196–7/§20)

Many questions are raised by the duplicitous Donestre, and are compounded by difficulties in translation and interpretation, but three in particular have exercised scholars. First, why are they called "Donestre"? What does this appellation denote? The word has no clear meaning in either Old English or Latin. One suggestion has been that the accompanying phrase in Latin accounts, "quasi divini," refers to this name, and that "Donestre" thus means "divine" in the creatures' own tongue.

Most commentators, however, have taken "quasi divini" to refer to the inhuman upper half of the Donestre's body, and this brings us to the second mystery. How, exactly, are the Donestre of "mixed nature"? What does it mean to record that, although human beneath, from head to navel they are "divine" or "prophetic," or, in the Old English version, that they have "grown like soothsayers" (*swa frihteras*)? Available illustrations provide only limited answers. In the oldest manuscript, the Donestre has a smooth, bestial head, with extended muzzle and bulging eye, reminiscent of some kind of dog. In the later manuscripts, however, the visage looks, more often than not, much more like a human face, with clearly defined nose and mouth, but now the monster has a long, flowing mane, like that of a lion.

Finally, and perhaps most perplexing of all, why do the Donestre weep? Are these false tears, evidence of further deception, as some writers have suggested? Are they insincere crocodile tears? Or are they real tears, which demonstrate genuine remorse at the monster's terrible act? As he cries over his victim's remains, the Donestre is portrayed with curved hand raised to the side of his cheek, a gesture depicted by Anglo-Saxon illustrators to indicate grief. It is possible, then, that the members of this fearful, monstrous race were taken to experience regret and sorrow at their dreadful deeds.

In all the many tracts and tomes of the period, the Donestre appear just twice, in two wonderfully peculiar compilations. The curious *Liber Monstrorum de Diversis Generibus* (Book of Monsters of Various Kinds) is a remarkable catalogue of nearly 120 creatures, gathered together, as the opening words tell us, from the deserts, islands, mountains and other "hidden parts of the world." The time and place of composition are unclear: scholars have suggested dates as wide-ranging as the sixth and tenth centuries CE, and a provenance that might be Irish but is more likely Anglo-Latin. Directly and indirectly, the *Liber Monstrorum* draws on a great number of earlier sources, both classical and Christian, including the work of Virgil (70–19 BCE) and Pliny (23–79 CE), Augustine of Hippo (354–430 CE) and Isidore of Seville (560–636 CE), and many others. It survives today in just five manuscripts, all dating from the ninth and tenth centuries.

The *Liber Monstrorum* is divided into three parts. The first recounts all manner of human monsters and half-human hybrids: **giants**, six-fingered men, wood-dwelling **fauns**, fish-tailed **sirens**, one-eyed **cyclops**, dog-headed Cynocephali, headless Epifugi, a race with turned-back feet, one-legged Sciapods, the three **Gorgons**, insatiable **harpies**, snake-haired Eumenides, and more. The second part lists wild beasts and terrifying cross-breeds, including lions, elephants, wild asses, tigers, lynxes, leopards, panthers, hippopotami, the **Chimera**, three-headed **Cerberus**, gold-guarding ants, **shapeshifters**, saw-horned antelope, and ferocious mice the size of foxes. The final part tells of serpents of all kinds, including the Lernaean **Hydra**, the Indian Stares with which Alexander waged war, the pepper-producing Corsiae, the fiery salamander, the horned Cerastes, the multi-colored Ophitae, and the deadly asp. The Donestre are described, but not named, in the first part of the *Liber Monstrorum*, immediately after the many-eyed giant Argus, and just before the innumerable monsters with human faces and animal bodies who live on the borders of the land of the sorceress-goddess **Circe**. The Donestre are here described simply as polyglots of mixed nature, living on their island in the Red Sea, who astonish and deceive those who come from afar before eating them raw.

No more is said of these devious hybrids until they appear in *The Wonders of the East*. Known also as *The Marvels of the East*, this much shorter compendium of extraordinary sights and beings was written in Latin and Old English. The longest of the three surviving manuscripts—which date from the turn of the millennium, from the eleventh, and from the twelfth centuries CE—contains fewer than 50 wonders. Where the *Liber Monstrorum* provides only textual accounts, however, the denizens of the *Wonders* manuscripts are accompanied in each instance by an illuminating illustration. And in among the horned donkeys, the headless men with eyes and mouths in their chests, the bird-legged Homodubii, the bearded huntresses, the gigantic **dragons**, the people with fan-like ears, the beautiful Catini, the jewel-producing trees, the tusked women, and the eagle-headed **griffin**, we encounter once more the Donestre. Still insular in habits and habitat, these mixed, multilingual monsters are now named for the first and last time. It is here that they are described as "quasi divini," or as having grown partially like soothsayers, and that we find illustrations depicting strange, bestial heads atop human bodies. And it is here we learn that it is not quite the whole traveler that is consumed, but that their severed head remains, over which the Donestre weeps, perhaps with remorse and perhaps not.

Tom Tyler

References and Suggested Reading

Friedman, John Block. *The Monstrous Races in Medieval Art and Thought*. Syracuse, NY: Syracuse University Press, 2000.

Kim, Susan M. "The Donestre and the Person of Both Sexes." *In Naked Before God: Uncovering the Body in Anglo Saxon England*, edited by Benjamin C. Withers and Jonathan Wilcox, 162–80. Morgantown: West Virginia University Press, 2003.

Mittman, Asa Simon, and Susan M. Kim. *Inconceivable Beasts: The "Wonders of the East" in the Beowulf Manuscript*. Tempe, AZ: ACMRS, 2011.

Orchard, Andy. *Pride and Prodigies: Studies in the Monsters of the Beowulf-Manuscript*. Cambridge: D.S. Brewer, 1995.

Tyler, Tom. "Deviants, Donestre and Debauchees: Here Be Monsters." *Culture, Theory and Critique* 49, no. 2 (Autumn 2008): 113–31.

DONKEY KONG—*see* Video games, Monsters In

DOPPELGANGER

The figure of the doppelganger (from German *Doppelgänger* or "double") may, of course, be more correctly identified as two figures in one. Raising questions as to the wholeness of the human subject, doppelgangers emerged as shadowy, disturbing alter egos in an age in which the Cartesian *cogito ergo sum* of the Enlightenment firmly established the individual and its intellectual powers of reason as the defining characteristic of mankind. Transcending the narrow borders of literature, the doppelganger has pervaded philosophical, visual, and literary discourses since the late 1700s when it became a key figure in portrayals of the complex psychological economy of the modern subject. More than most other fantastic figures and monsters, with the exception, perhaps, of the **werewolf**, the doppelganger has thus occupied a privileged position in psychoanalytical theory (as Otto Rank's groundbreaking 1914 study, *The Double* [not published until 1925], underlines).

Although it is by no means an invention of modern culture (there are numerous examples in ancient mythology and religion), its name points toward Germany as a privileged site of formation around 1800. The term was first employed by the German writer Jean Paul in his novel *Siebenkäs* (1796–97), in which he defined the "*Doppeltgänger*" as "*Leute, die sich selber sehen*" (people who see themselves) (66). From this modest beginning, the doppelganger found its way into various national literatures over the course of the eighteenth century and then experienced a new lease of life in the early cinematic era. Jean Paul's definition points towards a physical similarity of the doppelganger to the person who experiences it; there are, however, various other forms in which the double appears, such as automatons, puppets, living statues (see **Objects, Animate**), pictures and shadows, **golems**, **robots**, clones, **demons** and the **Devil** himself.

The Doppelganger in Literature

The doubles of mythology were figures of confusion, drawing on Platonic concepts of man's original multiplicity/dualism, as visible in theories of gender formation and in mythical twins or in figures such as Janus. While such doubles were considered confusing, they were not necessarily felt to be shocking, often connoting instead a helpful extension of the individual body. As Christof Forderer suggests, they were mythical figures used to depict "the manifoldness and complexity of mankind" (12). In late-Enlightenment and early-Romantic Germany, however, the doppelganger emerges as an unsettling figure because it renders problematic any fixed sense of individuality or subjectivity—it is a figure of identity as/in crisis.

In philosophy (for example, Johann Gottlieb Fichte's theories of the ego in *Foundations of Natural Right* [1796] and elsewhere) and politics (most notably in the principles of the French Revolution) around 1800, man was posited as a free-thinking subject and as a being capable of self-reflection. It is precisely this self-assuredness that German authors such as Jean Paul and E.T.A. Hoffmann (1776–1822) sought to unsettle with their doubles. Most notably in Hoffmann's Gothic novel *Die Elixiere des Teufels* (*The Devil's Elixir*) (1815–16) and his short tale "Doppeltgänger" (1821), a radical skepticism pertaining to the sovereignty and singularity of the human subject pervades. In the earliest German doubles, identity becomes malleable as hidden connections between seemingly different people exist through which they share thoughts, wishes, and identities unconsciously. In Romantic scientific discourse, by contrast, the doppelganger becomes encoded as a potentially positive figure that is initially shocking but that is actually an instance of the Romantic unconscious or of Schelling's "Weltseele" concept (world-soul) pervading every being. The disruption to the rational subject of the *homme machine* (Julien Offray de La Mettrie's famous phrase) through the doppelganger expresses doubt as to whether man may even be seen as a rationally functioning being whose powers of reasoning control and limit his body (Forderer 31–8). Viewed thus, the doppelganger goes beyond the initial shock to ultimately produce a euphoric moment: the destruction of the *homme machine*.

Hoffmann's later doppelganger fantasies draw widely on this thinking, although his figures are more obviously conceived in the shocking Gothic tradition than from his scientific sources. The shared identity of

Medardus and Viktorin in the *Elixir* shows people who are not "separated" from each other, but rather defenseless in the face of external factors and challenges. Psychical energies and thoughts can be transferred between different people who thereby disquietingly emerge as different versions of the same subject. Medardus, for example, feels how the voice of his doppelganger speaks through him on occasions, and a girl takes on a new personality through mesmerist hypnosis. The weakness of the subject, rather than its enlightened sovereignty and security, forms the basis of the doppelganger as a specifically modern monster.

These are issues that transferred easily to different national contexts. A late-Romantic story such as James Hogg's *The Private Memoirs and Confessions of a Justified Sinner* (1824) is obviously indebted to Gothic pre-texts such as Hoffmann's *Elixir* and Matthew Lewis's *The Monk* (1796). Hogg also focuses prominently, and famously, on a religious theme in order to render a subject that is fundamentally unstable and transformed by the experiences of strangers. The ultra-rationalist, protestant Wringham experiences himself as a possessed, doubled being because he feels emotions and urges which he—as Calvinist elect—should not be suffering. Hogg develops a conflict between a socially sanctioned *ideal* of the subject and the often base reality in which this subject actually experiences life: "I had heart-burnings, longings and yearnings, that would not be satisfied ... I was a being incomprehensible to myself. Either I had a second self, who transacted business in my likeness, or else my body was at times possessed by a spirit over which it had no countroul [sic], and of whose actions my own soul was wholly unconscious" (125). Wringham then experiences this "second self" as a devil-like figure who appears to him in the perverted guise of a religious zealot.

Hogg's text is closely related to a series of thematically and intertextually linked German, French, and English novels of the late 1790s and early 1800s in which the doppelganger is articulated in terms of a pact with the Devil. Most famously developed in Johann Wolfgang von Goethe's two *Faust* plays (1808; 1832)—the various versions of which between 1770 and 1832 roughly mark the start and end of the era of Romantic doppelganger—the Devil as doppelganger is also central to less canonized texts such as Lewis's *The Monk* and Charles Robert Maturin's ***Melmoth the Wanderer*** (1820), both of which are heavily indebted to Goethe. In Goethe's plays, the striving academic Faust signs a pact with Mephisto (see **Mephistopheles**) in the hope of gaining infinite knowledge. Mephisto employs his magical powers and scrupulous intelligence in order to fulfill all of Faust's intellectual and corporeal desires, while Faust is chained to Mephisto by virtue of the pact. In the course of the first and particularly the second part of Goethe's play, both figures seem on occasions to swop roles and become increasingly indistinguishable, emerging as devilish doubles of the other.

One of the most disturbing doppelganger texts of the mid-nineteenth century was written by an American who famously felt the necessity to distance himself from German literature, namely Edgar Allan Poe. "William Wilson" (1839) draws openly on the Gothic violence of his German predecessors, but Poe is certainly more radical in the consequences of this violence than even Hoffmann, with a key moment of the text lying in the narrator William's efforts brutally to end his relationship with his double Wilson. This act of violence turns out to be equally destructive for William as the dying Wilson seemingly merges with him in what ultimately seems to be an act of suicide: "In me didst thou exist—and, in my death, see by this image, which is thine own, how utterly thou hast murdered thyself" (641). For Poe, the doppelganger is most obviously the embodiment of suppressed elements of the subject itself—perhaps even of the "conscience grim" of which the story's epitaph speaks.

In Fyodor Dostoevsky's "The Double" ("Dvoinik"; 1846), the doppelganger seems to be inseparable from the rhythms and demands of modern commercial and urban life. For Goliadkin, successful bureaucrat, his doppelganger is not simply the uncanny, romantic specter of earlier tales; he is rather an actual person who takes over Goliadkin's responsibilities and fundamentally undermines his authority, both at work and in society. At the heart of Goliadkin's horrific experiences is the sense he gains of modern individuality in the city as that of unimportant anonymity in the masses. While society emphasizes individuality, Goliadkin sees how the hierarchical and commercial nature of modern society actually undermines this ideal through increasing processes of homogenization (see **Dvoinik**).

The confrontation between the ideal orderly, bourgeois identity and its horrifying alter ego dominated by base drives lies at the heart of the most famous doppelganger story of all, Robert Louis Stevenson's *The Strange Case of Dr Jekyll and Mr Hyde* (1886). In this hybrid mix of Victorian science fiction and Gothic novel, the gentleman scientist Dr Jekyll develops a drug that transforms him into the decrepit and stunted body of **Mr Hyde**. In his account of his earlier life, Jekyll points towards the duplicity of his identity which leads to his scientific fantasies: "it came about that I concealed my pleasures; and that when I reached years of reflection, and began to look round me and take stock of my progress and position in the world, I stood already committed to a profound duplicity of life" (55). Hyde is the monstrous embodiment of those elements of Jekyll's personality that were not sanctioned by society—violence, sexual wantonness, egotism. Although this thematic focus merely repeats the earlier concerns of Hoffmann or Hogg, the psychological intensity of the story alongside its dual criminological and scientific imaginary make it the epitome of fears of degeneration of the modern subject common during the *fin de siècle*. Stevenson's novel is also profoundly visual, drawing heavily on the phantasmagoric imagery and effects of photography and proto-forms of cinema.

The Doppelganger in Film

Dr Jekyll and Mr Hyde subsequently became one of the most filmed literary texts in early cinema history. The double once again grew in importance around 1900, not least because photography and film had made it possible to create real and later moving images of people remarkably similar to Jean Paul's idea of "people seeing themselves." The spectacular nature of early cinema lent itself to such fantastic, Gothic stories of man's duplicity, as shown by the countless doppelgangers of the period, such as Wiene's *The Cabinet of Dr Caligari* (1920) and Lang's *Dr Mabuse* (1922). In Expressionism, film became an important medium for articulating modernism's discontent with modernity itself, focusing on fragile identities in the form of doppelganger fantasies and hypnotic mind-control (see Andriopoulos). In this respect, many films of the period returned to figures such as **Hyde**, **Frankenstein**, and **Dracula** and to stories about animated statues, **golems**, **robots**, and pacts with the Devil from the literary archive of the doppelganger. In Max Mack's *Der Andere* (*The Other*, 1913), for example, starring Albert Bassermann in the leading role of Dr Hallers, Hallers experiences a schizophrenic "splitting" of his identity into what his acquaintance Justice Arnoldy (Emmerich Hanus) terms a "double being," following a fall from a horse.

If Poe's aforementioned story "William Wilson" highlighted a violent and ultimately suicidal obsession with the self as Other/the Other as self, another of his stories, "The Man of the Crowd," can be seen as the prototype for a long line of detective figures in literature and film in which detective and suspect take on the character of uncanny doubles. Poe's nameless narrator initially seems to be a thoroughly unassuming, rational observer who takes up the trail of a suspicious looking man on the busy city streets; however, the very measure of pursuing his "suspect" turns the narrator into an obsessive stalker figure whose actions in turn appear criminal. Such an obsessive hunting down of one's arch-nemesis, only to find oneself tainted by the Other's criminality, is inherent to the father of all film detectives, Sherlock Holmes. Whether in the initial classical series of 12 films (1939–46) starring Basil Rathborne as Holmes, or in the countless remakes up to Guy Ritchie's *Sherlock Holmes* (2009) with Robert Downey, Jr in the lead-role, Holmes's pursuit of the dastardly Moriarty reveals two main doppelganger constellations that remain central in later Hollywood detective thrillers. Initially the relationship between Holmes and Moriarty appears to repeat the basic mirror-image dichotomy of good/evil, reason/desire familiar from Stevenson's *Jekyll and Hyde*. On closer inspection, however, an uncanny merging of identities takes place with Holmes always walking the line between legal and illegal action and frequently getting on the wrong side of the law himself; indeed the need to adopt a criminal mind in order to uncover his nemesis' plans shows a disturbing similarity between, or even the fusion of, both figures. This is a form of alter ego identities that continues to inform Hollywood cinema to the present day.

The doppelganger continues to exert a fascination in contemporary cultural production. Hollywood cinema in particular has continuously revisited and plundered early cinema history in a series of remakes and adaptations of stories of doubles in the widest sense. Films such as Don Siegel's *Invasion of the Body Snatchers* (1958), Alfred Hitchcock's *Psycho* (1960), Ridley Scott's *Blade Runner* (1982), Avi Nesher's *Doppelganger—The Evil Within* (1993), and even Spike Jonze's self-reflexive meta-film *Being John Malkovitch* (1999) all show a continuing fixation with the doppelganger as a cultural trope. In suspense and horror films in the 1980s and 1990s, such as *Fatal Attraction* (1987) in particular, a fixation with the ability of one person first to mimic and then adopt another person's identity wholesale is notable. In the wake of the poststructuralist deconstruction of essential identity and the prospering of theories of social performativity that view identity as a mere bricolage-style performance of multiple stereotypes, intertexts, and ciphers, these films encapsulate the disturbance caused by the lost prospect of any authenticity of selfhood.

Perhaps the most successful doppelganger film of recent years is David Fincher's *Fight Club* (1999), which draws on this form of doubling while also reactivating both the self-reflexive doubles of early twentieth-century film and the fantasy of desire and corporeality inherent to Hofmann and Stevenson. While the appearance of Tyler Durden (Brad Pitt) as a rogue of almost Dionysian proportions confronts the *fin de siècle* ennui of Ed Norton's nameless narrator figure with the desired authenticity of bodily pain, sexual pleasure, and criminal thrills, Norton's "Everyman" suspects and accuses Tyler of stealing his identity. His suspicions are well founded, the close of the film reveals, quite simply because he and Durden *are* indeed alter egos, a fact that becomes clear through the gunshot that wounds Norton's character himself, recalling the end of Poe's "William Wilson." When the film then cuts to show a different version of earlier key scenes, this time without Pitt in shot however, Fincher returns to the self-reflexive fixation with film itself as the means of generating experiences of doubling familiar from early Weimar cinema.

As a figure of doubling that is itself seemingly endlessly reproducible, the doppelganger lends itself to re-actualization in various historical periods as a core figure for the expression of general social fears and issues of identity politics, psychological disturbance, and unsanctioned or unconscious human desires.

Barry Murnane

References and Suggested Reading

Andriopoulos, Stefan. *Possessed: Hypnotic Crimes, Corporate Fiction, and the Invention of Cinema*. Chicago and London: University of Chicago Press, 2008.

Dryden, Linda. *The Modern Gothic and Literary Doubles: Stevenson, Wilde and Wells*. Basingstoke: Palgrave Macmillan, 2003.

Forderer, Christof. *Ich-Eklipsen. Doppelgänger in der Literatur seit 1800*. Stuttgart: Metzler, 1999.

Hoffmann, E.T.A. *The Devil's Elixir*. Guildford: Grosvenor House Publishing, 2007.

Hogg, James. *The Private Memoirs and Confessions of a Justified Sinner hrsg. v. P.D. Garside*. Edinburgh: Edinburgh University Press, 2001.

Miller, Karl. *Doubles: Studies in Literary History*. Oxford: Oxford University Press, 1985.

Paul, Jean. *Siebenkäs. Flegeljahre*, edited by Gustav Lohmann. Munich: Hanser, 1959.

Poe, Edgar Allan. "William Wilson." In *The Collected Tales and Poems of Edgar Allan Poe*, 626–42. New York: Modern Library, 1992.

Rank, Otto. *The Double* [1925]. Reprint, London: Karnac Books, 1989.

Stevenson, Robert Louis. *The Strange Case of Dr Jekyll and Mr Hyde and Other Tales of Terror*. London: Penguin, 2003.

Webber, Andrew. *The Doppelgänger: Double Visions in German Literature*. Oxford: Clarendon Press, 1996.

DRACULA

Dracula refers to the nickname of a fifteenth-century Romanian warlord, to the eponymous **vampire** in Bram Stoker's 1897 novel, and to any number of adaptations of Stoker's character in literature, film, video games, and other popular culture. It is no exaggeration to assert that Stoker's character is one of the first significant transformations of a primitive belief into a complex social metaphor. Thus, the belief that reanimated dead bodies return to suck the blood of the living changes in Dracula into a metaphor that addresses the apprehensions of people living in a scientific and secular world. Dracula in this respect is an example of a modern myth, the evolution of which parallels other significant cultural transformations.

Vlad Dracula

While Stoker's vampire count is fictional, the name Dracula is one of the nicknames of a historical person, Vlad III, a warrior and statesman, who lived from 1431 to 1476 and ruled Wallachia in 1448, 1456–62, and 1475. Vlad remains to this day a Romanian national hero, though he is also known in his homeland as Vlad Tepes, the Impaler, because of his preferred method for punishing enemies—impaling them on wooden stakes, a punishment that caused offenders to die in agony. A three-time voivode (or "warlord") of Wallachia, Vlad was known beyond Wallachia's borders as a fierce fighter against the Turks and as a ruthless ruler.

While the nickname Tepes comes from Vlad's treatment of his enemies, the nickname Dracula comes from the fact that his father, Vlad II (c. 1390 to 1447) called himself Vlad Dracul (Vlad the **Dragon**) after his initiation in 1431 into the Order of the Dragon, a chivalrous society dedicated to defending Christianity from non-Christians. His son consequently became known as Dracula, meaning son of Dracul or son of the dragon. While the term would have had positive connotations for both father and son, the fact that "dracul" also means "**devil**" in Romanian adds an additional intimidating connotation to the name.

Linking the name Dracula to the vampire legend was apparently Stoker's idea, as there is no indication that Vlad was connected to vampirism during his life. Indeed, there is some doubt whether Stoker knew anything about Vlad's connection to impalement.

Stoker's Sources

Stoker's notes for *Dracula*, collected and annotated in 2008 by Robert Eighteen-Bisang and Elizabeth Miller, reveal that he did research for the novel that became *Dracula* for seven years preceding its publication and that he probably did not decide to use the name Dracula until 1890, when he discovered a reference to the historical Dracula in the Whitby Library in England. He had imagined his vampire as an aristocrat along the lines of earlier Gothic villains such as Prince Manfred in Horace Walpole's *The Castle of Otranto* (1764), **Lord Ruthven** in John Polidori's "The Vampyre" (1819), and the Marquis de Montalt in Ann Radcliffe's *The Romance of the Forest* (1791), and his earliest notes refer to the vampire as a "Count" and occasionally as "Count Wampyr," a designation in lieu of the actual name. Miller and Eighteen-Bisang observe that he "began to use the name 'Dracula' during or shortly after the summer of 1890" (26). Indeed, Stoker copies almost verbatim from William Wilkinson's *An Account of the Principalities of Wallachia and Moldavia* (1820), where he learned of Vlad's cruelty and also that "Dracula" means "devil" in Romanian. Until shortly before publication, Stoker called his novel *The Un-Dead*, and one wonders whether Stoker or an editor decided to use the one-word *Dracula* as its title.

Stoker's Dracula

When asked to describe Dracula, most people in the twenty-first century would likely describe someone who resembles Bela Lugosi (who appeared in Tod Browning's 1931 *Dracula*), Christopher Lee (who appeared as Dracula in a number of films produced in the 1950s and 1960s by Hammer Film Productions), or Frank Langella (John Badham's 1979 *Dracula*), whose debonair evening dress suggests he is not spending his days in a box filled with his native soil. The practice of dressing Dracula in formal attire definitely preceded the Browning film, however. According to David Skal, in "Dracula on the Stage" (2005), Hamilton Deane, who first adapted *Dracula* for the stage, "conceived the now-familiar appearance of Dracula as a kind of devilish vaudeville magician in evening dress and an opera cloak" (304) and Deane's conception of Dracula has become so much a part of the popular imagination that even Count von Count, who teaches children their numbers on *Sesame Street*, and Count Chocula, the mascot for a brand of cereal, wear evening dress.

Stoker's Dracula, however, resembles his peasant ancestors, and the cover for the first paperback edition (published in 1901) presents a less cosmopolitan Dracula. Shown crawling barefoot down the castle walls while a horrified Jonathan Harker looks on, this Dracula looks more ready to hang in a cave than grace a drawing room. Indeed, Stoker says nothing about Dracula's sartorial choices, though Harker's initial description reveals strong features:

> *The mouth ... was fixed and rather cruel-looking, with peculiarly sharp white teeth; these protruded over the lips, whose remarkable ruddiness showed astonishing vitality in a man of his years ... his ears were pale and at the tops extremely pointed ... The general effect was one of extraordinary pallor ... As the Count leaned over me ... I could not repress a shudder. It may have been that his breath was rank, but a horrible feeling of nausea came over me, which, do what I would, I could not conceal.* (52)

At this point, Harker observes characteristics that later gain in significance, notably the sharp teeth, animal-like ears, and halitosis. Only later does he come to realize that Dracula is not merely foreign but is of a completely different order of being, a being that it is appropriate to hate:

> *It seemed as if the whole awful creature were simply gorged with blood; he lay like a filthy leech, exhausted with his repletion ... This was the being I was helping to transfer to London, where, perhaps, for centuries to come he might, amongst its teeming millions, satiate his lust for blood and create a new and ever-widening circle of semi-demons to batten on the helpless.* (100)

The other English characters are similarly repulsed, mostly by his animal behavior. Upon first seeing him in London, Mina Harker notices his cruel sensuality: "His face was not a good face; it was hard, and cruel, and sensual, and his big white teeth, that looked all the whiter because his lips were so red, were pointed like an animal's" (258). Consciously aware of these negative characteristics, Mina will observe, after Dracula visits her, something appealing about him: "I was bewildered, and strangely enough, I did not want to hinder him. I suppose it is a part of the horrible curse that such is, when his touch is on his victim" (396).

Mina's ambivalence becomes more important in subsequent adaptations of Dracula, but Stoker and his characters generally emphasize traits that make him easy to fear and hate. In a world that is proud of its scientific and technological prowess, Dracula is primitive and foreign, unable to use modern methods of communication and transportation. As a result, besieged by his modern adversaries, he retreats to his Transylvanian lair, where he is either dispatched by Jonathan Harker's Kukri knife and Quincey Morris's bowie knife, or he dissolves into mist, from which he will eventually plot a later attack. The ambiguity of the conclusion is one of the reasons for the plethora of sequels. Whatever Dracula's fate, however, Stoker's *Dracula* focuses on traits that cause his human characters to fear him. In an increasingly democratic world where middle class professionals are in the ascendancy, Dracula is an aristocrat who lives in a remote castle, mulling over the old days when warlords had total control. Indeed, Stoker's contemporaries feared what Dracula embodied, a way of life that seemed moribund. Needing to perpetuate his undead existence by draining the blood of the living makes him even more threatening. Furthermore, because he is also presented as a sexual predator and as an example of the racial and cultural Other, Stoker's Dracula lends himself to a variety of critical readings. Although many of his descendants are presented as sexually attractive and occasionally troubled by their need for blood, Stoker's Dracula is feared because his opponents see him as more animal than human. He can transform himself into wolf, dog, bat, and mist, and consequently is little troubled by conscience or any kind of inner life.

Dracula in Drama and Film

It is somehow fitting that Stoker, who began his writing career as a drama critic and spent most of his professional life as the business manager for the Lyceum Theatre, would be the first to dramatize *Dracula*. On 18 May 1897, 15 members of the Lyceum company staged a dramatic reading, *Dracula: or The Un-Dead*, largely to protect the novel's dramatic copyright.

Stoker worked to protect *Dracula*'s dramatic copyright, and his widow became involved in a bitter court battle with German filmmaker F.W. Murnau over ***Nosferatu*** (1922). Even though Murnau set *Nosferatu* in Bremen, Germany, renamed his vampire Count Orlock, and made him even more animalistic in the process by linking him to plague-carrying rats, the German court ordered him to destroy all copies. Fortunately, because not all copies were destroyed, it was subsequently possible to reconstruct *Nosferatu*, which is now admired as a significant example of German Expressionism. While Murnau makes significant changes in the names of the primary characters and even in plot details, casting Max Schreck as what James Craig Holte describes in "Film Adaptations of Dracula" (2005) as "a personification of plague-like evil" (319) reinforces Stoker's depiction of the vampire as more animal than human and as an undead body.

The first major transformation in Dracula's character occurred in the early 1920s when Florence Stoker granted Hamilton Deane a license for a stage adaptation of her husband's novel, and Deane's *Dracula*, which premiered in 1924, regularly appeared as a touring production until after World War II. Deane's decision to dress Dracula in evening clothes and to have him interact more directly with the human members of the cast was largely the result of his decision to reduce the novel's panorama to a limited number of scenes, a decision that has been followed by other dramatic (though not cinematic) adaptations. David Skal, in "Dracula on the Stage" (2005), observes that Deane's *Dracula* introduces the "standard trappings we now associate with Dracula" and that one "familiar costume detail, the exaggerated stand-up collar on Dracula's cape," was essential on stage to "hide the back of the actor's head while he slipped through a trap door or panel" (305), leaving others holding the empty cloak. Although practical, the formal clothing also helps to transform Dracula from primitive threat to attractive seducer.

Film versions of the novel continued with the development of more human and more sympathetic representations of Dracula. Certainly Lugosi's interpretation of Dracula is the one that has become most iconic. Hungarian by birth, Lugosi initially appeared in the 1927 Broadway production of *Dracula*. Because of the play's popularity, Universal Studios bought the film rights and hired Tod Browning as director and Lugosi as the title character. Cast as a Gothic seducer, Lugosi humanizes Dracula and makes him a credible sexual predator rather than a merely bestial one. The British company Hammer Films, with Christopher Lee as Dracula, continued to humanize Dracula. Beginning in 1958 with Terence Fisher's *Dracula* (released in the US as *Horror of Dracula*), Hammer released a series of eight films that present Dracula as a Gothic seducer clad in evening clothes and cape. John Badham's film with Frank Langella (*Dracula*, 1979) makes Dracula even more sympathetic by presenting him as a viable alternative to Lucy's rather dense human lover, and by characterizing his human opponents as either prosaic or preoccupied with food. Instead of being a predatory monster, he is now a romantic lead to whom the audience is expected to relate. Frances Ford Coppola's *Bram Stoker's Dracula* (1992) presents Dracula as a medieval warlord who is never at home in the modern world, despite the scene in which he has Dracula accompany Mina to the movies—more an homage to Coppola's film predecessors than a characterization of Dracula. Like Langella, Gary Oldman plays Dracula as a lover as well as a fighter. In addition to the films that can be characterized as more or less serious adaptations of Stoker's original demonic count, there are a number of humorous adaptations, including *Love at First Bite* (1979) with George Hamilton as Dracula, and Mel Brooks's *Dracula: Dead and Loving It* (1995). This list barely scratches the surface of the countless dramatic interpretations available in a variety of cultures and through a variety of different dramatic media that include film, television, and video games, as well as on-stage productions.

Literary Adaptations

Literary adaptations are even more numerous. In *The New Annotated Dracula* (2008), Leslie S. Klinger includes an Appendix, "Dracula After Stoker: Fictional Accounts of the Count," which includes "vampire tales with no direct reference to *Dracula*," as well as "serious works considering the events described in *Dracula* and later events" (527). While one of the earliest adaptations, Raymond Rudorff's *The Dracula Archives* (1971), depicts Dracula as something to fear, most subsequent interpretations are more sympathetic. Fred Saberhagen follows the events in *Dracula* very closely in *The Dracula Tape* (1975). By relating the events through Dracula's first-person point of view, he presents a character more sinned against than sinning and continues this approach in *The Holmes-Dracula File* (1978). Kim Newman has also created a series of novels featuring Dracula, including *The Bloody Red Baron* (1995) and *Dracula Cha Cha Cha* (2001). While the titles of some recent adaptations suggest a more sympathetic view (Karen Essex, *Dracula in Love*, 2010; R.H. Greene, *Incarnadine: The True Memoirs of Count Dracula*: Volume One, 2009; and Syrie James, *Dracula, My Love: The Secret Journals of Mina Harker*, 2010) and reveal that the monstrous count has become kinder and gentler in the twenty-first century, Stoker's great-grandnephew Dacre Stoker (with the assistance of Ian Holt) returns to a darker version in *Dracula The Un-Dead* (2010).

Dracula and the Critics

Fascination with Dracula has produced a body of secondary literature that is as monstrous as the Count himself. Not only do writers, filmmakers, and video game designers continue to create adaptations of Dracula, but scholars and critics have explored both the historical Vlad and his offspring ever since Montague Summers wrote *The Vampire: His Kith and Kin* in 1928. There are numerous annotated editions of Stoker's novel (Leonard Wolf, Leslie Klinger, and Nina Auerbach), biographies of the historical Vlad (M.J. Trow, and Florescu and McNally), analyses of film and television adaptations (Holte, Bignell, and Skal), and books and articles that focus on various aspects of Dracula, including his sexuality and his relationship to female sexuality (Craft, Griffin, and Senf), anti-Semitism (Halberstam), politics (Arata and Brantlinger, as well as books that explore his relationship to either Ireland or Romania), religious interpretations, narration (Seed and Senf), science and technology (Greenway and Jann), use of folklore, psychological interpretations of the literary figure or of one of his adaptations. There are also several excellent collections of essays (Carter, Davison, and Miller). Feminist, Freudian, Jungian, and Marxist interpretations abound. William Hughes's 2009 book publication, *Bram Stoker—Dracula: A Reader's Guide to Essential Criticism*, offers a useful overview of the extensive criticism on the work. It seems that each new critical methodology will find in Dracula something monstrous to explore.

Carol Senf

References and Suggested Reading

Arata, Stephen D. "The Occidental Tourist: Dracula and the Anxiety of Reverse Colonization." *Victorian Studies* 33 (1990): 621–45.

Auerbach, Nina, and David J. Skal, eds. *Dracula.* New York: Norton, 1997.

Bignell, Jonathan. "A Taste of the Gothic: Film and Television Versions of Dracula." In *From Page to Screen: Adaptations of the Classic Novel*, edited by Robert Giddings and Erica Sheen. Manchester: Manchester University Press, 2000.

Brantlinger, Patrick. "Imperial Gothic: Atavism and the Occult in the British Adventure Novel, 1880–1914." *ELT* 28 (1985): 243–52.

Carter, Margaret L., ed. *Dracula: The Vampire and the Critics*. Ann Arbor: UMI Research Press, 1988.

Craft, Christopher. "'Kiss Me With Those Red Lips': Gender and Inversion in Bram Stoker's Dracula." *Representations* 8 (1984): 107–33.

Davison, Carol Margaret, ed. *Bram Stoker's Dracula: Sucking through the Century, 1897–1997*. Toronto: Dundrun, 1997.

Eighteen-Bisang, Robert, and Elizabeth Miller. *Bram Stoker's Notes for Dracula: A Facsimile Edition*. Jefferson, NC: McFarland, 2008.

Florescu, Radu, and Raymond T. McNally. *Dracula: Prince of Many Faces*. Boston: Little, Brown, and Company, 1989.

Greenway, John L. "Seward's Folly: Dracula as a Critique of 'Normal Science.'" *Stanford Literature Review* 3 (1986): 213–30.

Griffin, Gail B. "'Your Girls That You Love Are Mine': Dracula and the Victorian Male Sexual Imagination." *International Journal of Women's Studies* 3 (1980): 454–65.

Halberstam, Judith. *Gothic Horror and the Technology of Monsters*. Durham, NC: Duke University Press, 1995.

Holte, James Craig. *Dracula in the Dark: The Dracula Film Adaptations*. Westport, CT: Greenwood, 1997.

———. "Film Adaptations of Dracula." In *Bram Stoker's Dracula: A Documentary Volume*, edited by Elizabeth Miller. Detroit: Thomson Gale, 2005.

Hughes, William. *Bram Stoker—Dracula: A Reader's Guide to Essential Criticism*. New York: Palgrave Macmillan, 2009.

Jann, Rosemary. "Saved by Science? The Mixed Messages of Stoker's Dracula." *Texas Studies in Literature and Language* 31 (1989): 273–87.

Klinger, Leslie S. *The New Annotated Dracula.* New York: Norton, 2008.

Miller, Elizabeth, ed. *Dictionary of Literary Biography: Bram Stoker's Dracula: A Documentary Volume*. Detroit: Thomson Gale, 2004.

Riquelme, J.P., ed. *Dracula: Complete, Authoritative Text with Biographical, Historical, and Cultural Contexts, Critical History and Essays from Contemporary Critical Perspectives*. Boston: Bedford/St Martin's Press, 2002.

Seed, David. "The Narrative Method of Dracula." *Nineteenth Century Fiction* 40 (1985): 61–75.

Senf, Carol. "Dracula: Stoker's Response to the New Woman." *Victorian Studies* 26 (1982): 33–49.

———. "Dracula: The Unseen Face in the Mirror." *Journal of Narrative Technique* 9 (1979): 160–70.

Skal, David. "Dracula on the Stage." In *Bram Stoker's Dracula: A Documentary Volume*, edited by Elizabeth Miller. Detroit: Thomson Gale, 2005.

——. *Hollywood Gothic: The Tangled Web of Dracula from Novel to Stage to Screen*. New York: Faber and Faber, 2004.

Stoker, Bram. *Bram Stoker's Dracula Unearthed*, edited by Clive Leatherdale. Westcliff-on-Sea, Essex: Desert Island Books, 1998.

Summers, Montague. *The Vampire: His Kith and Kin* [1928]. Reprint, Berkeley, CA: Apocryphile Press, 2011.

Trow, M.J. *Vlad the Impaler: In Search of the Real Dracula*. Gloucestershire: Sutton Publishing, 2003.

DRAGHIGNAZZO—*see* Demon

DRAGON

The dragon is a magnificent form of hybrid monster that has dominated the Western imagination since ancient times. Properly speaking, dragons are an Indo-European creation and play a foundational role in Indo-European mythology. Taking an historical approach, we see that dragons begin not as the winged, four-footed fire-breathing creatures we think of today but rather as monstrously large serpents. In the ancient Indian Vedas, for instance, the god Indra slays a serpent Vritra who has been keeping water from the world. In the Old Norse *Eddas*, the god Thor fights an apocalyptic battle against the Midgardsomr or World-Serpent. In ancient Greek myth, the god Apollo slays Python, the monstrous serpent who had been guarding the oracle at Delphi. Later on, as myth gives way to legend, heroic figures like Beowulf and Sigurd will gain enduring fame by one act above all others: the slaying of dragons.

Westerners have used the term "dragon" to describe other, unrelated creatures that they thought resembled their own favorite creation. As Lin Wang points out below, the Chinese "dragon," or *long*, to use its proper name, was famously described as made up of parts from nine different animals, among them the scales of a carp and the paws of a tiger. It is scaly because it is part fish! But going all the way back to Marco Polo, Westerners took one look at this monster as depicted in carvings and said, "Aha! It is a dragon, just like we have." Accordingly, in this entry we have treated the Asian dragon (for it is also found in Japan, Korea, and other East Asian countries) as a separate but important category.

Classical Dragons

Dragons in classical art (for example, in vase paintings) are depicted as large serpents, and not as the winged, limbed, and fire-breathing creatures we usually associate with the term today. When Apollo slays the "she-dragon" Python with his bow, a Homeric hymn (sixth century BCE) offers this description of her snaky death: "rent with insufferable pains, she lay panting fiercely and writhing on the ground. The din was ineffably awesome, and throughout the forest she rapidly thrust her coils hither and thither; with a gasp she breathed out her gory soul" (Athanassakis, 3.358–62). Herakles slays a hundred-headed dragon to recover the golden apples of the Hesperides, throwing its body up into the sky where it becomes the constellation *Draco*. Herakles slays another dragon, the **Hydra**, whose nine heads grow back in duplicate as soon as they are cut off. Jason has to defeat a dragon at Colchis to obtain the golden fleece; in vase paintings, the serpent is big enough to devour him. Jason also has to confront Medea, whose chariot is drawn by dragons. A few writers, including the Roman poet Ovid (*Metamorphoses*, 7.350; first century CE), say her dragons are winged, but they are usually depicted as monstrously large serpents with crests and little beards. The dragon slain by Jason and another slain by Cadmus share the feature that their teeth, after they have been sown in the ground, emerge as fighting warriors.

Roman culture transmits these myths and adds a new element, the dragon standard or banner. After the Romans defeated the Dacians in 106 CE in what is now Romania, they confiscated their vanquished enemy's weapons and the standards they had carried into battle. From visual depictions and one surviving medieval example, we can tell that these standards had metal dragon heads (with a crest, scales, and teeth) and a trailing windsock behind them. Writers like the fourth-century military historian Vegetius tell us that they were adopted as the ensign for individual cohorts of soldiers, even as the eagle was the ensign for the entire legion.

Late antique Roman and Greek culture also saw the development of bestiaries such as the *Physiologus* (second century CE; Latin translation eighth century) that classified different kinds of dragons, among them the *amphisbaena* that had another dragon head at the end of its tail. In his encyclopedia called the *Etymologies* (Book 12, 4:4–5), Isidore of Seville (c. 560–636) writes that:

> *The dragon (draco) is the largest of all the snakes, or of all the animals on earth. The Greeks call it drakon, whence the term is borrowed into Latin so that we say draco. It is often drawn out of caves and soars aloft, and disturbs the air. It is crested, and has a small mouth and narrow pipes through which it draws breath and sticks out its tongue. It has its strength not in its teeth but in its tail, and it causes injury more by its lashing tail than with its jaws. Also, it does not harm with poison; poison is not needed for this animal to kill, because it kills whatever it wraps itself around. Even the elephant with his huge body is not safe from the dragon, for it lurks around the paths along which the elephants are accustomed to walk, and wraps around their legs in coils and kills them by suffocating them. (255)*

Isidore's dragon, then, is a giant constrictor. For other authors, dragons are venomous; Ovid says of the dragon slain by Cadmus: "Its crest shone gleaming gold; its eyes flashed fire; its whole body was big with venom, and between its triple rows of teeth its three-forked tongue flickered ... Coil by scaly coil the serpent wound its way, and, rearing up, curved in a great arching bow, erect for more than half its length, high in the air" (*Metamorphoses* 3.33–46). [**PA**]

Medieval Dragons

The serpent dragon continues into the early Middle Ages and is seen, for instance, in the Old English *Wonders of the East*, one copy of which is found in the *Beowulf* manuscript from about the year 1000. It claims that in a certain country, "Dragons are born there, who are one hundred and fifty feet long, and are as thick as great stone pillars" (Orchard 194). But writers and artists begin to add other features to the dragon. In the *Letter of Alexander to Aristotle*, also in the *Beowulf* manuscript, these same large serpents have "three-pronged tongues, and when they breathed their breath came from their mouths like a burning torch" (Orchard 237); that is, they *almost* breathe fire. It may be the poem *Beowulf* itself that adds to the dragon both significant fire-breathing qualities (it burns down houses, for instance) and also the ability to fly. And yet epithets like *hringboga*, "ring-coiled one" (line 2561), suggest that this dragon still moves like a serpent when on land; it has no legs.

The unnamed *Beowulf* dragon is often compared to Fáfnir, a dragon killed by Sigurd in the Old Norse *Edda* (written down c. 1275 but from a much older tradition). Sigurd kills Fáfnir by digging a pit and then stabbing upward when the beast slithers over it, by which we should understand that Fáfnir, called an *ormr* (*wyrm*, serpent) in the *Edda*, is in form a giant, venomous serpent. Unlike any of the other dragons thus far mentioned, Fáfnir had been human (a dwarf) and turned into a dragon as his greed for a treasure hoard intensified (the motif is picked up with the character Eustace in C.S. Lewis's 1952 fantasy *Voyage of the Dawn Treader*). Fáfnir retains the ability to speak and converses with his killer, Sigurd, in the Eddic poem *Fáfnismál* (much as Smaug speaks with Bilbo in Tolkien's 1939 fantasy *The Hobbit* [**see Tolkien, Monsters In**]).

Two serpent dragons (one red, one white) figure briefly in Nennius's *Historia Brittonum* (c. 830, 2.42). They live under the foundation of a tower that King Vortigern has been trying to build. A boy named Ambrosius identifies the problem and also interprets the red serpent as the native Britons and the white one as the invading Anglo-Saxons. When this story is retold in Geoffrey of Monmouth's *Historia Regum Britannia* (c. 1136; Bk. 7, ch. 3), the serpents have now become fire-breathing dragons and Ambrosius has become Merlin (see **Witch/Wizard**). When Robert Mannyng (c. 1275–c. 1338) retells the story in Middle English, the dragons now have the power of flight (*The Story of England*, c. 1338, line 8190). In addition, Mannyng writes that King Arthur carries a dragon standard (line 13345). In the anonymous Middle English prose *Merlin* (c. 1450), Merlin also sets a dragon banner on a spear for King Arthur; it has a long tail and appears to breathe fire (*Merlin* 116). These traditions underlie the red dragon that appears on the national flag of Wales today.

Dragons in medieval art from about 900–1450 are usually depicted as serpents with wolf-like heads, feathery wings, and two front legs, and these legs are mentioned or can be inferred in some Middle English, Old French, and Old Norse romances. Of a dragon in the Norse *Thidreks Saga* (c. 1250), for instance, it is stated: "He was both long and stout, with thick legs and claws that were sharp and long, and his head was large and terrible. He flew along close to the ground and everywhere his claws touched the earth it was as if the sharpest iron had struck it" (ch. 105). It is not until later fifteenth-century art that familiar four-legged dragons, often with leathery, bat wings rather than feathered, avian wings, begin to appear.

The later Middle Ages also add another dragon-slayer to the pantheon. In the earliest Latin versions of his life, St George had nothing to do with dragons, but after the thirteenth century he becomes a holy dragon-slayer, his story turning up in Middle English poetic narratives like the *South English Legendary* in about 1400. An early modern work that looks back on this medieval tradition of St George is Edmund Spenser's *The Faerie Queene* (1590), in which the dragon allegorically represents sin and the error (from an English point of view) of Catholicism; the Redcross Knight (a version of St George and of England), by slaying this dragon, restores the one true faith. Spenser uses epic similes to suggest the dragon's vast size, as it belches flame like a volcano and crashes to its death, causing the very Earth to groan beneath its weight (Bk. I, Canto XI). [**PA**]

Early Modern and Victorian Dragons

Dragon lore continued to be transmitted from classical and medieval sources in the early modern and Victorian eras; Milton in *Paradise Lost* (1674; Bk. 10, line 530), for instance, compares Satan to Python. An encyclopedist like Edward Topsell in his *The Historie of Serpents* (1608) has to admit that: "There be some Dragons which haue winges and no feete, some againe haue both feete and wings, and some neither feete nor wings" (158). As a form of retronym, writers of heraldry like John Gibbon (*Introductio ad Latinum Blasoniam*, 1682) began to employ the term *wyvern* to distinguish the older two-legged dragon from the modern four-legged one. Legends of St George and of King Arthur (mainly derived from Caxton's 1485 printing of Malory's *Morte d'Arthur*) continued in popularity, with a resurgence in the Gothic revival of the Victorian era. In the 1860s, Pre-Raphaelite artists like Dante Gabriel Rossetti (1828–82), William Morris (1834–96), and Edward Burne-Jones (1833–98) tell stories of St George and the dragon in successive paintings or stained glass panels, a bit like modern graphic novels. The nineteenth century also sees the first translations of *Beowulf* and of the Old Norse legends of Sigurd the Dragon-Slayer, paving the way for the popularity of dragons among twentieth-century writers of fantasy (most notably the dragon Smaug in Tolkien's *The Hobbit*). [**PA**]

Dragons in Contemporary Fantasy Novels

Dragons have continued to preoccupy the human imagination and they have found congenial homes in modern fantasy literature and film. Among the most important representations in modern fantasy is that of Smaug in Tolkien's *The Hobbit*. Tolkien had read medieval works like the Old English poem *Beowulf* and the Old Norse *Poetic Edda* and drew on both for ideas and motifs. Like the dragon Fáfnir in the *Edda* and the unnamed dragon in *Beowulf*, Smaug guards a treasure hoard. Bilbo sneaks into the hoard and steals a cup, as the thief does in *Beowulf*, and speaks in riddles with Smaug, as Sigurd does with Fáfnir. Smaug flies and destroys towns with his fiery breath, as does the *Beowulf* dragon. A bird tells Bard how to slay Smaug, as birds had told Sigurd how to gain the hoard. All three dragons are killed by a wound from below, although Smaug's vulnerable spot is specified in more detail.

Tolkien wrote about and also made paintings of other dragons. In the mythologies developed in *The Silmarillion* (1977), Glaurung is said to be the first of a line of wingless dragons. Tolkien's verse retelling from Old Norse, *The Legend of Sigurd and Gudrún* (which includes a section on Sigurd and Fáfnir), was published in 2009, long after Tolkien's death. [**PA**]

An especially well-developed representation of dragons is contained within "The Dragonriders of Pern" series, which began with the publication of *Dragonflight* in 1967, and consists of 22 novels and several shorter works by Anne McCaffrey and her son Todd. The dragons depicted in the series are actually aliens (see **Extraterrestrial**), genetically modified long ago by human settlers to combat the natural hazards of their world, the planet Pern. This modification created beasts specifically bred to serve as mounts, making this series one of the first to feature the now popular trope of dragon riders, seen in fantasies like Christopher Paolini's 2003 novel *Eragon* (see below) and the film *Avatar* (James Cameron, 2009, although its creatures are more like pterodactyls). The dragons are naturally color-coded based on sex and strength, much as in the *Dungeons & Dragons* role-playing games (1974; see **Dungeons & Dragons, Monsters In**), and their riders are socially regimented based on these colorations. In McCaffrey's mythos, a dragon bonds with a pubescent human as soon as it hatches, effectively choosing its rider. From that point on, the bonded pair shares thoughts, emotions, and even sexual urges. If one dies, the other is driven to insanity and often commits suicide. The dragons also have the ability to access the Between, a hyperspace-like dimension that allows them to teleport and, in later books, time travel. [**RB**]

Drawing inspiration from McCaffrey, Christopher Paolini's best-selling *Eragon* (2003) tells the story of a boy, Eragon, who finds a dragon's egg and befriends the female blue dragon who hatches out of it, whom he names Saphira. Eragon (his name derives from the word "dragon" with only one letter changed) attempts to raise the dragon in secret, garnering advice from Brom the storyteller. Through their partnership with dragons, the dragon riders are given incredible powers. They operate as peacekeepers, together with their dragon allies. The symbiotic relationship between dragon and rider is indeed palpably similar to the dragon–rider relationship of Anne McCaffrey's "Dragonriders of Pern" series, while the mechanism of language-based magic takes its inspiration from Ursula K. Le Guin's depictions of wizards and their shaky relationships with dragons developed in her "Earthsea" novels (1968–2001). The relationship is no less troubled in Paolini's world, for it is one of the dragon riders, Galbatorix, driven mad by the death of his first dragon, who destroys the dragon rider order and becomes a fearful tyrant. The dragon Saphira and Eragon communicate telepathically; they become close, and eventually Eragon becomes a dragon rider himself. [**AC**]

In a more comical vein, dragons appear in two very distinct forms in Terry Pratchett's novel *Guards! Guards!* (1989). The book's swamp dragons, far from being intimidating monsters, are small, fussy creatures raised in kennels and treated much like lapdogs. They have malleable digestive systems, which they can change at will in order to produce flame from whatever they happen to eat. Most of the swamp dragons' mental power is taken up with controlling their complex digestion, so they are not terribly intelligent creatures, and they are liable to explode if they get too excited. In contrast to the swamp dragons, the noble dragon is a huge, fearsome creature that craves a treasure hoard and is capable of instantly burning people to ashes. It is cunning and vengeful, and appears to defy the laws of physics by flying gracefully despite its huge size. This anomaly is eventually explained when the characters discover that the dragon is in fact an imaginary creature, one which can be called into existence by magic. [**MM**]

Of course, no survey of magical creatures—including dragons—would be complete without some mention of the veritable bestiary that constitutes the world of J.K. Rowling's "Harry Potter" (see **Harry Potter, Monsters In**). Although dragons are mentioned in several of the volumes, they play the most important role in the fourth contribution to the series, *Harry Potter and the Goblet of Fire* (2000). Here, dragons are revealed to come in a variety of breeds and, as part of the Tri-Wizard Tournament, Harry is tasked with retrieving a golden egg from a nasty Hungarian Horntail dragon. Earlier, in *Harry Potter and the Philosopher's Stone* (1997; released as *Harry Potter and the Sorcerer's Stone* in the US, 1998), the character Hagrid serves as foster mother to a baby dragon which he names Norbert. [**TR**]

Dragons in Contemporary Films

Although the idea of the dragon stretches back many centuries, they are beasts that seem particularly well suited to modern cinematic special effects wizardry. In perhaps the tamest representation, Disney's *Pete's Dragon* (Don Chaffey, 1977), live action is mixed with animation as a young abused runaway (Sean Marshall) is accompanied by an invisible dragon until he finds a new, loving home. The dragon here serves as a psychological symbol of Pete's sense of wellbeing as he is threatened by abusive backwater foster parents, a snake-oil salesman, and more general fears of the unknown and of growing up. The dragon remains invisible to everyone but Pete (and occasionally to intoxicated characters) until the end and talks only in chirps and whistles. Even at its most angry, the dragon, Elliot, is non-threatening, bright green, plump, and can only produce a minimal flame. The dragon leaves at the end of the film when Pete is adopted. [**TR**]

More dramatic is Matthew Robbins's *Dragonslayer* (1981), an unusual collaboration between Disney and Paramount that features a sorcerer's apprentice who is tasked with hunting down a dragon that has been accepting virgin sacrifices in exchange for not attacking the king's people. The film is dark and fantastical, a precursor to the equally low-grossing and unpopular *The Black Cauldron* (Ted Berman and Richard Rich, 1985). Animatronics, puppets, and stop-motion animation were all used to create the special effects and most of the modern dragon characteristics are present: it is rendered with a serpent-like body and bat wings, and it is a hostile creature full of fire and vitriol, with a taste for virgins (a motif drawn from the St George legend). Sorcery, prevailing over the king's politics and the Church's supplications, is needed to defeat it. [**TR**]

In contrast to *Dragonslayer*, Rob Cohen's *DragonHeart* (1996) presents dragons as benevolent creatures and followers of the "Old Code" of chivalry. Draco (a computer-generated dragon voiced by Sean Connery) gives half his heart to the mortally wounded (and newly crowned) King Einon (David Thewlis), under the condition that the young boy renounce the ways of his tyrannical father. Draco's gift forms a magical link between himself and Einon; while Draco lives, Einon cannot be harmed. Einon fails to fulfill his oath and becomes just as tyrannical as his father. Einon's mentor, the knight Bowen (Dennis Quaid), believes that the dragon heart has corrupted the boy and vows to destroy every dragon. Many years later, Bowen encounters Draco who, at this point, is the last surviving dragon. During an attack on Einon's castle, Bowen reluctantly agrees to slay Draco, understanding that it is the only way Einon can be stopped. Draco in the film is a quadruped who can also fly with his leathery bat-like wings. Like many other dragons, he is capable of ejecting flame from his nostrils. [**AM**]

In the 2002 film *Reign of Fire* (Rob Bowman), fire-breathing dragons are awakened from hibernation and then raze the earth, creating a post-apocalyptic world. They have scaly ridges down their backs, two horns atop their heads, two hind legs, and two long, webbed forelimbs that serve as wings. Once the dragons are roused, they are represented primarily as aerial creatures that dominate the sky. They spawn quickly and "[swarm] like locusts, burning everything in their path." They starve, sleep, and repeat the cycle perpetually, subsisting on ash, which offers an evolutionary rationale for their ability to breathe fire. This ability is given a pseudo-scientific explanation: the dragons possess "two glands in the mouth [which] secrete separate chemicals." These chemicals "combine in exhalation" and become "nitro-napalm." Ultimately, the dragons' weakness lies in their inability to see well at dusk. In the "failing light" they are unable to focus, leaving the dragons susceptible to attack and destruction. [**MB**]

Two movies loosely based on *Beowulf* feature dragons. *The Thirteenth Warrior* (John McTiernan, 1999) follows its source novel (*Eaters of the Dead* by Michael Crichton, 1976) in rationalizing the dragon: it is really just a line of torches carried by primitive tribesmen on horseback. *Beowulf* (Robert Zemeckis, 2007), on the other hand, makes use of digital animation to stage an exciting dragon-fighting sequence in which Beowulf (Ray Winstone), who in this version has sired the dragon with Grendel's mother (Angelina Jolie), mounts the dragon as it flies toward the mead hall known as Heorot. In the end, Beowulf cuts out the dragon's heart. The makers of this movie follow a recent trend (seen also in *Reign of Fire* and the "Harry Potter" movies) of redesigning the dragon from an impossible **Chimera** (a snake with bird wings attached) to a creature that could physically fly, like a pterodactyl or a giant flying squirrel (with scales). [**PA**]

In keeping with films targeting younger audiences, Dreamworks' *How to Train Your Dragon* (Chris Sanders and Dean DeBlois, 2010) softens the representation of the dragon and delivers a lesson on the importance of being open-minded. This animated film, loosely based on the first of author Cressida Cowell's books in the series of the same name (published in 2003, itself an extension of Cowell's earlier picture book, *Hiccup the Seasick Viking* [2000]), treats dragons more as naturally occurring animals than as mythological creatures, and catalogues them in the manner of an encyclopedia or a role-playing game. Varieties include the Deadly Nadder, Gronckle, Hideous Zippleback, Monstrous Nightmare, Night Fury, and Terrible Terror. In a training scene, young would-be dragon slayers confront the various kinds of dragons that regularly attack the Viking village of Berk.

How to Train Your Dragon primarily develops the relationship between Hiccup, the movie's main character, and Toothless, a Night Fury wounded by Hiccup in an attack by dragons on Berk. Hiccup succeeds in rehabilitating the dragon from its injury and develops a friendship with the creature. Hiccup then helps the young dragon-slayer trainees tame and befriend their own dragons. As the movie builds to its climax, Hiccup and his friends, mounted on their dragons, fight against a gigantic dragon that has been keeping the other dragons living in fear and forcing them to raid Viking villages in order to feed the monster dragon's equally monstrous appetite. Like James Cameron's *Avatar*, *How to Train Your Dragon* explores the themes of overcoming prejudice and stereotypes, reinforcing the notion that underlying causes should be sought for destructive behavior. [**ME**]

Asian Dragons

Anyone who has seen Chinese "dragons" in the form of effigies during Chinese New Year parades would have to admit that the creature is lively and fascinating. But in origin, character, and behavior, the Asian monster is in fact quite different from the Western dragon to which it is often compared.

The Chinese "dragon," or *long*, is a mythical creature found across Asian cultures. Images of the *long* can be traced back to the Neolithic Yangshao culture dated from around 5,000 to 3,000 BCE. Jade carvings of *long* have also been discovered in the tombs of the Hongshan culture (c. 4700–2900 BCE). The pictograph for *long* is later found in the oracle bone script of the Shang dynasty (sixteenth to eleventh centuries BCE), the earliest form of Chinese writing. Both the jade carvings and the pictograph depict the creature in a coiled shape. Although depictions of *long* vary in ancient documents, the classic perception of the *long* is articulated by the Han dynasty philosopher Wang Fu (c. 90–165 CE) who is quoted in the Song dynasty scholar Luo Yuan's twelfth-century *Material Appended to the Er Ya* (*Er Ya Yi*), describing the shape of *long* as having nine anatomical resemblances: "the horns of a deer, the head of a camel, the eyes of a demon, the neck of a snake, the abdomen of a clam, the scales of a carp, the claws of an eagle, the paws of a tiger, and the ears of a cow" (297). As such, the *long* only superficially resembles the Western dragon. But as far back as Marco Polo in the late thirteenth century (who saw *long* depicted on the walls of Kubla Khan's palace), Westerners have identified the *long* with their own kind of dragon.

The Chinese *long* is seen as the embodiment of a dynamic, arousing, and creative force in the *Book of Changes* (*I Jing*, c. third or second century BCE) and has become predominantly the symbol of imperial authority since the Han dynasty (206 BCE–220 CE). The connection between the *long* and imperial power can be traced back to a number of Chinese legends that associate ancient sage kings such as Huangdi (who reigned c. 2696–2598 BCE) and Shun (who reigned c. twenty-third–twenty-second century BCE) with *long*. The mythological *long* is a benevolent and noble creature that symbolizes power and fortune.

In popular belief, the *long* can control weather and water, especially making rain in times of drought. The practice of making clay *long* and sacrificing to it is mentioned in Wang Chong's (c. 80 CE) essay "On Balance" (*Lun Heng*) as a way of invoking rain during the Han dynasty. The *long*'s power to manipulate water, however, can sometimes bring devastating results. Tales about flood *long* are found in many regions of China.

The *long* appears in a variety of novels and films. In one of the four great classic novels of Chinese literature, *Journey to the West* (*Xi You Ji*; c. 1590), the *Dong hai long wang* (Dragon King of the Eastern Seas) plays an important role in the tenth chapter in which the **Monkey King** Sun Wukong seizes the Dragon King's crown treasure: a gold-banded iron prod used as a pillar of the ocean. In the novel, one of the disciples of the main character monk Xuanzang, also known as Tripitaka, is the third prince of the *Xi hai long wang* (Dragon King of the Western Seas) who is condemned to serve Xuanzang in the transformed shape of a horse, because of his indiscretions in the celestial court. Dragon Kings also appear in *The Investiture of the Gods* (*Fengshen Yanyi*), a vernacular mythological novel written during the Ming dynasty (1368–1644), as the adversary of the boy-hero Nazhe. Another novel from the Ming dynasty (but based on earlier sources) tells the story of Hua Mulan, a young woman who fought as a warrior alongside men. In 1998, Walt Disney Pictures released the animated film *Mulan* (Tony Bancroft and Barry Cook), which features the legendary heroine Hua Mulan and her companion Mushu, a small and comical Chinese *long* (voiced by Eddie Murphy). Mushu appears again in the 2005 sequel, *Mulan II* (Darrell Rooney and Lynne Southerland).

The influence of the Chinese *long* has spread well beyond China's borders and across much of South and East Asia. In Vietnam, the *rồng* or *long* is similar to the Chinese *long* in appearance and behavior. It too controls rain and represents royalty and prosperity. In Thailand, the concept of the *Nāga* (a deity in the form of a snake) has been merged with the image of the Chinese *long*. The *Nāga* often has five heads and appears in the style of the Chinese *long* in front of Buddhist temples. The Korean *yong* and Japanese *tatsu* or *ryū* are generally comparable with their Chinese counterpart *long* in appearance and symbolic significance, and only differ in relatively insignificant details such as the nature of their beard and claws. Like the Chinese *long*, the Korean *yong* and Japanese *tatsu* or *ryū* are also considered symbols of royalty and power, and are associated with water and weather. They, too, make frequent appearances in literature, folklore and cinema. The eighth-century Japanese classics *Kojiki* (Records of Ancient Matters) and *Nihon Shoki* (Chronicles of Japan) both have multiple references to dragons.

In modern times, the concept of *ryū* plays an important role in Ryūnosuke Akutagawa's *Dragon: The Old Potter's Tale* (*Ryū*; 1919), a short story based on a thirteenth-century Japanese folktale. The plot revolves around a practical joke played by the monk E'in who claims that on a certain day of a month, a dragon will ascend to heaven from a local pond. On the day of the supposed event, many gather around the lake and wait for the spectacular event. As the sky darkens, all of them, including E'in, the fabricator of the rumor, believe that they see a dark dragon ascending towards the sky.

While the *ryū* only remains as the illusion of mass hysteria in Akutagawa's story, in Japanese films, especially the *Kajiu* (monster) films, dragons appear as concrete creatures with formidable power. Ishirō Honda's 1963 film *Atragon* and 1968 film *Destroy All Monsters* both feature Manda, a sea-dwelling dragon-like creature, as one of the antagonists. In Hayao Miyazaki's 2001 animated film *Spirited Away*, Haku, the friend of the main character Chihiro, is a white dragon in the guise of a human who can fly in his true form. In Korean folktales, the Dragon King (*yong-wang*) is a recurrent figure. In "Rabbit Visits the Palace of the Dragon King," for example, the Dragon King who falls ill and needs a rabbit's liver for cure is outsmarted by the rabbit. In another tale, "Dragon Carp," a poor fisherman hauls in a giant carp but releases it when it begs for mercy. The carp turns out to be the son of the Dragon King and the fisherman is greatly rewarded. The dragon also appears in Korean cinema. Shim Hyung-rae's 2007 fantasy film *Dragon Wars: D-War* revolves around a battle between two *Imugi* (mythological creatures that can transform into dragons). The benevolent *Imugi* and the evil *Imugi* compete for possession of the power by which one of them could become a true dragon. Ultimately, the evil *Imugi* is destroyed when the good one acquires the power and transforms into the Celestial Dragon.

Regardless of the region, the dragon has been an iconic figure in Asian cultures. Whether depicted as a benevolent creature or a fearsome beast, it is not only a recurrent motif in mythology, folklore, literature, and cinema, but also a common symbol of national identity among Asian countries.

[LW] **Paul Acker, Ruth Babb, Matthew Bardowell, Anthony Cirilla, Michael Elam, Melissa Mayus, Austin McIntire, Thomas Rowland, and Lin Wang**

References and Suggested Reading

Acker, Paul. "Dragons in the Eddas and in Early Nordic Art." In *Revisiting the Poetic Edda: Essays on Old Norse Heroic Legend*, edited by Paul Acker and Carolyne Larrington, 53–75. New York: Routledge, 2013.

Athanassakis, Apostolos N., trans. *The Homeric Hymns. 2nd edn.* Baltimore: The Johns Hopkins University Press, 2004.

Bates, Roy. *All About Chinese Dragons*. Beijing: China History Press, 2007.

De Visser, Marinus Willem. *The Dragon in China and Japan* [1913]. Reprint, New York: Philosophical Library, 1972.

Evans, Jonathan. *Dragons*. New York: Metro, 2008.

Isidore. *The Etymologies of Isidore of Seville*. Translated by Stephen A. Barney. Cambridge: Cambridge University Press, 2006.

Lionarons, Joyce. *The Medieval Dragon: The Nature of the Beast in Germanic Literature*. Enfield Lock: Hisarlik, 1998.

Luo Yuan. Er Ya Yi (Material Appended to the Er Ya). In *Congshu jicheng chubian* (Collected collectanea, 1st series), edited by Wang Yunwu. Shanghai: Shangwu Yinshu guan, 1936.

Merlin: or, the Early History of King Arthur: a Prose Romance, edited by Henry B. Wheatley. London: Kegan, Paul, Trench, Trübner, & Co., 1899.

Orchard, Andy. *Pride and Prodigies: Studies in the Monsters of the Beowulf-Manuscript*. Cambridge: Brewer, 1985.

Ovid. *Metamorphoses*. Translated by A.D. Melville. Oxford: Oxford University Press, 1998.

Riordan, James. *Korean Folk-Tales*. Oxford: Oxford University Press, 1994.

The Saga of Thidrek of Bern. Translated by Edward R. Haymes. New York: Garland, 1988.

Topsell, Edward. *The Historie of Serpents*. London: Wm. Jaggard, 1608.

Zhao Qiguan. *A Study of Dragons, East and West*. New York: Peter Lang, 1992.

DRYAD—*see* Elemental

DUESSA—*see* Demon

DULLAHAN—*see* Body Parts

DUNGEONS & DRAGONS, MONSTERS IN

Fig. 11 ***My Cave*** **by Erol Otus. © Wizards of the Coast, LLC. Image used with permission.**

In 1974, Gary Gygax and Dave Arneson published Dungeons & Dragons (D&D), the first fantasy role-playing game. The game's unique mix of wargaming, improvisation, adventure, magic, and monsters struck a popular culture chord, leading to a fad in the early 1980s. While its popularity has dwindled since, and the game has been eclipsed by video games, D&D has left its mark on the monsters of popular culture, video games, and fiction. In its early days, the monsters of D&D were an eclectic mix drawn from mythology, film, and fantasy and science fiction literature, but early in the game's history, monsters began to appear that were original to the game and particularly well suited to D&D's unique take on fantasy adventure gaming. In time, D&D came to influence creators of popular and literary works, and mythological beings in video games and much contemporary fantasy fiction often bear the influence of the D&D game.

Monsters have been essential to the D&D experience since their introduction in the fantasy supplement to D&D's precursor, the *Chainmail* wargame (1971), and were given a prominent place in the original version of the Dungeons & Dragons rules (1974). When it came time to release the first book in the Advanced Dungeons & Dragons (AD&D) game line, and the first hardcover book for Dungeons & Dragons, it was the *Monster Manual* (1977) that was released first, preceding both the *Player's Handbook* (1978) and *Dungeon Master's Guide* (1979). Further monster manuals followed, including the *Fiend Folio* (1981) and *Monster Manual II* (1983) for AD&D and the Monstrous Compendium series (beginning in 1989 and running to 15 volumes and four "annuals") for AD&D second edition.

Sources for D&D monsters are eclectic, including mythology as well as fantasy and science fiction literature, and even toys used by the designers as tokens for game play. Monsters from classical sources abound from the earliest versions of the game (**Medusa**, **Hydra**, nymph, **Minotaur**, **Centaur**, **satyr**, dryad), as do creatures from medieval bestiaries (**cockatrice**, **basilisk**, unicorn, and so on). Other monsters have closer ties to contemporary films. The D&D **vampire** and **werewolf** echo Universal Studio's 1930s and 1940s ***Dracula*** and *The Wolf Man* films, as well as Hammer Studios' *Horror of Dracula* (Terrance Fisher, 1958) and other monster movies. The D&D "flesh **golem**" clearly draws elements from Universal's version of **Frankenstein's monster** (James Whale, 1931), gaining power from electricity in a nod to the movies. D&D's large variety of monstrous oozes and slimes took their original inspiration from Irvin S. Yeaworth, Jr's ***The Blob*** (1958).

Many monsters were drawn from fantasy and science fiction literature. The gnoll originated in reference to Lord Dunsany's "How Nuth would have Practiced his Art upon the Gnoles" (1912), though the modern D&D gnoll no longer resembles Dunsany's creation. The displacer beast is inspired by the alien being the Couerl from A.E. van Vogt's 1939 short story, "Black Destroyer." D&D's regenerating **troll** is based on Poul Anderson's 1961 treatment of the monster in *Three Hearts and Three Lions*, also the origin of the D&D swanmay. J.R.R. Tolkien's (1892–1973) influence on monsters is clear (see **Tolkien, Monsters In**). The D&D tree monster, the treant, was originally called an ent; the Type VI **demon** (or balor) originally a Balrog; and the halfling originally appeared under the name hobbit. The orc and wight too originate in Tolkien's works and still bear the names given them by Tolkien. Other features of D&D monsters wed literary sources to wargaming directly, as stone **giants** in *Chainmail* blend a passing mention of stone giants hurling boulders in J.R.R. Tolkien's *The Hobbit* (1937) with the usefulness of mobile catapults in wargaming.

Alongside monsters adapted from outside sources, Dungeons & Dragons developed a set of uniquely weird monsters all its own, many of which were adapted to fit the ecology of the fantasy role-playing dungeon (an underworld full of traps, monsters, and treasure), as well as to suit the gaming table itself. The oozes, slimes, and molds took on the role of "dungeon clean up crew," a role played particularly well by the gelatinous cube, a nearly transparent ooze that takes the shape of a standard 10 feet by 10 feet dungeon hallway. The rust monster, whose appearance is based on a plastic toy from Hong Kong (as was the "bulette" or "land shark"), is adapted to the role of terrorizing heavily armored warriors and their players. The beholder, a spherical floating horror with a toothy maw, a large central eye, and ten smaller eyestalks, counters magic-using characters with its anti-magic gaze, while remaining a formidable threat to a party of adventurers, as each of its eyes has a different dangerous magical power.

Some classic D&D monsters function basically as traps or tricks rather than monstrous foes to be fought in battle, acting as a kind of dungeoneering cautionary tale and serving as punishments for the unwary or careless player. Examples include the cloaker (which looks like a cloak, but has teeth), the trapper (which looks like a floor and engulfs victims who step on it), the mimic (which looks like a treasure chest and eats those who try to open it), and rot grubs (waiting in corpses, infecting those who meddle with cadavers in their search for treasure). These monsters reflect a game in which players pit their wits against a trap-filled, dangerous, often surreal otherworld—a dungeon—an unforgiving place for the unwary. On another level, they echo the cautionary tales of some folklore and monster stories—as the monster in a slasher film punishes teens for having sex, or the malicious **fairy** ruins the life of the farmer for failing to keep his word. Unlike moral cautionary tales of folklore and film, D&D cautions players about carelessness or lack of cunning in game play. Their weirdness has inspired numerous online tributes such as Jared Hindman's "Dungeons

& Dragons: Celebrating 30 Years of Very Stupid Monsters" (2006) and Zach Parsons and Steve Sumner's "WTF, D&D?!" series (2009–present) at SomethingAwful.com.

While Dungeons & Dragons has been inspired by myth, literature, and film, it has also in its turn inspired subsequent literature, film, and art. The influence of D&D on monsters in modern fantasy literature is widespread, even beyond officially licensed D&D novels such as Margaret Weis and Tracy Hickman's "Dragonlance Chronicles" trilogy (1984–85) or R.A. Salvatore's *The Crystal Shard* (1988) and subsequent novels starring the D&D drow (dark **elf**) Drizzt. Indeed, even beyond these obvious examples, it is not always clear where Tolkien pastiche leaves off and Dungeons & Dragons pastiche begins in modern genre fantasy.

And the influence of D&D on fantasy fiction is not limited to pastiche. Fantasy author China Miéville (1972–) has noted: "I use AD&D-type fascination with teratology in a lot of my books, and I have the original *Monster Manual*, and the *Monster Manual* 2, and the *Fiend Folio*. I still collect role-playing game bestiaries, because I find that kind of fascination with the creation of the monstrous tremendously inspiring, basically" (Anders). Terry Pratchett has scattered D&D references throughout his "Discworld" novels (1983-present). Tony DiTerlizzi, the author and illustrator of *The Spiderwick Chronicles* (2003–2009) and *The Search for WondLa* (2010) got his start as a professional illustrator for Dungeons & Dragons, leaving his mark on D&D's *Planescape Campaign Setting* (1994) and the Advanced Dungeons & Dragons second edition *Monstrous Manual* (1993). In television animation, Pendleton Ward's television series *Adventure Time* (2010–present) makes numerous references to the D&D game, and iconic monsters such as the gelatinous cube and mimic have appeared on the show. Other literary works inspired by D&D include Belinda Rule's "The Secret of the Dark Elves" (2010) and Sam Lipsyte's "The Dungeon Master" (2010). New York's Allegra LaViola Gallery's panel "Dungeons and Dragons in Contemporary Art" testifies to the influence of the game on a number of contemporary artists, including participants Casey Jex Smith (1976–), Sean McCarthy (1976–), Ryan Browning (1981–), Chris Hagerty (1976–), Tim Hutchings (1974–), Mat Brinkman (1973–), and Zak Smith (1976–) (Allison et al.).

Finally, the Dungeons & Dragons creators and players have at times themselves been represented as monsters in popular culture, as the game was caught up in the "Satanic Panic" of the 1980s and was villainized by conservative Christian churches. At the time, the game was condemned as a doorway to witchcraft and demonology, and law enforcement agencies and the mass media outlets have implicated the game in crimes, especially suicides and murders. The height of public paranoia about satanic ritual abuse corresponded to the height of the D&D game's success as a fad, and the game came under particularly strong condemnation from Patricia Pulling (1948–97), whose son's suicide she blamed on the game. It was also the subject of Jack Chick's tract "Dark Dungeons" (1984), framing it as a recruiting tool for **devil** worship. Furthermore, it was implicated in the attempted suicide of James Dallas Egberd, III (1962–80) in the steam tunnels beneath Michigan State University, a story that was fictionalized in the book and TV film *Mazes & Monsters* (Steven Hilliard Stern, 1982), starring Tom Hanks. Much of this anti-D&D sentiment has abated, but the game still has the ability to draw attention. Wisconsin's Waupun prison has banned the play of the game by inmates, a ban that has been upheld by federal courts (Schwartz). The rationale for the ban is that the game promotes "gang activity," another hobgoblin of contemporary US society.

Richard W. Forest

References and Suggested Reading

Allison, Tavis, et al. "Dungeons and Dragons in Contemporary Art: A Panel Discussion." 2010. <http://muleabides.wordpress.com/2010/11/12/dd-in-contemporary-art-video-of-the-panel-discussion/>.

Anders, Lou. Interview with China Miéville. April 2005. <http://www.believermag.com/issues/200504/?read=interview_mieville>.

Harrigan, Pat, and Noah Wardrip-Fruin, eds. *First Person: New Media as Story, Performance, and Game*. Cambridge, MA: MIT Press, 2004.

——, eds. *Second Person: Role-Playing and Story in Games and Playable Media*. Cambridge, MA: MIT Press, 2007.

——, eds. *Third Person: Authoring and Exploring Vast Narratives*. Cambridge, MA: MIT Press, 2009.

Schwartz, John. "Dungeons & Dragons Prison Ban Upheld." *The New York Times, 26 January* 2010. <http://www.nytimes.com/2010/01/27/us/27dungeons.html?_r=0>.

DVOINIK

The dvoinik is a Russian variant of the double, partly influenced by the **doppelganger** found in eighteenth- and nineteenth-century German Romanticism. Yet the two are not identical; the dvoinik is first mentioned in medieval Slavic texts. Like the doppelganger, the dvoinik is usually male. It may take the form of a man, a **devil**, a shadow, or a mirror reflection, or it may appear as a detached body part (a nose in Nikolai Gogol's "The Nose" [1836], for example; see **Body Parts**). The dvoinik may regard its original as a friend, a servant, or a dangerous enemy. Conflicts between the original and the dvoinik often, but not always, end badly for the former. Sometimes the dvoinik lures the protagonist to madness or death, yet such tragic consequences are not inevitable. The Russian dvoinik is closely connected to the notion of individual fate.

The dvoinik, as Likhachev shows, was known as early as in the anonymous fifteenth-century poem "A Tale about Alcohol." It also appeared in several anonymous seventeenth-century tales, such as "A Tale of Misery and Ill Fortune" (rediscovered in 1856), in which it personifies Misery and represents an antagonistic force within the personality of the anonymous protagonist. The dvoinik in this tale cannot be banished, even by a suicide attempt. Rescue finally comes when the protagonist enters a monastery, where Misery cannot follow. By assuming responsibility for the hero's evil or mischievous deeds, the dvoinik stimulates the reader's sympathy with his original.

A new phase in the history of the dvoinik arrived with a short story collection entitled *The Double, or My Evenings in Little Russia* (1828) by Antonii Pogorel'skii (the pen-name of Aleksei Perovskii). The stories are united by a frame-tale featuring a provincial squire and his physically identical, good-natured dvoinik, who visits him at home in order to entertain him. They tell each other a series of linked fantastic tales. As they converse, each is represented not as human and demonic versions of the same personality, but rather as Romantic imagination (the dvoinik) versus skeptical intelligence (the squire). Pogorel'skii's book initiates the Russian vogue for *goffmaniada* (stories in the tradition of E.T.A. Hoffmann's [1776–1822] tales). Russian *goffmaniada* partially overlaps with the Gothic tale and develops juxtaposition between a fantastic or Utopian world and Russian actuality. Pogorel'skii's narrator alludes to the doppelganger, yet the Dvoinik (with capital D) explicitly rejects and differentiates himself from this German prototype on the grounds that he is a Russian patriot. He also debunks negative superstitions surrounding doubles, such as the notion that they portend death or fear cock-crow and certain times of day. Pogorel'skii's Dvoinik is clearly a positive figure, representing facets of the human personality that, far from being antagonistic, support and enrich each other.

Nikolai Gogol develops the dvoinik in several of his Gothic-fantastic short stories, especially "The Nose" (1836). The plot describes how Kovaliev, a petty official, mysteriously wakes up to find his nose missing. Kovaliev's barber finds the nose in his wife's homemade bread, recognizes it, and disposes of it in the river for fear of being blamed for cutting it off. Later Kovaliev encounters his own nose in the cathedral, now attired in the uniform of a senior official, and hence outranking him. Kovaliev's efforts to recapture his nose fail, but fortunately for him, a police officer arrests the nose (which is carrying a fake passport) and returns it to its owner. Eventually, the nose reappears on Kovaliev's face just as mysteriously as it had earlier vanished.

Scholars (for example, Meyer and Passage) agree that the nose represents Kovaliev's dvoinik. The story may be a general parody of Romantic fantasy, especially Hoffmann's *A New Year's Eve Adventure* (1815) and Chamisso's *Peter Schlemihl* (1814). Or it may lampoon the physical comedy found in Sterne's *Tristram Shandy* (1759–69) and in the popular culture of Gogol's Russia, in which anecdotes about noses abounded. Freudians such as P. Spycher liken Kovaliev's loss of his nose to impotence or castration, while another approach points to Kovaliev's social dilemma when his nose apparently outranks him (thus parodying Russia's rigid hierarchy of civil and military ranks). Gogol's dvoinik is an entirely random aberration—both an offshoot of absurd reality and a sign of a hidden, terrifying, transcendent world.

Fyodor Dostoevsky enhanced the dvoinik theme significantly in his novels *Dvoinik* or *The Double* (1846) and *The Brothers Karamazov* (1880). *The Double*'s hero, a clerk called Goliadkin (the surname connotes nakedness and poverty) aspires to marry the daughter of his former benefactor and superior, but is rejected in favor of a wealthier groom and subsequently ostracized by the family. Goliadkin imagines his place in society is being invaded by an impostor, identical to him in everything except conscience, which his dvoinik, Mr Goliadkin, Jr, appears to lack. After initially masquerading as his friend and protégé, the dvoinik soon supplants Goliadkin, Sr at work, in public, and in his private life. Forced by his rival's shameless behavior to re-evaluate his own flaws, which include servility, hypocrisy, and flattery, Goliadkin ultimately goes mad.

Ivan Karamazov, the anguished intellectual in *The Brothers Karamazov*, assumes moral responsibility for the parricide committed by his illegitimate brother (and partial dvoinik) Smerdiakov. Formerly a rational atheist, Ivan comes to believe in the **devil** (possibly a dvoinik of Ivan's own father); his sense of guilt drives him mad. The dvoinik here is not a symbol of universal evil, but merely a reflection of Ivan's troubled soul. Dostoevsky's characters can have more than one dvoinik, and several characters may share their dvoinik, as, for example, in *Crime and Punishment* (1866), in which Raskolnikov is doubled by the characters Svidrigailov, Luzhin, and Razumikhin.

Dvoiniks in twentieth-century Russian literature include several archetypes of Peter the Great in Andrei Bely's major novel *Petersburg* (1913; revised 1922) and several Hoffmannesque tales by the economist and architectural historian Aleksandr Chaianov, particularly "The Venetian Mirror, or The Strange Adventures of the Glass Man" (1923). In this story, the hero, Aleksei, a dilettante art collector, purchases an antique mirror. However, his reflection turns out to be both self-aware and malicious; it forces Aleksei to change places with it and, stealing his identity, causes havoc in the real world until Aleksei manages to escape from the mirror and restore order. Chaianov's plot is a reworking of the Symbolist poet Valerii Briusov's earlier short story "In the Mirror" (1903), which has a similar plotline with female characters.

Mikhail Bulgakov's early short story "Diaboliad" (1924) invokes the Gogolian and Dostoevskian pattern of a minor official supplanted by a more personable dvoinik: the petty clerk Korotkov is dismissed from his job for a minor error. Next, his money and documents are stolen, leaving him without a provable identity (a disaster in Soviet Russia). Both Korotkov and his oppressive boss Kalsoner acquire dvoiniks. Korotkov is duplicated at first by his libidinous alter ego Kolobkov, and then by his mirror reflection. The bald, close-shaven Kalsoner has a twin brother with an Assyrian beard, and Korotkov chases them both in an unsuccessful and progressively lunatic quest for reinstatement. Struggling to salvage his remaining dignity, Korotkov commits suicide.

The dvoinik is a recurring character in Russian literature to the present day. It frequently signifies the social alienation of the "little man," and/or his suppressed feelings of solitude or guilt.

Larisa Fialkova

References and Suggested Reading

Chizhevsky, Dmitri. "The Theme of the Double in Dostoevsky." In *Dostoevsky: A Collection of Critical Essays*, edited by René Wellek, 119–29. Englewood Cliffs, NJ: Prentice-Hall, Inc, 1962.

Frank, Joseph. *Dostoevsky: The Seeds of Revolt, 1821–1849*. Princeton: Princeton University Press, 1979.

Fusso, Susanne, and Priscilla Meyer, eds. *Essays on Gogol: Logos and the Russian Word*. Evanston, IL: Northwestern University Press, 1992.

Likhachev, Dmitriĭ. "Zhizn' cheloveka v predstavlenii neizvestnogo avtora XVII veka." In *Povest' o gore-zloschastii*, edited by D.S. Likhachev and E.I. Vaneeva, 89–105. Moscow: Nauka, 1984.

Meyer, Priscilla. "Supernatural Doubles: Vii and The Nose." In *The Gothic-Fantastic in Nineteenth-Century Russian Literature*, edited by Neil Cornwell, 189–209. Amsterdam and Atlanta: Rodopi, 1999.

Passage, Charles E. *The Russian Hoffmannists*. The Hague: Mouton & Co, 1963.

Rosenshield, Gary. "The Bronze Horseman and The Double: The Depoeticization of the Myth of Petersburg in the Young Dostoevskii." *Slavic Review* 55, no. 2 (1996): 399–428.

Spycher, Peter C. "N.V. Gogol's 'The Nose': A Satirical Comic Fantasy Born of an Impotence Complex." *The Slavic and East European Journal* 7, no. 4 (1963): 361–74.

DUPPY—*see* Ghost

DUST DEVIL—*see* Demon

DWARF

Old Norse mythology, the primary source for early Germanic dwarf lore, distinguished among gods, elves (see **Elf**), **giants**, monsters, dwarfs, and humankind. Dwarfs in Norse mythology and later folklore were smaller in stature than humans (although this feature was not consistently emphasized), so that the term "dwarf" was later applied to humans with genetic dwarfism. This entry treats mythological dwarfs primarily in Old Norse and their counterparts in the fantasies of J.R.R. Tolkien, with a brief discussion of dwarfs in contemporary popular culture at the end.

In the Old Norse *Poetic Edda*, copied down as a whole in Iceland c. 1275 but reflecting earlier beliefs, dwarfs are created from the blood and limbs of the primordial giant Ymir ("The Sybil's Prophecy," stanza 9). Their leaders are Motsognir and Durin. A long list of dwarf names follows, which was probably added from an earlier poem; many of these names were taken up by J.R.R. Tolkien (1892–1973) in his works of fantasy (see below). One of the dwarfs was called Dvalin; the text recounts that the descendants of Dvalin first lived in "halls of stone" (stanza 14). In the *Prose Edda*, composed c. 1230 but drawing on earlier versions of poems from the *Poetic Edda*, Icelandic mythographer Snorri Sturluson (1179–1241) adds that the dwarfs first lived as maggots in Ymir's flesh and then were given intelligence and human shape by the gods. According to Snorri, dwarfs live in the earth and in rocks.

In another mythological poem from the *Poetic Edda*, "The Sayings of All-Wise," a dwarf named All-Wise (Alvíss) plays a major role. He lives below the earth under a rock and is pale and ugly as a *thurs* (**troll**). He has taken Thor's daughter and will give her back only if Thor can tell him the names of things from all the world's regions, in the languages of men, gods, giants, elves, and dwarfs. Thor does so, saying, for instance, that the dwarfs call the sun "Dvalin's deluder," apparently referring to a myth in which Dvalin was betrayed by the sun. Such a betrayal in fact happens in this poem, for in the end Thor says that day has dawned and (we infer from other sources) the dwarf is transformed into a rock. (The motif is applied to trolls in later Icelandic folklore and in Tolkien's 1937 fantasy *The Hobbit*.)

Other dwarfs are said to be craftsmen; according to the *Poetic Edda*, the sons of the dwarf Ivaldi made Skidbladnir, the best of ships, for the god Frey ("Grimnir's Sayings," stanza 43). Snorri adds that these same dwarfs also made the spear Gungnir for Odin and silver hair for Thor's wife Sif. Further, two dwarfs named Brokk and Eitri (sometimes called Sindri) made a magic ring for Odin, a shining boar for Frey, and the famous magic hammer Mjolnir for Thor (Snorri 96–7). The dwarfs Fjalar and Galar brewed a magical drink called the mead of poetry from the blood of a being named Kvasir (Snorri 62), whom they had killed.

In the legendary-heroic poems written down in the second half of the *Poetic Edda*, the young hero Sigurd is fostered by Regin, who was skillful at making things (he forges a sword for Sigurd) and also "a dwarf in height; he was wise, ferocious, and knowledgeable about magic" ("The Lay of Regin," introductory prose, *Poetic Edda* 51). The gods had taken gold from a dwarf named Andvari and then given it to Regin's father (the gold includes a ring upon which Andvari had placed a curse). Regin and his brother Fafnir kill their father for the gold but Fafnir refuses to give Regin any of it. Fafnir turns into a large serpent-**dragon**, lies down upon the gold, and hoards it until Sigurd kills him, thus earning the name Sigurd Fafnir's-Bane. Sigurd also kills the dwarf Regin (Fafnir's brother), who had been plotting to get the gold for himself.

The story of Sigurd is told briefly by Snorri in his *Prose Edda* (99–105) and then anonymously in *The Saga of the Volsungs* (written c. 1270), which quotes from and adapts the *Poetic Edda*. On the model of that saga, Icelanders composed a number of *fornaldar* sagas, sagas of ancient times, some of which included dwarfs as characters. In the anonymous *The Saga of Án Bow-bender* (late fourteenth century), for example, the hero, while still a young man, goes into a forest. He prevents a dwarf named Litr from returning into a large stone where his home was, and so the dwarf, in order to earn his way back home, makes a mighty bow for Án (the name Litr is probably taken from Snorri's *Edda*, in which a dwarf named Litr runs in front of Baldr's funeral pyre and Thor kicks him into the flames [Snorri 49]). In other *fornaldar* sagas, dwarfs forge excellent swords for the heroes (see Battles 41–4), as Regin had done for Sigurd. In *The Tale of Sorli*, some dwarfs live inside a rock; we are told that they "mixed with people more in those days than now" (chapter 1). Freyja, here called Odin's mistress rather than a goddess of fertility, comes upon the rock when it is "open" and sees the dwarfs forging a gold necklace. She covets the necklace, which they give to her on the condition that she sleep with each of them.

Dwarfs in Other Traditions

While other areas of Northern Europe do not preserve Germanic mythological information as well as Old Norse does, dwarfs do figure in medieval literary narratives, especially Middle High German ones like the *Nibelungenlied* (c. 1200). Some of these episodes parallel the Sigurd material, and others center on another hero, Dietrich von Bern (see Battles 50–67). Sometimes the dwarfs live in hollow mountains, a motif that eventually turns up in the Grimm Brothers' fairytale "Snow White and the Seven Dwarfs" (published 1812).

Dwarfs figure in medieval Arthurian romances by authors such as Chrétien de Troyes (late twelfth century) and Thomas Malory (late fifteenth century). These dwarfs may be evil, ugly antagonists; companions of fair maidens; or hunchback spies. In origin, some of them may derive (if rather obscurely) from Irish and/or Welsh mythology, as Vernon Harward argues. **[PA]**

Dwarves in Tolkien

J.R.R. Tolkien draws upon dwarf-lore found in the Old Norse *Poetic Edda* in creating the dwarves of Middle Earth, especially from that part of the mythological poem, "The Sybil's Prophecy," known as *Dvergatal* or "the catalog of dwarfs" (see **Tolkien, Monsters In**). From this source, Tolkien adapts the names of the dwarves first introduced in *The Hobbit* (Dwalin, Balin, Fili, Kili, Dori, Nori, Ori, Oin, Gloin, Bifur, Bofur, Bombur, and Thorin Oakenshield; 16–18), and whose history and lineage continue through its sequel, the three-volume *The Lord of the Rings*, published in 1954 and 1955. (From the same Eddic list, Tolkien also takes the name Gandalf, but he applies it to a **wizard**.) The development of dwarves in Tolkien's fiction combines ancient source material with idiosyncratic preference. This can be seen in Tolkien's pluralization of the word *dwarf*. Despite objections from his publisher Rayner Unwin, he insisted on using the form *dwarves* rather than *dwarfs* (presumably on the analogy of forms like *wharfs/wharves*), even though he knew it was linguistically incorrect (largely because the Old English word for dwarf ended in a *g*, rather than an *f*). He called it a "piece of private bad grammar" (*Letters* 17). The irony is, however, that many Tolkien readers have assumed that he was correct and have adopted the form *dwarves* themselves (we use it in this entry only when referring to Tolkien's own dwarves).

Dwarves in Tolkien's cosmology are created before any of the other creatures known as the children of Ilúvatar (the supreme deity of Middle Earth). At first there is a great void (compare the Old Norse primordial void *Ginnungagap*; Snorri 9–10) that is yet to be populated. Aulë, a minor deity, fashions the dwarves in darkness in order to fill this void. Tolkien attributes the irregular appearance of the dwarves to Aulë's inability fully to comprehend Ilúvatar's vision for the creatures who will eventually inhabit Middle Earth. Because Aulë's act is premature, it is transgressive. In an act of repentance, Aulë, who is a smith, raises his hammer to destroy the dwarves, but Ilúvatar takes compassion on his earnestness and humility and gives the dwarves life (*Silmarillion* 43–4).

From this origin, Tolkien establishes the nature of the dwarves. They dwell under stone, excavating and inhabiting mines. They are "stone-hard," stubborn in character, and make loyal friends as well as bitter enemies (*Silmarillion* 44). They are, like their creator Aulë (and like some Old Norse dwarfs), skilled smiths. Because of the transgressive nature of their creation, there is an enmity between them and the other children of Ilúvatar. A specific example of this enmity (and also of the dwarves' fierce loyalty) can be seen in the relationship between the dwarf Gimli and the elf Legolas featured throughout *The Lord of the Rings*.

Dwarves figure prominently in *The Hobbit*, in which Gandalf the wizard cajoles the stay-at-home hobbit Bilbo Baggins into accompanying 13 dwarves on a mission to the Lonely Mountain. There they must retrieve their hoard of gold, which is guarded by the dragon Smaug. The dwarves wear colorful hoods and grow long beards, which are a point of pride among them. While the dwarves all, to varying degrees, exhibit the qualities common to their race, their characters range rather broadly—from the comic Bombur to the noble Thorin. In *The Lord of the Rings*, Gimli, son of Gloin, is the only dwarf to be included in the fellowship of the ring.

In the appendices to *The Lord of the Rings*, Tolkien develops a focused history of the dwarves as a race. Durin is the most famous of the dwarves originally created by Aulë. He established a great society of dwarves in the mines of Moria. This society thrives until the dwarves' desire for precious metal causes them to delve too deeply into the mine, awakening a Balrog of Morgoth. The creature kills their ruler and brings their civilization in Moria to an end. From there, the dwarves settle in the north by the Lonely Mountain where they discover a large jewel they call the Arkenstone (*LOTR* 1045–53). This jewel, along with other treasure, would eventually entice the dragon Smaug to drive the dwarves from the Lonely Mountain and claim the hoard for himself, an event that forms the background for the plot in *The Hobbit*.

The only female dwarf mentioned in Tolkien's work is Dís, daughter of Thráin II. Female dwarves are said to be scarce; male dwarves outnumber them three to one. The female dwarves seldom walk abroad and when they do, they are so similar in appearance to male dwarves that they are difficult to identify. Their scarcity and similarity in appearance to male dwarves is said to account for the erroneous belief that female dwarves do not exist and that, in order to reproduce, dwarves merely "grow out of stone" (*LOTR* 1053). [**MB**]

Dwarfs in Contemporary Popular Culture

In addition to Tolkien's novels and their various cinematic adaptations, the twenty-first-century understanding of dwarfs has largely been shaped by Disney's animated *Snow White and the Seven Dwarfs* (David Hand et al., 1937) and contemporary role-playing and video games. Based on the fairytale by the Brothers Grimm, Disney's *Snow White and the Seven Dwarfs*, which has the distinction of being the first full-length cel-animated feature in cinematic history, presents dwarfs as kindly and industrious. While Snow White keeps house, they mine for jewels by day, whistling while they work, and sing and dance at night. It is fair to say that all subsequent popular culture representations of dwarfs are forced to contend with this representation by either replicating the saccharine quality of Disney's dwarfs or, more frequently, turning it on its head by rendering them as grumpy—for example, the character Hoggle in Jim Henson's *Labyrinth* (1986)—or menacing, as are, for example, the **zombie** dwarves in Don Coscarelli's cult-film favorite, *Phantasm* (1979).

Both helpful dwarfs and treacherous ones exist in the world of C.S. Lewis's (1898–1963) Narnia. Called "sons of earth" by Aslan (as opposed to men, which are referred to as "sons of Adam"), they come in two varieties differentiated by the color of their hair and their disposition. Red Dwarfs are generally kind and helpful, and ally themselves with Aslan; Black Dwarfs, in contrast, are typically selfish and serve in the White **Witch**'s army in *The Lion, The Witch and the Wardrobe* (1950). In the film *Snow White and the Huntsman* (Rupert Sanders, 2012), the dwarfs have scruffy beards and hair, Celtic names (many are names for letters in the Ogham alphabet), and are survivors from a once populous race of gold miners.

Dwarfs in contemporary role-playing and video games are obvious outgrowths from Tolkien's fiction. In *Dungeons & Dragons*, introduced in 1974, dwarfs are a humanoid race available as character types for players (see **Dungeons & Dragons, Monsters In**). In keeping with Tolkien, they distrust elves. The dwarf is also a character type in the *Warcraft* (introduced in 1994) and *Warhammer* (introduced in 1983) universes. In each, they are stout and sturdy craftsmen (see **Video Games, Monsters In**). The animated program *South Park* gently satirized online gamers in the 2006 episode "Make Love, Not Warcraft," in which the character Cartman adopts as his avatar a dwarf very much resembling Gimli (John Rhys-Davies) in Peter Jackson's *Lord of the Rings* films. Also derived from Tolkien are the dwarfs who appear in fantasy author Terry Prachett's "Discworld" series, begun in 1983 and currently numbering 39 volumes.

[JW] **Paul Acker, Matthew Bardowell, and Jeffrey A. Weinstock**

References and Suggested Reading

Acker, Paul. "Dwarf-lore in Alvíssmál." In *The Poetic Edda: Essays on Old Norse Mythology*, edited by Paul Acker and Carolyne Larrington, 213–28. New York: Routledge, 2002.

Battles, Paul. "Dwarfs in Germanic Literature: Deutsche Mythologie or Grimm's Myths?" In *The Shadow-Walkers: Jacob Grimm's Mythology of the Monstrous*, edited by Tom Shippey, 29–82. Tempe, AZ: Arizona Center for Medieval and Renaissance Studies, 2005.

Harward, Vernon. *The Dwarfs of Arthurian Romance and Celtic Tradition*. Leiden: Brill, 1958.

Hughes, Shaun F.D. "The Saga of Án Bow-Bender." In *Medieval Outlaws: Twelve Tales in Modern English Translation, revised edition*, edited by Thomas H. Ohlgren, 290–337. West Lafayette, IN: Parlor, 2005.

Jakobsson, Ármann. "The Hole: Problems in Medieval Dwarfology," *Arv 61* (2005): 53–76.

The Poetic Edda. Translated by Carolyne Larrington. Oxford: Oxford University Press, 1996.

Snorri Sturluson. *Edda*. Translated by Anthony Faulkes. London: Dent, 1987.

Tolkien, J.R.R. *The Hobbit* [1937]. Boston: Houghton Mifflin, 1978.

———. *The Letters of J.R.R. Tolkien*, edited by Humphrey Carpenter. Boston: Houghton Mifflin, 2000.

———. *The Lord of the Rings* [1954]. Boston: Houghton Mifflin, 1994.

———. *The Silmarillion. Boston: Houghton Mifflin, 2000.*

DWELLER ON THE THRESHOLD

The Dweller on the Threshold is a malevolent spectral entity appearing in the 1842 occult romance *Zanoni*, by the novelist Edward Bulwer-Lytton (1803–73). To attain true magical power, an initiate must confront and defeat the Dweller. Attempting this confrontation too early in one's training, or while distracted by mundane concerns, allows the Dweller to haunt or possess the would-be magus. The Dweller tempts its victim to debase and destroy himself further, and can only be banished by a higher, more powerful spirit.

The most arresting and terrifying features of the Dweller are its "malignant eyes" (296) of "livid and demoniac fire" (242). Bulwer-Lytton variously describes the Dweller as a "mistlike, formless thing" (296) and as a humanoid being of "female" outline that nonetheless "seem[s] rather to crawl as some vast misshapen reptile" (242). Its true form and face (though not the intensity of its "burning glare") remain disguised by a mist or "filmy veil" (242). Its true nature is likewise uncertain: "the shadowy Horror was not all a spirit, but partook of matter enough, at least, to make it more deadly and fearful an enemy to material forms" (243). It is "a thing not of earth" (296) and a member of "the tribes of space" (266)—although it comes not from outer space but from a magical plane it calls "the immeasurable region" (243). At one point, the Dweller reveals itself unveiled to its invoker Glyndon, but Bulwer-Lytton explains that it is "forbidden for the hand to record" (272) what Glyndon sees and hears.

The Dweller's gaze "can haunt, but it cannot harm" (266). However, it shows its victim such horrors, and whispers such temptations, that even the immortal Rosicrucian **wizard** Zanoni is nearly undone by it. If the haunted one drowns himself in animalistic or base pleasures and passions, the Dweller does not appear. It manifests only to bar the way to any sort of spiritual enlightenment, including artistic or scientific pursuits. The Dweller guards the Threshold of initiation against trespassers, and drives would-be adepts back down into the material mire, but also seems to take genuine delight in spiritually destroying and enslaving its victims. At the final extremity, however, Zanoni's ultimate act of self-sacrifice summons the benevolent spirit Adon-Ai and banishes the Dweller.

The indescribable, implacable Dweller on the Threshold, whose power dwarfs even the mightiest human wizards, can be seen (despite Bulwer-Lytton's morality-restoring ending) as the first cosmic horror in literature, and as the spiritual and artistic progenitor of any number of Lovecraftian monsters (see **Lovecraft, Monsters In**). August Derleth, for example, likely took the title of his Cthulhu Mythos novel *The Lurker at the Threshold* (1945) from Bulwer-Lytton's specter. Derleth's titular Lurker is Lovecraft's creation Yog-Sothoth, similarly veiled and formless, invoked by unwise or arrogant magi.

Zanoni was not only the first cosmic horror novel, but also the first occult romance. A sensational best-seller, it influenced other novelists as well as occultists in Bulwer-Lytton's circle of friends, such as the spiritualist Daniel Dunglas Home (1833–86) and the ceremonial magician Eliphas Levi (1810–75). Bulwer-Lytton filled his novel with asides and lectures on all manner of arcane subjects, and his mystically minded readership imported *Zanoni*'s metaphysics—including the Dweller—into their own theories and publications. The humanist mystic Rudolf Steiner (1861–1925) repurposed the Dweller as the Guardian of the Threshold; his 1913 play *The Guardian of the Threshold* presents a spirit more inclined to lecture than to haunt.

Helena Petrovna Blavatsky (1831–91), the founder of theosophy, typifies this response. She admits that Bulwer-Lytton invented the Dweller on the Threshold, but maintains that the monster represents a real class of being—specifically "certain maleficent astral doubles of defunct persons" (106). This notion of the Dweller as evil double animates Robert Hichens's 1911 novel *The Dweller on the Threshold*, in which a séance accidentally creates a dominant, forceful shadow personality inside a meek curate.

Aleister Crowley (1875–1947), the magician and self-proclaimed Antichrist, repeatedly referenced the Dweller in his writings, usually quizzically or ironically. Many of his disciples missed the joke and took the Dweller more seriously. The painter Austin Osman Spare (1886–1956) repeatedly depicted the Dweller as a formless, malevolent silhouette in his occult artworks and, like other Crowleyans, identified the Dweller with Crowley's own threshold **demon** Choronzon (a name lifted from the Elizabethan magus John Dee's [1527–c. 1608] occult texts). The occult film *Choronzon (Dweller on the Threshold)* (2009), by the experimental filmmaker Raymond Salvatore Harmon, also makes this association.

Kenneth Hite

References and Suggested Reading

Blavatsky, H.P. *The Theosophical Glossary.* London: The Theosophical Publishing Society, 1892.

Bulwer-Lytton, Edward. *Zanoni.* Estes and Lauriat edn, 1842. Reprint, Boston: Estes and Lauriat, 1892.

Godwin, Joscelyn. *The Theosophical Enlightenment.* Albany: State University of New York Press, 1994.

Hichens, Robert. *The Dweller on the Threshold.* London: Methuen, 1911.

Lachman, Gary. *A Dark Muse.* London: Dedalus, 2003.

DYBBUK

"Why has the soul descended from the high castle to the lowest dungeon? Every ascent requires a descent." These words, the epigram beginning S. An-sky's play *The Dybbuk, or Between Two Worlds* (1914), exemplify the world between worlds in which the restless soul that will become a *dybbuk* (literally, something that "attaches" itself to something else, plural *dybbukim*), a type of **ghost**, must dwell. Often characterized as malicious, *dybbukim* more accurately represent the manifestation of the longing of a soul for fulfillment that it was unable to achieve in the world of the living. Unfulfilled vows, unaccomplished tasks, incomplete religious pledges—any of these can cause a soul to wander, seeking attachment to a body in order once again to be able to engage in the physical actions necessary to complete the requisite tasks.

Dveykut, a state of "clinging" or "attachment"—from the same root as "*dybbuk*"—is a state devoutly aspired to by Jewish mystics, a connection (though not a union) between the soul and God, a condition that mystics attempt to initiate via meditation, chanting, the use of music, movement, dance, and the study of esoteric texts. But every positive mystical state has its negative shadow, and while *Dveykut* is elusive and desirous to achieve, and can only come about at the instigation of the mystic, there is a dangerous sort of *Dveykut*—in this case, spirit possession—that comes upon the individual unawares, and often not through her or his initiation at all; this form of *Dveykut* can be described as a sudden infection in which something slips through the cracks—often literally, since these spirits are believed to enter and leave the body through the small toe of the left foot.

Dybbukim generally manifest as being of a different gender than the body they possess. That is, the body of a man will be possessed by a female *dybbuk*, or (and this is vastly more common) the body of a woman will be possessed by a male *dybbuk*. *Dybbukim* hold the body captive, as it were, threatening not to release the victim until some *tikkun* or correction of sins of commission or omission in life takes place that can only be effected via a living body. One does not have to be a master of psychology to understand that a woman being possessed by a male *dybbuk* in a pre-modern society—or indeed, in any postmodern society in which women are second-class citizens—could empower her through the assumption of a male voice, vocabulary of gesture, masculine prerogatives, and masculine power.

Much of the material on *dybbukim* in Jewish mystical literature arises from developments in the town of Safed, in northern Israel, in the sixteenth century. After the expulsion of the Jews from Spain in 1492, many Jews, including the mystically inclined, made their way to this area. Under the direction of mystical masters like Isaac Luria (1534–72), these spiritual seekers built a kabbalistic culture that had much to do with the discovery by mystical means of the graves of the ancient, righteous rabbis that had, until that point in time, been neglected, forgotten, or hidden from view. This culture of contacting, celebrating, and becoming intimately involved with the world of the dead was also one that revived and intensified interest in reincarnation and spirit possession. Gradually, in seventeenth- and eighteenth-century Kabbalah, standard *modus operandi* of spirit possession and exorcism developed, reaching their most baroque development in the Hassidic culture in Eastern Europe in the nineteenth century.

Accordingly, a titration of all things related to *dybbukim* and the manner in which they operate is wonderfully manifest in An-sky's play, based as it is on his ethnographic survey of East European Jewish folk beliefs he believed to be on the brink of extinction—concerning, among many other things, the occult and the world of the dead. An-sky's play was mediated to popular culture in a variety of contexts, but justifiably most celebrated is the 1937 Yiddish language film, *The Dybbuk*, directed by Michał Waszyński.

The plot elements of An-sky's play contain all the rudiments of a spirit possession case history: in a small East European town, Khonen, a poor yeshiva student, falls in love with Leah, a rich man's daughter. In truth, these two had been promised to each other by a vow sworn years before by their fathers, who had been best of friends. But after his friend's death and the descent of the family into poverty, Leah's father conveniently forgets his promise to his friend and rejects Khonen's proposal. Leah is pledged to the son of a rich merchant. Khonen becomes despondent, then desperate, attempting to win Leah's love by the use of Kabbalistic love spells, which end up sapping his spiritual strength and he dies in the attempt. Just before Leah's wedding to the merchant's son, Khonen's spirit enters Leah in the form of a *dybbuk*, ensconcing itself there and refusing to depart. The wonder-rabbi of Miropol is called in on the case, and the unfulfilled vow made between Leah and Khonen's fathers before their children's births is recalled by the *dybbuk*, who demands justice for the spirit of Khonen's father, lest he continue to possess Leah. Since the spirit will broach no compromise, an exorcism is undertaken, and in a charged atmosphere replete with black candles and the sound of the shofar, the wonder-rabbi drives the *dybbuk* from Leah's body. But the banished spirit, who cannot now claim his beloved's body, returns and possesses her soul, snuffing out her life in the process. Not all possessions by *dybbukim* end so badly as in the case of Leah and Khonen. In most cases, once the victim has sufficiently empowered her- or himself to achieve whatever it is that is demanded, an exorcism will have the effect of bringing the situation back to *status quo*.

An-sky's *Dybbuk* has seen productions in many languages. An opera based on the play was written by Lodovico Rocco in 1934 after Arthur Hammerstein and George Gershwin had abandoned similar projects in 1926 and 1929 respectively. Since Lodovico's 1934 opera, countless recensions have appeared including danced versions (1974's *Dybbuk Variations*, a collaboration between Jerome Robbins and Leonard Bernstein), Tony Kushner's 1997 restaging of the play at New York's public theater, Shulamit Ran's 1997 operatic version, and a Polish stage version produced by Krzysztok Warlikowski in 2003 in which contemporary Polish-Jewish novelist Hanna Krall's post-Holocaust-themed 1996 short story, "The Dybbuk," was interwoven with An-sky's drama. *Dybbukim* have featured in radio drama, including versions of An-sky's play adapted in 1960 by Sidney Lumet, for CBS Radio Mystery Theater in 1974, and in a version (now lost) for BBC Radio 4 in 1979. DC Comics incorporated the entity through the character Dybbuk, an artificial intelligence who was created to serve as a member of Israel's team of superheroes. Dybbuk's superpower was the ability to control any computer, or machine that was run by a computer, by "attaching" itself to the machine in the manner of a *dybbuk* possessing a body.

Modern literary adaptations include Michelene Wandor's *Guests in the Body* (1986), a work that features interlinked stories about the exploits of *dybbukim*, and Ellen Galford's 1998 novel, *The Dyke and the Dybbuk*, which queers the equation with a lesbian possession set in New York City during and after the Stonewall riots, and then in early 1980s Britain. Finally, a novella called *The Dybbuk in Love* by Sonya Taaffe appeared in 2007. Each of these fictional approaches draws on the melodrama and plays off the sexual tension and frisson of danger in which the *topos* of spirit possession tends to be steeped, accomplishing on the more localized scale of Jewish mythology what the various **vampire** novels of the last 20 years have achieved in adapting the ancient and medieval topos of the vampire lover for the postmodern age.

Marc Michael Epstein

References and Suggested Reading

Chajes, J.H. *Between Worlds: Dybbuks, Exorcists, and Early Modern Judaism.* Philadelphia: University of Pennsylvania Press, 2003.

Goldish, Matt, ed. *Spirit Possession in Judaism: Cases and Contexts from the Middle Ages to the Present.* Detroit, MI: Wayne State University Press, 2003.

Neugroschel, Joachim, and S. An-sky. *The Dybbuk and the Yiddish Imagination: A Haunted Reader.* 1st edn. Syracuse, NY: Syracuse University Press, 2000.

ECHIDNA—*see* Cerberus; Chimera

ELEMENTAL

An elemental is a magical spirit, being, or **demon** that inhabits one of the four natural elements: water, fire, air, or earth. It can manifest on its own or be summoned and manipulated by elemental masters, also called benders or weavers.

The first extensive account of elementals is provided by the sixteenth-century Swiss-German alchemist Philipus Aureolus Theophrastu Bombastus von Hohenheim (1493–1541), known as Paracelsus. In his treatise, *De Nymphis, Sylphis, Pygmaeis et Salamandris* (c. 1566), Paracelsus identifies four kinds of beings, or *ding*: pygmies (also called *gnomi*), nymphs (*udina*), sylphs (*sylvestres*), and salamanders (*vulcani*). Each type of ding inhabits its *chaos*—that is, the element to which it is attuned. According to Paracelsus, ding are not spirits; while not endowed with souls, they are at least partly corporeal, resembling people both in outer appearance and in their propensity for hunger and disease (hence Paracelsus's tendency to call ding mountain, water, air, and fire people).

Paracelsus's ideas about elementals were much later developed by the Canadian writer and mystic Manly P. Hall (1901–90).

In *The Secret Teachings of All Ages* (1928), Hall adapts and broadens Paracelsus's terminology and provides details concerning the elementals' typology and alleged appearance and habits. Thus, as maintained by Hall, earth elementals (gnomes) include pygmies who work with stones and metals, as well as tree and forest spirits such as **satyrs**, **pans** or dryads. Gnomes can change their size and stature and are generally considered malicious, distrustful, and secretive. Described as more anthropomorphous than gnomes, undines are friendly but highly temperamental. Grouping them according to the types of water that they inhabit, Hall enumerates, among others, fountain nymphs, wave oceanids, stream naiads, nereides, mountain oreades, limoniades, and **mermaids**. Sylphs and female slyphids are what Hall calls "elemental nomads" (297). Although they reside in the clouds and near mountain tops, they are born wind wanderers. In disposition they are like the wind—joyful and capricious. Salamanders are approximately foot-long, glowing lizard-shaped creatures curling in the flames. Other fire elementals include flaming **giants** and globe-like *acthnici*—known to sailors as St Elmo's fire.

Numerous references to the traditional tetrad of elementals appear in the fiction of Algernon Blackwood (1869–1951). Calling elementals "the active force[s] behind the elements" (127), Blackwood describes them as impersonal, but susceptible to outside manipulation. This image corresponds with the views of the occultist Aleister Crowley (1875–1947) who, in *Moonchild* (1917), depicts elementals as imperfect beings, which unlike souls are just "illusions, things merely three-dimensional, with no core of substance in themselves" (141). Purely amorphous and non-animate representations of elementals are, however, fairly rare. Among them are fire beings that take the form of mindless thunderbolts in Roger Zelazny's *Lord of Light* (1967) and the floating radiant orbs (translucent or opaque) from Joseph Delaney's *The Spook's Sacrifice* (2009). Delaney also mentions fully shaped lizard-like salamanders and *asteri*, five-armed fire elementals that resemble burning sea stars.

In Robert A. Heinlein's "Magic, Inc." (1940), elementals take the concrete shapes of undines, salamanders, and gnomes, yet they remain little more than simple forces of destruction. Quite frequently, however, elementals in fiction exhibit rather high levels of sentience and cognition. Gaining temporary independence from its energy matrix, the salamander in Poul Anderson's *Operation Chaos* (1971) is not only consciously intent on gaining maximum strength but also able to speak. Communicative skills among non-anthropomorphic elementals also appear in Jo Clayton's "The Immortals" tetralogy (1992–96) and Diane Duane's *The Door into Fire* (1979). Unlike water elementals, which feature mainly as delicate beings poking their heads above the surface, earth elementals in Clayton's *Wildfire* (1992) engage in direct non-linguistic communication, interacting with those they serve through a succession of silent gestalts. Enraged, they take the form of shapeless gray serpents whose roars, although silent, reverberate nonetheless not in human ears but minds. Duane's *The Door into Fire*, on the other hand, introduces Sunspark, a fire elemental in the shape of a blood-colored horse with golden mane and tail—a fully cognizant being, which communicates through silent "bespeaking."

Elementals' complexity or bearing on the plot often increases together with their level of anthropomorphization and their divergence from the traditional tetrad. In Bradley P. Beaulieu's (1968–) *The Winds of Khalakovo* (2011), spirits called *hezhan* relate to five distinct elements—*surra* (fire), *jala* (water), *hava* (wind), *vana* (earth) and *dhosha* (stuff of life). Hezhan are "spirits from beyond the aether" which appear of their own volition or are summoned by the Aramahn people. Masters of the hezhan are known as *qiram*—hence a vanahezhan is controlled by a vanaqiram, a dhoshahezhan by a dhosaqiram, and so on. The forms of hezhan vary from amorphous (water whirlpool, vortex of air and mist) to vaguely humanoid (slender fire figure, wide child-like pool of water, massive gray rock beast with two legs, four arms, and a glittering dark torso). In Tanya Huff's (1957–) *Sing the Four Quartets* (1994), elemental spirits are called *kigh*. Summoned or "sang" by the bards of Shkodar, who use music to lure and control them, kigh are rather small and rarely of discernible shape. Yet some of them, especially water kigh, though lustrous and translucent, appear fairly human-seeming. In Diana Wynne Jones's (1934–2011) *Howl's Moving Castle* (1986), a fire elemental, or **demon** as it calls itself, appears as a face in the hearth, to which it is bound by a magic contract. Similar although much more menacing elemental manifestation features in Pittacus Lore's *I Am Number Four* (2010), where one of the Lorien children seems to awaken a sort of all-encompassing weather elemental, which takes the form of an old, bearded face twisted in wrath and malice, and materializing in the sky. Jim Butcher's (1971–) "Codex Alera" series focuses, on the other hand, on people skilled in *furycrafting*, that is, drawing power from, forming bonds with, and "manifesting" six types of elementals (**furies**): those of earth, water, wind, fire, wood and metal. While the majority of furies are shapeless, one of the supreme ones, Alera, who combines the properties of different elements, assumes the shape of a young woman. Similarly, in Phyllis Eisenstein's (1946–) *The Crystal Palace* (1988), a fire demon, Gildrum, shapeshifts from a ball of fire into a full-grown young man; and in *The Chronicles of Riddick* (2004), the humanoid envoy Aereon, played by Judi Dench, is presented as an elderly gray-haired woman who dissolves into and glides through air. In *The Red Hawk* (1984), Elizabeth A. Lynn (1946–) introduces five air elementals, each of which controls one type of wind. Whereas south wind is governed by a red-maned horse, four remaining elementals are clearly anthropomorphic: a golden cherub (east wind), a demon-like boy with green eyes (west wind), a pale warrior (north wind), and a clawed, winged man (wind of the heights). Also humanoid are the sea **troll** Tethis and *gnolls* in Terry Pratchet's (1948–) novels *Colour of Magic* (1983) and *Jingo* (1997). Whereas the blue-colored and slightly phosphorescent Tethis resembles an old but rather pleasant-looking man, soil elementals, gnolls, look like somewhat disfigured people with rubbish and compost attached to their back.

Variations on the traditional Paracelsian elementals include beings derived from different natural formations and phenomena, as well as elemental materializations of certain abstract concepts and ideas. In *Changeling Earth* (1973), Fred Saberhagen (1930–2007) introduces sand, desert, prairie, and forest elementals (pathmakers). Most novel of the four are the penultimate ones, whose characteristics include tangled grass, recurrent gusts of wind, dreariness, and the tendency to expand the distance between the travelers and their destination. A whole array of elementals also appears in China Miéville's (1972–) "New Crobuzon" novels, *Perdido Street Station* (2000), *The Scar* (2002), and *Iron Council* (2004). Undines (or undine familiars) resemble waves and water pillars, and are usually controlled and used as a form of live moisturizer by the aquatic people *vodyanoi*. Still, the majority of Miéville's elementals serve as weapons and are called and unleashed by a group of thaumaturges, called *elementarii*. Among them are: *fulmen* (lightning), *shunders* (stone), *luftgeists* (air), dog- and ape-shaped *yags* (fire), a whole group of wood, metal, concrete, and glass elementals, as well as *proasmae* and *fegkarions* (the former being skinless, amoeboid flesh elementals born from inside corpses and capable of adopting almost human, child-like shapes; the latter known as moon elementals, beast-like, phosphorous and shape-changing). Diverging even further from the traditional four, Miéville also mentions the elementals of history, beings whose elemental standing remains open to debate. Finally, in *The Traveller in Black* (1971), John K.H. Brunner (1934–95) introduces elementals of oblivion (Laprivan of the Yellow Eyes) and repetitive deceit (Farchgrind), known as the fellow-natures of a supreme spirit called the One.

Examples of worldly or earthbound supernatural imagery, elementals feature almost exclusively in fantasy and horror. Oriental undertones in most of their names point toward their being more at home in exotic, foreign locations, rather than in technology-oriented Western culture characterized by a general alienation from the natural world.

Julia Nikiel

References and Suggested Reading

Beaulieu, Bradley P. *The Winds of Khalakovo*. San Francisco: Night Shade Books, 2011.

Blackwood, Algernon. "Nemesis of Fire." In *Three John Silence Stories*. Boston: IndyPublish.com, 2010.

Crowley, Aleister. *Moonchild*. York Beach: Samuel Weiser, Inc., 2000.

Hall, Manly P. *The Secret Teachings of All Ages*. Radford: Wilder Publications, 2009.

Sigerest, Henry, ed. *Four Treatises of Theophrastus Von Hohenheim Called Paracelsus*. Baltimore: The Johns Hopkins University Press, 1996.

EMIM—*see* Giant

ELF

The word *elf* comes from Common Germanic, the ancestor language of English, German, and the Scandinavian languages. Our earliest solid evidence for beliefs about elves comes from the second half of the first millennium CE, in texts written by churchmen in Germanic languages. Narratives featuring elves as protagonists are few, however, until the early modern period: in medieval texts, elves most often appear in passing, often as potential causes of illness, in prayers and medical texts. Even in the rich traditional poetry of medieval Iceland, elves mostly appear fleetingly, in poetic formulas as companions of the Æsir (the pagan gods), or in metaphors for male warriors.

Throughout recorded history, elves have often been linked with the **demons** of Judaeo-Christian-Mediterranean tradition (alongside the similarly unpleasant figure of the mare, female supernatural beings who crush people in their sleep). The Old English poem *Beowulf* lists elves among the **monstrous races** springing from Cain's murder of Abel; the late thirteenth-century *South English Legendary* explains elves as **angels** that sided neither with Lucifer (see **Devil, The**) nor with God, and were banished by God to Earth rather than Hell; while in the late fourteenth-century *Wife of Bath's Tale*, Geoffrey Chaucer equates male elves with **incubi**. Seeking traditions uninfluenced by Christianity, nineteenth-century scholars looked to the *Prose Edda*, an early thirteenth-century mythography by the Icelander Snorri Sturluson. Snorri wrote of *ljósálfar* ("light elves") living in the heavens and *døkkálfar* ("dark elves") living under the earth, and scholars interpreted these as evidence for elves as pre-Christian deities of the sun, fertility, and/or death. However, it is clear that Snorri's elves are at least partly based on angels and demons, and need not reflect pre-Christian traditions. During the early modern period, confessions of dealing with elves were often taken in Scottish witchcraft trials as evidence of dealings with the Devil (see **Witch/Wizard**), and efforts to fit elves into Christian worldviews sometimes led to theological treatises, as in the Icelandic *Tíðfordrif* (1644) by Jón Guðmundsson lærði and, in Scotland, Robert Kirk's *Secret Commonwealth of Elves, Fauns and Fairies* (1691).

However, in Britain and Scandinavia, there is extensive evidence for alternative traditions in which elves were essentially people, a distinct ethnic group living alongside human communities, similar to the *fatae* ("fates") mentioned in some medieval Latin texts, French *fées* ("**fairies**," a term derived from *fatae*), and the Irish *áes síde*. This may represent a pre-Christian tradition general to Western European cultures. The earliest hint of elves' human-like character comes in personal names: the word *elf* is used in names (for example, the Gothic *Alboin*, etymologically "elf-friend") where words for monsters are not. In Old English, the plural *ælfe* ("elves") is grammatically an ethnonym. In the second half of the twentieth century, most scholars imagined that elves in the Anglo-Saxon tradition were small, invisible, demonic beings, causing illness with arrows (which the scholars, but not the texts, labeled "elf-shot"). But there is no actual evidence for any of this, and it is more likely that Anglo-Saxon elves were like people. Certainly, elves appear as human-like neighbors in early modern Scottish evidence and in nineteenth-century Scandinavian folklore (where they also appear under names such as the Icelandic *huldufólk*—"hidden people"). Indeed, stories told about elves in nineteenth-century Denmark were later transferred to other ethnic groups such as Greenlanders and Turkish immigrants.

Where elves appear in narratives, they often threaten people, either by causing illness or by seduction/sexual aggression—but out of personal motivation rather than because of a malignant disposition towards humanity in general. Debate is ongoing as to whether the group of Norse gods labeled by Snorri Sturluson as *Vanir* are the same as the *álfar*; if so, then the god Freyr may have been an elf. Otherwise, the earliest narrative that fairly certainly features an elf as a protagonist is the Old Norse poem *Vǫlundarkviða* ("the poem of Vǫlundr"), first attested in the late thirteenth century but probably older. Vǫlundr lives outside the normal human community, but is abducted into it. He avenges his imprisonment by seducing and/or raping his abductor's daughter before magically escaping. Elves are certainly viewed as seductive outsiders in the *South English Legendary* and the fourteenth-century Icelandic poem *Gullkársljóð*. This conception continues in ballads attested from the early modern period, most influentially the Scandinavian tradition known as "Sir Olaf and the Elves," in which Sir Olaf rebuffs the advances of an elf-maid and, on granting her one kiss, is stabbed by her to the heart, subsequently dying. This story was popular among Romantic thinkers, inspiring Johann Gottfried von Herder's poem *Erlkönigs Tochter* (1778) and through it Goethe's celebrated *Der Erlkönig* (1782). Most English-language equivalents of "Sir Olaf" feature a **mermaid** instead of an elf, but elves do appear in other ballads, for example, the Scottish ballad *Tam Lin*, which dates back at least to the sixteenth century. Folktales collected in the nineteenth and twentieth centuries, particularly in Scandinavia, continue the seduction narratives, though many other narratives also appear, including benevolent deeds by elves; the tale "midwife to the fairies," in which people are brought temporarily into the elves' world to deliver difficult births; and stories of changelings, in which elves abduct healthy human children, replacing them with old or malformed beings. Hints of most such narratives are present in medieval texts, but seldom do the narratives appear in full.

In European traditions, oral and literary, supernatural beings tended to diminish (in size and significance) from the sixteenth century onwards, reflecting a general reassessment of such traditions as superstitions and/or fantasies—a trend epitomized by Shakespeare's *A Midsummer Night's Dream* (c. 1590–96). By the nineteenth century in England, the word *elf* had largely been superseded by the French loan *fairy*, and was likewise being displaced in much of Scandinavia by terms/beings like the *nisse* (Denmark) and *tomte* (Sweden). Thus, the German folktale *Die Wichtelmänner* (where *Wichtel* means "little creature" and *Männer* "men"), first published by the Grimm Brothers in 1812, was translated by Margaret Hunt in 1884 as "The Elves and the Shoemaker." As American Christmas traditions crystallized in the nineteenth century, the anonymous 1823 poem "A Visit from St Nicholas" (widely known as "'Twas the Night before Christmas") characterized St Nicholas himself as "a right jolly old elf" (line 45), but it was the little helpers that were later attributed to him to whom the name stuck. This development seems to have prompted the unfounded scholarly assumption that Anglo-Saxon elves were small, demonic sprites.

However, the term *elf* and its cognates were given a new lease of life by early twentieth-century fantasy writers, who made elves a stock genre feature. Leading figures here were Lord Dunsany in his 1924 *The King of Elfland's Daughter* and J.R.R. Tolkien, most importantly in his *The Lord of the Rings*, published in 1954–55 (see **Tolkien, Monsters In**). Both drew on nineteenth-century folklore and Romantic texts like von Herder's *Erlkönigs Tochter*; Tolkien's work in particular also shows a deep indebtedness and sensitivity to medieval traditions. In these texts and much of the fantasy literature they inspired, elves are once more human-like in form and size, enjoying superior wisdom, immortality, and an aloofness from human affairs. Translations of *The Lord of the Rings* into other Germanic languages in turn used *elf*'s old cognates. Drawing on Snorri Sturluson, Tolkien distinguished between "light elves" and "dark elves," but attached no moral significance to the terms; however, many subsequent fantasy writers present a distinction between races of good and bad elves in these terms. In works where elves are the main characters, such as Tolkien's *The Silmarillion* (published posthumously in 1977) or Wendy and Richard Pini's comic book series *Elfquest*, published from 1978 to 2007, elves exhibit a similar range of behavior to a human cast, distinguished largely by their superhuman physical powers. However, where narratives are more human-centered, elves sustain their role as powerful, sometimes threatening, outsiders. Later fantasy literature has continued to draw on a diverse range of earlier images of elves, as with J.K. Rowling's use of the *Wichtelmänner* as inspiration for her "house-elves" in the "Harry Potter" series (see **Harry Potter, Monsters In**).

Narratives indicate that elves have always had a role in constructing norms of sexual propriety, right up to Tolkien's Galadriel and the sexually liberated world of *Elfquest*. Older texts also suggest a role in probing gender norms more generally: male elves do not always seem to behave in very "manly" ways. This is arguably true of Vǫlundr; Anglo-Saxon elves are associated with *siden*, apparently a kind of magic that, in its Norse guise as *seiðr*, was particularly opprobrious for men to perform; Chaucer's self-portrait in the prologue to the *Tale of Sir Thopas* in *The Canterbury Tales* (1387) characterizes him both as "elvish" and a cuddly "popet" ("doll"). Meanwhile, later narratives give elves a role in demarcating normal people's religious identity, and constructing threats to reproduction.

Alaric Hall

References and Suggested Reading

Alver, Bente Gullveig, and Torunn Selberg. "Folk Medicine as Part of a Larger Concept Complex." *Arv* 43 (1987): 21–44.

Hall, Alaric. *Elves in Anglo-Saxon England: Matters of Belief, Health, Gender and Identity: Anglo-Saxon Studies*. Woodbridge: Boydell, 2007.

Jonsson, Bengt R. "Sir Olav and the Elves: The Position of the Scandinavian Version." *Arv* 48 (1992): 65–90.

Purkiss, Diane. *Troublesome Things: A History of Fairies and Fairy Stories.* Harmondsworth: Penguin, 2000.

Tangherlini, Timothy R. "From Trolls to Turks: Continuity and Change in Danish Legend Tradition." *Scandinavian Studies* 67 (1995): 32–62.

Wade, James. *Fairies in Medieval Romance.* Basingstoke: Palgrave Macmillan, 2011.

EMPOUSA

The empousa was a creature in ancient Greek folklore responsible for killing children. Empousae were believed to be the spirits of women who had died childless and who wanted to harm infants out of revenge or spite. The Greeks believed in several types of child-killing monsters; in addition to empousae, the stories speak of **lamia**, a child-eating **demon**; gello, a female demon or revenant that causes infant mortality and infertility; and mormo (or mormolyke), a spirit who bit bad children. There was often conceptual overlap, with the empousa being considered a type of lamia or, more frequently, vice versa: the empousa, for example, like the lamia, was known not only for killing children but also for seducing and eating young men. Empousa folklore eventually spread throughout the Roman Empire.

The infant mortality rate in antiquity was quite high, so mothers felt a terrible anxiety over the lives of their children. Parents often hung amulets meant to protect against empousae. At the same time, mothers and nurses would often discipline children by threatening that an empousa would take them away if they did not behave. These largely female concerns are often dismissed as mere superstition in the surviving Greek and Roman literature, as by Plato in his late fifth-century or early fourth-century BCE *Crito* (46C). Even so, the Greeks imagined the physical appearance of an empousa in various ways. One of the earliest surviving descriptions of an empousa appears in *Frogs*, by the fifth-century BCE comic playwright Aristophanes. In this play, the god Dionysus and his servant Xanthias, traveling to the Underworld, suddenly see a "huge beast" that shape-shifts into an ox, a mule, a dog, and a lovely woman with a face blazing as if on fire. She has one leg of bronze. "This is surely Empousa!" cries Dionysus (289–94). The second-century CE satirist Lucian, in his *True Histories* (2.46), describes a race of donkey-legged women that seems intentionally based on the legends of the lamia and empousa (Georgiadou and Larmour, 229). These beautiful women, wearing tunics that reach the ground, welcome travelers seductively. But one traveler notices that an alarming number of human bones and skulls are lying around on the ground, and then he sees that his hostess has "the legs not of a woman but of an ass!" She admits that they get men drunk and then eat them as they sleep. This race of women is called the Onoskeles ("ass-legs"), and Onoskelis was also the name of an empousa (Georgiadou and Larmour, 230).

Given that both Aristophanes and Lucian are satirists, they may have been exaggerating the empousa's characteristics as a way to mock superstitious beliefs. Thus, the tenth-century Byzantine encyclopedia known as the *Suda*, though not a major literary text, is nevertheless an important source of information for the empousa because its author had access to a vast body of literature that is lost to us. Its entry on "Empousa" describes her as a monstrous attendant of the Greek goddess Hecate, but makes no mention of empousa as a threat to infants.

In modern literature, two empousae take the form of cheerleaders intent upon killing Percy Jackson in Rick Riordan's *The Battle of the Labyrinth* (2008); in *The Last Olympians* (2009), the empousa, though seductive, is less threatening. Empusa is the main antagonist in the novel *Grecian Rune* by James Matthew Byers (2004). Neil Gaiman's novel *Stardust* (1998) includes three unnamed **witches** who, in the 2007 film version (Matthew Vaughn), are called Empusa, Mormo, and Lamia.

Bradley Skene

References and Suggested Reading

Georgiadou, Aristoula, and H.J. Larmour. *Lucian's Science Fiction Novel True Histories: Interpretation and Commentary*. Leiden: Brill, 1998.

Johnston, Sarah Iles. "Defining the Dreadful: Remarks on the Greek Child-Killing Demon." In *Ancient Magic and Ritual Power*, edited by Marvin Meyer and Paul Mirecki, 361–87. Leiden: Brill, 2001.

ENCANTADO—*see* ShapeShifter

ENT—*see* Tolkien, Monsters in

EPHIALTES—*see* Dante, Monsters In

ESHU—*see* Demon

EVIL OTTO—*see* Video Games, Monsters In

EXTRATERRESTRIAL

Fig. 12 ***Illuminator on Aix*** **by John Adastra**

Creatures from other planets have been widely used as monsters in literature and film throughout the twentieth and twenty-first centuries. As the ultimate foreigner, extraterrestrials come in many different varieties and from a host of different places, including moons, planets, black holes, parallel universes, and alternate dimensions. Unlike other monsters such as **vampires**, **ghosts**, and **sea monsters**, extraterrestrials are hindered by very few generic rules. They can be microscopic or immense, humanoid or non-humanoid, or even entirely devoid of corporeal bodies. They can communicate through speech or different modes. Their social and biological development may approximate that of human beings or be radically different, depending upon their creator's vision. While the extraterrestrials in world literature and film originate in the human imagination, speculation persists that varying sorts may exist on other planets.

The increasing use of extraterrestrials in fictional narratives stems in large part from several interwoven elements of the twentieth century. Though humans had always looked to the sky for meaning and inspiration, it was the twentieth century that took humanity from the airship of the 1800s to airplanes in the early 1900s, to spacecraft in the 1950s, and to human space-travel in the 1960s. These developments were increasingly linked with advances in a range of astronomically related sciences. All of this pushed to the forefront questions about humankind's place in the universe and the potential for the existence of non-terrestrial intelligent species. Many extraterrestrial narratives address the theoretical and hypothetical questions about how first contact and interstellar relations with an alien species might manifest.

Coupled with a better understanding of the larger universe was the rise of mysterious or indeterminate phenomena that left many wondering if humans are truly alone. Incidents such as the purported crashing of an unidentified flying object (UFO) at Roswell, New Mexico in 1947 raised questions for, and sparked the imagination of, many creators through the twentieth century. Unexplained crop circles (and their hoaxes) increased attention toward atmospheric phenomena such as meteorites. Substantive evidence of potential life-yielding planets encouraged many to think about and project a galaxy filled with other life forms.

Twentieth- and twenty-first-century human rights movements also arguably have contributed to the increase of narratives about extraterrestrials. Such narratives allow for a displaced discourse on cultural otherness. The increasing popularity of such stories, particularly ones in which humans and aliens negotiate the same cultural spaces, speaks to the challenges of an increasingly globalized world in which individuals with different cultural backgrounds and belief systems confront the challenges of coexistence. In addition, the conceptualization of planet Earth as a closed system in which humans must find equilibrium with nature and natural forces also prompted speculation about how alien species from other planets would grapple with these demands or how humanity might colonize other planets in pursuit of more resources.

Though some narratives featuring extraterrestrials predate H.G. Wells's *War of the Worlds* (1897)—such as *L'Autre Monde: où les États et Empires de la Lune* (*The Other World: The States and Empires of the Moon*, 1657) by Cyrano de Bergerac, and "The Unparalleled Adventure of One Hans Pfaall" (1835) by Edgar Allan Poe—Wells's novel serves as a touchstone text for many extraterrestrial narratives, particularly those premised upon invasion and post-invasion themes. The novel features an unnamed narrator who retells the story of an invasion from Mars by a series of spaceships carrying Martians, who attack humans through a variety of means including mechanical tripods, heat rays, and poisonous black gas. The narrator recounts how the Martians ravaged London and other towns and cities. Though humans attempted to fight back, the British military (at the height of its power in the late nineteenth century) was ineffectual against the Martians. In the second half of the novel, the narrator details his movements through an England that can best be described as post-apocalyptic. In the end, the Martians are defeated not by man, but by bacteria, against which the Martians have no immunity.

This entry will address narratives of extraterrestrials in terms of four at times overlapping categories: narratives involving alien invasions and ensuing conflict; stories of first contact; "multicultural" tales of coexistence among humans and aliens; and humorous representations of aliens. What such accounts make clear is that, although extraterrestrials in fiction and film come from outer space, they nevertheless always stand in for very terrestrial issues and concerns. Some nations, most notably Russia, have developed distinctive science fiction traditions as a vehicle not only for terrestrial, but for coded political concerns. The Aesopian role played by Russian and Soviet science fiction will be discussed in a separate section.

Alien Invasion

Many narratives of extraterrestrials operate as allegories of human conflict in which aliens substitute for some human anxiety or concern. Difference from the human—which at least initially defines the alien—serves as a major source of tension and conflict in such narratives. As noted above, Wells's *The War of the Worlds* is the seminal narrative of extraterrestrial invasion and conflict—and addresses real-world anxieties concerning technology and the clash of cultures. The expectation of domination on the part of alien life forms with advanced technology reflects the history of colonization in which civilizations with more resources and advanced technology came to dominate other civilizations.

Wells's novel also serves as an example of invasion literature reflecting threats to a nation's perception of elevated cultural status. Often this threat manifests in the loss of the civilization's "true" people or by means of barbaric and foreign infiltrations and attacks. Beyond the physical and technological might of the Martians, the narrator discovers that the Martians had come to Earth to round up humans in order to feast on their blood, literally draining the British citizenry of its life-force. In the same year that Wells was serially publishing his novel (1897), Bram Stoker published ***Dracula***, a novel about an inhuman foreigner from the border between Europe and the Ottoman Empire who invades the heart of England also to feast on blood and to undermine the prestige of the British Empire. In both cases, the foreign power seeks to feed upon the rich resources and destroy the formidable power of the elite civilization; it is a theme repeated throughout the extraterrestrial invasion narrative.

The iconic status of Wells's novel is testified to by its unofficial sequels, radio productions, comic book adaptations, and repeated cinematic renderings (Bryon Haskin, 1953; Piotr Szulkin, 1981; Steven Spielberg, 2005). Among the most notable adaptations was the famous radio dramatization performed by the Mercury Theater and directed by Orson Welles on 30 October 1938. Welles repositioned the narrative to take place in New York and New Jersey, and spliced it together as a series of news accounts from reporters and witnesses. Welles's masterfully crafted production frightened a significant portion of the residents in the New Jersey and New York area into seeking confirmation of the alien invasion or even fleeing their homes.

Many subsequent narratives about aliens follow Wells's theme of direct confrontation between humans and extraterrestrials. Alex Raymond's comic strip, *Flash Gordon*, was launched in 1934. It continued as a comic strip in various runs from the 1930s to the early 2000s. The main story arc of protagonist Flash Gordon dealt with his being cast out into the stars to do battle with Ming the Merciless, evil ruler of Mongo, who had attacked and all but destroyed Earth. Flash Gordon proved an early and popular icon in the space-opera narrative. His popularity led to several films over the years, including three film serials—*Flash Gordon* (Frederick Stephani, 1936), *Flash Gordon's Trip to Mars* (Ford Beebe et al., 1938), and *Flash Gordon Conquers the Universe* (Ford Beebe and Tay Taylor, 1940); as well as several live-action and animated television shows, several books, and a campy 1980 remake (Mike Hodges).

Deriving influence from Wells, John Wyndham in his 1953 novel *The* ***Kraken*** *Wakes* presents alien spaceships landing in Earth's oceans and eventually directly attacking humans. Wyndham here uses the extraterrestrial invasion narrative to comment on 1950s politics, especially the Cold War between the Soviets and Americans. More optimistic concerning the possibilities of human co-operation, Harry Turtledove's "Worldwar" novels (1994–96) situate a massive alien invasion in the midst of World War II. Unlike Wyndham's novel, the different countries in Turtledove's novels are able to bind together to fight off the menace, and humanity eventually confronts the aliens on their home world.

Turtledove is not the only author to follow in the tradition of Flash Gordon, in which an attack on Earth is met with an intergalactic war and the eventual discovery of the alien's home world for confrontation. Robert Heinlein's *Starship Troopers* (1959) and its later film adaptation by Paul Verhoeven (1997) present an alien attack leading to a full-fledged military assault on the aliens' home world. Orson Scott Card's *Ender's Game* (1985) follows this tradition by taking the militaristic themes present in *Starship Troopers* and applying them to children as they work through battle school. Believing he is fighting against a simulation, Ender, the school's best student, unknowingly destroys the aliens' (known as the Formics) home world and, essentially, the entire species. In later books of the series, Ender pontificates upon the actions he has taken and if there could have been another way of mitigating the differences between humans and Formics. Greg Bear's *The Forge of God* (1987) and *Anvil of Stars* (1992) also follow this formula and present humankind as nearly wiped out by a forward fleet of machines sent to terraform Earth. The survivors seek out the home of the alien but, as in Orson Scott Card, their ensuing battle creates moral quandaries around the idea of actually destroying an entire alien race—particular in this instance in which destroying one race has a cascading effect, leading to the destruction of many other alien races.

Across the Pacific, Japan, too, regularly produced alien invasion films, including *The Mysterians* (Ishirô Honda, 1958). The story depicts an alien race demanding that Earth relinquish some territory. The humans resist and are forced to confront an overwhelming force. The idea of a foreign force demanding land usage when there is little land available had larger cultural implications in a country occupied by US forces. Other Japanese alien invasion films include *Battle in Outer Space* (Ishirô Honda, 1960), *Invasion of the Neptune Men* (Koji Ota, 1961), and *Gamera vs. Viras* (Noriaki Yuasa, 1968).

One of Japan's most popular science fiction film franchises also pitted super-powered aliens against one of its own super-powered beings. In transforming **Godzilla**, the giant lizard who breathes atomic rays, from villain to protagonist, the franchise relied upon the introduction of several alien races and monsters against which Godzilla focuses his violence in lieu of humans. Starting with *Ghidorah, the Three-Headed Monster* (Ishirô Honda, 1964), Godzilla faced off against a series of monsters from other planets—including Ghidorah, a three-headed space-dragon; Hedorah, an alien smog-monster (Yoshimitsu Banno's *Godzilla vs. Hedorah*, 1971); and Mechagodzilla, an alien-created robot version of Godzilla (Jun Fukuda's *Godzilla vs. Mechagodzilla*, 1974)—to protect Earth. Alien races and monsters attacking Earth would continue to feature prominently in Godzilla films through the rest of the series, including the last film, Ryuhei Kitamura's *Godzilla: Final Wars* (2004).

Recent films such as *Independence Day* (Roland Emmerich, 1996), *Signs* (M. Night Shyamalan, 2002), *Cloverfield* (Matt Reeves, 2008), *Skyline* (Colin Strause and Greg Strause, 2010), and *Battle Los Angeles* (Jonathan Liebesman, 2011) further develop the cinematic history of alien invasions resulting in battles with humankind. Renewed interest in this plot line coincided with the development of more sophisticated special effects. A heightened tension around illegal immigration ("illegal aliens") in the last 30 years in the United States and elsewhere, however, has also influenced the cultural prominence of these invasion narratives.

Alien Infiltration

While massive alien invasions often make for spectacular storytelling, a significant number of alien invasion narratives do not operate on the epic scale of Wells's tradition, but instead follow a pattern of discovery as the aliens to some degree covertly invade the Earth. The aliens often attempt to take over the Earth by infecting humans, mutating humans to meet alien needs, or "passing" as humans. In such narratives, an individual or group of humans becomes aware of the alien invasion and looks to stop it or expose it. Often, the discoverers will not be believed by their society until it is almost too late.

John W. Campbell's *Who Goes There?* a novella published in the magazine *Astounding Science Fiction* in 1938, is a prime example of what one may refer to as the "alien infiltration narrative." The story follows a group of scientists at an Antarctic base as they uncover an alien spaceship and defrost an alien species. The adaptive nature of the alien allows it, after killing and absorbing a being, to morph into it and mimic that being's thoughts and actions. Any time a piece of the alien (for example, body parts or blood) is separated, it develops its own consciousness and sense of self-preservation (see **Body Parts**). Slowly, the alien takes over a large portion of the crew before the leader, McReady, devises and executes a plan to expose the alien. The narrative, as suggested by its title, is driven by the fear and paranoia of a closed system (Antarctica or Earth) with things that look like humans but differ in some significant way; the ubiquity of this theme in mid-twentieth-century America reflected the Cold War mentality and anxieties about the infiltration of communist ideas. Campbell's novella has spawned three related films: Howard Hawkes's *The Thing from Another World* (1951), John Carpenter's *The Thing* (1982), and Matthijs van Heijningen Jr's prequel to Carpenter's film, *The Thing* (2011).

The rise of the "Red Scare" and McCarthyism in American society in the 1950s generated a host of alien invasion narratives in which aliens slowly take over human society. Three significant narratives, all of which have been repeatedly adapted over the last 60 years, that invoke the communist threat (and later, terrorist threat) are the film *Invaders from Mars* (William Cameron Menzies, 1953), the 1954 novel *The Body Snatchers* by Jack Finney, and the 1956 novel *The Midwich Cuckoos* by John Wyndham. In all three, aliens attack not just the city, but penetrate suburbia and the countryside as well. *Invaders from Mars* tells the story of a boy, David (Jimmy Hunt), who discovers that Martians have crashed and are bringing humans into their spaceship and changing them from their normal selves. Adapted numerous times into film (1956 and 1978 as *Invasion of the Body Snatchers* [Don Siegel and Philip Kaufman respectively], 1993 as *Body-Snatchers* [Abel Ferrara], and 2007 as *The Invasion* [Oliver Hirschbiegel]), *The Body Snatchers* focuses on Miles and a small cohort within his town as they uncover humans being replaced by aliens who must morph into the humans they are replacing. This is the origin of the famous "pod people" reference throughout science fiction as the aliens are initially faceless beings that must develop into humans. Also regularly adapted (1960 as *The Village of the Damned* [Wolf Rilla], a sequel film *Children of the Damned* in 1963 [Anton Leader], and a remake of *Village of the Damned* by John Carpenter in 1995), *The Midwich Cuckoos* explores the concept of an alien changeling. Nine months after the appearance of an unidentified object, scores of women in a British village give birth at the same time to boys and girls who eventually have golden hair and eyes, and supernatural abilities such as group telepathy.

Evoking a sense of paranoia similar to that of *Invasion of the Body Snatchers* is Robert Heinlein's 1951 novel *The Puppet Masters* (and its cinematic adaptation by Stuart Orme, 1994). Within the narrative, Heinlein explicitly compares the mind-controlling parasitic aliens (see **Parasite**) that invade Earth to Soviet communists. These aliens take the form of slugs that attach to the back of human necks in order to control their minds. Many other narratives, including the British film *Quatermass 2* (1957), follow this idea of alien contamination. An inverse to the parasitic alien is present in ***The Blob*** (1958). In this film, an amoeboid "blob" from outer space terrorizes the small town of Phoenixville, Pennsylvania, seeking to absorb everyone it encounters.

In 1988, director John Carpenter returned to the theme of an alien infiltration in *They Live*. In the film, a nameless drifter (referred to as Nada [Roddy Piper]) dons a pair of black sunglasses that reveal many humans to be aliens in disguise, slowly taking over the Earth. Nada bands together with other humans who have realized the infiltration to fight the aliens by destroying the signal that generates their disguises. In the documentary, *Nightmares in Red, White and Blue: The Evolution of the American Horror Film* (Andrew Monument, 2009), Carpenter explains that *They Live* is a critique of 1980s consumer culture and, in particular, of the particular political ideals valued under President Ronald Reagan. David Twohy's 1996 film *The Arrival* follows a similar pattern of discovery and an attempt by a small group of humans to reveal alien disguises through broadcast media.

Another more local variant of the alien invasion narrative pits a person or a small group of humans against aliens. These narratives typically stick to a plot in which the aliens and humans are antagonistic toward each other and remain so until one group has been sufficiently subdued, exiled, or destroyed. However, in these narratives, the alien(s) is not a threat en masse to humanity. They are not harbingers of an ensuing invasion, but loners, exiles, or visiting of their own accord. Some of the aliens in such narratives are **shapeshifters** who kill human beings in order to occupy their bodies. These aliens are dangerous both in their murderous intent and in their ability to disguise themselves as human. In *The Hidden* (Jack Sholder, 1987), two FBI agents, Gallagher (Kyle MacLachlan) and Beck (Michael Nouri), are on the hunt for an alien who kills and occupies the bodies of humans and dogs alike. Gallagher turns out to be a shape-shifting alien seeking revenge against the alien who killed his family. Similarly, in *Dreamcatcher* (Lawrence Kasdan, 2003), based upon the 2001 Stephen King novel, aliens with the ability to occupy bodies wreak havoc upon four childhood friends on their annual hunting trip. When the group takes in a frostbitten man, a worm-like alien with razor sharp teeth exits the man's body. Later in the narrative, another alien referred to as "Mr Grey" is introduced. Although there is a military expedition seeking to quarantine anyone who has come into contact with the aliens, the aliens are really only concerned with this group of friends. They seek access to the friends' memories of Dudits (Donnie Wahlberg), a mentally challenged boy that the friends had protected when they were young and with whom they remain close. Dudits, it turns out, is actually an alien.

In *Predator* (John McTiernan, 1987), a large and imposing alien targets a military special operations team that is attempting to free hostages in Central America. The humanoid-looking creature possesses advanced technology, and has the ability to use thermal imaging and to camouflage itself. At the close of the film, the subdued alien pushes a self-destruct button on itself that triggers an explosion tantamount to a nuclear bomb. Little is revealed about the alien besides the fact that it operates as a hunter, seeking out trophies (as revealed in Stephen Hopkins's 1990 sequel, *Predator 2*). After acquiring the comic book rights for both the "Predator" and the "Alien" series, Dark Horse Comics generated a popular series of crossover comics in the 1990s that led to several video games and eventually two crossover films: *AVP: Alien vs. Predator* (Paul W.S. Anderson, 2004) and *AVPR: Alien vs. Predator: Requiem* (Colin Strause and Greg Strause, 2007).

Alien Abduction

Another classic theme of conflict within extraterrestrial narratives is the alien abduction story. In these tales, individual human beings or groups are taken by aliens, either temporarily or for longer durations, to be used for a variety of purposes including as test subjects, conscripted labor, food, and entertainment. In Anne McCaffrey's "Freedom" series of novels, human beings are taken from Earth and brought to a slave colony by aliens known as the Catteni. Beginning in the first book in the series, *Freedom's Landing* (1995), humans are herded like cattle into Catteni ships and then brought to slave colonies in outer space. When Kris Bjornsen and others attempt to organize an escape, they are exiled to an unnamed planet. What complicates this series is that the Catteni also exile aliens to this strange planet and, in order to survive, humans must work side by side with aliens who look just like the terrifying creatures who captured and enslaved them. The other three books in the series, *Freedom's Choice* (1997), *Freedom's Challenge* (1998), and *Freedom's Ransom* (2002), chronicle the transformation of this planet into a home that they name Botany and their struggles to defend this home at all costs.

In the film *Dark City* (1998), the Strangers are endangered extraterrestrial parasites who come to Earth to study human beings by bringing them onto their ship in a virtual space. These aliens share a collective consciousness and seek to analyze the individuality of human beings in order to save their race. At midnight of each evening, they put human beings into a comatose state to perform their experiments.

The 1990s saw an upsurge of alien abduction stories that were in part influenced by the success of the TV show *The X-Files* (1993–2002), which spawned a secondary TV series (*The Lone Gunmen*, 2001) and two films (*The X-Files*, Rob Bowman, 1998, and *The X-Files: I Want to Believe*, Chris Carter, 2008). The series followed two FBI agents, Mulder (David Duchovny) and Scully (Gillian Anderson), as they encountered strange cases. The series also included an ongoing story arc focusing on the alien abduction of Mulder's younger sister and the invasion of Earth by aliens. Films playing on the alien abduction theme include *Fire in the Sky* (Robert Lieberman, 1993), *Progeny* (Brian Yuzna, 1999), and *Night Skies* (Roy Knyrim, 2007). Building upon the popularity of the trope of "discovered footage" popularized in horror films like *The Blair Witch Project* (see **Blair Witch**), *Cloverfield*, and the "Paranormal Activity" series, Olatunde Osunsanmi's *The Fourth Kind* (2009) combines "recovered" video recordings of people discussing their alien abduction experiences with re-enacted scenes to piece together an "authentic" account.

Human Encroachment

Although many narratives featuring extraterrestrials focus on aliens invading Earth or human space, another variant presents humans encountering, encroaching, or invading alien habitats, homelands, and dimensions. Overwhelmingly, these tales still represent aliens as antagonistic and humans as innocent or justified in their actions. In such narratives, humans venture out into space and confront aliens or intentionally or unintentionally bring the extraterrestrial back to Earth. Here again, H.G. Wells provides a template for this form of human/alien encounter with his 1901 novel, *The First Men in the Moon*. This story depicts two humans visiting the Moon who are captured by the insectoid Selenites. They break free but only one returns to Earth, while the other remains stranded and finds peace with the alien race. Georges Méliès's French film, *Trip to the Moon* (1902), blended Wells's novel with Jules Verne's *From the Earth to the Moon* (1865) and provides the first cinematic rendering of hostile alien confrontation.

Among the most complex approaches to human colonization of other planets and encounters with aliens is Ray Bradbury's *The Martian Chronicles* (1950), a loosely connected group of short stories relating humans' exploration and colonization of Mars after greedy and selfish earthlings have devastated their own planet through atomic warfare. Published episodically in the late 1940s, these stories show the conflict between the colonizing earthlings and Mars's original inhabitants. For instance, in the critically acclaimed "Mars is Heaven" (1948), Captain John Black and his men arrive on Mars in the year 1960, but are told by the inhabitants that they are in 1926 Illinois. As the men begin to encounter deceased relatives, they question whether Mars is some kind of heaven or if this is an alien mind control trick. The latter is shown to be true, as alien tricksters, who have the ability to morph into images of loved ones, murder all of the invading men. Bradbury's *Chronicles* engages in an imaginative and sophisticated way with the colonization and eradication of Native Americans in the new world by European settlers.

Other narratives dealing with humans encountering aliens on other planets are critical of the method or assumptions of colonization. In "A Martian Odyssey" by Stanley G. Weinbaum (1934), the space explorer Jarvis is rescued by the friendly Martian Tweel. Tweel, an archetype for the friendly alien in science fiction, proves himself to be both an intelligent creature and loyal friend. Tweel teaches Jarvis many things about Mars, and Jarvis repays his kindness by absconding back to Earth with a crystal that might have healing powers. In Lisa Tuttle's "Wives" (1979), men from Earth fight a war on another planet and force the native species to become their wives. These wives are neither male nor female, but must wear "skintights," and dress and act like 1970s housewives. When one of the native aliens, Susie, tries to rebel against the men, the other wives have no choice but to eat her. This story critiques androcentricism and reflects the heightened awareness of gender politics in the 1970s.

More militant and action-packed is Ridley Scott's "Alien" series (1979–2007), which served as a major influence on the development of the alien confrontation tale and spawned a franchise of comics, video games, and books. The initial 1979 offering follows a crew in stasis, awoken when their spaceship is contacted by a nearby planet. When they venture out to find the source, a crew member is attacked and the crew unwittingly brings an incubating alien on board. After famously exploding from the chest of its host, the alien quickly works its way through the humans until only Ripley (Sigourney Weaver) remains, who manages to fend off the alien before escaping. The film's mix of genuine horror and substantive science made it a hallmark of the extraterrestrial narrative.

Confrontation narratives of Earth's expansion into the universe and encounter with alien life repeatedly brings to the forefront questions of historical colonization. Though not explicit in the initial film, the television series derived from the film *Stargate* (Roland Emmerich, 1994) certainly raised such questions repeatedly. As recently as James Cameron's *Avatar* (2009), the concern about how humans interact with aliens has been raised and, increasingly, colonizing humans are presented as antagonists rather than protagonists.

First Contact

First contact narratives differ from invasion narratives involving conflict in that they usually focus on an individual being (human or alien) or small group that encounters another individual, small group, or in some cases, society. Humans or aliens can sit on either side of this formula and, though there may be tension about the encounter, it is not necessarily antagonistic but an attempt for both human and alien to understand one another.

The context of where these encounters occur shapes the larger ramifications within the fictional universe that the narrative inhabits. When the encounter occurs on Earth, it is often a result of an alien purposely or accidentally arriving on Earth. The power imbalance is usually tipped in favor of the aliens since they are the ones with space-travel technology. The novella *Farewell to the Master* (1940) by Harry Bates, and its cinematic adaptation *The Day the Earth Stood Still* (Robert Wise, 1951; also remade in 2008 by Scott Derrickson), remains one of the most interesting first contact narratives. When an alien spaceship lands on Earth, a **robot** and humanoid alien emerge. Humankind's hostility and violence towards the alien almost kills it and, before it departs, it warns humanity that other alien life is watching and judging Earth for its propensity for violence, coupled with its increasing technology. Clifford Simak's novel *Way Station* (1963) also raises the question of Earth's place in the larger universe. After granting Enoch Wallace near immortality and the responsibility of guarding an alien transportation center on Earth, the government becomes increasingly suspicious of Wallace as time passes. The tactics by humankind towards Wallace and what they discover to be aliens leaves Earth's future in doubt.

In a similar vein, the 3D *It Came From Outer Space* (Jack Arnold, 1953) depicts aliens crashing to Earth and, though benign, manipulating the local population long enough to distract them while making the necessary repairs. Despite the aliens' harmless intentions, their superior abilities still make them menacing. Sir Fred Hoyle's novel *The Black Cloud* (1957) illustrates benign aliens unknowingly causing harm to humankind. A sentient space-cloud encircles the sun, resulting in climatic disruption on Earth. Only after the world's leading scientists learn that it is sentient and communicate with it does the cloud move on, beginning the process of recovery for Earth.

Other narratives use aliens as a superficial plot device akin to the monster in the cave or woods scenario when characters set off into the unknown. *Rocketship X-M* (Kurt Neumann, 1950) is an early example of this subgenre wherein humans set off into space, crash on Mars, and encounter hostile, though primitive, Martians. They escape to Earth with little harm done.

First Contact and Gender

Gender politics can sometimes present an interesting twist in first contact narratives. Since women are themselves "Other" in a patriarchal society (see **Women, Monstrous**), they often do not oppose the alien Other. For instance, in James Tiptree, Jr's (pseudonym for Alice Sheldon) "The Women that Men Don't See" (1973), Ruth and Althea Parsons find life for women on Earth to be so grim that, when the plane they are on crashes in the Yucatan, they choose to leave their planet with aliens they know nothing about rather than remain in a patriarchal society. In another Tiptree short story, "With Delicate Mad Hands" (1981), CP is a female space pilot whose role is to take care of the emotional and sexual needs of the men on board. After being used and abused by all the human men she meets, she goes mad and spirals her ship towards the voice of a loving and accepting alien. The women in Carol Emshwiller's "The Start of the End of the World" (1981) are divorcees who help aliens take over the world because they are fed up with the men on Earth. They eventually tire, however, of the aliens' controlling ways and rebel against them too.

In Gwyneth Jones's "Aleutian" trilogy, alien invaders are warmly welcomed on Earth after gender-based riots. In the first novel, *White Queen* (1991), which is set in 2038, the existence of human beings on Earth has become so dire that when human-looking aliens arrive, they are welcomed as potential saviors. Much like the Gethenians of Ursula le Guin's *Left Hand of Darkness* (1969), however, the Aleutians are neither male nor female. The inability of Aleutians and humans to understand the gender identities (or lack thereof) of the opposing group leads to the heartbreak of the novel's protagonist, Johnny Guglioli, thereby prompting him to join a fringe group that is determined to uncover the aliens' true intentions. The other two books in the series, *North Wind* (1994) and *Phoenix Cafe* (1997), explore the increasing conflict between the humans and the Aleutians, but a full-blown confrontation is always avoided.

First Contact and Contagion

Another major theme within narratives representing first contact between human beings and alien species is that of infection and contagion. This fear reflects and inverts Wells's *deus ex machina* in which the aliens die of bacterial infection. One of the earlier renderings of this approach is Val Guest's film *The Quatermass Xperiment* (1955) in which an astronaut returns to Earth with a **virus** that risks infecting the rest of the planet. In Michael Crichton's novel *The Andromeda Strain* (1969) and its film adaptation (Robert Wise, 1971), extraterrestrial micro-organisms contaminate human blood, causing deadly clots in most and insanity in others. The irony is that these micro-organisms originated from a space satellite whose purpose was to collect micro-organisms to use as biological weapons.

Other narratives that premise extraterrestrial life as infection include *Space Master X-7* (Edward Bernds, 1958), and David Brin's short story, "The Giving Plague" (1987). Robin Cook's *Invasion* (1997), along with its made-for-TV film counterpart (Armand Mastroianni, 1997), offered a blended rendering of the alien contagion narrative. Cook's narrative follows the course of an alien virus that slowly infects much of the human population, but small enclaves of humanity avoid being infected long enough to develop a cure. The title and initial plot execution mimic and overlap with the *Invasion of the Body Snatchers* narrative. Here, however, humans are converted into aliens by the virus.

Optimistic First Contact Narratives

Despite the abundance of first contact stories resulting in antagonism between humans and aliens, a significant number of positive or neutral first encounter narratives also exist. Many of these films reflect poorly on humankind's ability to think beyond its own individualized self-interest. Walter Tevis's 1963 novel *The Man Who Fell to Earth* (and its later film adaptation, Nicolas Roeg, 1976) follows an alien who arrives on Earth and works diligently to facilitate bringing the survivors of his dying world to Earth. He hopes that with the heightened intelligence of his race and humankind's resources, they will be able to avert the tragedy that his home world has suffered and Earth is in the process of enacting. Other optimistic first contact narratives include *Starman* (John Carpenter, 1984), *Cocoon* (Ron Howard, 1985) and its sequel *Cocoon: The Return* (Daniel Petrie, 1988), and astronomer and physicist Carl Sagan's 1985 novel *Contact* and its film adaptation (Robert Zemeckis, 1997).

Stephen Spielberg's *Close Encounters of the Third Kind* (1977) is an optimistic first contact narrative in which an electrician, Roy Neary (Richard Dreyfuss), is forever altered after an encounter with a UFO. After his initial contact, Neary becomes further interested in UFOs to the point of alienating his family. His dedication, however, leads him to an actual meeting with the aliens, face-to-face, who invite him onto their mothership. Released five months after George Lucas's *Star Wars* (1977), Spielberg's film traded the action and adventure of Lucas's film for a more nuanced exploration of what it means to meet an entirely foreign entity.

Still other narratives entail aliens coming to Earth seeking human aid from other threats. Nick Castle's *The Last Starfighter* (1984) follows Alex Rogan (Lance Guest) as he goes from trailer park resident to galactic hero after an alien race enlists him to fight against a dominating alien empire. Terry Pratchett's novel *Only You Can Save Mankind* (1992) is another example in which a video-game playing youth is pulled into the world within the game to aid an alien race being decimated by humans. "The Barsoom" book series (1912–43) by Edgar Rice Burroughs (discussed below) also has its hero, John Carpenter, called upon repeatedly to help the aliens of Mars.

First Contact as Critique

First contact also operates as a critique of human relations. At times, it can contemplate the issues of colonization as mentioned above, but it also looks to contextualize the various ways in which individuals and groups first encounter difference of any sort, and how humans properly or improperly respond to it. Stanislaw Lem's 1961 novel *Solaris* has been adapted to film several times (Boris Nirenburg, 1968; Andrew Tarkovskly, 1972; Steven Soderbergh, 2002) and presents one of the more challenging narratives regarding first contact with an utterly foreign life form. The story centers around humans coming into contact with a sentient liquid mass covering a planet. Despite years of study, there seems to be no conventional or direct way of communicating with the life form. While some narratives bypass the challenges of communication with the use of a universal translator, narratives like *Solaris* re-emphasize the limitations of communication—not only between different species, but between human beings as well. China Miéville's novel *Embassytown* (2011) focuses on this idea by presenting a setting in which humans need to be genetically engineered in order to communicate with an alien race.

In Robert Heinlein's *Stranger in a Strange Land* (1961), Martians have a profound effect on Earth without visiting the planet. Valentine Michael Smith is a human child raised by Martians after he was stranded there when his astronaut parents and entire crew were killed during an expedition. Smith possesses both psychic abilities and superhuman intelligence, which he eventually uses to begin his own church. He teaches his followers the language of Martians and how to acquire and use psychic abilities. Smith is trying to create a superior race of humans able to defend themselves against a Martian attack. Smith is killed by members of the religious cult the Fosterites. Humans rejecting or misusing the aid given to them by extraterrestrials is a common theme that relates back to *The Day the Earth Stood Still*.

Other narratives of first contact occur in space, upon asteroids, space stations, or among spaceships. With first contact in space, there remains reasonable opportunity for equal footing between the two parties; however, just as often, this lays the grounds for contrasting levels of technology and resources. A.E. van Vogt's *The Voyage of the Space Beagle* (1950) is a collection of adventures experienced by Dr Elliott Grosvenor aboard the *Space Beagle* (alluding to Charles Darwin's famous voyage aboard the *Beagle* that lasted from 1831 until 1836) as they move through space, encountering new alien races that continually cause problems aboard the ship. In Murray Leinster's "First Contact" (1945), the crew of the *Llanvabon* makes first contact with an alien ship in the Crab Nebula. After initially reacting in fear, the two groups realize they are not so unlike; however, they cannot trust one another with the locations of their home planets. They come to a compromise that involves the swapping of ships. The story ends with the human and alien astronauts exchanging dirty jokes. This story also contains the first instance of a "mechanical translator" that makes communication (friendly or otherwise) between human beings and alien species possible.

In some cases, alien contact narratives eschew direct alien encounters in favor of exploration of alien artifacts and remnants of their societies. These narratives often focus on what would happen if humans came across forbidden or powerful knowledge beyond the realm of normal human activity. Fred Wilcox's *Forbidden Planet* (1956) explores what occurs when humans stumble upon an alien machine from a dead planet that physically manifests the thoughts of the subconscious. By contrast, Arthur C. Clarke's novel *Rendezvous with Rama* (1972) sends humans to explore an unmanned spaceship. Believing the ship to be a threat, the government plans to destroy it, but the ship leaves before it can be destroyed, only to return in later books in the series. In Alex Cox's cult film *Repo Man* (1984), the bodies of four dead aliens are stolen and placed inside a 1964 Chevy Malibu. The bodies emit enough radiation to drive a person insane, and the scientist who has stolen the bodies of the aliens and is now driving them around Los Angeles has already been driven mad by the effects of alien radiation.

Coexistence

More fiction than film has been devoted to the idea of peaceful coexistence among humans and extraterrestrials, with the main exception coming from serial films (for example, *Star Wars, Men in Black*) or television/novel-derived films (for example, *Star Trek, Transformers*). Fiction that depicts what human and alien coexistence might look like often also explores the related themes of miscegenation, parasitism, symbiosis, and interdependence. The fiction of Octavia Butler, for example, depicts the necessity of human beings coexisting on other planets with aliens because they have destroyed their own. Coexistence, however, comes at a price: the wombs of human beings will be used to give birth to non-human beings. Butler first plays with this concept in her short story "Bloodchild" (1985), in which human beings are under the charge of giant bug-like creatures called Tlics. Tlics bond with their human families and feed them eggs that have both narcotic and healing properties, but at a gruesome cost. Certain human males are selected to have their stomachs be incubators for the small worm-like offspring of Tlics. When the Tlic grubs are mature enough, the human is anesthetized by a sting from his Tlic so that the worms can be cut out of his stomach and transferred to an animal carcass. This story explores power dynamics, miscegenation, and the parasitic nature of childbirth in general.

Although the aliens in "Bloodchild" resemble giant bugs, the story is often seen as a precursor to her "Xenogenesis" trilogy (1987–89), which deals with more traditional-looking aliens. The trilogy centers on an African-American woman who awakens in a post-apocalyptic future where human beings have destroyed their own planet and must either mate with the gene-trading alien Oankali and give birth to a new hybrid human–Oankali species, or remain sterile and let the human race die out altogether. The Oankali's reasoning for wanting to create an Oankali–human species is twofold: (1) Oankali crave and collect difference; (2) they see human beings as innately hierarchical and they want to breed out that impulse so humans do not destroy each other once again. As an African-American female, the irony of the situation is not lost on **Lilith**, and she compares the situation to both Nazi Germany and what went on during the days of African-American slavery.

Coexistence between humans and extraterrestrials on Earth usually involves plots in which a single or small groups of extraterrestrials come to the planet. Several months before Orson Welles's radio broadcast, one of the most famous fictional examples of human–extraterrestrial coexistence was launched. In June 1938, DC Comics published *Action Comics* #1, featuring Superman, an alien from another planet sent to Earth. In the ensuing comics, books, TV series, and films, Superman has been an icon of peaceful coexistence with Earth.

Some coexistence narratives posit Earth as an intergalactic hangout or rest stop. Similar to Simak's *Way Station*, Spider Robinson's "Callahan Place" stories and novels depict a terrestrial bar that acts as a magnet for intergalactic and interdimensional travelers, making for many numerous and often bemusing tales. Directed by Barry Sonnenfeld, the *Men in Black* (1997–2012) film franchise explores the idea of Earth inhabited by numerous peaceful aliens, with the Men in Black present to deal with any aliens who violate the peace treaties among human and alien civilizations.

There are few stories in which large alien populations peacefully coexist on Earth, since fear of overpopulation and limited resources remains consistent in the world. Arthur C. Clarke's *Childhood's End* (1953) is an early example in which extraterrestrials visit Earth and help to improve and evolve the human race. Though this idea is offered in much fiction and film, it is usually upended by a revelation that the aliens are in fact hurting humans. For instance, in Damon Knight's short story, "To Serve Man" (1950), an alien race comes to Earth with promises of benevolent intentions and the desire to share innovative technology. When a group of linguists gets together to crack the aliens' language and translate a book entitled *To Serve Man*, the double meaning of the title is discovered, as it is famously revealed to be a cookbook. The story was later adapted into an episode of Rod Serling's *The Twilight Zone* that aired in 1962.

Graham Baker's film *Alien Nation* (1988) offers an interesting look at a formerly enslaved alien race arriving on Earth and being slowly integrated into modern day society. Though tension exists between the humans and the Newcomers, they manage to get along despite their differences. Nearly 20 years later, Neill Blomkamp's *District 9* (2009) offers a much darker consideration of human and alien coexistence on Earth. Here, the formerly enslaved aliens arrive in a spaceship, but instead of entering US airspace, they hover above South Africa. Unlike the Newcomers of *Alien Nation*, these aliens are insectoid creatures rather than humanoid and they cannot speak human languages. Coexistence seems implausible and the aliens are ghettoized in what is essentially a concentration camp.

Gareth Edwards's *Monsters* (2010) overlaps with elements of *District 9* but to different ends. When an Earth space probe crashes in Central America, it contains an alien species that quickly spreads and comes to dominate much of Mexico before being quarantined. Despite the quarantine, a photographer and his ward cut through with the help of smugglers. Though the overwhelming depiction of the aliens is negative, in the penultimate scene of the film, the two protagonists witness a moment of intimacy expressed between two aliens, implying that coexistence may be possible—a possibility subsequently undercut by the film. Many narratives focused on peaceful coexistence between humans and extraterrestrials occur on other planets. One of the earliest depictions of this is Edgar Rice Burroughs's "Barsoom" series, which includes a series of humans, starting with John Carter, coming to Mars and becoming involved in various wars and political battles between different factions of Martian life forms.

Many extraterrestrial narratives emphasizing a universe populated by different alien species are positioned within the broader context of interstellar civilizations and warfare—often with planets and species paralleling Earth's nations and races. The more than 20 books in David Weber's "Honorverse" series (1992–present) follow the exploits of Honor Harrington in epic space battles with both human and alien forces alike. E.E. Doc Smith's "Lensman" series (1948–60) provides a more complex rendering of human–alien relations as two feuding alien life forms manipulate and position humans to be key figures in their centuries-long feud. In contrast, James White's "Sector General" series (1960–99) builds in the opposite direction. After humans recover from their earlier follies in space exploration and warfare, they build an intergalactic hospital to meet the needs of numerous alien life forms. David Brin's "Uplift Universe" series (1980–98) offers yet another take on the galactic civilization. In this series, more developed alien species contract with those who are less advanced in a form of indentured servitude in order for the less advanced society to receive the benefits. When Earth bypasses this process, however, it creates tension and problems.

The two most iconic representations of the galactic coexistence of humans and aliens are the two primary space opera franchises: *Star Trek* and *Star Wars*. *Star Trek* began as a television series (1966–69), but branched into a series of films (1979–2009), comics, video games, and hundreds of books. The franchise largely focuses on a galactic federation of human and alien worlds and the starship known as *The Enterprise* as it voyages through space, encountering rivals, new life forms, and other phenomena. One of *Star Trek*'s most influential, though not entirely original, ideas is that of the "Prime Directive," restricting officers from providing advanced technology to less advanced civilizations that they encounter. While *Star Wars* started as a film series (1977–2008), it has gone on to spawn television series, comic books, and several hundred novels. It deals with the rise of a sinister empire among the known planets within the Galactic Republic, and each film and novel is filled with a variety of humanoid and non-humanoid species such as Wookies and Ewoks working together with human beings (see Weinstock). [**LE & LC**]

Science Fiction as Trojan Horse

As mentioned above, in some countries—principally those of the former Soviet bloc—science fiction has acted as a "coded" genre to discuss political and social concerns without attracting the attention of censors. The first well-known extraterrestrials in Russian literature appear in the short story "Dream of a Ridiculous Man" (1877) by Fedor Dostoevsky, a writer long accustomed to steering acerbic social commentary past government censorship. Dostoevsky's embittered hero, in the very act of committing suicide, is transported to a faraway planet by an **angel**. There he discovers a race of innocent human-like beings, only unintentionally to infect their paradise with his egoism and hypocrisy. Once their culture has transformed into a simulacrum of terrestrial society, he miraculously wakes up on Earth and devotes the rest of his life to preaching fraternal love.

In the early twentieth century, extraterrestrial civilizations (usually Martian) continued to be radically different from (and usually superior to) their Earthly equivalents. In *Red Star* (1908) by the Marxist philosopher and scientist Aleksandr Bogdanov, a socialist activist is whisked from revolutionary Russia to Mars. There he encounters a technocratic utopia in which decisions are made by consensus, resources are shared fairly, and even external gender distinctions between the tall, slender, large-eyed Martians are largely absent. *Red Star* had a prequel, *Engineer Menni* (1913), which studied the roots of Martian society. In contrast, the Mars discovered by Engineer Los and his ex-soldier sidekick Gusev in A.N. Tolstoy's *Aelita* (1923) is a technocratic dystopia inhabited by diminutive humanoids, where the proletariat are exploited by an oligarchic Council of Engineers. Los and Gusev briefly lead a workers' revolution, but are forced to flee back to communist Russia. Both *Aelita* and its film adaptation (Yakov Protazanov, 1924) were successful exercises in pro-Soviet propaganda.

Later Soviet writers explored more universal perspectives: Ivan Efremov's *The Andromeda Nebula* (1957) marked the renaissance of Soviet science fiction in the aftermath of Stalinist repression. In this epic of interstellar exploration, characters encounter deadly aliens, but also exchange data with peaceful extraterrestrial races via a radio network called "The Great Ring." Beginning in 1958, the brothers Boris and Arkady Strugatsky published novels set in the near future, where unknown aliens stop off on Earth as if for a picnic, leaving behind a "Zone" polluted by otherworldly refuse (*Roadside Picnic*, 1971; filmed as *Stalker* [1979] by Andrei Tarkovsky), or where Martians take over Russia and replant agricultural land with blue wheat. Farmers, lulled by the invaders' generous handouts, allow themselves to be milked for their stomach juices, essential to the Martian metabolism (*The Second Martian Invasion*, 1968). The Strugatskys' most famous non-humanoid entities are the hyper-evolved "Wanderers" who foster the development of other species, including humans, through technological and genetic enhancement and occasional direct interventions.

In a striking departure from the extraplanetary topoi of most Russian science fiction, the dissident writer Abram Terts (Andrei Siniavskii) wrote a short story, "Pkhents" (1957), satirizing the isolation of Soviet intellectuals in society. "Pkhents" is a word from the language of a cactus-like alien, stranded in Soviet Russia after crash-landing in the tundra. Improvising a "human" appearance (as a reclusive hunchback), he inhabits a collective apartment, struggling to preserve his privacy and dignity and also to blend in as a Soviet citizen. The cult film *Kin-dza-dza* (Georgii Danielia, 1986 [the title is the local name for a distant galaxy]) comically describes the adventures of an ordinary Muscovite and a Georgian student accidentally teleported to the inhospitable and barbaric planet of Pliuk, where the telepathic inhabitants have only two spoken words (one of which is gravely offensive).

While Soviet writers produced a diverse array of alien entities, from the translucent beings of Genrich Altov and Valentina Zhuravleva's "Ballad of the Stars" (1960) to the **cyborg**-like entities in Sergei Snegov's "People Like Gods" series (1966–77), the majority imitate H.G. Wells (1866–1946), Jules Verne (1828–1905), Robert A. Heinlein (1907–88), and others. The chief interest of late twentieth-century Soviet and Russian science fiction lies in its value as political allegory. [**MM**]

Entertaining Aliens

From family-oriented TV shows such as *Lost in Space* (1965–68), *Mork & Mindy* (1978–82), *Alf* (1986–90), and *3rd Rock From the Sun* (1996–2001) to a host of cartoon series from the 1960s onward, like *The Flintstones*' (1960–66) The Great Gazoo, *Looney Tunes*' (1930–69) Marvin the Martian, and ZIM from *Invader ZIM* (2001–2003), aliens have been a mainstay of family entertainment, especially as represented in films such as *E.T. the Extra-Terrestrial* (Steven Spielberg, 1982), *Flight of the Navigator* (Randal Kleiser, 1986), *Mac and Me* (Stewart Raffill, 1988), and *Lilo & Stitch* (Dean DeBlois, 2002). While many are non-threatening and comical, antagonistic aliens exist in family entertainment as well, as in Bruce Coville's "My Teacher Is an Alien" novels (1989–92) and the films *Space Jam* (Joe Pytka, 1996) and *Jimmy Neutron: Boy Genius* (John A. Davis, 2001). The 2000s saw a host of CGI films oriented towards children with aliens in increasingly sympathetic roles, including *Planet 51* (Jorge Blanco, 2009), *Monsters vs. Aliens* (Rob Letterman, 2009), and *Mars Needs Moms* (Simon Wells, 2011).

Given the success of alien contact and alien invasion films, parodies mocking conventions and aspects of the extraterrestrial narrative were, of course, also inevitable; numbered among this group are *Abbott and Costello Go to Mars* (Charles Lamont, 1953) and Frederic Brown's novel, *Martians, Go Home* (1955). Douglas Adams's *The Hitchhiker's Guide to the Galaxy* (1979), its various sequels, and its later cinematic rendering (Garth Jennings, 2005) also operate as parodies, with ridiculous alien characters such as Eccentrica Gallumbits, the Triple-Breasted Whore of Eroticon Six, and Great Green Arkleseizure, an alien purported to have sneezed out the galaxy. Mel Brooks's *Spaceballs* (1987) took its lead from the *Star Wars* films; Dean Parisot's *Galaxy Quest* (1999) played off of *Star Trek*'s fame and fandom; and David Zucker's *Scary Movie 3* (2003) mocked, among many other films, M. Night Shyamalan's *Signs*.

Humor notably became increasingly prominent within the extraterrestrial narrative from the 1980s onward. These narratives still attempt to tell a serious story but regularly mock the same tradition and conventions on which they build. The 1986 *Critters* (Stephen Herek), the first of a four-film series, features flesh-devouring creatures that wreak havoc in a small town in Kansas until two space bounty hunters help destroy them. Tim Burton's *Mars Attack!* (1996) provides a satire of the alien invasion story. With an all-star cast including Jack Nicholson, Glenn Close, Annette Bening, and Pierce Brosnan, the film plays out the traditional alien invasion narrative. Only when it is discovered that the aliens will explode when exposed to a particular country song are the humans able to fight back against the Martian horde. In Robert Rodriguez's *The Faculty* (1998), mind-controlling parasites have taken over the faculty and staff at Herrington High School and comments are included within the film highlighting the similarities of *The Puppet Masters* and *Invasion of the Body Snatchers* to the students' own battle against a similar threat. Although this film does not have the Cold War context of the other two works, it does play off of the distrust between teenagers and adults, another common theme of 1950s science fiction and horror films. Similarly, James Gunn's *Slither* (2006) is a comedic horror movie that blends the narrative of *The Blob* with conventions from **zombie** films. In this film, the Long One is an alien parasite that arrives on Earth within a meteor. When it takes over someone, it absorbs both memories and consciousness, and the people affected by the parasites eventually turn into mindless beings performing on behalf of the Long One. Other films use aliens to jab at modern life, such as *Meet the Applegates* (Michael Lehmann,1990), *Suburban Commando* (Burt Kennedy, 1991), and Saturday Night Live's skit-turned-film, *The Coneheads* (Steven Barron, 1993), which figures the nuclear family, middle-class values, and suburban life as alien and incomprehensible.

Extraterrestrials continue to be a mainstay of entertainment, from fiction to comics to television to film. From their abundance in media, it is clear that humans continue to be curious about the universe beyond Earth and to ask what life would be like if humans were to encounter other sentient species. Until contact with extraterrestrials happens, narratives featuring them will continue to represent decidedly human anxieties and desires.

[LE & LC] Lance Eaton, Laurie Carlson, and Muireann Maguire

References and Suggested Reading

Barr, Marlene S. *Lost in Space: Probing Feminist Science Fiction and Beyond*. North Carolina: University of North Carolina Press, 1991.

Booker, M.K. and Anne-Marie Thomas. *The Science Fiction Handbook*. Chichester, UK: Wiley-Blackwell, 2009.

Cartmell, Deborah. *Alien Identities: Exploring Differences in Film and Fiction*. London: Pluto Press, 1999.

Kuhn, Annette. *Alien Zone: Cultural Theory and Contemporary Science Fiction Cinema*. London: Verso, 1990.

Landon, Brooks. *Science Fiction After 1900: From the Steam Man to the Stars*. New York: Routledge, 2002.

Larbalestier, Justine. *Daughters of Earth: Feminist Science Fiction in the Twentieth Century*. Middletown, CT: Wesleyan University Press, 2006.

Loughlin, Gerard. *Alien Sex: The Body and Desire in Cinema and Theology*. Malden, MA: Blackwell, 2004.

Lucanio, Patrick. *Them or Us: Archetypal Interpretation of Fifties Alien Invasion Films*. Bloomington: Indiana University Press, 1987.

Maddrey, Joseph. *Nightmares in Red, White, and Blue: The Evolution of the American Horror Film*. Jefferson, NC: McFarland, 2004.

Matthews, Melvin E. *Hostile Aliens, Hollywood, and Today's News: 1950s Science Fiction Films and 9/11*. New York: Algora, 2007.

McGuire, Patrick. *Red Stars: Political Aspects of Soviet Science Fiction*. Ann Arbor, MI: UMI Research Press, 1985.

Melzer, Patricia. *Alien Constructions: Science Fiction and Feminist Thought*. Austin: University of Texas Press, 2006.

Monk, Patricia. *Alien Theory: The Alien as Archetype in the Science Fiction Short Story*. Lanham, MD: Scarecrow Press, 2006.

Sardar, Ziauddin, and Sean Cubitt. *Aliens R Us: The Other in Science Fiction Cinema*. London: Pluto Press, 2002.

Suvin, Darko. *Metamorphoses of Science Fiction: On the Poetics and History of a Literary Genre*. New Haven, CT: Yale University Press, 1979.

Weinstock, Jeffrey Andrew. "Freaks in Space: 'Extraterrestrialism' and 'Deep-Space Multiculturalism'." In *Freakery: Cultural Spectacles of the Extraordinary Body*, edited by Rosemarie Garland Thomson, 327–37. New York: New York University Press, 1996.

Zinoman, Jason. *Shock Value: How a Few Eccentric Outsiders Gave Us Nightmares, Conquered Hollywood, and Invented Modern Horror*. New York: Penguin Press, 2011.

FAIRY

A fairy is a type of supernatural being that inhabits a parallel realm to that of humans. The term can include a wide range of magical creatures, but it most commonly refers to a legendary group of beings found in European folklore and romance whose appearance and social structure closely mirror that of humans.

The term *fairy* and its European cognates is likely derived from the Latin *fata*, a personification of fate suggesting a guardian or tutelary spirit. Fairy roles overlap with those of other supernatural beings, such as **witches**, **angels**, **demons**, and **ghosts**. The ambiguity surrounding the function of fairies may account for the unusually varied terminology applied to them, which includes euphemistic names such as the mother's blessing (Welsh, *bendith y mamau*), the good neighbors (Gaelic, *an daoine shidhe*), the good people (Irish, *na daoine maithe*), and ladies from outside (Sicilian, *donas de fuerra*), as well as more literary ones such as *Tuatha Dé Danann* (the people of the goddess Danu, Ireland) and *y tylwyth teg* (the fair family, Wales). Traditions about Irish fairies, for example, overlap with those of other supernatural beings like the Irish Tuatha Dé Danann, descendants of the gods in early Irish tales. Early collectors of Irish folklore, such as William Butler Yeats (1865–1939) and Lady Jane Wilde (1821–96) often equated the two.

Particular historical or ideological perspectives often shaped theories about the origins of fairies. Medieval chronicle writers such as Gervase of Tilbury (c. 1150–c. 1228), Walter Map (1140–c. 1210), and Gerald of Wales (c. 1146–c. 1223) scripted accounts of meetings between fairies and mortals to include cautionary morals. In the seventeenth century, the existence of fairy beings was used to counter the secularizing tendency of Enlightenment rationality. The treatise on Scottish fairy lore, *The Secret Commonwealth* by Robert Kirk (1644–92), regarded contact between fairies and humans as proof of the existence of a spiritual world. The folklorist David MacRitchie, writing at the end of the nineteenth century, rationalized fairy traditions as race memories of pre-Iron Age peoples forced underground or into remote areas to escape the superior iron weaponry of later invaders. Lucy Allen Paton attributed the origins of fairy stories to Celtic myths that had been corrupted and misunderstood through continuous oral transmission. For W.Y. Evans Wentz, fairy lore was evidence of the paranormal powers inherent in peoples such as the Celts, while Lewis Spence regarded fairy traditions as the remnants of shamanic ancestor cults.

In appearance, fairies generally resemble humans but with some exaggerated features. Depending upon the source, they are taller, shorter, more beautiful, or less attractive than humans. Some fairies are invisible. In the Irish tale of Connla (*Echtra Condhla*, twelfth century), the entire court can hear the fairy mistress, but only Connla can see her. In some accounts, such as Robert Kirk's *The Secret Commonwealth and A Short Treatise of Charms and Spells* (1692), those with second sight can see fairies, while John Rhŷs reports that an invisible fairy island can be seen from a particular point on the Pembrokeshire coast in Wales. The idea of winged fairies is rare before the changes brought about by Elizabethan literature and Victorian art, but the *sluagh*, a group of fairies common in Scottish Gaelic tradition and in parts of Ireland, travel through the air. Travelers caught up by the *sluagh* find themselves the next morning miles from where they started.

Diminutive fairies emerged in English literature in the late fifteenth and early sixteenth centuries, often as a means of satirizing social norms. Edmund Spenser's complex allegory in his epic poem *The Fairie Queene* (1590–96) equates Queen Elizabeth I with the queen of the fairies. Shakespeare's *A Midsummer Night's Dream* (1690–96) contains both human-sized and miniature winged creatures drawn from a variety of sources. Titania and Oberon derive from Ovid's first century CE *Metamorphoses* and medieval French romance respectively, while Puck comes from English fairy tradition. Michael Drayton wrote a mock heroic poem, "Nymphidia, the Court of Faery" (1627), in which Oberon and Mab as fairy king and queen, together with the **elf** knight Pigwiggin, preside over a miniature fairy world.

The miniaturized fairies of the Elizabethan world were a major inspiration for Victorian art and literature. Fairies in visual art are rare before the late eighteenth century and are linked with the early nineteenth-century interest in Shakespeare and Gothic fiction. Small winged creatures predominate and are depicted in contexts that range from cute to erotic. Among the most striking depictions of fairies are the almost surrealistic creatures of Richard Dadd (1817–86) and John Anster Fitzgerald (1819–1906). This type of art reached a peak in the 1840s, although it remained prominent in book illustration until World War II.

The late nineteenth- and early twentieth-century Irish literary revival (nicknamed the Celtic Twilight) influenced the appearance of another type of fairy art with more mystical and human-sized fairy beings. *The Riders of the Sidhe* (1911) by the Scottish artist John Duncan depicts beautiful Celtic fairies riding through a misty light. The Celtic Twilight is an important influence on contemporary perceptions of fairies, especially their mystical nature characteristic of many twentieth- and twenty-first-century renderings.

Fairy worlds exist in parallel with the ordinary human world, under water or in a mound or below ground. Fairy abodes can appear as ordinary houses or as elaborate palaces. Fairies and the worlds they inhabit, however, are frequently deceptive and a visitor who falls asleep in a beautiful fairy world may awaken surrounded by twigs and leaves. Descriptions of the fairy world can resemble the *locus amoenus* (the sweet place) of medieval poetry, but with some significant differences. The locations in the accounts from medieval chronicle writers such as Walter Map (*De nugis curialium*), Gerald of Wales (*Itinarium Cambriae, Journey through Wales*), and Gervaise of Tilbury (*Otia Imperialia*) are places of perpetual spring lit by a mysterious, supernatural light. In a sixteenth-century account of the life of a Welsh saint, Gwyn ap Nudd, the leader of the Welsh fairies, invites St Collen to visit a beautiful world under Glastonbury Tor, but the saint dispels the apparent beauty of the feast with holy water (see Rhŷs). A common fairy narrative from Great Britain concerns a midwife who attends a fairy mother and accidentally rubs her eye with ointment intended for the fairy child. She realizes that the fairy world is an ugly cave, but the fairy husband destroys her accentuated power of perception by blinding her. This deceptive quality of fairies is also illustrated by the beliefs associated with their gifts. Fairy money can turn to brass or even excrement, and beautiful fairy palaces revert to rocks and dirt at daybreak.

In special circumstances, fairies and humans are able to cross the boundaries that normally separate their worlds. Hunting in the forest, traveling at night, crossing a stream, entering a cave or mound, being on a beach or any place at a social or geographic periphery provides an opportunity to enter the fairy world, as do transitional times such as midsummer, Halloween, Christmas, midnight, and noon. Both men and women are lured into fairy dances, usually in remote places or at night, but the fairy mistress figure usually appears when a man is pursuing his daily business such as hunting, fishing, or tending his flock. Fairies are frequently associated with animal husbandry and farming. They reward humans who keep clean houses, farms, and dairies, but fairy gifts are lost if the owner reveals their source. Fairy wives often bring prosperity in the form of cattle that have red (that is, russet) ears. These cattle produce copious amounts of milk until the fairy wives are offended (see Wood).

Of particular note in relation to the convergence of mortal and fairy spheres is the phenomenon of the Wild Hunt in which fairies or other supernatural creatures are encountered in vigorous pursuit of their quarry. References to the Wild Hunt appear in the *Anglo-Saxon Chronicle* (1127) and this phenomenon is known elsewhere in Britain and Europe. The Wild Hunt could be a portent of death or disaster. The twelfth-century Norman/Welsh cleric Walter Map included an account of the Wild Hunt led by King Herla, a mythical British king, in his chronicle *De nugis curialium* (*A courtiers' trifles*).

Interactions between fairies and mortals follow well-established narrative patterns in which abduction and marriage are common themes. Women, children, and, occasionally, men are kidnapped to become part of fairy society. Yeats's poem "The Stolen Child" (1886) on the theme of fairy abduction, for example, contains the famous refrain "Come Away O Human Child." Fairies in such tales seem to desire human company, although it is possible to rescue the kidnapped wife, lover, or child. Walter Map records a story of a knight whose wife has apparently died but is later rescued from the fairies. The medieval English romance *Sir Orfeo* (fourteenth century) tells a similar tale and, in the Scottish Border ballad *Tam Lin* dating at least to the sixteenth century, the hero Tam Lin is rescued from the Queen of the Fairies by his sweetheart. Sometimes the kidnapped person can win his or her own freedom, as is the case for Thomas of Erceldoune in the eponymous fifteenth-century Scottish romance in which Thomas's fairy mistress rewards him with the gift of prophecy because he has abstained from fairy food and remained silent during his stay with her. Other traditions concern a fairy bride whose marriage ends when her mortal husband violates a taboo. Well-known tales about this figure include Macha, an Irish otherworld wife who appears in the twelfth-century *Book of Leinster* ("The Debility of the Ulsterman"); the wife of Wild Edric (Walter Map); Mélusine, a figure from medieval French romance (*Chronique de Mélusine*, Jean d'Arras, fifteenth century); and the Lady of Llyn Y Fan Fach in Wales (*The Physicians of Myddfai*, 1866). In a variation on this theme, the fairy mistress in *Lai de Lanval* (twelfth century), an Anglo-Norman poem composed by Marie de France, forgives the lover who reveals her identity and they return to her otherworld home.

The reality of fairies became a subject of controversy in the modern era when, in 1917, two cousins photographed supposedly real fairies near their home in Yorkshire. The controversial photographs of the Cottingley Fairies, as they came to be known, were shown to the theosophist Edward Gardner who attempted to authenticate them, and to Arthur Conan Doyle, whose spiritualist interests inclined him to view the pictures as concrete evidence for psychic phenomena. Doyle's article for the Christmas edition of *The Strand Magazine* (1920), and his subsequent book *The Coming of the Fairies* (1922), brought the pictures to a wider public. In the 1980s, the photographs were revealed as a hoax based on cutouts from a children's book, but the events surrounding the pictures have been the basis for several contemporary reinterpretations. In the film *Photographing Fairies* (Nick Willing, 1997), a photographer (Toby Stephens), grieving for his dead wife, is given photographs of supposed fairies taken by some young girls. Under the influence of a hallucinogenic flower, he believes he can see fairies and contact his dead wife. *Fairy Tale: A True Story* (Charles Sturridge, 1997) is also loosely based on the Cottingley hoax, while an episode of the cult science fiction/supernatural television series *Torchwood* presents a sinister reworking of the Cottingley incident ("Small Worlds," season one, 2006) in which supernatural beings described as "creatures from the dawn of time" abduct a young girl. Fantasy artist Brian Froud's 2005 publication *Lady Cottington's Pressed Fairy Book* provides a light-hearted visual homage to the Cottingley Fairies.

Modern fantasy literature, film, and television draw on the ambiguous nature of fairies for dramatic effect. John Keats's poem "La Belle Dame sans Merci" (1819) describes a knight seemingly trapped for eternity in a barren landscape after an encounter with a beautiful "faery" woman. The poem inspired numerous paintings by artists such as John William Waterhouse (1883) and Frank Dicksee (1902). Christina Rosetti's use of the motif of eating fairy food in "The Goblin Market" (1862) has been interpreted in terms of addiction, the allure of the forbidden, and a proto-feminist critique on Victorian attitudes to female sexuality. Despite her dainty stature and Victorian prettiness, J.M. Barrie's Tinker Bell, the companion of Peter Pan, is capricious and jealous (1904, 1911; see also **Pixie**). The fairies in Eoin Colfer's "Artemis Fowl" series (eight volumes, 2001–12) are an amalgam of supernatural and science fiction elements that has special appeal for an audience of younger readers. Charlaine Harris attributes the telepathic abilities of her heroine, Sookie Stackhouse, in *The Southern Vampire Mysteries* to fairy heritage. In an episode of the television adaptation, *True Blood*, Sookie (Anna Paquin) avoids the consequences of eating fairy food during a visit to the fairies' world ("She's Not There," season 3, episode 1). The consequence of eating food in the otherworld is also a key event in Ofelia's (Ivana Baquero) journey in *Pan's Labyrinth* (Guillermo del Toro, 2006). Susanna Clarke's novel *Jonathan Strange & Mr Norrell* (2004) is set in an alternative nineteenth-century England in which the magician, Gilbert Norrell, summons a fairy who brings a lady back from the dead with unforeseen consequences. In the film *Hellboy II: The Golden Army* (Guillermo del Toro, 2008), the comic book superhero becomes involved in an ancient feud between greedy humans and a complex supernatural realm that includes small deadly tooth fairies and elegant Celtic fairy beings. The deceptive nature of fairies is highlighted in Neil Gaiman's "The Sandman" graphic novel series in which the attractive appearances of fairies are revealed to be façades obscuring a more mundane reality.

Juliette Wood

References and Suggested Reading

Ashliman, D.L. *Fairy Lore: A Handbook*. Westport, CT: Greenwood, 2006.

Briggs, Katharine Mary. *The Anatomy of Puck: An Examination of Fairy Beliefs Among Shakespeare's Contemporaries and Successors*. London: Routledge and Paul, 1959.

———. *The Vanishing People: A Study of Traditional Fairy Beliefs*. London: Batsford, 1978.

Henderson, Lizanne, and Edward J. Cowan. *Scottish Fairy Belief: A History*. East Linton: Tuckwell Press, 2001.

Maas, Jeremy, Pamela White Trimpe, Charlotte Gere, et al. *Victorian Fairy Painting*. London: Merrell Holberton 1997.

MacRitchie, David. *Finns, Fairies and Picts*. London: Kegan Paul, Trench, Trübner & Co. Ltd, 1893.

Narvaez, Peter. *The Good People, New Fairylore Essays*. New York: Garland, 1991.

Paton, Lucy Allen. *Studies in the Fairy Mythology of Arthurian Romance* [London, 1903]. Reprint, New York: General Books, 1960.

Purkiss, Diane. *Troublesome Things: A History of Fairies and Fairy Stories*. London: Allen Lane, 2000.

Rhŷs, John. *Celtic Folklore Welsh and Manx*. 2 vols. Oxford: Clarendon Press, 1901. Facsimile Reprint, London: Wildwood House, 1980.

Sanderson, Stewart F. "The Cottingley Fairy Photographs: A Re-appraisal of the Evidence." *Folklore* 84 (1973): 89–103.

Silver, Carole G. *Strange and Secret Peoples: Fairies and Victorian Consciousness*. Oxford: Oxford University Press, 1999.

Spence, Lewis. *The Magic Arts in Celtic Britain* [1948]. Reprint, London: Constable, 1995.

Wentz, W.Y. Evans. *The Fairy-faith in Celtic Countries*. London: H. Frowde, 1911.

Wood, Juliette. "The Fairy Bride Legend in Wales." *Folklore* 103 (1992): 56–72.

FAUN AND SATYR

Satyrs, as well as fauns with which they are associated, are Greek and Latin, respectively, demigods with male human torsos and heads and animal legs; the faun has goat legs and cloven hooves, the satyr originally was said to have a horse's hind legs and a horse's tail, but at times it is described as having goat legs—as in Lucretius's first century CE *capripedes satyros* (*De Rerum Natura* 4.580). The faun, in addition, has goat horns on its human head, while the satyr has no horns, but horse ears. Often, however, fauns and satyrs were depicted as having human legs and feet, both in vase paintings and in sculpture (see plates in Keuls). Both fauns and satyrs were associated with powerful sex drives, although they were not always successful in their pursuit of nymphs or human women, and both types of demigods dwelt in woodlands. Satyrs followed the wine-god Dionysus, also referred to as Bacchus, who was tutored by an elder satyr named Silenus when he was first brought to Mount Nysa; Silenus then became one of the god's most devoted followers, staying perpetually drunk.

A remark by the philosopher Aristotle in his *Poetics* (fourth century BCE) has led many to believe that Greek tragedy grew out of the satyr play, which was an ancient comedy in which the chorus was composed of satyrs—presumably actors wearing horse tails and ears. The philosopher Friedrich Nietzsche, in his 1872 *Birth of Tragedy*, develops this satyr chorus into the embodiment of the Dionysiac spirit, which is the immersion of humans in the intoxication of nature, as represented by the "natural man" of the satyr, half-human and half-beast. However, the only extant complete satyr play, the *Cyclops* by Euripides (late fifth century BCE), is a broad burlesque in which the confrontation between the hero Odysseus and the **Cyclops** Polyphemus, from Homer's eighth-century BCE *Odyssey*, has Silenus as "father" to a group of satyrs, all of which have already been trapped and put to work by Polyphemus. Silenus tries to play Odysseus and Polyphemus off against each other for his own advantage—chiefly getting wine to drink—but Odysseus manages to blind the Cyclops and escape with all but a few of his men, as in the Homeric epic.

Faunus, one of the oldest of the native Roman gods, was associated in Latin literature with the Greek **Pan**, as in Ovid's *Fasti* (early first century CE), in which the "two-horned Faunus" was said to have been worshiped in Arcadia as Pan (2.268–271). Ovid explains that the ancient pastoral festival of the Lupercalia requires the young men who run in it to be nude because the god himself is nude (2.287), and Ovid relates how Faunus attempted to rape the Lydian princess Omphale while she was sleeping near Hercules; unfortunately for him, they had exchanged clothing, and Faunus was thrown to the ground by Hercules. This, jokes Ovid, is why Faunus prefers nudity to clothing. Faunus appears in Virgil's first-century BCE *Aeneid* as the grandfather of Lavinia, whom Aeneas marries, and as an oracle. Suetonius (late first–early second century CE) states that Faunus was supposed to have been the ancestor of Vitellius, the eighth Roman emperor (*Vitellius* 1.2).

Lucretius, in his *De Rerum Natura* (*On the Nature of Things*, first century BCE), states that people think goat-footed satyrs and nymphs live in mountains, as well as fauns, making music with stringed instruments and pipes (4.580–589). Here, as in many other places, the individual god Faunus is replaced by the category of goat-legged demigod *fauni*, or fauns. In the *Metamorphoses* (first century CE), Ovid has the Roman king of the gods, Jupiter, remark concerning the viciousness of early humanity that nymphs, fauns, and satyrs—demigods who live in woods and mountains—deserve a place where they can dwell in safety apart from men (1.192). Ovid ties in the element of music with his tale of the satyr Marsyas who challenged the god Apollo to a musical contest; Apollo, on his lyre, won against Marsyas on the flute and as punishment flayed the satyr's skin (6.382–400). In the twentieth century, the American poet James Merrill wrote a sonnet about this contest, "Marsyas" (1959), although his identity as a satyr is not mentioned.

Macrobius, in his fifth-century CE work *The Saturnalia*, derives both the words "Saturn" and "satyr" from the Greek word for "penis," explaining that, in the case of satyrs, it refers to their sexual lewdness (1.8.9). Macrobius also goes on to identify the god Apollo with the god Dionysus, and reports that on Mount Parnassus every other year a festival of Bacchus is held in which many satyrs are seen and their music is heard (1.18).

As classical culture was revived in the Renaissance, the faun and the satyr made their reappearance in art. One famous example is the figure of a faun standing at the base of the main figure in Michelangelo's sculpture *Bacchus* (1497). As with many representations of the faun both in classical antiquity and in the modern era, he has a mischievous grin as he eats from the bunch of grapes hanging from the drunken god's hand.

Jumping ahead to the nineteenth century, Nathaniel Hawthorne's *The Marble Faun* (1860) features an Italian count, Donatello, who remarkably resembles a sculpture of a faun by the ancient Greek sculptor Praxiteles (fourth century BCE). The count's carefree nature and his sexual attraction to an American woman, Miriam, further link him to the sculpted figure. Stéphane Mallarmé's 1876 poem "The Afternoon of a Faun" is narrated by the faun himself, and recounts his attempt to kiss two nymphs while they are sleeping in each other's arms; he startles them and they fly away in the form of white water birds, leaving him to play the Syrinx (panpipes) that he has carved from two reeds. Claude Debussy composed a tone poem, *Prelude to the Afternoon of a Faun*, which was first performed in 1894; this, in turn, was choreographed for ballet by Vaslav Nijinsky, who danced the role of the faun in 1912. The highly erotic nature of the choreography and the performance, said to have been masturbatory, created a scandal in Parisian society. The production was re-enacted in the 1980 film *Nijinsky* (Herbert Ross), in which Nijinsky, played by George de la Peña, is shown to actually masturbate on stage at the climax of the dance.

The 1940 Walt Disney film *Fantasia*, in which several pieces of classical music are set to animated visual dramatizations, has Beethoven's Symphony Number 6, the "Pastoral" (1808), manifest visually as a mythic celebration in an idealized Arcadian environment. In addition to male and female centaurs in a courting ritual, unicorns, winged horses in families, cupids, and a drunken Bacchus, there are numerous fauns, whose goat legs come in various bright pajama-like colors—though they all have black cloven hoofs—with pointed ears and horns, and who play panpipes following the woodwinds in the Beethoven score. They are mischievous, one of them playing "hide-and-seek" with a young unicorn by imitating a faun sculpture atop a pedestal. They are also complicitous with the cupids in "throwing together" various pairs of centaurs, but are not overtly sexual in themselves.

Mr Tumnus is a faun in C.S. Lewis's 1950 children's story *The Lion, the Witch and the Wardrobe.* He is shaped like a man from his waist up, but has goat legs covered with glossy black hair and cloven hoofs; in addition, he has a long tail—long enough for him to be carrying the end draped over an arm to keep it from dragging in the snow. He wears a scarf and carries an umbrella, since Narnia, the land where he lives, is experiencing eternal winter because of the White Witch, who rules it. In his cozy little cave, he has a bookcase with such titles as *The Life and Letters of Silenus*, *Nymphs and their Ways*, and *Is Man a Myth?* Having promised the Witch that he would kidnap any Son of Adam or Daughter of Eve whom he met and deliver him or her to the Witch, he entertains the first child to enter Narnia, Lucy, in the hopes of putting her to sleep and thus capturing her, but he has an attack of bad conscience and guides her back to the place where she can return to her own world. In a later visit, they find that he has disappeared, and still later see that he has been transformed into a sculpture for his disobedience.

In the 2010 novel *The Lightning Thief*, and in subsequent novels in the series "Percy and the Olympians" by Rick Riordan, the protagonist's best friend, Grover Underwood, is called a satyr and described as having goat legs, pointed ears, and horns.

Like Mr Tumnus, he lacks the lewd sexuality of many of the earlier fauns and satyrs, and does his inept best to protect his charge, Percy Jackson, who is the son of Poseidon and a mortal woman.

Don Riggs

References and Suggested Reading

Keuls, Eva C. "Male-Female Interaction in Fifth-Century Dionysiac Ritual as Shown in Attic Vase Painting." *Zeitschrift für Papyrologie und Epigraphik* 55 (1984): 287–97.

Lissarague, François. "The Sexual Life of Satyrs." In *Before Sexuality*, edited by John J. Winkler and Froma I. Zeitlin, translated by David M. Halperin and D. Lyons, 53–81. Princeton: Princeton University Press, 1991.

Munro, Thomas. "'The Afternoon of a Faun' and the Interrelation of the Arts." *The Journal of Aesthetics and Art Criticism* 10, no. 2 (1951): 95–111.

Sorabella, Jean. "A Satyr for Midas: The Barberini Faun and Hellenistic Royal Patronage." *Classical Antiquity* 26, no. 2 (2007): 219–48.

FELIX—*see* Demon

FETCH—*see* Wraith

FIR DARRIG—*see* Leprechaun

FIREBIRD—*see* Phoenix

FLAGG, RANDALL—*see* Demon

FLY, THE

"The Fly," a story by Paris-born British writer George Langelaan (1908–69 or 1972, date disputed), first appeared in the June 1957 issue of *Playboy* magazine. The plot, about a scientist who develops a matter teleportation device and accidentally merges his own molecular structure with that of a fly, combines elements of science

Fig. 13 ***The Fly Having Milk Laced With Rum at His Lab Desk*** **by John Adastra**

fiction, horror, and romance. The story also serves as a cautionary tale about the potential dangers of scientific curiosity. "The Fly" rapidly gained a wide audience and still maintains a strong cultural presence.

The story opens with Francois Delambre, brother of the scientist Andre Delambre, receiving a call from his sister-in-law Helene saying that she has killed Andre at the family's factory. She will not explain why. Francois and Police Commissaire Charas arrive to find Andre's head and right arm crushed under a steam-hammer. Helene's reticence and her sudden obsession with houseflies result in her being committed to an institution for the criminally insane. Helene finally explains her behavior via manuscript, writing that Andre had discovered how to transmit matter by disintegrating it in one place and reintegrating it in another. He had succeeded after several unsettling failures, including an unfortunate attempt to transmit the family cat. But Andre had a horrible accident when testing the device on himself: his molecules became scrambled with those of a housefly, turning him into a monstrous hybrid with the head and right arm of the fly—the fly ending up with Andre's head and arm. Andre hoped to restore himself by going through the transmitter with the fly again, but the fly proved impossible to find and Andre, unwilling to exist as a monstrosity, resolved to destroy himself. Helene describes how she aided Andre by working the steam-hammer controls after he placed himself under the mechanism. Unable to live with what she has seen and done, Helene swallows cyanide. After Charas reads the manuscript, he concludes that Helene had indeed been insane, but the story ends with Francois telling Charas that he had recently killed a fly whose head was "all white."

The strange story quickly caught Hollywood's attention, and Kurt Neumann's 1958 movie *The Fly* followed Langelaan's narrative quite closely. The film, however, also showed Andre (played by David Hedison) slowly losing his mind, becoming less human and more fly-like. Helene (Patricia Owens) does not commit suicide in the film, but instead is proven sane by the discovery of the white-headed fly in what is perhaps the most significant departure from Langelaan's story. Rather than Francois alone finding the fly, he (here played by Vincent Price) and Charas (Herbert Marshall) together come upon it caught in a spider's web. Both hear the movie's most famous addition, the fly's tiny, terrified cries of "Help me ... help me!" Rather than Francois, it is Charas, horrified, who kills the fly.

In Edward Bernds's 1959 sequel *Return of the Fly*, Andre's son (Brett Halsey) continues his father's experiments. Don Sharp's 1965 *Curse of the Fly* also focused on teleportation experiments but with little reference to the original characters. *The Fly*, David Cronenberg's critically acclaimed 1986 "remake," updated various technological aspects of the plot. Rather than having the scientist, Seth Brundle (Jeff Goldblum), emerge from the transmitter as a hybrid monster, the film lets Brundle's physical transformation proceed gradually and gruesomely as changes at the molecular-genetic level take effect. As in the 1958 film, the scientist—now sardonically calling himself "Brundlefly"—slowly loses his mind, ultimately begging his girlfriend (Geena Davis) to kill him. Chris Walas's 1989 sequel, *The Fly II*, revolves around corporate attempts to revive the teleportation experiments. Cronenberg turned his 1986 film into an opera, *The Fly*, which premiered in 2008 in Paris; its US debut occurred later that same year, performed by the Los Angeles Opera with Plácido Domingo (1941–) conducting.

The plot of "The Fly" spawned many television and film parodies. For example, in *The Simpsons* episode "Fly v. Fly" (*Treehouse of Horror VIII*, #9.4, 1997), Bart intentionally steps into a matter transporter with a fly, hoping for superpowers. In several episodes of *Teenage Mutant Ninja Turtles*, including "Enter: The Fly" (#2.7, 1988) and "Return of the Fly" (#3.31, 1989), the scientist Baxter, having accidentally merged with a housefly, suffers various misadventures. Other television episodes to parody *The Fly*'s teleporter accident include *Johnny Bravo* ("I, Fly," #2.7, 1999) and *SpongeBob Squarepants* ("SquidBob TentaclePants," #4.9, 2005), among many others. Movie references include *MANT!*, the film-within-a-film from Joe Dante's *Matinee* (1993), featuring a man with the head and arms of an ant; and the character Dr Cockroach in DreamWorks' *Monsters vs Aliens* (Rob Letterman and Conrad Vernon, 2009), a scientist whose experiment-run-amok left him with the head of a cockroach. Perhaps the most influential aspect of the 1958 film in particular has been the line "Help me ...

help me!" In Tim Burton's *Beetlejuice* (1988), for example, the title character (Michael Keaton) mockingly quotes the line just before eating a fly; and in Disney's *The Emperor's New Groove* (Mark Dindal, 2000), Kuzco sees a fly caught in a spider's web in the jungle crying "Help me! Help me!"

The fly's plaintive cry and other pseudo-scientific aspects of both the original story and the film versions have been criticized for their glaring scientific inaccuracies; both Andre and the fly should have died immediately after switching body parts, for example. But there is no disagreement about the story's essential themes. This particular tale of "metamorphic catastrophe" focuses on the dangers of faulty communication on both personal and technological levels (Clarke 174), as well as on the potential of science to elicit the desire for god-like powers (Telotte 180). Thus, in all versions, a scientist hubristically—albeit with good intentions—crosses dangerous boundaries in trying to create something that will vastly change human existence. The scientist lacks an understanding of his limits until too late, losing first his human identity and ultimately his life.

D. Felton

References and Suggested Reading

Clarke, Bruce. "Mediating the Fly: Posthuman Metamorphosis in the 1950s." *Configurations* 10, no. 1 (2002): 169–91.

Knee, Adam. "The Metamorphosis of *The Fly.*" *Wide Angle: A Film Quarterly of Theory, Criticism, and Practice* 14, no. 1 (1992): 20–34.

Pharr, Mary Ferguson. "From Pathos to Tragedy: The Two Versions of *The Fly.*" *Journal of the Fantastic in the Arts* 2, no. 1 (1989): 37–46.

Roth, Marty. "Twice Two: *The Fly* and *Invasion of the Body Snatchers.*" *Discourse* 22, no. 1 (2000): 103–16.

Telotte, J.P. *Science Fiction Film*. Cambridge: Cambridge University Press, 2001.

FOMORI—*see* Giant

FRANKENSTEIN'S MONSTER

Although Mary Shelley's *Frankenstein* (1818) takes its name from Victor Frankenstein, the scientist within her famous novel who constructs a monster out of pieces of corpses, nearly two centuries of popular culture references and representations have made the name nearly synonymous with Dr Frankenstein's creation, never named in Shelley's novel. The creature appears in fiction, comics, and graphic novels—in addition to scores of movies—that further develop the classic tale of its eponymous character.

Frankenstein is a complex epistolary structure of letters from Robert Walton to his sister, which itself frames Victor Frankenstein's narrative. After Walton's crew rescues Victor from the Arctic ice, he relates an account of his early life, his studies in Geneva, and his struggle to discover the secret of life. Within Frankenstein's narrative are the chapters in which the creature tells his own story, including his education in the De Lacey cottage and his rejection by society. Victor Frankenstein's story continues with the horror of the first murder, his conversation with the creature, the creature's plea for a mate, his agreement, and his final refusal. Although Victor's hubris is one of the most significant themes of *Frankenstein*, Shelley achieves much of the emotional impact of the novel by having Frankenstein's creation strip away his family and friends one by one. When the creature has killed everyone that Victor loves, Victor vows to find and kill the creature; however, he fails to catch the creature, dying after telling Walton his story. Then the creature breaks into Walton's cabin to weep over his creator, telling Walton he can die now—he plans to hurl himself onto his maker's funeral pyre. The inconclusiveness of this death scene has left room for later literary adaptations and sequels.

The Monster On Stage

The most direct outgrowths of Shelley's novel were the original stage adaptations—and, in fact, many subsequent literary and film adaptations have been derived not only from the original novel, but partly from early stage versions as well. The first and possibly most influential of these was Richard Brinsley Peake's *Presumption; or the Fate of Frankenstein*, which premiered in July 1823, with actor T.P. Cooke portraying the monster as an almost infantile mute—an interpretation that persisted well into the twentieth century. (Mary Shelley herself saw this production in August of 1823; her letters reveal that she was impressed by the intensity of the production and a little shocked to find herself suddenly famous.) Henry Milner's *Frankenstein, or the Man and the Monster* (1826) added another iconic scene, portraying the creation and awakening of the monster while borrowing the concept of "presumption" from Peake's play and adding it to one of Victor's monologues. Some of these creative choices may be attributed to the need to condense Shelley's complex novel—constraints that also affected the many films based partly on such adaptations. A much more recent stage adaptation, the Hammer films-inspired parody *The Rocky Horror Show* (1973), led to the wildly popular cult film *The Rocky Horror Picture Show* (Jim Sharman, 1975), which continues to be shown regularly in theaters.

The Monster in Political Discourse

As Elizabeth Young details in *Black Frankenstein: The Making of an American Metaphor*, in the wake of various stage adaptations of Shelley's novel, the term "Frankenstein" migrated from maker to monster as early as the 1830s (3) and was quickly utilized in political discourse to refer to any sort of policy or procedure with ominous implications or consequences. Language in the popular press, for example, likened Nat Turner, the orchestrator of a bloody slave revolt in 1931, to Frankenstein's monster created by the system of slavery (see Young, chapter 1). Susan Tyler Hitchcock notes the various ways in which the metaphor of Frankenstein's monster was utilized in the nineteenth century to refer to everything from steam engines and locomotives (101) to populist outbreaks and the threat of war. "References to Frankenstein and his monster seemed to shift from usage to usage, flinging associations hither and yon" (113).

The Monster in Literature

Literature was slower to appropriate and adapt Shelley's creation than political discourse. The plot of the novel, however, was so familiar to nineteenth-century readers that authors such as Honoré de Balzac (1799–1850), Charles Dickens (1812–70), and Nathaniel Hawthorne (1804–64) could make brief allusions to the work, "knowing that the full meaning would reverberate in every reader's mind" (Hitchcock 120). Actual adaptations of *Frankenstein* began to appear with some regularity in English around the turn of the nineteenth century, mostly in British and American magazines devoted to fantasy fiction. Donald Glut's extensive catalog of *Frankenstein* treatments notes, for example, "The New Frankenstein" by author E.E. Kellet, published around 1900, that likens the phonograph to a Frankenstein's monster, and Don C. Seitz's "The Frankenstein's Union Revolts" from 1926 that deals with thinking automobiles.

Across the twentieth century, a handful of recognizable writers and many lesser ones made use of Shelley's monster and themes. Robert Bloch tried his hand at it in the pulp magazine *Weird Tales* in 1939 with his story "Mannikins of Horror" about a scientist who animates a clay man. Bloch's story was adapted for film in 1972 as *Asylum* (Roy Ward Baker) and featured Peter Cushing. H.P. Lovecraft's 1921–22 "Herbert West—Reanimator" features a renegade doctor who develops methods of reviving corpses (see **Lovecraft, Monsters In**). In Kurt Vonnegut's "Fortitude," published in *Playboy* magazine in January of 1956, Dr Norbert Frankenstein falls in love with a disembodied head that he keeps alive with artificial organs.

Since the publication of the original novel, the creature has appeared in many crossover narratives with other iconic fictional monsters (such as the Wolfman [see **Werewolf**], **Dracula**, the Hunchback of Notre Dame, and Dr Jekyll and **Mr Hyde**). Adaptations have transplanted the creature to other times or places, explored the creature's relationships with other beings, or extended the creature's story into the present day. Notable science fiction writers have created variants: Brian Aldiss's *Frankenstein Unbound* (1973) and Arthur C. Clarke's *Dial "F" for Frankenstein* (1965) are two examples. The creature has even been the subject of some poetry, and Tom Disch wrote a libretto for an operatic version of the novel (1984).

While the science fiction and horror genres have both produced too many stories of technology run amok to mention, stories specifically drawing on Frankenstein's monster have proliferated since the early 1990s. Examples include Michael Bishop's 1995 baseball novel *Brittle Innings*, in which the creature appears as the hulking and strangely literate first baseman who calls himself Henry Clerval in a reference to Victor's boyhood friend. In Theodore Roszak's *Memoirs of Elizabeth Frankenstein* (1996), the monster befriends Elizabeth Frankenstein before ultimately murdering her. American science fiction and fantasy author John Kessel even connects the creature and his creator with Mary Bennet (from Jane Austen's 1813 novel, *Pride and Prejudice*) in "Pride and Prometheus," a 2008 novelette that manages to highlight some of the major themes of both source texts. The creature, true to Shelley's vision, is: "a face of monstrous ugliness" with "Yellow skin the texture of dried leather, black eyes sunken deep beneath heavy brows. Worst of all, an expression hideous in its cold, inexpressible hunger" (Kessel 72). Peter Akroyd's *The Casebook of Victor Frankenstein* (2008) re-imagines Victor himself, placing the doctor in the company of Mary Shelley, Percy, Byron, and Polidori in the chalet in Geneva on the night Byron proposed their game. Susan Heyboer O'Keefe's *Frankenstein's Monster: A Novel* (2010) is a direct sequel involving the later life of the monster and his pursuit by Robert Walton. Best-selling American science fiction and horror novelist Dean Koontz updated the character of Victor Frankenstein in a popular series of supernatural mystery novels (*Prodigal Son*, co-authored with Kevin J. Anderson, 2004; *City of Night*, co-authored with Ed Gorman, 2005; *Dead and Alive*, 2009; *Lost Souls*, 2010; and *The Dead Town*, 2011). *This Dark Endeavor: The Apprenticeship of Victor Frankenstein* by Kenneth Oppel (2011) deals with Victor's early studies and motivation.

The Monster in Film

Almost as soon as there was film, there were cinematic adaptations of Shelley's narrative. In the first cinematic representation of Frankenstein's monster, Thomas Edison's silent 1910 version directed by J. Searle Dawley, the creature's evil, or monstrosity, is attributed in intertitles to the evil of his creator: "Instead of a perfect human being, the evil in Frankenstein's mind creates a monster." The creature is cultured chemically in a vat as Frankenstein watches in horror; the viewer is told that "Frankenstein was appalled at the sight of his evil creation." Like many subsequent adaptations, this one diverges from the original narrative. In this case, the creature attacks Elizabeth but does not kill her. Instead, "The creation of an evil mind is overcome by love and disappears," leaving Victor Frankenstein behind in mystified despair or relief.

Several early films made by Universal Studios are notable for their cinematography, and for Boris Karloff (1887–1969) in the role of the creature. Karloff became the monster in his iconic form when Universal hired James Whale to direct *Frankenstein* (1931). The logic of Karloff's make-up, a design that has become instantly recognizable, was that Victor Frankenstein was no surgeon and would have selected the creature's skull size for convenience (Jameson 25). Shelley herself wrote that Frankenstein selected large body components to construct a being of unusual size—but Whale's visual interpretation is striking and has permeated popular culture. That Karloff was picked for his features is the stuff of Hollywood apocrypha, but we know two things: that Karloff's features "seemed likely to complement Pierce's makeup," and that his personality "suited the mixture of pathos and violence that Whale had decided formed the essence of the monster's character" (Jameson 25).

The second Karloff film, *Bride of Frankenstein* (1935), also directed by Whale, begins with the rampaging creature in classic form: an enormous, groaning, square-shouldered, dark-haired creature with electrodes in his neck and an awkward, stalking gait. The creature spends most of his on-screen time being chased by mobs and roaring inarticulately. He is captured, escapes, and meets an old man in the forest. When he is again captured and returned to the castle, his captors note that the old man has civilized him—so they offer him a bride. But when his bride greets him with revulsion, he speaks the classic line, "We belong dead."

Son of Frankenstein (1939), directed by Rowland V. Lee, was the last of the Frankenstein movies featuring Karloff as the creature. By then the creature had become a cash cow for the studio rather than a tragic icon. Perhaps furthest from the original tone of Shelley was the 1948 *Abbot and Costello Meet Frankenstein*, directed by Charles Barton, in which the creature was played for laughs, as he was decades later in Mel Brook's parody, *Young Frankenstein* (1974).

A new cycle of Frankenstein films was initiated in 1957 by England's Hammer Film Productions. Whereas Universal adapted *Frankenstein* from its source, it is more accurate to say that the Hammer films were only loosely inspired by Shelley. The Hammer films depict not a Romantic scientist carried away by the momentum of his vision, but a cynical one standing beyond the pale of society. Among the Hammer Frankenstein films are the minor classic *The Curse of Frankenstein* (Terence Fisher, 1957), featuring actor Christopher Lee as the monster, as well as the gory *Frankenstein Must Be Destroyed* (Terence Fisher, 1969) and the strange and lurid *Frankenstein and the Monster From Hell* (Terence Fisher, 1973). All Hammer's Frankenstein films were directed by Terence Fisher and all except for *The Horror of Frankenstein* (1970) star Peter Cushing as Victor.

After the Hammer era, it was probably inevitable that literary fans would want a faithful adaptation, something several films have claimed to be. One that comes reasonably close is *Mary Shelley's Frankenstein*, featuring Robert De Niro's interpretation of the creature under Kenneth Branagh's direction. The late eighteenth-century semi-fanciful realism of the apparatus, somewhere between a steampunk exhibit and authentic glassware used by the amateur scientists of the Lunar Society, resembles what might have been present in a real experimental laboratory of the era. Likewise, the creature is arguably the most realistic depiction on-screen visually. Branagh returns to Shelley's central theme, asking in the creature's voice during the confrontation on the glacier: "Did you ever consider the consequences of your actions?" Collectively, these depictions in fiction and film are a great expansion of how we think of Frankenstein and his creature; they form the bulk of popular interpretations of Shelley's work.

The Monster in Other Media

Frankenstein's monster has often appeared in comics and graphic novels, starting with a 1939 adaptation in DC's *Movie Comics* of the film *Son of Frankenstein*, followed by Dick Briefer's *Prize Comics* version (1940–49; revived 1952–54). Since then, there have been too many individual instances to list, but the monster prominently appears in the DC universe in Superman (1961), in Batman (1995), as part of a commando team tasked to save the world in *Creature Commandos* (1980), as a creation of Lex Luthor (1999), and as a member of the Teen Titans (2006). In the Marvel universe, the monster has been an antagonist to the X-Men (1968); the original novel was also adapted into a graphic novel by Bernie Wrightson, one of the major artists in the field (1983). Marvel's *The Monster of Frankenstein* series (1973–75) was reprinted in 2004 in the *Essential Monster of Frankenstein* collection, which consists of *The Monster of Frankenstein* (issues #1–5), *Frankenstein's Monster*, and three other series featuring the creature. This series was plagued by frequent staff changes in artists, writers, and inkers, and so suffered from the inconsistencies that afflict many comics. Though the original Marvel series portrays the monster as sadistic and brutal, in the series of graphic novels adapted from Dean Koontz's novels, he is a thinking, meditating being.

The monster has also had many roles in video and role-playing games, notably in the *Castlevania* series by Konami, and in the *Ravenloft* D&D campaign setting by TSR (see **Dungeons & Dragons, Monsters In**). The game *Mary Shelley's Frankenstein* (based on the 1994 film) was released for PC, Super Nintendo, and Sega Genesis; the original Nintendo system featured *Frankenstein: The Monster Returns*; and the Atari 2600 had *Frankenstein's Monster*. Homages to Shelley, Victor, and the monster appear in *Fable II* (2008), and the monster appears as a boss in the Wii game *MadWorld* (2009).

Parodies and Comic Adaptations

The Frankenstein narrative has also frequently been played for laughs. Two of the most significant parodies have been *The Rocky Horror Show* (in both stage and cinematic forms) and Mel Brooks's *Young Frankenstein* (1974), adapted into a musical in 2007. The monster appears as the bumbling but genial father played by Fred Gwynne in the short-lived sitcom *The Munsters* (1964–66), with a bride (Lily, played by Yvonne De Carlo), a werewolf son (Eddie, played by Butch Patrick), an "ordinary" niece (Marilyn, played first by Pat Priest, then by Beverley Owen), and a vampire father (Grandpa, played by Al Lewis). There have also been some attempts, mostly humorous, to market the monster to children: the General Mills cereal, Frankenberry, is notable in this respect, as is a series of children's books by Adam Rex featuring the titles *Frankenstein Makes a Sandwich* (2006) and *Frankenstein Takes the Cake* (2008).

Stacie Hanes

References and Suggested Reading

Baldick, Chris. *In Frankenstein's Shadow: Myth, Monstrosity, and Nineteenth Century Writing.* Oxford: Oxford University Press, 1990.

Bennett, Betty T., ed. *Selected Letters of Mary Wollstonecraft Shelley*. Baltimore: The Johns Hopkins University Press, 1994.

Glut, Donald F. *The Frankenstein Catalog.* Jefferson, NC: McFarland & Company, Inc., 1984.

Hitchcock, Susan Tyler. *Frankenstein: A Cultural History*. New York: W.W. Norton & Company, 2007.

Jameson, Robert. *The Essential Frankenstein.* London: Magna, 1992.

Kessel, John. "Pride and Prometheus." In *The Baum Plan for Financial Independence: and Other Stories,* by John Kessel. Easthampton, MA: Small Beer Press, 2008. <http://smallbeerpress.com/creative-commons/?did=27>.

Levine, George, and U.C. Knoepflmacher, eds. *The Endurance of Frankenstein: Essays on Mary Shelley's Novel.* Berkeley: University of California Press, 1974.

Turney, Jon. *Frankenstein's Footsteps: Science, Genetics and Popular Culture*. New Haven: Yale University Press, 1998.

Young, Elizabeth. *Black Frankenstein: The Making of an American Metaphor*. New York: New York University Press, 2008.

FRIEND, ARNOLD—*see* Demon

FURIES

In Greek mythology, the furies, goddesses of retribution, were known as the *Erinyes* ("the angry ones") and also by a euphemistic title, *Eumenides* ("the Kindly Ones"). Pausanias says, in his second-century CE *Descriptions of Greece*, that they were known in Athens as the "venerable goddesses" (*semnai theai*) (book 1, chapter 28), and in Roman mythology the more common term was *Dirae* or *Furiae*. Originally they were female Underworld deities who personified the anger of the dead for offenses committed against them in life.

Accounts of their origin reflect their primordial and ambiguous nature. According to Hesiod's *Theogany*, written in the eighth century BCE, they were born from the blood that dripped from the genitals of the castrated Uranus onto the earth-goddess Gaia. In Aeschylus, Ovid, and Virgil, sources dating from the fifth to the first century BCE, they are the offspring of Nyx (night). The discussion about the afterlife and the fate of the soul that precedes Socrates's suicide in Plato's *Phaedo* (fourth century BCE) claims that the dead had to placate the furies. Originally their number was unspecified, but eventually three figures emerge: Alecto ("unceasing"), Megaera ("grudging"), and Tisiphone ("avenger"). Their appearance varies in different accounts. Sometimes they are hag-like with heads and arms encircled by serpents or with eyes dripping blood. However, Pausanias observes that the cult statues at their sanctuary near the *Areopagus* at Athens were not frightening. In Greek art, they are often winged and dressed as hunters in short tunics and boots, to emphasize the swiftness of their retribution. An annual festival, the *Eumenideia*, was celebrated in their honour.

The furies were agents of cosmic retribution rather than human justice, and they embody implacable and relentless forces beyond even the ordered world of the Olympian deities. This is reflected in their sphere of activity. They avenged crimes that violated sacred or social norms—for example, perjury, the murder of parents and supplicants, and any violation of the obligations of hospitality. The implication is that these crimes might go unnoticed or appear to be justified, and therefore restitution was left to implacable beings who could strike against anyone, even powerful rulers and those favored by the gods. In the *Argonautica*, a Greek epic poem written in the third century BCE, Jason conspires with Medea to murder her brother. The author, Apollonius of Rhodes, says that one of the furies took note of the deed out of the corner of her eye (Book III, 470–80).

Their most famous appearance in classical literature occurs in the *Eumenides*, part of Aeschylus's fifth-century BCE trilogy, the *Orestaeia*, in which they seek retribution for the crime of matricide perpetrated by Orestes and his sister Electra. Clytemnestra murdered her husband, Agamemnon, in revenge for the death of their daughter, Iphigenia; in turn their son, Orestes, with the help of his sister, murders her. The goddess Athena breaks this cycle of vengeance and retribution that began with the crimes committed by Orestes's ancestor, Atreus. Athena and the Athenian court, the *Areopagus*, act together to acquit Orestes of matricide, thereby restoring the primacy of human justice and asserting the power of the Olympian gods. The goddess placates the furies by transforming them from goddesses devoted to vengeance into protective figures known as the Eumenides, and she creates an Athenian festival to honour them.

The tragedy of the house of Atreus has been frequently reinterpreted in art, literature, and popular culture. The three Greek tragedians, Aeschylus, Sophocles, and Euripides, each treated the theme in the fifth century BCE. The actions of the furies were an important aspect of Aeschylus's plays, whereas Sophocles and Euripides focused on the theme of retribution through the character of Electra. In Book XII of Virgil's epic poem written in the first century BCE, the *Aeneid*, Jupiter sends a fury against King Turnus and his sister Juturna. The fury takes the form of an owl and causes fear and confusion during the battle, while the mere sound of its wings brings Juturna to despair. In Dante's fourteenth-century epic poem, the *Inferno*, the furies are half-women, half-serpents who attempt to hinder Dante the Pilgrim and Virgil's journey as they attempt to enter the lower depths of Hell (Canto 9; see **Dante, Monsters In**).

Modern interpretations of furies often emphasize the effects of their actions, namely despair, guilt, and the threat of madness. In horror literature and film, the furies can be the personification of internal guilt, as in Edgar Allan's Poe's "The Telltale Heart" (1843). These qualities are also evoked in the studies of murderers pursued by menacing figures painted by the German Symbolists, such as Franz Stuck's *The Murderer* (1891) and Arnold Böcklin's *Murderer Pursued by Furies* (1870) at the end of the nineteenth century.

The tragedy of the house of Atreus has also been treated numerous times by modern authors and artists, such as in John Singer Sargent's mural, *Orestes Pursued by the Furies* (1921). In T.S. Eliot's *Family Reunion* (1939), the main character Harry sees the furies, who embody past family crimes. Eventually, like his classical counterpart, he finds redemption from his guilt. In Jean-Paul Sartre's existentialist play *Les Mouches* (*The Flies*) (1943), the furies are annoying perpetually buzzing flies that represent the inflexibility of official religion. Eugene O'Neill's *Mourning Becomes Electra* (1931) adopts a Freudian perspective on family guilt, with the American Civil War rather than the Trojan War as background. In Michael Mann's Western adaptation of the Atreus myth, *The Furies* (1950), the goddesses become identified with the land itself, a ranch that gives the film its title. The furies chase Dream (Sandman) in Neil Gaiman's *The Kindly Ones* (1996) because he has apparently killed one of his own family.

Sometimes the role of Electra as daughter is fused with the female furies as agents of retribution. In works as diverse as Richard Strauss's opera *Elektra* (1909) and the Marvel comic female assassin *Electra* (1981–2009), the desire for vengeance becomes a self-destructive force that threatens to engulf the heroine. Specific references to the furies appear with some regularity in contemporary fantasy literature and media. For example, Percy and his friends are pursued by a fury in Rick Riordan's *The Lightning Thief* (2005); in the television series *Xena: Warrior Princess*, Ares (Kevin Smith) sends the furies after Xena (Lucy Lawless); and in author Terry Brooks's "Shannara" novels (1977–2010), furies are essentially **demons** that have gone mad with bloodlust.

Juliette Wood

References and Suggested Reading

Edgeworth, Robert J. "Vergil's Furies." *The Harvard Theological Review* 76, no. 3 (1983): 365–7.

Hansen, William. *Handbook of Classical Mythology*. Santa Barbara: ABC-CLIO, 2004.

March, Jenny. *Cassell's Dictionary of Classical Mythology* [1998]. Reprint, London and New York: Cassell, 2001.

Morford, Mark, Robert J. Leonardon, and Michael Sham. *Classical Mythology*. 9th edn. Oxford: Oxford University Press, 2011.

GABRIEL—*see* Angel

GAMERA—*see* Godzilla; Sea Monsters

GANON/GANONDORF—*see* Video Games; Monsters In

GARGANTUA AND PANTAGRUEL

Gargantua and Pantagruel are two giants, father and son respectively, featured in the fictional works of French Renaissance writer, monk, and physician François Rabelais (c. 1494–1553). Their adventures are renowned for extreme consumption of food and wine, for jollity, for extraordinary tall-tale exaggerations, and for a philosophy encouraging the embracing of the pleasures of life, good companionship chief among them. These works have been put on the Roman Catholic Church's Index of Banned Books, have been widely appreciated by royalty and cardinals, and some scholars have seen in them esoteric philosophical wisdom hidden amid the apparent oral, anal, and genital fascinations of its author. The adjective "gargantuan" has come into the English language to signify anything enormous, but terms deriving from Pantagruel have been less widespread. Rabelais himself, in his "Author's Preface to the Fourth Book of the Adventures of Pantagruel," defines "pantagruelism" as "a certain gaiety of spirit, pickled in a disdain for fortuitous things" (*Oeuvres*, 826).

Of the five volumes narrating the adventures of Gargantua and Pantagruel, (published in 1532, 1534, 1546, and 1552, with the fifth book published around 1564, after Rabelais's death), what is now numbered as volume two was written first, and concerns the birth, education, and early years of Pantagruel; volume one, on the birth and education of his father Gargantua, was a prequel composed to counter other authors' inferior versions written to cash in on the popularity of the original novel. Volumes three and four, narrating the adventures of Pantagruel and his companions on an extended and evolving quest, followed, and the fifth volume, attributed to Rabelais, is usually included in publications of the complete adventures, although its authorship has been disputed.

The giant Grandgousier, or Bigthroat, and his wife Gargamelle, or Throatpipe, were the parents of Gargantua, whose name also derives from a word for "throat," as in the Spanish *garganta*. However,

Rabelais gives the origin of the giant's name in the exclamation "*que grand gars tu as*" (what a big boy you have) upon his birth; Pantagruel was born during such a severe drought that his name, which Gargantua coined from the Greek *Panta*, "all," and the Arabic *gruel*, "thirsty," stands for the circumstances of his birth. At the same time, Pantagruel is thirsty for all knowledge and a wide range of experience. Gargantua's early education is a parody of the medieval education and Gothic philosophy spurned by the new Renaissance scholars; he is sent to a new tutor, and a typical day under this regime epitomizes the new learning, which emphasizes wide reading in both Greek and Roman classics as well as other languages, such as Hebrew, Arabic, and vernacular European tongues, and a disciplined attention paid to the body and its health, along with the intellectual and spiritual aspects of a person. The education of Gargantua and Gargantua's letter to his son Pantagruel when the latter first goes to Paris to study are widely recognized as manifestos of the new Renaissance approach to learning.

The size of these two giants is never specified. They are small enough to sit at a table with regular human beings or to fit on shipboard, but at other times this would hardly seem possible. For example, when Pantagruel, having interrupted his studies to fight an enemy invading his home kingdom of Utopia, finds his army caught in a severe downpour, he sticks his tongue halfway out and shelters the entire force. Alcofribas Nasier, the narrator of *Pantagruel*, arrives late and finds there is no room for another person under the tongue, so he climbs into Pantagruel's mouth and discovers an entire society living in his mouth and throat. When he emerges six months later and tells Pantagruel about this, the giant asks him what he ate and where he excreted; when Nasier tells him that he ate what Pantagruel ate and excreted in him, the giant laughs good humoredly.

The generation of giants is outlined in a quasi-Biblical genealogy in the beginning of the second book: they resulted from ordinary humans eating apples that were enormous because they grew in earth soaked in the blood of the murdered Abel. Some of these people grew to an enormous size, and Rabelais explains that these giants survived the Flood because one of them, Hurtaly, although he was not *in* Noah's Ark, straddled it the way a child straddles his hobbyhorse, and so survived to propagate a line of giants culminating in Gargantua and Pantagruel. Another kind of monstrous generation occurs when Pantagruel farts: not only does the Earth shake for 29 miles around, but his fart creates 53,000 tiny men; a second fart creates a like number of tiny women, and together they constitute the race of Pigmies, whom Pantagruel moves to an island where they flourish, but engage in perpetual warfare with the cranes. Catherynne Valente, in her 2010 novel *The Habitation of the Blessed*, develops this motif and creates an interrelation between the pigmies' and cranes' war and reproductive cycles.

Monsters that Pantagruel encounters in his travels and campaigns include a werewolf—*Loupgarou* in French—who is not described as a werewolf as such, but as a giant wearing armor made of anvils. Pantagruel picks him up and uses him as a scythe to mow down the other giants in his army. A flying stone decapitates Pantagruel's tutor, Epistemon. After the battle, Pantagruel's friend Panurge uses various ointments to glue Epistemon's head onto his body, which he then sews on; Epistemon revives and recalls having spent some time in the Underworld, drinking with devils. This narrative about patching together parts of a corpse and reanimating it anticipates Mary Shelley's *Frankenstein* by nearly 300 years (see **Frankenstein's Monster**).

Books four and five chronicle Pantagruel's quest for the Oracle of the Bottle, which takes him through many strange lands. On the Island of Nowhere, he purchases a reindeer that is very large and that changes colors, not only according to its background, like the chameleon, but also according to its emotional state. Further on, their ships approach a gigantic whale, associated with **Leviathan**. Pantagruel arranges his ships in an *upsilon* formation, which was associated with Hercules's *bivium*, or crossroads choice between vice and virtue; Panurge runs below deck in great fear while Pantagruel takes the virtuous path and kills the whale with three well-aimed harpoons. On an island after their encounter with the monstrous whale, Pantagruel's company is attacked by an army of wild sausages, led by a giant brain sausage, and reinforced by blood puddings and patés. On another island, they encounter the giant Bringuenarilles, or Splitnostrils, who eats windmills and, having run out of these structures, has gone on to eat all of the stoves, pans, and other kitchenware on the island. Elsewhere, another giant, Quaresmeprenant, or Lent-holder, is described in a Surrealist fashion as a giant composed of a variety of mismatched objects, such as a tongue like a harp, a mouth like a blanket, a beard like a lantern, a perineum like a flageolet, and an optic nerve like a musket.

Urination plays a major recurring role in the saga of the giants; when the young Gargantua first arrives in Paris, he is so annoyed by the people's insolence that he urinates on the city, killing 260,418 people, not including women and children. When the survivors realize that it was a joke, and that the joke was on them, they say it was done *par ris*, for a laugh, thus giving the city its name, Paris. Pantagruel, counterattacking the army of the Dipsodes that has attacked his native land of Utopia, urinates on the enemy's camp, drowning all within a ten-mile radius. That the use of piss jokes is more than adolescent humor here is indicated by a study of the serious role that urine played in the medicine of Rabelais's day (see Persels 150–51).

Rabelais himself, in the Author's Prologue to the First Book, compares the adventures of Gargantua to a kind of box called a *Silenus*, which is made to look like the old satyr: grotesque, ugly, and humorous, but containing a valuable medication inside. In the same prologue, the author instructs the reader to emulate the dog who gnaws tirelessly on a bone, because the most nutritious meat is the marrow locked at its core. Paradoxically, Dr Rabelais's prescription for the reader, as stated in the Author's Prologue to the Fourth Book, is for moderation in all things. Appropriately enough, an author significantly influenced by Rabelais is the famously immoderate Alfred Jarry (1873–1907), whose King Ubu is modeled on the lovable coward Panurge.

The Russian literary critic and philosopher Mikhail Bakhtin (1895–1975) wrote a dissertation that has since been translated as *Rabelais and His World*, in which he argues that Rabelais's work is best understood as an outgrowth of the medieval Feast of Fools. In this non-canonical celebration, the roles of the official authorities and the lowest—and most ridiculed—members of society were reversed for a day; Bakhtin argues that this leveling was what Rabelais was doing in his works featuring Gargantua and Pantagruel. The physical body and bodily functions, such as eating, drinking, urinating, and excreting, were celebrated on the same level as the "higher functions" of thinking and feeling, and this celebration of the vital functions was embodied in the grotesque. This reversal of traditional categories, also known as the "World Upside-Down," and the exuberant valuation of the physical processes of life, together bound up in the "carnivalesque," has been highly influential in subsequent readings of Rabelais's work, and has been extended, although not without controversy, to other areas of study, such as folkloristic studies of the Mardi Gras.

Don Riggs

References and Suggested Reading

Bakhtin, Mikhail. *Rabelais and His World*. Translated by Helene Iswolsky. Cambridge, MA: MIT Press, 1968.

Masters, G. Mallary. *Rabelaisian Dialectic and the Platonic-Hermetic Tradition*. Albany: State University of New York Press, 1969.

Persels, Jeff. "Taking the Piss out of Pantagruel: Urine and Micturition in Rabelais." *Yale French Studies* 110 (2006): 137–51.

Rabelais, François. *Gargantua and Pantagruel*. Translated by Burton Raffel. New York: Norton, 1990.

——. *Oeuvres complètes*, edited by Guy Demerson [1975]. Reprint, Paris: Editions du Seuil, 1995.

GARGOYLE

A gargoyle is an animal statue, often in chimerical or monstrous form, which serves as a conduit for demonic energy, usually coming to life in the process. (An animated human statue is a **homunculus** or **golem.**) The monster takes its name and shape from the sculptures used as waterspouts and exterior ornaments in Gothic architecture.

Architectural gargoyles likely originated as devices to frighten birds away from nesting in rain gutters, given the strong similarities (large or prominent eyes, snarling mouths) of gargoyles in ancient Greece and China, and in medieval Europe. The earliest known medieval gargoyles appear on Laon Cathedral (c. 1200–1220) and Notre-Dame de Paris (c. 1225); the

Fig. 14 ***On My Head*** **by Anki King**

widely cited denunciation of gargoyles by St Bernard of Clairvaux (1091–1153) actually refers to carvings *inside* the church, or even to illuminated manuscripts. Much of the modern image of gargoyles comes not from authentic medieval statuary but from the wildly popular and much-imitated "reconstructions" sculpted in 1843–64 by Eugene Viollet-le-Duc (1814–79) for the cathedral of Notre-Dame de Paris.

Technically, the term "gargoyle" refers only to sculpted waterspouts, since the word comes from the French *gargouille*, meaning "throat." However, in horror the word denotes a wide variety of bestial sculptures, of three general types: constructs animated by sorcery, vessels for possession by **demons**, or a monstrous species resembling statues. (In pulp horror especially, it also denoted ugly or deformed villains, or racial minorities.) As with many other monsters, the overlap of horror and fantasy tropes, and the increasing market for juvenile "horror" fiction, have produced friendly gargoyles of all three types.

Evil Constructs

In "Maker of Gargoyles" (1932), Clark Ashton Smith introduces the gargoyle brought to supernatural life by evil. Medieval stonemason Reynard unconsciously infuses his hate and lust into two gargoyles that ravage the town of Vyones; when he tries to smash them, they push him off the roof. Fritz Leiber's novelette "Conjure Wife" (1943) (expanded to novel length in 1952) adds active sorcerous intent: a **witch** animates a **dragon** sculpture from the roof of Hemphill College and sends it to kill anthropology professor Norman Saylor. Leiber equates self-important, reactionary Victorian morals with overwrought twentieth-century Gothic architecture: when animated by hate and jealousy, both can kill. Sidney Hayers's 1962 film of the novel, *Night of the Eagle*, replaces the dragon with an eagle: like Smith's gargoyles, the film's eagle kills the witch who animates it. Dario Argento (as misdirection in his 1977 film *Suspiria*), Martin Campbell (straightforwardly in the 1991 HBO film *Cast a Deadly Spell*), and Colin Budds (adding a still-petrified flock of statues in *Curse of the Talisman* [2001]) all utilize this basic structure.

Variations include the science-fictional Bok in the 1971 *Doctor Who* episode "The Daemons" by Barry Letts and Robert Sloman, and the gargoyle sorcerer in *Reign of the Gargoyles*, a 2007 Sci-Fi original film by Ayton Davis. The alien "Daemon" Azal (see **Extraterrestrial**) animates Bok, an English stone gargoyle, using telekinesis, not magic. Davis's "horned king" was animated by pagans, but sculpted his own gargoyle army to kill his creators; when Nazi sorcerers reawaken the "bloodstone" beast, they suffer the same fate. Borrowing the contagious monster motif from **werewolf** and **vampire** films, the king gargoyle's creations only die when he is returned to stone by a blow from the Spear of Destiny.

Demonic Vessels

In "The Horn of Vapula" (1932) by Lewis Spence, the bishop Brachet makes a pact with Satan (see **Devil, The**), but reneges and binds his demon familiar Vapula into a horned and goatish gargoyle; it prowls the countryside by night for centuries until stopped by two adventurers. "The Cambridge Beast" (1988) by Mary Ann Allen presents the gargoyle as a moldering, corpse-like material **ghost** in the tradition of M.R. James. In Ivan Reitman's *Ghostbusters* (1984), two horned canine statues hold the demonic spirits Zuul and Vinz Klortho. They attack those demons' chosen human hosts, possess them, and then transform back into demon dogs.

Such "possessed" gargoyles can contain either demonic or human spirits, seemingly interchangeably. Isaac Christians, the Marvel Comics hero Gargoyle (created by J.M. de Matteis [1953–], first appearing in *Defenders* #94 [1981]), makes a deal with a demon in exchange for prosperity for his hometown. The demon transplants Christians's spirit into a gargoyle statue to kidnap a superhero. Thwarted by the Defenders, Christians rebels against the demon and becomes a superhero in his own right and a member of the Defenders. In later comics, he gains the ability to switch between human and gargoyle forms. The magical gargoyle in *Cursed* (a grade-Z 1990 Canadian horror film by Mychael Arsenault) contains both good and evil spirits, likely a reference to the folk theory that gargoyle statues protected the cathedral from demons (rather than protecting the walls from water damage). Coincidentally, under gargoyle influence, the film's scientist Vlad develops a protective molecule for resisting acid rain.

The line between human and gargoyle can blur still further. An artist sees a gargoyle murder his best friend in "Lover's Vow," the final segment of *Tales From the Darkside: The Movie* (John Harrison, 1990). It spares his life under the condition that he tell no one what he saw. The same night, he meets a beautiful woman and later marries her. When he shows her his gargoyle sculpture, she turns out to be the gargoyle, transformed to human. She (regretfully) kills him for breaking his promise, then returns to stone form. In "Grotesque," a 1996 episode of *The X-Files* by Howard Gordon, a barely sane artist claims a "gargoyle spirit" committed a series of brutal slayings. The episode ends ambiguously, hinting that the gargoyle spirit possessed the artist, the FBI investigator on his case, and (briefly) our hero Fox Mulder (David Duchovny).

The Gargoyle as Species

Bill L. Norton's 1972 CBS TV movie *Gargoyles* is the first work to present gargoyles as a species as opposed to solitary creatures. A race of reptilian creatures created by Satan to harry mankind at centuries-long intervals hunts for a gargoyle skull found by an anthropologist in a roadside exhibit; gargoyle statues, the film explains, are folk memories and warnings. That same year, the short story "Bleeding Stones" by Harlan Ellison depicted the gargoyles on St Patrick's Cathedral suddenly brought to life by industrial pollution; they rapidly massacre New York City and fly east toward Rome.

Less apocalyptically, gargoyles appear as a species in the earliest (1974) *Dungeons & Dragons* rulebooks (see **Dungeons & Dragons, Monsters In**). These cunning, reptilian, horned, fanged monsters can only be hit with magic weapons. A similar rule obtains in Jim Wynorski's film *Gargoyle* (2004): a race of demonic creatures driven almost to extinction in medieval times, gargoyles can only be killed by weapons coated with the blood of Christ (or the specially blessed blood of a priest). The heroes stop the last surviving gargoyle in Romania from hatching its eggs. The gargoyles in Bill Corcoran's film *Rise of the Gargoyles* (2009) are similarly oviparous, and blend into Parisian rooflines by day by turning into statues.

Friendly Gargoyles

These latter species almost certainly derive from the nocturnal, egg-laying protagonists of the animated Disney-ABC TV series *Gargoyles* (1994–97), created by Greg Weisman. Magically petrified, the heroic "Manhattan Clan" awakens when their Scottish castle is transplanted to the top of a millionaire's New York skyscraper. They resist this modern sorcerer's schemes and instead befriend a New York police officer, battling monsters for humanity. Fantasy novelist Katherine Kurtz (1944–) subverts the demonic vessel: one gargoyle lives in every church in modern Dublin, angelic observers who can move and talk on one moonless night a month. Her novel *Saint Patrick's Gargoyle* (2001) expands her short story "The Gargoyle's Shadow" (1998) in which a gargoyle and an elderly knight (of Malta) recover stolen church property.

All these domesticated gargoyles emphasize the folk belief of gargoyles as protectors. Piers Anthony also evokes the gargoyles' original hydraulic function in *Geis of the Gargoyle* (1995), in which Gary Gar is the guardian and purifier of a river. The gargoyles of Terry Pratchett's (1948–) Discworld (either urban **trolls** or accidentally animated statues) still function as waterspouts and as protectors: Constable Downspout (a secondary character in *Feet of Clay* [1996]) serves on the City Watch.

Perhaps the most original, and at the same time most traditional, friendly gargoyles are Hugo, Victor, and Laverne, the trio of singing, talking statues in the animated Disney feature *The Hunchback of Notre Dame* (1996) by Kirk Wise and Gary Trousdale. Carefully drawn replicas of Viollet-le-Duc's "restorations," they come to life only when alone with Quasimodo. Thus, they embody his subconscious desires and fears, much as Viollet-le-Duc's "re-created" gargoyles embodied the desires and fears of the Victorian age while shaping its medieval fantasies.

Kenneth Hite

References and Suggested Reading

Benton, Janetta Rebold. *Holy Terrors: Gargoyles on Medieval Buildings.* New York: Abbeville Press, 1997.

Camille, Michael. *The Gargoyles of Notre-Dame: Medievalism and the Monsters of Modernity.* Chicago: University of Chicago Press, 2009.

Kilpatrick, Nancy, and Thomas S. Roche, eds. *In the Shadow of the Gargoyle.* New York: Ace Books, 1998.

Leiber, Fritz. *Conjure Wife.* New York: Twayne, 1953.

Sheridan, Ronald, and Anne Ross. *Gargoyles and Grotesques: Paganism in the Medieval Church.* Boston: New York Graphic Society, 1975.

Wilks, Stephen R. *Medusa: Solving the Mystery of the Gorgon.* Oxford: Oxford University Press, 2007.

GELLO—*see* Empousa

GERYON—*see* Dante, Monsters in; Manticore

GHIDORAH—*see* Extraterrestrial

GHOST

The term "ghost," from the German *geist* ("soul," "spirit"), generally refers to the spirit of a dead person or animal, particularly one

Fig. 15 ***Waiting*** **by Anki King**

that manifests its presence to the living. In Western cultures, ghosts appear most frequently as insubstantial apparitions. In many other cultures, however, including those of Africa and Asia, ghosts take a variety of forms, some of them quite corporeal. Nevertheless, the reasons why these spirits of the dead appear to the living tend to be similar across the globe. Ghosts return to exact revenge, to complete unfinished business, to request proper burial, and to warn the living of danger. More generally, ghosts reflect human speculation as to whether the spirit survives bodily death and, if so, what forms and attitudes the spirit might exhibit. Literary and cinematic ghosts are also used to express a wide variety of societal concerns, often appearing in metaphorical and allegorical contexts intended to represent themes of cultural significance, such as political and economic criticism as well as larger issues of national identity. As liminal figures, ghosts often represent the experiences of displaced or marginalized peoples such as woman, immigrants, and various minority groups.

Literary ghosts have a long history. One of the earliest ghosts ever to appear in literature is that of Enkidu in the Babylonian/ Mesopotamian epic *Gilgamesh* (c. second millennium BCE), a story greatly concerned with the nature of mortality. A number of ghosts appear in Greek epic poems from the eighth century BCE, and the ghost of Samuel speaks warnings to Saul in the Old Testament (*Samuel* 1:28.13–20). In classical Greek and Roman literature, ghosts appear for many traditional reasons such as the desire for a proper burial, whereas in the largely Christian milieu of the Middle Ages, ghosts often remind the living of the perils of sin. Later European literature, as well as that of the Americas, presents more secular ghosts, but often also uses phantoms symbolically to represent cultural discontinuity in the face of frequently shifting national boundaries and immigrant populations. Ghosts eventually begin to represent more psychologically and morally complex concerns, and invariably say more about the mindset of the living than about that of the dead.

In various African and Asian countries, many types of ghost are corporeal rather than insubstantial, but they often represent the same issues as their Western counterparts. Ghosts in African literature frequently reflect concerns of the African diaspora and the lost histories of slave populations. Ghosts in Asian literature and cinema are predominantly female, usually angry and destructive after having suffered at the hands of men, returning primarily for vengeance.

D. Felton

Classical and Medieval

Ghosts appear as characters in many genres of literature surviving from the classical and medieval worlds, including epic poetry, tragedy, history, early church writings, and medieval chronicles. In the classical period, ghosts illustrated a number of traditional themes related to restless spirits, such as the desire for vengeance or for a proper burial. In the medieval period, ghosts were tied more closely to Christian themes such as spiritual salvation.

In the play *Eumenides* (458 BCE) by the Greek tragedian Aeschylus, for example, the ghost of Clytemnestra, murdered by her son Orestes, demands vengeance. In the works of the Roman historian Livy, the ghost of the slain Verginia never rests until all the people involved in her death are brought to justice (*Ab Urbe Condita* 3.58, c. 27–20 BCE). The rhetorician pseudo-Quintilian (first century CE) wrote a speech in which the ghost of a young man appears to his grieving mother each evening to comfort her (*Declamation X*; exact date uncertain). But the majority of ancient literary ghosts return to request a proper burial, because the Greeks and Romans strongly believed that the souls of those deprived of burial could find no rest in the afterlife. The earliest examples of such ghosts appear in the Homeric epics (eighth century BCE): the ghost of Patroclus, who died in battle, indicates to Achilles that once his body is granted funeral rituals he will no longer haunt the living (*Iliad* 23.75–6), while the ghost of Elpenor, who fell off a roof when drunk and broke his neck, tells Odysseus that he cannot enter Hades until his body is buried (*Odyssey* 11.52). According to the Roman biographer Suetonius, the assassinated emperor Caligula, whose corpse was only partially burned in a hastily built fire, haunted the area until his sisters dug up the body and gave it a proper ceremony (*Caligula* 59, c. 121 CE).

The most fully realized literary ghost story in classical literature—essentially a prototypical **haunted house** tale—comes from Roman author Pliny the Younger. A large house is haunted by the phantom of an old man rattling chains until the inhabitants all leave or die of fright and the house falls into disrepair. But finally a philosopher, unperturbed by the supernatural, faces the phantom and follows it into the courtyard, where it vanishes. When the spot is excavated, a body is found, entwined with chains. After the remains receive a public burial with proper rituals, the ghost never appears again (*Letter* 7.27, c. 100–109 CE).

To the early Christians, however, the Greek and Roman appeasement of the dead by funerary rites represented the kind of pagan superstition frowned upon by the Church (Joynes 3). Rather, in the Middle Ages, "a time of unquestioning religious faith," ghost stories tended to have exemplary purposes, with the intent of evoking a pious response from the audience (Joynes xii). The souls of the dead were restless because they had sinned, but they could be saved through prayer, as in works from the early Middle Ages such as the *Dialogues* of Gregory the Great, Book IV, Chapters XL and LV (593 CE). Bede's *Ecclesiastical History of the English People* (731 CE) also contains several stories of such ghostly visitations.

A number of texts from the high Middle Ages preserve ghost stories, including *Of Miracles* by French abbot Peter the Venerable, which presents various apparitions of the dead. The ghost of Baron Bernard le Gros, for example, appears to request that the local abbot pray for him (Book I, Chapter XI; second quarter of the twelfth century). The *Deeds of the English Kings* (c. 1127) by the English monk and historian William of Malmsbury contains, among other stories, one about the ghost of a sinful man who returns to warn his friend to lead a virtuous life (Book III, Section 237).

Icelandic sagas from the late Middle Ages present ghost stories that focus less on Christian redemption and instead contain troublemaking ghosts, such as a group of phantom fishermen in *Eyrbyggja Saga* (c. mid-thirteenth century) who, having been lost at sea, show up at their own funeral feast and do not leave until Snorri the Priest drives them away with an effective combination of Christian ritual and Icelandic law (Chaper 54; Joynes 156). The late medieval period also saw the development of a new theme: those who scorn love in this life are punished in the next. In the thirteenth-century French *Lay du Trot* ("The Song of the Jolting Horse"), for example, a knight sees a ghostly procession of suffering women and finds that they are thus tormented for disdaining their lovers during their lives. Likewise, Boccacio's *Decameron* (c. 1353) contains the story of a nobleman scorned by the woman he loved. The man killed himself out of despair, and his ghost explains that he is condemned to eternal suffering for the suicide. But the girl herself, never repenting her cruelty, was also condemned to Hell, and their joint punishment in the afterlife is for them to continually re-enact a scene in which he cuts out her heart and feeds it to his dogs (Fifth Day, Story VIII). Such stories were intended as warnings to the living, reminders of the brevity of life and the importance of even transitory pleasures (Joynes 206).

D. Felton

References and Suggested Reading

Felton, D. *Haunted Greece and Rome: Ghost Stories from Classical Antiquity.* Austin: University of Texas Press, 1999.

Hickman, Ruby Mildred. *Ghostly Etiquette on the Classical Stage.* Cedar Rapids, IA: Torch Press, 1938.

Joynes, Andrew. *Medieval Ghost Stories: An Anthology of Miracles, Marvels and Prodigies.* Woodbridge: The Boydell Press, 2001.

Europe and Russia

Ghosts and spirits have always held crucial symbolic value in the European cultural heritage. In medieval and Renaissance texts, their roles ranged from the spiritual and eschatological (as in medieval mystery plays) to the largely rhetorical, like the specter of Égée (Aegeus), whose declamation about an impending tragedy in the house of his son Theseus opens French dramatist Robert Garnier's play *Hippolyte* (1573). From the late eighteenth century, the Romantic reaction against Enlightenment rationalism provoked new trends in supernatural literature, including the German *Sturm und Drang* ("storm and stress"), the French *roman noir* (whose gruesome plotlines responded directly to the real-life horrors of the French Revolution), and the British Gothic novel, with its characteristically lurid neo-medieval tropes of ancestral ghosts, crumbling castles, and haunted rooms. Such literature, drawing on both regional folklore and individual psychology, created a new, secular type of ghost, often motivated by venal desires such as revenge, lust, or greed. Twentieth- and twenty-first-century cinema renewed Europe's fascination with the spectral, often casting the phantom as a symbol for absence, alienation, or cultural discontinuity. Today, European literary and cinematic ghosts continue to reflect personal and national traumas.

Germany

The famous phrase *die Todten reiten schnell* ("the dead travel fast") originated in Gottfried Bürger's 1773 ballad *Lenore* (line 134). This story of a young warrior slain in the Seven Years' War whose specter returns to claim his waiting bride was read, adapted, and translated throughout Europe, as, for example, in Russian poet Vasilii Zhukovskii's 1813 Russian version *Svetlana*, which influenced Aleksandr Pushkin's (1799–1837) supernatural fiction. Other foundational ghost stories include Friedrich Schiller's unfinished novel *The Ghost-Seer* (1786), Heinrich von Kleist's tale "The Beggarwoman of Locarno" (1810), in which an old woman's ghost revenges itself on an arrogant knight, and E.T.A. Hoffmann's "The Entail" (1817), featuring a spiteful ghost and an inheritance dispute. Later German writers refined the genre: in Theodor Fontane's major realist novel *Effi Briest* (1896), the haunting of her marital home foreshadows Effi's infidelity, while in Theodor Stern's unusual and atmospheric novella *The Rider on the White Horse* (1888), the ghost of a local dyke-builder and his spectral mount warn of imminent flooding on the Friesian coast. Franz Kafka's "Unhappiness" (1913) is a fragmentary ghost story about a spectral child. In Fritz Lang's 1922 silent film *Dr Mabuse the Gambler* and its sequels, the murdering Dr Mabuse is haunted by his victims' phantoms—or perhaps by his own psychotic hallucinations. Christian Petzold's widely acclaimed 2007 film *Yella* analyzes, via spectrality, the sense of dislocation experienced by citizens of the former East Germany.

Russia and Eastern Europe

German Romantic literature, particularly E.T.A. Hoffmann's Gothic-fantastic tales, enjoyed broad popularity in Russia, especially between 1800 and 1850. Unsurprisingly, therefore, scarcely any Russian writers of the late Romantic period failed to write at least one ghost story. Typical themes included gambling, unrequited love, extramarital passion, and social ambition.

In 1833, Aleksandr Pushkin penned the most famous ghost tale in Russian literature, "The Queen of Spades" (adapted as an opera by Petr Chaikovsky in 1890). In Pushkin's tale, Hermann, a young army officer, overhears that an elderly countess possesses the secret of three cards that, played in sequence, can win a fortune. Hermann deliberately initiates an affair with the

Countess's penniless ward in order to gain access to the old lady. Hoping to persuade the Countess to reveal her secret, he steals into her room at night and inadvertently frightens her to death. The Countess's ghost later visits Hermann and tells him the three winning cards, on the condition that he marry her ward. Using the supernatural formula, Hermann wins huge sums at the first two games of cards he attempts; but the third and final card—the Queen of Spades—proves false. Ruined, Hermann goes mad.

Two of Pushkin's younger contemporaries, Mikhail Lermontov and Nikolai Gogol, also wrote celebrated ghost stories, including Lermontov's 1841 "Shtoss." *Shtoss* was a popular Russian card game and, like "The Queen of Spades," this story, too, revolves around gambling, featuring a card-sharping specter who lures the hero to financial and psychological ruin. The ghost in Nikolai Gogol's "The Overcoat" (1842) has been famously interpreted by many critics as a powerful allegorical symbol of social justice for the browbeaten "little man." Gogol's anti-hero is Akakii Akakievich Bashmachkin, a poor clerk who dies of despair after his new overcoat—which he has starved himself for months to afford—is stolen. Akakii returns as a ghost who steals overcoats, targeting those who bullied or neglected him in his lifetime. These two stories, as well as "The Queen of Spades," are set on the foggy streets of St Petersburg, once described by Fyodor Dostoevsky (1821–81) as the most unreal city in the world, built on the bones of slave laborers and thus a foreordained locus for haunting.

Crime and Punishment (1866), one of Dostoevsky's most Gothic novels, includes several ghosts. The most prominent is Marfa Petrovna Svidrigailova, the wife of the hero Raskolnikov's amoral alter ego Svidrigailov, who may have murdered her (this remains unclear). She appears three times to Svidrigailov, each time with a remarkably trivial message: for example, like Tristram Shandy's mother in Laurence Sterne's novel (1759–67), she reminds her husband to wind up the clock. Dostoevsky's great literary rival, Ivan Turgenev, wrote several short supernatural tales, most famously "Phantoms" (1864) and "Klara Milich" (1882). Both feature young men seduced and emotionally exhausted by nocturnal, **vampire**-like female phantoms. In Anton Chekhov's short story "The Black Monk" (1894), the hero repeatedly sees a cowled phantom who promises him a brilliant future which is, ironically, destroyed by his growing insanity.

Few ghosts appear in twentieth-century Russian literature, although the re-emergence of specters in post-Soviet fiction shows modern Russian writers in dialogue with their revolutionary past. Such specters include the old Count's ghost haunting a modern family in Petr Aleshkovskii's *Vladimir Chigrintsev* (1997) and the shade of a Russian Civil War telegraph operator in Dmitry Bykov's *Living Souls* (2008), set in an imaginary future Russia.

Like Russian literature, Eastern Europe's spectral fiction has evolved from explicit horror to the use of haunting as a trope for memory. Famous Polish supernatural tales include Jan Potocki's *The Manuscript at Saragossa* (1804), a Gothic labyrinth of interweaving plots and multiple specters, and Witold Gombrowicz's ironic postmodern Gothic novel *Possessed, or, The Secret of Myslotch* (1939). Similarly ironic is Hungarian author Antal Szerb's *The Pendragon Legend* (1934) about a haunted Welsh castle. Hungarian dramatist Ferenc Molnár's play *Liliom* (1909), in which the hero, a carousel barker, is given one chance to undo as a ghost the evil he did as a man, was remade with a slightly happier ending by Rodgers and Hammerstein as the musical *Carousel!* (1945). Romanian author Doina Ruşti's novel *The Ghost in the Mill* (2008) exploits the device of haunting to revisit her nation's recent history, including the effects of the Chernobyl accident in Ukraine in 1986.

France, Italy, Spain, Portugal

Voltaire, the champion of Enlightenment rationalism, ironically created one of French drama's most famous ghosts in his play *Sémiramis* (1748; produced as the opera *Semiramide* by Rossini, 1823). Nino, the late king of Babylon, rises from his tomb to expose his murderers and prevent an incestuous marriage. French phantoms flourished in the nineteenth century; the vogue for Spiritualism inspired tales such as Théophile Gautier's novella *Spirite* (1866), a spectral love story plotted around automatic writing, and Villier de l'Isle-Adam's "Véra" (1874), in which a husband refuses to release his dead wife. Alsatian folklore informed the jointly written ghost tales of Émile Erckmann (1822–89) and Alexandre Chatrian (1826–90). The prolific Guy de Maupassant frequently used haunting as a trope for incipient insanity, most notably in his short stories "**The Horla**" (1887) and "Who Knows?" (1890); his "The Apparition" (1883), in contrast, is a brief Gothic mystery about a chateau haunted by a female revenant.

With rare exceptions, such as the few ghosts in Boccacio's *Decameron* (c. 1353), Italy lacks a literary tradition of haunting. In cinema, Italy's specters are generally familial or historical, such as the ghost of the family's stillborn son in *A Whisper in the Dark* (Marcello Aliprandi, 1976) and the Nazi phantoms that terrify two teenage couples at a remote villa in Lucio Fulci's *Sodoma's Ghost* (1988).

In Spain, many modern authors and directors have used phantoms to revisit cultural memories of the Spanish Civil War and the Franco regime, as in Galician writer Manuel Rivas's *The Carpenter's Pencil* (1998), in which the ghost of an artist executed by Falangist militia haunts a pencil (and its future user). Similarly themed cinema includes the Spanish-Mexican production *The Devil's Backbone* (2001) from Guillermo del Toro, set in a haunted Spanish orphanage during the Civil War, and the US-Spanish production *The Others* (Alejandro Amenábar, 2001), set in the British Crown Dependency of Jersey in 1945. Children's ghosts also feature in 2007's *The Orphanage* (Juan Antonio Bayona), while Pedro Almodóvar's 2006 film *Volver* subverts the entire genre with a false ghost (that nonetheless attempts to effect the traditional spectral tasks of revelation and reparation). The most notable ghost in Portuguese literature is the poet Fernando Pessoa, who affectionately haunts the title character of José Saramago's novel *The Year of the Death of Ricardo Reis* (1984).

Scandinavia

One of the earliest literary Scandinavian ghosts is Angantyr's ghost from medieval Old Norse epic poetry (the *Eddas*), who rises from his grave to give his warrior-daughter the **dwarf**-forged sword Tyrfor. This episode has been translated and adapted by many writers, including Leconte de Lisle and W.H. Auden. Danish author Hans Christian Andersen's tale "The Travelling Companion" (1835) features a grateful ghost who helps a traveler to defeat a magician and marry a princess, and many apparitions inhabit a Stockholm townhouse in Swedish playwright August Strindberg's experimental drama *The Ghost Sonata* (1907). In "The Supper at Elsinore" (1934), an elegiac tale by Danish author Isak Dinesen (Karen Blixen), two elderly sisters reunite with their brother's ghost—and with the truth behind his long-ago disappearance.

Muireann Maguire

References and Suggested Reading

Billiani, Francesca, and Gigliola Sulis, eds. *The Italian Gothic-Fantastic: Encounters and Rewritings of Narrative Traditions.* Madison, NJ: Fairleigh Dickinson University Press, 2007.

Chesters, Timothy. *Ghost Stories in Late Renaissance France: Walking by Night.* Oxford: Oxford University Press, 2011.

Cornwell, Neil, ed. *The Gothic-Fantastic in Nineteenth-century Russian Literature.* Amsterdam and Atlanta, GA: Rodopi, 1999.

Evans, David, and Kate Griffiths, eds. *Haunting Presences: Ghosts in French Literature and Culture.* Cardiff: University of Wales Press, 2007.

Maguire, Muireann. *Stalin's Ghosts: Gothic Themes in Early Soviet Literature.* Oxford: Peter Lang, 2012.

Simpson, Mark. *The Russian Gothic Novel and its British Antecedents.* Columbus, OH: Slavica Publishers, 1986.

Stiffler, Muriel W. *The German Ghost Story as Genre.* New York: Peter Lang, 1993.

Great Britain and Ireland

The British tradition of ghostly narratives long predates the familiar Victorian ghost story. In medieval Britain, ghosts populated both religious and folkloric narratives; they requested prayers, terrified their former companions, or merely served as a *memento mori* for the living. Most such narratives portray ghosts as souls in Purgatory, permitted to return to the living to seek repentance or confession for sins that prevented them from going to Heaven. Existing within this specifically Christian, specifically purgatorial construct of the afterlife, these ghosts were predictable and formulaic, acting in accordance with scripts already written.

By the sixteenth and seventeenth centuries, with less emphasis on the doctrine of Purgatory, ghosts' purposes among the living became less clear. Lacking a definite location from which to appear, and consequently lacking a definite set of rules governing their behavior, ghosts of this period began to appear for increasingly trivial reasons. They still confessed their sins, accused their murderers, or demanded revenge, but they also requested that relatives clear debts left outstanding at their deaths or revealed the location of hidden wills. Ghosts no longer needed the intercession of prayers to release them from Purgatory, but they remained unable to join the afterlife proper until the circumstances of their deaths had been resolved.

It is these ghosts whose echoes we see remaining in the Renaissance and early modern period, as Shakespeare's Richard III (1591) is condemned by the spectral forms of those whose deaths he caused, and as Macbeth (c. 1606) sees the ghost of his friend and victim Banquo. Hamlet's father's ghost (c. 1601) appears to his son rather than his murderer, but still to seek revenge. As with their medieval forebears, such ghosts act as symptoms of a greater problem, rather than as agents in their own right; they arise when the normal order of things—moral or metaphysical—is disrupted, and disappear once that order is restored.

Ghosts were frequent characters in Elizabethan and Jacobean dramas, fitting particularly well within the bloodthirsty conventions of the revenge tragedy, but it is the eighteenth-century Gothic novel that laid the foundations for the modern ghost story. The Gothic, with its emphasis on the archaic and supernatural, provided a counter to the forward-thinking rationality of the Enlightenment. Thus, Horace Walpole's *The Castle of Otranto* (1764) features a skeletal apparition as well as a ghostly disembodied armored hand and helmet, signifying the disruption of a noble family by usurpation and immorality. Matthew Lewis's *The Monk* (1796) provides a dramatic Gothic example in its frightening portrayal of a spectral nun.

Ghosts like these might serve pivotal roles, but they are not central to the narrative; rather, they illustrate the significance of plot elements, or act as macabre scenery in a genre that fetishized the horrific. Ghosts may have lost the highly structured conventions governing the narrative roles that the medieval worldview provided for them, but their conventional appearance as terrifying apparitions guaranteed them a place in Gothic literature.

With the growth of the short story form in the nineteenth century came the rise of the ghost story proper. The genre is often seen as a milder and more palatable successor to the Gothic, but its significantly different conventions and aims constitute a new form of supernatural narrative, one in which the ghost itself plays a central role. The 1820s saw several clear examples of a transition from the eighteenth-century Gothic to this newer form, and the increased popularity of ghost stories corresponded with the Victorian fascination with death and Spiritualism, with its claims to a new understanding and interaction with the afterlife.

W.H. Ainsworth's "The Spectre Bride" (1822), perhaps the most Gothic of these early nineteenth-century stories, is set in a seventeenth-century German castle. Its only true ghost is the skeletal form of the eponymous bride's father, come to warn her of her impending marriage to a mysterious demonic figure. Such overtly Gothic influences are more rare in later stories, with occasional exceptions such as Mrs Henry Wood's "Gina Montani" (1851). Still, echoes of the Gothic appear in gruesome depictions of ghosts such as Charlotte Bronte's "Napoleon and the Spectre" (1833). In Walter Scott's "The Tapestried Chamber" (1828), however, the conventions of what would become the Victorian ghost story emerge, presenting more realistic domestic settings and protagonists alongside ghosts who took a central role in the story. Although the ghost itself is terrifying and threatening, the house it haunts is unremarkable, and the supernatural events cease as soon as the protagonist leaves.

Another of Scott's stories, "Wandering Willie's Tale" (1832), features a mysterious figure rather than a ghost, but also presents a narrative framed in the first person by a protagonist relating the story to a small group of eager listeners. This convention became ubiquitous in later nineteenth-century ghost stories. Hence, in Irish author Joseph Sheridan Le Fanu's "An Account of Some Strange Disturbances in Aungier Street" (1853), the narrator bemoans the necessity of relating events on pen and paper rather than in person. The supernatural event occurs in an old mansion that once belonged to a particularly unpleasant judge; when the narrator and his friend spend the night there, the judge's ghost, as malevolent as he was in life, appears and intentionally torments them. As the housekeeper makes clear, the specter's malice is not the result of its supernatural nature, but reflects the personality of the man himself. Thus, the actions of the ghost are not driven by any conventions governing why and how the dead appear, as was the case in the early medieval narratives. Rather, a ghost's actions are motivated by its own personal circumstances.

Not all mid nineteenth-century ghosts showed as much individual agency. In Edward Bulwer-Lytton's "The Haunted and the Haunters" (1857), for example, a man and his faithful servant spending the night in a haunted house see its history played out before them, with the narrator later explaining that a ghost is not the soul of the departed, but rather "the eidolon of the dead form" re-enacting traumatic events (Bulwer-Lytton 236). Elizabeth Gaskell's "The Old Nurse's Story" (1852) makes its moral point particularly strongly: not only does a dead child return to haunt the family home from which she and her unmarried mother were cast, providing a constant reminder of her death and her family's culpability, but a ghostly tableau re-enacts the scene in which the mother's own father and sister refuse her pleas for mercy and send her and the child out into the snow.

Gaskell's story was published in the Christmas number of Dickens's *Household Words* magazine, a common venue for ghost stories in the mid nineteenth century and, most likely, the reason for the widespread Victorian association between ghost stories and Christmas. Dickens's *A Christmas Carol* (1843) presents one of the best known of all such ghosts in the form of Jacob Marley, held on Earth by chains of his own making, forged from the greed which marked his life. Marley's visit serves as Scrooge's call to repentance and reconsideration of his life. In this, perhaps, we can see a reflection of the ghosts of medieval narratives; Marley is, after all, trapped in a secular Purgatory, one that awaits Scrooge if he does not follow his former partner's warning. Notably, however, Marley's ghostly appearance is not visually horrific. For the most part, the narrative voice lingers on descriptions of the chains he wears as well as the groaning sounds he makes, identifying his role in the narrative without overemphasizing death and decay.

In this, Jacob Marley is a far more typically nineteenth-century ghost than Scott's or Le Fanu's. When Victorian ghosts appear, their presence itself is more often psychologically terrifying than visually horrifying. Indeed, they are often mistaken for the living, as with the ghost of the young Cathy appearing to Lockwood at the beginning of Emily Brontë's *Wuthering Heights* (1847). Existing outside the Gothic framework of their forebears, these ghosts are far more likely to materialize within an otherwise ordinary, domestic setting, with much of the power of their narratives resting upon the reader's identification with the world they disrupt. Along with the increasingly central roles they took in their own narratives, these ghosts were more individual, remaining identifiably the person they were in life rather than becoming one of the interchangeable dead.

With a greater sense of ghosts as individuals came less emphasis on narrative conventions governing the reasons they might appear. If a ghost is chiefly identified as one of the dead, its actions are governed by the spiritual laws regarding when and why it can appear. But a ghost more strongly identified with its living self may appear for any reason or motivation that appeals to that individual. As such, narratives guided by the clear metaphysical regulations of *A Christmas Carol* became less popular. Dickens's "The Signalman" (1866) contrasts the earlier story with an enigmatically disturbing ghost whose motivations are never revealed. A figure waving to the eponymous signalman in apparent warning, the ghost nevertheless gives him no opportunity to prevent the tragedies that follow, and he is left in traumatized confusion. Possibly the ghost is a premonition of the signalman's own death; possibly it is an echo of an earlier accident, one which the signalman unknowingly replicates. The story ends with no neat revelation, no discovery of an overarching truth governing the relationship between the natural and the supernatural.

By this stage in the ghost story's development, then, the form already demonstrates a far greater level of narrative and psychological complexity than was the case earlier in its history. Developments like this allowed for the possibility of the sympathetic ghost, and indeed the mid to late nineteenth century saw an expansion of the ghost story beyond the boundaries of a form designed to induce fear in the reader. Many ghosts demonstrate considerable psychological depth, as evident in the works of Mary Elizabeth Braddon (1835–

1915), Rhoda Broughton (1840–1920), Edith Nesbit (1858–1924), Dinah Mulock Craik (1826–87), and Sabine Baring-Gould (1834–1924), for example. Charlotte Riddell (1832–1906) wrote many supernatural stories featuring ghosts driven by their own emotions and motivations. Margaret Oliphant's novel *A Beleaguered City* (1880) portrays a French town from which a host of the dead expel the irreligious and unrepentant living. By the late nineteenth century, regardless of how formulaic many ghost stories may seem, it is no longer possible to describe the form using any one set of conventions. Even fear and pity were no longer the desired emotions; this period saw humor integrated into ghost stories, as, for example, in Oscar Wilde's "The Canterville Ghost" (1887), Jerome K. Jerome's collection *Told After Supper* (1891), and H.G. Wells's "The Inexperienced Ghost" (1902).

Although supernatural fiction remained quite popular in twentieth-century Britain, stories specifically featuring ghosts appeared far less frequently than they had in the Victorian period. Nevertheless, ghost stories were still written and read, with authors such as Algernon Blackwood (1869–1951) and Arthur Machen (1863–1947) blending ghosts with a wider range of supernatural terror in their novels and short stories. Richard Middleton (1882–1911), Violet Hunt (1862–1942), Walter de la Mare (1873–1956), and Oliver Onions (1873–1961), among others, continued the tradition of psychologically complex ghosts; in later decades, writers such as Joan Aiken (1924–2004) continued in that vein. That convention contrasted strongly with the work of M.R. James (1862–1936), whose collections of short supernatural fiction in the 1920s and 1930s evinced a clear return to the macabre. His ghosts are gruesome and terrifying relics of the Gothic past, and he had several imitators, including E.G. Swain (1861–1938) and R.H. Malden (1879–1951).

The ghost stories of more recent years have displayed a variety of ghostly conventions, from the Gothic macabre to the psychologically complex. Susan Hill's novel *The Woman in Black* (1983), adapted as a play by Stephen Mallatratt (1987), television series (Herbert Wise, 1989), and film (James Watkins, 2012), features a malevolent and terrifying ghost. The BBC film *Truly, Madly, Deeply* (Anthony Minghella, 1991) presents a more benevolent figure, with the ghost of an affectionate, although imperfect, husband appearing to his wife. Hogwarts Castle, the wizarding school in J.K. Rowling's "Harry Potter" series (1997–2007; see **Harry Potter, Monsters In**), is haunted by an assortment of ghosts, who are overall typically helpful to the protagonists and convivial in nature. The BBC television series *Being Human* (2009–) and its US adaptation of the same name (2011–) feature a ghostly protagonist, and combine older conventions, such as the inability of a ghost to move on to the afterlife proper until unresolved elements of its death are put to rest, with the psychological depth and complexity of the later ghost story. Given a possible renewed enthusiasm for ghosts, then, perhaps the ghost story will rise once again to its Victorian popularity; it would seem fitting, after all, that ghosts in British literature and film are not dead, but merely resting.

Jenny Bann

References and Suggested Reading

Briggs, Julia. *Night Visitors: The Rise and Fall of the English Ghost Story.* London: Faber and Faber Limited, 1977.

Bulwer-Lytton, Edward. "The Haunted and the Haunters: Or, The House and the Brain." *Blackwood's Edinburgh Magazine* (August 1859): 224–45.

Dickerson, Vanessa D. *Victorian Ghosts in the Noontide: Women Writers and the Supernatural.* Columbia and London: University of Missouri Press, 1996.

Finucane, R.C. *Ghosts: Appearances of the Dead and Cultural Transformations.* New York: Prometheus, 1996.

United States and Canada

Ghosts in literature and cinema of the United States and Canada, though often appearing for familiar reasons such as vengeance or lost love, quite frequently reflect larger thematic concerns unique to their eras. American ghosts tend in particular to mirror the immigrant experience, expressing the concerns of displaced or marginalized peoples and dealing with issues of national and ethnic identity.

Canada's literary ghost tradition is perhaps less strong than that of the United States, because for a long while Canada was considered "too new for ghosts." Settlers, particularly of French Canada, brought over their own familiar ghost stories from Brittany and Normandy (Manguel vii–viii). Nevertheless, Canadian writers offer a wide variety of unique ghosts. In Mavis Gallant's "From the Fifteenth District" (1979), for example, it is the living who haunt the dead. In W.P. Kinsella's story "Shoeless Joe Jackson Comes to Iowa" (1980, expanded into the novel *Shoeless Joe*, 1982; adapted in cinema as *Field of Dreams*, by Phil Alden Robinson, 1989), an Iowa farmer hears a mysterious voice telling him to build a baseball diamond in his cornfield, which then attracts the ghostly spirits of the 1919 Chicago White Sox team and, potentially, that of the man's father. Robertson Davies's collection *High Spirits* (1982) sets a number of humorous ghost stories in academia. In "The Ghost Who Vanished by Degrees," for example, the ghost of a graduate student who shot himself after failing his PhD orals cannot rest until he has passed his examinations.

Ghosts in early United States literature often reflect more specifically the nation's beginnings. Nathaniel Hawthorne used ghosts retroactively to reflect New England's Puritan origins, as in "The Gray Champion" (1837), but the dominance of Puritanism in actual colonial times meant that, although literature of that period was highly spiritual in nature, addressing concerns about the afterlife and the necessity of avoiding demonic influences (see **Demon**), it overall contained few literary ghosts. Not until the late eighteenth and early nineteenth centuries, under the influence of the European Gothic and Romantic movements, did ghosts start appearing regularly in American literature, and from then on writers have used ghosts to express concerns and tensions not only universal to the human condition but also unique to the nature of American settlement and expansion.

Initially, unlike many of their European counterparts, American ghost stories focused less on ghosts than on the protagonists' perception of those ghosts, expressing ambiguity as to whether the ghosts are "real" or whether a protagonist's state of mind is insufficiently able to distinguish reality from illusion. This ambiguity reflects the nineteenth century as "the scene of great debates between faith and doubt, religion and science" (Kerr, Crowley, and Crow 2–3). Such tensions frequently appear in the ghost stories of Washington Irving, most notably in "The Legend of Sleepy Hollow" (1820). The little village of Sleepy Hollow is itself "haunted" by its past, with its history of Indians, of early Dutch settlements, and the legend of the **Headless Horseman**. Irving implies that Brom Bones disguised himself as the Horseman to terrify Ichabod Crane, but Ichabod, strongly influenced by the history of the local landscape, believed he saw the famous ghost. Similarly, in "The Bold Dragoon" (1824) and "The Guests from Gibbet Island" (1845), while indicating that the protagonists believe they have seen ghosts, Irving leaves open the possibility that a more worldly explanation exists for what they have seen. The supernatural horror of Edgar Allan Poe surprisingly contains no apparitions per se, although he takes the concept of possession by the spirit of a dead woman to a particularly horrific conclusion in "Ligeia" (1838)—but here, as in the works of Irving, the state of mind of the opium-addicted protagonist results in ambiguity.

By the late nineteenth century, under the influence of Victorian-era Spiritualism, the growing feminist movement, and the rise of psychoanalytic theory, American literary ghosts reached a new height of popularity, reflecting a broad variety of societal issues. Mary E. Wilkins Freeman, for example, wrote a number of ghost stories dealing with dark family secrets, including "The Wind in the Rose-Bush" (1902) and "The Lost Ghost" (1903), in which the ghosts are those of young girls who had been abused by their stepmother and mother, respectively. The mother in the latter story, unsuited to and overburdened by the demands of motherhood, leaves her child to starve to death. Edith Wharton, in "Afterward" (1910), simultaneously critiques both the disempowered status of women and the exploitative nature of capitalism as protagonist Mary Boyne, either unaware of or refusing to acknowledge her husband's shady business dealings, unwittingly tells the ghost of her husband's cheated associate where to find him (Weinstock 99–103). Henry James's *The Turn of the Screw* (1898, and later film versions) leaves open the question of whether the governess really saw the ghosts of Peter Quint and Miss Jessel or whether she hallucinated them after succumbing to an imagination overwrought with repressed erotic fantasies.

More traditional, vengeful ghosts appear in the works of F. Marion Crawford (1854–1909). In "The Screaming Skull" (1908), the vindictive ghost of Mrs Pratt, murdered by her husband, animates her skull to kill him; and in "Man Overboard" (1903), the ghost of a man murdered by his brother returns to kill his murderer. Conversely, a unique ghost appears in "The Water Ghost of Harrowby Hall" (1894) by humorist John Kendrick Bangs. The ghost of a young woman who committed suicide by drowning haunts the owners of Harrowby Hall, not simply by appearing to them but by soaking everything in the room. The current owner confronts the ghost outside rather than inside the home, causing her to freeze solid, then transporting her to a fireproof cold-storage warehouse. In this instance, the ghost is conquered by modern technology (a theme taken to an even more irreverent conclusion in Ivan Reitman's 1984 film *Ghostbusters*).

The post-Civil War era also saw a rise in the ghost story as an expression of "cultural" haunting as authors sought to deal with the trauma of a national war, of the lost South, and of the legacy of slavery. The shock of the war inspired Ambrose Bierce to write a number of ghost stories in which the phantoms are those of soldiers who continue to perform their military duties even after they have died, often because they do not even realize that they have been killed, as in "A Man with Two Lives" (1905) and "A Baffled Ambuscade" (1906). The fallen South and its ghosts also figure in Sarah Morgan Dawson's "A Tragedy of South Carolina" (1895). A wealthy landowner before the war, the Colonel—now a widower and a drunk—has little left. Nevertheless, maintaining the arrogance of his previous status, he forces his terrified black slave to shoot his "cracker" neighbors, an impoverished mother and son, for letting their hogs trespass into his cotton. But the ghost of the murdered neighbor woman haunts him for years, finally driving him to shoot himself.

By the early twentieth century, ghosts were appearing less frequently in American literature and for different purposes. The suffering generated by the new technologies of World War I—particularly the use of gas and tanks—along with the spread of electric lighting may have temporarily lessened the impact of frightening literary ghosts (Brennan 253–8), and the main ghosts in this period tended instead to be humorous and benevolent, as in Thorne Smith's novel *Topper* (1926) and its sequels. In this series, later adapted for film, an uptight businessman is haunted by the ghosts of a convivial young couple, George and Marion Kerby, who cannot move on until they have done a good deed—in this case, teaching Topper to relax. Another friendly ghost, Casper, made his storybook debut in the 1930s and, from the 1940s on, became the subject of animated shorts and comic books (and of Brad Silberling's 1995 film). But one of the more notable literary ghosts from this period is also one of the most wistful, that of Emily in Thornton Wilder's play *Our Town* (1938). Emily dies during childbirth and her spirit, along with the other ghosts of the town dead, meditates on how futile life can be when we do not realize its value.

In the wake of World War II, the mid twentieth century saw a slight rise in ghostly characters in literature, and particularly in cinema. More than 100 films about ghosts were released during the 1940s alone (Edwards 84), including the humorous *The Ghost Breakers* (George Marshall, 1940), starring Bob Hope as a reporter helping an heiress explore her spooky mansion, and *The Uninvited* (Lewis Allen, 1944, based on the 1942 novel by British author Dorothy MacArdle), also about a haunted house. In one of the earliest films to depict a romance between a ghost and a living person, *The Ghost and Mrs Muir* (Joseph L. Mankiewicz, 1947), the ghost of a gruff sea captain tries to haunt the new owner of his house, but instead the two slowly fall in love.

By the end of the twentieth century, ghosts had regained a strong presence in American literature and film. One factor has been the frequent appearance of ghosts in immigrant fiction post World War II. Polish-born Isaac Bashevis Singer, for example, often used the supernatural to explore the psychic devastation of the Holocaust, as in "The Cafeteria" (1970), in which a woman who had been in the German concentration camps thinks she sees Hitler and a group of Nazis meeting in a Jewish cafeteria on the East Side of New York. Later, the narrator, who doubted the woman's sanity, believes he has seen her ghost, reconsiders her story, and reflects on the nature of reality and perception. In Asian-American literature, ghosts are often metaphorical for the immigrant experience and the difficulties of cultural assimilation. In Maxine Hong Kingston's semi-autobiographical *The Woman Warrior* (1975), "ghost" has many meanings, including the spirits of the dead, but to Kingston's mother, "ghosts" are all the non-Chinese people in the unfamiliar culture of America, as they do not seem real or relatable to her. In Nora Okja Kellor's *Comfort Woman* (1997), a Korean-American woman "redefines her ethnicity by opening herself to the ghosts of her mother's Korean past" (Brogan 3).

Ghosts in contemporary African-American literature often provide an expression of how United States history is haunted by the legacy of slavery. Toni Morrison's *Beloved* (1987), set in 1873, centers around the ghost of Sethe's daughter, whom Sethe murdered to save from slavery. The ghost must ultimately be exorcised by a re-enactment of the murder scene (Brogan 7). In Gloria Naylor's *Mama Day* (1988), the spectral appearance of an enslaved African ancestor helps unravel the title character's family history, while in August Wilson's play *The Piano Lesson* (1990), the action revolves around the ghost of a murdered white slave-owner who haunts the descendants of his slaves (Brogan 1). Such ghosts signal an attempt "to recover and make social use of a poorly documented, partially erased cultural history" (Brogan 2).

Similarly, other ethnic groups use ghosts as a way to recall and prevent the potential loss of cultural identity, as well as to dramatize the divided cultural loyalties that immigrants often feel. Indian-born writer Bharati Mukherjee, in "The Management of Grief" (1989), drawing on a real-life event, tells the story of a Hindu Canadian woman who loses her husband and two sons in the 1985 bombing of Air India Flight 182, which was attributed to Sikh terrorists. Back in India to bury the dead, she sees the ghost of her husband who urges her to return to Canada and continue the life they had started there. The protagonist of Mexican-American writer Sandra Cisneros's short story "Woman Hollering Creek" (1991), relocated by her abusive husband from Mexico to Texas, obsesses about the ghostly **La Llorona** but, unlike that unhappy figure, saves herself—by moving back to Mexico.

In Native American literature, ghosts often provide a way for characters to realize the significance of their tribal origins. For example, in Leslie Marmon Silko's *Ceremony* (1977), the protagonist Tayo is haunted by his cousin and uncle's ghosts, as well as by a spectral lover, until he allows them to help him reconnect with the Laguna Pueblo people. Silko's *Almanac of the Dead* (1991) is filled with angry ghosts, especially those of various Native Americans calling for the destruction of European America (Bergland 162–8). In Susan Power's *The Grass Dancer* (1994), ghosts of the Sioux past serve to contrast spiritual Native American tradition with the rational mindset of modern Western society. A similar theme is developed in Michael Linn's 2007 film *Imprint*, in which ghostly voices and visions compel a Native American attorney to re-examine her traditional beliefs. These literary and cinematic ghosts also provide a rebuttal to the portrayal of Native Americans over the centuries by white American writers, who frequently depicted Indians as ghostly figures as a way to remove them from the landscape and establish American nationhood (Bergland 4–5).

But another common trope in ghost stories is the disturbance of an "Ancient Indian Burial Ground," leading to vengeful Native American spirits who refuse to be marginalized, as in Jay Anson's *The Amityville Horror* (1977, and later film versions), Tobe Hooper's 1982 film *Poltergeist* (see **Poltergeist**), and Stephen King's *Pet Sematary* (1983; film by Mary Lambert, 1989; see **Windigo**). Peter Straub's *Ghost Story* (1979; film by John Irvin, 1981), about a vengeful spirit, also draws on Native American beliefs (see **Manitou**). These works and others about haunted houses and haunted people, particularly Stephen King's *The Shining* (1977, and later film and television adaptations) were highly influential in the late twentieth-century rise in the pop-culture appeal of ghosts, especially in cinema, in which ghosts haunt for vengeance and justice in such films as *The Lady In White* (Frank LaLoggia, 1988), *Ghost* (Jerry Zucker, 1990), *Stir of Echoes* (David Koepp, 1999; based on Richard Matheson's 1958 novel), and *What Lies Beneath* (Robert Zemeckis, 2000). Hearkening back to Bierce, ghosts who do not realize they are dead appear in *Carnival of Souls* (Herk Harvey, 1962), *The Sixth Sense* (M. Night Shyamalan, 1999) and the US-Spanish production *The*

Others (Alejandro Amenábar, 2001), as well as in the recent television series *American Horror Story* (produced by Ryan Murphy and Brad Falchuk, 2011).

Advances in technology—and fear of those advances—are also significant factors in the renewed presence of ghosts in the late twentieth century. Modern special effects have provided not only new ways to represent ghosts in film and other media, but also new ideas about how ghosts might interact with and through such media. In *Poltergeist*, for example, angry spirits communicate through a family's television set. In *The Ghost in the Machine* (Rachel Talalay, 1993), the spirit of a serial killer is trapped in cyberspace by an electrical surge; it continues to kill through the electrical network and has to be "deleted." In Gore Verbinski's 2002 film *The Ring* (a remake of *Ringu*, see below), the furious ghost of a murdered girl kills people by crawling out of the television and terrifying them to death seven days after they watch an eerie video. Similarly, in *fear dot com* (William Malone, 2002), the ghost of a murdered girl takes vengeance through a website, while in 2006's *Pulse* (Jim Sonzero; a remake of 2001's *Kairo*, below), spirits of the dead find their way into the world of the living via certain electronic frequencies.

In short, ghosts may be even more prominent now in American film than in literature as special effects allow for various imaginings of apparitions. But the American love of cinema also plays a significant role in this shift, a relationship perhaps best exemplified by the merging of ghosts and cinema in Joe Hill's story, "20th Century Ghost" (2002), in which the apparition of a young woman who died of an aneurysm during a showing of *The Wizard of Oz* haunts the Rosebud theater until she finally gets to see the end of the film.

D. Felton

References and Suggested Reading

Bergland, Renée L. *The National Uncanny: Indian Ghosts and American Subjects*. Hanover, NH and London: University Press of New England, 2000.

Brennan, Joseph Payne. "Can the Supernatural Story Survive?" In *American Supernatural Fiction from Edith Wharton to the* Weird Tales *Writers*, edited by Douglas Robillard, 253–60. New York and London: Garland Publishing, Inc., 1996.

Brogan, Kathleen. *Cultural Haunting: Ghosts and Ethnicity in Recent American Literature*. Charlottesville and London: University of Virginia Press, 1998.

Edwards, Emily D. "A House That Tries to Be Haunted: Ghostly Narratives in Popular Film and Television." In *Hauntings and Poltergeists: Multidisciplinary Perspectives*, edited by James Houran and Rense Lange, 82–119. Jefferson, NC: McFarland, 2001.

Kerr, Howard, John W. Crowley, and Charles L. Crow, eds. *The Haunted Dusk: American Supernatural Fiction, 1820–1920*. Athens, GA: The University of Georgia Press, 1983.

Manguel, Alberto, ed. *The Oxford Book of Canadian Ghost Stories*. Toronto, Oxford, and New York: Oxford University Press, 1990.

Weinstock, Jeffrey Andrew. *Scare Tactics: Supernatural Fiction by American Women*. New York: Fordham University Press, 2008.

Latin America

In Latin America (the Spanish- and Portuguese-speaking nations of the Americas), ghosts in literature often represent contemporary philosophical or political concerns, while ghosts in horror films reveal social and moral dilemmas.

Outside of popular traditions, ghosts did not figure significantly in Latin American literature before the nineteenth century. Nineteenth-century ghost stories represented a challenge by Modernist writers, primarily concerned with spiritual, supernatural, and aesthetic phenomena, to the social prescriptions espoused by Positivist thinkers, who believed that biological, scientific, and material progress were paramount.

Related to this debate, early twentieth-century ghosts reflected questions about emerging technologies such as film. In several of his short stories, Uruguayan Horacio Quiroga (1878–1937) speculated on the impact of film technology on the actor's "original" soul. A technological specter appears in "El espectro" (1921), in which a dead actor's gaze breaks from the screen to stare accusingly at his wife and her lover in the audience. In "El puritano" (1926), dead actors relive their characters' traumas each time they are projected on screen. In "El vampiro" (1927), a man devises a way to extract a beloved film idol from the screen, but his spectral visitor cannot thrive until her carnal self, the Hollywood actress, is murdered.

Argentinean Adolfo Bioy Casares's novel *The Invention of Morel* (1940) also explores the destructive potential of cinematic recording. Morel creates a machine that literally captures a week in the life of his island guests, absorbing the life of his subjects as film absorbs light. Converted into phantoms by this technology, he and his guests must then relive their final week in a perpetually looping projection.

Mid twentieth-century ghosts appeared in allegories of political violence or trauma, reflecting the unrest and oppression common to many Latin American countries at that time. In Juan Rulfo's short novel *Pedro Páramo* (1955), Juan Preciado travels to the town of Comala in search of his father; he gradually discovers that all the town's inhabitants, with whom he converses and interacts, are ghosts, and that he himself may also be dead. The novel telescopes through Mexican history across a greater allegory of the Fall of Man. The muted, fragmented narrative communicates the ghostly populace's ongoing agonies under the rule of an archetypal strongman.

Writers of the Latin American *boom* (1960s and 1970s) often used ghosts to explore the imprint of the historical past on the modern present. In Carlos Fuentes's novella *Aura* (Mexico, 1962), historian Felipe Montero enters the household of an impossibly old woman, Consuelo Llorente, ostensibly to reconstruct the history of her long-dead husband, a general during the French Intervention (1861–67). Consuelo projects herself through her alluring, spectral niece Aura, achieving a carnality that allows her to seduce him. Aura is destroyed in their encounter and Felipe is bound to Consuelo in the guise of her dead husband.

Magical realist literature combines realistic narrative technique with both natural and supernatural plot elements, to illustrate the characters' everyday reality within a belief system that includes the supernatural as a matter of course. The ghosts of José Arcadio Buendía in Gabriel García Márquez's *One Hundred Years of Solitude* (1967) and Clara, the matriarch of Isabel Allende's *House of the Spirits* (1982), represent historical recurrence within the allegorical family.

Recent writers have used ghosts to explore subjective themes. In Argentine César Aira's novel *Ghosts* (1990), people and ghosts coexist casually, and an alienated teenager eventually "joins" the ghosts for a party, becoming a ghost herself. Mexican writer Carmen Boullosa places ghosts in many of her novels: a young girl's ghost in *Antes* (*Before*, 1989) explores the role of fear in identity; Moctezuma II, a fifteenth-century Aztec ruler, appears in modern-day Mexico in *Llanto, novelas imposibles* (*Tears*, 1992); and *El complot de los románticos* (*The Romantic Plot*, 2009) concerns an annual literary convention of dead writers, among them Dante, Mishima, and Goethe.

Mexico's long tradition of horror films often treats moral questions. Shortly after 1933's *La Llorona* (see **La Llorona**), Fernando de Fuentes's *The Phantom of the Convent* (1934) told the story of a couple and the husband's best friend, who happen on a mysterious convent; a night of harrowing events provides a cleansing lesson against adultery. In Chano Urueta's *The Witch's Mirror* (1962), a mother conjures the ghost of her daughter to torture the husband who murdered her. In Guillermo del Toro's *The Devil's Backbone* (2001), the ghost of a murdered child haunts an orphanage, his manifestation becoming the central mystery and metaphor of this allegorical film of the Spanish Civil War (1936–39).

Persephone Braham

References and Suggested Reading

Duncan, Cynthia. *Unraveling the Real: The Fantastic in Spanish-American Ficciones.* Philadelphia: Temple University Press, 2010.

Morales, Ana María, José Cardona López, and José Miguel Sardiñas, eds. *Rumbos de lo fantástico: actualidad e historia.* Palencia, Spain: Cálamo, 2007.

Africa and the Caribbean

In much of African and Caribbean literature, the boundary between the world of the living and the world of the dead is permeable. Spirits of the dead return easily, often, and in many forms. These ghosts are not always haunting or uncanny. Often they just go about their business, which differs slightly from that of living persons—their relationship to time is different, their ties to the past are stronger, and they may interact with supernatural forces. Prevalent as they are in African and Caribbean literature, ghosts are strikingly absent from African and Caribbean film, which tends to be starkly realist and not to engage with traditional belief systems or mythology.

Because they are generally embodied spirits of the dead rather than eerie apparitions, ghosts are not always immediately recognizable for what they are. The difficulty in determining whether an entity is a ghost thus provides a main theme in several important works. In Alejo Carpentier's *The Kingdom of This World* (Cuba, 1949), a crowd watches flames consume the rebel slave Mackandal's body, but then Mackandal helps to foment further revolts. Carpentier never clarifies whether Mackandal dies and returns as a ghost or employs magic powers to escape death. Jess, the protagonist in Helen Oyeyemi's *The Icarus Girl* (Nigeria, 2006), befriends Tilly Tilly and then realizes that no one else can see her; it remains unclear whether she is ghost, fantasy, disease, or something else entirely. In Wilson Harris's *The Infinite Rehearsal* (Guyana, 1987), the protagonist Glass meets a character called "Ghost," but recognizes it as a figure of indeterminacy between male and female, self and other, colonizer and colonized.

Although some writers, like Harris, use the term "ghost," others prefer words drawn from local languages. Duppies and jumbies, common in the Anglophone Caribbean, can be spirits of people who have died or manifestations of angry or tricky spirits. The duppies in Jamaica Kincaid's *At the Bottom of the River* (Antigua, 1983) go about their business just as they did when they were living. However, in Ismith Khan's *Jumbie Bird* (Trinidad, 1987) the jumbie is a bird who haunts the world of Jamini and his family stranded in Trinidad.

Ghosts not only experience the African diaspora, but also often serve as figures through which writers comment on immigration, return, and struggles in postcolonial nation-making. The inability of ghosts to cross the Atlantic causes sorrow for Tituba in Maryse Condé's *I, Tituba, Black Witch of Salem* (Guadeloupe, 1982), because once she has sailed from Barbados to Salem, she will no longer benefit from the advice of her dead friends and relatives. In Oyeyemi's *White Is for Witching* (Nigeria, 2009), the ghost Lily can cross the ocean, inhabiting the house that her children have emigrated to in England and occasionally conversing with them. When Bertram returns from England to a fictional Caribbean island in Caryl Phillip's *A State of Independence* (St Kitts, 1986), he finds his brother Dominic dead, but interacts with Dominic's ghost.

Just as ghosts can enter and exit the world of the living, so can the living enter and exit the world of ghosts. Achille voyages to Africa in Derek Walcott's epic poem "Omeros" (St Lucia, 1990) to visit his ancestors back in time, but also in the ghost-filled underworld that they inhabit. Perhaps most famously, the young protagonist in Amos Tutuola's *My Life in the Bush of Ghosts* (Nigeria, 1954) escapes human warfare and slavery by getting lost in the "bush of ghosts." There he finds gentle ghosts, like that of his dead cousin, but also terrible ones who enslave him.

Often more disconcerting than ghosts of the dead are those who become "ghosts" without leaving the world of the living. In Ama Ata Aidoo's plays *Dilemma of a Ghost* and *Anowa* (Ghana, 1964 and 1970), characters who return to Africa are metaphorical ghosts, trying to come back to a "home" where they no longer belong. In Aminata Sow Fall's *Le revenant* (Senegal, 1976), Bakar fakes his own death and then "returns," his face bleached white, to appear at his own funeral.

In contrast, the rebel leader Martial in Sony Labou-Tansi's *Life and a Half* (Congo, 1979) undergoes a real and unwanted death when the dictator of the imaginary African nation of Katamalanasie slices his throat and cuts him in half, but Martial lingers for generations, haranguing brutal dictators and complicit subjects alike. Labou-Tansi thus harnesses the power of the ghost for cultural critique and political activism.

The ghosts of earlier colonial encounters, of those drowned in various slave trades, often haunt African and Caribbean literature. Dionne Brand's *A Map to the Door of No Return* (Trinidad, 2001) explores Caribbean and African diasporic identity, reaching back to lives and histories that haunt us precisely because they have been irrecoverably lost. In Yvette Christianse's *Unconfessed* (South Africa, 2007), Sila, a Mozambican slave barely surviving in nineteenth-century South Africa, maintains lyrical thought-conversations with other women who did not survive. In Fred D'Aguiar's historical novel *Feeding the Ghosts* (Guyana/Britain, 2006), one of the main characters, Mintah, feeds the ghosts of those drowned in the Middle Passage with stories that keep them around. In contexts where peoples' spirits regularly return after their bodies die, the absence of ghosts can be more troubling than their presence.

Ghosts appear regularly in high life, reggae, calypso, and other African and Caribbean popular music. Only a few have passed through their literary manifestations into pop culture, especially Western pop culture. A notable exception is David Byrne and Brian Eno's album *My Life in the Bush of Ghosts*, inspired by Tutuola's novel.

Keja Valens

References and Suggested Reading

Johnson, Erica L. *Caribbean Ghostwriting*. Madison, NJ: Farleigh Dickinson University Press, 2009.

Khair, Tabish. *The Gothic, Postcolonialism, and Otherness: Ghosts from Elsewhere*. New York: Palgrave Macmillan, 2009.

South Asia

As in East and Southeast Asia, ghosts in India fall into several categories, which are further distinguished by regional (and thus dialectal) differences. They include, among others, *bhut/bhoot* (Hindi for ghost), *poochandi* (Tamil for bogeyman), *payee* and *aavi* (Tamil for spirit), *pisaase/pisaci/pisache* (Hindi for spirit), and *mohini* (Sanskrit), which originally referred to a female avatar of Lord Vishnu, but which is now also believed to be the soul of a dead woman who has become a **succubus**. Corresponding to the country's religious traditions, these entities are not, unlike in the West, viewed as "other" to the living, but rather as part of a continuum of the living. This is unsurprising since Hinduism, the principal religion, does not distinguish between different planes of "being," but considers all sentient forms as part of existence. In fact, Hinduism posits that existence is fundamentally an illusion (*māyā*), which must nevertheless be brooked in order for the devotee to overcome ignorance (*avidyā*) and arrive at reality (*atman*). Based on this principle, ghosts (here strictly defined as spirits of dead persons) and the living are not located at binary opposites, but are plotted along a continuum that summarily relegates them as unreal.

Although South Asian countries such as India, Nepal, and Pakistan have long folk traditions of supernatural lore, as a constituent of literary fiction, ghosts are a colonial heritage. Indian author Ruskin Bond posits that the ghost story was introduced to India by Rudyard Kipling in 1888 (Bond xii). One early practitioner was S. Mukerji, whose *Indian Ghost Stories* (1914) underwent two editions, but his stories were largely anecdotal, aped the discursive style of Victorian literature, and replicated the ennoblement of Western rationalism and civilization through discrimination against the superstitious, ghost-fearing "natives." There seems to have been little development in the genre since Mukerji's work, as evident in Bond's *The Penguin Book of Indian Ghost Stories* (1993), whose title's claim is significantly undermined by two problems: half the tales are by British, not Indian, writers; and many of them are clearly not about ghosts. Moreover, those that do fulfill both criteria sound curiously English in tenor, deploying overused tropes, especially the haunted manor (Satyajit Ray's "AnitBabu's Terror" and Jug Suraiya's "A Shade Too Soon"), rather than anything distinctly Indian. A later exception is the Rajasthani writer Vijaydan Detha's "Duvidha" ("The Dilemma," 1997), a literary retelling of a folktale in which a ghost falls in love with a newlywed woman and assumes the guise of her husband when the latter goes away on business. Detha's story was adapted for the 2005 Hindi film, *Paheli* (Amol Palekar), but the film's ending differs in that the bride chooses to remain with her ghostly lover, even after discovering its real identity. The folktale was also the basis for the 1973 Hindi film *Duvidha* (Manil Kaul).

Other Indian writers who have produced ghost narratives include Malayalam author Vaikom Muhammad Basheer, whose short story "Neelavelicham" ("The Blue Glow," 1952), about a female ghost who haunts a house, was later adapted for the 1964 Malayalam film *Bhargavi Nilayam* (A. Vincent). Bengali author Upendrakishore Ray (AKA Upendrakishore Raychoudury, 1863–1915) wrote a popular ghost story for children, *Goopy Gyne Bagha Byne* ("The Adventures of Goopy and Bhaga"), which became the basis for the 1968 film of the same title, directed by his famous grandson, Satyajit Ray.

If Indian cinema fares better than literature in terms of its output in narratives featuring ghosts, it is only slightly and in terms of quantity. Bollywood has always made forays into the horror genre, but the first successful Indian movies featuring ghosts are the Hindi film *Gerahyee* (Vikas Desai and Aruna Raje, 1980) and the Tamil film *Pillai Nilla* (Manobala, 1985), both involving vengeful female spirits who take possession of children to cause destruction. Since the late 1990s, Bollywood has witnessed an explosion of horror films, but they tend to be highly formulaic. A prevalent feature is the relationship among ghost, family, and house: the ghost is somehow connected to a dark family secret encrypted within the house. And although Bollywood is more balanced in gendering its ghosts and victims (unlike its East Asian counterparts, which largely relegate both roles to women), it nevertheless rehearses distinct gender roles that reflect deep-seated stereotypes. For example, the female ghosts in the Hindi films *Raaz* (Vikram Bhatt, 2002) and *Bhoot* (Ram Gopal Varma, 2003) are more destructive and bear greater menace than male ghosts in Indian cinema, thus suggesting their weaker ties to virtues such as temperance, moderation, and stoicism. Male ghosts, in contrast, were once victims of oppression; as ghosts, they become hyper-masculinized and are able, at last, to defeat the real evil, as, for example, in the Tamil film *Muni* (Raghavendra Lawrence, 2007) and the Hindi *Raaz 2: The Mystery Continues* (Mohit Suri, 2009).

Andrew Hock Soon Ng

References and Suggested Reading

Bond, Ruskin. *The Penguin Book of Indian Ghost Stories.* New Delhi, India: Penguin, 1993.

Deb, Swagata, trans. *Goopy Gyne Bagha Byne: The Magical World of Upendrakishore Roychoudhury.* New Delhi, India: Penguin, 2004.

Mukerji, S. *Indian Ghost Stories.* BiblioBazaar, 2007. Accessed 1 July 2011. <http://www.gutenberg.org/ebooks/17113>.

Southeast Asia

In Southeast Asia, "ghost" refers to a large variety of supernatural creatures, comprising such diverse entities as Buddhist ghosts, certain monsters, and spirits of the dead. Female ghosts predominate; seen as particularly powerful, they are primarily the spirits of mothers and pregnant women who died horrible deaths at the hands of men. Commonly associated with the destructive powers of nature, these ghostly, long-haired women often inhabit banyan trees, wailing for their dead babies and using their charms to lure unsuspecting bystanders into danger. Although known by different names in each region and derived from separate mythologies, their portrayal in film and literature as a fascinating combination of sorrowful vulnerability and predatory instincts is relatively similar.

One such spirit in Thai tradition is the notorious Mae Nak, a faithful wife who refused to be parted from her husband after her death in childbirth. As a fearsome *phii tai tham klong* ("ghost that died with a baby in its womb"), ripping to pieces everybody who stands in her way, she has been immortalized in over 20 Thai films, most notably Nonzee Nimibutr's *Nang Nak* (1997); a musical (*Mae Nak*, Takonkiet Viravan, 2009); and an opera (*Mae Nak*, Somtow Sucharitkul, 2003). The Malaysian *pontianak*, another vengeful female spirit, returns in Tunku Halim's novel *Dark Demon Rising* (1997), and in Shuhaimi Baba's *Pontianak: A Scent of the Tuberose* (2004)—a film that brought horror back to Malaysian cinemas after 30 years of absence. Rizal Mantovani's film *Kuntilanak* (2004) uses a modern rendition of the *kuntilanak* legend—about a malevolent female spirit known for her foreboding laughter—to focus on the question of Indonesian identity and relationship with history.

Perhaps the most extreme example of a Southeast Asian female ghost is the spirit best described as a flying head that can detach itself from its body and move through the air, trailing its exposed organs behind. Sometimes referred to as "the filth ghost," it is drawn to women in labor and feeds on their placenta, blood, and unborn fetuses. Variants of this creature appear throughout Southeast Asia; memorable examples include a *penanggalan* created out of an American student of the occult by an Indonesian **witch** in *Mystics in Bali* (H. Tjut Djalil, 1981); *manananggal* in the similarly titled segment of a Filipino movie *Shake, Rattle & Roll* (Peque Gallaga, 1984); and its Thai equivalent, *phii krasue*, from Yuthlert Sippapak's *Krasue Valentine* (2006).

Female spirits are occasionally portrayed in connection with baby spirits, known as *kuman tong* or *tuyul*. A nineteenth-century Thai epic poem, *Khun Chang Khun Phaen* (*Phaen and Chang*), mentions a rather gruesome ritual of creating a *kuman tong*: a fetus is cut out of its mother's womb, chargrilled, and contained within an amulet. Meant to ensure prosperity of their keepers, baby ghosts are valuable commodities in Southeast Asia and frequent causes for maternal vengeance, as in *The Mother* (Bandit Thongdee, 2005). The Filipino *tiyanak*, an evil child spirit said to be a miscarried or aborted fetus, inspired David Hontiveros's novella, *Craving* (2005), which draws upon the anxieties of pregnancy and the bond between the mother and her unborn child. Additionally, female grudge-bearing spirits of the violently dead are a great favorite with Thai horror directors, as in *Shutter* (Parkpoom Wongpoom and Banjong Pisanthanakun, 2004).

Also prominent in Southeast Asia are the so-called "hungry ghosts." These vary greatly in conception. In "*The Novice*" segment of *Phobia 2* (Paween Purikitpanya, 2009), an unruly boy turns into a tall pin-mouthed Buddhist ghost, known as *phii pret*, in punishment for his rudeness and greed. Chinese "hungry dead" feast for a month in the Singaporean film *The Maid* (Kelvin Tong, 2005), and another class of "hungry ghosts" includes a ravenous, liver-eating *phii pob*, a never-ending source of fear and laughter in Thai horror-comedies, portrayed more seriously in *P* (Paul Spurrier, 2005). Many stories of hungry ghosts recall Chinese ancestor worship, still practiced today in most Chinese communities. Some particularly haunting Chinese ghost stories appear in Singaporean short story collections, such as Catherine Lim's *They Do Return ... But Gently Lead Them Back* (1983) and *The Howling Silence: Tales of the Dead and Their Return* (1999), and in movies, such as *Where Got Ghost?* (Jack Neo and Boris Boo, 2009).

Katarzyna Ancuta

References and Suggested Reading

Heeren, Katinka van. *Contemporary Indonesian Film: Spirits of Reform and Ghosts from the Past.* Doctoral Thesis, Leiden University, 2009. <https://openaccess.leidenuniv.nl/handle/1887/13830>.

Knee, Adam. "Thailand Haunted: The Power of the Past in the Contemporary Thai Horror Film." In *Horror International*, edited by Steven Jay Schneider and Tony Williams, 141–62. Detroit: Wayne State University Press, 2005.

China

Despite a skeptical tradition well established by the mid first millennium BCE and repeated in well-known injunctions from Confucius (traditionally 551–479 BCE) to "keep ghosts and spirits at a distance" (*Analects* 7.22), ghosts abound in Chinese literature. Fueled in part by practices of ancestor worship and the belief that spirits of the departed continue to need the attentions of surviving family members, ghosts are an integral part of traditional cultural life and consequently appear as characters in stories, plays, novels, and films.

Identifying ghosts in Chinese materials is complicated both by Taoist notions of transformation and by Chinese Buddhist ideas about transmigration of the soul. Extended biographies that include progressions such as animal to **demon** to human, or human to ghost to god, are common in Chinese histories and fiction. As a result, the distinctions among ghosts, demons, deities, animals, humans, and sometimes even plants and stones are particularly murky. Regular conflation of different orders of being is also demonstrated in the treatment of "hungry ghosts," a level of rebirth in Buddhist thought in which beings are punished for karmic failures by insatiable hunger and thirst. While distinct from returning or unsettled specters, hungry ghosts are often included in accounts of vengeful spirits.

Typically, Taoist and Buddhist themes use ghosts to educate and convert audience members. Well known among these is the story of the monk Mulian (Maudgalyāyana) rescuing his mother, whose tale is told in Tang period (618–907) transformation texts and later ritual dramas. Mulian's mother, having committed crimes during her lifetime, is reborn in the Underworld as a hungry ghost. She is brought out of one of the many Buddhist hells where punishment for misdeeds in life is meted out and saved by her pious son, a monk, who braves the horrors of the Underworld and appeals directly to the Buddha for her release.

Ghosts regularly come back to right some wrong or demonstrate loyalty to family or country. In the Ming historical novel and in dramatic versions of the cycle of the fourteenth-century *Romance of the Three Kingdoms*, Zhang Fei and Guan Yu visit their sworn brother Liu Bei as ghosts. Yue Fei, the Song martial hero who in life defended China from northern invaders, appears as a ghost to Monkey in the sixteenth-century novel *Journey to the West* (see **Monkey King**). Zhong Kui, a minor deity with powers to subdue demons, is also a ghost with a human biography. Accounts of his origin vary, though many include the Tang Emperor seeing the demon catcher in a dream. Zhong Kui cures the Emperor of an illness by capturing the demons causing it, and thereafter images of Zhong Kui were reproduced and used as talismans against illness and bad luck. Zhong Kui thus appears in popular plays and tales from the twelfth century onward.

In one of the most celebrated pieces of the traditional opera corpus, the thirteenth-century *The Injustice to Dou E* by Guan Hanqing, the ghost of the wrongly executed widow Dou E haunts her estranged father, a judge, demanding that her flawed court case be re-examined and her family reunited. Dou E is unlike most other female ghosts, who become increasingly popular subjects of theater and story from about the sixteenth century onwards and are, for the most part, concerned with romance rather than revenge or righteousness. In earlier Six Dynasties (220–589) and Tang tales, female ghosts are known to be dangerous sexual predators whose relations with any human man may case his untimely death, but there are also, throughout the tradition, notable exceptions of loyal ghost wives and lovers. In a number of plays republished through the Ming and Qing, young women die—sometimes at the hands of others, though also by an excess of romantic feeling—before they are able to make a fated marriage. Through dizzying chains of circumstance that may involve journeys to Hell or wandering souls made to reanimate bodies not their own, female ghosts in dramas are typically united with their destined partners in marriage. Most well known among these is Du Liniang in Tang Xianzu's poetic opera *The Peony Pavilion* (1598), who dies of love-longing, haunts her lover as a ghost, and, after much adventure and the help of a Taoist monk, is reincarnated in order to consummate a fated marriage.

Ghost characters have been especially prevalent in Hong Kong films, and themes from Ming and Qing period drama and stories regularly form the basis for movie plots. Famous examples include Ching Siu-tung's (Cheng Xiaodong) *A Chinese Ghost Story* (1987) in which the female ghost protagonist Nip Siu-sin (Nie Xiaoqing) is controlled by an evil tree demon. The story in Pu Songling's *Strange Stories from a Chinese Studio*, on which the plot of the film is loosely based, features an identically named female protagonist, also a ghost, who, as the devoted wife of the living man who saves her from a demonic power, bears him two illustrious sons. Fleur, the female ghost in Stanley Kwan's *Rouge* (1987), comes to the world of the living in search of her erstwhile lover who failed to complete his side of a double suicide pact. More recent Hong Kong productions include ghosts in a variety of themes and genres, such as horror films and depictions of vampires.

Karin Myhre

References and Suggested Reading

Doré, Henri. *Researches into Chinese Superstitions*. Shanghai, 1914. Reprint, Taipei: Ch'eng-wen Publishing Co., 1966.

Groot, J.J.M. de. *The Religious System of China*. 6 vols. Taipei, Taiwan: Southern Materials Center, 1982.

Poo, Mu-chou. "The Concept of Ghost in Ancient Chinese Religion." In *Religion and Chinese Society*, edited by John Lagerwey, 173–91. Hong Kong: The Chinese University Press, 2004.

Japan

The stereotypical image of the Japanese ghost—most commonly referred to today as a *yūrei* (literally, "hazy spirit")—is of a woman with long, black, disheveled hair and no feet wearing a traditional white death robe. The absence of feet is a feature that often distinguishes a *yūrei* from living beings, especially in early *ukiyo-e* prints and folktales. The basic characteristics of this image were established during the Tokugawa period (1600–1867) through innumerable literary, theatrical, and pictorial depictions. This image has survived largely unchanged to the present day. Even the ghost in Nakata Hideo's film *Ringu* (*The Ring*, 1998) still draws heavily on the conventional imagery, although her clothing has been updated.

Prior to the Tokugawa period, ghosts were a notable presence in the noh theater. During the late fourteenth and early fifteenth centuries, the dramatist Zeami developed a style called "dream plays" in which a traveling monk encounters a stranger who later turns out to be the ghost of a widely known figure. Typically, in the second half of the play, the monk has a dream or vision in which the stranger appears in his or her true form to enact an important moment from the past and ask the monk to pray for him. As seen in Zeami's *Atsumori* and *Kiyotsune*, noh plays are filled with ghosts of warriors whose deaths during a twelfth-century war between the Minamoto and Taira clans have been frequently retold in various genres. Also, in many plays notable female characters return as ghosts; in Konparu Zenchiku's *Nonomiya* (*The Shrine in the Fields*), for example, the ghost is Lady Rokujō, a character in *The Tale of Genji* who was tormented by jealousy even after her death.

Ghosts emerged as a topic of particular interest during the peaceful centuries of the Tokugawa period, when printing and popular urban culture flourished. The new literary and cultural focus on commoners rather than on warriors and historical figures established the image of ghosts who appear in ordinary white death robes. Representations of female spirits had been common since the Heian period (794–1185), but in the Tokugawa period, the association of ghosts with women grew stronger as long-held Buddhist beliefs that women were subject to dangerous excesses of attachment and jealousy led to the creation of popular works featuring female ghosts bent on vengeance (Tsutsumi).

Tokugawa representations were strongly influenced by Chinese ghost narratives of the Ming (1368–1644) and early Qing dynasties (1644–1912). Ueda Akinari's *Tales of Moonlight and Rain*, the most famous Tokugawa collection of ghost tales, took much of its material from Chinese vernacular fiction, but infused the stories with imagery from classical and ancient Japanese literature. "Mudan dengji" ("The Peony Lantern"), from Qu You's *Jiandeng xinhua* (*New Tales Under the Lamplight*, 1378)—a Chinese tale of an amorous ghost who drains the life from her mortal lover—was adapted many times during the Tokugawa period and beyond, notably by Asai Ryōi in *Otogi bōko* (*Hand Puppets*, 1666). Sanyūtei Enchō's *Kaidan botan dōrō* (*Peony Lantern Ghost Story*, 1884), a rewriting for the performative genre of *rakugo* (oral storytelling) that drew on Tokugawa adaptations of the story, gave the name Otsuyu to the amorous ghost; the work was also published, and the name was fixed in the Japanese cultural memory.

The genre that contributed most to the establishment of the visual image of the female ghost was the kabuki theater. The early nineteenth-century playwright Tsuruya Nanboku IV (1755–1829), in particular, created horrific spectacles featuring ghosts deeply rooted in urban legends. Using special effects, real water, and a newly invented technique for representing blood, he brought to the stage many female ghosts of women who were wronged and returned after death to give vent to their suffering. For example, "Kasane," from *Kesakakematsu narita no riken* (*The Pine Tree of the Priest's Robe and the Sharp Sword of Narita*, 1823), features Kasane, a disfigured woman who returns as a ghost after her lover kills her with a sickle on a riverbank. Another canonical ghost is Okiku, a servant who is tortured and thrown into a well for breaking a plate in a set her master treasured; Okiku emerges from the well every night to count the plates until she drives her master to madness. Reworking Asada Icchō's puppet play, *Banshū sarayashiki* (*The Plate-Counting Mansion of Banshū*, 1741), kabuki plays including Nanboku's *Iroeiri otogi zōshi* (*Illustrated Fiction in Vivid Colors*, 1808) and Kawatake Mokuami's *Shin sarayashiki tsuki no amagasa* (*A New "Plate-Counting Mansion": An Umbrella on a Moonlit Night*, 1883) adapted images of this female ghost.

The most canonical ghost of all is Oiwa, from Nanboku's kabuki play *Tōkaidō Yotsuya kaidan* (*Eastern Seaboard Highway, Ghost Tales at Yotsuya*, 1825), which, like the stories of Kasane and Okiku, has its roots in both fictional and documentary sources. Oiwa, the virtuous wife of a masterless samurai, is given a disfiguring poison by a neighbor who schemes to have his granddaughter marry Oiwa's husband, Iemon. After Oiwa learns of her husband's betrayal, she further disfigures herself, dies a horrific death, and returns as a vengeful ghost to mercilessly murder everyone responsible for her downfall.

Oiwa, Okiku, and Otsuyu remain popular in modern times, and have appeared in many horror films, including Fuyushima Taizō's *Banchō sarayashiki* (*The Plate-Counting Mansion of Banchō*, 1937) and Yamamoto Satsuo's *Botan dōrō* (*The Peony Lantern*, 1968). Until the 1940s and 1950s, Japanese horror cinema often drew on materials from traditional theater and oral storytelling, a trend that continued to some extent even into the 1970s. According to the kabuki scholar Yokoyama Yasuko, more than 30 films featuring Oiwa appeared between 1910 and 1994. Nakagawa Nobuo's *Tōkaidō Yotsuya kaidan* (*Ghost Story of Yotsuya*, 1959) is a representative example. There is also a corpus of artistic films drawing on traditional ghost narratives, such as Mizoguchi Kenji's *Ugetsu* (1953), inspired by *Tales of Moonlight and Rain*, and Kobayashi Masaki's *Kwaidan* (1965), based on Lafcadio Hearn's (1850–1904) collections of pre-modern folktales.

Even today, Japanese ghosts remain indebted to characters created during the Tokugawa period. Sadako in the film *Ringu* (based on a 1991 novel by Suzuki Kōji) is a perfect example: her gender, her association with the well and water, her white clothing and long hair, and the emphasis the film places on urban legend and the circulation of stories, all link her to the kabuki ghost-play lineage. Images of water, black hair, and a female ghost also play an important role in Nakata Hideo's *Dark Water* (2001). At the same time, these horror films from the 1990s onward use ghosts in a new way, connecting them to the fear of technology and a sense of alienation in the urban environment, and develop a new visual language for representing the physicality of ghosts, as seen in the vaguely digital ghosts in Kurosawa Kiyoshi's *Kairo* ("Circuit," 2001). These innovative approaches to an old trope have had an influence even beyond Japan through the global circulation of these films and their Hollywood adaptations.

Satoko Shimazaki

References and Suggested Reading

Addiss, Stephen, ed. *Japanese Ghosts and Demons: Art of the Supernatural.* New York: G. Braziller, Inc., 1985.

Tsutsumi, Kunihiko. *Nyonin jatai: henai no Edo kaidanshi.* Tokyo: Kadokawa gakugei shuppan, 2006.

Yokoyama, Yasuko. "Yotsuya kaidan eiga no Oiwa tachi." In *Kaiki to gensō e no kairo: kaidan kara jei horā e*, edited by Uchiyama Kazuki, 145–70. Tokyo: Shinwasha, 2008.

GHOUL

Often lumped together with other fictional monsters like **ghosts** and **vampires**, the figure of the ghoul has a long and particular heritage of its own. Lingering around the corpses of the recently dead and their places of rest, the ghoul is neatly summed up in the epigraph seen at the start of Freddie Francis's 1975 film, *The Ghoul*, in which the creature is described as "a person of revolting inhuman tastes supposed in the East to haunt burial places and feed on the dead."

Some Origins: Evil from the East

The ghoul originates in the Arab world of antiquity; the term is derived from the Arabic word *ghala*, meaning "to seize," and traditionally was used to describe a supernatural being that inhabits burial grounds and feeds on the flesh of corpses. Several tales featuring ghouls appeared in the many European adaptations of *The Thousand and One Nights* (see **Arabian Nights, Monsters In The**), which followed Antoine Galland's first French editions published in twelve volumes between 1704 and 1717. By the beginning of the nineteenth century, the concept of the ghoul had become well established in Western literature; William Beckford's *Vathek* (1786) includes references to *gouls* and Lord Byron's poem *The Giaour: A Fragment of a Turkish Tale* (1813) also evokes the Eastern desecrater of graves: "Wet with thine own best blood shall drip / Thy gnashing tooth and haggard lip; / Then stalking to thy sullen grave, / Go—and with Gouls and Afrits rave; / Till these in horror shrink away / From Spectre more accursed than they!" (781–6).

Subsequent literary representations of the ghoul during the late nineteenth and early twentieth centuries continued to locate such stories in the exotic setting of the East, many of them drawing upon *The Thousand and One Nights* for inspiration. Both Edward Lucas White's "Amina" (1906) and Clark Ashton Smith's "The Ghoul" (1934) borrow the name of Amina from the "Tale of Sidi Nouman." In White's story, the Yankee explorer Waldo comes across a strange woman wandering in the Persian desert. Following her back to her shadowy lair full of strange bestial children, he is saved from attack by his more knowing companion who shoots the woman dead as she is about to strike. Waldo, sickened by the deformities of the woman's corpse and skeptical that he has just encountered a ghoul, is told gravely by his friend: "I can believe that there are none in Rhode Island ... [but] this is Persia, and Persia is in Asia" (73).

The Gothic Ghoul, Lovecraft, and Beyond

The association between the ghoul and the exotic East continued to shape stories well into the twentieth century, even when such tales began to be situated in Western settings. Particularly influential in this sense is Henry S. Whitehead's story, "The Chadbourne Episode" (1933). Whitehead's tale features a pack of Persian ghouls who have relocated to London, bringing "home" the ghastly creatures from the East. In a similar vein, Clark Ashton Smith's "The Nameless Offspring" (1932) tells the story of a respected English family cursed by the oriental ghoul. The narrator of Ashton Smith's story, Henry Chaldane, becomes embroiled in the travails of the Tremoth family during a motorcycle holiday in the English countryside. The death of Sir John Tremoth reveals the "thing" he has been sheltering in his country home—the horrific offspring of his deceased wife, Lady Agatha, and a strange beast that attacked her some years before. The narrator is disturbed by the sound of "bestial, diabolic scratching" (21) as the hungry "thing" tries to get close to the corpse of Sir John. Eventually, the horrific nature of this beast is revealed: "the corpse-devouring demon of Oriental tales and legends ... the *ghoul*" (16).

Ashton Smith was clearly influenced by his contemporary H.P. Lovecraft (1890–1937; see **Lovecraft, Monsters In**) who arguably did the most to decouple the notion of the ghoul from its colonial context and instead to embed it in the Western Gothic tradition. Several of Lovecraft's early tales seem to suggest the presence of ghouls, although there is no explicit naming of them as such. In "The Statement of Randolph Carter" (1920), a disembodied voice from the grave may well be that of a ghoul, and the tragic narrator of "The Outsider" (1926) may also be one of their kith and kin. These tales represent the more traditionally Gothic of Lovecraft's stories, as does "The Rats in the Walls" (1924) in which the implied ghoulishness of the narrator—who is found "crouching over the plump, half-eaten body of Capt. Norrys" (104)—is perhaps one of the most chilling pay-offs in his early works.

It was not until the publication of "Pickman's Model" in 1927 that Lovecraft explicitly points to the figure of the ghoul, which is represented in the disturbing and unearthly paintings of the Salem painter Robert Upton Pickman. While investigating the disappearance of the shunned artist of such unsettling works as *Ghoul Feeding*, the narrator of this story discovers that Pickman has been working not from figures of his imagination, but from real models he has discovered living in the subterranean tunnels in the sinister North End of Boston. It is in this story that Lovecraft establishes a number of distinctive notions associated with the figure of the ghoul, and his description of the "dog-like features" of such creatures obviously influenced other writers such as Clark Ashton Smith. In Ashton Smith's "The Nameless Offspring", the description of the ghoulish offspring of the Tremoths ("a huge, whitish, hairless and semi-quadruped body, of canine teeth in a half-human face, and long hyena nails at the end of forelimbs that were both arms and legs" [23]) owes much to the portrayal of such creatures in both "Pickman's Model" and Lovecraft's novella-length, *The Dream-Quest of Unknown Kadath* (1927), in which Pickman reappears, himself transformed into a ghoul.

Pickman's transformation in *Unknown Kadath* develops Lovecraft's consideration of the possible origins of the ghoul by suggesting that such creatures could evolve (or devolve) from humankind. As the narrator of "Pickman's Model" relates, his invitation to view one of the painter's secret works, *The Lesson*, reveals the horrific implications of the intermingling of humans and ghouls. In the painting he sees: "a squatting circle of nameless doglike things in a churchyard teaching a child how to feed like themselves ... I began to see a hideous relationship in the faces of the human and non-human figures. He was, in all his gradations of morbidity between the frankly nonhuman and the degradedly human, establishing a sardonic linkage and evolution. The dog-things were developed from mortals!" (195).

Lovecraft's representation of ghouls also had an important effect on the kind of stories published in the influential *Weird Tales* magazine (originally published from 1923 to 1954 and subsequently revived several times). Writers and acolytes of Lovecraft such as Robert Bloch ("The Grinning Ghoul," 1936) and the aforementioned Clark Ashton Smith produced several stories about ghouls in this tradition during Lovecraft's short lifetime and beyond. Perhaps the most effective of these is Robert Barbour Johnson's "Far Below" (1939), a story that takes its cue directly from one of the descriptions of Pickman's paintings, *Subway Accident*, that depicts an attack by ghouls on a crowd of commuters on the Boston underground. Johnson's tale describes the activities of a covert police squad as they attempt to contain the activities of a race of ghouls residing in a section of the New York subway and further draws on the legacy of Lovecraft by tracing the ancient lineage of this tribe back into antiquity. Despite this, Johnson's tale brings the figure of the ghoul firmly into the modern metropolis of the twentieth century, mixing the traditional image of the Eastern ghoul with elements of traditional Gothic narrative and contemporary urban myths of strange creatures living "far below" in the tunnels and sewers of our cities.

Ghouls on Screen

Although both "Far Below" and "Pickman's Model" were made into adaptations for television (the former for *Monsters* in 1990 [season 2, episode 19, directed by Ernest D. Farino] and the latter in Rod Serling's *Night Gallery* in 1971 [airdate 1 December 1971, directed by Jack Laird]), representations of ghouls on film are relatively scarce.

There have been many depictions of ghoulish characters and their nefarious activities throughout film history that do not depict ghouls in the traditional sense. The practice of grave-robbing is a theme explored in several films, inspired either by the fictional misdeeds of mad scientists such as Victor Frankenstein (see **Frankenstein's Monster**) or the true life crimes of the notorious "resurrection men" Burke and Hare. This gruesome pair murdered over a dozen victims in nineteenth-century Edinburgh in order to profit from the sale of corpses for medical dissection, and their oft-told story is most effectively conveyed in Robert Wise's *The Body Snatcher* (1945) and John Gilling's *The Flesh and the Fiends* (1953). These films do not represent ghouls themselves; instead, they focus on certain elements of ghoulish behavior, characterized by the grave-robbing practices of murderous opportunists and ambitious doctors.

There are two films bearing the name of *The Ghoul*, the first directed by T. Hayes Hunter and starring Boris Karloff in 1933, and the second directed by Freddie Francis and starring Peter Cushing in 1975. Both of these films draw upon the tradition of ghoul stories related to the colonial encounter with the East. The 1933 film features Boris Karloff as the fatally ill Egyptologist Professor Henry Morlant who returns to England with the ancient secret of resurrection in his grasp. Upon his death, he is cheated of his proper rebirth by the theft of a sacred jewel and returns **zombie**-like from the grave to exact his revenge on the living. The film bears very little resemblance to any recognizable ghoul mythology other than a storyline involving death and burial grounds, and is rather an attempt to exploit the success of the earlier Karloff vehicle, *The* ***Mummy***, released the previous year. Universal's *The Mad Ghoul* (James P. Hogan, 1943), made a decade later, also has very little to do with established ghoul-lore, and features George Zucco's mad doctor zombifying his unsuspecting assistant with Mayan nerve gas.

Freddie Francis's 1975 film starring Peter Cushing as the troubled ex-priest, Dr Lawrence, is more closely linked with the Eastern mythology of the ghoul. The plot bears a strong resemblance to Clark Ashton Smith's "The Nameless Offspring," with the widowed Dr Lawrence harboring something sinister in his attic room. Now a retired colonial missionary, Lawrence lives alone in his isolated house on the moors of south-west England, save for his Indian ayah (Gwen Watford) and unstable groundskeeper (John Hurt), until a group of young fops and flappers arrive to disturb his melancholy peace. The visitors soon become prey to Lawrence's hideous cannibalistic son (Don Henderson) who somehow "went bad" over in India. Once his son is eventually revealed as a shambling and rotting ghoul, Lawrence is forced to shoot his offspring and then himself in order to end the Eastern curse. The only explanation given for this ghoulish transformation is a reference to the influence of the local Raja's son on Lawrence's wife and child while they were in India, again illustrating the horrific and corrupting dangers of the East.

In the Amicus Productions portmanteau horror film, *The Monster Club* (Roy Ward Baker, 1981), ghouls appear prominently on the monster genealogical chart discussed between a vampire (Vincent Price) and his recovering victim (John Carradine). The final story features Stuart Whitman as a location-scouting movie director trapped in a village full of ghouls, and focuses on the figure of the "Humghoul" (half-human, half-ghoul), particularly the innkeeper's daughter Luna (Lesley Dunlop) who sacrifices herself so that Whitman can (seemingly) escape. This segment contains some effective and haunting moments, particularly in the illustrated back-story that explains the coming of the ghouls to the village. The images of ghouls spotted "squatting behind tombstones" and "gnawing on bones" as they feed on the corpses of the dead neatly epitomize all of the familiar characteristics of the Gothic ghoul. There are various knowing nods to existing ghoul-lore, such as the reference by Luna to the underground railway which she has been told offers "good feeding"—a reference perhaps to Johnson's "Far Below," or maybe to the subterranean cannibals found living in the London tube network in Gary Sherman's film, *Death Line* (1973).

Since the later decades of the twentieth century, the flesh-eating characteristics of the ghoul have gone on to shape new variations of cinematic and literary monsters. Perhaps the most widespread and enduring example of the modern ghoul-like monster can be found in the tradition of the George Romero zombie. Arguably, the resurrected, flesh-eating undead of Romero's horror films bear a much closer relationship to the ghoul than the traditional zombie of Haitian mythology. First introduced in 1968 in *Night of the Living Dead*, Romero's ghoulish undead have swept all before them and continue to spawn countless stories, novels, comics, movies, and television programs, such as the hugely successful graphic novel-inspired cable series, *The Walking Dead* (2010–present).

Ghouls Gone Bad, Made Good

The advent of the zombie-ghoul has not meant that ghouls proper have disappeared from popular literature and film altogether; in recent years, the ghoul has become widely incorporated into a wide range of entertainment forms. The transition of the ghoul from the limited confines of the Gothic tradition into more mainstream forms of entertainment reflects wider processes of commercialization of the horror genre itself. The origins of this more acceptable face of horror could be said to reach back to the horror comics of the 1950s such as the then controversial titles produced by EC such as *Tales From the Crypt* (1950–55). Although these titles caused widespread moral panic on both sides of the Atlantic, the jokey (as well as horrific) approach taken by the three "ghoulunatic" "hosts" of the EC titles has done much to shape the more acceptable face of popular horror. Stories like "Midnight Snack" (Issue 24, June/July 1951) and "Swamped" (*The Haunt of Fear*, September 1954) tell horrific tales of carrion-eating ghouls, but at the same time temper these comic strips with sardonic commentary and tasteless puns. Although these comics were said to be aimed at adults, they were also hugely popular with younger readers and the knowing sensibility of these tales has since become a familiar mode of address. The HBO series based on the comic books ran for seven seasons (1989–96) and included the episode "Mournin' Mess" (Episode 34, air date 31 July 1991, directed by Manny Coto), which featured a corporate band of ghouls feeding on the corpses of the homeless. The success of children's stories featuring ghouls, such as several titles written by R.L. Stine (1943–) of "Goosebumps" fame and the all-conquering "Harry Potter" series of books by J.K. Rowling (1965–), has placed the ghoul at the heart of mainstream film and literature. The somewhat anodyne depiction of ghouls in these titles is tempered by more grisly children's tales such as those penned by Gris Grimley (his 2007 short film *Cannibal Flesh Riot* tells the story of two redneck grave-robbing ghouls), and the horror and fantasy genre has continued to throw up more adult-orientated material such as Brian McNaughton's *The Throne of Bones* (1997) and Brian Keene's novel *Ghoul* (2007).

Rehan Hyder

References and Suggested Reading

Byron, George Gordon. *The Giaour: A Fragment of a Turkish Tale*. Whitefish, MT: Kessinger Publishing, 2011.

Connors, Scott. "The Ghoul." In *Icons of Horror and the Supernatural: An Encyclopedia of Our Worst Nightmares*, edited by S.T. Joshi. Connecticut: Greenwood, 2006.

Johnson, Robert Barbour. "Far Below." In *Far Below and Other Horrors from the Pulps*, edited by Robert Weinberg. Gillette: Wildside Press, 2003.

Lovecraft, Howard Phillips. "Pickman's Model" and "The Rats in the Walls." In *Necronomicon: The Best Weird Tales of H.P. Lovecraft*. London: Gollancz, 2008.

Smith, Ashton Clark. "The Nameless Offspring." In *The Abominations of Yondo*. St Albans: Panther, 1974.

White, Edward Lucas. "Amina." In *The House of Nightmare*. Seattle: Midnight House, 1946.

GIANT

From fairytale to fantasy fiction, Greek mythology to Hollywood film, the giant is a familiar figure. Almost every culture possesses some version of this monster, probably because the giant amounts to nothing more than a body enlarged to the point at which the human figure becomes estranged. Looming over our diminished selves, the giant makes evident our frailty, our mortality. Giants typically elicit terror, as in Francisco Goya's famous painting *Il Colosso* (c. 1808), in which a panicked mob flees the monster's towering form. Some, however, offer an invitation to corporeal pleasure: food, sex, mirth. The giant is therefore an ambivalent monster, combining fear of self-annihilation with an undercurrent of desire, forces of domination with possibilities of subversive celebration. Because only size need distinguish giants from humans, the line separating these groups is easily traversed. Even when giants are imagined as a separate, monstrous race, humans sometimes intermingle with them. Thus the Biblical Goliath is a Philistine; the **Cyclops** Polyphemus is famous for his love of a normally proportioned woman, Galatea; Cain was sometimes held to be the father of monsters, including giants; medieval Norse giants were often lovers for gods and humans; the offspring of giants are sometimes depicted as ordinary in size. For all their monstrous excess, giants are in the end rather human.

The giant has long haunted the Western imagination. Greek myth, the earliest verses of the Hebrew Bible, early Christian interpreters of that text, and Irish, Welsh, and Icelandic stories record the monster's ancient presence. The giant pervades every level of society, from popular culture and folklore to self-consciously artistic literature and scholarly discourse. With some notable exceptions, the giant is strongly gendered male. He often figures the masculine body out of control, demarcating a cultural boundary not to be traversed. The giant is foundational. The world may have been created from the body of a giant, as in Norse fable; or the body of the Earth may spawn giants, as in classical tradition. He is so elemental that humanity cannot escape his abiding presence. His reality is often attested through the landscape he has supposedly reconfigured, so that his name becomes attached to mountains and rock formations. The giant therefore often serves an etiological function.

Fig. 16 ***Giant*** **by Scott Ogden**

Greek and Roman Myth

Classical giants are an autochthonous order of beings associated with the brute forces of the Earth. They are monsters that must be eradicated so that humans—and the anthropomorphic gods who watch over them—may flourish. Hesiod's *Theogony* (c. 700 BCE) describes how the emasculation of rapinous Uranos ("Sky") by his son Cronus engendered the giants, a race of pernicious creatures who eventually attempt to overthrow the gods by storming Olympus. This battle against Zeus was called the Gigantomachia and was frequently depicted in literature and painted on vases. Virgil (70–19 BCE) and Ovid (43 BCE–17/18 CE) both refer to the war, describing the giants' monumental feat of stacking the mountain Ossa atop Pelion in order to reach the home of the gods. Other classical giants include the **Titans**; the sons of Aloeus, who likewise attempted a divine assault; Argus Panoptes, the hundred-eyed giant who served as Hera's watchman; and Briareus, who possessed a hundred hands. All of these monsters possessed long afterlives. Briareus, for example, appears in the ninth circle of Dante's *Inferno* (c. 1308–21; see **Dante, Monsters In**), the windmill episode of *Don Quixote* (v. 1, 1605), the Dungeons & Dragons *Monster Manual* (1977; see **Dungeons & Dragons, Monsters In**), and *The Battle of the Labyrinth* (2008) by Rick Riordan.

One-eyed giants also appear frequently. Homer (c. eighth century BCE) describes the Cyclopes as solitary beings, lacking the laws that form communities and the technology necessary for agriculture. When the itinerant hero Odysseus requests food and shelter from Polyphemus, the most famous of their kind, the monster responds by cannibalizing his men. Odysseus's blinding of the giant's single eye is a rebuke to the creature's worldview, one in which the sacred bond between host and guest may be ignored.

These classical giants were eventually conflated with similar monsters from the Hebrew Bible, with whom they share several traits, especially hostility towards the divine (see **Bible, Monsters In The**). As early as the writings of the Jewish historian Josephus (first century CE), the murderous spawn of Uranos were linked to the Nephilim of Genesis.

Biblical Giants

Following the precedent set by Latin translations of the Bible, in English versions the term "giant" quietly collects a variety of Hebrew words, creating a false impression of unity, as if all the Biblical giants constituted a single race. The first mention of giants occurs in a mysterious passage from Genesis, which states "giants [*Nephilim*] were upon the earth in those days" (6:4). These monsters are the apparent offspring of the "sons of God" (sometimes understood to be the mortal children of Seth, at other times fallen **angels**) and the "daughters of men" (usually glossed as the offspring of Cain, exiled for murdering his brother). The Flood follows shortly after the appearance of the Nephilim, implicitly linking the birth of these creatures with a mysterious miscegenation and a subsequent proliferation of earthly evils. The passage is obscure enough never to have found a definitive interpretation. It eventually yielded the medieval idea that a giant might be the child of an **incubus** (a kind of fallen angel) and a mortal woman. Though the giants of Genesis 6:4 should have been wiped from the Earth as a result of the Deluge, moreover, they also appear well after the story of Noah. They therefore posed a difficult problem for rabbinical interpreters as well as Christian exegetes. The Talmud developed a complete mythology for the giant Og of Bashan (Deuteronomy 3:11), a post-diluvian giant destroyed by the Israelites. Supposedly he made a pact with Noah and submitted himself and his children to slavery to board the ark.

Giants enter the Biblical narrative a second time in Numbers, after which their presence proliferates. When Moses sends spies into the Promised Land, they return to the waiting Israelites with a report of a land flowing with milk and honey. Canaan also holds inimical giants (Anakim, said to be descendants of the Nephilim) "in comparison to whom we seemed as locusts" (Numbers 13:28–34). These monsters appear to represent indigenous peoples, figured as inhumanly vast to convey the difficulty of settling the territory and dispossessing them of a claim to their land. Other Biblical groups assimilated into the Latin and English categories of "giant" include similarly aboriginal peoples, the Emim (Deuteronomy 2:10) and the Zamzummim (Deut eronomy 2:20). The giant (*raphah*) Goliath of Gath, defeated by the young David, is a lone monster rather than a member of a group or race. The young warrior's defeat of that giant and display of his severed head became so iconic that the expected fate for almost all giants in Western texts is decapitation. The vivid encounter between David and Goliath (I Samuel 17) intermingles the theological with the nationalistic. Goliath curses his opponent by his gods, while the boy replies with his faith in a single deity. The humiliation of the giant is a gleeful disparaging of his polytheism: a shepherd boy too young to wear armor, carrying a staff, which his enemy bemoans as grossly insulting, defeats the monster with a well-aimed stone from a slingshot. Called the *nanus contra gigantem* ("boy against the giant") theme, the scene of David's victory would become among the most frequently illustrated Biblical episodes. Caravaggio (1571–1610), Michelangelo (1475–1564), Titian (c. 1448–1576), and Rubens (1577–1640) created famous depictions.

Medieval and Early Modern Giants

The medieval Irish imagined that their island had once been held by the Fomori, a primordial race who were disfigured and bellicose. Though not originally imagined as giants (Old Irish *aithech*), over time their size was exaggerated in order to render them more fearsome. They were associated with stonework and caves, their historical presence readable from the landscape. The famous Giant's Causeway in County Antrim is supposed to have been their handiwork. These frozen sprays of lava, jutting from the sea in weirdly architectural black columns, are called by the Irish *Clochán na bhFomharaigh*, "the stepping stones of the Fomori." Various Neolithic edifices were also associated with this race. For the Irish—as for many other cultures—the primeval race of giants served an explanatory function, anchoring present landscape to an origin in the distant past. Nearby Wales told stories of more singular giants, such as Ysbaddaden, a foe of Arthur who withholds his daughter from marriage and is, when overcome, shaved to the skull and decapitated. Bran the Blessed is another important Welsh giant. King of Britain, he possesses a magic cauldron that can restore vitality to the dead. Mortally wounded in Irish battle, Bran instructs his men to cut off his head and return it to his island. The severed head retains its ability to speak for seven years, after which it is interred in London at the site of the future White Tower. Supposedly the giant's head kept Britain free from invasion so long as it remained buried.

According to Norse mythology, the Earth itself was fashioned from the corpse of the giant Ymir. Elemental and rather primitive, giants might inhabit a distant geography (Glasisvellir or Jotunheim), but also mingle freely with humans as they wander the world. Norse giants are frequently female, and often intermarry with gods and men.

Odin is the son of a giantess named Bestla. Although they could be fierce, the Norse *jötnar* are more ethically complex than other traditions of giants: chaos-loving, perhaps, but rather indifferent to binaries like good versus evil, wildness against civilization. Giants were especially associated with stone and topography. Boulders, ruined buildings, and mountains indicated their former presence. This etiological function is shared by giants in Old English literature, which frequently refers to ancient structures like Roman walls as *enta geweorc*, the work of giants. Though never precisely described, the monster **Grendel** and his mere-dwelling mother appear to both be giants. Enormous, humanoid, and children of Cain, they share the same fate, decapitation.

In his *History of the Kings of Britain* (c. 1136), the text that bestowed to the future the mythic King Arthur we know today, Geoffrey of Monmouth imagined that the island of Britain was originally settled by an exiled Trojan named Brutus. His only impediment to making a kingdom of the new land was its current occupants, giants who attack Brutus's men and are exterminated as a result. Like the Biblical Anakim, these giants represent in monstrous form native peoples and the challenges of conquest. Later mythology would develop the idea that these giants were the spawn of incubi or devils and Greek princesses exiled to Britain for their crimes. In a culminating moment of the *History of the Kings of Britain*, moreover, Geoffrey will have Arthur defeat a menacing but lone giant on Mont Saint Michel in Normandy. A rapist and a cannibal, this monster is the male body out of control. He harkens from Muslim Spain, aligning him with non-Christian others at a time not long after the First Crusade. Giants, like all monsters, tend to gather to themselves all the contemporary signifiers of otherness and difference. Whereas Arthur fights with his famous sword, the giant wields a primitive club. After the king defeats the brute, he orders the head displayed, Goliath-like, to his men to announce the triumph. This scene of warrior against giant set the stage for many similar combats in the chivalric romances of the Middle Ages. Overcoming the giant became a way for the young knight to demonstrate that he had overcome the monster within, that he could control his body sexually and martially.

In the *Inferno*, as Dante prepares to descend into the Ninth Circle of Hell, he spots what appears to be a tower but is in fact a giant, interred from the waist down. The monster bellows gibberish at the poet. His guide Virgil reveals that this is Nimrod, architect of the tower of Babel. Though this episode takes great liberties with the Biblical narrative, it demonstrates the creativity to which giants spurred medieval authors, and the tendency of these monsters to lurk darkly at foundational moments in human history. Giants could easily be allegorized. They were often associated with pride, inspiring Edmund Spenser's Orgoglio in the *Faerie Queene* (v. 1 1590; v. 2 1596). Yet not all giants were depicted so negatively. St Christopher was often believed to have been a converted giant. Medieval romances offered comic giants like Ascopart and Rainouart, whose attempts to become Christian knights lead to ridiculous scenes of horse riding, jousting, and baptism gone wrong. Geoffrey Chaucer provides a comedic version of the monster in *The Canterbury Tales* (1387) with "The Tale of Sir Thopas," which features an inept knight threatened by the three-headed Sir Olifaunt. François Rabelais's beloved **Gargantua and Pantagruel**, depicted in a connected series of five sixteenth-century novels, celebrate bodily excess. Their merry presence inspired the Russian literary theorist Mikhail Bakhtin (1895–1975) to develop the idea that such seemingly folkloric figures pose a carnivalesque challenge to domineering, official culture.

Giants made frequent appearances in travel literature. The enormously popular *Book of John Mandeville* (c. 1357) is typical, describing giants that clothe themselves in the skin of beasts and devour raw flesh, including humans that they snatch from ships. Jonathan Swift will reverse this negative depiction with the cultured Brobdingnagians of *Gulliver's Travels* (1726; see **Swift, Jonathan, Monsters In**), whose king declares Europeans to be the savages. Patagonians, giant denizens of the New World, were reported by Ferdinand Magellan (c. 1480–1521) and Francis Drake (1540–96).

Contemporary Giants

Giants are familiar figures in films, novels, comic books, and fairytales. As the cloud dweller in "Jack in the Beanstalk," he invites children to the rewards of self-assertion over parental obedience. In the form of **bigfoot** or the yeti, the giant reassures that the world has not been completely mapped, that some wild remnant remains. As a corporate emblem, the monster promises us that our frozen and canned vegetables taste fresh (the Jolly Green Giant, mascot in the employment of General Mills) and that our processed paper products arrive with a patina of wilderness (the fakelore figure of Paul Bunyan, promulgated by a logging company). The vast, humanoid trees called Ents in J.R.R. Tolkien's *Lord of the Rings* (1954–55; see **Tolkien, Monsters In**) similarly connect giants and ecological concerns. The science fiction thriller *Attack of the Fifty Foot Woman* (Nathan R. Juran, 1958) originally encoded a social anxiety about the women's movement with its depiction of a huge housewife run amok, but today that figure has become more campy feminist heroine than crazed and fearful horror. Another contemporary film, *The Amazing Colossal Man* (Bert I. Gordon, 1957), features an army colonel exposed to plutonium who rapidly grows to 60 feet tall. Brain damage causes him to become insane, and after a rampage through Las Vegas, he is killed by the army atop the Hoover Dam. Victor **Frankenstein's monster** in Mary Shelley's *Frankenstein* (1818) and Arnold Schwarzenegger's Terminator in the series of films beginning with *The Terminator* in 1984 (James Cameron; see **Cyborg**) may not precisely be giants, but they both invoke that monster's mythology as they come to embody anxieties about technology's ability to enable humans to exceed their traditional limits. A wrestler named André the Giant played Fezzik in the *The Princess Bride* (Rob Reiner, 1987), an enduringly popular film that attempts to re-enchant a cynical world. Hagrid, a central character in the "Harry Potter" series of books begun in 1997 by J.K. Rowling, is half giant in descent. He likewise figures in a magical landscape that offers an alternative to the impoverished one of contemporary adulthood. Giants can be spotted in video and role-playing games as well.

Varied as they are, these modern instances suggest that, although some monsters vanish as the fears, anxieties and desires that engendered them change, the giant never departs for long. Perhaps giants are such intimate monsters because their forms are so familiar. Many writers placed giants at the origin of the human, arguing that our stature had declined over time. A figure of chaos and merriment, severity and celebration, life as well as death, the elemental giant is a constant companion, a version of the human writ so large that our own monstrousness is vividly displayed in his form.

Jeffrey Cohen

References and Suggested Reading

Asma, Stephen T. *Monsters: An Unnatural History of Our Worst Fears.* Oxford: Oxford University Press, 2009.

Bakhtin, Mikhail M. *Rabelais and His World.* Translated by Hélène Iswolsky. Bloomington, IN: Indiana University Press, 1984.

Cohen, Jeffrey Jerome. *Of Giants: Sex, Monsters, and the Middle Ages.* Minneapolis, MN: University of Minnesota Press, 1999.

Friedman, John Block. *The Monstrous Races in Medieval Art and Thought.* Cambridge, MA: Harvard University Press, 1981.

Stephens, Walter. *Giants in Those Days: Folklore, Ancient History, and Nationalism.* Lincoln, NE: University of Nebraska Press, 1989.

Stewart, Susan. *On Longing: Narratives of the Miniature, the Gigantic, the Souvenir, the Collection.* Durham, NC: Duke University Press, 1993.

GIBBELIN

The Gibbelins are monsters created in the story "The Hoard of the Gibbelins" by Anglo-Irish writer Lord Dunsany (Edward John Moreton Drax Plunkett, 18th Baron Dunsany, 1878–1957).

Dunsany gained instant celebrity with such works of high fantasy as *The Gods of Pegāna* (1905), *Time and the Gods* (1906), *The Sword of Welleran* (1908), and *A Dreamer's Tales* (1910). In the first two of these volumes, Dunsany created an imaginary realm called Pegāna peopled with its own gods, demigods, and worshippers. For Dunsany, this realm served as a symbol for the unity with the natural world that he believed contemporary humanity was on the verge of losing.

With *The Book of Wonder* (1912), Dunsany took a different tack. Many of the stories in this collection were written around paintings by the celebrated British artist Sidney H. Sime (1867–1941), who had illustrated several of Dunsany's previous volumes. Both the stories and the illustrations were commissioned by a popular fashion magazine of the day, *The Sketch*; "The Hoard of the Gibbelins" appeared in that magazine on 18 January 1911. Since the illustrations came first and the story afterward, the latter sometimes have very little to do with the former. In "The Hoard of the Gibbelins," the Gibbelins are in fact never described; it is merely said of them, in the opening sentence: "The Gibbelins eat, as is well known, nothing less good than man" (44). The absence of description of the entities may reflect the fact that Sime's drawing does not depict any monsters; instead, it shows only a man attempting to penetrate a forbidding castle in the forest. (The illustration appears only in *The Sketch* and in the first British and American editions of *The Book of Wonder.*)

In Dunsany's story, the Gibbelins attract their human dinner with a hoard consisting of emeralds, rubies, and other precious gems. Alderic, "Knight of the Order of the City and the Assault, hereditary Guardian of the King's Peace of Mind" (44), decides to storm the Gibbelins' castle in an unorthodox manner: he persuades a **dragon** to fly him over the Forest Impassable, then swims across the river separating the castle from the lands occupied by humans; then, with a pickaxe, he makes a hole in the castle under the water line, swimming into the castle's cellar and coming upon the jewels stored there. But just as he is about to take some of them in a satchel, the Gibbelins appear, "with torches in their hands ... and, without saying a word, *or even smiling*, they neatly hanged him on the outer wall" (49).

The tale is told with the owlish gravity of all the narratives in *The Book of Wonder*, suggesting that Dunsany was not taking himself very seriously. Aside from stating that the Gibbelins had come from the Moon, we are offered no information about them. *The Book of Wonder* contains other self-parodic tales of the same sort, including "How Nuth Would Have Practised His Art upon the Gnoles," in which the Gnoles (whom Nuth seeks to rob) are similarly undescribed. Later works by Dunsany, including the scintillating novel *The King of Elfland's Daughter* (1924), return to the tone of high fantasy of his earlier writing.

S.T. Joshi

References and Suggested Reading

Amory, Mark. *Biography of Lord Dunsany*. London: Collins, 1972.

Dunsany, Lord. *The Book of Wonder* [with *Time and the Gods*]. New York: Modern Library, 1918.

Joshi, S.T. *Lord Dunsany: Master of the Anglo-Irish Imagination*. Westport, CT: Greenwood Press, 1995.

Schweitzer, Darrell. *Pathways to Elfland: The Writings of Lord Dunsany*. Philadelphia: Owlswick Press, 1989.

GLAISTIG—*see* Banshee

GNOLL—*see* Dungeons & Dragons, Monsters In; Elemental

GNOME—*see* Elemental; Gremlin; Harry Potter, Monsters In

GOBLIN

Fig. 17 ***Goblin*** **by Aeron Alfrey**

The goblin's origin is ancient and diverse. The *Oxford English Dictionary* speculates that the Old French word *gobelin* (the first recorded use of which is from the sixteenth century, but a twelfth-century record mentions *Gobelinus* as a spirit plaguing Évreux in northern France) may have originated from the ancient Greek word *kobalos*, signifying "rogue" or "wicked sprites invoked by rogues," and made its way into French by way of the Middle Latin transliteration *cobalus* or *covalus*, meaning "mountain sprite." In the folkways of Europe, the goblin, generally understood as a type of **fairy**, is a trickster figure, small and humanoid in form, mischievous, mercurial, spiteful, and cunning in nature.

In some parts of Europe, goblins were known as household sprites that would, in secret, perform small labors unless insulted or neglected, in which case their services would end and punishments begin. In France, goblins especially favored wine and pretty children. They would ride the family's horses but tangle their manes. If they became too troublesome, goblins could be driven off by sprinkling flaxseed on the floor: the goblin would pick it up, seed by seed, and then abandon the home, exhausted.

German kobolds, which are closely connected to goblins and may share a common root (kobold and goblin being cognates), also have qualities of a household sprite. Their name may have originated in medieval High German (rather than from the ancient Greek) as a compound of *kobe* for "house" and *hold* for "friendly" or *walten* for "to rule." In a home or aboard ship, kobolds provided services. In the mines, however, their forms and natures twisted, harkening back to the **dwarfs** of Germanic mythology: cunning and greedy, though less clever with crafting.

In Great Britain, goblins are closely connected with the Scottish boggle, the Lancashire boggart, and the English hobgoblin (literally, "hearth" goblin, although in *Deutsche Mythologie* [1835], Jacob Grimm claimed the prefix "hob" reinforced the goblin's comic nature, as Hob was the name for a stock rustic clown). The goblin was also linked to the **pixie** (or *piskie*) and puck (akin to the Welsh *pwca* or the Cornish *bucca*), both types of mischievous sprites that favor dark and lonely places: woodlands, coastlands, and depths. In Welsh folklore, a goblin king (rather than a fairy queen) ruled fairy-kind. In the legend of St Collen, Grwyn ap Nudd summons the saint to his court to answer for having denounced him as a devil (see **Devil, The; Demon**), accusing him of ruling over Hell as well as the otherworld, Annwn, as both are subterranean. St Collen vanquishes all with holy water.

As goblin-kind evolved from oral folkways to the commercial literary ways of early modern literature and theater, writers became more self-conscious of the goblin's chimerical nature. In *Greene's News Both from Heaven and from Hell* (1593; authorship disputed), a goblin brags of his varied exploits: he might get travelers drunk to cause them to lose their way; disguise himself as the mischievous sprite Robin Goodfellow to seduce women; or assume the mantle of each occupation and station to encourage vice from within. Similarly, in *A Midsummer Night's Dream* (dated between 1690 and 1696), Shakespeare's Robin Goodfellow serves as jester of the fairy court ("hobgoblin" to that royal hearth). He closes the play with a conventional apology that relies upon the audience's believing him an "honest Puck," itself an oxymoron. Given his pagan associations and tendency to mischief, Robin Goodfellow's name became a euphemism for the Devil (in England, *pouke* was already a synonym) and "goblin" an adjective that denoted evil.

As the Enlightenment took hold of Europe, goblins became synonymous with superstitions fit only to frighten the peasantry. For centuries, the goblin had figured in cautionary tales told to children; it was the bogey-man who would steal and devour them if they misbehaved. Tales told in service to this "pedagogy of fear" (Tatar 22 and *passim*) were sometimes called "goblin-stories" and the foolish belief in them was referred to as "nursery goblinism."

The Antiquarian movement in Europe from the late eighteenth century onward led to a renewed dissemination of goblin-kind in written folktale form and to a cataloguing of types and characteristics dependent on people and region (see, for example, Sikes). The Romantic movement provided additional impetus, repackaging fairy-kind as agents of a liberating imagination and encouraging throughout nineteenth-century Europe fairytales and fairy fantasies both within and without the nursery.

Two important works of goblin-haunted Victorian fantasy are Christina Rossetti's *Goblin Market* (1862) and George MacDonald's *The Princess and the Goblin* (1872). Rossetti's poem tells of two sisters whom goblin men try to tempt into buying the luscious fruits they market to wandering maidens. A girl may only buy once, in exchange for a lock of her hair, after which she cannot again hear goblin voices calling her to buy. The exchange echoes at once the danger of fairy food under the hill enslaving humans who eat of it, Eve's tasting of the forbidden fruit in the Biblical Fall, and the Mephistophelean accord of selling one's soul to the Devil in exchange for worldly wants, only to receive instead hard-bought wisdom (see **Mephistopheles**). One of the two sisterly protagonists, Laura, falls prey to the goblin market, while the other, Lizzie, resists, ultimately saving her sister.

MacDonald's *The Princess and the Goblin* features goblins as the chief antagonists of a mountainous human kingdom, with a plan to tunnel into the palace, kidnap eight-year-old Princess Irene, and wed her to Prince Harelip, heir to the goblin throne. The goblins were once human but have deformed as a result of living in "unnatural" conditions. They are hideous and dwarfed, with soft feet, hard heads, and strength equal to their cunning. To their subterranean homes they have stolen land-dwelling creatures and tamed them as helpmates. These, too, have deformed, now resembling something human, while the goblins resemble something animal. As reflects their depravity, MacDonald's goblins fear the sunlight and can be driven off by song, both of which are expressions of a vital divinity. Even so, they are not portrayed without sympathy: goblins contribute to a class allegory, as the reader is told that they originally sought refuge below to escape persecution by an unjust king. At the end of the story, those who survive become much like "Scotch **brownies**," with softer skulls and hearts, and harder feet, enabling peaceful co-existence with humankind and good industry.

As in these two instances, original Victorian fairytales tended to depict goblins as agents of moral reform, even if the goblins were degenerate: Dickens wrote a Christmas story ("The Story of the Goblins Who Stole a Sexton," published as part of the serial *The Pickwick Papers*, 1837) about goblins—stout, foppish, and cheerfully malicious—who punish a morose sexton who cannot abide merriment in others and is stuck in an unseasonably grim job (burying the dead). By the *fin de siècle*, goblins were also used as figures of disorderly fun, with spectacular Christmas pantomimes bearing names such as *The Grim Goblin* (H. Spry and G. Conquest, 1876) and *The Goblin Bat* (F. Bowyer, 1886). In the early twentieth century, goblins made the leap from the stage to early cinema, in translations of Shakespeare and pantomime.

In the mid twentieth century, goblins underwent another transformation, as they became a major race (or racial group) within high fantasy narratives, proliferating in fiction, film, games, comics, and more. These goblins owe their origin to J.R.R. Tolkien (1892–1973), a philologist with a keen interest in Northern European folklore and myth (see **Tolkien, Monsters In**). In the Author's Note to the revised edition of *The Hobbit* (1951), Tolkien writes: "Orc is not an English word. It occurs in one or two places but is usually translated goblin (or hobgoblin for the larger kinds). Orc is the hobbits' form of the name given at that time to these creatures" (1). Tolkien's neologism, "orc," is derived from the Anglo-Saxon word for monsters or demons (*orcnéas*), which had been associated in the Old English epic poem *Beowulf* (composed sometime between the eighth and eleventh centuries) with a monstrous race descended from the Biblical Cain.

By his admission, Tolkien's goblins were also influenced by George MacDonald's, but they lack the comic homeliness. Rather, Tolkien's orcs represent the savage, invading Other, a cannibalistic horde, as he describes in a letter: "squat, broad, flat-nosed, sallow-skinned, with wide mouths and slant eyes

... degraded and repulsive versions of the (to Europeans) least lovely Mongol-types" (Carpenter 293). Like folkloric goblins, Tolkien's smaller, crooked-legged goblins shun the sun, and often dwell in the depths, as in Moria.

Tolkien's orcs are the literary precursor to the goblins (and orcs) found in fantasy gaming culture (which has itself influenced further literary treatments and films), beginning with the role-playing game Dungeons & Dragons in 1974 (see **Dungeons & Dragons, Monsters In**). The Warhammer fantasy setting (which has evolved since 1983 from tabletop miniatures to pen-and-paper role-playing to massively multiple online role-playing) later united a number of "goblinoid races" (a term for savage demihumans derived from Dungeons & Dragons) under the label Greenskins (goblins, orcs, snotlings, hobgoblins, and gnoblars), and is now widely credited with having separated the smaller, smarter goblins and bigger, stronger orcs into distinct races and fixed them with the green skin so common thereafter. The Greenskins share a war-like, tribal culture. Like Tolkien's orcs, they are incapable of positive creation or civilization, and it is unclear whether they have females.

Other fantasy games that have depicted goblins in Warhammer's direct line of influence include 1993's *Magic: The Gathering* (see, for example, the Goblin Mob *Scourge* Theme Deck of 2006) and 2004's *World of Warcraft*. In the Warcraft fantasy universe, goblins and orcs remain separate races, with goblins and many orcs green-skinned. Goblins, however, have become a race of merchants and inventors, ruled by trade princes and engaged in immoral capitalist practices such as deforestation and slaving. Both goblins and orcs include females as active player options, a singular development.

Beyond fairy fantasy and high fantasy, goblins have proliferated across contemporary fantastic fiction, from steampunk (see Maureen Doyle McQuerry's *The Peculiars* [2012] and William Alexander's *Goblin Secrets* [2012]) to paranormal romance (see Shona Husk's "Shadowlands" series begun in 2011) to urban fantasy (see Charles DeLindt's *Jack of Kinrowan* [1995]) to children's picture books (see Pamela Jane and Jane Manning's *Little Goblins Ten* counting book [2011]) and young-adult fantasy fiction. In young-adult narratives, goblins are often portrayed as objects of prejudice, and so resonate sympathetically with marginalized protagonists (for example, pre-adults, singular talents, practitioners of forbidden magic). The goblins in J.K. Rowling's "Harry Potter" series (1997–2007)—short, pink-skinned, long of hand and feet, pointy eared and nosed, and universally male—have earned a place in wizarding society through their skill with finance and metal-smithing, largely controlling the economy (right down to minting the coin of the "realm") and overseeing Gringotts Wizarding Bank (see **Harry Potter, Monsters In**). Yet, they remain outsiders, speaking Gobbledegook and possessing their own magic, the secrets of which they conceal from wizards, who will not allow goblins to carry wands and consider them subservient. To those in the mainstream, even their goblin notion of ownership reads like a rationale for thievery, for they believe it is retained by the maker of an item, regardless of who comes to possess it. In another example, Hilari Bell's "Goblin Wood" trilogy (2003–11), twelve-year-old hedgewitch Makenna makes an alliance with an army of clever goblins, sharing in common their status as misunderstood outcasts who are denied their magic by the Decree of Bright Magic, which dictates that only human high priests may practice the arts (see **Witch/Wizard**).

Goblins also have a place in Western comic book culture and, as a result, now appear in Eastern comic book culture (particularly in Japanese manga) through adaptations of and original works inspired by Western fantasies. In Western comic book culture, perhaps the most infamous goblins have appeared in *The Amazing Spider-Man* storylines. The original Green Goblin (there have been at least three since) appeared in Marvel's *The Amazing Spider-Man* #14 (1964) as the Halloween-themed alter ego of industrialist Norman Osborn, whose chemically induced insanity led him to transform himself into the monster he had most feared as a child. Others include Hobgoblin, Grey Goblin, and the goblin-themed Menace of Manhattan.

Goblins have appeared in contemporary cinema, too, through film adaptations of works by MacDonald (*The Princess and the Goblin*, József Gémes, 1991), Tolkien (Rankin/Bass's animated *The Hobbit*, 1977; Ralph Bakshi's animated *Lord of the Rings*, 1978; and Peter Jackson's *Lord of the Rings Trilogy*, 2001, 2002, 2003), and Rowling. Other important, original goblin instances in fairy-themed film include David Bowie as Jareth the Goblin King in *Labyrinth* (Jim Henson, 1986) and the Lord of Darkness' motley goblin henchmen in *Legend* (Ridley Scott, 1985). Brian Froud's (1947–) depictions of goblins in art books and films (he provided the concept art for *Labyrinth*) have also widely influenced their representation in the contemporary fantastic, from the animal-inspired goblins that range from endearing to fierce to the often comic, almost-human grotesques, with their oversized gear.

Goblins have even become a stock monster in B-horror movies, including the cult classic *Troll 2* (Claudio Fragasso, 1990), with fans insisting that the menacing forest creatures in the film are goblins rather than **trolls**. In horror narratives and fantasy films influenced by tales of dark fairies, goblins often figure as child snatchers. An example may be found in the first book (*The Field Guide*, 2003) of Tony DiTerlizzi and Holly Black's "The Spiderwick Chronicles," and in the film adaptation of those first five books (Mark Waters, 2008). Like traditional fairies, Spiderwick goblins are invisible to the unaided human eye; they are forced, however, to make or find their own teeth.

Kelly Searsmith

References and Suggested Reading

Carpenter, Humphrey, ed. *The Letters of J.R.R. Tolkien*. Boston: Houghton Mifflin, 1981.

Froud, Brian, and Ari Berk. *Brian Froud's Goblins!* New York: Harry N. Abrams, 2008.

"Goblin." *Funk & Wagnalls Standard Dictionary of Folklore, Mythology and Legend* [1949]. Reprint, edited by Maria Leech, San Francisco: Harper/Collins, 1984.

MacDonald, George. *The Princess and the Goblin* and *The Princess and Curdie*, edited by Roderick McGillis. New York: Oxford University Press, 1990.

Rossetti, Christina. *Goblin Market and Other Poems*. Cambridge: Macmillan, 1862.

Scott, Charles C.G. "The Devil and His Imps: An Etymological Inquisition." *Transactions of the American Philological Association* XXVI (1985): 79–146.

Sikes, Wirt. *Folk-lore British Goblins: Welsh, Fairy Mythology, Legends and Traditions.* London: S. Low, Marston, Searle, and Rivington, 1880. Internet Sacred Text Archive, edited by Phillip Brown. 15 July 2012. <http://www.sacred-texts.com/neu/celt/wfl/wfl01.htm>.

Tatar, Maria. *Off with Their Heads!: Fairy Tales and the Culture of Childhood*. Princeton, NJ: Princeton University Press, 1992.

Thoms, William J. *Three Notelets on Shakespeare*. London: J.R. Smith, 1865.

Tolkien, J.R.R. "Author's Note." In *The Hobbit*. 2nd edn. St Louis, MO: Turtleback, 2002.

GODZILLA

Godzilla is a gigantic, bipedal, and amphibious beast that first appeared in the Japanese science fiction film *Godzilla* (1954), directed by Ishirō Honda and released by Tōhō Studios in Japan. Its body resembles a **dinosaur** with jagged dorsal fins and fierce claws; its skin is invulnerable to artillery shells. Lumbering and thrashing its trail, Godzilla is powerful, aggressive, and destructive, spewing radioactive rays. The original black-and-white film was a blockbuster, which prompted Tōhō to produce other Godzilla-featured films and introduce other giant monsters. The name Godzilla, or *Gojira* in Japanese, derives from the words "gorilla" (*gorira*) and "whale" (*kujira*). In Japan, the film is regarded as the first of the well-established *kaijū* (giant monster) genre. Since its inception, the Godzilla series has been globally circulated, adapted, and enjoyed, attracting international fans and cult followers. Today, Godzilla is one of the world's most well-known pop icons.

The first *Godzilla* film reveals the basics about the titlular monster's place of origin and his characteristics. The story begins with a Japanese boat in the Pacific Ocean. A glaring flash of light from under the sea blinds the crew and the boat bursts into flames and sinks. Similar shipwrecks follow and the rural residents of Ōdo Island are assailed by a mysterious, enormous creature. Paleontologist Professor Kyōhei Yamane (Takashi Shimura) and his group investigate the disaster site on the island and find a now-extinct marine arthropod Trilobite and several radioactive footprints. From these findings, Yamane concludes that both disasters were caused by a prehistoric dinosaur creature that has survived since the Jurassic period and has mutated through a series of hydrogen bomb experiments conducted in the Pacific Ocean. The creature's name, Godzilla, was taken from Ōdo folklore about a deep-sea monster and has been passed on from generation to generation. Regardless of Yamane's efforts to keep Godzilla alive for further research, the Japanese government prepares to attack the creature. When Godzilla emerges from Tokyo Bay, the government attempts to kill the monster, mobilizing its military. Yet Godzilla defies such resistance and rampages toward downtown Tokyo, demolishing high-rise buildings and terrorizing citizens. Eventually, a secret weapon called the "Oxygen Destroyer," invented by scientist Daisuke Serizawa (Akihiko Hirata), destroys Godzilla. Worried about the misuse of such a powerful weapon, Serizawa sacrifices himself to kill Godzilla under the sea, letting the knowledge of this deadly technology die with him. The film ends with Yamane proclaiming that there will be other Godzillas who will appear if humans keep using nuclear weapons.

At the initial stage of production, producer Tomoyuki Tanaka's plan was to make a deep **sea monster** movie, possibly inspired by Eugène Lourié's *The Beast from 20,000 Fathoms* (1953) and the re-release of the 1933 Hollywood film ***King Kong***, directed by Merian C. Cooper and Ernest B. Schoedsack, in the same year in Japan. Tanaka assigned popular fiction writer Shigeru Kayama to compose the original story, hiring Ishirō Honda as the director and Eiji Tsuburaya as a special effects artist. It is important to note that Kayama's original story and Tanaka's adaptation of the film were responses to the sense of urgency at play in the social and historical situation of Japan at the time. The film was in production only two years after the end of the US occupation. Despite the restoration of Japan's sovereignty, the nation remained unavoidably involved in the high politics of the Cold War due to the US–Japan security treaty signed in 1951, which allowed the

US military to remain stationed within Japan. This complex political position caused apprehension among the Japanese, reminding them of the deployment of atomic bombs in Hiroshima and Nagasaki nine years earlier; in particular, the Japanese were anxious about a series of nuclear tests in the South Pacific. In addition, on 1 March 1954, a Japanese tuna fishing boat crew on the *Lucky Dragon 5* (*daigo fukuryū maru*) were exposed to nuclear fallout from the US nuclear experiment at Castle Bravo on Bikini Atoll, which caused the death of the crew due to radiation sickness. Along with the grave anxiety over polluted fish in the market, the radiation-exposure victims triggered public discussion on the use of nuclear technology and weaponry. Indeed, throughout *Godzilla*, several explicit social and political allusions are made that reflect the trauma of the Japanese toward the nuclear holocaust and World War II: a character refers to surviving the atomic bomb in Nagasaki and a girl is examined with a Geiger counter to determine the degree of her radiation exposure. In addition, the Godzilla-devastated Tokyo scenery in the film evokes the image of Tokyo in ruins as a result of US air raids during the end of the war. These historical and political elements in the film make Godzilla both a *Japanese* and *atomic age* monster.

The success of *Godzilla* was also due to the talented creators and production staff. Among them, the film's special effects (*tokusatsu*) technician was Eiji Tsuburaya, whose artwork is highly regarded. Tsuburaya is famed as the founder of the Japanese special effects studio Tsuburaya Productions, inaugurated in 1961, and he developed the popular TV superhero show *Ultraman* (1966) and other sequels with similar superheroes. In *Godzilla*, Tsuburaya introduced a new technique for animating monsters. Unlike the stop-motion animation used in Hollywood monster movies, Tsuburaya employed the use of human-sized suits for animating monsters. Dubbed as "suitmation," Godzilla actors wore rubber suits and performed in elaborately crafted miniature sets to create the illusion of Godzilla's enormity. Godzilla's monstrosity is also underscored by the creature's trademark jarring roar and the lumbering sound of its footsteps. Composer Akira Ifukube, who also composed the score of the film's memorable main theme, created the sound of Godzilla's roar by rubbing a loosened string of a double bass with a glove; the sound of footsteps was produced by bashing an amplifier box.

In the midst of the film's popularity, Tōhō Studios immediately prepared a sequel, which resulted in the Motoyoshi Oda-directed *Godzilla Raids Again* (*Gojira no gyakushū*) in 1955. In this film, Godzilla reappears along the coast of Japan, but this time it attacks Osaka. The film features another giant monster named Anguirus (*Angirasu*) and Godzilla battles it. This element—giant monsters fighting each other—became a recurrent, popular format in later Godzilla series, including 1962's *King Kong vs. Godzilla* (Ishirō Honda), the highest-grossing film in the series. As the series progressed, the size of Godzilla increased as Japan constructed higher buildings in its urban areas, and the characterization of the monster also shifted, sometimes from the ultimate enemy of humanity to the savior of the people, or even a friendly companion to children.

In Japan's postwar cinema industry, the financial success of *Godzilla* and later sequels triggered the boom of *kaijū* genre films. Japanese film companies began to create similar *kaijū* genre films, featuring different giant monsters such as Rodan, Mothra, King Ghidorah, and Gamera, to name a few. In 1956, Tōhō released another giant monster film, *Rodan* (*Radon, the Flying Monster*), also directed by Honda. Like

Godzilla, the film features a flying monster named Rodan that resembles an extinct, enlarged winged-reptilian Pteranodon. In fact, the original Japanese name of the monster Rodan is "Radon," a contracted word from "petranodon." One of the key characteristics of the Rodan is to be able to fly with supersonic speed, which creates a destructive sonic boom. In 1961, Tōhō also introduced another monster named Mothra. Mothra is an enormous moth-like creature, the existence of which is explained as resulting from anomalous climate conditions in the southern Pacific. Like a moth, Mothra metamorphoses through egg, larva, pupa, and ultimately matures into its moth-like form. While in the larva stage, Mothra has the ability to attack its enemy by spraying silk, while the matured Mothra creates windblasts with its large wings. Unlike other *kaijū*, Mothra is always associated with femininity or motherhood, and it appears as a "guardian deity" in every Mothra film. Within Japan, Godzilla, Rodan, and Mothra are categorized as the "three greatest monsters" (*san dai kaijū*). Observing the popularity of monster films, Daiei Motion Picture Company (now Kadokawa Shoten Pictures, Inc.) followed suit in creating monster films. In 1965, Daiei released a giant monster film, *Gamera* (Noriaki Yuasa). Gamera is a giant turtle monster with fierce fangs that stick out of its lower jaw. Gamera has an extremely solid and hard shell that resists missiles and other artillery, and is capable of flying in the air and even in outer space. Due to the characterization of the monster as a children's hero, Gamera gained popularity among the young Japanese audience.

Today, Godzilla is one of the world's most internationally well-known monsters. Two years after the release of the Japanese original, Hollywood adapted the film and created *Godzilla, King of the Monsters!* (1956), which has a different plot for American audiences. The adaptation contains English-dubbed, edited scenes of the original film directed by Honda, which are combined with newly shot sequences directed by Terry O. Morse and starring Raymond Burr. Despite receiving lousy reviews, this American film was a box office hit, grossing more than $2 million in its initial run. As the Godzilla series began to circulate worldwide, several similar films were made in different countries, such as Eugène Lourié's *Gorgo* (1961) in England; a Danish-American co-production, *Reptilicus* (Sidney W. Pink, 1961); Kim Ki-duk's *Yongary* (1967) in South Korea; and *Pulgasari* (Chong Gon Jo and Sang-ok Shin, 1985) in North Korea. In 1998, Hollywood attempted to re-make Godzilla with computer-generated special effects (*Godzilla*, directed by Roland Emmerich), but it was a critical flop.

Even in the new millennium, Godzilla-inspired imagination and creativity continues. In recent years, there have been two internationally circulated Godzilla films: the South Korean *The Host* (2006), directed by Bong Joon-Ho, and the American *Cloverfield* (2008), directed by Matt Reeves. Following the spirit of the original *Godzilla*, both films offer social and political commentaries, responding to the contingencies at play in their national contexts: the former on the presence of the American military in South Korea; the latter on the 9/11 terrorist attack in the US.

C.J. Suzuki

References and Suggested Reading

Allison, Anne. *Millennial Monsters: Japanese Toy and the Global Imagination*. Berkeley: University of California Press, 2006.

Berra, John. *Directory of World Cinema: Japan*. Bristol, UK: Intellect, 2010.

Igarashi, Yoshikuni. *Bodies of Memory: Narratives of War in Postwar Japanese Culture, 1945–1970*.

Princeton, NJ: Princeton University Press, 2000.

Ryfle, Steve. *Japan's Favorite Mon-Star: The Unauthorized Biography of "The Big G."* Toronto: ECW Press, 1998.

Yomota, Inuhiko. "The Menace from the South Seas: Honda Ishirō's *Godzilla* (1954)." In *Japanese Cinema: Texts and Contexts*, edited by Alistair Phillips and Julian Stringer. New York: Routledge, 2007.

GOG—*see* Bible, Monsters In the

GOKUSOTSU—*see* Demon

GOLEM

Questions of human usurpation of divine prerogative in the creation of artificial life, the limitations of such life, and the parameters of artificial intelligence were as intriguing to rabbinic Judaism as they are to postmodernity. In the Babylonian Talmud (Sanhedrin 65b) we read a refreshingly matter-of-fact description of the creation of "a man" by the third-century sage Rava. When he sends the man to his colleague, Rav Zeira, Rav Zeira speaks to him, but he returns no answer. Rav Zeira then suspects that he has been created by magical means and orders him to return to dust. Tradition has it that this man is a "Golem" (Hebrew for "unformed") and he is the first of a panoply of artificial humanoids of varying powers and capacities alleged to have been created by holy men throughout the history of the Jews in their diasporas.

Although the word "Golem" has the implications of incompleteness, lack of development, and gross brutishness on the physical and intellectual planes, legend always has the creators of Golems striving for refinement on a variety of levels. First of all, not anyone can animate a Golem. The creator has to be an extremely refined and pious individual. There is a belief among Jewish mystics that the book called *Sefer Yezirah*, the *Book of Formation*, which discusses aspects of the Hebrew alphabet as the foundation of creation, is, in fact, a blueprint for the creation of life, Golems included. Golems, like the primeval Adam, are created from the dust of the Earth, from clay molded into the rough parameters of the human form. They are animated via the recitation of Biblical verses, magical formulae, and various Names of God in combination and recombination. In some tales, the Golem has the Name of God inserted into it or placed in its mouth. In others, the Name, or the word EMET ("truth"), is inscribed on its forehead. When the Name is removed, or in the case of the word EMET, the first letter (aleph, the first Hebrew letter, representing the First Principal—God) is erased, leaving the word MET ("dead"), the being returns to its inanimate state.

The most famous Golem is the one allegedly made by Judah Loew ben Bezalel (c. 1520–1609) of Prague, called the Maharal (an acronym for "*Moreinu ha-Rav Loew*," "Our Teacher, Rabbi Loew"). This story, in which the Golem is created to save the Jews of Prague from a blood libel against them, is most likely an invention of nineteenth-century German literature, arising from several sources—the earliest around 1837. The tale of the Maharal's Golem was not a part of Prague lore before the early nineteenth century. It was known neither to Rabbi Yedidiah Tiah Weil (1721–1805), who wrote in Prague and described the creation of Golems (including one allegedly created by Rabbi Avigdor Kara, 1389–1439, who himself dwelled in Prague) nor to Rabbi Meir Perels, the author of a biography of the Maharal published in 1745.

In this tale, circulated in German literature and then in the form of an "authentic manuscript" by Rabbi Yudl Rosenberg, a 1909 forgery that purports to be the testimony of the Maharal's son-in-law, the Golem protects but then begins avenging the Jews, killing non-Jews and terrorizing even the innocent. Some versions have the Golem spurned in its attempts to love the rabbi's daughter and turning to violence; others have it eventually turning on the Maharal and other Jews.

The tale has antecedents in other Golem stories, most directly from those circulating around Rabbi Elijah of Chelm (1550–83), which academic scholars of Kabbalah view as the earliest written accounts of the creation of a Golem involving a known historical figure. This version has several elements—including the use of the word EMET to animate and decommission the Golem, and the precipitous growth of the Golem, which necessitates its destruction—that anticipate and are incorporated into the account of the Maharal. The Maharal Golem tale was sufficiently popular to become, within a generation, an "authentic tale of Prague" and to influence other, subsequent treatments, from the story of a Golem created by Rabbi Elijah of Vilna (1720–97) to the Golems in contemporary science fiction and literature.

Golems are to their creators as humans are to God, but also as children are to parents; thus, they enable the human-divine/creator-created parent-child dynamic to be played out in microcosm. Accordingly, all the inherent complications of both relationships are manifest in the stories of such being—projection, hubris, over-reaching. Although Golems should theoretically obey their masters perfectly, the imperfection of even the most saintly masters can create problems in the relationship that cause it to end badly in most cases. The creators of Golems ostensibly operate for the good of their communities, creating these beings when Jews are threatened with destruction and when no champion seems to be available to defend them. Yet many are inevitably drawn to the misuse of the creatures—exploiting them as servants or neglecting them so that others with less insight exploit them, projecting their own desires onto their creations and descending into hubris. Consequently, these creatures, like any supernatural beings who are inherently unstable in the sensate universe, may carry out instructions too literally—ordered to chop wood and then neglected or forgotten about, they will chop and chop everything within reach without ceasing (akin to the "Sorcerer's Apprentice"). Or, like **Frankenstein's monster**, they will rebel and become uncooperative, ultimately turning on their creators, who attempt to return them to dust at the last minute, succeeding in most cases, but failing in at least one—the case of Elijah of Chelm, who was crushed by the Golem he created in the process of deactivating it.

Golems entered Western popular consciousness via tales of the magic and mysteries of Prague. Gustav Meyrink's 1914 novel *Der Golem* is a bizarre expressionistic occultist novel that is only peripherally inspired by the Jewish tales of the Golem. Paul Wegener's series of German expressionistic silent films followed—there were three, of which only the first one, *The Golem: How He Came Into the World* (1920), survived. Other films followed, including Julien Duvivier's 1936 Wegener sequel *Le Golem*, and *It!* (1966), a pulp sensational film starring Roddy McDowall.

The Golem features in contemporary fiction, notably in Marge Piercy's novel *He, She and It*, a futuristic romance that interweaves the tale of the coming into consciousness, the loves, and the losses of a **cyborg** named Yod, whose tale is interwoven with that of the Golem of Prague. Michael Chabon's *The Amazing Adventures of Kavalier & Clay* (2001) charts the origins of an imagined comic book superhero in the experiences of Josef Kavalier, a stage magician who smuggles himself out of Nazi-occupied Europe along with the Golem of Prague. In fantasist China

Miéville's *Iron Council* (2004), protagonist Judah Low becomes a master at conjuring Golems from a variety of raw materials, ultimately including time itself. Golems have also featured in several of Terry Pratchett's "Discworld" novels, including *Feet of Clay* (1996), in which Golems attempt to liberate themselves. Both Isaac Bashevis Singer and Elie Wiesel wrote versions of the tale (both entitled *The Golem*, the former published in 1969, the latter in 1983) intended for children. Jonathan Stroud's 2004 novel, *The Golem's Eye*, finds Bartimeus, the **demon** protagonist, struggling against a magic-sapping Golem.

Golems appear as comic book characters as well. Swamp Thing #153 ("Twilight of the Gods" by Mark Millar and Chris Weston, DC, 1995) features an imagined alternative history wherein a triumphant Nazi regime is pitted against a US president who seeks to reactivate the Golem in order to destroy the world. Marvel Comics introduced "The Golem" as a recurring character in its *Strange Tales* series of comics in 1974. Perhaps most notably, in *The Simpsons* Halloween Treehouse of Horror episode XVII (2006), Bart discovers the Golem of Prague in Krusty the Clown's storeroom and animates it by placing written commands in its mouth. Also on television, *The X-Files* episode "Kaddish" (1997) featured a Golem-like creature.

Golems, as artificial people, raise questions of what it means to be human—what is a soulless, yet anthropoid creature in comparison to a "fully" human being? They highlight issues of who is within and without the community—can a Golem be counted for a prayer quorum when the requisite for such a group is ten adult Jewish men? Is he a Jew? Is he a man? Because they raise issues like these, Golems are "good to think with" regarding **robots**, androids, artificial intelligence, and a host of other issues faced by humankind in postmodernity.

Marc Michael Epstein

References and Suggested Reading

Idel, Moshe. *Golem: Jewish Magical and Mystical Traditions on the Artificial Anthropoid.* New York: State University of New York Press, 1990.

Morris, Nicola. *The Golem in Jewish American Literature.* New York: Peter Lang Publishing, 2007.

Neugroschel, Joachim. *The Golem: A New Translation of the Classic Play and Selected Short Stories.* New York: W.W. Norton & Company, 2006.

GOLIATH—*see* Giant

GOLLUM—*see* Tolkien, Monsters In

GONG GONG—*see* Demon

GOOMBA—*see* Video Games, Monsters In

GORGONS

In the most widespread tradition derived from Hesiod's *Theogony* (c. 700 BCE), the Gorgons consist of three winged supernatural female creatures, powerful and monstrous. "Gorgon" derives from the Greek word *gorgós*, which means "dreadful." Their individual names are Euryale, Sthenno, and **Medusa**, and of the three, only Medusa is mortal. Their parents in some tellings are Ceto and Phorcys and in others Ceto and Gorgo Aix. In Greek myth, Medusa was killed by Perseus with Athena's help and her head was mounted on Athena's shield.

As opposed to the more common understanding of the Gorgons as three sisters, some early sources refer to only one Gorgon, Gorgo Aix, the daughter of the sun god Helios. Gorgo Aix in Greek myth is killed by Zeus during the war of the **Titans** and Zeus uses her skin to create his famous Aigis cape. Homer in his *Odyssey* (c. eighth century BCE) writes only about one Gorgon who is among the dreadful spirits that reside in Hades, the Greek Underworld.

In Hesiod's *Theogony*, the Gorgons live in the Western Ocean, not far from the Hesperides (nymphs who tend a blissful garden in a far western part of the world). Consistent with age-old connections between femininity and water, Hesiod treats the Gorgons as nymph-like water creatures with the ability to create underwater reefs. Herodotus in *The Histories*, composed in the fifth century BCE, instead places their home in northern Africa. In later traditions, the Gorgons are figured as chthonic monsters connected to the Underworld. Aristophanes in *The Frogs* (405 BCE) and Virgil in his *Aeneid* (29–19 BCE) both place them in Hades alongside various other mythical creatures.

In neither art nor literature is there one coherent description of the Gorgons. Most commonly they are featured as females with golden wings, brazen claws, snake-like fangs or tusks, and serpents curling in their hair or in their hands. They possess a petrifying gaze and can turn their victims to stone. Because of this power, the Gorgons (or just their heads) became a protective symbol and a charm against evil. Their representations were placed on gates, walls, floors, coins, armors and shields, graves, and even pottery and daily use items. The *Gorgoneion*, originally an apotropaic pendant showing the Gorgon's head, was often used as a motif on shields and armor. Its function was to repel bad luck and frighten the enemy. In addition, according to myth Gorgon blood had amazing powers of healing. Blood from the right side of a Gorgon's body could heal wounds and even resurrect the dead. Blood from the left side was lethal. Asclepius, the god of medicine, received the healing blood of a Gorgon from Athena.

Gorgons were interpreted in various ways by the ancient Greeks themselves. Athenaeus reports in *Deipnosophistae* (c. 200 CE) that the Gorgons were exotic animals living in Africa called "downlookers" that appeared somewhat like wild sheep or calves. They had poisonous breath, long hair that hung from the forehead over the eyes, and if one looked directly at a human being, it killed him instantly. He said that the soldiers of Marius, during the expedition against Jugurtha in the late second century BCE, ambushed and killed an African Gorgon. Other writers such as Euripides in his play *Heracles* (c. 416 BCE) suggested that such creatures were the personification of madness. People possessed by mania were sometimes named *gorg opis*, meaning "gorgon-eyed."

According to the German classical scholar Wilhelm Roscher in his 1896 study, *Ausführliches Lexikon der griechischen und römischen Mythologie*, it is possible to distinguish three separate stages in the development of pictorial representations of the Gorgons. The oldest so-called "archaic" stage lasted from the eighth century to the fifth century BCE, making the Gorgons among the earliest motifs to appear in Greek painting. These early representations of Gorgons, like the one described in the Greek poem "The Shield of Hercules" (c. sixth century BCE, author uncertain), have giant, round hypnotic eyes, wide faces, and open mouths full of teeth and large fangs. The tongues protrude and their noses are wide and flat. Short curly hair hangs around their faces. The ears are not hidden by the hair and may be pierced with small round earrings. Round faces are adorned with beards, sometimes blending with the hair flowing down from the heads.

These early paintings of Gorgon faces probably derive from symbolic theatrical or cult masks and are inconsistent when rendering the body. Several early representations present Gorgons with bird or horse bodies, similar to **centaurs**, **sirens**, and **harpies**. Snakes are already connected with the Gorgons in this period; however, none of the three sisters has snakes for hair. They are represented instead holding snakes in their hands, with snakes entwined in their hair, or with them wrapped around their waists. In ancient Greece and Rome, pictures of Gorgon heads were placed on the tops and necks of vases and jars; Gorgons' heads adorned soldiers' shields to arouse fear and to paralyze enemies. The pictures placed over doors served to scare away spirits and **demons**, and to assure the safety of the household.

The middle stage in the development of Gorgon images lasted from the fifth century to the second century BCE. In representations from this period, the head is smaller, the wild nature and evil appearance of the Gorgon is toned down, and the demoniac aspect is softened. The appearance is considerably more human and serves as a transition to the later phase in which the Gorgon emerges as a beautiful woman. It is also during this period that snakes become a constant attribute of the Gorgon's head, replacing hair entirely.

The third and final stage of Gorgon artistic evolution emerged in the second century BCE. The emphasis in this period was on Medusa, not on her sisters. The mortal Gorgon was humanized and shown as a beautiful woman with a rounded face, snakes for hair, and a pair of small wings growing from the brow, shown in three-quarter view.

Representations of Gorgons in the Middle Ages were relatively uncommon. Interest in them redeveloped during the Renaissance, in some instances associating them with thunder, lightning, and stormy clouds. Gorgons also became a prominent motif in art. The snake-haired decapitated head of Medusa was painted by Leonardo da Vinci (1452–1519), Carravaggio (1571–1610), and Peter Paul Rubens (1577–1640).

In contemporary culture, Gorgons appear in games, comic books, and movies. A Gorgon named Megaera is the monster at the center of Hammer Studios' 1964 production, *The Gorgon*, directed by Terrance Fisher. Seventeen years later in *Clash of the Titans*, director Desmond Davis presented a memorable half-snake half-human image of Medusa based on the snake dancer from Nathan Juran's *7th Voyage of Sinbad* (1958). Gorgons and Medusas as a race also appear in one of the most famous video game series, *Heroes of Might and Magic*.

Marcin Konrad Kaleta

References and Suggested Reading

Garber, Marjorie, and Nancy J. Vickers, eds. *The Medusa Reader*. New York: Routledge, 2003.

Mode, Heinz. *Fabulous Beasts and Demons*. London: Phaidon, 1975.

Murgatroyd, Paul. *Mythical Monsters in Classical Literature*. London: Duckworth Publishing, 2007.

Wilk, Stephen R. *Medusa: Solving the Mystery of the Gorgon*. New York: Oxford University Press, 2000.

GRABOID—*see* Cryptid

GRAY, DORIAN

Dorian Gray is the central character of Oscar Wilde's only published novel, *The Picture of Dorian Gray* (1890), a primary example of the *fin de siècle* Gothic. Like Robert Louis Stevenson's *The Strange Case of Dr Jekyll and Mr Hyde* (1886; see **Hyde, Edward**), Wilde's novel explores the ethical and aesthetic depths of good and evil embodied in a dark **doppelganger** figure. Dorian's doppelganger is a portrait, which bears the marks of his sins and ages in his place, while Dorian remains eternally young and beautiful. This exchange is achieved by a Faustian bargain, in which Dorian offers his soul in exchange for the eternal youth.

The Picture of Dorian Gray describes Dorian's gradual descent into monstrosity. As a young, innocent man, he is seduced by the admiration of the painter Basil Hallward and the aesthetic theories of the jaded aristocrat Lord Henry Wotton, who convinces him that the only things worth possessing are youth and beauty. As Eve Kosofsky Sedgwick argues in *Epistemology of the Closet*, the novel's plot is one of "male-male desire" (160), which is, however, translated into narcissism and, ultimately, into a dark obsession with the picture that contains Dorian's soul. The homosocial subtext was, as Andrew Smith points out, designed to remain largely invisible to the dominant culture of the time (151)—so invisible, in fact, that many film adaptations still seem to feel the need to add a second heteronormative love story to the original plot, possibly in an attempt to cater to the tastes of a larger audience (an exception to this rule is the 1970 *Dorian Gray* directed by Massimo Dallmano, which is openly queer). While it can be argued that Wilde's original novel also introduces a heterosexual love story, it seems significant that Dorian falls in love with an actress, admiring her portrayal of various theatrical heroines more than herself.

As a true aesthete, Dorian is "poisoned by a book" (116)—an unnamed "yellow book" (100) given to him by Lord Henry, which is, allegedly, based on Joris-Carl Huysman's scandalous novel *À Rebours* (1884). The influence of French decadent literature is undeniable, especially in chapter 11, which reads like "a textbook of psychology of fin de siècle economic man" (Gagnier, 22), but Lord Henry's hedonism also draws heavily on the influential but disputed "Conclusion" to Walter Pater's essay collection, *The Renaissance* (1873). Wilde's novel can be read as a "dark, revealing double" of Pater's theory (Riquelme 609). However, Pater, whom Wilde had met at Oxford, was apparently quick to distance himself from Lord Henry's position—claiming that Lord Henry's attempt at Epicureanism lacked "moral sense" (Riquelme 613).

Lord Henry's theories, often expressed in the witty paradoxes typical of Oscar Wilde's style, remain theoretical and vague, whereas Dorian actually begins to act on them. In the pursuit of pure aestheticism, even the suicide of his first love—the young, naïve actress Sybil Vane—seems justifiable, as Dorian loses interest in her once she falls in love with him and neglects her acting. The young woman's death, caused by Dorian's callousness, marks the point of no return in his monstrous career. After that, he does not shrink from murder to protect his decaying portrait from discovery. When the painter Basil Hallward wants to exhibit his creation, Dorian stabs him in a fit of rage.

Reflecting Victorian double standards, Dorian's crimes largely remain in the dark, hidden behind the façade of youth and beauty. However, Dorian's deal with the **Devil** is a treacherous one as it binds him to his dark doppelganger, the portrait he keeps locked away in the psychologically symbolic space of the attic. The most recent film adaptation by Oliver Parker (2009) stresses the importance of the attic room by subtly introducing a traumatic background of child abuse and letting the film begin with the pivotal murder scene, which also takes place in the attic. Basil Hallward's blood-smeared, yellow shawl and the sound of flapping wings work as subtle links between the spectacular opening scene and the other attic scenes in the film. Dorian's first exploration of the attic space is also significant, as the scene is interrupted by flashback images of a scared child—presumably a younger Dorian—and introduces a broken mirror, which reflects a disrupted and multifaceted image of Dorian.

In both the novel and its various film adaptations, the eponymous picture, which shows the signs of Dorian's depravity, establishes a link between ethical and aesthetic corruption, evoking and challenging nineteenth-century theories of physiognomy such as Sir Francis Galton's (1822–1911) attempt to define physiognomic characteristics of criminality by superimposing photographs of criminals, or Cesare Lombroso's (1835–1909) work in anthropological criminology, which was based on the assumption that a criminal disposition was hereditary and would show itself in the features of an individual. While the picture is gradually destroyed by a strange kind of corruption, eating at it from the inside, Dorian's monstrosity remains well hidden. This contrast is also taken up by various adaptations of the novel: Oliver Parker's 2009 film version shows the picture oozing blood and maggots. Albert Lewin's 1945 film version uses Technicolor shots of the painting inserted into an otherwise black-and-white film to enhance its eerie effect. The portrait was produced and altered during the filming by American artist Ivan Albright (1897–1983) to show Dorian's gradual descent into depravity. It is now part of the Art Institute of Chicago's collection. In the pivotal murder scene, the bright horror of the painting is contrasted with a stark sequence of light and shadow, cast by a swinging lamp, which alternatingly shows Dorian's expressionless, white face and the shadow of the dead body of Basil Hallward behind him on the wall. The dominant imagery of light and darkness and the contrast of the wild, decaying painting and the smooth surface of Dorian's ageless face underline the aesthetic ambiguity of the central character.

The picture also plays an important role for another Dorian Gray, as the character appears in Stephen Norrington's 2003 film adaptation of *The League of Extraordinary Gentlemen*. Although he does not feature in Alan Moore's original series of graphic novels, the film adaptation introduces Dorian Gray (Stuart Townsend) in the role of an ambiguous villain, who is ultimately destroyed by meeting "his **demon**" (his disfigured picture) in the hands of the vampiric femme fatale Mina Harker (Peta Wilson). The film also features a memorable line of dialogue: when Dorian is hit by several bullets at very close range and the bullet wounds heal in a manner of seconds, his adversary is amazed. "What are you?" he asks, to which Dorian replies, "I'm complicated."

The 2009 *Dorian Gray* provides another answer to the same question: here, Dorian (Ben Barnes) lays the blame at Lord Henry's (Colin Firth) door, claiming: "I am what you made me." It thus seems appropriate that it is also Lord Henry who ends it by setting fire to the picture, which has come to life and is trying to strain out of its frame. The underlying love story between Dorian and Lord Henry's daughter Emily (played by Rebecca Hall; Emily is not a character from the novel) makes Dorian's suicide seem more heroic than it is in the original text.

The somewhat melodramatic subject matter and bold aestheticism of Wilde's novel also lend themselves well to be set to music, and there have been several successful international musical adaptations—among them Canadian, Hungarian, and Czech productions—as well as a number of theater adaptations. While most of these seem to stage the story in the original time frame of *fin-de-siècle* England, Matthew Bourne's contemporary dance adaptation, *Dorian Gray* (2008), successfully transfers the novel's aesthetics to the twenty-first century.

Indeed, the novel's main theme—the celebration of an aesthetic hedonism, which values youth and beauty above anything—has lost none of its relevance in today's visually oriented culture. Although not an adaptation of Wilde's novel, Bret Easton Ellis's *American Psycho* (1991) explores a similar combination of violence and aestheticism. While modern adaptations of *Dorian Gray*, like Will Self's 2002 novel *Dorian, an Imitation* and Oliver Parker's 2009 film *Dorian Gray*, are more explicit in their depiction of Dorian's deeds, the original novel often remains vague, leaving ample room for speculation. This effect is underlined by the novel's ambiguous moral message. The controversial preface is a manifesto of aestheticism, claiming that "[t]here is no such thing as a moral or an immoral book. Books are well written, or badly written" (Wilde 3). But the story seems to take a moral stance. In the end, Dorian is punished for his crimes in an act of poetic justice: when he tries to destroy the picture to free his soul, the killing of his dark double turns into a suicidal act. The picture remains intact, miraculously young again, while the aged and decaying body of Dorian Gray is found dead in an attic room. The novel's moral ambiguity and homoerotic undertones contributed to its success, as well as its author's notoriety.

Anya Heise-von der Lippe

References and Suggested Reading

Gagnier, Regenia. "Wilde and the Victorians." In *The Cambridge Companion to Oscar Wilde*, edited by Peter Raby. Cambridge: Cambridge University Press, 1997.

Riquelme, Jean Paul. "Oscar Wilde's Aesthetic Gothic." *Modern Fiction Studies* 46, no. 3 (2000): 609–31.

Sedgwick, Eve Kosofsky. *Epistemology of the Closet*. Berkeley: University of California Press, 1990.

Smith, Andrew. *Victorian Demons*. Manchester: Manchester University Press, 2004.

Wilde, Oscar. *The Picture of Dorian Gray*. New York: Norton, 2007.

GREENSKIN—*see* Goblin

GREMLIN

Before being popularized as the mischievous, rule-breaking punishment for feeding Gizmo, the adorable mogwai, after midnight in Joe Dante's 1984 movie of the same name, gremlins had a rich history as part of American popular culture developing out of World War II. In the accounts of American airmen from the conflict, gremlins were represented as a form of diminutive gnome or **imp**-like creature that created mechanical havoc aboard the flying air machines—most often causing problems to their weapons, motors, or instrument display panels. The history of the gremlin, however, goes back further in the twentieth century: British aviators from the Royal Naval Air Service and, later, the Royal Air Force reported the devilish little creatures as early as World War I. The word "gremlin" itself, according to E.T. Bryan, was coined by British airmen stationed in India in the late 1930s.

In keeping with its depiction in the famous 1963 episode of *The Twilight Zone* written by Richard Matheson and starring William Shatner ("Nightmare at 20,000 feet")—or its incorporation into the 1984 movie remake directed by Joe Dante and starring John Lithgow—gremlins were frequently reported on the wings of aircraft and causing general technological disturbances. In such accounts, their appearances range from being mere inches in height to larger **goblin**-like breadths, commensurate with *The Twilight Zone*'s depiction of something approximating a rabid gorilla. Variant descriptions of gremlins indicate that they may have green skin or be blue, have reptilian features or be hairy (or some combination of both), with accoutrements varying from horns to gnarled teeth concealed within a diabolic smile. Regardless of depiction, they mainly functioned as an alibi for the failed upkeep of the first highly mechanized combat airplanes put into military service by

British and American forces alike. Gremlins, in practical history, seem to be scapegoats for human and mechanical error.

Significant in developing the popular idea of the gremlin was British author Roald Dahl's 1943 work, *The Gremlins* (his first children's book). Walt Disney Studios arranged for publication of the book through Random House, and it became an international hit with its story of Gus, a Royal Air Force airman, who convinces gremlins to cease plaguing the Allies and to redirect their mischief against Adolf Hitler and the Germans. Disney, who had originally planned a live-action film for the adaptation, actually only used the story as a backdrop for a series of nine animated shorts from 1943 to 1944 staring "Gremlin Gus." Over at Warner Bros Studios, in the Bob Clampert-directed episode of *Merrie Melodies* entitled "Falling Hare" (1943), the gremlin troubling Bugs Bunny is little more than a sickly green, **elf**-like creature with a clown's trademark red nose and a period-appropriate flight mask. This character, who otherwise stagnated throughout the remainder of the twentieth century, was later re-appropriated in the twenty-first-century video game *Epic Mickey*, in which Gus is oddly reworked into a conscience figure and traveling companion for Mickey Mouse, akin to Jiminy Cricket's characterization in the Disney version of *Pinocchio* (Norman Ferguson, 1940).

The most popular modern version of the gremlin tale is undeniably the 1984 feature film that largely passes over the history, legends, and fiction connected with the gremlin in order to reinvent the monster. Divorcing the gremlin from established folklore and World War II associations (aside from a brief throw-away history from Murray Futterman [Dick Miller] who is a World War II veteran), *Gremlins* recasts the creatures as the unintended evolution of a more docile and domesticated creature, the mogwai—a specimen of which happens to be living in an old curiosity shop that Randall Pelzer (Hoyt Axton) visits while searching for a last-minute Christmas present for his son Billy (Zach Galligan). In this scenario, the gremlin is curiously orientalized as the proprietor of the Chinatown shop, Mr Wing (Keye Luke), refuses to sell the mogwai due to the dangers of the creature. Unfortunately, Mr Wing's shop is old, broke, and in severe disrepair; his less scrupulous grandson (John Louie) decides to sell the mogwai to Pelzer with three grave restrictions: do not expose it to bright light, particularly sunlight which will kill it; do not get it wet; and, most ominously, never feed the creature after midnight.

What Pelzer and Billy discover is that getting a mogwai wet prompts a process of asexual reproduction resulting in multiple offspring, and that feeding a mogwai after midnight triggers their bizarre transformation into green, scaly, reptilian gremlins. As opposed to the classic World War II interpretation of the creature, Dante's gremlins are not only mischievous, but actually quite vicious and deadly. They also spread like a virus: at one point, Stripe, the gremlin leader, immerses himself in a pool, spawning hundreds of new gremlins that terrorize the town. From this point forward, the movie teeter-totters between horror and dark, parodic humor: the newly hatched gremlins actually take over a bar at one point and begin to act as humans might in a similar situation, drinking away the holiday blues. Ultimately, the swarm of gremlins finds itself in a movie theater where, perhaps not coincidentally, a showing of Disney's *Snow White and the Seven Dwarves* (William Cottrell, 1937) happens to be playing. Billy and his love interest, Kate Beringer (Phoebe Cates), blow up the theater to kill all of them before any further damage can be done. Stripe survives but is ultimately dispatched by Gizmo who lures him into sunlight.

A sequel to the original *Gremlins* entitled *Gremlins 2: The New Batch* was released in

1990. Also directed by Dante, it was a critical and commercial failure that added little to the history, aside from ratcheting up the comic valences even further.

Joseph Michael Sommers

References and Suggested Reading

Bryan, E.T. "Gremlore." *Gremlin Trouble*. 1995. <http://www.gremlintrouble.com/html/body_gremlore.html>.

Dahl, Roald. *The Gremlins* [1943]. Reprint, Milwaukie, OR: Dark Horse Books, 2006.

Miller, Kristine. "Ghosts, Gremlins, and 'the War or Terror' in Children's Blitz Fiction." *ChLA Quarterly* 34 (Fall 2009): 272–84.

Sloane, Eric. *Gremlin Americanus: A Scrap Book Collection of Gremlins*. New York: B.F. Jay & Co., 1942.

GRENDEL AND GRENDEL'S MOTHER

In the Old English poem *Beowulf*, composed sometime between the eighth and eleventh centuries CE, Grendel and his mother are two of the three monsters that the hero Beowulf must overcome (the third is a **dragon**). After the Danish king Hrothgar builds an impressively large mead hall named Heorot to celebrate his rise to power, the monster Grendel is enraged by the sounds of joy coming from the hall. From his home beyond the fens and moors, Grendel attacks Heorot and drags away the bodies of 30 warriors. For twelve years he rules the hall at night, killing all who come his way. From his home in Sweden (Geatland), young Beowulf hears of Hrothgar's monster troubles and sails to Denmark. He has heard specifically that Grendel devours his victims and uses no weapons to overcome them, so he vows to face the monster with nothing but his own strength and his experience in fighting monstrous creatures. Beowulf and his men await Grendel's attack, as the beast crosses the moors in the darkness and then flings open the hall door, tearing it off its hinges, an evil light shining from his eyes. Grendel snatches up a man and devours him, right down to his hands and feet, crunching his bones and drinking his blood. Beowulf steps forth and grasps the arm of the monster, who soon discovers he cannot break free, except by struggling so hard that his arm detaches at the shoulder. Grendel slinks off to his "joyless home," where he will die of his wound. In the morning, men follow his bloody track back to a mere (or lake) still seething with his blood.

Grendel's arm is hung up as a trophy in the hall, on which one could see his nails like claws or talons. The warriors celebrate, but then, while Beowulf is sleeping elsewhere, Grendel's mother attacks the hall to avenge her son, seizing one of the Danes and carrying him off to the fens. Only now does Hrothgar mention that his people had seen *two* large human-shaped creatures stalking the moors, one of them female. They called the larger one Grendel, and no one knew its father. Beowulf rides again to the mere and dives into it to find the Grendel-kin's cavernous lair. He swings at the *mere-wif* ("lake-woman") or *brim-wylf* ("sea-she-wolf") with his sword but its edge fails; she then stabs at him with a short sword but his chain mail protects him. He sees and takes from the cave wall a sword made by **giants** and cuts off her head with it, and then does the same to Grendel's corpse lying nearby. Grendel's head is so big that it takes four men to carry it back to Hrothgar's hall.

When Beowulf reports back to his king in Sweden, he adds that Grendel carried a pouch made of dragon skins in which he would stuff his victims. Otherwise we mainly know only that Grendel and his mother are of human shape but larger than men. Earlier the poet narrator (a Christian, unlike the pagan Scandinavians he describes) had said that God condemned Grendel as one of the kin of Cain, perhaps one of the "giants in the earth" mentioned in Genesis, a few of whom escaped Noah's flood according to some traditions. More broadly speaking, Grendel and his mother would seem to be the legendary lone survivors of a monstrous race of humans, like the yeti and sasquatch (see **Bigfoot**) of tales from other peoples. Depending on whether we align Grendel and his mother more with humans or with monsters (the poem does both), they are either cannibals or man-eating predators, both of which provide effective sources of horror in monster tales. Grendel's mother gains added *frisson* as an avenging female, like the cobra Nagaina in Rudyard Kipling's story "Rikki-Tikki-Tavi" (1894) or the egg-laying **extraterrestrial** mother-creature in James Cameron's film, *Aliens* (1986).

Grendel does not seem to have been known outside the poem, unless a few place names in England commemorate him (see Fulk, 293–4). In modern literature, he mainly inspires John Gardner in the novel *Grendel* (1971) and Michael Crichton in *Eaters of the Dead* (1976). Gardner tells the story in first person from Grendel's point of view. His mother, however, does not speak and seems to be more bestial than he is. The novel encourages us to sympathize somewhat with Grendel as an antihero who recognizes the follies of humans, except that in his philosophizing he cannot find any morality to counterbalance random murder. The novel was made into an animated film called *Grendel Grendel Grendel* (Alexander Stitt, 1981).

In *Eaters of the Dead*, Michael Crichton begins with the historical account of an Arab, Ibn Fadlan, who encountered Vikings in what is now Russia. To this account Crichton appends a rationalized version of the Beowulf story, in which Grendel is not a monster but a primitive tribe called the Wendol, apparently a group of surviving Neanderthals, hairy with toes like claws. They attack Rothgar's hall and drag men away, devouring them in their cave home. The Wendol are a matriarchal clan, carrying idols that Crichton, in his notes, likens to the historical Venus of Willendorf figurine. Later Buliwyf (that is, Beowulf) and his men seek out the marauding tribe and encounter them worshiping an old woman, the "mother of the Wendol," who corresponds to Grendel's mother. Buliwyf kills her but not before she stabs him with a poisoned pin, from which wound he dies in the end.

Four films adapted from *Beowulf* were released between 1999 and 2007, including *The Thirteenth Warrior* (John McTiernan, 1999), an adaptation of Crichton's novel. In *Beowulf* (Graham Baker, 1999), Grendel is able to change his shape like the chameleonic alien hunter in *Predator* (John McTiernan, 1987). His mother first appears as a seductress with whom Hrothgar fathers Grendel; she then turns into a many-clawed **demon** whom Beowulf fights and defeats. In *Beowulf and Grendel* (Sturla Gunnarsson, 2005), Grendel is called a **troll** but may just be an oversized and extra hairy human. Hrothgar killed Grendel's father, so when the troll grows to adulthood, he attacks Hrothgar's men. Occasionally the white arm of a "sea hag" arises out of the ocean; she corresponds in a not very compelling way to Grendel's mother. Finally, the motion-capture animated film *Beowulf* (Robert Zemeckis, 2007) expends no little effort in making its monsters satisfying to a contemporary horror film audience. Grendel is an "embodiment of pain," his eardrum throbbing in close-up when he first hears the reveling in Heorot. Perhaps because he grows larger when enraged, his skin appears to be pulling away from his flesh. Beowulf, stripped naked, defeats Grendel in the hall, slamming his arm in the doors. Grendel's mother, played by Angelina Jolie, is a creature of the gold-hoard, her voluptuous body naked save for a thin layer of gold film. Her clawed feet resemble high-heeled shoes, and her long braid coils around behind her like a snake. She is in fact a lizard-like creature who adopts a human form to seduce her mates, so that Hrothgar fathers Grendel with her, and Beowulf does the same for a "golden boy" who becomes the dragon. She is not killed in the end but lives on to look seductively upon Beowulf's sidekick, Wiglaf.

Paul Acker

References and Suggested Reading

Acker, Paul. "Horror and the Maternal in *Beowulf*." *PMLA* 21 (2006): 702–16.

Crichton, Michael. *Eaters of the Dead* [1976]. Reprint, New York: Ballantyne, 1992.

Fulk, R.D. *Klaeber's Beowulf*, edited by Robert E. Bjork and John D. Niles. 4th edn. Toronto: University of Toronto, 2008.

Gardner, John. *Grendel*. New York: Knopf, 1971.

GRIFFIN

The griffin or gryphon is a monstrous hybrid with the body of a lion and the head and wings of an eagle. The name may derive from the Latin *grypho* (to grasp) and from the Greek *grypos* (curved). Sometimes the entire forepart of this animal resembles an eagle with curved beak, talons, wings, and feathers, and only the hindquarters resemble a lion. At other times, it is a flying quadruped with legs like a lion and the head and wings of an eagle. In heraldry, this type is called an *opinicus*. An interesting feature of the griffin is the addition of ears, which may be a development from an earlier crest or from the dog aspect of the Persian *simorgh* (see **Birds, Giant**), which was a similar composite of bird and quadruped.

Bird–lion hybrids appear in ancient Mesopotamian and Egyptian art from as early as 3000 BCE. They often act as guardians of deities and sacred places and frequently occur in pairs, symbolic of the struggle between opposing forces. Griffins appear battling other animals with claws barred or as recumbent peaceful guardians, such as those with crests and stylized wings dating to around 1700 BCE in the "throne room" at Knossos (the largest Bronze Age archeological site on Crete). The half-eagle and half-lion type, associated with the Greek god of the sun Apollo, began to appear frequently in Greece around the eighth century BCE as an adornment in pottery, metalwork, and architecture. In the Greek *Physiologus*, a compendium of bird and animal symbolism written in the fifth century CE, a pair of griffins catches the rays of the morning sun and flies across the sky, echoing both Apollo and the ancient guardian solar griffins associated with him.

In classical Greek mythology, the griffins' home was a country rich in gold close to Scythia (southern Ukraine) or India. The Hereford Mappamundi—the largest medieval map still existing—provides a detailed visual representation of the medieval world c. 1300 CE and places a griffin fighting an Arimaspian (a legendary people of northern Scythia and the traditional enemy of the griffins) in the eastern section of the map. The fight between the griffins and the neighboring Arimaspians who rode swift horses and attempted to steal the griffins' gold is one of the oldest traditions associated with these beasts. The story appears in Herodotus's fifth-century BCE *Histories* and is attributed to an even older source, the seventh-century BCE poet and traveler, Aristeas of Proconnesus. According to Herodotus, the struggle for gold accounts for the hostility between the horse and the griffin. This tale is repeated with added details by other writers such as Ctesias in the *Indica*, a compilation of geographic and travel lore written in the fourth century BCE, who says that griffins in India guard treasure. Aelian, in the second century CE, describes the mountain lair of the winged lion-like Indian griffin, guarding his gold hoard.

Griffins were important artistic and literary motifs. They were carved on Greek and Roman tombs as symbolic guardians of the dead. Herodotus describes a bronze vessel in the temple of Hera adorned with griffins' heads, and Strabo's first-century CE *Geography* mentions a painting of the goddess Artemis borne aloft by griffins. In the tragedy *Prometheus Bound*, attributed to Aeschylus (c. fifth century BCE), griffins are called the sharp-beaked hounds of Zeus.

The *Natural History* of Pliny the Elder, written in the first century CE, synthesizes existing information and provides a major source for subsequent descriptions, notably that of the seventh-century CE encyclopedist Isidore of Seville, who describes the griffin as a feathered quadruped with the body of a lion that is hostile to both men and horses. Much the same description appears in the thirteenth-century account of Bartholomeus Anglicus, who mentions in his compendium *De proprietatibus rerum* (*On the Properties of Things*; c. 1240) that the griffin's egg protects against poison. In the medieval bestiary tradition, the griffin is usually shown with a large animal, like an ox, in its claws.

In the *Alexander Romance*, a recording of the adventures of Alexander the Great popular from the fourth to the sixteenth centuries, griffins are harnessed to a chair to create a flying machine. Chunks of meat are suspended just out of the griffins' reach. Consequently, they fly upwards, lured by the bait, and carry Alexander into the air. This episode became a popular subject for manuscript illustrations and misericord carvings in medieval churches. In *Huon of Bordeaux*, a thirteenth-century *chanson de geste* (author unknown), Huon is carried off to a griffin's nest. He kills the young birds and is attacked by the mother. Later, he presents the Emperor Charlemagne with a griffin's claw. Such literary references emphasize the wildness and strength of the creature and its defeat by heroic forces. In Dante Alighieri's *Divine Comedy* (1308–21), the hybrid nature of the griffin represents the dual nature of Christ's humanity and divinity. Beatrice flies to paradise on a griffin to lead Dante on the final stage of his journey (see **Dante, Monsters In**). By contrast, John Milton's *Paradise Lost* (1667) invokes the legend of the griffin's pursuit of its stolen gold as a metaphor for Satan's relentless pursuit of mankind (see **Devil, The**).

As a combination of eagle and lion, kings of birds and beasts respectively, the griffin was a symbol for royalty and courage, while its size and the magic stone egg that protected against poison made it a good symbol for protection, both literal and figurative. Heraldic griffins are usually depicted in a sergeant posture, standing with one leg raised and claws displayed. A series of heraldic beasts sculpted for the coronation of Queen Elizabeth II in 1953 included a heraldic griffin. The merchant guilds of Perugia in central Italy advertised their reputation for safe trading with a griffin *sergeant* on a bale of cloth.

Not every classical authority accepted the reality of griffins. Both Pliny the Elder and Strabo questioned their existence and, throughout the seventeenth century, exploration and the rise of natural history writing based on observation undermined belief in them. In a description of the northern world published in 1518, the Polish writer Matias Michovius found no evidence for the griffin. Italian naturalist Ulisse Aldrovandi echoed this skepticism in 1599 by including the griffin among the fabulous birds listed in his *Ornithlogiae*. English author Thomas Browne's *Popular Errors* (1646) devoted an entire chapter to disproving its existence. Alexander

Ross, chaplain to Charles I, in turn upheld classical and scriptural authority against the new science in *Arcana Microcosmi* (1652) and vigorously defended "ancient" writings about the griffin. Skeptics explained the griffin as a misunderstanding of some other animal such as a large bird, like the eagle, while the nineteenth-century antiquary John Timbs, in *Arcana of Science and Art* (1828–38), attributed the griffin to a misunderstanding of the South American tapir. Griffins' eggs and claws, in reality ostrich eggs and exotic animal horns, are found in collections of medieval and Renaissance curiosities. More recently, the classical scholar Adrienne Mayor suggested that **dinosaur** fossils from central Asia gave rise to stories about griffins as guardians of gold treasure. She points out in *The First Fossil Hunters* (2000) that fossils are frequently associated with gold-bearing ores, and that the living dinosaurs laid eggs in nests and had beaked faces.

The griffin has retained its position in both art and literature. It remains a popular heraldic beast and, since the 1920s, has provided a logo for the Vauxhall Motor Company. Griffins also feature in modern role-playing and video games. As characters in fantasy literature and children's books, however, some of their fierceness has dissipated. Griffins do fight in Aslan's army in C.S. Lewis's "The Chronicles of Narnia" (1939–49) and the young King Arthur and Kay battle a griffin with the help of Robin Hood in T.H. White's *The Once and Future King* (1958). Lewis Carroll's *Alice's Adventure in Wonderland* (1865) gently satirizes the dual nature of the griffin who speaks half to itself and half to Alice, while Frank Stockton's "The Griffin and the Minor Canon" (1885) turns the death of the last griffin into a parable against intolerance. Gillian Bradshaw's *Beyond the North Wind* (1993) reworks the story of Aristeas and his "lost" poem as a fantasy in which a young magician goes on a quest to save the griffins. A griffin called Skandranon is one of the lead characters in the fantasy trilogy, *The Black Gryphon* (1995), *The White Gryphon* (1997), and *The Silver Gryphon* (1997), co-written by Mercedes Lackey and Larry Dixon. Diana Wynne Jones's distinctive fiction creates appealing fantasy worlds while at the same time satirizing the modern fantasy genre. Two of her books, *The Dark Lord of Derkholm* (1998) and *The Year of the Griffin* (2000), concern a gentle **wizard** who breeds fantastic animals. His five griffins and two human children later have their own adventures at university.

Juliette Wood

References and Suggested Reading

Borges, Jorge Luis, and Margarita Guerrero. *The Book of Imaginary Beings*. London: Vintage, 2002.

Cherry, John, ed. *Mythical Beasts*. San Francisco: Pomegranate and British Museum Press, 1995.

Goldman, Bernard. "The Development of the Lion-Griffin." *American Journal of Archaeology* 64, no. 4 (October 1960): 319–28.

Hansen, William. *Classical Mythology: A Guide to the Mythical World of the Greeks and Romans* [2004]. Reprint, Oxford: Oxford University Press, 2005.

March, Jenny. *Cassell's Dictionary of Classical Mythology* [1998]. Reprint, London and New York: Cassell, 2001.

Mayor, Adrienne. *The First Fossil Hunters: Paleontology in Greek and Roman Times* [2000]. Reprint, Princeton, NJ: Princeton University Press, 2011.

GRINDYLOW—*see* Harry Potter, Monsters In; Sea Monsters

GRUE—*see* Harpy

HABETROT—*see* Brownie

HARPY

The harpy is most commonly depicted as a carrion bird with a woman's face. It is insatiably hungry, constantly screeching, filthy in its appearance and habits, and pollutes everything it touches. The name comes from Greek *harpezein* meaning "snatcher." Originally, the harpies were the offspring of sea and weather deities. As such, they personified winds and storms, and their appearance was that of winged women with unbound hair. Eventually, they became a trio of monsters—known as the "hounds of Zeus"—called Aello (Storm Swift), Celaeno (Dark), and Podarge (Fleet Foot). In heraldry, the harpy, sometimes referred to as the "maiden eagle," is represented as a vulture with a woman's head and neck. As a figure in contemporary art, film, and literature, it is usually a monstrous female creature.

The story of Phineus and the harpies is the most persistent tradition associated with them. It is recounted in detail in the *Argonautica*, a Hellenistic romance written in the third century BCE by Appolonius of Rhodes. Phineus, king of Thrace, was a prophet who revealed too much and angered the gods. He was blinded and exiled to an island where the harpies stole the tempting food laid out for him. When Jason and the Argonauts arrived, the *Boreads*, Cailas and Zetes, winged sons of Boreas the north wind, drove the harpies away. Their lives were spared because their sister, Isis, goddess of the rainbow, promised that Phineus would be left alone, and the harpies settled on the Strophades Islands. In gratitude, Phineus revealed how the Argonauts could avoid further dangers on their journey. A piece of Greek pottery from the fifth century BCE shows Phineus tormented by the harpies in the form of winged women, rather than monsters. On the other side, the king acknowledges the *Boreads*. In Book III of Virgil's *Aeneid* (c. 20 BCE), the harpies take the more familiar form of vultures with women's faces when they attack the feasting Trojans on the Strophades Islands. The Trojans defeat them, causing their leader, Celaeno, to prophesy that Italy will be their destination, but not before they suffer further hunger and tribulation.

Other traditions reflect the association between harpies and the winds. Thaumos, an ancient sea-god whose names translates as "wonder," and his wife Electra, who was associated with clouds, are appropriate parents for the stormy whirlwind aspect of the harpies and for their sister, the rainbow goddess Isis, since rainbows typically follow storms. Achilles's preternaturally swift horses were the offspring of the harpy Podarge and Zephyrus, the west wind. The winged sons of Boreas, the north wind, are able to drive the harpies from their feast and threaten them with destruction until Iris intervenes. There is also a link between the harpies and the **furies** as both are associated with retribution and the dead. Homer, in *The Odyssey* (c. eighth century BCE), says the harpies carried off the daughters of King Pandareus to become handmaidens to the furies.

Harpies are also associated with other supernatural beings, the **sirens**. Both are linked with storms at sea and both are depicted as birds with women's faces, although the harpy has a harsh voice, while the sirens sing beautifully. These similarities can cause confusion in visual contexts. The elaborate fifth-century BCE Lycian "Harpy tomb" depicts bird-like creatures with women's breasts and faces carrying away small female human figures, but it is not clear whether they are harpies snatching the daughters of Pandareus, or conveying the souls of the dead to the afterlife, or an entirely different creature such as sirens. Because of their associations with the dead, some scholars suggest that the harpies have links with the ancient Egyptian *ba* or soul bird that became manifest at the point of death and was depicted as a bird with a human head.

In post-classical literature, harpies are usually characterized as monstrous creatures with female heads and torsos, but with clawed hands and the bodies of birds. In Dante's description of the wood of the suicides in Canto 13 of his fourteenth-century *Inferno*, harpies make their nests in the trees which enclose suicides (see **Dante, Monsters In**). The story of a king tormented by the harpies and rescued by heroes is told in the sixteenth-century epic *Orlando furioso* by Ludovico Ariosto. In Shakespeare's *The Tempest* (1610–11), Prospero makes an ironic comment on the gracefulness exhibited by Ariel when the spirit snatches food from the shipwrecked nobles in the form of a harpy (III.iii.83).

In medieval bestiaries, the harpy can be a male figure symbolizing greed. By contrast, harpies in medieval Islamic art and literature were usually female and had a positive connotation. Both male and female harpies appear in medieval church carvings, especially carved misericords and columns, as warnings against greed or as representations of monstrosity. The harpy was one of many images that embodied monstrosity and all that deviated from the natural order. An illustration of a harpy and her prey appeared in a late fifteenth-century edition of *Hortus Sanitatis* (*Garden of Health*), the most popular herbal of its time. Two influential seventeenth-century works, Ulisse Aldrovandi's history of monsters, *Monstrorum Historia*, and John Johnston's *Historiae naturalis*, depict harpies with human female heads on realistic eagle bodies. Occasionally bestiaries used a harpy-like creature to illustrate the *serra* or *sawfish*, a destructive winged **sea monster** that destroyed ships. Links between harpies, sirens, and extreme weather seem to provide the context for this identification, and this continued even after the bestiaries ceased to be an important source for meaning. For example, an eighteenth-century pamphlet now in the Bodleian Library describes an amphibious monster "harpy" seen off the coast of Spain ("A Harpy Drawn From Life.")

Dramatic incidents involving harpies recorded in classical and medieval works such as the story of Jason and the Argonauts, the *Aeneid*, and the *Divine Comedy* continue to provide inspiration for art. The *Boreads Chasing the Harpies* by Jan Erasmus Quellinus (1630) is now in the Prado Museum (Spain). The fight between the harpies and Aeneus and his companions is the subject of a heroic classical painting by the seventeenth-century French artist Francois Perrier, and the confrontation between Dante, Virgil, and the harpies has also been the subject of striking illustrations by Sandro Botticelli (1445–1510), Gustave Doré (1832–83), and Salvador Dalí (1904–89). A fourteenth-century copy of Dante's *Divine Comedy* owned by the Earls of Leicester contains a miniature illustration of Dante and Virgil's encounter with the harpies (MS Holkham misc. 48 p. 19). In his illustrations for Dante's work in the 1820s, William Blake depicted the harpies as owl-like creatures with human faces and women's breasts. Artistic depictions of the harpies also evoked their symbolic associations. Andrea del Sarto's *Madonna of the Harpies*, a sixteenth-century altarpiece for an Italian convent, depicts the Virgin and child standing on a classical pedestal adorned with carved harpies. For the Norwegian artist Edvard Munch (1863–1944), the harpy had overtones of death-like sexual predation in a lithograph of 1898. Harpies evoke greed in all its aspects in the satirical *Los Caprichos* (1899) by the Spanish artist Francisco Goya.

Special effects creator Ray Harryhausen gave the harpies cinematic life in *Jason and the Argonauts* (Don Chaffey, 1963). The theme of the harpy as destructive female was reworked in *Harpya* (Rauol Servais, 1979) in which a man rescues a harpy, only to find himself overwhelmed by her insatiable appetite. The harpy Celaeno is treated more sympathetically in *The Last Unicorn* (Peter S. Beagle, 1968). The unicorn discovers that she and Celaeno are the only real mythical creatures held captive by a sorceress. Once freed, Celaeno kills their tormentor. Harpies have a more traditional role in Philip Pullman's fantasy trilogy, *His Dark Materials*. In *The Amber Spyglass* (2000), harpies guard the Underworld and guide the spirits of the dead, until Lyra persuades them to lead the spirits to a more peaceful afterlife.

Harpies also feature in anime films, manga art, and role-playing games such as *World of Warcraft* in which they appear as winged females with talons for feet. Harpy images proliferate in the fan art and merchandising that accompany these phenomena, and are also influenced by the work of contemporary fantasy and comic book artists like Frank Frazetta (1928–2010) and Boris Vallejo (1941–).

Juliette Wood

References and Suggested Reading

Baer, Eva. *Sphinxes and Harpies in Medieval Islamic Art: An Iconographical Study*. Jerusalem: Israel Oriental Society, 1965.

Borges, Jorge Luis. *The Book of Imaginary Beings*. Translated by Andrew Hurley. New York: Penguin, 2006.

Cherry, John, ed. *Mythical Beasts*. London: British Museum Press, 1995.

Tasker, Edward G., and John Beaumont, eds. *Encyclopedia of Medieval Church Art*. London: B.T. Batsford, 1993.

Tritsch, F.J. "The Harpy Tomb at Xanthus." *The Journal of Hellenic Studies* 62 (1942): 39–50.

HARRIS, JAMES—*see* Demon

HARRY POTTER, MONSTERS IN

Author J.K. Rowling (1965–) populates her magical world with widely disparate creatures and successfully mines mythology and folklore for monsters best suited to her story's needs. At times, she modifies existing tropes, providing garden gnomes with pointy teeth, but also invents her own monsters, such as thestrals and blast-ended skrewts. Although monsters in the films usually function as vehicles for special effects and lively soundtracks, throughout the novels they serve a wider range of purposes. They highlight the fantastic nature of the series while serving as analogies for realistic challenges, representing inner and outer dangers that readers might encounter in daily life, and adding to both plot and character development. Most importantly, they reinforce a sense of reader empowerment by illustrating G.K. Chesterton's (1874–1936) observation that "[t]he objection to fairy stories is that they tell children there are dragons. But children have always known there are dragons. Fairy stories tell children that dragons can be killed" (Pratchett 205). Rowling invokes Greek and Roman mythology with creatures including a sphinx, a basilisk, and a phoenix, along with a wide range of monsters appearing in folklore. In addition to dragons and giant spiders (see **Animals, Monstrous**), she brings in lesser-known entities from British and Japanese folklore like Boggarts, Grindylows, and **Kappas**. Other traditionally frightening creatures do not appear so in her hands: these include spectral monsters like **ghosts**, **poltergeists**, and **ghouls**, and other non-traditional presentations like **kraken**, **hippogriffs**, **centaurs**, and **shapeshifters**. The series also incorporates a vast array of monstrous people, including **trolls**, merpeople (see **Mermaid/Merman**), **goblins**, **giants**, **werewolves**, **vampires**, inferi, and dementors, many (though not all) of which Rowling utilizes to develop her pervading theme of multiculturalism. Her own inventions complement this theme, but her real masterpiece is the villain Voldemort, who inhabits a number of monstrous guises and whose connections with serpents reinforce his remorseless evil nature.

Greek and Roman Monsters

Greek and Roman myths are popular choices for Rowling's inspiration. Both Fluffy, Hagrid's choice of guardian for Hogwarts' tunnels in *Harry Potter and the Sorcerer's Stone* (1998; published as *Harry Potter and the Philosopher's Stone* in 1997 in Britain and other English-speaking countries), and **Cerberus**, Greek myth's guardian of the approaches to the Underworld, are three-headed dogs who can be lulled by music. Likewise, the sphinx, a mythical being with the body of a lion and the head and torso of a human, figured prominently in Greco-Roman myth after being borrowed from ancient Egypt, where it was an icon of royalty, fertility, and immortality. The riddling sphinx in the third task of the Triwizard Tournament in *Harry Potter and the Goblet of Fire* (2000) evokes the Greek account of the riddle contest between the sphinx and Oedipus; Argus, the namesake of Hogwarts' caretaker Argus Filch, appears in both Greek and Roman tales as a hundred-eyed sentinel (as in Ovid's presentation of him in his first century CE *Metamorphoses*, where he is sent by Juno to watch Io). Defense Against the Dark Arts' Professor Quirrell's dual-faced form (*Sorcerer's Stone*) is perhaps more specifically a Roman image, echoing the two-faced Roman god of beginnings, Janus.

The figure of the basilisk, which guards the Chamber of Secrets in *Harry Potter and the Chamber of Secrets* (1998) and occasionally roams through Hogwarts' pipes searching for victims, first appears in first-century Roman author Pliny the Elder's *Natural History* as a lethal snake native to North Africa; known as the king of serpents because of its crown-like head markings, it was believed to approach its victims upright and to be able to set fire to bushes or break stones by breathing on them. Rowling's basilisk is powerful enough that its direct stare is fatal, and even an indirect glimpse—in a watery reflection (Filch's cat Mrs Norris), in a mirror (Penelope Clearwater and Hermione), through a camera lens (Colin Creevey), or through a ghost (Justin Finch-Fletchley)—induces a frozen, coma-like state evocative of the **Medusa**'s ability to turn victims to stone. While Rowling presents this petrification as curable by the root of the mandrake (a plant that traditionally can kill by screaming), the only antidote for her basilisk's venom is the tears of a phoenix. The venom is also presented as strong enough to destroy Horcruxes, vessels containing fragments of a human soul, and thus forms a vital plot element. The film's basilisk in *Harry Potter and the Chamber of Secrets* (Chris Columbus, 2002) is much more active than the book's, chasing Harry down a corridor to add cinematic excitement.

Folkloric Monsters

Rowling draws much inspiration from both traditional folklore and mythology, occasionally adding embellishments to create the creature best suited to her story. **Dragons** from both western and eastern mythology appear throughout the series. Hagrid hatches Norwegian Ridgeback Norbert from a dragon's egg procured from a stranger in a bar, but when Norbert becomes too large to manage, Hagrid sends him to dragon-minder Charlie Weasley in Romania (*Sorcerer's Stone*). Four dragons form the first task of the Triwizard Tournament—a Swedish Short-Snout, a Common Welsh Green, a Chinese Fireball, and a Hungarian Horntail—and Harry's mission is to steal the egg of the latter; the cinematic dragons in *Harry Potter and the Goblet of Fire* (David Yates, 2005) add even more action as Harry falls off his broomstick while distracting the Horntail. While the dragon guarding the **goblin**-run **wizards**' bank Gringotts is blind, this does not impede its mobility when Harry, Ron, and Hermione free it and break out of Gringotts after having stolen the Hufflepuff Cup from Bellatrix Lestrange's vault in *Harry Potter and the Deathly Hallows* (2007). Mary GrandPré's cover illustration for the deluxe edition of *Deathly Hallows* (Scholastic, 2007) features this dragon.

The Acromantula Aragog, a "monstrous eight-eyed spider capable of human speech" (*Fantastic Beasts* 1), has roots in the African folktale of Anansi the spider, a trickster and story-keeper providing the link between humans and the gods. He tells Harry and an arachnophobic Ron Weasley in *Chamber of Secrets* how twelve-year-old Hagrid rescued and hatched his egg; later, after Hogwarts' student Myrtle was killed by the basilisk, Aragog was blamed for the murder and Hagrid was expelled. Aragog settled in the Forbidden Forest and raises his family there; though they agree not to harm Hagrid, they do not extend this agreement to other humans and try to attack Harry and Ron. After Aragog's death in *Harry Potter and the Half-Blood Prince* (2005), Hagrid honors him by hosting his funeral, which Professor Horace Slughorn attends to procure Aragog's valuable venom for his Potions class. One of Aragog's children appears during the third task of the Triwizard Tournament, and when Voldemort forces the Acromantulae out of the Forbidden Forest, they invade Hogwarts (evoking memories of the 1975 B-movie *The Giant Spider Invasion* [Bill Rebane]) and eventually fight in the Battle of Hogwarts in *Deathly Hallows*. Literary precedents appear with Shelob in J.R.R. Tolkien's *The Two Towers* (1954; see **Tolkien, Monsters In**).

Numerous lesser-known monsters from British folklore appear during Defense Against the Dark Arts (DADA) classes. Boggarts, shape-shifting spirits from northern English tradition, are dark and hairy creatures connected with the bogeyman, a supernatural being who lurks under beds or in cupboards. Their name has roots in the Scots version of Bogeys, which "come to our consciousness through visualization above all: one's inward eye sees them, but so vividly that they appear before the eyes of the body, too, as in phantasms" (Warner 43). Boggarts literally embody their victims' worst fears and can be vanquished only by the magical charm, *Riddikulus*. Grindylows, small, horned water **demons** of Yorkshire myth, have long fingers and fangs and were mentioned to frighten children away from unsafe places; several of them try to trap Harry during the second task of the Triwizard Tournament. Eight-inch-tall electric blue Cornish **pixies** wreak havoc during Professor Lockheart's first DADA class in *Chamber of Secrets*; this incident provides immense comic relief, particularly in the film. Hinkypunks, from southwestern English folklore, lurk in bogs and other remote places and light lanterns to startle travelers and lure them to their doom. One of the few non-British DADA monsters is the Kappa, an intelligent Japanese water spirit that drags its victims into water to drown and mutilate them.

Spectral Monsters

Although spectral phenomena appear throughout the series, they rarely seem frightening to the characters. Ghosts including Nearly Headless Nick (AKA Sir Nicholas de Mimsy-Porpington), the Bloody Baron, the Grey Lady, the Fat Friar, Professor Binns, and Moaning Myrtle help strengthen the tales' fantastic flavor and add comic relief, as with Nick's Deathday party (*Chamber of Secrets*) or Professor Binns's dull lectures, or provide important information to advance the plot. Moaning Myrtle helps Harry realize that it was young Voldemort who first opened the Chamber of Secrets, and, in *Goblet of Fire*, suggests that Harry open the egg containing the clue to the second Triwizard task underwater in order to understand its song. In *Deathly Hallows*, the Grey Lady reveals herself as Helena Ravenclaw, daughter of one of the original founders of Hogwarts, and gives Harry the details he needs to locate one of the Horcruxes. Similarly, Peeves the poltergeist is a source of continual annoyance to students and teachers alike, tattling to Filch about student misdemeanors and accidents; however, due to the castle's magical nature, his typical behavior of overturning furniture and making loud sounds does not have the usual frightening effect. **Ghouls**, monsters that consume human flesh, also exist in the wizard world, but the one that lives in the Weasleys' attic is not particularly dangerous: while it moans and can throw things, it successfully impersonates Ron to keep Voldemort's Ministry of Magic from realizing that he accompanies Harry on his journey in *Deathly Hallows*.

Non-Traditional Presentations

Like these spectral phenomena, other entities that might usually appear monstrous are not always frightening: Rowling often reverses expectations by modifying the nature of a monster to grab readers' attention. The giant squid that lives in the lake might resemble a kraken, but it is harmless and tosses Dennis Creevey back into the boat when he falls out during his first year (*Goblet of Fire*). Hippogriffs, which first appear in Ariosto's *Orlando Furioso* (1516), result from the union of a male **griffin** (half-eagle and half-lion) and a female horse and have an eagle's head and beak, a lion's front legs and talons, feathered wings, and a horse's body; they fly faster than birds and dive like thunderbolts. Buckbeak the hippogriff is one of Hagrid's many magical creatures; though friendly to Harry and his friends, after being provoked he attacks Draco Malfoy and is sentenced to execution in *Harry Potter and the Prisoner of Azkaban* (1999). In this book, Harry and Hermione use the time-turner to save both Buckbeak and Sirius Black, the titular character and Harry's godfather, and the two become fellow fugitives before Buckbeak's return to Hagrid in *Half-Blood Prince*. While centaurs, half-human half-horse beings from Greek mythology, are not always friendly towards humans and attack Professor Umbridge, Hogwarts' newly installed DADA professor and eventually Hogwarts' High Inquisitor and temporary headmistress (*Harry Potter and the Order of the Phoenix* [2005]), the centaur Firenze consents to work as the Divination teacher at Hogwarts, and later the centaurs join Harry during the Battle of Hogwarts.

Other creatures that might traditionally be viewed as monsters include shapeshifters. Animagi, wizards who can change into animals, include Transfiguration professor and Head of Gryffindor Professor McGonagall (cat), Sirius (dog), Harry's father James Potter (stag), *Daily Prophet* newspaper reporter Rita Skeeter (beetle), and the traitor Peter Pettigrew (rat). Other kinds of shapeshifters include metamorphmagi like auror Nymphadora Tonks, who can change her appearance at will, or wizards who can perform a transfiguration spell, as Durmstrang student and Bulgarian Seeker Victor Krum attempts during the Triwizard Tournament when he partially transforms himself into a shark. Another common type of shapeshifting appears via the Polyjuice potion, a Jekyll and **Hyde** formula that allows wizards to assume temporarily the appearance of someone else. Harry and Ron use Polyjuice potion to impersonate Crabbe and Goyle when investigating the identity of the heir of Slytherin (*Chamber of Secrets*);

during this episode, Hermione develops cat features after inadvertently misconcocting her potion. They use it again in *Deathly Hallows* to infiltrate the Ministry of Magic and to break into Gringotts. Barty Crouch Jr, one of Voldemort's most loyal Death Eaters, employs it to switch places with his dying mother and escape from Azkaban, the wizard prison, and again to impersonate DADA professor Mad-Eye Moody in *Goblet of Fire*. Crabbe and Goyle take it in *Half-Blood Prince* to masquerade as younger female students guarding the Room of Requirements while Draco Malfoy smuggles Death Eaters into Hogwarts. Either transfiguration or the Polyjuice potion may be involved in Fred and George's Canary Creams, which temporarily transform unsuspecting consumers into canaries, in *Half-Blood Prince*. Finally, the combination of the Furnunculus Curse and the Jelly-Legs hex results in Malfoy sprouting facial tentacles, a typical indication of monstrosity (*Goblet of Fire*).

Monstrous People

Monsters with human-like appearances pervade the series. Some stay within traditional bounds, like the troll that invades Hogwarts in *Sorcerer's Stone*: the dispatch of this enormous, clumsy creature that mindlessly destroys property and attacks humans functions as a plot device that solidifies the friendship between the boys and Hermione. Merpeople, mythical aquatic people with fish-tails, threaten Harry during the second task of the Triwizard Tournament, and sing a mournful lament at Dumbledore's funeral (*Half-Blood Prince*), reinforcing the series' growing theme of cultural pluralism. Rowling extends others beyond their stereotypes, like Veela. In Eastern European folklore, these beautiful female shapeshifters have such intoxicating effects on the young men who encounter them dancing that the men are forced to dance until they die of exhaustion. Rowling considerably softens this effect: Fleur Delacour, Beauxbatons' Triwizard champion who marries Bill Weasley in *Deathly Hallows*, appears in the traditional form of a beautiful young girl with long, flowing hair, but lacks both the Veela's mythical gifts for healing and prophecy, and the ability to shapeshift at will.

Rowling's modification of human-like monsters serves to further the multicultural theme she develops throughout the series. Goblins are traditionally fierce, avaricious, lascivious, and treacherous, like the Victorian goblins of Christina Rossetti (1830–94) and George MacDonald (1824–1905), and the twentieth-century goblins of Tolkien or David Bowie's goblin-king in the film *Labyrinth* (Jim Henson, 1986). Despite repeated mentions of historical Goblin Rebellions, Rowling's goblins work alongside the wizards, maintaining and guarding Gringotts, and are renowned craftspeople. While Harry, Ron, and Hermione are wary of the goblin Griphook, in *Deathly Hallows* he helps them break into Gringotts before reclaiming the goblin-made sword of Gryffindor, exemplifying Bill Weasley's observation that goblins hold different notions of ownership than humans and regard the maker of an object as its rightful owner. Like other non-wizards, goblins are oppressed figures who do not enjoy full rights in the magical world.

Rowling's stance against intolerance appears especially in her portrayal of giants, werewolves, and vampires, all of whom are similarly subjugated. Ron's perception of giants epitomizes the wizard community's opinion of them as gruesome and brutal, and Beauxbatons headmistress Madame Maxime accordingly denies her own giant heritage. While the half-giant Hagrid, who shares his name with a Celtic giant and champion of animals, is unashamed of his heritage, his misguided love for dangerous beasts that the rest of the wizard world considers monsters might indicate his status as other in their world. In many ways Hagrid acts as a kind of a bridge between species, spanning the realms between the magical world and "the monster realm" (Neumann 165). Though his attempts in *Order of the Phoenix* to align the giants with Dumbledore fail and many of the giants eventually join Voldemort, Hagrid's half-brother and full giant Grawp joins him, moving to the Forbidden Forest and fighting with Hagrid in the Battle of Hogwarts. Werewolves are similarly reviled by the majority of the wizard community, at times justifiably as a result of such figures as Fenrir Greyback, who attacks as many victims as possible in both *Half-Blood Prince* and *Deathly Hallows*, before being defeated by Neville Longbottom and Ron. However, Remus Lupin, Harry's third-year DADA teacher, illustrates that not all werewolves are vicious: though he fell victim as a boy to Greyback, Lupin eventually controls his monthly transformations into a vicious half-wolf, half-human with the Wolfsbane potion, which allows him to keep his human consciousness during his transformations. His name evokes the Roman myth of Romulus and Remus—twins suckled by a wolf—and *lupin*, the Latin word for wolf. Even vampires are accepted: the vampire Sanguini attends Slughorn's Christmas party in *Half-Blood Prince*, albeit satirized as an intriguing, handsome stranger who must be watched so as not to abscond with any of the girls.

Rowling does not make a similar case for Inferi and Dementors. A type of **zombie** or undead creature, Inferi are corpses reanimated by dark magic. Inferi awakened by Voldemort attack Harry and Dumbledore as they escape from the cave concealing the fake Horcrux in *Half-Blood Prince*, and formed part of young Grindelwald's plans for world domination (*Deathly Hallows*). Dementors, who seem clearly influenced by Tolkien's *nazgul* and whose name has roots in the Latin *dementatus*—to make mad—wear dark, hooded cloaks, and have no eyes, gaping holes for mouths, and decomposing, skeletal hands. Their horrific ability to remove their victims' happy memories culminates in the Dementor's kiss, which sucks out their victims' souls. Dementors make their victims feel as though they will never be happy again, symptoms which in the real world mirror the onset of clinical depression. Their inclusion in the series might indicate that "mental illness, like so many other 'complex' issues, was a taboo subject for children's literature in the past; but increasingly, the monsters are being let out of the closet, and exceptional award-winning literature is being written as a result" (Barton 37). However, they function more as a representation of symptoms rather than actual mental illness, since the defense against Dementors is casting a Patronus—an animal-shaped apparition created by calling upon one's happiest memories, although chocolate can help alleviate the symptoms caused by exposure—rather than receiving treatment for the real disease.

Rowling's Inventions

The series includes a few monsters of Rowling's own invention. First appearing in the mention of horseless stagecoaches in *Chamber of Secrets* but not becoming visible to Harry until *Order of the Phoenix*, Thestrals, from the Old English *thestri*, meaning dark, are skeletal flying horses with dragonish heads and leathery wings, and are visible only to those who have seen death. Perhaps inspired by **Pegasus**, the winged horse of Greek mythology, Rowling has developed them into something unique. Similarly, the Whomping Willow on the Hogwarts' grounds evokes the tree spirits of Greek mythology, as well as Tolkien's Ents, yet takes on its own identity: planted over the entrance leading to the Shrieking Shack, this giant tree guards the passageway from curious intruders and thus allowed Lupin to endure his monthly werewolf transformations in relative safety (see **Plants, Monstrous**). It destroys Mr Weasley's flying Ford Anglia in *Chamber of Secrets* and nearly injures Harry and Hermione when they are pursuing Sirius in dog-form after he has captured Ron in *Prisoner of Azkaban*. Blast-ended skrewts, a cross between a **manticore** and a fire-crab—another fictional Rowling creation, identified as a beast resembling a large tortoise native to Fiji with rear-shooting defensive flames (*Fantastic Beasts* 17)—appear during the third task of the Triwizard Tournament, and are bred by Hagrid against Ministry of Magic regulations; while not actively malevolent, they sting, bite, and burn anyone who stumbles on them. Erumpents, large, rhinoceros-like beasts, are believed to possess a deadly horn containing a lethal explosive fluid; these monsters are rare since "males frequently explode each other during the mating season" (*Fantastic Beasts* 16). Xenophilius Lovegood keeps an Erumpent horn on his wall, mistaking it for a Crumple-Horned Snorkack horn, which explodes and causes great chaos; *Harry Potter and the Deathly Hallows: Part 1* (David Yates, 2010) vividly shows the Lovegoods' home being blown apart.

Rowling's most powerful monster is über-villain Voldemort, whose name comes from the Old English word for land or will and the Middle English word for death or corpse. He inhabits a plethora of forms through the series: the **parasite** on Professor Quirrell (*Sorcerer's Stone*); the embodied memories of Tom Riddle (*Chamber of Secrets*); the **wraith**-like creature possessing frail arms and legs just strong enough to wield a wand (*Goblet of Fire*); the reanimated man with snake-like features, a soul split into eight fragments, who can fly (*Order of the Phoenix* and *Deathly Hallows*); and the flayed child at King's Cross Station (*Deathly Hallows*). The true heir to Salazar Slytherin, by blood as well as inclination, Voldemort aspires to domination of both the wizard and muggle worlds, and envisions ruling over a kingdom of pure-blooded wizards free of muggle connections. Entirely amoral, he is incapable of remorse, torturing and murdering anyone who stands in the way of his arrogant goal to conquer death. Signs of his unwavering identification with evil appear in his red eyes (a traditional fairy tale signifier), his desire to cause his victims to suffer and admit his superiority before their death, and his connection with serpents. A Parselmouth, someone who can communicate with snakes, Voldemort is sorted into Slytherin, and later makes his enormous pet snake Nagini the receptacle of one of his Horcruxes. Nagini provides physical sustenance for Voldemort before his re-embodiment and she becomes an active force of Voldemort's evil actions: she attacks Arthur Weasley (*Order of the Phoenix*), and in *Deathly Hallows* she devours Charity Burbage, the teacher Voldemort has murdered, inhabits the corpse of Bathilda Bagshot in order to attack Harry at Godric's Hollow, and kills Severus Snape. The fiendfyre in the Room of Requirements in *Deathly Hallows* takes on the forms of fiery serpents, **Chimeras**, and dragons, and Part 2 of the film renders this most convincingly.

Regardless of their forms, monsters throughout the series function as metaphors for inner fears as well as external challenges. Some represent wizard society's pariahs and the need to overcome negative stereotypes, while others evoke the sublime resulting from the juxtaposition of terror and beauty. As *The Monster Book of Monsters*—Hagrid's textbook for his Care of Magical Creatures class, which attempts to bite Harry and then scuttles under his bed when he first opens it (*Prisoner of Azkaban*)—demonstrates, the art of the monsters in the "Harry Potter" series lies in Rowling's gift for creating and presenting the unexpected.

Anne Hiebert Alton

References and Suggested Reading

Barton, Julie. "The Monsters of Depression in Children's Literature: Of Dementors, Spectres, and Pictures." *The Journal of Children's Literature Studies* 2, no. 1 (2005): 27–39.

Dendle, Peter. "Monsters, Creatures, and Pets at Hogwarts: Animal Stewardship in the World of Harry Potter." In *Critical Perspectives on Harry Potter*, edited by Elizabeth E. Heilman, 163–76. 2nd edn [2003]. Reprint, New York: Routledge, 2009.

Eccleshare, Julia. *A Guide to the Harry Potter Novels*. London: Continuum, 2002.

Gilmore, David D. *Monsters: Evil Beings, Mythical Beasts, and All Manner of Imaginary Terrors*. Philadelphia: University of Pennsylvania Press, 2003.

Kronzek, Allan Zola, and Elizabeth Kronzek. *The Sorcerer's Companion: A Guide to the Magical World of Harry Potter*. 3rd edn [2001]. Reprint, New York: Broadway, 2010.

Neumann, Iver B. "Naturalizing Geography: Harry Potter and the Realms of Muggles, Magic Folks, and Giants." In *Harry Potter and International Relations*, edited by Daniel H. Nexon and Iver B. Neumann, 157–75. Lanham, MD: Rowman & Littlefield, 2006.

Pratchett, Terry. "Let There Be Dragons." In *Only Connect: Readings on Children's Literature*, edited by Sheila Egoff, Gordon Stubbs, Ralph Ashley, and Wendy Sutton, 201–5. 3rd edn. Toronto: Oxford University Press, 1996.

Rowling, J.K. *Fantastic Beasts and Where to Find Them. By Newt Scamander*. London: Bloomsbury, 2001.

Tolkien, J.R.R. "On Fairy Stories." In *Tree and Leaf*, 11–72. London: Unwin, 1964.

Warner, Maria. *Monsters of Our Own Making: The Peculiar Pleasures of Fear*. Lexington: University of Kentucky Press, 2007.

HARUT—*see* Angel

HAUNTED HOUSE

A haunted house is a dwelling in which a generally evil and ostensibly supernatural entity, traditionally a **ghost**, manifests itself. Classical Greek, Roman, and Middle Eastern literature contain references to haunted houses, but as the motif developed over later centuries, the dwelling often evolved from functioning as a setting to assuming an active or even predominant role in the haunting. While the motif is one of the most durable in supernatural literature and cinema, it has also grown to be one of the most hackneyed, and the success of later treatments has often depended upon the introduction of inventive variations.

An Emerging Pattern

William Shakespeare's play *Hamlet* (c. 1600) presents a castle that is, in a sense, haunted by the ghost of the murdered Danish king, although it is perhaps more accurate to say that it is Hamlet, the king's son, who is haunted. The play influenced Horace Walpole, whose novel *The Castle of Otranto* (1764) is credited with inspiring the Gothic movement in literature. The corridors and dungeons of Walpole's castle may be read as symbolic counterparts to Count Manfred's murderous and incestuous impulses, although the supernatural apparatus of the short novel, including a ghost of enormous stature, is bound to strike modern readers as puerile. Nevertheless, Walpole and his many imitators established the importance of placing a haunting presence, either natural or supernatural, in a symbolically appropriate setting.

Edgar Allan Poe's "The Fall of the House of Usher" (1839) is the first work to exploit the possibilities of the haunted house motif in a manner that is both literarily and psychologically satisfying. The story's narrator makes a clear identification of the Usher house with the Usher family, while the narrative itself makes an implicit identification of the bleak dwelling with Roderick Usher's troubled mind. However, it is not a ghost that haunts the house but Usher's unnaturally intense regard for his twin sister and, ultimately, his fear that he has buried her alive.

While Poe's fellow countryman Nathaniel Hawthorne embedded a kernel of the supernatural in *The House of the Seven Gables* (1851), his novel is above all else a notable example of a house blighted by the evil deeds of its builder. Colonel Pyncheon's framing of Matthew Maule for witchcraft and his subsequent usurpation of Maule's land on which to build the eponymous house result in the horrible death of the colonel and, ultimately, that of his descendant, Judge Jaffrey Pyncheon (see **Witch/Wizard**).

Edward Bulwer-Lytton's "The Haunted and the Haunters; or, The House and the Brain" (1859) is probably the most influential story of its kind ever written, and introduced an important element that would be taken up by later writers—an individual who conducts an investigation of the haunted house. In this case an occult apparatus is discovered through which a magician who had committed two murders in the house continues to work his evil will. The long story contains several other features, such as doors that open and shut of their own accord, that would become commonplaces.

Variations on a Motif

The decades following the publication of Bulwer-Lytton's landmark work were rich ones for supernatural fiction in general and the haunted house motif in particular. Outstanding short examples include "Ghost Stories of the Tiled House" (1861) by Joseph Sheridan Le Fanu, in which a spectral, disembodied hand makes repeated attempts to enter the house in question before finally succeeding. (see **Body Parts, Animate**). "Vaila" (1896; revised as "The House of Sounds," 1911) by M.P. Shiel is set in a brass mansion chained to a storm-swept island in the North Atlantic and doomed by an age-old curse. Modeled on "The Fall of the House of Usher," it is written in a style even more florid than Poe's.

In Henry James's notoriously ambiguous short novel *The Turn of the Screw* (1898), the ghosts of two depraved servants may or may not be haunting a country house in order to harm the two children living there. With "The Mezzotint" (1904), M.R. James introduced a creative twist to what was becoming a very common motif; while the story describes what is indeed a ghostly crime in a country house, it is a *print* of the house that is haunted. An air of abandonment and desolation hangs over the haunted American dwellings described by Ambrose Bierce; typical of Bierce's approach is "A Vine on a House" (1905), in which the supernatural presence has incorporated itself into a monstrous plant (see **Plants, Monstrous**).

A writer succumbs to the sensual charms of a ghost in "The Beckoning Fair One" (1911) by Oliver Onions, while the spectral inhabitants of a room in an Italian villa—huge, loathsome invertebrates with the pincers of crabs—give guests cancer in E.F. Benson's "Caterpillars" (1912). Henry James's friend Edith Wharton provided a feminist perspective in such works as "Miss Mary Pask" (1925), which is set in an isolated cottage in Brittany haunted by a lonely old woman. But is she a ghost? The supernatural presence is more pronounced in haunted house stories by Wharton such as "Kerfol" (1916) and "Afterward" (1910) that explicitly connect ghosts to the disempowerment or disenfranchisement of women.

Besides being a landmark in supernatural fiction, William Hope Hodgson's novel *The House on the Borderland* (1908) is easily the period's most original treatment of the haunted house motif. The dwelling in question is an aged stone house in Ireland that lies on the "borderland" between our world and another dimension in which good and evil have a literal, cosmological existence. In some of the novel's episodes the house is beset by loathsome swine-like creatures from a pit beneath it, and in another the narrator witnesses the death of our solar system in the distant future.

Modern Masterpieces

During the latter half of the twentieth century, five highly talented writers reinvigorated the motif with fully developed, character-driven works. And with only a single exception, their novels involve haunted houses that are unquestionably malignant, if not inherently evil.

The Haunting of Hill House (1959) by Shirley Jackson appeared exactly 100 years after Bulwer-Lytton's story, but in this case the haunted has evolved into the haunter. The novel features another occult investigator, two psychically receptive guests, a member of the owner's family, and the investigator's meddlesome wife. One of the guests, Eleanor Vance, has led a cruelly sheltered life, and the novel dramatizes her mental deterioration under the influence of Hill House. The novel's famous opening and closing paragraphs describe the house as "not sane." Its designer ensured that all its angles are "wrong" and its doors off-center, and over the years it appears to have accumulated the pain and misery of its residents.

The setting of *The Green Man* (1969) by Kingsley Amis, a pleasant British inn, stands in benign contrast to Hill House. Yet the novel's troubled protagonist is nearly as vulnerable as Eleanor Vance. Hotelier Maurice Allington is an irrepressible womanizer, but he is also alcoholic and cripplingly afraid of dying—weaknesses that have made him particularly subject to the machinations of the ghost that haunts his inn. The specter is that of Dr Thomas Underhill, a seventeenth-century occultist whose murderous attention has been drawn to Allington's pubescent daughter.

As Stephen King has acknowledged, *The Shining* (1977) was influenced by *The Haunting of Hill House*. The setting of King's own novel is the Overlook, an aging hotel where Jack Torrance has taken a job as winter caretaker. Like Hill House, the Overlook possesses a force that has been feeding for decades on the crimes and misfortunes of its owners and guests. And, like Maurice Allington, Torrance is an alcoholic. As Torrance's wife comes to realize, the Overlook is particularly interested in their psychically gifted son, Danny, but is working its will through the self-destructive caretaker.

The House Next Door (1978) by Anne Rivers Siddons features an attractive, architecturally striking residence with none of the trappings traditionally associated with haunted houses. Yet it is as evil as the Overlook, finding the weakest link in each family that lives in it. Near the novel's end, the narrator realizes that the architect, a seemingly normal young man, is "some kind of terrible carrier" of evil, but Siddons provides no further explanation.

In the richly imagined *Hawksmoor* (1985), Peter Ackroyd moves between two figures—an eighteenth-century London architect who consecrates his churches to Satan with human sacrifices, and a twentieth-century British detective investigating a series of murders in those same churches. Each seems somehow to be vaguely aware of the other's existence, but even though the detective senses a pattern in the murders, its actual configuration remains just beyond his reach.

In addition to these five works, two recent British novels—*The Woman in Black* (1983) by Susan Hill and *The Little Stranger* (2009) by Sarah Waters—illustrate the undiminished ability of the haunted house motif to dramatize the dead weight of the past upon the present. In the former the setting is remote Eel House, while in the latter it is deteriorating Hundreds Hall. The owner of Eel House has died, and it is the job of the narrator, a naïve young solicitor, to wrap up her affairs. *The Little Stranger* is narrated by an older doctor struggling to attend to the owners' wellbeing, but his naïveté is of a darker and more destructive strain.

Haunted (Movie) Houses

Haunted house films began to appear before the turn of the twentieth century, but the first example of any consequence is *The Fall of the House of Usher* (1928), a silent, atmospheric work directed by Jean Epstein and based on the story by Edgar Allan Poe. In this version, Roderick Usher's dying sister has, tellingly, become his wife, while the plot also draws upon an 1842 tale by Poe, "The Oval Portrait," for its treatment of a portrait that drains away the life of its subject.

Two more key works were adapted for equally important haunted house films—*The Haunting* (1963) and *The Shining* (1980). Directed by Robert Wise, the former is based on *The Haunting of Hill House* by Shirley Jackson and stars Julie Harris as Eleanor Lance (her surname altered slightly from the novel). Although the black-and-white film successfully recreates the book's tone, screenwriter Nelson Gidding changed the character of the investigator's wife considerably, allowing for a more dramatic climax. Meticulously directed by Stanley Kubrick and based on the novel by Stephen King, *The Shining* (1980) is generally regarded as one of the most successful supernatural films ever produced. Jack Nicholson's over-the-top performance as Jack Torrance became one of the most famous of his career, but King expressed disappointment in seeing his sympathetic caretaker depicted in such overtly sinister terms.

Although supernatural films of the late twentieth and early twenty-first centuries relied increasingly on spectacular special effects, *The Others* (2001) and *The Orphanage* (2007) derive their power from careful plotting, deliberate pacing, and largely traditional elements. The work of Chilean-Spanish director Alejandro Amenábar, *The Others* stars Nicole Kidman as the mistress of a manor house on the island of Jersey at the end of World War II. While ghosts do indeed haunt the isolated residence, the revelation of their identity forces viewers to re-evaluate everything they have seen.

The Orphanage, a Spanish-language film directed by Juan Antonio Bayona, dramatizes the efforts of a grown woman (played by Belén Rueda) to turn the orphanage where she grew up into a home for disabled children. But the disappearance of her own adopted son, who had found companionship with what were assumed to be imaginary playmates, sidetracks her plans and ultimately destroys her.

[Rec] (2007) and *Paranormal Activity* (2009) share a new, faux-documentary style popularized by *The **Blair Witch** Project* (1999). Directed by Jaume Balagueró and Paco Plaza, the Spanish-language *[Rec]* dramatizes a series of bizarre and increasingly violent events in a Barcelona apartment house, ostensibly as recorded on a shaking camcorder by a member of a television news team. The key to the events turns out to lie in a room once occupied by an agent of the Vatican investigating a biological basis for demonic possession (see **Demon**).

Paranormal Activity is made up of footage ostensibly shot by a young man sharing a newish—but somehow disturbed—house in San Diego with his lover. At night the camera is mounted on a tripod and records inexplicable movements, some minor but others frighteningly unnerving. Although the film suggests that the woman has brought some sort of haunting presence with her, writer-director Oren Peli leaves the question open. Like other notable films of the twenty-first century, *Paranormal Activity* reverts to the use of the house as setting, albeit one with an important symbolic role.

Grove Koger

References and Suggested Reading

Ackroyd, Peter. *The House of Doctor Dee.* London: Hamilton, 1985.

Amis, Kingsley. *The Green Man.* London: Cape, 1969.

Bailey, Dale. *American Nightmares: The Haunted House Formula in American Popular Fiction.* Bowling Green, OH: Bowling Green State University Popular Press, 1999.

Bulwer-Lytton, Edward George. *The Haunted and the Haunters; or, The House and the Brain.* London: Gowans & Gray, 1905.

Duvall, Daniel S. "Inner Demons: Flawed Protagonists and Haunted Houses in *The Haunting* and *The Shining.*" *Creative Screenwriting* 6, no. 4 (1999): 32–7.

Hodgson, William Hope. *The House on the Borderland.* London: Chapman and Hall, 1908.

Jackson, Shirley. *The Haunting of Hill House.* New York: Viking, 1959.

King, Stephen. *The Shining.* Garden City, NY: Doubleday, 1977.

Poe, Edgar Allan. "The Fall of the House of Usher." In *Poetry and Tales*, 317–36. New York: Library of America, 1996.

Siddons, Anne Rivers. *The House Next Door.* New York: Simon & Schuster, 1978.

HEADLESS HORSEMAN, THE

Author Washington Irving's (1783–1859) creation, the Headless Horseman of Sleepy Hollow, is arguably the most famous **ghost** in American literature, despite the strong possibility that this decapitated spectral equestrian never actually materializes in the story introducing him, "The Legend of Sleepy Hollow" (1820).

"The Legend of Sleepy Hollow," included along with "Rip Van Winkle" in Irving's collection, *The Sketch Book of Geoffrey Crayon, Gent.* (1820), remains one of the earliest examples of American fiction still enjoyed today. The story centers on protagonist Ichabod Crane, a generally unlikeable schoolmaster with a pronounced taste for tales of **witches** and ghosts. Ichabod competes for the affections of the attractive and rich Katrina van Tassel—who seems to encourage his suit with the primary intention of inflaming the passions of Ichabod's competitor, the rough and rowdy Abraham "Brom Bones" Van Brunt. Following a festive gathering culminating in the telling of supernatural tales (including several featuring the Headless Horseman) and then the probable dismissal of Ichabod as a suitor by Katrina, the superstitious Ichabod—his imagination already excited by the spooky stories told earlier—has an encounter with the Headless Horseman in the woods and disappears. While the narrative implies that, rather than an ectoplasmic assailant, Ichabod was in fact harassed by a disguised Brom Bones, the "old country wives ... who are the best judges of these matters," explains the narrative, "maintain to this day that Ichabod was spirited away by supernatural means" (73).

While Ichabod is the story's protagonist, the imaginative focus and true star of the piece is, of course, the story's "dominant spirit" (5), the spectral Headless Horseman. What the reader learns at the story's start is that the Sleepy Hollow region of New York State is an "enchanted region" (5) whose residents are "given to all kinds of marvellous beliefs; are subject to trances and visions; and frequently see strange sights, and hear music and voices in the air." The narrator explains that: "The whole neighborhood abounds with local tales, haunted spots, and twilight superstitions" (4). The "commander-in-chief" (5) of Sleepy Hollow's supernatural battalion, however, is the Headless Horseman, whose origin can be traced to decapitation by a cannonball "in some nameless battle during the revolutionary war" (5). According to the country folk and old wives, he rides forth at night to the scene of the battle in search of his head and must be back to the churchyard in which he is buried before daybreak.

Irving drew inspiration for the story not only from folklore current in rural New York about a spectral horseman, but also from the established tradition of folktales and poems involving supernatural chases. In particular, he appropriated from German legends about Rübezahl, a capricious and at times playful mountain spirit, as recorded by Johann K.A. Masaeus in *Volksmärchen der Deutschen* (1782: see Pochmann). Irving also seems to have drawn from Scottish poet Robert Burns's *Tam O'Shanter* (1790) about a man who drinks a bit too much in a public house and has a hallucinatory vision on his way home involving witches and the **Devil**, as well as from Gottfried August Bürger's *Der wilde Jäger* (*The Wild Huntsman*, 1796), a Gothic poem about an arrogant and irreverent earl who begins as a hunter and ends up as prey, eternally pursued by a demonic hunter (see **Demon**).

Irving, however—fully aware of his situation as an author in a newly established country without a literary tradition of its own—adapts his source material in the attempt to create a literary work with a uniquely American flavor. As in "Rip Van Winkle," the American landscape plays an important role—dark stretches of woods serve as a liminal space in which reality shades into fantasy; the story is populated by immigrant farmers and stereotyped black servants (who, interestingly, are paralleled with Ichabod throughout the story); and, most especially, the spectral Headless Horseman's origin is coincident with the founding of the country. As a German Hessian—a mercenary killed while fighting for the British during the American Revolutionary War—the Headless Horseman becomes the first ghost specific to the United States. Through the Headless Horseman, Irving works to populate the American landscape with supernatural creatures directly connected to the establishment of a new country.

This first ghost of the US has not ceased to haunt the American imagination, and Irving's story has been adapted repeatedly for screen, TV, and stage. Among the most notable movie and TV adaptations are the 1922 silent version directed by Edward Venturini, starring Will Rogers as Ichabod Crane; the 1949 Disney animated version narrated by Bing Crosby, who serves as the voice of Ichabod when he sings; and, more recently, the 1999 feature film version directed by Tim Burton and starring Johnny Depp. In Burton's reimagining of Irving's famous tale, Ichabod Crane (Depp) is a bumbling investigator sent from New York City to investigate recent murders in Sleepy Hollow—which turn out to be perpetrated by the Headless Horseman (memorably played by Christopher Walken) who is magically controlled by Lady Van Tassel (Miranda Richardson). A short-lived Broadway musical titled *Sleepy Hollow* was attempted in 1948 (music by George Lessner, book and lyrics by Russell Malony and Miriam Battista); it lasted only twelve performances.

Jeffrey Andrew Weinstock

References and Suggested Reading

Hoffman, Daniel G. "Irving's Use of American Folklore in 'The Legend of Sleepy Hollow.'" *PMLA: Publications of the Modern Language Association of America* 68, no. 3 (June 1953): 425–35.

Irving, Washington. "The Legend of Sleepy Hollow." Accessed 8 June 2012. <http://www.bartleby.com/310/2/2.html>.

Pochmann, Henry A. "Irving's German Sources in 'The Sketch Book.'" *Studies in Philology* 27, no. 3 (July 1930): 477–507.

Wilm, Jan. "'The Legend of Sleepy Hollow': Washington Irving's Short Story, Tim Burton's Film and Disney's Animated Version in Comparison." In *Crossing Textual Boundaries in International Children's Literature*, edited by Jan Wilm, 192–205. Newcastle upon Tyne, England: Cambridge Scholars Press, 2011.

HEDORAH—*see* Extraterrestrial

HELLKNIGHT—*see* Video Games, Monsters In

HERMAPHRODITE

The hermaphrodite, which possesses both male and female genitals, is the figure of hybridization par excellence. It is therefore a kind of monstrosity that points toward ambiguity, duplicity, transgression, and the violation of order, but also towards plenitude, coincidence of opposites, and rich potentiality.

A heterodox interpretation of Genesis 2.26–27 claims that Adam is originally both a male and a female. This apocryphal interpretation is developed within the esoteric, gnostic, and hermetic literary traditions. Several *midrashim* (commentaries on or interpretations of the Old Testament) present Adam as an androgyn. The originary union of Adam and Eve is followed by the theme of perfection within the return to unity that can be identified within the major literature as well, including St Paul's Epistle to the Galatians 3.28. Divinity itself, in this sense, is characterized by bisexuality, and God's perfection is in His being All and One.

Within Greek culture, Plato celebrates the hermaphrodite. In the *Symposium* (c. 385–380 BCE), the character of Aristophanes tells the story of beings who have both male and female natures. The hermaphrodites are terribly strong and vigorous, and in their immense pride, they decide to attack the gods. Zeus punishes them by dividing them in two parts. Since then, the male and the female parts have never ceased looking for each other and trying to reunite (189c–193e). This doctrine of a primitive unity introduced in Plato survived for many centuries. We find traces of it in the early Middle Ages, when Johannes Scotus Eriugena (ninth century), following Maximus the Confessor (seventh century), claims in his *Periphyseon* the necessity of a reunion of the universe within the original unity, which culminates in God being All and One.

Ovid hands down the most accomplished and elaborated version of the myth in his first-century CE *Metamorphoses*. The Naiad Salmacis falls in love with the beautiful god Ermaphrodite, son of Hermes and Aphrodite. She entices him on the bank of a spring in Caria, the present Turkey, and embraces him, begging the gods to make that moment eternal. The gods grant this wish by fusing them into a single bisexual being (IV, 285–388). Androgyny is not a departure here, but rather an arrival, the product of a metamorphosis. Ermaphrodite experiences this fusion as an impairment, and asks the gods to reserve the same fate—the loss of virility—to everyone who bathes in the same spring.

Ancient culture also develops a scientific interest in the bisexual being. Aristotle, for example, classes it among monstrosities in his *Generation of Animals* (c. fourth century BCE). Monsters are, for Aristotle, animals that are imperfect only compared with their own specific end (*telos*). They are a failure not for what concerns "Nature in her entirety and by necessity" (in this sense nothing happens against nature), but for what concerns "Nature in the generality of cases" (IV, 770b). Therefore, the hermaphrodite is a monster because it is infrequent and deviates from a being's end, which is to be *either* male *or* female. In *On Divination* (first century BCE), Cicero mentions the hermaphrodite as an "unlucky prodigy" (I, 43). Pliny the Elder, in his first-century CE *Natural History*, in turn observes that if hermaphrodites were once considered portents, they are now only sources of entertainment (VII, 34).

In the high Middle Ages, the hermaphrodite attracted theologians' and canonists' attention for its legal implications—in particular as regards the administration of the sacraments. If other kinds of anomalies undermine the decision concerning the humanity of the individual and therefore raise the specter of administering baptism to the "monster," the hermaphrodite presents other problems as well, particularly concerning marriage and ordination to the priesthood (that was reserved for males). This debate became part of the discourse of condemnation of homosexuality in the Middle Ages (see van der Lugt). The answer of Pierre le Chantre (twelfth century) is particularly meaningful and exemplary: the hermaphrodite will have to choose its own sex, the one with which he or she is more comfortable. However, if he or she tries to change his or her mind, punishment will result (Pierre Le Chantre, "Verbum abbreviatum," 148; *Patrologia Latina* 205, 333–5).

Within the Platonic renaissance of the fourteenth and fifteenth centuries, the metaphorical interpretation is revived. In his *Dialogues of Love* (1535), Leo the Hebrew tries to connect the Platonic myth with the Biblical theme of the fall, interpreted as a division of a primordial unity. In a fifteenth-century commentary upon Plato's *Symposium*, Marsilio Ficino gives an Orphic reading of the myth, in which the hermaphrodite represents the fusion of matter and spirit, natural and supernatural, moving toward the prelapsarian nature of man. A more material and licentious interest in the hermaphrodite is in the works of Pietro Aretino (*Lust Sonnets*, written in 1524, as a companion to the pornographic drawings of Giulio Romano, *The Ways* or *The Sixteenth Pleasures*), Pierre de Ronsard (*Amours de Cassandre*, 1552), and Edmund Spenser (*The Faerie Queene*, 1590), and in the art of Leonardo da Vinci (*Mona Lisa*, circa 1503, and *St John the Baptist*, 1513) and Raphael Sanzio (*Leda and the Swan*, 1507).

But the allegorical reading proclaiming the necessity of a recomposition was soon challenged by the crisis and degeneration of the political situation of Europe in the sixteenth century. The hermaphrodite was then charged with a peculiar political meaning, and the negative traits of doubleness, licentiousness, and debauchery become this character's attributes. In the midst of the Religious Wars, developing the theme of Machiavellianism as the degeneration of the traditional ethical values, Thomas Artus, in his 1605 pamphlet, *The Hermaphrodites*, makes the hermaphrodite the symbol of political monstrosity and suggests it is embodied by Henry III of Valois.

Artus's pamphlet was read and appreciated by King Henry IV of Navarre, and is considered a clever satire by seventeenth-century philosopher Pierre Bayle. The main character of Artus's story, François, is wrecked on a remote island inhabited by double beings who embody a long list of moral and material vices. The debauched Roman emperor Eliogabalus is the *pater patriae* of this population, whose days, customs, and licentious ceremonies are meticulously described. They do not believe in God or immortality. They do not love war, but foment civil division. Adultery, violence, and incest are badges of honor in this hyperbolic farce in which the hermaphrodite's double body is the symbol of degeneration and falseness of the soul.

The extraordinary voyage described in Gabriel de Foigny's *The Southern Land, Known* (1676) is more complicated. Following the same pattern, the main character Sadeur (upon which Pierre Bayle writes a long entry in his *Historical and Critical Dictionary*, 1695–97) is wrecked on an island exclusively inhabited by hermaphrodites. They usually kill anyone who is not a hermaphrodite, but by chance, Sadeur himself is one. A description of the customs of this people functions as a utopic fiction in which the "monsters" become the model of life for the European reader. Yet at the end of the story, Sadeur is involved in a war that the hermaphrodites fight against an enemy population of invaders. Not only does Sadeur consider horrible the hermaprodites' exterminating fury against the enemy, but he is also charmed by a young girl prisoner. Instead of killing her, he has sex with her. This provokes disgust and marginalization, and finally a death sentence is pronounced by the hermaphrodites against Sadeur. The utopia is reversed and becomes a dystopia, and Sadeur is forced to flee and go back to his country.

Between the sixteenth and seventeenth centuries, the hermaphrodite became a favorite subject for philosophical and scientific literature. It is an idea that challenges the conceptual tools of the new science. Ambroise Paré (*On Monsters and Marvels*, 1573), Jean Riolan (*Discourse on Hermaphrodites*, 1614), and Caspar Bauhin (*On Hermaphrodites*, 1614) deal with it, amongothers. OverthrowingtheAristotelian perspective, René Descartes (*Cogitationes circa generationem animalium*, early 1620s) denies the monstrous character of the hermaphrodite, and considers it an individual whose anatomy is a slight modification of the normal one.

In the eighteenth century, these monsters presumably should have disappeared and been absorbed within a general movement of rationalism and skepticism toward the mythical and fabulous attributes that have always been associated with this figure. In fact, however, hermaphrodites remained in the literary and philosophical visions of the period as a problem, an emblem, and a model of inspiration for enlightened conceptualization within the new vitalist movement. The hermaphrodite suggests, for example, to Denis Diderot (*D'Alembert's Dream*, 1769) and Jean-Baptiste-Claude Delisle de Sales (*The Philosophy of Nature*, 1770) the necessity of softening the rigid boundaries between sexes, both on conceptual and biological grounds.

The awakening of the myth of the androgyne continued in the nineteenth century, especially within Romanticism and Decadentism. German Romanticism in particular was charmed by the perfect man who, like Christ, reconciles oppositions. In Germany, Johann Wolfgang von Goethe (*Wilhelm Meister's Apprenticeship*, 1796) deals with the hermaphrodite, while in France, one should mention George Sand (*Gabriel*, 1839 and *The Countess von Rudolstadt*, 1844), Téophile Gautier (*Contralto*, 1852 and *Spirite*, 1866), and later *The Androgyne* (1891) by Joséphin Péladan. But the subject was especially developed by Honoré de Balzac in two of his novels, *Sarrasine* (1830) and *Séraphita* (1835).

Following Emanuel Swedenborg's (1688–1772) theory of the perfect man, Balzac develops the topic of the original androgyne as a state of perfection. In *Sarrasine*, bisexuality is the synonym for bitter sacrifice and suffering, linked to genius and artistic creation. Here the sculptor Sarrasine falls in love with Zambinella, a castrato and opera singer who tries to hide his sexual identity. Zambinella will be kidnapped by Cardinal Cicognara, who will also kill Sarrasine. In *Séraphita*, a mysterious character who lives in a castle loves Minna, to whom he appears like a man—Seraphitus—but also loves Wilfred, to whom she appears like a woman—Séraphita. The ultimate perfection, for Balzac, is a real love for two persons of different sexes in a relationship of complete fusion.

The subject acquires an even greater importance in the twentieth century, thanks to the psychoanalytic notion of bisexuality introduced by Sigmund Freud (1856–1939), following Wilhelm Fliess's (1858–1928) idea. According to Fliess, every individual carries an innate bisexuality. A certain degree of anatomical hermaphroditism, in fact, is normal in every developed individual, who always carries the traces of the genital apparatus of the opposite sex. Every organism, therefore, is originally bisexual but is eventually oriented toward monosexuality during its final development. Although building on this idea in his theory, Freud always criticized the reductionism implied by Fliess's theory. In Fliess, the psychological mechanism of repression of the recessive sexuality by the dominant sexuality can be entirely traced back to biological grounds. Repression, for Freud, is a more complex mechanism, but he still moves closer to Fliess's theories, especially in *Analysis Terminable and Interminable* (1937).

At the beginning of the 1960s, historian of religion Mircea Eliade situated the hermaphrodite within a necessary movement toward the opening of the Western spirit to the "other." At the crossroads of the inner discovery of the subconscious (Freud and Carl Jung [1875–1961] in particular) and the outer discovery of the stranger (the arrival of non-European people on the stage of "universal" history), the idea of the hermaphrodite is common to both Western and non-Western cultures and thus one of the myths and symbols through which a more complete knowledge of man in general is finally possible.

Within his wider project on the history of sexuality, French philosopher Michel Foucault (1926–84) dealt with the hermaphrodite—in particular in his introduction *Herculine Barbin: Being the Recently Discovered Memories of a Nineteenth-Century French Hermaphrodite* (1980). In this work, Foucault is interested in the shift of the discourse on hermaphroditism in the modern age. In the Middle Ages, as Foucault points out, the anatomically ambiguous individual was free to choose his or her own sex (and would then be tied forever to this choice). In the modern age, on the contrary, the necessity of an "expert" discourse in order to determine—beyond the individual's choice—the "true" sexual identity of the hermaphrodite acquired more importance. Herculine Barbin grew up as a girl, but s/he was eventually recognized and defined as a "true" boy. She was forced to live within this sexual identity that she did not feel as her own, and eventually committed suicide. Foucault compares the memoir to *A Scandal at the Convent* (1893), by the psychiatrist and writer Oskar Panizza. The memoirs of Herculine Barbin also inspired the film *Le Mystère Alexina* (René Féret, 1985).

Twentieth-century literature processes the theme of the androgyne in several different ways. Among the most famous we find *The* ***Golem*** (1915) by Gustave Meyrink, who reworks the hermetic origins of the theme (his hermaphrodite therefore encounters another kind of monster, the anthropomorphic being created from inert matter of the Cabalist tradition). Michel Tournier, in *Les Météores* (1975), explores the idea of fusion of individuals through a pair of twins. But the most powerful and insightful androgyne of the century is probably Virginia Woolf's Orlando. Written in 1928, *Orlando: A Biography* is a masterpiece of feminist and homosexual literature, in which Woolf also investigates the topics of metamorphosis, nomadism, and the voyage through time. The book was masterfully brought to the screen by Sally Potter in 1992. In the twenty-first century, Jeffrey Eugenides's Pulitzer Prize-winning *Middlesex* (2002) chronicles the effects of genetic mutations resulting in hermaphroditism on three generations of a Greek family.

In cinema, the self-declared hermaphrodite and artist Josephine Joseph (born 1913) appears as one of the characters in the monstrous circus in Tod Browning's masterpiece ***Freaks*** (1932). Gérard Curbiau's biographical movie *Farinelli* (1994) tells the story of the famous eighteenth-century opera singer and castrato Carlo Maria Broschi. The film focuses on the character's charm, which derives from his sexual ambiguity and the legendary aura that surrounds him. The hermaphrodite also appears in Federico Fellini's *Satyricon* (1969), loosely based on the first-century CE satirical novel by Petronius. The director's conceptual move is an attempt to bypass centuries of encrusted Catholic morality by reconstructing an original and mythical past in which love is finally experienced in its purest form. The hermaphrodite is exploited by Miklós Jancsó in *Private Vices, Public Virtues* (1976), an irreverent and iconoclastic reading of the Mayerling affair. Mary Vetsera, who was found dead together with Prince Rudolf of Austria, heir to the Habsburg throne, is represented here as a charming hermaphrodite. The couple's alleged and disputed suicide is read by Jancsó as a reaction of the power and reason of the State against a pure and irrepressible quest for freedom through sexual desire. The theme of sexual "choice" is also used by Lucia Puenzo in *XXY* (1997), in which a young Alex is looking for his own—not only sexual—identity. Intersexuality here becomes a metaphor for the conflicts that the "other" can generate in every community.

Filippo Del Lucchese

References and Suggested Reading

Aa.Vv. *L'androgyne dans la litterature.* Paris: Albin Michel, 1990.

Aristotle. *Generation of Animals*, IV, 770 b. Cambridge, MA: Harvard University Press.

Aurnhammer, Achim. *Androgynie. Studien zu einen Motiv in der europaeischen Literatur.* Cologne: Böhlau, 1986.

Barbin, Herculine. *Herculine Barbin: Being the Recently Discovered Memoirs of a Nineteenth-Century French Hermaphrodite.* New York: Harvester Press, 1980.

Brisson, Luc. *Sexual Ambivalence: Androgyny and Hermaphroditism in Graeco-Roman Antiquity.* Berkeley and London: University of California Press, 2002.

Cantarella, Eva. *Bisexuality in the Ancient Word.* New Haven: Yale University Press, 1992.

Daston, Lorraine, and Park, Katharine. "Hermaphrodites and the Orders of Nature." *Gay and Lesbian Quarterly* 1 (1995): 419–38.

Delcourt, Marie. *Hermaphrodite: Myths and Rites of the Bisexual Figure in Classical Antiquity.* London: Studio Books, 1961.

Eliade, Mircea. *The Two and the One.* New York: Harvill Press, 1965.

Ficino, Marsilio. *Commentary on Plato's Symposium on Love.* Dallas, TX: Spring Publications, 1985.

Foigny, Gabriel de. *The Southern Land, Known.* Syracuse, NY: Syracuse University Press, 1993.

Leo the Hebrew. *Dialogues of Love.* Toronto: University of Toronto Press, 2009.

Long, Kathleen P. "Sexual Dissonance: Early Modern Scientific Accounts of

Hermaphrodites." In *Wonders, Marvels, and Monsters in Early Modern Culture*, edited by Peter G. Platt, 145–63. Newark, DE: University of Delaware Press, 1999.

Lugt, Maaike van der. "L'humanité des monstres et leur accès aux sacrements dans la pensée medieval." In *Monstres et imaginaire social. Approches historiques*, edited by Anna Caiozzo and Anne-Emmaunelle Demartini, 135–62. Paris: Créaphis, 2008.

Vasarri, Fabio. "Androgino." In *Dizionario dei temi letterari*, edited by Remo Ceserani, Mario Domenichelli, and Pino Fasano, vol. 1, 75–8. Torino: UTET, 2007.

HINKYPUNK—*see* Harry Potter, Monsters In

HIPPOGRIFFIN

According to tradition, the hippogriffin, the half-**griffin**/half-horse product of the unlikely mating between a griffin and a mare, hatches from an egg and possesses the eagle-like head and lion-like forequarters of the griffin and the hindquarters of a horse. Like its father the griffin, it is a creature from the northern edge of the world. It is wild and spirited and can be tamed only by a hero.

This magical beast makes its first literary appearance in the epic poem *Orlando furioso* by Ludovico Ariosto (the poem initially appeared in 1516 but was not published in its complete form until 1532). In this text, the hippogriffin is first tamed by the **wizard** Atlantes and then ridden by the heroic knights, Ruggiero and Astolpho. Ariosto's description of the origin and nature of the hippogriffin reflects the first-century BCE poet Virgil's metaphor for the marvels and perils of love, as well as griffin lore and classical, medieval, and Eastern material about magic mechanical horses and the flying horse, **Pegasus**.

The most pertinent classical reference influencing the creation of the literary hippogriffin occurs in Virgil's *Eclogues* (c. 38 BCE) in which the poet refers to horses mating with griffins (VIII.26–28) as a metaphor for the impossible—specifically ill-fated love. Commentators on Virgil note that griffins and horses were natural enemies—horses being attacked by griffins appear on Scythian gold objects such as an elaborate gold collar dated to the fourth century BCE; therefore, such an unlikely mating would be a marvelous event. The ironic tone of the metaphor as an image of love, as well as its classical heritage in the work of Virgil, would have appealed to Ariosto and his Renaissance audience, and the hippogriffin in *Orlando furioso* is a symbol for the contradictory forces of love and desire.

Beyond Virgil, Ariosto drew additional inspiration from a variety of places. A capital on a Romanesque column from Autun Cathedral (France), for example, shows a damaged figure riding an eagle-horse hybrid that conforms closely to Ariosto's description. Matteo Boiardo's unfinished poem, *Orlando Innamorato* (c. 1486), which was completed by Ariosto, includes several magic horses. The intelligent steed Bayard, whose size could accommodate every rider, was already part of the *chanson de geste* tradition of epic poems describing heroic deeds, and Boiardo added Rabicano, a supernatural horse born of a fiery mare and the wind. In addition, two thirteenth-century romances, *Cleomades* and *Méliacin ou le Cheval de Fust*, feature flying mechanical horses, and these reflect the influence of Eastern narratives like the automata in the ***Arabian Nights***. The winged horse Pegasus is clearly also an influence on the hippogriffin—indeed, in Ariosto's poem, a hippogriffin assists one of the central characters in rescuing a maiden from a **sea monster**, thereby fulfilling exactly the same role that Pegasus does in the Greek myth of Perseus's rescue of Andromeda. The northern home of the hippogriffin, the land of the Hyperboreans, is redolent with mythical equine associations. The god of the north wind, Boreas, mysteriously fertilized mares and produced unusually swift horses. He gave his father-in-law, King Erekhtheus of Athens, two immortal horses sired in this way.

The result of these multiple and varied influences is a creature that plays an important role in late chivalric romance that incorporates characters from the *chanson de geste* adventures of Charlemagne and his paladins. *Orlando furioso* is a complex tale about restoring the sanity of the hero, Orlando, who has been driven mad for love of the lady Angelica. Woven into this tale are the adventures of other heroes. The hippogriffin is first tamed by the wizard Atlantes, who wishes to prevent the marriage between the Saracen knight Ruggiero and the Christian Bradamante. Eventually Ruggiero escapes on the back of the hippogriffin and learns how to tame the creature, a symbol of Ruggiero's unconquered desire. As noted, in an episode that parallels the Perseus story, Ruggiero rides the hippogriffin when he rescues Angelica from a sea monster. In another episode, Ruggiero attempts to tether the fractious hippogriffin to a myrtle tree. The tree is actually a transformed knight, Astolfo, who in turn rides the hippogriffin to the Earthly Paradise, and eventually the Moon, in his search for Orlando's lost wits. Finally, Astolpho removes the hippogriffin's bridal and sets it free.

Sixteenth-century editions of Ariosto's poem show it as a flying horse with an eagle's head, wings, and front claws. This creature appears in several nineteenth-century illustrations drawn by Gustave Doré (1832–83) for Ariosto's poem. The episode in which Ruggiero rides the hippogriffin to rescue Angelica was a popular subject for artists from Girolamo dei Carpi in the sixteenth century to Auguste Ingres and Odilon Redon in the nineteenth.

In the seventeenth century, Thomas Blount, a barrister of the Inner Temple, London, published his *Glossographia* (1656), a dictionary of foreign words in English usage. He described the *Hippogryph* as a "feigned beast" part horse, part griffin. Ambrose Bierce, in his *Devil's Dictionary* of 1906, used the hippogriffin to satirize American materialism. The hippogriffin also appears in modern fantasy literature, especially among writers who favor picaresque adventures. Merlin becomes involved with a hippogriffin in the sprawling political satire *Merlin l'enchanteur* (1860), written by the nineteenth-century French writer Edgar Quinet. A chapter entitled "How One Came, as was foretold, to the city of Never" is part of the *Book of Wonder* (1912), by the Anglo-Irish fantasy writer, Lord Dunsany. The central character has a magic halter that can tame any fantastic beast such as "the hippogriff Pegasus" (28). Dunsany's piece is more a prose meditation than a tale and contains descriptions of hippogriffins dancing in the air in an ethereal ballet. One of the characters in *The* ***Witch****-Woman: A Trilogy About Her* (1948) by the American fantasy writer James Branch Cabell is a hero mounted on a hippogriffin searching for the elusive ideal woman. The fantasy novelist E.R. Eddison used the hippogriffin in his 1926 novel *The Worm Ouroborus*. Lessingham, the narrator, is conveyed to the planet Mercury in a chariot drawn by a hippogriff. The tale revolves around four hero-brothers. The central character learns that the only way to rescue his imprisoned older brother is with the aid of a hippogriffin hatched from an egg at the bottom of a lake. A herd of hippogriffin lives in the forest surrounding Hogwarts School in J.K. Rowling's "Harry Potter" series (see **Harry Potter, Monsters In**). Buckbeak is the favorite of the gentle **giant**, Hagrid. The creature is depicted as strong and proud, but loyal, even when threatened with execution. In an echo of Ariosto's Ruggiero, it helps Harry's godfather, Sirius Black, to escape. A themed rollercoaster ride, the Flight of the Hippogriff, has been installed in the Wizarding World of Harry Potter at Universal Parks and Resorts in Orlando, Florida. In Neil Gaiman's "Sandman" series, a hippogriffin is one of Dream's gatekeepers, together with a griffin and a wyvern, a two-legged **dragon**.

Like so many mythical creatures, the hippogriffin features in modern fantasy role-playing and video games. A variant of the hippogriffin, with leonine front legs, equine back legs, and the head and wings of an eagle, serves as war mounts of Breton knights in *Warhammer*, and they were among the earliest mythical beasts introduced into the ***Dungeons & Dragons*** Universe.

Juliette Wood

References and Suggested Reading

Ariosto, Ludovico. *Orlando furioso*. Translation and introduction by Barbara Reynolds. London and Harmondsworth: Penguin, 1975.

Blount, Thomas. *Glossographia; or, A Dictionary Interpreting the Hard Words of Whatsoever Language, Now Used in Our Refined English Tongue*. N.p., 1656.

Borges, Jorge Luis, and Margarita Guerrero. *The Book of Imaginary Beings*. Translated by Norman Thomas di Giovanni. London: Vintage, 2002.

Cabell, James Branch. *The Witch-Woman: A Trilogy*. New York: Farrar and Straus, 1948.

Cherry, John, ed. *Mythical Beasts*. London: British Museum Press, 1995.

Dunsany, Lord. "How One Came, as was Foretold, to the City of Never." In *The Book of Wonder: A Chronicle of Little Adventures at the Edge of the World*, 28–30. London: William Heinemann, 1912.

Eddison, E.R. *The Worm Ouroboros* [1926]. Reprint, New York: Ballantine Books, 1975.

Gygax, Gary, and Arneson, Dave. *Dungeons & Dragons*. Lake Geneva, WI: TSR Hobbies, 1974.

Kisacky, Julia. *Magic in Boiardo and Ariosto*. New York: Peter Lang Publishing, 2000.

Quinet, Paul. *Merlin l'enchanteur*. 2 vols. Paris: Levy, 1860.

Rowling, J.K. *Fantastic Beasts and Where to Find Them. By Newt Scamander*. London: Bloomsbury, 2009.

HIPPOCAMP—*see* Animals, Monstrous

HOBGOBLIN—*see* Brownie; Goblin

HODAG—*see* Cryptid

HOMUNCULUS

Fig. 18 ***Homunculus*** **by Riley Swift**

In alchemy, literature, and cinema, a homunculus (Latin for "little human") is an artificially created person, usually but not always described as being tiny in stature. Although its nature differs somewhat from work to work, the homunculus is closely related in concept to such creatures as the **golem** and **Frankenstein's monster**. The creation of such a being, which takes place without the participation of God or woman, carries with it connotations of both blasphemy and homosexuality.

It is possible to trace the concept of the alchemical homunculus as far back as mystics Simon Magus (c. first century CE) and Zosimos of Panopolis (c. late third/ early fourth century CE). Our modern understanding of the monster, however, is derived primarily from a passage attributed to alchemist Aureolus Philippus Theophrastus Paracelsus Bombast von Hohenheim (1493–1541), commonly known simply as Paracelsus. In *Concerning the Nature of Things*, he argues that a man may "be begotten without the female body and the natural womb" (124). He goes on to provide instructions that involve putrefying human semen in a sealed flask with matter from a horse's womb for 40 days, or until it begins to live and move. At this point the creature will resemble a human being, although, rather confusingly, it has no body. After being kept warm for a suitable period and fed a concentration of human blood, the homunculus will become a tiny, living infant. Paracelsus adds that homunculi can grow into any number of marvelous and powerful creatures who "know all secret and hidden matters" (124).

Thomas Browne makes a passing reference to Paracelsus and the homunculus in *Religio Medici* (1642), but the first significant use of the creature in literature occurs in *The Tragedy of Faust, Part II* (1832) by Johann Wolfgang von Goethe. Here a Puckish character named Homunculus is brought to life by a former student of Faust's through a different alchemical process—within a glass phial heated in a furnace. Homunculus has a sense of humor and is capable of speech, flight, and mind-reading, but longs to break free of his glass prison—a goal he finally achieves by throwing himself into the sea.

W. Somerset Maugham based the protagonist of his melodramatic novel *The Magician* (1908), Oliver Haddo, on occultist Aleister Crowley (1875–1947). Haddo is determined to create homunculi, information about which Maugham apparently gleaned from an English translation of *The Life of Philippus Theophrastus, Bombast of Hohenheim, Known by the Name of Paracelsus* (1886) by Franz Hartmann. Maugham made particular use of one of the book's footnotes, which repeated a passage from a Viennese journal of freemansonry, *Die Sphinx*, describing the creation of ten homunculi in the eighteenth century by a Tyrolean count and an Italian Rosicrucian. Haddo succeeds in bringing a series of misshapen humanoid creatures to life but is murdered by an arch-enemy, who then proceeds to destroy the homunculi by setting fire to Haddo's mansion. (Crowley himself would write about what he called a homunculus in his didactic 1929 novel *Moonchild: A Prologue*, but its generation involves the impregnation of a woman by a being from another dimension.)

Lawrence Durrell acknowledged borrowing and expanding the footnote from Hartmann's biography of Paracelsus for a *jeu d'esprit* in his novel *Clea* (1960), the final volume of "The Alexandria Quartet." Incorporated into a letter written by the character Capodistria during the closing days of World War II, the passage follows the account in *Die Sphinx* closely. In Durrell's version, it is an Austrian Baron who produces the homunculi, which eventually are able to prophesy the future. As in the original account, a king homunculus escapes from his canister and attempts to liberate his queen before being recaptured. The experiment comes to a halt, however, when rumors that the Baron is a spy begin to circulate, leading him to poison the homunculi. The passage reflects Durrell's lifelong interest in human simulacra and can be read as a lighthearted commentary on the relationship between the writer and his characters.

Sven Delblanc combines myth, satire, metaphysical speculation, and the clichés of espionage fiction in *Homunculus: A Magic Tale* (1969). His protagonist Sebastian Verdén is an alcoholic chemistry teacher who struggles to assert his humanity against the forces of destruction by fashioning a homunculus, more or less according to the instructions of Paracelsus, in his bathtub. The unlikely experiment works, and Verdén is then delighted to discover that he is able to suckle the resulting creature—which he names Bechos—at his breast. A struggle involving the United States, the Soviet Union, and Sweden ensues as the powers attempt to obtain Sebastian's secret.

The most comprehensive treatment of the homunculus in literature is *The House of Doctor Dee* (1993) by Peter Ackroyd. This densely imagined novel consists of two storylines, one of which is set in the sixteenth century and concerns alchemist John Dee, a character based on the real-life John Dee (1527–1608). However, Ackroyd's character departs from what is known about the real Dee in several important respects. On his way to meet Paracelsus, the fictional Dee visits the scene of the death of Johann Georg Faust—the real-life figure on whom Goethe's Faust is based. This visit signals Dee's turn away from natural philosophy toward magic, and eventually leads to his subsequent attempts to create a homunculus in a kind of blasphemous mimicry of God's creation of man.

A second storyline in Ackroyd's novel concerns a resident of late twentieth-century London, Matthew Palmer, whose father leaves him a house said to have been Dee's. Palmer's sense of his own unreality leads him to believe that he may be the homunculus that Dee created centuries before, and there are hints throughout the novel that characters in the two storylines are sometimes dimly aware of each other. However, Palmer's dissociative state may be the result of sexual abuse by his father—that is, in a psychological sense he may represent the fulfillment of the Paracelsian dream of creating a human being without the involvement of a woman. The novel derives its power from the reader's sense that each of these interpretations is tenable.

There are very few instances of true homunculi in cinema, the only notable example being the six-part, black-and-white Duetsche Bioscope serial *Homunculus* (1916–17). Directed by Otto Rippert, photographed by Carl Hoffmann, and starring popular Danish actor Olaf Fønss, the work was the most popular serial in Germany during World War I. According to Martin Burgess Green and John C. Swan in *The Triumph of Pierrot: The Commedia dell'Arte and the Modern Imagination*, it even shaped fashion trends in Berlin. (While only the film's fourth episode and section of its fifth are preserved in European archives, a tinted Italian print derived from a shortened 1920 version was discovered in 2002 and exhibited the following year.)

Created by Dr Hansen and an assistant, Homunculus discovers his true identity—and his lack of a soul—only when he is an adult. Understanding why he is incapable of love, he proceeds to drive Hansen's daughter to her death and wreak vengeance on the world. Subsequent episodes chronicle the monster's world travels, his futile attempts at love, and his growing hatred for mankind. Although Homunculus develops a chemical capable of destroying the world, he decides instead to consolidate political power in order to sow havoc. In the final episode, Hansen creates a second homunculus and the two creatures engage in a struggle; the original emerges as the victor, only to be struck by a bolt of lightning.

While *Homunculus* is one of the most influential works of German Expressionist cinema, influencing the style of many of the better-known films that followed it, the serial and its vengeful, embittered protagonist owe as much to Mary Shelley's novel *Frankenstein* (1818) as they do to the tiny creatures described centuries before by Paracelsus. In addition, striking parallels between Homunculus's proclivities and those of German dictator Adolf Hitler have been drawn by later commentators.

Grove Koger

References and Suggested Reading

Ackroyd, Peter. *The House of Doctor Dee*. London: Hamilton, 1993.

Ferreira, Maria Aline Salgueiro Seabra. *I Am the Other: Literary Negotiations of Human Cloning*. Westport, CT: Praeger, 2005.

Gibson, Jeremy, and Julian Wolfreys. *Peter Ackroyd: The Ludic and Labyrinthine Text*. Houndmills, Basingstoke, England: Macmillan, 1999.

Lembert, Alexandra. *The Heritage of Hermes: Alchemy in Contemporary British Literature*. Berlin: Galda and Wilch Verlag, 2004.

Maugham, W. Somerset. *The Magician, a Novel; Together with a Fragment of Autobiography*. Garden City, NY: Doubleday, 1957.

Paracelsus. *The Hermetic and Alchemical Writings of Aureolus Philippus Theophrastus Bombast, of Hohenheim, called Paracelsus the Great*. Translated and edited by Arthur Edward Waite. Berkeley, CA: Shambhala, 1976.

Quaresima, Leonardo. "*Homunculus:* A Project for a Modern Cinema." In *A Second Life: German Cinema's First Decades*, edited by Thomas Elsaesser and Michael Wedel, 160–67. Amsterdam: Amsterdam University Press, 1996.

HOP-FROG

Hop-Frog is the protagonist of Edgar Allan Poe's short story "Hop-Frog; Or, the Eight Chained Ourangoutangs," first published in the 17 March 1849 edition of the weekly Boston-based "story paper," *The Flag of Our Union*. The story, like the more famous "The Cask of Amontillado" (1846), can be classified as a revenge tale in which an arrogant despot and his retinue receive an especially violent comeuppance from the eponymous court jester.

Within the story, Hop-Frog is both a **dwarf** and a cripple who serves as "fool" for an unnamed king and his seven ministers—all, like the king, "large, corpulent, oiley men, as well as inimitable jokers" (899). One evening, Hop-Frog—who has little tolerance for alcohol—is commanded to drink wine and then to assist the king and his ministers in deciding upon costumes for a masquerade. When the bewildered Hop-Frog hesitates and is upbraided by the king who orders him to drink more wine, the similarly dwarfish but nevertheless lovely Trippetta intercedes on Hop-Frog's behalf and has wine thrown in her face for her trouble. This callous treatment of Trippetta—with whom Hop-Frog is enamored—prompts him to propose the jest of "the Eight Chained Ourangoutangs," in which the king and his ministers will dress as orangutans and, chained together, rush into the masquerade en masse, scaring the attendees. The plan is gleefully adopted, but in the midst of the ensuing chaos after the men enter the party, the disguised men find themselves hoisted aloft by a chain descending from the ceiling. The revelers consider this a "well-contrived pleasantry" (906), until Hop-Frog sets the men on fire. He and his co-conspirator Trippetta then make good their escape, while "[t]he eight corpses swung in their chains, a fetid, blackened, hideous, and indistinguishable mass" (908).

Poe's achievement in the story is to create sympathy for the monstrous Hop-Frog, despite his horrific appearance and the especially violent form of retribution he visits upon his abusers. Hop-Frog, the reader learns, is the name conferred upon the dwarf because of a physical handicap preventing him from walking in the usual fashion. His movement, the reader is told, is "something between a leap and a wriggle" and only accomplished "with great pain and difficulty" (900). Like Trippetta, Hop-Frog originates from "some barbarous region ... that no person ever heard of" (900) and was "forcibly carried off" from his home and sent to the king as a prize. In contrast to the corpulent king and his oily ministers who are "afforded illimitable amusement" (900) by the handicaps, embarrassment, and abuse of others, Hop-Frog—whose grinding teeth signal his otherwise suppressed rage and malevolent intent—finds little humor in abusing others, which is highlighted in his ironic final pronouncement. Surveying the trapped king and his ministers prior to their immolation, he states that he now sees distinctly "a king who does not scruple to strike a defenceless [*sic*] girl, and his seven councilors who abet him in the outrage." He then concludes: "As for myself, I am simply Hop-Frog, the jester—and *this is my last jest*" (908).

There has been a good deal of speculation on Poe's inspiration for the story, as well as commentary on its themes. Satwik Dasgupta, citing both Kenneth Silverman and Arthur Hobson Quinn, notes two possible sources for the tale. The first is an article entitled "Chronicles of Froissart," printed in the *Broadway Journal* of 1 February 1845 (shortly before Poe purchased one-third interest in that periodical). It relates an incident that occurred at the court of Charles VI of France, during which a Norman squire suggested that King Charles and five others dress as **satyrs** with pitch and flax covering their clothes. Accidentally set aflame, the king barely escaped with his life by leaping into a pool of water. Another source may be a story titled "Frogere and the Emperor Paul," printed in the *New Monthly Magazine* in 1830 and signed "P." It is the story of a court jester exiled by the Emperor of Russia to Siberia. Tricked by a long ride in the countryside, the jester is ultimately returned to the Emperor's court and later becomes a participant in the death of the Emperor. In addition, one of the more popular "spectacles" of the New York stage during Poe's time was *Jocko! The Brazilian Ape*. John Bryant notes that the actor Joseph Marzetti "played the role of the ape so convincingly that he became identified with the role" (30), and Poe likely knew of Marzetti's performance. Another possible source is the character of **Quasimodo** in Victor Hugo's *The Hunchback of Notre-Dame* (1831).

The topic that has received the most attention in the body of critical literature addressing the story is its connection with American slavery. Hop-Frog and Trippetta, originating in a foreign land and brought in chains to serve the king, are essentially slaves who, in an ironic reversal, cast the king and his ministers as orangutans in chains—the ape and the African having a well-established connection in pseudo-scientific racist discourse (see Dayan; Kennedy and Weissberg).

While "Hop-Frog" does not seem to have inspired much in the way of literary homage, it has been adapted for film, TV, radio, and symphony. The earliest cinematic adaptation is the 1910 silent version directed by Frenchman Henry Desfontaines, and Eugene Cools composed a symphony in 1926 inspired by "Hop-Frog." Director Roger Corman's 1964 adaptation of Poe's "The Masque of the Red Death"

(1842) interpolates "Hop-Frog" in the form of "Hop-Toad," played by Skip Martin. Julie Taymor directed a short film in 1992 entitled *Fool's Fire*, based on "Hop-Frog," for American Public Broadcasting, and the story is included as part of musician Lou Reed's 2003 album, *The Raven*.

Jeffrey Andrew Weinstock

References and Suggested Reading

Bryant, John. "Poe's Ape of UnReason: Humor, Ritual, and Culture." *Nineteenth-Century Literature* 51, no. 1 (June 1996): 16–52.

Dasgupta, Sawik. "The Anthropocentric Vision: Aesthetics of Effect and Terror in Poe's 'Hop-Frog'." *Journal of Philosophy: A Cross Disciplinary Inquiry* 6, no. 15 (Spring 2011): 43–55.

Dayan, Joan. "Amorous Bondage: Poe, Ladies, and Slaves." In *The American Face of Edgar Allan Poe*, edited by Shawn Rosenheim and Stephen Rachman, 179–209. Baltimore: The Johns Hopkins University Press, 1995.

Kennedy, J. Gerald, and Liliane Weissberg, eds. *Romancing the Shadow: Poe and Race*. Oxford: Oxford University Press, 2001.

Poe, Edgar Allan. "Hop-Frog." In *Poe: Poetry, Tales, and Selected Essays*, 899–908. New York: Library of America, 1996.

HORLA, THE

The title character of the 1887 short story "Le Horla" by French author Guy de Maupassant (1850–93) is described by the story's narrator as an invisible, **vampire**-like being that subsists not only on milk and water but also on the life force of its victim. The Horla, whose name probably translates as "out there" (Showers 147), may be a new species of being on Earth, possibly even a species from beyond Earth, and either way is an entity superior to mankind, capable of dominating him (see **Extraterrestrial**). As the narrator's sanity is frequently in question, de Maupassant left open the possibility that the Horla is merely a symptom of the man's increasingly delusional state. This ambiguity contributes to the particularly disturbing horror the creature evokes in both the narrator and the reader.

The story's events occur over approximately four months, as told in the form of the anonymous narrator's journal. Watching boats sailing by on the Seine, the narrator salutes a grand Brazilian vessel. Shortly thereafter he falls ill. Soon, in an increasingly nervous and alienated state of mind, he experiences sleep paralysis and nightmares, imagining that someone is kneeling on his chest and strangling him. He finds his water and milk gone though he had not drunk them, and seriously questions his own sanity. But after seeing a rose stalk bend and break as if plucked by an unseen hand, he believes "that there exists close to me an invisible being that lives on milk and water, that can touch objects, take them and change their places ... although it is imperceptible to our senses" (461).

His fears seem confirmed when he reads of "an epidemic of madness" in São Paulo, Brazil (466). The inhabitants are deserting their villages, pursued by "invisible, though tangible, beings, a species of vampires, which feed on their life while they are asleep" (466). Remembering the Brazilian ship he had greeted before falling ill, the narrator is now convinced that he had inadvertently summoned one such creature to his home. Rebelling against its triumphant taunting, he determines to kill it. Thinking he has trapped the Horla in his bedroom, the narrator burns down his own house, forgetting to warn his servants, several of whom die in the conflagration. Suddenly seized by crushing doubt that the Horla really is dead, the narrator concludes: "Then—I suppose I must kill *myself*!" (472).

The earliest known story to feature an invisible, malevolent entity is Fitz-James

O'Brien's "What Was It?" (1859), which may have influenced de Maupassant's Horla; "The Horla" in turn probably influenced Ambrose Bierce's "**The Damned Thing**" (1893; Showers 147–8). Another such creature appears in M.R. James's "Oh, Whistle, and I'll Come to You, My Lad" (1904): it remains unseen until covered with a sheet. "The Horla" also greatly impressed H.P. Lovecraft (1890–1937), who considered the story a masterpiece of terror (Lovecraft 49; see **Lovecraft, Monsters In**). Manly Wade Wellman incorporated "The Horla" into several of his works, including "The Theater Upstairs" (1936). In Jonathan Straud's *Bartimaeus* fantasy series (2003–2005), horlas appear as shadowy spirits causing madness in humans.

The dozens of cinematic adaptations of "The Horla" include *Zlatcha Notch* ("The Terrible Night," Evgueni Bauer, 1914) and *Para Gnedych* ("Diary of a Madman," Yakov Protazanov, 1915). *Diary of a Madman* (Reginald Le Borg, 1963), a relatively loose adaptation starring Vincent Price, features an invisible being called a "horla" that controls its victims, who think they are going mad. The many shorter film versions include *Le Horla* (Jean-Daniel Pollet, 1966), *El Horla* (Antonio Castro, 1969), and *Le Horla* (Boris Labourguigne, 2009). The story was also adapted for a 1962 Québécois television series (*Le Horla*, Guy Hoffmann). Production company Les Films Du Horla, created in 1987 to make documentaries about the real and the unreal, was inspired by de Maupassant's story. On the audio side, Peter Lorre narrated the story for his 1947 radio series *Mystery in the Air* (episode 3; available in MP3 format), and The Box, a new wave band from Montreal, released a 2009 album "d'apres Le Horla De Maupassant," the tracks of which correlate to different episodes within the story.

D. Felton

References and Suggested Reading

Lovecraft, Howard Phillips. *Supernatural Horror in Literature* [1927]. Reprint New York: Dover Publications, Inc., 1973.

Maupassant, Guy de. "The Horla." In *Great Tales of Terror and the Supernatural*, edited by Herbert A. Wise and Phyllis Fraser, 447–72. New York: The Modern Library, 1944.

Showers, Brian J. "The Horla." In *Encyclopedia of the Vampire: The Living Dead in Myth, Legend, and Popular Culture*, edited by S.T. Joshi, 146–8. Santa Barbara: Greenwood, 2011.

HOUYHNHNMS—*see* Swift, Jonathan, Monsters in (*Gulliver*)

HUNCHBACK OF NOTRE DAME—*see* Quasimodo

HUORN—*see* Tolkien, Monsters In

HYDE, EDWARD

Edward Hyde is the immoral **doppelganger** of Dr Henry Jekyll in the novella *The Strange Case of Dr Jekyll and Mr Hyde*, written by Robert Louis Stevenson and published in 1886. Hyde serves as a character of mystery and uncertainty within the original story. Often described as a person of small size who unsettles those who look upon him, Hyde has an unclear relationship with Jekyll throughout most of the story that the characters, particularly Jekyll's lawyer, Utterson, find alarming. Utterson learns of Hyde from his friend, Enfield, who witnesses Hyde trample a little girl with no apparent remorse. Upon meeting Hyde, Utterson becomes determined to figure out who he is. Later, following Hyde's impulsive killing of Sir Danvers Carew, he disappears, only subsequently to be discovered by Utterson dead in Jekyll's laboratory after swallowing cyanide. The major plot twist is revealed within the chapter "Dr Lanyon's Narrative," in which Lanyon witnesses the transformation of Hyde into Jekyll. In the final chapter, Jekyll confesses that Hyde is the product of his experimentation and attempt to divide the dual moral nature of man.

The character of Hyde was inspired by Deacon William Brody of Scotland (1741–88) who was an exemplary citizen by day and burgled many upper-class homes by night. Hyde was also born out of a series of dreams that Stevenson experienced, which drove him quickly to write the first draft within a few days (Stevenson and Linehan). Hyde's persistence as an influential monster stems from Stevenson's well-crafted mystery and the narrative tension between the respectable Jekyll and notorious Hyde in Victorian London.

The first serious dramatic adaptation of Stevenson's novel appears to have been the Boston stage play, *Dr Jekyll and Mr Hyde*, mounted in 1887. It starred English actor Richard Mansfield (1857–1907), who continued to play the roles of both Jekyll and Hyde until his death in 1907. Evidence also indicates that several short films based around the novella were made in the 1900s, although no actual films survive. The first feature-length production, the silent *Dr Jekyll and Mr Hyde* directed by John S. Robertson and starring John Barrymore (1882–1942), was released in 1920 and more than 60 cinematic and televisual adaptations have followed. Retellings of the story, however, have largely taken their lead from the early dramatic adaptations that introduced a love interest for Dr Jekyll, and sometimes a sexual partner for Hyde. Many of these adaptations take for granted that the audience knows Jekyll is Hyde, which also speaks to the narrative's popularity. Therefore, the dramatic emphasis switches from the relationship between Jekyll and Hyde to a focus on how far Hyde will go before Jekyll stops him—assuming he can. In later adaptations, Hyde's villainy is often accentuated by an increased number of murders and sexual violence. Adaptations that do focus on the revelation of the Jekyll/Hyde persona do so largely by renaming the narrative, as seen in such films as *Fight Club* (David Fincher, 1999) and *Secret Window* (David Koepp, 2004).

Hyde's influence also extended into comics with the creation of Batman's enemy, Two-Face, whose first appearance in *Detective Comics* #66 in 1942 directly invokes Dr Jekyll and Mr Hyde. A year later, the Gilberton Company adapted the novella into comic form for *Classics Comics* #13. Among the most lasting and significant Hyde-inspired creations has been the Incredible Hulk from Marvel Comics. Since *The Incredible Hulk* #1 in 1962, the Bruce Banner/Hulk dynamic has served as an ongoing narrative of a Hyde-like character that has changed contemporary perspectives of Hyde. Films featuring Hyde such as *The League of Extraordinary Gentlemen* (Stephen Norrington, 2003), which rather bizarrely turns Hyde into a hero, and *Van Helsing* (Stephen Sommers, 2004) feature Hyde characters that more physically resemble the Hulk than the original Hyde.

"Jekyll and Hyde" has also come to serve as cultural shorthand for describing a split personality, often with psychopathic overtones. Real-world serial killers such as Jeffrey Dahmer (1960–94) and Ted Bundy (1946–89), as well as fictional serial killers such as **Hannibal Lecter** in the series of horror novels by Thomas Harris (1940–) and Dexter Morgan in the works by Jeff Lindsay (born Jeffry P. Freundlich, 1952–), are often described in a way eliciting comparisons to Jekyll and Hyde, even when they are not explicitly invoked.

Lance Eaton

References and Suggested Reading

McNally, Raymond T., and Radu Florescu. *In Search of Dr Jekyll & Mr Hyde*. London: Robson, 2001.

Rose, Brian A. *Jekyll and Hyde Adapted: Dramatizations of Cultural Anxiety.* Westport, CT: Greenwood Press, 1996.

Stevenson, Robert Louis. *The Strange Case of Dr Jekyll and Mr Hyde: An Authoritative Text, Backgrounds and Contexts, Performance Adaptations, Criticism,* edited by Katherine Linehan. New York: Norton, 2003.

Tithecott, Richard. *Of Men and Monsters: Jeffrey Dahmer and the Construction of the Serial Killer.* Madison: University of Wisconsin Press, 1997.

HYDRA

Originating in classical mythology, the Hydra was a multi-headed snaky monster that lived in the swamp of Lerna in southern Greece. As Lerna was a region of many springs and lakes, the water-dwelling Hydra took her name from the Greek root for water, *hydr-*. The Hydra appeared mainly in the myth of the Greek hero Heracles (Hercules, to the Romans) but has lived on in the popular imagination throughout the centuries, particularly as a symbol for uniquely difficult-to-overcome problems.

According to the poet Hesiod in his *Theogony* (c. 700 BCE), the "baneful" Hydra was the offspring of the monsters Echidna and **Typhoeus**, making her the sibling of **Cerberus** and the **Chimera**. The goddess Hera, who bore a longstanding grudge against Heracles, nourished the Hydra herself, intending the creature as a future threat to the hero (313–14). The Hydra ravaged the countryside around Lerna, destroying crops and livestock. Some ancient authors simply refer to the Hydra as "many-headed," and writers who assigned a specific number of heads did not agree: estimates ranged from one to at least one hundred. But the most popular tradition in antiquity gave the Hydra an immense body with nine heads, eight of which were mortal; the middle head was immortal. When any of the eight heads

Fig. 19 ***Hydra*** **by Scott Ogden**

was destroyed, two new heads sprang up in its place. The Roman author Hyginus (first century BCE or later) adds that the Hydra's breath was so poisonous that the lingering vapor killed anyone who came across her tracks, even if she was asleep (*Fabulae* 30).

The most complete version of Heracles's encounter with the Hydra appears in pseudo-Apollodorus (*Bibliotheca* 2.5.2, date uncertain, but most likely first century CE). Heracles had been assigned twelve dangerous Labors to atone for killing his wife and children in a fit of madness induced by Hera. His first Labor was to kill the Nemean Lion, a huge feline with invulnerable skin. Heracles had to strangle the beast with his bare hands. His second Labor was to rid Lerna of the Hydra. Arriving there with his nephew Iolaüs, Heracles discovered the

Hydra in its den by the swamp. He forced the creature to come out by shooting fiery arrows at it. But Heracles was unable to accomplish anything by smiting the Hydra's heads with his main weapon, a club, since when one head was smashed, two sprang up in its place. Complicating the problem, a huge crab that also lived in the swamp came to help the Hydra by biting Heracles's foot. He was able to kill the crab, but the Hydra was starting to overcome him until he called to Iolaüs for help. The young man set fire to a piece of wood and whenever Heracles crushed one of the Hydra's heads, Iolaüs burned the stump. This cauterization prevented new heads from sprouting. Heracles then chopped off the one immortal head and buried it under a huge rock. Various ancient authors say that Hera put the Crab (*Cancer*) among the constellations for its bravery, next to the Nemean Lion (*Leo*); she put the constellation Hydra nearby. A minor mythological tradition holds that after the Hydra was destroyed, her shade went to Hades to help guard the Underworld, keeping company with Cerberus.

This was not the last of the Hydra, however. Heracles had slit open the Hydra's body and dipped his arrows in the creature's poison. Thus, any wounds Heracles inflicted with his arrows were utterly incurable. In a battle against hostile **centaurs**, Heracles slew many of them with these poisoned arrows. Later, as many ancient authors tell us, the Hydra's poison was responsible for the death of Heracles himself. Heracles and his new wife, Deianeira, were traveling home when they came to a wide river. The centaur Nessus offered them passage on his back; taking Deianeira across first, he then tried to rape her. Hearing her cries, Heracles shot Nessus with one of his arrows. As Nessus was dying, he exhorted Deianeira to take some of his blood to use as a love potion if Heracles's affections ever strayed. The girl believed the treacherous centaur and not long after, when Heracles indeed fell in love with another woman, Deianeira tried to regain his love by sending him a tunic smeared with Nessus's blood. As soon as the tunic touched Heracles's skin, the poisoned blood began to burn like acid and, desperate to die, he threw himself on a pyre. When Deianeira realized the true nature of the "love potion," she killed herself.

A number of later Greek and Roman writers presented rationalizing versions of the Hydra. For example, the heads that renewed themselves were interpreted as actually referring to the marshes of Lerna, because when anyone tried to drain the marshes, the water seeped back. The deadly poisonous breath of the Hydra was really the vaporous swamp miasma. In another interpretation, Lernus was a king and Hydra the name of his capital city. Lernus had as bodyguard a troop of 50 archers, and whenever one of them was killed, another immediately replaced him (Grimal 17).

The Hydra herself does not appear prominently as a specific monster in literature of the medieval and Renaissance periods but, along with the many other serpentine and multi-headed monsters of Greek myth, as well as beasts from the Bible (such as that in Revelation 13:1; see **Bible, Monsters In The**), was essentially a type of **dragon**. This interpretation of the Hydra continued into the modern period as, for example, in the 1963 film *Jason and the Argonauts* (Don Chaffey). The film depicts the dragon guarding the Golden Fleece as a seven-headed hydra, which Jason kills with a sword thrust to its heart (no head re-growth involved). Heracles regains his role as the Hydra's opponent in Disney's *Hercules* (Ron Clements and John Musker, 1997). Here, however, the Hydra starts out with only one head, but when the hero cuts that one off, *three* new heads spring up in its place. This continues until the monster has dozens of heads. Hercules finally kills the Hydra by crushing it with a rockslide. In the second book of Rick Riordan's "Percy Jackson and the Olympians" series, *Sea of Monsters* (2006), Percy and his friends face and defeat an acid-spewing Hydra; in the film adaptation of the Percy Jackson series, though, a fire-breathing Hydra appears in the first installment, *The Lightning Thief* (Chris Columbus, 2010).

The Hydra seems to have had a stronger presence in art than in literature across the centuries. Illustrations of the Labors of Heracles, including his encounter with the Hydra, were common in Greek vase paintings from the seventh century BCE on, particularly in southern Greece (Venit 100–101) where the Hydra was regularly depicted with nine heads. Greek myth was a popular subject for artists in the Renaissance, a number of whom saw the conflicts between Greek heroes and monsters as representing the battle of good versus evil, or of civilizing forces taming uncivilized nature. Thus, Heracles and the Hydra provided subject matter for Antonio del Pollaiolo (1475) and Guido Reni (1620), among others. Nineteenth-century French Romantic/Symbolist artist Gustave Moreau employed a more specific, contemporary political allegory in his *Hercules and the Lernaean Hydra* (1869–76). Moreau presents a youthful Hercules, club in hand, confronting a seven-headed Hydra, while the Hydra's victims lie strewn about the swampy landscape. Moreau associated Hercules, whom he regarded as a civilizing influence, with French patriotism; his painting likely symbolized the struggle between France, personified by Hercules, and the neighboring Prussians, represented as the multi-headed monster (Lacambre 136–42). Other examples of the Hydra's popularity in art include a monumental bronze statue of Hercules and the Hydra by Danish Symbolist artist Rudoph Tegner (1818) that stands on the coast of Helsingør, north of Copenhagen. American artist John Singer Sargent produced a large mural, *Hercules and the Hydra* (1922), based on the constellation Hercules.

The Hydra appears in a number of other media as well. In science, the creature gives its name to a genus of tube-shaped freshwater animal having a mouth surrounded by one to twelve thin tentacles. The Hydra also features in a variety of fantasy-based video games, including *Age of Mythology*. The monster appears as a character in various songs by different bands, as in the compilation album "Teeth of the Hydra" (1989) by the heavy metal rock band Omen; the title song describes a seven-headed hydra guarding the Golden Fleece, as in Chaffey's film.

The peculiar difficulty in killing the Hydra—that the monster keeps growing new heads—led to an expression in ancient Greek, *hydran temnein*, "to cut off a hydra," said of undertakings that were considered hopeless. The word "hydra" in modern English usage retains a similar meaning, referring to any persistent dilemma that does not have an easy solution.

D. Felton

References and Suggested Reading

Grimal, Pierre. *The Dictionary of Classical Mythology.* Translated by A.R. Maxwell-Hyslop. Oxford: Blackwell, 1996.

Lacambre, Geneviève. *Gustave Moreau: Between Epic and Dream.* Chicago: The Art Institute of Chicago, 1999.

Venit, Marjorie Susan. "Herakles and the Hydra in Athens in the First Half of the Sixth Century BC." *Hesperia* 58, no. 1 (1989): 99–113.

IFRIT—*see* Div; Djinn and Genie; Koran, Monsters In The

IGNEUM—*see* Demon

IKTOMI—*see* Shapeshifter

IMP

From the Old English word for a sapling or young tree, imps are small creatures, ugly in appearance and mischievous by nature. Often confused with other supernatural beings such as **goblins** or **elves**, imps are usually described by name as companions or offspring of the **Devil** or Satan, as familiars of **witches**, or as small devils or **demons** who play tricks and harass humankind. Imps can be bound to serve an individual or to inhabit an object, usually a bottle.

The word imp, as used to describe a particular creature, appeared in print as early as 1584, in Reginald Scot's *The Discoverie of Witchcraft*, a work that attempts to debunk the existence of witches and the practice of magic. Imps are also discussed in seventeenth-century treatises insisting on the reality of witchcraft and the supernatural. In *An Antidote Against Atheism* (1652), the British poet and philosopher Henry More writes of witches conversing with imps; they also appear as witches' familiars in British philosopher Joseph Glanvill's *Some philosophical considerations touching the being of witches and witchcraft* (1667) and the anonymous *A Pleasant Treatise of Witches* (attributed to "A, pen near the covent of Eluthery," 1673). In *Wonders of the Invisible World* (1693), American minister Cotton Mather's account of the Salem witch trials, the author describes imps as feeding from secret teats on witches' bodies—so-called witches' marks—and even sinking ships at the behest of their masters.

Later writers expanded upon the portrayal of imps as tempters and mischief-makers. Edgar Allan Poe's "The Imp of the Perverse" (1845) explores and explains the metaphorical imp inside human beings that causes us to act rashly and often self-destructively; in the narrator's case, the imp provokes an unsought confession of a murder. Leo Tolstoy's 1886 short story, translated as "The Imp and the Crust," recounts an imp's ultimately successful efforts to win a poor man's soul for the Devil. In "The Bottle Imp" (1891) by Robert Louis Stevenson, the imp grants wishes from inside a cursed bottle. The story's two central characters, Keawe and Kokua, eventually overcome the curse through self-sacrifice. "The Bottle Imp" was made into a 1917 silent film directed by Marshall Neilan, as well as a 1909 short film called *The Imp of the Bottle* produced by the inventor Thomas Alva Edison's Edison Manufacturing Company. Edison's company made at least two other short films featuring imps, including *Pluto and the Imp* (1900), in which an imp serves the lord of the Underworld, and *Lovers and the Imp* (1903), with the creature causing trouble for a courting couple.

Across the twentieth and into the twenty-first centuries, literary and filmic imps take on a variety of narrative roles, often in what could be called exploitation films. In Roger Corman's *The Undead* (1957), actor Billy Barty plays an imp who can change into a bat. This film may be best known today as the subject of a 1997 episode of the cult television program *Mystery Science Theater 3000* (created by Joel Hodgson, the program aired from 1988 to 1999). In the 1988 B-movie, *Sorority Babes in the Slimeball Bowl-O-Rama* (David DeCoteau), a murderous imp is accidentally released from the trophy to which he has been magically bound. *Imp of Satan*, a 2008 underground short horror satire with gay themes, directed by Flynn Witmeyer, features a killer imp terrorizing a young apartment dweller. A 1978 episode of the television series *The Man from Atlantis* depicts an imp wreaking havoc in an underwater research station ("Imp," directed by Shimon Wincelberg; season 2, episode 11); and in Jesse Bullington's novel *The Enterprise of Death* (2011), the alchemist

Paracelsus tells of exorcizing an imp from the pommel of a sword. Imp is also an epithet used to describe the clever but short-statured Tyrion Lannister in George R.R. Martin's "Song of Ice and Fire" series of novels (1996–2011), as well as the related television series, *Game of Thrones* (created by David Benioff and D.B. Weiss, 2011).

Imps show up as mischief-makers in a number of books and films for children, such as Allan Baillie's *Imp* (2002)—part of the "Aussie Bites" collection of books for young readers—in which an Australian child encounters an imp in his new home. Lawrence Yep's *The Imp that Ate My Homework* (2000) depicts a boy and his grandfather battling a troublemaking green imp in Chinatown. *The Lincoln Imp* (2009), by British author Sue Hampton, is a children's book based on folktales surrounding a stone imp that resides in England's Lincoln Cathedral. In the illustrated storybook *Perry the Imp* (Will and Nicholas, 1956), an imp causes trouble in the town of Dopple, and in *Fia and the Imp* (Lauren Mills and Dennis Nolan, 2002), the titular creature haunts a woodland. *Dorrie and the Witch's Imp* (Patricia Coombs, 1975) gently employs the theme of imp as witch's familiar. Children's films that feature imps include *Jack the **Giant** Killer* (Nathan Juran, 1962) and the Disney animated movie *Hercules* (Ron Clements and Jon Musker, 1997), in which the god Hades has an imp as a sidekick. In the animated television program *She-Ra: Princess of Power* (created by Lou Scheimer, 1985–87), Imp is the companion or familiar of the villain Hordak. The British animated television series *The Imp* (created by Andy Fielding, 2006) features the tagline "Short, Cute, Evil" and humorously follows an imp's attempts to spread his wickedness throughout the world.

Regina Hansen

References and Suggested Reading

Baskin, Leonard. *Imps, Demons, Hobgoblins, Witches, Fairies and Elves.* New York: Pantheon Books, 1984.

Kesson, H.J. *The Legend of the Lincoln Imp.* Lincoln: J.W. Ruddock, 1948.

Mather, Cotton. *Wonders of the Invisible World: Being an Account of the Trials of Several Witches Lately Executed in New England* [1693]. Reprint, Nashville, TN: General Books, LLC, 2009.

INCUBUS/SUCCUBUS

Incubi (masculine) and succubi (feminine) are demonic beings (see **Demon**) that seek sexual union with humans of the opposite sex. The words "incubus" and "succubus," from Latin, literally mean "one who lies on" and "one who lies under" respectively. In most traditions, the goal is to generate either demon children or humans with warped natures of some sort. For the purposes of this entry, this will exclude sexual liaisons with primary gods, which often result in demigod children (like Heracles). It is necessary, however, to recognize that in many traditions the exact dividing line between primary gods and the lesser figures that populate the supernatural world is hazy.

Significant characters in mythology are often given a divine parent, partly to explain why they are able to do things of which regular mortals are incapable. Not all come from primary deities, however, and morally ambiguous characters are all the more likely to come from lesser spiritual entities or even demons. So, for example, Gilgamesh's father was a supernatural being named Lilu, who was a lower-level god whose role was to impregnate human women. He was, for all appearances, the Sumerian equivalent of an incubus (Irdu lili was another). There were also Sumerian succubus-like equivalents: Lilitu and Ardit lili ("lil" means "air, wind"). In Genesis 6, the Nephilim (usually translated as "**giants**") were similarly fathered by "the sons of God" (called the "watchers" in later Jewish literature). The difference lies in that, whereas Gilgamesh's engendering was approved by the Sumerian deities, the actions of "the sons of God" met with divine disapproval and may have been the root cause of the flood.

Excepting the Virgin Mary, Christian and Jewish thought would consider all such human–supernatural unions inappropriate and assign them to the demonic world. Medieval Christians came to call all children of such unions "cambions." Famous cambions from fiction and legend include **Caliban** from Shakespeare's *The Tempest* (1610–11) and Merlin of Arthurian legend, who is described as the offspring of a nun seduced by an incubus who dwells between the Earth and the Moon in Geoffrey of Monmouth's *History of Kings* (c. 1136).

Cambions must, of course, come from the union of incubi with human women, since succubi are presumably unable to have human children. Catholic theology from the time of Thomas Aquinas (1225–74) did not believe that demon seed could impregnate human women either, so a double process was required in which a succubus collected semen from a human male, which was then used to impregnate a human female. Aquinas believed that the demons were hermaphroditic (see **Hermaphrodite**), so that the same demon could perform both functions. Others came to disagree, asserting (as does the *Malleus Maleficarum* [1436]) that the demonic world was gendered, in which case two demons and some sort of transfer method was required to complete the transaction. The process somehow damaged the human male contribution such that the resulting children were marred—physically or spiritually—thus finding reasons in a single explanation for the existence of both birth defects and nasty people.

The Jewish community had the equivalent of incubi and succubi, but not cambions. Rather, sex with demons, male or female, resulted in demon children. The most famous succubus was **Lilith**, queen of demons. She later came to be viewed as the first wife of Adam, but in earlier traditions she functions more like a second wife. After their expulsion from Eden, Adam and Eve separated for 130 years, during which time both were visited by supernatural lovers—Adam by Lilith (Talmud Tract Erubin 18b) and Eve by unnamed incubi. Numerous demon children ensued. The classes of sexual demons are called "lilin" and "liliot" (plural forms, male and female respectively). Besides Lilith, Samael (the **Devil**) has three other succubus wives: Naamah, Agrat bat Mahlat, and Eisheth Zenunim. Agrat had mated with King David and produced Ashmodai (Asmodeus in Greek), prince of demons, who is portrayed trying to continue the family tradition in the book of Tobit (unsuccessfully, as it turns out).

Liliths (collectively), while they usually mate with humans at night, through dreams, nocturnal emissions, or masturbation, may also collect semen from marital intercourse, if the couple does not elevate it above base desires (and with the lights out). In the Latin Vulgate translation of Isaiah, the single Biblical occurrence of the word "Lilith" is translated "**Lamia**," although the concept of Lamia has its own history in Greek thought.

Cultural Variations

In Greek myth, Lamia had been a Libyan queen and paramour of Zeus. Jealous Hera compelled her to kill and eat her own children so she, driven mad, set out to murder other women's children (Horace, *Ars Poetica* l.340; c. 18 BCE). In time her name came to refer to a class of **vampire**-like females who, similar to the child-eating **empousa** of Greek mythology, devoured young men, sexually and literally (Philostratus, *Apollonius* 4.25; 217–38 CE). Since Lilith also had a reputation for killing babies, making the connection between the two did not seem that far-fetched. Medieval representations of Lamia in art often provided them with a snake's torso (sometimes with two tails). This may have influenced the appearance of female-headed serpents in many Renaissance paintings of the temptation of Adam and Eve, although there are also reasons to connect the serpent with Lilith.

In Islam, the *qarîn* is a sort of demonic alter ego that accompanies each person through life. These entities are part of the pre-Islamic tradition and are mentioned in the **Koran**, although nothing there refers to their sexual roles. Tradition has it, however, that men get a qarîna (feminine) and women a qarîn (masculine) that comes into being at, or soon after, the person's birth. Part of this spirit companion's role is sexual, with the resulting coupling taking place in dreams. Such unions may result in children, presumably demonic. They are jealous of their human's natural spouse, and the male variety is jealous of its partner's children (and will sometimes kill them). A very powerful qarîna may prevent her man from marrying (See **Koran, Monsters In The**).

Naturalist Explanations

In many ways, attempts to explain the phenomena as natural fundamentally miss the religious dynamic. Belief in evil, personified in supernatural villains, is a part of most religious systems. People tend to be protective of their sexuality, so having a class of supernatural sexual assailants seems to be a natural development. Particularly where sexuality is seen as especially sinful, such as in a monastic community, some explanation may be needed for such things as erotic dreams and nocturnal orgasms.

In the Chiloé province of Chile, an incubus-like creature called a "trauco" magically seduces women (sometimes in their sleep, sometimes not). Since the trauco's lure cannot be resisted, women are held blameless if he impregnates them. Other cultures have similar stories. As in the case of the trauco, it can be convenient in some societies to have a ready-made explanation for unexpected pregnancies, particularly among unmarried women. The victims of incubi in most cultures may not even be aware that they have been attacked, or not until it is too late, so they cannot usually be blamed (although the inquisition did just that in the case of "**witches**" who they felt were willing participants). This could function as an easy explanation for sleep-rape or for girls unwilling to identify their lovers. In some cases, the lover or rapist could have sufficient social standing, so that prosecution was undesirable to the community leaders. In any case, the demons could disguise themselves as real people, such that an apparent malefactor could be justifiably regarded as innocent.

A popular explanation is to associate these attacks with sleep paralysis. Sleep paralysis is usually characterized by the sense of a presence, a feeling of weight on the chest (with difficulty breathing), and panic. It is sometimes accompanied by a vision/hallucination of the assailant. As the name implies, it is associated with waking from a light sleep. However, other than the fact that women usually perceive their attackers as male, there is rarely any sexual component, and it may be argued that such sexual experiences are something other than sleep paralysis, which is more likely related "mares" in Germanic folklore (and other names elsewhere). Supernatural sexual assault is *always* perceived as sexual (when it is perceived at all). This is not to argue that it defies psychological explanation, just that sleep paralysis is not the correct one.

Fiction

In 1492, Angelo Poliziano published his Latin poem, *Lamia*, but it was John Keats's poem of the same name (1819) that inspired artists and writers of the Romantic era. The story attempts to redeem the main character of the Greek myth (Philostratus's version) described above. It was followed by Honoré de Balzac's short story, "The Succubus" (1837), about the 1271 trial of a succubus disguised as a woman. Dante Gabriel Raphael popularized Lilith in two poems (*Lilith*, 1868, and *Eden's bower*, 1869). *Lilith* was accompanied by a painting. Various academic-style painters, such as John Collier (1850–1934), attempted to portray the heroine of Keats's *Lamia*. 1899 brought an opera by August Enna (libretto by Helge Rode), based on the Greek myth, and reused the now-popular title.

In the twentieth century, a significant number of tales use the terms "incubus" or "succubus" without reference to the traditional meaning. In these stories, such a character is likely simply to be a demonic character or a vampire (as in Marion Crawford's short story, "For the Blood is the Life" [1905]). Exceptions include the following: British poet Arthur Symons makes Lilith the mother of Lamia in "The Avenging Spirit" (1920). In his 1962 short story, "The Likeness of Julie," Richard Matheson follows Balzac in having his succubus character take on flesh in the seduction of a teenage boy. Of course, human–devil cross-breeding is the theme of Ira Levin's *Rosemary's Baby* (1967) (and *Son of Rosemary* in 1997), provided we consider the Devil an incubus. Poul Anderson's novel, *Operation Chaos* (1971), has a hermaphroditic sex demon try to seduce both members of a pair of newlyweds. In Kenneth Johnson's *The Succubus* (1979), a man suffers under the wiles of Lilith, and Piers Anthony populates Hell with succubi (*For Love of Evil*, 1988). A witch calls on a succubus to persuade the hero to do her bidding in Orson Scott Card's *Treasure Box* (1996). Richelle Mead regales us with a series of books (six so far) in which an ordinary girl seems to have a side-job working as a succubus (complete with demonic wings and tail), beginning with *Succubus Blues* (2007). Lacey Reah introduces us to a bisexual succubus in *Fireflies* (2011), and Jackie Kessler's "Hell on Earth" series (2007–present) currently has five books (so far) about a succubus leaving her career in Hell for a more upright job as an exotic dancer.

In cinema, *Rosemary's Baby* (above) became a film directed by Roman Polanski in 1968, but before that, in 1966, *Incubus* (Leslie Stevens) gave us the story of a succubus who falls in love and turns to God. In *Devil's Nightmare* (Jean Brismée, 1971), lost tourists are seduced and killed by a succubus. 2006 brought *Succubus: The Demon* (Sami Haavisto), in which a man tries to raise his deceased wife and gets a succubus instead. *Jennifer's Body* (Karyn Kusama, 2009) vaguely recalls Matheson's "The Likeness of Julie," in which a succubus-cheerleader goes on a boyfriend killing spree.

There are two orchestral symphonic poems related to succubi, one by Edward MacDowell ("Lamia," Op. 29, 1888) and the other by Frederick Zeck ("Lamia," 1926). There is also a popular goth/pagan band named Inkubus Sukkubus (formed in 1989), and a rock band just named Incubus (formed in 1991).

Alan Humm

References and Suggested Reading

Boyarin, Daniel. *Carnal Israel: Reading Sex in Talmudic Culture*. Berkeley: University of California Press, 1993.

Graves, Robert. *Greek Myths*. London: Penguin, 1955.

Lawson, John C. *Modern Greek Folklore and Ancient Greek Religion: A Study in Survivals.* New York: New York University Books, 1964.

Melton, Gordon J. *The Vampire Book: The Encyclopedia of the Undead.* Detroit: Visible Ink Press, 1999.

Roth, John E. *American Elves: An Encyclopedia of Little People from the Lore of 380 Ethnic Groups of the Western Hemisphere.* Jefferson, NC: McFarland, 1997.

Russell, Jeffrey B. *Lucifer: The Devil in the Middle Ages.* Ithaca, NY: Cornell University Press, 1984.

Stephens, Walter. *Demon Lovers.* Chicago: The University of Chicago Press, 2002.

Zwemer, Samuel M. *Studies in Popular Islam: Collection of Papers Dealing with the Superstitions and Beliefs of the Common People.* London: Sheldon Press, 1939.

INFERI—*see* Harry Potter, Monsters In

INVISIBLE MAN, THE

A popular concept in modern literature and film most readily associated with the science fiction of author H.G. Wells, the invisible man has classical origins. In Book 2 of the *Republic* (360 BCE), Plato refers to the mythical Ring of Gyges that enables its holder to become invisible at will in order to examine how invisibility might loosen the moral responsibility of the subject. Modern literature and film often links the attainment of invisibility to the creation of an unethical monstrosity, although writers and filmmakers have explored other ramifications of invisibility. The invisible man provides a narrative trope for exploring various forms of otherness (notably, class and racial) and the notion of corporeal invisibility encapsulates the fears, preoccupations, and anonymity of modernity.

The most famous invisible man appears in Wells's *The Invisible Man: A Grotesque Romance* (1897). In this early work of scientific fiction (Wells preferred the term "scientific romance"), the protagonist Griffin, one of the most gifted scientists of his generation, discovers the secret of corporeal invisibility. In the first half of the novel, Griffin arrives in the Sussex village of Iping. Wells's admiration for the detective fiction of Arthur Conan Doyle is apparent as the villagers make a series of guesses as to the identity concealed by the stranger's bandaged condition—hypothesizing, for example, that he is a criminal in disguise and that he is a "piebald" of mixed race. Having burgled the local vicarage, and now unable to pay for his upkeep, Griffin reveals his invisible persona when publicly confronted by his landlady. Griffin then flees Iping, committing random acts of violence. He coerces Mr Marvel, a superstitious tramp, into helping him, though Marvel escapes with the books containing Griffin's secret of invisibility. Escaping from the authorities, Griffin accidentally stumbles upon the home of his once fellow student Dr Kemp, to whom he recounts the narrative of his adventures. Wells himself noted the importance of "scientific patter" in upholding the illusion of scientific marvels, and references to scientific principles grant verisimilitude to his protagonist's invention. Griffin recounts his initial elation upon becoming invisible. His elation is soon deflated as he is confronted with the realities of being an invisible man in bustling central London. Indeed, as Griffin confronts the disadvantages of being invisible, he is forced to assume a disguise, making him grotesquely visible and reinforcing the otherness he had felt as a working-class albino. He then retires to Iping to discover a means of restoring himself to visibility. Griffin's narrative highlights the moral regression associated with the invention of invisibility, especially in his lack of remorse after his theft of money results in his father's suicide. Kemp, alarmed by Griffin's immorality, alerts the authorities, while Griffin attempts to enlist him as a confederate in establishing a new "Reign of Terror." Following his betrayal, Griffin escapes and declares the Epoch of the Invisible Man. After an unsuccessful attempt to kill Kemp, Griffin goes on the rampage, murdering Mr Wickstead, a benevolent gentleman. Griffin is eventually cornered and beaten to death by an angry mob. The novel ends with Mr Marvel, now the owner of an inn called *The Invisible Man*, secretly poring over the dead man's books.

The Invisible Man is typically considered to be a fable warning of the dangers of scientific over-reaching. Critics such as Robert Sirabian and Steven McLean have debated how *The Invisible Man* examines the complexities inherent in the relationship between scientist and society. They have also examined how *The Invisible Man* enacts nineteenth-century debates over the scientific method and how the concept of an invisible man relates to the increasingly invisible (or microscopic) objects of scientific study. Commentators like Keith Williams have noted the cinematic prescience of Wells's novel, perhaps explaining the enormous appeal that *The Invisible Man* has for filmmakers.

One of the most famous adaptations of Wells's novel is James Whale's *The Invisible Man* (1933). Whale retains essential plot elements and the historical setting of Wells's story. The stranger, renamed Dr Jack Griffin (Claude Rains), arrives in Iping and reveals his invisible persona after his unsociable behavior leads to a confrontation with the innkeeper and his wife. In Whale's film, Griffin forces Kemp (William Harrigan) to be his confederate, and Griffin has a fiancée (Flora, played by Gloria Stuart). The film depicts Griffin murdering Kemp following his betrayal. Rather than being beaten to death, Griffin is tracked to a barn and is mortally wounded as police see his footprints in the snow (much as the inhabitants of central London had inferred Griffin's presence in Wells's story). Whale overcomes the technical challenge of portraying on-screen invisibility through the use of wires, and by using a body cask of Claude Rains and then treating the film in a laboratory to achieve the illusion of Griffin's becoming invisible. Whale retains essential themes of Wells's novel, particularly the association of invisibility with moral regression (the new "monocane" drug that renders Jack Griffin invisible causes insanity). As Griffin lies on his death-bed, he confesses to Flora that he had been seduced by a dangerous branch of science—thus making overt the theme of scientific over-reaching implicit in Wells's novel.

Other Hollywood appropriations of *The Invisible Man* are not so explicit about their Wellsian source. Paul Verhoeven's *Hollow Man* (2000) relocates the story to modern-day America, although the theme of megalomania remains an integral plot-device. Adaptations like the 1950s British TV series *The Invisible Man* explore the implications of invisibility for espionage. Finally, it is worth noting that Ralph Ellison's novel *Invisible Man* (1952) appropriates the notion of the invisible man for political purposes, highlighting the plight (or "invisibility") of African-Americans under racial segregation.

Steve McLean

References and Suggested Reading

Fleissner, Robert F. "H.G. Wells and Ralph Ellison: Need the Effect of One Invisible Man on Another Be *Itself* Invisible?" *Extrapolation* 33, no. 4 (1992): 346–50.

McLean, Steven. *The Early Fiction of H.G. Wells: Fantasies of Science*. London: Palgrave Macmillan, 2009.

Sirabian, Robert. "The Conception of Science in H.G. Wells's *The Invisible Man.*" *Papers on Language and Literature* 37 (2001): 383–402.
Williams, Keith. *H.G. Wells, Modernity and the Movies.* Liverpool: Liverpool University Press, 2007.

JABBERWOCK

Fig. 20 *Jabberwock* by John Tenniel (1871). Image courtesy of the Clarke Historical Library, Central Michigan University.

Titular beast of Lewis Carroll's poem "Jabberwocky" in his *Through the Looking Glass and What Alice Found There* (1871), the Jabberwock is characterized by its biting jaws, catching claws, and "eyes of flame"; it whiffles and burbles through the "tulgey wood" before being beheaded by the poem's hero. The initial verse first appeared as "A Stanza of Anglo-Saxon Poetry" in *Misch-Masch,* one of Carroll's private family periodicals, in 1855; while the title invokes earlier heroic adventures entailing monsters such as **Grendel** from the Old English heroic poem *Beowulf* (arguably composed during the first half of the eighth century), the poem was probably inspired by the 1846 translation of German Friedrich de la Motte-Fouqué's poem "The Shepherd of the Green Mountains." Carroll's tale includes elements of the quest motif such as the father warning his son to beware the ferocity of the Jabberwock, the Jubjub bird, and the Bandersnatch; and the son using his "vorpal sword" to slay the monster and return with its head. The poem has been translated over 42 times into 16 different languages, with Latin and Greek being perennial favorites. Nevertheless, the Jabberwock, while recognizable, has not entered the English language as a proper noun but instead remains identified with Carroll's poem. Considered one of the most familiar works of English language nonsense poetry, "Jabberwocky" is an excellent example of the genre, which works with firm logical rules and a high degree of intellectual sophistication. The poem's imaginative coinage has provided material for considerable linguistic and language-based research. Its many neologisms include "chortle" and "galumphing," and the word "jabberwocky" has been extended to mean invented language or nonsensical behavior.

Though John Tenniel's original illustration, which Carroll approved before publication, remains the most familiar image of the Jabberwock, the poem has spawned numerous stand-alone picture books, including traditional romantic renditions by Graeme Base (1989), Nick Bantock (1991), and Joel Stewart (2003). Other artists have regarded Carroll's flexibility of language as a creative springboard: Stephane Jorisch (2004) uses the backdrop of a surreal modernist landscape to recast the story as a conflict between a young soldier and a horrific war-mongering beast, while

Christopher Myers (2007) depicts a dramatic basketball game against an enormous opponent. The poem also inspired Daniel Coleman's novel *Jabberwocky* (2011), numerous stage and musical versions, and Terry Gilliam's (of *Monty Python* fame) heroic film of the same name (1977). Tim Burton's *Alice in Wonderland* (2010) presents the gold standard for CGI imagery, with "the jabberwocky" appearing as an enormous winged red-eyed **dragon** spewing purple laser fire, with razor-sharp teeth and the voice of Christopher Lee. After pursuing it through Acropolis-like ruins, Alice slays it at the top of a tower and is rewarded with a vial of its purple blood, which sends her home. Carroll's use of nonsense and portmanteau words was influential over James Joyce's composition of *Finnegans Wake* (1939), and some of the anthropomorphized characteristics from Tenniel's illustration are mirrored in Maurice Sendak's *Where the Wild Things Are* (1963; see **Wild Things**).

Anne Hiebert Alton

References and Suggested Reading

Carroll, Lewis. *The Annotated Alice: The Definitive Edition*. Illustrated by John Tenniel, edited by Martin Gardner. New York: Norton, 1999.

Collingwood, Stuart Dodgson. *The Life and Letters of Lewis Carroll: Rev. C.L. Dodgson* [1898]. Reprint, Detroit: Gale, 1967.

JACK THE RIPPER

"Jack the Ripper" is the name by which the serial killer who murdered Mary Ann Nichols, Annie Chapman, Elizabeth Stride, Catherine Eddowes, Mary Jane Kelly, and possibly other women in and around London's Whitechapel district in 1888 is popularly known. The identity of the killer has never been confirmed, and the name "Jack the Ripper" originated in a letter to the press that police at the time suspected was written by a journalist rather than the actual murderer.

The rise in mass media newspapers and the global reach of telegraph cables meant that the news of the Whitechapel murders could spread quickly. The *New York Times* wrote about the death of Mary Ann Nichols on 1 September, the day after she was killed, and by 11 September reports of the Whitechapel murders were appearing in newspapers as far away as Australia. Relatedly, the popular demand for mass market fiction meant that works of fiction capitalizing on the Whitechapel murders could appear with an unprecedented speed. The first work of fiction about Jack the Ripper was John Francis Brewer's Gothic novel *The Curse Upon Mitre Square* (1888). In the sixteenth century, the south corner of Mitre Square, where Catherine Eddowes was murdered, was a part of the cloister of Holy Trinity Priory, Aldgate, but beginning in 1536 Henry VIII disbanded various English, Welsh, and Irish religious institutions. *The Curse Upon Mitre Square* claims that this act brought a curse down upon Mitre Square, and that Catherine Eddowes's murder was a part of this curse.

The Curse Upon Mitre Square, published only six weeks after the first Whitechapel murder, began the trend of portraying Jack the Ripper as a being of more-than-human evil. Whether or not the late nineteenth-century reading audience truly believed that there was something superhumanly monstrous about Jack the Ripper, the trend over the next 20 years was to portray Jack the Ripper in that fashion. This was true in Great Britain and abroad: the anonymously written 1900 Polish dime novel *Duch Zemsty* portrayed Jack the Ripper as a being who sold his soul to Satan (see **Devil, The**) in exchange for superhuman abilities, and Norbert Sévestre's "Tserpchikopf, le Sanglant Hypnotiseur" (1909) portrayed Jack the Ripper as a creature of superhuman mesmeric abilities who is a match for the superhuman psychic abilities of Sévestre's series hero, Sâr Dubnotal.

This trend began to change in 1913 with the publication of Marie Belloc Lowndes's *The Lodger*. The novel, set in Victorian London, is about the Buntings, an elderly couple who rent out the upper half of their house to Mister Sleuth, a polite but secretive young man who the couple soon begins to suspect is "The Avenger," the man who is murdering drunken women. Mister Sleuth is eccentric but kindly in manner to Ellen Bunting, and although her suspicions of him are confirmed, she still views him somewhat positively. Lowndes's version of Jack the Ripper is neither supernatural nor superhuman. Lowndes's Jack the Ripper is a religious fanatic, and the final impression left by Sleuth is of an ordinary man with a ghastly secret.

The Lodger was filmed in 1927, 1932, 1944, 1953, and 2009, and made into an opera in 1960. Lowndes's novel was a critical and popular success, as was the 1927 film (made by Alfred Hitchcock), and Lowndes's version of Jack the Ripper would prove to be the dominant model over the next three decades. G.W. Pabst's film *Pandora's Box* (1929) features a remorseful and obsessed Jack the Ripper, similar to Lowndes's character but more psychologically tormented, but *Pandora's Box* was not a popular success on its release and was soon forgotten about until its rediscovery in the 1950s.

The international rise in pulp fiction, both as a medium and as an aesthetic, led to an increased usage of Jack the Ripper as a villain in stories with the pulp aesthetic or characterized by the pulp fashion. Typical of the German *heftromane* ("hero books," or dime novels) was Elisabeth von Aspern's 1938 story "Der Kleine Jack," in which the German consulting detective Tom Shark, one of Germany's most popular *heftromane* characters, travels to London to solve a series of crimes committed by "the Little Jack," son of the original Jack the Ripper. The story repeatedly emphasizes the fact that such crimes are peculiar to England and a part of the English national character, and could never take place in Nazi Germany. In the United States, Robert Bloch's "Yours Truly, Jack the Ripper" (1943) was widely reprinted and broadcast on the radio. Bloch's Jack is a psychiatrist in Chicago who in personality is close to ordinary, but whose secret is that he sacrifices victims to dark gods in return for eternal life.

The portrayal of Jack as an ordinary Englishman began to change in 1959, with Robert S. Baker and Monty Berman's film *Jack the Ripper*, which was the first film to put Jack in his now-customary top hat and opera cloak. This change in the iconography of Jack the Ripper was followed by a change in his character. In British popular culture during the 1960s and 1970s, Jack the Ripper was no longer an ordinary Englishman, but a member of the upper classes, typifying the predatory practices of the aristocracy. The most prominent example of this trend was the 1972 Peter Medak film *The Ruling Class*, in which the insane 14th Earl of Gurney comes to believe that he is Jack the Ripper and commits a Whitechapel-style murder. The 1979 Bob Clark film *Murder By Decree*, in which Sherlock Holmes pursues Jack the Ripper, portrays a conspiracy of the aristocracy and the political and social elite that protects Jack.

However, in the United States, Jack the Ripper became a more generalized horror icon. The "Wolf in the Fold" episode of *Star Trek* (1967), written by Robert Bloch, puts Jack the Ripper into twenty-third-century space opera and portrays him as an alien being who lives on the fear of other beings, taking possession of creatures and forcing them to commit murders. Bloch also wrote "A Toy for Juliette" (1967), a science fictional horror story in which Juliette, a young woman in a far-future decayed Earth, gets pleasure from raping and torturing boys and men taken from Earth's past. Juliette's latest victim is Jack the Ripper, who kills her before she can kill him. Harlan Ellison wrote a sequel, "The Prowler in the City at the Edge of the World," in which Jack, still in Juliette's world, is manipulated by the citizens of the City to commit atrocities for their amusement. "The Prowler" is both science fiction and Grand Guignol horror. And in the Nicholas Meyer film *Time After Time* (1979), Jack the Ripper is the cause of a timeslip romance, as H.G. Wells pursues Jack the Ripper into the twentieth century and falls in love with a modern woman.

This trend has continued. Iain Sinclair's *White Chappell, Scarlet Tracings* (1987) is a metaphysical detective novel in which the Whitechapel murders are counterpointed by the pursuit by second-hand book dealers of rare Victorian editions. Jack the Ripper becomes intertwined with both London and Sherlock Holmes, the quintessential British detective, and an investigation into the Whitechapel murders becomes an investigation into both the basic assumptions of detective fiction and the psychology and geography of London itself. And Alan Moore and Eddie Campbell's *From Hell* (1988–98) is a meticulously detailed examination of the Whitechapel murders, theorizing that the physician William Gull initially committed the murders at the behest of Queen Victoria as a way to protect Prince Eddy, but that Gull went further as part of a mystical ritual and was ultimately protected by his fellow Freemasons. In *From Hell*'s second appendix, "Dance of the Gull Catchers," Moore and Campbell portray Ripper theorists, including themselves, as complicit in the victimization of the original Whitechapel dead: "Five murdered paupers, and one anonymous assailant. This reality is dwarfed by the vast theme-park we've built around it" (II: 22).

But more common is the approach taken by Roger Zelazny in *A Night in the Lonesome October* (1993). Zelazny's Jack the Ripper is the novel's protagonist and hero, and the novel as a whole is a humorous fantasy in which various famous fictional monsters, including **Dracula**, the Wolfman, and **Frankenstein's monster**, attempt to create or prevent the summoning of a Lovecraftian Elder God (see **Lovecraft, Monsters In**). Zelazny's Jack the Ripper has no symbolic, historical, or moral meaning apart from being a cultural icon. Like many modern authors, Zelazny makes the Whitechapel murderer into an unserious plug-and-play monster, completely severed from his serious real-life associations.

The figure of Jack the Ripper has become an icon of horror in literature, film, and popular culture. Originally a symbol of both supernatural evil and urban danger in late-Victorian London, he has become divorced from history and changed into a cultural icon suitable for use in any genre, format, or time period. In the words of Alan Moore, "Jack mirrors our hysterias. Faceless, he is the receptacle for each new social panic" (II: 22).

Jess Nevins

References and Suggested Reading

Bloch, Robert. "A Toy for Juliette." In *Dangerous Visions: 33 Original Stories*, edited by Harland Ellison, 115–27. Garden City, NY: Doubleday, 1967.

——. "Yours Truly, Jack the Ripper." *Weird Tales* 36, no. 12 (July 1943): 83–95.

Brewer, John Francis. *The Curse Upon Mitre Square*. London: Simpkin, Marshall and Co, 1888.

Ellison, Harlan. "The Prowler in the City at the Edge of the World." In *Dangerous Visions: 33 Original Stories*, edited by Harland Ellison, 128–54. Garden City, NY: Doubleday, 1967.

Lowndes, Marie B. *The Lodger*. London: Methuen & Co, 1913.

Sévestre, Norbert. "Tserpchikopf, le Sanglant Hypnotiseur." *Sâr Dubnotal* 7 (July 1909): 1–24.
Sinclair, Iain. *White Chappell, Scarlet Tracings.* Uppingham: Goldmark, 1987.
Zelazny, Roger, and Gahan Wilson. *A Night in the Lonesome October.* New York: William Morrow and Co, 1993.

JENKINS, ANYA—*see* Demon

JERSEY DEVIL—*see* Cryptid

JIANGSHI—*see* Demon

JIGSAW—*see* Psychopath

JISH-IN-UNO—*see* Sea Monsters

JOHNSON, HENRY

Henry Johnson is the title character of "The Monster," a novelette by Stephen Crane (1871–1900), published in *The Monster and Other Stories* (1899). An African-American, Johnson maintains the horses and carriage of Dr Trescott, one of the physicians of Whilomville. He is a friend to Trescott's young son, Jimmie, is regarded with condescending tolerance by the white community, and is a popular bachelor among Whilomville's black residents. Johnson, however, is transformed while successfully rescuing Jimmy from a fire in the Trescott home. Overcome by smoke, Johnson falls beneath a table in Dr Trescott's laboratory and, in a memorable sequence, caustic liquid from a burst container flows onto Johnson's upturned face, resulting in hideous deformity.

"The Monster" is a study in the ways monstrosity is created and defined. The injured Johnson is restored to life by Dr Trescott, who must repay the rescue of Jimmie, even though advised by his friend the judge that it would be kinder to let Johnson die. The recreated Johnson, product of a laboratory accident and the doctor's intervention, is clearly intended to recall the monster of Mary Shelley's *Frankenstein* (1818; see **Frankenstein's Monster**). The now feeble-minded Johnson is also monstrous in the sense that, with his face burned away, he is hideous to look at, inspiring revulsion in everyone. His friends attempt using a hood to conceal his appearance, but the hood also inspires fear.

Most importantly, Johnson is a black man in a racist society. As long as he was recognized as the harmless, if vain and slightly comical, employee of a respected physician, he enjoyed a safe position within Whilomville. In an early scene, he is watched by a barber and several customers as he approaches and passes the barber shop. The men speculate about the identity of the elegantly dressed black man, before agreeing that he is, indeed, Henry Johnson. Once his face is burned away, however, this safe identity is lost and Johnson becomes just a hideous black man, onto whom racist fears and stereotypes are projected. In other stories by Crane, Whilomville is presented as an idyllic community, repository of a passing simple way of life, as its name suggests. In this story, in true Gothic fashion, the narrative of small town virtue is disrupted. When Johnson unintentionally frightens a little girl, he is nearly lynched and the Trescotts are boycotted by the community. Thus, though the title of "The Monster" refers directly to Henry Johnson, the real source of monstrosity is Whilomville itself, which projects its fears upon this innocent scapegoat.

Charles L. Crow

References and Suggested Reading

Asma, Stephen T. *On Monsters: An Unnatural History of Our Worst Fears.* Oxford: Oxford University Press, 2009.
Crane, Stephen. *The Monster and Other Stories.* New York: Harper and Brothers, 1899.

JOHNSON, RUFUS—*see* **Demon**

JÖRMUNGANDR—*see* **Animals, Monstrous**

JORŌGUMO—*see* **Shapeshifter**

JUMBIE—*see* **Ghost**

KABOUTERMANNEKIN—*see* **Brownie**

KAITABHA—*see* **Demon**

KAPPA

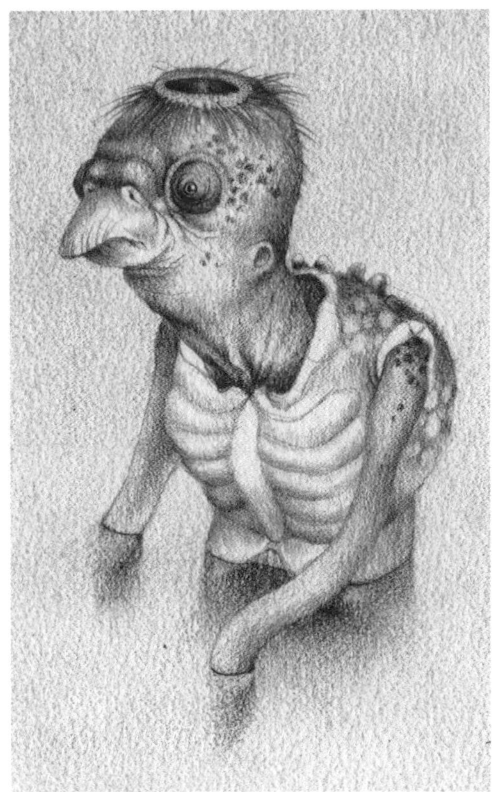

Fig. 21 ***Kappa*** **by Allison W. Sommers**

A well-known supernatural water creature of Japanese folklore, the kappa has become a popular character in literature, film, manga, anime, commercial iconography, and other forms of popular culture in Japan. Historically, the kappa was known by a number of regional variant names, such as *kawatarō, mizuchi, suiko, enkō,* and *garappa*. While these names still have meaning in local legend and belief systems, and description and characteristics vary from region to region, a somewhat generic version of the kappa has become the most commonly articulated image in literature, film, and popular culture.

The kappa is associated with water, usually rivers, ponds, or swamps. It is scaly or slimy, greenish in color, with webbed feet and hands, and a carapace on its back. Sometimes characterized like a monkey, sometimes more like a frog or turtle, the kappa is generally the size of a young child, but disproportionately strong. It has a small concave indentation or saucer on the top of its head containing water; if this water is spilled, the kappa loses its superhuman strength. Kappa are notorious for pulling horses and cattle into the water and drowning them; they also drown young children and extract their internal organs through their anuses.

Despite these murderous proclivities, however, kappa are also known to be both playful and exceedingly honest. They especially enjoy sumo wrestling, often challenging passers-by to a match. One tactic for defeating a kappa in sumo is simply to bow; the kappa will bow in response, spilling the strength-giving liquid from its saucer. In local legend, folktale, and belief, therefore, the kappa is both a dangerous, demonic monster (see **Demon**)—a reason to warn children from swimming in the water—and also an amusing, if disgusting, water sprite. While Chinese lore has certainly influenced its development, and comparable water creatures exist elsewhere in world folklore, the kappa as described above is generally considered to be a distinctly Japanese monster.

In local rituals and festivals, particularly in agricultural communities depending on water for irrigation, kappa may be celebrated as water deities (*suijin*). When properly pacified and treated appropriately, they ensure ample water for irrigation; if neglected or treated badly, they can cause flooding or drought. This folkloric version of the kappa is frequently characterized as having a penchant for certain foods including melons, eggplant, and most notoriously, cucumbers. In fact, the kappa's love of cucumbers is reflected throughout contemporary Japan, and much of the rest of the word, with the word *kappa maki*, or kappa roll: roll sushi made with cucumbers.

The earliest written reference to a kappa-like creature is found in one of the oldest extant texts in Japan, the mytho-historical *Nihonshoki* (*Chronicles of Japan*, 720 CE), in which it is explained that a snake-like water creature called a *mizuchi* had been killing travelers near a particular river. Although kappa-related legends and beliefs presumably persisted in oral form for hundreds of years after this, the creature does not appear regularly in literary and artistic contexts until the Edo period (c. 1603–1868), with its efflorescence of inexpensive commercial woodblock prints (*ukiyo-e*), popular books, and graphic literature. The earliest known mass-produced image of the kappa appears in the *Wakansansaizue* (c. 1713) encyclopedia under the label "kawatarō"; a kappa is also among the first monsters noted in *Gazu hyakkiyagyō* (1776), a famous illustrated catalog of supernatural creatures by Toriyama Sekien (1712–88). During this period, kappa increasingly began to appear as protagonists in graphic literary works, precursors to contemporary manga, such as the *kibyōshi* ("yellow-covers") genre that flourished between 1775 and 1806. Through such inexpensive and widely circulated formats, the image of the kappa became relatively standardized. While variations still thrived in localized folk belief, this "character" version of the kappa, often deployed as a proxy human for purposes of satire or comic entertainment, gradually came to inform the modern Japanese understanding of the creature.

In the twentieth century, the most famous literary treatment of the kappa is Akutagawa Ryūnosuke's short novel, *Kappa* (1927), a Swiftian social satire narrated by a human who journeys to a land of kappa. In his depiction of kappa characters, with their similarities and differences to humans, the author poignantly skewers modern Japanese society. Akutagawa was already well known when he wrote *Kappa*; his suicide soon after its appearance brought attention not only to him, but also to the satirical contents and kappa characters of his final novel. Kappa also appear in minor works by other canonical modern authors such as Izumi Kyōka (1873–1939) and Ibuse Masuji (1898–1993), in numerous children's stories, in detective fiction, and extensively in the fiction of Hino Ashihei (1907–60).

The visual image of the kappa also continued to develop throughout the twentieth century. In the artwork of Ogawa Usen (1868–1938), kappa were depicted pastorally, frolicking joyfully in nature. The creature's role as symbolic human came to the fore in comics (manga), particularly the work of Shimizu Kon (1912–74), whose *Kappa tengoku* (*Kappa Heaven*), complete with she-kappa (a rarity in folklore) and "salaryman" kappa, began nationwide circulation in the *Asahi Weekly* (magazine) in 1953. Kojima Kō (1928–) followed in Shimizu's footsteps and also illustrated naked female kappa, with pink nipples and thick eyelashes, indistinguishable from humans but for their patterned carapaces and delicate head-top saucers. Images by both artists were used in advertising campaigns, most famously by Kizakura Saké. The kappa's role as a national icon, a stand-in for the Japanese consumer, persists today—for example, in the kappa's use (along with another common folkloric creature, the **tanuki**) as a mascot figure for the DC (credit) Card.

The kappa's commercial appeal was also recognized on the local level. In the 1970s and 1980s, rural communities throughout Japan began to develop local kappa-lore for "village revitalization" (*mura-okoshi*) projects; in response to Japan's postwar prosperity and increasing urbanization, these efforts drew on the kappa's traditional association with agriculture and a rapidly disappearing rural lifestyle. Similarly, once considered a terror to people and animals venturing near the water, in the late twentieth century the kappa began to morph into a symbol of pristine nature; today cutesified kappa images are posted near rivers throughout Japan, imploring people not to spoil the environment.

Concurrent with the revaluation of local folkways during Japan's postwar period of high economic growth, kappa also continued to feature in popular media. In the 1960s, Mizuki Shigeru (b. 1921), one of Japan's foremost manga artists (known especially for his depiction of Japanese monsters or *yōkai*), published a serialized manga titled *Kappa no Sanpei* (*Sanpei the kappa*). Kappa also appeared in popular monster films such as *Yōkai daisensō* (1968; *Great Yōkai War*), where the creature is portrayed as a somewhat comical member of a gang of monstrous heroes.

After the bursting of the Japanese economic bubble in the late 1980s, kappa emerged as even more of a presence in popular media, especially in film. Mizuki's *Kappa no Sanpei*, for example, returned as an animated series in the 1990s, and a kappa played a starring role in the *E.T.*-inspired feature film *Kappa* (Tatsuya Ishii, 1994). The early twenty-first century is also witnessing a proliferation of kappa-related films, such as a totally revised version of *Yōkai daisensō* (Miike Takashi, 2005; *Great Yōkai War*); *Death Kappa* (Tomo'o Haraguchi, 2009), starring a mammoth mutant kappa stomping through Tokyo and harkening back to Japan's long monster movie (*kaijū eiga*) tradition; and Imaoka Shinji's *Onna no Kappa* (2011; *Underwater Love*), a fantasy musical in the *pinku* (Japanese soft porn) genre. In contemporary media, the kappa remains a vibrant and versatile character, more often than not providing satirical, if not frightening, commentary on contemporary human society.

Finally, as one of the most recognized of Japan's many monsters, the kappa has ventured onto the international stage, notably making an appearance in J.K. Rowling's *Harry Potter and the Prisoner of Azkaban* (1999) in which Professor Snape mistakenly explains that kappa are found in Mongolia. This error is then comically corrected in Rowling's bestiary *Fantastic Beasts & Where to Find Them* (2001); in the entry for "Kappa," the word "Japanese" is underlined and the comment "Snape hasn't read this either" (23) is scribbled in the margins. With its humble beginnings as a repulsive water creature in a Japanese river, the kappa has proven itself a mutable signifier, recognized around the world perhaps, but still identified with Japan.

Michael Dylan Foster

References and Suggested Reading

Foster, Michael Dylan. "The Metamorphosis of the *Kappa*: Transformation of Folklore to Folklorism in Japan." *Asian Folklore Studies* 57, no. 1 (1998): 1–24.

Iikura Yoshiyuki, ed. *Nippon no kappa no shōtai.* Tokyo: Shin Jinbutsu Ōraisha, 2010.

Nakamura Teiri. *Kappa no Nihonshi.* Tokyo: Nihon Editaasukūru shuppanbu, 1996.

Rowling, J.K. *Fantastic Beasts & Where to Find Them. By Newt Scamander.* London: Scholastic Press/Arthur A. Levine Books, 2001.

KELPIE—*see* Shapeshifter

KETOS—*see* Animals, Monstrous

KIKIMORA—*see* Demon

KILLMOULIS—*see* Brownie

KING KONG

King Kong, the 50-foot giant ape of the eponymous 1933 film directed by Merian C. Cooper and Ernest B. Schoedsack, was first released to the world in a promotional novel published in 1932, written by Edgar Wallace and Merian C. Cooper. The cinematic premiere occurred in March 1933.

Within the narrative, King Kong initially inhabits the mysterious Skull Island, supposedly located somewhere off the western coast of Sumatra. He lives in a jungle filled with prehistoric **dinosaurs**, and the human inhabitants of the island sacrifice women to him during a ritual that entails dressing up in ape-like wardrobe, dancing, and chanting. When director Carl Denham (Robert Armstrong), his film crew, and the crewmen of the *SS Venture* encounter the island, the natives find the blonde white female actress Ann Darrow (Fay Wray) appealing. They kidnap her and bind her to the ritual site, which stands inside the jungle behind giant wooden gates. Kong takes Darrow, so Denham and his crew must go into the jungle to rescue her. Within the jungle, Kong fights several beasts, including a Tyrannosaurus Rex and a serpentine creature. Darrow is rescued by her love interest, First Mate John "Jack" Driscoll (Bruce Cabot). With her disappearance, Kong races back and breaks through the wooden gates. He wreaks havoc on the villagers, some of which are consumed by him, until Denham uses bombs to knock Kong unconscious and capture him. Denham then carries him back to New York City where Kong is to be displayed as the "Eighth Wonder of the World." On opening night, the camera flashes and Darrow's presence cause the chained monster to break free. He rampages through New York and eventually kidnaps Darrow. While swatting at airplanes atop the Empire State Building, Kong falls to his death.

The inspiration for King Kong was largely derived from Sir Arthur Conan Doyle's *The Lost World* (1912), its cinematic adaptation by Harry O. Hoyt in 1925, and Edgar Rice Burroughs's "Caspak" trilogy, beginning with *The Land That Time Forgot* (1918). *King Kong* was followed by *The Son of Kong* in December 1933 (Ernest B. Schoedsack), which was not nearly as financially successful. The sequel's story centers on Denham's (again played by Robert Armstrong) return to Skull Island to meet the friendlier, smaller Son of Kong, who sacrifices his life to save Denham and others in the end. *King Kong* was later re-released to theaters in 1938, although scenes included in the original 1933 release were censored by the new Motion Picture Production Code, including a scene of Kong removing Ann's clothing and all scenes showing Kong biting or stomping on people. The film was periodically re-released into theaters through the 1940s and 1950s, and in the 1940s, Cooper wrote and produced *Mighty Joe Young* (Ernest B. Schoedsack, 1949), an analogous film featuring a large ape brought from the wild that goes rampaging in the US.

The re-releases and other renditions on King Kong led to the epic confrontation of *King Kong vs.* ***Godzilla*** (Ishirô Honda, 1962) and *King Kong Escapes* (also Ishirô Honda, 1967). Both films were produced in Japan by Tōhō Studios, who licensed the character from RKO Radio Pictures. They each positioned Kong as a protagonist or generally sympathetic character—especially the latter, since it was based in part upon an American/Japanese cartoon show called

The King Kong Show that aired from 1966 to 1969 (and which has the distinction of being the first anime series produced in Japan for an American company). Director John Guillermin and producer Dino De Laurentiis launched a remake of *King Kong* in 1976 and followed it with a sequel, *King Kong Lives* (1986), which tells of Kong's survival and pairing with a female Kong. A second animated series was produced in 2000–2001, *Kong: The Animated Series*, which had two direct-to-DVD sequels (*Kong: King of Atlantis* directed by Patrick Archibald [2005] and *Kong: Return to the Jungle* [director unknown, 2006]). The most impressive retelling of *King Kong*, however, is producer, writer, and director Peter Jackson's 2005 remake. Jackson remained faithful to the characters, plot, and progression of the original film (unlike the De Laurentiis production), but brought to bear updated and spectacular special effects.

A notable feature of the monstrous King Kong is the ambivalence that audiences feel in regard to the giant ape. Though ostensibly pitted as the villain of the narrative who disrupts the budding romance between Jack Driscoll and Ann Darrow, Kong is nevertheless often viewed in a sympathetic or even heroic light at times. Particularly during the escapades on Skull Island, Kong's villainy as kidnapper of Darrow is offset and undercut by his protection of her from various monsters. Later, Kong's shackled exhibition in New York elicits pity from the viewing audience. Even Denham's famous final words in the film, "Oh no, it wasn't the airplanes. It was beauty killed the beast," imply that Kong was more victim than villain.

A central criticism of the film and its various adaptations over the years has been the racism embedded within the story and symbolically present within Kong's narrative arc. The natives of Skull Island closely approximate stereotyped representations of Africans, despite being located somewhere within the Pacific Ocean. Their depiction unmercifully presents them as ignorant and buffoonish savages. Kong himself, however, is most notably racially charged, given that anxieties concerning the potency of the African-American male's sexual desire for white women was a repeated theme in literature and then film throughout the nineteenth and early twentieth centuries. As a large dark ape, Kong lives contentedly in his jungle enjoying sacrifices from the natives. The offering and rescinding of the blonde-haired, white Darrow sends him into a rampage, in which he breaks down the previously confining walls. It takes the ingenuity of the Westernized men to conquer Kong, eventually chaining him up and putting him on display for the civilized world to see. His breaking free from his chains and persistence in recapturing Darrow only further develops this racialized subtext, which is then hammered home with his death and Denham's eulogy.

Lance Eaton

References and Suggested Reading

Andriano, Joseph. *Immortal Monster: The Mythological Evolution of the Fantastic Beast in Modern Fiction and Film*. Westport, CT: Greenwood Press, 1999.

Bellin, Joshua D. *Framing Monsters: Fantasy Film and Social Alienation*. Carbondale: Southern Illinois University Press, 2005.

Maddrey, Joseph. *Nightmares in Red, White, and Blue: The Evolution of the American Horror Film*. Jefferson, NC: McFarland, 2004.

Morton, Ray. *King Kong: The History of a Movie Icon from Fay Wray to Peter Jackson*. New York: Applause Theatre & Cinema Books, 2005.

Skal, David J. *The Monster Show: A Cultural History of Horror*. New York: Faber and Faber, 2001.

KIRTIMUKHA—*see* Body Parts

KITSUNE

The Japanese word for "fox," a kitsune is one of the most ubiquitous animals in the Japanese cultural imagination. Along with the **tanuki**, it is commonly viewed as a **shapeshifter** and a trickster, a *yôkai* (folkloric monster) that can transform into human beings and various objects. It is also closely associated with the Shinto deity Inari and the Buddhist deity Dakininten, and is often depicted as their animal messenger.

The etymology of the name "kitsune" is believed to come from the phrases meaning "come and sleep" (*kite neru*) or "come always" (*ki-tsune*). *Nihon Ryôiki* (787–824) contains the first Japanese fox legend in which a fox wife tells her human husband: "Between you and me a child has been born, therefore I cannot forget you. *Come always and sleep with me*" (quoted in de Visser 20). However, the kitsune also goes by other names such as *ninko* (man fox) in Izumo, *yako* (field fox) in Kyûshu, *osaki* (split tail) in Kantô, and *kuda* (pipe fox) in Shizuoka, Nagao, and Yamanashi.

A kitsune can be of various colors and types, and can possess up to nine tails; it is also a harbinger of both auspicious and inauspicious omens. Two of the earliest fox references are listed in *Nihon shoki* (*The Chronicles of Japan*, 720); it is noted that, in 657, a white fox (*byakko*) was spotted and interpreted as an auspicious sign; however, in 659, another white fox was sighted and was considered inauspicious. In contrast, all nine foxes mentioned in *Shoku Nihongi* (*Continuation of the Chronicles of Japan*, 797) are auspicious, and *Engi shiki* (*Regulations and Laws of the Engi Era*, 927) lists three types of lucky foxes: white, black (*kuroko*), and nine-tailed. In these tales, however, ordinary field foxes (*yakan*) that invade palaces or howl outside of temples are seen as inauspicious.

The older the fox, the more powerful it becomes. It is said that when a fox reaches 50 years of age, it can transform into a woman, at 100 it can be a beautiful female or a man and also spiritually possess human bodies, and at 1,000 it turns into a celestial fox (*tenko*), a fox that can ascend to heaven. The nine-tailed fox (*kyûbi no kitsune*) is seen as the shapeshifting kitsune's final stage, as it requires 10,000 years. The most infamous nine-tailed fox in Japanese legends is Tamamo-no-mae, consort to the Cloistered Emperor Toba (cloistered 1129–56). According to legend, she controlled the country through the emperor and his son, killing countless people, and when the emperor mysteriously fell ill, her true form—a white, nine-tailed fox with golden hair—was uncovered by the famous Yin Yang master Abe no Seimei (921–1005). After she was pursued and finally killed, she turned into a poisonous stone called a "murder stone" (*sesshôseki*) and continued to kill those that approached her, until the stone was finally destroyed by Sôtô Zen priest Gennô in 1385.

As the story illustrates, a kitsune is associated with feminine yin power and often appears as a seductress or a domestic wife. In ancient China, the fox was a beast that conducted shamanistic soul journeys to the Underworld, and it was believed that the bad foxes sucked human yang energy by means of sexual intercourse, in order to use this essence to facilitate their magic and to metamorphose; they possessed a human through his or her organs (see **Incubus/Succubus**). In Japan as well, the kitsune was thought to be the cause of spirit possessions of women, as well as of psychological conditions like schizophrenia and hysteria that were interpreted to be "fox possessions" (*kitsune-tsuki*) throughout the modern period (1868–1945). Fox possession came to be described as mental illnesses that are hereditarily transmitted through the female line. Pre-modern (pre-1868) tales identify "fox handlers" (*kitsune-tsukai*) as people trained to conduct exorcisms, but these sorcerers (see **Witch/Wizard**) also sometimes manipulated the foxes for their own money-making schemes. Eighteenth-century anthologies like *Tales of Human Fox* (*Ninko monogatari*, 1787) contain cases in which foxes possessed not only individuals but large groups of people, leading to witch hunt-like accusations against these fox-owners.

The kitsune is also associated with fire and is said to produce "fox fire" (*kitsune-bi*), often during possessions. The kitsune is often depicted with globes of fire, which can look like jewels or luminous pearls in its tails. In China, these pearls were thought to be the foxes' souls or source of power, and it was said that if one were to attain this pearl, one would gain the fox's magical powers. In Japan, the jewel has special powers like transformation, wealth, or intelligence. There are many folktales in which people steal the jewel, but they are either tricked by the fox to return them, or they return the ball on their own accord—an act that is rewarded by the fox's protection and gratitude.

In a religious context, the kitsune is strongly associated with Inari shrines. Inari has been worshipped since the eighth century on the sacred mountain of Fushimi and is generally understood to be a Shinto deity; Dakininten is its Buddhist equivalent. Since Inari's origin story does not have a fox, the question of how the deity became associated with the kitsune is a contested question in Inari studies. In ancient times, foxes were thought to be servants of field deities, and the fact that Inari is associated with fertility and rice may suggest one link. The Buddhist explanation is that the fox imagery came in with the worship of Dakininten, who is depicted as a female bodhisattva flying with a white fox, which was a female **demon** that was converted to Buddhism by Dainichi, the central buddha of Shingon. When Shingon priests began the Dakini cult in the 800s, the practice included sorcery; since native fox sorcery was already well established, some elements could have become conflated. The kitsune could also have become a substitute for the Indian jackal, the animal associated with the Dakinin in India. The association of the kitsune to Inari is so strong that the fox is often seen as Inari and vice versa. People still give offerings of *oage* (fried tofu), said to be the fox's favorite food, and they rub the fox statues at the local Inari shrines to cure their illnesses. If one suffers from *kitsune-tsuki* (fox possession), the patient comes to an Inari shrine for exorcism. The main center of Inari worship, the Fushimi Inari Shrine, however, denies any association of Inari with foxes.

On top of the older folklore and legends, the twentieth century produced its own literature surrounding the kitsune. Niimi Nankichi is known for two famous children's tales: *Gon, the Little Fox* (*Gongitsune*, 1932) is about a fox who gives a villager various gifts in order to make up for stealing the eel the villager meant to feed his dying mother; *Buying Mittens* (*Tekubukro o kaini*, 1943) is an endearing story about a mother fox and a baby fox who decide that they must journey to the village in order to buy mittens for the baby's freezing hands. Miyazawa Kenji also wrote a couple of children's tales, including "Snow Crossing" (*Yukiwatari*, 1921) in which a little kitsune named Konzaburô convinces two children that foxes are not tricksters at all, and "Earth God and the Fox" (*Tsuchigami to kitsune*, 1934), which tells of a love triangle between a kitsune, a birch tree, and an earth deity, in which the deity ends up killing the kitsune out of jealousy. In 1999, Amano Yoshitaka, the famed artist of the video-game series *Final Fantasy*, also collaborated with Neil Gaiman for the illustrated book

Sandman: The Dream Hunters, which focuses on a love story between a Buddhist monk and a kitsune. All the tales above thus depict a benevolent kitsune (*zenko*).

In recent years, the kitsune has continued to appear across various media. In the ongoing manga and anime series *Naruto* (1997–) written and illustrated by Masashi Kishimoto, a nine-tailed fox demon is sealed within the body of the protagonist Naruto Uzumaki and becomes the source of his ninja power. Another popular series, Takahashi Rumiko's *Inuyasha* (1996–2008), had a young fox demon named Shippô, who could shapeshift and use fox-fire magic. The creator of the successful Nintendo video-game series *Star Fox*, Miyamoto Shigeru, has stated that design for the leading character Fox McCloud is based on the figure of a kitsune at the Fushimi Inari Shrine near Nintendo's main building. Films featuring the kitsune are countless, but a notable one is the scene about a fox's wedding in Akira Kurosawa's *Dreams* (1990). The light novel (*raito noberu*) by Jin Shibamura, *Our Home's Fox Deity* (*Waga ya no oinarisan*, 2003–) has a female fox deity Kûgen Tenko, who protects the male character Takagami Tôru from monsters.

Miri Nakamura

References and Suggested Reading

Bathgate, Michael. *The Fox's Craft in Japanese Religion and Folklore*. New York and London: Routledge, 2004.

Blacker, Carmen. *The Catalpa Bow: A Study of Shamanistic Practices in Japan*. London: George Allen and Unwin Ltd, 1975.

De Visser, Marinus Willem. "The Fox and the Badger in Japanese Folklore." *Transactions of the Asiatic Society of Japan* 36, no. 1 (1908): 1–159.

Foster, Michael. *Pandemonium and Parade: Japanese Monsters and the Culture of Yôkai*. Berkeley: University of California Press, 2009.

Heine, Steven. *Shifting Shape, Shaping Text: Philosophy and Folklore in the Fox Kôan*. Honolulu: University of Hawaii Press, 1999.

Jordan, Brenda. "The Trickster in Japan: Tanuki and Kitsune." In *Japanese Ghosts and Demons: Art of the Supernatural*, edited by Stephen Addiss, 129–68. New York: George Braziller, Inc., 1985.

Kang, Xiaofei. *The Cult of the Fox: Power, Gender, and Popular Religion in Late Imperial and Modern China*. New York: Columbia University Press, 2006.

Li, Michelle. *Ambiguous Bodies: Reading the Grotesque in Japanese Setsuwa Tales*. Stanford: Stanford University Press, 2009.

Smyers, Karen A. *The Fox and the Jewel: Shared and Private Meanings in Contemporary Japanese Inari Worship*. Honolulu: University of Hawaii Press, 1999.

KOBOLD—*see* Goblin

KOOPA—*see* Video Games, Monsters In

KORAN, MONSTERS IN

The Koran is not a book of monsters. It does, however, draw from the world of pre-Islamic Arabia, which was populated by spiritual nasties of various varieties. Except for a few, they are organized in subgroups under the larger category of "djinn" (see **Djinn and Genie**). This entry will focus on descriptions of the spiritual underworld as it is portrayed in the Koran and in a handful of passages from early Hadith (the written remembrances of Mohammed's companions). Citations below without named references are to passages in the Koran. A fuller discussion, particularly as regards later developments in this area of Muslim thought and culture, will be found in the separate article, Djinn and Genie (see also **Arabian Nights, Monsters In The**).

The Koran distinguishes three classes of created sentient beings: **angels**, humans, and djinn. Angels (made from light) do not have free will and can only do what God (Allah) commands. Humans and djinn, however, although they were created to worship God (51.56) may choose between obedience and rebellion (in spite of this apparent free will, according to 7.179, some were created for Hell). For humans, belief generally precedes obedience, and this is the primary dividing point between the faithful (Muslims) and the unbelievers (although it is possible to believe and still choose to disobey). Unbelief among the djinn is not generally an issue (37.158)—they choose disobedience in spite of their knowledge, but unlike the **demons** of Christian theology, some djinn are faithful to the creator (the first group of these, in fact, was converted when they heard Mohammed's preaching, so God's mercy and forgiveness are available to them as well [46.30; 72.1]).

Djinn

The djinn (the word means "invisible," although they can take animal form—especially snakes) were created from smokeless (or scorching) fire (55.15; humans were made from black clay). The first djinni (singular of djinn) to be created was Iblis, and he is the ancestor of all the djinn. As in some post-Biblical Christian mythology, Iblis was offended when God asked the heavenly assembly to bow down to Adam, even though Adam had demonstrated his admirable prophetic skills by naming them (that is, the angels—a variation of the Genesis account where he names the animals). God was not pleased but grants him an indulgence until the final judgment. Iblis, in his rebellion, promises to do his best to lead humankind astray from the creator. Adam and Eve taste from the tree (of the knowledge of good and evil) against God's command, as in Genesis, and become aware of either their "shameful parts" which, apparently, they had not yet noticed, or their "evil intentions," depending on the translation (7.11–27). Iblis comes to be known as Shayṭān ("mischief," cognate with the Hebrew, Satan [accuser]), but lower level djinn can be referred to as shaytans as well if they are functioning to lead people astray. In this role they may also be called "whisperers," although the **Devil** is the prime whisperer, whispering even into the hearts of djinn (114.4)

Djinn come in a variety of types, a few of which are mentioned in the Koran. An *ifrīt* is an extremely powerful and clever type. **Ghosts** fall into this category in modern belief, but their only mention in the Koran is associated with Solomon (27.39–40). As suggested in earlier Jewish pseudepigrapha (*The Testament of Solomon* [date uncertain, sometime between the first and fifth century CE]), Solomon was able magically to impress the demon world into a labor force. An ifrīt volunteers to fetch the Queen of Sheba's extremely heavy throne and bring it to Solomon. Later, after Solomon dies, the djinn continue on his projects for a while, unaware that the magic that compelled them has now dissipated. When they do discover their error, they are embarrassed and depart from his service (34.14).

Mārid are a class associated with the sea, and play a large role in the *Arabian Nights* but appear once in 37.6–7 (not mentioned by name in most translations). The Sunan of Abu-Dawood 5088 (told by Aisha, one of Mohammed's wives) refers to an otherwise unknown type. Mohammed asks if any *mugharribun* have been seen, and when prompted he says that they are a type of djinn. In addition to these, Iblis has several sons, famous for various forms of mischief: Zalambur (who oversees fraudulent business deals [and in the modern world, traffic]), Awar (encourages depravity), Dasim (marital discord), Sut (lies), and Tir (disasters). In one tradition, claiming to date from the seventh or eighth century, another son, Khannas, gets eaten by Adam and Eve (in the body of a goat), which enables him to work with his father to tempt humans from within.

A *qarîn* (also called *hamzaad*) is a peculiar type of djinn that is created each time a human is born. They function as devilish versions of guardian angels, although they are even more intimately connected to their assigned human. They appear several times in the Koran (for example, 41.25; 43.36–39; 37.51–55), and most English translations call them "companions" (which is a proper translation—the word can also refer to people). Their job is generally to try to lead their assigned humans astray. They continue with them throughout life and are with them before God at the judgment. Humans who are not faring well at that point will often try to blame their qarîns, who in turn will testify that they did not compel their humans to do anything—they only whispered suggestions to which the humans complied from their own will (50.27). If someone rebels from God, a shaytan is appointed for him as a qarîn (43.36; this implies a slightly different model for the qarîn than is generally accepted). Since all humans have a qarîn, Mohammed was asked how he managed with his. He responded that, in his case, his qarîn had been converted and was a Muslim, enabling him to be free from error (Sahih Muslim [a collection of Hadith], 2814). Jesus apparently had the same advantage, as perhaps did other prophets as well.

The idea of the qarîn certainly existed in pre-Islamic Arabia, and some Egyptologists have speculated that its origins are in the Egyptian concept of the Ka (sometimes translated "soul," although this hardly does it justice). Like humans, djinn are gendered, and sex between them and humans is a possibility. Early on, traditional Islam viewed the qarîn as inversely connected to their human partner by gender, so that a woman receives a qarîn (masculine) and a man a qarîna (feminine—although note that Mohammed referred to his qarîn as masculine). In adulthood, they often mate sexually, usually in dreams, with their human partner; resulting children are composite in some way. Both varieties will be jealous of their human's physical spouse; the man's qarîna might attack her. A bachelor is sometimes said to be married to his qarîna (see **Incubus/Succubus**). Qarîn are particularly bothered by their woman's natural children, so infant deaths may be blamed on the mother's djinn companion.

"Monsters" Other than Djinn

Since angels have no free will, they cannot be in rebellion against God. This does not mean that all their activities are positive from a human point of view. The two angels of Babylon, Harut and Marut, apparently taught magic to both humans and djinn, intentionally trying to lead people astray, which, in this case, must have been God's intention. Careful to protect God from the accusation of misdirecting people, they always accompanied their deception with the warning, "We have been sent to deceive you" (2.102). Apparently, however, their dupes were not listening during the disclaimer portion of their presentations.

The angel Malik also does God's will, so the faithful would have no issue with him. The damned (both humans and djinn), however, are not so understanding, since he is the warden of Hell (43.77, where the damned ask to be annihilated, but are compelled to live on in torment). Modern Christian folklore, of course, assigns this role to the Devil, but Biblical Christianity and Islam agree that he will be one of the suffering damned rather than ruling. Malik does not work alone; he is accompanied by 18 other angels (74.30). There is also an angel of death (32.11), whose actions are not generally welcome (see **Death, Personified**).

Although not particularly monstrous, 27.82ff contains what may be a version of the Beast in the *Revelation of John* (certainly monstrous there). He appears, turned into a final messenger, just before the end, to remind people that they have erred in not accepting God's revelations.

In most of the Koran, false gods are simply idols, and the point is frequently made that they cannot in any way assist those who believe in them. But there is a group of passages (for example, 28.63) that have the gods themselves denying on the day of judgment that they were truly worshipped, although they do admit that they led people astray. A few passages in Hadith also seem to animate the gods occasionally. These beings are usually called "partners" and may have independent existence. The angels deny that it is they that are being worshipped, saying it was the djinn (34.4 of; see also 6.100). There is no other indication that these gods were seen as having any real existence, even as sub-deities.

In Fiction

Djinn have been hugely popular as fictional villains, usually with only the faintest allegiance to Islamic beliefs regarding them. For a more general summary, the reader is referred to the article on djinn. This list will be limited to cases where one of the discussed sub-categories is specifically mentioned (not expecting such portrayals to be any closer to tradition). Neil Gaiman's 2001 novel *American Gods* contains a scene in which a taxi-driving ifrīt switches identities with a passenger. *Slaves of Sleep* and *Masters of Sleep* (two connected novels) by L. Ron Hubbard (1939) feature ifrīts. Wes Craven's film *Wishmaster* (1999) is worth mentioning only because it illustrates the traditionally valid principle that the djinn may give you what you ask for, but you will not get what you expected. Not surprisingly, Salman Rushdie's 1988 *Satanic Verses* features its contingent of djinn as well.

Alan Humm

References and Suggested Reading

Hughes, Thomas Patrick. *A Dictionary of Islam.* London: Allen, 1895.

Lebling, Robert. *Legends of the Fire Spirits: Djinn and Genies from Arabia to Zanzibar.* London: I.B.Tauris, 2010.

Macdonald, Duncan B. *Haskell Lectures in Comparative Religion.* Lecture 5, 130–56. University of Chicago, 1906.

Stevens, Ethel S. *Folk Tales of Iraq.* London: Oxford, 1931.

Zwemer, Samuel M. *Studies in Popular Islam: Collection of Papers Dealing with the Superstitions and Beliefs of the Common People.* London: Sheldon Press, 1939.

KOROV'EV—*see* Demon

KRAKEN

A kraken is a giant **sea monster**, usually represented in literature and film as an octopus-like creature, characterized by powerful tentacles and vast size sufficient to sink ships. Despite the long-established literary presence of multi-limbed sea terrors such as Scylla in Homer's *Odyssey* (c. eighth century BCE; see **Scylla and Charybdis**), the kraken is a relatively modern monster; the word was first used in the 1750s by Bishop Pontopiddan of Bergen (1698–1764) to describe creatures reported in the seas around Norway. While deep-sea dwelling giant (*Architeuthis*) and colossal (*Mesonychoteuthis*) squid may account for sightings, the kraken is notable as a mythological, as well as a biological, monster in folklore, literature, and later in film. Its mythology inflects literary and cinematic

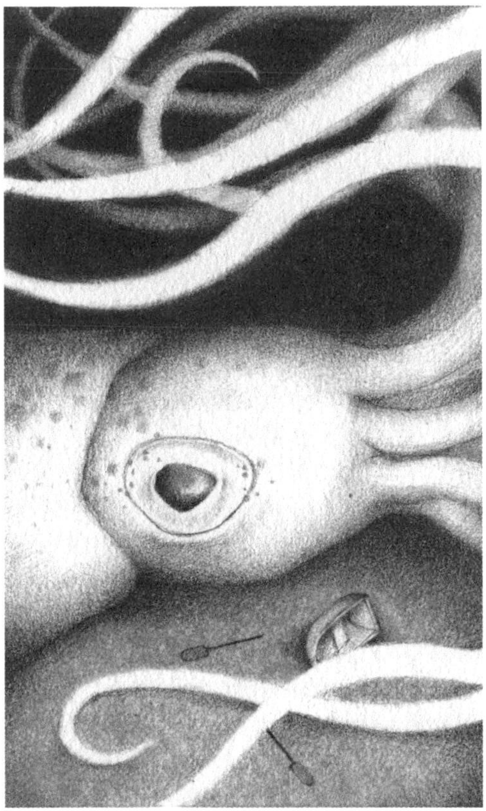

Fig. 22 ***Kraken* by Allison W. Sommers**

representations, both of cephalopods and more fantastical tentacular monsters. It is often presented as aggressive and hostile to humans, particularly in horror narratives, but can also represent the primordial natural world and the dangers of excessive scientific or exploratory curiosity. In literature and film, both literally and metaphorically, the kraken slumbers beneath the sea, heralding terror and apocalypse when it awakes or is disturbed.

The kraken was a popular subject for nineteenth-century literature, earning a place in novels by Sir Walter Scott (1771–1832) and Thomas Love Peacock (1785–1866), as well as coverage in folklore and fairytale, and in numerous scientific accounts. Scott's *The Pirate* (1821) includes a description of the influence of Norse sagas on Shetland culture; boatmen flee the sight of a kraken in the fog in case it should drag away their ship. In "The Kraken" (1830), Alfred Lord Tennyson made the kraken the focus of the poem: "Far, far beneath in the abysmal sea, / His ancient, dreamless, uninvaded sleep / The Kraken sleepeth" (lines 2–4). The kraken here is a primeval, distant presence, destined to lie until the end of the world when it will rise and die on the surface of the sea. Tennyson blends nineteenth-century biological science in his representation of the deep sea, its sponges and polypi, with the mythical power of the kraken legend (see Maxwell). The kraken appears metaphorically in other poems, such as J.R. Lowell's "Ode to France" (1848), in which the myth of the kraken being mistaken for an island stands for deceptive stability, and Henry Wadsworth Longfellow's "The Cumberland" (1863), in which the iron ship destroying the Cumberland is compared to a kraken. Tennyson's poem, however, set the tone of the kraken legend in literature for many subsequent texts.

In narratives maintaining a degree of biological verisimilitude (with varying degrees of accuracy), the kraken often features as a giant squid or cuttlefish. In Melville's ***Moby-Dick*** (1851), a white squid with tentacles "like a nest of anacondas" is briefly mistaken for the whale itself and Ishmael speculates that giant squid form the origin of the kraken myth (see especially 231–2). In Victor Hugo's *Toilers of the Sea* (1866), Gilliatt, after a shipwreck, is attacked by a cephalopod armed with powerful suckered tentacles. The monster is cast as a malignant creature in a category of its own; after a brief violent struggle, Gilliatt kills the creature with his knife.

Jules Verne's *Twenty Thousand Leagues Under the Sea* (1869) (and Disney's 1954 film adaptation directed by Richard Fleischer) includes a battle with several giant squid that latch onto the *Nautilus* (itself named after a cephalopod); one sailor is snatched up and dragged underwater despite seven of its eight arms being hacked off by the crew and "squirm[ing] like serpents all over the platform" (Verne 349). Despite its questionable zoology, Verne's novel invigorated public interest in cephalopods in the nineteenth century (see Stott). This period marks a turning point for fictional monsters, including the kraken, as evolutionary theory was used to validate a range of physically monstrous creatures (such as H.G. Wells's octopus-like Martians; see **Extraterrestrials**), in contrast to the human villains of the traditional Gothic. In this new literature, the tentacle, the kraken's hallmark, became "the default monstrous limb-type" of weird fiction (Miéville 512).

H.G. Wells's "The Sea Raiders" (1896) describes the discovery by a Devon tourist of human-eating octopus-like creatures, predatory and intelligent: *haploteuthis ferox*. Later, these aggressive monsters are sighted in the coastal waters; they attack the investigating boat and gnaw off the boatman's arm. The shoal harries the south coast; eventually the raids cease, although whether due to death or departure is deliberately left uncertain. William Hope Hodgson (1877–1918), British sailor turned horror-writer, produced a number of stories in which kraken-like terrors assail boats. Hodgson uses the legendary weed-world of the Sargasso Sea as a breeding ground for giant monsters, including cephalopods that pluck sailors from ships, as in "From the Tideless Sea" (1907). The Watcher in the Water in J.R.R. Tolkien's *The Fellowship of the Ring* (1954), and Peter Jackson's 2001 film adaptation, is another kraken-like monster, grabbing hobbits in its tentacles (see **Tolkien, Monsters In**). In H.P. Lovecraft's "The Call of Cthulhu," Cthulhu has a "cephalopod head" (72) resembling an octopus and, like the kraken, sleepeth, awaiting its time (see **Lovecraft, Monsters In**).

Other texts adopt the name of the kraken to denote hostile alien beings, accompanied by kraken-like features such as associations with invertebrate physiology or dormancy disturbed, including John Wyndham's *The Kraken Awakes* (1953) and Jay Williams's *The Time of the Kraken* (1977). In Wyndham's novel, alien ships land and vanish into the deepest oceans, until, perhaps aggravated by American bombing, they attack ships and islands worldwide. The aliens are never seen, but their tank-like constructions explode with cilia that drag away several people. After retaliation from human armies and navies, the aliens melt the ice caps. The increasing water level causes worldwide social and political breakdown, until it stops after rising 100 feet; Japan develops an ultrasonic weapon to kill the aliens underwater.

Hugh Cook's 1977 poem, "The Kraken Wakes," is partly a modern retelling of Tennyson's "The Kraken." In Cook's poem, the deep-sea **giant**, representing our planet's ecological balance, is fatally disturbed by the damaging consequences of human civilization, even while it participates in its destruction. In Jim Lynch's *The Highest Tide* (2005), the discovery by a teenage boy of a giant squid with eyes the size of hubcaps, washed up on an American shore, initiates a coming-of-age story told through his relationships with other characters and his deep love of the marine environment. China Miéville's *Kraken* (2010) blends a number of facets of the kraken's history. After a specimen *Architeuthis* mysteriously vanishes from London's Natural History Museum, curator Billy is drawn into a kraken-worshiping cult and London's dangerous occult web. Miéville incorporates the existing texts by Tennyson, Lynch, and Cook into his fictional kraken mythos.

The kraken has appeared numerous times in films, especially horror or disaster movies. The kraken is usually antagonistic, either actively predatory or defensive when disturbed. In *It Came From Beneath the Sea* (Robert Gordon, 1955), an irradiated monster affected by nuclear weapons testing rises from the sea bed to attack ships and later San Francisco itself with vast and powerful tentacles, recasting the sleeping kraken's awakening for an atomic age. In *Clash of the Titans* (Desmond Davis, 1981), the kraken is one of two monsters (the other is **Medusa**) battled by Perseus in his efforts to save Andromeda. The kraken is represented as a multi-limbed reptilian sea-monster. A remake, directed by Louis Leterrier, followed in 2010. In Disney's 2006 *Pirates of the Caribbean* sequel *Dead Man's Chest* (Gore Verbinski), a kraken is the monstrous pet of Davy Jones (Bill Nighy) and follows his bidding to hunt Captain Jack Sparrow (Johnny Depp), dragging him into the Underworld. Davy Jones himself has a cephalopod head reminiscent of Cthulhu. In the third film, *At World's End* (Gore Verbinski, 2007), Davy Jones is forced by Lord Beckett (Tom Hollander) to kill the beast, the last of its kind.

The kraken possesses a unique mystique as a sea monster, only loosely based on a known zoological source, which itself remains one of the modern mysteries of the deep sea. As a result, the kraken's shape, behavior, motivation, and significance are all up for artistic interpretation. A creature rich in both literal and metaphorical potential, the kraken is a versatile monster well adaptable to such a range of environments of genre and form.

Emily Alder

References and Suggested Reading

Heuvelmans, Bernard. *The Kraken and the Colossal Octopus*. Letchworth: Kegan Paul, 2003.

Lovecraft, Howard Phillips. *The Call of Cthulhu and Other Weird Tales*. London: Vintage, 2011.

Maxwell, Richard. "Unnumbered Polypi." *Victorian Poetry* 47, no. 1 (2009): 7–23.

Melville, Herman. *Moby-Dick* [1851]. Reprint, Ware: Wordsworth, 2002.

Miéville, China. "Weird Fiction." In *Routledge Companion to Science Fiction*, edited by Mark Bould, Andrew Butler, Adam Roberts, and Sherryl Vint, 510–16. London: Routledge, 2009.

Stott, Rebecca. "Through a Glass Darkly: Aquarium Colonies and Nineteenth-Century Narratives of Marine Monstrosity." *Gothic Studies* 2, no. 3 (2000): 305–27.

Tennyson, Alfred Lord. "The Kraken." In *Selected Poems*, edited by Christopher Ricks, 7. London: Penguin, 2007.

Verne, Jules. *Twenty Thousand Leagues Under the Sea*. London: Penguin, 1994.

KRUEGER, FREDDY

The creation of Wes Craven, Freddy Krueger is the recurring antagonist of the "Nightmare on Elm Street" franchise and is a being who inhabits a dream world in which he is capable of physically murdering children while they sleep. Krueger's distinctive look is introduced in Craven's *A Nightmare on Elm Street* (1984): he wears an old hat and a red and green striped jumper, is horrifically burnt and scarred, and kills with a glove that has razor sharp claws on each finger. It is revealed that, while still alive, he was believed to have murdered over 20 children, but his trial was thrown out of court due to a legal technicality. The children that Krueger preys on in the film are those of the parents who formed a mob and burnt him alive. Much of Krueger's menace is linked to our vulnerability while sleeping and he uses memories and phobias to torment his prey. Played with great relish by actor Robert Englund (b. 1947), the character is infused with a sense of mischievous fun and his crimes are fiendishly inventive, perhaps explaining why such a seemingly unsympathetic character went on to build a huge international fan base.

The first film features one intended victim, Nancy Thompson (Heather Langenkamp), attempting to fight back and kill Krueger by drawing him into the real world. In order to figure out how to survive his attacks, Nancy deprives herself of sleep, blurring the lines between wakefulness and lucid dreaming. She appears to be victorious in the last act of the film, before the final scene inevitably shows that Krueger remains at large. This becomes a recurrent narrative arc, with Krueger always able to find a way to return in order to continue the franchise. In *A Nightmare on Elm Street Part 2: Freddy's Revenge* (Jack Sholder, 1985), teenager Jesse Walsh (Mark Patton) and his family move into Nancy's old house, 1428 Elm Street. Jesse starts to dream about Krueger, who breaks down the barriers of his mind so that he can use the boy's body to kill adults and children alike. This is the first of many significant additions to the abilities of the character.

A Nightmare on Elm Street 3: Dream Warriors (Chuck Russell, 1987) focuses on a group of children at the Westin Hills Psychiatric Hospital who share recurrent nightmares about Krueger. This film accentuates the fantastical elements of Freddy's dream world, as he is able to possess and transmogrify any object or piece of technology with which to torture and kill the teenagers. *Dream Warriors* introduces the ghost of Krueger's mother, Amanda, who was a nun at the hospital who became trapped in the wing for the criminally insane one holiday and was raped by the inmates. Amanda dubs Krueger "the bastard son of a hundred maniacs." The children of *Dream Warriors* fight back in the dream world and the three who survive are carried forward into *A Nightmare on Elm Street 4: The Dream Master* (Renny Harlin, 1988). When they are killed, Krueger moves on to the dreams of one of their friends, Alice Johnson (Lisa Wilcox), who is the only character in the series able consciously to bar the killer from her dreams. In *A Nightmare on Elm Street 5: The Dream Child* (Stephen Hopkins, 1989), Krueger kills once again, through the dreams of Alice's unborn child, who ultimately helps his mother defeat the dark presence inside them both. *Freddy's Dead: The Final Nightmare* (Rachel Talalay, 1991) sees Krueger ostensibly meet his ultimate demise, only for the character to be resurrected for *New Nightmare* (Wes Craven, 1994), in which Krueger becomes the vehicle for an ancient evil that can only be laid to rest by continuing to tell stories about him.

Krueger's popularity as an icon of horror cinema led to the film *Freddy vs. Jason* (Ronny Yu, 2003), in which he battles against another franchise villain, **Jason Voorhees**; commercial interests in both series dictated an inevitable stalemate. With the 2010 remake of *A Nightmare on Elm Street*, directed by Samuel Bayer, Jackie Earle Haley was cast as the new Freddy Krueger. His performance eschews the comedic elements of the previous Krueger, replacing it with a furious intensity. Its box office success has ensured the continuation of the series, with a sequel in production.

David McWilliam

References and Suggested Reading

Schoell, William, and James Spencer. *The Nightmare Never Ends: The Official History of Freddy Krueger and the "Nightmare on Elm Street" Films*. New York, NY: Citadel Press, 1992.

KUBERA—*see* Mahābhārata, Monsters In

KUEI—*see* Demon

KUTSA—*see* Demon

LAMIA

In ancient Greek folklore, *Lamia* was a name often given to a kind of spirit that was believed to kill infants, similar to and sometimes identified with the **empousa**. The origin of the name remains a matter of controversy, but may derive from the Greek for "gullet," in reference to the belief that this entity devoured its victims; or the name may have its roots in ancient demonology relating to Lamashtu and **Lilith**, child-killing **demons** in Mesopotamian and Babylonian folklore (Resnick and Kitchell 80–81). Indeed, many of the rituals used to protect children against the attacks of such spirits were borrowed by the Greeks from the Near East. Lamia was the best-developed figure from the world of child-killing spirits in Greek thought, and has been the most influential on later literature.

Ancient Greek literary references to Lamia, though frequent, lack detail until the Hellenistic period, when Lamia began to figure prominently in a story known as the "Libyan myth," which became increasingly elaborate throughout the Roman era. In the story's oldest attestation, found in the Greek historian Diodorus Siculus (20.41.1–6, first century BCE), Lamia was originally the daughter of the Syrian god Belos and the African nymph Libya, and became queen of Libya. The god Zeus fell in love and had an affair with her, but an envious Hera, wife of Zeus, killed all of Lamia's children. Driven to hide in a cave, Lamia became a monster that emerged only to seize and devour as many children as she could. The only relief the Libyans had came when she slept. Initially, Hera had further punished Lamia by denying her the ability to sleep, but Zeus took pity on Lamia by giving her the power to remove her eyes and replace them at will, thus letting her sleep when she took her eyes out.

Child-killing spirits such as Lamia were originally used as bogeymen to frighten children into obedience. Thus, the Libyan myth form of her story became a commonplace during the Roman Empire, not only in the nursery but also in classrooms, as reflected in the surviving writings of scholars and teachers such as Diodorus and Plutarch (*Moralia*, 515F–516A; c. first century CE), who tell the story because a moral can be drawn from it, as from the fables of Aesop (c. 620–564 BCE). They rationalized the supernatural elements of the Libyan myth so that, for instance, the removal of her eyes is interpreted as Lamia passing out from drunkenness.

By the early Roman Empire, Lamia had changed in the literature from an infant-killing spirit to a sexual monster that seduced and devoured young men. For example, the Sophist Dio Chrysostom (c. 40–112 CE) devoted his entire fifth *Oration* to such a retelling of the Libyan myth. In Dio, the lamia is a savage animal native to Libya that preys upon shipwrecked sailors. Dio describes the *lamiae* as having the face of a woman, along with a woman's neck and breasts. But the lower part of her body was that of a snake. The lamiae would lure men closer by revealing at first only their upper, female parts, but as soon as a man came close enough, the creature would sting him with poison and then devour him. A king of Libya once waged war to wipe these monsters out, but he and his army were destroyed instead. Finally, the hero Hercules was able to eradicate the lamiae. The moral of Dio's story is that only the heroic virtue taught by philosophy can overcome the baser human instincts. Dio's version of the Lamia story was loosely adapted for the television series *Hercules: The Legendary Journeys*, in *The Wrong Path* (#1.1, 1995).

Another Sophist, Philostratus (c. 170–250 CE), in his *Life of Apollonius of Tyana* (4.25), transports the Lamia story from Libya to the Greek city of Corinth. In this version, the young Cynic philosopher Menippus is seduced by a lamia who wishes to "fatten him with pleasures" before devouring him. He abandons the philosophical school and moves into her palace, which is an illusion of luxury created by her magic. But the heroic philosopher Apollonius discerns the lamia's true nature. He tells Menippus that his lover is a serpent, but the young man is too smitten, or too enchanted, to believe it. So Apollonius comes to the wedding feast where he dispels the lamia's illusory banquet and breaks her spell over the youth using reason, saving Menippus from becoming the main course. The moral once again is that only philosophical discipline can triumph over the allure of pleasure.

Interest in the lamia as a monster for didactic use was renewed among Christian authors, and natural philosophers of the medieval period recorded many legends about the lamia (Resnick and Kitchell 83–4; 91–2). But it was Philostratus's story that most greatly influenced later literature, particularly two major poems of the Romantic movement: Wolfgang von Goethe's *The Bride of Corinth* (1797) and John Keats's *Lamia* (1821). In *The Bride of Corinth*, Goethe uses Philostratus's tale to make an ironic attack against Christianity. His hero unwittingly consorts with a lamia in Corinth; the creature reveals that she died childless and is therefore doomed to existence as a man-eating **vampire** because her Christian mother made her become a nun. Goethe implies that the ascetic strain of Christianity is unnatural and destructive for human beings. His lamia is definitely interested in drinking her lover's blood rather than eating him; Goethe intended this to be satirical of the Christian sacrament of communion, but the act establishes an important element of the modern vampire myth. Goethe's poem is the link that establishes the figure of the lamia as the ancestor of the vampire.

Keats's long poem *Lamia* probably provides the version of the Lamia story most familiar to modern readers. He follows Philostratus's plot very closely, but transforms the tone of the story. Keats's Lamia genuinely loves the philosopher Lycius and uses her illusory spells to shield him from the forces of the outside world that would separate them. Apollonius's discernment of the truth that causes the illusions to vanish becomes a symbol for the modern forces of reason and science that have destroyed the traditional world of myth.

Keats's poem directly inspired several substantial works of modern literature, including A.S. Byatt's "A Lamia in the Cévennes" (1995). In the story, a lamia, in the form of a snake, turns up in the swimming pool of a British painter living in southern France. Ironically, he would rather paint the creature as a serpent than make love to it and enable it to become human. After the lamia manages to cast her spell over a friend of his on a visit, the painter reflects that Keats was wrong: understanding the natural world through science makes the world more numinous, not less. Byatt's lamia thus serves as a symbol of the irrational become insignificant in the modern world.

Tim Powers's fantasy novel *The Stress of Her Regard* (1989) set the tone for much of the lamia's reception in modern popular culture. The main character, Michael Crawford, is a classmate of John Keats in medical school circa 1816. In this novel, the lamiae are essentially vampires as understood in modern horror films: they drink the blood of their victims and induce an intense erotic euphoria. They kill their victim's family members, including children, out of jealousy. Keats, along with the Romantic poets Percy Shelley (1792–1822) and Lord Byron (1788–1824), belongs to a secret society devoted to exterminating the lamiae.

Lamiae indistinguishable from vampires commonly appear in later fantasy novels and other media. Ken Russell adapted Bram

Stoker's 1911 novel, *The Lair of the White Worm*, into a film in 1988; the novel had been loosely based on the Lambton Worm of English folklore, but Russell's transformation of the story incorporated many themes from the Lamia tradition, creating a highly sexualized, devouring monster that could transform between human and serpentine forms. In "The Muse" episode of the television series *Star Trek Deep Space Nine* (#4.21, 1996), the character Jake Cisco (Cirroc Lofton) is attacked by a creature based on the Leanan Sidhe, a **fairy** creature from Irish mythology who inspires poets but also drains their life away. In the episode, this creature is specifically said to have killed John Keats; thus, the episode interprets Keats's Lamia as a kind of destructive muse who drains her victims' life force rather than their blood. This further development of the lamia sometimes appears in other brief references to the creature in fantasy works in various media, such as Neil Gaiman's television series *Neverwhere* (Dewi Humphreys) and its concurrent novelization (1996), and the film version of his *Stardust* (Matthew Vaughn, 2007), wherein the witches Lamia (Michelle Pfeiffer), Mormo (Joanna Scanlan), and Empusa (Sarah Alexander) need to eat the heart of a fallen star to replenish their youth and magical powers.

Bradley Skene

References and Suggested Reading

Anderson, Graham. *Philostratus: Biography and Belle Letters in the Third Century A.D.* London: Croom Helm, 1986.

Daruwala, Maneck H. "Strange Bedfellows: Keats and Wollstonecraft, Lamia and Berwick." *Keats-Shelley Review* 11 (1997): 83–132.

Johnston, Sarah Iles. "Defining the Dreadful: Remarks on the Greek Child-Killing Demon." In *Ancient Magic and Ritual Power*, edited by Marvin Meyer and Paul Mirecki, 361–87. Leiden: E.J. Brill, 1995.

Resnick, Irven M., and Kenneth F. Kitchell, Jr. "'The Sweepings of Lamia': Transformations of the Myths of Lilith and Lamia." In *Religion, Gender, and Culture in the Pre-Modern World*, edited by Alexandra Cuffel and Brian Britt. Basingstoke: Palgrave Macmillan, 2007.

LANGSUYAR—*see* Women, Monstrous

LEATHERFACE—*see* Psychopath

LECTER, HANNIBAL

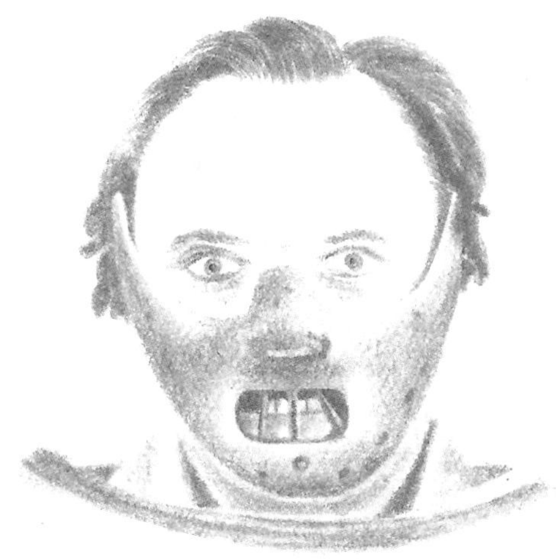

Fig. 23 ***Hannibal Lecter*** **by Robyn O'Neil**

Chosen in 2003 as the American Film Institute's number one villain, the cannibalistic serial killer Hannibal Lecter is a character in a series of novels by Thomas Harris (1940–) and in the films adapted from them. Introduced in the 1981 book *Red Dragon*, the brilliant psychiatrist Lecter is already incarcerated for murder but is consulted by his nemesis, FBI agent Will Graham, for help in catching "The Tooth Fairy." It is a pattern echoed in the novel's sequel *The Silence of the Lambs* (1988), in which trainee FBI agent Clarice Starling consults with an incarcerated Lecter in order to catch "Buffalo Bill," a serial killing transsexual who, having been refused gender reassignment surgery, sets about constructing a "woman suit" from the flayed skin of his victims. Lecter will echo this practice, with greater success, at the end of the novel when he escapes captivity by wearing the face of a prison guard as disguise. Thus free, Lecter moves to center stage in *Hannibal* (1999), which opens with him living in Florence under an assumed name and working as an eminent curator at the Uffizi gallery. Having outwitted and destroyed a revenge-seeking former victim, Lecter drugs and then seduces Starling; the novel ends some three years later with the lovers living together in Argentina. In 2006, Harris would revisit the Lecter story in *Hannibal Rising*, a prequel that expands on *Hannibal*'s account of Lecter's cannibalistic origins at the hands of Nazi collaborators who butcher and eat his sister in the final years of World War II.

The first cinematic adaptation of *Red Dragon* was Michael Mann's *Manhunter* in 1986, starring Brian Cox in the role of the incarcerated psychiatrist. A second cinematic version of the novel was released in 2002 as *Red Dragon*, with Anthony Hopkins reprising the role for which he had won an Oscar in Jonathan Demme's filmic adaptation of *The Silence of the Lambs* (1991). Ridley Scott's *Hannibal* (2001) replaced Jodie Foster with Julianne Moore as Starling and proved to be hugely profitable, with a final domestic gross standing at an impressive $200,000,000—an American box office record for any non-action movie (Shaw 10). Balking at the controversial Starling love plot, however, the film has Lecter escape alone. By 2007, the killer's appeal was waning; Harris's novel *Hannibal Rising* and its filmic adaptation of the same year, directed by Peter Webber, received a panning at the hands of critics and achieved comparatively miniscule box-office returns.

Having saturated the popular cultural consciousness to an unprecedented degree, the Lithuanian-Italian Lecter, as played by Welsh and Scottish actors, has become an unlikely American icon. He has been affectionately parodied in animations such as *The Simpsons* ("Stark Raving Dad," season 3, episode 1 [1991]), *South Park* ("Toilet Paper," season 7, episode 3 [2003]), and *Family Guy* ("Stuck Together/Torn Apart," season 3, episode 19 [2002]), and films such as *The Cable Guy* (Ben Stiller, 1996), *Cats and Dogs* (Lawrence Guterman, 2001), and *Austin Powers in Goldmember* (Jay Roach, 2002). And although the films excise his ancestry, which can be traced to the Florence of Dante, his unapologetic rejoicing in the decadence of the Old World is most certainly a large part of his charm. Fond of *cordon bleu* cuisine, the music of Bach, and the art and architecture of the Renaissance, Lecter's surname is Italian for "scholar." What is more, his given name is that of the Carthaginian general who took on the might of the Roman Empire in utterly individual fashion by crossing the Italian Alps on elephants. Certainly, in the novels, Lecter's academic and high-cultural tendencies can be seen in his intimate familiarity with the work of T.S. Eliot (1888–1965), John Donne (1572–1631), Marcus Aurelius (121–180 CE) and Shakespeare (1564–1616), the paintings of Duccio (c. 1255–1318), and the motions of the stars. This is a sadistic serial killer notable both for his utter sadism and his intellectual acuity, taste, and sophistication: a potent and unique combination.

A medical doctor and psychiatrist still eminent in his field, Lecter is what the Behavioral Science Unit (BSU) of the FBI would term a highly "organized" offender, selecting his victims in advance, engaging in elaborate planning, and executing his crimes and his victims with utterly ruthless efficiency. As such, he is what the BSU would term a "hedonistic power/control killer" whose acts in the novels (though excised from the films) have included the purposeful release of violent criminals into the community, the murder of an ex-patient, and the arrangement of the victim's body as a tableau representing the sixteenth-century "wound man" (originally illustrating the mishaps to which the human frame is prone on the field of battle). In the films, these acts have included the infamous consumption of a census-taker with *legumes* and a decent Italian red, and the administration of hallucinogenic drugs that cause a pedophile ex-patient to feed his own face, in slivers, to two hungry dogs. In none of the films, however, do we receive any easy or reductive explanations as to Lecter's motivations. The FBI may be able to explain the motivations of a Tooth Fairy or a Buffalo Bill, but they are entirely incapable of offering either a clinical or sociological explanation for Lecter's crimes. Certainly, until the final disappointing installment, Lecter himself provides no explanation as to his own nature, preferring to revel in the infamy of irrational evil rather than participate in the behaviorist rationalizations of second-rate therapists such as the asylum head Dr Chilton (played by Anthony Heald in *Silence of the Lambs* and *Red Dragon*), whom Lecter subsequently hunts down and kills. As such, Hannibal Lecter can be plausibly seen as the embodiment of the very paradox that has informed America's mission into the wilderness since the seventeenth century. He is cultured, intellectually brilliant, witty, and charismatic. He is, to all intents and purposes, "civilization" incarnate. And yet, like the harbingers of American civilization who tamed a wilderness through slaughter of its native people, the decimation of its ecosystem, and the wholesale enslavement of the African-American race, he is capable of acts of enormous and seemingly barbaric savagery—an American icon indeed.

Linnie Blake

References and Suggested Reading

Greig, Charlotte. *Evil Serial Killers: In the Minds of Monsters*. London: Arcturus Publishing, 2009.

Ressler, Robert, et al. *Sexual Homicide: Patterns and Motives*. New York: Free Press, 1988.

Shaw, Daniel. "The Master of Hannibal Lecter." In *Dark Thoughts: Philosophic Reflections on Cinematic Horror*, edited by Stephen Jay Schneider and Daniel Shaw, 10–24. Lanham, MD: Scarecrow Press, 2003.

Simpson, Philip L. *Psycho Paths: Tracking the Serial Killer Through Contemporary American Fiction*. Carbondale: Southern Illinois University Press, 2000.

LEPRECHAUN

The Leprechaun is a diminutive, solitary species of Irish **fairy**, known first and foremost for his hoard (or crock) of gold, which humans may gain as ransom if they manage to capture and hold onto him. The often red-bearded figure, with green, buckled top-hat, shoes, and waistcoat, has become so ubiquitous in his present-day kitsch manifestations, including film appearances, cartoons, and St Patrick's Day-related paraphernalia, as to lose any sense of continuity with his mythological origins in pre-Christian Ireland. He (for most Leprechauns are described as male in existing literature) is certainly the most successfully exported Irish fairy.

The historical origins of the Leprechaun are multifaceted and contradictory. Various accounts of Irish folklore maintain that the modern English word "Leprechaun" is derived from one of the following translations from the original Irish. T. Crofton Croker, one of the most often cited nineteenth-century authorities, claims that the term may be a Leinster provincialism of *Luacharma'n*, the Irish word for pygmy (96). Douglas Hyde, however, a founding member of the Gaelic League, maintains that the term derives from the Irish *leith bhrogan*, the "one shoe maker," due to the creature's predisposition towards the cobbling trade (quoted in Briggs 264). Contemporary folklorist James MacKillop definitively dates the term from the Middle Irish word *luchorpán*, meaning "small body." The term is originally ascribed to water-sprites who carry Fergus over the water in the eighth-century text *Echtra Fergusa maic Léti* (*The Adventures of Fergus Son of Leti*) (263). The word *luchorpán* then evolved into the modern Irish name for the shoe-making, gold-hoarding fairy, which has many regional spellings and pronunciations, but is most often rendered in modern Irish as *leipreachán* or *luprachán*, subsequently anglicized to the current spelling of this entry. Leprechauns in Irish mythology are traditionally associated with the Irish landscape itself, specifically raths (ruined, Iron-age earth-forts), remains of castles, forests, and depressed places in the earth.

One of the most important sources for the Leprechaun's dissemination outside Ireland was the 1825 work by T. Crofton Croker, *Fairy Legends and Traditions of the South of Ireland*. He notes that various regional legends from around Ireland seem to coalesce in or around a single type of fairy: "the Cluricaune of the County of Cork, the Luricaune of Kerry," he notes, "appear to be the same as the Leprechaun or Leprochaune of Leinster, or the Loghery-man of Ulster" (96). His description of the Cluricaune seems the most like the modern Leprechaun, for he is a solitary fairy who is a "maker of shoes." He sports "huge silver buckles" on his own shoes, and possesses a "pruned, ruddy face and a twinkle in his eye" (82–3). If the Cluricaune can be caught, he or she who accomplishes the feat shall have "money enough always" (95). Croker also describes a third spirit, the Fir Darrig, or "red man," most often envisioned as a tiny, red-clad practical joker, also potentially related to the modern Leprechaun, given its "delight in mischief and mockery," which Croker compares to "other [foreign] sprites such as Robin Goodfellow or the German Kobold" (284). Poet and amateur folklorist William Butler Yeats opined, after reading Croker, as to whether these three fairies (the Leprechaun, the Cluricaune, and the Fir Darrig) are in fact "one spirit in different forms and shapes" (Yeats 80). This theory seems supported by John Winberry, who provides a map indicating that the Cluricaune was traditionally associated with southern Ireland, and the Leprechaun with western Ireland (65), an area massively depopulated by emigration in the nineteenth century, both during and after the Great Famine. This fact might help to explain the dominance of the latter term among Irish immigrants.

In addition to Croker's volume, William Allingham's popular mid-nineteenth-century poem entitled "The Leprechaun; or Fairy Shoe-maker" also helped to reinforce many of the details we associate with the modern fairy, as is aptly demonstrated by the following excerpt:

> *Lay your ear close to the hill*
> *Do you not catch the tiny clamour,*
> *Busy click of an elfin hammer,*
> *Voice of the Leprechaun singing shrill*
> *As he merrily plies his trade?*
> *He's a span*
> *And a quarter in height.*
> *Get him in sight, hold him tight,*
> *And you're a made man!*

The poem goes on to relate how the creature is found in a "castle-ditch," is bespectacled, and wears silver buckles and a leather apron (Yeats 82–3). Croker and Allingham both helped to refine the image of the Leprechaun as an earth-bound cobbler of shoes who, like other fairies, frequents raths and other ruined places, and has the ability to bring great wealth to the one who catches him. However, Leprechauns are not so easy to capture or to hold, as they are well known for their deceit and trickery.

Lady Wilde (1821–96), the mother of Oscar Wilde and an avid Irish folklorist, appears to be the first to mention the Leprechaun as being "dressed all in green," also noting that he wore a "leather apron, drab clothes and buckled shoes" (Briggs 266). In her 1888 work, *Ancient Legends, Mystic Charms and Superstitions of Ireland*, she also expands on the other themes, especially the crock of gold itself and the Leprechaun's wily nature with regard to it. The Leprechaun, she maintains, is not only the tailor and cobbler to the fairy gentry, but also the treasurer of their hoard of gold, who, if captured, will guide the captor to the fairy rath where the treasure lies buried. She then relates the story of a family from Castlerea (Ireland) who purportedly came by their fortune in such a manner: a young member of the family, himself suspected of being a "fairy changeling," was as a result capable of outwitting a Leprechaun and securing its crock of gold. He then took the treasure to Dublin and placed it in a bank where the fairies could not reacquire it (Wilde 56–7). Not all people have such extraordinary luck, she maintains, as Leprechauns can be "bitterly malicious if offended, and one should be cautious in dealing with them" (57).

Leprechauns' popularity again grew when they became primary characters in Irish author James Stephens's novel *The Crock of Gold* (1923), in which they are featured as wily tricksters and antagonists to the protagonists of the novel, the Philosopher and his wife, the Thin Woman of Inis Magrath. Unlike previous incarnations of the myth, we here encounter an entire underground community of Leprechauns, who have been hoarding gold for "many thousands of years" (30). They also hold the couple's children hostage after the Philosopher reveals the crock's location to a third party, who then steals it. Stephens explains that the gold has been obtained over centuries by theft and is needed for ransom if one of their number is captured. Most, he qualifies, however, escape because "men are fools" (73) and are easily duped by the mischievous fairies.

Given their adaptability to a variety of different contexts, as well as their association with avarice, Leprechauns have found a ready home in American mass media. Two decades after the publication of Stephens's book, the 1947 musical *Finian's Rainbow* became a hit on Broadway, and was later made into a 1968 movie directed by Francis Ford Coppola and starring Fred Astaire as Finian, an Irish immigrant who comes to the United States with a crock of gold, pursued by its owner, the Leprechaun Og (Tommy Steele). As well as introducing countless Americans to the myth of the Leprechaun, the work also offered a subtle critique of current politics and race relations in the United States. Leprechauns continue to enjoy widespread success in the film industry, ranging in genre from the 1959 Disney hit comedy, *Darby O'Gill and the Little People* (Robert Stevenson), to the 1993 horror film, *Leprechaun*, directed by Mark Jones and featuring Warwick Davis, who plays the Irish fairy as a sadistic monster bent on murder to regain his gold.

Many of these filmic representations, along with the various other iterations of the modern Leprechaun, from Halloween costume to St Patrick's Day parade staple, have essentialized the character, marketing him as yet another example of the "nostalgia and innocence in which Irishness is so often embedded in the United States" (Negra 354). The modern figure of the Leprechaun has in many ways become, as filmmaker Bob Quinn has remarked about

Ireland itself, "a figment of the American imagination" (Meaney 255), quite divorced from the ancient fairy legend with which it originated.

Michael Jaros

References and Suggested Reading

Briggs, Katherine. *An Encyclopedia of Fairies.* New York: Pantheon, 1976.

Croker, Thomas Crofton. *Fairy Legends and Traditions of the South of Ireland.* London: John Murray, 1834.

Hyde, Douglas, ed. and trans. *Beside the Fire: A Collection of Irish Gaelic Folk Stories.* London: David Nutt, 1890.

Koch, John T., ed. "Tuath De." In *Celtic Culture: A Historical Encyclopedia: Vol 5*, 5 vols, 1693–95. Santa Barbara, CA: ABC-CLIO, 2006.

MacKillop, James. *Dictionary of Celtic Mythology.* Oxford: Oxford University Press, 1998.

Meaney, Geraldine. "Dead, White, Male. Irishness in *Buffy the Vampire Slayer* and *Angel.*" In *The Irish in Us: Irishness, Performativity, and Popular Culture*, edited by Diane Negra, 254–81. Durham, NC: Duke University Press, 2006.

Negra, Diane. "Irishness, Innocence, and American Identity Politics Before and After September 11." In *The Irish In Us: Irishness, Performativity, and Popular Culture*, edited by Diane Negra, 354–72. Durham, NC: Duke University Press, 2006.

Stephens, James. *The Crock of Gold.* New York: Macmillan, 1923.

Wilde, Lade Jane Francesca. *Ancient Legends, Mystic Charms and Superstitions of Ireland.* Revised edition. London: Chatto and Windus, 1925.

Winberry, John T. "The Elusive Elf: Some Thoughts on the Nature and Origin of the Irish Leprechaun." *Folklore* 87, no. 1 (1976): 63–75.

Yeats, William Butler, and Lady Augusta Gregory. *A Treasury of Irish Myth, Legend and Folklore* [1888]. Reprint, New York: Avenel Books, 1986.

LESHCHII—*see* Demon

LESTAT DE LIONCOURT

Lestat de Lioncourt is the **vampire** protagonist of several novels by author Anne Rice (1941–) in her "Vampire Chronicles" series. Initially presented to readers through the eyes of his longtime companion Louis in *Interview with the Vampire* (1976), Lestat figures prominently in five subsequent novels: *The Vampire Lestat* (1985), *The Queen of the Damned* (1988), *The Tale of the Body Thief* (1992), *Memnoch the Devil* (1995), and *Blood Canticle* (2003). He also appears in Rice's *Blackwood Farm* (2002), a novel that combines the storylines of her "Vampire Chronicles" and "Lives of the Mayfair Witches" series. The tremendous popularity of Rice's books (most of which have been best-sellers) speaks to the continuing appeal of the Gothic novel, as well as to the specific appeal of the vampire Lestat character.

Lestat is first introduced in *Interview with the Vampire* from the perspective of Louis, who is being interviewed by a young reporter. Lestat is portrayed as vain, sadistic, and uncaring, in contrast to the sensitive Louis. The early life of Lestat de Lioncourt is narrated in the novel presented as Lestat's autobiography, *The Vampire Lestat*. Lestat tells the reader that he began life in eighteenth-century France as the son of an ailing landowner. He soon departed for the delights of Paris with his friend Nicolas and there was hunted and eventually transformed into a vampire by the ancient vampire Magnus. His new status as vampire alienated Lestat from his friends and family but endowed him with strength, wealth, and a new appreciation for and perception of existence. Lestat famously describes the world he sees before him as a "savage garden"—a phrase that has resonated with readers and fans over the years. When Lestat meets other vampires, he begins to discover their long history and embarks on a quest to learn more about his powers and the origins of vampires.

The plot of *The Vampire Lestat* concerns Lestat's rise to rock stardom and the publication of his autobiography—actions that anger many other vampires who see his revelation as a violation of their community's ancient secrets. The story of Lestat's quest for vampire origins is continued in *The Queen of the Damned* when he discovers the resting place of "Those Who Must Be Kept," the ancient Egyptian forebears of all vampires. While *Interview* depicts Lestat as particularly cold and cruel, further novels privilege Lestat's point of view and position him as a beautiful, arrogant, and long-suffering outsider.

Of note concerning Rice's representations of vampires is their sexual celibacy—all sensuality is transferred to the drinking of blood and the appreciation of the sights, textures, and smells of the "savage garden" around them. Nevertheless, Lestat is presented as a powerfully sensual creature who forms highly eroticized relationships with both men and women. This has led to a great deal of academic criticism focusing on the representation of homosexual desire between male characters in Rice (see, for example, Hodges and Doane; Haggerty). Interpretation of Rice's vampire series has also focused on the ways in which the characters are shown creating alternative kinship networks through vampirism (see Gelder; Wasson).

Given the popularity of Rice's vampire novels, cinematic adaptations were inevitable and Neil Jordan made the first attempt with *Interview with the Vampire* in 1994, starring Tom Cruise as Lestat—a casting decision that sparked a good deal of controversy among fans and conflict between Rice and the film producers. In 2002, a film adaptation of *Queen of the Damned* directed by Michael Rymer appeared, with Stuart Townsend playing Lestat. While Jordan's film did eventually garner some financial and critical success, *Queen of the Damned* was poorly received and overshadowed by the untimely death of the singer Aaliyah, who played Queen Akasha in the film. The two screen versions of Lestat are quite different; in *Interview with the Vampire*, Cruise delivers a highly theatrical performance in a film by a director whose work has been characterized as possessing a flair for dark fantasy (see Zucker). In *Queen of the Damned* (an adaptation that also encompasses much of the plot events of *The Vampire Lestat*), Townsend comes closer to capturing Lestat's elegance and appeal through his more natural performance style, and the film is greatly influenced by the alternative music and goth sub-cultural styles of the late 1990s and early 2000s. In addition to the two films, there was also a short-lived musical adaptation—*Lestat The Musical*—that ran in San Francisco and New York in 2005 and 2006 and featured music by Elton John.

Lestat's impact on the image of the vampire in popular culture cannot be underestimated, as evidenced by the line uttered in 2000 in the first episode of season 5 of the vampire-themed program, *Buffy the Vampire Slayer* ("Buffy vs. Dracula"): "I've fought more than a few pimply, overweight vamps who called themselves Lestat." Mitchell (Aidan Turner) in the BBC's *Being Human* and Eric Northman (Alexander Skarsgård) of Showtime's *True Blood* are both arguably figures indebted to Lestat. All these adaptations and homages reflect the popularity of the Lestat character and a desire to see him brought to life beyond the page—a desire shared by the New Orleans-based Anne Rice's Vampire Lestat Fan Club, which maintains an active online presence and organizes an annual Vampire Ball and Undead Con.

S. Artt

References and Suggested Reading

Gelder, Ken. *Reading the Vampire*. Abingdon, Oxon: Routledge, 1994.

Haggerty, George E. "Anne Rice and the Queering of Culture." *Novel: A Forum on Fiction* 32, no. 1 (1998): 5–18.

Hodges, Devon, and Janice L. Doane. "Undoing Feminism in Anne Rice's Vampire Chronicles." In *Modernity and Mass Culture*, edited by James Naremore and Patrick Brantlinger, 158–75. Bloomington and Indianapolis: Indiana University Press, 1991.

Hoppenstand, Gary. *The Gothic World of Anne Rice*. Bowling Green, OH: Bowling Green State University Popular Press, 1997.

Wasson, Sara. "The Coven of the Articulate: Orality and Community in Anne Rice's Vampire Fiction." *The Journal of Popular Culture* 45, no. 1 (2012): 197–213.

Williamson, Milly. *The Lure of the Vampire: Gender, Fiction and Fandom from Bram Stoker to Buffy*. London: Wallflower Press, 2005.

Zucker, Carole. *The Cinema of Neil Jordan: Dark Carnival*. London: Wallflower Press: 2008.

LEVIATHAN

The Leviathan is mentioned only six times in the Hebrew Bible and once in a pre-Biblical written source. He nevertheless reached the status of a paradigmatic monster in post-Biblical times and in Western culture.

In the cuneiform inscriptions from ancient Ugarit (second millennium BCE), mention is made of "the fugitive serpent Litanu." The inscription mentions that Litanu was killed by a god, most probably by the storm god Baal, and that the sea god Yammu will take revenge for the smiting of his helper who is also called "wriggling serpent" and "mighty one with the seven heads" (De Moor 69–71). Litanu/Leviathan is here clearly cast in a role of a chaotic monster that threatens the balance in cosmos and civilization.

In the Hebrew Bible, Leviathan is only mentioned in poetic texts. The six occurrences do not reveal a single homogenous portrait of the monster. In Psalm 74, a poem lamenting the destruction of the temple by inimical powers, the Israelites are summoned to trust in YHWH and his kingship that is "of old." His kingship is demonstrated by references to victories over the sea and the **dragons**. In this context, God is seen as a deity who had crushed the head of the Leviathan and had given him as food to the creatures of the wilderness (Psalm 74:14). The same reflection of the ancient combat myth is present at Isaiah 27:1. God will destroy Leviathan who is mentioned here twice and described in words common to the Ugaritic depiction as "the fugitive serpent," as well as the "wriggling serpent." The most elaborated image is found in Job 41:1–34, as a monstrous beast without a rival, full of strength and power. This beast is stronger than iron and his breath sets coals ablaze. He cannot be tamed by human beings, only by God, his maker. Within the dialogues in the Book of Job, this description functions to demonstrate to Job the futility of questioning God, who alone has created these beings and who alone can contend with them. The concept of God as creator of the Leviathan recurs in Psalm 104:26, where the beast stands in parallelism to ships, indicating his connection with the sea. Job 3:8 depicts some unfaithful people as having the ability to rouse Leviathan.

According to Jewish tradition, both Leviathan and **Behemoth** were created on the fifth day but soon separated and were sent to different domains (4 Esdras 6:49–52; 1 Enoch 60:8–90). Strangely enough, Leviathan is here a female dragon. (See also the *Apocalypse of Abraham* 21:4, where the monster is construed as a fierce beast from the sea whose aim is to destroy civilization up to today.) All efforts definitively to associate Leviathan with an existing creature—for example, a hippopotamus, or crocodile—

have failed; however, some Creationists believe that the Leviathan is identical to a **dinosaur** that became extinct after the great flood, or to a giant whale.

Very influential on the general conception of Leviathan is Thomas Hobbes's famous book that was written in the aftermath of the turmoil of the English Civil War in the middle of the sixteenth century. Hobbes's *Leviathan*, in fact, is a political philosophy tract on the question of power. The title of the work is derived from the Biblical **sea monster**. Hobbes construes Leviathan as a very powerful creature controlling the world around him. That is exactly the role of the state in a world in despair. He sees this creature as the embodiment of the collected power of a nation and construes him as a mortal god. Under the guidance of the immortal god, people owe peace and deference to Leviathan. A Dutch historian has recently adopted Hobbes's title in his sketch of the struggle for liberal politics in Europe in the nineteenth and early twentieth centuries (Lamberts).

In *The Satanic Bible* (1969), the fifth book is entitled "The Book of Leviathan." This book is composed as a compendium of ritual instructions containing all sorts of incantations. Interesting is the "Invocation to Satan" that is to be performed at the outset of each ritual. Leviathan is here connected with the world of dark water and functions as an apotropaic feature against the good things in life.

In modern literature, several novels are named Leviathan. Most famous is Paul Auster's 1992 novel. The opening scene narrates how the main character, Leviathan, accidently blows himself up with a bomb. The story seeks for the why of this action and it turns out that the "Phantom of Liberty" has been blowing up replicas of the Statue of Liberty all over the country. The novel toys with Hobbesian ideas on the power of the state. Less well known, and also less elegantly written, are Warren Tute's *Leviathan* (1962) about a fictional ocean liner; Philip Hoare's *Leviathan* (2008), which tells stories about whales; Robert Anton Wilson and Robert Shea's *Leviathan* (1975), the third part of their science fiction work "The Illuminatus! Trilogy"; and Scott Westerfeld's *Leviathan* (2009), a steampunk retelling of the Great War (1914–18) in which Leviathan refers to the great British airbeasts.

The concept of the Leviathan has received various treatments in film and on TV. The science fiction television series *Farscape*, which aired from 1999 to 2003, is set in a different universe accidentally reached by the main characters through a wormhole. One of the races that inhabits this universe is the Leviathans, a species of **cyborgs** that was constructed by the main inhabitants of Farscape, the Builders. Leviathans are not always monstrous. In 1989, George Pan Cosmatos directed the science fiction horror movie *Leviathan*. In this film, geologists assisting in an underwater mining operation discover the remains of a Russian ship, *The Leviathan*, with all its crew dead from a mysterious decease.

In the horror comic *Leviathan*, created by Ian Edginton and D'Israeli, *The Leviathan* is the largest ship ever built. It took ten years to build the mile-long ship apparently modeled after *The Titanic*. On its first trip in 1928, it disappeared with 30,000 passengers on board and now dwells in a never-ending ocean where no other forms of life are present. The passengers on the upper decks are unaware of what is going on; nevertheless, on occasion they hear strange sounds. Of quite a different character is *Leviathan*, a comic strip by Peter Blegvad that appeared in the review section of the British newspaper *The Independent on Sunday* during the 1990s. Leviathan is here shortened to Levi, who is drawn as a baby without a face accompanied by a stuffed toy that goes under the name Bunny or Rabbit. The pet cat Cat is never far away and eager to give advice. The fabric of the strip is philosophical discussions on the incomprehensibility of reality. Many features in this strip remind one of the comic *Calvin and Hobbes*.

In 2008, fossil remains of an extinct whale were found in the highlands of Peru. In view of its size, the species was called *Leviathan melvillei*. In this, the name of the Biblical monster is connected to Herman Melville, the author of **Moby-Dick**.

Bob Becking

References and Suggested Reading

Auster, Paul. *Leviathan*. New York: Viking, 1992.

Beal, Timothy K. *Religion and its Monsters*. New York: Routledge, 2002.

Birmingham, John. *Leviathan: The Unauthorised Biography of Sydney*. London: Vintage, 1992.

Dimovitz, Scott A. "Portraits in Absentia: Repetition Compulsion and the Postmodern Uncanny in Paul Auster's 'Leviathan'." *Studies in the Novel* 40 (2009): 447–64.

Hobbes, Thomas. *Leviathan: Or the Matter, Forme, and Power of a Common-Wealth Ecclesiasticall and Civill*, edited by Ian Shapiro. New Haven, CT: Yale University Press, 2010.

Lambert, Olivier. "The Giant Bite of a New Raptorial Sperm Whale from the Miocene Epoch of Peru." *Nature* 466, no. 7302 (2010): 105–8.

Lamberts, Emiel. *Gevecht met Leviathan: een verhaal over de politieke ordening in Europa, 1815–1965*. Amsterdam: Prometheus Bv Vassallucci, Uitgeverij, 2011.

LaVey, Anton. *The Satanic Bible*. New York City: Avon, 1969.

Moor, Johannes C. de. *An Anthology of Religious Texts from Ugarit*. Leiden: Brill Archive, 1987.

Sussmann, Naomi. "How Many Commonwealths Can Leviathan Swallow? Covenant, Sovereign and People in Hobbes's Political Theory?" *British Journal for the History of Philosophy* 18 (2010): 575–96.

Uehlinger, Christoph. "Leviathan." In *Dictionary of Deities and Demons in the Bible: Second Extensively Revised Edition*, edited by Karel van der Toorn, Bob Becking, and Peter W. van der Horst, 511–15. Leiden: Brill; Grand Rapids: Eerdmans, 1999.

LICTOR—*see* Demon

LILITH

Lilith is the primary representation of the demonic feminine in Jewish lore (see **Demon**; **Women, Monstrous**). Her main function is to attack family life and particularly the things traditionally valued by women. So on the one hand, she is associated with infant death, and to a lesser extent threatens women's health in childbirth. On the other hand, she acts as a seductress, leading men away from their wives, but more importantly into disfavor with God. She also uses this opportunity to steal men's semen and bear numerous demon children.

Her relation to older demonic figures from Mesopotamia is disputed but probable. Certainly the Mesopotamians (Sumerians, Assyrians, Babylonians) had evil feminine spirits whose functions closely parallel Lilith's, but the exact nature of the relationship has not yielded scholarly consensus. She does, however, give her name to a class of similarly functioning spirits called "liliths" (actually three differently formed plurals in Hebrew). It may not always be clear when her name in texts refers to her or one of her minions. But her earliest undisputed literary references are to "liliths" (2 Baruch 10:8, and in the Dead Sea Scrolls, 4Q510 *fr.* 1). She also makes a few appearances in the Talmud (tractates Erubin 100b; Nidda 24b; Shab. 151b; and one of her "sons" is referenced in Baba Bathra 73a–b).

Her one cameo in the Bible (Isaiah 34:14), however, is disputed. The context has a *lylyt* haunting desert places in the company of other animals, and a *sa'ir* (calling to his companions). *Sa'ir* can mean "goat," but it is used in other Biblical contexts for a type of demon (or possibly a **satyr**); *lylyt* occurs nowhere else in scripture. If the *sa'ir* is a demon, then the *lylyt* probably refers to our demoness (given the Mesopotamian parallels and her clear role in later Judaism), but if he is a goat, then *lylyt* is most likely an otherwise unknown animal name (probably an owl, judging from the immediate context).

In the ancient world, Lilith appears in magical texts and on amulets and other prophylactics intended to thwart her activities, but we see somewhat more of her in late Roman and early medieval Judaism. She appears frequently on magical bowls (buried under thresholds to keep various unwanted spirits out). These protective methods are most frequently intended to thwart her role as a threat in childbirth and infancy, although they may also protect against her sexual attacks. She is often countered by invoking the powers of her nemesis **angels**: Snvi, Snsvi, and Smnglof.

In the late Talmudic period, *Genesis Rabbah* (a collection of commentaries on the Book of Genesis) tells us that Eve had a predecessor—that she was Adam's second wife, although the first wife is never named (18.4; 22.7). Between the eighth and tenth centuries CE, however, Lilith shows up in a satirical work entitled the *Alphabet of Jesus Ben Sira*. At this point the connection is made between Eve's predecessor and the already well-known baby-stealer. She is created at more or less the same time as Adam, but because she tries to assert her equality, and is rebuffed by Adam's own self-assertion (the issue is really about dominance in sexual intercourse), she ends up escaping from Eden and being replaced by the more submissive Eve. Lilith now adopts her new persona as baby-stealer and mother of demons. She makes a deal in which she promises to leave babies alone if they are protected by amulets with the names of the three angels mentioned above.

Jewish mystical literature (Kabbalah) plays down the "first wife" aspect of the Lilith tradition and focuses instead on her role as Samael's (Satan) wife (see **Devil, The**). She participates in the Temptation of Eve in Naftali Bacharach's seventeenth-century *Emeq haMelekh* 23c–d and then, after the Fall, sleeps with Adam for a time, making many demon babies. In some traditions, she has been rendered infertile in order to prevent her from filling the world with her progeny.

She is a major player in Jewish supernatural folklore, most of which focuses on her role as the Devil's queen or as a sexual temptress. She is the mistress of illusion and a personification of temptation, seeking to entrap even the righteous, killing them and bringing them to God for judgment if they fall. In her role as **succubus**, she has, of course, particular control over nightmares and erotic dreams. She also rules a horde of other succubi and **incubi**.

In many Renaissance paintings of the temptation of Adam and Eve, the serpent is given a woman's head and often a full **mermaid**-like body (half-snake, rather than half-fish). This feminizing of the serpent may simply represent a general feminizing of personified Sin, also seen in Milton (1608–74), but may alternatively (or also) reflect Lilith's function in the Temptation, as described in Kabbalah. We do know that there was some intellectual crosstalk between the Kabbalists and a parallel Christian scholarly movement (usually spelled Cabala), which may have, in turn, influenced art, although medieval portrayals of **Lamia** frequently had serpentine torsos.

The Vulgate translation of the Bible uses *lamia* to translate *lylyt* in the Isaiah passage (discussed above). The distinctions between the Greco-Roman Lamia and the Jewish Lilith may be fairly subtle anyway (see **Incubus/Succubus**), so it is not particularly surprising that the two concepts merged in nineteenth-century art and literature. Her transition into the modern world began with a brief appearance in Goethe's *Faust* (1808) in which she is portrayed as irresistibly sexual. She then returns eleven years later in John Keats's poem *Lamia*, in which readers are reminded of her connection to the snake. Poet-artist Dante Gabriel Rossetti added a painting (*Lady Lilith*, 1868) and two poems (*Lilith* [renamed *Body's Beauty*], 1868, and *Eden's Bower*, 1869). There followed Robert Browning's *Adam, Lilith, and Eve* (1883), and several paintings by John Collier (1850–1934).

Although the para-Biblical myth occasionally surfaced (see, for example, George MacDonald's *Lilith*, 1885) as the nineteenth century progressed into the twentieth, Lilith/Lamia usually represented the feminine dark side (the part that men subliminally fear) in both literature and art. This is what lies behind Carl Jung's (1875–1961) use of her as the prime expression of the *anima* in men (the suppressed *femme* within), or for a maladaptive behavior in a woman that seeks to destroy other women's marital happiness. The best monograph on her still belongs to a disciple of Jung, Siegmund Hurwitz (1980).

With the feminist movement, particularly beginning in the latter third of the twentieth century, Lilith has been escorted through another shift in persona. The story in the medieval *Alphabet of Jesus ben Sira*, written from a man's perspective, paints a picture of Lilith's lack of submission to Adam as the root cause of her transition from Eden to the demonic. Read subversively, however, feminists find a heroic story of one woman's escape from oppression to independence; Lilith becomes the first feminist, sacrificing even the paradise of Eden as the necessary cost of freedom and equality. Of course, her role as baby-stealer and her marriage to the Devil are usually down-played (or assigned to a patriarchal layer of the tradition). Her assertion of sexual equality is held up as a model for women's sexual independence and self-awareness. Some neo-pagan groups have taken up her cause as well, either accepting her dark nature as part of a larger sacred reality (a Kali-type goddess), or finding the erotic goddess within by removing the clutter of what they argue are patriarchal and monotheistic condemnations.

Art and literature have generally followed suit. Most graphic images try to portray her as unapologetically sexual. Another significant group focuses on her as a dark goddess, or in a few cases as powerful and unyielding. Of course, para-Biblical images continue to abound (see, for example, contemporary artist Lilian Broca's "Lilith" series, begun in 1994). Novels and poetry (including songs) often focus on retelling the *Alphabet* story, often with some clever twist, as in Eduard Le Compte's 1988 *I, Eve*, which focuses on Eve's response to Lilith's role as Adam's lover after Eden; there are, however, a number of offerings, usually from a magical point of view, that reassert her demonic nature, such as in Donald Tyson's *The Tortuous Serpent* (1997).

Finally, she has a place in **vampire** lore, either as the first and most powerful of the vampires, or at least as their queen. She is sometimes presented as the daughter or the consort of **Dracula**. She plays this role in Marvel Comics' *Tomb of Dracula* series (1972–79), and it has been her primary guise in various films including *Bordello of Blood* (Gilbert Adler, 1996). This and her demon persona have not surprisingly proved fruitful ground for the creators of role-playing and video games such as *Darkstalkers*, in which she is a vampire/succubus alter ego to the character Morrigan (either to be played or fought).

Alan Humm

References and Suggested Reading

Humm, Alan. "Lilith." Published 1995–2011. <http://www.jewishchristianlit.com/Topics/Lilith/lilith.html>.

Hurwitz, Siegmund. *Lilith—The First Eve: Historical and Psychological Aspects of the Dark Feminine*. Translated by Gela Jacobson. Einsiedeln, Switzerland: Daimon Verlag, 1992.

Patai, Raphael. *The Hebrew Goddess*. New York: KTAV Publishing House, 1978.

Pereira, Filomena. *Lilith: The Edge of Forever*. Las Colinas, TX: Ide House, 1998.

Scerba, Amy. "Changing Literary Representations of Lilith and the Evolution of a Mythical Heroine." 1999. <http://feminism.eserver.org/theory/papers/lilith/index.html>.

Schwartz, Howard. *Lilith's Cave: Jewish Tales of the Supernatural*. Oxford: Oxford University Press, 1989.

LINOGE, ANDRÉ—*see* Demon

LA LLORONA

La Llorona, La Gritona, the Weeping Woman, the Wailer, and the Woman in White are different names for the same mythical woman cursed to haunt a place, usually by a body of water, weeping for her dead children or seeking to punish wayward men for her suffering (see also **Women, Monstrous**). The depiction of La Llorona dates back to early indigenous mythology in Mexico prior to the Spanish colonization, but different versions of this myth not only populate contemporary Mexican culture but also circulate through the southern United States. Some variants of the myth depict her as the monstrous mother who kills her children by drowning them, while others focus on her victimization at the hands of patriarchal society because of her racial and/or social inferiority.

Some sources for the legend of La Llorona include the Biblical figure of Rachael, Medea in Greek mythology, and even some **vampiric** figures such as the Malaysian *langsuyar* or the Greek **Lamia** that kidnap children after losing their own. The Mexican traditions of this legend date back to pre-colonial roots in the Aztec mythological figures of Coatlicue and Cihuacoatl. Both of these goddesses appeared to Monctezuma I dressed in white in 1452, and it is said the Cihuacoatl also appeared in the Aztec city of Tenochtitlan in 1502, dressed in white and wailing, "Dear children, soon I am going to abandon you!" (Read and González 149)—a wail that is said to have prophesied the fall of the indigenous people to the Spanish.

These indigenous roots of La Llorona are then blended with the historical figure of La Malinche (c. 1496 or 1505–c. 1529 or 1550), an Aztec princess given to the Spanish conquistador Hernán Cortés (1485–1547) as a gift on his arrival in the New World in 1519. She became not only Cortés's translator but also his lover and mother to his child in 1521. La Malinche, feeling guilty for having "aided" Cortés in the murder of her people, prays to her gods for guidance and they tell her that her son would continue the massacre if she allowed him to leave for Spain with Cortés. At this point legend and history blend together: it is said that La Malinche escaped one night to the lake and stabbed the child in the heart before dropping his lifeless body into the water and crying out "Oh, hijo mío" ("Oh, my son"). Oral tradition has it that La Malinche can be seen at the lake's edge crying out for her dead child—the distinctive epigraph of many accounts of La Llorona.

Another origin story for the legend refers to the case of the *mestiza* girl Doña Luisa de Olveros who lived in Mexico City around 1550 (see Norman). Like La

Malinche, she falls in love with a Spanish captain and has his children, but she is never given the legal recognition of being his wife. When her Spanish lover admits to her that he will never marry her because of her race, she kills all three children with a dagger. She is subsequently condemned to death and is said to roam moonlit streets dressed in white and crying for her children.

Modern-day versions of the legend function as bogeyman stories told to children. One variant tells the story of a young wife, abandoned by her husband because she is no longer beautiful, who attempts to recapture her husband's love by drowning her children in the Rio Grande since they were to blame for her diminished beauty. Overwrought with guilt and haunted by her children's screams, she drowns herself in the same river, and legend has it that along that spot of the Rio Grande one can hear her wailing: "*¡Ay, mis hijos! Aquí los eché, aquí los eché, ¿dónde los encontraré?*" ("I left you here, I left you here. Where am I going to find you?")

The legend also extends into the US. In the short story "Woman Hollering Creek" (1991), Chicana writer Sandra Cisneros adapts the story such that the body of water does not represent the site of infanticide and suicide but rather one of liberation—a rebirth. As a reflection of Coatlicue's power, the creek is named *La Gritona*, or Woman Hollering Creek, rather than *La Llorona*, Woman Wailing Creek. Cisneros's rewriting of the legend changes La Llorona's wail or cry into a holler and a shout of female empowerment and self-esteem.

Other variants insert a revenge-seeking component into the legend associated more with the **sirens** of Greek mythology and the Mexican goddesses of Coatlicue and Chalchiuhtilycue. These punitive versions involve the figure of La Llorona haunting a river, wailing for her children, and enticing men into the water to save her, only for them to reach her exhausted and be drowned by the **ghost**. In another variant, the La Llorona figure entices unfaithful or drunk men to follow her into the winding streets of the dark city to get lost and die—a variant picked up in the pilot episode, "The Woman in White" (2005), of the television series *Supernatural*. This vindictive La Llorona is popular in horror films such as *La maldición de La Llorona* (*The Curse of the Crying Woman*; Rafael Baledón, 1963), *La venganza de La Llorona* (*Vengeance of the Crying Woman*, Miguel M. Delgado, 1974), *Wailer* (Andrés Navia, 2006) and *Wailer II* (Paul Miller, 2007), *J-ok'el: La Llorona—The Curse of the Weeping Woman* (Benjamin Miller, 2007), and *The Cry* (Bernadine Santistevan, 2007). La Llorona is also popular in musical lamentations by such artists as Chavela Vargas and Lhasa de Sela, to name a few.

Cristina Santos

References and Suggested Reading

Anzaldúa, Gloria. *Borderlands/Frontera: The New Mestiza*. San Francisco: Aunt Lute Books, 1999.

Aragon, Ray John de. *The Legend of La Llorona*. Santa Fe, NM: Sunstone Press, 2006.

Norman, Michael. *Haunted Homeland: A Definitive Collection of North American Ghost Stories*. New York: Tor Books, 2007.

Perez, Domino Renee. *There Was a Woman: La Llorona from Folklore to Popular Culture*. Austin, TX: University of Texas Press, 2008.

Read, Kay Almere, and Jason J. González. *Mesoamerican Mythology: A Guide to the Gods, Heroes, Rituals and Beliefs of Mexico and Central America*. New York: Oxford University Press, 2000.

LOCH NESS MONSTER

While cryptozoologists (see **Cryptid**) still search for the Loch Ness monster, in popular culture it is the most domesticated

Fig. 24 ***Loch Ness Monster*** **by Robyn O'Neil**

of cryptids, more likely to be depicted as a delightful oddity, charming and even cute, than as scary or even representative of what is unknown and alien to mankind. Lake monsters in general are often depicted as hidden and elusive but not enigmatic or awe-inspiring. For instance, in a 1999 episode of the TV show *South Park*, the parents of the character Chef say that the Loch Ness monster keeps asking them for $3.50 (as the parents say, "tree-fitty"), a request that always gets turned down. One can hardly imagine many cryptids other than perhaps **bigfoot** being depicted this mundanely. Affection for fresh-water monsters is strong enough that legislation protects them, whether they exist or not: the Loch Ness monster, Champ in Lake Champlain, and Arkansas's White River monster are all explicitly covered by conservation laws.

There are, however, exceptions. Especially in films, the Loch Ness monster and its fresh-water kin are occasionally threats. Sometimes they represent nature, as something to be protected or something to be overcome or just survived. Especially as a character in children's books and films, however, they are approachable and even, paradoxically, more human than genuinely humanoid cryptids such as bigfoot. Films and novels in which the Loch Ness monster is scary tend to give zoological explanations for its existence that are quantifiable and natural—a huge eel, a relict **dinosaur**—making it less bewildering and shocking. Perhaps the name Nessie and similar ones for other lake monsters make them more familiar, almost homey. In any event, the creature from the Scottish loch has been a part of folk culture for many centuries and has passed from being a terrifying monster through joking reference to become a more pliable figure than any other cryptid.

History and Science

Stories of lake and **sea monsters** stretch back to the first sailors. The lore of cultures around the world features water monsters, including those of ancient Mesopotamia, Japan, Sweden, Ireland, West Malaysia, and the Lakota people of America. The Vikings (700–1100 CE) recorded stories of sea serpents; in *Carta Marina*, published in 1539, Olaus Magnus describes many types of sea monsters. Zoologist Antoon Cornelis Oudmann, in *The Great Sea Serpent* (1892), studied 166 sightings. Actually, "serpent" is a misnomer, since many look more like crocodiles, pinnipeds (aquatic mammals such as the sea lion), or even the finned equivalents of centipedes. In any form, the sea monster is an enduring figure.

Apart perhaps from the **kraken**, however, twentieth- and twenty-first-century interest settled more on their land-locked cousins, the lake monsters—especially Nessie. *The Life of St Columba*, written in the seventh century by Adomnán, reports that the Irish monk saw a "water beast" by the River Ness while spreading Christianity in Scotland. Modern interest in the loch really began in July of 1933 when a couple named Spicer saw an "extraordinary creature"—25 feet long with a thin, ten-to-twelve-foot-long neck—cross the road in front of them near the loch. Sporadic sightings continued, and in 1963 a poor-quality film appeared. Some evidence has later been exposed as hoaxes, including a supposed photo of the creature's head and neck from 1935, admitted in 1979 by Christian Spurling to be a toy submarine with a head and neck he had sculpted. Films like that by engineer Tim Dinsdale in 1960, however, and results from sonar such as in the LNPIB (Loch Ness Phenomena Investigation Bureau) study in 1967–68, have kept interest alive. Groups led by Robert H. Rines produced photos in 1972, 1975, 2001, and 2008. However, a BBC expedition in 2003 regretfully concluded that the Loch Ness monster is only a myth.

Various cryptozoologists have suggested that something unknown may live in the loch, but it could be a giant sturgeon, catfish, crocodile, eel, pinniped, or even, according to Oberon Zell-Ravenheart (1942), founder of the Ecosophical Research Association that explores the truth behind myths, a slug-like shell-less mollusk. Many suggest that it is a surviving dinosaur, especially a plesiosaur. The biggest problem for such cryptozoologists is that Loch Ness is too small for a breeding population of any huge animal. More mundane explanations include schools of fish blurred together by sonar, optical effects of weather, and half-submerged tree trunks.

Films and Television

The Nessie aficionado often cannot know until the end of a film or text whether the monster is truly involved. For instance, in "The Convenient Monster," a 1959 short story by Leslie Charteris featuring British thief Simon Templar, an alleged monster attack is proven to have a human culprit, whom the real monster attacks. The same pattern—suggest, disprove, reveal—is used by *The X-Files* episode "Quagmire" (directed by Kim Manners, 1996) with a lake monster in Georgia, and even by *Scooby-Doo! and the Loch Ness Monster*, a 2004 direct-to-video film (Scott Jeralds and Joe Sichta).

The term "Loch Ness monster" itself, which became popular in 1933, assures that some versions of Nessie will be truly monstrous—that is, threatening to human beings. *Beyond Loch Ness*, also called *Loch Ness Terror*, is a 2008 made-for-TV horror film directed by Paul Ziller, in which Brian Krause plays James Murphy, a cryptozoologist whose family was killed by Nessie during a trip to Scotland when Murphy was a boy. Thirty years later, when the same monster shows up in Lake Superior, Murphy and a local youth destroy the monster, a 60-foot plesiosaur. Similarly, in *Beneath Loch Ness* (Chuck Cominsky, 2002), after the monster kills people, it is dispatched by an eccentric hermit who has lost his son to the monster and is blamed for that death. In *The Loch Ness Horror*, directed by Larry Buchanan (1981), the monster kills swimmers, but its scientist nemesis is insane, not a hero as in the previously mentioned films.

While other lake monsters are more likely to be friendly, the titular creature in *The Crater Lake Monster* (William R. Stromberg, 1977) is a relict plesiosaur, its egg hatched by the heat of a meteorite, which preys on nearby Oregonians. Some horror movies do not refer to Nessie or another famous lake monster but present the same situation, such as *Razortooth* (Patricia Harrington, 2007), about a huge super-eel eating people in the Florida everglades.

These monster films, however, are the minority, and in most films the monster is either a neutral force of nature or a likeable, often intelligent animal. *7 Faces of Dr Lao* (George Pal, 1964) provides an interesting middle ground: the mysterious circus manager says that a tiny fish in a bowl is actually the Loch Ness monster, and indeed, when town ruffians break the bowl, it grows into something like a dinosaur and then sprouts whiskers like a Chinese **dragon**. Although it grabs Dr Lao (Tony Randall) and one of the ruffians in its mouth, they are released unharmed. This movie also provides one solution to the breeding-population problem: the creature is a sea serpent that visits the loch but breeds in the ocean.

Some films depict the Loch Ness monster as a friend, especially to children. In *Mee-Shee: The Water Giant* (John Henderson, 2005), a creature in a Canadian lake does kill people, but only because the people have netted its child. The human hero, the son of a US oil man sent there to investigate a broken drill, rescues the younger mee-shee after it is harpooned. The film is based on **Ogopogo**, a lake monster in Canadian folklore, but after complaints by leaders of native Canadians, including Penticton chief Stewart Phillip, the makers deleted specific references to this creature. Earlier, Henderson directed *Loch Ness*, a 1996 family drama starring Ted Danson and Joely Richardson, in which the loch is home to surviving plesiosaurs. A cryptozoologist, eager to prove the existence of the monster, is influenced instead to keep the species secret to protect it. A Canadian lake monster named Orky, in *Magic in the Water* (Rick Stevenson, 1995), is possessing people to tell humanity that toxic waste in the lake is killing him; a brother and sister, Ashley (Sarah Wayne) and Joshua (Joshua Jackson), discover Orky's message and expose a businessman doing illegal dumping.

In one film, the creature goes beyond being a friend to being a pet. *The Water Horse: Legend of the Deep* (Jay Russell, 2007) is based on the children's novel *The Water Horse*, written by Dick King-Smith and illustrated by David Parkins (2000). In Scotland in 1942, on the shores of Loch Ness, young Angus McMorrow (Alex Etel) finds a mysterious egg that hatches into a creature that he names Crusoe. It is explained to him that the loch contains one "water horse," which asexually produces an egg and then dies. After growing huge, Crusoe is released into the lake, but is wounded by a British cannon meant to stop German U-boats. While others try to exploit or kill Crusoe, Angus convinces Crusoe to safely live in the wider sea. The term "water horse" shows the connection in popular culture and by some cryptozoologists between the Loch Ness monster and the kelpie, a shape-shifting water monster from Scottish legend (see **Shapeshifter**).

The ultimate making-familiar of the Loch Ness monster is *Happy Ness: The Secret of the Loch*, a 1996 movie of a 1995 children's show in which children encounter the underwater race of helpful, multicolored Nessies—including Brave Ness, Silly Ness, Forgetful Ness, and others—who teach them moral lessons.

The most unusual film about the Loch Ness monster is *Incident at Loch Ness* (2004), directed by Zak Penn, starring Penn himself and honored German director Werner Herzog. Like a Russian nesting doll, this film is about the making of two films, *Herzog in Wonderland*, a documentary by John Bailey about Herzog's career, and *Enigma of Loch Ness*, a documentary that Herzog is filming about the creature. Penn upsets Herzog by secretly hiring actors as a fake sonar operator and cryptozoologist, yet Herzog encounters what might be a real monster in the lake. Nessie is primarily an occasion for a metafictive film that completely confounds usual standards of truth and fiction.

An entire television series, *Surface*, concerns a species of huge creatures that can live in both salt and fresh water. Comprising 15 episodes that aired on NBC in 2005–2006, the show was created by Jonas and Joshua Pate. In its two interwoven plots, it demonstrates the flexible nature of the water monster: one plot concerns a government conspiracy to keep the dangerous and scientifically valuable creatures hidden and the oceanographer who wants an open investigation; the other concerns a teen boy who finds an egg, hatches it, and keeps the result as a pet. Although the creatures turn out to be genetically engineered, the show thoroughly depicts a truly scientific investigation of cryptids.

Fiction

Two common kinds of fiction featuring the Loch Ness monster are books for children or young adults and novels in cryptofiction series. Authors of the latter include Douglas Tanner, Lee Murphy, and Tabitca Cope. While *The Loch* (2005) is not part of a series, author Steve Alten also wrote the "Meg" series about huge prehistoric sharks in the present era. *The Loch,* a story of revenge by a marine biologist on the creature, was adapted into the movie of the same name (see above). Horror author Jeffrey Konvitz's 1982 *Monster: A Tale of Loch Ness* is early cryptofiction in which the monster is a plesiosaur that spawns at sea.

Popular children's fiction about the Loch Ness monster includes *Luck of the Loch Ness Monster: Tale of a Picky Eater* (2007), written by Alice Weaver Flaherty and illustrated by Scott Magoon. When a little girl on a ship to Scotland throws her oatmeal overboard every day, a tiny worm swimming alongside eats it and grows to be the Loch Ness monster. In *The Mysterious Tadpole,* by Steven Kellogg, a boy's uncle brings him a tadpole from Loch Ness that the boy must take care of as it grows and grows. The book was first published in 1977 and an anniversary edition with some edits came out in 2002. Poet Ted Hughes wrote *Nessie the Mannerless Monster* (1992 edition illustrated by Gerald Rose), in which the monster causes trouble and goes to London for an audience with the queen. *The Ogopogo: My Journey with the Loch Ness Monster* (1983) by Harry Horse (pseudonym for Richard Horne) became the first children's book to win the Scottish Arts Council Award.

Other children's books about Nessie include *The Lough Neagh Monster,* written by Sam McBratney and illustrated by Donald Teskey (1994), and *Nessie and the Little Blind Boy of Loch Ness* by Ken Anderson (1992). The Loch Ness monster also appears in the series featuring Wiggles the Flying Pig (*Wiggles and the Loch Ness Monster,* writer John Gatehouse, illustrator Dave Windett, 2011) and in the final volume of the decades-spanning Little Toot series, finished after author Hardie Gramatky's death (*Little Toot and the Loch Ness Monster,* 1989). *Nessie the Loch Ness Monster* by Richard Brassey (1997) is a non-fiction explanation for middle-school readers of the creature as a surviving aquatic dinosaur. These are only some of the works about the denizen of Loch Ness itself: other lake monsters also appear in children's and young adult books, such as Champ, the Lake Champlain monster, in *Champ and Me by the Maple Tree* (writer Ed Shankman, illustrator Dave O'Neill, 2010). In *Loch: A Novel* by Paul Zindel (1995), surviving dinosaurs in Lake Alban in Vermont devour people, but the 15-year-old protagonist and his sister save a young monster they call Wee Beastie.

Other novels and short stories often propose various explanations for the Loch Ness monster besides the usual cryptozoological ones or fanciful ones from children's novels. In some works, the Loch Ness monster is a purely supernatural creature: a steed that draws the chariot of the Celtic sea-god Lir in Roger Zelazny's short story "The Horses of Lir" (1981); a shape-shifting creature trapped in one form in *The Boggart and the Monster* by Susan Cooper (1997); a dragon who is given human form in the paranormal romance *Dragon in the Mist* by Nancy Lee Badger (eBook 2011); another shape-shifting dragon in Keri Arthur's *Destiny Kills* (2008); and the world's largest kelpie in J.K. Rowling's *Fantastic Beasts and Where to Find Them* (2001), a companion to her "Harry Potter" series. Conversely, in the 1973 short story "The Monster of

Loch Ness" by Sir Fred Hoyle and Geoffrey Hoyle—known for both science non-fiction and science fiction—the "monster" is the ship of **extraterrestrials** that have been recuperating and manufacturing fuel from the loch's water.

Bernadette Bosky

References and Suggested Reading

Coleman, Loren, and Jerome Clark. *Cryptozoology A–Z.* New York: Simon and Schuster, 1999.

Ellis, Richard. *Monsters of the Sea.* Guilford, CT: The Lyons Press, 2000.

Harrison, Paul. *The Encyclopaedia of the Loch Ness Monster.* London: Robert Hale, 2000.

Zell-Ravenheart, Oberon. *A Wizard's Bestiary: A Menagerie of Myth, Magic, and Mystery.* Franklin Lakes, NJ: New Page Books, 2007.

LORNE—*see* Demon

LOVECRAFT, MONSTERS IN

Fig. 25 *The Black Goat of the Woods* by Erol Otus. © Wizards of the Coast, LLC. Image used with permission.

The American writer H[oward] P[hillips] Lovecraft (1890–1937) was a pioneering figure in the literature of supernatural horror. In a literary career spanning less than 20 years in the 1920s and 1930s, Lovecraft revolutionized the field by transferring the locus of horror from the Earth to the boundless universe. His monsters are of a highly original and distinctive sort and have exercised a tremendous influence on subsequent writing in the fields of horror and science fiction.

At the very outset of his career, Lovecraft appears to have determined that the monsters that had populated previous supernatural fiction—**vampires**, **ghosts**, **werewolves**, **witches**, and the like—were outmoded in his day. The advance of science, in his judgment, had rendered these entities so implausible that they were of little aesthetic value in literature. A student of chemistry, astronomy, and physics since his early youth, Lovecraft adopted an atheistic and materialistic worldview that rejected the Christian dualism of body and spirit. Accordingly, he was compelled to create entities that largely conformed to the most advanced theories in biology, physics, and other sciences, and he also came to be a highly articulate spokesman for the kind of "weird fiction" that he wished to write. He did not enunciate his views until the late 1920s, but his radical view of monsters appears evident in the earliest stages of his mature literary career.

"Dagon" (1917) envisions the upheaval of a land mass in the Pacific, revealing an immense entity with "webbed hands and feet, shockingly wide and flappy lips, glassy, bulging eyes, and other features less pleasant to recall" (*Dagon* 18). (This entity is not the Dagon of the title, or even a prototype of that Phoenician god, but a worshipper of that prototype; but it appears that the worshipper is similar in physical form to the prototype.)

Later stories continue the trend of fashioning innovative monsters. In "Beyond the Wall of Sleep" (1919), a cosmic entity, never fully described, finds itself trapped in the body of an ignorant denizen of rural New York State. "From Beyond" (1920) shows us shapeless entities that pass through objects without harm—reflecting the views of contemporary physicists that what we think of as solid matter is really largely empty space.

Another group of early stories take as their starting point Darwin's theory of evolution and render the conception hideous. In "Facts Concerning the Late Arthur Jermyn and His Family" (1920), a noble family, many of whose members have peculiar physical characteristics, is shown to be the offspring of miscegenation between a human being and a curious white ape found in the African jungle. "The Lurking Fear" (1922), although something of a potboiler, is entertaining in its display of legions of mole-like creatures—again the products of unwholesome inbreeding in a family in upstate New York. The culmination of Lovecraft's ruminations on this topic occur in "The Rats in the Walls" (1923) in which an American man who retires to England and rebuilds a family mansion discovers to his horror that his ancestors were cannibals; as a result of that knowledge, he himself descends abruptly on the evolutionary scale, speaking in increasingly archaic language and finally reverting to cannibalism himself.

The quasi-scientific thread that we have seen in "Dagon" and "From Beyond" comes to a head in "The Shunned House" (1924), in which Lovecraft makes some of his most significant statements regarding the radical nature of his monsters. What would seem like a conventional tale of a haunted house, apparently inhabited by a vampire, becomes something much more daring and unconventional. Set in an actual colonial house in Lovecraft's native Providence, Rhode Island, "The Shunned House" depicts a centuries-old entity that, while being largely material, exercises a kind of psychic vampirism over the minds of the denizens of the house, causing them to speak in a debased form of French, even though they do not know the language. This entity is finally dispatched, not by a cross or a stake through its heart, but by immense quantities of hydrochloric acid.

In the course of "The Shunned House," Lovecraft's protagonists express startling views on the nature of the entity and its philosophical basis:

> *We were not ... in any sense childishly superstitious, but scientific study and reflection had taught us that the known universe of three dimensions embraces the merest fraction of the whole cosmos of substance and energy ... To say that we actually believed in vampires or werewolves would be a carelessly inclusive statement. Rather must it be said that we were not prepared to deny the possibility of certain unfamiliar and unclassified modifications of vital force and attenuated matter; existing very infrequently in three-dimensional space because of its more intimate connexion with other spatial units, yet close enough to the boundary of our own to furnish us occasional manifestations which we, for lack of a proper vantage-point, may never hope to understand ... Such a thing was surely not a physical or biochemical impossibility in the light of a newer science which includes the theories of relativity and intra-atomic action.* (*At the Mountains of Madness* 251–2)

This appeal to Einstein and Max Planck's quantum theory ("intra-atomic action") renders the tale an early experiment in science fiction.

Lovecraft attained his greatest celebrity—although much of that celebrity was posthumous—and, simultaneously, his greatest innovations in the creation of monsters in the tales of his final decade of writing. These tales are now designated under the rubric "Cthulhu Mythos"—a term that was coined by Lovecraft's colleague and early publisher August Derleth only after Lovecraft's death, and one that perhaps Lovecraft would not have approved. The name was devised chiefly because the first tale to outline what would become a detailed pseudomythology was "The Call of Cthulhu" (1926). In this tale, evidence is gradually pieced together of the existence of an immense creature of eccentric shape that has highly anomalous physical properties, such as the ability to recombine disparate parts of itself—the narrator, speaking of a statue of the entity, states: "If I say that my somewhat extravagant imagination yielded simultaneous pictures of an octopus, a **dragon**, and a human caricature, I shall not be unfaithful to the spirit of the thing" (*Dunwich Horror* 127). This creature came from the depths of space millions of years ago but was accidentally trapped in the underwater city of R'lyeh in the South Pacific. The crux of the narrative is the emergence of R'lyeh from the waves, allowing for a momentary glimpse of Cthulhu; but an earthquake sends the monster and its city back under the waves again. Through this scenario, Lovecraft suggests the fragile tenure of human beings on this Earth: were it not for the accident of that earthquake, our very existence would be jeopardized by the incalculable power of Cthulhu and its minions.

Lovecraft continued to elaborate upon this mythology for the remainder of his brief career, although he did so haphazardly and without having an overall plan at the start. The core of the Cthulhu Mythos is the existence of a whole pantheon of **extraterrestrial** entities who have, by a series of accidents, come to Earth at various points in the past and who make themselves visible in remote corners of the Earth. Such entities include Nyarlathotep (originally created in the prose-poem "Nyarlathotep" [1920] and there depicted as a kind of Pharaoh figure who foments the entropic destruction of the universe), Yog-Sothoth (an entity sometimes seen as a series of intertwined ropes and at other times as a congeries of iridescent bubbles), Shub-Niggurath (apparently a fertility goddess), and, at the pinnacle of the pantheon, Azathoth, a blind and mindless creature at the center of chaos—an obvious symbol for the ultimate meaninglessness of the cosmos. These creatures, and their human or alien servitors, are depicted in a series of novellas and short novels that, although few in number, were enormously rich in intellectual and aesthetic substance and of vast influence on subsequent writing in the field: "The Colour out of Space" (1927), "The Dunwich Horror" (1928), "The Whisperer in Darkness" (1930), *At the Mountains of Madness* (1931), "The Shadow over Innsmouth" (1931), "The Thing on the Doorstep" (1933), and "The Shadow out of Time" (1934–35).

It may seem peculiar that an avowed atheist would be so prodigal in the invention of these "gods." But what is of interest is that, right from the beginning, these "gods" are only seen as such by their human followers, who perhaps seek to gain a privileged place in any new earthly society once these entities rid the Earth of the great majority of the human beings who reside on it. Cthulhu itself is clearly just an extraterrestrial, and many of the other "gods"—with perhaps the exception of Azathoth, who always remained largely a symbol—become increasingly "demythologized" as each story is written. Similarly, the occult books that claim to provide esoteric information on these "gods"—such as, most famously, the *Necronomicon* of the mad Arab Abdul Alhazred—are shown to be mistaken as to the basic nature and function of these entities. The most explicit statement occurs in *At the Mountains of Madness*, where barrel-shaped "Old Ones," who had manifestly come to Earth from outer space and settled in Antarctica, are identified with identical creatures cited in the *Necronomicon*: "They were the makers and enslavers of [Earth] life, and above all doubt the originals of the fiendish elder myths which things like the Pnakotic Manuscripts and the *Necronomicon* affrightedly hint about" (*At the Mountains of Madness* 59).

In many ways, the stories of Lovecraft's later decade are recapitulations of conceptions that he had broached nebulously in earlier work. The hybrid entities in "The Shadow over Innsmouth"—half-fish and half-frog, who mate with the human beings in a small town on the Massachusetts coast to produce still more loathsome hybrids—are a reprise of the entity found in "Dagon"; the Great Race—a group of mental entities who, millions of years ago, occupied the bodies of a race of rugose cone-shaped creatures and who have discovered the ability to fling their minds through space and time into the bodies of nearly every species throughout the universe—is a radical revision of the idea of psychic possession tentatively outlined in "Beyond the Wall of Sleep." In "The Whisperer in Darkness," half-animal, half-vegetable creatures who have descended from the planet Yuggoth (equated with Pluto, then just discovered) have highly anomalous properties: they cannot be photographed with an ordinary camera, and when they die they dissolve into a hideous pool of greenish ichor.

It is difficult to speak in small compass of these later narratives by Lovecraft. They constitute the pinnacle of his literary achievement, and they embody in full the philosophical and aesthetic theories he had been evolving over a lifetime of scientific study and diligent reading in supernatural literature. In 1931, just as he was embarking upon the writing of *At the Mountains of Madness*, he articulated his views in a letter to fellow writer Frank Belknap Long: "The time has come when the normal revolt against time, space, & matter must assume a form not overtly incompatible with what is known of reality—when it must be gratified by images forming *supplements* rather than *contradictions* of the visible & measurable universe. And what, if not a form of *non-supernatural cosmic art*, is to pacify this sense of revolt—as well as gratify the cognate sense of curiosity?" (*Selected Letters* 295–6). This view makes it evident that Lovecraft was seeking to go beyond traditional supernatural horror and more in the direction of the new genre of science fiction.

Lovecraft's subsequent influence on the field, in spite of the fact that he published no collection of his stories in his lifetime, has been immense. In his own lifetime and in the first few decades after his death, several of Lovecraft's colleagues and disciples added their own monsters to his pantheon: Clark Ashton Smith (1893–1961; responsible for the toad-god Tsathoggua, the primal entity Ubbo-Sathla, and others); Robert E. Howard (1906–36; Gol-Goroth and others); and, most prolifically, August Derleth (1909–71; the fire-god Cthugha and many others). Derleth, however, was guilty of a severe misconstrual of the basic thrust of Lovecraft's pseudomythology: he believed it to be a reflection of a cosmic good versus evil struggle, similar to that found in Christianity (and, accordingly, he devised out of his own imagination a group of "Elder Gods," representing the forces of good, to battle against the "evil" Old Ones), and also believed that Lovecraft's gods were **elementals**. This deformed view of the Cthulhu Mythos had the effect of causing many subsequent writers (most notably the prolific Brian Lumley [1937–]) to imitate Derleth rather than Lovecraft. But as new scholarship in the 1970s and 1980s pointed out the errors of Derleth's interpretation, creative writers began returning to the cosmic sources of Lovecraft's own vision, and today such writers as Caitlín R. Kiernan (1964–) and Laird Barron (1970–) are using the framework of the Cthulhu Mythos for their own individual and highly imaginative tales and novels.

Film adaptations of Lovecraft's stories, beginning in the 1960s, have been generally disappointing, chiefly due to budgetary constraints and the impoverished imaginations of screenwriters and directors. A new direction was taken in 1984 with *H.P. Lovecraft's Re-animator*, directed by Stuart Gordon, a rollicking and half-parodic adaptation of "Herbert West—Reanimator" (1921–22), in which an unscrupulous scientist seeks to revive the dead. Few films, however, have attempted to depict the cosmic entities of Lovecraft's Mythos, although such films as *Alien* (Ridley Scott, 1979) and *The Thing* (John Carpenter, 1982), while not being explicit adaptations of Lovecraft, nonetheless feature monsters that are strongly Lovecraftian in appearance and behavior. Lovecraft has also been adapted for a popular role-playing game (*Call of Cthulhu*, published by Chaosium), and his influence on video games, rock music, and other media has also been detected. In general, depictions of his monsters in these media focus relentlessly on tentacles and other superficial elements, but even so they suggest the degree to which Lovecraft's work departed from the stock monsters of previous horror literature and opened up new imaginative vistas that a wide variety of artists have exploited.

S.T. Joshi

References and Suggested Reading

Burleson, Donald R. *H.P. Lovecraft: A Critical Study.* Westport, CT: Greenwood Press, 1983.

Joshi, S.T. *H.P. Lovecraft: The Decline of the West.* Mercer Island, WA: Starmont House, 1990.

——. *I Am Providence: The Life and Times of H.P. Lovecraft.* 2 vols. New York: Hippocampus Press, 2010.

Lévy, Maurice. *Lovecraft: A Study in the Fantastic.* Translated by S.T. Joshi. Detroit: Wayne State University Press, 1988.

Lovecraft, H.P. *At the Mountains of Madness and Other Novels.* Sauk City, WI: Arkham House, 1985.

——. *Dagon and Other Macabre Tales.* Sauk City, WI: Arkham House, 1986.

——. *The Dunwich Horror and Others.* Sauk City, WI: Arkham House, 1984.

——. *Selected Letters: 1929–1931.* Sauk City, WI: Arkham House, 1971.

Schultz, David E., and S.T. Joshi, eds. *An Epicure in the Terrible: A Centennial Anthology of Essays in Honor of H.P. Lovecraft.* Rutherford, NJ: Fairleigh Dickinson University Press, 1991. Reprint, New York: Hippocampus Press, 2011.

Waugh, Robert H. *The Monster in the Mirror: Looking for H.P. Lovecraft.* New York: Hippocampus Press, 2006.

LUCIFER—*see* Devil, The

MADHU—*see* Demon

MAENAD

Also called bacchae, bacchantes, or bassarids, maenads are female companions and sometime priestesses of Dionysus, the Greek god of wine (known as Bacchus to the Romans). The maenads worship in the open air, in fields and forests, dressed in animal skins, crowned in vines, and carrying decorated sticks known as thyrsi. Maenads are represented in literature as human women driven by intoxication to both ecstatic celebratory dancing and fits of murderous violence, tearing apart animals, and sometimes people, and consuming their raw flesh (see also **Women, Monstrous**).

In 406 BCE, the Greek dramatist Euripides devoted his final play, *The Bacchae*, to these women. In it, Dionysus arrives with his followers in the city of Thebes, only to be rebuffed by the city's king, Pentheus. In retaliation, Pentheus is attacked and torn apart by the frenzied bacchae, led by Pentheus's own mother,

Agave. Maenads or bacchae also appear in various retellings of the death of Orpheus. After failing to bring his wife Euridyce out of Hades, Orpheus travels the land of Thrace in sorrow, playing his lyre and foregoing human company. Maenads set upon him and decapitate him, throwing his head into the river. The earliest known account of the murder is probably from *Bassarides*, a lost work by the Greek dramatist Aeschylus (c. 525–455 BCE). The story is also fully told in two Latin works: book 4 of the *Georgics* (37–30 BCE) by the poet Virgil; and Book 11 of Ovid's *Metamorphoses* (8 CE).

Maenads make occasional appearances in nineteenth- and twentieth-century poetry. In Percy Shelley's "Ode to the West Wind" (1820), the lightning signaling an oncoming storm is compared to a maenad's hair. The maenads are also seen mourning the titular god of the poem "The Dead Pan," published in 1844 by Elizabeth Barrett Browning. Sylvia Plath's poem "Maenad" (1959) is told in the voice of a once-innocent girl transitioning to adulthood, and perhaps madness. There are also some twentieth-century novel references. Maenads, though not very fierce, accompany a jolly Bacchus through Narnia in C.S. Lewis's children's fantasy *Prince Caspian* (1951). In her 1985 novel *The Handmaid's Tale*, Canadian author Margaret Atwood alludes to the maenads' murderous frenzies in a scene describing the public execution of a falsely accused rapist. The scene is also central to the 1990 film version of the book, directed by Volker Schlöndorff. *Fables and Reflections* (1993), volume 7 of Neil Gaiman's "Sandman" series of graphic novels, retells the story of the maenads' murder of Orpheus.

Maenads or bacchae turn up in a number of films, often those based directly on Greek and Latin originals. These include a 2002 film version of Euripides's *The Bacchae*, directed by Brad Mays, and a 2010 filmed version of a live performance by the National Theater of Northern Greece, directed by Bruno Coppola. The 1961 Italian film *Le Baccanti*, with the improbable English language title *Bondage Gladiator Sexy*, is a contemporary updating of Euripides's play using much of the dramatist's original dialogue, with additional scripting by the director Giorgio Ferroni. In 1991, the television series *The Storyteller: Greek Myths*, from Henson Productions and director Anthony Minghella, combined live action and puppetry in a retelling of "Orpheus and Euridyce" that includes the murder of Orpheus by maenads. A 1996 episode of the series *Xena: Warrior Princess*, entitled "Girls Just Wanna Have Fun," alludes to the Orpheus myth and portrays the god Bacchus (Dionysus) trying to turn young women, including lead character Xena, into **vampire**-like bacchae. The second season of the HBO television series *True Blood* (2009) focuses on Michelle Forbes as maenad Maryann Forrester, and is loosely based on Charlaine Harris's Sookie Stackhouse novel *Living Dead in Dallas* (2002), in which the character is called Callisto.

Regina Hansen

References and Suggested Reading

Goff, Barbara E. *Citizen Bacchae: Women's Ritual Practice in Ancient Greece.* Berkeley: University of California Press, 2004.

Graves, Robert. *The Greek Myths.* New York: Penguin Books, 1992.

Hamilton, Edith. *Mythology.* New York: Warner Books, 1999.

Seaford, Richard. *Dionysos (Gods and Heroes of the Ancient World).* New York: Routledge, 2006.

MAGOG—*see* Bible, Monsters In The

MAHĀBHĀRATA, MONSTERS IN

Within the ancient Sanskrit epic, monstrous figures such as Rākṣasas, Gandharvas, and

Yakṣas are often found living in the untamed forest. The text's central characters, the royal Pāṇḍava brothers named Yudhisṭhira, Bhīma, Arjuna, Nakula, and Sahadeva, encounter these creatures while in exile from their kingdom. Though diverse, the monsters—which are often translated as **demons** or **ogres** in English—frequently display supernatural abilities, such as extreme feats of strength and the power to drastically alter physical appearances.

During the Pāṇḍavas' first sojourn into the forest, brother and sister Rākṣasas Hiḍimba and Hiḍimbā spy on the princes as they sleep. The text describes Hiḍimba as "a cruel Rākṣasa who ate human flesh—powerful and strong, malformed, yellow-eyed, tusked, and loathsome to the eye" (Mbh 1.139.1). Hiḍimbā is sent by her brother to capture the Pāṇḍavas, but instead falls in love with Bhīma. She transforms herself into a beautiful maiden, but fails to win her beloved's heart. Hiḍimba learns of this betrayal and attempts to murder his sister. Bhīma wrestles with the monster, kills him, and then turns toward the sister. Yudhiṣṭhira intervenes, chiding Bhīma for his threat to harm a woman. Instead, Hiḍimbā and Bhīma are promptly married and go on to make love all over the world. Immediately afterwards, their son Ghaṭotkaca is born as "Rākṣasa women give birth the day they conceive" (Mbh 1.143.32). This child, also described as a Rākṣasa (Mbh 1.143.37), goes on to play a key role in the Great War, saving the Pāṇḍavas from certain death during battle. The narrative makes no mention of Hidimbā's whereabouts as the forest is left behind.

Baka

Following the events in the forest, the Pāṇḍavas seek shelter in a small town. There they learn that a man-eating Rākṣasa named Baka, living on the outskirts, has been exploiting the town, consuming its residents and their rations while claiming to protect them from outsiders. Bhīma takes a cart of food to the forest to appease the demon, but stops short to feed himself. Baka sees his spoils being ingested, becomes enraged, and attacks Bhīma; but the prince remains indifferent and continues to eat. The Rākṣasa then uproots a tree and sets upon Bhīma (Mbh 1.151.12), at which point the two begin an earthquake-inducing battle. Bhīma breaks Baka's spine, killing him. Afterwards, Bhīma instructs the Rākṣasa's family to do no harm to the townspeople and the village persists in peace. Later in the Mahābhārata (3.12), Baka's brother, Kirmīra, attempts to avenge his defeat, but is similarly killed by Bhīma.

Citraratha

The Pāṇḍavas eventually leave the small town to return home through the untamed forest. Along the way, they enter the territory of the Gandharva king Citraratha, who quickly attacks the princes with burning arrows for breaching land unfit for humans. Arjuna is able to subdue the monstrous king with divine weaponry. Defeated, Citraratha bestows magical gifts upon the five brothers and offers them sagely advice on the importance of traveling with a priest, to avoid aggression from other Gandharvas as the brothers continue their journey.

Kubera

During their twelve-year exile in the forest, narrated throughout the Mahābhārata's third book, the Pāṇḍava brothers experience regular run-ins with the monsters that inhabit the landscape. Early on, Kubera, chief of the Rākṣasas, sends an army of both Rākṣasas and Yakṣas to kill Bhīma. After Bhīma slaughters scores of demons, Kubera thanks the Pāṇḍava, as Bhīma's actions helped to lift a curse placed upon the Rākṣasa. The monster follows up his expression of gratitude by providing Yudhiṣṭhira with a lesson on dharma and a promise to protect the brothers with his remaining army (Mbh 3.159.11).

The Yaksa's Questions

Toward the end of their time in the forest, Nakula finds a water source and attempts to quench his thirst. A Yakṣa asks the Pāṇḍava to first answer a series of questions before he partakes. Nakula ignores the request and falls unconscious upon drinking the water. The same series of events is repeated with each brother until Yudhiṣṭhira arrives at the lake and agrees to answer the Yakṣa's questions. The Yakṣa proceeds to interrogate Yudhiṣṭhira extensively with 18 questions on the nature of dharma. Satisfied with Yudhiṣṭhira's answers, the Yakṣa revives his brothers and reveals himself to be the god Dharma, Yudhiṣṭhira's father. The god then bestows boons upon the Pāṇḍavas, effectively ending their exile in the forest.

Sthūna

Vowing revenge against the man who kidnapped her from her fiancé, Śikhaṇḍī lives for many years disguised as a male, so that she might meet her captor on the battleground one day. When her true sex is discovered, Śikhaṇḍī flees into the forest to commit suicide. There she encounters a Yakṣa named Sthūṇa who, observing her distress, immediately offers to fulfill any wish she might desire. Śikhaṇḍī recounts her plight and the Yakṣa offers to switch sexes with the woman by trading sexual organs for only as long as it takes for Śikhaṇḍī to avenge her injustice (Mbh 5.193.1). Thereupon, Śikhaṇḍī becomes the male Śikhaṇḍin and goes off to seek revenge. Kubera later arrives at Sthūṇa's home, but the Yakṣa fails to properly greet the Rākṣasa chief, ashamed by her new appearance. Off-put by this lack of hospitality, Kubera curses Sthūṇa to remain fixed in female form, thus rendering Śikhaṇḍin permanently male.

Dan Rudmann

References and Suggested Reading

Doniger, Wendy. *Splitting the Difference: Gender and Myth in Ancient Greece and India.* Chicago: University of Chicago Press, 1999.

Hiltebeitel, Alf. *Dharma: Its Early History in Law, Religion, and Narrative.* New York: Oxford University Press, 2011.

Van Buitenen, J.A.B. *The Mahabharata.* 5 vols. Chicago: University of Chicago Press, 1978.

MAHISHASURA—*see* Demon

MALACODA—*see* Demon

MALAK AL-MAUT—*see* Angel

MALINCHE, LA—*see* Women, Monstrous

MAMI WATA—*see* Demon

MAMMON—*see* Angel

MANITOU

Manitous are spirits in the belief system of Anishanaabe (Ojibwe) and other Algonquian peoples of North America. There are numerous manitous; no one representation accounts for all manifestations of the phenomenon. The complexity of the Ojibwe language makes translations into English imprecise and suggests that the simple equation of the terms "manitou" and "spirit" is insufficient to capture all possibilities. Illustrating this complexity, Basil Johnston offers multiple definitions: "Mystery, essence, substance, matter, supernatural spirit, anima, quiddity, attribute, property, God, deity, godlike, mystical, incorporeal, transcendental, invisible reality" (242).

One reason why Western conceptions of the manitou are problematic has to do with accounts of contact by fifteenth- and sixteenth-century European explorers to North America. Hearing the indigenous peoples refer to them as "manitou," and limiting their understanding of that term to "God," these early explorers believed that First Nations peoples thought of them as gods. However, while one might translate the term "manitou" as "god," one should not mistake manitous for gods. Manitous are not divinities in the Western sense, although they do command reverence and respect. Haefeli cites mistranslation to account for the confusion: "The native accounts never claimed the Europeans were gods in any Christian sense of the term. Instead, their words (in this case Manitou) reflected an understanding of the power and danger of the encounter that the actual experience confirmed" (407).

One of the more interesting treatments of the manitou occurs in Brian Moore's 1985 novel *Blake Robe*, adapted by director Bruce Beresford in the film *Black Robe* (1991), which takes up the theme of contact, casting a convincing Lothaire Bluteau as young seventeenth-century Jesuit missionary, Father Jean Laforge. The Wendat (Huron) characters who guide him on his journey through remote Quebec speak of the proselytizing priest as a manitou, not a god: he is considered either as a benign but problematic spirit or an evil and dangerous one, depending on the political disposition of the observer.

Manitou is not the One True God; manitous are not **angels** or stewards of the One True Manitou. Neither are they evil spirits, though some are monstrous. Following tradition, Basil Johnston categorizes them "according to the sequence in which the manitous appeared and performed services in the development and growth of the [Ojibwe] nation" (xiii). Kitchi-Manitou is the creator of the physical world and the beings in it. Muzzu-Kummik-Quae is Earth Woman or Mother Earth. The manitou Ae-pungishimook, the West, who is old age and death, mated with the human woman Winonah to produce four half-manitou, half-human sons: Maudjee-kawiss was a great hunter and warrior and the first leader of the nation; Pukawiss brought the people dance and theater; Cheeby-aub-oozoo gave the people vision, dream quest, music, and poetry; Nana'b'oozoo, fourth and youngest son, is an everyman, "the prototype of all Anishinaubaek and of all human beings" (B. Johnston 116). Additional manitous are associated with places or seasons, such as forest manitou Gawaunduk, the Spirit of the Spruce, and meadow manitou Maundau-meen, the Spirit of Corn; the nebaunauquaewuk and nebaunaubaewuk, **mermaids** and **mermen**; manitoussiwuk, or sprites, such as the maemaegawaehnse (little people) who guard over children; and auttissookaunuk, the muses of the north, south, east, and west, who help storytellers. Personal manitous, such as thunderbirds and eagles, influence destinies and serve as the patrons of individual people. Pauguk, the Flying **Skeleton** or "outcast," is so called by the manitous of the Underworld who would not accept his spirit after death because of the crime he committed in life. **Windigo** (Weendigo), the cannibal **giant**, serves to warn against greed and excess. These are a few of many manitous (see B. Johnston for amplification).

Excellent examples of how Ojibwe people conceived of manitous as natural elements of their everyday lives can be found in the oral stories of Maggie Wilson, which relate the history of the Rainy River Ojibwe of northwestern Ontario and northern Minnesota in the nineteenth and early twentieth centuries. "She Knew That This Woman She Dreamed Was the Bear," for example, speaks of *manitokaso*—taking on the spiritual power of a manitou "by one's own authority" (Wilson 216)—as an ordinary practice. Wilson's stories are refreshing because they are memoir, in contrast to horror films and novels that misrepresent manitous as evil spirits or the ghosts of dead Indians.

The standout Hollywood offering is director William Girdler's *The Manitou* (1978), adapted from Graham Masterson's novel. It features an accomplished cast: Tony Curtis, Susan Strasberg, Michael Ansara, Stella Stevens, and Burgess Meredith. Let the plot synopsis offered by the film company suffice: "A psychic's girlfriend finds out that a lump on her back is a growing reincarnation of a 400-year-old demonic Native American spirit ... an ancient evil and enraged beast known as THE MANITOU." Masterson's novel was published in Great Britain in 1975 and in the United States in 1976, first in a series that has established precedent for many subsequent applications of the manitou motif. In the debut novel, pseudo-psychic Harry Erskine outsmarts the evil sorcery of Misquamacus, the greatest medicine man to ever live, who is now trying to reincarnate through the tumor on Harry's girlfriend's neck, so that he can exterminate the white race. Victorious, Harry moves on in Masterson's follow-up novel, *The Djinn* (1977), to perform the same service, this time dispatching another culture's evil spirit, the Islamic **djinn** or **genie**. Masterson's novels appeal because they are outlandish and exciting, which is sufficient for many fans. Masterson's follow-up exploitation of the djinn brings to mind Darlene Johnston's research, which praises one seventeenth-century French missionary for translating "manitou" as "Genie" and recognizing that manitous are not de facto evil (12). The comparison between manitous and djinn is apt. Whether or not Masterson was aware of this linkage, the pattern of appropriating the beliefs of other cultures as myths and transforming myths into monsters is a longstanding template for commercial success. Masterson renews this pattern in *Revenge of the Manitou* (1987), which exploits the Windigo manitou motif paralleling the **vampire** tradition, and again in *Burial: A Novel of the Manitou* (1994), in which Misquamacus returns from the Underworld with back-up: a voodoo priest who shares his lust for revenge against the white race. Masterson's proponents praise these tales for bringing the colonial abuses of the past to light in gritty detail.

The revenge motif often appears in literary treatments of this figure, as in prolific pulp writer Guy N. Smith's *Manitou Doll* (1985), and in Ernest Hemingway's "Judgment of Manitou" (1916), written when the Nobel Laureate was still in high school. Rather than holding one group accountable for transgressions against another, however, Hemingway invokes the manitou as a governing spirit that punishes an individual crime. The reputation of manitous fares better in young adult fiction which preserves the manitou as guide, guardian, or Great Spirit. Notable examples include Charles De Lint, *The Dreaming Place* (1990) and Stella Calahasen, *Dream Catcher* (2009). Manitous exhibit their staying power even in e-reader publications, where Lexus Luke's 2011 *Manitou: The Sky People Saga* advertises its intention to rival J.K. Rowling's "Harry Potter" series (see **Harry Potter, Monsters In**).

Grace L. Dillon

References and Suggested Reading

Haefeli, Evan. "On First Contact and Apotheosis: Manitou and Men in North America." *Ethnohistory* 54, no. 3 (Summer 2007): 407–43.

Johnston, Basil. *The Manitous: The Supernatural World of the Ojibway*. New York: HarperCollins, 1995.

Johnston, Darlene. "Respecting and Protecting the Sacred." Accessed 17 July 2012. <http://www.attorneygeneral.jus.gov.on.ca/inquiries/ipperwash/policy_part/research/pdf/Johnston_Respecting-and-Protecting-the-Sacred.pdf>.

Wilson, Maggie. "She Knew That This Woman She Dreamed Was the Bear." In *Rainy River Lives: Stories Told by Maggie Wilson*, edited by Sally Cole, 191–6. Lincoln: University of Nebraska Press, 2009.

MANTICORE

Perhaps invented to strengthen the image of the mighty tiger in the ancient world, the manticore is a mythical creature whose name is derived from the ancient Persian word *martiora*, meaning "man-eater." It most closely resembles the Egyptian **Sphinx**, though with stark differences (Topsell 144). The actual beast is said to come from the forests of Central Asia (India is most often mentioned) and to eat man's raw flesh. In most descriptions, it has the face of a man, three rows of razor sharp teeth, and the body of a lion. Sometimes winged and horned, it attacks its victims fiercely and swiftly with a stinger-lined scorpion-like tale that is sometimes venomous (Nigg). The manticore's body is blood red, it has pale gray or blue eyes, and can leap far distances. Its voice resembles the sound of a trumpet or a whistle. Although its literary origins harken back more than two millennia, it remains popular in contemporary culture where it shows its gruesome face in fiction, comic books, television, film, video games, and social media such as Facebook.

The manticore is first mentioned in the fifth century BCE by Ctesias the Cnidian (c. 441 BCE), a Greek physician at the Persian Court of King Artaxerxes II (c. 435–358 BCE). In his work the *Indica*, he describes "a red lion-sized monster with a man's face, ear, and eyes, and a tail like a scorpion" (Nigg 5, 42). Although Ctesias wrote numerous texts about the cultures of India and Persia, they did not survive except as interpolations within other texts. The most famous of these is by the Byzantine scholar Photius I (c. 815–97 CE). In the years between Ctesias and Photius, the existence of the manticore as an actual creature that roams the Earth was fiercely debated by ancient scholars. This can be seen in the work of the Greek philosopher Aristotle (384–322 BCE) who makes reference to Ctesias and the manticore in his *Historia Animalium*, which is a work that led to the development of zoology as a science. In this work, Aristotle includes the manticore in his list of worldly creatures, but also questions the viability of the creature and the authority of Ctesias (Nigg 47–8). Pliny the Elder makes reference to the manticore in his *Historia Naturalis* (77 CE) and one can also find mention of the manticore in the Greek geographer Pausanias's *Description of Greece* (mid second century CE). Pausanias is of the opinion that it is really a tiger whose description has merely been exaggerated by Ctesias. The Greek writer Flavius Philostratus (c. 170–247 CE) grapples with existence of the manticore in his second-century CE book, *The Life of Apollonius of Tyana*—ultimately not deciding for either side of the argument.

Of the many texts that reference or discuss the manticore, it was Pliny's description of the beast that most strongly influenced the literature about it that arose in the medieval world in Europe. Yet the manticore became an altogether different creature as it passed through the ages and entered the literature of Western Europe, where it came to be seen as an evil omen and to be associated with the **Devil** in medieval bestiaries. This association helped the creature grow in mythical stature and devilish reputation, and served as a basis for its insertion into different contexts. For example, in the thirteenth century, French scholar Bartholomaeus Anglicus mentions the manticore in Book 18 of his proto-encyclopedia, *De proprietatibus rerum.*

The manticore is mentioned in several anonymous romances about Alexander the Great written in the thirteenth and fourteenth centuries (see Stoneman). One of these stories recounts how Alexander lost men to various beasts during his campaigns, including the terrifying man-eating manticore. Notable from the Middle Ages is the appearance of Geryon, the **giant** and grandson of **Medusa** in Greek mythology, in Dante Alighieri's *Divine Comedy* (1308–21 CE; see **Dante, Monsters In**). This character is an unforgettable manticore-like creature called the "Monster of Fraud" that lives between the circles of Violence and Fraud in Dante's *Inferno* and plays a significant role in the narrative as he conveys Dante the Pilgrim and his guide, the poet Virgil, between circles. During the sixteenth century, the manticore was used in heraldry, but not extensively because it retained some of its malevolent features from the medieval age in Europe. Over the next 300 years, the manticore was occasionally mentioned in literature but, in keeping with the significant surge in the popularity of Egyptian antiquities in Europe and a new-found interest in the texts of the ancient world, it more often made appearances in art as a Sphinx-like creature.

The manticore has been included in some of the greatest writing of the twentieth century, including the work of Argentine Jorge Luis Borges who includes an entry about it in his *Book of Imaginary Beings* (1957). It is also featured in *The Manticore* (1972) by Robertson Davies, which is the second book in his "Deptford Trilogy" (1970–75). Influenced by Borges and the Greek classics, Ecuadorian author Alfredo Pareja Diez Canseco published his book about magical realism and myth, *La Manticora* (*The Manticore*) in 1974. Nobel prize-winning author Salman Rushdie's novel *The Satanic Verses* (1988), about the life of Mohammed, features the manticore in the opening chapter in which British authorities turn immigrants into manticores, snakes, and water buffalo (see Finney). There is also a play on words in the novel when a police force is called the "manticorps." In 2005, Indian fantasy writer Samit Basu titled the second novel in his "GameWorld" trilogy *The Manticore's Secret* (2005). Recent additions to the compendium of works that feature the manticore as a main character in the plot include the Gothic **vampire** story *Manticore Reborn* (2006) by Peter Evans, in which the main character can only save herself by locating an artifact called the "manticore," and the juvenile science fiction novel *Island of Fog* (2009) by Keith Robinson, in which children who live on a secluded island defy their parents to find out what is beyond the foggy horizon.

The manticore has also found a comfortable home in Western popular culture where its immortality has been secured by its inclusion in mainstream literature such as J.K. Rowling's novels *Harry Potter and the Prisoner of Azkaban* (2004), in which the main characters read about a manticore that killed someone in the thirteenth century but was never caught, and *Harry Potter and the Goblet of Fire* (2005), in which Hagrid breeds the manticore with Fire Crabs to create a Blast-Ended Skrewt (see **Harry Potter, Monsters In**). It has also appeared in several American television shows, including the briefly aired cyberpunk series *Dark Angel*, in the episode entitled "Cold Comfort" (season 1, episode 8, 2000; directed by Jefery Levy); in the series about good witches, *Charmed* (season 6, episode 8, 2003; directed by James L. Conway); and in the *Scooby-Doo! Mystery Incorporated* episode "Menace of the Manticore" (season 1, episode 21, 2011; directed by Curt Geda). It rears its fearsome head in feature-length films including the animated *The Last Unicorn* (Jules Bass and Arthur Rankin, Jr, 1982) based on the 1968 novel by Peter S. Beagle; the comedy *Napoleon Dynamite*, directed by Jared and Jerusha Hess (2004); and the 2005 science fiction cult classic *Manticore* (Tripp Reed) about US army commandos in Iraq who go in search of terrorists, only to come up against a man-eating monster. The image of the manticore persists in new media where it makes appearances in such diverse spaces as an online flash game called *Which Way Adventure*, in the role-playing game *Dungeons & Dragons* (see **Dungeons & Dragons, Monsters In**), and in the Facebook game *Superhero City* in which players go on a mission in virtual Athens, where they must overcome the wily manticores to win.

Stephenie Young

References and Suggested Reading

Borges, Jorge Luis. *The Book of Imaginary Beings*. Translated by Peter Sís. New York: Penguin Classics, 1996.

Finney, Brian. "Demonizing Discourse in Salman Rushdie's *The Satanic Verses*." 1998. <http://www.csulb.edu/~bhfinney/rushdiesat.html>.

Hassig, Debra. *The Mark of the Beast: The Medieval Bestiary in Art, Life, and Literature*. New York: Routledge, 2000.

Nigg, Joe. *The Book of Fabulous Beasts: A Treasury of Writings from Ancient Times to the Present*. New York: Oxford University Press, 1999.

Stoneman, Richard. *The Greek Alexander Romance*. New York: Penguin, 1991.

Topsell, Edward. *Topsell's Histories of Beasts*. Chicago: Nelson-Hall, 1981.

MARSH, ARABELLA

Arabella Marsh is the female protagonist in Bram Stoker's lesser known Gothic novella, *The Lair of the White Worm* (1911). Arabella is a shapeshifting, supernatural, primordial monster that lurks beneath the undergrowth of England's remote countryside landscape, but she is also the beautiful femme fatale of the tale. It is this incongruity that lies at the heart of this Gothic tale of mystery and suspense.

Set in 1860, *The Lair of the White Worm* employs a rather convoluted and elaborate plot. The tale tells the story of a young man, Adam Salton, who arrives in the historic "ancient Kingdom of Mercia" (Stoker 16) to visit his great uncle. Adam has traveled from his native Australia with the understanding that he will inherit his great uncle's estate upon his death. His great uncle's friend, Sir Nathaniel de Salis, soon befriends Adam and the two embark on a quest to unravel the meaning of local folklore. The land upon which Adam's uncle's estate lies has great historic significance and, early in the tale, Sir Nathaniel encourages Adam to take note of this prehistoric setting as a way of exploring some of the area's local superstitions and legends. Before long, Adam and Sir Nathaniel turn their attentions to Lady Arabella Marsh, whom they believe to be implicated (though at first they know not how) in the peculiar goings on in the region.

Meanwhile, the novella relates the ambitions of Arabella. Her desire, it appears, is to marry Edgar Caswall, the heir to a local estate called Castra Regis. Like Adam, Caswall is a newcomer to the region, having been born and brought up in Africa. Following Caswall's appearance, and as Adam and Sir Nathaniel delve ever further into the possible veracity of local legends, it gradually becomes apparent that sinister forces are at work. Among other strange happenings, Adam witnesses Caswall's black African servant Oolanga being murdered by Arabella; Caswall uses his mesmeric techniques on Lilla, the cousin of Adam's fiancée, to devastating effect; and Adam and

Sir Nathaniel observe (and only just escape) the legendary white worm stalking in the forest at night. These bizarre events lead the men to the rather disturbing conclusion that the shapeshifting primordial monster that plagues the countryside of mid-nineteenth-century England is none other than Lady Arabella Marsh, the blonde-haired, blue-eyed beauty of the tale.

This mutational and hybrid human-worm figure—a composite of advanced and primitive biological forms—functions as a nightmarish phantom that literally incorporates the past and present at once. She stands metonymically for the process of human evolution over vast tracts of time and space. Significantly, this monster has acquired, over time and by ontogeny rather than phylogeny, the ability to shapeshift (see **Shapeshifter**) between human and worm. Stoker's human/worm is a "technological" shapeshifter, a monster that has, in accordance with Darwin's theory of natural selection, adapted in order to survive in the modern world (needing, in this case, to be both human and animal).

There has been very little criticism published on *The Lair of the White Worm* and when it is discussed, critics tend to discard the novel as a failure, or provide a sweeping overview of the text. Maud Ellmann argues in her introduction to the Oxford Classics *Dracula* that *Lair* is Stoker's most "startlingly demented novel" (xiii), while the Gothic critic David Punter understands Arabella to be a solely mythical creature (176). Yet, despite the novella's shortcomings, it is fascinating in its complexities. By combining the snake of ancient religious myth with the biological framework of the modern woman, Stoker imagines an evil monster that slithers out of the past and into the present, seeking financial collateral in order to secure its (biological, that is to say, material) future at the cost of those around her.

Within the realms of this Gothic tale, Arabella is simultaneously human, worm, snake, and **dragon**. However, she is, of course, none of these: she is simply one of the monstrous Others in Stoker's Gothic stories. The novel's plot may be weak, but the concept of such a human/animal monster existing and functioning in the modern world reveals deep-rooted anxieties about humankind's place in the natural world. A 1988 cinematic adaptation of the novel was directed by Ken Russell, and Dutch death metal band God Dethroned used *The Lair of the White Worm* as the title of their sixth album, released in 2004.

Claire McKechnie

References and Suggested Reading

Ellman, Maud. Introduction to *Dracula*, by Bram Stoker, vii–xxviii. Oxford: Oxford University Press, 1996.

Hurley, Kelly. *The Gothic Body: Sexuality, Materialism, and Degeneration at the Fin de Siècle*. Cambridge: Cambridge University Press, 1996.

Punter, David. "Echoes in the Animal House: *The Lair of the White Worm*." In *Bram Stoker: History, Psychoanalysis and the Gothic*, edited by William Hughes and Andrew Smith, 173–87. Basingstoke: Macmillan Press, 1998.

Stoker, Bram. *The Lair of the White Worm* [1911]. Reprint, London: Penguin, 2008.

MARUT—*see* Angel

MATILDA

Matilda, a **demon** who assumes the form of a beautiful woman, seduces the vain but pious abbot Ambrosio, the title character of the eighteenth-century novel, *The Monk* (1796). A popular best-seller in its day, leading to its author being nicknamed Matthew "Monk" Lewis (1775–1818), it remains an important landmark in the Gothic literary tradition.

Matilda first appears in the novel disguised as the young monk Rosario. She thus manipulates her way into Ambrosio's arms, unveiling her womanly features, which have been modeled on those of a portrait of the Madonna that the abbot admires. His desire awakened through a number of ruses, Ambrosio breaks his vow of chastity; his desire sated, he soon loses interest in Matilda, now lusting after the pure and innocent Antonia. Since Matilda's charge is to corrupt the holy monk, she agrees to help him seduce the maiden, who is later revealed to be his sister. She partially reveals the extent of her evil, admitting that her "invisible servants" (Lewis 214) have observed his every move; through a magic mirror, Ambrosio and Matilda watch Antonia enter her bath. Matilda needs assistance, though, summoning Lucifer to help Ambrosio gain entrance to Antonia's chamber.

Unfortunately, Antonia's mother suspects the monk's evil intentions. When she confronts him prowling through her apartment in the middle of the night, Ambrosio strangles her. Matilda helps him to cover up this crime, and subsequently to kidnap and ravish Antonia. Meanwhile, a parallel set of crimes in the neighboring nunnery has been discovered and the ensuing ruckus leads Ambrosio to panic; fearing his own capture, he stabs Antonia with Matilda's dagger. Discovered, arrested, and brought before the Inquisition, Ambrosio is offered one last hope by Matilda: selling his soul to the **Devil**. The weak-willed monk agrees, and in the final pages of the novel he learns Matilda's true identity. As Lucifer explains: "I saw that you were virtuous from vanity, not principle, and I seized the moment of seduction. I observed your blind idolatry of the Madona's [*sic*] picture. I bade a subordinate but crafty spirit assume a similar form, and you eagerly yielded to the blandishments of Matilda" (350).

Matilda belongs to the long literary tradition of the **succubus**, a female demon who preys sexually upon men; her immediate literary precursor is Biondetta, the demon-temptress featured in *The Devil in Love* (1772) by Frenchman Jacques Cazotte (1719–92). *The Monk*'s frank portrayal of sexual crimes made it a *succès de scandale* and its detractors included the great English Romantic Samuel Taylor Coleridge (1772–1834) (Thomas, in Lewis vi). More recently, literary critics have examined Matilda's "rhetoric of deceit" as a demon (Grudin) and her role as a cross-dresser through the lens of queer and gender studies theory (Brewer; Fincher). As William Brewer points out: "[t]he disruptive power of Matilda ... derives from her unsettling ability to take on both masculine and feminine identities in her relationship with Ambrosio" (192–3). Lewis's novel has often been analyzed within the context of the English Protestant critique of Catholicism in the Gothic genre as a whole (McAloney).

Amy J. Ransom

References and Suggested Reading

Brewer, William. D. "Transgendering in Matthew Lewis's *The Monk*." *Gothic Studies* 6, no. 2 (2004): 192–207.

Fincher, Max. "The Gothic as Camp: Queer Aesthetics in *The Monk*." *Romanticism on the Net* 44 (2006). <http://www.erudit.org/revue/ron/2006/v/n44/013997ar.html>.

Frank, Fred, ed. *Matthew Lewis's* The Monk. Special issue of *Romanticism on the Net* 8 (1997). <http://www.erudit.org/revue/ron/1997/v/n8/index.html>.

Grudin, Peter. "*The Monk*: Matilda and the Rhetoric of Deceit." *Journal of Narrative Technique* 5 (1975): 136–46.

Lewis, Matthew. *The Monk* [1796]. Reprint, New York: The Modern Library, 2002.

McAloney, Regina. "The Catholic Monster in the Gothic Novel: Matthew G. Lewis's *The Monk* and Ann Radcliffe's *The Italian*." *Crossings: A Counter-Disciplinary Journal* 5–6 (2002): 175–207.

Macdonald, D.L. *Monk Lewis: A Critical Biography*. Toronto: University of Toronto Press, 2000.

MECHAGODZILLA—*see* Extraterrestrial

MEDEA—*see* Circe; Witch/Wizard; Women, Monstrous

MEDUSA

Fig. 26 *Medusa* by Christopher Mir

Medusa is one of the three **Gorgons**: winged chthonic female monsters. While her two sisters, Euryale and Sthenno, are immortal beings, Medusa is mortal and can be killed. In Greek myth, the parents of the Gorgons are either Phorcys and Ceto or Gorgo Aix and Ceto, and the Gorgons are figured as female water creatures with the ability to create underwater reefs. In later narratives, which focus much more fully on Medusa than on her two sisters, Medusa is presented as an Underworld monster connected to death. Ancient poets from Homer (c. eighth century BCE) onwards place her in Hades alongside other dangerous mythical creatures. All three Gorgons are presented in myth as having female forms, golden wings, snake-like fangs or boar-like tusks, brazen claws, and serpents curling in their hair or in their hands. They each have a petrifying gaze that can turn their victims to stone; Medusa, however, is the most famous of the Gorgons and, according to some narratives, was the first to obtain the power of petrifaction.

Two separate origin stories exist for Medusa. In the first, according to Apollodorus (second century BCE) she and her two sisters are born as monsters; in the second, which is included in Hesiod's *Theogony* (c. 700 BCE) and Ovid's *Metamorphoses* (8 CE), Medusa is presented as originally having been a beautiful maiden and priestess of the goddess Athena. Her beauty was so extraordinary that the king of the seas, Poseidon, was captivated by her charm and tried to violate her. Medusa hid herself in Athena's temple, but Poseidon could not be deterred and Medusa was raped in front of her goddess's altar; as if this was not enough, Athena then punished her for violating the chastity of her sanctuary by changing Medusa into a monster so ugly that she could transform humans into stone. Pseudo-Apollodorus also suggests in the *Bibliotheca* (first century BCE) that Medusa was punished by Athena because her beauty rivaled that of the goddess.

In the best-known versions of the legend, Medusa is killed by the Greek hero Perseus (son of Zeus and the mortal Danaë), who was sent by King Polydectes to behead her. In order to accomplish this, Perseus receives divine help during his quest. The goddess Athena directs him to the Hesperides, nymphs who tend a blissful garden in the western corner of the world, who supply him with winged sandals, a sword, a cap of invisibility, and a mirrored shield. By looking at Medusa's reflection in this shield, he is able to behead her without being turned to stone. After Medusa's head is severed, two creatures are born from her blood: the winged horse **Pegasus** and the **giant** Chrysaor. After her death, Medusa becomes a guardian in Hades, the land of the dead. It is there that Hercules later meets her.

The death of Medusa, however, is not the end of her tale as her severed head in myth continues to retain its petrifying power and her blood has many uses. According to Ovid and Apollonius, when Perseus flies on Pegasus with the monster's head still dripping with blood, he fails to notice that every drop of black ichor that falls to the ground creates serpents of many kinds. This is why, according to the ancients, northern Africa had a high population of serpents. In a similar manner, the coral reefs of the Red Sea were created by Medusa's blood that covered seaweed during Perseus's venture in Ethiopia. The power of the beheaded Gorgon also petrified the **Titan** Atlas when Perseus flew past him. And while her looks could kill, her blood could restore life. Medusa's blood possesses amazing powers of healing and is given by Athena to the god of medicine, Asclepius. With its help, he could even bring the dead back to life.

Medusa's head also plays a pivotal role in the saving of Princess Andromeda. After the killing of the Gorgon, Perseus discovers Andromeda chained to a coastal rock. She is to be sacrificed to the **sea monster** Cetus that has been plaguing the kingdom of Ethiopia. When the horrid beast appears, Perseus turns it to stone using the petrifying power of Medusa's head. Then he sets the princess free and proposes marriage. Andromeda, however, has already been promised to another man. When the young hero learns that her previous fiancé is plotting against him, he shows the Gorgon's head to all of the conspirators, turning them to stone. Following this sequence of events, the hero gives the Gorgon's head to the goddess Athena, who places it in the center of her Aegis (shield or breastplate), creating a *Gorgoneion*. Throughout the ancient world, representations of the Gorgon's head appeared on armor and weapons, gates, walls, coins, and pottery. The *Gorgoneion*'s function was to repel bad luck and petrify the enemy.

As with the other Gorgons, the earliest images of Medusa in art come from the eighth century BCE and it is possible to distinguish three stages in the representations of her appearance. The oldest stage presents her and her sisters with big, round hypnotic eyes, a wide face, a mouth full of teeth and fangs, a protruding tongue, and a wide, flat nose. The hair is short and curly, and is sometimes connected with a beard that adorns the face. The Gorgons were painted mostly as a full face staring directly at the viewer. The middle stage lasted from the fifth century until the second century BCE and during this period the wild nature and evil appearance of Medusa are toned down and she begins to transform into a beautiful woman. The final stage of the Gorgon's visual evolution began in the third century BCE and focused increasingly on Medusa to the exclusion of her sisters. During this stage, she was painted as a young maiden with a round face, a pair of small wings growing from her brow, and snakes in her hair. These portraits are often shown from a three-quarter view.

Relatively little attention was given to Medusa during the Middle Ages; however, she was "rediscovered" during the Renaissance. As is the case with many fantastic creatures of ancient myth, Medusa appears in **Dante**'s *Divine Comedy* (1308–21) where she acts as an allegorical symbol for the soul frozen or stuck in sin. Italian painter, writer, and historian Giorgio Vasari (1511–74) notes in his biography of Leonardo da Vinci (1452–1519) that da Vinci painted a portrait of Medusa's severed head on a wooden shield in his youth (this portrait does not survive). A variety of other paintings of Medusa followed, such as those by Michelangelo (1475–1564), Caravaggio (1571–1610), and Peter Paul Rubens (1577–1640). Each of these painters represents Medusa as a young woman with snakes for hair, with her head slightly turned so she cannot change the viewer to stone. Benvenuto Cellini's (1500–1571) famous bronze statue represents Perseus with a sword in his right hand and Medusa's head in his left. In the seventeenth and eighteenth centuries, Medusa often appeared in literature, mostly in poetry such as Pierre de Ronsard's "Second Livre des Amours" (1555) or Philippe Desportes's Amours d'Hyppolite" (1573).

In the nineteenth century, Medusa was a symbol used by the Romantics, who considered her a mysterious, fascinating Dark Woman and the personification of **Death**.

This fascination is evident in the first part of Goethe's *Faust* (1808), in which she is presented as a dangerous and seductive creature, as well as in Charles Baudelaire's *Les fleurs du mal* (1857), in which she represents the attractions and dangers of feminine sexuality.

Since the start of the twentieth century, Medusa has appeared in a variety of different contexts and media. Films featuring Medusa include Alberto De Martino's *Medusa Against the Son of Hercules* (1962) and George Pal's *7 Faces of Dr Lao* (1964), the cinematic adaptation of Charles G. Finney's 1935 novel, *The Circus of Doctor Lao*. Probably the best-known adaptation of the Perseus and Medusa myth occurs within Desmond Davis's *The Clash of the Titans* from 1981 and its remake by Louis Laterrier in 2010. This production is arguably responsible for the modern appearance of Medusa. She was introduced by Davis as a half-woman, half-snake figure.

Early in the twentieth century, scholars such as A.L. Frothingham considered Medusa as a symbol of fertility and examined the Perseus story as an allegory for the passage of seasons, or for the ending of drought and the beginning of new life. Later in the century, Medusa's visage was adopted by many feminists and modern women as a symbol of female rage and its power—notably French feminist Hélène Cixous who turned to the Gorgon in her 1975 feminist manifesto, "The Laugh of the Medusa"—and Medusa's head appeared on the covers of feminist books and magazines such as Anne Devane's *Female Rage: Unlocking Its Secrets, Claiming Its Power* (1994). In the twenty-first century, Medusa appears regularly in video games, including the *Kid Icarus* and *Castlevania* series, and is featured in both the literary and cinematic versions of author Rick Riordan's *The Lightning Thief* (2005), the first entry in the popular "Percy Jackson" fantasy series. In the Chris Columbus film (2010), she is played by Uma Thurman.

Marcin Konrad Kaleta

References and Suggested Reading

Brunel, Pierre, ed. *Companion to Literary Myths, Heroes, and Archetypes*. New York: Routledge, 1996.

Frothingham, A.L. "Medusa, Apollo, and the Great Mother." *American Journal of Archaeology* 15, no. 3 (July–September 1911): 349–77.

Garber, Marjorie, and Nancy J. Vickers, eds. *The Medusa Reader*. New York: Routledge, 2003.

Mode, Heinz. *Fabulous Beasts and Demons*. London: Phaidon, 1975.

Murgatroyd, Paul. *Mythical Monsters in Classical Literature*. London: Duckworth Publishing, 2007.

Ogden, Daniel. *Perseus*. London: Routledge, 2008.

Wilk, Stephen R. *Medusa: Solving the Mystery of the Gorgon*. New York: Oxford University Press, 2000.

MELMOTH THE WANDERER

Melmoth the Wanderer is the title character of an 1820 Gothic novel by Anglo-Irish cleric Charles R. Maturin (1780–1824). Having sold his soul, the eponymous Melmoth is doomed to wander forever, unless he can find a victim to take his place, swapping heavenly salvation for eternal life on Earth. Cruel and sardonic, ever mocking mortal man's folly and weakness, Melmoth's cursed existence makes him a monstrous figure. And yet he earns sympathy as well. He is the hero of a romantic love story and the curse of his longevity—like that of today's **vampires** in the fiction of Anne Rice or Charlaine Harris—renders him a victim to be pitied or a superhuman to be envied.

Melmoth's monstrous characteristics include his intensely disturbing eyes, a strange music that may accompany his arrival, his uncanny tone of voice, and his ability to arrive in and depart from the most impenetrable locations suddenly and without notice. The most disturbing, however, appears in his constant allusion, as one victim describes it, "to events and personages beyond his *possible memory* ... this perpetual reference to events long past, and men long buried" (Maturin 228). This last trait is due, of course, to his immortality.

Set in 1816, *Melmoth the Wanderer* opens with the arrival of Trinity College student John Melmoth at his ancestral home to attend the death of his uncle; as he inherits the family manor, he also inherits its dark secret, the existence of his demonic ancestor and namesake. Typical Gothic devices—a portrait and a moldy manuscript—offer John the first pieces of the Wanderer's story, portions of which are told by different narrators. First, the housekeeper's hints at "an *odd story in the family*" (22) and a visit to Biddy Brannigan, the local herbal-healer/fortune-teller, pique the young man's curiosity, which soon becomes an obsession. Brannigan explains that John's ancestors settled in Ireland during Oliver Cromwell's (1599–1658) time, but one of them had left and "resided so long on the Continent, that his family had lost all recollection of him" (26). Referred to as "the traveller," "he was never heard to speak, seen to partake of food, or known to enter any dwelling but that of his family," and "his late appearance boded no good either to the living or the dead" (27).

John reads the ancient manuscript, in which one John Stanton describes an encounter with the former's ancestor. During his travels to Spain in 1677, a local woman told Stanton the gruesome tale of a bridal party attended by "an Englishman of the name of *Melmoth*, a traveller" (32), which ended with the priest killed and the groom mad after waking to find the bride dead in his arms. Horrified but fascinated, the enigma of Melmoth obsesses Stanton almost to the point of madness, and he is committed to an insane asylum where he has written the narrative now in John's hands.

John's own first glimpse of the mysterious Melmoth, a man alive in 1677 and still so in 1816, occurs amid the terrible chaos of a shipwreck on a stormy night. Rushing to the aid of victims desperately fighting to reach the rocky coast behind his estate, John hears a demoniacal laugh and, turning toward it:

> *just then he descried, standing a few yards above him on the rock, a figure that shewed neither sympathy or terror,—uttered no sound,—offered no help. Melmoth's surtout, in spite of his efforts to wrap it around him, was fluttering in rags,—not a thread of the*

> *stranger's garments seemed ruffled by the blast. But this did not strike him so much as his obvious insensibility to the distress and terror around him.* (66)

The shipwreck's sole survivor, the Spaniard Don Alonzo di Monçada, tells John much more about the mysterious Wanderer.

The novel's famously complex narrative—a trait attributed by Sharon Ragaz to Maturin's piecemeal submissions to his editor—involves the embedding of several additional tales, those of other individuals whose destiny it has been to cross Melmoth's path. Brought to the Melmoth estate to recover, Monçada relates the first of these framed narratives, "The Tale of the Spaniard." Rebelling against his family's wishes that he become a monk, the young nobleman encounters Melmoth the Wanderer in the midst of a terrible fire in the prison of the Spanish Inquisition, which allows him to escape.

Monçada's escape is only temporary. He finds refuge in the city's Jewish quarter where he hears "the Tale of the Indian, – the victim of Melmoth's passion" (534). In this tale-within-a-tale-within-a-tale, Immalee, a pale-skinned woman abandoned on a remote island in the Indian Ocean, falls in love with Melmoth when he appears as the first human she meets. He teaches her about the world beyond and then disappears after whetting her thirst for knowledge. Their acquaintance is renewed three years later in Spain: Immalee, actually Isidora di Aliaga, the lost child of a wealthy Catholic family, has been rescued. They are secretly married and Melmoth wonders at the fact that she can love him, hinting at his curse of eternal life, frightening her with sardonic utterances that her innocence prevents her from understanding.

Two more episodes in which Melmoth plays a dastardly role, "The Tale of Guzman's Family" and "The Lovers Tale," intervene before the climax of "The Tale of the Indian" with the death of Isidora and her infant daughter in the prisons of the Spanish Inquisition. The novel itself concludes with Melmoth's interview with his great-great-grand-nephew, John. The former's eyes are now dead, their eerie light extinguished, and he proclaims that: "Your ancestor has come home ... his wanderings are over" (537). The conclusion remains a literal cliff-hanger. While Melmoth has clearly admitted that "none have consented" to take his place (537), it seems that his wanderings may come to an end and that he is about to die. The next morning he has disappeared, leaving behind signs of a struggle that John and Monçada follow to the edge of a cliff. The only remaining trace of the Wanderer is his handkerchief hanging from a rocky crag.

The nineteenth-century French novelist Honoré de Balzac (1799–1850) leaves no doubt about the Wanderer's fate in his sequel to Maturin's novel, "Melmoth Reconciled" (1835). Balzac magnifies Melmoth's supernatural powers to equal those of Satan (see **Devil, The**), but he depicts the monster's redemption, as a mediocre Parisian cashier, Castanier, accepts taking his place. *Melmoth the Wanderer* inspired other great literary figures, including French poet Charles Baudelaire (1821–67), founder of Surrealism André Breton (1896–1966), and Irish novelist James Joyce (1882–1941). Indeed, when he traveled to France after his imprisonment in 1897, Irish writer Oscar Wilde (1854–1900) assumed the name of "Sebastian Melmoth"; Dave Sim (b. 1956) produced a graphic novel account of Wilde's last days, titled *Melmoth* (1991), book six of the *Cerebus* series illustrated by Gerhard. More recently, Hugh Sykes Davies (b. 1909) penned *The Papers of Andrew Melmoth* (1960); however, its title character only vaguely echoes the monstrous anti-hero of Maturin's novel.

Amy J. Ransom

References and Suggested Reading

Balzac, Honoré de. "Melmoth Reconciled" [1835]. Translated by Ellen Marriage. *Project Gutenberg*, 2010. <http://www.gutenberg.org/ebooks/1277>.

Brown, Marshall. *The Gothic Text*. Stanford: Stanford University Press, 2005.

Lanone, Catherine. "Verging on the Gothic: Melmoth's Journey to France." In *European Gothic: A Spirited Exchange, 1760–1960*, edited by Avril Horner, 71–83. Manchester: Manchester University Press, 2002.

Maturin, Charles. *Melmoth the Wanderer* [1820]. Reprint, edited by Douglas Grant, Oxford: Oxford University Press, 1998.

Ragaz, Sharon. "Maturin, Archibald Constable, and the Publication of *Melmoth the Wanderer*." *Review of English Studies: The Leading Journal of English Literature and the English Language* 57, no. 230 (2006): 359–73.

MEMNOCH—*see* Angel

MEPHISTOPHELES

The **demon** Mephistopheles, famous for his sly rhetoric and base tomfoolery, has been a popular preoccupation of literature, drama, film, and opera for nearly 500 years. Made famous by Christopher Marlowe's *Doctor Faustus* (1604) and Johann Wolfgang von Goethe's *Faust* (Part I, 1806; Part 2, 1832), Mephistopheles was one of the first literary **devils** established as a character in his own right, not simply a mere servant of Satan sent to do his diabolical master's bidding on Earth. From his very inception, Mephistopheles has been associated with curiosity, with intellectual and artistic advancement at whatever cost, serving as an unlikely mirror for the desires and ambitions of every age.

While demons have been a key feature of literature since the Middle Ages, the devil Mephistopheles is purely a Renaissance invention as the Renaissance emphasis on individual character seems to extend to devils as well as humans. The origins of the name are as complex and multifaceted as the character itself and have baffled philologists for centuries (Goebel 148). Parts of the name translate into Hebrew, Persian, Greek, or Latin (Butler 131–2), all with relevant meaning. In Greek, the components "*me*," "*phos/photos*," and "*philos*" translate as "he who is not a lover of light"; "*Mephitis*" in Latin translates as "pungent, sulfurous, stinking"; while the Hebrew word "*tophel*" means "liar"—all of which are entirely appropriate for a servant of Satan (Russell 61). As Jeffrey Brown Russell points out, "that the name is a purely modern invention of uncertain origins makes it an elegant symbol of the modern Devil with his many novel and diverse forms" (61).

The first records of one George or John Faust first appeared in the early sixteenth century, denoting a charlatan reputedly endowed with supernatural skill. In the 1540s, Faust was linked with the demonic pact, and the first reference to Faust's personal demon, "Mephistophilis," appeared in 1587 in the first *Faustbook*. This episodic chapbook proved one of the most popular books of its day and the speed at which it was printed and reprinted, translated, and disseminated across Europe is astonishing. Sometime between 1588 and 1592, Marlowe brought Faust's devil from folklore into drama by adapting the story for the Elizabethan stage. *Doctor Faustus* was one of the most popular and influential plays of its time and spawned a series of devil dramas, although nothing that followed produced a devil as compelling or developed as Mephistopheles.

Intrinsically connected to the humanist desire to know more, Marlowe's Mephistopheles is a devil that caters to the Renaissance humanist thirst for knowledge, fueling curiosity by promising to lay bare the secrets of the world and thus enabling man to achieve his full intellectual potential though magic. This is an empty bargain, however; Mephistopheles repeatedly outsmarts his human counterpart, overcoming Faustus with dazzling rhetoric and visual distractions to disguise the limitations of his powers, as Mephistopheles is also a Protestant devil, limited to base tricks and wonders but nothing miraculous. He appears in various guises, first as something too terrible for Faustus's liking and then as a Franciscan friar at Faustus's request. This human-like guise serves to enhance his very human qualities, for this demon is an alluring character in his own right and worthy of audience sympathies in the regret he expresses over his unfortunate fall with Lucifer. As Dorothy L. Sayers points out, "it is his dark angelic melancholy that makes the splendor of Marlowe's Mephistopheles" (*Devil to Pay* 8). Marlowe assimilates the characteristics of man and demon in identifying the humanistic side of an unredeemable devil, a trope developed in later works such as John Milton's *Paradise Lost* (1667). In fact, Marlowe's Mephistopheles initiated a change in the literary devil as "he is at least a little sympathetic with his victim, and he shows some small signs of introspection, including a hint of regret for his own rebellion" (Russell 64).

While Marlowe's Mephistopheles epitomizes Renaissance humanist ideals and the consequences of curiosity, Goethe's *Faust* is equally a product of its age, embodying both Enlightenment and Romantic views of the world and thus encompassing the dramatic changes in science, politics, philosophy, technology, and the increasing secularization of society that rendered the presence of an external devil preying upon spiritual morality and weakness redundant. The product of 60 years' work, Goethe's two-part drama was first published in 1806 (Part One) and 1832 (Part Two). From the very beginning of the drama it is unclear whether Mephistopheles is serving Satan or God or acting as a free agent, for he appears "both as an opponent of God and as the instrument of the divine will; as the creator of the material world and as God's subject; as the principle of matter against the principle of spirit; as evil against good; as chaos against order; as a stimulus to creativity; and in many other aspects" (Russell 158). In fact, Goethe's theology hints at a Manichean duality with the Devil as an essential component of God's power.

The Prologue opens with a dialogue between Mephistopheles and God, alluding to the bargain made between God and Satan in Job in which Satan is allowed free-reign over enticing the pious Job to evil. Mephistopheles is similarly granted this latitude over the devout Faust without heavenly intervention. This Mephistopheles also exhibits the characteristics of traditional devils, lying, cheating, casting illusions, and shapeshifting (see **Shapeshifter**). Yet, unlike Marlowe's Mephistopheles who uses visual tricks to distract Faustus from the intellectual quandaries he is unable to solve, Goethe's Mephistopheles leaves Faust deliberately dissatisfied. He does not feed Faust's illusions; rather, he shatters them, foiling the scholar's zealous enthusiasm. The pair is ostensibly bound to each other for eternity, for Mephistopheles promises to serve Faust during his lifetime if Faust promises to serve Mephistopheles afterwards in Hell. Goethe's play has significantly different eschatological implications to the traditional Faust story for this Mephistopheles fails; Faust escapes to Heaven while his demon is distracted by beguiling **angels**. Faust's sins are redeemable, his devil ultimately ineffectual.

The Faust myth has continued to feature in popular literature, although in more recent retellings the Mephistopheles character is not strictly associated with forbidden knowledge. Instead, he has come to represent an illicit key to success, tricking the ambitious in exchange for their souls in what is later revealed to be a hollow bargain. Louise May Alcott's 1877 novel *A Modern Mephistopheles* depicts a writer who sells his soul in order to be a successful poet—a pact also explored in Max Beerbohm's 1916 short story "Enoch Soames." Similarly, in John Banville's 1986 novel *Mefisto*, the mathematician Gabriel Swan is coerced into a Faustian bargain of sorts by the mysterious Felix who promises to unveil the world's numerical mysteries. In a similar bid for genius, the protagonist of Thomas Mann's 1947 novel *Doktor Faustus* intentionally contracts syphilis with the idea that the subsequent madness will allow him to produce extraordinary music. The resulting madness leads him to strike a bargain with a Mephistophelean character of his own invention. In Oscar Wilde's *The Picture of* **Dorian Gray**, the eponymous character makes a Faustian pact for eternal youth with no devil present whatsoever. Here the demonic pact is completely internalized, with Mephistopheles incorporated into the psyche of the Faustian figure. The external, physical devil is not required, as human becomes both Faust and Mephistopheles. Magician and devil are also combined in the magical feline "Mr Mistoffeelees" by T.S. Elliot in *Old Possum's Book of Practical Cats*.

Dramatic adaptations of the Faust story have also continued to fascinate theater and cinema audiences. In 1939, Dorothy L. Sayers adapted the Faust story into a new play, *The Devil to Pay*, a more traditional version of the story. Mephistopheles also appears in Vaclav Havel's play *Temptation* (1968), as a disgusting tramp named "Fistula" who offers Foustka an escape from the banal rationalities of daily life with promises of magic and creative escape. The Faustian bargain is also a popular trope in film, with Mephistopheles figures called upon to help protagonists with a variety of unattainable prizes including getting the girl in *Bedazzled* (Stanley Donen, 1967; remade by Harold Ramis in 2000), a job in a successful law firm in *The Devil's Advocate* (Taylor Hackford, 1997), or beating a professional baseball team in *Damn Yankees* (George Abbott and Stanley Donen, 1958). These devil characters are rarely called "Mephistopheles," however, and are seldom developed as three-dimensional characters. They usually represent Satan himself, with none of the individualistic character attributes of Marlowe's and Goethe's respective demons. Marlowe's and Goethe's versions have also been adapted several times into film, most famously in Richard Burton's 1967 adaptation of the Elizabethan play and by Czech director Jan Svankmajer with puppets in the 1994 *Faus*—a film that draws on the long tradition of Faustus puppet adaptations staged in Europe since the Renaissance.

Bronwyn Johnston

References and Suggested Reading

Butler, Elizabeth M. *The Fortunes of Faust*. Stroud: Sutton Publishing, 1998.

Goebel, Julian. "The Etymology of Mephistopheles." *Transactions and Proceedings of the American Philological Association* 35 (1904): 148–56.

Russell, Jeffrey Brown. *Mephistopheles: The Devil in the Modern World*. Ithaca: Cornell University Press, 1986.

Sayers, Dorothy L. *The Devil to Pay*. Canterbury: H.H. Goulden, 1939.

——. *The Poetry of Search and The Poetry of Statement and Other Posthumous Essays on Literature, Religion, and Language*. London: Victor Gollancz Ltd, 1963.

MERL—*see* Demon

MERLIN—*see* Witch/Wizard

MERMAID/MERMAN

Mermaids and **mermen** are fictional aquatic beings with the upper bodies of humans and fish-like tails. These human–aquatic hybrids are known collectively as merfolk and are frequently represented as both beguiling and dangerous.

The Origin of the Mermaid

Sea-dwelling deities, part-human and part-fish, in Near Eastern and Indian mythology influenced the development of the mermaid. The Mesopotamian deity Oannes embodied the sea itself and may date back as far as 5000 BCE. Matsya is the fish incarnation of the Hindu god, Vishnu, while Levantine moon deities, such as Atargatis and Derceto, were depicted with female and piscine elements. Triton, the son of the god and goddess of the seas in Greek and Roman traditions, was usually a benevolent presence to those who treated the sea with respect. Like many sea deities and maritime spirits, he was associated with storms, abundant fish, and shipbuilding.

The mythical **siren** who lured mariners to their deaths also influenced the image of the mermaid. Classical sirens were bird-like, but their connection with the sea anticipates their eventual transformation into mermaids. Funeral votives from the seventh and sixth centuries BCE depicting female-headed bird sirens also suggest a connection with the afterlife. Descriptions given by classical writers from Homer and Hesiod (seventh century BCE) to the tenth-century CE Byzantine Encyclopedia known as the *Suda* suggest that the sirens' power derived from their ability to prophesy and to grant knowledge. The names of the sirens recorded by writers such as Hesiod, including Parthenope (splendid or maiden voice) and Ligea (clear-toned), invoke the sound of the voice and singing is their cosmological function in Plato's Myth of Er (*The Republic*, Book 10, fourth century BCE). During the sixth and fifth centuries BCE, depictions of Ulysses tied to a ship's mast listening to winged, female-headed sirens appeared on Greek pottery. Homer noted their fatal singing and their connection with the sea, and he says they drowned themselves in despair when Odysseus escaped (*Odyssey*, Book 12). Song is also central to their power in Apollonius of Rhodes's *Argonautica* (third century BCE), but Jason and the Argonauts are saved because Orpheus's music is stronger than the siren's song (Book 4, lines 892 ff). The location of temples and cult sites dedicated to the sirens also strengthens their connection with the sea. Leucosia, whose name may refer to the white tips of storm waves, had an island cult site off the coast of Italy (Pliny the Elder, *Natural History*, Book 3 chapter 85, first century CE).

The qualities passed by the siren to the mermaid include song, knowledge of the future, and a link with the sea. Pliny records a sighting of both male and female sirens on the Nile (*Natural History*, Book 10, chapter 70). In the *Etymologies* of Isidore of Seville (Book 11, chapter 3, sections 30–31, seventh century), sirens still retain avian characteristics, while the *Suda* links the sirens' song with sexuality.

Medieval bestiaries, which presented allegorical interpretations of animal behavior to encourage Christian virtue, were popular during the twelfth and thirteenth centuries. The siren illustrated in the Anglo-Norman *Bestiary of Philippe de Thaon* (twelfth century) has both claws and fish tail, but the fish-tailed mermaid eventually became dominant in European art and literature. They appear in medieval church architecture as double-tailed sirens and as fish-tailed mermaids. They adorn misericords, columns, doorways, and roof bosses, holding a comb and a looking glass, playing an instrument, or clutching a fish in one hand. In this ecclesiastical context, they symbolize the dangers of women and of worldly pleasures in general. In a Renaissance painting, the sixteenth-century *St Nicholas of Bari Rebuking the Storm* by Bicci di Lorenzo, the patron saint of sailors flies towards a foundering ship, while directly below him, a mermaid swims in the opposite direction.

Mermaids, and related sea people, are always peripheral figures. A famous sighting of a mermaid and merman, which allegedly took place in the Nile river, remained part of mermaid lore for centuries. Ulisse Aldrovandi in his *History of Marvellous Creatures* (1581) interpreted this sighting as a warning prodigy. In Zennor church in Cornwall, a carving on a fifteenth-century wooden bench depicting a mermaid with a looking glass and a comb has given rise to a popular folktale: in the nineteenth century, the Cornish folklorist William Bottrell included a tale about a mermaid who attended Zennor church in order to seduce one of the choristers. The carving undoubtedly predates the legend, but the link between the church carving and the Mermaid of Zennor tale has become part of romantic Cornish lore and the church a popular tourist attraction. Even when mermaids remain on dry land, they are never fully integrated into the human world. In his apocalyptic history of the world, *Speculum Mundi* (1635), John Swan adopted a critical attitude to the existence of some fabulous beasts, but nevertheless recorded an incident in 1402 in which a mermaid was washed through the dyke near Edam in the Netherlands. Eventually, she was captured, became a Christian and learned to spin, but never spoke.

Mermaids in Folklore, Literature, and Popular Culture

Mermaids are an established feature of European folklore and literary tradition. They are beautiful but can cause storms and shipwrecks and affect the availability of fish. A fisherman who releases a captured mermaid will be successful and will be warned of approaching storms. A Greek folk legend influenced by the *Alexander Romance* (third–fourteenth centuries) concerns a mermaid in the Black Sea who brings good luck to sailors who correctly answer a riddle about Alexander the Great.

Several prominent medieval mer-creatures have more specialized features, possibly as a result of local traditions being absorbed into older material. The beautiful Mélusine, the subject of a fourteenth-century romance (Jean d'Arras, *La noble histoire de Lusignon* [*The Noble History of the Lusignan Family*]) has wings and a serpent-like tail. When her husband violates a taboo against interrupting her Saturday bath, she flies out of the window, but her cries are heard before a death in the family. Mélusine's wings and her association with water and death echo the siren figure, while the terms of her marriage suggest a connection with a class of hybrid supernatural beings able to assume human form in order to become temporary brides of mortal men. Cola Pesce (Nicolas, the fish) is related to the popular Mediterranean saint Nicholas of Bari, patron of sailors. He is a kind of merman, although without a tail, who dies once he is taken away from the sea (Walter Map, *De Nugis Curialium*, twelfth century).

In Irish mermaid folktales, a fisherman can compel a "merrow" (mermaid) to marry by hiding one of her possessions. The children of these marriages have special qualities inherited from their non-human mother. However, the merrow returns to the sea when she finds her stolen possession. By contrast, the mermaid Liban becomes a saint after the overflowing of Lough Neath in Ireland drowns her father's palace and she is transformed (*The Book of the Dun Cow*, eleventh century). Eventually Liban gives up the longevity of a supernatural creature to be baptized as Muirgen (sea-born) and becomes a Christian saint.

Literary references to mermaids draw on both the classical heritage of these creatures as well as common folklore characteristics. In Luis Vaz de Camoes imaginative reworking of Portuguese history, *Os Lusíadas* (1572), mermaids called nereids rescue Vasco da Gama's fleet and prophesy the country's future glory (canto 2, 10). The theme of a sea woman married to a mortal is rooted in traditional legend motifs, but the plight of a mermaid or merman caught between the sea and the human world also struck a chord with Romantic writers in the nineteenth century, and the tragic outcome of mermaid tales continues to appeal to contemporary writers. *Undine* (1811), a German romantic novella by Friedrich de la Motte Fouqué, uses the traditional motif of the mermaid's desire for an immortal soul to express core romantic concerns with yearning and frustrated desire, as well as images of femininity, mutability, and death. The water-nymph heroine lacks a traditional mermaid tail, but wants to marry a mortal in order to gain a soul; her failure results in her lover's death. Hans Christian Andersen's *The Little Mermaid* (*Den lille havfrue*, 1837) is more conventional in appearance, but she too desires a soul and a husband. Anton Dvořák's opera *Rusalka* (1911) also uses the theme of a water-nymph who falls in love with a human, but draws as well on Slavic traditions about female river spirits who can cause death. In each of these three instances, the mermaid's desire to transcend her nature leads to tragedy.

Other literary interpretations vary the dynamic between the sea creatures and their human counterparts, although they focus on the tension and disruption that these contacts cause. Matthew Arnold's poem "The Forsaken Merman" (1849) reflects the poet's concern with shifting moral norms. It is based on a Danish ballad in which the human wife abandons her merman husband and their children. The central character in Oscar Wilde's literary fairytale *The Fisherman and his Soul* (1888) also reverses the usual narrative pattern. It is the human character, a fisherman, who wishes to sell his soul to a **witch** in order to live with a mermaid. Pierre Loti's novel *Pecheur d'islande* (*Iceland Fisherman*, 1886), set in Brittany, expresses a quintessential romantic conflict between necessity and desire as a conflict between a fisherman's love for a beautiful woman and his fatal attraction to the mysterious sea. The Irish poet Nuala Ní Dhomhnaill (1952–) uses the mermaid to explore contemporary themes of femininity, sexuality, and culture identity. In her *The Fifty Minute Mermaid* (2008), the main character is presented as a conflicted figure only able to live on land if she forgets the sea. In a short story by Jane Yolen, "The Lady and the Merman" (1977), a seemingly unattractive young woman longs for the love of a merman. In the end, she follows him into the sea, finally beautiful in death. Sue Monk Kidd's novel *The Mermaid Chair* (2005) reworks the Zennor mermaid tale in terms of the marital and emotional conflicts experienced by a contemporary middle-aged woman. In J.K. Rowling's popular "Harry Potter" series, merpeople populate the lake outside of Hogwarts (see **Harry Potter, Monsters In**).

The popularity of mermaid traditions is also reflected in stage plays and film productions, with Hans Christian Andersen's *Little Mermaid* being one of the most frequent sources of inspiration. The

Australian swimmer Annette Kellerman created several water ballet films using the mermaid theme, including 1911's *Siren of the Sea* (director uncredited). Other adaptations include "The Little Mermaid" ballet in the film biography of *Hans Christian Andersen* (Charles Vidor, 1952), Walt Disney's upbeat animation of Andersen's tale (Ron Clements and John Musker, 1989) and its spin-offs, and a Japanese anime version *Ponyo on the Cliff by the Sea* (Hayao Miyazaki, 2008). *Undine*, de la Motte Fouqué's novella, has been adapted as a stage play by Jean Girardeau (1956), and as a ballet, *Ondine* (1958, choreographer Sir Frederick Ashton).

Curtis Harrington's *Night Tide* (1961) reworks the sea-siren myth in which a naive young sailor (Dennis Hopper) falls in love with a strange girl who works as a mermaid at a carnival (Linda Lawson). She is tormented by the idea that she is actually a siren who kills her lovers, but tragically it is she, rather than the lover, who drowns during a storm. In some instances, contemporary films often shift the focus from the mermaid as a figure of tragic love to the mermaid as a potential victim of scientific exploitation. In the comedy films *Miranda* (Ken Annakin, 1948) and *Mad About Men* (Ralph Thomas, 1954), Glynis Johns plays a flirtatious mermaid who finds love and escapes the scientific and commercial interests which would exploit her. In *Splash* (Ron Howard, 1984), a mermaid (Daryl Hannah) saves a young boy from drowning. Later, he (Tom Hanks) falls in love with her and protects her from exploitation. A mermaid is at the center of M. Night Shyamalan's *Lady in the Water* (2006), and the 2011 installment of the *Pirates of the Caribbean* franchise (Rob Marshall) restores an element of danger to the mermaid as they first appear as alluring, then turn monstrous.

Non-European Mermaids

Not all mythical sea creatures conform to European ideas about mermaids and many are no doubt independent of the Western mermaid tradition. The Amazonian myth of Serek-A concerns an unhappy wife who dives into a river and becomes half-woman and half-snake. She is associated with the rainbow, the bridge between life and death, and is the mother of the anaconda, a powerful creature in Amazonian mythology who inhabits both the land and the river. Another Amazonian creature, the boto, is able to shapeshift between river dolphin and human forms (see **Shapeshifter**). In human form, he seduces young women, but always returns to his own world.

The Inuit mother figure Sedna is associated with control of the weather and the availability of game. She is known by many names and was not a mermaid originally, but rather a woman who married a supernatural bird. Her father threw her out of his kayak and, as she clung to the side, chopped off her fingers, causing sea creatures such as fish, whales, sea birds, and so on, to flow from her bleeding hands. As art has replaced spiritual traditions like shamanism in contemporary Inuit culture as a way of representing the world of non-human beings, Sedna is increasingly depicted as mermaid-like. In the ancient Sanskrit epic the *Ramayana*, Rama and the monkey-god Hanuman set out to rescue Rama's wife from the island fortress of the **demon** king, Ravana. Hanuman and his monkey army attempt to build a bridge, but every day Ravana's mermaid daughter scatters the stones. Hanuman's courtship of the mermaid is a popular episode in the masked court dance drama of Thailand and in the popular shadow puppet theater throughout Malaysia.

Juliette Wood

References and Suggested Reading

Andersen, Hans Christian. *Andersen's Tales for Children*. Translated by Alfred Wehnert. London: Bell and Daldy, 1866.

Bottrell, William. *Stories and Folk-Lore of West Cornwall*. Penzance, 1880. Reprint, Whitefish, MT: Kessinger Publishing, 2009.

Kidd, Sue Monk. *The Mermaid Chair*. New York: Viking Press, 2005.

Laugrand, Frédérick, and J.G. Oosten. *The Sea Woman: Sedna in Inuit Shamanism and Art in the Eastern Artic*. Fairbanks: University of Alaska Press, 2008.

Mindlin, Betty, and Indigenous Storytellers. *Barbecued Husbands and Other Stories From the Amazon*. Translated by Donald Slatoff. New York: Verso, 2002.

Murphy, Maureen. "Siren or Victim? The Mermaid in Irish Legend and Poetry." In *More Real Than Reality: The Fantastic in Irish Literature and the Arts*, edited by Donald E. Morse and Csilla Bertha, 29–40. New York: Greenwood Press, 1991.

Ni Dhomhnaill, Nuala. *The Fifty Minute Mermaid*. Translated by Paul Muldoon. Loughcrew, Ireland: Gallery Press, 2008.

Pollard, John. *Seer Shrines and Sirens*. London: George Allen & Unwin, 1965.

Rachewiltz, Siegfried de. *De Sirenibus: An Inquiry Into Sirens From Homer to Shakespeare*. New York: Garland, 1987.

Stoneman, Richard. *Alexander the Great: A Life in Legend*. New Haven and London: Yale University Press, 2008.

Thompson, C.J.S. *Mystery and Lore of Monsters* [1930]. Reprint, Whitefish, MT: Kessinger Publishing, 2003.

Wright, Herbert. "The Source of Matthew Arnold's Forsaken Merman." *Modern Language Review* 13 (1918): 90–94.

Yolen, Jane. *The Lady and the Merman*. Easthampton, MA: Pennyroyal Press, 1977.

MESTACLOCAN—*see* Shapeshifter

METATRON—*see* Angel

MICHAEL—*see* Angel

MICROMÉGAS

Micromégas travels to Earth from a planet in the star system of Sirius in the eponymous tale written by eighteenth-century French philosopher François-Marie Arouet de Voltaire (1694–1778). Measuring 120,000 feet in height and still a young man at the age of 700 years, the **giant** Micromégas appears monstrous because of his extraordinary size and his extreme longevity. Having been banished after publishing a literary work critical of his world's ruler, he travels from planet to planet to learn as much as he can. On Saturn, Micromégas encounters a fellow traveler who, at only one mile tall, appears almost a dwarf in comparison. Together they jump on the tail of a comet and, via the aurora borealis, arrive on the northern shore of the Baltic Sea on 5 July 1737. With its **extraterrestrial** main character and interplanetary odyssey, "Micromégas: A Philosophical Story" (1751) represents an early text in the development of science fiction.

In spite of the monstrous size, longevity, and extraordinary diet—he eats mountains for dinner—of his protagonist, Voltaire's philosophical tale seeks to illustrate "the prodigious differences which nature has contrived between all her creatures" (17). In fact, the story is an exercise in proportion, as the philosopher calculates that, given the Sirian's size in relation to that of a man (five feet), his planet must be immense: 1,600,000 times greater than the circumference of Earth. To provide an intermediary figure for comparison, Voltaire introduces the inhabitant of Saturn, a planet "barely nine hundred times the size of the Earth" (19). Micromégas's traveling partner explains that Saturnians possess 72 senses. Further examples of nature's great variety appears in the Sirian's revelation that, because of the reddish-cast of his sun, on his planet 39 primary colors can be perceived, and that during his interstellar travels, he has discovered 3,000 new elements.

In addition to the obvious motifs of interplanetary travel by extraterrestrials, "Micromégas" resembles later works of science fiction in its active engagement with scientific extrapolation. Not only does Voltaire show off his mathematical skills in calculating proportions, but he directly engages recent scientific discoveries of the Enlightenment, specifically mentioning a number of astronomers and natural scientists, as well as their detractors. These include the seventeenth- and eighteenth-century Dutchmen Jan Swammerdam (1637–80; discovered the life cycle of insects), Antonie von Leeuwenhoek (1632–1723) and Nicolaas Hartsoeker (1656–1725; both pioneers of the microscope), as well as the French Jesuit Louis-Bertrand Castel (1688–1757; author of treatises on gravity and mathematics), and Anglican vicar William Derham (1657–1735; amateur astronomer and naturalist).

While Voltaire clearly seeks to showcase the state of modern science in his era, he lampoons its philosophers. As a *conte philosophique*, the tale's goal is as much to critique contemporary society's flaws as it is to instruct about its virtues, a trait it also shares with much science fiction. The tale concludes with a satirical debate between Micromégas, his companion from Saturn, and a bevy of terrestrial philosophers—who appear as "microbes" to the extraterrestrials—about the nature of the soul. The latter cite near contemporaries René Descartes (1596–1650), Nicolas Malebranche (1638–1715), Gottfried Leibniz (1646–1716), and John Locke (1632–1704), as well as the Greek Aristotle (384–322 BCE). Voltaire's satire of contemporary philosophy is clear, as one scholar concludes his argument with the point that "one should always cite what one does not understand in the language one least understands" (Voltaire 33). In the end, Voltaire's monster Micromégas is the least monstrous character in the tale.

Amy J. Ransom

References and Suggested Reading

Braun, Theodore. E.D. (2004). "*Micromégas*: Voltaire's Interstellar Conte, a Model for the Future?" In *The Enterprise of Enlightenment*, edited by Terry Pratt and David McCallam, 195–210. New York: Peter Lang, 2004.

Engstrom, Alfred G. (1950). "Lucretius and Micromégas." In *Romance Studies: Presented to William Morton Dey*, edited by Urban Tigner Holmes, 59–60. Chapel Hill: University of North Carolina Press, 1950.

Morrow, James. "Extrapolations of Things Past: A Barbarously Brief Account of European Science Fiction, from Micromégas to Microchips." *New York Review of Science Fiction* 19, no. 9 (2007): 1, 8–11.

Voltaire. "Micromégas" [1751]. In *Micromégas and Other Short Fictions*, edited by Haydn Mason, translated by Theo Cuffe, 17–35. London: Penguin, 2002.

MINOS—*see* Dante, Monsters In

MINOTAUR

The Minotaur is a monster from Greek mythology composed of a man's body and a bull's head and tail. Images of the Minotaur survive on Greek vase paintings from the eighth century BCE on, whereas the first surviving literary reference appears in the works of the sixth-century BCE poet Sappho (fragment 206). The primary myths about the creature concern its birth and death. Born as the hybrid offspring of the Cretan queen Pasiphae and a bull, the Minotaur dwelled in the Cretan Labyrinth, where it eventually met its demise at the hands of the Athenian hero Theseus.

As told by many ancient authors, such as Pseudo-Apollodorus (*Bibliotheca* 3.1; first century CE) and Plutarch (*Life of Theseus*; first century CE), the Minotaur's unusual conception resulted from a hubristic act by Minos of Crete. Minos, son of the god Zeus and the mortal Europa, claimed the kingship over Crete. He asked Poseidon to send him a bull from the sea as a sign that he deserved the kingship, declaring that he would sacrifice it to the god in thanks. Poseidon agreed, sending a bull so magnificent that Minos could not bear to kill it. Instead, breaking his vow, he sacrificed a lesser bull. As a punishment, Poseidon made Minos's wife Pasiphae lust after the bull. Pasiphae had the architect Daedalus craft a hollow wooden cow and, concealing herself inside it, mated with the bull, conceiving the Minotaur—the "Bull of Minos," sometimes called Asterion. Minos confined Pasiphae's monstrous offspring in the Labyrinth, a maze-like prison designed by Daedalus.

When his son was killed by Aegeus, the king of Athens, Minos declared war on Athens. Unable to conquer the city, he prayed to the gods, who afflicted Athens with a plague. The Delphic Oracle declared that the plague would be lifted if the Athenians sent seven youths and seven maidens to be fed to the Minotaur every ninth year. Depending on the account, Aegeus's son Theseus either volunteered to be one of the seven or was selected by Minos as recompense for his son's death. Minos's daughter Ariadne fell in love with Theseus when he arrived, and promised to save him if he would elope with her. She gave him a ball of thread to tie to the entrance to the Labyrinth and unroll as he went through, so that he could retrace his steps. Reaching the innermost part of the Labyrinth, Theseus killed the Minotaur. Many Greek paintings depict Theseus slaying the beast with a sword; some literary accounts say he used a club (Ovid, *Heroides* 4.115; c. 20 BCE) or his bare hands (Pseudo-Apollodorus, *Bibliotheca* E1.9).

At the end of the sixth century BCE, the Athenians carefully crafted Theseus to become their national hero, lending new significance to his defeat of the Minotaur, a victory that was reinterpreted in terms of Athenian dominance over neighboring city-states. Depictions of Theseus fighting the Minotaur therefore became particularly popular in the fifth century BCE, and the state commissioned a statue of the conflict to be erected atop the Acropolis in the 450s. The tale of the victorious hero became historicized as Theseus was reconfigured as an Athenian founding figure. Fourth-century Athenian historians eventually rationalized the Minotaur as an officer in Minos's army named Tauros whom Theseus defeated in a naval battle.

The story of the Minotaur entered the consciousness of the Middle Ages and Renaissance primarily via authors such as Catullus (poem 64; first century BCE), Ovid (*Metamorphoses* 8), Plutarch (*Life of Theseus*), and Pseudo-Apollodorus (*Bibliotheca*), always in connection with Theseus. In the fourteenth century CE, Dante's *Inferno* (Canto 12, 11–15) broke this pattern by focusing on the Minotaur alone, assigning the Minotaur as the guardian of the Seventh Circle of Hell, which housed the violent. Dante highlighted the Minotaur's bestial nature by connecting the creature with the sin of violence. Geoffrey Chaucer's *The Legend of Good Women* (c. 1385 CE) featured the Minotaur as a "wikked beste" who was killed by a lump of wax that Theseus threw into its throat. Alexander Ross, in his 1647 *Mystagogus Poeticus*, allegorized Theseus as Christ and the Minotaur as Satan; Ariadne's thread became the word of God that guides humans through the labyrinth of life. For several hundred years afterwards, artists focused on the romance between Theseus and Ariadne rather than on the hero's victory over the Minotaur.

In the 1930s, the Minotaur re-entered the public imagination thanks to a series of excavations begun in 1900 at Knossos, Crete by Sir Arthur Evans, who published his findings in *The Palace of Minos* (1921–35). Evans discovered a palace complex at Knossos that he believed represented the Cretan Labyrinth. Evans also found many bull images, most notably the so-called "Toreador Fresco" which depicts a human figure apparently leaping over a bull. Evans imagined that this was a literal representation of an actual Minoan ritual, and that the myth of the Minotaur eating the Athenian youths and maidens recalled this dangerous practice. J. Alexander MacGillivray argues that Evans did not so much discover his findings as invent them, saying that Evans has led scholarly investigation astray (6–8). Although MacGillivray may be right, Evans's discoveries and ideas evoked a reawakening of the story of the Minotaur in the minds of visual, literary, and cinematic artists.

The twentieth century presented some particularly creative interpretations of the myth. From 1933 to 1939, the French avant-garde journal *Minotaure*, a publication devoted to the Surrealist movement, used the Minotaur as a symbol of humanity and bestiality, sexuality and violence; images of the Minotaur by such artists as André Derain (1880–1954), Marcel Duchamp (1887–1968), Max Ernst (1891–1976), Joan Miró (1893–1983), Salvador Dalí (1904–89), Henri Matisse (1869–1954), René Magritte (1898–1967), and Diego Rivera (1886–1957) regularly graced its covers. The political unrest in Europe at the time led to a chilling appropriation of Theseus as a racially pure hero triumphing over the hybrid beast. For the Surrealists, for example, in André Masson's 1930 painting *The Minotaur and the Labyrinth*, the Minotaur was a symbol of the unconscious mind and ultimate freedom. Pablo Picasso's intensely personal understanding of the Minotaur led to its use as a symbol of rejuvenated animal energy and violence, often erotic, best seen in the numerous prints in his *Suite Vollard* of the 1930s.

Twentieth-century literature also pushed the boundaries for interpreting the Minotaur. In F.L. Lucas's epic poem *Ariadne* (1932), the Minotaur was revealed as Minos himself wearing a bull mask, a reading based on some scholars' views that a sacred priest wore a bull mask at Knossos. W.H. Auden's long poem "New Year Letter" (1940) politicized the image of the Minotaur as representing various tyrants and dictators. In "The Minotaur" (1944), poet Muriel Rukeyser depicts the monster as betrayed and filled with loneliness. Jorge Luis Borges's short story "The House of Asterion" (1947) is a monologue from the point of view of Asterion, the Minotaur, who argues against the claims of his defamers. In Nikos Kazantzakis's drama *Theseus* (1949), the hero combats the Minotaur, who represents the three branches of the subconscious: animal, man, and god. Theseus frees the Minotaur from its bestial nature and the monster is reborn as Kouros, a handsome youth.

Even though the plural form "Minotaurs" had existed at least since William Shakespeare's *Henry VI* (V.III.189) in 1623, the twentieth century innovated a race of Minotaurs in fantasy novels. For example, the White Witch in C.S. Lewis's *The Lion, the Witch and the Wardrobe* (1950) allied with a race of Minotaurs. Mary Renault's historical novel *The King Must Die* (1958) removes all supernatural elements, and accordingly the Minotaur—named Asterion—is simply the human son of Pasiphae, who had an affair with a bull-leaper. More recently, the Minotaur has appeared as a border-guarding monster in two of Rick Riordan's "Percy Jackson and the Olympians" series, *The Lightning Thief* (2005) and *The Last Olympian* (2009), and in the 2010 film version of the former, directed by Chris Columbus.

Cinema has appropriated the Minotaur in various ways. The 1960 sword-and-sandal film *Minotaur, the Wild Beast of Crete* (Silvio Amadio) features Theseus killing a shaggy all-bull Minotaur. A satanic cult worships the Minotaur as a god in Kostas Karagiannis's *Land of the Minotaur* (1976). In Terry Gilliam's 1981 fantasy *Time Bandits*, a young boy travels back in time to find a different hero, Agamemnon, battling a Minotaur. The 1994 made-for-TV movie *Hercules in the Maze of the Minotaur* (Josh Becker) presents the Minotaur as the son of Zeus and the half-brother of Hercules, while the 2006 horror film *Minotaur* (Jonathan English) portrays the Minotaur as a giant skeletal bull. "Minotaur" is an energy drink in David Wain's 2007 comedy *Role Models*, hawked with the tagline "Taste the Beast" by Minotaur Man, the product's mascot—a man in a Minotaur suit. For most of these literary and cinematic artists, the Minotaur's semi-bestial nature inspired introspection on the nature of humanity.

Craig Jendza

References and Suggested Reading

MacGillivray, J. Alexander. *Minotaur: Sir Arthur Evans and the Archaeology of the Minoan Myth*. London: Pimlico, 2001.

Ward, Anne G., ed. *The Quest for Theseus*. New York: Praeger, 1970.

Ziolkowski, Theodore. *Minos and the Moderns: Cretan Myth in Twentieth Century Literature and Art*. New York: Oxford University Press, 2008.

MOBY DICK

Herman Melville's huge novel, *Moby-Dick; or, The Whale*, first published in 1851,

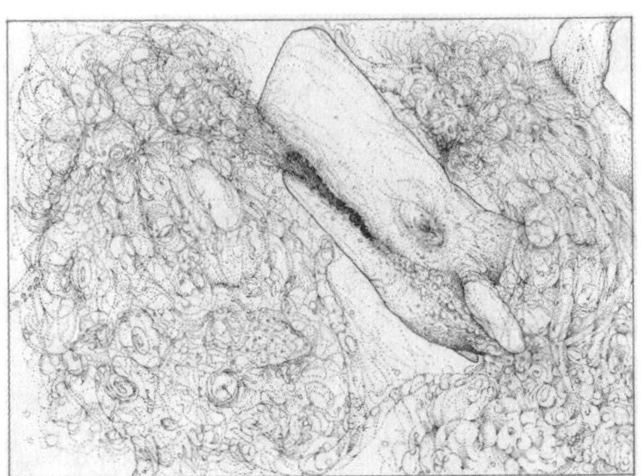

Fig. 27 ***Ambergris* by Sean McCarthy**

combines a dramatic story of maritime adventure and revenge with a remarkable range of interpolated information disliked by many readers. These interpolations constitute an encyclopedia of whale lore, including cetology and whale biology, paleontology, art criticism, political satire, anthropology, folklore study, and detailed descriptions of whaling sociology and technology, among other subjects. These sections are essential dimensions of the book's project: an exploration of the true nature of whales, especially of the great white whale Moby Dick.

Melville drew inspiration for the story from the sinking of the Nantucket ship *Essex* in 1820 after it was rammed by a sperm whale off the western coast of South America, and from the alleged killing in the 1830s of a legendary albino sperm whale, christened Mocha Dick, that was fabled for attacking whaling ships with premeditated ferocity. The May 1839 issue of the American periodical *The Knickerbocker* included an article by explorer Jeremiah N. Reynolds (1799–1858) detailing one such encounter. Melville, who himself had served upon a whaling vessel before jumping ship in the Marquesas Islands in 1842, also drew upon his own experience in crafting the novel.

The plot of *Moby Dick* concerns the voyage of the New England whaling ship *Pequod*, its monomaniacal captain,

Ahab, who lost a leg to Moby Dick in a previous encounter with the whale, and its multicultural and multiracial crew. The narrator, Ishmael, signs aboard as a common sailor, but possesses an uncommon education and the ability to meditate on the action, even as he is caught up in it. As the story opens, Ishmael is seeking to ship out on a Nantucket whaling ship, looking for excitement and a chance to see the world. He meets Queequeg, a skilled "harpooneer" from a cannibal South Seas island culture, and they become close friends. The two of them sign on aboard the ship *Pequod*, captained by Ahab. The storyline follows the relationships among the men on the ship, Ahab's increasing power over the crew, and the various events of their voyage. Although the trip is supposed to be a for-profit whaling expedition, it soon becomes evident that Ahab's desire for revenge against the whale is distorting the mission of the voyage and coloring his view of the universe, as well as his relations with his crew.

The *Pequod* meets and exchanges information with a number of other ships on its voyage, during social occasions called "gams." Some captains and crews have tried to kill Moby Dick and experienced his ferocity. They are now happy to leave him in peace. Only Ahab thirsts for a second opportunity to try to destroy him. The whale does not actually appear until late in the novel, so that the reader's sense of him is strongly colored by his ferocious reputation and especially by Ahab's perspective. He first appears in Chapter 51, "The Spirit Spout," as a series of moonlit apparitions. These may be sightings of a different whale or even hallucinations, but they seem to be luring the *Pequod* to its destruction. The story culminates in the crew's catastrophic effort to kill the great white sperm whale, Moby Dick.

The white whale called Moby Dick easily qualifies as a monster. A member of a species whose size, intelligence, and ferocity are a matter of record, Moby Dick within the novel has become legendary among the whalers of his time. He is huge even for a sperm whale, and also stands out for his unusual color, uncanny intelligence, and destructive prowess when defending himself against whalers. He is often perceived as malevolent by those who have encountered him. The novel as a whole explores whether the whale Moby Dick is a natural or unnatural phenomenon. The storyline seems to support Ahab's view that it is demonic, while the inserted encyclopedic material argues for the various ways in which the whale is simply a whale, a natural creature whose species includes even tender nursing mothers.

The source of Moby Dick's complexity as an entity in the novel is that—standing in for all whales—it is simultaneously an innocent natural creature, a natural resource exploited by human beings, an economic powerhouse, a Biblical metaphor, a valiant defender of its kind against predators (including whalers), the subject of high art, scholarship, and folk crafts, the focus of aboriginal worship, and the center of both "civilized" and "savage" ways of life. The whale and nature itself are alternately or sometimes simultaneously monstrous (whether sublime/divine or demonic/terrifying) and utilitarian, suitable to be exploited without hesitation or guilt. Through Ishmael, Melville makes clear his intentions to present Moby Dick as both a whale and much, much more. Ishmael, meditating on the whiteness of the whale, ponders:

> *Is it that by its indefiniteness it shadows forth the heartless voids and immensities of the universe, and thus stabs us from behind with the thought of annihilation, when beholding the white depths of the*

milky way? Or is it, that as in essence whiteness is not so much a colour as the visible absence of colour; and at the same time the concrete of all colours; is it for these reasons that there is such a dumb blankness, full of meaning, in a wide landscape of snows—a colourless, all-colour of atheism from which we shrink? ... And of all these things the Albino whale was the symbol. Wonder ye then at the fiery hunt? (Melville 165)

Captain Ahab—who himself has monstrous qualities—sees the whale as his personal adversary. He has been physically and psychologically scarred by the loss of his leg to the whale, and he also carries a mark on his face like a lightning strike, a symbol of accursedness. Once a handsome and good man, he has become a grotesque. He feels that the ills he has suffered are somehow purposeful strikes of the evil universe against him in particular; in response, he is willing to strike Heaven itself. In his rebellion against the ordinary "thumps" all men receive, Ahab enacts the very satanic energy that he attributes to the white whale. He is willing to sacrifice not only his own life but that of his entire crew in the service of his obsession. His charisma, like the whale's, draws people to him, even against their wills.

The monstrous element in the novel has provided material for a number of films, comic books, and TV series. None of these reflect the complexity of the original, following instead the sea-adventure plot. The first cinematic adaptation took place in the silent 1926 feature, *The Sea Beast* (Millard Webb), starring John Barrymore as the heroic Ahab with an evil brother. It was remade in 1930 with sound (Lloyd Bacon) in a version in which Ahab (also John Barrymore) kills the whale and returns home to the woman he loves (played by Joan Bennett). Perhaps the most famous cinematic version is the 1956 adaptation directed by John Huston and starring Gregory Peck as Ahab; the screenplay was written by Ray Bradbury. *Moby Dick* was adapted for film again in 2010 by Trey Stokes, with Barry Bostwick in the Ahab role. A 1998 TV mini-series version of *Moby Dick*, directed by Franc Roddam, starred British actor Patrick Stewart as Ahab and included Gregory Peck in the role of Father Mapple, for which he won a Golden Globe award for Best Supporting Actor. A 2011 TV mini-series version, directed by Mike Barker, cast William Hurt as Ahab.

The influence of Melville's novel and its eponymous monstrous whale has entered the English language through the understanding of a "white whale" as an obsession that takes over one's life. Ishmael's speculation that the whiteness of the whale allows it to serve as a sort of template on which meaning is inscribed seems borne out by the continual acts of appropriation and revisioning that allow meaning and significance of Melville's text to be repeatedly adapted into new contexts.

Judith B. Kerman,
with Andrew Brusso

References and Suggested Reading

Barrenechea, Antonio. "Conquistadors, Monsters, and Maps: *Moby Dick* in a New World Context." *Comparative American Studies* 7, no. 1 (March 2009): 18–23.

Bezanson, Walter E. "*Moby Dick*: Work of Art." In *Moby Dick: Centennial Essays*, edited by Tyrus Hillway and Luther S. Mansfield, 30–58. Dallas: Southern Methodist University Press, 1953.

Hayford, Harrison. "'Loomings': Yarns and Figures in the Fabric." In *Moby-Dick. A Norton Critical Edition*, edited by Hershel Parker and Harrison Hayford, 657–69. New York: Norton, 2002.

Kaplan, Carter. "Jules Verne, Herman Melville, and the 'Question of the Monster'." *Extrapolation* 39, no. 2 (1998): 139–47.

Melville, Herman. *Moby-Dick; or, The Whale* [1851]. Reprint, edited by Hershel Parker and Harrison Hayford. New York: W.W. Norton, 2002.

MOLOCH

Traditionally, (the) Moloch has been construed as a monstrous and pagan god whose wrath could only be appeased by the sacrifice of a child. In 1935, the German scholar Otto Eissfeldt offered a very different interpretation. Informed by Punic inscriptions excavated at, for instance, ancient Carthage (near Tunis in North Africa), he arrived at the conclusion that the Hebrew word *mlk*, traditionally vocalized as *molek*, should be read as *molk* or *mulk*. In his view, the word did not refer to a divine being but a specific kind of offering, sacrificing human children as a *molk* to a god, be it Yahweh in Israel or Tannit in Carthage.

His views have been challenged in the last decades by John Day and George C. Heider. Biblical scholars now think that Moloch was originally a chthonic deity connected with the netherworld. Mesopotamian god-lists mention a deity, *Maliku*, who was connected with the cult of the dead ancestors. In ancient Ugarit (a Mediterranean port city located in what is today Syria), a divine being *mlk* was known (evidenced in a snake-bite incantation). He probably was the afterlife shade of a king who played a role in the cult for the dead ancestors.

The instances in the Hebrew Bible where Moloch occurs can easily be understood in this connection. Leviticus 20:2–5; 2 Kings 23:10, and Jeremiah 32:35 can be understood as condemning the cult of an ancestral deity. Whether or not children really were sacrificed to the Moloch is still debated. The Biblical phrase "to make your children pass through the fire" (2 Kings 16:3, 17:17) could also be construed as a reference to a purification rite. The same is probably true for the expression "to give your children to Moloch" (Leviticus 20:2–4). Remarks in classical authors such as Diodorus Siculus and Plutarch on the practice of child-sacrifice among Semitic-speaking people, however, have fuelled the idea that Moloch was a god devouring children, as can be observed in the Rabbinic tradition. In the Koran (Sura 43:77), Moloch, here called Malek, is depicted as an archangel (see **Angel**) governing the damned on behalf of Allah. This might be a late reflection of the idea of Moloch as a chthonic deity connected with the netherworld.

Western culture sees Moloch as "that horrid king besmeared with blood" (Milton, *Paradise Lost*, I, 392). In Milton's famous seventeenth-century poem, Moloch is cast in the role of one of the most important warriors of the falling angels who, under the leadership of Satan (see **Devil, The**), tempts Adam and Eve to give up their trust in God. In *Paradise Lost* II, 43–105, Moloch delivers a speech at the parliament of Hell where he argues for immediate warfare against God. Later, the monster Moloch becomes revered as a pagan god on Earth. It is interesting to read this speech in connection with Milton's political activities during the English Civil War. *Paradise Lost* can be read as a theodicy, a text that defends God against incriminations from the existence of evil on Earth.

Around the turn of the twentieth century, a group of bohemian artists gathered around the mystic Alfred Schuler (1865–1923), the so-called Munich Cosmic Circle. They were of the opinion that Western civilization was plagued by degeneration that was caused by a rationalistic view. In their writings, Moloch occurs as a symbolic name for a person whose rationalism was emotionally cold and hence hostile to life as they saw it. Bertrand Russell (1872–1970) used the name Moloch in *A Freeman's*

Worship (1923) to depict a specific kind of religion that can be found among the savage people of the Earth. He refers specifically to the cruelty of sorts of rituals and offerings that were applied to appease the wrath of the gods and forces of nature. This "observation" then functions in an atheistic discourse against religion. In "The War of the Newts," a 1936 satirical science fiction story by Czech author Karel Capek, the discovery of the Newts is narrated. This species lived in the waters of the Pacific. After being enslaved, they acquire human traits and begin to rebel against the humans. They counter the attempt by Christians to convert them by constructing the religion of the Moloch. He is construed by them as a giant Newt with a human head, dwelling in the waters. In the second part of Allen Ginsberg's poem "Howl" (1955), Moloch is addressed and accused. Moloch is construed as the dehumanizing dark side of industrialized capitalism—especially its American variant. In Wayne Barlow's *God's* ***Demon*** (2007), Moloch is portrayed as the head of the armies of the city of Dis, the capital of Hell. He is represented as a fierce and merciless warrior. Strangely enough, he goes without legs, since they were set on fire while falling from Heaven.

In two movies, Moloch plays the role of a devouring being: *Cabira* by Giovanni Pastrone (1914) and Fritz Lang's *Metropolis* (1927). In this latter movie, Freder (Gustav Fröhlich)—the son of the head of Metropolis—has a nightmare in which the M-machine (the central power station in the city) comes alive as a monster. Alexander Sokurov's 1999 biographical film about Adolf Hitler is revealingly entitled *Moloch*. In the episode "I, Robot ... You, Jane" from the first season of the television series *Buffy the Vampire Slayer* (1997), the main character Willow (Alyson Hannigan) flirts with a mysterious boy Malcolm (Mark Deakins) over the internet. Meanwhile a demon, Moloch the Corruptor, has been freed after five centuries.

In the comic series *Watchmen*, Moloch the Mystic is cast in the role of an underworld leader and a crime boss. The video game *Assassin's Creed: Bloodlines* contains as one of its characters the antagonist Moloch "the Bull," a tall armed man. The role-playing game *Dungeons & Dragons* can be played in various ways. Quite often its settings contain Moloch cast in the role of the arch-devil of Hell (see **Dungeons & Dragons, Monsters In**).

Bob Becking

References and Suggested Reading

Beal, Timothy K. *Religion and its Monsters*. New York: Routledge, 2002.

Day, John. *Molech: A God of Human Sacrifice in the Old Testament*. Cambridge: Cambridge University Press, 1989.

Heider, George C. "Molech." In *Dictionary of Deities and Demons in the Bible*, 2nd edn, edited by Karel van der Toorn, Bob Becking, and Pieter W. van der Horst, 581–5. Leiden: Brill, 1999.

Raskin, Jonah. *American Scream: Allen Ginsberg's Howl and the Making of the Beat Generation*. Berkeley: University of California Press, 2004.

MONKEY KING

The Monkey King, or *Sun Wukong* (Sun, Awakened-to-Vacuity), is the lively questing protagonist of the sixteenth-century Chinese novel (*xiaoshuo* "unverified narrative") *Xiyou ji* (*The Journey to the West*), which is widely but improbably attributed to Wu Cheng'en (c. 1500–1582). Arguably the best-known popular culture figure in East Asia, the Monkey King (Monkey hereafter) is prominent in traditional popular cultures of Japan, Korea, Vietnam, and Tibet.

Monkey is entering Western and global culture in part as an element of multicultural diversity, but also because of the attraction of his impetuous vital energy and the adaptability of the episodic structure of his quest. Recent cinematic and literary adaptations make use of the Monkey figure in martial arts adventures, as a form of subversion of everyday or orthodox culture, or as a type of spiritual transformation. By far the most common reworking of the Monkey King utilizes the dynamism of his original persona.

The novel *Xiyou ji* is a culmination of centuries of storytelling and dramatic performances loosely based on the historical account of the monk and translator Xuan Zang (602–664 CE). In the novel, the earliest manuscript for which dates to 1592, the role of the Monkey takes prominence over the monk. Monkey appears in a leopard-skin robe, carries with him a marvelous staff or cudgel that can transform to any size from a needle to an enormous pillar, and wears a gold fillet about his head. His eyes are red from an encounter in a heavenly elixir-producing furnace. Among his many powers and attributes, he has the ability to perform 72 transformations, to perceive disguised **demons**, to out-perform the highest skills of martial artists, and to transforms bits of his hair into multiple forms of himself. According to the novel, he is born from a stone egg imbued with generative powers from earth and sky. He then seeks for immortality and increasing power, which leads to his wreaking havoc in the bureaucratic palaces of Heaven, after which the Buddha subdues him and sends him to accompany Xuan Zang, otherwise known as Tripitaka, to retrieve Buddhist scriptures from India. Along the way, he battles demons and overcomes obstacles, including conflict among his fellow pilgrims. Eventually, they obtain the scriptures and achieve divine titles.

The novel derives from earlier Chinese and possibly Indian sources. Chinese appropriations of the novel include a sequel by Dong Yue (1620–86) suggesting Monkey's subjection to passion (*qing* or desire). *Xiyou ji* may have also influenced the archetypal frame of *Honglou meng* (*Dream of Red Mansions* [c. 1640]). Both novels begin with magical stones and may constitute a spiritual quest.

Initial literary Western appropriation of Monkey favors the portrayal of subversive energy. Arthur Waley's translated abridgement *Monkey*, published in 1943, conveys a lively and engaging depiction of Monkey and his antics. Possible suggestions of alchemical transformation are diluted in Waley's abridgement as he omits poems that interlace the original and imply allegorical reference. This version probably contributed to multicultural literary adaptations such as Maxine Hong Kingston's *Tripmaster Monkey* (1989) in which the protagonist resolves his Chinese-American identity by means of the figure of Monkey. Gerald Vizenor incorporates the Monkey King into his multicultural narrative *Griever: An American Monkey King in China* (1987). The idea of an individualistic, subversive Monkey promises to continue in a personal narrative by Neil Gaiman, *Monkey and Me*, about his discovery of China. A number of children's books address Monkey as a model of determination for children, apparently providing for multicultural literacy. Among many scholarly works, Anthony Yu's full and detailed translation of *The Journey to the West* (1983) contextualizes Monkey as a personal spiritual quest.

The undercurrent of games and television productions may additionally propel the cultural expansion of Monkey. Anime and comic book series have developed out of Monkey's episodic quest and martial arts antics, such as the "Dragonball" series that initially began as a manga comic series by Akira Toriyama in 1984 and have been adapted into three animated television series and other features. Numerous electronic games also make use of Monkey's episodic quest and martial arts dynamism.

East Asian television series and film versions tend to emphasize Monkey as a representative of national culture, while recent feature film accommodations emphasize his energy. In 1961, China produced a carefully animated Monkey, impetuous but lovable, in *Da nao tiangong* (*Uproar in Heaven*, directed by Wan Laiming). From 1979 through 1987, extensive television series in Japan and China also showcased Monkey as a cultural resource. In contrast, Hallmark's television feature *The Lost Empire* (Peter MacDonald, 2001) does little more than expose a setting for Monkey's quest. The 2008 film *Forbidden Kingdom* (Rob Minkoff) references Monkey only as a goal for a martial arts-fighting Bostonian named Tripitaka. In contrast, the 2007 opera *Monkey: Journey to the West*, conceived by Chinese actor and director Chen Shi-zheng, constitutes a significant effort at a fuller telling.

Carl Robertson

References and Suggested Reading

Dudbridge, Glen. *The Hsi-yu Chi: A Study of Antecedents to the Sixteenth-Century Chinese Novel*. Cambridge: Cambridge University Press, 1970.

Kingston, Maxine Hong. *Tripmaster Monkey: His Fake Book*. New York: Knopf, 1989.

Vizenor, Gerald. *Griever: An American Monkey King in China*. Minneapolis: University of Minnesota Press, 1987.

Waley, Arthur. *Monkey*. New York: Grove Press, 1953.

Yu, Anthony, ed. and trans. *The Journey to the West*. 4 vols. Chicago: University of Chicago Press, 1977–83.

MONONOKE—*see* Demon; Oni

MORGAN, DEXTER—*see* Psychopath

MORGAN LE FAY—*see* Shapeshifter; Witch/Wizard

MORMO/MORMOLYKE—*see* Empousa

MORRÍGAN—*see* Shapeshifter

MOTHMAN—*see* Cryptid

MOTHRA—*see* Godzilla

MUMMY

Fig. 28 ***Mummy* by Christopher Mir**

The mummy is a corpse, preserved by natural desiccation or embalming. In horror, the mummy comes to life, often to fulfill a curse on those who desecrate its tomb or to pursue its reincarnated lover in the modern world. Although cultures all over the world practiced mummification—ancient Celts and medieval Aragonese, Tocharians in Xinjiang, Buddhist monks in Vietnam, Inca and pre-Inca civilizations in South America, Anasazi and Mound Builder tribes in North America—the best-known mummies in horror and popular science alike are Egyptian.

Mummification in Egypt began around 3400 BCE, becoming common for pharaohs and other exalted personages by early in the third millennium BCE. By about 1200 BCE, the techniques and rituals reached a peak of refinement: natron desiccated the body more efficiently than sand, oils and resins preserved the grave cloths and flesh, and organs overly conducive to putrefaction were ceremonially removed and placed in canopic jars. The mummy's wrappings contained specialized amulets to ensure the continued life and health of the soul, while the ritual "Opening of the Mouth" (often depicted on tomb walls) allowed the mummified dead to continue breathing in the afterlife. Such amulets and rituals, found millennia later by Arabic and European travelers and scholars unable to read hieroglyphics, gave rise to legends of the reanimated dead. By the Hellenistic era (330–31 BCE), mummification had spread to virtually every class of citizen, and even to pets, although such mass embalming was much cheaper and less effective than Middle Kingdom practices. The millions of mummies buried during this period fed a medieval market for excavated mummies and for ground mummy powder, used as medicine, pigment, and magical ingredient from Persia to England.

Rise of the Mummy

Such traffic serves as the background for the first horror story involving mummies, an anecdote related by Louis Penicher in his 1699 *Traité du Embaumements* (*Treatise on Embalming*). In it, a Polish merchant buys two mummies in Egypt, but must throw them overboard to end a series of hauntings on his ship; Penicher's offhand treatment of the tale implies such stories were common at the time. It was Napoleon Bonaparte's invasion of Egypt a century later that launched modern Europe's first true Egyptomania, driving fashions in costume, painting, furnishings, and architecture. This Egyptomania sparked a fad for public unrolling of Egyptian mummies in the 1830s and 1840s, inspiring a tongue-in-cheek quasi-hoax by Edgar Allan Poe, "Some Words With a Mummy" (1845), in which a galvanically revived mummy mocks the unrollers.

The first full-fledged mummy fiction, *The Mummy! A Tale of the Twenty-Second Century* (1827) by Jane Webb Loudon, forsakes its moment of horror for moral and social commentary as a resurrected pharaoh Cheops rebuilds society in futuristic London. Théophile Gautier (1811–72) introduced the theme of love across the centuries: both his novel *The Romance of the Mummy* (1856) and his comic story "The Mummy's Foot" (1840) feature the doomed love of man for mummy princess, although only in the second tale does the mummy reanimate. Louisa May Alcott was one of the first to re-introduce Penicher's motif of the cursed mummy, although her 1869 tale "Lost in a Pyramid, or, The Mummy's Curse" implicates a mysterious vampiric plant grown from seeds fallen from a burned mummy's wrappings (see **Vampire**).

Sir Arthur Conan Doyle added the immortal sorcerer trope to the mix, although the sorcerer in "The Ring of Thoth" (1890) seeks only to die in the arms of his true love, a recently excavated mummy (see **Witch/Wizard**). With Doyle's "Lot No. 249" (1894) appears the first sinister mummy in fiction: Edward Bellingham, a student, reanimates a mummy and sends it to murder his enemies. *Iras, A Mystery* (1896), by H.D. Everett, features a revived Egyptian mummy who falls in love with an English Egyptologist, while Guy Boothby's *Pharos the Egyptian* (1899) is a more sinister immortal sorcerer, who must safeguard his own mummy while spreading plague in England. (Boothby's "A Professor of Egyptology" [1904] has no mummy, but does have a reincarnated heroine.) The occult detective Flaxman Low discovers a British mummy with vampiric tendencies in

"The Story of Baelbrow" (1898) by Hesketh V. Prichard and his mother, Kate O'Brien Ryall Prichard. Algernon Blackwood's "The Nemesis of Fire" (1908) succeeds thanks to Blackwood's skill rather than the originality of the plot, in which a mummy brought from Egypt turns out to be the cause of mysterious fires in an English house.

This burst of late-Victorian mummy fiction may have derived from British nervousness at the new prevalence of imports, spectacle, and machined goods. Alternately, it may just be further working-out of the sexual, racial, and cultural tensions of Orientalism, itself a seemingly inescapable product of Empire.

From Stoker to Hammer

Bram Stoker connected the reincarnated princess to the reanimation theme, adding a major piece to the mummy corpus in his 1903 novel, *Jewel of Seven Stars*. Tera, an Egyptian princess, has been reincarnated as Margaret, an Egyptologist's daughter. To reanimate her body, brought to England, she must find her missing hand, on which rests the titular jewel. In the 1903 version, her attempts end in death and catastrophe; in a 1912 revision, Margaret survives and marries the narrator. The mummy's beautiful, perfectly preserved body disappears.

The global sensation surrounding the 1922 discovery of the tomb of Tutankhamun, and the hysteria about the "Mummy's Curse" following the sudden death of the dig's sponsor, Lord Carnarvon (1866–1923), increased public appetites for Egyptian thrills. Notable mummy tales of the pulp era include: H.P. Lovecraft and Hazel Heald's "Out of the Aeons" (1931) in which the image reflected in the cornea of a mummy from Mu can mummify onlookers as well (see **Lovecraft, Monsters In**); Victor Rousseau's "Curse of Amen-Ra" (1932); Clark Ashton Smith's "Empire of the Necromancers" (1932) featuring heroic mummies who earn peace for their kind by killing the titular black magicians; E.F. Benson's "Monkeys" (1933); Robert E. Howard's *The Hour of the Dragon* (1935) in which his hero Conan battles the reanimated necromancer Xaltotun; Donald A. Wollheim's "Bones" (1941); Seabury Quinn's "The Man in the Crescent Terrace" (1946); and Lester Dent's Doc Savage yarn *Resurrection Day* (1936) wherein Doc accidentally resurrects the mummy of Typhon instead of King Solomon!

Robert Bloch wrote several mummy stories, among them two featuring the immortal mummy of the god Sebek ("The Secret of Sebek" [1937] and "The Eyes of the Mummy" [1938]) and one creeper ("Beetles" [1938]), later adapted for television as a 1987 episode of *Tales from the Darkside*. Bloch would use the mummy symbol powerfully in his later novel *Psycho* (1959). (It's not impossible that the pun-loving Bloch decided to play on "mummy" and "mommy," either.) The mummy of **Norman Bates**'s mother (revealed with shocking effect in Alfred Hitchcock's 1960 film of the book) may not come alive in a supernatural sense, but she clearly animates Norman's homicidal rampages, and her Freudian curse lingers over her son well after her death.

Hitchcock's film was far from the first mummy movie: that honor goes to Georges Méliès's *Cleopatre* (1899). At least three dozen mummy films appeared during the silent era, featuring reanimated princesses, stolen rings, and Napoleon Bonaparte. Charles Calvert's loose adaptation of Stoker's novel *The Wraith of the Tomb* (1915) was probably the first full-length British horror picture. Cinema influenced mummy fiction in its turn: Burton Stevenson set the action of his novel *A King in Babylon* (1917) among a film crew making a mummy movie at an Egyptian dig site.

Karl Freund directed *The Mummy* (1932) for Universal, creating the core mummy narrative of a resurrected mummy sorcerer, his search for his reincarnated love, and his murderous vengeance on those who opened his tomb. Star Boris Karloff's presence and Freund's stark cinematography drive the film. Universal's second mummy picture, *The Mummy's Hand* (Christy Cabanne, 1940) replaces Karloff's suave Imhotep with a new villain, the mute and bandaged Kharis, reanimated not by the Scroll of Life, but by "tana leaves." Rather than use Imhotep's sorcery, Kharis killed his foes by strangling them. Wartime censorship made Egyptian villains more problematic, hobbling the action in *The Mummy's Tomb* (Harold Young, 1942). This may have been one factor in the decision to move the setting to New England in that film and its sequel, *The Mummy's Ghost* (Reginald LeBorg, 1944), and to Louisiana for the series' coda, *The Mummy's Curse* (Leslie Goodwins, 1944).

Postwar mummy stories were generally forgettable, often played for humor. "The Next in Line" (1947) by Ray Bradbury is a rare exception, albeit one with no overtly supernatural element: a tourist couple visits a Mexican town on the Day of the Dead and the wife dies there. The mummies of Guanajuato, vividly depicted in the tale, embody both the protagonist's fear of death and her desire to belong.

Hammer Studios reanimated the mummy film, as it had other classic supernatural monster movies, with a 1959 Terence Fisher remake of Freund's picture, inserting elements of the later Universal stories. Fisher's *Mummy* starred Christopher Lee as Kharis, and broke box-office records set by Fisher and Lee's ***Dracula*** (1958). Two later mummy films, *Curse of the Mummy's Tomb* (Michael Carreras, 1964) and *The Mummy's Shroud* (John Gilling, 1967), focused more on the mummy's revenge and less on its search for love. The final Hammer mummy film, *Blood From the Mummy's Tomb* (Seth Holt, 1971), was another version of Stoker's novel. Although an artistic success, audiences had tired of the classical mummy legend, and Hammer discontinued the series.

The Postmodern Mummy

Following the end of the Hammer cycle, creators began combining mummy horror with other genres. Steve Gerber's (1947–2008) Marvel Comics hero N'kantu the Living Mummy (debuting in *Supernatural Thrillers* #5, August 1973) combined mummies, black-power politics (N'kantu had been mummified for leading a slave revolt in ancient Egypt), and superheroics. The mummies in the "Pyramids of Mars" (1975) episode of *Doctor Who* turn out to be **robot** servants of the alien Sutekh, last of the Osirans (see **Extraterrestrial**). T.W. Hard introduced the mummy into the medical thriller with *SUM VII* (1979), in which doctors resuscitate an intact mummy (later revealed to be an alien) by blood transfusion. John Bellairs added occult Egyptology to juvenile fiction in the 1983 novels *The Curse of the Blue Figurine* and *The Mummy, the Will, and the Crypt*. Michael Slade's torture-horror crime novel *Death's Door* (2002) makes explicit the subtext of necrophilia in the mummy legend.

Other creators tried returning to the original sources. In 1989, Anne Rice resurrected the Victorian mummy as a romantic hero. The immortal title character of *The Mummy, or Ramses the Damned* reanimates his lost lover, Cleopatra, but she remains hideous and brain-damaged while he walks the Earth. In the revival spirit, director Stephen Sommers contented himself with adding computer special effects, chase scenes, and the Ten Plagues of Egypt to his loose, retro-adventure remake of Freund's *The Mummy* (1999). Its wild success spawned an immediate sequel, *The Mummy Returns* (2001).

More interesting is Joe R. Lansdale's short story "Bubba Ho-Tep" (1994), featuring Elvis Presley and a black John F. Kennedy protecting their fellow nursing-home inhabitants from a soul-sucking mummy. Although the tale is gripping and effective (as is the 2002 Don Coscarelli film of it), the symbolic parallel of an anonymous mummy with the senescent Elvis and JFK embalmed in their own legends gives the story its true depth.

Postmodern mummy stories also increasingly utilize non-Egyptian monsters. Rafael Portillo's film *Aztec Mummy* (1957) essentially recapitulates the Universal films in his native Mexico, complete with cursed treasure and reincarnated princess, but adds a costumed villain, the Bat. His sequels, *Curse of the Aztec Mummy* (1957) and *Robot vs. Aztec Mummy* (1958), add a masked wrestler (a common hero in Mexican adventure films) and the titular robot to the mix. Repackaged for late-night American television, the latter two films made the Aztec mummy a staple of B-horror, appearing in a 1975 episode of *Kolchak: The Night Stalker* ("Legacy of Terror"). Alexander C. Irvine's historical horror-fantasy novel *A Scattering of Jade* (2002) and Jeff Burr and Chip Gubera's superheroic wrestler film *Mil Mascaras vs. the Aztec Mummy* (2007) both demonstrate that the Aztec mummy can supersede mere camp.

All five of the stories original to editor Bill Pronzini's 1980 anthology *Mummy!* centered on non-Egyptian mummies, and the trend has only grown since then. The "Inca Mummy Girl" episode (1997) of *Buffy the Vampire Slayer* effectively reworks the by now centuries-old theme of the mummy as immortal seductress. The third film in the revived *Mummy* franchise, Rob Cohen's *The Mummy: Tomb of the Dragon Emperor* (2008), features Chinese mummies reanimated by Jet Li as the revived "Emperor Han."

Even now, the mummy film is far from creatively dead. In *Loft* (2005), Kiyoshi Kurosawa uses the mummy's symbolic erasure of time, and its connection with love and death, to subtle effect. Writer's block leads Reiko to a remote town where an anthropologist has stolen a mummy found in a nearby swamp. The mummy acts as a catalyst, triggering love, terror, and possibly paranoia in the couple, who see the **ghost** of another writer murdered in the house where Reiko is staying. The one scene in which the mummy awakens may be another delusion; Reiko and the anthropologist burn the mummy at the end, more to keep it from being displayed than to defeat it. The uncanny and the documentary combine here, as they did for Louis Penicher at the dawn of the Enlightenment, and indeed for the Egyptian priests who first composed the rituals to keep mummies alive forever.

Kenneth Hite

References and Suggested Reading

Briefel, Aviva. "Hands of Beauty, Hands of Horror: Fear and Egyptian Art at the Fin de Siècle." *Victorian Studies* 50, no. 2 (2008): 263–71.

Brier, Bob. *The Encyclopedia of Mummies.* New York: Facts on File, 1998.

Daly, Nicholas. "That Obscure Object of Desire: Victorian Commodity Culture and Fictions of the Mummy." *NOVEL: A Forum on Fiction* 28, no. 1 (1994): 24–51.

Davies, David Stuart, ed. *Return from the Dead: Classic Mummy Stories.* London: Wordsworth, 2004.

Frost, Brian J. *The Essential Guide to Mummy Literature.* Lanham: Scarecrow Press, 2008.

Guran, Paula. "The Mummy." In *Icons of Horror and the Supernatural: An Encyclopedia of Our Worst Nightmares*, vol. 2, edited by S.T. Joshi, 375–407. Westport, CT: Greenwood Press, 2007.

Haining, Peter, ed. *The Mummy: Stories of the Living Corpse.* London: Severn House, 1998.

Pringle, Heather. *The Mummy Congress: Science, Obsession, and the Everlasting Dead.* New York: Hyperion, 2001.

Rice, Anne. *The Mummy, or Ramses the Damned.* New York: Ballantine, 1989.

Stoker, Bram. *The Jewel of Seven Stars* [1903], edited by Kate Hebblethwaite. Harmondsworth: Penguin, 2008.

MUTANT AND FREAK

There is a complex relationship between freaks and mutants; both terms are used to describe biologically abnormal creatures. Here they will be distinguished in the following way: "freak" is a culturally constructed concept that indicates someone or something somatically abnormal, while "mutant" follows the *Oxford English Dictionary* definition of "an individual imagined as having arisen by genetic mutation, esp. one with freakish or grossly abnormal anatomy, abilities, etc." Not all freaks are mutants, as one can be rendered freakish by accident or design (like the tattooed lady of nineteenth- and early twentieth-century freak shows). Similarly, not all mutants are freaks because genetic mutations need not be physically visible. While there is an embedded historical attitude of distrust towards both freaks and mutants as malign, they may in fact be benign and even self-sacrificing for the general human good; many superheroes are freaks or mutants (a prime example being the X-Men, created by Marvel Comics in 1963 and perpetuated in a series of films beginning in 2000, whose heroic stunts are intended to redeem the public image of mutants). This entry will explore the status of human and humanoid freaks and mutants in popular culture, from classical times to the cult cinematic franchises (such as the *X-Men* series) of the present day.

History of Mutants

Cultural fascination with freaks and mutants is as old as recorded history; according to Greek legend, Hephaestus, the Greek god of fire, was born with a deformed foot (and shunned by the other gods on behalf of his lameness). The first century CE Roman scholar Pliny the Elder created a fantastic world geography in his *Naturalis Historia*, describing and locating mutant human communities such as the one-eyed **Cyclops**, the acephalic Blemmyae, and the one-legged Sciopods (see **Races, Monstrous**). (Both of the latter feature in Umberto Eco's novel *Baudolino* [2000]; the Sciopods reappear as Monopods in C.S. Lewis's *The Voyage of the Dawn Treader* [1952].) Medieval geographies perpetuated Pliny's mutants, and mutant animal births were frequently interpreted as omens (meteorological or political). The mutant-filled canvases of the Dutch artist Hieronymous Bosch (1450–1516) and publications by scientists like the French surgeon and obstetrician Ambroise Paré (1510–90), whose illustrated pamphlets on genetic and surgical freaks helped inform the early modern cultural imagination, reflected the contemporary fascination with teratology (see Asma 141–62).

Scientific advances post-Enlightenment, perhaps surprisingly, fostered rather than banished this preoccupation with freakish, mutated bodies; the trope proliferated in nineteenth-century British fiction. From Mary Shelley's *Frankenstein* (1818) near the beginning of the century (see **Frankenstein's Monster**) to Bram Stoker's ***Dracula*** (1897) at the end, a wide array of unusually shaped creatures abounded. Some could change shape—magically, if not genetically (genetics was a term not yet used and a concept not yet known)—while others were frozen inside their freak-like frames (see **Shapeshifter**). Throughout the eighteenth and nineteenth centuries, those with unusually shaped bodies were put on display and paraded before the public for entertainment. This was one of the few ways that disabled people could survive in a non-welfare state, and the representation of freaks in fiction plays on a morally tenuous culture in which people sought pleasure and amusement in the misfortune of their fellow human beings.

Mutants and freaks also find their place in the work of Richard Marsh, a lesser known but important Gothic writer at the *fin de siècle*. In Marsh's best-known novel, *The Beetle* (1897), a monstrous human-beetle invades London from the East in an act of revenge against one of the novel's main characters. Able to metamorphose at will between human and beetle, the mutant creature terrifies observers with its transformations. In Marsh's *The Joss: A Reversion* (1901), a man is transformed into a shape-changing "joss" after being physically tortured by the inhabitants of a far-away island who believe he is a god. Benjamin Batters is a deformed creature with long dangling arms and wheels for legs, who tricks everyone around him to gain his own ends. As a malevolent force throughout the novel, Batters is symbolic of the kind of greed and materialism associated with freak culture during the nineteenth century. Another significant Gothic writer during this period, Arthur Machen, imagined monstrous half-human hybrids in two of his stories. *The Great God Pan* (1890) and *The Three Impostors* (1895) explore the possibility of radically dysmorphic human physical alteration (see **Pan**). Both tales feature human characters capable of morphing into monstrous creatures.

One of the most well-known scientific romances of the nineteenth century to feature radical biological change is Robert Louis Stevenson's *The Strange Case of Dr Jekyll and Mr Hyde* (1886; see **Hyde, Edward**; **Doppelganger**). In this study of chemical and biological horror, Stevenson examines the idea of the alter ego. The mutational potential of Jekyll is revealed in his animalistic and degenerative Other self—Hyde—and by drinking a particular potion, he can transform himself into this other person. The result is a terrifying experiment upon the nature of humanity itself, as the fiendish Hyde rages through London, causing disorder wherever he goes.

One lesser known Victorian writer also interested in in-between species was William Hope Hodgson (1877–1918). In *The Boats of the "Glen Carrig"* (1907), amphibious humans prey on shipwrecked sailors on a deserted island. In a post-Darwinian "biology gone wrong" tale of horror, Hodgson imagines the popular degeneration theories of Cesare Lombroso (1835–1909) and Max Nordau (1849–1923) in action. Cannibalistic and predatory in nature, the amphibious humans in Hodgson's fiction are a terrifying reminder of the mutational possibilities of the organic biological form. (For more on these "abhuman" or "Gothic" bodies in Victorian fiction, see Kelly Hurley's *The Gothic Body*.)

In mainstream popular fiction of the nineteenth century, disabled and freakish bodies abound. From the dwarfish eccentric Miss Mowcher in *David Copperfield* (1850) to the evil, grotesquely deformed Daniel Quilp in *The Old Curiosity Shop* (1840), to the wooden-legged opportunistic Silas Wegg in *Our Mutual Friend* (1865), freaks play a major role in Charles Dickens's novels. Similarly, Dickens's close friend Wilkie Collins also exploited this trope in his sensation fiction. In *The Law and the Lady* (1875), the eccentric detective Miserrimus Dexter is remarkable for the contrast between his handsome face and his missing legs. Trapped in a wheelchair, Dexter is described in the novel as a "monstrous frog" (244), thus animalizing him and emphasizing his otherness. Furthermore, in *No Name* (1862),

Collins portrays a giant woman named Mrs Wragge whose bosom is described as an "Enormous Mistake" (460); *Poor Miss Finch* (1872) features a blue-skinned man.

At the end of the nineteenth century, H.G. Wells visualized numerous freakish, mutant bodies. From the post-human types in *The Time Machine* (1895), to Moreau's Beast People in *The Island of Dr Moreau* (1896), to the monstrous aliens in *The War of the Worlds* (1898), Wells examined the malleability of the organic body. One of Wells's lesser known novellas, *The Food of the Gods* (1904), explores the idea of metabolic change while putting a political spin on scientific knowledge. Here, those who are fed on special food chemically designed to make **giants** are regarded as outsiders and are treated harshly by their "normal" counterparts. Arguably, all the above nineteenth-century mutants reflect a cultural shift from fear of nature's disruptive potential (as depicted in medieval and early modern teratologies) to a genuine fear of how man, armed with scientific tools, may mutate himself. This distrust of science continues to feature in many modern productions, notably David Cronenberg's film *The Fly* (1986) (in which a scientist experimenting with a prototypical teleporter accidentally merges his own DNA with that of a housefly, triggering a disastrous mutation [see **Fly, The**]), and various films on the theme of mutation by David Lynch, including *Eraserhead* (1977) and *The Elephant Man* (1980), the latter based on the story of a real-life Victorian-era "freak."

Twentieth-Century Mutants

The twentieth century was marked by a sustained cinematic interest in freaks, most famously in the film *Freaks* (Tod Browning, 1932) in which a mercenary, normal-sized blonde attempts to marry into a community of circus freaks in order to defraud her future husband. *Freaks* was especially notable for the fact that none of the "freak" actors were fakes; all—including the Siamese twins (Daisy and Violet Hilton) and the man with no limbs (Prince Randian)—were genuinely deformed. The film features the famous chorus "One of us! One of us!" with which the false bride is ironically welcomed into the freakish "family."

In keeping with *Freaks*—and in contradistinction to twentieth-century literature that tended to emphasize hyper-evolved mutants—twentieth-century cinema emphasized regressive mutation. Examples of degeneration vary widely. In the 1977 Wes Craven horror film *The Hills Have Eyes*, for example, the Nevada desert is home to mutant cannibals. In Andrei Tarkovsky's *Stalker* (1979; based on the novel *Roadside Picnic* [1971] by Boris and Arkady Strugatsky), an alien visitation despoils large tracts of land across the planet and leaves a legacy of genetic damage in those most exposed (see **Extraterrestrial**). The eponymous Stalker, who regularly enters the affected Zone, has a daughter who, although born normal, gradually transforms into a monkey-like creature with psychokinetic powers. Neil Marshall's 2005 film *The Descent* describes the adventures of six female hikers as they explore underground caves inhabited (unbeknownst to them) by blind, semi-human, cannibalistic mutants. A similarly themed episode of The X-Files, "The Jersey Devil" (season 1, episode 5, 1993; Joe Napolitano), features a colony of wild cannibals in a New Jersey forest (***see Cryptid***). Katherine Dunn's controversial 1989 novel *Geek Love* echoes Freaks by describing a tightly bonded family of performing freaks; this family, however, is not only self-contained but self-sustaining, as the freaks' parents and siblings have deliberately used drugs and radiation to mutate their children.

In contrast to the emphasis on degeneration in twentieth-century film, hyper-evolved freaks or mutants predominate in literature. One popular culture example is Steven King's *Firestarter* (1980), the story of Charlie, a girl with pyrokinetic ability born to parents who participated in government-funded experiments (and who each subsequently developed psychic abilities). Not only is Charlie able to generate heat equivalent to solar energy, but her intelligence and empathy are also unusually developed. Other examples of "positive" mutation include Charlie Gordon, hero of Daniel Keyes's 1966 novel *Flowers for Algernon*. Charlie, a severely mentally handicapped youth, undergoes experimental surgery which drastically alters his mental powers, tripling his IQ; unfortunately, just as Charlie's intelligence peaks, he perceives that a flaw in the original experiment dooms him to regression to his former state. Charlie's brief intellectual parabola demonstrates the troubled dynamic between intellect and emotion, and the equally fraught status of the mentally disabled in society. Theodore Sturgeon's 1953 novel *More Than Human* introduces homo gestalt—an advanced organism created by psychically bonding two or more human beings—as a potential next step in human evolution. Each of the six individuals who form the gestalt organism in Sturgeon's novel by "bleshing" (a compound word derived from "blending" and "meshing") is individually inadequate or outcast; once united, their unique gifts combine into a superhuman being.

Human–Animal Mutants

Mutant animals and human–animal combinations, because of their threatening nature, occupy an important place in the literature of mutation (see Animals, Monstrous). In the twentieth century, such mutants function as symbols of social repression; real issues of racial injustice are transferred onto imaginary, part-human races. As genetic engineering has become increasingly viable, authors and directors have responded with increasingly radical, and challenging, hybrids. The Czech writer Karel Ĉapek's satirical account of tensions between humans and giant, intelligent newts in his novel *War with the Newts* (1936) reflects real inter-racial and inter-ethnic tensions in the explosive inter-war decades. Humans, having set out to enslave the mutant newts, find themselves on the brink of eradication after the newts assimilate human culture and fight back, reducing the Earth's land masses to a newt-friendly marine environment. In Soviet Russia, Mikhail Bulgakov's novella *Heart of a Dog* (1925), which ostensibly describes the surgical transformation of a dog into a human being, pokes fun at the accelerated transformation of Russian society into a Marxist meritocracy. In *The Amphibian Man* (1926; revised 1938), which became a classic of Russian children's fiction, Aleksandr Beliaev explores the same topic of somatic transformation: a brilliant doctor implants a shark's gills into a human child, creating the world's first amphibious man. Unfortunately, the doctor is put on trial for vivisection and blasphemy, while his creation, Ikhtiandr, is forced to flee permanently into the ocean. Beliaev's novel concludes that the world is not yet ready for such experimental surgery—a conclusion that could equally well refer to the even more radical experiment of Soviet Russia. H.P. Lovecraft's story "The Shadow over Innsmouth" (1931) also features human–piscine hybrids; these, however, result from demonic inbreeding (see **Demon**) rather than surgical grafting (see **Lovecraft, Monsters In**). Both newts and sharks recur in South Korean director Bong Joon-ho's 2006 cult horror film *The Host*. When American military personnel dump a formaldehyde-like chemical into a river, an ordinary newt mutates into an amphibian, shark-like monster that devastates a South Korean city, and one family in particular. Bong Joon-ho exploits the monster scenario to teach the importance of family ties and mutual compassion in the emotionally vitiated modern city.

English-language science fiction abounds in genetic and surgical human–animal hybrids. Cordwainer Smith's "The Ballad of Lost C'Mell" (1962), with its feline–human protagonist, describes a fictional universe in which the mixed-species "underpeople" have organized a resistance movement against their human oppressors. Will Self's darkly comic science fiction satire *The Book of Dave* (2006) envisions an extremist religious community of the distant future, living on (and off) semi-human evolved pigs known as "motos." Margaret Atwood's future dystopia, described in *Oryx and Crake* (2003), presents a society in which almost all humans have been killed off by epidemics, but communities of semi-intelligent, biologically engineered animals (including the human-like "Crakers") continue to thrive (see **Animals, Monstrous**). Begun in 2000, China Miéville's "New Crobuzon" series of fantasy novels features a variety of mutants referred to as "remades," who have achieved hybrid bodies as forms of punishment for an assortment of transgressions against the state.

Many films about mutants, especially human–animal mutants, dwell on the superiority (often in terms of intellect and emotional acuity) of such creatures over the pure human genotype. While plots typically end in tragedy, there are exceptions. Dean R. Koontz's *The Watchers* (1987; filmed by Jon Hess in 1988) follows a boy's successful attempt to protect a hyper-intelligent Golden Retriever dog, an escapee from a top-secret research laboratory, despite the efforts of sinister government agents to destroy all evidence of the dog's existence. Secret military research laboratories recur in the television series *Dark Angel* (James Cameron and Charles H. Eglee, 2000–2002), in which twelve fugitives, each sharing genetic material with one or more animals in order to enhance their fighting or espionage ability, struggle to survive in a dystopian near-future America. Wolverine, although he has been mutated by heavy metal implants like the other X-Men, has strong connections with both wolves and wolverines; he preserves the ethos of a lone wolf, defying authority and defending individual autonomy. In *Splice* (Vincenzo Natali, 2009), a broody female scientist combines her own genes with material taken from chickens, fish, and other animals to create an unexpectedly charming, highly intelligent entity (named Dren). Dren matures at an accelerated rate, and her unexpected sexual desires (and attributes) have disastrous consequences for all concerned. In contrast to earlier narratives on the "secret research project" theme, the Dren project is funded by private enterprise rather than the government—a possible indicator that public fears about social and genetic engineering have shifted from Big Brother to big business.

Muireann Maguire and Claire McKechnie

References and Suggested Reading

Asma, Stephen T. *On Monsters: An Unnatural History of Our Worst Fears*. Oxford: Oxford University Press, 2009.

Bogdan, Robert. *Freak Show: Presenting Human Oddities for Amusement and Profit*. Chicago: University of Chicago Press, 1990.

Collins, Wilkie. *The Law and the Lady*. London: Penguin, 1998.

——. *No Name*. Oxford: Oxford University Press, 1998.

Fiedler, Leslie. *Freaks: Myths and Images of the Secret Self*. New York: Simon & Schuster, 1978.

Hurley, Kelly. *The Gothic Body*. Cambridge: Cambridge University Press, 1996.

Leroi, Armand Marie. *Mutants: On The Form, Varieties and Errors of the Human Body*. London: Harper Collins, 2003.

Thomson, Rosemarie Garland, ed. *Freakery: Cultural Spectacles of the Extraordinary Body*. New York: New York University Press, 1996.

MYERS, MICHAEL

Fig. 29 *Michael Myers* by Robyn O'Neil

Michael Myers is the relentless killer who terrorizes the teenagers of Haddonfield, Illinois throughout the "Halloween" slasher film series that was inaugurated in 1978 and currently consists of ten films.

Michael's story can be summarized as follows: on Halloween night 1963, six-year-old Michael Myers killed his 17-year-old sister, Judith. Michael was subsequently institutionalized at Smith's Grove Sanatorium, where he remained for the next 15 years under the care of Dr Samuel Loomis (Donald Pleasence). On 30 October 1978, Michael escaped and returned to his hometown, where he terrorized babysitter Laurie Strode (Jamie Lee Curtis) and murdered three of her friends on Halloween. Dr Loomis saved Laurie by shooting Myers six times, but he survived and disappeared into the night. It is later revealed that Laurie is the younger sister of Michael Myers and that he has an obsession with killing all remaining members of his family, along with anyone else who gets in his way.

Michael was introduced to the world in the low-budget, independent horror film *Halloween* (John Carpenter, 1978). The character has a distinctive appearance, including a gray boiler suit and an expressionless white mask, made by altering and repainting an existing mask of *Star Trek*'s original captain, James T. Kirk (William Shatner). Michael frequently uses kitchen knives and other sharp instruments to stab or impale his victims, but turns to other objects and brute force when necessary. Michael is in fact not named but rather listed solely as "The Shape" in the credits for *Halloween* and *Halloween II* (Rick Rosenthal, 1981)—a name used to refer to the character in the original *Halloween* screenplay. "The Shape" reflects the way that Myers is represented on screen; he does not speak and is frequently depicted as an ominous black form at the edges of shots, or obscured by shadows in the background. His presence is usually signified by point-of-view camera shots and a recurrent musical theme originally composed by John Carpenter.

Within the film series, multiple attempts are made to destroy Michael, but he has an unnatural capacity for survival that renders him virtually indestructible. Dr Loomis obsessively pursues Michael over the course of five films, shooting, burning, and beating him to no avail. In *Halloween H20: 20 Years Later* (Steve Miner, 1998), Michael appears to be decapitated by his sister Laurie (Jamie Lee Curtis), but she attacks the wrong man, and in *Halloween: Resurrection* (Rick

Rosenthal, 2002), Michael finally succeeds in killing Laurie (Curtis again in the role).

The obsession with killing family members is not the only explanation that the series offers for Michael's violent behavior. It also suggests that his periodic killing sprees coincide with Samhain, a Druid festival that provided the origins for modern Halloween celebrations. In Rob Zombie's 2007 remake of *Halloween*, it is suggested that a dysfunctional and aggressive childhood contributed to the character's violent behavior. Zombie continued to explore the character's psychological dimension in *Halloween II* (2009), suggesting that he was encouraged to kill by visions of his dead mother.

Michael appears in all the *Halloween* films produced to date, with the exception of *Halloween III: Season of the* ***Witch*** (Tommy Lee Wallace, 1982), which is unrelated to the other films in the series. Numerous actors and stuntmen have played Michael Myers, but only two have played the character in more than one film: George P. Wilbur in *Halloween 4: The Return of Michael Myers* (Dwight H. Little, 1988) and *Halloween: The Curse of Michael Myers* (Joe Chappelle, 1995); and Tyler Mane in *Halloween* (2007) and *Halloween II* (2009).

Michael Myers has made a number of appearances beyond the screen, including featuring in film novelizations by Curtis Richards (*Halloween*, 1979), Jack Martin (*Halloween II*, 1981), and Nicholas Grabowsky (*Halloween IV*, 1988); in a short series of young adult novels by Kelly O'Rourke (*The Scream Factory*, 1997; *The Old Myers Place*, 1997; and *The Mad House*, 1998), and in a number of comic books, including series published by Chaos Comics and Devil's Due Publishing. The character also inspired the 2003 song "Michael Myers" by British band The Meteors. Myers is the subject of an array of merchandise including Halloween costumes and masks, and collectibles such as action figures, bobble-heads, and plush toys. Michael Myers is a firmly established presence within popular culture, and his position as the figurehead of one of the most successful film franchises in horror cinema has seen him emerge as an iconic figure of the genre.

Liz Dixon

References and Suggested Reading

Dika, Vera. *Games of Terror: Halloween, Friday the 13th and the Films of the Stalker Cycle*. London: Associated University Press, 1990.

Harper, Jim. *Legacy of Blood: A Comprehensive Guide to Slasher Movies*. Manchester: Headpress/Critical Vision, 2004.

Rockoff, Adam. *Going to Pieces: The Rise and Fall of the Slasher Film, 1978–1986*. Jefferson, NC: McFarland & Co. Inc., 2002.

Worland, Rick. "*Halloween* (1978): The Shape of the Slasher Film." In *The Horror Film: An Introduction*, edited by Rick Worland, 227–42. Oxford: Blackwell Publishing, 2007.

NĀGA—*see* Shapeshifter

NAGUAL—*see* Shapeshifter

NAMUCI—*see* Demon

NANABOZHO—*see* Shapeshifter

NAZGUL—*see* Tolkien, Monsters In

NECROMORPH—*see* Video Games, Monsters In

NEMESIS—*see* Video Games, Monsters In

NEPHILIM—*see* Bible, Monsters In The; Giant; Incubus/Succubus

NEREID—*see* Mermaid/Merman

NICK OF THE WOODS

Nick of the Woods is the title of an 1837 novel by American author Robert Montgomery Bird (1806–54) and the name of the fictional Indian-killer who spends his life avenging the native slaughter of his mother, wife, and children. In his lifetime, Bird produced several critically and popularly acclaimed novels and plays portraying Aztecs and Incans as noble savages, but he was far less sympathetic to the native peoples of North America. Offended by James Fenimore Cooper's portrayal of Native Americans in the "Leatherstocking" books, Bird responded by writing *Nick of the Woods*, which portrayed Native Americans, specifically the Shawnee of Kentucky, in unrelentingly hostile terms. *Nick of the Woods* was Bird's most successful novel. It was profitably dramatized and a best-seller in its German translation.

Nick of the Woods tells the story of a group of pioneers from Virginia and Kentucky who come into conflict with the Shawnee in 1782. Roland Forrest and his cousin Edith travel to Bruce's Station, a fort in northern central Kentucky. Colonel Bruce, commander of the station, tells them both about "Nick of the Woods," a mysterious figure, dressed like a monster, whom the native peoples call the "Jibbenainosay" or "Spirit-Who-Walks." Nick of the Woods kills and scalps every native he finds and is regarded by them as an evil, supernatural creature. Roland and Edith leave the fort and are joined by Ralph Stackpole, a horse thief, and Nathan Slaughter, a wandering Quaker hunter who is mocked as "Bloody Nathan" by the pioneers, because of his pacifist ways.

Nathan helps Roland and Edith escape from a native attack by leading them to an old cabin where they can safely spend the night. However, the Shawnee attack the cabin and capture Edith and Roland, although Ralph escapes. Nathan rescues Roland and the pair attempt to rescue Edith. Nathan and Roland are recaptured by Wenonga, the "Black Vulture," but a band of Kentuckians attacks the Shawnee village and Nathan reveals himself to be Nick of the Woods and kills Wenonga, who was responsible for the murder of Nathan's family.

Written during a decade of violence between white settlers and Native Americans, *Nick of the Woods* successfully reframed the literary portrayal of Native Americans from Fenimore Cooper's noble savages to something far more brutal and sub-human. Bird's counter-narrative, with its blanket absolution and justification of white violence toward Native Americans, proved as popular and influential as Fenimore Cooper's, while also establishing (though not creating) the archetype of the "Indian-hater" character who believes that the best native is a dead one and is eager to put that belief into practice. In the titular character, Bird further creates the character type of the costumed adventurer who leads a double life, as an ordinary civilian and as a costumed vigilante. With its ancient, ruined cabin, haunted landscape, and mysterious protagonist, *Nick of the Woods* is also a prominent example of the American Gothic form.

Jess Nevins

References and Suggested Reading

Dahl, Curtis. *Robert Montgomery Bird*. New York: Twayne Publishers, 1963.

Hoppenstand, Gary. "Justified Bloodshed: Robert Montgomery Bird's *Nick of the Woods* and the Origins of the Vigilante Hero in American Literature and Culture." *Journal of American Culture* 15, no. 2 (Summer 1992): 51–61.

Slotkin, Richard. *Regeneration Through Violence: The Mythology of the American Frontier, 1600–1860*. Middletown, CT: Wesleyan University Press, 1973.

NIMROD—*see* Dante, Monsters In

NIXIE—*see* Shapeshifter

NO.1—*see* Demon

NOSFERATU

The etymologically dubious "nosferatu" was popularized by author Bram Stoker in his 1897 novel ***Dracula*** as the Romanian name for the vampiric undead. The film *Nosferatu* (also translated as *Nosferatu, A Symphony of Horror* and *Nosferatu, A Symphony of Terror*) is a silent German production of 1922, directed by F.W. Murnau (1888–1931) and starring Max Schreck (1879–1936). An unauthorized adaptation of the Stoker novel, *Nosferatu* renames many of *Dracula*'s central characters, with the exception of Van Helsing who is entirely absent. It also gives us the first cinematic representation of many of the novel's now iconic scenes: the rural inn full of superstitious locals, the howling of wolves across bleak mountains, the Count's terrifying black carriage, and the **vampire**'s fatal sea voyage. Unsurprisingly, Stoker's widow successfully sued for copyright infringement, forcing the film's production company, Prana, into liquidation.

Certainly, *Nosferatu* makes a significant formal contribution to the Dracula mythos. Written by Henrik Galeen (1881–1949), who had already worked on the classics of German Expressionist cinema *The Student of Prague* (Stellan Rye and Paul Wegener, 1913) and *The* ***Golem*** (Carl Boese and Paul Wegener, 1920), it is a highly stylized evocation of alienated German subjectivity in the years following World War I. Its *chiaroscuro* depictions of the bald, long-fingered Count Orlock ascending a stair in silhouette, looming over the deck of the plague ship, or rising supernaturally from his coffin have become iconic of vampire horror. They also bespeak a protean anti-Semitism: the hook-nosed, talon-fingered, and rapaciously lecherous Orlock having much in common with anti-Semitic stereotypes of Jews that would be subsequently encapsulated in films such as the Nazi-sponsored propaganda piece *The Eternal Jew* (Fritz Hippler, 1940).

Over time, *Nosferatu* has inspired a number of homages and revisionings. Among them, the 1979 American TV movie *Salem's Lot* (Tobe Hooper) models its vampiric Kurt Barlow (Reggie Nalder) on Orlock, and Werner Herzog's *Nosferatu the Vampire* (1979) remakes the original while reverting to Stoker's original names. Most interestingly, *Shadow of the Vampire* (E. Elias Merhige, 2000) retells the history of the making of the 1922 original, but asserts that Max Schreck (played here by Willem Dafoe) was himself a vampire and that F.W. Murnau (John Malkovich) was aware of the fact.

Nosferatu remains a hugely watchable yet technically innovative work that excites even contemporary audiences through its use of superimposed images, negative film stock, and variable film speed, linked together with irises, wipes, and fades to evoke a disturbed and disorientating world of social disease and alien infection. These are themes, of course, that haunt the Gothic horror film even to the present day. The film can be downloaded free from: http://www.archive.org/details/nosferatu.

Linnie Blake

References and Suggested Reading

Eisner, Lotte. *The Haunted Screen* [1952]. Translated by Roger Greaves. Reprint, New York: Thames and Hudson, 1969.

Isenberg, Noah, ed. *Weimar Cinema: An Essential Guide to Classic Films of the Era*. New York: Columbia University Press, 2009.

Kracauer, Siegfried. *From Caligari to Hitler: A Psychological History of the German*

Film [1947]. Reprint, Princeton: Princeton University Press, 2009.

Roberts, Ian. *German Silent Cinema: The World of Light and Shadow*. London: Wallflower, 2008.

Scheunemann, Dietrich, ed. *Expressionist Film: New Perspectives*. New York: Camden House, 2003.

OBJECTS, ANIMATE

Humans have long demonstrated a readiness to attribute human-like character and motivation to everyday objects, sometimes for allegorical purposes, sometimes for amusement, and sometimes in fear. Written records of talking objects go back at least to the Sumerian genre of disputations, such as the disputation between the hoe and the plow—a debate about rural versus urban life between inanimate objects, probably written for amusement. The attribution of human-like or animal behavior to everyday things can be played for amusement, and often is, from the dishes and spoons running away together in Mother Goose rhymes, to Disney's use of comic relief clocks, teakettles, and wardrobes in *Beauty and the Beast* (Gary Trousdale and Kirk Wise, 1991), the "pet" flying carpet in *Aladdin* (Ron Clements and John Musker, 1992), and even the exuberant weirdness of Chairry (Alison Mork) and Mr Window (voiced by Ric Heitzman) in *Pee Wee's Playhouse* (1986–90). However, this personification can take on a much more sinister tone when everyday tools and domestic objects are possessed by evil spirits or an ill will. It is then that the animate object can be considered a monster.

Animate objects can be catalogued in a variety of ways. One consideration is the source of their unnatural animation. Some objects, though animate, retain their essential nature as tools, their movements controlled by an external force such as sorcery or psychic power (see **Witch/ Wizard**). They may appear animate but actually be guided by the invisible hand of a spirit, whether it be a car with a ghostly driver or doors closing and objects rearranging themselves due to a spirit like a **poltergeist**. The next stage in animacy toward internal animation is possession by an evil spirit or **ghost**, a theme common with human-like objects. More internal yet are those items that are not controlled by an outside force but have awakened or been awakened to a malicious consciousness. It is not uncommon for tales of animate objects to leave the nature of the object's animacy somewhat ambiguous, and it may be impossible to say whether the object is manipulated externally by a spirit, is possessed by a ghost, or possesses a spirit all its own.

More concretely, animate objects can be categorized according to the nature of the objects themselves. Indeed, every object has its own affordances and connotations, and when animate, an object's behavior typically embodies the object's uses and cultural associations. This embodiment may be a very direct extension of the object's attributes, as is the case for a sword that craves blood or the magic mirror of the Snow White tale, which tells the truth, though it may lead to monstrous ends. However, the object's actions may also invert the typical relationship between the object and its user. An example of extension might be the malevolent shoes in Hans Christian Andersen's "The Red Shoes" (1845), which force their wearer to dance until eventually her feet need to be chopped off to release her from their hold. There is inversion here as well, as it is normally not the shoes that decide but the dancer. More striking inversions can be found in the realms of animate ventriloquist's dummies and puppets which, when animate, become the master over their ventriloquist or puppeteer, who is then relegated to a role as accomplice or helpless bystander. This tendency of the animate object to embody the physical affordances or cultural associations of the object itself makes it particularly striking when the object behaves in a markedly different way, as when the painting gets down off the wall on its own in Horace Walpole's *The Castle of Otranto* (1764). Here the weirdness of the animate object is joined by the inexplicability of its movements.

Common Things

Thus, in keeping with the principle that animate objects embody their uses and cultural associations, it is typical that animate weapons be attributed with a suitably violent spirit. In the Finnish epic poem *The Kalevala* (1835), the hero Kullervo's sword desires the taste of blood so much that it is happy to taste the blood of its own master. The spear of the Irish hero Lugh fights alongside him, and Cuchulain's sword speaks boastfully of prowess in battle. Elric of Melniboné's demon sword "Stormbringer" in Michael Moorcock's fantasy series built around the character first introduced in 1961 is the inheritor of this tradition, granting Elric the strength to win victory in battle.

As weapons seek battle, books can invade the mind, and sometimes have minds of their own. While the movements of a book may be limited and subtle, such as being found open when thought closed, or opening to specific passages, their danger is that they give the reader ideas—ideas best left unknown. In Margaret Irwin's "The Book" (1930), a book with subtle movements begins to have a dark influence on its reader, Mr Corbett, ultimately leading to his death when he attempts to destroy it; and in Oscar Wilde's *The Picture of Dorian Gray* (1890), the title character falls under the influence of a "poisonous" French novel (see **Gray, Dorian**). In the "Harry Potter" series by J.K. Rowling, Tom Riddle's journal in *Harry Potter and the Chamber of Secrets* (1998) directs Ginny Weasley to dark ends (see **Harry Potter, Monsters In**). It is not the only animated book in the series, and indeed not even the most animate: *The Monster Book of Monsters*, a textbook used by Rubeus Hagrid, is itself a kind of monster, animate and aggressive towards the reader—not unlike many of the magic books in Unseen University's library in Terry Pratchett's "Discworld" series, initiated in 1983. And though H.P. Lovecraft's (1890–1937) creation *The Necronomicon* is not animate in Lovecraft's works, in Sam Raimi's 1992 film *Army of Darkness*, its threat is more material, biting with the monstrous face on its cover (see **Lovecraft, Monsters In**).

It is perhaps arguable whether all the above books and weapons are monsters, and many are only barely animate. In contrast, the Japanese monsters called "tsukumogami" are premier examples of everyday tools that have become animate and monstrous. Tsukumogami are animated tools, said to awaken one hundred years after their creation, and can include objects as varied as umbrellas, scrolls, prayer beads, clubs, and musical instruments. They are typically portrayed as malevolent spirits that seek revenge against the humans who have abandoned them, even killing and feeding on humans (see Reider; Lillehoj). The key features of tsukumogami were in place by the Japanese medieval period, and they have maintained a presence in contemporary Japanese comic books, video games, and films such as *The Great Yōkai War* (Takashi Miike, 2005). Their portrayals in art are often darkly humorous, but their behavior can be quite gruesome. Tools are typically simply used by people and discarded when no longer needed—but tsukumogami tales suggest that our tools may come to resent us for such neglect.

Domestic objects also feature in European, English, and US sources as ghosts or monsters, sometimes with a humorous touch. Brooms possessed by summoned spirits reel out of control in Goethe's *Der Zauberlehrling* (*The Sorcerer's Apprentice*, 1797), and while they ultimately do no harm, only the words of the master sorcerer can bring them back under control. Perhaps the most famous contemporary retelling of the poem is Disney's *Fantasia* (segment directed by James Algar, 1940), which presents an animated interpretation of the poem that alternates between the dramatic, amusing, and didactic potential of the work. The haunted chair in Charles Dickens's *Pickwick Papers* (1836–37 serial) remarks freely on Tom Smart's drinking while giving him wooing advice. More darkly, Margery Lawrence's "The Haunted Saucepan" (1926) features a pan that brings itself to a sinister boil, a ghostly echo of its former use by a woman to brew poison to murder her husband. And an entire room full of ordinary objects animates in mocking laughter in Sam Raimi's *Evil Dead II: Dead by Dawn* (1987), including a mounted deer head, lamps, books and book cases, a clock, and even sofa cushions. A final example of an animate object that is both a monster and comic relief is the luggage of Terry Pratchett's "Discworld" series, a sentient many-legged case with dangerous proclivities.

A major class of animate object in contemporary film and literature is the animate vehicle, in particular the automobile. One of the earliest examples is E. Nesbit's "The Violet Car" (1910), which features a ghostly automobile without a driver, the car itself an apparition. Antonia Fraser's "Who's Been Sitting in my Car?" (1976) offers an alternative take on the notion, with a ghostly driver of a very real car whose jealousy makes him a very real threat to the protagonist's children. Theodore Sturgeon's "Killdozer!" (1944), published in *Astounding Science Fiction*, provides an alien source to the animation of construction equipment. Stephen King's novel ***Christine*** (1983) is probably the most famous example, both in print and film (the film version was directed by John Carpenter in 1983), with its presentation of a murderous, implacable car that is personified as a jilted lover. Film and television treatments of murderous cars are numerous. These include Steven Spielberg's *Duel* (1971), adapted from Richard Matheson's 1971 short story, in which an enormous truck with a mysterious driver menaces travelers. The driver remains unknown, and it is the truck that is the monster. Jerry London's *Killdozer* (1974) adapts Sturgeon's short story to the screen. Elliot Silverstein's *The Car* (1977) also has a mystery driver, but it is the titular car that kills. In addition to John Carpenter's *Christine* adaptation, Stephen King directed *Maximum Overdrive* (1986), in which the monster is a truck. More recently, Eric Valette's film *Super Hybrid* (2010) includes yet another killer automobile. The evil car theme is blended with the **werewolf** legend in season 2, episode 18 of the TV series *Futurama*, titled "The Honking" (Susie Dieter, 2000). In this episode, the **robot** Bender is cursed to transform into a murderous automobile. Season 5, episode 134 of the *Twilight Zone* TV series, "You Drive" (Brahm, 1964), features an animate car that hunts down its driver, nearly killing him—but its purpose is to bring the driver to the police station to turn himself in for having hit and killed a young boy and driven away. Here, the driver is the monster and the animate car an agent of justice.

Simulacra

Another class of animate objects is the human simulacrum. Suits of armor, statues, puppets, dolls, toys, scarecrows, and mannequins all simulate the human form and have a long tradition of monstrous or magical forebears. Idols stand in symbolically and ritually for the gods, and statues of guardian spirits adorn temples worldwide. Popular culture's conception of the "voodoo doll," while of dubious authenticity, reflects a long history of attributing power to representations of humanity, a history attested by such diverse objects as prehistoric "Venus figurines," West African fetishes, and religious idols with human forms. It is no wonder that objects with human forms abound among the class of animate objects. Empty suits of armor haunt folklore and fiction, from the mysterious empty armor in C.S. Lewis's *The Silver Chair* (1953) and Poul Anderson's *Three Hearts and Three Lions* (1961), to the faux ghosts of the *Scooby Doo* children's cartoon franchise (1969–present, in various forms). Like suits of armor, statues can come to life and prove a danger to those around them. Prosper Mérimée's 1837 short story "The Venus of Ille" provides the example of a statue that comes to life, threatening the protagonist. A statue comes to life and drags Don Giovanni to Hell in the climax of Mozart's 1787 opera of the same name. Of course, statues brought to life need not always lead to dark ends, as the classical Greek myth of Pygmalion shows. In this tale, the sculptor Pygmalion falls in love with a statue carved by his own hand, and the goddess Venus grants his wish by bringing it to life. Yet just as often, living statues prove harmful. Robert E. Howard's barbarian Conan encounters animate iron statues in "Iron Shadows in the Moon" (originally published as "Shadows in the Moonlight," 1934). Paul Wegener's 1915 silent film *The Golem* (*Der Golem*), based on the 1913–14 serial (1915 novel) of the same name by Gustav Meyrink, describes an animate statue of a kind, destructive to those around it if not intrinsically malevolent. **Golem** stories had a particularly full publishing history in nineteenth-century Germany, but it was this film that brought the tales to a wider audience. A giant animate bronze statue, Talos, threatens Jason and his crew in Don Chaffey's *Jason and the Argonauts* (1963).

There is often an ambivalence about human simulacra, raising as they sometimes do the question of what it means to be human. Simulacra need not be unambiguously malevolent to be treated as monsters, though their unnaturalness may be unsettling and they may even prove destructive to body or mind. Yet for all that, they may also be victims. E.T.A. Hoffmann's 1817 story *The Sandman* (*Der Sandmann*) includes an automaton, Olimpia, whose nature contributes to the descent into madness of the protagonist. In Nathaniel Hawthorne's "Feathertop" (1852), an animate scarecrow with the guise of a man causes such fear in his beloved Polly that he destroys himself, but he is not malevolent. This ambivalence is also reflected in that modern form of human simulacra, the **robot**.

More often sinister and unambiguously monstrous are animate puppets and dolls. Animated puppets abound in film and television, frequently in tales which invert the relationship between puppet and puppet master. The *Twilight Zone* features two episodes devoted to ventriloquist's dummies: Abner Biberman's 1962 "The Dummy" (season 3, episode 98), in which the dummy switches places with its ventriloquist; and Robert Butler's 1964 "Caesar and Me" (season 5, episode 148), in which the dummy drives its ventriloquist to commit crimes. Films featuring evil ventriloquist's dummies include James Cruze's *The Great Gabbo* (1929, a film alluded to in the final episode of season 4 of *The Simpsons*, in which a ventriloquist's dummy named Gabbo is featured [season 4, episode 22; David Silverman, 1993]), Alberto Cavalcanti's *Dead of Night* segment "The Ventriloquist's Dummy" (1945), Lindsay Shonteff's *Devil Doll* (1964),

Richard Attenborough's *Magic* (1978), David Schmoeller's *Puppetmaster* (1989), and James Wan's *Dead Silence* (2007). In nearly all such films, the dummy either exerts a dark influence on the ventriloquist or represents the ventriloquist's darker impulses.

Even when used to less sinister ends, the question of who is master—puppet or puppeteer—remains. Carlo Collodi's 1883 novel *The Adventures of Pinocchio*, a reinterpretation of which was later animated as *Pinocchio* (Ben Sharpsteen et al., 1940) by Walt Disney Studios, introduces a puppet that is brought to life by the puppet master Geppetto. Pinocchio's misbehavior leads to bad ends for those around him, particularly in Collodi's earlier telling, where Pinocchio's actions even lead to deaths. Bill Willingham's comic book series *Fables* (2002–present) revives the monstrous potential of Pinocchio's animacy, while simultaneously putting the puppet-master back in control. In the comic book series, Gepetto becomes an evil overlord with a puppet army, and Pinocchio is forced to choose between his evil father figure (and wooden soldier "brothers") and the good of the other "fables" (fairytale and other fabulous beings). An ambiguously animate—but thoroughly monstrous—puppet can be found in the *Saw* franchise (James Wan, 2004). These films prominently feature Billy, the serial killer Jigsaw's puppet, through which he communicates with his victims. It is left unclear how the dummy moves as freely as it does.

Animate dolls play on the juxtaposition of childhood and the trappings of childhood with evil and monstrosity. The most iconic animate doll in recent horror cinema is **Chucky**, the serial killer doll in the *Child's Play* films (1988–2004, with *Curse of Chucky* released in 2013), which variously embrace the gruesome humor of the monstrous doll convention. Earlier takes on monstrous dolls include, again, the *Twilight Zone*, with a particularly memorable example in Richard C. Sarafian's 1963 "Living Doll" (season 5, episode 126). The doll, Talky Tina, is supernatural, evil, and apparently indestructible. Monster dolls feature in Kevin Connor's *From Beyond the Grave* (1973), and Tobe Hooper's *Poltergeist* (1982) includes both a monstrous clown doll and a jack in the box.

Animate toys feature in film and television as well, including season 5, episode 10 of *The X-Files*, titled "Chinga" (1998), co-written by Stephen King and Chris Carter, with a cursed doll that causes gruesome suicides. Disney's *The Princess and the Frog* (Ron Clements and John Musker, 2009) includes evil spirits in the form of voodoo dolls that drag the villain to Hell. A murderous Zuni fetish doll is featured in "Amelia," a segment of the TV horror anthology film *Trilogy of Terror* (Dan Curtis, 1975). This segment was adapted for television by Richard Matheson from his 1969 short story "Prey." Stephen King uses toys in "The Monkey," a short story first published in 1980, in which a cymbal monkey tolls death. Toys play the roles of both heroes and villains in a number of sources, prominent examples of which include Pixar's *Toy Story* films (1995–2010) and precursors such as the operetta *Babes in Toyland* (adapted multiple times to film). A humorous take is featured in season 5, episode 14 of the TV series *Angel*, "Smile Time" (2004), which inverts the convention by transforming the protagonist Angel, himself a **vampire**, into an animate puppet in an episode in which he must stop a group of murderous puppets.

Richard W. Forest

References and Suggested Reading

Gross, Kenneth. *Puppet: An Essay on Uncanny Life*. Chicago: University of Chicago Press, 2011.

Kuznets, Lois Rostow. *When Toys Come Alive: Narratives of Animation, Metamorphosis, and*

Development. New Haven: Yale University Press, 1994.

Lillehoj, Elizabeth. "Transfiguration: Man-Made Objects as Demons in Japanese Scrolls." *Asian Folklore Studies* 54 (1995): 7–34.

Nelson, Victoria. *The Secret Life of Puppets*. Cambridge: Harvard University Press, 2001.

Papapetros, Spyros. "Malicious Houses: Animation, Animism, Animosity in German Architecture and Film—From Mies to Murnau." *Grey Room* 20 (2005): 6–37.

Pringle, Patricia. "Scampering Sofas and 'Skuttling' Tables: The Entertaining Interior." *Interiors: Design, Architecture and Culture* 1, no. 3 (2010): 219–43.

Reider, Noriko T. "Animating Objects: Tsukumogami ki and the Medieval Illustration of Shingon Truth." *Japanese Journal of Religious Studies* 36, no. 2 (2009): 231–57.

OBOROTEN'

The oboroten' is the Russian equivalent of the were-animal; the term includes all creatures capable of switching between human and animal form. The most common types of oborotni in literature and folklore include were-bears, were-cats, were-hares, and of course, lycanthropes (the Russian word *vurdalak* can mean either a **werewolf** or a **vampire** [**upyr'**]).

The earliest literary depictions of the oboroten' in Russian literature represent ferocity in battle. The anonymous twelfth-century narrative poem "The Song of Igor's Campaign" evokes an eleventh-century Kievan Prince, Vseslav the Sorcerer, who is said to prowl in wolf shape at night and to loot conquered cities in the form of a "savage beast" (line 532). The soldiers of the poem's hero, Prince Igor, are described as "grey wolves bounding in the field" (line 93).

By the Romantic period, literary oborotni had degenerated into comic or grotesque foils to love stories. In Orest Somov's "Oboroten'" (1829; usually translated as "The Werewolf"), a clever peasant girl outwits a sheep-stealing sorcerer to make an advantageous marriage. In Anton Pogorel'skii's "The Lafertovo Poppy-Seed Cake Seller" (1828), a witch transforms her black cat into a louche, ingratiating civil servant who woos her niece. In Somov's story, the girl marries the (repentant) werewolf; in the second tale, the feline oboroten', as an obstacle to true love, is repulsed.

Later in the nineteenth century, oborotni acquired symbolic currency in social and political satire. In Aleksandr Sukhovo-Kobylin's satirical play *The Death of Tarel'kin* (1869), the title character fakes his own funeral and appropriates the papers of a recently deceased clerk, hoping to evade his debts while blackmailing superiors from the safety of his stolen identity. When his deception is uncovered, he is arrested: his equally venal prosecutors cannot decide whether Tarel'kin is an oboroten' or a vurdalak, but agree that he is an unnatural monster. As such, Tarel'kin embodies the corruption endemic within, and parasitic upon, the Russian imperial bureaucracy. As one official remarks: "I am now of the opinion that our entire nation is nothing but a pack of wolves, snakes, and hares, suddenly transformed into people, and I suspect everybody; and that's why one has to establish a rule and put everyone under arrest!" (Act III, Scene 2). A more specific use of the oboroten' to indict a particular class occurs in Anatoly Lunacharsky's screenplay for the film *The Bear's Wedding* (Konstantin Eggert and Vladimir Gardin, 1926). A wealthy landowner (played by Eggert) who periodically transforms into a savage bear (apparently because his mother was startled by a bear while pregnant) tragically takes ursine form on his wedding night and mauls his lovely bride (Vera Malinovskaya) to death. Anatoly Lunacharsky (1875–1933) was the Soviet Commissar of Enlightenment at this time, and the film unsubtly reflects typical Soviet prejudices against the old nobility.

Begemot, the enormous black cat who accompanies the demon Woland in Mikhail Bulgakov's magical realist novel *The Master and Margarita* (1940), is endowed with both the ludic and satirical functions of the oboroten'. The name Begemot is derived from the Books of Job and Enoch, in which Begemoth (**Behemoth**) is described as a vast monster capable of devouring all of creation, were he not restrained by God. According to Sokolov (1996), Bulgakov may have based Begemot's personality on his own cat, Fliushka. While greed is one aspect of the fictional Begemot's character, he is more notable for his charm, zany humor, and universal ability. Acting as Woland's page and jester, Begemot alters from an oversized, walking, talking cat to a small, fat, and greedy man (his original form, glimpsed at the end of the book, is that of a slender, demonic page boy [see **Demon**]). In the course of the novel, Begemot beheads an obstreperous Master of Ceremonies, stages a bloodless shoot-out with police, and sets fire to the Moscow Literary Institute. He also helps arrange Woland's Satanic Ball. Begemot remains one of the most popular characters in Bulgakov's novel, which enjoys cult status in Russia. Begemot features on the covers of both Western and Russian editions of the book; statues in Moscow and Kiev commemorate his character; and in the 2005 television production of *The Master and Margarita* (Vladimir Bortko), his stunts were recreated by a 100 cm high (about 39 inches) actor in a feline costume (played by Vano Miranian).

The most significant recent satirical use of oborotni occurs in Viktor Pelevin's (1962–) prolific postmodernist texts. In "A Werewolf Problem in Central Russia" (1998), a student wandering through the Russian provinces accidentally discovers a secret partisan army, each member of which is able to transform into a specific animal (including snakes and wolves). One of their leaders reveals that they constitute a vital, if top secret, military reserve, and that the Bolsheviks' victory in the Civil War was aided by the intervention of oboroten'-soldiers. Pelevin's oborotni can be interpreted as a satire on modern Russia's vociferous cohorts of backwards-looking National Bolshevists and other nationalist political groupings. In Pelevin's *The Sacred Book of the Werewolf* (2005), the werewolf character Sasha Seryi (literally, Sasha Gray) works as a general in the FSB, Russia's post-Soviet replacement for the KGB. He and his fellow officers, some of whom have to be injected with ketamine in order to complete the transformation, boost crude oil production by howling at pumping machinery in the Siberian tundra. Sasha's lover (and the book's narrator) is a 1,200-year-old Buddhist were-fox who works as a high-class prostitute, selling her clients obscene hallucinations instead of sex. Pelevin censures the modern obsession with glamor and possessions through her meditations on the illusory nature of perception and the transience of reality.

Shape-changing magicians are glamorous characters in Sergei Lukianenko's popular "Night Watch" tetralogy (1998–2005), which describes the struggle between two opposing orders of supernatural beings or "Others," the benign Night Watch and the sinister Day Watch, in contemporary Russia. Lukianenko's novels distinguish two types of **shapeshifters**, each of which can transform at will into a certain type of animal. The first category consists of magicians who can choose their own animal avatars, which then become fixed: the aptly named Bear and Tiger Cub serve in the Night Watch, as does the sorceress Olga, who can transform into an owl. The second category, collectively and pejoratively known as oborotni, largely belong to the Day Watch and have fewer magical powers; they are unable to select their avatar (wolves and predatory cats predominate among them). In several of Lukianenko's novels, vampires also transform into bats or hares.

Muireann Maguire

References and Suggested Reading

Brougher, Valentina. "Werewolves and Vampires: Historical Questions and Symbolic Answers in Petr Aleshkovsky's 'Vladimir Chigrintsev'." *The Slavic and East European Journal* 45, no. 3 (Autumn 2001): 491–505.

Sokolov, Boris. *Entsiklopediia Bulgakovskaia*. Moscow: Lokid-Mif, 1996.

OG—*see* Giant

OGOPOGO

Ogopogo is one of several lake monsters that have occasionally figured in film and literature. Based on a cryptozoological creature (see **Cryptid**) believed to live in Lake Okanagan in the Canadian province of British Columbia, Ogopogo resembles a sea serpent and is reported to measure some 40 to 50 feet long. In Salish Native American tradition, the monster is called Naitaka or N'ha-a-tik. Explanations for sightings range from misidentification of a large fish, eel, or even an aquatic mammal such as a seal, to the continued survival of such prehistoric creatures as the plesiosaur or zeuglodon (Coleman and Huyghe 83–5; see **Dinosaur**).

The creature designed by Jim Hensen's workshop for *Mee-Shee the Water* ***Giant*** (John Henderson, 2005) represents Ogopogo; the film depicts a caring monster who saves several people from death in the deep waters. More recently, a computer-generated image of Ogopogo appears fleetingly in *The Beast of Bottomless Lake* (Craig March, 2010), a satire about a "scientific" team's search for the monster. The Scooby-Doo crew also encountered a Canadian lake monster in season Three, episode 15, "The Beast is Awake in Bottomless Lake" (1978).

Literary interpretations of lake monsters appear relatively rarely in adult fiction. Canadian science fiction and fantasy writer James Alan Gardner includes Ogopogo in his delightful story "All the Cool Monsters At Once," a veritable beast fest, which situates Ogopogo as the first Canadian monster, and also mentions Manipogo, a legendary denizen of Lake Manitoba. Robert Sampson's "The Silver Face" (1992) offers an eerie take on an unidentified creature in Ontario's Sully Lake.

Lake monsters occur slightly more frequently in young adult and children's literature. Youth novels featuring Ogopogo include *Ogopogo, the Misunderstood Lake Monster* (1985) by Don Levers, *Ogopogo: Dead or Alive* (1988) by Penny Smith, and more recently the "Box Car Kids" mystery, *The Creature in Ogopogo Lake* (2006) by Gertrude Chandler Warner. Other lake monsters include Champ—believed to inhabit Lake Champlain on the New York/Vermont border—the subject of *Champ—Wave of Terror* (2006) by K.B. Brege and *The True Story of Champ* (2006) by Marc Hughes, a book tie-in for the Burlington, VT Lake Monsters minor league baseball franchise. The most famous of these cryptids remains, of course, the **Loch Ness monster** in Scotland, featured in Paul Zindel's novel *Loch* (1994), as well as in the adult horror novel *Monster (A Tale of Loch Ness)* (1982) by Jeffrey Konvitz.

Such water serpents appeared in Native American lore before the arrival of Europeans; Abenaki legends refer to Champ as Tatoskok (Shovlin 42) and also reference Gitaskog, while the Penobscot speak of Aglebemu ("Native"). The Mishegenabig, "monstrous sea serpents," were reported by early folklorist William Schoolcraft (quoted in Colombo 19), and in Ojibwa legend Nanabozho is considered to be the son of Winona and grandson of Nokomis.

In addition to these lake monsters in North America and the British Isles, sightings of **sea monsters** off the coast of Canada have been reported in historical literature since the first explorers came from Europe, including what the Mi'kmaq called the "Gou-gou," a sea monster that Samuel de Champlain reported seeing in the Chaleur Bay off the coast of New Brunswick (Lambert 181). Cadborosaurus, nicknamed "Caddy," is named after Victoria, British Columbia's Cadboro Bay where it, too, has been sighted since pre-contact times, known in native Manhousat lore as *hiyitl'iik* and called *Numkse-lee kwala* in native Comox lore.

Amy J. Ransom

References and Suggested Reading

Coleman, Lauren, and Patrick Huyghe. *The Field Guide to Lake Monsters, Sea Serpents, and Other Mystery Denizens of the Deep*. New York: Penguin, 2003.

Colombo, John Robert, ed. *Windigo: An Anthology of Fact and Fantastic Fiction*. Saskatoon, Saskatchewan: Western Producer Prairie Books, 1982.

Gaal, Arlene B. *In Search of Ogopogo: Sacred Creature of Okanagan Waters*. Surrey: Hancock House, 2001.

Gardner, John Alan. "All the Cool Monsters At Once." In *Mythspring*, edited by Julie Czerneda and Genevieve Kierans, 33–50. Markham: Red Deer Press, 2007.

Lambert, Richard Stanton. *Exploring the Supernatural: The Weird in Canadian Folklore*. London: Arthur Baker, 1955.

Sampson, Robert. "The Silver Face." In *Northern Frights*, edited by Don Hutchison, 189–203. Oakville, Ontario: Mosaic, 1992.

Shovlin, Paul. *Lake Monsters: Fact or Fiction?* Detroit: Thomson/Gale, 2005.

OGRE

Large, strong-bodied, lumbering imaginary beings, ample-bellied, and often sporting prodigious hair and beard, ogres have earned mythological and literary distinction due to their predilection for violence and insatiable appetite. Though often described as **giants**, they vary in size from human height to hundreds of feet tall, but are uniformly infamous for their hideous appearance and cruelty. Principally occupying far reaches of the forest, living in isolation from humankind, ogres possess a dark reputation for, in particular, victimizing, feeding upon, and/or devouring humans, especially the small or vulnerable. For their prey, they display a special preference for children. Ogres favor raw flesh. Numbered among the dubious list of accomplishments are spousal and child abuse, sexual predation, cannibalism, and infanticide. Ogres demonstrate an excellent sense of smell and poor eyesight, and hence are a reminder of our lingering reptilian brain and, perhaps, a vestige of some formidable previous humanoid race. Ogres may have preoccupied the human imagination for so long because they so accurately depict the darkest parts of humanity—traits and impulses of which we may ultimately be most afraid.

The prevalence of ogres in so many different cultures testifies to the powerful fears and fantasies inspired in humankind by cannibalism. For all their depravity and transgressions, however, ogres are tailor-made victims and scapegoats; in their simple, single-minded pursuit of their desires, they bear a resemblance to an overgrown version of the very children upon which they prey. In the Western tradition, their conventionally ungainly forms once dominated the imagined landscapes of unexplored, mysterious regions in Europe and Asia, but in more modern literature, the villainous ogre enters the urban milieu and has become increasingly complex and multidimensional. Though contemporary ogres have proven a potent trope for authors who wish to address Nazism, totalitarianism, and the notion of the scapegoat, ogres have, on occasion, won the role of modern heroes. They and their female counterpart, the ogress, appear in varied contemporary media, including cinema, juvenile literature, video games, and comic books.

In French Tradition

The Latin term *orcus*, the Italian terms *orco* or *orgo*, and the later French word *ogre* may derive from an Etruscan name for a fearsome god of the Underworld—a wrathful, hairy giant who guarded a cave. Orcus became a Roman deity of the Underworld, principally worshipped in rural areas. *Ogre* entered the French language as a twelfth-century word. The earliest known reference to ogres comes from the twelfth-century poetry of Chrétien de Troyes, whose unfinished Arthurian verse, *Perceval, or the Story of the Grail*, includes the lines:

> *And it is written that there will come an hour*
> *When the whole kingdom of Logres*
> *Which was once the land of ogres,*
> *Will be destroyed by that lance.* (*Perceval* 6168–71)

The passage refers to a "bleeding spear dripping a single unstoppable drop of blood" prophesied to deliver ruin to the Arthurian Kingdom and perhaps return it to its past uncivilized state, when it was "governed" by the ogre.

The name and reputation of the ogre gained considerable infamy from its dark profile in the seventeenth-century French fairytales of Charles Perrault. In Perrault's tales, heroes and heroines can be common people who must outwit cruel, evil beings. In "Little Thumbling," an ogre threatens the resourceful Tom Thumb and his band of small children, as it attempts to slay and devour them in the middle of the night, only mistakenly to slaughter his own daughters. The ogress Queen Mother of "Sleeping Beauty" directs her cook to prepare her princely stepson's grandchildren for dinner with a brown mustard sauce. The "eerie" and "cold-blooded" blue of his beard have led Jungian critics such as Verena Kast to characterize the murderous husband of "Bluebeard," an aristocrat who has taken to hanging his slain wives from the ceiling of a secret locked room in his basement, as an otherworldly being, perhaps descended from a far more primitive god of death.

Apart from Perrault, Marie Catherine Jumelle de Bernville, Comtesse d'Aulnoy (1651–1705) played a role in familiarizing the world with the profile of the ogre. She composed aristocratic fairytales richly furnished with ogres, notably *The Bee and the Orange Tree*. This tale begins when its protagonist, an infant princess named Aimée, survives a tempestuous shipwreck and floats in her cradle to the shore of a beautiful country tormented by Ravagio and Tourmentine, an ogre and ogress who respectively harvest and devour the few unlucky human inhabitants. Her fair features allow Aimée to escape ogreish appetites and remain uneaten for the time being; however, at adulthood, she has been promised as a bride to the eldest of the ogre brood. To escape the ogres and regain her palatial status, Aimée must steal a magic wand from the ogress and escape her cannibalistic surrogate family by using this wand to transform herself into a bee and the prince into an orange tree.

Asian Creation Myths and Folktales

Asian mythology features innumerable cruel and memorable humanoids. Japan is home to some of the most colorful and morphologically diverse ogres in the world. David Gilmore suggests in *Monsters: Evil Beings, Mythical Beasts, and All Manner of Imaginary Terrors*, that the many foreign influences on the island and myriad religions may have been partially responsible for this diversity. Japanese **oni**, variously translated as **demon**, **devil**, ogre, or **troll**, are muscular **shapeshifters** that at first appear human but turn purple, black, or blue when overtaken by their volatile temper. Some possess two horns, a third eye, and extra fingers or teeth. They wear tiger-skin loincloths and threaten peasants with iron clubs called *kanabō*. Harbingers of natural disasters, their favorite activity seems to be tormenting human beings. In the Japanese fairytale "The Ogre of Rashomon," for instance, the ogre or oni of the tale (the words are used interchangeably) waits by the Gate of Rashomon after sunset, seizes passersby, and greedily devours them. The ogre of Rashomon demonstrates abilities as a crafty shapeshifter: after a valorous Kyoto knight, Watanabe, slices off its arm, the beast appears in the slight form of an old woman and successfully retrieves its missing limb, escaping knightly justice at the close of the story. Another tribe of Japanese ogre, the Shokera (meaning roughly "roof **devil**") lurks upon rooftops and uses its roost to spy on households, which it then invades, frightening tenants to death. The oni may have originated in China, whose ogres display simian characteristics, taking the shape of threatening apes that are perhaps distant ancestors to the yeti or abominable snowman (see **Bigfoot**). Such beings may be descendants of a primordial simian ogre with supernatural powers, the Kung-kung, who rebelled against the gods in the earliest Chinese creation myths.

Contemporary Ogres

Modern ogres are both formidable and surprising and have made a dramatic reappearance in literature after an absence of nearly two centuries. As examined by Jonathan Krell in *The Progress of Ogres*, French novelists, including Emile Zola (1840–1902), Michel Tournier (1924–), Pierette Fleutiaux (1941–), Sylvie Germain (1954–), and Pascal Bruckner (1948–), make frequent use of the ogre as a metaphor in their work. The ogre menaces these tales in many varied shades. In *The Belly of Paris* (1873), Zola unfolds a sophisticated metaphor: Paris is an ogre and the Parisian market its belly and digestive cavity. With a feminist flair, Fleutiaux overturns the patriarchal narratives and characterizations of the Perrault fairytale in "La Femme de l'ogre" (1984), empowering the ogre's wife who runs away with Tom Thumb. In his acclaimed novel *The Ogre* (1970), Tournier describes the fate of narrator Abel Tiffauges. An innocent from the wilderness drawn to the sinister and ancient forces in his life, Tiffauges becomes entangled with the Nazi movement. Learning all too late about the hidden, genocidal agenda of the holocaust, he endeavors to save a child who has escaped from Auschwitz.

In late twentieth- and twenty-first century representations, the ogre appears as an important trope for representing the most disturbing urges of humanity and as a protagonist who no longer needs seven league boots of Perrault's "Little Thumbling" to travel great distances. It is not necessarily isolated, inarticulate, or ugly, and is more than capable of entangling us in intimate relationships. It may have abandoned its cavernous lair and become a denizen of the city; in fact, it might even be the city itself, as in Zola's *The Belly of Paris*, or the father pursuing you under your own roof, as in Muriel Cerf's *Ogres et Autre Contres* (1997). It might be the fetishistic, photography-obsessed girlfriend that readers encounter in Tournier's "Veronica's Shrouds" (1978). As Jonathan Krell has discovered in *The Ogre's*

Progress, the modern day author finds that the most frightening ogres are those very close to ourselves. Perhaps most surprisingly, in the manner of Chrétien's own Perceval, who aspires to and attains knighthood after a childhood spent in the remote forests of Wales, the ogre has even evolved on occasion into a protective or heroic figure. In Japan, it is now not uncommon to encounter oni who guard the thresholds of household doorways.

The most notable instance of the rehabilitation of the fairytale ogre is the popular series of *Shrek* films distributed by DreamWorks Pictures (*Shrek*, 2001, directors Andrew Adamson and Vicky Jenson; *Shrek 2*, 2004, directors Andrew Adamson, Kelly Asbury, and Conrad Vernon; *Shrek the Third*, 2007, directors Chris Miller and Roman Hui; and *Shrek Forever After*, 2010, director Mike Mitchell). These films subvert the traditional role of the ogre as villain, simply driven to satiate its worst, most taboo desires. Instead, the ogre protagonist Shrek (voiced by Mike Myers) assumes the role of hero and marries Princess Fiona (voiced by Cameron Diaz) who chooses to transform into an ogress. Jack Zipes has characterized the original screenplay as a "mock fairy tale" that questions conventions and invites reconsideration of evil and beauty. The popularity of these films attests to the compelling complexity and transformative power of the ogre metaphor.

Matthew Schumacher

References and Suggested Reading

Asma, Stephen. *Monsters: An Unnatural History of our Worst Fears*. Oxford: Oxford University Press, 2009.

Gilmore, David. *Monsters: Evil Beings, Mythical Beasts, and All Manner of Imaginary Terrors*. Philadelphia: University of Pennsylvania Press, 2003.

Jacoby, Mario, Verena Kast, and Ingrid Riedel. *Witches, Ogres, and the Devil's Daughter: Encounters with Evil in Fairy Tales*. Boston: Shambhala Publications, 1991.

Krell, Jonathan. *The Ogre's Progress*. Newark: University of Delaware Press, 2009.

Tournier, Michel. *The Ogre*. Baltimore: The Johns Hopkins University Press, 1997.

Troyes, Chrétien de. *Perceval, or the Story of the Grail*. Translated by Burton Raffel. New Haven: Yale University Press, 1985.

Zipes, Jack. *Breaking the Magic Spell: Radical Theories of Folk and Fairy Tales*. Lexington: The University Press of Kentucky, 1979.

OGUN—*see* Demon

OLVIKAN—*see* Demon

ONI

The most prominent of Japanese monsters, *oni* lurk in all types of literature, art, theater, and film. They are typically portrayed as having large muscular humanoid bodies, round eyes, wild hair, fangs, an odd number of eyes, fingers with sharp nails, and horns. They may wear a cloth or tiger-skin loincloth and carry an iron club. Their skin is often red but can vary in color. Such representations appear in the Heian period (794–1185) as the warders of Buddhist hells (*gokusotsu*), who administer punishments to sinners in *Jigoku zōshi* (*Hell Scrolls*, late twelfth century) and similar works. Bovine and equine-headed *oni* exist in Hell, but rarely appear in this world. In collections of *setsuwa* (short didactic tales compiled predominately in the ninth through fourteenth centuries) such as *Miraculous Stories from the Japanese Buddhist Tradition* (*Nihon ryōiki*, c. 823), *oni* sometimes assist Enma-ō (Yama), King of Hells, by fetching people (Book 2: 24 and 25).

According to the first dictionary of the Japanese language, *Wamyō ruijushō* (c.

930), the term "*oni*" comes from a Chinese character meaning "to hide," homophonous with the "on" of "*oni*." Whether or not this theory is accurate, *oni* prefer to remain invisible. They usually materialize at twilight or night and in liminal or marginal spaces: abandoned buildings such as Kawara Mansion (once located beside the Kamo River on the east side of the capital, Kyoto, and famous for its garden), city gates like Rashōmon, bridges, and riverbanks. That *oni* can appear anywhere at anytime renders them even scarier.

Oni eat humans, as depicted first in *Izumo no kuni fudoki* (*The Topography of Izumo*, c. 733) when a single-eyed *oni* consumes a farmer. However, the mythical *Yamata no orochi*, a giant serpent in the *Kojiki* (712) and *The Chronicles of Japan* (*Nihon shoki*, 720), is the first flesh-eating creature recorded. While he consumes what is likely the flesh of gods—seven daughters of two earthly deities—the motif recurs in Japan of a monster threatening families and society by consuming cherished daughters, who also serve as political pawns through marriage arrangements. An *oni* impersonating a groom devours his bride, to the grief of her parents (*Miraculous Stories of Japan*, c. 823, 2:33, and *Konjaku monogatari shū* [*Tales of Times Now Past*], c. 1120, 20:37). The *oni* **Shuten Dōji** abducts and eats young noblewomen from the capital in *Ōeyama ekotoba* (*The Tale of Mount Ōe in Pictures and Words*), a fourteenth-century *otogizōshi* ("companion tales"—illustrated stories from the Muromachi period, 1392–1573) and elsewhere.

As similarities in the stories of Yamata no orochi and Shuten Dōji suggest (in addition to consuming daughters, both are slain when inebriated), *oni* can be linked to mythological figures. The goddess Izanami sets *Yomotsu shikome* (ugly women of Yomi or the land of the dead) on the god Izanagi when he defies her wishes and looks at her decaying body. The displeasure of an *oni* in female form is similarly dangerous. Moreover, *shikome* are considered prototypes of *oni*.

Oni were also shaped by Chinese concepts of spirits, the worship of *kami* (gods) (Shintoism), Hindu demonology (see **Demon**), Buddhism, and Onmyōdō (the Japanese adaptation of Ying-yang/Taoist practices). The Japanese appropriated the Chinese understanding of the Chinese character for *oni* as restless spirits of the dead. *Oni* called *rasetsu* and *yasha*, with *nyo* often added to indicate "female," drew from *rākṣasī* and *yakṣinī*, Buddhist-appropriated Hindu demonesses. In a *setsuwa* with Indian origins, which acquired broad cultural significance in Japan, *rasetsu* and *yasha* inhabit an island in the South Seas. Impersonating beautiful women, they seduce and eat men (*Konjaku* 5:1 and *Tales of Uji*, tale 91). *Oni* was also a way of understanding disease and other destructive natural forces, including thunder and lightning. Avenging enemies, the spirit of scholar Sugawara no Michizane appears as the god of thunder and lightning, Raiden, in the form of an *oni* in *Illustrated Legends of the Kitano Shrine* (*Kitano tenjin engi emaki*, thirteenth century) and the noh play *Raiden* (c. late fourteenth century). Other *oni* were possibly once unruly gods that resisted subjugation through worship. Scholars have also associated *oni* with mountain people, **giants**, and, because some are beneficent, auspicious visitors (*marebito*). Because of the blending of concepts, however, it is usually impossible to trace a given creature to a single origin.

Oni in Nara period (710–794) texts have a corporeal presence. In *Topography of the Land of Hitachi* (c. 713), *oni* called *chimi* in the village of Koko gaze at their reflections in the smooth surface of a mirror-like rock, but become extinct because mirrors ward off evil. An *oni* watching the funeral of Empress

Saimei in *The Chronicles of Japan* (720) wears a large hat. People from remote or foreign places, such as the seafaring Mishihase, are called *oni*. The association of "others," such as enemies and colonized people, with *oni* persists throughout history, notably in revisions of the folktale about Momotarō, a boy demon-queller found inside a giant peach, from the late nineteenth century through World War II.

In the Heian period, *oni* developed together with concepts of *mononoke*, invisible malevolent spirits causing illness, death, natural disasters, and strange phenomena. *Mononoke* include vengeful spirits of the dead (*onryō* or *goryō* when worshipped) and spirits of living people (*ikiryō*) who leave the body to possess and kill others. Many *oni* are *onryō*. In *Nihon ryōiki*, an *oni* who murders acolytes at Gangō Temple is the spirit of a wicked slave (1:3). Elsewhere, a lustful holy man wills himself to die and become an *oni*. The creature charms Empress Somedono into sex and performs in front of the emperor and imperial court, thereby undermining them (*Konjaku*, 20:7). *Oni* are often employed in narratives that challenge authority, as is also evident in episode six of *The Tales of Ise* (c. 905) and a related *setsuwa* (*Konjaku*, 27:7), when Ariwara no Narihira defiantly abducts a woman of the dominant family, the Fujiwara, only to have an *oni* consume her. (In history, she becomes an imperial consort.)

The Lady of the Bridge at Uji, Hashihime, is in poetry and legend a lonely woman longing for her lover, but was later re-imagined as an *oni*. A vengeful noblewoman spurned by her husband transforms into an *oni* in *Kankyo no tomo* (*A Companion in Solitude*, c. 1222, tale 2:3), *The Tale of the Heike* (mid thirteenth century), and the noh play *The Iron Crown* (*Kanawa*, late fourteenth/early fifteenth century). While considered a prototype of the *Heike* Hashihime story, the tale of the *oni* at Agi Bridge (*Konjaku*, 27:13) does not ascribe any motives to the *oni*. The protagonist of the short story "One Day in Spring" (1906) by Izumi Kyōka imagines himself as the horseman who encounters the *oni* impersonating a forlorn woman at the bridge. The noh and kabuki plays *Rashōmon* (fifteenth century) and *Modori-bashi* (*The Modori Bridge*, late nineteenth century) are based on the *Heike* Hashihime story, in which the warrior Watanabe no Tsuna severs the arm of the *oni*. However, the *oni* is Ibaraki Dōji, a retainer of Shuten Dōji.

Mononoke or *oni* sometimes possess objects (*Konjaku*, 27:18 and 19; see **Objects, Animate**). More often, objects transform into monstrous forms. In the illustrated *Tsukumogami-ki* (*Record of Tool Specters*, c. late fifteenth century), tools, containers, and instruments, resentful at having been discarded after serving people for nearly a century, transform themselves into vengeful beings, but are later converted to Buddhism. Processions and banquets of *oni* occur in *setsuwa*. *Hyakki yagyō* or *yakō emaki* (*Illustrated Handscrolls of the Night Procession of One Hundred Demons*, Muromachi period and later) depict various creatures in the festive march.

Associations of the aged with the demonic can be found elsewhere in Japanese culture as well. The old mountain crone or demonic hag can nurture or devour people. Called Yamauba, Yamanba or Onibaba, she emerges in many places, beginning with *setsuwa* (*Konjaku* 27:15), but most memorably in the noh masterpiece *Yamamba* (fifteenth century) in which she embodies the Buddhist truth of non-dualism. A simpler demonic old woman appears in another play, *Kurozuka* (*Black Tomb*), also called Adachigahara (*The Adachi Moor*, fifteenth century). Yamauba can be young and beautiful. In the late seventeenth century, she is recast as the sensual mother of the superhuman child Kintarō in *bunraku*, *kabuki*, and *ukiyo-e* (woodblock prints). The short stories "The Holy Man of Mt Kōya" by Izumi Kyōka (1900) and "The Smile of the Witch" by Ōba Minako, as well as *Onibaba* (1964) directed by Shindō Kaneto, exemplify modern works involving her.

In the Edo period (1603–1867), *oni* were often tamed through humor and science. Some, including those in "The Kibitsu Cauldron" and "The Blue Hood" by Ueda Akinari (*Tales of Moonlight and Rain*, 1776), retain their fearsomeness. In modern fiction, *oni* sometimes refers to evil people such as Takegorō in *Kotō no oni* (*Demon of a Solitary Island*, 1929–30) by Edogawa Ranpo. Tanizaki Ichirō, Oda Sasunosuke, and Enchi Fumiko, among others, have treated *oni* as part of the human psyche. However, the connection between human emotion and *oni* is made in *The Tale of Genji* (c. 1011) and Heian poetry, for example, in the phrase "kokoro no oni" (demon of the heart). Writers such as Nakagami Kenji and Yumemakura Baku reflect a modern sensibility in emphasizing the suffering of *oni*. Yet, before leaping into flames, the *oni* in the previously mentioned *Kankyo no tomo* tale about a spurned woman addresses an angry mob, describing her pain and expressing the desire that her spirit be assisted through ritual.

Michelle Osterfeld Li

References and Suggested Reading

Kawashima, Terry. *Writing Margins: The Textual Construction of Gender in Heian and Kamakura Japan*. Cambridge, MA: Harvard University Asia Center, 2001.

Kimbrough, R. Keller, trans. "The Demon Shuten Dōji." In *Traditional Japanese Literature: An Anthology, Beginnings to 1600*, edited by Haruo Shirane, 1123–38. New York: Columbia University Press, 2007.

Li, Michelle Osterfeld. *Ambiguous Bodies: Reading the Grotesque in Japanese Setsuwa Tales*. Stanford: Stanford University Press, 2009.

——. "Human of the Heart: Pitiful Oni in Medieval Japan." In *The Ashgate Research Companion to Monsters and the Monstrous*, edited by Asa Simon Mittman with Peter Dendle, 173–96. London: Ashgate Publishing, 2012.

Moerman, D. Max, "Demonology and Eroticism: Islands of Women in the Japanese Buddhist Imagination." *Japanese Journal of Religious Studies* 36, no. 2 (2009): 351–80.

Reider, Noriko T. *Japanese Demon Lore: Oni, from Ancient Times to the Present*. Logan, Utah: Utah State University Press, 2010.

Watson, Burton, trans. and Haruo Shirane, ed. *The Demon at Agi Bridge and Other Japanese Tales*. New York: Columbia University Press, 2011.

ONIBABA—*see* Demon

ONOSKELIS—*see* Empousa

ORC—*see* Goblin, Tolkien, Monsters In

OUROBOURUS—*see* Cockatrice

PADFOOT—*see* Brownie

PAN

Pan is the Greek god of shepherds and their flocks, a horned, goat-legged wanderer of woodland thickets and cliffs, and a companion to the nymphs; depictions of Pan tend to be cognate with those of **satyrs**, **fauns**, and the **Devil**. Mythical reckonings of his geniture vary, with several classical sources assigning him different Arcadian mothers, but most accounts agree that he is descended from Hermes, the cunning messenger of the gods. According to *The Homeric Hymns* (anonymous, c. seventh century BCE), Pan was "from birth monstrous to behold" as a result of his caprine features (62); nevertheless he delighted the Olympians, and Dionysus, the god of wine and revelry, found him especially pleasing. As is the case with many Greek deities, Pan may be best remembered for his amorous escapades, especially his pursuit of the nymphs Echo, Pitys, and Syrinx. From Syrinx, who pleaded to be transformed into marsh reeds in order to defend her chastity against his advances, Pan devised the pipes customarily associated with him.

Myriad variations on the figure of Pan appear prior to the nineteenth century, most of which situate him in pastoral contexts. Some, however, explore the tension between his human and animal halves, especially in light of conflicting Christian and pagan imperatives. In these treatments Pan takes on several monstrous qualities: a capacity to inspire terror, an unchecked lustfulness, and an undomesticated bestiality. In her seminal study *Pan the Goat-God* (1969), Patricia Merivale suggests that John Milton's works summarize these precedent approaches to the deity and express the full range of Pan's figurative potential at the end of the early modern era. Milton's Pan (in *Paradise Lost* [1667], "On the Morning of Christ's Nativity" [1645], and other verse) is at times a sylvan, generative, benevolent god, yet he can also be beastly, disruptive, and devilish. Discussion of Pan as a literary monster tends to arise from this duality.

Writers in the eighteenth century elaborated on classical themes, but in some of their comedic works Pan occurs as a caricature of untutored rusticity. The Romantics, in contrast, emphasized the positive prospects inherent in the notion of the god. In the poetry of William Wordsworth (1770–1850), John Keats (1795–1821), and Percy Bysshe Shelley (1792–1822), Pan appears as a source of inspiration and revelation, as an energy that permeates nature. When Keats invokes Pan in "Endymion" (1818), for example, the god occurs as the "Dread opener of the mysterious doors / Leading to universal knowledge" and "a symbol of immensity" (288–9, 299). Intimations of his animalistic aspect tend to be eclipsed by reflections on an energetic, enigmatic potential. The Victorians in turn focused on Pan's physicality, and in their hands a coarser, more menacing vision of the god emerges. In the verse of Walter Savage Landor (1775–1864), Elizabeth Barrett Browning (1806–61), and Alfred, Lord Tennyson (1809–92), Pan—split into the creative deity and the lascivious satyr—vivifies and terrifies. Robert Browning would describe a similarly dualistic Pan, one who inspires awe and at times reminds the reader of the grosser claims of flesh. In his "Pan and Luna" (1880), a retelling of a story from Virgil, Browning's "half-god half-brute" schemes against the virtue of his victim (82), ultimately clutching the maiden moon against his bristled body.

According to Merivale, a fully sinister Pan emerges at last at the close of the Victorian era and the start of the twentieth century. Arthur Machen's short novel *The Great God Pan* (1894) acts as a bellwether for a shift in representational possibilities. While the figure of Pan had been recruited previously to elicit dread in a number of capacities, Machen's story involves the penetration of the secular sphere by the terrifying presence of the primeval deity. Rather than existing as a property of mythology or as an abstraction confined to the arena of ideas, this version of Pan intrudes on the everyday and overwhelms whoever he encounters. Subjected to a perceptual experiment by the coldly clinical Dr Raymond, a woman named Mary, the initial focus of the story, faces the deity himself; she is at first wonderstruck, then terrified, and the encounter destroys her mind. At the conclusion of the narrative the reader learns that Helen, a woman connected to several intervening episodes of carnality, madness, and suicide, is the child born of the union of Mary and the god. Helen's death involves an astonishing degeneration, a dissolution that a witness describes as a horrific conflation of the masculine and the feminine, the human and the bestial. In essence, Machen translates Pan's rapacity into a realistic context, converting the classical pattern into an act of fleshly trespass and appalling transformation.

Treatments of Pan in the modern era often emphasize the complexity of this dualistic dynamic, the tension between the natural and the unnatural, the spiritual and the secular, the generative and the malevolent—what Ronald Hutton calls "the shocking, menacing, and liberating aspects of the god's image" (46). In Aleister Crowley's "Hymn to Pan" (1913), for example, the speaker prays for Pan to ravish him, unconcerned whether the object of his incantation is diabolical or godly. In another elusive evocation, e.e. cummings depicts a "goat-footed / balloonMan" in his poem "in Just-" (1920). The figure whistles his way around children busily at play, yet the indefinite depiction could call to mind Pan, a satyr, or the Devil equally well; the cloven-hoofed visitor seems both frolicsome and ominous. Variations on this theme appear in the writing of authors as diverse as Algernon Blackwood (1869–1951), D.H. Lawrence (1885–1930), E.M. Forster (1879–1970), Saki (Hector Hugh Munro, 1870–1916), and Stephen King (1947–), a testament to the provocative combination of divinity and monstrosity associated with the woodland god.

William H. Wandless

References and Suggested Reading

The Homeric Hymns. Translated by Apostolos N. Athanassakis. Baltimore: The Johns Hopkins University Press, 1976.

Hutton, Ronald. *The Triumph of the Moon: A History of Modern Pagan Witchcraft*. Oxford: Oxford University Press, 1999.

Machen, Arthur. *The Great God Pan* [1890]. Reprint, Freeport, New York: Books for Libraries Press, 1970.

Merivale, Patricia. *Pan the Goat-God: His Myth in Modern Times*. Cambridge, MA: Harvard University Press, 1969.

PARASITE

In biology, parasitism is a type of symbiotic relationship in which one organism, the parasite, increases its own biological fitness at the expense of the host, whose fitness decreases, although in certain cases hosts may also benefit. In science fiction, fantasy, and horror, monstrous parasites—both physical and psychic—represent a much wider spectrum of exploitative relations. Given the ubiquity of the parasite in fiction and film, it is more productive to view this particular monster in terms of metaphoric clusters reflective of contemporary cultural moments. Parasites, therefore, will be addressed below in light of their relationships to their human hosts (both hostile and occasionally beneficial), as well as metaphorical embodiments of anxieties concerning human autonomy, carnality, and infection.

Science fiction texts in which parasites figure as elements of fantastic ecosystems, such as Stanley G. Weinbaum's "Parasite Planet" (1935), A.E. van Vogt's *The Voyage of the Space Beagle* (1950), or Brian Aldiss's "Poor Little Warrior" (1958), do not usually posit parasites as monsters *per se*. Rationally explained, they are at best positioned as painful reminders that size and high intelligence are not automatic prerequisites of humanity's biological primacy and survival. Somewhat less rigorously science fictional, George R.R. Martin's *A Song for Lya* (1974) features a race inhabiting the planet Shkeen who at some point in their lives willingly accept a parasitic animal and become wandering pilgrims in a drug-like state of bliss, only to be eventually devoured by much larger versions of the parasite.

As in nature, parasites are occasionally presented as advantageous for their hosts. For example, Hal Clement's debut novel *Needle* (1949) pits two intelligent alien parasites against each other in an insular community on Earth. One of the two is a criminal and the other is a policeman of sorts named the Hunter. The aliens inhabit the bodies of a father and his young son respectively. In the end, the boy and the Hunter manage to drive out the malign parasite from Mr Kinnaird's body and eliminate it. This reversal, as well as the happy ending, can be largely explained by the fact that *Needle* and its sequel *Through the Eye of the Needle* (1978) were marketed as children's science fiction and young adult fiction. This is not the case with Damon Knight's trilogy consisting of *CV* (1985), *The Observers* (1988), and *A Reasonable World* (1991), in which an alien **virus** infects humans, altering their personalities and making them incapable of violence. More ambiguously, Octavia Butler's "Blood Child" (1985) constructs the complexity of parasitical relations, both biological and social, between humans and the alien race of the Tlic as expressive of racial, gender, and family relations.

Parasitism has long been a metaphor for control. The title of Arthur Conan Doyle's *The Parasite* (1894) alludes to such a variety of telepathic vampirism exercised by a female character on young men. In Colin Wilson's *The Mind Parasites* (1967), the eponymous parasites are renegade fragments of the human unconscious draining people of energy and creativity. Psychic parasitism can also be found in Ramsey Campbell's *The Parasite* (1980), which, playing with occultism, ultimately posits the possessive spirits as manifestation of human evil, and *Dark City* (Alex Proyas, 1998), in which the race of hive-mind alien Strangers not only uses corpses as their hosts but also experiments on humans to discover the mystery of individuality.

The writer who literalized parasitic imagery the most extensively and systematically was William S. Burroughs, whose *Naked Lunch* (1959), *The Ticket that Exploded* (1962), and *Nova Express* (1964) show the human race at the mercy of alien parasites using media and drugs as their means of control. For Burroughs, most forms of control, exploitation, and enslavement are caused by literal (in his fiction) and mental (in both fiction and non-fiction) parasites—a belief most expressly articulated in *The Place of Dead Roads: A Novel* (1983): "evil is quite literally a virus parasite occupying a certain brain area" (155).

More physical parasitic controllers can be found in pulp fictions such as Harl Vincent's "Parasite" (1935), in which invading aliens attach themselves to humans and control their thoughts, but the motif emerged as particularly resonant in the Cold War era. Invisible and yet leeching on vital powers, parasites became perfect expressions of the period's paranoia and suspicion of hidden agendas of otherwise normal-looking individuals. Robert A. Heinlein's *The Puppet Masters* (1951), as well as its 1994 film adaptation, are exemplars, in which alien parasites take over the neural system and turn humans into dummies. Variations of this motif can be found in many films such as *Invaders from Mars* (William Cameron Menzies, 1953), *The Brain Eaters* (Bruno VeSota, 1958), *Star Trek II: The Wrath of Khan* (Nicholas Meyer, 1982),

The Hidden (Jack Sholder, 1987), and *Dark Breed* (Richard Pepin, 1996). In more recent films, including *Alien Raiders* (Ben Rock, 2008) or *Splinter* (Toby Wilkins, 2008), possessing alien parasites tend to transform the body, turning their hosts into bloodthirsty predators. Although technically not featuring a commensal relationship between the parasite and the host, a significant group of "body-snatching" narratives, including Jack Finney's *The Body Snatchers* (1955) and its four filmic adaptations, *The Thing* (John Carpenter, 1982), and *The Astronaut's Wife* (Rand Ravich, 1999), can also be read as representing extreme forms of exploitation of the human. Like **vampires** and **zombies**, somatic and mental parasites become visible emblems of alienation and the loss of self, arguably some of the crucial themes in the literatures of the fantastic.

Truly monstrous parasites are central to body horror, the convention whose parameters are well exemplified by David Cronenberg's *Shivers* (1975), in which a strain of parasites, artificially developed by a researcher believing that humanity needs to reconnect with carnality, induce uncontrollable sexual desire in hosts. Cronenberg's parasites proved to be so repulsive and their ingress—either oral or vaginal—so nauseating that the film provoked a public debate concerning its harmful influence. The film's parasites function as uneasy reminders of the physiology of sexuality writ monstrous, but also visibly emblematize modern horror's reliance on the abject themes and motifs. In retrospect, *Shivers* was indeed one of the first in a long line of international horror films that use the parasitic motif to showcase increasingly disgusting and gory scenes of violence, such as *Parasite* (Charles Band, 1982), *Parasite Eve* (Masayuki Ochiai, 1997), *Sexual Parasite: Killer Pussy* (Takao Nakano, 2004), and *Slither* (James Gunn, 2006). The body horror imaginary has been most famously deployed in the *Alien* series: *Alien* (Ridley Scott, 1979), *Aliens* (James Cameron, 1986), *Alien³* (David Fincher, 1992), and *Alien: Resurrection* (Jean-Pierre Jeunet, 1997). While the parasitic stage is only one of the forms of the titular entity, its spectacular chest- or stomach-bursting transition to a fully developed form has become universally recognizable.

In the last two decades parasitic metaphors have become increasingly co-opted by infection narratives that often blur the boundaries between parasites, microbes, and viruses. A clear counterbalance to the gory excesses of body horror productions, infection novels, and films reflects both the increasing importance of such disciplines as genetic engineering, biochemistry, and virology and the growing social anxieties regarding micro rather than macro threats. These concerns inform a number of episodes of *The X-Files*—"Ice" (1994), "The Host" (1995), "Firewalker" (1995), "F. Emasculata" (1995), and "Roadrunners" (2000)—all of which revolve around various parasitic entities. More recently, bridging body horror and somewhat more disciplined science fictional storytelling, *Growth* (Gabriel Cowan, 2010) exploits cultural disgust with slug-like parasites while delivering the parable of the dangers of unsupervised scientific research. On the other hand, *The Thaw* (Mark A. Lewis, 2009) dispenses entirely with gory theatrics, concentrating on the parasitic/viral threat brought about by global warming—a prehistoric parasite released from the carcass of a woolly mammoth. The film's ambiguous conclusion contributes to the sense of terror—albeit of an entirely different order from that found in Cronenberg and his followers.

While parasites have featured in both literary and cinematic narratives, it is not a coincidence that moving image texts constitute the majority of the examples above. Culturally constructed as distasteful and disgusting, the negative visual appeal of parasites, particularly those suggestive of worms or larvae and characterized by mucosity, is best conveyed visually and most effectively in film or television, which additionally extend the space of disgust to aural effects.

Paweł Frelik

References and Suggested Reading

Burroughs, William S. *The Place of Dead Roads: A Novel*. New York: Picador, 1983.

Glassy, Mark C. *The Biology of Science Fiction Cinema*. Jefferson, NC: McFarland & Co, 2001.

Parker, Helen N. *Biological Themes in Modern Science Fiction*. Ann Arbor: UMI Research Press, 1984.

Sinclair, Alison. "Parasites." In *The Greenwood Encyclopedia of Science Fiction and Fantasy: Themes, Works, and Wonders*, edited by Gary Westfahl, 586–8. Westport, CT: Greenwood, 2005.

Stableford, Brian. "Parasitism and Symbiosis." In *The Encyclopedia of Science Fiction*, edited by John Clute, David Langford, Peter Nicholls, and Graham Sleight, 2011. <http://www.sf-encyclopedia.com/entry/parasitism_and_symbiosis>.

PARI—*see* Div; Djinn and Genie

PAZUZU—*see* Demon; Devil, The

PEGASUS

Pegasus, a divine, winged horse from Greek mythology, appears in several legends, most notably those of the hero Bellerophon. The myths record that Pegasus was born either from **Medusa**'s neck when the hero Perseus beheaded the **Gorgon**, or from drops of Medusa's blood that fertilized the Earth when she was killed (Grimal 349). Pegasus, whose name may derive from the Greek word for "fountain" or "spring" (*pêgê*), was connected with several famous springs throughout Greece, particularly those sacred to the Muses. Thus, poets have frequently drawn upon the Hippocrene ("horse-fountain," a fountain sacred to the Muses on Mt Helicon in Greece, presumed to have been formed by the hooves of Pegasus) and Pegasus for inspiration. Another tradition describes an entire race of winged horses (as in Plato's fifth-century BCE dialogue, *Critias* 116e) but does not relate them to Pegasus.

The poet Hesiod writes in his *Theogony* (c. 700 BCE) that after Pegasus's birth, the horse flew to Olympus to bring thunder and lightning to Zeus (284–6). Subsequently, Pegasus met Bellerophon, and the myths vary on the specifics of the encounter. The late eighth-century or early seventh-century BCE *Catalogue of Women*, frequently attributed to Hesiod, states that Bellerophon's father Poseidon gave him Pegasus as a gift (fragment 7), while the sixth-century BCE poet Pindar says that Bellerophon subdued the horse at the spring of Peirene with a golden bridle he received from the goddess Athena (*Olympian* 13.65–73). The second-century CE travel writer Pausanias suggests in his *Description of Greece* that Athena bridled Pegasus for the hero (2.4.1). But Strabo, a first-century BCE geographer, records simply in his *Geographica* that Bellerophon, unaided, caught Pegasus while the horse was drinking at Peirene (8.6.21).

Sources agree that Bellerophon and Pegasus then traveled to the court of King Proetus of Tiryns, where his wife Stheneboea attempted to seduce the young man. When he rejected her advances, she accused him of rape. Therefore, Proetus asked his father-in-law Iobates, king of Lycia, to kill Bellerophon. Assuming Bellerophon would die in the attempt, Iobates sent him to slay the monstrous **Chimera**. Riding on Pegasus, Bellerophon killed the Chimera either with a sword, with arrows, or by breaking off the lead point from his spear in the Chimera's mouth; the lead then melted in the monster's fiery breath, suffocating it (Grimal 75, 100). Afterwards, Iobates sent Bellerophon against an obscure tribe, the Solymoi, and the Amazons, a race of female warriors, whom he conquered with the assistance of Pegasus (Pindar, *Olympian* 13.87–90). Having convinced Iobates of his merits, Bellerophon obtained Iobates's daughter in marriage and inherited his kingdom (see Pseudo-Apollodorus's first-century CE *Bibliotheca*, 2.3.2). According to Euripides's fragmentary play *Stheneboea* (fifth century BCE), Bellerophon and Pegasus later returned to deal with the treacherous queen, and after luring her atop Pegasus with him, Bellerophon pushed her to her death.

The hero's last exploit was a misguided attempt to fly Pegasus to Mt Olympus. The Greek comic playwright Aristophanes parodied this deed when the protagonist in his *Peace* (421 BCE) rides a dung beetle instead of Pegasus up to Mt Olympus. Various ancient authors describe how, for his hubristic act, Pegasus threw Bellerophon down to the Earth either voluntarily or because Zeus sent a gadfly to sting the horse. Bellerophon survived due to his divine blood, though he ended up a cripple. Upon leaving Bellerophon, Pegasus returned to the heavens. According to the myths, a singing contest between the daughters of Pierus and the Muses' singing had caused Mt Helicon to swell with joy; because Helicon was about to reach the heavens, Poseidon ordered Pegasus to strike the mountain with his hoof to reduce it to its normal size. The mountain receded, but the Hippocrene fountain gushed forth where Pegasus's hoof had struck. Pindar says that after this, Pegasus brought thunder to Zeus (*Olympian* 17.92). Ultimately Zeus honored Pegasus by placing him in the sky as a constellation (see the *Astronomica* attributed to the first-century BCE Hyginus, 2.18).

Pegasus, like many mythological monsters, became a subject for the rationalists and allegorists. Palaephatus, a fourth-century BCE mythographer, thought Bellerophon was an actual person who had traveled to Lycia on a speedy ship named *Pegasus* (*Peri Apiston* 28). According to Plutarch (first century CE), Bellerophon sailed a ship named *Pegasus* and defeated a pirate named Chimarros who had a ship with a lion on the prow, a goat on the sail, and a snake on the stern, making it a sort of Chimera (*Moralia* 247F–248D). In *On Astrology*, Lucian, a second-century CE satirist, explained Bellerophon as an astronomer who reached the heavens with his intellect rather than his volatile horse (section 13). Claudian, a Roman court poet in 398 CE, appropriated the symbol of Pegasus to honor the Roman emperor Honorius (384–423), having him, rather than Bellerophon, ride the divine steed (*On the Fourth Consulship of Emperor Honorius* 558).

Parallelism between the exploits of the heroes Perseus and Bellerophon led to a gradual conflation of their myths that culminated during the medieval period: Perseus, rather than Bellerophon, was now the tamer of Pegasus and slayer of the Chimera. Perseus was already associated with Pegasus because he had slain Medusa, thereby causing the birth of the horse. Ogden (60–62) notes that both heroes conquer monsters with characteristics of snakes—Bellerophon kills the Chimera, and Perseus kills not only Medusa but also Ceto, a snake-like **sea monster**—and that Perseus had slain Ceto while flying on winged sandals, parallel to Bellerophon flying on Pegasus. The two heroes eventually became so conflated that, according to the First Vatican Mythographer (c. ninth to eleventh centuries CE), Perseus was also known as Bellerophon and was sent against both the Chimera and Medusa. In his encyclopedic *On the Genealogy of the Gods of the Gentiles* (1360–74 CE),

Boccaccio states that Perseus rode Pegasus. This became common knowledge in the Renaissance and consequently Bellerophon became a side note, if not forgotten entirely. Thus, when Shakespeare mentions Pegasus in 1623's *Troilus and Cressida* (I.iii.42), it is as Perseus's horse. In Pierre Corneille's play *Andromède* (1650), Perseus rescues Andromeda on Pegasus (portrayed on stage with a live horse lofted into the air by a custom harness). The episode was depicted frequently in Renaissance art, exemplified by Peter Paul Rubens's paintings *Perseus and Andromeda* (1621) and *Perseus Liberating Andromeda* (1622). Pegasus became increasingly less identified with Bellerophon solely, and more of a helper figure for heroes in general.

The symbolism of the white winged horse has lent itself to interpretations of peacefulness and serenity in the modern period. For Picasso, Pegasus was a representation of man's innocence and peaceful existence in his "War and Peace" panels (1952). This interpretation also prevailed in *The Pastoral Symphony* segment of Disney's *Fantasia* (1940), which features fabulous creatures from Greek mythology including a variety of multi-colored Pegasi. A number of other children's media showcase Pegasus as a symbol of innocence, such as Greg Richardson's film *Barbie and the Magic of Pegasus* (2005).

Other films present Pegasus as an aid to heroes; interestingly, Bellerophon is absent entirely. In Desmond Davis's 1981 film *Clash of the Titans* and its 2010 reworking by Louis Leterrier, both loosely based on Greek mythology, Pegasus helps Perseus in his adventures. Pegasus has appeared as an assistant to Heracles as well, mainly in Disney's 1997 animated film *Hercules* (John Musker). In this movie, Zeus describes Pegasus as "a magnificent horse with the brain of a bird," and Frank Welker, the voice actor playing Pegasus, highlights the duality of horse and bird with a combination of whinnies and chirps, producing an effect of comic relief.

From antiquity, the horse has been an inspiration for poets; modern literature is no different. Henry Wadsworth Longfellow's poem "Pegasus in Pound" (1850) allegorizes his distaste for materialism by describing how some schoolboys—rather than being awed by the amazing golden-maned horse (and the arts that the creature represented)—capture Pegasus on the village common and put him up for sale. The horse is gawked at but neglected, and finally, as he bursts forth from his chains and soars away, his hoof creates a fountain in the Earth to gladden the region. Longfellow thus indicates that appreciation of the arts strengthens society. Rick Riordan's series *Percy Jackson & the Olympians* (2005–2009) features a number of Pegasi, especially Blackjack who often provides crucial transport for Percy (short for Perseus). Pegasi guide a carriage of Beauxbatons students to the Triwizard Tournament in J.K. Rowling's *Harry Potter and the Goblet of Fire* (2000) and in the 2005 film version (Mike Newell).

As a winged creature, Pegasus symbolized soaring through the skies; consequently *USS Pegasus* is the name of a starship on *Star Trek: The Next Generation* (1987–94), as well as of a spacecraft in the 1978 television series *Battlestar Galactica* and its 2004 re-imagining. A Turkish aircraft fleet is called Pegasus Airlines. The sublime vision of Pegasus is one of the most vivid in our imaginations today.

Craig Jendza

References and Suggested Reading

Baldwin, T.W. "Perseus Purloins Pegasus." *Philological Quarterly* 20 (1941): 361–70.

Gantz, Timothy. *Early Greek Myth: A Guide to Literary and Artistic Sources*. Baltimore: The Johns Hopkins University Press, 1993.

Grimal, Pierre. *The Dictionary of Classical Mythology*. New York: Blackwell, 1986.
Ogden, Daniel. *Perseus*. New York: Routledge, 2008.
Yalouris, Nikolas. *Pegasus: The Art of the Legend*. London: Westerham Press, 1977.

PENANGGALAN—*see* Body Parts

PHANTOM OF THE OPERA, THE

The Phantom of the Opera refers to the central character in *Le Fantôme de l'Opéra*, a novel by French writer Gaston Leroux, first serialized in a French newspaper (*Le Gaulois*) from 23 September 1909 to 8 January 1910. This mysterious individual, living in the depths of the Opera House in Paris, is consumed by bitterness and passion. It is easy to categorize him as a monster because of his scarred face, dark temper, and dwelling, but the hideousness of his face is counterpoised by his talent and refinement. He is thus a freakish but ambiguous creature, exerting magnetic power over the reader and the other protagonists of the story.

The book starts with a preface in which the narrator (Gaston Leroux himself), 30 years after the events, describes his research about the Phantom of the Opera. The story proper begins with the retirement of the former directors of the Paris Opera House. At the retirement party, Christine Daaé, a chorus girl, replaces the Prima Donna (also called la Carlotta) who has strangely fallen ill at the last minute. She makes a dazzling performance and draws everybody's attention. The Viscount Raoul de Chagny, whom she had already met before, falls in love with her. Christine has reached heights of mastery in the art of singing because she has actually been trained and taught by a strange voice that speaks and sings to her in the Opera. This magnetic and unearthly voice belongs to Erik, the Phantom of the Opera, but she first believes she has met what her deceased father called the Angel of Music:

> *The voice without a body went on singing; and certainly Raoul had never in his life heard anything more absolutely and heroically sweet, more gloriously insidious, more delicate, more powerful, in short, more irresistibly triumphant. He listened to it in a fever and he now began to understand how Christine Daaé was able to appear one evening, before the stupefied audience, with accents of a beauty hitherto unknown, of a superhuman exaltation, while doubtless still under the influence of the mysterious and invisible master.* (190)

The new directors of the Opera House are warned about the existence of the phantom and his demands: 20,000 francs and a permanent reservation of Box 5, which must be available for him at all times. They mistake this for a joke and fail to respect the requirements. As a result, the lead singer la Carlotta loses her voice, and the chandelier crashes into the audience, killing one woman and injuring several people. Erik then kidnaps Christine, with whom he is madly in love. She eventually comes back from the depths of the Opera where he has kept her prisoner, hoping she will eventually love him in return. She is scared but also fascinated. As she later tells her beloved Raoul, she feels both repulsion and pity for Erik.

The Phantom of the Opera can be both delicate and violent. He continuously hides from the whole world because of a hideous face whose horrific description calls to mind characters like Robert Louis Stevenson's Mr **Hyde** in *The Strange Case of Dr Jekyll and Mr Hyde* (1886) or the portrait of the depraved **Dorian Gray** in Oscar Wilde's *The Picture of Dorian Gray* (1890). When the songstress pulls away his mask and discovers the face behind it, he is all rage and pain, and the young woman is petrified with terror: "Yes, if I lived to be a hundred, I should always hear the superhuman cry of grief and rage which he uttered when the terrible sight appeared before my eyes" (253).

Erik eventually releases Christine, on her promise to be faithful to him. After hearing Christine's confession to Raoul, he abducts her again. He wants to marry her and threatens to kill everyone in the Opera with explosives. Out of despair, she wants to die. Raoul and "le Persan" (the Persian, an old acquaintance of the phantom) try to rescue her and are locked in the Phantom's so-called Chamber of Tortures, a room whose walls are covered with mirrors in order to create the illusion of being trapped. The replication of the image of trees, together with a heated environment, is meant to convince the prisoners that they are lost in a deep African forest, thus driving them mad. The only possible way to save them is for Christine to agree to be Erik's "femme vivante" (living bride), whereupon the phantom rescues both men just in time. He is totally shattered because, for the first time in his whole life, a woman has allowed him to kiss her. As he confesses later, even his mother refused physical contact with him. Because the songstress cries and feels pity for him, and because she gives him a kiss too, he sets her free again and allows her to leave with the man she loves.

Suffering from physical deformity, Erik was born disfigured but he is gifted with intelligence, talent, and creativity. (Many cinematic adaptations present him as disfigured as the result of having acid thrown on his face.) His most earnest wish is to be like everybody else but he is unfortunately doomed and thus decides to hide in the eerie depths of the Paris Opera House, where he has created a magical dwelling: a lake and a home for himself in which he can shun humanity. The cellars will be his grave too, as Christine has agreed to come back and bury him after his death. The book concludes by insisting on how unlucky and unhappy the Phantom of the Opera was. According to Leroux, one has to feel more pity than disgust for him:

> *Poor, unhappy Erik! Shall we pity him? Shall we curse him? He asked only to be "someone," like everybody else. But he was too ugly! And he had to hide his genius OR USE IT TO PLAY TRICKS WITH, when, with an ordinary face, he would have been one of the most distinguished of mankind! He had a heart that could have held the empire of the world; and, in the end, he had to content himself with a cellar. Ah, yes, we must needs pity the Opera ghost.* (497–8)

The novel has inspired many cinematographic adaptations, including: the eponymous 1925 silent version directed by Rupert Julian and starring Lon Chaney; the 1949 version directed by Arthur Lubin and staring Nelson Eddy, Susanna Foster, and Claude Rains; the Hammer Film Productions version in 1962 directed by Terence Fisher; and the gory 1989 version directed by Dwight H. Little. The story of the Phantom has also been adapted for the stage, including musicals such as the loose musical film adaptation by Brian de Palma, *Phantom of the Paradise* (1974), and notably the record-breaking musical, *The Phantom of the Opera*, by Andrew Lloyd Webber (1986). The latter was in turn adapted into a film by Joel Schumacher in 2004.

In 1990, Susan Kay wrote a book, *Phantom*, based on Gaston Leroux's work. Erik's life is imagined here from early childhood to his installation in the Paris Opera House and through to his meeting with Christine Daaé, with whom he conceives a child. Terry Pratchett had fun making a parody of *The Phantom of the Opera*, called *Maskerade* (1995). Children's books have been based on the novel (*Phantom of the Auditorium* by R.L. Stine [1995]), as have comics and even manga (*The Opera House Murders*, story by Yozaburo Kanari and art by Fumiya Sato in "The Kindaichi Case Files" series, 2003).

The character of Erik is an intricate maelstrom of contradictions: ghostly life and appearance, yet a creature of flesh and bones; pain and violence endured and inflicted; romantic impulses and criminal behaviors. This characterizing tension, together with the aesthetic of his mask and his subterranean dwelling, have inspired and enthralled many. The secrecy and mystery of this personality, mixed with his inescapable fate, his crushed dreams, and the unbearable ugliness of his face, make him an ambiguous and alluring monster, now deeply rooted in popular culture.

Valérie Charbonniaud-Doussaud

References and Suggested Reading

Hall, Ann C. *Phantom Variations: The Adaptations of Gaston Leroux's* Phantom of the Opera, *1925 to the Present*. Jefferson, NC: McFarland & Co Inc., 2009.

Hogle, Jerold E. *The Undergrounds of the Phantom of the Opera: Sublimation and the Gothic in Leroux's Novel and Its Progeny*. New York: Palgrave, 2002.

Hopkins, Vicki. *Lessons from "The Phantom of the Opera."* Bloomington, IN: Xlibris Corporation, 2009.

Leroux, Gaston. *Le Fantôme de l'Opéra. Le Gaulois* [1909–10]. Reprint, Paris: Le Livre de Poche, 1959.

PHOENIX

A sacred firebird whose multivalent origins can be traced separately to the ancient mythologies of the Egyptians, Persians, Chinese, Romans, and Greeks, the phoenix is most often depicted as a majestic avian fire spirit with red and gold plumage. In many traditions, the phoenix possesses tremendous longevity, living for 500 to 1,000 years. At the end of its life, the phoenix of Western and Middle Eastern traditions constructs a nest of sticks and branches that catches fire and incinerates the bird. From the ashes, a new, young phoenix rises, ready to begin its life cycle again. Thus, the phoenix is often considered a symbol of resurrection and immortality.

In Egypt, the phoenix is known as the Bennu, a heron-like reincarnation of the Sun god Ra. In the *Book of the Dead*, the Bennu says, "I am the Bennu, Soul of Ra, Guide of the Gods ..." (23). In Greek mythology, however, the phoenix is more aquiline. In his *Histories* (fifth century BCE), Herodotus writes, "I have not seen it myself, except in a picture. Part of his plumage is gold-colored, and part crimson; and he is for the most part very much like an eagle in outline and bulk" (Bulfinch 383). Thus, phoenix can be translated as "crimson" in Greek. A benevolent creature subsisting on dew alone, its hauntingly beautiful song prompted Sun god Apollo to pause to listen along his celestial career. Similarly, in Arabian lore, the phoenix made its home near a well or oasis, from which it emerged every morning to sing.

The firebird of Russian lore is a more nebulous presence, at once a blessing and a curse to its captor. Widely portrayed in Russian fairy-tales, the firebird, with its long tail and glowing feathers, has long been a source of wonder. In one common version, Young Prince Ivan first plucks a feather from the firebird's tail during the magnificent avian's nightly raid on the Tsar's tree of golden apples; then, with the help of a sagacious gray wolf, he captures the firebird. Inspired by the mythical creature,

Igor Stravinsky composed a ballet named *The Firebird* in 1910.

An avian composite featuring aspects of the golden pheasant, the rooster, the swallow, the crane, the parrot, and the peacock—with a serpentine neck and an ichthyic tail—the scintillating Chinese *fenghuang* (Japanese ho-o), the mythological emperor among birds, is generally rendered as "phoenix." Perhaps bearing closer kinship to the Persian simurgh (see **Birds, Giant**), the East Asian phoenix may be a bird of a different feather than its Western and Middle Eastern cousins. Both an auspicious symbol and a token of power, this phoenix, with its flute-like melodious voice, was associated with harmony and harmonious rule. In one of the earliest texts of antiquity, *The Book of Documents*, a passage ends: "when pipes and the ritual bells are used in timely fashion, birds and beasts come rapidly; when the flute harmonizes the nine achievements, the phoenix comes and regulates" (5.127). A symbol of harmonious order, the phoenix was a regulator. When ceremonial specialists in early China learned to use ritual instruments to harmonize men and spirits, the technique was called "regulation of the phoenix."

Like the emperor among men, as avian sovereign the phoenix set a pattern for other avians to follow. Thus, in Chinese lore, the numinous phoenix is often followed by hundreds of thousands of flocking sparrows, lesser birds magnetized by its splendor and grace. In the late Tang dynasty (618–907), poet-official Li Ao, in his "Discourse on Recognizing a Phoenix," remarked on the sublime silence of the avian sovereign, dark blue in color and shaped like a magpie or turtle-dove, moving among other birds "like a sage amidst other men" (Spring 139), its incomparable regal comportment naturally drawing the fealty of more ordinary birds.

The male phoenix in the Chinese tradition is called the *feng*. The female phoenix is called *huang*. Combined, *feng* and *huang* can intimate connubial harmony. At some juncture in early imperial China, however, this initial distinction became blurred. *Fenghuang* or *fengniao* became a female imperial symbol to complement the male dragon. With this inbuilt imperial element, the phoenix was well suited as a symbol of female imperial power. During the reign of Wu Zhao (690–705 CE), China's first and only female ruler, the phoenix appeared frequently in titles, architecture, and as an auspicious omen. Finally, the East Asian phoenix is identified with the Vermilion Bird, an apotropaic creature complementing other guardians of the cardinal directions like the White Tiger of the West and the Azure Dragon of the East.

The phoenix plays a colorful, recurring role in Western literature. It appears in *The Annals* of Tacitus (c. 117 CE) and Ovid's *Metamorphoses* (8 CE). The *Aberdeen Bestiary*, a twelfth-century English compendium, draws an allegorical parallel between the phoenix and Jesus, stating: "Our Lord Jesus Christ displays the features of this bird ... the phoenix can also signify the resurrection of the righteous who, gathering the aromatic plants of virtue, prepare for the renewal of their former energy after death ... Faith in the resurrection to come is no more of a miracle than the resurrection of the phoenix from its ashes" (*Aberdeen Bestiary Project*, Folio 55v).

Shakespeare alludes to the phoenix in several works. In *Timon of Athens* (1623), the eponymous hero is referred to as "a naked gull which now flashes a phoenix" (*Timon* ii. 1). The firebird also appears in *The Tempest* (1623) and in one of his lesser known poems, "The Phoenix and the Turtle" (1601). In the iconic Spanish novel *Don Quixote* (vol. 2, 1615), Cervantes writes, "The phoenix hope, can wing her way through the desert skies, and still defying fortune's spite; revive from ashes and rise" (vol. 2, 285). During the Enlightenment,

French philosopher Voltaire provided a detailed description of the phoenix in his *The Princess of Babylon* (1768). In the classic Chinese novel of the eighteenth century, *Dream of Red Mansions* (c. 1750), the flamboyant, cheeky and eminently capable Wang Xifeng, literally "Splendid Phoenix," is a central character and one of the Twelve Beauties of Jinling.

Over the past century, the phoenix has maintained a consistent presence in literature, from making magical cameos in C.S. Lewis's *The Magician's Nephew* (1955) and *The Last Battle* (1956), to symbolizing the cyclical nature of history in Ray Bradbury's famous social commentary, *Fahrenheit 451* (1953). Bradbury compared society's inevitable patterns to the phoenix's life cycle, writing: "[t]here was a silly damn bird called a phoenix back before Christ, every few hundred years he built a pyre and burnt himself up. He must have been first cousin to Man. But every time he burnt himself up he sprang out of the ashes, he got himself born all over again" (158). In Sylvia Plath's famous "Lady Lazarus" (1962), she connects failed suicide to resurrected Lazarus and the ascendant phoenix. The last lines of her poem read: "Out of the ash / I rise with my red hair / And I eat men like air." Indeed, in both classical and contemporary writing and speech, to "rise from the ashes [of the phoenix]" has come to mean making a miraculous comeback, overcoming an extreme setback or disaster to become something great.

In recent years, J.K. Rowling's immensely popular "Harry Potter" series features a phoenix named Fawkes (see **Harry Potter, Monsters In**). In Harry Potter's magical world, the pearly tears of the benevolent phoenix possess tremendous healing properties, while Fawkes's song encourages the true of heart and wards off evil. The seventh and final book of the series, *The Deathly Hallows* (2007), poses the riddle: "Which came first: The phoenix or the flame?" The correct answer is that it is "a circle that has no beginning."

The phoenix has also been portrayed in film. In Walt Disney's *Fantasia 2000* (segment directed by Paul and Gaëtan Brizzi), a phoenix rises in time to Stravinsky's *Firebird*. In both the 1965 and 2004 versions of *Flight of the Phoenix* (directed by Robert Aldrich and John Moore respectively), crews of a cargo plane downed in the Sahara desert miraculously salvage the wreckage and rebuild the plane. At the denouement, like the phoenix, the plane flies again, "reborn" from the twisted wreckage of the crash. Film adaptations of *The Chronicles of Narnia* and "Harry Potter" both draw upon the phoenix myth. In C.S. Lewis's *The Lion, the Witch and the Wardrobe* (Andrew Adamson, 2005), a phoenix swoops in during the final battle and creates a protective wall of fire against the army of the sinister White Witch. And in the film adaptation of *Harry Potter and the Chamber of Secrets* (Chris Columbus, 2002), Fawkes swoops in at a critical juncture, saving Harry and his friends from the venomous **basilisk**.

In recent decades, the phoenix has risen afresh in popular culture. In a *Star Trek* fan series, the first spacecraft made by humans capable of traveling faster than light is named *The Phoenix*, representative of hope for a rebirth of humanity at a time when Earth was recovering from the mass destruction of World War III. The French-based alternative rock group Phoenix won a Grammy in 2009. In China, the Hong Kong-based Phoenix network is a powerful media conglomerate. A Korean TV drama *Phoenix* (2004), about star-crossed lovers from opposites sides of the tracks, aired on MBC in 2004. Thus, the phoenix has been a great and enduring symbol of hope, rebirth, and immortality in cultures all over the world. While the beast itself is perhaps mere legend, its myth has certainly achieved immortality.

Norman Harry Rothschild

References and Suggested Reading

Andrews, Tamar. *A Dictionary of Nature Myths*. New York: Oxford University Press, 1998.

Ashton, John. *Curious Creatures in Zoology*. New York: Cassel Publishing, 1890.

Bradbury, Ray. *Fahrenheit 451* [1953]. Reprint, New York: Simon and Schuster, 1993.

Brooks, Dan. *Love Birds: Unlocking the Secrets of the Emperor's Bird Scroll*. New York: D. Brooks, 1995.

Bulfinch, Thomas. *The Age of Fable or Beauties of Mythology*. Philadelphia: Henry Altemus, 1897.

Cai Yi'an. *Long-Feng tu dian* (*Images of Dragons and Phoenixes*). Zhengzhou: Henan Art Press, 1996.

Cao Xueqin. *The Story of the Stone*, vol. I. Translated by David Hawkes. New York: Penguin Books, 1974.

Cervantes, Miguel. *The History of the Ingenious Gentleman, Don Quixote de la Mancha*. Translated by Peter Anthony Motteux. Boston: Little, Brown and Co., 1845.

Clark, William, and Meredith T. McMunn, eds. *Beasts and Birds of the Middle Ages: The Bestiary and its Legacy*. Philadelphia: University of Pennsylvania Press, 1989.

Gilchrist, Cherry. *Russian Magic: Living Folk Traditions of an Enchanted Landscape*. Wheaton, IL: Quest Books, 2009.

Harrison, Thomas P. "Bird of Paradise: Phoenix Redivivus." *Isis* 51, no. 2 (1960): 173–80.

Lum, Peter. *Fabulous Beasts*. New York: Pantheon Books, 1951.

Nigg, Joseph. *Wonder Beasts: Tales and Lore of the Phoenix, the Griffin, the Unicorn, and the Dragon*. Santa Barbara, CA: Libraries Unlimited, 1995.

Payne, Anne. *Medieval Beasts*. New York: Amsterdam Books, 1990.

Shangshu zhengyi (*The Book of Documents*). Beijing: Beijing University Press, 1990.

Spring, Madeline. *Animal Allegories in T'ang China*. New Haven, CT: American Oriental Society, 1993.

The University of Aberdeen. *The Aberdeen Bestiary Project: Phoenix*. 1995. <http://www.abdn.ac.uk/bestiary/translat/55r.hti>.

Williams, Charles Alfred Speed. *Chinese Symbolism and Art Motifs*. Edison, NJ: Tuttle, 1974.

Wilson, Epiphanius, and Wallis Budge. *The Book of the Dead According to the Theban Recension*. Colonial Press, 1901. Reprint, Pomeroy, WA: Health Research, 1968.

Zvorykin, Boris, and Jacqueline Kennedy Onassis. *The Firebird and Other Russian Fairy Tales*. New York: Viking Press, 1978.

PINHEAD

Pinhead is the name attributed to Doug Bradley's **Cenobite** character in the *Hellraiser* films due to his striking appearance: his corpse-pale, hairless head is scarified by a grid of horizontal and vertical lines, with a nail extending outward at each intersection. In Clive Barker's novella *The Hellbound Heart* (1986), the character is rather different, a member of a group with no particular dominance over his associates. The most significant cinematic alteration to the character is the change from the "light and breathy ... voice of an excited girl" of the novella (8) to the ominous, deep timbre of Bradley's vocal delivery. Despite his short screen time in *Hellraiser* (Clive Barker, 1987), Pinhead—initially credited as the Lead Cenobite—was immediately popular. This melancholic, mysterious figure would become the only character to appear in all eight *Hellraiser* films released to date.

Unlike the other Cenobites, Pinhead appears to have a degree of autonomy from the dictates of his god, **Leviathan**. In the original film and novella, he is willing to bargain with Kirsty Cotton (Ashley Laurence) after she opens the puzzle box (known as the Lament Configuration), in exchange for her uncle Frank (Sean Chapman), who has escaped the torments of Hell. In *Hellbound: Hellraiser II* (Tony Randel, 1988), Pinhead stays the hands of his minions when puzzle-obsessed child Tiffany (Imogen Boorman) opens one of Dr Channard's Lament Configurations at his behest, claiming that another will had summoned them. Later in the film, Kirsty passes him a photograph of the man he was before he became a servant of Hell, Captain Elliott Spencer. The revelation causes Pinhead to revert to his former human self, allowing the Channard Cenobite (see **Cenobites**) to kill him. Nevertheless, Pinhead returns once more in *Hellraiser III: Hell on Earth* (Anthony Hickox, 1992), as his Cenobitic essence has become divided from the spirit of Spencer. He begins the film trapped in the Pillar of Souls, an artifact that was created at the end of *Hellbound*, and needs humans to supply him with blood and flesh in order to escape. Bradley plays Pinhead as a Mephistophelian seducer (see **Mephistopheles**), offering power to the weak if they will submit to his commands. By his will alone, Pinhead can create innovative weapons, as well as his characteristic hooks and chains, with which to slay masses of victims. In this film, Pinhead is less interested in torture than bloodletting, bringing him closer to slasher icons such as **Freddy Krueger**, **Michael Myers**, and **Jason Voorhees** than the disciplined priest of pain of the first two films. *Hell on Earth* ends with Pinhead and Spencer merging once more, essentially resetting the character.

Hellraiser: Bloodline (Kevin Yagher and Joe Chappelle, 1996) follows the story of the dynasty of the Lemarchand family, initially responsible for creating the means of summoning the Cenobites but now intent on making a device that will annihilate them. Pinhead is destroyed on a space station in the twenty-second century by a trap that can maintain strong light indefinitely. This still leaves many years for Pinhead to torment those who use the Lament Configuration, and in *Hellraiser: Inferno* (Scott Derrickson, 2000), he takes the role of the mysterious Engineer who is tracked by protagonist Detective Joseph Thorne (Craig Sheffer) as part of a murder investigation. Following what becomes a pattern for the remaining four films, Pinhead delights in revealing himself at the end, after his victims have irrevocably damned themselves, taking on a moralistic tone absent in the original concept. In *Hellraiser: Hellseeker* (Rick Bota, 2002), Pinhead once again allows Kirsty to save herself, this time in return for the souls of five others. In *Hellraiser: Deader* (Bota, 2005), he tracks down a cult that has defied death, killing them all mercilessly with hooks and chains. In *Hellraiser: Hellworld* (Bota, 2005), Pinhead is presented as a fictional character until the denouement, when he visits retribution on a man who attempts to murder four young people.

With the recent low-budget *Hellraiser: Revelations* (Victor García, 2011), a new comic book series launched in the same year by BOOM! Studios in association with Barker, and the resurrection of the author's long-awaited *Scarlet Gospels*, which pits Pinhead against Harry D'Amour (another iconic character created by the author), interest in the character remains strong.

David McWilliam

References and Suggested Reading

Barker, Clive. *The Hellbound Heart* [1986]. London: Harper Voyager, 2008.

Jones, Stephen, ed. *Clive Barker's Shadows in Eden*. Lancaster, PA: Underwood Miller, 1991.

Kane, Paul. *The Hellraiser Films and their Legacy*. Jefferson, NC: McFarland, 2006.

Timpone, Anthony, ed. *Fangoria: Masters of the Dark*. New York, NY: Harper Prism, 1997.

PIXIE

The pixie (also piskie, pigsy, and pixy) is a small, winged creature that finds its origin in the folk traditions of south-east England, particularly the marshy regions of Cornwall and Devon. While "pixie" is sometimes synonymous with **fairy**, pixies are said to be a class of Cornish fairy in English folklore, along with the small people, spriggans, and knockers. There are a number of legends related to the origin of pixies, with the most prevalent being that they are the spirits of stillborn or unbaptized babies. Still others believed that they were an ancient race of man.

Pixies can range in size, but are understood to be considerably smaller than a child. Some tales have them measuring nearly a foot in height, others suggest that they are small enough to fit through a keyhole, while still others maintain that they are too small to be seen with the naked eye. Typically, they are said to have pointed ears and noses, green clothing, and of course wings. There is little agreement regarding their aesthetic qualities, with just as many reports of their ugliness as their beauty. They are consistently believed to have exuberant energy, have a fondness for song and dance, and are always laughing. They love water and dwell in solitary places like hills, pathless woods, and riverbeds, often making their homes inside rocks.

The threat that a pixie represents, most often, is general mischief, and they are commonly presented as a household pest like insects or rodents. Many precautions could be taken to safeguard one's home against potential pixie havoc. For example, Cornish farmers might place pieces of lead on their roofs to discourage pixie dancing. Special protection could also be arranged for livestock, as pixies tormented and teased cows and horses while their owners slept. Solitary travel is a dangerous prospect for those who fear pixies, due to their fondness for "mazing," or casting prankish spells on lonely travelers. The most common spell is for a group of pixies to change the direction of a path, looping it around to its origin, which can be remedied by the traveler turning his or her clothes inside out. There are, occasionally, more disturbing dangers. The phosphorescent lights seen over the marshlands were believed to be caused by dancing pixies, luring curious men into the murky water like a **siren**'s song. Cakes are to be brought to Cornish baptisms as a charm to protect the newly christened child from pixies, and babies were sometimes pinned to their cribs by their bedclothes to prevent pixies from abducting them in the night, replacing them with their own offspring. There can also be harsh punishment for humans who gaze upon a pixie, most severely with the perpetrator losing his or her eyesight.

There are many occasions, however, on which pixies are celebrated and welcomed. Ruth Manning-Sanders's collection of Cornish folktales, *Peter and the Piskies* (1958), includes a number of stories in which pixies are a force for social good. In the tale "Betty Stogs' Baby," pixies abduct an infant from his lazy parents. They bathe and care for the child before returning him to his family, with the warning that they will steal him away permanently should they find him dirty again. Pixies thresh a farmer's corn in "The Piskie Thresher" in exchange for a new set of clothes, and a pixie disguises herself as an old beggar woman in "Saint Margery Dew" to test the kindness of mankind. In this tale, when the title character sells her own bed to help the beggar woman, the pixie leaves her milk and food each night.

A number of eighteenth- and nineteenth-century writers produced poetry inspired by pixies, including Samuel Minturn Peck (1854–1938), Nora Chesson (1871–1906), and Samuel Taylor Coleridge (1772–1834). In Peck's poem "The Pixies" (1881), he claims they can ease all ills. In Chesson's poem of the same name, published in 1902, she depicts them as ageless, fearless, and lovers of humanity. Coleridge's "Songs of the Pixies" (1793) declares that pixies own the powers of night, and references a cell "Where the blameless Pixies dwell" (line 90). In 1854, Anna Eliza Bray published *A Peep at the Pixies: or, Legends of the West*, a book of the folklore of both Cornwall and Devon that features pixie lore extensively. The aforementioned *Peter and the Piskies* by Ruth Manning-Sanders includes many stories of pixies, and the author's note claims that the tales in the collection were given to her by an old woman who heard them from the pixies dwelling in her garden.

The most famous pixie in popular media is undoubtedly Tinker Bell of Disney's *Peter Pan* (1953), a slight divergence from the 1904 J.M. Barrie play on which the film is based, in which she is a fairy. Disney's Tinker Bell, or "Tink" as Peter Pan often calls her, is rendered in garb befitting a traditional Cornish Pixie—in green pointed clothing with a trail of "pixie dust" behind her that also helps humans fly. When she gestures with her head or arms, the sound of jingling bells can be heard, which is evidently how she communicates with both Peter Pan and Captain Hook. In the film, she is portrayed as a bit vain; she becomes distracted by her reflection in a hand mirror when she and Peter are searching for his lost shadow. She is also very jealous of Peter's attention to other females, specifically Wendy. She pulls Wendy's hair when she tries to kiss Peter Pan, and she lies to the Lost Boys, prompting them to attack Wendy with wooden swords and rocks. She also reveals the secret location of Peter's hideout to Captain Hook, after Peter has banished her from the Hangman's Tree. Nonetheless, Tinker Bell redeems herself when she takes a bomb blast intended for Peter, and she proves herself helpful in Peter's final stand-off with Captain Hook aboard his ship. Since this film, Tinker Bell has become an international symbol for the magic of Disney. She is featured flying above the Magic Kingdom in the opening credits of all Disney films, has spawned her own series of feature-length films, and earned a star on Hollywood's Walk of Fame.

Pixies are sporadically featured in a number of contemporary fantasy series geared toward young adults, such as the "Artemis Fowl" series of Eoin Colfer (1965–) and the "Harry Potter" series of J.K. Rowling (1965–; see **Harry Potters, Monsters In**). A pixie named Opal Koboi is a prominent villain in two of the "Artemis Fowl" books. She is described as a mad genius, plotting rebellions against the humans who have forced magical creatures into exile. Pairing high intelligence with a ferocious temper, Opal often acts on impulse and to settle long-standing grudges. She destroys her father's business because he tried to stop her from studying engineering, and has a bitter rivalry with a **centaur** who defeated her at their university science fair. She appears as the primary antagonist in *The Opal Deception* (2004) and *The Time Paradox* (2008). Cornish pixies are the focus of a Defense Against the Dark Arts lesson in the second novel of the Harry Potter series, *Harry Potter and the Chamber of Secrets* (1998; film directed by Chris Columbus, 2002). In the film, the pixies are quite small, electric blue, and aggressive. The novel reports that they are eight inches in height, with pointed faces and shrill voices. Once released, they wreak general havoc on the room—stealing wands, breaking windows, shredding books and paper, and so on. While most of their behavior is merely pesky, they suspend Neville Longbottom from a chandelier. The pixies return briefly in the final film installment, *Harry Potter and the Deathly Hallows Part 2*, directed by David Yates (2011), in the Room of Requirement.

Rather than use pixie and fairy interchangeably, or present pixies as a type of fairy, the Nickelodeon cartoon series *The Fairly Odd Parents* distinguishes between the two. While fairies in the series are brightly colored and vivacious, pixies are shown as drab bureaucrats who wear gray and carry cell phones instead of wands.

Every year in June, the town of Ottery St Mary in Devon, England celebrates "Pixie Day," which commemorates the eradication of a pixie menace from the town on Midsummer's Day, 1454. According to the legend, local pixies were driven from the town and forced to live in "Pixie Parlour," caves on the banks of the Otter River. Today, the locals celebrate by dressing as pixies and re-enacting the Pixie Revenge, in which they unsuccessfully tried to reclaim the town from the townspeople.

Erin Gore

References and Suggested Reading

Bray, Anna Eliza. *A Peep at the Pixies: or, Legends of the West*. London: Grant and Griffith, 1954.

Courtney, Margaret Ann. *Cornish Feasts and Folk-lore* [1890]. Reprint, Totowa, NJ: Rowman and Littlefield, 1973.

Deane, Tony, and Tony Shaw. *The Folklore of Cornwall*. Totowa, NJ: Rowman and Littlefield, 1975.

Manning-Sanders, Ruth. *Peter and the Piskies: Cornish Folk Tales*. New York: Roy Publishers, 1958.

PLANTS, MONSTROUS

The monstrous plant—whether an entirely invented anthropomorphic vegetable entity or a creative extrapolation based on a real carnivorous plant species like the Venus flytrap—has proven an enduring object of fascination in literature and film, appearing everywhere from traditional folklore to contemporary horror, and from high fantasy to hard science fiction. Although there is incredible diversity among the hundreds of carnivorous plant species on the planet, the monstrous plants of fiction almost invariably exceed the size of even the largest of these, possess a much higher degree of mobility, and, rather than settling for a diet of insects and the occasional frog, often prove capable of consuming prey as large as *Homo sapiens*—sometimes the only acceptable food. (For further discussion of the basis of fictional monstrous plants in actual species, see Supper.) The man-eating plant, long the grail of cryptobotany, has roots in several folkloric traditions and especially in travelers' tales: thus, Indo-Arabian legends tell of the Waq-Waq Tree, which bears fruit in the shape of human bodies or heads, whether or not (depending on the version) it is also dangerous to humans and, as recently as the nineteenth century, European visitors to remote locales like Madagascar describe terrifying anthropophagous trees. Humanoid plants and other plant-animal hybrids form a separate lineage, with examples proliferating after the 1971 introduction of DC Comics' Swamp Thing, a man turned plant **elemental**. Yet this tradition, too, extends far back, even beyond H.P. Lovecraft's part-plant, plant-animal Old Ones from the 1931 novella *At the Mountains of Madness* (see **Lovecraft, Monsters In**). Finally, we should place in yet another category the many anthropomorphic or otherwise animate trees, with varying degrees of sentience, that populate fairytales and contemporary heroic fantasy, where they are sometimes known as "treants" or "treefolk," and which may behave either benevolently (Tolkien's Ents) or monstrously (Tolkien's Old Man Willow, the Fighting Trees of Oz) (see **Tolkien, Monsters In**).

Regardless of where one sets the boundaries of the category, it is clear that monstrous plants come in almost as many forms as do their non-monstrous counterparts—and their non-plant counterparts, for that matter. Nevertheless, despite this diversity of shapes, a distinct type of stock non-woody plant monster has come to dominate literature and film, a type that derives largely from a few influential examples, like the titular ambulatory plants of John Wyndham's 1951 novel *The Day of the* ***Triffids***, and Audrey, Jr, the bloodthirsty potted shrub first made famous by Roger Corman's 1960 film *Little Shop of Horrors*. This stock plant monster out for human blood has become such a staple of horror narrative that it now appears regularly in comedic contexts—as in lighter young adult fictions like Nancy McArthur's *The Plant That Ate Dirty Socks* (1988)—and it has also pollinated other media: the most immediately recognizable species of carnivorous plant in popular culture is probably the sharp-toothed flora of the pipes in the *Mario* video game universe. Indeed, the presence of the deadly exotic plant in genre fiction came to be so ubiquitous that the plant monster was formalized as a creature type unto itself in ***Dungeons & Dragons*** (3rd edition; see **Dungeons & Dragons, Monsters In**). Regardless of its shape, the attributes of any given monstrous plant are generally drawn from a shared pool of common characteristics—tentacular appendages, toxic excretions, spines, regenerative capabilities, insatiable appetite, and so on—but it can be difficult to classify them further, since the traits appear in different combinations that do not necessarily correspond to different kinds of narratives. Accordingly, the following sections will discuss the monstrous plant in the genres of science fiction, horror, and fantasy and folklore, but one must keep in mind that these categories often overlap when a monstrous plant takes a central role in the story.

Alien Plants and Mad Science

Some works of science fiction take the subject of vegetable intelligence quite seriously, although it also inspires humor: in Christian Nyby's 1951 film *The Thing from Another World*, one character, contemplating the plant-like horror, quips: "An intellectual carrot. The mind boggles." Indeed, many works of fiction ascribe intelligence to monstrous plants in order to deepen the terror. In Wyndham's *The Day of the* ***Triffids***, for example, the narrator's friend (correctly) suggests that triffids communicate with one another, and (again correctly) predicts that they would dominate mankind were the advantage of eyesight removed: a meteor shower soon blinds almost everyone on the planet, permitting the cunning triffids to wreak apocalyptic havoc. Of course, not all intelligent plants play the role of monster; for example, in David Brin's *Uplift* novels, beginning with *Sundiver* in 1980, the Kanten race is a sentient plant species friendly to humans.

In science fiction, therefore, we can observe two opposing trends: the use of a demonic plant to inject novelty into the typical monster movie plot or to offer a serious meditation on the relationship between plant and animal. Sometimes, as in Kazuki Omori's 1989 film ***Godzilla*** *vs. Biollante*, both impulses are present: the plant monster Biollante arises after a failed attempt to genetically engineer a wheat–cactus hybrid able to survive in the Middle Eastern desert. As this premise suggests, monstrous plants are ideally situated to address environmental anxieties, which we see unmistakably in the 2009 BBC adaptation of *The Day of the Triffids* (Nick Copus). In Wyndham's novel, the plants had been cultivated for food but, in the new rendering, humans gamble on the perilous undertaking of triffid-farming because it promises an alternative fuel supply that will end global warming. Today, plants frequently participate in so-called "revolt of nature" scenarios that were once the special province of outsized animals, like the nuclear ants of Gordon Douglas's 1954 film *Them!* or the monster of the original *Godzilla*, released the same year (Ishirō Honda). The best example of this trend is M. Night Shyamalan's 2008 film *The Happening*, in which Earth's plants release a chemical that drives humans to suicide, seemingly in a deliberate effort to cleanse them from the planet. Filmmakers' priorities have clearly changed a great deal since Steve Sekely's 1962 film version of *The Day of the Triffids*, in which the monstrous plants absorbed all the clichés of the B-movie tradition; nowhere is this plainer than in the film's poster, which preposterously puts a plant in the place of the classic ape/robot/Martian abducting a woman.

The triffid, then, adaptable to new circumstances in each successive incarnation, remains the monstrous plant *par excellence*, continuing to inspire homages like Simon Clark's 2001 sequel *Night of the Triffids*, and to permeate culture at large: the word "triffid" has entered the *Oxford English Dictionary*, according to which it may refer to any large plant or invasive species. Moreover, the ever-shifting nature of the triffid in literature and film—here **extraterrestrial** in origin, there a scientific abomination, here a vehicle for social commentary, there drive-in titillation—can stand in for all monstrous plants in their infinite variety and adaptability. With no uniform function in science fiction, the monstrous plant spans the century and a half between one of the earliest instances of the "mad scientist" in literature, Nathaniel Hawthorne's 1844 short story "Rappaccini's Daughter" (included in Arment, *Flora Curiosa*), and Steven Spielberg's 2002 blockbuster *Minority Report*, which features an attack by a poisonous plant. Likewise, the inertness of the vegetable offered a powerful metaphor for the deadening political climate of 1950s America in the form of the emotionless "pod people" from Don Siegel's 1956 film *Invasion of the Body Snatchers*, just as the sinister red weed accompanying the Martians in H.G. Wells's 1898 novel *The War of the Worlds* had literalized the creeping fear of invasion common to many works of the time. More recently, beginning in 1983, David Gerrold's "Chtorr" novels carry the idea of the literally "invasive" plant species to extremes, in that an entire alien biosphere supplants the Earth's native flora and fauna; like any monster, the monstrous plant remains an evocative symbol in many different contexts and periods.

From Horror to Dark Comedy

Science fiction featuring monstrous plants understandably overlaps with horror, and indeed the horror genre has long reveled in these prodigies, which play a minor role in one of the first horror films, F.W. Murnau's *Nosferatu* (1922). Midway through the film, we see a close-up of a Venus flytrap in action, and a lecturing professor marvels, "Isn't it—like a vampire!" Later monstrous plants are often described in vampiric terms, and the bloodthirsty plant continues to fascinate: in 2008, Carter Smith released *The Ruins*, a film that combines several monstrous plant tropes to meet the expectations of modern horror audiences. In a Mayan temple, leafy vines slowly stalk a group of tourists using sophisticated sound mimicry; their tendrils can also "infect" victims and squirm underneath their skin, offering a healthy dose of body horror. The film also relies on the psychological horror that the innocuous plants induce, and recalls the infamous rape scene from *The Evil Dead* (Sam Raimi,

1981), a sequence in which trees possessed by demonic powers graphically assault a woman lost in the woods: again, otherwise unassuming foliage becomes inimical.

Despite several such rather grave examples, the monstrous plant is far more prominent in horror narratives that border on black comedy, perhaps due to the incongruity of imagining a monstrous plant at all, since most are sessile and harmless—to quote the 1962 *The Day of the Triffids*: "There's no sense in getting killed by a plant!" For instance, John De Bello's *Attack of the Killer Tomatoes* (1978), far from earnestly imagining a plant-led "revolt of nature," spoofs the absurdity of such films precisely by inserting a vegetable into the monster-of-the-week slot. Furthermore, Audrey II, one of the most memorable monstrous plants, consistently stars in comedies, first in Corman's darkly comic *Little Shop of Horrors*, and then in its musical stage production and ensuing 1986 film version by Frank Oz. In all versions, hapless floral shop employee Seymour Krelborn raises an increasingly ravenous man-eating plant, but comedy abounds, as when Oz's Seymour, baffled at Audrey II's speech, punningly stammers, "You opened your trap!" Corman's *Little Shop of Horrors* also influenced the gruesome-but-droll tone of Czech director Oldřich Lipský's retro-pulp adventure *Dinner for Adele* (*Adéla ještě nevečeřela*, 1977), on which Jan Švankmajer worked as an animator for the plant. Švankmajer went on to direct his own surrealistic "dark plant comedy," *Little Otik* (*Otesánek*, 2000), based on a Czech folktale. "Little Otik" is a tree stump that a childless couple begins to raise, and—like Audrey, Jr with its imperative "Feed me!"—Otik quickly gains monstrous appetites—and proportions. Annie Proulx has even transplanted this same narrative germ to the American west in her 2008 tall tale "The Sagebrush Kid," perhaps testifying to a deep resonance between anxieties over nurturing a child and uncanny monstrous growth.

Cryptids and the Fantastic Hothouse

Little Otik is far from the only contemporary instance of a monstrous plant narrative based in traditional folklore. For example, in the first paragraph of Jasper Fforde's 2009 novel *Shades of Grey*, the narrator finds himself trapped in the digestive juices of a "yateveo tree" (Spanish for "I can see you"), a man-eating variety described in J.W. Buel's 1887 illustrated handbook of exotica, *Sea and Land*. Works like Buel's represent a transitional stage between (alleged) native legends of monstrous plants and their appropriation by the Western fantastic tradition; Frank Aubrey's 1896 romance *The Devil-Tree of El Dorado* serves as a good example of a fiction from this period that differs little from accounts purported to be true. (For a comprehensive discussion of such plant **cryptids**, see Shuker 108–26 ["Man-Eating Trees and Vampire Plants"].) The abundance of tentacles in the accounts that Shuker compiles suggests a relationship between monstrous plants and the tentacle horror associated with octopoid monsters, and indeed the two traditions flourished together in the heyday of the "weird tale" that would come to be defined by H.P. Lovecraft's work, creative and critical. In *Supernatural Horror in Literature* (1927, revised 1933–34), for instance, Lovecraft praises William Hope Hodgson's 1907 novel *The Boats of the Glen Carrig* (see also his "The Voice in the Night" in Arment, *Flora Curiosa*), and Algernon Blackwood's story of cosmic horror from the same year, "The Willows" (also in Arment, *Flora Curiosa*), both of which feature monstrous plants. Since Blackwood, who also wrote the eerie tale of terminal dendrolatry "The Man Whom the Trees Loved" (1912; in Arment, *Flora Curiosa*), evil trees have sufficiently established themselves in fantasy to merit a mention in Diana Wynne Jones's *The Tough Guide To Fantasyland*, where she cannily classifies them as prehensile, mobile, poisonous, or "[a]ll these things at once" (207). For a typical example, see the tangle trees of Piers Anthony's "Xanth" series that drag unsuspecting humans into their gaping mouths.

The path from folklore to fantasy is often a tangled one itself and, while the folkloric influence on the earlier weird tales was pronounced, "traditional" accounts of monstrous plants were often manufactured in order to meet the tremendous demand for such narratives. Commentators on Corman's film advance John Collier's 1931 story "Green Thoughts" (in Arment, *Flora Curiosa*) as an obvious source, but a thriving tradition preceded Collier: luminaries like Ambrose Bierce (1842–1913 [?]), Arthur Conan Doyle (1859–1930), Lord Dunsany (Edward John Moreton Drax Plunkett, 18th Baron of Dunsany, 1878–1957), E. Nesbit (1858–1924), and H.G. Wells (1866–1946) all penned stories about monstrous plants (see Arment, *Flora Curiosa*). Collier's tale remains significant, however, for its use of the Waq-Waq legend; the story typifies the Western tendency to combine the essential feature of the Waq-Waq Tree, its human fruit, with the man-eating tree motif. Corman preserves this aspect of the tale, as Audrey's buds open to reveal the victims' faces; likewise, in fantasy author China Miéville's bestiary of a secondary world, Bas-Lag, there dwells a sentient race of cactus people, as well as a man-eating "wake-tree" that, after devouring prey, grows "prey-fruit" in the shape of human heads (Miéville 124). Finally, Yann Martel's 2001 novel *Life of Pi* combines the aspidochelone myth—the island-sized animal on which sailors unthinkingly land—with a version of the Waq-Waq Tree: Pi realizes that the entire island is a carnivorous plant when he discovers a human tooth in a fruit. And, like Martel's unlooked-for tooth, finding a monstrous plant of legend hidden in contemporary literature or film forces us to reflect anew on this most unlikely and unexpected of monsters.

T.S. Miller

References and Suggested Reading

Arment, Chad, ed. *Botanica Delira: More Stories of Strange, Undiscovered, and Murderous Vegetation*. Landisville, PA: Coachwhip Publications, 2010.

——. *Flora Curiosa: Cryptobotany, Mysterious Fungi, Sentient Trees, and Deadly Plants in Classic Science Fiction and Fantasy*. Landisville, PA: Coachwhip Publications, 2008.

Cassaba, Carlos, and Michel Parry, eds. *Roots of Evil: Beyond the Secret Life of Plants*. London: Corgi, 1976.

Jones, Diana Wynne. *The Tough Guide to Fantasyland*. New York: Firebird, 2006.

Ketterer, David. "The Genesis of the Triffids." *New York Review of Science Fiction* 16, no. 7 (2004): 11–14.

Laumer, Keith, et al., eds. *Dangerous Vegetables*. Riverdale: Baen, 1998.

Lovecraft, H.P. *The Annotated Supernatural Horror in Literature*, edited by S.T. Joshi. New York: Hippocampus Press, 2000.

Miéville, China. *Iron Council*. New York: Ballantine, 2004.

Osborn, Chase S. *Madagascar, Land of the Man-Eating Tree*. New York: Republic Publishing Company, 1924.

Pharr, Mary. "Different Shops of Horrors: From Roger Corman's Cult Classic to Frank Oz's Mainstream Musical." In *Modes of the Fantastic: Selected Essays from the Twelfth International Conference on the Fantastic in the Arts*, edited by Robert A. Latham and Robert A. Collins, 212–29. Westport: Greenwood, 1995.

Price, Laurence. "Messrs Wells and Conan Doyle—Purveyors of Horticultural Curiosities and Proto-Triffids." *Wellsian* 21 (1998): 35–44.

Shuker, Karl. *The Beasts That Hide from Man: Seeking the World's Last Undiscovered Animals*. New York: Paraview Press, 2003.

Supper, Judith. "Botanischer Horror: Vom Woher und Wohin tödlicher Pflanzen in der phantastischen Literatur" ("Botanical Horror: From Whence and Whither Deadly Plants in Fantastic Literature"). *Quarber Merkur* 109/110 (2009): 181–96.

Wyndham, John. *The Day of the Triffids*. Harmondsworth: Penguin Books, 1951.

POKEMON—*see* Video Games, Monsters In

POLYPHEMUS—*see* Cyclops

POLTERGEIST

A poltergeist is a particular type of **ghost** supposedly responsible for unexplained physical disturbances such as loud noises and the movement of objects. The term, from the German *poltern* ("to make noise") and *geist* ("spirit") first appeared in the writings of the sixteenth-century German religious leader Martin Luther, who used it to designate events that, as was popularly believed, were caused by disembodied spirits. Well before the term was coined, narratives about unexplained physical disturbances had existed for centuries and included the following common characteristics: disembodied sounds, such as knockings or scratching; the movement or breakage of furniture and other objects; lithobolia ("stone-throwing," that is, showers of stones); spontaneous fires; and personal assaults such as slaps and shoves (Machado 228). Visible apparitions are notably absent from poltergeist disturbances. The manifestations usually center on a particular person, with an adolescent often serving as the focus; many of the most famous poltergeist cases, however, are firmly associated with locations rather than individuals. Throughout the centuries, many poltergeist cases have been reported from all over the world and have often been included in collections of folktales. Descriptions of "true" poltergeist activity in literature and cinema are surprisingly rare, however, largely because in these media the poltergeist activity is inevitably accompanied by an apparition or turns out to be the work of specific demonic (see **Demon**) or disturbed spirits, whereas in historically reported cases of poltergeist activity, the cause of the disturbances, though often believed to be spiritual in nature, is either never discovered or is proven to be a hoax.

Poltergeists are regularly reported from medieval times onward. One of the earliest accounts appears in *The Annals of Fulda*, a ninth-century CE Frankish historical record. The report describes how, in the year 858 on an estate near Bingen in Germany, an unseen "evil spirit" threw stones and banged on walls, making "a nuisance of himself to the people living there." Then the spirit seemed to focus its attention on one man, causing "every house which the man entered to catch fire." This went on for three years until the unexplained phenomena suddenly ceased (Reuter 44).

After Martin Luther brought attention to the phenomena, reports of poltergeist activity became more frequent. Some of the best-known cases occurred in England in the eighteenth and nineteenth centuries and, because of their popularity, appear frequently in **haunted house** anthologies. One classic case is the haunting of Epworth Parsonage, a rectory in the small town of Epworth, England, notable for being the home of the Reverend Samuel Wesley, grandfather of the founder of Methodism. In December 1716, the Wesleys' maidservant heard mysterious groans; a few nights later, several family members heard loud knocking sounds. Soon the disturbances became quite frequent: footsteps in empty rooms, noises like glass being smashed. The phenomena never became harmful, and the family good-humoredly named the poltergeist "Old Jeffrey." The disturbances ceased after two months, and although the family suspected a connection with Samuel Wesley's teenage daughter Hetty, the true cause was never discovered (Wilson 124–5).

The Epworth case was notable for its absence of physical phenomena. Similarly, the most notorious eighteenth-century poltergeist case, that of the "Cock Lane ghost," was characterized almost entirely by auditory disturbances. It began with knocking noises in the home of Richard Parsons in Cock Lane, London, in 1759. Rapping and scratching noises continued through 1762, becoming increasingly violent, and seemed to be associated with Parsons's daughter Elizabeth. Unsubstantiated rumors of murder connected with the house led to the "ghost" becoming famous throughout London. A formal committee, including Dr Samuel Johnson (1709–84), was sent to observe the phenomena and concluded that the poltergeist was a hoax, though the disturbances continued for many more months. Ultimately, the public agreed that Elizabeth had produced the ghostly phenomena at her father's bidding, and Mr Parsons was convicted of fraud (Wilson 129–30; Finucane 13). The case, and Dr Johnson's role in it, was spoofed by English satirist Charles Churchill in his 1762 play *The Ghost*, though the playwright, who bore a grudge against Johnson, depicted him as credulous rather than skeptical. Similarly, the English actor and playwright David Garrick satirized the Cock Lane affair in *The Farmer's Return from London* (1762), in which the no-nonsense farmer mocks the credulity of supposedly sophisticated Londoners. Charles Dickens referenced the "Cock-lane Ghost" in several of his works, including *Nicholas Nickleby* (1838; Chapter 49) and *A Tale of Two Cities* (1859; Chapter 1).

One of the first poltergeist cases to be more widely disseminated into literature and eventually cinema was the Tennessee **Bell Witch** disturbance of 1817–21. Another was an Australian case that occurred in the town of Guyra, New South Wales, in 1921. The Bowen family home was plagued for several weeks by unexplained thumping noises and showers of stones. Attention focused on their daughter Minnie (age 12), as the phenomena seemed to follow her around, but no human agency was ever proven. The events inspired an early Australian film, *The Guyra Ghost Mystery* (John Cosgrove, 1921), and prompted Australian poet Colin Newsome to write his collection *Minnie Bowen: The Guyra Ghost* (1993). In the United States, the now infamous 1848 case of the three Fox sisters, whose claims to have experienced poltergeist-like activity and to have actually contacted the spirit world were eventually admitted to be fraudulent, has not been greatly influential on literature but was largely responsible for the rise of the Spiritualist movement in America.

More recently, there has been the case of the so-called "Enfield poltergeist" of London, England, an incident that lasted for several months during 1977–78. A mother and her four children (ages seven to thirteen) experienced mysterious scuffling sounds, beds shaking, furniture sliding across the floors, and books and toys being flung around the rooms. The disturbances became increasingly violent. Investigators suspected fraud and centered their suspicion on daughter Janet (age eleven), but a satisfactory explanation was never found (Wilson 235–49). The Enfield case inspired the 1998 film *Urban Ghost Story* (Genevieve Jolliffe), which transplants the events to Glasgow.

The most well-known film to center on poltergeist activity is undoubtedly the aptly named *Poltergeist* (Tobe Hooper, 1982), in which a family moves into a home in a new development, only to be terrified by inexplicable phenomena. The disturbances begin with chairs and other objects moving around. But soon youngest daughter Carol Anne (Heather O'Rourke), who had secretly been communicating with indistinct voices emanating from the television set, is sucked through an inter-dimensional portal in her bedroom closet. At this point, the action has departed vastly from traditional poltergeist activity, despite the presence of parapsychologists and a medium (Zelda Rubinstein) who assert that the home suffers from a poltergeist infestation. The medium explains (contrary to established poltergeist lore) that multiple restless spirits inhabit the house and have taken Carol Anne, drawn to her life force. The group rescues the girl successfully from the spirit dimension, and the family discovers that the house had been built directly over a cemetery. The film's success spawned two sequels (*Poltergeist II: The Other Side*, Brian Gibson, 1986; and *Poltergeist III*, Gary Sherman, 1988) and a television series (*Poltergeist: The Legacy*, 1996–99, created by Richard Barton Lewis). Additionally, the film has been much parodied; see, for example, *The Simpsons: Treehouse of Horror* "Bad Dream House" episode (#1.2, 1990).

Another film series to feature poltergeist activity, ultimately attributing it to a demonic spirit, is *Paranormal Activity* (Oren Peli, 2007) and its prequels, *Paranormal Activity 2* (Tod Williams, 2010) and *Paranormal Activity 3* (Henry Joost, 2011). In the first film, a young woman named Katie (Katie Featherston) believes that an evil spirit has followed her and her boyfriend to their new home, and they set up a video camera to record any unusual events. Initially, the audio records unseen footsteps. Then the noises grow louder, and objects such as the planchette on an Ouija board move with no apparent cause; eventually, Katie is pulled across the floor by an unseen force. The film implies that the phenomena are caused by a demon who ultimately possesses Katie. In the first prequel, which begins two months before the original film, the poltergeist-type activity includes kitchen cabinets opening suddenly, pots falling down, scratches appearing on the basement door, and large pieces of furniture moving across the room. In the second prequel, set during Katie's childhood, the phenomena are more clearly caused by an invisible being.

In literature, a large number of haunted house novels describe poltergeist-like activity, including Shirley Jackson's *The Haunting of Hill House* (1959) and Richard Matheson's *Hell House* (1971). Terry Pratchett's 1991 novel *Reaper Man* includes a good deal of poltergeist and other ghostly phenomena, and poltergeist activity also features prominently in the Japanese novel (1989–94), manga (1998–2010), and anime (2006–2007) series *Ghost Hunt*. In J.K. Rowling's "Harry Potter" books (1997–2007), a ghostly character named Peeves is often referred to as a poltergeist because of his propensity for hurling objects around Hogwarts School, but because he usually presents simply as a rather chatty and mischievous apparition, he does not fit the mold of the traditional poltergeist (see **Harry Potter, Monsters In**).

D. Felton

References and Suggested Reading

Carrington, Hereward, and Nandor Fodor. *The Story of the Poltergeist Down the Centuries*. London: Rider, 1953.

Finucane, Ronald C. "Historical Introduction: The Example of Early Modern and Nineteenth-Century England." In *Hauntings and Poltergeists: Multidisciplinary Perspectives*, edited by James Houran and Rense Lange, 9–17. Jefferson, NC: McFarland, 2001.

Machado, Fátima Regina. "A New Look at Haunting and Poltergeist Phenomena: Analyzing Experiences from a Semiotic Perspective." In *Hauntings and Poltergeists: Multidisciplinary Perspectives*, edited by James Houran and Rense Lange, 227–47. Jefferson, NC: McFarland, 2001.

Reuter, Timothy, trans. *The Annals of Fulda*. Manchester: Manchester University Press, 1992.

Wilson, Colin. *Poltergeist! A Study in Destructive Haunting*. London: Llewellyn Publications, 2000.

PSYCHOPATH

Unlike many of the monsters detailed in this volume, the psychopath in crime and horror is predominantly a mundane, human antagonist. Their monstrous otherness ostensibly arises from the notion that their lack of pity for the victims they torture and kill is a form of radical evil. It is important to note that this view is challenged by many academics: for example, Simon Baron-Cohen's psychological theory outlined in *Zero Degrees of Empathy* that such individuals are at one end of a scale that positions everyone on a continuum of empathy erosion, manifesting in psychopaths as a "willingness to do *whatever it takes* to satisfy their desires. This might take the form of a hair-trigger violent reaction to the smallest thing that thwarts them. Or it might take the form of cold, calculated cruelty" (43). The psychopath as literary and cinematic monster is often synonymous with serial murder and/or torture. In reality, not all psychopaths are serial killers and not all serial killers are psychopaths. Like the majority of real-life serial killers, most monstrous psychopaths in literature and cinema are white, male Americans.

There have been tales of depraved murder throughout human history, but the psychopath as a distinct category of villain is foreshadowed in the late nineteenth century by the **Jack the Ripper** murders of 1888 in Whitechapel, London, and the crimes of serial killer H.H. Holmes (1861–96) in Chicago during the 1890s. The former was never caught, quickly passing into legend as the pre-eminent symbol of motiveless evil, whereas the latter horrified because of his ability to blend into society while dispatching victims in the "Murder Castle" that he had created behind the seemingly respectable exterior of his home. These cases emerged at a time when criminal activity began to be pathologized, with concepts like "moral insanity" entering wide use. An early attempt to grapple with this notion of a psychological wellspring of monstrous malice hidden within otherwise admirable characters can be found in Robert Louis Stevenson's *The Strange Case of Dr Jekyll and Mr Hyde* (1886), in which the scientist Dr Jekyll finds a means of allowing his dark desires and wrath to walk the streets, free from the risk of blemishing his reputation (see **Hyde, Edward**). The Holmes case has recently been explored in Erik Larson's 2003 non-fiction book, *The Devil in the White City: Murder, Magic, and Madness at the Fair That Changed America*.

Fiendish criminals and compassionless villains can be found throughout the early twentieth century, but it is not until the noir fiction of the 1950s that we see recognizably psychopathic figures emerge as monstrous anti-heroes/protagonists, most notably in Jim Thompson's *The Killer Inside Me* (1952) and, to a lesser extent due to his occasional feelings of guilt, Patricia Highsmith's Tom Ripley in *The Talented Mr Ripley* (1955) and its sequels. This was to re-emerge as a dominant movement in the late twentieth century with the figure of **Hannibal Lecter**, but was superseded for a long period by the role of psychopath as monstrous antagonist in the wake of the sensational success of Alfred Hitchcock's filmic adaptation of Robert Bloch's *Psycho* (1959) in 1960. A dark crime narrative, *Psycho* sets up **Norman Bates** of the Bates Motel as a radically schizoid murderer who has internalized the overbearing voice of his psychologically abusive mother to the extent that his mind is now split between mother and son. Most famous for the knife murder of a young woman who had aroused taboo thoughts in Norman, set to shrieking violins, *Psycho* lays the groundwork for the slasher sub-genre of horror that emerges in the 1970s.

Beginning with Bob Clark's *Black Christmas* (1974), the slasher film is established around the figure of an implacably malevolent antagonist who hunts down his (often young) victims and kills them with a knife or other hand-held weapon. *Black Christmas* augments the anonymity of the serial killer by refusing to show his face. Instead, it uses the camera to indicate his point of view, combining with his deranged laughter and disturbing phone calls to terrorize a sorority house of female university students. Slashers found a wider audience with the release of John Carpenter's *Halloween* (1978), which focuses on the masked figure of **Michael Myers**. Myers, a psychopath that his own psychiatrist views as the embodiment of evil, escapes from an asylum in order to slaughter teenage girls in his former neighborhood. Myers's eerie mask and slow, methodical movements set up one of the key tropes of slasher cinema: the iconic image of named-yet-unknowable monstrous evil. Spawning a series of sequels, the success of *Halloween* encouraged the creation of numerous similar franchises around such figures as **Jason Voorhees** in the *Friday the 13th* series initiated in 1980 and **Freddy Krueger** in the *A Nightmare on Elm Street* films that premiered in 1984. The recurrent theme of killers punishing teenage transgression has laid the slasher film open to accusations of a reactionary conservatism, while its emphasis on gore and nudity has been the source of campaigns against its malign influence.

Another significant representation of the psychopath as monster in the cinema of the 1970s is Tobe Hooper's *The Texas Chainsaw Massacre* (1974), which was loosely based on the crimes of Ed Gein (1906–84). It was discovered in 1957 that Gein had murdered and mutilated women from Waushara County, Wisconsin. This serial killer used the body parts of his victims and corpses exhumed from local graves in order to fashion furniture and clothing, which decorated his dilapidated farmhouse. Hooper's film replaces the lone figure of Gein with a cannibal family that waylays those traveling on a nearby highway in order to subject them to a similarly grisly fate. The iconic psychopath from this franchise is Leatherface: a hulking, chainsaw-wielding figure who wears a mask of human skin. This notion of the psychopathic rural poor also generated a small sub-genre, such as Wes Craven's *The Hills Have Eyes* (1977) and its sequels, as well as the *Wrong Turn* series initiated in 2003.

The next major incarnation of the monstrous psychopath appears in Thomas Harris's novel *Red Dragon* (1981), which introduces the figure of Dr Hannibal Lecter. Lecter is an ex-psychiatrist criminal genius, whose psychopathic cannibalism is presented as a symbol of his decadent disdain for the rules and conventions of human society. His powerful insight into the criminal mind makes him perennially useful to the FBI, which asks him for help in capturing serial killers still at large, such as the titular character of this novel or Buffalo Bill in the internationally best-selling sequel, *The Silence of the Lambs* (1988). David Schmid, in his essay "The

Devil You Know: *Dexter* and the 'Goodness' of American Serial Killing," identifies Lecter as part of a process of making serial killers into charismatic anti-heroes in mainstream culture by creating "audience sympathy for the 'good' serial killer by contrasting him with a 'bad' serial killer" (140). Lecter's formidable intellect makes him a master manipulator, a point that is foregrounded by Anthony Hopkins's career-defining performance in Jonathan Demme's 1991 film adaptation. Hopkins's charismatic Lecter eclipses the central crime narrative through his cat and mouse engagement with FBI agent Clarice Starling (Jodie Foster). Arguably, Hopkins's performance influenced Harris's follow-up, suitably named *Hannibal* (1999), in which the doctor takes center stage. Lecter is no longer contrasted with a rival serial killer, but rather the petty political machinations of Starling's superiors, allowing him to win her over into his world of opulent depravity.

During the course of Lecter's rise to stardom, public interest in serial killers became increasingly difficult to separate from the celebrity culture that now dominates the American media landscape. This is the central theme of David Schmid's *Natural Born Celebrities*, in which he analyzes the response to the fame of such criminals and the role played by an often salacious news media. Two key films that explore this fascination are Dominic Sena's *Kalifornia* (1993) and Oliver Stone's *Natural Born Killers* (1994). In the former, David Duchovny plays a young liberal writer who wants to understand what motivates serial murder in order to write a book about it, while in the latter Woody Harrelson and Juliette Lewis play a couple of murderous psychopaths on a bloody road trip across America, gathering frenzied media coverage in the process. Another method of satirizing America in late capitalism via the figure of the psychopath is presented in Patrick Bateman from Bret Easton Ellis's *American Psycho* (1991). Bateman is the hollowed-out representative of the corporate excesses of the USA in the 1980s, a man who speaks almost entirely in clichés and only finds differentiation from his peers by murdering others. It is left unresolved as to whether his crimes are real or imaginary, but the novel suggests that the mechanisms of high finance would not allow themselves to be disrupted by his indiscretions.

Keying into the pre-millennial sense of a culture on the point of destruction, numerous representations of psychopaths in the 1990s show serial killers reflecting back their society's perceived moral decay. David Fincher's *Seven* (1995) is a noir thriller that follows the murders of the visionary John Doe (Kevin Spacey), whose victims die in a manner akin to each of the Catholic Seven Deadly Sins, as he seeks to make the ultimate denunciation of the world in which he finds himself. Heavily inspired by *Seven*, Chris Carter's television series *Millennium* (1996–99) sees retired FBI agent Frank Black (Lance Henriksen) drawn back into solving serial murder cases when he is hired by the mysterious Millennium Group. As the series progresses, Frank's parapsychological skill of seeing trace images of crimes when scanning the scene of a murder reveals some form of metaphysical evil, suggesting a satanic power behind the rising tide of corpses piling up in preparation for some apocalyptic future event.

Literary and cinematic psychopaths continue to fascinate in the twenty-first century. Perhaps the dominant filmic representation of sadistic serial murder of the century thus far is the *Saw* franchise begun in 2004, in which the killer Jigsaw's malice is generated by a brain tumor, leading him arbitrarily to pick those he views as responsible as victims for his elaborate revenge. James Wan's original film draws on the murders of Fincher's John Doe, as the killer's victims are placed in deadly situations and faced with the choice between carrying out horrific tasks or certain death. The film's sequels led to the popularization of the horror sub-genre derogatively known as "Torture Porn," in which it is argued that the focus is on damaged bodies as the source of pleasure for the viewer, exemplifying what Mark Seltzer defines as America's "wound culture" in *Serial Killers*: "a collective gathering around shock, trauma, and the wound" (1). This has paralleled a wider interest in the physicality of psychopathic crimes in the shift from psychological profiling, as favored by Lecter and Black, to the rapidly developing discipline of forensic science in shows such as *CSI: Crime Scene Investigation* that premiered in 2000, and its numerous spin-offs and imitators. Here, the graphic images of the deceased are perhaps used to reassure viewers of the power of the police in tracing the killer from their morbid creations.

If Hannibal Lecter marks an early sign of the acceptance of serial killers, then, as Schmid notes, Dexter Morgan from Jeff Lindsay's novel *Darkly Dreaming Dexter* (2004) and its sequels goes even further in rehabilitating this monstrous figure. Best known from Michael C. Hall's performance of the role in Showtime's adaptation of the novels for television, begun in 2006, Dexter is a blood-spatter analyst in the Miami Metro Police Department who moonlights as a serial killer. It is revealed that Dexter witnessed his mother's murder as an infant—a psychical trauma that his foster father, the policeman who found Dexter in a pool of blood, believes has molded him into a future serial killer. Rather than seek psychological treatment for his son, Harry instead trains him to channel his urges by tracking down and killing those who escape justice that, as Schmid argues, further rehabilitates the image of serial murderers. In many respects, Dexter is the culmination of previous developments of the psychopath on page and screen, confronting contemporary American society with a physical incarnation of the death penalty.

David McWilliam

References and Suggested Reading

Baron-Cohen, Simon. *Zero Degrees of Empathy: A New Theory of Human Cruelty*. London: Allen Lane, 2011.

Fox, James Alan, and Jack Levin. *Extreme Killing: Understanding Serial and Mass Murder*. Thousand Oaks, CA: Sage, 2005.

Larson, Erik. *The Devil in the White City: Murder, Magic, and Madness at the Fair That Changed America*. New York: Crown Publishers, 2003.

Schmid, David. "The Devil You Know: *Dexter* and the 'Goodness' of American Serial Killing." In *Dexter: Investigating Cutting Edge Television*, edited by Douglas Howard, 132–42. London: I.B. Tauris, 2010.

——. *Natural Born Celebrities: Serial Killers in American Culture*. Chicago: University of Chicago Press, 2005.

Seltzer, Mark. *Serial Killers: Death and Life in America's Wound Culture*. New York: Routledge, 1998.

Simpson, Philip L. *Psycho Paths: Tracking the Serial Killer through Contemporary American Film and Fiction*. Carbondale, IL: Southern Illinois University Press, 2000.

PÚCA—*see* Shapeshifter

PUG—*see* Demon

PYRAMID HEAD—*see* Video Games, Monsters In

QILIN

The *Qilin*, also known as *Kirin* in Japan, and sometimes the "Chinese Unicorn" in the West, is a mythical Chinese creature that appears throughout East Asian cultures. The description of the appearance of the *Qilin* varies in different times. In Lu Ji's third-century CE *Explanatory Notes on the Plants, Trees, Birds, Quadrupeds, Insects and Fish in Mao's Version of the Book of Songs* (*Mao shi caomu niaoshou chongyu shu*), the *Qilin* is said to have the body of a deer, the tail of an ox, the hooves of a horse, yellow fur, and a single flesh-covered horn on its head. The depiction of the physical features of the *Qilin* changed in later times. According to anthropologist Schuyler Cammann, by the Ming dynasty (1368–1644), the *Qilin* had evolved from the single-horned creature to one that has the head of a **dragon** with a pair of horns. Although horned, the *Qilin* is a compassionate and benevolent creature that walks rhythmically without treading on insects or damaging the grass. Together with the **phoenix**, dragon, and tortoise, the *Qilin* is one of the Four Supernatural Creatures (*Si ling*) and symbolizes virtue and prosperity. Its appearance often coincides with the arrival of a sage or virtuous ruler. In folklore, the *Qilin* is believed to bring talented children to families. The image of an infant riding on a *Qilin* is a motif that prevails in Chinese art.

One of the earliest references to the *Qilin* appears in the *Book of Songs*, also known as the *Book of Odes* (*Shijing*), the oldest existing collection of Chinese poems, parts of which date to the Shang dynasty (approximately 1600 BCE–1046 BCE). In one of the songs, "*Qilin's* Hooves" (*Lin zhi zhi*), the physiology of the *Qilin* is moralized and compared to the sons and grandsons of King Wen, the *virtuous* founder of the Zhou dynasty. Other early records of the *Qilin* include the *Spring and Autumn Annals* (*Chunqiu*), the first Chinese chronological history traditionally attributed to Confucius in the fifth century BCE. The *Annals* ends with the entry that states that a *Qilin* was captured in 481 BCE during a hunting expedition. According to the *Gongyang Commentary on the Spring and Autumn Annals* (*Chunqiu gongyang zhuan*), composed sometime between the fifth and third centuries BCE, Confucius grieved about the untimely arrival of the *Qilin*. The capture of the *Qilin* was conventionally credited as the reason that Confucius stopped writing the *Annals*.

In classical Chinese poetry, the *Qilin* frequently appears as the symbol of serenity and virtue. The Han poem, "Regretting the Oath Betrayed" (*xishi*) by Jian Yi in the second century BCE, mourns the loss of morals in the society of the time and the evasiveness of the *Qilin*. The *Qilin* also often appears as the symbol of bureaucratic success, as it has been used on robes as a badge of high-ranking officials since the Tang dynasty. The prominent eighth-century Tang poet Du Fu's "Beyond the Frontier, the Third Poem" depicts the bloody cost of gaining fame and fortune in wars: "Merit and fame are pictured in the figure of *Qilin*, when the bones of war quickly decay" (line 4). In one of the four great classical novels of Chinese literature, *Water Margin* (*Shui Hu Zhuan*), attributed to author Shi Nai'an (date disputed; likely fourteenth century CE) Lu Junyi, one of the 108 outlaws depicted in the novel, is given the nickname the "Jade *Qilin*" for his physical attractiveness, charisma, and martial arts skills.

In more modern works, the nature of this originally gentle creature becomes ambiguous. Some literary and cinematic works describe it as an aggressive monster with supernatural power. In the 2010 novel *Riju: A Kaiju Hunter Novel* by K.H. Koehler, for instance, the *Qilin* is a powerful shapeshifting monster that is capable of destroying New York City (see **Shapeshifter**). The Hong Kong comic series *Storm Rider* (*Fung Wan* in Cantonese or *Feng Yun* in Mandarin) and its film adaptation *The Storm Rider* by Andrew Lau (1998) also feature a *fire*-breathing *Qilin* whose blood can unleash the power of a magical sword. The monster *Qilin* also frequents other media: in the *Final Fantasy* video game universe, *Kirin* is one of the summoned monsters that pose serious threats to its *adversary*. Others representations still regard the *Qilin* as the symbol of peace and kindness. In 2003, Japanese author Hitomi Kanehara wrote the award-winning novel *Snakes and Earnings* in which a tattoo of *Kirin* is given to the protagonist Liu by tattoo artist Shiba-san, who explains the compassionate nature of *Kirin* to her. The film version of this novel was directed by Yukio Ninagawa and released in 2007.

Lin Wang

References and Suggested Reading

Cammann, Schuyler. "Some Strange *Ming Beasts*." *Oriental Art* 2, no. 3 (Autumn 1956): 99–100.

Du Fu. "Beyond the Frontier." In *Dushi xiangzhu* (*Du's Poems*, with detailed commentary), vol. 1, edited by Qiu Zhao'ao, 120. Beijing: Zhonghua shuju, 1979.

Knapp, Ronald G. *China's Living Houses: Folk Beliefs, Symbols, and Household Ornamentation*. Honolulu: University of Hawai'i Press, 1999.

Mei, Xianmao. "Talk about *Qilin*." *Wenshi zhishi* (*Chinese Literature and History*) 6 (1991): 116–21.

Robert, Jeremy. *Chinese Mythology A to Z*. New York: Chelsea House, 2010.

QUARIN/A—*see* Incubus/ Succubus; Koran, Monsters In The

QUASIMODO

Quasimodo is a central character in *Notre-Dame de Paris* (known in English as *The Hunchback of Notre-Dame*), a romantic novel written by French novelist and playwright Victor Hugo in 1831.

In fifteenth-century Paris, Quasimodo is left abandoned on the steps of Notre-Dame Cathedral because of his deformity. Claude Frollo, the Archdeacon of Notre-Dame, adopts the little boy and gives him the name of Quasimodo, after the name of the day when he was found (first Sunday after Easter, according to Catholic liturgy). The hunchback becomes the bell-ringer of the cathedral, where he finds refuge. Because of his frightening appearance, he is feared by people and seen as a freakish creature. Frollo, madly attracted to a Gypsy dancer called Esmeralda, orders Quasimodo to kidnap her, but the beautiful girl is rescued by Phoebus de Châteaupers (Captain of the Royal Archers). She falls in love with this handsome man, although he is already engaged to his fiancée Fleur-De-Lys.

Quasimodo is arrested for trying to abduct Esmeralda and punished at the pillory. His feelings for Esmeralda grow into genuine love as she feels pity for him by showing him human kindness and giving him water. The jealous Archdeacon stabs Phoebus, who had arranged to meet Esmeralda, and lets the innocent girl be accused of attempted murder (and witchcraft). She is taken to Notre-Dame to make amends. Deeply attached and enamored with Esmeralda, Quasimodo carries her off into the sanctuary of the cathedral in a desperate attempt to protect her. But Esmeralda, after refusing Frollo's compromising protection, is eventually captured and hanged.

Finally understanding the role played by his master, Quasimodo murders Frollo by pushing him off the heights of the cathedral. He then chooses to stay with his beloved for eternity, clutching the lifeless body of the young dancer in the graveyard of Montfaucon, where she lies with the other corpses of condemned people. When his body is found, years later, he is still in close embrace with Esmeralda, and crumbles into dust when his skeleton is pulled away.

Quasimodo has become the archetypal figure of the monster with a human heart—a poignant union of sublime and grotesque. A monster on the outside, a tender soul on the inside, he is a symbol of social injustice, physical rejection, and abnormality. (In fact, the "Quasimodo Complex" was first coined by two physicians in 1967 to describe a personality disorder produced by emotional reaction to physical deformity.) The hunch-backed bell-ringer also personifies devoted, passionate love. Although he does not receive tender feelings in return, he fights like a lion and commits murder for his beloved, hence transforming into a tragic hero. Nevertheless, "quasi" means almost, and the character is doomed from the beginning: he will never be considered as completely human. His appearance seals his fate as a monster. In French culture and language, Quasimodo generally refers to a person of ugly appearance.

Hugo's narrative has inspired many adaptations and has been brought to life in various cinematic versions, including the silent film *The Darling of Paris* (J. Gordon Edwards, 1917), *The Hunchback of Notre Dame* (Wallace Worsley, 1923) with Lon Chaney, and the famous 1939 version directed by William Dieterle, with Charles Laughton. The first color version was made by Jean Delannoy in 1956, with Anthony Quinn starring as Quasimodo. The novel was also adapted into a Disney animated feature in 1996 (Diane Eskenazi) with a softer beginning (a loving mother for Quasimodo) and a child-friendly happier ending. A sequel was made in 2002 (*The Hunchback of Notre Dame II*, directed by Bradley Raymond). A very popular French-Canadian musical was also created in 1998 (music composed by Richard Cocciante and lyrics by Luc Plamondon).

Valérie Charbonniaud-Doussaud

References and Suggested Reading

Gleizes, Delphine. *L'œuvre de Victor Hugo à l'écran. Des rayons et des ombres.* Paris: L'Harmattan, 2005.

Hugo, Victor. *Notre-Dame de Paris* [1831]. Translated by I.F. Hapgood. Project Gutenberg, 2009. <http://www.gutenberg.org/ebooks/2610>.

Nourisson, Didier. "La caméra explore le temps: Notre-Dame de Paris." In *Littérature et cinéma, écrire l'image*, edited by Jean-Bernard Vray, 145–56. Saint-Étienne: Publications de l'Université de Saint-Étienne, 1999.

Robb, Graham. *Victor Hugo: A Biography.* New York: W.W. Norton, 1997.

QWAN—*see* Demon

QWEFFOR—*see* Demon

RACES, MONSTROUS

The concept of the monstrous race was developed and popularized in the ancient and medieval world and today has a strong foothold in science fiction. Themes inherited from ancient mythology, travelers' tales infused with fantastic motifs, beliefs in the actual existence of ideas that were in fact allegorical or metaphoric, as well as many other cultural and discursive elements underlay beliefs in the existence of different and "other" races one step removed from the human. Poised at the boundaries of animality and monstrosity, the "humanity" of such races was always scrutinized and questioned.

The first problem that the concept of the "monstrous race" presents is the conjunction of two signifiers that are themselves problematic: what do authors mean by "race"? And what do they mean by "monstrous"? The problem of a monstrous race is linked to the fact that the individuals who are imagined to belong to it cannot be perceived as completely "other." A **dragon** arguably has very little in common with humans. It is completely on the side of either animality or monstrosity. But what about the traditional monstrous race of the Sciopods—one-legged beings who spend their days lying on their backs protecting themselves from the sun with a great single foot—as mentioned in Pliny the Elder's first-century CE *Naturalis Historia* (*Natural History*)? Are they human? Or something else?

The problem of their "monstrosity" is just as complex given that monstrosity is an ambiguous and shifting concept. The Blemmyae, for example—people without heads and necks and with their faces on their chests, as mentioned by the first-century BCE/first-century CE Greek geographer Strabo and others—are certainly monstrous, but what about Pliny the Elder's Speechless Men, who only communicate by gesturing, and the Raw Meat Eaters, who live by eating only raw meat and honey, who are considered monstrous in some regions and periods, but not in others? Such considerations reveal that the concept of monstrosity is inevitably relational and context dependent.

Monstrous Races in the Ancient World

Greek and Latin cultures were preoccupied with the question of whether monstrous races exist. Debates thus focused on the reliability of the authors mentioning them, the tradition of the tale, the likelihood of their physical existence, and so on. Those races posed scientific and ontological questions to philosophers and historians: do they really exist? How can they survive and how do they reproduce? Why do they live only in some parts of the world? The geographical element was extremely important. The traditional location of monstrous races was in remote lands such as India, Ethiopia, Libya, and the uncharted deserts and forests of the whole world. These lands were supposed to be extremely prolific and fertile; here, nature plays with species: hybrids and violations of a normal order are more frequent. A chaotic fecundity is manifested in these extreme regions, where nature is richer in marvels to be admired.

Monstrous races with specific traits appear very early in Greek literature, with Homer's **Cyclops** and lotus-eaters in *The Odyssey* (c. eighth century BCE). Ancient historians and ethnographers were also important in developing and disseminating the concept: Ctesias of Cnidus (*Indica*, fifth century BCE), Herodotus (*The Histories*, fifth century BCE), and Megasthenes (*Indica*, between the third and second century BCE) all speak about India as a fabulous land of monstrous races. The Greek heritage of monstrous races was formalized in Latin by Pliny the Elder, whose *Natural History* was widely read in the following centuries. Pliny collects and describes a long list of monstrous beings and races, including the Sciopods, Blemmyae, Speechless Men, and Raw Meat Eaters already mentioned. His point of view is encyclopedical: he is interested in listing and describing rather than offering erudite interpretations or allegorical explanations. Moreover, the many monstrous beings that appear in the *Natural History* are scattered throughout the different volumes and incorporated next to normal beings and phenomena; monstrosity is not, for Pliny, a category of organization, but rather a phenomenon that deserves to be included in a wide and exhaustive description of the universe.

Of particular note are the Blemmyae, introduced in the *Natural History* as a headless people bearing their faces on their chests, said to live south of Egypt. Although based on actual Nubian tribes, the Blemmyae quickly entered fiction and common belief as monstrous beings and are featured in works of fact and fiction throughout the ensuing centuries. Sixteenth-century cartography, for example, frequently featured Blemmyae: Martin Waldseemüller's world map of 1507 and Johann Schöner's globe of 1515 find places for them. William Shakespeare's *Othello* (c. 1603) mentions the Blemmyae, as does Sir Walter Raleigh when reporting his findings in *The Discovery of Guiana* (1596). In Umberto Eco's contemporary novel *Baudolino* (2000), the protagonist encounters various monsters, among them Blemmyae and Sciopods.

Important, too, are the Sciopods (Greek for "Shadow-Feet") and the Cynocephali, men with the heads of dogs. Sciopods, who despite having only one leg were allegedly capable of moving at incredible speed, were placed by Pliny and Ctesias in India; several tenth- and thirteenth-century maps of the world, so-called "mappaemundi," show Sciopods inhabiting Ethiopia. Cynocephali, who appear in Egyptian religion as the dog-headed gods Hapi and Anubis, are also situated in India by Ctesias and Megasthenes.

Monsters in Christian Culture

For early and medieval Christians, the problem was to know not only where monstrous races were located, but when and how they entered into history and why. These meditations center around the roles that the Christian assigns to himself and his God within the larger context of the whole of creation—a creation that should be seamless, with even the oddest and most curious aspects having an explanation. For the theologian and the believer, the questions shift to: do members of monstrous races have souls? Are they rational? Are they descended from Adam? How did they survive the Deluge? How do they also express the will of God and what do they mean for the Christian? Can they be converted to Christianity? A theological consensus developed around the idea that the proliferation of monstrous races was the consequence of the divine punishment at the time of Babel.

The *Physiologus* (between the second and the fourth century), written by an unknown Alexandrian author, clearly shows the shift in emphasis from classical thinking about monstrous races to early Christian preoccupations. The monstrous races discussed become an instrument for a better knowledge of God and the universe that he has created, as well as a means of avoiding evil. The encyclopedic attitude exemplified by Pliny moves into the background, and the ethical interpretation linked to spiritual truth takes center stage.

Augustine of Hippo (St Augustine) devotes a good deal of space to the monstrous races, including Cynocephali, in his *City of God* (early fifth century). In Book 16, monstrosity is fully integrated within the divine design. The seemingly monstrous character of these beings, for Augustine, results from human ignorance about the correspondence of the individual parts of the universe to the whole, as well as the limits of the human intellect in grasping all God's works. In his fourth-century BCE text *De generatione animalium* (*Generation of Animals*), Aristotle had described monstrosity as the result of the resistance of matter to take its appropriate form and therefore as a partial failure of the teleological process that governs everything in nature. Augustine rejects this view: as the teleological process is in fact directed by God, nothing can be a failure in it. We do not have to find a justification for the failures—that is, monstrosities—in nature, because God and his design are perfect. The question for Augustine is not where monsters come from, but what they mean and how they fit into the larger whole of God's divine plan. Monsters might, for example, be the sign of a divine punishment for our corrupted nature after original sin and serve to remind us of our condition of misery. An apocryphal Augustinian sermon (*Ad Fratres in Eremo Sermo*, c. 900 CE) goes so far as to praise the pious life of the monstrous races, compared with the corrupted one of many Christians.

Isidore of Seville in his *Etymologiae* (seventh century) again situates monsters within the Christian narrative of history. The encyclopedical collection of knowledge is important for Isidore, as it was for Pliny, yet division and organization of the races into categories is even more critical, as these races are an active part of the divine design and should be interpreted as such. Isidore also develops the theme proposed by Hippocrates (c. 460–c. 370 BCE) of the link between the occurrence of monstrous races and the climatic conditions of the lands they inhabit, which will become widely accepted.

Monstrous Races in the Medieval World

The concept of monstrous races received additional elaboration and development during the Middle Ages. Although not in the traditional form or with one of the "known" races, the theme is clearly fundamental to *Beowulf* (composed some time between the eighth and eleventh centuries; see **Grendel**). More traditional monstrous races are present in many of the most important early and high medieval documents, such as the *Liber monstrorum* (seventh/eighth century), *Alexander the Great's Letter to Aristotle* (tenth century), the *Wonders of the East* (eleventh century), and the *Letter of Prester John* (twelfth century). The differences in the judgments that different authors make concerning monstrous races are the most important feature of these texts. Monstrous races are sometimes potentially good Christians (anticipating the early modern myth of the Good Savage), sometimes good Christians in actuality (by virtue of the evangelization of the apostle Thomas, for example), and sometimes threatening and evil beings who only deserve to be conquered, submitted, or exterminated—as Alexander did in his Eastern enterprises.

Particularly notable is Gerald of Wales's *The Topography of Ireland* (twelfth century), as here the monsters are not located in exotic and remote lands, but rather at the gate. Descending from the Scythians, who had monstrous customs themselves, the Irish deserve to be colonized and civilized through violence. The boundary between an individual monster and a whole race of monsters is blurred: the countless deformed people who live on the island, according to Gerald, testify to their violations of natural laws. Following a model deriving from the literature on Alexander's mission in the East, monstrosity is here enlisted to justify the imposition of "civilized" values and customs on the Irish barbarians.

A different conception that might be defined as relativistic, in contrast, starts to develop in works including Marco Polo's *The Million* (thirteenth century) and Mandeville's *The Travels of Sir John Mandeville* (fourteenth century). Monstrous races embody a difference that is no longer only a sign of inferiority. Nor is it exploited for the explanation of a divine design centered on Christianity and the West. Jacques de Vitry, for example, claims in his *Historia Orientalis* (thirteenth century) that our astonishment about monstrous races is not different from the one that they would have in meeting our race, or that a people of **dwarfs**, or **giants**, or black-skinned people would have in meeting Western people. On this ground Jacques maintains the full humanity of monstrous races.

The profound moral implications that result from a relativization of the concept of monstrosity and from the historical and ontological contextualization of the observer within the observed environment are developed even before the Renaissance. In the third book of his *Opus de natura rerum* (thirteenth century), called *Book of Monstrous Men of the Orient*, Thomas de Cantimpré explicitly claims that monstrous races are our "other" and that our moral behaviors can be even worse than theirs. Although Cantimpré does not recognize monstrous peoples as fully human, he highlights their proximity to us and puts into question a rigid separation. Going back to Isidore's *Etymologies*, Cantimpré also gives a thoughtful explanation of the difference between the monstrous individual and the monstrous race. Only the former is a violation of natural order, while the latter is certainly part of the way nature follows its own laws.

Monstrous Races in the Renaissance and Early Modern Period

In the early Renaissance, before the discovery of the New World and the initial studies of modern anatomy, variations on the theme of monstrous races were mainly developed from moral and theological perspectives. A meaningful change in the attitude toward monstrous races does not become evident until the sixteenth century, when the belief in the real existence of these races waned and monsters were put back into the scientific domain and studied as anomalies rather than allegories. The humanist Joachim Vadianus clearly claims in his *Epitome trium terrae partium* (1534) that "monstrous men do not exist," and the Franciscan André de Thevet repeats this idea in his *Cosmography of the Levant* (1554) and *Universal Cosmography* (1575).

A further step is taken by Antoine Fumée who, in his *Histoires* (1574), definitively dissociates the history of nature and the history of men. Diversity of customs, for example, does not have anything in common with anatomical diversity. Therefore, Fumée does not ask whether monstrous races represent the divine punishment after Babel, or if they contribute to the beauty of the world, as did Augustine. Monsters instead should be referred to the science of nature rather than to theodicy. An individual monster can be generated as a consequence of a single and peculiar event in nature. This, however, will never change God's primary disposition and laws. Properly speaking, therefore, "monstrous" races do not exist. There are only individual anomalies due to nature and its variety.

In the same period, Michel de Montaigne writes arguably the most famous assertion of skepticism and relativism of the early modern period, precisely on the topics of monstrosity, in his *Essays* (1572–92)—in particular in *On Cannibals* and *An Apologie of Raymond Sebond*. The savage, Montaigne explains, is the one who is a stranger to us. With a subtle criticism of the totalitarian claims of reason, which are no less dangerous than those of theology, Montaigne appreciates Pliny for his intellectual curiosity and his openness toward the other. We should think that monstrous races exist, explains Montaigne, not out of gullibility, but because they are the sign and the metaphor of a conception of a rich, powerful, and diverse nature. Montaigne intends to reduce the claim of the centrality of man in nature, not by accepting the existence of monstrous races, but by skeptically attacking those who deny them on the basis of reason.

Early modern literature exploits the potentialities of monstrosity in multiple directions. Monstrous races are in Shakespeare, both, as noted, in *Othello* and in the more disturbing and subversive project of populating an island with a monstrous race when **Caliban** rises against the usurper Prospero in *The Tempest* (1610–11).

Monstrous Races in the Modern Era And Beyond

Monstrous races appear in seventeenth-century utopian and extraordinary voyages such as Cyrano de Bergerac's *The Other World: The States and Empires of the Moon* (1657) and *The States and Empires of the Sun* (1662), and in Gabriel de Foigny's *The Southern Land, Known* (1676), which imagines a whole continent populated with a hyper-rational race of **hermaphrodites**. Augustinism slowly waned during the seventeenth century and so did the traditional Augustan position on monstrous races. The new philosophical discourse tended to eliminate the belief in monstrous races and their supposedly theological functions within the universe. In its place, new scientific and anthropological discourses developed, such as the early modern primatology of Olfert Dapper (*Description of Africa*, 1668). Ancient individuals belonging to monstrous races were sometimes "translated" into the new beings encountered in the New World. The chimpanzee corresponds, for example, to the "Indian Satyre" in Nicolas Tulp's *Observationes Medicae* (1641), and the baboon corresponds to the cynocephali of the ancients in *The Anatomy of a Pygmie Compared with that of a Monkey, an Ape, and a Man* by Edward Tyson (1698).

Monstrous races, however, continued to have an ontological significance extending beyond purely scientific interest. Early modern reflections on the nature of animal species and, in particular, on the evolution of living beings are full of philosophical and theological implications. Inspired by Epicurism, Benoît de Maillet, in his *Telliamed* (c. 1722), develops a curious theory on the marine origin of the human race in which humans evolved from fish. The book is full of digressions that, although fabulous, open the way to subsequent transformational theories. The idea of an almighty nature, unconscious of its own ends and generating diverse beings by trying multiple combinations, was slowly formed. From such a perspective, the world evolves constantly and vicious combinations of matter (such as Empedocles's oxen with human faces, mentioned in the collected fragments of his fifth-century BCE teachings) eliminate themselves. Nature is not perfect and it produces monsters. These ideas will be developed by the major philosophers of the period, including Pierre Louis Maupertuis (*Vénus physique*, 1745), Julien Offray de La Mettrie (*Machine Man*, 1748 and *The System of Epicurus*, 1750), and Denis Diderot (*D'Alembert's Dream*, 1769).

As in seventeenth-century utopian literature, the moral implications of the encounter with the other—both imagined and actually met—are of great significance. The most famous example in travel literature with fantastic themes is Jonathan Swift's *Gulliver's Travels* (1726; see **Swift, Jonathan, Monsters In**). "A Voyage to the Country of the Houyhnhnms"—part 4 of *Gulliver*—directly exploits the idea of a monstrous race in the form of the yahoos, beings tied to representations of "savages" and **troglodytes**; but at the same time Swift represents the failings of the human race when compared with the noble equine race of the Houyhnhms. Developing a deep aversion toward the yahoos, Gulliver is compelled by these juxtapositions to recognize the misery of the human condition.

Within the scientific literature, the encounter with the other prompted the elaboration of a theory earlier promulgated by Isidore that today appears curious but was maintained by the most serious social scientists of the period, including Montesquieu—namely the theory of climate. Just as the theory of astral influences had formerly held great influence, the theory of climate becomes widespread in the eighteenth century. Geography, and climate in particular, of remote regions, so different from those of the temperate regions of Europe, was proposed as the cause of social, political, and moral differences of other people. This theory was exploited to maintain the superiority of the Europeans over other races, and to explain Eastern despotism or to justify the forced labor of African people.

In the nineteenth century, ancient monstrous races seemed to be a legacy of the past. Yet the anxiety and tensions that they provoked from theological, anthropological, and social points of view did not fade away. Gustave Flaubert mentions them in *The Temptation of Saint Anthony* (1849) and they are exploited in both H.G. Wells's *The Time Machine* (1895), which contrasts troglodytish Morlocks with the more ethereal Eloi, and Edward Bulwer-Lytton's *The Power of the Coming Race* (1871), in which the narrator discovers a subterranean world populated by a race called the Vril-ya who resemble **angels**.

The theme of the monstrous race is also present in the two most famous and successful monster tales of the century: *Frankenstein; or, The Modern Prometheus* by Mary Shelley (1818) (see **Frankenstein's Monster**); and ***Dracula*** by Bram Stoker (1897). Both monsters—the creature fabricated and eventually repudiated by Dr Frankenstein and the aristocratic undead Transylvanian Count Dracula who threatens Western civilization—cultivate projects of "reproduction" to propagate their race. The creature asks Frankenstein for a female companion, thus making the threat of an autonomous reproduction concrete. The attempt of Count Dracula to infiltrate civilized London is grounded on a project of contamination by, and therefore reproduction of, vampires.

Between the nineteenth and twentieth centuries, the theme of monstrous races was further transformed and tragically embodied in the "monstrification" of some human "races." Although, on the one hand, scientific knowledge progressively put into question the possibility of using the concept of race itself for humans, on the other hand, the pseudo-scientific idea of race was increasingly established in the public discourse and in literature. In his *Orientalism* (1978), Edward Said traces the development of this pseudo-scientific discourse within the Western colonial project. Following a long and inveterate tradition, the monstrous "race" par excellence became in this period the Semitic. The process of monstrification of this race and of many other subjects (homosexuals, the handicapped, communists, and so on) reached its climax in the Nazi extermination project.

A proper cinema of monstrous races, in the classic and medieval sense, does not really exist. Yet the themes of monstrous races and the encounter with the other, anomalous and monstrous, span the whole history of cinema, starting from the Selenites of George Méliès's *A Trip to the Moon* (1902), considered the first science fiction movie (see **Extraterrestrial**). Monstrous races are reworked in particular in "contagion" (see **Virus**) and "alien race" cinema. Whether presenting humanoid creatures with ulterior motives or entirely monstrous, inhuman entities, science fiction persistently represents the opposition between the human and the monstrous other. That this engagement is frequently displaced to non-terrestrial environments perhaps reflects the fact that scientific knowledge no longer permits the belief in monstrous races on this planet. A prime example of the direct transition from Earth to outer space is the cantina scene in George Lucas's *Star Wars Episode IV: A New Hope* (1977), populated by a varied assortment of monstrous aliens. Among the most famous and important cinematic and televisual representations of extraterrestrial monstrous races, monstrous races derived from extraterrestrial contact, or the monstrification of the human as a result of a virus or diseases are Don Siegel's *Invasion of the Body Snatchers* (1956), Wolf Rilla's *The Village of the Damned* (1960), Ubaldo Ragona's *The Last Man on Earth* (1964), Boris Sagal's *The Omega Man* (1971), George Romero's "Dead" movies, Ridley Scott's *Alien* (1979) and, more recently, David Cronenberg's *Slither* (2006), Neill Blomkamp's *District 9* (2009), Michael Haneke's *The White Ribbon* (2009), and Breck Eisner's *The Crazies* (2010). Monstrous races from outer space have also threatened the human characters in several television series such as *Star Trek* (1966–69) and its spin-offs, *V* (1984 and the 2010 remake), and *Falling Skies* (2011–present).

Filippo Del Lucchese and Jana Toppe

References and Suggested Reading

Asma, Stephen T. *On Monsters: An Unnatural History of Our Worst Fears*. Oxford: Oxford University Press, 2009.

Baltrusaitis, Jurgis. *Le Moyen-Âge fantastique. Antiquités et exotismes dans l'art gothique*. Paris: A. Colin, 1955.

Beal, Timothy K. *Religion and Its Monsters*. New York: Routledge, 2002.

Bildhauer, Bettina, and Robert Mills, eds. *The Monstrous Middle Ages*. Cardiff: University of Wales Press, 2003.

Céard, Jean. *La Nature et les prodiges, l'insolite au XVIe s., en France*. Geneva: Droz, 1977.

Friedman, John B. *The Monstrous Races in Medieval Art and Thought*. Syracuse: Syracuse University Press, 2000.

Greenblatt, Stephen. *Marvelous Possessions: The Wonder of the New World*. Chicago: University of Chicago Press, 1991.

Said, Edward. *Orientalism*. London: Routledge, 1978.

Verner, Lisa. *The Epistemology of the Monstrous in the Middle Ages*. New York: Routledge, 2005.

RAHAB—*see* Bible, Monsters In The

RĀKSASAH—*see* Demon; Shapeshifter

RASALOM—*see* Demon

RASETSU—*see* Demon

RAVANA—*see* Demon

RAW MEAT EATER—*see* Races, Monstrous

REDCAP—*see* Brownie

REVENANT—*see* Video Games, Monsters In

RINGWRAITH—*see* Wraith

ROBOT

Robots are artificially intelligent machines created by mankind or other sentient life and often humanoid in appearance. The concept of the robot largely emerges from the industrial revolution. Typically, their two distinguishing characteristics are a physical body and some degree of autonomy. The autonomous artificial intelligence with a physical body differentiates robots from artificially intelligent computers, machines, weapons, and other mechanical objects. A robot's autonomy or sentience is often the center of tension within robot narratives, which directly invokes a master–slave relationship, thereby contemplating humankind's role with regard to god(s), each other, and material objects.

The robot's origin mirrors many human origin myths, from the Bible to Greek mythology to Chinese folklore, in which a being is formed from inanimate materials, but given life by some higher being. While these origin myths answer the question of where humans come from, they also provide an early example of the unnatural birth. The unnatural birth remains a common element within horror and science fiction. It has provided a means for vilifying the monster—in particular, robots—since its existence subverts the natural order of procreation. In many stories, this unnatural creature challenges or disobeys its creator, which can be seen as a parallel between humankind and its mythic creator. Robot narratives thus lead us to ponder the autonomy of humankind and the responsibility of and to a creator.

Precursors

Mary Shelley's *Frankenstein* (1818) bridges the gap between man-made beings and robots (see **Frankenstein's Monster**). Victor Frankenstein's creation of a life, assembled piecemeal and sewn together, echoes robots that are manufactured and held together with nuts and bolts. Victor's relationship with his creation directly mirrors the relational tension present in John Milton's *Paradise Lost* (1674) between humankind and God, as well as between Satan and God (see **Devil, The**). The creature experiences rejection, rebels against its master, and longs to procreate, which are dominant themes within robot narratives. The creature's appearance as an eight-foot tall, yellow-skinned humanoid with significant strength and speed introduces uncanny elements that are also present in many robot narratives. As with robots, he is quite humanlike in his appearance, but varies in ways that disincline a human to perceive him as such. This difference between appearance and perception creates a rift and stimulates repulsion in humans.

Besides Frankenstein's monster, several other tales influence the robot narratives of the twentieth century. A Jewish folkloric creature, the **golem**, provides an early example of man creating a life without procreation. The golem legend tells of a rabbi who forges the golem from earth, just like the Biblical Adam. In some versions, the golem serves as protector of the Jews and is eventually put to rest, while in others, he rebels against his maker. In the early nineteenth century, E.T.A. Hoffmann also produced several stories featuring automatons, humanoid robots controlled by others, including "The Sandman" (1817) and "Automata" (1819); the former became a focal point for Freud's essay on the uncanny. Fitz-James O'Brien's "The Wondersmith" (1859) also features dolls under the control of malicious gypsies, which could also be seen as a precursor to robots.

Positive depictions of robots existed in the nineteenth century. Carlo Collodi's *The Adventures of Pinocchio* (1883) features a puppet brought to life through magic (see **Objects, Animate**). Pinocchio's humanization and acceptance invokes the benevolent robot narrative in which the robot is ultimately accepted by humans through its dedication to humanity. (The connection between Pinocchio and the robot is made clear in Stephen Spielberg's *A.I. Artificial Intelligence* [2001], a film about a robot child that wishes to be human.) In the latter half of the nineteenth century, American dime novel publishers released several prototypical robot series. Edward F. Ellis's *The Steam Man of the Prairies* (1868) provided the starting point for several mechanical men series, including *Frank Reade and His Steam Man of the Plains* (1876) by Harry Enton and a follow-up series by Luis P. Senarens about the adventures of boy inventor Frank Reade, Jr. Though the mechanical men had the potential to be manipulated for evil ends, they were largely creations of the protagonist and coexisted reasonably with humankind; another theme that still permeates robot narratives.

The Robot Menace

Three major themes dominate the hostile or evil robot narrative. The first theme is the creation of robots for maniacal purposes. These robots tend to be two-dimensional and represent science used in the wrong hands. The second theme explores the loss of control between the creator and the created. The evil or malfunctioning robot reflects mankind's follies and hubris, creating life and losing control of it in some manner. The robot often perpetrates some violence directly upon the creator in its attempts to break free. This theme blends together fears of technology, offspring, and the other. The final theme, the robot revolt, largely extends from the second. It relies upon the same fears as the rebel robot, but also evokes class and racial tensions, given that the relationship between humans and robots is always hierarchical. It is not coincidental that robot narratives emerged during the late nineteenth and early twentieth centuries when mechanization, workers' rights movements, and racial tension were clear stress points within society.

American author Ambrose Bierce's short story "Moxon's Master" (1893) keenly illustrates the clashes intertwined into the robot narrative. The story follows a conversation between the narrator and Moxon, a scientist. They debate the relationship between man and machines. Moxon argues that there is no difference between machines and humans while the narrator disagrees. Later, the narrator witnesses Moxon playing chess against a humanoid machine. When the machine loses, it kills Moxon. The narrator's refusal to recognize sentience within machines parallels the debates surrounding African Americans that Bierce witnessed in the lead-up to the American Civil War (1861–65). The language of intelligence and competence that dominated the race debates from the Civil War to the late 1890s permeates the short story. Having witnessed a time in which an entire group of people were considered property and not competent, Bierce brings that discussion to the center of this story about the place of machines in an increasingly mechanized world.

The 1920 Czech play *R.U.R.* (Rossum's Universal Robots) by Karel Čapek marked the first use of the term robot and featured the robot-revolt narrative. The dystopian play reveals a future in which robots are mass produced to meet every need. Humankind soon becomes incapable of reproducing, while the robots demand either to live longer or to be capable of reproducing. The robots of Capek's play featured few mechanical characteristics and were barely distinguishable from humans. However, their mass production and hierarchal relationship to humans clearly commented on the role of class in the modern world. The robot revolt and revolution continued to strike chords within literature, including Fred Saberhagen's "Berserker" series (1967–2005), which posits a robot race known as the Berserkers whose mission entails wiping out all sentient life in the universe. *The Butlerian Jihad* (2002) and other books in Frank Herbert's "Dune" series explore a robotic enemy that had tried to wipe out humans within the universe.

With limited variation, the nefarious robot plots continued throughout the mid twentieth century. It was not until the late 1960s, as science fiction took on more sophisticated ideas in the writing of authors such as Robert Heinlein (1907–88) and Philip K. Dick (1928–82), that the robot narratives gain further complexity. Dick's *Do Androids Dream of Electric Sheep* (1969; adapted as *Blade Runner* in 1982 by Ridley Scott) raises questions about what happens when technology delivers robots that are indistinguishable from humans. Others, such as Ira Levin's *The Stepford Wives* (1973), asked just how much can robots and technology replace real live experiences such as love.

Until the 1960s, there were few films featuring menacing robots. Maria, a robot directed to create insurrection among workers in Fritz Lang's *Metropolis* (1927), was the first major cinematic robot. *Gog* (Herbert L. Strock, 1954) features two robots, Gog and Magog, that are programmed by the villain to do harm but are stopped from killing the protagonists at the last moment. *Creation of the Humanoids* (Wesley Barry, 1962) offers a sophisticated consideration of robots. In the post-nuclear war world, humans are slowly dying away and increasingly rely upon robots to be their caretakers. When a doctor perfects the transplant of human consciousness into robots, humans become increasingly angst-ridden about their robot companions.

Westworld (Michael Crichton, 1973) and *The Stepford Wives* (Bryan Forbes, 1975) are iconic works of the 1970s that consider how robots would exist as entertainment and domestic figures. *Westworld* presents a future in which people can entertain their carnal desires in an amusement park filled with robots. Eventually, the robots resist their programming and attack humans. *The Stepford Wives* features a suburban enclave in which the men replace their wives with perfectly well-behaved women and the protagonist, Joanna (Katherine Ross), discovers the conspiracy. Both films participated in a discussion about how robots could be used to supplement human entertainment and, in some ways, these films were also part of the discussion stimulated by second-wave feminists about the place of women in society.

From the 1980s to the 2000s, four films represented the serious tension and fears that robots exemplified. In 1982, Ridley Scott's *Blade Runner* (based upon *Do Androids Dream of Electric Sheep*) revealed a future in which robots do human labor and are entirely human-like, except that they lack empathy. A group of robots rebels and a blade runner (one who hunts robots, played by Harrison Ford) must catch them. *The Terminator* (James Cameron, 1984) features a time-traveling robot sent to the past from a future in which the raging war between humans and robots has nearly destroyed all vestiges of human civilization (see **Cyborg**). *The Matrix Trilogy* (Andy and Lana Wachowski, 1999–2003) inverts the human–robot relationship by presenting a world in which human existence is a computer program created by robots to keep humans alive, in order to fuel robot existence. When some humans break past the matrix programming and see the real world, it becomes their mission to overthrow the machines. By contrast, *I, Robot* (Alex Proyas, 2004—named after, but not actually based upon, Isaac Asimov's 1950 collection of stories of the same name) presents a future world in which robots became mass produced and replace many human jobs. However, the controlling artificial intelligence computer changes the programming and comes close to realizing a robot-controlled world, before being stopped by the protagonist (played by Will Smith). Together, these films reflect the arc of technological change as the world emerged into the digital age marked by increasing reliance upon artificial intelligence.

Robot Coexistence and the Friendly Robot

With some exceptions, such as Tik-Tok from Frank L. Baum's *Oz* series (1900–1920), robots were largely villainous or despised until the end of the 1930s, when several stories emerged that turned the robots into protagonists. Raymond Z. Gallun's "Derelict" (1934) features an alien robot healer, while Lester del Rey's "Helen O'Loy" (1938) stages a love story between a human and a robot.

Eando Binder's "I, Robot" (1939) features Adam Link, a sentient but misunderstood robot, who is hunted by humans as a result of being perceived as a threat.

It was Isaac Asimov (1920–92), however, who most substantially influenced the direction of the robot narrative. In 1940, his short story "Strange Playfellow" (later republished as "Robbie") marked the start of his remolding of the robot narrative. By 1942, Asimov had established the influential three laws of robotics that drive a robot's "positronic" brain. The laws, which are outlined in *I, Robot* (1950), have been used directly or indirectly throughout literature and film. The three laws are:

1. A robot may not injure a human being or, through inaction, allow a human being to come to harm.
2. A robot must obey the orders given to it by human beings, except where such orders would conflict with the First Law.
3. A robot must protect its own existence as long as such protection does not conflict with the First or Second Laws.

Asimov returned to these laws in *Robots and Empire* (1985) to add the zero law: "A robot may not harm humanity, or, by inaction, allow humanity to come to harm." This law supersedes the others and came after four decades of Asimov, among other writers, creatively challenging the premises of the first three laws.

In the mid twentieth century, many authors contemplated neutral or positive robots. Lester del Rey wrote a series of sympathetic robot stories, as well as ones in which human–robot relational complexity was further explored, including *Into Thy Hands* (1945), "A Code for Sam" (1966), and *Vengeance Is Mine* (1964). Clifford D. Simak also presented positive robots in novels such as *Cosmic Engineers* (1939), *City* (1952), *Time and Again* (1951), and *A Choice of Gods* (1973).

During the late twentieth and early twenty-first century, robots increasingly became protagonists and a normalized part of society. David Gerrold's *When HARLIE Was One* (1972) considers the question of at what point a robot becomes human. In his "Hitchhiker's Guide to the Galaxy" series (1979–2009), Douglas Adams created Marvin the Paranoid Android, a depressed robot who moves through the stories constantly moping about his pointless existence.

The alien robot, Gort, from *The Day The Earth Stood Still* (1951—based upon *Farewell to the Master* by Harry Bates, 1940) may be considered a predecessor to the benign robot since the audience's allegiance was with the alien protagonist, Klaatu. Cinematically, the good robot narrative begins with Robbie from *Forbidden Planet* (Fred M. Wilcox, 1956). With the same name as Asimov's first robot character, the robot indirectly invokes the laws Asimov had set up and would make later appearances in other television series and films. Beginning with *Star Wars* (1977), George Lucas's "Star Wars" series (1977–2005) expanded upon the characteristics of Robbie with a universe in which "droids" exist and in some cases—such as R2D2 and C3PO—feature fully developed personalities. Though Lucas's second trilogy positioned droids as enemies, it is clear within the films that they are not inherently evil. Throughout the 1980s, comedies and family films such as *D.A.R.Y.L.* (Simon Wincer, 1985), *Weird Science* (John Hughes, 1985), *Short Circuit* (John Badham, 1986), and its sequel *Short Circuit 2* (Kenneth Johnson, 1988) made robots cute and playful, which coincided with a rise in robotic and electronic games and toys.

Throughout the 1990s and 2000s, several popular films presented a series of sympathetic and self-sacrificing robot protagonists, such as *Edward Scissorhands* (Tim Burton, 1991), *Bicentennial Man* (Chris

Columbus, 1999—based upon Asimov's 1976 novel), *The Iron Giant* (Brad Bird, 1999—based upon Ted Hughes's *The Iron Man* [1968]), and *A.I. Artificial Intelligence* (Stephen Spielberg, 2001). Into the 2000s, robot narratives also became part of children's entertainment with the release of several CGI films including *Robots* (Chris Wedge and Carlos Saldanha, 2005), *Wall-E* (Andrew Stanton, 2008), and *9* (Shane Acker, 2009). These stories made the robots the protagonists, in some cases excluding humans entirely, and sometimes, such as *Wall-E*, with humans as part of the problem that the robots need to fix. Finally, the "Transformers" series (Michael Bay, 2007–11), based upon the 1980s television series, presents Transformers as aliens whose only difference from humans is that their bodies are entirely machine-based. By the late twentieth and early twenty-first century, the traditional robot themes within literature faded significantly. As real-world technology caught up with and in some cases surpassed the fictional expectations, the idea of robots became less frightful.

Lance Eaton

References and Suggested Reading

Alkon, Paul K. *Science Fiction Before 1900: Imagination Discovers Technology*. New York: Twayne, 1994.

Asimov, Isaac. *I, Robot*. New York: Bantam Books, 2004.

——. *Robots and Empire*. Garden City, NY: Doubleday, 1985.

Asma, Stephen T. *On Monsters: An Unnatural History of Our Worst Fears*. Oxford: Oxford University Press, 2009.

Freud, Sigmund. *The Uncanny* [1918]. Reprint, New York: Penguin Books, 2003.

Graham, Elaine L. *Representations of the Post/human: Monsters, Aliens and Others in Popular Culture*. Manchester: Manchester University Press, 2002.

Halberstam, Judith. *Skin Shows: Gothic Horror and the Technology of Monsters*. Durham, NC: Duke University Press, 1995.

Kelley, Leo P. *Themes in Science Fiction: A Journey into Wonder*. New York: McGraw-Hill, 1972.

Pierce, John J. *Great Themes of Science Fiction: A Study in Imagination and Evolution*. New York: Greenwood Press, 1987.

Riley, Dick. *Critical Encounters: Writers and Themes in Science Fiction*. New York: Ungar, 1978.

Rose, Mark. *Alien Encounters: Anatomy of Science Fiction*. New York: ToExcel, 1999.

Schelde, Per. *Androids, Humanoids, and Other Science Fiction Monsters: Science and Soul in Science Fiction Films*. New York: New York University Press, 1993.

Telotte, J.P. *Replications: A Robotic History of the Science Fiction Film*. Urbana: University of Illinois Press, 1995.

ROC—*see* Animals, Monstrous; Birds, Giant

RODAN/RADON—*see* Godzilla

RUTHVEN, LORD

Lord Ruthven is the central figure in Dr John Polidori's (1795–1821) short story "The Vampyre," which first appeared in April 1819 in the *New Monthly Magazine*. Lord Ruthven is generally acknowledged as the first definitive appearance of the **vampire** in English literature. The story was immensely popular at the time of its publication and remains widely read.

The story itself is narrated by a young man named Aubrey who encounters the aristocratic Lord Ruthven and accompanies him on a journey around Europe and into Greece. On their travels, they encounter European superstitions regarding vampires: undead creatures who resemble humans and must feed on human blood to survive. While they are still in Greece, Ruthven mysteriously falls ill and seems to die, but not before exacting a promise from Aubrey: that he will conceal his death for some time on his return to England. A distraught Aubrey returns home and becomes gravely ill. When he recovers, he discovers that his sister has become engaged to a young aristocrat—who turns out to be Lord Ruthven. Throughout the story, Aubrey is horrified at Ruthven's evil powers of seduction. Upon hearing tales of vampires, he begins to suspect Ruthven, but it is not until the final moments that Ruthven is declared a vampire in the story's revelatory final line. While Ruthven is never actually seen to drink blood, it is clearly implied when Aubrey discovers the lifeless corpse of Ianthe, the Greek maiden who tells him about vampires and with whom he has fallen in love: "upon her neck and breast was blood, and upon her throat were the marks of teeth having opened the vein" (Polidori 12).

Much like later figures of the vampire in English literature and on screen, Ruthven is an aristocratic and dissipated figure. Aubrey is a clear predecessor to both Renfield and Jonathan Harker in Bram Stoker's ***Dracula*** (1897), in the sense that he begins as an unwary companion and helpmeet to Ruthven, whom he later turns against.

The figure of Lord Ruthven is said to be based in some measure on Lord Byron (1788–1824), due in part to the name Ruthven, initially "coined by Lady Caroline Lamb to satirize Byron in her novel *Glenarvon*" (Twitchell 108). The story's genesis is now the stuff of legend: it was begun during the ghost story competition among Percy Shelley (1792–1822), Lord Byron, and Mary Shelley (1797–1851) during their sojourn near Geneva in the summer of 1816—the competition that led most famously to Mary Shelley's novel *Frankenstein* (1818; see **Frankenstein's Monster**). John Polidori was also present on this occasion as he was traveling with Byron as his private physician. Various accounts (substantiated by Polidori's diary) show that Polidori also tried his hand at creating a ghost story for the competition, although "The Vampyre" emerged later. Polidori's association with Byron and the story's mysterious publishing history—there is no original manuscript for "The Vampyre" and Byron's name was attached to the story when first published—led to both Ruthven and the story being permanently linked to Byron's reputation, and resulted in an accusation of plagiarism being brought against Polidori, an event that some scholars, including Twitchell, Rigby, and Macdonald, speculate may have contributed to Polidori's early suicide at the age of 25. Byron had also published a similar tale, "Augustus Darvell: A Fragment," in 1819 and "The Vampyre" was seen as being characteristic of some of Bryon's previous work. Indeed, some scholars and readers continue to attribute "The Vampyre" at least in part to Byron, despite the consensus attributing it to Polidori (see Twitchell, Rigby, Gelder, and Praz).

Ruthven's appearance as the first definitive vampire in English literature gives the story a clear place in the Gothic canon. In spite of its landmark status, however, "The Vampyre" has never been adapted for the screen. (John Polidori, in contrast, is played by Timothy Spall in Ken Russell's 1986 film *Gothic*, which is loosely based on the legendary ghost story competition.) Other iterations of the Lord Ruthven character have appeared in fiction and in the theater. Nineteenth-century stage versions in both France and Britain were extremely popular. In France, the notoriety of "The Vampyre" was enhanced by Cyprien Bérard's extended novel adaptation, *Lord Ruthven ou les vampires* (1820), as well as by numerous theatrical adaptations and parodies. Charles Nodier's 1819 play *Le Vampire* is generally acknowledged as the more faithful stage adaptation, where others insert the Lord Ruthven character into various Gothic narratives. J.R. Planche's English stage melodramas featuring Lord Ruthven initially appeared in 1820 but were so popular that they ran regularly into the 1870s. In more recent fiction, Lord Ruthven appears in Kim Newman's "Anno Dracula" series (1992–)—an alternate history vampire saga stretching from the Victorian period to the 1980s.

S. Artt

References and Suggested Reading

Frayling, Christopher. *Vampyres: Lord Byron to Count Dracula*. London: Faber and Faber, 1991.

Gelder, Ken. *Reading the Vampire*. Abingdon, Oxon: Routledge, 1994.

Macdonald, David Lorne. *Poor Polidori: A Critical Biography of the Author of The Vampyre*. Toronto: University of Toronto Press, 1991.

Polidori, John. "The Vampyre." In *The Vampyre and Other Tales of the Macabre*, edited by Robert Morrison and Chris Baldick, 1–24. New York: Oxford University Press, 2008.

Praz, Mario. *The Romantic Agony*. Translated by Angus Davidson. New York: Oxford University Press, 1970.

Rigby, Mair. "'Prey to some cureless disquiet': Polidori's Queer Vampyre at the Margins of Romanticism." *Romanticism on the Net* 36–37 (November 2004–February 2005). <http://www.erudit.org/revue/ron/2005/v/n36-37/011135ar.html>.

Senf, Carol A. *The Vampire in 19th Century English Literature*. Bowling Green, OH: Bowling Green State University Popular Press, 1988.

Twitchell, James. *The Living Dead: A Study of the Vampire in Romantic Literature*. Durham, NC: Duke University Press, 1981.

SALAMANDER—*see* Elemental

SAMAEL—*see* Angel; Devil, The; Incubus/Succubus; Lilith

SAMSA, GREGOR

Gregor Samsa is the central character of "The Metamorphosis" ("Die Verwandlung"), published in 1915 by the modernist Franz Kafka (1883–1924). Samsa awakes one morning having "found himself"—the passive construction is central to his monstrosity—"transformed in his bed into a horrible/monstrous insect-like figure" (115). This apparent metamorphosis forms the core of the subsequent narrative, as Gregor and his family readjust their bourgeois domesticity to deal with this monstrous son, first by confining Gregor to his bedroom, before finally rejecting him outright. The story ends with Gregor's silent demise and the apparent return of his family to normalcy. Owing both to the narrative focalization through Gregor and to the family's progressively negligent behavior towards him, his monstrosity increasingly renders him as a figure to be pitied more than abhorred.

Kafka openly plays with issues of Gregor's monstrosity, even if the text stops short of depicting his monstrous body in the usual manner of traditional horror or fantastic texts. The "found himself" of the first sentence merely presents the *possibility* of a metamorphosis, so that the monstrous here seems rather to be the result of the story's polyvalent and ambiguous modernist style. Reactions to Gregor throughout the text slowly suggest that something awful has indeed happened, however. Even ignoring the references to his multiple small legs and to various bodily fluids as signs of an actual metamorphosis, the story presents a disturbed relationship to the human body that is constantly coded by Gregor and the others in terms of the monstrous. Gregor's appearances invoke the traditional affective responses to the monstrous—he causes wonder, anger, and even horror, with the agent sent by his employer, for example, running away in disgust. In focusing on these responses, "The Metamorphosis" not only depicts a monster, but also thematizes the processes of encoding the body by which monstrosity is always defined. If Gregor initially *feels* as though he is a "monstrous vermin," by the end of the story he *has* become completely encoded as an "old dung beetle" (179).

Kafka's story both thematically and stylistically deems problematic the seemingly simplest of ontological questions pertaining to the definition of the human and the animal. In an almost freak-show scene shortly before his death, Gregor is tempted out of the isolation of his bedroom by his sister playing her violin for three lodgers that the family has taken in order to make ends meet. Aroused by the music, Gregor fantasizes about leaving his isolation and convincing his sister to come and join him in his bedroom; he declares: "for the first time" his "horrifying figure" could be of use to him—he "wanted to be at every door of his room at once to hiss and spit at his attackers" (186). With the music in the background, Gregor creeps slowly towards the others and shocks and disgusts them. The lodgers are at first bemused and then bitterly complain about the "repugnant conditions" in the Samsa household, at which stage the father drives Gregor back into his room in an almost choreographed dance. In a curious mixture of reported speech and narratorial commentary, the text finally asks the question: "Was he an animal if music could move him thus?" (185), highlighting the key issue in the text and a central problem of the monstrous: namely the difficulties in defining the normal and abnormal, the human and animal, and orderly and disorderly behavior.

Despite the masses of criticism that Kafka's story has attracted, the jury is still out on whether or not Gregor's monstrous metamorphosis genuinely occurs. The text blurs the borders between the metaphorical and the factual, the form of depiction and the depicted—thereby rendering any definitive interpretation problematic. At the very least, the metamorphosis of the title refers to an extreme feeling of estrangement that Gregor harbors towards his own body, so that both he and his family experience him as strange. The real scandal of Gregor's corporeality derives from Kafka's disruption of the borders between the human and the animal, that is, between the concept of humanity based on the rational control of the body by its intellect and its naked corporeality. As Frank Möbus has remarked, "man can barely become less human than Gregor Samsa sees himself and he is portrayed" (71).

Fittingly, Gregor's transformation into this atavistic corporeality goes hand in hand with his leaving all the trappings of modernity behind. When he stays in bed and misses his train, he slips out of the machine-based rhythms of modern life (alarm clock ... train ... sales ... sleep) that had previously defined his daily life as a sales rep. Whether the metamorphosis is the result of this modern life itself or of Gregor's refusing to adhere to its rhythms any longer is a matter of debate in Kafka studies; there is broad consensus, however, that his identity becomes more and more defined by his animal urges.

"The Metamorphosis" plays with these fears, drawing on a specifically post-Darwinian discourse of the monstrous body, according to which the intellectual barriers seemingly dividing humans from animals are less certain than believed. If the corporeal had previously been demonized in relation to mankind's intellect, it now returns into view as a primitive, tabooed form of naked existence. Gregor too loses control over his own body, develops "the voice of an animal" (131), loses the capacity to communicate and relies increasingly on his basic senses (smell, touch, and taste). The constant references to bodily mucus and brown juices flowing from his mouth denote this corporeality as a degenerative process. This points towards a monstrous state in which the brutal forces of man's animal impulses, the animalistic within the human being itself, become the basis of a daily threat to human identity. This is the monstrous disruption at the core of Kafka's and Gregor's text.

When the protagonist of William Gibson's novel *Idoru* (1996), Colin Laney, walks into a bar called "Death Cube K" in post-apocalyptic, twenty-first-century Tokyo, it is obvious that Gregor's monstrosity is a part of popular consciousness. Alongside references to other Kafka texts such as "In the Penal Colony," the bar includes insect-like mandibles overhead and chairs molded from a brown, chitinous resin. Alongside countless literary references, "The Metamorphosis" has also been adapted for stage and film productions, as well as graphic novels. In 1969, Steven Berkoff performed a legendary stage adaptation in London; in 1983, Brian Howard used Berkoff's script as a libretto for his opera version of the story. Film adaptations have traditionally struggled to cope with the complex, ambiguous narrative voice of the pre-text that requires either an intense use of point-of-view camera perspectives or suitable voice-overs, as Jan Němec's 1975 *Die Verwandlung* can illustrate. David Cronenberg's *The Fly* (1986; see **Fly, The**) includes a tongue-in-cheek reference to its literary predecessor when Seth Brundle (Jeff Goldblum) remarks shortly before the end of his transformation: "I'm an insect ... who dreamt he was a man." There have been many graphic novels and comic adaptations based on Gregor Samsa, most notably those by US artists Robert Crumb and David Zaine Mairowitz (1993), and Peter Kuper (2003). Samsa's problematic relationship to his own corporeality and the resulting nightmarish monstrosity seem to resonate still in late twentieth- and early twentieth-first-century thought and culture.

Barry Murnane

References and Suggested Reading

Anderson, Mark M. *Kafka's Clothes: Ornament and Aestheticism in the Habsburg Fin de Siècle*. Oxford: Clarendon Press, 1992.

Brady, Martin, and Helen Hughes. "Kafka Adapted to Film." In *The Cambridge Companion to Kafka*, edited by Julian Preece, 226–41. Cambridge: Cambridge University Press, 2002.

Corngold, Stanley. *The Commentator's Despair: The Interpretation of Kafka's Metamorphosis*. London: Kennikat Press, 1973.

Kafka, Franz. "The Metamorphosis." In *Schriften. Tagebücher. Briefe. Kritische Ausgabe: Drucke zu Lebzeiten*, edited by Wolf Kittler et al., 113–200. Frankfurt am Main: Fischer, 2002.

——. "The Metamorphosis." In *The Metamorphosis*, edited and translated by Stanley Corngold, 1–42. New York: W.W. Norton, 2006.

Möbus, Frank. *Sündenfälle. Die Geschlechtlichkeit in Erzählungen Franz Kafkas*. Göttingen: Wallstein, 1994.

Murnane, Barry. "Ungeheuere Arbeiter: Moderne Monstrosität am Beispiel von Gregor Samsa." In *Monster*, edited by Roland Borgards, Christiane Holm, and Günter Oesterle, 289–307. Würzburg: Königshausen & Neumann, 2009.

Robertson, Ritchie. *Kafka: Judaism, Politics and Literature*. Oxford: Clarendon Press, 1985.

SANDMAN, THE

The Sandman is an imaginary character who sprinkles magic sand into the eyes of good children to bring them pleasant dreams. He is also a bogeyman used to frighten naughty children. He first appeared as a literary figure in E.T.A. Hoffmann's short story "Der Sandmann" (1814). Another author of literary fairytales, Hans Christian Andersen, wrote about the dream **elf**, Ole Lukoje, and his brother, death (see **Death, Personified**) in "Ole Lukøje" (1841), and this tale appeared in English as "The Sandman" (1861). More recently, the contemporary writer Neil Gaiman produced a series of graphic novels that revolved around a figure called *Sandman* (DC Comics, Vertigo, 1989–96).

The Sandman figure combines aspects of mythological beings connected with sleep, dreams, and death, as well as traditional bogeymen figures and nursery lore. In Hoffmann's "Der Sandmann," the protagonist Nathaniel identifies a sinister scientist, Coppelius, who constantly frustrates his attempts to marry with a nursery bogeyman known as the Sandman who throws sand in the eyes of children who refuse to sleep and causes their eyes to fall out. He collects these eyes as food for his children who live in an iron nest on the moon. Hoffmann's source may be the famous medieval treatise on demonology, *Malleus Malificarum* (*The Hammer of the Witches*, 1486), which describes how witches collect human penises and place them in a nest (Part II, Question I, Chapter VII). Hoffmann's tale is discussed in detail in Sigmund Freud's 1919 analysis of "Das Unheimliche," the uncanny, the effects of which, according to Freud, are associated with repressed feelings induced by sexual anxiety.

Hans Christian Andersen's elf-like protagonist Ole Lukøje ("eye-closer") is a less overtly threatening figure who eventually reveals that his name is Morpheus; Thanatos (death) is his brother. Translated as the Sandman in English, he brings dreams to good children but punishes naughty children with dreamless sleep. Eighteenth-century references to this figure predate the tale, and in 1840 Andersen wrote to a Swedish friend comparing the sleep-inducing powers of Ole Lukøje and the German Sandman (see *Anderseniana*, 3. rk. II, 2, 1975, s. 146f).

The Sandman is one of several nursery lore figures related to dreaming, but clear references to the Sandman in English do not appear to predate the translation of Hoffmann's tale. The two figures came to be further identified once Andersen's tale was translated into English, and the use of "the Sandman" as a translation for Andersen's character may suggest that the term referred to a nursery lore figure at an earlier period.

The Sandman has played a variety of roles in contemporary popular culture. A vigilante detective known as "the Sandman," who wears a gas mask to protect his identity and subdues criminals with a sleeping-gas gun, appeared in DC Comics of the 1930s and 1940s. In the 1960s, DC Comics' competitor, Marvel Comics, introduced a **shapeshifter** named Sandman with the ability to turn himself into sand, who served as first an antagonist toward, and then an ally of, Spider-Man. He plays an antagonist in 2007's *Spider-Man 3* (performed by Thomas Haden Church; film directed by Sam Raimi). A long-running German language children's program, *Der Sandemanchen*, was created in the 1950s, based on Hans Christian Andersen's figure. In *Logan's Run*, a dystopian science fiction novel by William F. Nolan and George Clayton Jones (1967; film directed by Michael Anderson, 1976), the police enforcers are euphemistically called "Sandmen." The main character, Logan, is a "Sandman" who eventually defies the dystopian authorities. In the animated film *The Sandman* (Paul Berry, 1991), based on E.T.A. Hoffmann's story, a small boy makes his way up to bed through a Gothic house followed by a sinister and mysterious entity. Perhaps closest to the dream-like erosion of reality found in Hoffmann's tale is the world of Neil Gaiman's graphic novel hero, the Sandman (also called Dream and Morpheus), who is lord and personification of dreams and has several siblings referred to as "the Endless," including his sister, Death.

Juliette Wood

References and Suggested Reading

Andersen, Hans Christian. *Andersen's Tales for Children*. Translated by Alfred Wehnert. London: Bell and Daldy, 1866.

Hoffmann, E.T.A. "The Sandman" [1814]. In *Tales From the German*, translated by John Oxenford and C.A. Feiling, 140–64. London: Chapman and Hall, 1844.

"Motif *Ole Lukoie, the sandman* in Hans Christian Anderson's fairy tales and stories." *Hans Christian Andersen Center*. Updated 26 June 2012. <http://www.andersen.sdu.dk/forskning/motiver/vismotiv_e.html?id=77>.

Simpson, Jacqueline, and Steve Roud. *A Dictionary of English Folklore*. Oxford: Oxford University Press, 2003.

Tatar, Maria M. "E.T.A. Hoffmann's 'Der Sandmann': Reflection and Romantic Irony." *MLN* 95, no. 3 (1980): 585–608.

Taylor, Archer. "Raw Head and Bloody Bones." *The Journal of American Folklore* 69, no. 272 (1956): 114–75.

Widdowson, John. "The Bogeyman: Some Preliminary Observations on Frightening Figures." *Folklore* 82, no. 2 (1971): 99–115.

SASQUATCH—*see* Bigfoot

SATAN—*see* Demon; Devil, The

SAURON—*see* Tolkien, Monsters In

SCHONSPIGEL—*see* Demon

SCIOPOD—*see* Donestre; Mutant and Freak; Races, Monstrous

SCREWTAPE—*see* Demon

SCYLLA AND CHARYBDIS

Scylla and Charybdis are rocky cliffs marking the narrow Straits of Messina between Italy and Sicily. In classical mythology, Scylla was a ravening **sea monster** and Charybdis was a surging vortex or whirlpool; to navigate between them meant certain death. The phrase "between Scylla and Charybdis" describes a choice between two equally undesirable, dangerous alternatives.

The daughter of the primordial earth-goddess Gaia and Poseidon or Pontos, Charybdis was hurled into the sea by Zeus as punishment for her rapacious nature. There she became a belching whirlpool who thrice daily sucks down the surrounding waters and then vomits them forth. Charybdis is associated with the tides and with the marine goddess of the sea monsters Ceto/Crataeis or Ceto-Trienos (also known as **Lamia** and Hecate).

The eight-century BCE poet Homer describes Scylla as the daughter of Crataeis (*Odyssey*, Book 12). Later commentators describe her as the daughter of Crataeis and her brother Phorcos, "the old man of the sea" (Pliny, *Natural History* 3.73, first century CE; Hyginus, *Fabulae*, Fable 199, and Pseudo-Apollodorus, *Library* E7.20, both second century CE); or the offspring of Typhon and Echidna, the primordial snake goddess (*Fabulae* 151).

In Ovid's *Metamorphoses* (first century CE), Scylla is not born a monster, but a beautiful maiden with whom the sea-god Glaucus falls in love. He implores the enchantress **Circe** to make Scylla reciprocate his affection. Circe, who craves Glaucus's attentions for herself, instead poisons Scylla's bathing cove, and Scylla metamorphoses into a vicious, yelping sea monster with six mouths. According to two sources, Scylla was ultimately slain by Heracles (Lycophron, a Greek poet of the third century BCE, and Pseudo-Hyginus, a

Roman mythographer of the second century CE). Ovid writes that Scylla is transformed into a rock (*Metamorphoses* 14.70–76). In John Keats's poem "Endymion" (1818), after a thousand years of age and pain, Glaucus restores the drowned (not monstrous) maiden Scylla to life and recovers his own youth.

Three mythological heroes braved the passage between Scylla and Charybdis: Odysseus, Aeneas, and Jason. On Odysseus's journey from victory in Troy to his home in Ithaca, the goddess **Circe** instructs Odysseus how to navigate the narrows between the homicidal monster Scylla and Charybdis, a heaving whirlpool beneath a cliff planted with a large fig tree. She warns him that Scylla is cruel and invincible, and that he must inevitably fail in trying to pass through safely with all his men. Indeed, as Odysseus and his mariners attempt to steer away from the sucking whirlpool, Scylla darts from her cave to seize six of his strongest men, one in each mouth. Odysseus is sickened by their pitiful cries as each is dashed against the rocks and devoured before his eyes (*Odyssey* 12.210–259). After escaping, Odysseus and his remaining mariners are trapped by ill winds on the island of Thrinacia, where the sun god Helios keeps his flocks. Disobeying Odysseus, the men kill and eat the sacred animals, upon which Zeus destroys them and their ship. The sole survivor, Odysseus, is blown back to Charybdis; she sucks his raft down but he survives by clinging to the branches of the overhanging fig tree until she belches it forth again.

The Trojan wanderer Aeneas was more fortunate than Odysseus. Setting forth after his city's defeat to found a new home, he is warned by Helenus the prophet to make a wide berth of Scylla and Charybdis, and his ships are driven to safety by the north wind (Virgil, *Aeneid* 3.655 ff, first century BCE). The text is not completely clear as to whether the Trojans actually navigate through the passage itself or circumnavigate as they were advised, but Ovid is definite that they survive the passage, because Scylla had been previously transformed into a rock (*Metamorphoses* 14.70–76). Jason and his Argonauts are more fortunate still: the goddess Hera commands the sea-nymph Thetis to guide them through the strait (Apollonius of Rhodes, *Argonautica* 4.825, third century BCE).

Homer describes Scylla as having twelve misshapen feet and six long necks, each ending in a head with three rows of sharp teeth (*Odyssey* 12.54). Scylla appears in fourth-century BCE Greek art with a woman's upper body, a sea serpent's long tail, and six slavering dog's heads at her waist, described by Ovid as "hell-black waist with raging dogs" (*Metamorphoses* 14.1). According to Virgil: "Scylla guards the right shore, insatiable Charybdis the left ... But Scylla lurks unseen in a cavernous lair, from which she pushes out her lips to drag ships onto the rocks. Her upper part is human—a girl's beautiful body down to the privates; below, she is a weird sea-monster, with dolphin's tail and a belly of wolverine sort" (*Aeneid* 3. 420 ff).

In James Joyce's *Ulysses* (1922), the chapter "Scylla and Charybdis" represents competing interpretations of Shakespeare's *Hamlet*, through which the intellectually ambitious young Stephen Dedalus must navigate in his precarious passage towards acceptance among Dublin's literary elite. The mythologist Joseph Campbell (1904–87) identifies Scylla as "the rock of logic" and Charybdis as the "vortex of mysticism" (101), following Francis Bacon (1561–1626) who wrote of the virtue of intellectual moderation: "in every knowledge and science, and in the rules and axioms appertaining to them, a mean must be kept between too many distinctions and too much generality" (*Of the Wisdom of the Ancients* XXVII). Stephen's elders appear to concede the worth of his interpretations, saying "the truth is midway" (9.1017) before dashing his hopes on the metaphorical rocks.

Scylla and Charybdis appear in *The Sea of Monsters* (2006), the second book of Rick Riordan's children's series, "Percy Jackson and the Olympians." On a quest to find the Golden Fleece and rescue their friend from the one-eyed **giant** Polyphemus, the teenaged demi-god Percy enters the Bermuda Triangle with his friends: Scylla attacks the crew, Charybdis destroys their ship, and all of their companions apparently perish.

Persephone Braham

References and Suggested Reading

Bacon, Sir Francis. *Of the Wisdom of the Ancients* [1609]. Reprint, New York: Garland, 1976.

Campbell, Joseph. *Mythic Worlds, Modern Words: On the Art of James Joyce*. Lovato, CA: New World Library, 1993.

Joyce, James. *Ulysses* [1918–20]. Reprint, New York: Vintage, 1990.

Murgatroyd, Paul. *Mythical Monsters in Classical Literature*. London: Duckworth, 2007.

Ovid. *Metamorphoses*. Translated by A.D. Melville. Oxford: Oxford University Press, 1986.

Virgil. *The Aeneid*. Translated by Cecil Day-Lewis. Oxford: Oxford Paperbacks, 1998.

SEA MONSTERS

The ocean environment offers tremendous potential for monstrosity: more unfathomable and mysterious than outer space, even to modern science, the deep sea is an alien world cradling unknown life, sometimes hostile, sometimes profound, sometimes enlightening. Literary sea monsters originate in mythology and folklore, which themselves derive from anecdotal sightings of sea serpents, **dragons**, and **kraken**, arguably accounted for by the scientifically confirmed existence of animals such as whales, oar-fish, basking sharks, and giant or colossal squid. In literature and film, sea monsters are often portrayed as aggressive or threatening, represented as reptiles, amphibians, mollusks, or mammals, and sometimes an amalgamation of multiple categories. Thus, the fictional sea monster often possesses biologically plausible origins, blended with fantastical representation and a symbolic narrative purpose. These features exist on a spectrum, with some monsters used purely for horror, for example, and others represented with close attention to known science.

Sea monsters have a lot in common with other freshwater-dwelling monsters such as the **Loch Ness monster**, the **Ogopogo**, the **kappa**, and the **Creature from the Black Lagoon** in terms of their general biological classifications, mysterious habits or origins, and ambivalent or hostile attitudes to humans. However, sea monsters tend to be less individualized than these localized monsters (**Godzilla**, for example, is an exception), instead sharing some broad generic functions and often forming species or categories of monster (krakens, **mermaids**, serpents) rather than named individuals. Sea monsters (particularly whales, kraken, and serpents) are catalogued early in natural histories, notably by Aristotle (fourth century BCE), Pliny the Elder (23 CE–79 CE), Olaus Magnus (1490–1557), and Bishop Erik Pontoppidan (1698–1764). They also feature in medieval bestiaries and later in innumerable nineteenth- and twentieth-century newspaper reports and scientific accounts.

Sea and water monsters have a strong mythological presence in cultures worldwide, often blamed for tidal waves, earthquakes, or lost ships, although in modern literature and cinema they are often instead disturbed *by* earthquakes (or by human interference). The Japanese

Jish-in-uno is a type of 700-mile cod, and Maori legend tells of the lurking Tipua (a kind of **demon** or uncanny thing). In Greek mythology, Hercules and Perseus both battle and kill sea monsters. Norse mythology contributes Jörmungandr, the submerged world serpent clasping the globe. Giant cetaceans feature in the Hebrew Talmud; **Leviathan** and Jonah's whale in the Bible; and **Tiamat**, dragon-goddess of the sea, in Babylonian creation myth. Millennia of mythology and anecdotal sightings of giant serpents, krakens, or unidentified monsters find their way into early and modern creative literature.

Particularly in early writing, it is not always easy to distinguish between myth, natural history, and fiction. The *Arabian Nights* story of Sinbad landing on a giant whale mistaken for an island is a recurring sea monster myth, as well as featuring in historical anecdotes (see **Arabian Nights, Monsters In The**). The **sirens** in Homer's *Odyssey* (c. ninth century BCE) can be seen as a type of mermaid, as can the fish-god Dagon (also appearing in the work of John Milton [1608–74], and a 2001 film [*Dagon*, directed by Stuart Gordon] based on a 1919 story of the same name by H.P. Lovecraft [see **Lovecraft, Monsters In**]). Odysseus also braves the monster and whirlpool duo, **Scylla and Charybdis**. In Virgil's first-century BCE *Aeneid*, sea serpents are sent to kill the Trojan Laocoön and his sons.

In medieval, early modern, and Renaissance literature, sea monsters begin to be presented as natural creatures, albeit seen as freakish and frightening. Spenser's *The Faerie Queene* (1590) includes a catalogue of sea monsters, presented as the deformed products of nature, from "spring-headed hydres" to "greedy rosmarines with visages deforme" (Book II, Canto XII, l.204–26; see **Hydra**). Sea monsters also appear as amalgamations of human and animal; in Shakespeare's *The Tempest* (c. 1611), Trinculo views **Caliban** as somewhere between a man and a fish, while the medieval German poem "Das Meerwunder" (reworked by German author Gerhart Hauptmann in 1934) involves the monstrous offspring of a queen and a monster from the sea. P'u Sung-Ling's "Football on the Tung-T'ing Lake" (c. 1679) recounts a game with marine monsters shaped like men; a severed arm becomes a fin in the morning. Jonas Lie's "The Fisherman and the Draug" (1870) exemplifies a recurring fairytale in which denizens of the sea shift between human and animal shapes: a fisherman unknowingly attacks the Draug in its seal form; the Draug revenges itself by drowning his family at sea (see **Shapeshifter**).

In Christian culture, the Biblical Leviathan influences literature and serves in the political theory of Thomas Hobbes (1588–1679) as a metaphor for strength and power, as well as denoting a whale. The Leviathan is glimpsed in William Blake's *The Marriage of Heaven and Hell* (1790), and is evoked by Ishmael in Herman Melville's ***Moby-Dick*** (1851). The latter's great white whale marks the beginning of modern literary beast monsters, represented demonically as the focus of Ahab's obsession, and as a natural mammalian creature (see Andriano). In Jules Verne's *Twenty Thousand Leagues Under the Sea* (1869), not only is the submarine *Nautilus* attacked by giant squid, but the ship itself is initially taken for a sea monster. Observed spouting water and air, and estimated at 350 feet long, the *Nautilus* is thought to be a kraken or a giant whale. Rudyard Kipling's "A Matter of Fact" (1893) describes a steamer to Southampton caught in the vast swells generated by an underwater volcanic eruption. Chill water and sediment from the ocean floor are flung up to the surface, along with a monstrous sea serpent: white, eyeless, and unearthly. Ejected violently from its usual habitat, the creature is injured and helpless; crew and passengers watch its death throes with pity, as it is joined by its mate, unable to help it. In England, no one will believe the tale, and the journalist witnesses are forced to sell the story as fiction.

H.G. Wells's "The Abyss" (1896) concerns a deep-sea exploration project: an explorer, Elstead, is lowered to the sea floor in a specially designed steel sphere. On his return, Elstead is bruised and traumatized, and recounts his discovery of strange quasi-human sea creatures, bipedal and combining reptilian, amphibian, and piscine features. The creatures tow his sphere to a phosphorescent underwater city, where they worship their discovery, until the cord attaching him snaps and he floats back to the surface. On a second expedition, Elstead does not return. William Hope Hodgson (1877–1918) includes several sea monsters in his novels and short stories, often combining human, amphibious, and invertebrate features in Gothic distortions of mermen (see **Mermaid/Merman**). A giant sea serpent attacks in "A Tropical Horror" (1905), as do cephalopods in "From the Tideless Sea" (1906). In "Out of the Storm" (1909), the sea itself becomes a hellish monster, the breaking waves its teeth; Hodgson's most striking sea monsters, however, are those that blur conventional boundaries. In "The Derelict" (1912), an old ship found adrift in the Indian Ocean has kept its wooden shape but has transformed into a creature part animal, part fungus, whose substance attacks and consumes sailors careless enough to board it. The transformation is attributed to a natural combination of conditions and materials.

While nineteenth-century literature tends to present sea monster stories from the human perspective, twentieth-century fiction also presents a non-human point of view, or encourages empathy with the creature. In Ray Bradbury's "Undersea Guardians" (1944), drowned men and women live on in the sea, attacking German U-boats and preserving Allied convoys. Mermaid-like, they also resemble underwater **zombies**, their dead white flesh revivified. The heroine, Alita, sacrifices herself to prevent a torpedo sinking the ship on which her beloved still lives. In Bradbury's "The Fog Horn" (1951), the calling of a lighthouse's foghorn attracts the attention of a lonely monster from a million years of deep-sea slumber, pitied by the lighthouse workers even as it destroys the tower in its anguish.

Sea monsters are common features of children's literature and film, as objects of friendship as well as fear. The Gift in *A Gift from Winklesea* (Helen Creswell, 1969), friendly and intelligent, is monstrous by reason of its indeterminate species rather than its appearance or behavior: it hatches from an egg, is compared to a sea lion ("a *rare* kind of sea-lion" [74]), but is apparently amphibious. It leaves its human family to return to the sea just before its rapid growth causes serious problems. Friendly monsters in children's literature often occupy such interstitial positions between fear and empathy, engaging with child and adult characters in different ways; the marginal position of the monster enables a bond with a marginalized or disempowered child. The serpent in the Maori tale *Nuki and the Sea Serpent* (Ruth Park, 1969) is both a friend to Nuki, evicted from his village for telling "lies," and an object of terror to the village elders, until they accept the value of storytelling. While Nuki's monster is a personified fantasy, such monsters can also be biological and symbolic, like Kahu's whale in Witi Ihimaera's *Whale Rider* (1987). In Kipling's "The Crab who Played with the Sea," from *The Just So Stories* (1902), and Ted Hughes's "How the Whale Became" (1963), the creatures undergo transformations that blend fantasy with biology to create modern myths of origin.

Science fiction also transforms sea creatures into new roles. Arthur C. Clarke's *The Deep Range* (1957) imagines a future in which whales are farmed for food and milk; despite extensive human control, monsters still lurk in the ocean depths and a giant squid is captured. China Miéville's *The Scar* (2002) contains a range of marine creatures and hybrids: the "Remade" prisoner Tanner Sack has tentacles grafted to his chest as a punishment and later undergoes surgery to become fully amphibian; the floating city of Armada is towed by a captured avanc, a sea monster loosely based on Welsh myth; and Silas Fennec is hunted by grindylow. (Grindylow are traditionally lake-dwelling water demons, also appearing in J.K. Rowling's "Harry Potter" series [1997–2007]; in Miéville's novel, they are an intelligent amphibious race.)

In novels such as Christopher Moore's *The Lust Lizard of Melancholy Cove* (1999) and Ben H. Winters's *Sense and Sensibility and Sea Monsters* (2009), monsters are played for comedy. Winters recasts Austen's story in a scenario of a long-standing feud between people and sea creatures. Marine monster sequences are interpolated into Austen's tale; Willoughby becomes a deep-sea diver, Colonel Brandon has tentacles, and characters are attacked by octopi, sharks, and sea serpents.

Modern literature and film also continue to use sea monsters for terror. In the 1970s and 1980s, Peter Benchley wrote several sea monster thrillers using dangerous sea creatures, including a squid, a manta ray, a killer whale, and a great white shark (see **Animals, Monstrous**). In *Beast* (1991), a giant squid is disturbed by human activity. Several of his books were adapted into films, notably Steven Spielberg's famous suspenseful thriller, *Jaws* (1975). In the film, the predatory monster, a 20–25-foot great white shark, is presented as more sinister and intelligent than a normal animal. The shark harries a small American island resort before it is eventually blown up.

Numerous films visualize sea monsters, adapting classic tales such as *Moby-Dick* and Verne's adventures, or inventing new monsters. These are often enormous mollusks, reptiles, amphibians, or fish, or an indeterminate combination to create something uniquely strange and terrifying. In *Deep Rising* (Stephen Sommers, 1998), thieves hijack a cruise ship and become prey for a fanged kraken monster with Hydra-like serpents for tentacles. Gore Verbinski's *Pirates of the Caribbean: Dead Man's Chest* (2006) and *At World's End* (2007) feature a kraken as the pet of Davy Jones (Bill Nighy), himself a sort of tentacle-headed sea monster who is later forced to kill it.

In post-World War II films, the monster is often disturbed or affected by atomic bombs or weapons testing, and is sometimes an alien (see **Extraterrestrial**) or a type of **mutant**; others are presented as naturally occurring. These are often disaster movies belonging to an extended family of sequels, imitations, and rivals. The ***Creature from the Black Lagoon*** (Jack Arnold, 1954), although a river monster, inspired a spate of imitations using a Gill Man character, such as *Creature from the Haunted Sea* (Roger Corman, 1961), a horror send-up with a rubbery and vaguely humanoid Caribbean sea monster. ***Leviathan*** (George P. Cosmatos, 1989) uses a scientific premise: "Leviathan" is the name of a wrecked Russian ship, and the "monsters" are the humans who find it and fall victim to the mutagenic experiments it conceals.

A number of films are built around urban destruction by a giant sea monster. Bradbury's "The Fog Horn" is the story behind Eugène Lourié's *The Beast from 20,000 Fathoms* (1953); nuclear testing disturbs a long-slumbering **dinosaur**, which awakes to threaten the east coast of the USA. Similar plots follow in several other films, including ***Behemoth** the Sea Monster* (Douglas Hickox and Eugène Lourié, 1959). Lourié directed another giant lizard film, *Gorgo* (1961), in which London is attacked by an angry mother in search of her captured son. The most famous monster of this kind, however, is **Godzilla**. The original Japanese movie *Gojira* (Ishirô Honda, 1954) was released in America as *Godzilla, King of the Monsters* (1956), with an American hero. A sort of giant amphibious dinosaur, Gojira is unleashed from hibernation by atomic bomb tests and proceeds to destroy Tokyo before its defeat. More than a dozen sequels followed, often with Gojira/Godzilla pitted against other monsters such as Gorgo. Tōhō, the production company behind *Gojira*, produced many other monster films, including *Kaitei Gunkan* (Ishirô Honda, 1963) about a giant sea serpent, Manda. *Gamera* (Noriaki Yuasa, 1966) was produced by rival studio Daiei Motion Pictures, about a giant prehistoric turtle, accidentally awakened from hibernation to terrorize Japan. Later movies offer innovations on this theme: *Cloverfield* (Matt Reeves, 2008), in which a monster is disturbed from underwater slumber, is shown from the point of view of victims, rather than survivors, their story recorded on video.

Emily Alder

References and Suggested Reading

Andriano, Joseph. *Immortal Monster: The Mythological Evolution of the Fantastic Beast in Modern Fiction and Film*. Westport, CT: Greenwood, 1999.

Baker, Margaret. *Folklore of the Sea*. Newton Abbot: David & Charles, 1979.

Cresswell, Helen. *A Gift from Winklesea*. London: Hodder, 1999.

Ellis, Richard. *Monsters of the Sea*. New York: Knopf, 1994.

Glut, Donald F. *Classic Movie Monsters*. Metuchen, NJ: Scarecrow, 1978.

Heuvelmans, Bernard. *The Kraken and the Colossal Octopus*. Letchworth: Kegan Paul, 2003.

Spenser, Edmund. *The Faerie Queene*. Edited by Thomas P. Roche. London: Penguin, 1987.

SELKIE—*see* Shapeshifter

SEREK-A—*see* Mermaid/Merman

SHAPESHIFTER

The shapeshifter—an entity with the power to change its shape, size, species, or even sex—features prominently in secular and religious stories dating to thousands of years ago and continues to populate the popular media of today. Although involuntary transformation is a common theme in many stories, especially punitively—consider the story of Arachne, transformed by the goddess Athena into a spider, or the plight of Eustace Scrubb, who is transformed into a **dragon** in C.S. Lewis's *Voyage of the Dawn Treader* (1952)—true shapeshifters are those beings able to *control* their form to some extent, whether this is achieved through biological or magical means. For the purposes of this entry, changes brought about by using objects, such as drinking a potion or donning a cursed mask, do not truly make the user or victim a shapeshifter. This entry will first survey shapeshifters found in traditional stories from regions spanning the globe and how these creatures have persisted through time, and then cover shapeshifters' appearances by genre in more recent media.

Greco-Roman Mythology

The earliest examples of shapeshifters in literature stem from mythology. Many gods and goddesses in the Greco-Roman pantheon can change their shapes at will. Zeus takes forms ranging from a bull to a shower of gold to the goddess Artemis, often for the purpose of forced sexual congress. Zeus, however, runs afoul of a fellow shapeshifter: while trying to destroy the titaness Metis (see **Titan**) to forestall a prophecy, Zeus tricks her into becoming a fly and consumes her. Metis is hardly daunted by this and cranially impregnates Zeus with the unborn Athena. Zeus's transformations have even influenced other imaginative works, such as William Butler Yeats's sonnet, "Leda and the Swan" (1924). Poseidon, too, changes form in many tales, such as while pursuing Demeter. From Proteus, who appears as the shapeshifting sea god that Menelaus defeats in Homer's *The Odyssey* (c. eighth century BCE), we get the word protean, used to describe things as extremely versatile, variable, or capable of changing shape. While completing his eleventh labor, Hercules must grapple the sea god Nereus—who changes through a variety of animal forms—to learn the location of the Garden of the Hesperides. Ovid's narrative poem *Metamorphoses* (first century CE) collates and expands upon numerous myths and legends related to shapeshifting and other transformations, influencing countless adaptations, including versions in poetry, drama, and even music.

In Religious Traditions

Many early examples of shapeshifters stem from religion-linked mythologies. In the realm of Christian occult practices, various **demons** are believed capable of changing form, including Satan himself (see **Devil, The**). A shapeshifting Satan posing as a pitiable prisoner convinces a man to release him in an episode of *The Twilight Zone* called "The Howling Man" (season 2, episode 41, 1960; director Douglas Heyes). In Islamic culture, spirits classified as djinn and ifrit (see **Djinn and Genie**) are sometimes portrayed with shapeshifting powers, appearing in numerous tales in the collection of folktales, *One Thousand and One Nights*, compiled in Arabic and dating back to the tenth century CE (see **Arabian Nights, Monsters In The**). The Genie of Disney's *Aladdin* (Ron Clements and John Musker, 1992), famously voiced by Robin Williams, is a modern incarnation of this category, and after becoming a genie himself, Jafar (voiced by Jonathan Freeman) demonstrates similar powers in *The Return of Jafar* (Toby Shelton et al., 1994). Hindu tradition is rich with tales of shapeshifting beings, including the categories of rākṣasaḥ and asura, two types of generally evil supernatural entities. In the ancient Sanskrit *Rāmāyaṇa* epic (c. 4000 BCE), the powerful shapeshifting demon Rāvaṇa leads the evil rākṣasaḥ forces, and even sends the shapeshifting rākṣasaḥ Mārīcha in the form of a deer to lure away the heroine Sītā. The heroes of the *Rāmāyaṇa* are aided by the vānara, a race of shapeshifting monkeys led by Hanumān. The *Rāmāyaṇa* has seen numerous adaptations across Asia in a variety of media, from the Japanese animated film *Ramayana: The Legend of Prince Rama* (Yugo Sako and Ram Mohan, 1992) to the comic book series *Ramayan 3392 AD* (2006–2007), written by Shamik Dasgupta and illustrated by Abhishek Singh. Finally, the nāga is a serpentine being from Hindu folklore that changes between snake and human form in some tales.

The Americas

Trickster figures from folk stories of the Americas frequently appear as shapeshifters. Mayan stories describe the being Mestaclocan who could change his form, while tales of naguals—powerful shamans who can transform into animals—

derive from the Mexican Olmec tradition. The encantado is a bestial Brazilian shapeshifter—usually delphine, though some are serpentine—able to take human form, often to abduct people. The indigenous peoples of North America tell tales revolving around a number of shapeshifting entities: Nanabozho is a shapeshifting Ojibwa trickster that often takes the form of a rabbit, while the Lakota trickster Iktomi prefers an arachnid form. The shapeshifting tricksters Raven and Coyote appear in the mythologies of various First Nations peoples, with Coyote even appearing in contemporary novelist Neil Gaiman's *American Gods* (2001). The skin-walker is a person able to transform into an animal and remains a popular figure in modern American media, featuring in comic books, short stories, and even a feature film—*Skinwalkers* (James Isaac, 2006). However, the term has been co-opted in popular culture to refer to **werewolves** and other were-animals, rather than the traditional figures from Native American folklore. The **Windigo**—an evil spirit able to possess and sometimes transform into people—also features as a shapeshifter that has gained popularity in contemporary culture, appearing in such works as the 2001 film, *Wendigo* (Larry Fessenden).

East Asia

East Asian folklore contains many shapeshifters based on real animals, a theme persisting in modern media. An example from Chinese literature is Sūn Wùkōng, the simian protagonist of the novel *Journey to the West*, written by Wú Chéng'ēn near the end of the sixteenth century (see **Monkey King**). Born a regular monkey, Sūn Wùkōng acquires superpowers through Daoist techniques, including the ability to shapeshift into various animate and inanimate forms. Sūn Wùkōng stars in numerous literary, television, film, and comic incarnations, from the Chinese animated film *Havoc in Heaven* (Wan Laiming, 1961) to the live-action Japanese TV series *Saiyūki* (creator Wu Cheng'en, 1978–80), and even informed the character Son Goku in the *Dragon Ball* franchise of manga and anime. Another shapeshifter story popular during the Ming dynasty was the "Legend of the White Snake," in which a man falls in love with the titular creature who has turned into a beautiful woman. This tale has generated numerous adaptations, including E. Hoffman Price's 1979 novella *The Devil Wives of Li Fong*, and even the 2011 film *The Sorcerer and the White Snake* (Siu-Tung Ching) starring Jet Li. The fox spirit is an especially prolific shapeshifter, known variously as the *húli jīng* (fox spirit) in China, the ***kitsune*** (fox) in Japan, and the *kumiho* (nine-tailed fox) in Korea. Although the specifics of the tales vary, these fox spirits can usually shapeshift, often taking the form of beautiful young women who attempt to seduce men, whether for mere mischief or to consume their bodies or spirits. In Japan, fox spirits even feature in Shinto religious rites, as they are considered the servants of Inari, an androgynous *kami* (spirit/god) associated with fertility and rice planting.

Fox spirits are not the only animalistic beings with the power to shapeshift in Japanese stories, however. The *jorōgumo* is an arachnid *yōkai* (**demon**/spirit/monster, referring to a type of creature from Japanese folklore) that can transform into a beautiful woman to lure in prey. The *bakeneko* (monster cat) is a feline yōkai sometimes able to take the form of a human female and even become the **doppelganger** of a woman it kills. The bakeneko, however, is not always a mischievous or antagonistic character, and at times helps humans. The ***tanuki*** (raccoon dog), an animal indigenous to Japan, features in yōkai stories ancient and modern as another morally ambiguous shapeshifter.

Unlike the other animal spirits mentioned previously, the tanuki commonly transforms into a much wider range of forms—even inanimate objects such as statues and tea kettles (see **Objects, Animate**). The tanuki is renowned for its colossal testicles, which are fully transformable into things ranging from umbrellas and drums to entire rooms. This creature endures in modern popular media. For example, in the 1988 video game *Super Mario Bros 3*, the player can find a tanuki suit power-up, allowing the character Mario to fly and transform into a statue for protection (see **Video Games, Monsters In**). The 1994 animated Japanese film *Heisei Tanuki Gassen Ponpoko* (Isao Takahata), usually shortened in English to *Pom Poko*, focuses on a group of tanuki who must fight to protect their natural environment. The tanuki even stars in non-Japanese media, making appearances in works ranging from the Korean massively multiplayer online role-playing game (MMORPG) *Ragnarok Online* to Tom Robbins's 2003 novel, *Villa Incognito*. Other shapeshifting yōkai have experienced a similar popularity in film and literature, such as the various creatures in the 1968 film *Yōkai Daisensō* (*The Great Monster War*, Yoshiyuki Kuroda), for example, remade by Takashi Miike in 2005.

European Folklore

Shapeshifting entities are prominent in traditional European folklore, with some varieties—notably **vampires** and werewolves—spawning innumerable adaptations. Indeed, werewolves and other were-creatures are part of a wider tradition of therianthropy (metamorphosis of humans into animals) explored in other sections of this entry. Vampires, commonly portrayed as shapeshifting into bats, wolves, and other forms, also fall into this tradition. Although lycanthropes, vampires, and their ilk are especially prominent in pop culture today, there are many more European creatures able to shapeshift between humanoid and animal forms. In Norse mythology, both Odin and Loki change into a variety of human and bestial forms, but Loki does so much more frequently, usually in pursuit of mischief. Various types of **fairies** and spirits appear as shapeshifters in traditional tales, including the Cornish spriggan, the Welsh púca, the Germanic nixie, and the Celtic kelpie—an aquatic horse able to change into a beautiful woman in order to lure men to their doom. The selkie, a pinniped (fin-footed) creature from Northern European folklore capable of shedding its skin to become human—usually female and attractive—and re-donning it to regain animal form, appears in modern media ranging from folk music to A.E. van Vogt's novel *The Silkie* (1969). A similar shapeshifter is the swan maiden, which changes between avian and human form, featured famously in Tchaikovsky's 1876 opera *Swan Lake* and adapted into the 1994 animated film *The Swan Princess* (Richard Rich). Often, however, the shapeshifting creature is the antagonist of a folktale. In the classic fairytale "Puss in Boots," the finely shod feline must outwit an **ogre** who takes various forms. Disney's adaptation of another Mother Goose fairytale, *Sleeping Beauty* (Clyde Geronimi, 1959), features the villainess Malificent (voiced by Eleanor Audley) transforming into a **dragon** in a last-ditch bid to defeat the heroes.

British Literature

Many tales from the British Isles deal with humanoid shapeshifters, including deities, spellcasters, and even poets. In the Irish epic *Táin Bó Cúailnge*, dating in writing to the twelfth century, the protagonist Cú Chulainn is a shapeshifter and experiences changes called *ríastrad* (warp spasm) in battle, which cause a host of gruesome physiological transformations, compelling the hero to fight furiously. (A similarly involuntary metamorphosis is seen in the Marvel character Bruce Banner, who transforms into the superhuman Hulk when enraged.) Cú Chulainn's archnemesis is Morrígan, a powerful shapeshifting sorceress who changes into everything from a beautiful woman to an eel (see **Witch/ Wizard**). Another formidable female with shapeshifting powers is Morgan le Fay—whose origins may lie in common with Morrígan—featured in various retellings of Arthurian legend. Geoffrey of Monmouth describes Morgan turning into a bird in his *Vita Merlini* (1150), while Thomas Malory tells of Morgan self-petrifying in *Le Morte d'Arthur* (1485). Merlin himself appears as a shapeshifter, as in T.H. White's *The Sword in the Stone* (1939), where Merlin transforms himself and the protagonist Wart into animals, and even fights the witch Madam Mim in a magical shapeshifting duel, a memorable scene in the 1963 animated film adaptation (Wolfgang Reitherman). Another shapeshifter battle appears in Welsh folklore, when a boy named Gwion Bach attempts to evade the enchantress Ceridwen—after illicitly tasting of a wisdom and knowledge-granting potion she was brewing—by transforming into a series of agile animals, which she counters by turning into various predators. Finally, Ceridwen consumes him and later births him, but is unable to kill him because he becomes such a beautiful baby. Numerous other stories abound involving witches, **wizards**, druids, and other spellcasters changing their form through magical means.

Modern Fantasy

Many modern works of fantasy feature shapeshifters, who are often wielders of magic. The wizards of Ursula K. Le Guin's "Earthsea" novels (1964–2002) are able to transform into animals, as can the Immortals of Tamora Pierce's series by the same name. The magician Dolph, from Piers Anthony's "Xanth" novels (1977–present), can transform into many different forms, humanoid and animal. Various magic-wielding shapeshifters appear in Tolkien's Middle-earth books as well. In *The Silmarillion* (1977), Sauron appears as a powerful shapeshifter, able to transform into a werewolf, an immense bat, and others. In *The Hobbit* (1937), Beorn can change into a powerful bear-form, drawing Gandalf to speculate that he is the last of a race able to shapeshift into animals (see **Tolkien, Monsters In**). Finally, in "The Fellowship of the Ring" (1954), Gandalf implies that another wizard, Radagast, has the power to change shape. J.K. Rowling's "Harry Potter" books (1997–2007) contain two varieties of shapeshifting wizards: the animagus, who can transform into a specific animal at will, and the metamorphmagus, who can morph his or her body to look like anyone, or even adopt animal features (see **Harry Potter, Monsters In**). The Helghasts, which appear in Joe Dever's "Lone Wolf" series (1984–98), are fairly unusual in that they are undead shapeshifters, immune to most physical assault and able to psychically attack their victims. The Goblin King Jareth from *Labyrinth* (Jim Henson, 1986), played by David Bowie, can shapeshift into various forms, including a barn owl. The African trickster figure Anansi—portrayed as a shapeshifter in a variety of tales encompassing comedy, ribaldry, and didactics—appears as a heroic helper in several modern fantasy novels, including China Miéville's novel *King Rat* (1998) and Neil Gaiman's *American Gods* (2001) and *Anansi Boys* (2005).

Horror

The shapeshifter is not limited to appearances in high fantasy, but also appears in works of horror, as humans naturally fear the formless. The malevolent god Nyarlathotep, first appearing in an eponymous 1920 prose poem by H.P. Lovecraft, appears in various incarnations—some of which are shapeshifters in and of themselves—throughout Lovecraft's oeuvre (see **Lovecraft, Monsters In**). That this powerful being is immune to definition or delineation makes it all the more terrifying. Stephen King has also penned several tales dealing with powerful, otherworldly shapeshifters. The most famous is his 1986 novel *It*, adapted as a televised mini-series in 1990 (Tommy Lee Wallace), centered around a small town besieged by an inter-dimensional horror able to change into its victim's worst fear. The being famously takes the form of Pennywise the clown, and also appears as a hobo, werewolf, **mummy**, **Frankenstein's monster**, brobdingnagian eyeball, giant spider, and even a glowing cloud of light in outer space, believed to be its true form. Rowling employs a similar device in the "Harry Potter" books; the boggart is a creature able to take the form of its viewer's worst fear. Finally, to move deeper into the abstract, Robert Louis Stevenson's novella *The Strange Case of Dr Jekyll and Mr Hyde* (1886) uses the idea of shapeshifting to illustrate the duality inherent in human nature (see **Hyde, Edward**).

Science Fiction

Shapeshifting beings, both earthly and alien, appear in many works of science fiction that explore the boundaries of humanity (see **Extraterrestrials**). One of the most famous science fiction shapeshifters is the alien being from Joseph W. Campbell's novella "Who Goes There?" (1938). This malevolent extraterrestrial, found frozen in the wastes of Antarctica, has the ability to transform into a perfect copy of any living thing it consumes. Campbell's novella has been adapted for the screen numerous times, beginning with the 1951 film *The Thing from Another World* (Christian Nyby), followed by John Carpenter's 1982 cult classic *The Thing*, and influencing a 2011 prequel, also entitled *The Thing* (Matthijs van Heijningen, Jr). Many science fiction shapeshifters function by mimicking humans via psychically gained information, as is the case with the shapeshifting imposter in Ray Bradbury's short story "The Martian" (1949). Here, a Martian shapeshifter appears in a human settlement and empathically changes into the forms of people remembered by other characters, such as lost family members, until it ultimately expires from the effort of maintaining these forms. Shapeshifting aliens are a recurring threat to the crew of the *USS Enterprise* in *Star Trek*. In "The Man Trap" (Marc Daniels, 1966), the first episode aired, the crew faces a salt-seeking creature able to transform into a person with which its victim has a strong emotional connection. Again, shapeshifting is portrayed as a physically demanding process, and the creature dies from repeated exertions of its powers. Another psychically talented shapeshifter with unusual appetites appears in an episode of *Red Dwarf*, tellingly entitled "Polymorph" (season 3, episode 15, 1989; directed by Ed Bye). The creature takes forms ranging from a basketball to a kebab, and feeds on the emotions of the crew of the *Red Dwarf*. Several shapeshifters appear in *Doctor Who*, such as the monstrous Prisoner Zero, from "The Eleventh Hour" (episode 203, 2010; directed by Adam Smith), able to transform by creating a psychic link with its target, and the Tesselecta, a tessellationally transforming robot—able to copy people it scans—piloted by miniaturized time travelers from the futuristic Justice Department, in "Let's

Kill Hitler" (episode 218, 2011; directed by Richard Senior).

Frank Herbert depicts a different sort of shapeshifting alien in his "Dune" series (1965–2007): the face dancers, created as a powerful servant race. First appearing in *Dune Messiah* (1969), these beings are able to morph their bodies to mimic other people's appearances to the point of replicating physical, sex-based traits, making them invaluable for espionage. One of the best known technologically enabled shapeshifters in modern film is the liquid alloy construct T-1000 from *Terminator 2: Judgment Day* (James Cameron, 1991), able to transform into humans, turn its extremities into useful tools, and even function in a fluid form. Another type of shapeshifting assassin is the Alien Bounty Hunters from *The X-Files*, first appearing in "Colony" (season 2, episode 16, 1995; directed by Nick Marck), sent by their alien overlords to eliminate opposition. Other *X-Files* shapeshifters include Marty (Darin Morgan) from "Gender Bender" (season 1, episode 14, 1994; directed by Rob Bowman), who can change sex at will (male Marty is played by Peter Stebbings; female Marty is played by Kate Twa), and the criminal Eddie Van Blunt from "Small Potatoes" (season 4, episode 20, 1997; directed by Cliff Bole), who can transform into other people. Another criminal who shapeshifts selfishly before getting his just desserts appears in the *Twilight Zone* episode, "The Four of Us Are Dying" (season 1, episode 13, 1960; directed by John Brahm). In this episode, con man Arch Hammer (Harry Townes), who can change his appearance to resemble anyone he chooses, is gunned down mistakenly. To return to the subject of shapeshifting servants, the diabolic agents in the Wachowski brothers *Matrix* films (1999–2003) use their transformational abilities to carry out the wills of their machine overlords within the titular computer simulation. Another science fiction shapeshifter functioning in a virtual world appears in the 2010 film *Inception* (Christopher Nolan): the character Eames (Tom Hardy) is a forger who can freely take the form of any person in the dream world.

Paul T. Beattie

References and Suggested Reading

Campbell, Joseph. *The Hero with a Thousand Faces*. Novato: New World Library, 2008.

Chalker, Jack L. *Dance Band on the Titanic*. New York: Del Rey, 1988.

Coville, Bruce, ed. *Bruce Coville's Shapeshifters*. New York: HarperCollins, 1999.

Foster, Michael Dylan. *Pandemonium and Parade: Japanese Monsters and the Culture of Yokai*. Berkeley: University of California Press, 2008.

Gilman, Laura A., and Keith Decandido, eds. *Otherwere: Stories of Transformation*. New York: Ace Books, 1996.

Hyde, Lewis. *Trickster Makes This World: Mischief, Myth, and Art*. New York: North Point Press, 1999.

Ovid. *Metamorphoses (Oxford World's Classics)*. New York: Oxford University Press, 2009.

Radin, Paul, Karl Kerényi, and C.G. Jung. *The Trickster: A Study in American Indian Mythology*. New York: Schocken Books, 1972.

Royall, Tyler. *Japanese Tales*. New York: Pantheon, 2002.

Skipp, John, ed. *Werewolves and Shape Shifters: Encounters with the Beasts Within*. New York: Black Dog & Leventhal Publishers, 2010.

SHELOB—*see* Animals, Monstrous; Tolkien, Monsters In

SHEMJAZA—*see* Angel

SHUTEN DŌJI

Shuten Dōji is the single most notorious ***oni*** **(demon)** in medieval and early modern Japan. His name has been written with a variety of characters, the most common of which can be read to mean "saké-

Fig. 30 *The shogun Tokugawa Yoshinobu Drawn as the Demon Shuten Dōji.* From the woodblock-printed broadsheet "Driving Out the Morning Drunkard of Mount Ōe" (Ōeyama Chōdon Dōji taiji no zu), 1868. Private collection.

drinking boy." During the tenth and early eleventh centuries—the supposed reign of his terror—the shapeshifting Shuten Dōji is reported to have traumatized the people of the Heian capital (contemporary Kyoto) by repeatedly flying into the city, abducting beautiful young noblewomen, enslaving them in a kind of pseudo-sexual bondage in his palatial mountain fortress, and then squeezing them for their blood and eating them alive. Several of the scenes in illustrated renditions of the demon's principal tale are iconic, including generally standardized depictions of a cannibalistic feast and set paintings of Shuten Dōji's own violent, bloody end.

Shuten Dōji's story dates to the fourteenth-century Ōeyama ekotoba (The Tale of Mount Ōe in Pictures and Words), which tells of how the historical warrior Minamoto no Yorimitsu (also known as Raikō; 948–1021) and his small band of loyal retainers used a combination of cunning, bravery, and divine assistance to infiltrate Shuten Dōji's mountain lair and cut off the demon's head. The story was widely reproduced in illustrated scrolls, painted screens, woodblock-printed texts, and theatrical productions (in the noh, puppet, and kabuki theaters) from the fourteenth through early twentieth centuries. Today, Shuten Dōji's tale is best known to Japanese and English-reading audiences through annotated and translated editions of the eighteenth-century bookseller Shibukawa Seiemon's woodblock-printed *Shuten Dōji*, published in his *Otogi bunko* "Companion Library" anthology of medieval fiction (c. 1716–29). In addition, the demon has been depicted by some of the greatest artists of Japan, including Kanō Motonobu (1476–1559), Hishikawa Moronobu (c. 1630–94), and Utagawa Hiroshige (1797–1858), enhancing his fame both in Japan and abroad.

Shuten Dōji is arguably the first great antihero of Japanese literature. His story inspired a plethora of prequels and sequels telling of his birth and childhood, and even alluding to his postmortem conquest of Hell. For example, a set of sixteenth- or seventeenth-century illustrated scrolls in the British Museum, titled *Ibuki Dōji* (The Child of Mount Ibuki), explains how Shuten Dōji was born to an excessively carnivorous, saké-drinking human father, and how later, as a small child, he was abandoned in the woods for being constantly drunk and deranged. He is then raised by animals in the wild and eventually attains supernatural powers. In a puppet play titled *Shuten Dōji wakazakari* (Shuten Dōji in his Prime), published in 1660, the as-yet human Shuten Dōji is sent to a temple school at the age of 13 so that he might mend his evil ways, but instead he kills 160 monks and acolytes in a murderous rampage and burns their temple to the ground. Later, he is kidnapped by the famous Chinese **tengu** Zegaibō and transformed into an *oni*.

Among *Shuten Dōji* sequels, the sixteenth- or early seventeenth-century *Rashōmon* (The Rashōmon Gate) tells of how Watanabe no Tsuna (953–1025), one of

Raikō's retainers from the original *Shuten Dōji* story, killed Shuten Dōji's demon retainer Ibaraki Dōji at a famous gate in the capital after he escaped the carnage at Shuten Dōji's mountain fortress. Likewise, the parodic seventeenth-century *Yoshitsune jigoku yaburi* (Yoshitsune's Harrowing of Hell) describes how the dead twelfth-century Genpei War hero Minamoto no Yoshitsune invaded Hell with an army of deceased Taira and Minamoto warriors (former adversaries in the human realm) and killed the dead Shuten Dōji there. Shuten Dōji stories and parodies continued to be produced through the nineteenth century, and in 1989, the demon was again reincarnated—literally delivered to Earth from outer space—in Nagai Gō's anime *Shuten Dōji*.

The name of the contemporary saké "Onigoroshi" (Demon Slayer), produced in different varieties by different distilleries throughout Japan, is allusive to the magical saké that Raikō and his men are said to have used to poison Shuten Dōji before slaughtering him in his bed. As evidence of Shuten Dōji's enduring influence on Japanese popular culture, the labels of some of the bottles sport an image of Shuten Dōji's flying, decapitated head.

R. Keller Kimbrough

References and Suggested Reading

Reider, Noriko T. *Japanese Demon Lore: Oni from Ancient Times to the Present*. Logan, UT: Utah State University Press, 2010.

Shirane, Haruo, ed. "The Demon Shuten Dōji." In *Traditional Japanese Literature: An Anthology, Beginnings to 1600*. Translated by R. Keller Kimbrough, 1123–38. New York: Columbia University Press, 2007.

"*Shuten Dōji*: Drunken Demon." Translated by Noriko T. Reider. *Asian Folklore Studies* 64, no. 2 (2005): 207–31.

SILKY—*see* Brownie

SIMORGH—*see* Animals, Monstrous; Birds, Giant; Phoenix

SIREN

In ancient Greek mythology, the sirens were three sea-nymphs who inhabited the island of Anthemoessa in the Mediterranean Sea. The daughters of the primordial river-god Achelous or of the sea-spirit Phorcus (the father of **Scylla**), and Terpsichore, Melpomene, or Gaia, their names are most commonly given as Parthenope, Ligeia, and Leucosia. The sirens' irresistible song enticed passing mariners to shipwreck on the rocky island.

In Homer's *Odyssey* (eighth century BCE), Odysseus defeats the sirens by plugging his crew's ears with wax and having himself bound to the mast so that he may hear their song without succumbing (XII.166). Jason and his Argonauts also escape the sirens with the help of Orpheus, who drowns out the sirens' music with his own (Apollonius Rhodius, *Argonautica* 4.885, third century BCE). In Euripides's tragedy *Helen* (fifth century BCE), the Trojan maiden invokes the sirens to accompany her in her lamentations (167). According to the Latin mythographer Hyginus (first century CE), Demeter, the goddess of the harvest, transformed the nymphs into monstrous bird-women as punishment for allowing Hades to carry off her daughter, Persephone, to the Underworld (*Fabulae* 141); Hyginus's contemporary Ovid wrote that they requested wings to aid their search for Persephone (*Metamorphoses* V.552). The sirens' song lured the **Centaurs** to their deaths (Lycophron, *Alexandra* 648, third century BCE); but they were defeated in a singing contest by the Muses, who plucked their feathers for crowns (Pausanius 9.34.3, second century CE). Plato (fourth century BCE) had them harmonize with the Fates to accompany the movement of the stars and planets around the Earth (*Republic* 10.616 ff). Several tales are told of sirens committing suicide after Odysseus defeats them; others that they killed his son Telemachus in revenge.

The siren's hybridity signals the transgression of boundaries between air, earth, and water. The Latin orator Cicero (first century BCE) wrote that their song promised memory and forbidden knowledge (*De Finibus* 5.18.49). According to the Greek philosopher Plutarch (c. 46–120 CE), their song offered a path to transcendent knowledge through union with the divine (*Morals* III; *Symposiacs* IX.XIV). Natural philosophers such as Pliny the Ender (first century CE) began to question the existence of sirens and other **monstrous races**, placing them in faraway lands such as India (*Natural History* 10.70), and by the fourth century CE, Augustine of Hippo (354–430 CE) would describe them as pernicious remnants of secular history (*City of God* 16.8).

Medieval Christians easily mapped Odysseus's journey onto the Christian passage through trial and temptation, and his ship's salvation onto the triumph of Christian virtue. Accordingly, in medieval bestiaries, sirens represent vanity, avarice, sexual perfidy, and corruption. The seventh-century bishop Isidore of Seville describes them as *meretrices* or harlots (*Etymologies* XI.iii.30). Sometimes associated with the serpent or the eel, sirens were depicted attacking their victims, as active allies of the hostile sea and the Underworld (Cambridge bestiary, twelfth century). In Dante's *Purgatorio* (c. 1308–21 CE), the poet has a vision of a siren. She is rendered powerful by the heat of his desire, but her true, vicious nature is exposed by her stinking belly or *ventre*. As Dante's guide Virgil uncovers the fetid parts, he exhorts the poet to look instead for the entrance to paradise (Canto 19; see **Dante, Monsters In**).

The prevailing image of sirens was part bird and part woman until roughly the seventh century CE, after which (by easy association with Eve and the serpent, the fish-tailed tritons, and female fish and snake hybrids such as the **Hydra**, Echidna, **Lamia**, and the Nereids) sirens were increasingly described as maidens (or virgins) above the waist and fish below. Numerous versions of the Alexandrine *Physiologus* (second or third century CE) give conflicting information on the siren's anatomy. The Anglo-Saxon *Liber Monstrorum* (ninth or tenth century CE) describes sirens as maidens with a fish tail. Philippe de Thaon's twelfth-century *Bestiaire* gives both wings and a fish's tail (666), while thirteenth-century didacts such as Guillaume le Clerc (*Bestiaire* XII.1000) and Bartholomaeus Anglicus (*De proprietatibus rerum*, 18) limit them to the fish tail. The linguistic conflation of sirens (part woman, part bird or fish) with **mermaids** (beautiful maidens with fish tails) is sometimes attributed to Chaucer, who explains: "Though we mermaids call them here ... Men call them sirens in France" (*Romaunt of the Rose*, 682–4, c. 1366). Boccaccio's fourteenth-century *Genealogy of the Gentile Gods* (VII.20) and Boiardo's fifteenth-century *Orlando Innamorato* (II. 4.36) also describe the siren as half-woman and half-fish. In 1493, Christopher Columbus reported dispiritedly that the three sirens he sighted in the Indies were not as beautiful as they had been painted (*Diary of the First Voyage*, 9 January).

Sirens in sixteenth- and seventeenth-century English literature are celebrated for their beautiful music. In William Shakespeare's *A Midsummer Night's Dream* (1590s), the **fairy** king Oberon recalls having "heard a mermaid on a dolphin's back / Uttering such dulcet and harmonious breath / That the rude sea grew civil at her song" (II.1.150). Milton's sirens tamed the **sea monsters**: "Scylla wept, / And chid her barking waves into attention, / And fell **Charybdis** murmured soft applause" (*Comus* 252; 1634). In Spanish Golden Age literature, Calderón's zarzuela *El golfo de las Sirenas* (1657) retells Odysseus's encounters with Scylla, Charybdis, and the sirens as a parable on the senses. Sir Francis Bacon returned to the moral interpretation in his *Wisdom of the Ancients* (1609), equating sirens with "the pernicious incentives to pleasure," driving otherwise rational men to perdition. Even their bone-strewn islands "do not sufficiently deter us from the wicked enticements of pleasure" (420 ff).

The nineteenth century again became preoccupied with sublime or forbidden knowledge associated with sirens. In the second part of Goethe's *Faust* (1832), the Homeric sirens tempt the protagonist with knowledge, but he is warned off by the **Sphinxes** (II.ii.7155 ff). Victorian writers saw sirens as the symbol of Italy, the source of sublime aesthetic experience. Thomas Adolphus Trollope (a less famous brother of Anthony Trollope) lived much of his life there, and his novel *A Siren* (1870) recounts the travails of a beautiful, gifted young opera singer. The English Pre-Raphaelite artists were devoted to sirens, in particular Dante Gabriel Rossetti—whose 1869 outline of a libretto for a "lyrical tragedy," *The Doom of the Sirens*, accompanies his famous drawing *Ligeia Siren* (1873)—and John William Waterhouse, who painted Odysseus's passage (1891). French Decadent poet Charles Baudelaire represented sirens as relentlessly sensual avatars of forbidden knowledge, decadence, and degeneration, bent on transforming the male impulse toward the sublime into devastating erotic desire (*Fleurs du mal*, 1857).

In the twentieth century, Rainer Maria Rilke's poem "The Sirens' Island" (1907) depicts sirens whose silent menace suffocates passing sailors with dread. In Franz Kafka's story "The Silence of the Sirens" (1917), the sirens turn the tables on the hero by refusing to sing; his ears plugged with wax, he remains ignorant of their silence. James Joyce's *Ulysses* (1922) casts the sirens as black-clad barmaids in the Hotel Ormond. Leopold Bloom warns that these emancipated working girls are not easy sexual victims but careful manipulators: "Fellows shell out the dibs. Want to keep your weathereye open. Those girls, those lovely. By the sad sea waves. Chorusgirl's romance. Letters read out for breach of promise. From Chickabiddy's owny Mumpsypum. Laughter in court" (11: 1077–80). Kurt Vonnegut's *Sirens of Titan* (1959) are robot-built sculptures of frighteningly beautiful women, whose image the protagonist uses to sell cigarettes. This alludes to the Mermaid Tobacco poster that Bloom notices in the Ormond bar: "a swaying mermaid smoking mid nice waves. Smoke mermaids, coolest whiff of all. Hair streaming: lovelorn. For some man" (11: 299–301). T.S. Eliot writes of mermaids who ignore a sad old man: "I do not think they will sing to me" ("The Love Song of J. Alfred Prufrock," line 124, 1920). Max Horkheimer and Theodor W. Adorno's 1947 *Dialectic of Enlightenment* reinterprets Ulysses as a symbol of the ruling class, who must protect his enslaved workers from the forbidden song of enlightenment. And the Coen Brothers' 2000 film *O Brother, Where Art Thou?* returns to the *Odyssey*, set in the Depression-era southern United States. Three fugitives come across the sirens washing clothes on the rocks. The sirens seduce them with liquor, sex, and song, depriving even the loquacious Ulysses Everett McGill (George Clooney) of words.

Persephone Braham

References and Suggested Reading

Joyce, James. *Ulysses: The 1934 Text, as Corrected and Reset in 1961*. New York: Random House, 1961.

Lao, Meri. *Sirens: Symbols of Seduction*. Rochester, VT: Park Street Press, 1998.

Mustard, Wilfred P. "Siren-Mermaid." *Modern Language Notes* 23, no. 1 (January 1908): 21–4.

Williams, David. *Deformed Discourse: The Function of the Monster in Medieval Thought and Literature*. Montreal: McGill-Queen's University Press, 1996.

SKELETON

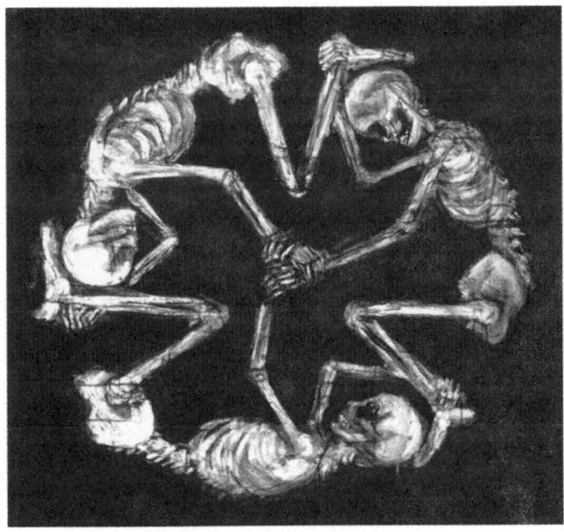

Fig. 31 ***Circle III*** **by Anki King**

The skeleton is a common monster archetype found across various media, including literature, film, comic books, and video games. Although the skeleton can be the bony structure of any creature, real or imaginary, it usually refers to the animated human skeleton. Like **zombies**, the animated skeleton is a form of the undead that straddles the boundary between the living and the dead.

A walking skeleton has been a popular culture image in the West since the Middle Ages. The allegorical figure of Death—the Grim Reaper—is often depicted as a walking skeleton cloaked in a black hood and carrying a large scythe (see **Death, Personified**). In German painter Hans Holbein the Younger's representation of the *Dance of Death* (1538), for example, Death is personified as a skeleton. The Flemish painter Pieter Bruegel the Elder also depicted an army of skeletons slaughtering people in his 1562 painting *The Triumph of Death*.

In addition to being a popular motif in drawings and paintings, the animated skeleton also makes its way into literature. In the Brothers Grimm fairytale "The Boy Who Wanted the Willies" (1812), a boy named Hans dances with a group of dancing skeletons. In 1908, the English writer and journalist Perceval Landon published "Thurnley Abbey" in his short story collection *Raw Edges*. In the story, a ghost appears in the form of a skeleton, part of which is still covered by dry skin. The walking skeleton also appears in Terry Pratchett's "Discworld" series of novels begun in 1983, in which Death is a seven-foot tall skeleton that sits astride a pale horse. Although a symbol of death, in Terry Pratchett's novels, the skeleton develops a fascination with humanity and often meddles in human affairs.

In modern fantasy films, the appearance of animated skeletons is often attributed to the use of black magic. In Gore Verbinski's 2003 film *Pirates of the Caribbean: The Curse of the Black Pearl*, the crew members of the *Black Pearl* transform into skeletons when exposed to moonlight as a consequence of having stolen the cursed treasure in a chest of Aztec gold. Skeletons can also be summoned by their masters, be they humans with supernatural powers or other powerful undead. In such cases, skeletons are mindless sets of bones, simply following the orders given to them. Because they have no will of their own, no fear of death and are difficult to destroy, skeletons are perfectly obedient soldiers. In his *The 7th Voyage of Sinbad* (Nathan H. Juran, 1958) and the film adaptation of the legend *Jason and the Argonauts* (Don Chaffey, 1963), animation expert Ray Harryhausen (1920–2013) brought the living-dead skeleton warriors to vivid life employing stop motion. Harryhausen's animated skeletons have had a direct influence on how skeletons are portrayed later on the screen. Sam Raimi's *Army of Darkness* (1992), Robert Rodriguez's *Spy Kids 2: Island of Lost Dreams* (2002), and Rob Cohen's *The* ***Mummy****: Tomb of the* ***Dragon*** *Emperor* (2008), for example, all emulated Harryhausen's skeleton soldiers.

Skeleton warriors have also appeared frequently in various *other media* formats, such as video games and television series. In *Dungeons & Dragons*, the animated skeleton was one of the earliest creatures introduced in the game (see **Dungeons & Dragons, Monsters In**). In the first-person shooter game series *Serious Sam*, initially released in 2001, skeletons from Planet Kleer are one of the most frequently encountered, and one of the most dangerous, enemies of all. In 1993–94, a 13-episode cartoon series, *Skeleton Warriors*, was aired on CBS. The story revolves around the conflict between Baron Dark, the show's main villain, and his brother Prince Lightstar over the control of the ancient Lightstar Crystal. The half of the crystal that Baron Dark has obtained not only turns him into a living skeleton but also makes his followers skeleton warriors. Along similar lines, in the cartoon series *He-Man and the Masters of the Universe* (1983–85), He-Man's chief adversary is Skeletor, a blue-skinned villain with a yellow skull for a head.

Although deeply rooted in Western culture, the skeleton is not a monstrous figure unique to the West. In Japanese folklore, the dancing skeleton is the embodiment of a vengeful soul that awaits its opportunity to seek justice. Variants of this motif are found in Keigo Seki's *Folktales of Japan*, published in 1963. In China, the most well-known skeleton is probably the White Bone **Demon** (*Bai gu jing*) that appears in the classical Chinese novel *Journey to the West* by Wu Cheng-en (c. 1506–82). The White Bone Demon is a metamorphic skeleton that can alter its original physical shape and take on human form (*see* **Shapeshifter**). In the novel, it transforms into an innocent young maiden, the maiden's mother, and the maiden's father to deceive its target—the monk Xuanzang, also known as Tripitaka—in order to achieve immortality by consuming his flesh. Its disguises are so convincing that only Tripitaka's superhuman disciple Monkey can see through them with his magical eyes (see **Monkey King**). Monkey fights the demon until it appears in its true form of a skeleton and perishes. This story has inspired numerous films, television shows, and musicals. In 1966, the Shaw Brothers Studio produced Princess Iron Fan, which features two sister White Bone Demons. One of the most recognizable depictions of the White Bone Demon appeared in the tenth episode of the 1988 television series Journey to the West produced by CCTV, China Central Television. In Peking Opera, "Monkey Subdues the White Bone Demon Three Times" has become a staple (see, for example, the Peking opera entitled *Zhi Ji Mei Hou Wang* [Agitating Monkey King with Wit], first produced by the celebrated opera singer Li Shaochun in 1938).

The skeleton is a monstrous figure found both in the West and the East. This fear-inspiring monster is not only a recurrent motif in folklore, video games, literature, and cinema, but also an iconic cultural image that constantly reminds us of the fluid boundary between the living and the dead.

Lin Wang

References and Suggested Reading

Seki, Keigo. *Folktales of Japan*. Chicago: University of Chicago Press, 1963.

Westfahl, Gary, ed. *The Greenwood Encyclopedia of Science Fiction and Fantasy: Themes, Works, and Wonders*. Westport, CT: Greenwood Press, 2005.

Yu, Anthony C., trans. *Journey to the West*. Chicago: University of Chicago Press, 1983.

SKIN-WALKER—*see* Shapeshifter

SKUNK APE—*see* Bigfoot

SOUKOUGNAN—*see* Demon

SPEECHLESS MEN—*see* Races, Monstrous

SPHINX, THE

The Sphinx (Greek for "strangler") is a monster from ancient Near Eastern and Mediterranean culture, with a lion's body, a human head, and, often, a bird's wings. Sometimes ancient and modern authors also describe the creature as having a snake's tail. (Composite monsters having a human head on a lion's body appear in Asian culture as well, where they are called by many different names.) While the Greek Sphinx, which dwelled near Thebes, invariably has a woman's head, the Egyptian Sphinx is often (though not always) male. The Theban Sphinx challenges men—most notably Oedipus—with a riddle, killing them if they fail to answer correctly. The Egyptian Sphinx, on the other hand, which usually has the role of benevolent guardian, is famously silent.

The Theban Sphinx first appears in Hesiod's poem, *Theogony* (c. 700 BCE), as the offspring of the monsters Echidna and Orthus. Pseudo-Apollodorus (second century CE) states that she was born of Echidna but sired by **Typhoeus**. One tradition explaining the Sphinx's presence at Thebes holds that the king of that city, Laius, Jocasta's first husband and Oedipus's father, heard a prophecy that his son would kill him. In attempting to avoid having such a son, he raped a young boy, Chrysippus. For this, Hera, goddess of marriage, sent the Sphinx to Thebes as punishment (Edmunds 53). This use of the Sphinx as the punisher of sexual transgression paradoxically meshes with the partly sexual nature of the monster, which has not only the head of a woman but, in many works of art both ancient and modern, breasts as well (Regier).

This Sphinx punished Thebes by decimating the city's population through a particularly insidious method. The monster would waylay travelers to the city and especially Theban youths, forcing them to answer a riddle that they could not solve: "What walks on four legs in the morning, two legs at noon, and three legs in the evening?" The Sphinx then devoured anyone who could not answer the riddle correctly. Many ancient Greek vase paintings and relief sculptures show the Sphinx on a hillock or pedestal facing a young man, apparently posing her question; many others show a young man lying on his back before the Sphinx, evidently after her attack; some even show the Sphinx raking a youth's chest with her lion's claw.

Thebes was saved by the hero Oedipus who, confronted by the Sphinx, said the answer to her riddle was "Man," because as a baby a man crawls upon all fours, as an adult he walks upright, and in old age he aids himself with a cane. Upon being bested by Oedipus, the Sphinx killed herself by leaping from the Theban acropolis; other accounts have Oedipus slay her (Regier 205). Surprisingly little of this story is told in Sophocles's play *Oedipus the King* (fifth century BCE), but in Seneca the Younger's tragedy *Oedipus* (first century CE), Oedipus describes the Sphinx readying her wings, lashing her lion-like tail, and tearing at the rocks with her claws while waiting impatiently for his answer. He also describes the bloody remains of previous men who have failed to answer the riddle correctly.

On one of the paws of the Egyptian Sphinx at Gizeh, an inscription in Greek points out that this is not the same sphinx that Oedipus faced at Thebes (Regier 22). As opposed to the Theban Sphinx, who asks riddles, the Great Sphinx at Gizeh is silent, displaying a close-lipped, mysterious smile. The inscription indicates an early association of—or confusion between—the two sphinxes, and later writers have often continued to make this association, or have even deliberately blended the Theban and Egyptian sphinxes (Suhr 97).

As early as the fourth century BCE, Palaephatus, a writer who explained myths as exaggerations of historical facts, rationalized the myth of the Sphinx by stating that she was in fact an Amazon whom Cadmus, the founder of Thebes, had brought home as a bride. When he took an additional wife, Sphinx rebelled and, with some of the townspeople, went up the mountainside and from there waged a guerilla war. Oedipus, in this interpretation, was a young hero who ambushed and killed her, thus ending the insurgency (Edmunds 51). Similarly, the second-century CE geographer Pausanias wrote that the Sphinx was a pirate, or else she was a natural daughter of Laius, who told her to ask all young men arriving at Thebes a question that only those in the royal line would know. Oedipus had been told the answer in a dream, so she had to let him through (9.26.2–4).

The tendency to rationalize or allegorize the Sphinx has recurred down the ages. Francis Bacon, in his essay "Sphynx or Science" (1619), interpreted her as a symbol of science, or knowledge, explaining that she has two kinds of riddles: one about the nature of things and the other about the nature of man. Command over the various aspects of the world, such as bodies, medicines, and mechanical power, is the admirable object of natural philosophy. But solving the second riddle—having insight into the nature of man, as Oedipus did—makes one an effective leader. Bacon recalls that Augustus Caesar's (63 BCE–14 CE) personal seal was a sphinx, which indicated that his genius was in the science of ruling men.

Alternatively, the Sphinx was sometimes seen as a symbol of the erotic. One of Oscar Wilde's most famous poems, "The Sphinx" (1894), which also reflects the Victorian era's Egyptomania, describes a visit to the poet by this "inviolate and immobile" being, "this curious cat" who is "half woman and half animal" (lines 3–12). In addition to acknowledging her great antiquity—she led the Holy Family to safety on the flight to Egypt, she can read the Hieroglyphs, she knew the Labyrinth of the **Minotaur**—the poet wonders about her lovers who, he suggests, may have included the **Chimera** and Ammon, the Egyptian sun god. The poet then urges her to go to Egypt to reanimate her lovers, or to take a lion as a lover. Wilde thus assigns the Sphinx, as a being with both human and animal parts, lovers both divine and bestial. Finally, the poet bids the Sphinx begone, saying "you wake in me each bestial sense, you make me what I would not be" (line 168). The Sphinx, here, is a fatal temptress, of the same order as the **sirens** or Lorelei.

In his play *The Infernal Machine* (1934), in a somewhat more modern take on the Sphinx, French author Jean Cocteau has The Voice that delivers the prologue refer to the Sphinx variously as a winged virgin, a singing dog, and a monster. This Sphinx, though, is essentially a young woman tired of killing. She wants Oedipus for herself, and so gives him the answer to her riddle in advance. Cocteau uses his Sphinx to suggest that certain demi-gods have sympathies and even longings for humans, of which the humans—like Oedipus—are unaware. Thus, Oedipus continues on his way and unknowingly marries his own mother.

A less sympathetic Sphinx appears in Esther Friesner's 1989 novel *Sphynxes Wild*. This Theban Sphinx alternates between her true shape—woman's head, lion's body, and wings—and that of a beautiful woman. She is a man-eater, both figuratively and literally, who first seduces and then devours human men. She intends to make humans extinct, but is defeated by a young couple in love. The Egyptian Sphinx in this novel takes the form of another woman, who tries unsuccessfully to battle with the Theban Sphinx. In a more comic vein, Rick Riordan's 2008 novel *The Battle of the Labyrinth* has the demi-gods Percy Jackson and Annabeth encounter the Sphinx in the Labyrinth, where Annabeth must answer 20 questions correctly or be eaten. The Sphinx here is a parody of standardized, trivial multiple-choice testing, rather than the philosophizing creature of Greek myth. Percy and his friends frustrate the Sphinx and continue on their way.

J.K. Rowling, however, effectively combines the various natures of the Sphinx in *Harry Potter and the Goblet of Fire* (2000; see **Harry Potter, Monsters In**). The creature confronts Harry in the maze at the Triwizard Tournament. She has a lion's body, with a lion's claws and tail, but a woman's head with "long, almond-shaped eyes" (628). She presents Harry with a complicated riddle based on wordplay. In this respect, Rowling's Sphinx is related to the Theban Sphinx; however, when Harry asks a rhetorical question about the last part of the riddle, the Sphinx "merely smiled her mysterious smile," in imitation of the Egyptian Sphinx (630).

Don Riggs

References and Suggested Reading

Edmunds, Lowell. *Oedipus: The Ancient Legend and Its Later Analogues*. Baltimore, MD: The Johns Hopkins University Press, 1985.

Regier, Willis Goth. *Book of the Sphinx*. Lincoln, NE: University of Nebraska Press, 2004.

Rowling, J.K. *Harry Potter and the Goblet of Fire*. New York: Scholastic, 2000.

Suhr, Elmer G. "The Sphinx." *Folklore* 81, no. 2 (1970): 97–111.

Wilde, Oscar. "The Sphinx." London and Edinburgh: Ballantyne Press, 1894. Reprint, *Connexions*. <http://cnx.org/content/m34206/latest/>. Accessed 1 September 2011.

SPRIGGAN—*see* Shapeshifter

SPRITE—*see* Elf; Goblin; Kappa; Leprechaun; Manitou

SWIFT, JONATHAN, MONSTERS IN (*GULLIVER*)

The anti-Whig (British political party) satire *Gulliver's Travels* (1726) presents the four fictional voyages of protagonist Lemuel Gulliver to the realms of Blefuscu, Brobdingnag, Laputa, and Glubbdubdrib, and the country of the Houyhnhnms, during which he encounters a variety of monstrous creatures, including giant humans (see **Giant**), diminutive humans, wasps (see **Animals, Monstrous**), eagles (see **Birds, Giant**), immortals ostracized by their community due to their age, deformed and savage humans called Yahoos, and Houyhnhnms, the intelligent horse-like creatures completely ruled by logic. An immediate success due to its sensational nature, the novel was quickly adapted into chapbooks and subsequently into other abridged versions for children, including a 1913 edition illustrated by artist Arthur Rackham. Lilliputian (tiny people) and Brobdingnagian (giants) motifs appear throughout literature, with notable examples including T.H. White's *Mistress Masham's Repose* (1946), which mentions the descendants of Lilliputians, and Mary Norton's *The Borrowers* (1955) about tiny people who inhabit people's homes and "borrow" things, while the eighteenth-century English folktales *Jack and the Beanstalk* and *Tom Thumb* have clear Brobdingnagian antecedents. Most animated and live-action film adaptations of *Gulliver's Travels* include only the initial one or two voyages, though a 1996 television mini-series, directed by Charles Sturridge and starring Ted Danson, includes all four journeys. Three of Swift's words from the novel entered the language: "Lilliputian," denoting "a person of diminutive size, character, or mind" (*OED*); "Brobdingnagian," meaning "of huge dimensions; immense; gigantic" (*OED*); and "Yahoo," which has become "a common name for the wilder, more uncivilized forms of humanity, and for savage and uncouth customs and behavior" (Rawson 3).

Eighteenth-century monster lore about giants often involved notions of large, misshapen humanoid creatures thought to live on the extreme borders of Europe; due to their size, these "vastly, grotesquely oversized" people (Gilmore 175) were regarded as gods and thus, in addition to becoming objects of power, awe, worship, respect, and reverence, they were also sources of fear. Swift's portrayal of giants overturns this stereotype, both in how Gulliver is viewed by the Lilliputians, the diminutive people he meets during his first voyage, and in how he regards the Brobdingnagians, the giants he meets during his second voyage. The Lilliputians are initially frightened of Gulliver because he is roughly twelve times their size, and they subdue him by tying him up and drugging him with wine. However, they quickly come to call him a Man-Mountain, and he becomes a member of their community rather than being treated as a monster. This is reinforced by the Lilliputians' treatment of him after he helps them in their conflict against their neighbors, the Blefuscudians, but refuses to completely subdue them: he is charged with treason and sentenced to blinding—a horrific judgment, but the same penalty the Lilliputians would enact upon any of their citizens. Similarly, though Gulliver initially assumes that the giant human inhabitants of Brobdingnag are monsters because they are 60 feet tall, he gradually overcomes his feelings of horror about their size and starts identifying with them, because they act like his English compatriots, with all of their virtues and flaws. He identifies so strongly with them that, after he returns home to England, he continues to behave as though he is the size of a Brobdingnagian rather than an Englishman, perceiving everything as much smaller than its actual size.

In Brobdingnag, it is the dangerously large size of animals and insects, and even a giant baby, in relation to Gulliver's tininess that makes them monstrous. A giant frog seems deformed to him because of its size, and he loathes its odious slime. He considers giant flies merely a nuisance, but the sight of the gigantic lice on the beggars horrifies and nauseates him. When giant wasps, whose humming sounds like droning bagpipes, attack his honey cake, he slays them and draws out their stingers, which are an inch and a half long, and keeps them to donate as curiosities to the Royal Society of London for Improving Natural Knowledge, reflecting the eighteenth century's fascination for curiosities from abroad. His encounter with rats the size of large mastiffs brings out his combative nature as he kills them with his sword. Though Gulliver claims that his masterful attitude towards animals is enough to keep them subdued, citing his intimidation of a giant cat, he hastily retreats after shaking his weapon at an enormous kite, and receives a beating from the wings of an oversize bird that steals his food. A giant spaniel retrieves him like a bird and carries him to its master; though Gulliver is not harmed, it renders him helpless. Later, a giant monkey belonging to one of the kitchen clerks grabs Gulliver and carries him to the roof, where it force-feeds him and nearly squeezes him to death, and he has a similar experience with a Brobdingnagian baby that picks him up and treats him as a pacifier before dropping him. Eventually the specially constructed box in which he resides is grabbed by a gigantic eagle and subsequently dropped into the sea when the eagle is attacked by other giant birds.

Gulliver meets other creatures that could be considered monsters during his voyages, including the **ghosts** and immortals he encounters during his third journey. On Glubbdubdrib, the island of sorcerers or magicians, he sees domestic specters that serve as attendants to the ruler, and when dining with the governor, he notices that the wait-staff are ghosts that vanish into thin air when finished with their tasks. Gulliver quickly learns not to fear them, and eventually assents to the governor's invitation to call up the spirits of the dead to ask them questions, who will tell the truth since lying is no longer of any use to them. The ensuing hero parade is significant for its sheer range of figures, including the spirits of Alexander the Great, Hannibal, Caesar, and Pompey; the Senate of Rome, Brutus, and several Roman emperors; Homer and Aristotle; Didymus and Eustathius; Descartes and Gassendi; Agrippa; and Eliogabalus's cooks, followed by several English yeomen. Shortly thereafter, Gulliver meets the Struldbruggs, immortals who continue to age and suffer from all of the complications of aging, stereotypically presented by Gulliver to include such human flaws as vanity, covetousness, moroseness, and talkativeness. Their cantankerous dispositions are exacerbated by their people's treatment of them as monsters, for they are declared legally dead at the age of 80 and cannot own property, marry, or participate in any meaningful way in society.

During his fourth and final voyage Gulliver meets the Yahoos, deformed and savage humans he considers to be monstrous beyond all reason. The Yahoos live in subservience to the Houyhnhnms, sentient horse-like creatures ruled totally by logic who adhere to the principles of temperance, industry, exercise, and cleanliness; in their language, the word "Houyhnhnm" means "perfection of nature." In contrast, the Yahoos demonstrate crude, vulgar, and coarse behavior; Gulliver refers to them as monsters and beasts, likening them to monkeys or jackdaws. The Yahoos are covered with hair, have a disagreeable smell, and are not housebroken; their sharp-pointed, hooked claws enable them to climb trees easily, and they can bound, spring, and leap like wildcats. Gulliver decides that they are not teachable due to their violent and perverse dispositions, and the Houyhnhnms use them as beasts of labor, as well as make shoes out of their skins. Though Gulliver reviles them as disgusting creatures, especially when a female Yahoo pounces on him and attempts to mate with him, the Houyhnhnms eventually decide that Gulliver is merely a "perfect" Yahoo and banish him from their land, because they believe that he must be a danger to society. Upon his return home, Gulliver regards his fellow humans—including his wife and children—with disgust, considering them no more than slightly civilized Yahoos, and spends the rest of his life living in the stable with his horses.

Despite the novel's satirical tone, since its publication critics have objected to Swift's misanthropy, particularly in relation to the Yahoos, and note problems with his treatments of race and gender. Certain scenes reproduce "the historical relationship between imperialist exploitation abroad" (Brown 137; see **Races, Monstrous**), and Rawson convincingly argues that the Yahoos are simply a stripped-down version of the ugly Irish paradigm that was popular throughout eighteenth- and nineteenth-century British literature. The identification of monsters, whatever their forms, throughout *Gulliver's Travels* is predicated on Gulliver's consideration of them as other, initially in relation to their appearance but eventually in relation to their behavior; by the end of the narrative, Gulliver considers monsters to be any creatures that he perceives to exhibit and embrace flawed moral characteristics.

Anne Hiebert Alton

References and Suggested Reading

Brown, Laura. "Reading Race and Gender: Jonathan Swift." In *Critical Essays on Jonathan Swift*, edited by Frank Palmeri, 121–42. New York: G.K. Hall, 1993.

Gilmore, David D. *Monsters: Evil Beings, Mythical Beasts, and All Manner of Imaginary Terrors*. Philadelphia: University of Pennsylvania Press, 2003.

Rawson, Claude. *God, Gulliver, and Genocide: Barbarism and the European Imagination, 1492–1945*. Oxford: Oxford University Press, 2001.

Rielly, Edward J. *Approaches to Teaching Swift's* Gulliver's Travels. New York: MLA, 1988.

Taylor, Aline. "Sights and Monsters and Gulliver's Voyages to Brobdingnag." *Tulane Studies in English* 7 (1957): 29–82.

SYCORAX—*see* Caliban

SYLPH—*see* Elemental

TANNIN—*see* Bible, Monsters In The

TANUKI

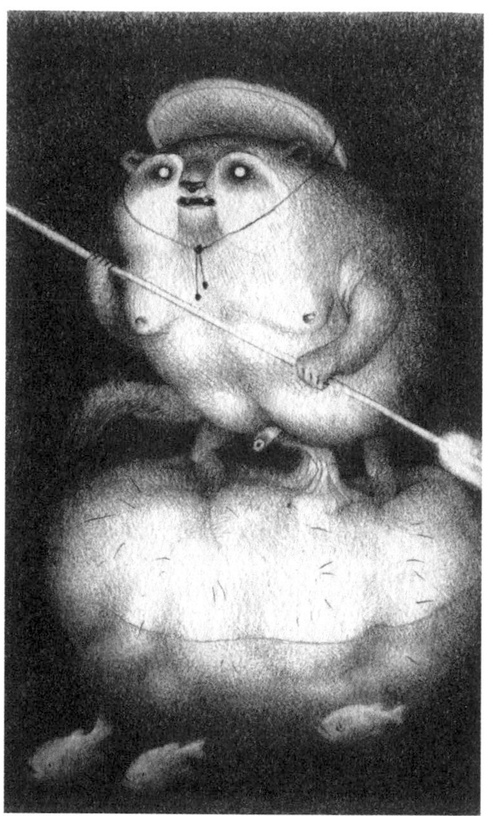

Fig. 32 ***Tanuki*** **by Allison W. Sommers**

One of the best known creatures of Japanese folklore, the tanuki has long been a presence in Japanese literature and art, and more recently in films, anime, video games, and other forms of popular culture. While often considered an example of *yōkai* or *bakemono*, both translatable as "monster," tanuki are commonly characterized as ambiguous supernatural trickster figures, mischievous but not necessarily murderous. Zoologically speaking, tanuki are real animals found throughout East Asia; they are generally nocturnal, omnivorous mammals similar to raccoons in both appearance and size. In Japanese, this same creature is sometimes referred to as a *mujina*, but *tanuki* has come to be the more common term. In English, tanuki is sometimes translated as badger or raccoon, but "raccoon dog" is a more accurate label in terms of the creature's Linnaean classification as a canid (*Nyctereutes procyonoides*). Similar to raccoons, possums, foxes, and coyotes in other parts of the world, the tanuki is a wild animal that occasionally makes brief mischievous intrusions into areas inhabited by humans.

The tanuki of folklore is accordingly a liminal trickster figure, often portrayed as somewhat bumbling and pot-bellied, with a penchant for drinking sake, changing shape, and impersonating a Buddhist monk. The tanuki often performs its shapeshifting (see **Shapeshifter**) through the machinations of its gigantic scrotum—numerous woodblock prints and other images attest to the protean abilities of this magnificent physical feature. Not surprisingly, one of the many roles the tanuki plays in contemporary Japan is that of fertility symbol in the realm of commerce, a function transferred into a sign of prosperity and good fortune in the guise of ceramic tanuki figurines placed in front of restaurants and shops throughout the country.

From a literary perspective, the tanuki makes its first documented appearance (called *mujina*) in the mytho-historical *Nihonshoki* of 720 CE. During the Heian (794–1185) and Kamakura (1185–1333) periods, tanuki begin to appear in *setsuwa* (short tales), such as the thirteenth-century *Uji shūi monogatari shū* (*A Collection of Tales from Uji*), in which a mountain hermit, after years of deep devotion, begins to receive nightly visits from the Bodhisattva Fugen on his white elephant. One evening a hunter stays to witness the holy vision. But when Fugen appears, radiating a beautiful light, the hunter is suspicious and shoots an arrow at the image. The light goes out and a crashing sound is heard. In the morning, hunter and hermit follow a trail of blood to the bottom of a ravine where they find a dead tanuki with an arrow in its chest.

Historically, the image of the tanuki was sometimes combined with that of the fox, or ***kitsune***, and tales associated with the two creatures are often interchangeable. Indeed, a common term for the two together was *kori* (Chinese *huli*), a combination of the two Chinese characters that has come to refer to all manner of supernatural occurrences. While it is difficult to generalize, kitsune-related narratives (sometimes directly influenced by Chinese folk and literary motifs) tend to portray a seductive, sly, and dangerous creature, often assuming the shape of a seductive woman. Broadly speaking, tanuki tend to be more comical than foxes; as in the medieval-period narrative related above, they often end up dead, despite the temporary success of their transformations. In local folklore, tanuki were particularly known for leading people astray by imitating sounds or creating uncanny drumming noises by thumping their bellies (known as *hara tsuzumi*).

As lore relating to the tanuki continued to develop during the long Edo period (c. 1600–1868), a time of relative political stability, the light-hearted image of a somewhat inept shapeshifter circulated. For example, in the popular folktale of the *Bunbuku-chagama*, a tanuki is unable to sustain a transformation into a teapot; his head, limbs, and tail disobediently pop out of his teapot body, a humorous dilemma that makes for wonderful imagery in woodblock prints (*ukiyo-e*) and other visual forms. Indeed, the Edo period witnessed the flowering of a rich visual and print culture of woodblock prints, *kabuki* drama, *bunraku* puppet theater, and numerous forms of graphic literature, such as *kibyōshi* ("yellow-covers"), that featured light-hearted, often satirical, stories with detailed illustrations. In these formats, traditional tanuki folklore intersected dynamically with popular cultural concerns, veiled political sentiments, and commercial and artistic interests. In most cases, tanuki were portrayed as comical and fun-loving rather than overtly monstrous. At the same time, however, tanuki also continued to appear in *kaidan*, or spooky narratives, related in oral tale-telling sessions known as *hyaku-monogatari*, and then published in collected form. In one 1677 tale, for example, a tanuki assumes the form of a lonely samurai's dead wife, appearing to him seductively at night. The samurai musters up the courage to stab the apparition in his bedroom, and the next morning an old tanuki is found dead outside.

With the advent of the Meiji period (1868–1912) and Japan's abrupt rush into modernity, folkloric tanuki continued to appear in newspapers and oral tales. In one widely distributed legend, tanuki articulated a voice of resistance against the onslaught of the steam train; running through the countryside, a train is approached by another train coming toward it from the opposite direction. Miraculously, no collision occurs, but in the morning light, a dead tanuki is found on the tracks.

As the twentieth century progressed, tanuki also became common commercial characters, appearing as ceramic figurines in front of shops and more recently as mascot figures, for example, for the DC (credit) Card (along with the ***kappa***, another common folkloric creature). In literature, the creature has played a minor role in modern fiction, appearing, for example, in a 1905 short story "Koto no sorane" (English title: "Hearing Things") by one of the most famous of all modern Japanese authors, Natsume Sōseki (1867–1916), and featuring prominently in *Fukkoki*, a 1985 novel by the renowned satirical author, Inoue Hisashi (1935–2010).

The tanuki's long history in visual representations has continued in contemporary Japan, in manga and anime, and most famously in the 1994 animated feature film, *Heisei tanuki gassen: Pompoko*, known in English simply as *Pompoko*, directed by Takahata Isao. While the film was well received in Japan, its references to tanuki lore and explicit portrayal of the creature's gigantic scrotum may have put off wider distribution; it was not released internationally on DVD until 2005. The film's story takes place in the late 1960s, during a period of rapid economic growth and urbanization, and revolves around the plight of a tribe of tanuki living in the Tama Hills on the outskirts of Tokyo. Humans are planning to build a new suburb in the hills, destroying the tanuki's native home. In a desperate attempt to thwart the encroachment of human civilization, older tanuki teach younger ones the shapeshifting magic of old and together they create illusions and roadblocks in order to stop the construction of the suburb. In this contemporary popular culture characterization, then, the mischievous tanuki invokes traditional shapeshifting talents in a battle against humans, but here assumes the explicit role of proxy for a disappearing natural environment.

The tanuki also stars in an experimental musical film, *Operetta tanuki goten* (*Princess Raccoon*) directed by eclectic filmmaker Suzuki Seijun, which premiered at the Cannes Film Festival in 2005. On an international level, the tanuki has received popular attention as a character in the Mario Bros video game franchise, where a raccoon-like figure with various magical abilities is called "Tanooki." In the early twenty-first century, the creature has even infiltrated American popular literature, as a big-balled protagonist in Tom Robbins's 2003 novel, *Villa Incognito*.

The tanuki has a long history in Japan, in folklore, art, literature, and, more recently, manga, animation, and digital media. As a "monster," it is particularly remarkable for its ability to change shape, a trait it not only performs within narratives and visual contexts, but also by conforming through time to diverse media and different historical and social contexts. In today's Japan, the tanuki is simultaneously a real animal, a fun-loving supernatural trickster, a nostalgic icon of rural Japan, a commercial mascot, and a mutable character for creative filmic and digital experimentation.

Michael Dylan Foster

References and Suggested Reading

Casal, U.A. "The Goblin Fox and Badger and Other Witch Animals of Japan." *Folklore Studies* 18 (1959): 1–93.

De Visser, M.W. "The Fox and Badger in Japanese Folklore." *Transactions of the Asiatic Society of Japan* 36, part 3 (1908): 1–159.

Hisashi, Inoue. *Fukkoki*. Tokyo: Shinchōsha. 1985.

Robbins, Tom. *Villa Incognito*. New York: Bantam Books, 2003.

Sōseki, Natsume. *Ten Nights of Dream, Hearing Things, The Heredity of Taste*. Translated by Aiko Itô and Graeme Wilson. Vermont: Charles E. Tuttle, 1974.

Teiri, Nakamura. *Tanuki to sono sekai*. Tokyo: Asahi shinbun sha, 1990.

TASH—*see* Demon

TEHOM—*see* Bible, Monsters In The

TENGU

Tengu, written with two Chinese characters meaning "celestial dog," are a kind of flying **demon**-bird people known for living deep in the mountains. They are a specifically

Fig. 33 ***Minamoto no Yoshitsune and the Great Tengu of Mount Kurama.* From a seventeenth-century *Tengu no Dairi (The Palace of the Tengu)* picture scroll. Private Collection.**

Japanese, rather than pan-Asian, monster; although pre-modern Japanese sources speak of famous Chinese and Indian tengu, such creatures are unknown in the literature of those lands. (In China, the same written characters have been used to denote a type of mountain dwelling raccoon-dog apparently unrelated to the Japanese tengu.) Tengu are typically portrayed with human arms and legs, wings, and either a hawk-like beak or a long red nose. They are famous for their magical powers, martial skills, and antagonism to Buddhism. Tengu often disguise themselves as other birds—particularly kites (*tobi*)—and in human form they usually dress as *yamabushi* mountain ascetics. They are attracted by excessive human pride, especially that of arrogant Buddhist monks, whom they seek out to murder, abduct, or simply deceive.

The earliest reference to a tengu appears in *Nihon shoki* (*Chronicles of Japan*), compiled in 720 CE, although the term is used there to refer to a thunderously noisy shooting star. As fully formed monsters, tengu begin to appear in Japanese textual sources from around the early twelfth century, particularly in the encyclopedic tale anthology *Konjaku monogatari shū* (*Tales of Times Now Past*, c. 1120). There, tengu are described as evil enemies of Buddhism. *Konjaku* 20:1, for example, tells of an unnamed Indian tengu who once heard a Buddhist verse echoing across the ocean; recognizing its profundity, he is said to have followed it to Mount Hiei in Japan (headquarters of the Japanese Tendai Buddhist sect) in order to make it stop. He tries and fails, and is converted instead. Likewise, according to *Konjaku* 20:2, the Chinese tengu Chirayōju once traveled to Japan to test his strength against the Buddhist monks of that land—we are told that he had already subdued all of the monks in China—and he, too, is defeated. Based on these and other early tengu tales, the scholar Komine Kazuaki argues that, because tengu are always eventually thwarted by the Buddhist forces whom they oppose, their stories function to validate Buddhist authority rather than to diminish or undermine it in any way (36).

In the thirteenth and later centuries, the dangers of tengu extended beyond external attack to include human-tengu transformations. In 1296, for example, an unknown artist (or group of artists) created a set of satiric picture scrolls titled *Tengu zōshi* (*The Book of Tengu*), which describes how the monks of several great temples in Japan had all metamorphosed into tengu as a result of their conceit. As the scholar Abe Yasurō has explained, by depicting Buddhist monks as tengu, *Tengu zōshi* attempted "to articulate the diverse forms of arrogance that constituted the condition of corrupt monks" (217). According to the c. 1309–10 "Engyōbon" variant of *Heike monogatari* (*Tales of the Heike*), the great deity of the Sumiyoshi Shrine once explained that many scholars and wise men become tengu after they die—not because of ignorance, but because, in addition to being arrogant, they lack Buddhist passion or devotion (*dōshin*, literally "a heart for the Way"). The Sumiyoshi Deity reveals that, as "celestial demons" (*tenma*, a synonym for *tengu*), they will have the faces of dogs, the bodies of humans, and wings, and that in addition to being able to fly, they will be cognizant of events spanning a hundred years in both the past and the future (Kitahara and Ogawa 223). Among Buddhist divinities, the Mantra King Fudō (Fudō Myōō; Acala Vidyārāja) is especially well known for protecting against tengu; *Tengu zōshi* includes his name in a tengu's list of "frightening things" in a transcription of a tengu song (Umezu 91c).

There were many famous tengu in medieval Japan (c. twelfth through sixteenth centuries), but three of the most celebrated are Zegaibō of China, Tarōbō of Mount Atago (outside of Kyoto), and the so-called Great Tengu of Mount Kurama (outside of Kyoto). Zegaibō is best known in Japanese literature as the protagonist of the picture scroll *Zegaibō-e* (*Pictures of Zegaibō*; c. 1308), and as the protagonist (*shite*) of the noh play *Zegai*, attributed to Takeda Jōsei (1421–1508) and apparently inspired by the earlier painted scroll. According to *Zegaibō-e*, the story of which is based upon the aforementioned tale of the Chinese tengu Chirayōju (*Konjaku* 20:2), the tengu Zegaibō first came to Japan in 966 CE in order to obstruct local Buddhist practice. The noh play *Zegai* explains that, upon arriving in Japan, Zegaibō immediately visited Tarōbō on Mount Atago to seek his advice. (In *Zegaibō-e*, Zegai visits a tengu named Nichirabō on Mount Atago.) Tarōbō directs Zegaibō to Enryakuji Temple on Mount Hiei, where he suffers a series of comical and ignoble defeats. Although Zegaibō may be the greatest tengu in China, he is shown to be no match for the Tendai Buddhist monks of Japan, and as he flies home at the end of the play, he cries out that he "will never come back again" (Koyama 532).

Tarōbō and the Great Tengu of Mount Kurama are also popular figures in medieval and early modern fiction. Tarōbō appears at a famous gathering of tengu in the Miidera scroll of *Tengu zōshi* (Nezu Art Museum); in the noh play *Kuruma-zō* (*The Handcart Priest*; first recorded performance in 1514), as well as a sixteenth- or early seventeenth-century work of short illustrated fiction titled *Kuruma-zō sōshi* (*The Tale of the Handcart Priest*), he engages an itinerant Zen monk—the eponymous Handcart Priest—in a debate on the nature of Buddhist truth. In the "Engyōbon" variant of *Heike monogatari*, the Sumiyoshi Deity describes Tarōbō as "the greatest tengu in all of Japan" (Kitahara and Ogawa 226), while the fourteenth-century *Taiheiki* (*A Chronicle of Peace*) refers to him as a tengu "of whom everyone speaks" (Gotō and Okami 65). Nevertheless, he is little match for the Handcart Priest. The Great Tengu of Mount Kurama is best known for befriending the twelfth-century Genpei War hero Minamoto no Yoshitsune when he was a boy, protecting him and teaching him fighting skills in the tengu's invisible palace on Mount Kurama to the north of Kyoto. The early sixteenth-century *Tengu no dairi* (*The Palace of the Tengu*), which survives in numerous lavish picture scrolls and woodblock-printed editions in libraries and museums around the world, depicts the Great Tengu's wondrous palace and introduces readers to his formerly human wife, whom he is said to have kidnapped from the human realm. It also describes how the Great Tengu kindly led Yoshitsune on a sightseeing tour of the realms of Hell, hungry **ghosts**, *ashura* (a world of never-ending battle), and the Western Pure Land Paradise, where Yoshitsune is able to meet his own dead father.

The Japanese Buddhist monk Keisei claimed to have interviewed the Great Tengu of Mount Hira on three occasions in the fifth month of 1239 when it possessed a 21-year-old woman in the household of Keisei's younger brother, Kujō Michiie. A transcript of Keisei's interview survives as *Hirasan kojin reitaku* (*Oracles of an Elder of Mount Hira*, 1239). Speaking through the body of the young woman, the tengu explains that it is "the arrogant, and those with deep attachments" who are prone to become tengu (Koizumi 472). The Great Tengu further relates that his own spouse is "already more than 400 years old," and that tengu children tend to be "cute when they're small" (Koizumi 471). In the seventeenth century, the Confucian scholar and governmental advisor Hayashi Razan wrote at length about tengu in his *Honchō jinja-kō* (*A Consideration of the Shinto Shrines of Japan*, c. 1638–45); and in the early nineteenth century, the nationalist intellectual Hirata Atsutane declared that he had learned the secrets of the supernatural "Other World" from a 14-year-old tengu boy named Kozō Torakichi, who claimed to have been born human and raised by tengu.

In the modern period, tengu have taken on a generally benevolent form. Today they are best known for their long red noses—a symbol of their own overweening pride—and for their large, feathery fans (*ha-uchiwa*), which they sometimes wave to stir up blustery storms. Tengu have become a staple of contemporary Japanese film, manga, anime, and video games, including television and film adaptations of Osaragi Jirō's *Kurama tengu* (*The Tengu of Mount Kurama*), the NHK anime *Zenmai zamurai* (*Wind-up Samurai*), Kabuto Mushitarō's manga and anime *Benben hantā kotengu Tenmaru* (*Monster Hunter: Tenmaru the Little Tengu*), and Terasawa Buichi's manga and anime *Karasu tengu Kabuto* (*Crow Tengu Kabuto*).

R. Keller Kimbrough

References and Suggested Reading

Abe, Yasurō. "The Book of *Tengu*: Goblins, Devils, and Buddhas in Medieval Japan." Translated by Toyosawa Nobuko. *Cahiers d'Extrême-Asie* 13 (2002–2003): 211–26.

Bialock, David T. "Outcasts, Emperorship, and Dragon Cults in *The Tale of the Heike*." *Cahiers d'Extrême-Asie* 13 (2002–2003): 227–310.

Gotō, Tanji, and Masao Okami, eds. *Taiheiki 3*. Nihon koten bungaku taikei, vol. 36. Tokyo: Iwanami Shoten, 1967.

Hansen, Wilburn. *When Tengu Talk: Hirata Atsutane's Ethnography of the Other World*. Honolulu: University of Hawaii Press, 2008.

Kimbrough, R. Keller. "Battling Tengu, Battling Conceit: Visualizing Abstraction in *The Tale of the Handcard Priest*." *Japanese Journal of Religious Studies* 39, no. 2 (2012): 275–305.

Kitahara, Yasuo, and Eiichi Ogawa, eds. *Engyō-bon Heike monogatari: honbun hen*. Vol. 1. Tokyo: Benseisha, 1990.

Koizumi, Hiroshi, et al., eds. *Hōbutsushū, Kankyo no tomo, Hirasan kojin reitaku*. Tokyo: Iwanami Shoten, 1993.

Komine, Kazuaki. *Setsuwa no mori: tengu, tōzoku, igyō no dōke*. Tokyo: Taishukan Shoten, 1991.

Koyama, Hiroshi, ed. *Yōkyokushū 2*. Tokyo: Shōgakukan, 1998.

Li, Michelle. *Ambiguous Bodies: Reading the Grotesque in Japanese Setsuwa Tales*. Stanford: Stanford University Press, 2009.

Shibata, Mitsuhiko. "Tengu." In *Nihon denki densetsu daijiten*, edited by Katsumi Inui, 619–20. Tokyo: Kadokawa Shoten, 1986.

Umezu, Jirō, ed. *Tengu sōshi, Zegaibō-e*. Tokyo: Kadokawa Shoten, 1978.

Wakabayashi, Haruko. "The Dharma for Sovereigns and Warriors: Onjō-ji's Claim for Legitimacy in Tengu zōshi." *Japanese Journal of Religious Studies* 29, nos 1–2 (2002): 35–66.

——. *The Seven Tengu Scrolls: Evil and the Rhetoric of Legitimacy in Medieval Japanese Buddhism*. Honolulu: University of Hawaii Press, 2012.

THESTRAL—*see* Harry Potter, Monsters In

TIAMAT

Tiamat is one of the main characters in the Babylonian Epic of Creation, *Enuma Eliš*. Within Mesopotamian mythology, this is a relatively late text composed in the second half of the twelfth century BCE to undergird the Babylonian quest for world dominance. Tiamat in *Enuma Eliš* should not be construed as a **sea monster** or a serpent. She is presented as the primordial goddess of the ocean. In a sacred marriage with Abzu, the god of fresh water, she produced many younger gods. Although she gave birth to all sorts of monsters and **dragons**, scorpion men and merpeople (see **Mermaid/Merman**), she herself cannot be seen as a dragon. Her depiction in *Enuma Eliš* is rather anthropomorphic. Later on in *Enuma Eliš*, animosity between her and Marduk—the Babylonian god whose rise to power is reflected in this myth—arises, leading to a chaos war in which Marduk defeats Tiamat in single combat: "And the lord stood upon Tiamat's hinder parts, And with his merciless club he smashed her skull. He cut through the channels of her blood, And he made the North wind bear it away into secret places" (*Enuma Eliš* IV: 129–33).

Marduk splits Tiamat's body into two parts: the upper parts are used in the construction of the firmament; the other parts become the Earth. A mountain is placed on her head and her eyes become the source for two rivers: the Euphrates and the Tigris. Construing the Earth as the remains of a threatening goddess—in combination with the concept of humankind as being created out of clay and the blood of the rebellious god Kingu—the Babylonian epic gives a mythic explanation for the presence of evil in the universe and in the human body.

Outside of the *Enuma Eliš*, Tiamat is hardly referred to in Mesopotamian sources, which has given rise to the idea that this combat myth was not an indigenous element of Mesopotamian culture. The battle between Marduk and Tiamat is beautifully depicted on a peristyle from the temple of Bel—a later name for Marduk—in Palmyra (Syria). Slightly older fourteenth-century BCE inscriptions from the ancient Mediterranean port city of Ugarit (northern Syria) mention a battle between the rising god Ba'lu and the god of the sea Yammu. Although this myth does not parallel the account in the *Enuma Eliš* in all detail—Yammu is not completely destroyed, but confined to his sphere of origin—the Ugaritic tale most probably served as a mold for the Babylonian myth. In addition, new finds and analyses of the Ugaritic inscriptions have revealed that the inhabitants of that old harbor city feared the deified deep waters referred to by the name *thmt*, which is clearly a cognate of Tiamat.

In the Hebrew Bible, some 35 occurrences of the proper noun *tehôm*, "the deep (water)," are attested. Although connections with Tiamat and Ugaritic *thmt* are clear, the deep (water) is depicted in the Hebrew Bible as some sort of geographical entity, but never deified. Nevertheless, texts like Genesis 1 and Isaiah 13 can be seen as late reflections of the Tiamat story, although in a more secular form.

In Berossus's first volume of a universal history dating to the third century BCE, it is narrated that in primordial times, when gods, men, and animals were mingling, a woman was in control of everything: "named Omorka, who in Chaldean is named Thalath (Tiamat) but in Greek her name is translated as Thalassa" (Komoróczy 131–3). In the eyes of this Hellenistic historian, Tiamat could be equated to the Greek primordial goddess of the sea, Thalassa. A late echo of this can be found in the sixth-century CE Greek author Damascius who, in his *Difficulties and Solutions of First Principles*, states that: "there being two principles at first called Tauthe and Apason, and these producing Moymis, but in the Creation tablet the first existence is called Mummu Tiamatu, a name meaning the 'sea-water' or 'sea chaos'" (Doria and Lenowitz 136). After Damascius, Tiamat seems to have disappeared from the consciousness of Western culture until the recovery of the Babylonian clay tablets in the nineteenth century. Therefore, she does not play a role in Hobbes's political analyses, unlike **Leviathan** and **Behemoth**.

In modern culture, author Zecharia Sitchin construes Tiamat to predate the Earth in his "Earth Chronicles" series (1976–2007). In a fabricated tale presented as based on real clay tablets dictated by the Sumerian god Enki to his scribe Endubšar, Sitchin constructs a strange cosmology, allegedly based on tales of astronauts from the twelfth planet Nibiru. Sitchin assumes that one of Nibiru's moons hit the Earth in the Pacific Basin. The merger of this moon, called the North Wind—a clear reference to *Enuma Eliš* IV—with Tiamat formed the Earth with all its life and gave it its present orbit. The novelist Joan D. Vinge wrote two books that are set on the planet Tiamat (*The Snow Queen* [1980] and *The Summer Queen* [1991]), where the population tries to survive, despite the misconduct of the reigning queen.

Outside of literature, Tiamat appears in the role playing game *Dungeons & Dragons* (see **Dungeons & Dragons, Monsters In**), in which she is presented as the offspring of Io, the dragon creator deity. This greedy, vain, and arrogant goddess is in continuous rivalry with her brother Bahamut, probably a reference to Behemoth. Tiamat is represented by the image of a five-headed dragon. She also appears in a similar role in many other role-playing and video games, including *Final Fantasy Tactics*, *Dark Queen of Krynn*, **Ogre** *Battle: March of the*

Black Queen, and *League of Legends*. In the internet action game *Diablo II*, "Tiamat's Rebuke" is a valuable dragon shield with good defensive qualities. There is a Swedish gothic metal band named Tiamat whose songs contain all sorts of references to the dark side of creation (see, for instance, their song "Church of Tiamat," from the album *Skeleton Skeletron* [1999]).

Bob Becking

References and Suggested Reading

Alster, Bernd. "Tiamat." In *Dictionary of Deities and Demons in the Bible*, 2nd edn, edited by Karel van der Toorn, Bob Becking, and Pieter W. van der Horst, 867–9. Leiden: Brill, 1999.

Beal, Timothy K. *Religion and its Monsters*. New York: London, 2002.

Dirven, Lucinda. "The Exaltation of Nabû: A Revision of the Relief Depicting the Battle against Tiamat from the Temple of Bel in Palmyra." *Welt des Orients* 28 (1997): 96–116.

Doria, Charles, and Harris Lenowitz, eds. *Origins: Creation Texts from the Ancient Mediterranean*. New York: Anchor Books, 1976.

Geyer, John B. "Twisting Tiamat's Tail: A Mythological Interpretation of Isaiah XIII 5 and 8." *Vetus Testamentum* 37 (1987): 164–79.

Jacobsen, Thorkild. "The Battle between Marduk and Tiamat." *Journal of the American Oriental Society* 88 (1968): 104–8.

Komoróczy, Géza. "Berosos and the Mesopotamian Literature." *Acta Antiqua Academica Scientiarum Hungarica* 21 (1973): 125–52.

Sitchin, Zechariah. *The Lost Book of Enki: Memoirs and Prophecies of an Extraterrestrial God*. Rochester, VT: Bear & Company, 2004.

Vinge, Joan D. *The Snow Queen*. New York: Dial Press, 1980.

——. *The Summer Queen*. New York: Tor Books, 1991.

TIPUA—*see* Sea Monsters

TITAN

The Titans appear in Greek mythology and are the children of Gaea, the female personification of Earth, and Uranus, the male personification of Sky. Originally twelve in number, they were chiefly nature deities that were later supplanted by the Olympian gods who defeated them in an epic battle known as the Titanomachy. The most famous of the Titans are Cronus, Atlas, and Prometheus.

In the Greek creation myths, Gaea and Uranus had three groups of children: the **Cyclops**, three in number and known for their skills as smiths and their one eye; the Hecatonchires, the hundred-handed **giants**; and the Titans. Uranus imprisoned all of his children within Gaea. Gaea sought to end her pain and help her children, so she created a sickle of adamant and asked one of her children to use it to overthrow Uranus. Cronus, the youngest of the Titans, agreed to do it. When Uranus came to Gaea that night, Cronus seized his genitals and castrated him, throwing the severed genitals into the sea.

The Titans then came into power. They were originally six males and six females, usually paired. Cronus married his sister Rhea, an earth goddess. There were also Oceanus, Tethys, Hyperion, Theia, Crisus, Coeus, Iapetus, Themis, Phoebe, and Mnemosyne. Oceanus and Tethys were the parents of the Oceanids and the spirits of springs, rivers, and waters. Hyperion was a sun deity, as was his son, Helius. Selene, the goddess of the moon, and Eos, goddess of the dawn, were also his children. Iapetus was the father of Atlas, Prometheus, and Epimetheus, with some accounts listing Themis as their mother and others the nymph Clymene.

After overthrowing his father, Uranus and Gaea informed Cronus that he too would be overthrown by one of his children. Because of this prophecy, he swallowed his children when they were born. Pregnant for the sixth time, Rhea went to her parents for advice. They aided her and she gave birth to Zeus. Instead of giving him to Cronus to swallow, she gave her husband a stone wrapped in baby clothing. Cronus was deceived and Zeus reached adulthood, protected by nymphs.

Zeus and his mother tricked Cronus into then regurgitating his elder siblings: Hestia, Poseidon, Hades, Hera, and Demeter. Zeus also freed the Cyclops and the Hecatonchires, which Cronus had failed to do. The Cyclops forged Zeus's thunderbolt for him, and in some versions, Poseidon's trident and Hades's helm of invisibility. The Hecatonchires proved a fierce ally in the battle with the Titans, being able to throw 300 rocks at once. The Titans were defeated and, according to the Greek poet Hesiod in his *Theogony* (c. 700 BCE), were imprisoned in Tartarus, a place of darkness beneath the Earth guarded by the Hecatonchires.

Atlas, the son of Iapetus, was sentenced to hold up the vault of Heaven. He appears in versions of the myth of Perseus and Hercules. When Hercules has to fetch the apples from the garden of the Hesperides, he asks Atlas to get them for him and takes the burden of the sky on his shoulders while Atlas does the task. Atlas tries to leave Hercules with the burden, but the hero tricks Atlas into taking back the weight. In some versions, Perseus flies past Atlas with the head of **Medusa** and transforms him into a mountain.

Prometheus, along with Themis, sided with the gods in the Titanomachy. He helped create mankind and stole fire to give to them. He was punished by being chained to a rock and having his liver eaten by an eagle. He was later freed by Hercules. His brother Epimetheus, though warned by Prometheus not to accept any gifts from Zeus, does so when he takes Pandora as his wife. Pandora was also given a jar that contained all the ills of the world and releases them to plague mortals forever.

Other versions of the myths show Cronus, or Saturn, the Roman name for the Titan, in a different way. In Ovid's first-century CE *Metamorphoses*, Saturn rules over the Golden Age of Mankind. Other myths also have him ruling over the Elysian Fields in the afterlife.

In general, the interpretation of the victory of the gods could represent the victory of the forces of civilization over the more savage time before it. The Titanomachy may also represent the dominance of the Indo-European invaders, who worshipped Zeus, as they spread into the Greek peninsula and supplanted the local deities who were once worshipped there.

In the mystery religion associated with Orpheus, the Titans play a different role. In that tradition, Zeus and Kore, another name for Persephone, mate and she gives birth to Dionysus. The Titans kill the infant Dionysus, dismember him, and feast on the body. Zeus eradicates them with his lightning, reducing them to ashes. From these ashes, mortals arise, made from the evil Titans but still keeping part of the divine Dionysus in their nature.

Prometheus becomes perhaps the most important of the Titans, though not as a monstrous figure. The fifth-century BCE *Prometheus Bound*, attributed to the Greek playwright Aeschylus, elaborates his story. Percy Bysshe Shelley also interpreted the myth in his play *Prometheus Unbound* (1820). Mary Shelley's *Frankenstein* (1820) also bore the second title of *A Modern Prometheus*.

Though the 1981 film *The Clash of the Titans* (Desmond Davis) and its remake of the same title in 2010 (Louis Leterrier) both have mythological inspiration, neither actually features characters that are Titans. The **Kraken**, the monster of both movies, is not counted among the Titans, nor is the **gorgon Medusa**. Rick Riordan, in his mythological young adult series "Percy Jackson and the Olympians," uses the Titans, and particularly Cronus, as the main villains. Cronus is trying to return and overthrow Zeus and the Olympians. In the final book of the series, Percy Jackson is instrumental in defeating Cronus and his Titan army. However, in the movie version of the first novel, *Percy Jackson and the Lightning Thief* (Chris Columbus, 2010), the rise of Cronus was eliminated from the storyline.

P. Andrew Miller

References and Suggested Reading

Hesiod. *Hesiod and Theognis*. Translated by Dorothea Bender. New York: Penguin Classics, 1973.

Morford, Mark P.O., Robert J. Lenardon, and Michael Sham. *Classical Mythology*. 9th edn. Oxford: Oxford University Press, 2011.

Ovid. *Metamophoses*. Translated by Samuel Garth, John Dryden, et al. *The Internet Classics Archive*. <http://classics.mit.edu/Ovid/metam.1.first.html>. Accessed 31 July 2012.

Riordan, Rick. *The Last Olympian*. New York: Scholastic Books, 2010.

TOLKIEN, MONSTERS IN

When Illuvatar, the Creator-god of J[ohn] R[onald] R[euel] Tolkien's (1892–1973) imagined Middle-earth, started his act of creation through singing, Tolkien tells us in *The Silmarillion* (1977) that Melkor (who subsequently became Morgoth), one of the Ainur (the earliest, **angel**-like race), repeatedly sang dissonances to the first melody in competition with the Creator. All of the monsters of Middle-earth were subsequently produced—either created or transformed—by Morgoth or his followers as perversions or distortions of natural beings. Some, such as the Maiar Sauron (a lesser Ainur) and the **wizard** Saruman, started out, like Melkor, as potentially good beings who were then corrupted. Others are simply bestial or "born bad."

Although Tolkien himself rarely gives detailed descriptions of monsters, instead using a few descriptive words in order to allow the reader to imagine the worst according to his or her imagination, the various film adaptations of Tolkien's works have created indelible images of Tolkien's monstrous creations. The Arthur Rankin Jr/Jules Bass animated film *The Hobbit* (1977), Ralph Bakshi's animated and rotoscoped film *The Lord of the Rings* (1978), and Peter Jackson's film trilogy of the same name (2002–2004) have each given these monsters specific form, as have many illustrators in their drawings and paintings.

Demons

The chief source of evil in *The Lord of the Rings* is Sauron. He is originally one of the elder race of the first beings, the Ainur, from that division called the Maiar, cognate to the Christian conception of angels. He was the chief servant of Melkor, and on Melkor's death Sauron became the chief Lord of Darkness. He tricked the Elvish smith Celebrimbor (see **Elf**) into teaching him the secret of making Rings of Power, and Sauron forged the One Ring to rule the Nine and the Seven, the rings made seemingly to empower but really to entrap men and **dwarves**, respectively. The Three Rings for Elven Kings were never shown to Sauron, so he had no power over them. Sauron is called the Necromancer when he is dwelling in Mirkwood, before his expulsion from that wood and subsequent return to Mordor, and is referred to as such by Gandalf in *The Hobbit* (1937) upon his return to the company of the dwarves. The Necromancer's presence in Mirkwood is what has allowed the giant spiders to take up residence there and for shadow to gather in the wood (see **Animals, Monstrous**). Although the archvillain of *The Lord of the Rings* trilogy (*The Fellowship of the Ring*, 1954; *The Two*

Towers, 1954; *The Return of the King*, 1955), he did not originate evil, nor did evil end with his destruction, which occurred when the One Ring, in which Sauron had put his power, was destroyed.

Balrogs are another form of **demon** who came from the Maiar, and who were twisted into creatures of darkness by Morgoth. They are described as having streaming manes of fire and breathing flame, being surrounded by clouds of darkness, and using many-thonged whips of fire in addition to flaming swords. One balrog that survived the First Age by taking refuge at the root of a mountain was disturbed by dwarves delving too deep in the mines of Moria, and this balrog killed Durin (one of the seven kings of the Dwarves)—hence was known to the dwarves as Durin's Bane—and killed the dwarves that had settled in Khazad-dum. This balrog is defeated by Gandalf in *The Fellowship of the Ring*. It is depicted as having great wings in Bakshi's animated adaptation (which would raise questions as to why it would fall into the chasm beneath the Bridge of Khazad-Dum); in Jackson's *The Fellowship of the Ring*, it is shown as a large, two-armed and two-legged devilish creature whose open mouth glows as intensely as a superheated blast furnace; it has no discernible wings.

Among minor demonic beings are the Barrow-wights, ghostly beings that dwell in barrows, or earth-mounds, raised to hide hoards of gold or other treasure. Early in the *Fellowship*, one captures Merry, Pippin, Sam, and Frodo and starts a ritual to entrap them, but Frodo calls the mysterious Tom Bombadil to break the spell and save them. Other demonic beings include the Silent Watchers, two great stone statues guarding the pass of Cirith Ungol, at the back entrance to Mordor. Each has some spirit within it that is aware of anything living that passes. The orcs' name for them is the Shriekers.

Humanoid Monsters

While demons such as balrogs are spectacular manifestations of monstrosity, monsters in Tolkien's world of Middle-earth are more commonly humanoid in appearance. Most threatening are the Black Riders, or Nazgul, which constitute the physical form that the Nine Ringwraiths take when they issue forth from Mordor to seek Frodo Baggins and the One Ring. Originally human kings, they accepted the Nine Rings made for mortal men by Sauron, and as a result their lives were extended by him so that, as **wraiths**, they became undead and under his control. As they are blind to the world of sunlight, their horses must guide them; they are invisible, so can be seen only as shapes beneath their cloaks, except when Frodo puts on the Ring and thereby enters their shadow realm of existence. They miss capturing Frodo at the Inn at Bree through a stratagem of Strider's (AKA Aragorn); they corner and wound Frodo at Weathertop, then miss capturing him at the Ford of Bruinen when the river—through the white magic of Elrond Halfelven and Gandalf—rises up to drown their horses and carry the Riders south. As with their horses, the winged beasts they subsequently ride—serpentine creatures akin to **dragons**—are vulnerable to arrows. The Captain of the Black Riders is the **Witch** King of Angmar, who is also the general of Sauron's army in the assault on Gondor.

Another group of undead is led by the King of the Dead, the surviving form of the King of the Mountains who had sworn allegiance to Elendil to fight against Sauron. When the war came, he and his men avoided service, having worshiped Sauron in the interim. Elendil's son Isildur laid a curse that he and his men would not truly die until they had returned to fulfill their pledge in the last fight against Mordor. Aragorn, instead of riding with Theoden and the Riders of Rohan to the direct aid of Gondor after the victory at Helm's Deep, takes instead the Paths of the Dead to collect on this long-delayed promise and, after their service in battle, they wish for nothing more than to be allowed at last to die.

Just as the Nazgul and the Dead are twisted and preserved forms of men, enslaved by their Rings or a curse, Gollum is the preserved and diminished form of Smeagol, a hobbit who stole the One Ring from his friend Deagol, whom he strangled. He used the invisibility made possible by the Ring to steal and kill, and his community banished him. For 500 years, he lived by a lake under the Misty Mountains, sustained but vitiated by possession and use of the Ring. He represents a shadow figure for both Bilbo in *The Hobbit* and Frodo in *The Lord of the Rings*, and the two Bagginses are seen to grow morally as they come to pity Gollum and learn from his affliction. His absolute addiction to the power of the Ring is what ultimately causes it, ironically, to be destroyed. Leading up to the casting of the Ring in the fires beneath Mount Doom, Gollum is Frodo and Sam's guide into and along the back ways of Mordor. Slinker and Stinker are Sam Gamgee's nicknames for Gollum's two sub-personalities—one a fawning, subservient creature, the other a spiteful creature that threatens the hobbits—observed during Frodo and Sam's voyage into Mordor.

Orcs were made in mockery of the elves by Sauron and form the mass of Sauron's army. They are described as having long arms and fangs, but Tolkien gives little further exact description, except for details about individuals such as the "huge orc-chieftan, almost man-high" who attacks Frodo in the Chamber of Mazarbul: "His broad flat face was swart, his eyes were like coals, and his tongue was red" (*Fellowship* 317). The word "orc" is cognate to "**ogre**" and is an Old English word for "demon." Most orcs cannot stand to be out in the sunlight, but Sauron (Saruman, in Jackson's adaptations) developed larger orcs that could travel in daylight, called the "Uruk-hai." This is the kind of orc that captures Merry and Pippin near Amon Hen, killing Boromir as he valiantly defends the hobbits. The orcs loyal to Sauron argue with the Uruk-hai loyal to Saruman over where the hobbits are to be brought, Mordor or Isengard, and in part this infighting allows Merry and Pippin to escape into the forest of Fangorn. Similarly, it is infighting and bickering among orc guards at Cirith Ungol that allows Sam to rescue Frodo, so that they can make their way into Mordor. In Bakshi's film version of *The Lord of the Rings*, the orcs are actors wearing masks, furs, capes, and horned headdresses, and are colored in so darkly that the only details that can be seen are white protruding fangs and glowing red eyes. In Jackson's films, the orcs are depicted as humanoid with grossly distorted facial features and misshapen bodies.

Goblins is the term used for orcs in *The Hobbit*. The lexicographical identity of "goblins" with "orcs" is established through the Elvish sword named *Orcrist*, which is translated in the common tongue as "Goblin-cleaver." Goblins are referred to once in *The Fellowship of the Ring* as storytale bogeymen with which to scare children. The goblins under the Misty Mountains were animated by Rankin and Bass as fat, bulldog-like creatures with protruding fangs, though they are not described in any detail in the text. Tolkien may have derived his goblins in part from George MacDonald's *The Princess and the Goblin* (1872), but distanced himself from the earlier author as his career progressed.

Just as orcs were made in mockery of the elves, **trolls** are dim-witted mockeries of the tree-like ents. They are unable to withstand sunlight and, when exposed, they revert to the stone out of which they have been fashioned. Three such trolls are encountered by Bilbo and the dwarves, but Gandalf tricks them into arguing till sunrise turns them to stone. Trolls also wield the battering ram in *The Return of the King* that smashes the Great Gate of Gondor. Though a "cave-troll" attempts to kill Frodo in Jackson's version of *Fellowship*, there are no trolls mentioned in the Moria chapters in the original novel.

Animal Monsters

Tolkien also populated his world of Middle-earth with a variety of non-humanoid monstrous creatures. Dragons are large lizards with wings and legs with claws. Tolkien wrote that dragons were, in medieval literature, emblems of *malitia*, or ill-will (see Kaske 303, n. 76). They brood atop hoards of gold and other riches, killing the original owners and any who happen upon the hoard. Such treasure, long coveted by dragons, has great power to enchant dwarves and others with gold-lust. Ancalagon the Black was the mightiest dragon of the First Age of Middle-earth; Smaug is the dragon who is central to *The Hobbit*; Chrysophylax Dives in Tolkien's 1949 fable "Farmer Giles of Ham" is a somewhat less dire monster than these first two, but deadly nonetheless to those without the magic sword Caudimordax (AKA Tailbiter). Smaug was based in part on the unnamed dragon in the Old English saga of *Beowulf* (dating to somewhere between the eighth and eleventh centuries), which Tolkien criticized as being too generic a dragon, and on Fafnir from the Icelandic *Volsunga Saga* (late thirteenth century), whose personality informed Tolkien's depictions of both Smaug and Chrysophylax Dives. Tolkien also depicted Smaug in a water color, in which the dragon lies upon a pile of gold; this painting may have in part inspired Rankin and Bass's animated Smaug.

Shelob is a giant spider, daughter of the greatest giant spider of all, Ungoliant, of the First Age. Shelob settled in the mountains of Mordor, near the pass known as Cirith Ungol, the Pass of the Spider (see **Animals, Monstrous**). There for untold ages she was feared by the orcs and anyone else who had heard of her, but she is defeated by Samwise Gamgee, who stabs her with his sword Sting. She drags herself off in defeat, apparently to die. Some giant spiders, although smaller than Shelob, have settled in the Greenwood and spread the nets of their darkness until it becomes known as the Mirkwood, the dark wood. A group of these captures the twelve dwarves following the dwarf Thorin Oakenshield and binds them in their webs; one starts to entrap Bilbo, but he awakes in time to free himself and then the dwarves.

Wolves are always portrayed as evil in Tolkien. The Wolf of Angband is the wolf sent by Morgoth to kill the human Beren in revenge for his having stolen one of the Silmaril, or jewels, from Morgoth's crown. **Werewolves** are wolves possessed by tortured spirits through sorcery; these, under their Chief, Draugluin, served Sauron in the First Age, but were defeated by Huan, the Wolfhound of the Valar. After Draugluin's death, Sauron shifted his shape to become a werewolf himself, but Huan defeated him as well. In *The Hobbit*, when Gandalf, Bilbo, and the dwarves emerge from the tunnels through the Misty Mountains, they stumble across a meeting of mountain wolves; these are joined after nightfall by goblins who ride them.

A warg is a wolf of a particularly evil kind, which can only take physical form at night, as it cannot exist in daylight. The Fellowship of the Ring is attacked by wargs before they arrive at Moria; the elf Legolas shoots one with an arrow, which he finds on the hillside the next day, not having lodged in flesh or bone. This tips off Gandalf that their nocturnal attackers were not flesh-and-blood living things, but the product of enchantment.

Finally, the Watcher in the Water is a **kraken**-like beast that inhabits the pool near the West Gate of Moria. Disturbed by the presence of the Fellowship trying to open the gate, the Watcher catches Frodo with a long, sinuous tentacle and starts to pull him into the lake; Sam cuts the tentacle with a knife and frees him, but 20 more tentacles emerge as the Fellowship escapes into the just-opened portal to Moria; these tentacles smash the stone door shut and bury it in an avalanche.

Plant Monsters

In the Old Forest—where the trees, having been beaten back from encroaching on the Shire in Buckland, hate all who walk on two legs—Old Man Willow is the center of the darkness. Rooted on the shore of the Withywindle River, he ingests Merry and Pippin when they are sleeping at his roots; his roots also push Frodo into the river and hold him underwater. Huorns are tree-like beings, possibly ents, that have slowed down to become almost completely like trees. After the battle of Helm's Deep, a forest composed of huorns suddenly appears behind Saruman's orc army and kills all orcs that try to run through it.

Influences

The monsters in Tolkien's literary oeuvre have been replicated repeatedly in high-fantasy literature and films that have either aped or rebelled against the model provided by *The Lord of the Rings*. Terry Brooks's *The Sword of Shannara* (1977) features an arch-villain, Brona, known as the Warlock Lord, who believes he has conquered death; his most trusted servants, the Skull Bearers; and a Gollum-like gnome named Orl Fane, who covets the titular Sword. Tad Williams's trilogy "Memory, Sorrow and Thorn" (*The Dragonbone Chair*, 1988; *Stone of Farewell*, 1990; and *To Green Angel Tower*, 1993) features a race of men who have supplanted a much older race called the Sithi, who in many ways parallel Tolkien's elves; a group of these elder beings, the Norns, and their leader, Ineluki the Storm King, plot the overthrow of the realm of men by using black magic and many monsters reminiscent of the various beasts and humans who have been drafted into Sauron's forces, such as the sea serpent *kilpa* and the Diggers. Furthermore, Ineluki, having died, is seeking a living mortal to possess, thus giving him physical presence in the world; in this, he is like Sauron, who in *The Lord of the Rings* has not yet been able to attain physical form.

In addition to fantasy novels, Tolkien's monsters have been concretized in films, the most influential of which has been Peter Jackson's *The Lord of the Rings* trilogy. A number of both parodies and straight homages use Jackson's visual style, including the depiction of orcs which figure significantly in the fan films *Born of Hope* (Kate Madison, 2009) and *The Hunt for Gollum* (Chris Bouchard, 2009). There have also been many games, both role-playing games such as Dungeons & Dragons (released by Gary Gygax and Dave Arneson, 1974; see **Dungeons & Dragons, Monsters In**)—although Gygax claimed that Tolkien's influence on the game was minimal—and video games, including a 1990 game using clips from Ralph Bakshi's film, and games developed since the release of Peter Jackson's trilogy using the imagery from those films. In all, at least 20 action or role-playing electronic games based on aspects of Tolkien's work have appeared, including a Lord of the Rings pinball game in 2003.

Don Riggs

References and Suggested Reading

Day, David. *Guide to Tolkien's World: A Bestiary*. New York: Metro Books, 2010.

Haber, Karen, ed. *Meditations on Middle-earth*. New York: St. Martin's Press, 2001.

Kaske, R.E. "*Sapientia et Fortitudo* as the Controlling Theme of *Beowulf*." In *An Anthology of Beowulf Criticism*, edited by Lewis E. Nicholson, 269–310. Notre Dame: University of Notre Dame Press, 1963.

Long, Josh. "Clinamen, Tessera, and the Anxiety of Influence: Swerving from and Completing George MacDonald." In *Tolkien Studies: Annual Scholarly Review VI*, edited by Douglas A. Anderson, Michael D.C. Drout, and Verlyn Flieger, 127–50. Morgantown, WV: West Virginia University Press, 2009.

Tolkien, J.R.R. "*Beowulf*: The Monsters and the Critics." In *An Anthology of Beowulf Criticism*, edited by Lewis E. Nicholson, 51–103. Notre Dame: University of Notre Dame Press, 1963.

——. *The Hobbit: or, There and Back Again* [1937]. New York: Random House, 1996.

——. *The Lord of the Rings*. New York: Houghton Mifflin, 1994.

——. *The Silmarillion*. Boston: Houghton Mifflin, 1977.

——. *The Tolkien Reader*. New York: Ballantine, 1966.

Tyler, J.E.A. *The Tolkien Companion*. New York: St. Martin's Press, 1976.

TRAUCO—*see* Incubus/Succubus

TRIFFID

The triffid is a species of monstrous plant (see **Plants, Monstrous**) first featured in the 1951 novel *The Day of the Triffids*, by John Wyndham. Their name comes from the Latin for "divided into three," referring to the ambulatory plant's three rudimentary feet. Carnivorous and predatory, the triffids rapidly adapt to a global outbreak of blindness brought on by a meteor shower. In the chaos that follows, civilization collapses and the triffids remorselessly rise to the top of the food chain. In so doing, they display evidence of communication, cooperation, and perhaps a communal intelligence.

In temperate countries, triffids grow to a height of seven feet; tropical triffids are taller. The triffid's stem rises from a thick, nearly spherical bole covered with rootlet hairs. The triffid's feet protrude from the lower surface of the bole, lifting the plant about twelve inches off the ground when it moves, which it does at the speed of a walking human. At other times, the triffid roots itself in the soil and waits for prey. The triffid disables or kills its prey with a ten-foot sting, whipping out from a frond at the top of the stem carrying enough venom to kill an adult human. The triffid cannot lift an animal body with this sting, but it can tear decomposing flesh from the corpse and deposit such food in the trumpet-shaped cup of petals atop its stem. This cup resembles the "mouth" of the Venus fly-trap, containing a sticky substance and digestive fronds. (It also sprays triffid seeds when it reproduces.) Like the fly-trap, it also lures insects, which the triffid subsists upon in the absence of larger game. At the base of the stem are three stiff, stick-like projections that sometimes drum against the stem, producing a clattering sound that carries a good distance. Triffids are drawn towards sound, especially regular or constant noises like engines or radios.

The origin of the triffids varies. In their first appearance in "Revolt of the Triffids" (1951), a condensed version of Wyndham's novel in *Collier's* magazine, they originated on the planet Venus, where it is speculated that they grow to enormous size (see **Extraterrestrial**). By the time of the novel's unabridged publication, their origin had become terrestrial. The result of Soviet genetic engineering (the 1954 edition of the novel implies that the Stalinist crank Trofim Lysenko [1898–1976] created them), triffids were first grown at an experimental station in Kamchatka. (Wyndham's unpublished novel, *Plan for Chaos*, written at the same time as *The Day of the Triffids*, does not mention the triffids specifically but hints that Nazi geneticists engineered them.) They had been bred for their oils, which were nutritionally far superior to all others. A failed attempt to steal a box of triffid seeds released them into the jet stream, and they rained down all across the globe, first growing to maturity in the tropics and then raised as garden specimens in the temperate world. Garden triffids have their stings pruned every year; this dilutes the oil too much to be practicable for industrial agriculture.

By the time of the novel's action, triffids are a valuable crop where cultivated, and a dangerous menace in the wilderness. Their woody make-up and lack of vital organs make triffids fairly resistant to firearms, so agronomists and jungle adventurers settle on a kind of boomerang gun that shoots razor-sharp discs capable of severing a triffid stem. Triffids are also vulnerable to fire, as befits their vegetable composition.

In Steve Sekely's 1962 film *The Day of the Triffids*, the triffids are once more extraterrestrial: *Triffidus celestus* ride down to Earth on the meteor shower that blinds humanity. (One scene, however, implies that Earth plants mutate into triffids.) They more closely resemble ambulatory broccoli, and rather than stinging, they shoot a wad of venom from their cup. They are never cultivated and resemble standard "alien invaders" of the period, rather than Wyndham's carefully plotted Darwinian nightmare. Like Wells's Martians, Sekely's triffids have a crippling weakness: Earth's seawater dissolves them. Wyndham's triffids, by contrast, take immediate advantage of human weaknesses: even before the Blinding, they always aim for the humans' eyes or hands, attempting to negate human advantages in evolutionary competition. In the authorized 2001 sequel by Simon Clark, the novel *The Night of the Triffids*, the triffids have further mutated to amplify their intelligence, and some varieties have grown to monstrous size.

Generally, the triffids in both BBC television productions (Ken Hannam, 1981 and Nick Copus, 2009) more closely resemble Wyndham's triffids, although the 1981 BBC triffids replace the "drumming sticks" with claws and the 2009 BBC triffids have extensible vines that grab and pull their victims to their death. (Gerry Ordway's comic book adaptation of the novel, in Marvel Comics' *Unknown Worlds of Science Fiction* #1 [October 1974], followed Wyndham almost exactly, down to the Wyndham-derived artwork by Ross Andru [1925–93], Ernie Chua [1940–], and Rico Rival [1940?–].) The 2009 triffids also cannot perceive people blinded by diluted triffid venom, which makes little logical sense, even in the context of that production.

As Wyndham's novel combined postwar famine fears and indictment of the Cold War arms race (the global blindness and plagues, he implies, come from malfunctioning weapons satellites), other triffids fuel other terrors. The 1962 triffids fit that era's invasion fears and growing technophobia, adding a scene on a doomed airliner. The 2009 triffids are genetically engineered not to replace food stocks but as fuel, now that global warming (the 2009 Blindness comes from a solar flare) replaces global famine in the audience's consciousness.

Kenneth Hite

References and Suggested Reading

Ketterer, David. "The Genesis of the Triffids." *New York Review of Science Fiction* 16, no. 7 (2004): 11–14.

———. "John Wyndham: The Facts of Life Sextet." In *A Companion to Science Fiction*, edited by David Seed, 375–88. Malden, MA: Blackwell, 2005.

Sawyer, Andy. "'A Stiff Upper Lip and a Trembling Lower One': John Wyndham on Screen." In *British Science Fiction Cinema*, edited by I.Q. Hunter, 75–87. London: Routledge, 1999.

Wyndham, John. *The Day of the Triffids*. Harmondsworth: Penguin, 1954.

TROGLODYTE

The term "troglodyte" or "troglodytae" literally means "cave dweller" in Greek, and it can refer to any primitive creature that inhabits a cavern or natural dwelling; the term is often used as a synonym for the stereotypical Neanderthal "cave-man" or prehistoric human. It can also, however, refer to a mythical humanoid cave monster and is often used as a derogatory slur to define a person (or group) as backward, primitive, monstrous, and/or unenlightened.

According to the *Histories* of Herodotus (c. 440 BCE), ancient Greek explorers referred to the inhabitants of upper Egypt, Ethiopia, and the west coast of the Red Sea as troglodytes because of their earthen dwellings, and the Greek geographer Agatharchides used the label "Troglodytice" in the second century BCE to describe the Red Sea coast. Ancient Greeks regarded the foreign peoples of these areas as primitive and barbarous: in Book five of *On the Erythraean Sea* (c. second century BCE), Agatharchides describes them as naked, licentious beasts who murder their sick and elderly. Some explorers described the Ethiopian troglodytes as wild in appearance and marveled at their ability to run more swiftly than horses; Herodotus also suggests that Ethiopian cave dwellers ate lizards and reptiles and spoke a language that resembled the twittering of bats.

European scholars and explorers in the early modern period also referred to North African peoples as troglodytes: Johann Boemus, a German ethnographer, refers to troglodytes as ground-dwellers in his anthropological study *Fardle of Facions* (1555), and Sir Walter Raleigh's *History of the World* (1614) describes North Africa as the land of Prester John and the Troglodytes. Carl Linnaeus, the Swedish scientist who pioneered the modern nomenclature of taxonomy, uses the term *Homo troglodytes* in his 1758 *Systema Naturae* to describe the supposedly primitive inhabitants of foreign lands and to distinguish them from contemporary humans or *Homo sapiens*.

The first significant literary reference to troglodytes appears in Montesquieu's *Persian Letters* (1721), which portrays the fictional correspondences of two Persian noblemen travelling through France. Contemplating the question of whether human happiness originates from sensory pleasure or from the practice of virtue, one of the nobles (Usbek) offers a fable concerning a mythic Arabian people he calls the Troglodytes. In the fable, which Montesquieu deploys to refute Thomas Hobbes's (1588–1679) view of social contract theory, the Troglodytes overthrow their foreign king and decide to follow their own passions without law or government. Soon most of the Troglodytes are ruined; thinking only of themselves, the majority of them fail to recognize their dependence on others for resources and protection. After most perish, a small number of virtuous Troglodytes band together to build a new society, and they are successful because of their commitment to social responsibility.

Despite Montesquieu's assertion of the possibility of virtuous utopian troglodytes, the majority of subsequent portrayals depict the creatures in derogatory terms and they are often presented as sub-human monsters. Sir F.C. Burnand's theatrical *Acis and Galatea, or, The Nimble Nymph and the Terrible Troglodyte!* was first performed in the Royal Olympic Theatre in London in April 1863, and according to the *Oxford English Dictionary*, the term "troglodyte" was recognizably used in English as a slanderous epithet during this time. The stereotype of the "cave-man" as a monstrous anachronistic antagonist was firmly established in Western popular culture by the early twentieth century, and troglodytes appear as prominent villains in Sir Arthur Conan Doyle's *The Lost World* (1912), Edgar Rice Burroughs's *The Land That Time Forgot* (1915), and D.W. Griffith's film, *Man's Genesis* (1912). The cave-dwelling Morlocks of H.G. Wells's 1895 novel, *The Time Machine*, can also be considered a species of troglodytes.

The most monstrous portrayal of the troglodyte appears in the *Dungeons & Dragons* role-playing game (see **Dungeons & Dragons, Monsters In**). In the first D&D *Monster Manual* (1977), Gary Gygax goes beyond the typical depiction of the troglodyte as a "cave-man" to imagine troglodytes instead as chaotic lizard-men with offensive odors who dwell underground, who worship evil gods, and who indiscriminately slaughter humans and other good creatures. This fanciful approach to troglodytes can also be observed in the horror film *Troglodyte* (Paul Ziller, 2008; released on DVD in 2009 as *The Sea Beast*), which depicts the creature as an invisible poisonous subterranean reptile.

In popular culture, troglodytes are sometimes portrayed in a celebratory or humorous (rather than monstrous) light. The Jimmy Castor Bunch released a funk song in 1972 called "Troglodyte" that narrates the tale of a cave-man who seeks out a primeval woman in order to persuade her to dance with him; elements of the song have been widely sampled by artists such as N.W.A., Phil Collins (1951–), and Christina Aguilera (1980–). Other humorous depictions of cave-men appear in the comic strips *B.C.*, *Alley Oop*, and *The Far Side*, and in the animated television series *The Flintstones*.

David M. Higgins

References and Suggested Reading

Crisafulli, Alessandro S. "Montesquieu's Story of the Troglodytes: Its Background, Meaning, and Significance." *PMLA* 58, no. 2 (June 1943): 372–92.

De Montesquieu, Charles. *Persian Letters* [1721]. Translated by John Davidson. Lawrence, KS: Digireads Publishing, 2010.

Herodotus. *The Histories*. Translated by Aubrey de Selincourt. New York: Penguin, 2003.

TROLL

Fig. 34 ***Norwegian Forest Troll with Digging Machine*** **by John Adastra**

An ancient, primeval monster and denizen of northern mountains and forests, the troll has a history as old as its home. As Scandinavian legend and folklore came with the Vikings and their forebears into what would become the English-speaking world, so did stories of trolls; today, their folkloric origins are revised and supplemented by novels, short stories, films, and television shows. The troll may be a creature of the past, but it has found a comfortable home in the present.

Trolls in Folklore

Norwegian and northern Swedish folklore distinguishes between the large, brutal, and stupid troll and the smaller, cunning, human-like *huldrefolk* or *vitterfolk*. In southern Sweden and Denmark, the term "troll" applied to the latter, while the former were known as **giants** (jätte). "Troll" can also be used as a generic term for any magical or supernatural being and, in more recent centuries, the terms "troll" and "**ogre**" are sometimes used interchangeably. The flexibility permitted by these varying conventions has arguably contributed to the survival of the troll as a literary and filmic figure, but for the most part it is the troll of Norwegian legend—giant, brutish, destructive, and ferocious—that continues to carry the name.

In the best known of all troll fairy tales, "Three Billy Goats Gruff," the troll antagonist threatens three goats who must cross the bridge under which it lives in order to graze on the other side. The tale was first collected in Asbjørnsen and Moe's *Norske Folkeeventyr* (*Norse Fairytales*) in 1845, and translated into English by Sir George Webb Dasent in 1859. It has since become so well known as to create its own archetype, repeated countless times in whole or part in later stories, with the predatory troll outwitted by its intended prey. In the original story collected by Asbjørnsen and Moe, the first and smallest goat convinces the troll to allow him to pass and instead to eat the plumper goat following him; the second goat does the same, leaving the third and largest goat to hurl the greedy troll into the river with his horns.

The fondness of trolls for meat in general, and human flesh in particular, is a common thread throughout stories of trolls, and their great strength is typically destructive in its focus. Folkloric trolls are most often depicted as being armed with axes or clubs, emphasizing the threat of the brutal, if unsophisticated, violence they pose. Fortunately, however, they are far from invincible. Most trolls are portrayed as animalistic and of limited intelligence, allowing a cunning hero to easily outwit them. Further, they are creatures of the night in the strictest sense, typically turning to stone when sunlight hits them.

Trolls in Literature

In literature, trolls have an illustrious heritage, arguably reaching back to the Old English epic poem *Beowulf*. While the appearance of the monstrous **Grendel** is never directly described other than a reference to his humanoid form, he is a malevolent and destructive being, attacking a mead hall and feeding on the warriors he finds there. Although the term "troll" does not appear in most English dialects until the nineteenth century, a number of modern translators have used the word to describe Grendel, suggesting a connection between Grendel and the trolls of Scandinavian folklore (see the translations of *Beowulf* by Lehmann and Alexander).

J.R.R. Tolkien, familiar as he was with Scandinavian and Old English traditions, would no doubt have been aware of the folkloric history of the trolls when he penned *The Hobbit* (1937; see **Tolkien, Monsters In**). Here, Bilbo Baggins narrowly escapes being eaten by three trolls when they are tricked by Gandalf into arguing until the sun rises, turning them to stone. Tolkien's trolls are giant humanoid figures, stupid and vicious but strong and, at least in *The Hobbit*, capable of communicating in a thickly accented language; the trolls that appear in the "Lord of the Rings" trilogy (1954–55) seem more animalistic in nature and serve the villain Sauron. In Tolkien's wider mythology, trolls are described as being created from stone or from lesser animals by the evil god-figure Melkor as a mockery of the tree-like Ents (Tolkien 414).

Trolls are popular figures in the genre of Tolkien-esque fantasy that followed the publication of *The Lord of the Rings*, and are typically portrayed with the great strength and low intelligence that Tolkien depicts. Some authors, however, do add variations. In Tad Williams's "Memory, Sorrow, and Thorn" trilogy (1988–93), trolls are fairly small in stature, riding goats in their native mountains; their own name for themselves is the "Qanuc," and their society is a complex tribal one, resembling indigenous Arctic and sub-Arctic groups as much as anything from folklore. Terry Pratchett's 1992 story "Troll Bridge" echoes earlier folklore more directly. Pratchett's story, however, features not a protagonist outwitting the troll, but rather an aged hero seeking out bridge-dwelling trolls to defeat. Instead of fighting him, however, the troll he finds is overjoyed by such a well-known hero visiting its small and unremarkable bridge, and brings its wife and children out to be introduced. While the troll regales the hero concerning the bridge's illustrious history, its wife complains about the obvious poverty of the hero and describes various brothers-in-law who have left the bridge business and gone into various forms of industry. The confused hero hands over his own treasure to the troll and goes on his way.

Pratchett's "Troll Bridge" ostensibly takes place within the fictional universe of his comedic "Discworld" novels (1983 to present), a fantasy world in which magic coexists with industrial technology. Pratchett's trolls are no more threatening than other species, with their great strength typically channeled into manual labor and working as bouncers at the city's inns. As stone-based creatures, they eat rocks and cannot digest living beings (although it is suggested that some try nevertheless); their silicon-based brains conduct poorly unless the temperature is very cold, leading to their general perception as intellectually challenged, but they have personalities and even occasionally appear as protagonists.

In Neil Gaiman's short story, also titled "Troll Bridge" (appearing in his 1998 collection of short stories, *Smoke and Mirrors*), the troll seeks not flesh but rather something more ephemeral: the life, measured in some indefinable sense, of the child who crosses its path. The boy convinces the troll to let him go, and to eat him later once he has lived more fully, a scene repeated in the boy's teenage years. Finally, as a grown man, the protagonist returns to the bridge, mourning his life of lost chances and offering it to the troll. As the troll devours his life, the two exchange bodies, and the protagonist retreats from society under the bridge while the troll walks away into the world, whistling as it goes.

Urban fantasy and young adult literature have, in recent years, seen more inventive experimentations with the conventions of troll appearance and behavior. Sometimes they are still adversaries, abducting children in Ursula K. LeGuin's "A Ride on the Red Mare's Back" (1992), and exchanging a human baby for one of their own in Rose Estes's *Troll-Taken* (1993). More commonly, however, they are fully realized characters within a complex world. Nancy Farmer's fantasy trilogy, consisting of *Sea of Trolls* (2004), *The Land of the Silver Apples* (2007), and *The Islands of the Blessed* (2009), is set in a world of Norse mythology, where two young children are kidnapped by Vikings and taken to the kingdom of King Ivar the Boneless and his half-troll queen. Although the trolls might seem initially threatening, they are also members of a sophisticated society, playing chess and throwing banquets, and the troll queen herself befriends the children.

Further, trolls in such literature need not be threatening at all. John Vornholt's *Troll King* (2002) features trolls that, while gigantic and ugly, are sympathetic and pitiful characters, slaves to the ogres and sorcerers who rule their world. In Holly Black's *Valiant: A Modern Tale of Faerie* (2005), a bridge-dwelling troll named Ravus is also a healer by trade and a fully textured character in his own right. Although Val, the heroine of the story, initially finds Ravus hideous in appearance, her views begin to change after she learns more about him. Ravus has been framed for murder, and Val, determined to prove his innocence, ends up falling in love with him before clearing his name. In Charles Coleman Finlay's *The Prodigal Troll* (2005), the protagonist is again human, but this time raised by trolls from infancy. The trolls themselves have a complex democratic society seemingly based on Neolithic practices. In J.K. Rowling's "Harry Potter" series (1997–2007; see **Harry Potter, Monsters In**), trolls are again large, violent, and stupid creatures who communicate with a series of grunts, but as a result are the subject of some debate regarding their proper treatment and rights in the wizarding world.

Modern trolls, in addition, no longer require a strictly fantastical setting. T.H. White's 1935 story "The Troll" is set in northern Sweden, where the narrator is staying at a remote hotel while on a fishing holiday. After a terrifying dream involving blood pouring down a connecting door between his room and the next, the man wakes and investigates the room by peering through the keyhole, only to view a gigantic and grotesque troll eating a woman alive. The troll is described as eight feet tall, hideous in appearance, and possessing a fiery, infernal mouth that burns up any remaining traces of blood from its victim. The narrator's eyes meet those of the troll and the narrator quickly retreats to his bed.

Inquiring about the room's inhabitants the next day, he learns that they are a young professor and his wife, but that the wife has gone missing at some point in the night. The narrator begins to believe that the professor himself is a shapeshifting troll (see **Shapeshifter**)—an impression confirmed when he sees the man transform into a troll again in the hotel dining room. Although the other diners do not seem to notice, the narrator confirms his own suspicions by shaking the troll's hand, which burns and blisters his own. The troll threatens to eat him as well, and the narrator spends the day in a state of near-delirium in the remote and isolated town; eventually, he returns to his room, but keeps a set of rosary beads in the pocket of his pajamas. When the troll comes for him at night, its hands touch the rosary beads and it shrieks in pain, shrinks in size, and flees through the window. The next morning, the narrator hears that the professor's body has been found in a nearby lake. The story ends there, without any definite explanations, and with the narrator's own confusion and uncertainty lingering with the reader.

Björn Kurtén's novel *Dance of the Tiger* (1980) removes even the supernatural context of trolls. The novel is set in the Ice Age, where the "trolls" are the Neanderthals living alongside the Cro-Magnon protagonists. Kurtén, a palaeontologist himself, subscribes to the theory that the trolls of folklore may be a distant ancestral memory of another human species, and as a result his trolls are no less human than his other protagonists. Kurtén's work is, however, an anomaly in this regard, and most literary trolls remain in a context at least somewhat fantastic in nature.

Trolls in Film

Film and literature have also made liberal use of older folkloric conventions regarding trolls. Trolls' weakness to sunlight forms a significant point in one episode of the 1990s television series *The Outer Limits*, "Under the Bed" (Rene Bonniere, 1995), featuring a shapeshifting troll that steals children. Its nature is discovered by a police detective (Barbara Williams), who finds that its blood left on a broken window turns into a sand-like substance when exposed to daylight; together with the father of one missing child, she finds the troll and drags it into the daylight to be turned to stone.

The troll that appears in the BBC television series *Merlin* (2008–present) is also a shapeshifter, although this time an intelligent one using magical trickery to deceive the king into falling in love with her (see the two-part episode "Beauty and the Beast" [season 2, episodes 5–6, 2009; directed by David Moore and Metin Huseyin respectively]). A similar shapeshifting and deceptive troll and her father appear in an episode of Jim Henson's series *The Storyteller* (season 1, "The True Bride," 1988; directed by Peter Smith), this time explicitly based in Germanic folklore.

Not all trolls in film and television are particularly threatening figures. The animated film *A Troll in Central Park* (Don Bluth, 1994) features a troll who is both friendly and sympathetic. *Buffy the **Vampire** Slayer* features a troll transported from a parallel dimension in the episode entitled "Triangle," which aired in 2001 (season 5, episode 11; directed by Christopher Hibler). This troll (played by Abraham Benrubi) is also violent, destroying buildings with its hammer, although its mock-Viking speech patterns and enquiries about where it can find babies to eat are played for comedic value. A 2008 BBC televisual adaptation, *Billy Goats Gruff* (directed by Jeremy Dyson), plays with the conventions of the earlier folktale by transforming the setting into a contemporary landscape and presenting the troll itself as a pitiful and sympathetic figure.

The Norwegian film *The Troll Hunter* (André Øvredal, 2010) takes the form of pretend "found footage" sent anonymously to a film company, telling the story of three students filming their unofficial investigation into a man they suspect to be killing bears (Hans, played by Otto Jespersen). He turns out to be a government-employed troll hunter, killing giant, violent, and sometimes multi-headed trolls whose existence has been concealed by the government. These trolls are animalistic and lacking in intelligence, with the film emphasizing their natural behavior and providing a pseudo-scientific gloss for their intolerance of sunlight. As Hans warns the students, however, the trolls are angered by Christian blood; at one point, he even uses a bucket of the substance to lure a troll closer.

With such a variety of troll appearances and behaviors, it is at times difficult to decide where trolls end and other supernatural creatures begin. However, this same adaptability ensures the troll's continued existence and relevance.

Jenny Bann

References and Suggested Reading

Beowulf: A Verse Translation. Translated by Michael Alexander. New York: Penguin, 2003.

Beowulf: An Imitative Translation. Translated by Ruth P.M. Lehmann. Austin: University of Texas Press, 1988.

Kvideland, Reimund, and Henning K. Sehmsdorf. *Nordic Folklore: Recent Studies*. Bloomington, IN: Indiana University Press, 1990.

Pratchett, Terry. "Troll Bridge." In *After The King: Stories in Honor of J.R.R. Tolkien*, edited by Martin H. Greenberg and Jane Yolen, 34–43. New York: Tor, 1994.

Simpson, Jacqueline. *Scandinavian Folktales*. New York: Penguin, 1990.

Tolkien, J.R.R. *Morgoth's Ring: The Later Silmarillion, Part One*. New York: HarperCollins, 1994.

White, T.H. "The Troll." In *The Oxford Book of Modern Fairy Tales*, edited by Alison Lurie, 278–88. New York: Oxford University Press, 2003.

TSUKUMOGAMI—*see* Demon

TUTIVILLUS—*see* Demon

TYPHOEUS

In Greek mythology, Typhoeus (or Typhon) is chaos personified, a force of nature whose untamable energy threatens the order of the universe as upheld by the god Zeus. His very being attests to the cosmic struggles between generations of gods old and young. For after Zeus has vanquished her **Titan** children and confined them to the dusky realms of Tartarus—the bowels of the universe, where Zeus keeps his enemies imprisoned—Gaea makes one last effort to topple her grandson's rule. She gives birth to Typhoeus, a monster that the Greek poet Hesiod (c. 700 BCE) describes as "spouting a hundred terrifying snake-heads from his shoulders, their black tongues flickering" and "flashing fire from his eyes" (*Theogony* 824–8). He is the ultimate test of Zeus's disaster-preparedness. Had the Olympian not taken notice, this monster surely "would have ruled over mortals and immortals," succeeding Zeus as king of the cosmos (*Theogony* 837).

Part man, part beast, and part god, Earth-born Typhoeus is a study in corporeal dissonance. According to pseudo-Apollodorus in his *Bibliotheca* (c. first century CE), he sits taller than the tallest mountain, his head scraping the stars. Human from the thighs up, his torso is also winged, but snaky coils take the place of legs (1.6.3). Indeed, his anguiform limbs are an easy identifying marker for Typhoeus in Greek art, where he is shown in several black-figure vase paintings facing off against Zeus. His snake-legs also call to mind the Babylonian chaos-monster prototype **Tiamat**. But Typhoeus is aurally as well as visually monstrous, with a cacophony of voices that can produce "every imaginable kind of indescribable sound," not to mention the bellowing of bulls, lions, and a pack of hounds (*Theogony* 830–35). While the other gods flee, Zeus battles solo with Typhoeus for control of the universe, relying on his thunderbolts. At one point Typhoeus wrests control of the match: capturing Zeus in the firm grip of his abundant extremities, he imprisons the god in a cave at Delphi. But Zeus fights back, eventually pursuing Typhoeus around the Mediterranean, across mountain ranges, and finally to Sicily, where he buries him under Mt Etna; the myth thus provides an etiology or explanatory narrative of that volcano's eruptions (see Ovid's first century CE *Metamorphoses* 5.346–78). Some ancient authors trace Etna's volcanic blasts directly to the thunderbolts that Zeus victoriously hurled at his enemy (Pseudo-Apollodorus, *Bibliotheca* 1.6.3).

After he has been defeated, Typhoeus evolves into a permanent facet of the natural world, making his presence felt by hurling up from Tartarus terrible blasts of wet winds, which "blow haphazard at sea," scattering ships and drowning their sailors, and generally wreaking havoc on land (*Theogony* 869–80). In essence, he is a personification of the Earth's "terrifying natural phenomena, particularly volcanoes" (Tripp 595). The name Typhoeus/Typhon evokes *typhos*, the Greek word for "smoke." "Hundred-headed" Typhoeus is the father of nameless winds, but also of several monstrous mythological offspring that are eventually slain by Heracles and other heroes. His children, many of whom are also hybrid monsters, include **Cerberus**, **Hydra**, **Chimera**, and the **Sphinx** (*Theogony* 306–15).

If Typhoeus is a force of chaos and volcanic disruption, he has also been seen as epitomizing the last hope for the chthonian (Earth-born) gods to resist and forestall the relentless rise of Zeus and the ouranian (sky) gods. Zeus, who is frequently named as "father of gods and men" in early Greek sources, is the ruler of the younger generation of Olympian gods, who have suppressed older female goddesses such as Gaea and her Earth-born children—the **Giants**, **Furies**, and Titans. But for Zeus to remain in power, Gaea and Typhoeus must both be subdued. The battle between Zeus and Typhoeus represents the last challenge to Zeus's pre-eminence and consequently to patriarchy, which in its original sense means "the rule of the father." In neutralizing Typhoeus, Zeus also causes the Earth irreparable pain and scarring. Much of her surface is scorched—and thereby rendered infertile—by the preternaturally powerful blast of Zeus's thunderbolt (*Theogony* 854–64), guaranteeing that Olympus will face no further chthonian challenges. Patriarchy has won. There are variations on this gender-inflected clash of the gods; in the *Homeric Hymn to Apollo* (sixth century BCE), for example, Hera gives birth to Typhaon (a variant on Typhoeus) to get revenge on Zeus for fathering Athena on his own. But in all versions of the myth, Zeus emerges victorious, and Typhoeus is either banished to Tartarus or buried under Mt Etna.

Typhoeus's afterlife in literature is less colorful than that of many other monsters of classical antiquity. When he resurfaces, it is in the guise of the irrepressible force of nature that threatens to overturn the work of civilization, turning the clock back to an earlier moment in cosmic history. Typhoeus appears in Dante's fourteenth-century *Inferno* in the Ninth Circle of Hell (the Circle of Treachery), where he keeps company with other fiery-breathed giants such as Briareus and Tityus who offended the Olympians (Canto 31; see **Dante, Monsters In**). In popular culture, Typhoeus, played by actor Glenn Shadix, has featured in episodes of the television series "Hercules: The Legendary Journeys" (1995–99) where he is imprisoned by Hera (Meg Foster) and rescued by Hercules (Kevin Sorbo). In Rick Riordan's *The Last Olympian* (2009), Typhon fights on the side of Kronos and his army of Titans, who invade Olympus with the intent of overthrowing Zeus. Poseidon ambushes him at the Hudson River and the Olympians exile him to Tartarus.

Melissa Mueller

References and Suggested Reading

Clay, Jenny Strauss. *Hesiod's Cosmos*. Cambridge: Cambridge University Press, 2003.

Hesiod. *Theogony and Works and Days*. Translated by M.L. West. Oxford: Oxford University Press, 1988.

Ovid. *Metamorphoses*. Translated by Charles Martin. New York: W.W. Norton & Co., 2004.

Tripp, Edward. *The Meridian Handbook of Classical Mythology*. New York: Plume, 1974.

UNDINE—*see* Elemental

UNICORN—*see* Cryptid

UPYR'

The Russian **vampire** (*vampir*), the "upyr'" is deeply rooted in national folklore. The first fictional portraits of upyri, which emerged in nineteenth-century Romantic fiction, both enlarged upon and satirized traditional Slavic legends. Thus, Aleksandr Pushkin's 1834 poem "The Vurdalak" pokes fun at peasant superstition about the undead. (Russians make little distinction between vampires and were-creatures—both are assumed to drink human blood—and the term "vurdalak" is often used interchangeably for both [see **Oboroten'**].) In the poem, Vanya (a typical peasant name) is fearfully crossing a cemetery late at night when he hears the sound of growls and crunching bones. Expecting to confront a "red-lipped vurdalak" (line 8), Vanya finds instead an ordinary dog chewing a bone.

Two short stories by Aleksei Konstantinovich Tolstoy (a relative of the more famous Leo Tolstoy), "The Family of the Vurdalak" (1839) and "Upyr'" (1841), describe essentially the same supernatural creatures, despite the different nomenclature. The first story is narrated by a French officer who, on his way to take up a diplomatic posting in Moldavia, is forced by bad weather to spend several nights with a Serbian family in a remote village. He falls in love with their daughter Adenka, but witnesses a bizarre family drama: the father of the family returns from ten days' absence in the forest, apparently transformed into a vampire. Shortly after his return, he disappears again, and his grandson's body is found drained of blood. The officer continues his journey. Almost a year later, he learns from a local innkeeper that Adenka's entire village has been killed off by vurdalaks, here defined as living corpses who return from their graves to suck the blood of family members. The officer risks revisiting the place to find Adenka, who has become even more beautiful than before. After initially warning him to flee, she seductively urges him to stay. Realizing in time that the vurdalaks are waiting to devour him, he escapes on horseback, pursued by Adenka and her malevolent vampire siblings. By contrast, the narrative of "Upyr'" is complex to the point of confusion: part Gothic parody, part society tale, it is never clear whether its vampires are paranoid hallucinations on the part of the morbidly inclined hero Runevskii, or genuine undead sustained by a demonic pact. These upyri are especially pernicious because they have seamlessly integrated into the Moscow *haut monde*, one posing as a brigadier's widow (and grandmother to Dasha, the girl Runevskii loves), the other as a retired state councillor. "Upyr'" criticizes contemporary social mores directly (by depicting the spite and jealousy that almost prevent Runevskii and Dasha from marrying) and also implicitly. In both these stories, the theme of grandparents who drink their grandchildren's blood represents the unjust restriction of the younger generation's civic liberties by the government—an issue close to Tolstoy's liberal heart.

In the twentieth century, Russian writers and journalists exploited the vampire as a symbol of corruption and moral exhaustion. The poet Aleksandr Blok, an admiring reader of Bram Stoker's ***Dracula*** (1897), lambasted Russia's reactionary Tsarist administration by depicting leading councillors as bloodsucking vampires in his 1908 essay, "The Sun Over Russia"; similarly, Maksim Gorkii, the godfather of Stalinist Socialist Realism, portrayed a conservative judge and jury slavering hungrily over the young revolutionary prisoner in the dock, in *Mother* (1907). In Mikhail Bulgakov's novel *The Master and Margarita* (1940), the **demon** Woland arrives in Stalinist Moscow to turn Soviet society topsy-turvy. Amid the chaos he creates, the manager of the Variety Theater is bitten by the vampire Hella (the only female member of Woland's suite, also a **witch**) and (temporarily) becomes a vampire in his turn. Bulgakov probably intended to lampoon the grasping and unreasonable ways of theater administrators, who had frustrated many of his dramatic projects between 1926 and 1938.

Continuing Blok's use of vampirism as social polemic, Viktor Pelevin's *Empire V* (2006) attacks the commercialism and superficiality of human culture. The young protagonist of *Empire V* discovers that he is really a vampire and therefore part of a secret hierarchy of supernatural demi-gods, who have been absorbing human life-force and energy (materialized in the form of money and other cultural products) for millennia. This empire of vampires (hence the title) is maintained by the vampires' ability to manipulate human aspirations through "glamor" and "discourse." In Sergei Lukyanenko's tetralogy of "Night Watch" novels (1998–2005), set in contemporary Moscow, vampires of a humbler and less contentious stripe abound. As essentially penumbral creatures, they are associated with the powers of darkness, but are not inevitably evil. Lukyanenko's hero Anton even makes friends with a young vampire, Kostia Saushkin, until he accidentally alienates the latter by killing another vampire in self-defence. Vampires are allowed to feed on human blood, under strict legal controls; a vampire caught hunting without an official licence may be destroyed. However, they are also capable of good actions; some choose to drink only donated blood or animal blood. (In the 2004 film version of *Night Watch* [Timur Bekmambetov], Kostia's parents run a butcher shop.) Petr Aleshkovskii's 1997 novel *Vladimir Chigrintsev* (shortlisted for the Russian Booker Prize) describes the decline of the noble Derbetevs and their country estate near Moscow. Because of an ancient crime, each successive head of the family is suffocated on his deathbed by an upyr'. This ancestral upyr' still haunts the Derbetev estate, accompanied by ghostly hunting dogs, in modern times, appearing to trusted descendants and retainers. Despite its gruesome function, the upyr' is ultimately welcomed by the family as a benign figure, symbolizing continuity and stability (much as Irish families were supposed to prize their **banshees**). Like the oboroten', the upyr' is an originally negative archetype that has gradually become a symbol of national coherence and ethnic renewal.

Muireann Maguire

References and Suggested Reading

Mandelker, Amy, and Roberta Reeder. *The Supernatural in Slavic and Baltic Literature: Essays in Honour of Victor Terras*. Columbus, OH: Slavica, 1988.

Minto, Marilyn. *Russian Tales of the Fantastic*. London: Bristol Classical Press, 1994.

Perkowski, Jan L. *Vampires of the Slavs*. Cambridge, MA: Slavica, 1976.

Phillips, Delbert D. *Spook or Spoof? The Structure of the Supernatural in Russian Romantic Tales*. Washington, DC: University Press of America, 1982.

VAMPIRE

The history of the vampire is as long as that of Western culture. Elements peculiar to this monster also appear in non-Western cultures. Given the tremendous geographic and chronological extension of its existence, transforming itself through different ages and places, a univocal definition of the vampire is impossible; nevertheless, the basic kernel of this monster can be summarized in its being a reanimated corpse ("undead") that rises from its grave to suck the life force (usually blood) of living beings. The most accomplished formalization of this monster is in Bram Stoker's *Dracula* (1897; see **Dracula**). Stoker's novel is both a culmination, summarizing a very long tradition of vampires, and a starting point that will make available precise characteristics to the ensuing cinematic and literary interpretations. Stoker's vampire has become an inescapable point of reference for all subsequent reworkings that, as Nina Auerbach has shown, respond to the anxieties and fears of different epochs: every period has its own vampires.

Characteristics of the Vampire

The vampire is certainly one of the most successful monsters in the whole history of horror culture and literature. Its success derives from the complexity and quantity of theoretical subjects metaphorically involved in its character. The vampire indeed is poised at the crossroads of religious, social, sexual, medical, and ontological preoccupations. It encompasses in itself a multiplicity of themes that provides authors of different epochs and environments with the possibility of working out a multitude of theoretical and cultural problems. First and foremost, the vampire is "undead." If other undead creatures, such as **zombies** and, to a lesser extent, **ghosts**, live passively with this condition, the vampire feels more actively its status of not-alive-anymore, but not yet dead. Although still active (as it threatens, seduces, attacks, retreats, resists), it is often unhappy about its situation. It must therefore be helped to die definitively and make the final transition toward the other world. The unhappy death is thus one of the characteristic, although not omnipresent, features of the vampire.

The theme of blood is of course a trait that distinguishes it from other kinds of undead creatures. The vampire subsists by drinking its victims' blood. The blood is the symbol of life and purification in many ancient cultures, especially Greek and Christian. In Homer's *Odyssey* (eighth century BCE), Odysseus offers the sacrificial victim's blood to the souls of the dead to help them recover their memories. In the Gospels (first century CE), Christ's blood is the symbol of purification, forgiveness, and union of the Christians' community. Thus, in different ways, blood is the metaphor of eternal life and the connection with the afterlife, as St Paul explains in the Epistle to the Hebrews 9–10 (first century CE).

Sexuality is an equally important dimension of the relationship between the vampire and its victims. Although undead (and possibly because of this), the vampire has an extraordinary ability to charm its victims, explicitly thematized in several literary versions. The act through which the vampire sucks its victim's blood is a sexualized exchange. Although contagious and deadly, the sexuality that the vampire seems to carry is often more attractive than the one that the victims experience in their normal lives.

Yet the relationship between the vampire and its victims also reveals and expresses anxieties linked to the social role of sexuality. Homosexuality is explicitly mentioned in many vampire stories. In fact, whatever their physical sex might appear to be, vampires are often interested in victims of both sexes and ignore social boundaries that prevent and condemn homosexuality. Vampires are often openly bisexual beings, as depicted in the "Vampire Chronicles" series of Anne Rice (1976–2003) and in the recent collections of stories edited by Pam Keesey, *Daughters of Darkness* (1993) and *Dark Angels* (1995). The sexuality implied by the vampire's seduction of its victims, moreover, introduces anxieties connected to impurity and contagion. Different pathologies (syphilis or AIDS, for example) become the main threats conveyed by sexuality in different periods (Stoker himself contracted syphilis in the early 1890s). Thus, the vampire also works as a metaphor of sexual infection and represents the curse attendant on a forbidden carnal exchange that is punished with contagion.

Fears and anxieties created by the claim for an active feminine sexuality seem to be among the most important topics conveyed by the vampire as a sexual metaphor. Elisabeth Bronfen has shown that, through the centuries, the female body has been used to represent both the supreme space of alterity, and the relationship—both threatening and desired—with death. In Romanticism in particular, the female vampire is charged with fatal passions and embodies the erotic and sexual threat. Geraldine in Samuel Taylor Coleridge's *Christabel* (1797–1800), as well as John Keats's "La Belle Dame Sans Merci" (1819) and ***Lamia*** (1819), are seminal representations of the femme fatale, followed by Clarimonde in Theophile Gautier's "La Morte Amoureuse" (1836), the nymphomaniac of Baudelaire's "Metamorphosis of the Vampire" (1857), and Joseph Sheridan Le Fanu's ***Carmilla*** (1872).

The vampire also evokes the threat to Christian religion of primitive forces that draw their impetus from the sphere of sacredness, or rather from the pagan and profane overthrowing of its values. Vampires often embody the exotic threat of an archaic and savage religion that penetrates the social and religious sphere of the West by subverting its most sacred values. The theme of religious alterity is then connected with anthropological alterity. As Stephen Arata has developed in relation to Stoker's *Dracula*, vampires belong to another race, a monstrous race that threatens the West from the outside through a movement of imaginary counter-colonization that reverses the real historical one. Vampires carry the values of a pagan, Oriental, and barbarically aristocratic society.

All these themes—blood, sexuality, religion, ceaseless desire, anthropological alterity—arguably refer to a Manichean universe in which Western civilization has to resist the assault of a counter-civilization carried by vampires. The binary structure of this universe is developed through the oppositions pure/impure, heterosexual/homosexual, sacred/profane, rational/passional, civilized/barbarian. And yet Manicheism is only rarely the characterizing dimension of the vampire. More interesting is the way that, beyond these binary oppositions, the vampire unhinges rigid distinctions and blurs boundaries. The attraction of the vampire, not only for its victims but also for readers and viewers, depends mainly on the capacity to stimulate the ambiguities that undermine every possible Manicheism.

Historical Vampires

It is difficult, if not impossible, to trace back an historical origin for the belief in vampires. Their existence seems to be transcultural, as elements characterizing them appear in the most diverse environments and cultures, including China, India, Polynesia, and pre-Colombian America. As mentioned above, Greek and Latin mythology is already aware of the theme. An extremely important archetype is the character of **Lilith** in Jewish folklore, beginning with the eighth century, which is rooted in many diverse and more ancient mythological traditions. Lilith is Adam's first wife, created from the same earth from which he was created, rather than his rib. She is a rebellious wife who does not submit to him, and therefore is repudiated and substituted with the more accommodating Eve. In the Babylonian Talmud (sixth–eighth centuries CE), she is originally an evil spirit and a **demon** carrying disgraces and disasters. In the development of her character, she becomes more similar to a vampire, as she is characterized in Mesopotamian mythology, for example, by an anthropophagous (cannibalistic) passion for children and the desire to suck men's blood.

In the New Testament, blood becomes the sign of the connection between Christ and the Christian community, through the redemption and the forgiveness that saves sinners. The Christian theme of blood as the sacred liquid runs through the Middle Ages, along with the legend of the Holy Grail. Yet an imprudently literal interpretation of the text encourages an anthropophagic tendency and an excessive material conception of the blood as a redemptive drink during the first centuries of the Christian age. Although Catholicism negates every literal interpretation, the ambiguity seems to be implicit in the dogma of transubstantiation as it was reaffirmed by the Council of Trent (1545–63): the body and blood of Christ are *really* present within the bread and the wine during the Eucharist. The myth of the vampire will play with this ambiguity, developing the opposition between the sacred transubstantiation and the unholy drinking of blood by the vampire. Around blood there is a space of ambiguity between the natural and the supernatural, where tormented beings struggle on the edge of the two worlds, in an undecidability that provokes anxieties and opens the space for different materializations of the myth in the late Middle Ages.

In the fourteenth century, vampires begin to proliferate beyond the edges of a Europe both physically and culturally threatened at its Eastern boundaries. The vampire becomes the typical monster of the age of the great plague outbreaks, when contagion and pollution haunt the shattered imaginary of the period. Mythical and religious themes blend with more earthly and secular ones, such as in the Siena fresco on the *Allegory and Effects of Good and Bad Government* (1338–39) by Ambrogio Lorenzetti, in which the image of the tyrant, with his sharp teeth, announces already the evil and modern image of the vampire.

One of the most famous cases of vampirism in this period is that of Gilles de Montmorency-Laval (1404–40). A wunderkind of noble origins, the Baron of Rais was Joan of Arc's fellow soldier in the campaign against the English. Devoted to occultism, Gilles was eventually put on trial and confessed to the brutal killing of hundreds of children and youngsters, offered to the **Devil** with the help of his accomplices. Rais was accused of cannibalism and necrophilia, and became one of the early modern prototypes of the vampire through the literary reworkings by Charles Perrault and Joris Karl Huysmans, whose depictions of Bluebeard in *Histories or Fairy Tales from Bygone Eras* (1697) and *Là-bas* (1891) respectively were inspired by Gilles. Another famous and influential early modern case of vampirism is that of the Hungarian "Blood Countess" Elizabeth Bathory (1560–1614), accused of the killing of hundreds of young girls at the beginning of the seventeenth century. As a result of the sensational claims surrounding her—among them that she bathed in the blood of her victims—**Countess Bathory** has served as a point of reference for many contemporary vampire narratives.

The most important historical reference in the development of the concept of the vampire, however, is certainly Vlad III, Prince of Wallachia (1431–76), who inspired Stoker and is remembered for the resistance against the Ottoman Empire that was putting pressure on the Eastern boundaries of Europe during the fifteenth century. He is also famous for the cruelty exerted against his enemies, for which he was posthumously dubbed Vlad the Impaler. This reputation helped make him the archetype of the cruel and bloodthirsty aristocrat, which eventually converged into the myth of the vampire coming from the East.

Interest in vampires, the undead, and threatening creatures that inhabit the boundaries between life and death was also widespread during the sixteenth century. The texts of this period fluctuate between a folkloric interest in the myth of the vampire, its origins, and its religious meanings on the one hand, and a scientific interest on the other, trying to answer questions about the ontological and medical distinction between life and death. One of the most influential works of the period is the *Dissertatio Historico-Philosophica de Masticatione Mortuorum*, or *On the Chewing Dead* by Philip Rohr (1679). In this work, Rohr develops an inquiry into the belief in the resurrection of corpses that then devour their own shrouds and gnaw nearby corpses. Vampires are also mentioned by the Neo-Platonist Henry More in his *An Antidote against Atheism, or an Appeal to the Naturall Faculties of the Minde of Man, whether there be not a God* (1653).

In the eighteenth century, despite the Enlightenment emphasis on rationality, vampires nevertheless spread in European culture, as attested by influential texts such as the *Dissertatio Physica de Cadaveribus Sanguisugis* by Johan Christian Stock (1732) or the *Dissertatio de Vampiris Serviensibus* by Johann Heinrich Zopft (1733). Both offer detailed characterizations of vampires, including physical and behavioral traits as well as weaknesses. Two of the most famous books of the period were written by a Benedectine monk, Antoine Augustin Calmet. In his *Treatise on Vampires and Revenants* (1751) and then the *Dissertations upon the apparitions of angels, dæmons, and ghosts, and concerning the vampires of Hungary, Bohemia, Moravia, and Silesia* (1759), Calmet is ambiguous about the existence of vampires, and the long list of cases he mentions suggests his influential and authoritative belief in the possibility rather than the impossibility of their existence.

In his *Philosophical Dictionary* (1764), Voltaire writes that in the 1730s the existence of vampires was often debated. Voltaire places the vampires' origin in Christian and schismatical Greece, where followers of the Byzantine Rite imagine that the dead bodies of the followers of Latin Rite do not decay, as they have been excommunicated. For Western Christians, Voltaire underlines, the belief is the opposite, as it is the corpses of the blessed souls and not the damned ones who do not decay. The opposition of these two beliefs, both superstitious for Voltaire, develops into the myth of the vampire. Vampires, Voltaire maintains, were widespread in Hungary, Poland, and Moravia, but not in Paris or London, which were, on the contrary, full of usurers and speculators—that is to say, another form of vampire. Thus, the skepticism of Voltaire's satire anticipates the idea of the social profiteer as a vampire that will have to be defeated by reason. The appearance of vampires as a mere fabrication is also the opinion of one of the most erudite Catholics of the period, the Italian Giuseppe Davanzati, who spotlighted the elements of popular imagination in early modern Europe, among them the vampire, in his *Dissertazione sopra i vampiri* (1740).

Romanticism and Vampires

The Romantic renaissance of the vampire is rooted in this proliferation of eighteenth-century treatises and reflections, either theological or pseudo-scientific. It appears quite early in literature, not in prose but in poetry, with the short German poem "The Vampire" (1748) by Heinrich August Ossenfelder, and later in "The Bride of Corinth" by Johann Wolfgang von Goethe (1797). The erotic-seductive element of the vampire is already present in both works. The vampire emerges from its own grave, ceaselessly looking for the satisfaction of its desire, and offering to its victims, at the same time, a pagan horizon with the indulgence in pleasures of the flesh that Christian morality and asceticism cannot match.

In the Gothic ballad *Christabel* by Samuel Taylor Coleridge (1800), the eponymous protagonist meets the vampire Geraldine, whose body bears a terrible, yet not particularly specified, mark. Coleridge establishes an argument of fundamental importance for the eventual development of the character, namely acceptance: the vampire has to be invited and accepted by its victim. The contamination always happens through an exchange that takes place at night when the faculty of reason is weaker and does not resist the attack of the monstrous irrational.

The Giaour (1813) by George Gordon Byron is the tale of an impossible love between the slave Leila, one of the Pasha Hassan's wives, and the giaour, or "infidel"—one of the prototypes of Byron's *homme fatal*. Leila is punished by death for her infidelity, and the giaour takes revenge by killing Hassan, eventually becoming a monk out of remorse. Yet under the monk's cassock, an evil flame keeps burning. One of the narrators of the story suggests that the giaour's destiny is to become a vampire after life, coming back to suck the blood of his beloved ones in a ceaseless spiral of agony. Good and evil merge in the giaour, and the vampire here becomes the cursed hero that will crucially inspire Romantic literature.

One of the authors influenced by the character of the giaour was John William Polidori (1765–1821), who cultivated a conflicted friendship with Byron. Polidori's tale "The Vampyre" was published in 1819, but was famously conceived in May 1816, during the fruitful encounter at Villa Diodati between Lord Byron (1788–1824), Percy Bysshe Shelley (1792–1822), and Mary Wollstonecraft Godwin (1797–1851), future wife of Shelley, who imagined the plot of *Frankenstein* (1818—see **Frankenstein's Monster**) on the same occasion. The story of "The Vampyre" develops the character of **Lord Ruthven**, the prototype of the vampire as the cold and aristocratic persona with sharp eyes and ghostly pallor.

Ruthven suddenly appears in the London salons, where he meets the young Aubrey. They travel together to Italy, where they split, eventually meeting again in Greece. Here Aubrey learns about the existence of vampires from the young Ianthe, who is found dead shortly after, in conjunction with the re-appearance of Ruthven. After being attacked by bandits, the apparently mortally wounded Ruthven asks Aubrey to keep the secret of his imminent death for at least one year. But when Aubrey goes back to London, a healthy Ruthven reappears again and seduces Aubrey's sister. Their marriage is planned for precisely the day that the oath about Ruthven's death is due to expire. Aubrey senses the evil nature of Ruthven, but is unable to resist him, and the attempt to save his sister fails: she is reached just too late by her brother's letter in which the evil identity of Ruthven is revealed. She is found dead on the night of the marriage, while the vampire disappears again. One of the major themes developed by Polidori is the dominion of and fight over time between the vampire and its victims: the vampire moves quickly and anticipates them, being able to dominate the chronological dimension of the struggle between good and evil.

A female vampire, Aurelia, appears in *Vampirism*, or *Tale of a Vampire* (1819) by E.T.A. Hoffmann. The vampire is the monstrous feminine, divided between an erotic desire in the form of a perverse necrophagy, and an impossible love that spiritually destroys her partner. Hoffmann's main interest is not in developing the archetype of the vampire that is being shaped in the Romantic literature of the period. Rather, vampirism, necrophagia, and necrophilia are merged in the story in order to suggest dark aspects of eroticism in the relationship between the vampire and its victims.

Théophile Gautier reworked the theme of seduction in the short story "La Morte Amoureuse," published in *La Chronique de Paris* in 1836. Romuald is due to become a priest, but the beautiful courtesan Clarimonde attempts to seduce him, and eventually succeeds in bringing him with her to Venice to live a life of debauchery. Romuald finally realizes that Clarimonde survives by drinking his blood at night, and yet he neither disowns nor regrets his own choice to leave with her, until another priest, Sérapion, intervenes to destroy the vampire by scattering holy water on its body lying in the coffin. The theme of erotic seduction as a devilish weapon to separate believers from Christianity is clearly present, together with the open and active acceptance by the victims of their evil destiny.

The now-familiar elements of the vampire story were further solidified by James Malcolm Rymer, whose long "penny dreadful" novel, ***Varney the Vampire****; or, the Feast of Blood* (1845–47), features a young and beautiful girl who struggles to wake up from an evil and erotic dream and is unable to resist when a tall and pale character with a sharp glaze enters from the window. The vampiric possession resembles more a rape than a kiss here, with sensationalist attention paid to the sensual aspects of the encounter. The girl is eventually assisted by a stranger, who embodies the male principle of resistance to the evil and seductive monster.

Charles Baudelaire also engages with the topic in "The Vampire" and "Metamorphoses of the Vampire" in *The Flowers of Evil* (1857). Baudelaire's misogynistic treatment of this topic centers on the female vampire's overwhelming sexuality, which renders her victims powerless due to the combination of utter beauty and evil.

The final formalization of the elements that will converge in the brilliant reworking by Stoker comes in 1872 with the publication of ***Carmilla*** by Joseph Sheridan Le Fanu. Set in Styria (part of Austria), the tale tells the story of Laura who remembers an encounter when she was a child with a young girl kneeling by her bed, who caressed her until she fell asleep. The narrator eventually meets a child named Carmilla who was injured in an accident. As it turns out, both girls remember each other from the aforementioned encounter during early childhood. Due to her injury and her mother's urgent travel plans, Carmilla stays with Laura and her father. The smile of understanding between them is the sign of acceptance and invitation. The girls are charmed by each other, in an ambiguous mix of attraction, repulsion, and unavowed homoerotic love. As time progresses, Laura suffers nightmares of being bitten by a beast and gradually becomes ill. It is revealed later that she is in fact being bitten by the vampire Countess Mircalla Karnstein, who disguised herself as the girl Carmilla.

Dracula

At the end of the nineteenth century, the Irishman Bram Stoker wrote his masterpiece *Dracula* (1897). *Dracula* is the apotheosis of the romantic cycle of the vampire, giving to the monster the accomplished form that it will have from then on. One of the brilliant inventions of Stoker is the insertion of mythical elements within the modern reality and everyday life of the English reader, and the former's aggression against the latter. All the rationalistic and scientific presuppositions of the modern world seem to be threatened by contagion from the outlandish reality of the stranger that the vampire represents. Thus, Stoker portrays the crisis of the social and scientific pillars of respectable society, provoked by the re-emergence of a disturbing fantastic that was supposed to have been repressed and overcome.

Dracula is organized as an epistolary novel in which the different characters tell the adventures of the horrible aggression of the Count against Western civilization. In the first part of the novel, Dracula receives in his castle in the Carpathian Mountains the young solicitor Jonathan Harker, there to deal with the last details of the Count's definitive move to London. Harker soon finds himself a prisoner and victim of this strange creature, whose distinctive vampiric features are slowly disclosed. Leaving the barely alive Harker behind, the Count manages to land in England, on board the ship *Demeter*, whose entire crew is found dead, exterminated by a horrible presence. Dracula now focuses on Jonathan's fiancée, Mina Harker, and her young and sensual friend Lucy Westenra.

Lucy is about to choose her husband from three suitors: Dr John Seward, director of an insane asylum (where the vampire has made the inmate Renfield his acolyte); Texan Quincey Morris; and Arthur Holmwood, the future Lord Godalming. Arthur is chosen and, tragically, he himself will have to kill his young and beautiful wife following her seduction and transformation into a vampire by Dracula. Once these characters, helped by Dr Abraham Van Helsing, begin to understand the features of their enemy and the nature of the threat it represents, they are able to organize a plan for the ultimate defense against the Count's evil plans. The group manages to destroy all the Count's London shelters so that Dracula is forced to flee back to his own land. He is pursued by Van Helsing and his group, who also succeed in saving Mina—already partially contaminated—from vampirization. The Count is finally killed in the concluding struggle and the threat is averted.

Dracula represents the projection and anxieties raised by the repressed desires of the Victorian age. It is the myth of the violation of order and boundaries. The Count perversely seduces his victims and makes them part of his pagan and aristocratic race. Stoker brilliantly portrays all the elements of the previous vampire literature, especially insisting on the class nature of the threat (the aristocratic Count against the bourgeois Van Helsing and company); on its sexual nature, as well as on the patriarchal dominion over the female bodies by the civilized suitors and saviors (rightfully famous in this context is the scene of the group's collective killing of the vampirized Lucy, which really resembles a gang rape); and the Oriental, archaic, and pagan nature of the vampire, which threatens the Western, modern, and Christian values of Victorian society.

From Nineteenth- to Twentieth-Century Representations

Before leaving the nineteenth century, one needs to mention the vampire as a metaphor for the capitalist, largely exploited by Karl Marx. The horror of the working class's conditions of life is a recurring theme within the pages of *Capital* (1867). The bourgeois class, frequently compared to a vampire, sucks the blood of the workers. Responding to Adam Smith (1723–90), Marx suggests that capital is not the lifeblood of society. On the contrary, capital sucks it, by exploiting the workers: "capital is dead labour which, vampire-like, lives only by sucking living labour, and lives the more, the more labour it sucks" (Karl Mark, *Capital*, I, 10, section 1). Through the image of the vampire, Marx develops the political and conflictual opposition between living labor and dead labor which, within the capitalist regime, refuses death and needs to feed itself on someone else's life.

The twentieth century inherits Stoker's imagery and develops the vampire by adapting it to the most diverse cultural and social frameworks, as well as to the most diverse fantasies and anxieties. Richard Matheson's *I Am Legend* (1954) develops the theme of the destruction of humanity through contagion and disease. Robert Neville is the only survivor of an apocalyptic plague that destroyed life on earth. Yet he is not alone: the planet is infested by a race of undead vampires that come at night and try to kill him. In the novel's famous ironic conclusion, Neville realizes that it is he, the lone human on a planet full of vampires, who is the monster.

Stoker's imagery becomes more distorted and re-appropriated as the twentieth century progresses. Suzy McKee Charnas's collection of five novellas, *The Vampire Tapestry* (1980), features a highly modernized vampire that strays from the stereotype of the blood-sucking aristocrat in two important ways. Dr Edward Weyland, as the protagonist is called, is not a count or a mysterious traveler, but rather an anthropology professor. Furthermore, he is not a vampire due to infection by bite and blood exchange, but rather for biological reasons not further explained and unknown to Weyland. Instead of being part of a vampire family or community, he is a lone creature of a separate species. One of the main topics in the novellas is the difficult relationship between the empathic Dr Weyland and his prey.

Jewelle Gomez transfers vampire lore to a modern setting as well, re-appropriating and expanding the mythology with a lesbian and feminist perspective in *The Gilda Stories* (1991). The life of the protagonist Gilda, a woman of African descent who is turned into a vampire in the nineteenth century, is depicted over the course of 200 years, beginning with her life as a (not yet vampiric) runaway slave. The story uses this multiracial and feminist perspective as a backdrop for a vampire romance novel.

Culturally significant and at the same time hotly debated works of literature were penned by Anne Rice and Stephenie Meyer. Rice's best-known work, *Interview with the Vampire* (1976), was turned into a Hollywood blockbuster starring Tom Cruise, Brad Pitt, and Antonio Banderas (*Interview with the Vampire*, Neil Jordan, 1994). It was followed up by several sequels, commonly referred to as "The Vampire Chronicles," among them *The Vampire* ***Lestat*** (1985), *The Queen of the Damned* (1988, with an unsuccessful Hollywood adaptation by Michael Rymer in 2002), and *Memnoch the Devil* (1995). While Anne Rice's oeuvre has been noted for its eroticism, Stephenie Meyer's best-selling "Twilight" series (2005–10) has been heavily criticized for its promotion of abstinence and uncritical depiction of an abusive relationship. Despite this criticism of the devoutly Mormon author, both the novels and the film adaptations (2008–12) of the "Twilight" series have become hugely popular with teenagers, the films grossing over $2 billion worldwide as of 2012.

Instead of advocating conservative values, Octavia E. Butler uses the genre's bloodthirsty protagonists to examine contemporary values from a more liberal stance. Her 2005 novel *Fledgling* addresses issues of race and sexuality. Stephen King also exploits the theme, without a pronounced agenda such as the exploration of modern values, in many of his novels, including *Salem's Lot* (1975), *Wolves of the Calla* (1993), *Song of Susannah* (2004), and *The Dark Tower* (2004); here, the vampire is part of an arsenal of fantastic creatures, rather than a means of criticizing the status quo or propagating opinions.

The Cinematic Vampire

In addition to literary explorations of the vampire in the twentieth century, cinema has begun to cultivate new ways of speaking about the monster and its constellation of associated themes. The great classics of early twentieth-century cinema freely and unconventionally rework the theme of the vampire, introducing original rhetorical and formal elements for their success. Friedrich Wilhelm Murnau adapts Stoker's story in the visionary *Nosferatu: A Symphony of Horror* (1922), a milestone of German expressionism, with the unforgettable Max Schreck playing Count Orlok. Murnau, who studied art history, was a pioneer in the exploitation of camera movement in order to maximize the rhetorical effect of *unheimlich* or uncanny—in particular, he emphasizes the lifeless becoming alive or the dead claiming life, as in the sequence of the vampire coming out of the shadow and slowly filling the screen with its horrific glance. Seventy-eight years after Murnau's seminal film, E. Elias Merhige draws on this topic (with a grain of salt) in his film *Shadow of the Vampire*. The film purports to be a documentation of the making of *Nosferatu*, and in the course of the action exposes Max Schreck as an actual vampire.

The vampire is also a milestone of the post-1929 stock market crisis in the United States. Delivering some of the most astonishing monster movies of the era, director Tod Browning contributes, with his *Dracula* (1931), not only to the success of this monster, but also to that of the unforgettable Hungarian actor Bela Lugosi (1882–1956), whose face would become the paradigmatic icon of the Transylvanian Count for decades. Terence Fisher followed with his *Horror of Dracula* (1958) for England's Hammer Film Productions, starring Christopher Lee (1922–) as the Count, while other successful interpretations include Werner Herzog's *Nosferatu the Vampyre* (1979), with a memorable performance by Klaus Kinski, and Francis Ford Coppola's *Dracula* (1992).

Along with these more or less unconventional reworkings of Stoker's classic, there is a whole minor genre where the multiplication of vampires responds to the commercial necessity of repeating the ingredients of a horror character within a recognizable framework. Even so, sometimes original developments are to be found here, such as in Jesús Franco's *Count Dracula* (1970), with Christopher Lee again playing the Count; Harry Kümel's *Daughters of Darkness* (1971), with a modern version of Countess Bathory luxuriously played by Delphine Seyrig; Roger Vladim's *Et Mourir de Plaisir* (1960), based upon Le Fanu's *Carmilla*; and finally *Dance of the Vampires* (1967), a musical remake by Roman Polanski of his earlier film of the same name (released in the United States as *The Fearless Vampire Killers* [1967]).

Among the more recent versions, notable contributions include Abel Ferrara's *The Addiction* (1995), in which vampirism suggests the epidemic of AIDS in the early 1980s, but in which the horror of war and the commodification of society are also exploited as the crisis of modern values opens the door to the orgiastic violence of the new vampires. Guy Maddin's *Dracula: Pages from a Virgin's Diary* (2002) is a poetic and visionary homage, in the form of dance, to Stoker's masterpiece. More realistic is Thomas Alfredson's *Let the Right One In* (2008)—remade in English as *Let Me In* by Matt Reeves (2010)—in which the vampire is the metaphorical embodiment of alienation and the rejection of dominant values that produce the misery of society and conformism.

Social tensions are increasingly addressed in the modern vampire film. The tradition set forth by some "Blaxploitation" films of the 1970s, such as *Blacula* (William Crain, 1973) and *Ganja & Hess* (Bill Gunn, 1973), which deliver a racialization of the vampire, is continued by the *Blade* trilogy (1998–2004), as well as modified metaphorically in the *Underworld* films (2003–12). Blade, the son of a female human and a male vampire, cannot be integrated into either of the two worlds, and can be seen as a parable on the problematic social tensions for people with a biracial background. The action films in the *Underworld* series pit vampires (depicted as aristocratic and white) against **werewolves** (depicted as "proletarian" and even black—see Weinstock).

Whereas vampires were rare characters on television shows in the past, with *Dark Shadows* (Dan Curtis, 1966–72) being an exception, the vampire has lately had a tremendous success in television. TV series such as *Blood Ties* (2007), *True Blood* (first series in 2008, rewarded with an Emmy and a Golden Globe)—which also examines social tensions with special attention to gay rights and interracial dating—and *The Vampire Diaries* (first series in 2009) have successfully broadcast the vampire into millions of homes. The three hugely successful motion pictures in *The Twilight Saga* (2008–10), which have been addressed earlier, also helped to increase the attractiveness of the vampire genre for mainstream audiences.

Filippo Del Lucchese and Jana Toppe

References and Suggested Reading

Arata, Stephen. "The Occidental Tourist: *Dracula* and the Anxiety of Reverse Colonization." In *Dracula by Bram Stoker*, edited by Nina Auerbach and David J. Skal, 462–70. New York: W.W. Norton & Co., 1997.

Auerbach, Nina. *Our Vampires, Ourselves*. Chicago: University of Chicago Press, 1995.

Bronfen, Elisabeth. *Over Her Dead Body*. Manchester: Manchester University Press, 1992.

Douglas, Mary. *Purity and Danger*. New York: Routledge and Kegan Paul, 1966.

Du Boulay, Juliet. "The Greek Vampire: A Study of Cyclic Symbolism in Marriage and Death." *Man* 17, no. 2 (1982): 219–38.

Eisner, Lotte H. *L'écran Démoniaque: Influence de Max Reinhardt et de l'Expressionisme*. Paris: Editions Andre Bonne, 1952.

Harrison, Robert P. *The Dominion of the Dead*. Chicago: University of Chicago Press, 2003.

Hurwitz, Siegmund. *Lilith, die erste Eva: eine Studie uber dunkle Aspekte des Wieblichen*. Zurich: Daimon, 1980.

Lecouteux, Claude. *Histoire des vampires: Autopsie d'un mythe*. Paris: Imago, 1999.

Mascetti, Manuela Dunn, ed. *Vampire: The Complete Guide to the World of the Undead*. London: Aurum, 1994.

McNally, David. *Monsters of the Market: Zombies, Vampires and Global Capitalism*. Leiden: Brill, 2011.

Neocleous, Mark. *Monstrous and the Dead: Burke, Marx, Fascism*. Cardiff: University of Wales Press, 2005.

Skal, David J. *Hollywood Gothic: The Tangled Web of Dracula from Novel to Stage to Screen*. New York: Norton, 2004.

———. *The Monster Show: A Cultural History of Horror*. New York: Norton, 2001.

Weinstock, Jeffrey Andrew. *The Vampire Movie: Undead Cinema*. New York: Columbia University Press, 2012.

VĀNARA—*see* Shapeshifter

VARFOLOMEI—*see* Demon

VARNEY THE VAMPIRE

Varney the Vampyre is the title of an 1845–47 "penny dreadful" by James Malcolm Rymer (1814–84). *Varney* is considered the first **vampire** novel and was influential on later vampire fiction, contributing several tropes to the corpus, including the concept of vampires creating further vampires through feeding on them. Varney, a guilt-ridden vampire who both searches for victims and loathes his undead existence, is among the most emotionally recognizable and compelling monsters of nineteenth-century fiction.

Rymer was a professional writer of serialized fiction for the penny weeklies, but his previous work had been sensational melodrama modeled after the novels of Charles Dickens (1812–70) and Sir Walter Scott (1771–1832). The supernatural was new territory for Rymer, but Edward Bulwer-Lytton's *Zanoni* (1842) had created a great enthusiasm for tales of the occult and Rymer was quick to capitalize on it. Rymer was familiar with the basics of vampire lore from John Polidori's "The Vampyre" (1819) and from Eastern European folklore. *Varney*, like most of Rymer's work, displays the pronounced influence of late eighteenth- and early nineteenth-century Gothic novels, a genre in which Rymer had already published with *The Black Monk, or, The Secret of the Grey Turret* (1844).

In *Varney*, English noblewoman Flora Bannerworth is attacked by a vampire, but he is driven off by the arrival of her brothers Henry and George and her best friend Charles Holland. They soon suspect that their new neighbor, Sir Francis Varney, is the vampire, and further that he is Marmaduke Bannerworth, one of Flora's ancestors. Charles challenges Varney to a duel but is kidnapped by Varney before the duel can take place. Varney visits Flora and proposes marriage to her, but she declines in a friendly fashion, and when Henry challenges Varney to a duel, Varney spares his life. Varney's origin is later revealed as the narrative becomes increasingly complicated: in the early seventeenth century, Varney accidentally killed his son in a moment of fury, and was cursed by God to exist forever as a doomed, accursed creature as a result. The local villagers attack Varney's house and pursue him relentlessly. Varney releases Charles, who with Flora tries to stop the mob from killing Varney, even going so far as to hide him in their house, but ultimately the mob finds him and kills him. After his burial, he is disinterred and revived by the moonlight, and he begins a series of schemes that will allow him to marry a young virgin and then drain her. Each time the scheme is foiled. He apparently dies several times, by suicide and murder, but each time fate conspires to bring him back. After attending a vampire gathering, he tries to drown himself, but is rescued. Finally, he climbs Mt Vesuvius in Italy and throws himself into its live heart, permanently destroying himself.

Varney the Vampyre is written in the Gothic mode but functions as a satirical commentary on contemporary society. Nina Auerbach describes the predatory activities of the mob and notes the appearance of a metafictional element in the appearance of a "Count Polidori," who is one of several figures who attempt to force their daughters to marry Varney, and concludes that, "from mob to middle class to monarchy, Varney is only one increasingly weary member of a predatory society, the paradigmatic citizen of a decade that named itself the 'Hungry '40s'" (31).

Jess Nevins

References and Suggested Reading

Auerbach, Nina. *Our Vampires, Ourselves*. Chicago: University of Chicago Press, 1995.

Hackenberg, Sara. "Vampires and Resurrection Men: The Perils and Pleasures of the Embodied Past in 1840s Sensational Fiction." *Victorian Studies* 52, no. 1 (2009): 63–75.

Nevins, Jess. "Sir Francis Varney." In *The Encyclopedia of Fantastic Victoriana*, by Jess Nevins, 892–5. Austin, TX: MonkeyBrain, Inc, 2005.

VAUGHAN, HELEN

One of literature's great *femmes fatales*, Helen Vaughan is the central figure of Arthur Machen's *The Great God* **Pan** (1894), a novella of supernatural mystery. Influenced by Robert Louis Stevenson's *The Strange Case* *of Dr Jekyll and Mr* **Hyde** (1886), the story has an ingenious Chinese-box structure: its initially disconnected narratives all relate to the life of Helen Vaughan, who brings terror to Caermaen in Wales and to London society. The narrative's mingling of sex and horror shocked Victorian sensibilities. The story was published in tandem with *The Inmost Light*, which also combined science and supernaturalism.

In the opening chapter, "The Experiment," Dr Raymond conducts an operation on his ward, the significantly named Mary. A rearrangement of her brain cells allows Mary to gaze upon the god Pan, the Greek god of wild places and rustic music—a sight that leaves her an imbecile. This first chapter was originally published as "The Great God Pan" in June of 1890 in *The Whirlwind*, a short-lived periodical. Machen subsequently wrote seven further chapters. In the second chapter, set years later, Clarke, a connoisseur of the occult who has witnessed Raymond's operation on Mary, records a strange story about a sinister young woman known as Helen V, who creates alarm in the isolated village where she is sent to live. In the unnamed forest of Wentwood, near Machen's birthplace of Caerleon-on-Usk in Monmouthshire, Helen consorts with the **fauns** and weird creatures of the other world that will populate Machen's later stories. Initially, this account appears to have no connection with the opening chapter's events. The reader finally realizes that Helen is the demonic offspring of Mary and Pan (see **Demon**).

Emerging in London society under various aliases, Helen is described as the most beautiful and simultaneously the most repulsive woman people have ever seen—an opposition reflecting Machen's accomplished blend of beauty and horror. In the third chapter, an Oxford graduate, Charles Herbert, who has become a vagrant, describes to Villiers, one of Clarke's friends, how he has been ruined and corrupted by his marriage to Helen Vaughan. Villiers and his associate Austin become fascinated by a wealthy hostess, Mrs Beaumont, who seems connected to a rash of suicides of society gentlemen. Of course, Mrs Beaumont is Helen Vaughan. After Villiers forces Helen to hang herself, a doctor witnesses her body's transmutation: "I saw the form waver from sex to sex, dividing itself from itself, and then again reunited. Then I saw the body descend to the beasts whence it ascended, and that which was on the heights go down to the depths, even to the abyss of all being" (100).

Machen presents Helen's character obliquely: she is depicted only through the eyes of those encountering her. Helen herself has only a single line of dialogue, relating to the thousand-year-old wine of Avallaunius that she serves at her gatherings. Some readers find this distancing alienating, but Machen's admirers rejoice in this subtle approach, in which his horrors are characteristically veiled. In his 1927 treatise on horror, *Supernatural Horror in Literature,* H.P. Lovecraft wrote of *The Great God Pan*: "the charm of the tale is in the telling ... Melodrama is undeniably present, and coincidence is stretched to a length which appears absurd upon analysis; but in the malign witchery of the tale as a whole these trifles are forgotten" (90; see **Lovecraft, Monsters In**). Lovecraft himself used the theme of a demonic birth in "The Dunwich Horror" (*Weird Tales*, 1929) and Helen Vaughan may have influenced the character of Rebecca de Winter in Daphne du Maurier's novel *Rebecca* (1938). Rebecca's confession of the truth about herself to her husband on her honeymoon (Chapter XX) echoes the scene described by Charles Herbert in *The Great God Pan*. The story is acclaimed as a masterpiece in Carl Van Vechten's satirical novel *Peter Whiffle: His Life and Works* (1922). Whiffle says: "[Machen] keeps the thaumaturgic secrets as the alchemists were bidden to do. Instead of raising the veil, he drops it. Instead of revealing, he conceals" (206). Ira Levin's *Rosemary's Baby* (1968) may have been influenced by *The Great God Pan*; horror author Peter Straub has acknowledged Helen Vaughan as an influence on the character Alma Mobley, the **shapeshifting** entity in his novel *Ghost Story* (1979); and, in his study *Danse Macabre* (1981), Stephen King ranks the novella with *The Turn of the Screw* (1898) by Henry James and Lovecraft's *At the Mountains of Madness* (1936).

Roger Dobson

References and Suggested Reading

Lovecraft, H.P. *Supernatural Horror in Literature* [1927]. Reprint, New York: Dover Publications, Inc., 1973.

Machen, Arthur. *The Great God Pan and The Inmost Light*. London: John Lane, 1894. Reprint, London: Simpkin, Marshall, Hamilton, Kent & Co., 1915.

Michael, D.P.M. *Arthur Machen*. Cardiff: University of Wales Press, 1971.

Reynolds, Aidan, and William Charlton. *Arthur Machen: A Short Account of His Life and Work*. London: The Richards Press, 1963. Reprint, Oxford: Caermaen Books, 1988.

Sweetser, Wesley D. *Arthur Machen*. New York: Twayne Publishers, 1964.

Van Vechten, Carl. *Peter Whiffle: His Life and Works*. New York: Alfred A. Knopf, Inc., 1922.

VEELA—*see* Harry Potter, Monsters In

VIDEO GAMES, MONSTERS IN

Monsters are ubiquitous in video games, featured in nearly all gaming genres, from text adventure games such as *Zork* (1980) to first-person shooters like *Doom* (1993) and survival horror games like *Silent Hill* (1999). Video game monsters are drawn from diverse sources, but are heavily influenced by monsters in popular culture in the United States and Japan, two historically fertile places for digital game development. Typical gaming monsters include **extraterrestrials**, fantasy creatures inspired by *Dungeons & Dragons* (see **Dungeons & Dragons, Monsters In**), and monsters drawn from horror films and fiction, especially **zombies**.

Fig. 35 ***Ganon* by Aeron Alfrey**

The basic functions of video game monsters are not unlike those of other environmental features of the video game: they add a challenge to the gameplay experience, and they do so in a way that is consonant with the game's fictional content and atmosphere. Insofar as monsters are environmental challenges, they differ little from other aspects of a game's design: both a pit in the darkness and the slavering fangs of a lurking monster are essentially challenges. Both force players to bring light into dark places in the game. Indeed, the infamous grue of the *Zork* series is exactly that: a replacement for the pits that served as obstacles in *Zork*'s predecessor *Colossal Cave Adventure* (originally written by Will Crowther and developed by Don Woods, 1976). Aesthetically, however, they differ more significantly: a pit is little more than an obstacle, static and without any fictional pretense of hostility. A monster, in contrast, is actively hostile. The pits of *Colossal Cave Adventure* are largely forgotten, but the grue still haunts the dark places of the digital gaming psyche, and many gamers today still recognize the warning: "It is pitch black. You are likely to be eaten by a grue." In addition, from a game design perspective, monsters offer more dynamic challenges. And due to these aesthetic and dynamic features, monsters are often memorable, defining elements of the games in which they feature.

One key function of the monster is the "boss monster" role. Video games are organized into levels, and the end of a level features a boss: a particularly powerful, dynamic villain or monster that the player must defeat to complete the level. The boss is the most challenging part of the level, an aggressive challenge that the player must both outplay and outsmart to continue. Often, boss monsters are accompanied by cut scenes (short scenes that the player watches like a film rather than actually plays). Such scenes dramatize the entry of the boss monster and serve to emphasize the monster's prominence in the game's fiction. Indeed, in addition to adding an exciting and dynamic challenge at the end of a level, boss monsters also fulfill a classic role that would be well recognized by **Cerberus**: standing guard at the threshold. Level bosses are found throughout games at the end of each level, and a final boss is found at the end of the game. These bosses regularly become icons of the games that feature them. Examples are easy to find: Ganon/Ganondorf, the boar monster and wizard of the *Legend of Zelda* series (1986); the koopa king Bowser, the **dragon**-turtle brute of the *Super Mario* games (1985); and Pyramid Head, the gruesome torturer introduced in *Silent Hill 2* (2001) are all examples of monsters that double as icons of their respective games. Indeed, some games go so far as to be titled for the monsters rather than the heroes. The giant ape Donkey Kong (a humorous paean to the iconic **King Kong**) is the star of the eponymous game, overshadowing the hero Mario. Great care is placed on the development of strong, dynamic boss monsters, and a game famed for impressive boss battles (like the *God of War* series [2005], in which gamers fight and kill Greek gods and monsters) is a game certain to meet acclaim from the gaming press. In some games, such as *Rampage* (1986), the players take on the roles of giant monsters reminiscent of King Kong and **Godzilla**; gameplay focuses on stomping cities to rubble.

Indeed, it is possible to take the boss battle to its logical conclusion, creating a game in which the only monsters are bosses and the typical convention of the monster-filled game level is itself subverted. Battling the massive constructs that give their name to Team Ico's *Shadow of the Colossus* (2005) is an example of the boss fight taken to its ultimate conclusion. These huge beings are monstrous in all the ways a video game boss is monstrous: they are huge, among the largest boss monsters ever to feature in games at the time; they are challenging and complex, requiring extended puzzle solving and action routines to defeat; they are dynamic, striding across the landscape and responding to player actions. However, they stand apart from classic boss monsters as well—for their monstrosity is ambiguous. As the game progresses, the player kills more and more of these giant beings, but their minds are unknown and unknowable, and it becomes ambiguous whether the hero is indeed a hero at all for destroying them. Team Ico's follow-up game, *The Last Guardian* (2014), explores the relationship between monsters and the player again—this time through a boy and a **griffin**-like monster that appears to act as his ally and friend.

What makes a video game monster memorable is difficult to pin down, but some common features can be identified. One is design, as is the case of the constructs of *Shadow of the Colossus* or Pyramid Head of the *Silent Hill* (1999) franchise. Another is persistence: monsters like Nemesis in *Resident Evil 3* (1999) and Evil Otto of *Berzerk* (1980) hunt the player through the game, attacking repeatedly and regenerating or otherwise resisting destruction. Alongside persistence is difficulty, with particularly difficult monsters and boss monsters often becoming icons of their games. And a monster can be memorable simply because it works directly against the basic goals of a particular game, as is the case of the Creepers of the indie game *Minecraft* (2009). In this game, where building is a primary activity, the stealthy, mindless thing that rushes hissing toward the player and explodes presents a memorable monstrous problem.

Monsters of gaming differ in source and style, depending on the gaming genre. The role-playing game (RPG) genre, based on the *Dungeons & Dragons* (D&D) game, owes a very heavy debt to the table-top D&D game for its monsters. Indeed, the influence of *Dungeons & Dragons* is so strong on the RPG genre that many monsters of Japanese RPGs show clear roots in D&D's mélange of monsters drawn from classical, medieval, and fictional sources. Games taking influence from D&D include RPG variants like *Rogue* (1980) and *Nethack* (1987), action games like *Gauntlet* (1985) and *Diablo* (1997), and massive multiplayer online RPGs (MMOs) like *Ultima Online* (1997), *Everquest* (1999), and *World of Warcraft* (2004). Indeed, it is no exaggeration to state that fantasy games from *The Bard's Tale* (1995) to the *Elder Scrolls* (1994), *Dragon Age* (2009), and *Fable* (2005) series all owe a greater debt to *Dungeons & Dragons* than to any other single source of monsters and fantasy conventions. It is no surprise that D&D itself has seen numerous successful computer gaming adaptations, including *Pool of Radiance* (1988), *Eye of the Beholder* (1990), *Baldur's Gate* (1998), and *Neverwinter Nights* (2002).

There are few genres in gaming that do not feature monsters of some kind. Sidescrolling platformers (games presented from a side view that "scrolls" along as one moves through the level) such as *Super Mario Bros* (1985), *Sonic the Hedgehog* (1998), and action games typically present a mix of obstacles and monsters, some unique and others drawn from the wider culture. The *Super Mario Bros* games feature an array of strange creatures, including the mushroom-like goombas, turtle-like koopas, and toothed piranha plants. ***Ghosts 'n Goblins*** (1985) and its sequels use horror stories as inspiration for their monsters, including zombies, ghosts, and **demons**, eventually pitting the player against Lucifer (see **Devil, The**). *Prince of Persia* (1989) features **skeletons** reminiscent of Ray Harryhausen's famous skeletal warriors from *Jason and the Argonauts* (1963). The *Castlevania* (1986) series features Count **Dracula** as the end boss, and it is Dracula's castle that presents the challenges for the players to navigate. The breakthrough first-person shooter *Wolfenstein 3D* (1992) featured a blocky **robot** with Hitler's head as its end boss. The game's successor, *Doom* (1993), puts the players up against hordes of demons spilling out of portals to Hell discovered on the moons of Mars. *Doom* is particularly renowned for its monster design, with monsters like the revenant, hellknight, and the end boss Cyberdemon regularly noted as iconic monsters of video gaming.

Monsters have even made it into the martial arts-inspired fighting game genre. The fame of *Mortal Kombat* (1992) is due to its mix of blood, gore, and kung fu magic, as well as its monstrous elements like the four-armed, half-dragon boss Goro or the undead ninja fighter Scorpion. Capcom's *Darkstalkers* (1994; titled ***Vampire*** in Japan) series features many classic monsters of film and literature as its fighters, including clear counterparts to Dracula, the wolf man (see **Werewolf**), **Frankenstein's monster**, **the**

mummy, and the **Creature from the Black Lagoon**, alongside a yeti (see **Bigfoot**), an Aztec **robot**, more than one **succubus**, and Little Red Riding Hood as an uzi-toting monster hunter.

The survival horror genre is another home to monsters. Following the release of *Alone in the Dark* (1992), a survival horror and mystery game inspired by the works of H.P. Lovecraft (see **Lovecraft, Monsters In**), survival horror has grown to become one of the major genres in contemporary gaming, sometimes in combination with third- and first-person shooters. The *Resident Evil* (1996) series was an early entry, and a successful franchise that has spawned numerous sequels as well as films. Its most-talked-about monster is the relentless, seemingly unstoppable Nemesis, which hunts the player throughout *Resident Evil 3*. The atmospheric *Silent Hill* (1999) series has produced some of the most iconic monsters of horror gaming, from the terrifying torturer Pyramid Head to the medical horrors of its faceless nurses. Themes from survival horror have branched out into related genres. One striking example is the atmospheric first-person shooter *F.E.A.R.* (2005), featuring the ghostly Alma, a monster reminiscent of Samara from *The Ring* (Gore Verbinski, 1998). The *Left 4 Dead* (2008) franchise successfully introduced team-based play to a zombie survival horror game, as well as memorable zombie variants such as the **witch**. The third-person shooter *Dead Space* (2008) brings survival horror to a mining ship in space, filled with monstrous corpses called necromorphs. Zombies reemerged as iconic monsters of popular culture in the 1990s, a trend which shows no signs of abating in video game circles.

Finally, the enormously successful *Pokemon* (1996) franchise deserves mention in any treatment of monsters in video games. Short for "Pocket Monster," a pokemon is a small monster that can be housed in a ball and called forth by the owner (and pokemon trainer) to do battle with other pokemons, in a cartoonish version of callous practices such as dog- and cock-fighting. Originating in video games, Pokemon has grown into a franchise that includes television, film, collectible card games, and many other forms of entertainment product.

Richard W. Forest

References and Suggested Reading

Carr, Diane. "Play Dead: Genre and Affect in *Silent Hill* and *Planescape Torment*." *The International Journal of Computer Game Research* 3, no. 1 (May 2003). <http://www.gamestudies.org/0301/carr/>.

Donovan, Tristan. *Replay: The History of Video Games*. Lewes, UK: Yellow Ant, 2010.

Krzywinska, Tanya. "Hands-on Horror." In *Screenplay: Cinema/Videogames/Interfaces*, edited by Geoff King and Tanya Krzywinska, 206–23. London: Wallflower, 2002.

Perron, Bernard, ed. *Horror Video Games: Essays on the Fusion of Fear and Play*. Jefferson, NC: McFarland & Company, 2009.

Perron, Bernard, and Mark J.P. Wolf, eds. *The Video Game Theory Reader*. New York: Routledge, 2003.

———, eds. *The Video Game Theory Reader 2*. New York: Routledge, 2008.

Spittle, Steve. "'Did This Game Scare You? Because It Sure as Hell Scared Me!' F.E.A.R., the Abject and the Uncanny." *Games and Culture* 6 (2011): 312–26.

VII—*see* Demon

VIRUS

A virus is a sub-microscopic infectious agent that causes disease and can multiply only in the cells of humans, animals, and plants. The term stems from the late fourteenth-century Latin *virus*, meaning "poison," "slime" or "ooze," connoting foul-smelling

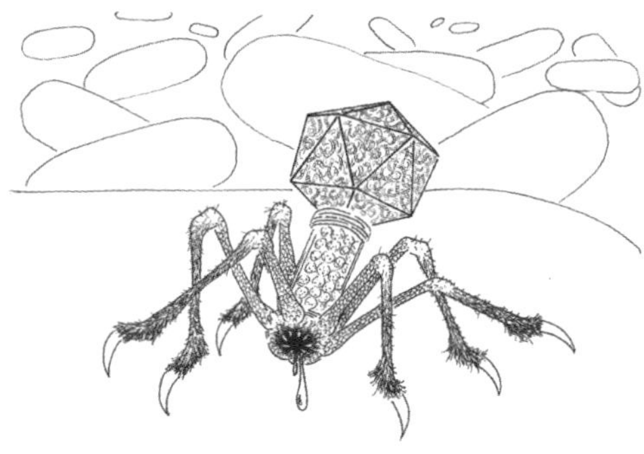

Fig. 36 ***Virus* by Risa Puno**

liquids. In 1892, the Russian biologist Dimitri Iwanowski discovered viruses while investigating an infection of tobacco plants. The germ theory of disease, which was prominent at this point, theorized that diseases are caused by specific micro-organisms that can be identified through microscopes, oftentimes cultivated in vitro and retained by filtration. Iwanowski found that the agent causing tobacco mosaic disease, which at the time spread rampantly, could neither be seen nor cultivated, and remained infectious even after filtration, thereby distinguishing it from bacteria (bacterial viruses were not discovered until 1915). The use of the word "virus" as the cause of an infectious disease was popularized after 1898, when the Dutch microbiologist Martinus Beijerinck (1851–1931), upon repeating Iwanowski's experiment and reporting his conclusion, named these infectious agents *contagium vivum fluidum*.

Since these early days of virology, rapid progress has been made in researching and identifying viruses. Millions of viruses exist in total, since every species can be infected by a specific range of viruses. The human species alone can be infected by more than 5,000 known pathogens. As opposed to the general assumption about viruses, these pathogens do not necessarily harm or even kill their hosts. In fact, only when the host–virus relationship—like a virus transitioning from one species to another—is an entirely new one does the infection kill a large percentage of hosts; over time, peaceful co-existence ensues. Therefore, the aggressive, deadly new relationship is the exception to the rule, though emerging virus infections such as Ebola, SARS, and H1N1 serve as reminders of how dangerous this relationship can be.

Within literature and film, viruses appear both as literal threats and as metaphors underlining a society's symptoms of decay or pointing towards specific social issues. Metaphorically, the virus can take on a range of pejorative meanings revolving around corruption, moral decline, and anti- as well as inter-human threats. Viruses invade the body and can use the host body to multiply and infect other bodies, transforming regular people into irrational and unpredictable monsters on a massive scale. Though the source of the infection is explicable, the virus' tendency to remain undefeated can have apocalyptic ramifications. They can disable human beings, reduce them to their most primitive instincts, and in some scenarios even awaken the dead (see **Zombie**). Similar to the plague, these microbes are now, despite their small size, the biggest threat to man's future. Cultural productions have put forth a set of four distinctive narratives regarding the virus, which serve the purpose of expressing skepticism, critiquing aspects of society, or admonishing the fragility of human life. These narratives can be categorized as: (1) skepticism about science, (2) skepticism about governmental forms of abuse, (3) body horror and breakdowns of bodily integrity, and (4) the virus as precursor for post-apocalyptic scenarios.

Skepticism about Science

Oftentimes, the outbreak of a virus-induced disease relates to modern skepticism regarding technological and scientific advancements. As early as 1826, Mary Shelley inquired about the functionality of medicine and science in her apocalyptic novel, *The Last Man*, which spotlights a world being decimated by the plague. Even a world rapidly progressing and developing sophisticated technology at a rapid pace can easily succumb to an uncontrollable enemy such as a virus.

This plot often plays out in narratives in which scientists experiment with sub-microscopic weapons in laboratories, wiping out mankind in the process. This kind of aversion to scientific hubris can be seen in many installments of popular culture, for instance Stephen King's novel *The Stand* (1978), in which the outbreak of a laboratory virus brings about an apocalyptic stand-off between good and evil, or Danny Boyle's film *28 Days Later* (2002), in which a "Rage" virus escapes from a laboratory, causing uncontrolled aggression.

Even the goodwill of the scientific community can lead to death and destruction; while trying to invent a type of vaccine against violent behavior, which would save a world infected with terror and violence, one of the protagonists in Steven King's short story "The End of the Whole Mess" (1986) brings about the end of mankind. The protein he isolates is not a virus; rather, violence is the virus that is running rampant in the world. This scientific endeavor to bring goodwill to all mankind via vaccine backfires as the protein liquidates the human brain. Margaret Atwood's 2003 novel *Oryx and Crake* features this type of "mad science" as well when the character Jimmy devises a viral pandemic to obliterate most of the human species, which he considers unworthy. The episode "TS-19" of the graphic novel-turned-television series *The Walking Dead* (Robert Kirkman and Frank Darabont, 2010–present) shows the Center for Disease Control (CDC) in Atlanta to be a highly inefficient institution: when all the other members have become infected, the last remaining scientist commits suicide.

Skepticism about Governmental Forms of Abuse

There exists a strong connection between the body politic and the virus, which can be seen in the actions taken by governments to contain the epidemic. The outbreak of a deadly virus results in chaos, not simply due to the massive and seemingly arbitrary decimation of a population, but also because of the enormous amounts of mobilization required to combat it. Governments and their agencies, as well as the military, are called upon to handle the crisis, and success is never guaranteed. Governments have to make decisions that threaten entire populations, such as clean-sweep operations designed to wipe out affected areas, no matter the cost. The divide between healthy and infected also becomes a categorization into desirable and undesirable, dangerous, and strange bodies. Moreover, governments make risky decisions regarding viruses: as discussed earlier, science is misused to develop viral weapons, and governments are depicted as selfishly aggressive institutions that value the possession of a new defense mechanism over the protection of their people.

Michael Crichton's *The Andromeda Strain* (1969) tells just such a tale of a government that neglects to take precautions and decides to explore **extraterrestrial** pathogens, causing the outbreak of an unknown virus. A filmic example of this outside of the fantastic realm is Wolfgang Petersen's 1995 film *Outbreak*, which focuses heavily on the inhumane treatment of the infected. The *Resident Evil* films (Paul W.S. Anderson, 2002–12), in contrast, show the absolute incompetence of government agencies and the dominance of large corporations—in this case the Umbrella Corporation, whose scientists manipulate the human body and ruthlessly experiment with viruses. Most films revolving around social breakdown caused by rampant viral infections stress the military's ineffectiveness in buffering against attack or further spread of the infection. Military bases are either overrun by the infected (for instance, Zack Snyder's *Dawn of the Dead* remake [2004], as well as *The Walking Dead*) or turn into inhumane, despotic gatherings that have sworn off mutual aid and only focus on survival, as in Danny Boyle's *28 Weeks Later* (2007).

Contagious Bodies: Body Horror and Breakdowns of Bodily Integrity

The virus is often the facilitator of a world in which mankind is stripped to its bare essentials. In most cases, it is human behavior, reaction to threat, and communal instincts that are emphasized by this life-threatening, world-changing herald of death. The body is the virus' battleground, upon which it unleashes its powers. Capitalizing on the fear of blood and other bodily fluids, in fictional virus narratives the virus becomes more than just a health hazard; it transforms human beings into viral bombs, creatures both alive and dead, as is the case in the zombie narrative. The infected lose their personality and all that makes them human, and are turned into instinct-driven, infectious monsters.

Films focusing on this physical fragility tend to feature extensive scenes displaying the disintegration of the infected, as exemplified in *Cabin Fever* (Eli Roth, 2002). Here, a flesh-eating virus disintegrates the bodies of the infected, which is focused upon heavily in many scenes. The French zombie film ***Mutants*** (David Morlet, 2009) examines physical fragility as well. The infected protagonist appears as a man with a degenerative disease who is being cared for by his partner, who watches his identity rapidly fade, to give way to an unknown, altered being. The outbreak of such viruses in fiction tends to point out the fragility of modern societies: once social regulation is gone, everyone has to fend for him- or herself.

Viral Societies: The Virus as Precursor for Post-Apocalyptic Scenarios

Fending for oneself entails the categorization of good and evil, with survival being only one motivator in the scenario; ideological battles follow closely. The aforementioned *The Stand* posits good against evil among the few remaining survivors of a viral outbreak; here, and in many cultural productions of this genre, the virus functions as the means to an end, the root of this post-apocalyptic status quo in which mankind is forced to rely on its bare essentials. A catalyst for states of emergency, the virus is a common denominator in many post-apocalyptic genre films and novels focusing on human behavior and social restructuring. An early example of this trope is *The Scarlet Plague* by Jack London (1912), set in a world decimated by a plague some 60 years prior. The characters are faced with preserving knowledge and history for the Earth's few remaining inhabitants.

In the novel that inspired George A. Romero's first zombie film, Richard Matheson's *I Am Legend* (1954), it is actually a strain of bacteria that infects and changes humans into **vampires**, who establish a vampiric counter-culture overrunning those not infected. The 2007 filmic adaptation by Francis Lawrence changed the infectious agent to a mutated measles virus that was intended to cure cancer and instead causes these mutations, turning into a rampant plague. While Matheson's novel identifies bacteria as the source of infection, most succeeding works that follow this pattern of infection threatening humans feature viruses as causal agents.

When infection spreads and individuals begin attacking each other, society is submerged into chaos. David Cronenberg's *Rabid* (1977) shows an entire city succumbing to the bloodthirsty infected, when a viral outbreak is started by one woman's newly acquired lust for blood. Since her condition is brought about by experimental surgery, this film also expresses serious skepticism regarding modern technology and scientific advancements. The infected city is also the setting of Guillermo del Toro's vampire book trilogy (*The Strain* [2009], *The Fall* [2010], and *The Night Eternal* [2011]).

The topic of human beings regressing to a primitive, aggressive state due to a virus is explicitly tackled in George A. Romero's *The Crazies* (1973). In addition, Romero's zombie films (*Night of the Living Dead* [1968], *Dawn of the Dead* [1978], *Day of the Dead* [1985], *Land of the Dead* [2005], *Diary of the Dead* [2008], *Survival of the Dead* [2010]) all build on the virus background, using the disease as a facilitator to make statements about political or social situations. Though originally brought about by radiation, the resurrection of the dead in *Night of the Living Dead* then goes on to spread like a virus: the living are infected through bites and bodily fluids, which cause them to die and be resurrected as a brain-dead, instinct-driven threat. The virus as a catalyst of the Apocalypse and determinant of the post-apocalyptic society is also prominent in the television show *Supernatural* (2005–present), which features the "Croatoan" virus. This blood-borne virus is of demonic origin and leads to fits of rage in the infected, causing widespread death and destruction. It is part of Lucifer's plan to rid the world of humanity and therefore fits into an actual Biblical Apocalypse rather than the man-made cataclysm often related to virus fiction.

M. Night Shyamalan's *The Happening* (2008) is somewhat of an exception to the "man versus man" theme, since this fictional epidemic—postulated as a response by nature to man's assaults on the environment—leads the characters to kill themselves rather than each other. Nonetheless, regrouping and organizing to survive becomes necessary. In Terry Gilliam's *12 Monkeys* (1995), surviving humans have been forced underground as a result of a virus decimating the planet. Convicted prisoner James Cole (Bruce Willis) is sent back in time to gather information on the virus and its release. *The Walking Dead* also spotlights human relations in an infected, post-apocalyptic world, highlighting the difficulties of retaining democracy and basic human rights in a world where civilization seems to have become extinct.

As mentioned above, viral threats also function to insinuate the morbidity and decay of a certain age or locality. For instance, Thomas Mann's Bildungsroman *Der Zauberberg* (*The Magic Mountain*, 1924), which is set in a sanatorium for tuberculosis patients, as well as his novel *Der Tod in Venedig* (*Death in Venice*, 1912), which takes place in a cholera-addled Venice, make use of this motif. Given the increasingly connected world in which we live, the threat of viruses—both real and fictional—will certainly continue to preoccupy the contemporary imagination.

Jana Toppe

References and Suggested Reading

Dimmock, Nigel J., and Sandy B. Primrose. *Introduction to Modern Virology*. 6th edn. Boston: Wiley-Blackwell, 2007.

Garrett, Laurie. *The Coming Plague: Newly Emerging Diseases in a World out of Balance*. New York: Penguin, 1995.

Matheson, Richard. *I Am Legend* [1954]. Reprint, New York: Orb Books, 1997.
Mayer, Ruth, and Brigitte Weingart, eds. *Virus! Mutationen einer Metapher*. Bielefeld: Transcript, 2004.
Wald, Priscilla. *Contagious: Cultures, Carriers, and the Outbreak Narrative*. Durham, NC: Duke University Press, 2008.
Weinstock, Jeffrey Andrew, ed. *Critical Approaches to the Films of M. Night Shyamalan: Spoiler Warnings*. New York: Palgrave Macmillan, 2010.

VOLDEMORT—*see* Demon; Harry Potter, Monsters In

VOORHEES, JASON

Jason Voorhees is the mass murderer at the center of the *Friday the 13th* slasher film franchise (1980–2009) that as of 2012 consists of twelve films. He is known for his iconic hockey mask and for stalking and killing teenagers in the area surrounding Crystal Lake.

Jason's back-story can be summarized as follows: in the summer of 1957, eleven-year-old Jason Voorhees drowned at Camp Crystal Lake. Over 20 years later, his mother, Pamela Voorhees (Betsy Palmer), murders a group of teenagers attempting to re-open the camp before she is decapitated by the sole survivor, Alice Hardy (Adrienne King). Unknown to Alice, Jason is actually alive, and witnessing the death of his mother triggers a reign of murderous terror in which he becomes determined to slay those who invade his territory at Crystal Lake.

Jason Voorhees (Ari Lehman) first appears as a child in Sean S. Cunningham's *Friday the 13th* (1980), but it is not until *Friday the 13th Part 2* (Steve Miner, 1981) that the character transforms into a killer. Jason is usually portrayed wearing a hockey mask, which conceals his severe facial disfiguration. Although the mask has become a defining part of Jason's image, it was not introduced until *Friday the 13th Part III* (Steve Miner, 1982), when Jason takes it from teenage character Shelly (Larry Zerner). Prior to wearing the hockey mask, Jason uses a white sack to conceal his face.

Jason frequently uses a machete to kill his victims, but he also makes creative use of spears, harpoons, axes, and other objects. In one example from *Freddy vs. Jason* (Ronny Yu, 2003), a crossover film with **Freddy Krueger** from the *Nightmare on Elm Street* franchise (1984–2010), Jason finds the character Trey (Jesse Hutch) lying in bed and stabs him repeatedly with a machete before folding the bed—and Trey along with it—in two. Jason's presence is most frequently signified by the eerie sound cue: "Ki-ki-ki, Ma-ma-ma." In the documentary *His Name Was Jason: 30 Years of Friday the 13th* (Daniel Farrands, 2009), Harry Manfredini, film composer for *Friday the 13th*, explains that this effect is derived from the phrase "Kill her, Mommy," spoken by the increasingly unbalanced Pamela Voorhees in the first *Friday the 13th* film.

Jason has been destroyed and resurrected a number of times, indicating that the character has supernatural abilities. This becomes most apparent in *Jason Goes to Hell: The Final Friday* (Adam Marcus, 1993), in which the evil spirit of Jason has the ability to move between different bodies. In *Friday the 13th: The Final Chapter* (Joseph Zito, 1984), Jason is hacked to death by 12-year-old Tommy Jarvis (Corey Feldman), one of the few recurrent characters in the series, but soon returns to life in *Friday the 13th Part VI: Jason Lives* (Tom McLoughlin, 1986) when a lightning bolt hits a metal post that Tommy has driven through Jason's corpse. Other methods used to bring Jason back to life include psychokinetic resurrection in *Friday the 13th Part VII: The New Blood* (John Carl Buechler, 1988), electricity in *Friday the 13th Part VIII: Jason Takes Manhattan*

(Rob Hedden, 1989), and reanimation by nanobots in the futuristic *Jason X* (James Isaac, 2001), which transforms Jason into a powerful **cyborg** known as Uber-Jason. In Marcus Nispel's new version of *Friday the 13th* (2009), all references to Jason's supernatural capabilities are removed and he is reinterpreted as a significantly more resourceful and intelligent character.

Jason Voorhees appears in all the *Friday the 13th* films, but is seen only in flashbacks and hallucinations in *Friday the 13th: A New Beginning* (Danny Steinmann, 1985), due to the fact that the killer in this film is a Jason imposter (the character Roy Burns, played by Dick Wieand). The role of Jason has been played by several different actors and stuntmen; Kane Hodder has assumed the role most often, featuring in four films in the series.

Beyond the screen, Jason Voorhees has had a significant influence on popular culture, appearing in novels, comic books, and video games. He also inspired the songs "He's Back (The Man Behind the Mask)" by Alice Cooper, and "Mr Voorhees" by German heavy metal band Capricorn. The list of merchandise featuring the character is vast and ranges from t-shirts, baseball caps, and Halloween costumes, to collectible action figures, plush toys, and dioramas. The widespread popularity of Jason Voorhees has transformed the character into a celebrity, as demonstrated at the 1992 MTV Movie Awards, when he became the first fictitious character to receive a Lifetime Achievement Award.

Liz Dixon

References and Suggested Reading

Bracke, Peter M. *Crystal Lake Memories: The Complete History of Friday the 13th*. London: Titan Books, 2006.

Conrich, Ian. "The *Friday the 13th* Films and the Cultural Function of a Modern Grand Guignol." In *Horror Zone: The Cultural Experience of Contemporary Horror Cinema*, edited by Ian Conrich, 173–90. London: I.B. Tauris & Co. Ltd, 2010.

Crane, Jonathan Lake. "Jason." In *Terror and Everyday Life: Singular Moments in the History of the Horror Film*, edited by Jonathan Lake Crane, 133–58. London: Sage Publications, 1994.

Dika, Vera. *Games of Terror: Halloween, Friday the 13th and the Films of the Stalker Cycle*. London: Associated University Press, 1990.

Grove, David. *Making Friday the 13th: The Legend of Camp Blood*. Surrey, England: FAB Press, 2005.

VRITRA—*see* Demon

VURDALAK—*see* Upyr'

WAG-AT-THE-WA'—*see* Brownie

THE WANDERING JEW

The Wandering Jew is a mythical figure of Christian medieval folklore with its origins in the thirteenth century. As a punishment for mocking Jesus on his way to crucifixion, this man was cursed to wander the Earth until the end of time when Christ returns. A cobbler by trade, he had stood with one of his children in his arms to watch the crucifixion. "Go on quicker," he is alleged to have said to Jesus, who is said to have replied, "I go, but thou shalt wait till I return," meaning the Second Coming. Upon putting his child down, he followed Jesus to the crucifixion and never saw his wife or children again. He believed the purpose of his roving to be the restoration of the faithless to God and the bringing of penitence to the unrepentant. He was characterized by abstinence, taking in very little food and drink, and rarely accepting the money he was offered. Fluent in the languages of all countries he crossed, he was able to communicate with anyone he met. Some legends claim he had a burning cross impressed upon his forehead so as to mark and identify him, which he then covered with a black bandage.

The name given to the figure differs from country to country, depending on whether his task of wandering or the duration of his punishment is being stressed. Teutonic languages emphasize his eternal task: there he is known as the "eternal" or "everlasting" Jew (*Der Ewige Jude*). In Romance languages, on the other hand, the wanderings are stressed: the French, for instance, refer to him as *le Juif errant*, while the Spanish term is *Juan Espera en Dios* or *judio erante*. The same goes for the English language as well.

The first published account of this tale is found in Roger of Wendover's thirteenth-century *Flores Historiarum* (*Flowers of History*), whereas the first legend of the Wandering Jew was recorded as early as 1228 at the Monastery of St Albans where monks relayed the tale to a visiting Archbishop of Armenia Major. This first legend depicts the Wandering Jew as a penitent figure, not a vengeful, demonic creature; this theme stretches through the centuries. While differing versions of the tale existed throughout the Middle Ages, the next important written account of it was not related until 1697 in Barthélemy d'Herbelot's *Bibliothèque orientale*, in which he appears under the name of Bassi Hadhret Issa, introducing himself to an Arab named Fadhilah who is leading a troop of horsemen.

The name Ahasverus for the Wandering Jew appeared first in Europe in several urban legends around 1602, in which the Bishop of Schleswig, Paul von Eitzen, encounters this ragged, sad figure in Hamburg, Germany in 1542. This man introduces himself as "eternal" and doomed to walk the Earth until the Second Coming. The content of these urban legends is the basis for the majority of succeeding tales. According to this legend, Ahasverus considered Jesus a heretic and is said to have been involved in Jesus's prosecution in the Sanhedrin trial (the Sanhedrin is a Jewish judicial body) and his crucifixion as ordered by Pontius Pilate.

The figure of the Wandering Jew circulated steadfastly in folk legends from the sixteenth to the nineteenth centuries and was often incorporated into fiction, especially by nineteenth-century Romanticists. In Matthew Lewis's famous 1796 Gothic novel *The Monk*, he is referred to as the "Great Mogul" (108) and later characterized as "being the celebrated character known universally by name of *Wandering Jew*" (115). He helps Don Raymond exorcize a supernatural being, a **ghost** called the Bleeding Nun, by revealing the burning cross on his forehead (112). English clergyman George Croly's three-volume novel *Salathiel* (1829) actually speaks of its protagonist's life and hardships and ends on the revelation that he will be doomed to walk the Earth for eternity. In France, Éugène Sue published the novel *Le Juif errant* (1844), which represents the Ahasverus figure as doubly cursed. Not only is he damned to be immortal, he also causes a cholera epidemic wherever he goes. A fellow Frenchman, Gustave Doré, published a book with twelve intriguing engravings of the Wandering Jew in the 1840s, each illustration adorned with a couplet beneath it. These engravings influenced subsequent cultural representations, such as George MacDonald's *Thomas Wingfold, Curate* (1876), which includes an episode featuring the Wandering Jew, referring intertextually to Doré's engravings. Further appearances in nineteenth-century English literature can be found in Percy Bysshe Shelley's *Queen Mab: A Philosophical Poem* (1813), which features the character Ahasuerus; Charles Robert Maturin's 1820 novel ***Melmoth the Wanderer***; and Lew Wallace's *The Prince of India* (1893), which follows the character through the ages and shows how he helps shape history.

In the twentieth century, Bernard Capes presents the Wandering Jew as a figure for the Antichrist in his 1902 novel *The Accursed Cordonnier*. The German-American poet and Nazi sympathizer George Sylvester Viereck composed two variations of the theme in cooperation with American poet and novelist Paul Eldridge: *My First Two Thousand Years: The Autobiography of the Wandering Jew* (1928) and *Salome: The Wandering Jewess* (1930). Even comical adaptations of the theme appear, such as Mary Elizabeth Counselman's "A Handful of Silver" (original publication date unknown; republished 1964), which fuses together the legend of the Wandering Jew with that of Judas.

German poetry of the nineteenth century was rife with the image of the cursed wanderer as well: Nikolaus Lenau ("Ahasver. Der Ewige Jude," 1827–31; "Der Ewige Jude," 1836), Julius Mosen ("Ahasverus," 1838), Christian Friedrich Daniel Schubart ("Der ewige Jude. Eine Lyrische Rhapsodie" ["The Eternal Jew: A Lyrical Rhapsody"], 1783), and Ludwig Köhler ("Der neue Ahasver" ["The New Ahasver"], 1841) are just a few prominent poets that included the Wandering Jew in poems, while Ernst August Friedrich Klingemann (*Ahasver*, 1827) and Achim von Arnim (*Halle und Jerusalem*, 1811) featured him in their respective tragedies. German fantastic literature in particular was smitten by the tale of the cursed wanderer: E.T.A. Hoffmann's *Die Elixiere des Teufels* (*The Devil's Elixir*, 1815), which is in fact based on Matthew Lewis's *The Monk*; Gustav Meyrink's *Das grüne Gesicht* (*The Green Face*, 1916); and Leo Perutz's *Marques de Bolibar* (1920) make use of the legend.

The Wandering Jew remained present well into the twentieth century. For instance, the Belgian author August Vermeylen makes use of it for his novel *De wandelende Jood* (*The Wandering Jew*) in 1906. In 1923, British director Maurice Elvey produced the cinematic adaptation of the story in his silent film *The Wandering Jew*. During the Third Reich, the legend was then re-appropriated and used to entitle a propaganda film (*Der Ewige Jude* [*The Eternal Jew*], Fritz Hippler, 1940) intended to prepare the citizens for the beginning of the Holocaust. Yet even after these horrors, the legend of Ahasverus remained alive: German author Stephan Heym tells Ahasverus's tale in his 1981 novel *Ahasver*. Even popular film makes use of the legend in the late twentieth century: for example, *The Seventh Sign* (Carl Schultz, 1988) touches upon the legend with the character Father Lucci (Peter Friedman), a Roman guard of Pontius Pilate condemned to walk the Earth for striking Jesus; and *The Gathering* (Brian Gilbert, 2003) features individuals bound to eternal life for watching the crucifixion of Christ out of sheer curiosity.

Jana Toppe

References and Suggested Reading

Hasan-Rokem, Galit, and Alan Dundes, eds. *The Wandering Jew: Essays in the Interpretation of a Christian Legend*. Bloomington: Indiana University Press, 1986.

Joshi, S.T., ed. *Icons of Horror and the Supernatural: An Encyclopedia of Our Worst Nightmares*. Santa Barbara, CA: Greenwood, 2006.

Körte, Mona. *Die Uneinholbarkeit des Verfolgten. Der Ewige Jude in der literarischen Phantastik*. Frankfurt: Campus, 2000.

Körte, Mona, and Robert Stockhammer, eds. *Ahasvers Spur. Dichtungen und Dokumente vom Ewigen Juden*. Leipzig: Reclam, 1995.

Lewis, Matthew Gregory. *The Monk* [1796]. Reprint, Mineola, NY: Dover Publications, 2003.

Russell, W.M.S., and Katharine M. Briggs. "The Legends of Lilith and of the Wandering Jew in Nineteenth-Century Literature." *Folklore* 92, no. 2 (1981): 131–40.

Fig. 37 *Transformation* by John Adastra

WAQ-WAQ TREE—*see* Plants, Monstrous

WARG—*see* Tolkien, Monsters In

WATCHER IN THE WATER—*see* Tolkien, Monsters In

WATCHERS, THE—*see* Angel

WEREWOLF

Typically defined as a human being who transforms into a large and bloodthirsty wolf, the werewolf's variable nature has inspired numerous films and literary works. As the result of a magic spell or potion, a curse, or an attack by another werewolf, the victim usually undergoes this metamorphosis unwillingly, sometimes only at the time of the full moon. Prior to transformation, the werewolf must often remove his clothing; when in human form it is sometimes said that his wolf skin remains on the inside. While in the shape of the wolf, he (or, more rarely, she) becomes a dangerous predator who ravages animal and human prey with the monster's hallmark savagery. A werewolf can be distinguished from a regular wolf by a number of traits, especially his glowing eyes and excessive size, or by his hybrid form that blends human and lupine features. Certain remedies protect against werewolf attacks, such as the Christian cross or the herb wolfsbane; in most cases, only a silver bullet or fire can destroy a werewolf. Upon death, the werewolf resumes his or her human shape, thus revealing the identity of the cursed individual.

In addition to the supernatural form of the monster described above, a psychological disorder called lycanthropy sometimes provides a rational explanation for the werewolf's activities. In this case, a human being simply believes that he has become a wolf and exhibits such symptoms as walking on all fours, craving raw meat or blood, howling, and so on. In extreme forms, the victim disinters buried bodies to consume them or violently attacks humans and animals for the same reason. The lycanthrope may remain completely unaware of his bizarre behavior, in essence leading a double life. On occasion, an extremely large wolf whose cunning and ferocity appear supernatural may also be called a werewolf.

Scholars attribute deep psychological and social meaning to the monster; Charlotte Otten asserts that: "[w]erewolf fiction is not a breeding ground for trivial or sensational or blood-curdling stories but is a deep pool that mirrors aspects of human life that can only be faced by looking into that pool" (xi). Half-man, half-beast, the Wolf Man reminds us of the violent animal hidden beneath our civilized veneer. This bestiality links the werewolf to sexuality as an expression of our animal nature, a destructive force to be feared or, more recently, as an exotic object of desire. In contrast with this image of the werewolf as the beast within, this monster may also arrive from a foreign land, symbolizing the threatening Other. Some werewolf tales foreground our admiration for the beast's power and nostalgia for the freedom and simplicity of a wolf's life in comparison to the complications of human society. As Carolyn Walker Bynum points out, the theme of metamorphosis addresses our deepest fears about identity and change.

The Werewolf in Ancient and Medieval Texts

The term lycanthrope derives from the Greek *lycos*, wolf, and *andros*, man; similarly, the English term "werewolf" combines the animal's name with the Old English *were*, man. The latter may be derived from the latin *vir* (pronounced like "we're"), but Sarah L. Higley also relates it to the "Old High German *warg*, Old English *wearg*, and Old Norse *vargr*," all of which referred to criminals, outcasts, or cursed beings as wolves (335–6). Indeed, the Icelandic sagas written in Old Norse represent a major source for the werewolf in literature. In *The Edda* (c. thirteenth century), Odin punishes the trickster/**shapeshifter** Loki by transforming his son into a wolf. The late thirteenth-century *Saga of the Völsungs* includes three werewolves: Siggeir's mother, Sigmund, and Sinfjötli, while *Egils Saga* (c. 1220–40) describes the hero Kveldulf, which translates as Night Wolf, and his friend Kari as *berserkers*, warriors who wore bear-skin or wolf-skin shirts and went into deadly rages on the battlefield.

Unlike its confederates in monsterdom, **Dracula** and **Frankenstein's monster**, the Wolf Man has no single literary text to which we can trace its origins; as a shapeshifter, however, the werewolf belongs to a long lineage of supernatural beings from indigenous traditions and classical Greek and Roman literature. In *The Metamorphoses* (c. 8 CE), Ovid recounts how the god Zeus punished the barbarous Lycaon by turning him into a wolf. In the *Eclogues* (38–39 BCE), Virgil depicts Moeris transforming into a wolf by using a concoction of herbs, and Petronius tells of the slave Niceros watching his master transform in the first century AD *Satyricon* (Higley 348).

During the Middle Ages, purportedly "real" werewolves were tried and executed for witchcraft (see Summers; see **Witch/Wizard**); at the same time a more sympathetic image of the werewolf as victim developed. In several texts, such as Marie de France's "Bisclavret" (c. 1165) and the anonymous "Biclarel" (c. 1350), the hero's wife tricks him into becoming a werewolf using a magic ring, rod, or potion. Through his loyalty and submission to the king, his humanity wins out over his beastly appearance and his unfaithful spouse is punished. The early thirteenth-century *The Lay of Melion* and fourteenth-century *Arthur and Gorlagon* identify King Arthur as the werewolf's savior, and Sir Thomas Malory's *Le Morte d'Arthur* (1485) mentions a werewolf, Sir Marrok. The anonymous romance *William and the Werwolf* (c. 1195; trans. c. 1350) describes how Prince Alphonse of Spain, transformed into a werewolf by his wicked stepmother's magic, kidnaps the title hero in order to save him from a murderous plot.

Werewolves in Literature from the Seventeenth to the Early Twentieth Centuries

During the Renaissance and Enlightenment, writers like Shakespeare (1564–1616) employed wolf metaphors (Robisch 231), but his contemporary John Webster presents an early case of literary lycanthropy in *The Duchess of Malfi* (1623). *A History of the Ridiculous Extravagancies of Monsieur*

Oufle (1711) by the Abbé Laurent Bordelon depicts its gullible title character running through town howling, believing himself transformed into a werewolf.

An object of ridicule during the rationalist eighteenth century, the werewolf slowly regained popularity during the Gothic and Romantic eras. The motif of a cursed soul tormented by violent desires appealed to writers obsessed with extreme emotions. Lord Byron asserts in his epic, but unfinished, poem "Don Juan" (parts of which were first published in 1819) that "*lykanthropy* / I comprehend, for without transformation / Men become wolves on any slight occasion" (Canto IX, strophe xx). Charles R. Maturin, author of the Gothic classic ***Melmoth the Wanderer*** (1820), includes a lycanthrope episode in *The Albigenses* (1824; vol. II, ch. 13). The French Romantic Petrus Borel (1809–59) called himself "Le Lycanthrope," and his compatriot, associated with the later Decadent movement in literature, Rachilde (b. Marguerite Eymery, 1860–1953) flaunted the family legend that "as the great-granddaughter of a defrocked priest, she had inherited the traits of a werewolf" (Finn 29). During this century, several plays featuring werewolves appeared in France and England.

As literacy increased across the nineteenth century, so did the demand for popular literature, and werewolves began to appear in the short stories and serialized novels of periodical fiction. In *The Essential Guide to Werewolf Literature* (2003), Brian J. Frost catalogues some dozen werewolf texts published in the US and UK during the period 1828–99 (55–91). Described as "[t]he first novel to have a werewolf as its principal character" (Frost 63), George W.M. Reynolds's *Wagner the Wehr-Wolf* (1846–47) borrows devices from Gothic fiction. Its original contribution lies in the detailed description of transformation as a painful, traumatic event. Catherine Crowe's "A Story of a Weir-Wolf" (*Hogg's Weekly Instructor*, 16 May 1846) exploits a recurring motif, revealing the monster's identity when the human bears an injury obtained while in wolf form. However, Mrs Crowe introduces the new device of explaining away her suspected werewolf; just as the suspect, a beautiful young girl, is about to be executed, her cousin drags in the actual injured wolf. Perhaps the most lyrical werewolf story of the period, Clemence Housman's novella *The Were-Wolf* (1896), introduces the notion of a beautiful female werewolf's sex appeal.

The Victorian and Edwardian eras blended an ongoing curiosity about the supernatural with a desire to prove its existence scientifically—attitudes reflected in the work of several well-known British and American writers. Rudyard Kipling's "The Mark of the Beast" (1890), adapted to film in 2012 (directed by Jonathan Gorman and Edward Thomas Seymour), portrays an Englishman transformed into a werewolf after insulting the monkey-god Hanuman in India. Saki (H.H. Munro) authored three werewolf tales: "Gabriel-Ernest" (1910) features one of the first young adult werewolves in literature; "The Wolves of Cernogratz" (1924) employs the family curse motif; and "The She-Wolf" (1914) initiates a new development in the genre—satire. Lampooning popular obsession with the supernatural, Munro's recurring *trouble-fête* Clovis Sangrail tricks a would-be magician by substituting a real wolf for his host's wife. One of England's most prolific and respected authors of **ghost** stories, Algernon Blackwood, penned one of the most effective literary accounts of the **Windigo** legend, as well as five werewolf-related tales. "The Camp of the Dog" (1908) offers a "modern" interpretation of lycanthropy, explaining it as an individual's astral double, which splits off from the sleeping self to express unconscious, animal desires, while

"Running Wolf" (1920) links the werewolf to the Native American tradition.

During the early twentieth century, werewolves figured in a growing number of novels, most often as a metaphor for man's dual nature, as in German Nobel laureate Hermann Hesse's *Steppenwolf* (1927), or as a red herring in popular mysteries, as in Albert Machard's *The Wolf Man* (1923) and Charles Lee Swem's *Werewolf* (1929). American writer Frank Norris's first novel, *Vandover and the Brute*, written in 1894 but not published until 1914, describes its protagonist as suffering from actual fits of lycanthropy.

Werewolf Pulp Fiction

Beginning in the 1920s, magazines specializing in science fiction and fantasy began to appear, with *Weird Tales*, the initial print run for which lasted from 1923 to 1954, as the best known of these. During the period 1919–49, nearly a hundred werewolf stories appeared in such "pulp" magazines, most by authors who published a single tale (Frost 106–43; 157–72); however, several prolific writers contributed multiple quality werewolf stories, including Greye La Spina (1880–1969), Seabury Quinn (1899–1969), H. Warner Munn (1903–81), Manly Wade Wellman (1903–86), and Robert E. Howard (1906–36).

Quinn's eight werewolf tales include "The Phantom Farmhouse" (1923) and "The Wolf of St Bonnot" (1930). "The Thing in the Fog" (1933) features his recurring detective Jules de Grandin and the *vrykolakas* of Greek lore. "The Gentle Werewolf" (1940) is about a noblewoman in the medieval Holy Land, cursed by a beggarwoman but eventually saved by her knight errant. Greye La Spina also deserves mention for her werewolf-themed texts first published in *The Thrill Book* and its competitor *Weird Tales*. La Spina's Russian werewolves are also sexual predators in "Wolf of the Steppes" (1919) and *Invaders from the Dark* (1925), while "The **Devil**'s Pool" (1932) employs the notion that magical water brings on the werewolf's metamorphosis. Most of the stories included in Munn's *The Werewolf of Ponkert* and *Tales of the Werewolf Clan* (both published in 1979) first appeared in *Weird Tales* between 1925 and 1931. The cycle recounts how an **extraterrestrial** transforms Hungarian Wladislaw Brenryk into a werewolf, cursing his family until his descendant Adam Grant banishes him from Earth.

Through the 1940s the werewolves depicted in pulp tales revisited their medieval origins, haunted the woods of North America, occasionally appeared in science fictional settings, and were also topically linked to the anti-German sentiments of the World War II era, as in "The Compleat Werewolf" (1942) by Anthony Boucher. Fritz Leiber's "The Hound" (1942), set in an urban, industrial environment, however, marks a turning point in the modernization of the werewolf. "The first pulp story to challenge the stereotypical image of the werewolf" (Frost 168), its werewolf appears with "red eyes like thickly scummed molten metal ... the jaws slavered with thick black oil" (Leiber, quoted in Otten 153).

From the 1950s through the 1970s, in spite of new periodicals like *The Magazine of Fantasy and Science Fiction* (1950 to present) and a new generation of writers nourished on *Weird Tales* in their youths, the boom of the pulp era declined and, with it, the number of werewolf stories. Yet writers like Robert Bloch (1917–94), Philip José Farmer (1918–2009), Jerome Bixby (1923–98), and Poul Anderson (1926–2001) updated the Wolf Man, ever seeking original approaches to the timeworn monster. Bixby's "The Young One" (1953) depicts its werewolves as immigrants to the United States; instead of demonizing the new arrivals like previous texts, the Kovacs adapt to their new life by eating raw beef rather than raw humans, and their neighbors accept them by minimizing their difference. This trend continued into the subsequent decades, as seen in Peter S. Beagle's "Lila the Werewolf" (1974), which satirizes the werewolf genre à la Woody Allen. A modern girl in New York City, Lila undergoes analysis, rebels from her mother and lives with her boyfriend (the narrator), takes pills to control her urges to mate when in wolf form, but, unable to handle the stress, finally goes home to her overprotective mother.

The Werewolf in Film History

First Werewolves on Film

The first werewolf film, a silent short called *The Werewolf* (Henry McRae, AKA MacRae, 1913), drew upon Native American lore, as did the now lost *The White Wolf* (1914; director uncertain) (Glut 1–2). They thus differed greatly from the bulk of the films that followed. The 1924 film *The Wolf Man* (Edmund Mortimer) represents the earliest appearance of a lycanthrope in a full-length feature film in English; however, two European films predate it: a 1917 Italian silent film, *Il lupo* (Giulio Antamoro) and the French *Le Loup-Garou* (Pierre Bressol, 1923). Based on the Alfred Machard novel, which uses the werewolf metaphorically to represent an escaped convict's inner struggle against his violent urges, the French film introduces the werewolf simply as a bogey-man (Glut 7). Lycanthropy had to wait until the 1940s to come into its own on celluloid.

The Universal Werewolves (1930–49)

In the 1930s, Universal Studios created a new genre of Gothic-style horror films, featuring their signature figures: Frankenstein's monster, Dracula, and the Wolf Man. The first film of the Universal werewolf cycle, *The Werewolf of London* (Stuart Walker, 1935), stars Henry Hull as Dr Glendon and introduces the element of a rare plant, the *mariphasa lumina*, which provides a temporary remedy for werewolfery. Jack Pierce designed the distinctive make-up for that film and its more famous follow-up, *The Wolf Man* (George Waggner, 1941), starring Lon Chaney, Jr. Since this film, Larry Talbot has become the paradigm for the werewolf as tormented victim, stressing this notion with the folkloric verse: "Even a man who is pure in heart and says his prayers at night, may become a wolf when the wolfsbane blooms and the autumn moon is bright." Attacked by the gypsy Bela (Bela Lugosi) and now cursed himself, the son of Sir John Talbot seeks every means possible to convince skeptics of his condition and to find a cure. While his father gives him peace by striking him with a silver-headed cane, Universal Studios resurrected Larry for a number of sequels, most written by Curt Siodmak and all featuring Chaney, Jr: *Frankenstein Meets the Wolf Man* (Roy William Neil, 1943), *House of Frankenstein* (Erle C. Kenton, 1944), and *House of Dracula* (Erle C. Kenton, 1945). The actor later reprised his famous role, playing a mummified werewolf in the Mexican/US production *Face of the Screaming Werewolf* (Gilberto Martínez Solares, 1964).

Drawing on its prior success, Universal produced *The She-Wolf of London* (Jean Yarbrough, 1946), starring June Lockhart as an heiress led to believe she is a werewolf by a greedy housekeeper. Other studios also tried to cash in on the werewolf's popularity; Fox's *The Undying Monster* (George Brahm, 1942; based on a Jessie Douglas Kerruish novel) exploits a family curse and a case of psychological lycanthropy. The B-movie *The Mad Monster* (Sam Newfield, 1942) offers a science fictional take, as a mad scientist

(George Zucco) transforms his mentally challenged handyman (Glenn Strange) into a werewolf, to take revenge on his professional rivals. The proliferation of monster-meets-monster films led to parodies in which monsters meet comedy teams. In *Abbott and Costello Meet Frankenstein* (Charles Barton, 1948), the comedy duo also encounters the Wolf Man and Dracula, while the Three Stooges meet the werewolf in *Idle Roomers* (Del Lord, 1943).

Hammer and AIP Werewolves

Perhaps because of its being overworked to the point of absurdity, the 1950s marked a lull in the werewolf's film appearances. Nonetheless, independent filmmakers cranked out low-budget fare like *The Werewolf* (Fred F. Sears, 1956), appealing to a growing teenage audience. American International Pictures (AIP) released *I Was A Teenage Werewolf* in 1957, starring Michael Landon (Gene Fowler, Jr), spawning a series of teenage monster films. AIP also produced *The Cry of the* ***Banshee*** (Gordon Hessler, 1970), in which Vincent Price appears in his only werewolf film, cast as Lord Edward Whitman, a witch-hunting magistrate in Elizabethan England. His family has been cursed by a pagan witch, who controls their servant Roderick's (Patrick Mower) transformation into a werewolf.

In the 1960s and 1970s in Great Britain, Hammer Films successfully revived the classic film monsters with their vivid technicolor productions. Director Terence Fisher's *The Curse of the Werewolf* (1961) transposes the story of Guy Endore's novel *The Werewolf of Paris* (1933) to late eighteenth-century Spain. A beggar unjustly imprisoned by an evil lord transforms over time into a hairy beast; when he rapes his jailer's beautiful but mute daughter, their child eventually becomes a werewolf. While his foster parents try to protect the innocent and loving child, his beastly nature will out, and he must face his tragic identity when he leaves home as a young man and murders a woman during the full moon. The related company Amicus featured werewolves in the first episode of the omnibus picture *Dr Terror's House of Horrors* (1964), *The Beast Must Die* (Paul Annett, 1974, AKA *The Black Werewolf*), based on James Blish's much-admired story "There Shall Be No Darkness" (1950), and *Legend of the Werewolf* (Freddie Francis, 1975).

In the 1970s, television offered a new venue for the werewolf, often exploiting contemporary culture: ABC's *The Werewolf of Woodstock* (John Moffitt, 1975; see Deal 195–6) places the monster at the popular rock festival of 1969; and the satirical *The Werewolf of Washington* (Milton Moses Ginsberg, 1973) targets the Watergate scandal of 1972. The ABC Gothic soap opera *Dark Shadows* (1966–71) also featured a werewolf character, Quentin Collins (David Selby), in addition to the better known **vampire** Barnabas (Jonathan Frid; see **Collins, Barnabas**).

Through the 1960s until the very end of the 1970s, most big-screen werewolf films were made abroad, like Italy's *Werewolf in a Girl's Dormitory* (Paolo Heusch and Richard Benson, 1961) and *The Werewolf Woman* (Rino di Silvestro, 1976). Indeed, the most famous film werewolf of this period comes from Spain. Paul Naschy (born Jacinto Molina Álvarez, 1934–2009), "known as the Spanish Lon Chaney" (Lázaro-Reboll 131), starred (and often wrote and directed) in twelve werewolf films from 1967 to 2003. His sympathetic werewolf, Count Waldemar Daninsky, searches endlessly for a cure to his curse, often saving his beloved from other monsters along the way. The first of these was released as *Frankenstein's Bloody Terror* (Enrique López Eguiluz, 1968) in the US; several films, including *Curse of the Devil* (Carlos Aured, 1974), pit Daninsky against **Countess Elizabeth Bathory**, a real historical figure who allegedly bathed in her victims' blood.

The Contemporary Werewolf in Film and Literature

The late 1970s and early 1980s marked a veritable werewolf renaissance in film and literature. Gary Brandner's 1977 novel *The Howling* spawned an entire franchise of sequels, situating the monster within the context of contemporary anxieties about crime and sexuality, but adding little new to the lore. Joe Dante's film version, adapted for the screen by John Sayles and Terence H. Winkless, further updated the film by integrating the mass media into the action and adding a serial killer. Between 1985 and 1995, six sequels were filmed, some in the UK and one in Australia. Released on 10 April 1981, *The Howling* represented the first of three radically different werewolf films to debut that year. Its special make-up effects (created by Rob Bottin with Rick Baker as consultant) revolutionized the contemporary werewolf, offering the spectacle of the transformation in all of its gory glory as this type of monster film's signature sequence.

Wolfen (Michael Wadleigh), based on Whitley Strieber's 1978 novel, debuted on 24 July 1981. Eschewing the spectacle of transformation, its monsters are highly evolved biological wolves, rather than supernatural creatures. The film combines the sub-tradition of medieval werewolf lore about uncannily intelligent, man-eating wolves with contemporary concerns about urban renewal, competition for resources, and a growing sense of guilt about the destruction of wildlife habitat. It also introduces the Native American tradition of shapeshifting almost as a red herring.

The last released (on 21 August) of 1981's werewolf films, *An American Werewolf in London* (John Landis), pays homage to the pastoral tradition of the genre and its seminal work, *The Wolf Man* (1941). As two nice Jewish-American boys on a walking tour of northern England face the tight-lipped denizens of a country pub, the film's understated humor lends it a level of plausibility largely absent from a genre grounded in the seriousness of Gothic horror. David Kessler's (David Naughton) struggle with the reality of the attack, the violent death (and reappearance as a ghost) of his friend Jack Goodman (Griffin Dunne), and his own growing realization of what it really means to be a werewolf render this one of the most human and moving portrayals of the tradition of the sympathetic werewolf. Rick Baker won an Oscar for his extended, extremely realistic transformation sequences, which stressed the pain felt by the werewolf as victim, rather than monster.

In comparison to these three films that continue to leave their mark on the genre, Stephen King's *Silver Bullet* (David Attias, 1985) appears dated today. Based on his novella *Cycle of the Werewolf* (1983), published in a limited edition illustrated by Bernie Wrightson, the werewolf strikes terror into the heart of a small Maine town at the full moon of each month, until an unlikely hero discovers his identity.

Of more lasting significance are Angela Carter's three stories published in *The Bloody Chamber and Other Stories* (1979), which rewrite the book on the relationship between Red Riding Hood and the wolf, and mark the feminist revision of the werewolf motif. "The Werewolf" imagines the little girl arriving at grandmother's house to find the wolf in bed; in self-defense she attacks and hacks off its paw. In an astonishing reversal, the paw transforms into an aged human hand: the grandmother was a werewolf. "The Company of Wolves," which was adapted to film by Neil Jordan in 1984, offers several werewolf vignettes, culminating with Red Riding Hood seducing the wolf; and "Wolf-Alice" combines the werewolf motif with that of feral children.

During the 1980s, some 60 werewolf novels appeared in print, with that number doubling in the 1990s (Frost 201–11; 215–33). With the development of home video and cable television markets, the number of werewolf films also rose exponentially across those decades and into the third millennium. With such quantities, quality often suffered, as did originality. However, a handful of writers and filmmakers made significant contributions to the genre from 1990 to the present.

While the spectacle of the werewolf's violent destruction continued to sell, revised attitudes about wildlife and the environment expressed themselves in several kinder, gentler werewolves, like Maeniel, the hero of Alice Borchardt's trilogy consisting of *The Silver Wolf* (1998), its prequel *Night of the Wolf* (1999), and *The Wolf King* (2001). Sister of vampire novelist Anne Rice, Borchardt sets her story in the time of the Roman conquest of Gaul and Britain through the purported reign of King Arthur. Robert McCammon successfully blends the historical spy thriller with the werewolf genre through his sympathetic hero and shapeshifter Michael Gallatin in *The Wolf's Hour* (1989). McCammon's novel offers a rare exploration of the possibility of werewolf fertility and reflects on the question of "What is the werewolf in the eyes of God?" (364). The paranormal romance genre has led to a burgeoning of werewolf novels that focus on the sexual relationship of a human heroine with a werewolf, or on a female werewolf heroine's lifestyle, as in Kelley Armstrong's *Bitten* (2001) and Carrie Vaughn's *Kitty and the Midnight Hour* (2005), both of which have led to sequels.

In the 1990s, big-screen efforts like the Jack Nicholson vehicle *Wolf* (Mike Nichols, 1994) fell flat with werewolf fans, as did *An American Werewolf in Paris* (Anthony Waller, 1997). The monster's popularity, however, had grown to the extent that the first television series developed around the monster, Frank Lupo's *Werewolf* (1987) and the Canadian *Big Wolf on Campus* (Peter A. Knight and Christopher Briggs, 1999–2002), both aired. Vampire-centered TV series like Joss Whedon's *Buffy the Vampire Slayer* (1997–2003), airing on the WB network, and HBO's *True Blood* (2008–12) also include werewolves. *Being Human* (2008–12), developed by Toby Whithouse for the BBC and adapted to the North American market for Syfy network (2010–12), features a vampire, a werewolf, and a ghost as room-mates trying to live "normal" human lives.

Significant werewolf films of the first decade of the third millennium include a sensationally gory re-make of *The Wolfman* (Joe Johnston, 2010), in which the notion of Sir John Talbot (Anthony Hopkins) being a truly evil werewolf offers a new take on the legendary film. Apart from the *Twilight* saga (discussed below), the *Underworld* film franchise made perhaps the largest contribution to mainstreaming the werewolf as a contemporary popular culture icon. Across four films, the franchise develops the storyline of an 800-year war between vampires and werewolves. *Underworld* and *Underworld: Evolution* (both Len Wiseman, 2003 and 2006) follow the central character of Selene (Kate Beckinsale), a "Death Dealer" specializing in hunting down and killing werewolves, who falls in love with the first werewolf–vampire hybrid, Michael Corvin (Scott Speedman). As Selene discovers more about the past and the treachery of the vampire leadership, moral right shifts from the vampires to the werewolves. Set in the deep Middle Ages, the prequel, *Underworld: Rise of the Lycans* (Paul Tatapoulos, 2009), focuses on the werewolf slave uprising led by Lucian (played by Michael Sheen, who ironically is also cast as the vampire Aro of the Volturi clan in the *Twilight* saga).

Amid the glut of straight-to-DVD, near home-movie quality productions that exploit the werewolf motif, several foreign and independent films stand out, including *The Brotherhood of the Wolf* (Christophe Gans, 2001), which draws on the historical incident of the eighteenth-century Beast of Gévaudan. *Wolf Girl* (marketed on video as *Blood Moon*; Thom Fitzgerald, 2001) features a gentle young woman with hypertrichosis (a disorder involving excessive hairiness historically used to "explain" the werewolf phenomenon) who tries an experimental serum; but as she loses her hair and begins to look normal, her personality becomes bestial. Two productions set in remote areas of the British Isles offer effective reworkings of the myth: *Dog Soldiers* (Neil Marshall, 2002) pits a British army unit on routine maneuvers against a household of werewolves in the Scottish highlands, while *Wild Country* (Craig Strachan, 2006) features a group of Welsh teenagers, including an unwed mother who has just given her baby up for adoption, encountering wolf-like beasts on a hiking trip.

Young Adult Werewolves

With its allegorical relationship to the bodily changes that humans undergo during puberty and adolescence (bulging flesh and growing hair), it is no wonder that the werewolf has become an increasingly popular figure in young adult literature and film. Two blockbuster novel series for young adults, subsequently adapted to film, include werewolves: J.K. Rowling's "Harry Potter" series (see **Harry Potter, Monsters In**) and Stephenie Meyer's "Twilight" series.

Meyer's "Twilight" saga, consisting of *Twilight* (2005; film Catherine Hardwicke, 2008), *New Moon* (2006; film Chris Weitz, 2009), *Eclipse* (2007; film David Slade, 2010), and *Breaking Dawn* (2008; film Bill Condon, 2011–12), follows the story of Bella Swan (Kristen Stewart in the films) who has moved to the Pacific Northwest to live with her father. When she falls in love with vampire Edward Cullen (Robert Pattinson in the films), her friendship with Jacob Black (Taylor Lautner in the films) appears jeopardized because of an ancient feud between the Cullens and the Quileutes. A genetic mutation allows certain members of this Native American band to shapeshift into the form of giant wolves; however, the series' final volume distinguishes Jacob and his clan from European werewolves.

J.K. Rowling's *Harry Potter and the Prisoner of Azkaban* (novel 1997; film Alfonso Cuarón, 2004) introduces a central character who appears in the remaining novels and films of the series, Professor Remus Lupin (David Thewlis in the films), who suffers from lycanthropy. Hired to teach the "Defense against the Dark Arts" course at Hogwarts, Lupin's curse threatens his career in teaching, even though he can control it with a potion. An intimate friend of Harry's father, he works with the Order of the Phoenix to fight Lord Voldemort in subsequent novels and films. In addition, the Death Eater—one of Voldemort's followers—Fenrir Greyback (Dave Legeno in the films) bears the name of the ferocious wolf of Norse mythology.

The independent Canadian film *Ginger Snaps* (John Fawcett, 2000) offers a quirky but smartly humorous (rather than parodic) take on two goth sisters grappling with a werewolf attack. Its success led to sequel and prequel films, *Ginger Snaps: Unleashed* (Brett Sullivan, 2004) and *Ginger Snaps Back: The Beginning* (Grant Harvey, 2004).

With the burgeoning market for young adult literature, it would be impossible to name the numerous texts and series featuring werewolves. Notable contributions include Mary Stewart's *A Walk in Wolf Wood: A Tale of Fantasy and Magic* (1980) and "The Werewolf," an oral tale told by William Faulkner and published by his niece, Dean Faulkner Wells, in 1980. Jane Yolen and Martin H. Greenberg's anthology *Werewolves* (1988) offers an introduction to the werewolf short story for young people. Typical of contemporary young adult werewolf fiction, Edo van Belkom's *Wolf Pack* (2004) novels feature four teenage werewolves saved from a forest fire in infancy by British Columbian forest ranger Garrett Brock. Noble, Argus, Harlan, and Tora—the lone female of the pack—are clearly sympathetic figures, with their desire to protect the environment, and their own privacy and right to existence.

The *Loup-Garou* (French-Canadian, Cajun and Caribbean Traditions)

The werewolf in French Canada and Cajun Louisiana, or *loup-garou*, originates in French folklore but develops unique traits in North American French-speaking populations. One form of the *loup-garou* evolved in the lumber camps of the north woods through stories told around the campfire, then brought home, re-told, and eventually preserved in literary form. It assumes the shape of a large black dog or wolf, the size of a man, with long sharp fangs and burning red eyes. In this predominantly Catholic environment, those who fail to say confession and attend mass for seven years risk becoming a werewolf, but they may be cured quite easily, simply by being cut with a sharp object. Claude Janelle catalogues at least eight literary versions published in Québec between 1848 and 1900, with the best known of these being Louis Fréchette's "The Loup Garou," first published in English in 1899, in *Christmas in French Canada*.

In addition to Christmas—a holiday sometimes connected to the werewolf—the sacrament of marriage appears threatened in traditional tales of the *loup-garou*, like those from the Great Lakes region retold by Marie Caroline Watson Hamlin in *Legends of Le Détroit* (1884). Similarly, J.J. Reneaux's cajun tale, "The Werewolf Bridegroom" (1994), tells of a rivalry between two suitors, one of whom becomes a werewolf. The *loup-garou* also appears in the television film *Moon of the Wolf* (Daniel Petrie, 1970), set in the southern swamps.

A much transformed version of the *loup-garou* exists in the Caribbean where, in the absence of actual wolves, the term has come to apply to other supernatural creatures. In Haiti, it refers to a wide range of revenants, while Trinidad's *lagahoo* has become a trickster figure. In many regions where wolves do not exist, hybrid creatures of supernatural origin reflect the local wildlife, such as the were-tigers of India and the leopard men of Africa.

On the one hand, the periodicity of werewolf "outbreaks"—periods or regions in which the werewolf tale seems to proliferate more than in others—reflects the monster's flexibility, its ability to engage very specific cultural concerns. On the other, as an almost universal icon, the werewolf allows us to explore the limits of our humanity, to fantasize about a return to the perceived simplicity of life as an uncivilized beast, or to act out our most violent impulses. The werewolf's diversity and staying power demonstrate its status as an almost archetypal figure.

Amy J. Ransom

References and Suggested Reading

Bynum, Carolyn Walker. *Metamorphosis and Identity*. New York: Zone Books, 2000.

Deal, David. *Television Fright Films of the 1970s*. Jefferson, NC: McFarland, 2007.

Dziemianowicz, Stefan. "The Werewolf." In *Icons of Horror and the Supernatural: The Encyclopedia of Our Worst Nightmares*, edited by S.T. Joshi, 653–87. Santa Barbara, CA: Greenwood Press, 2007.

Finn, Michael R. *Hysteria, Hypnotism, the Spirits, and Pornography: Fin-de-Siècle Cultural Discourses in the Decadent Rachilde*. Newark: University of Delaware Press, 2009.

Frost, Brian J. *The Essential Guide to Werewolf Literature*. Madison: University of Wisconsin Press, 2003.

Glut, Donald F. "When the Wolf Man Prowls." In *Classic Movie Monsters*, by Donald F. Glut, 1–67. Metuchen, NJ: Scarecrow Press, 1978.

Higley, Sarah L. "Finding the Man Under the Skin: Identity, Monstrosity, Expulsion, and the Werewolf." In *The Shadow Walkers: Jacob Grimm's Mythology of the Monstrous*, edited by Tom Shippey, 335–78. Tempe: Arizona Center for Medieval and Renaissance Studies, 2005.

Huckvale, David. "Interlude: Werewolves." In *Touchstones of Gothic Horror: A Film Genealogy of Eleven Motifs and Images*, by David Huckvale, 134–45. Jefferson, NC: McFarland, 2010.

Indovino, Shaina C. *Dracula and Beyond: Famous Vampires and Werewolves in Film and Literature*. Broomall: Maston Crest, 2011.

Janelle, Claude, ed. *Le XIXe siècle fantastique en Amérique française*. Quebec: Alire, 1999.

Jones, Stephen, ed. *The Mammoth Book of Wolf Men: The Ultimate Werewolf Anthology*. London: Constable and Robinson, 2009.

Lázaro-Reboll, Antonio. "*La Noche de Walpurgis/Shadow of the Werewolf*." In *The Cinema of Spain and Portugal*, edited by Alberto Mira, 129–38. London: Wallflower, 2005.

Leiber, Fritz. "The Hound." *Weird Tales*, 1942. Reprinted in *The Literary Werewolf: An Anthology*, edited by Charlotte F. Otten, 151–64. Syracuse: Syracuse University Press, 2002.

McCammon, Robert R. *The Wolf's Hour*. New York: Pocket Books, 1989.

Otten, Charlotte F., ed. *The Literary Werewolf: An Anthology*. Syracuse: Syracuse University Press, 2002.

Robisch, S.K., *Wolves and the Wolf Myth in American Literature*. Reno: University of Nevada Press, 2009.

Summers, Montague. *The Werewolf* [1933]. Reprint, New Hyde Park: University Books, 1966.

Young, Erin S. "Flexible Heroines, Flexible Narratives: The Werewolf Romances of Kelley Armstrong and Carrie Vaughn." *Extrapolation* 52, no. 2 (Summer 2011): 204–26.

WILD THINGS

Wild Things are the inhabitants of the imaginary land in Maurice Sendak's 1963 award-winning picture book, *Where the Wild Things Are*. There are a total of ten different monsters pictured in the book, although several appear in only one picture. Nearly all are oversized, and all but one are land-dwelling monsters. Each monster is a unique hybrid of animal (duck, lion, goat, alligator, bull, and so on), classical monster (**ogre**, **Chimera**, **griffin**, **Minotaur**, **siren**, **Sphinx**, and so on), and human characteristics (most notably, feet and hairstyles). They all have "terrible eyes" and "terrible claws," which get specified in the illustrations as large round eyes and long pointy claws on hands/feet. Most of them are quite toothy, but one is beaked.

Where the Wild Things Are also categorizes its child character, Max, as a "wild thing," creating an affiliation between children and monsters, and/or certain types of behavior and monstrousness (see **Children, Monstrous**). Throughout the story, Max wears a wolf costume (of the footy-pajamas-with-a-hood ilk). After acting destructively and aggressively (he puts nails in the wall, hangs a teddy bear by its arm, chases his dog, and threatens his mother), his mother deems him a "WILD THING" and sends him to bed without dinner. A forest magically grows in his room, and then Max hops aboard a boat and sails "off ... to where the wild things are." There, he tames the Wild Things by staring into their eyes, at which point the creatures declare him "the most wild thing of all," and make him "king of the wild things." Max's first order of business is to decree a "wild rumpus."

At this point, the pictures, which have been growing in size, growing out of their frames, and pushing the words to the edge of the pages, take over the narrative completely, suggesting a victory for the monster, the monstrous, the imagination, and the child. The Wild Things—Max and the monsters together—defeat the control of words, rules, civilization, and adults. Max, however, finds this state of affairs "lonely," and decides to give up "being king of where the wild things are" and return home. There, he finds "his supper waiting for him. And it was still hot." In his choice to abandon the monsters and their wild ways, Max also abandons his own monstrous wildness, which the book emphasizes by picturing Max in his room with his wolf-hood pushed off his head. Through his choice, he becomes human again. Likewise, reversing the earlier triumph of the image over the word (that is, the Wild Things and their ways over rules and socially acceptable behavior), the book's final page has no images at all: only words.

Some of the initial responses to the book felt that the Wild Things might be too scary for children, and they expressed concern that children might emulate Max's wild behavior. Children's responses to the book were, however, generally enthusiastic, and the book won the American Library Association's very prestigious award for outstanding art, the Caldecott Award, in 1964. The scholarship that surrounds the now much-lauded and much-loved book includes studies of the book and its monsters in terms of a psychological enactment of childhood emotions and/or a process of socialization; explorations of the book's engagement with cultural and conventional myth; and investigations of the historical and socio-political implications of the book's definition of the "wild" and the "monster."

Where the Wild Things Are and its monsters have also been translated to stage, screen, and objects (puzzles, stuffed animals, balloons, wall decals, and so on). The book was turned into an animated short in 1973 (Gene Deitch) and this was updated with new music and narration in 1988. Throughout the 1980s, Sendak, working with composer Peter Schickele (1935–), adapted the story into an opera. As part of this effort, Sendak not only expanded the story but also named the Wild Things (Tzippy, Moishe, Bruno, Emile, and Bernard). Most recently (2009), Spike Jonze and Dave Eggers wrote and produced a live-action film version. The film met with mixed reviews: it was admired for its artistry, wondered at in its use of technologies, and deemed "both the purest kids' movie ever and the starkest big-screen betrayal of children's literature" (Gutierrez 14). Eggers also novelized the screenplay, and the book appeared in a special furry monster edition, as well as a trade edition. Parodies of the book—including a Lovecraftian *Where the Deep Ones Are* (see **Lovecraft, Monsters In**)—as well as humorous homages, have become increasingly common.

Gretchen Papazian

References and Suggested Reading

Cech, John. *Angels and Wild Things: The Archetypal Poetics of Maurice Sendak*. University Park, PA: Pennsylvania State University Press, 1995.

Gutierrez, Peter. "Where the Wild Things Are and the Concept of the 'Kids' Movie." *Australian Screen Educator* (Summer 2010): 14, 56.

Kushner, Tony. *The Art of Maurice Sendak: 1980 to the Present*. New York: Abrams, 2003.

Shaddock, Jennifer. "*Where the Wild Things Are*: Sendak's Journey into the Heart of Darkness." *Children's Literature Association Quarterly* 22, no. 4 (Winter 1997–98): 155–9.

Spufford, Francis. "The Forest." In *The Child That Books Built: A Life of Reading*, by Francis Spufford, 23–63. New York: Metropolitan Books, 2002.

WINDIGO

The figure of the Windigo is familiar to Native and First Nations Algonquin peoples and predominant in Anishinaabe (Ojibwe) and Cree literature. It goes by various names with variant spellings (see Colombo 2) but is most commonly rendered as Windigo, Wendigo, or Witiko. The Windigo is a malevolent **manitou** or spirit whose insatiable appetite for human flesh can never be satisfied. The Windigo also has the power to turn humans into cannibals who suffer from the same voracity.

Ojibwe storyteller Basil Johnston explains that Windigos "came into being in winter and stopped villagers and beset wanderers. Ever hungry, they craved human flesh, which is the only substance that could sustain them. The irony is that having eaten human flesh, the Weendigoes grew in size, so their hunger and craving remained in proportion to their size; thus they were eternally starving" (*The Manitous* 247). The Windigo's appearance reflects the bitter winters of the remote North, and its presence is often signaled by sudden cold and wind. Although it can take many forms, the Windigo is often depicted as "a giant spirit-creature with a heart and sometimes a body of ice," endowed with "prodigious strength" and able to travel "as fast as the wind" (Atwood 66–7). However, the assumption that the Windigo is exclusively malevolent is challenged by assertions that, "though Weendigo was fearsome and visited punishment upon those committing excesses, he nevertheless conferred rewards upon the moderate. He was excess who encouraged moderation" (Johnston, *Ojibwe Heritage* 167).

Colombo's research identifies the first recorded instance of the Windigo in Bacqueville de la Potherie's 1722 travel narrative (2). The journals and memoirs of Hudson Bay Company employees document cases beginning in the 1770s (Smallman 572). For four centuries, the legends grew, culled from Algonquian stories. The Windigo entered the mainstream through compilations, translations, and borrowings, including Mary Hartwell Catherwood's "The Windigo," from her 1894 book *The Chase of Saint-Castin, and Other Stories of the French in the New World*. Catherwood was among the first who purported to retell original Native tales. Other anthologies of "true Windigo stories" include Herbert T. Schwartz, *Windigo and Other Tales of the Ojibways* (1969) and Howard Norman, *Where the Chill Came From: Cree Windigo Tales and Journeys* (1982). Richard Erdoes and Alfonso Ortiz retell the Cree and Métis story "Wesakaychak, the Windigo, and the Ermine" in *American Indian Trickster Tales* (1999). Anne M. Dunn's Ojibwe stories collected in *Winter Thunder: Retold Tales* (2000) include "Snowbird and the Windigo."

John Robert Colombo's *Windigo: An Anthology of Fact and Fantastic Fiction* (1982) provides a good example of how indigenous stories and commercial fiction combine in the development of the Windigo as a literary motif. Colombo's anthology has it all: weird tales of the supernatural by authors like Algernon Blackwood, poetic parody by Ogden Nash, "scientific" analysis from anthropologists and sociologists Ruth Landes and Morton I. Teicher, and Native stories from Ojibwe artists including Basil Johnston and Norval Morrisseau. In "The

Voice of the Wendigo," from *Condor Tales of the Supernatural in Alaska and Canada* (2000), Jacques L. Condor himself offers a "true story of a man who spoke [the name Windigo] and did not live to speak any other" (257) that appeals like the best of pulp horror fiction.

Stephen King's *Pet Sematary* (1984), adapted to film by director Mary Lambert in 1989, mixes the Windigo with another familiar exploitation of Native elements, the idea of the "Indian burial ground" that acts as a conduit between realms of existence. Other important literary works include: Eden Robinson's "Dogs in Winter" from her collection *Traplines* (1999); Stephen Graham Jones's *The Fast Red Road: A Plainsong* (2000) and *All the Beautiful Sinners* (2003); Michael Jensen's *Fireland* (2004); Margaret Atwood's *Oryx and Crake* (2005); and Edmund Metatawabin's *Hanaway* (2006). Louise Erdrich's poem "Windigo" is often anthologized. Young adult offerings that popularize the Windigo include Kathrene Pinkerton's *Windigo* (1945), Jane and Paul Annixter's *Windigo: A Wilderness Story of Fear and Courage* (1963), and *Bone Chiller* (2008) by award-winning young adult mystery writer Graham McNamee.

Allegorical adaptations exploit the socio-political tensions of contact between Euro-Western imperialism and indigenous culture, as the Windigo has become synonymous with Western capitalistic expansion and cultural appropriation (see Forbes; Johnston, *The Manitous* 235–7; C. Richard King; Root). Forbes, who compares the Windigo to "a cannibal or, more specifically, to an evil person or spirit who terrorizes other creatures by means of terrible evil acts, including cannibalism," draws on the etymology of the Algonquian word "wétikowatisewin," an abstract noun referring to "diabolical wickedness or cannibalism," and concludes that "imperalism and exploitation are forms of cannibalism and, in fact, are precisely those forms of cannibalism which are most diabolical or evil" (24). Historical evidence establishes the connection between the proliferation of Windigos and colonization, as indigenous peoples were stressed by dwindling resources and deadly diseases introduced by European settlers. Goldman contends that, "as a result of these illnesses, kinship groups faced huge losses; hunters died, and without them, starvation was inevitable" (171). Following this chain of reasoning, starvation spawned the Windigo, and colonization caused starvation; therefore, colonization brought the Windigo into being. Ethnohistorians make this case emphatically. Smallman examines the historical reports of Windigos in the context of commerce, emphasizing that "explorers, fur traders, missionaries, the police, psychologists, and social scientists sought to understand, define, and use this 'disorder,' as companies and the state sought to assert their authority in Cree and Ojibwa communities. Accordingly, an imperial context shaped both the discursive and practical responses of non-Algonquians to the windigo" (571–2).

A metaphor of "colonialism as cannibalism," the Windigo trope can alternatively represent Euro-Western consumption of indigenous peoples, lands, and resources or judgment and justice, or revenge, upon colonizers for their greed and brutality. Characters suffering possession by the Windigo might represent either the colonizer or the colonized, as the roles of both imperialist conqueror and victim reflect states of excess and imbalance. This metaphor is consistent with the Algonquian identification of the Windigo as the personification of excess, greed, and gluttony (Johnston, *Ojibwe Heritage* 66).

Director Antonia Bird's film *Ravenous* (1999), for example, is a cautionary tale of manifest destiny in which white men become Windigos, and the metaphor of colonialism as cannibalism is literalized: America is eating its way west in the guise of cannibal Army officers. The Menominee character George (Joseph Runningfox) warns an incredulous Colonel (Jeffrey Jones) that a Windigo is threatening their company. George produces an image of the Windigo painted on leather but must resort to the Native language of the Ojibwe to describe its meaning. The Captain translates: "A man who eats another's flesh, usually an enemy, and he takes—steals—his strength, essence, spirit, and his hunger becomes craven, insatiable. And the more he eats, the more he wants, and the more he eats, the stronger he becomes." The Captain pauses and asks: "George? People don't still do that, do they?" George answers: "Like the white man eats the body of Jesus Christ every Sunday." In the end, the only survivor is another Menominee, George's sister Martha (played by Sheila Tousey).

Director Larry Fessenden's *The Last Winter* (2006) returns the role of the Windigo to a Native character, Dawn (Joanne Shenandoah, a Grammy award-winning singer and a Wolf Clan member of the Iroquois Confederacy). The story depicts nature's revenge on an American oil company that is exploring the Alaskan wilderness for its next fix, manifesting a mixture of spirit **ghosts** that protect Mother Earth from the invader; this time, it is the Native who goes Windigo, displaying the maniacal behavior of someone who has lost sovereignty over her own mental and spiritual being. In both of these adaptations, the characters who go Windigo adhere to historical accounts, remaining "generally rational except at short intervals when the paroxysms seize them: their motions then are various and diametrically contrary at one time to what they are the next moment—sullen, thoughtful, wild look and perfectly mute: [then] staring, in sudden convulsions, wild, incoherent and extravagant language" (Brown and Brightman 91).

Among more nuanced uses, Fessenden's earlier film *Windigo* (2001) provides a psychological take, as the Windigo spirit who takes revenge on a murderous woodsman seems to manifest in response to a young boy's depression and melancholia. Director Norma Bailey's film adaptation (2003) of Gordon Sinclair's *Cowboys and Indians: The J.J. Harper Story* (2000) introduces Windigo vengeance to the original story, the true account of Winnipeg Police Constable Robert Cross's murder of First Nations Chief J.J. Harper in 1988. Although the crime and Cross's secret are covered up, he is overcome with guilt and commits suicide. In the film adaptation, Harper's father James recognizes that Cross is being punished by a Windigo and recommends pity and compassion. Grant Harvey's *Ginger Snaps Back: The Beginning* (2004), the third installment and prequel in the *Ginger Snaps* (John Fawcett, 2000) and *Ginger Snaps: Unleashed* (Brett Sullivan, 2004) trilogy, traces the origins of **werewolf** sisters Ginger and Brigitte to the Windigo of the nineteenth-century Canadian frontier, casting the Windigo as a defender of indigenous territories against encroachment by European traders and settlers.

Indigenous artists who utilize the Windigo trope to explore long-standing issues of injustice include Armand Ruffo (Ojibwe) and Tomson Highway (Cree). Ruffo's film *A Windigo Tale* (2010) studies the damaging effects of the residential boarding school system on generations of Canadian First Nations peoples. Highway's autobiographically based tour-de-force novel *Kiss of the Fur Queen* (2008) also uses Windigo imagery to contextualize the experience of residential boarding school, where he and his brother were sexually assaulted as boys.

The Windigo's cannibalistic behavior recalls the **vampire**, the **zombie**, and the werewolf. "Like the vampire, it feasts on flesh and blood," writes Colombo. "Like the werewolf, it shape-changes at will. Like the **Medusa**, it may scare its victim to death" (2). Nelson even offers the intriguing intertextual assertion that J.R.R. Tolkien based the Nazgûl, who terrify Sauron's enemies in *The Return of the King*, on the Windigo (see **Tolkien, Monsters In**). The belief that a person under the Windigo's influence undergoes a metamorphosis from human to creature/monster and back again foregrounds the werewolf tradition; in fact, Métis and French Canadian voyageurs called the Windigo the *loup-garou*, the French word for "werewolf" (Podruchny 685–93). Despite resemblances to other members of the monster pantheon, however, the Windigo should be distinguished as a cultural icon unique to the indigenous peoples of North America.

Indigenous scholars emphasize that Western perspectives are incapable of accounting for the Windigo phenomenon, which can only be "analyzed from within northern Algonquian cosmologies rather than Western perspectives if it is to be adequately accounted for" (Carlson 355). In hegemonic Western discourse, Windigo is dismissed as a form of insanity, and Windigo stories are relegated to the status of myth or legends born of the harsh winters across North America, where food became scarce and people sometimes resorted to cannibalism to stay alive. The reality of the Windigo for indigenous peoples is much more complex. Waldram decries the long-standing Western tradition of attributing Windigo possession to a psychological disorder: "Early historic and ethnographic reports of wendigo lead to … the transformation of this folk belief into a bona fide mental disorder, windigo psychosis, considered by many to be a culture-bound syndrome. But no actual cases of windigo psychosis have ever been studied" (17). Resorting to a fitting monster analogy, Waldram cautions against the misunderstanding and appropriation that has troubled the exchange between indigenous and Western thinking from those by-gone days when missionaries first recorded their versions of Native presence: "Windigo psychosis may well be the most perfect example of the construction of an Aboriginal mental disorder by the scholarly professions, and its persistence dramatically underscores how constructions by these professions have, like **Frankenstein's monster**, taken on a life of their own" (17–18).

Grace L. Dillon

References and Suggested Reading

Atwood, Margaret. *Strange Things: The Malevolent North in Canadian Literature*. Oxford: Oxford University Press, 1996.

Brightman, Robert A. "The Windigo in the Material World." *Ethnohistory* 35, no. 4 (Fall 1988): 337–79.

Brown, Jennifer, and Robert Brightman. *The Orders of the Dreamed*. Winnipeg: University of Manitoba Press, 1988.

Carlson, Nathan D. "Reviving Witiko (Windigo): An Ethnohistory of 'Cannibal Monsters' in the Athabasca District of Northern Alberta, 1878–1910." *Ethnohistory* 56 (2009): 355–94.

Colombo, John Robert, ed. *Windigo: An Anthology of Fact and Fantastic Fiction*. Saskatoon, Saskatchewan: Western Producer Prairie Books, 1982.

Condor, Jacques L., and Maka-Tai-Meh. "The Voice of the Wendigo." In *Condor Tales of the Supernatural in Alaska and Canada*, by Jacques L. Condor and Maka-Tai-Meh, 255–98. Poughkeepsie, NY: Vivisphere Publishing, 2000.

Forbes, Jack. *Columbus and Other Cannibals: The Wetiko Disease of Exploitation, Imperialism and Terrorism*. New York: Autonomedia, 1992.

Goldman, Marlene. "Margaret Atwood's Wilderness Tips: Apocalyptic Cannibal Fiction." In *Cannibalism and the Boundaries of*

Cultural Identity: Eating Their Words, edited by Kristen Guest, 167–85. New York: State University of New York Press, 2001.

Johnston, Basil. *The Manitous: The Supernatural World of the Ojibway*. New York: HarperCollins, 1995.

——. *Ojibwe Heritage*. Lincoln: University of Nebraska Press, 1990.

King, C. Richard. "The (Mis)Uses of Cannibalism in Contemporary Cultural Critique." *Diacritics* 30, no. 1 (Spring 2000): 106–23.

King, Thomas. *The Truth about Stories: A Native Narrative*. Minneapolis: University of Minnesota Press, 2003.

Nelson, Dale. J. "Possible Echoes of Blackwood and Dunsany in Tolkien's Fantasy." *Tolkien Studies* 1 (2004): 177–81.

Podruchny, Carolyn. "Werewolves and Windigos: Narratives of Cannibal Monsters in French-Canadian Voyageur Oral Tradition." *Ethnohistory* 51, no. 4 (Fall 2004): 677–700.

Root, Deborah. *Cannibal Culture: Art, Appropriation, and the Commodification of Difference*. Boulder: Westview Press, 1996.

Smallman, Shawn. "Spirit Beings, Mental Illness, and Murder: Fur Traders and the Windigo in Canada's Boreal Forest, 1774 to 1935." *Ethnohistory* 57, no. 4 (2010): 571–96.

Waldram, James B. *Revenge of the Windigo: The Construction of the Mind and Mental Health of North American Aboriginal Peoples*. Toronto: University of Toronto Press, 2004.

WITCH/WIZARD

Medea, Merlin, Morgan Le Fey, Broom-Hilda, Harry Potter. Everyone has a favorite witch or wizard (male practitioner of witchcraft, also sometimes referred to as a warlock) story from his or her childhood. The concept of the individual able to perform "magic"—to harness the powers of other worlds and realms to prophesize or effect one's will through spells and other invisible means—spreads across time and cultures.

Fig. 38 *Baba Yaga* by Aeron Alfrey

In ancient Greek literature, the witch often embodied dangerous sexuality, as exemplified by **Circe** in Homer's *Odyssey* (c. seventh or eighth century BCE) and the vengeful Medea from Euripides's fifth-century BCE play. In medieval literature, witches appear in the European romances of the French troubadours, as well as in the various incarnations of Merlin who appears in Robert de Boron's twelfth-century poem of the same name and many other writings spanning the centuries. Tales of witches and wizards stretch across Europe during these centuries and include stories about Morgan in the works of Chrétien de Troyes (late twelfth century) and about Atlante in Ariosto's *Orlando Furioso* (1516) who carries humans away to his enchanted castle.

The witch was a malleable figure in eighteenth- and nineteenth-century European literature. Victor Hugo used the witch to emblematize the falsely accused, such as Esmeralda in *The Hunchback of Notre Dame* (1831; see **Quasimodo**). Older tales of witchcraft were also revived and recast, such as Charles Perrault's 1697 retelling of *Sleeping Beauty* and the many early nineteenth-century tales of the Brothers Grimm. In Russian literature, witches play important roles in Aleksandr Pushkin's poem "Ruslan and Ludmila" (1820) and Nikolai Gogol's collection of short stories, *Evenings on a Farm Near Dikanka* (1831–32).

The United States and Latin America, influenced by a more transnational perspective and also their own histories and cultures, have added substantially to the ever-growing compendium of tales about witches with supernatural abilities. In these works, as in the works of ancient Greece, the witch is often associated with sexual power, as in John Updike's *The Witches of Eastwick* (1984). In Latin America, witch-like characters are often wily seductresses, indigenous shamen, or, as in the novels of Gabriel García Márquez (1927–), shady political dictators.

In the contemporary world, the witch most often casts his or her spell through the media of film and television where the conjuror can be sinister, supernatural, playful, intellectual, or a hybrid of these types. Stories of witch-hunts and hangings have been dramatized repeatedly—most notably by Arthur Miller in his drama of Salem, *The Crucible* (1952), and its many cinematic and televisual adaptations. On the lighter side are TV sitcoms such as *Bewitched* (1964–72), *Charmed* (1988–2006), and *Sabrina, the Teenage Witch* (1996–2003), and films including *Bell, Book and Candle* (Richard Quine, 1958) and Disney's *Hocus Pocus* (Kenny Ortega, 1993). Of course, witches and sorcery are central to the "Harry Potter" series (see **Harry Potter, Monsters In**). Witches and wizards have a long and complicated history and continue to enchant readers and viewers around the world.

Stephenie Young

Witches and Wizards in European Literature and Film

Witches, variously referred to as sorcerers, enchantresses, wizards, warlocks, magicians, necromancers, and conjurors, have been a key feature of popular European literature from antiquity to the present day. The warlock, influenced by the Biblical Solomon, the apocryphal Simon Magus, and the classical deities Apollo and Dionysus, is often an ambivalent character who serves both good and evil. The witch has a less equivocal reputation, mainly due to the sinister command of Exodus 22:18: "Thou shalt not suffer a witch to live."

In the literature of the ancient world, witch figures are often autonomous, sexually dominant females who take mortal lovers and seek revenge when abandoned (see **Women, Monstrous**). Chiefly remembered from Homer's *Odyssey* (c. seventh or eighth century BCE), Circe is the sorceress skilled in potion-making who transforms some of Odysseus's companions into animals and attempts to seduce Odysseus himself. Circe advises Odysseus to travel to the Underworld to consult the **ghost** of the prophet Tiresias on how to appease the gods, thus enabling him to return home. Featured in Euripides's fifth-century BCE *Medea*, Apollonius's third-century BCE *Argonautica*, and Ovid's first-century CE *Metamorphoses*, the witch Medea, Circe's niece, is a priestess of the witch-goddess Hecate. Medea falls in love with Jason and aids him in his quest for the Golden Fleece, providing the crew with an ointment that makes them indomitable. According to Ovid, Medea can calm the sea, cause forests and mountains to quake, banish the Moon, and summon ghosts from their graves.

The witches and warlocks of medieval literature display the same ambivalence as their classical forbears. While many of the supernatural figures of the Middle Ages, including Merlin and Morgan Le Fay, are firmly fixed in the British popular imagination, their origins are in the European romances of the medieval French troubadours that abound with magical characters who complicate the plots with evil turns or empower protagonists with enchantments and magical gifts. Although first mentioned by the English Geoffrey of

Monmouth in *Vita Merlini* (1150), much of what we know of Merlin comes from these French romances. The enigmatic magician appears in Robert de Boron's twelfth-century poem "Merlin." The child of a **demon** and a virgin, Merlin is baptized immediately at birth, thus escaping his intended fate as the Antichrist. His hellish parentage enables his superhuman abilities, however, and in the various retellings of his history, he is usually bestowed with the power to transform himself into other humans and inanimate objects. In the thirteenth-century prose retelling of the story, the *Lancelot-Grail* (also known as the *Vulgate Cycle*), Merlin's ambivalence is more pronounced. His demonic heritage is emphasized and it is unclear whether or not he has been baptized.

The witch Morgain, Morgana, or Morgan le Fay also appears frequently in French medieval literature. Chrétien de Troyes writes about Morgan in *Erec and Enide* (c. 1170) and *Yvain, le Chevalier au Lion* (c. 1170), establishing the witch as a gifted healer and Arthur's sister. The *Vulgate* develops her story further, describing her magical education at a convent after Uther Pendragon murders her father to marry her mother. Sometimes recognized as the son of Morgana, Oberon, the magical king of the fairies (see **Fairy**), also originates from European rather than English literature. His name is the French translation of Alberich, a **dwarf**-sized sorcerer of the Merovingian dynasty in the *Nibelungenlied* (*The Song of the Nibelungs*), the epic poem written in Middle High German in the eleventh century. In the thirteenth-century *Huon of Bordeaux*, the eponymous character is assigned seemingly impossible tasks after killing the son of Charlemagne, eventually achieved with the assistance of Oberon.

The *Chansons de Geste*, epic French poems dating to the late eleventh century, feature another magician, Maugris, in the *Renaud de Montauban* cycle. A human raised by fairies, Maugris possesses supernatural abilities. He also appears in the romances of the Italian Renaissance, namely Matteo Mario Boiardo's *Orlando Innamorato* (1495) where he is renamed Malagigi. In this epic, he is a necromancer enlisted by Angelica to bring her lover to her magical island. Equipped with a book and a magic ring, Malagigi is skilled in disguise and putting people to sleep. Ludovico Ariosto's sequel *Orlando Furioso* (1516) features a similar magician, Atlante, who spirits humans away to his enchanted castle on a **hippogriffin**. Angelica is something of a Circe figure, using a combination of witchcraft and feminine wiles to divert Rinaldo to the opulent palace and gardens she has created on a deserted island. She later rescues the titular Orlando from the throes of another witch-like figure, Dragontina. Alcina in *Orlando Furioso* also has strong connections to Circe. Her island, where Ruggiero finds himself, is a sensual paradise, but populated by Alcina's former lovers transformed into inanimate objects.

The appearance of the Faust myth in the Renaissance called for a re-examination of magic in which the magical practitioner took center stage. Based on the myths surrounding the reputed magician Johannes Faust, the multitude of chapbooks published in the late sixteenth century detailed the exploits of the Wittenberg academic who sold his soul to the **Devil** for unlimited knowledge and power. Known as the *Faustbooks*, these German chapbooks were extremely popular and were translated and widely disseminated across Europe. The story was later immortalized by Marlowe for the English stage in *The Tragical History of the Life and Death of Doctor Faustus* (1604) and by Goethe in *Faust* (1806) (see **Mephistopheles**).

The witch figure became a key feature of European Gothic literature in the nineteenth century. Johannes Wilhem Meinhold's *Die*

Bernsteinhexe (*Amber Witch*, 1839) and *Sidonia Von Borcke* (1847) both tell the stories of witch figures. The latter narrates the life of Pomeranian Sidonia, beheaded and burnt for witchcraft in 1620. The equally popular *Amber Witch*, set in the Thirty Years War, concerns Maria Schweidler, wrongly accused of witchcraft and rescued at the last minute by her lover as she is about to be burned at the stake. The false accusation of witchcraft was a popular literary motif in nineteenth-century literature; it is the charge laid against Esmeralda in Victor Hugo's *Notre-Dame de Paris* (*The Hunchback of Notre Dame*, 1831 [see **Quasimodo**]).

The nineteenth-century revival of interest in folktales saw some of the most well-known witch and wizard stories in print for the first time, although this practice dates back to Charles Perrault whose fairytales were published in 1697. Perrault introduces the figure of the Wicked Fairy Godmother in *La Belle au Bois Dormant* (*Sleeping Beauty*), whose malevolent magic is fueled by revenge and exhibits a preoccupation with children that would continue to characterize the witches and wizards that populate folklore. In many of these stories, the magical characters serve as sinister figures to be overcome in order for good to triumph. One of German Romantic E.T.A Hoffmann's most grotesquely fascinating stories is "Der Sandmann" (1816; see **Sandman, The**), which presents an inversion of the friendly Sandman of children's tales; Hoffmann's Sandman steals the eyes of children who cannot sleep. In contrast, Hoffmann's Doctor Drosselmeyer from "Nusskracker und Mausekonig," a clockmaker and inventor, is a benevolent magician to his godchildren, gifting them with the nutcracker doll that sets Marie's adventures in motion. Appearing just a few years before Hoffmann's stories are the *Children's and Household Tales* (1812) by the Brothers Grimm, which feature the well-known witch from Hansel and Gretel who tempts the children with her house of sweets, only to imprison one and keep the other as a worker, fattening them up to be eaten. The enchantress in *Rapunzel* similarly acquires a child and imprisons the young protagonist in a tower, as does the titular witch in Hans Christian Andersen's *Snow Queen* (1845). Andersen's *Little Mermaid* retells the Faustian pact, as the **mermaid** exchanges the gift of speech for her human life, orchestrated by the sinister Sea Witch.

The popularity of these magical characters has persisted into the twentieth century, with witches and wizards featuring in many popular European films. The wizard of European cinema has often been a conjuror, performing tricks rather than engaging in more sinister, supernaturally powered magic, in keeping with a more secular, skeptical audience. One of the first French films ever made was *Le Magicien*, a silent film directed by Georges Méliès in 1898. The success of Ingmar Bergman's 1958 *Ansiktet* (*The Magician*) and the 2010 French film *The Illusionist* demonstrate a continuing fascination with these masters of visual tricks. Other warlock films include Ildiko Enyedi's Hungarian film *Simon Magus* (1997) about the Biblical conjuror, and the Kabbalistic magic of Rabbi Loew in three German films about the mystical **Golem** of Prague, *Der Golem* (*The Golem*; Henrik Galeen and Paul Wegener, 1915), *Der Golem und die Tänzerin* (*The Golem and the Dancing Girl*; Rochus Gliese and Paul Wegener, 1917), and *Der Golem, wie er indie Welt Kam* (*The Golem: How He Came into the World*; Carl Boese and Paul Wegener, 1920).

Treatment of witches in European film reveals a fascination with the dubious history of witch persecution. Released in 1922, the Scandinavian silent film *Häxan* is a curious mix of horror and documentary.

Directed by Benjamin Christensen, the film draws much from the *Malleus Maleficarum*, the notorious witch-hunting manual penned by Dominican inquisitor Heinrich Kramer in 1487. Based on the 1909 drama *Anne Pedersdotter* by Norwegian playwright Hans Weirs-Jenssen, Carl Theodor Dreyer's 1943 Danish film *Vredens Dag* (*Day of Wrath*) dramatizes the events surrounding a sixteenth-century Norwegian witch trial. Michael Armstrong's graphic 1970 film *Mark of the Devil* (*Hexen bis aufs Blut gequält*) focuses on the sadistic methods employed by witch-hunters, as does *Kladivo na čarodějnice* (*The Witch's Hammer*) a 1970 Czech film about the witch-hunts in Czechoslovakia. Directed by Otakar Vávra, the film is based on a 1963 novel of the same name by Václav Kaplicky. The 1952 Finnish film *Noita Palaa Elämään* (directed by Roland af Hällstrom) depicts the unnatural occurrences in a small village following the discovery of a witch's body buried in the bog three centuries earlier. There have also been explorations of witch trials that took place on foreign soil. In 1957 French director Raymond Rouleau adapted Arthur Miller's Salem drama *The Crucible* (1952) into the French film *Les Sorcières de Salem*, with a screenplay written by Jean-Paul Sartre.

Witches have also featured prominently in Italian horror films. A trilogy directed by Dario Argento (*Suspiria* in 1977, *Inferno* in 1980, and *Mother of Tears* in 2007) depicts some of the most powerful and terrifying witches to ever appear on screen. The first, a cult classic, features an American ballerina who discovers that her new dance school is run by witches. Other Italian witch films include *Don't Torture a Duckling* (Lucio Fulci, 1972) and *Baba Yaga* (Corrado Farina, 1973).

The folktale witch also continues to entertain European audiences, particularly the fairytale associations of witchcraft and beauty. In the 1960 film *Black Sunday* by Mario Bava, a beautiful young girl killed for witchcraft returns from the dead. The 1966 film *La Strega in Amore* (*The Witch in Love*, Damiano Damiani) features a witch obsessed with beauty who makes herself appear youthful to seduce a younger man. More recently, French director Catherine Breillat has adapted the fairytales of Perrault and Andersen into modern films, including *La Belle Endormie* (*The Sleeping Beauty*, 2010) in which the young Princess Anastasia (Carla Besnaïnou) is cursed by a witch-like fairy into an enchanted sleep.

Bronwyn Johnston

References and Suggested Reading

Butler, Elizabeth M. *The Fortunes of Faust*. Stroud: Sutton Publishing, 1998.

Kisacky, Julia. *Magic in Boiardo and Ariosto*. New York: Peter Lang, 2000.

Lovecraft, Howard Philips. *Supernatural Horror in Literature* [1927]. Reprint, New York: Dover Publications, 1973.

Ogden, Daniel. *Night's Black Agents: Witches, Wizards, and the Dead of the Ancient World*. London: Hambledon Continuum, 2008.

British Witches and Wizards

Great Britain has a well-established literary and cinematic tradition of female witches and, to a much lesser extent, male witches (warlocks or wizards). Accordingly, this discussion will first address witches and then wizards.

British Witches

Early modern England saw the female witch as part pathetic, part predator—a victim and an opportunist who used fear rather than kindness to ensure Christian charity. Legally, she was a felon: her *modus operandi*—curses, magic, and familiars—enabled her to damage, hurt, spread disease, and kill. Spiritually, she was corrupt: she swore, cursed, stole, and could not pray. Physically, she was monstrous: her skin numbed, flesh extended into witch's marks, bodies floated, eyes stopped shedding tears—all metamorphoses that might be undone through counter-magics (cutting, scratching, piercing, or killing the witch or the object she bewitched to break the magic's hold). Moreover, those accused of being witches were almost exclusively female: 80–90 percent of the approximately 1,000 individuals executed in England as witches were women. Women also acted as local arbiters of witch beliefs, they suffered as victims and mothers of victims, and served as witnesses, accusers, and witch-searchers. Although magic might run in families, it was facilitated by familiars. Predominately animal spirits—although a number of humanoid spirits also appear—familiars corporealized witchcraft and provided the amorphous spiritual energy needed to bewitch, albeit at a cost. They bargained for a witch's soul, nested in her home, consumed her like parasites, and marked her body.

Ideas about witchcraft worked to make sense of the unwelcome overlap between the natural and supernatural landscapes. These beliefs were not the exclusive purview of children, fools, melancholics, and Catholics, despite Reginald Scot's assertion to the contrary in his skeptical *Discovery of Witchcraft* (1584). Appearing across age, gender, education, and class divides, such beliefs were sustained by a myriad of popular pamphlets, sermons, treaties, and laws passed. Prohibitions against lyblacs (instrumental magics) and morth-dæds (necromancy) appear in the laws of Ælfrēd (849–899), Edward the Elder (c. 899–924), Æthelstan (c. 893/895–939), Æthelred (968–1016), and Cnut (c. 985/995–1035). English kings demanded the exile of witches, soothsayers, magicians, whores, and morth-workers. King Edgar (959–975), who specifically "forbid well worshipings and necromancies" and the "vain practices which are carried on with various spells" (Thorpe 249), found his prohibitions were firmly backed by Ælfric's Homily on St Bartholomew's Day, which cautioned those who sought health in "forbidden practices, or by accursed enchantments, or with any witchcraft ... so destroyed their souls" (Meaney 41). Henry I (c. 1068/1069–1135) enacted laws against malefic murder; in the reign of King John (1199–1216) we find gossipy examples of "normal" magical practices; and in the reign of Edward III (1272–1307) magical accounts get gorier. In 1371, a Southwark man was brought before John Knyvet in the King's Bench, having been found carrying a magical book as well as the head and face of a dead man in his bag; he denied practicing magic so, without an indictment to hold him, he was let out of prison but charged for the cost of burning his magical implements.

In these early contexts, we find an especially potent and provocative figure of a witch who is a healer, gardener, magician, mathematician, and necromancer: Morgan Le Fey. Appearing first in Geoffrey of Monmouth's *Vita Merlini* (c. 1150), she has the herbal skills of a cunning woman and the ability to shapeshift not seen again until Anne Bodenham appears accused as a witch who could shapeshift into a "mastive dog, a black lyon, a white bear, a woolf, a bull, and an cat" in the anonymous 1653 account, *Dr Lambs Darling* (7; see **Shapeshifter**). Her skills grow across Chrétien de Troyes *Erec et Enide* (c. 1165), where she continues to heal, and into the *Vulgate Cycle*, where she is first made wicked. In the late fourteenth-century *Sir Gawain and the Green Knight*, she is described as learned, committed, and masterful in her use of rare magic, and in Sir Thomas Malory's epic romance *Le Morte D'Arthur* (printed by William Caxton in 1485), she is a hereditary practitioner; she is

Arthur's sister and a student of the darkest arts "lerned so moche that she was a grete Clerke of Nygromancye" (Malory A2v).

In the early modern period, laws passed by Henry VIII (1509–47), Elizabeth I (1558–1603), and James I (1603–25) were designed to root out elements that supposedly tainted the female gender and polluted their homes. They gave neighbors and family a language to explain inexplicable misfortunes, were a means to address unresolved animosity, and were a way to highlight the state as arbiter of justice; most women admitted to witching only once in court. The most famous witches of the English stage might be William Shakespeare's wyrd sisters as they appear in *Macbeth* (1611), a play written to appeal to King James's heritage, his interest in witch-hunting as articulated in *Daemonologie* (1597), and his later interest in debunking bewitchments as imagined or faked. These fearsome stage crones are largely responsible for the idea of spellcraft as spoken in rhyming riddles and the preposterous notion that witches had the eyes of newts and toes of frogs on hand; the women hanged as witches in England would more likely bewitch by simply mumbling nasty barbs under their breath. The women who toyed with Macbeth were not Shakespeare's only witches, however. The damned and foul witch Sycorax is a powerful and absent figure in *The Tempest* (1611), and the role of Mother Prat—alternately known as the wise woman of Brainford or as a cozening queen—in *The Merry Wives of Windsor* (1597) is unwittingly and unwillingly played by Falstaff as comeuppance and comic relief.

Also for the stage, Thomas Dekker, John Ford, and William Rowley's tragic comedy *The Witch of Edmonton* (1621) is based largely on *The Wonderfull Discoverie of Elizabeth Sawyer* (1621), the published account of the interviews Henry Goodcole conducted with alleged witch Elizabeth Sawyer while she awaited sentencing in Newgate prison. The play presents a somewhat sympathetic vision of the early English witch as a woman treated, at best, shoddily by her neighbors and her walking, talking, smart-aleck dog-familiar Tom.

In 1641, the anonymous *Prophesie of Mother Shipton in the Raigne of King Henry the Eighth* (1641) welcomes England's most flexible figure of a prophetical witch to the literary record. Shipton's prophecies, which supposedly predict events past the Civil War (1642–51), was printed and reprinted for the next several decades and, as her words remained in circulation, she also became a literary figure and a star of the stage. Her life was first fictionalized in Thomas Thompson's play *The Life of Mother Shipton* (1670) or, depending on the dating, Richard Head's *The Life and Death of Mother Shipton* (the extant version is 1677, but the text mentions an early publication in 1667). Both play and pamphlet, fictional accounts of her supposed life at Knaresborough near the dropping well in Yorkshire, invoke the Devil as her husband or sire and make her more of a witch than a prophet, a quasi-monster in her ugliness. *The Strange and Wonderful History of Mother Shipton* (1686) further fictionalized her life, naming her Ursula Soothtell and marrying her off to a man named Tom Shipton. Mother Shipton continued to be invoked; she was made into a metaphor by the author of *The Story of the St Albans Ghost* (1712), a tract sometimes thought to be authored by John Arbuthnot (1667–1735), Daniel Defoe (c. 1659–1731), Jonathan Swift (1667–1745), and/or William Wagstaffe (1685–1725), and applied to Frances Jennings (c. 1647–1730), a notable figure at the English Restoration-era court, as a means of demeaning her over-reaching. Mother Shipton's "home" at Knaresborough has since spawned a tourist trade and she likely served as the inspiration for *The Nice and Accurate Prophecies of Agnes Nutter* in Terry Pratchett and Neil Gaiman's novel *Good Omens* (1990).

Although Jane Wenham (tried in 1712) might mark the end of the legal pursuit of witches as it appears in populous print, with another 60 years before George I repealed James I's law against witchcraft, the British witch continued to accumulate cultural cachet in novella-style accounts like Henry Durbin's 1880 *A Narrative of Some Extraordinary Things that Happened to Mr Richard Giles's Children* that told of the bewitching of Richard Giles's children. As told in the account, the mainly invisible apparition of a witch in a dirty chip hat and ratty brown dress tormented Molly and Dobby Giles (1761–62), constantly biting, scratching, pinching, pricking, piercing, slicing, beating, spanking, and levitating them, and communicated only through the sound of scratching and thudding. The girls were cured when, on the advice of a cunning woman, their urine was boiled into a rainbow haze in a witch-bottle.

As the eighteenth century became the nineteenth, Edgar Taylor's English translation of the Brothers Grimm's fairy tales (1832) made witch stories essential children's reading, and Elizabeth Linton's *Witch Stories* (1861) rolled out a quasi-academic anthology of earlier accounts of British witches. Palm reading, fortune telling, and other forms of prognostication—historically a side trade for witches—were claimed by the gypsy, at least as represented in novels like Charlotte Brontë's *Jane Eyre* (1874), although such practices continued to be illegal.

On the margins of the twentieth century, James Frazier's *The Golden Bough* (1890) surveyed geographically and temporally diverse magical systems to seek ancient origins of witchcraft, setting a course later followed by Leland Charles's *Aradia* (1899) and Margaret Murray's *The Witch-cult in Western Europe* (1921) and *The God of the Witches* (1933). Near the end of the century, Ronald Hutton's *The Triumph of the Moon* (1999) develops witchcraft myths—particularly witchcraft's tie to ancient pagan fertility tradition—as a new religion woven from numerous cultural histories. Together, these trends imagined the witch as a contiguous part of ancient, folkloric, and secretive elite traditions; and spiritual practices like Magick and Wicca, as they populate popular cultures, reshaped the witch from the irritating, mumbling, cursing crone—or naughty daughter of one—that she was historically seen as.

Bubbling and troubling us for almost 450 years in print, the witch in the twentieth century became a film star. The witch of the Brothers Grimm appeared as a crone, apple in hand, in Disney's early film *Snow White and the Seven Dwarfs* (William Cottrell et al., 1937), yet the tale arguably finds even earlier origins in the British tradition. In 1658, as reported by Joseph Glanvill, the witch Jane Brooks gave twelve-year-old Henry Jones "an Apple ... stroked him down on the right side, shook him by the hand, and so bid him good night" (118). The lad roasted and ate half the apple before he became "extreamly ill, and sometimes speechless" (118). If one of the most acclaimed British cinematic narratives about witches is Michael Reeves's film *Witchfinder General* (1968), a fictionalized account of witch-finder Matthew Hopkins's (c. 1620–c. 1647) exploits, then the bleak, cult classic movie *The Wicker Man* (Robin Hardy, 1973) made the pagan witch a cinematic staple.

The witch remained the purview of British children's authors in the twentieth and now twenty-first centuries with Roald Dahl's book (1983) and film (Nicolas Roeg, 1990) *The Witches*, and Jill Murphy's children's books and television series *Worst Witch* (ITV, 1998–2001). The witch appeared on the small screen with *Hex* (Sky One, 2004–2005), a story about the battle between a demonic entity and witches who oppose it in a rural English town. In contrast to the seeming tidal wave of pretty, young, and powerful witches dominating popular culture, Terry Pratchett's "Discworld" series (1983–present) presents the Lancre witches: Granny Weatherwax, whose identity is firmly planted in looking like a witch and "headology" (acting like a witch); the drinking, gossiping, and cat-loving midwife Nanny Ogg; and the painfully awkward Magrat Garlick (and, later, Agnes Nitt)—witches who seem more like their early predecessors.

The witch, as she straddles twentieth- and twenty-first-century popular culture, has been deafeningly defined by the best-selling books that become films that become merchandise. The seven books that make up Irish author C.S. Lewis's *The Chronicles of Narnia* (1950–56) have now produced a television series (Helen Standage, 1967), a cartoon (Bill Melendez, 1979), a BBC mini-series (Marilyn Fox, 1988–90), a play (Richard Williams, 1984), an RSC musical (Adrian Noble, 1998–2002), and three blockbuster films—*The Lion, the Witch and the Wardrobe* (Andrew Adamson, 2005), *Prince Caspian* (Andrew Adamson, 2008), and *The Voyage of the Dawn Treader* (Michael Apted, 2010). Although the White Witch Jadis appears in only some volumes, the staying power of *The Lion, the Witch, and the Wardrobe* means that this impossibly tall and beautiful witch maintains the idea of the witch begun with the oft-resurrected figure of Arthurian witch Morgan Le Fey. Le Fey continues to appear in films almost every decade since they became talkies and television shows since narratives were serialized, played by such renowned actress as Helen Mirren in the film *Excalibur* (1981), Candice Bergen in the television mini-series *Arthur the King* (1985), and Helena Bonham Carter in the television series "Merlin" (1998).

J.K. Rowling's "Harry Potter" books (1997–2007), eight cinematic representations (2001–11), children's toy tie-ins (including the infamously vibrating broomstick, wands, and Lego), and theme park (*Wizarding World of Harry Potter* at Universal Studios Florida) represents the most money ever made off the back of the witch (see **Harry Potter, Monsters In**). Reversing the trope, Rowling's magical world is entirely occupied by hereditary witches and wizards; Minerva McGonagall, especially skilled at transfiguration, is perhaps as powerful at magic as Albus Dumbledore and becomes headmistress of Hogwarts after his death. One might still become a witch, however, even if muggle-born, as Hermione Granger does. The series was criticized for promoting witchcraft but the controversy did little to quench the irrepressible interest in the witching world found beyond Platform 9¾, King's Cross Station, London.

The witch has recently returned to her roots, grounded in historical "reality." The excitement caused by the recent discoveries of Nehemiah Wallington's (1598–1658) diary recounting Matthew Hopkins's witch-hunts, a supposed witch's cottage at Pendle Hill, and a witch-bottle in Greenwich, demonstrate that, despite her long and shifting evolution from courtroom to the big screen, the early English witch remains now, as she always was, a popular-cultural figure we have simultaneously imagined, reshaped, and lived alongside.

British Wizards

Men of magical means appear across the annals of British history. Before natural philosophy was split up into different disciplines, and long before the term "wizardry" was in popular parlance, the definitional differences between unwitchers, wise-men, wizards, conjurers, cunning-men, quacks, jugglers, piss-pot prophets, astrological physicians, mages, negromancers, and necromancers, were in flux. What wove these magic men together was a belief that it was possible to do magic—be it curative or malefic, prognostic or prognosis. Magical power could be used to impose one's will on the natural and supernatural world.

Although done at night in stealth after elaborate ritual preparation and with specially prepared instrumentation, magic was one of England's worst kept secrets. Older than England itself, prohibitions against raising spirits, finding treasure, or causing harm appear in foundational records, as do accounts of its practitioners. There were arguably more people mentioning magic than practicing it, but the magic men who purportedly practiced appeared copied and recopied in collections of "secret books" of conjurations like the thirteenth-, fourteenth-, and fifteenth-century manuscripts of Solomonic magical work, *Ars notoria*; Honorius of Thebes's *Liber sacer sive juratus*; and John the Monk's *Liber visionum*. By the sixteenth century (or early seventeenth) descriptions of necromantic practices were increasingly elaborate.

With common knowledge of the antics of magical men and terms like "necromancer" in normative parlance—Elizabeth herself inquired to the French King, "My God, what necromancer has blinded your eyes"—the theater reflected the anxieties played out in London's streets (Elizabeth 337). The drama in John Skelton's *Nigramansir* (performed before Henry VIII and printed by Wynkin de Worde, 1504) was bookended by the antics of a necromancer who, at the beginning of the play, "the devil kicks" for "waking him so soon in the morning," and in the last scene, "the devil trips up" and "disappears in fire and smoke" (Warton 360, 363). Christopher Marlowe's *The Tragical History of Doctor Faustus* (1604/1616), inspired by the German academic John Faust (and perhaps a satire on sixteenth-century English mathematician, astrologer, occultist, and consultant to Queen Elizabeth, John Dee [1527–c. 1608]), became notorious with the apocryphal anecdotal/marketing claim that the "real" Devil was conjured at the first theatrical performance. Although just one of many English renditions, Marlowe's *Faust* solidified the necromancer's presence on stage. Shortly thereafter, in the immensely popular *The Merry Devill of Edmonton* (1608)—a play perhaps partially penned by William Shakespeare or Thomas Dekker (c. 1572–1632)—the character of the necromancer, Peter Fabell, owns a "Necromanticke chaire, / In which he makes his direfull invocations, / And binds the fiends that shall obey his will" (A3v). This prop also finds purchase in John Milton's *Maske Presented at Ludlow Castle* AKA *Comus* (1634), albeit for a different purpose: there the Lady is trapped in an enchanted chair held in the "necromancers hall" (Milton 12).

The trend of seeing wizards as theater continued throughout the eighteenth century, with books like Richard Neve's *Hocus Pocus* (1725) exposing magic as sleight of hand or downright fraud. Daniel Defoe, in *A Compleat System of Magick* (1729), wrote of England's magical men: "in the first ages they were Wise Men; in the middle Age, Madmen; in these later Ages, Cunning Men: In the earliest time they were honest, in the middle Time, Rogues, in these last times, Fools" (Defoe x). In collections like *The Complete Wizzard* (1770), magical accounts were folklore and fairytale. Mary Shelley's *Frankenstein* (1818), following a trend that may have begun with Swedish scientist, philosopher, and mystic Emanuel Swedenborg (1688–1772), reframes the wizard as a scientist (see **Frankenstein's Monster**). Imported from America, the nineteenth-century necromancer was also a spiritualist. Men like British author Charles Williams (1886–1945) were purveyors of rising and trembling tables, mysterious knocking noises and instruments playing, and vague written and spoken messages from the dead. Welsh social reformer and founder of utopian socialism Robert Owen (1771–1858) supposedly converted to spiritualism before his death and dictated the seven principles of spiritualism after it; Sir Arthur Conan Doyle (1859–1930), author of the Sherlock Holmes mysteries, was a public supporter.

As the nineteenth century turned towards the twentieth, British cinema presented a new view of magic and the warlock. In *The Waif and the Wizard* (1901), W.R. Booth and R.W. Paul merged stage magician back into the wizard, presenting an illusionist-healer; in *The Haunted Curiosity Shop* (1901), they show a merchant as an inadvertent necromancer, unwittingly summoning ghosts, **elves**, Egyptians, knights, **shapeshifters**, and **skeletons**. In the 1930s, Lothar Mendes and Alexander Korda's *The Man Who Could Work Miracles* (1936), based on H.G. Well's 1898 story, showcases an unwitting Faustian figure in George Fotheringay (Roland Young), whose poor judgment (and inadequate knowledge of astronomy) nearly destroys the world.

The release of Ealing Studio's anthology film *Dead of Night* (1945) wove the role of the preternatural into the fabric of the country's cinema. A decade later, Jacques Tourneur's *Night of the Demon* (1957) presents the now-all-too-familiar sights of Satanists, a mysterious parchment inscribed with runes, and a séance. *The Devil Rides Out*, first published by Dennis Wheatley (1934) and developed for the screen by Hammer Films (Terence Fisher, 1968), made magical practices into satanic schlock. Piers Haggard's *Blood on Satan's Claw* (1971) does similar work: staged in the seventeenth century, spiritual infection is spread not by a witch's familiar, but by a totemic demonic claw. Michael Reeves's *The Sorcerers* (1967), featuring Boris Karloff, uses technology to spy into and influence the spirit of men, as does, in part, Roy Ward Baker's portmanteau-style *Asylum* (1972).

Despite the sinister, symbiotic reproduction of Clive Barker's "Hellraiser" franchise (consisting of nine films, several graphic novels, and merchandise tie-ins; see **Pinhead**; **Cenobites**), the nearly unfathomable money made off the scarred forehead of Harry Potter (with the character of Voldemort successfully conjuring himself from death with unprecedented necromantic skill; see **Harry Potter, Monsters In**), and the disembodied Eye of Sauron as imagined by J.R.R. Tolkien (1892–1973) and reimagined by Peter Jackson (1961–) beaming out across movie screens as shoppers purchased commemorative rings of power (see **Tolkien, Monsters In**), the most significant British wizard is clearly Merlin. This son of an **incubus** has an unbreakable magical hold on the British book and film industry.

The thirteenth-century Old French prose cycle of Arthurian literature, the *Prose Merlin* (also referred to as the *Post-Vulgate Cycle*), provides a genesis for Merlin: a naughty pack of fiends wanted "a man of oure kynde that myght speke and have oure connynge and [maystrie] worke, and have the knowleche as we have of things that be don and seide, and of thynges that be past" (*Prose Merlin* lines 36–38). The devils waited until Merlin's would-be mother was helplessly distraught and then one lay with her while she was sleeping. Piety outwitted plotting, however, and the woman baptized the child and christened him after her fallen father, Merlin. Merlin prophesies through Geoffrey of Monmouth's twelfth-century *Historia Regum Brittaniae* and acts as a consultant through Thomas Malory's fifteenth-century *Le Morte D'Arthur*. Thereafter a staple of British literature, he appears in William Rowley's *The Birth of Merlin* as a sage (c.

1662), Jonathan Swift's *A Famous Prediction of Merlin, the British Wizard* (1709), William Wordsworth's "The Egyptian Maid" (1835), and Tennyson's "Merlin and the Gleam" (1889) and "Merlin and Vivien" (1859), the sixth poem in Tennyson's *Idylls of the King* (1856–85).

Although Merlin's first slated screen appearance was to have been in D.W. Griffith's *The Quest of the Holy Grail*, the film lost its financial backers and died on the shelf. Merlin would have to wait another few years before making his cinematic debut in Emmett J. Flynn's *A Connecticut Yankee in King Arthur's Court* (1921) based on Mark Twain's 1889 novel. He gained traction on the British screen in Cornel Wilde's *Lancelot and Guinevere* (1963) and Nathan H. Juran's *Siege of the Saxons* (1963), and sees significant screen time in Disney's *The Sword in the Stone* (Wolfgang Reitherman, 1963). Monty Python gave us a version of Merlin in the unforgettable "Tim the Enchanter" (played by John Cleese), whose only powers seem to be magically generating fire bombs and lagomorphic crypto-zoology, in *Monty Python and the Holy Grail* (Terry Gilliam and Terry Jones, 1975). Merlin appeared for a while in panned films like *Merlin and the Sword* (1982) and *October 32nd/ Merlin* (1992). The BBC's successful ongoing television series *Merlin* has done much to reinvigorate weekly interest in the wizard. His appearance on posters, comic books, as action figures, figurines, and the kitsch 1978 Parker Brothers' hand-held game, "Merlin the Electronic Wizard," makes the magical man one of Britain's most famous, most flexible, and possibly most profitable exports.

Kirsten C. Uszkalo

References and Suggested Reading

Defoe, Daniel. *The Novels and Miscellaneous Works of Daniel De Foe*. Vol XII. Oxford: D.A. Talboys, 1840.

Dr Lambs Darling. London: 1653.

Durbin, Henry. *A Narrative of Some Extraordinary Things that Happened to Mr Richard Giles's Children*. Bristol: 1800.

Elizabeth. "Elizabeth: March 1585, 6–10." *Calendar of State Papers: Foreign: Elizabeth*, vol. 19, edited by Sophie Crawford Lomas, 326–45. *British History Online*. <http://www.british-history.ac.uk/report.aspx?compid=79176>.

Glanvill, Joseph. *Saducismus Triumphatus*. London: 1681.

Malory, Thomas. *Le Morte D'Arthur*. London: 1485.

Meaney, Audrey. "Extra-Medical Elements in Anglo-Saxon Medicine." *Social History of Medicine* 24, no. 1 (2011): 41–56.

Merry Devill of Edmonton As it hath beene sundry times acted, by his Maiesties Seruants, at the Globe, on the banke-side, The. London: 1608.

Milton, John. *A Maske Presented At Ludlow Castle, 1634*. London: 1637.

Podmore, Frank. *Modern Spiritualism: A History and a Criticism*. Vol. 2 [1902]. Reprint, Cambridge: Cambridge University Press, 2011.

Prose Merlin. Edited by John Conlee. Michigan: Medieval Institute Publications: 1998. <http://www.lib.rochester.edu/camelot/teams/melbifr.htm>.

Scot, Reginald. *Discovery of Witchcraft*. London: 1581.

Thorpe, Benjamin. *Ancient Laws and Institutes of England*. Vol. 2. London: G.E. Eyre and A. Spottiswoode, 1840.

Warton, Thomas. *The History of English Poetry*. Vol. 2. London: 1778.

Witches and Wizards in Russian Literature and Film

Witches and wizards in Russian literature denote humans born with supernatural powers or acquired later, yet the two types are not necessarily negative. Although the stories take place in many different regions, they are most often connected with "Little Russia," which is now Ukraine.

Aleksandr Pushkin's poem "Ruslan and Liudmila" (1820) tells about the abduction of the young Kievan princess Liudmila on her nuptial night by the evil **dwarf** and wizard Chernomor, and of subsequent adventures that lead to her reunion with Ruslan. In his quest for Liudmila, Ruslan confronts both Chernomor and the evil witch Naina, but is helped by the kind wizard Finn. Alexander Ptushko produced a film adaptation of the same name (1973). In Antony Pogorel'skii's (pen name of Alexei Perovskii) *The Double, or My Evenings in Little Russia* (1828), the author shows how the failure of magic to control a girl's love was experienced by an evil witch who tried to bring about the marriage of her own black cat to her young relative.

The Russian prose tradition of linking monstrous characters with Ukraine started with Orest Somov in stories published in the 1820s and 1830s, and was fully developed by Nikolai Gogol in his collections of stories *Evenings on a Farm near Dikanka* (1831–32) and *Mirgorod* (1835). In Gogol's stories, witches and wizards are usually powerful and range from the relatively harmless middle-aged libidinous Solokha in *Christmas Eve* (1832), to several sinister characters: a bloodthirsty old witch who orders Petro to kill a child in return for a cursed treasure in *St John's Eve* (1830; reworked version 1831); a cruel stepmother able to transform herself into a cat and to make her stepdaughter commit suicide in *A May Night or the Drowned Maiden* (1831); and a Cossack captain's daughter who used to change her age to ride a man while flying in the air, and who succeeds in taking revenge on her killer Khoma Brut in *Viy* (1835; reworked version 1842). The malevolent incestuous wizard from *Terrible Vengeance* (1831) is both a perpetrator of evil and victim of the curse put on him for his ancestor's crime. Several directors made film adaptations of Gogol's stories. These include Alexander Rou's *Evenings on a Farm near Dikanka* (1961), Yuri Ilienko's *St John's Eve* (1968), Konstantin Ershov's *Viy* (1967), and Semien Gorov's *Evenings on a Farm near Dikanka* (2001).

Vladimir Odoevsky in *Salamander* (1841) shows the evolution of El'sa from a child with supernatural powers to a girl helping her beloved Iakko in his alchemic endeavors and, upon being betrayed, to an avenging witch. Alexander Kuprin's *Olesya* (1898) depicts witches as victims. The protagonist Olesya and her grandmother, both fortune-tellers and healers, are blamed for all the bad things that happen around them. Film adaptations were made by André Michel (*La sorcière*, 1956) and Boris Ivchenko (*Olesya*, 1971).

The twentieth century includes Alexei Tolstoy's character *Count Cagliostro* (1921) who brings to life the long-dead beauty Tulupova, materializing her from a portrait. The film adaptation entitled *The Formula of Love* was produced by Mark Zakharov (1984). One of the most sinister wizards is Count Yakov Brius in Alexander Chaianov's *Strange, but True Adventures of Count Fyodor Mikhailovich Buturlin* (1924). Mikhail Bulgakov's Margarita in *Master and Margarita* (shortened and censored version first published 1966–67; first full publication 1973) becomes a witch and a hostess at Satan's ball in 1930s Moscow to save her beloved Master. Several directors made film adaptations of this novel, including Andrzej Wajda's *Pilat i inni* (*Pilat and the Others*, 1971), Aleksandar Petrović (1972), Maciej Woityszko (1989), Yuri Kara (1994), and Vladimir Bortko (2005).

Literary witches and wizards have remained popular in contemporary Russian literature, as with Sergei Lukyanenko's fantasy novels *The Nightwatch* (1998), *The Daywatch* (with Vladimir Vasiliev, 2000), *The Twilight Watch* (2004), and *The Last Watch* (2006). These are popular **vampire** stories that focus on the struggle between forces of good and evil in contemporary Moscow. Film adaptations of the first two novels under the same titles were directed by Timur Bekmambetov (2004, 2006). Even more recent is Lada Luzina's (pen name of Vladislava Kucherova) ongoing "Kiev Witches" series of novels launched in 2005, in which three contemporary witches try to change Kiev's history.

Also deserving of mention here is Baba Yaga. Although Baba Yaga in Russian folklore is not considered or referred to as a witch, she has been translated as such in English. Rather than a human being with magical powers, Baba Yaga belongs instead to the marvelous realm of the fairytale. She lives deep in the woods in a hut standing on chicken legs. She never walks, but flies in a mortar or lies still on a bench. Although she is sometimes a mother of monsters, she is never a wife or a lover. While in some tales she is a villain (a cannibalistic abductor) or a warrior, in other cases she is a donor who, willingly or not, provides a hero or heroine with a magical helper or a magical object to further a quest.

In Russian literature, Baba Yaga appears in the prologue to the poem "Ruslan and Liudmila" by Pushkin, in the poem "A Tale about Ivan Tsarevich and a Grey Wolf" (1845) by Vasilii Zhukovskii, and in two stories by Alexei Remizov (1877–1957) written in the 1910s, "Glowing Skulls" and "Driving Rain." Baba Yaga makes an appearance in the novel *Monday Begins on Saturday* (1965) by Arkady and Boris Strugatsky in which she assists the protagonist Aleksandr Ivanovich Privalov (Sasha). She is a negative force in Vasilii Shukshin's story "Before the Third Roosters" (1975), and in Leonid Filatov's dramatized poem "The Tale of Fedot the Strelets" (1986). In the novel *The Return to Baba Yaga* (1993), author Anna Natalia Malakhovskaia (née Natalia Malakhovskaia) represents her as a powerful female goddess.

Baba Yaga is also widely represented in Russian films, especially those for children. The 1939 film *Vasilisa the Beautiful* (Aleksandr Rou) features male actor Georgii Millyar in a role he was to reprise in a number of films in the 1940s, 1950s, and 1960s. A very kind Baba Yaga was performed by actress Tatyana Pelttser in *Along Unknown Paths* (Mikhail Yuzovsky, 1982). Composer Modest Mussorgsky's 1874 piano suite *Pictures at an Exhibition* features "The Hut on Bird's Legs (Baba Yaga)" as its penultimate movement.

At least in part due to the incorporation of Baba Yaga as an antagonist to be encountered in the *Dungeons & Dragons* role-playing game, she has increasingly begun to show up in English language texts (see **Dungeons & Dragons, Monsters In**). For example, she appears in book three of the graphic novel *Books of Magic* by author Neil Gaiman (*The Land of Summer's Twilight*, 1990–91) and is employed to fight against the **ogre** Shrek in the film *Shrek Forever After* (Mike Mitchell, 2010).

Larisa Fialkova

References and Suggested Reading

Beaujour, Elizabeth Klosty. "The Uses of Witches in Fedin and Bulgakov." *Slavic Review* 33, no. 4 (1974): 695–707.

Bely, Andrei. *Gogol's Artistry*. Translated by Christopher Colbath. Evanston, IL: Northwestern University Press, 2009.

Johns, Andreas. *Baba Yaga: The Ambiguous Mother and Witch of the Russian Folktale*. New York: Peter Lang, 2004.

Krys, Svitlana. "Allusions to Hoffmann in Gogol's Early Ukrainian Horror Stories." *Canadian Slavonic Papers* (June–September 2009): 243–66.

Mersereau, John. "Orest Somov: An Introduction." *The Slavonic and East European Review* 43, no. 101 (1965): 354–70.

Witches and Wizards in US Literature and Film

Witches and wizards in American literature and film stem largely from British and other European traditions, although recent works come from a wider range of influences, including Asian, Caribbean, and African-American traditions. In the United States, witches and wizards tend to be categorized into four types: supernatural creatures, human beings who call on supernatural beings, human beings who use magical forces, and human beings who transform themselves so that they achieve a trans- or superhuman perspective, becoming one with the universe and hence able to change reality.

In some books and films, American witches are supernatural, but appear as human beings. An example of this is the male and female witches in *Bell, Book, and Candle*, a 1958 film directed by Richard Quine and starring Jimmy Stewart and Kim Novak. The main characters appear human but lack human attributes; they cannot cry and lose their powers if they fall in love. In the television series *Bewitched* that ran from 1964 to 1972, witchcraft is an inherent characteristic, passed along genetically. The witches of the Oz books, including L. Frank Baum's *The Wonderful Wizard of Oz* (1900), appear to be born supernatural creatures.

Other American works show the witches' power stemming from partnership with some supernatural being; among those that are concerned with witches' and wizards' pacts with demons and devils is *Magic, Inc.*, a novella by science fiction writer Robert A. Heinlein (1940). Nathaniel Hawthorne uses the witches' Sabbath ambiguously in "Young Goodman Brown" (1835), while perhaps the best cinematic witches' Sabbath is the "Night on Bald Mountain" section of Disney's movie *Fantasia* (section directed by Wilfred Jackson, 1940). H.P. Lovecraft replaced the Devil and demons with gods, coldly indifferent rather than evil, such as Yog Sothoth, who is invoked by Joseph Curwen in "The Case of Charles Dexter Ward" (1943), and Old Wizard Wilbur Whateley in "The Dunwich Horror" (1929; see **Lovecraft, Monsters In**).

Since the 1980s, many witches are benign, even benevolent people whose power comes from a goddess or goddesses that they worship, as in the Bast series by Rosemary Edgehill, set among contemporary neo-pagans, beginning with *Speak Daggers to Her* (1994). The Mayfair Witches series by Anne Rice—*The Witching Hour* (1990), *Lasher* (1993), *Taltos* (1994), and *The Blood Canticle* (2003)—is a crossover with her vampire series. It draws on the inherently supernatural approach: the rich, powerful, and incestuous family, whose women keep the name Mayfair, use the power of and are manipulated by a creature named Lasher, but he gains power from the witches, some of whom are naturally more adept than others.

There are also works that present witches and wizards as rational beings who use magic as a technology to accomplish otherwise impossible or mundane tasks. In the 1960s, science fiction writer Larry Niven paralleled the contemporary energy crisis with a world depleting its magic in the "Warlock" stories, including *Not Long Before the End* (1969). Many stories of this type occur in fantasy worlds in which magic is presented as an accepted part of reality and include such works as Lyndon Hardy's trilogy that begins with *Master of the Five Magics* (1980). The work of L. Sprague de Camp also focuses on the relationship between wizardry and technology, as in the novella *The Roaring Trumpet* (1940). This is the first book in a series that features the character Harold Shea, a mathematician who uses symbolic logic to project himself into magical universes.

Magic can also depend on the consciousness of the witch or wizard, which must be expanded until the magus understands, and hence can control everything. This type of magic, widespread in the Hermetic tradition, appears in Peter Straub's novel *Shadowland* (1980), a depiction of initiation influenced by John Fowles's mimetic novel *The Magus* (1966). The protagonist, Tom Flanagan, must accept all aspects of his psyche and conflate what is inside him with the universe outside to attain mastery over both.

America's most famous witches, executed in Salem, Massachusetts in 1692, often show up in American works. Sometimes the Salem witches are inimical, as in the 1993 Disney film *Hocus Pocus* (Kenny Ortega). More often, these witches are presented as victims who are not supernaturally powerful, as in Frank Lloyd's 1937 movie *Maid of Salem*, Elizabeth Gaskell's novella *Lois the Witch* (1859), and Arthur Miller's play *The Crucible* (1952). The eponymous heroine of René Clair's film *I Married a Witch* (1942) is a witch killed at Salem who returns from the dead to torment the descendant of her accuser, but instead falls in love with him.

In general, American witches and wizards are more apt to be benevolent than in other parts of the world, but they often still show an evil side. In Fritz Leiber's novel *Conjure Wife* (1953), all women practice magic; the male protagonist wants his wife to stop but needs the magic for protection. Evil witches are present in Rebecca Ore's *Slow Funeral* (1995) and in works by Stephen King such as *Thinner* (1984), which focuses on a gypsy curse. Child witches are often evil, including the young girl in T.E.D. Klein's novel *The Ceremonies* (1984), while teen witches are more often sympathetic protagonists, as in the 1998–2006 TV show *Charmed*.

American witches often embody female power, for good or ill, as in John Updike's *The Witches of Eastwick* (novel 1984; George Miller film 1987) in which the devil figure helps the witches realize their own capabilities. The witch may be linked to female sexuality in a darker way, as in Robert Frost's poem "The Witch of Coos" (c. 1922). In Elizabeth Hand's *Waking the Moon* (1994), the female goddess worshippers fight the male, rational Benandanti.

Another theme present in American literature is the capitalistic witch or wizard. Heinlein's *Magic, Inc.*, shows how magic can be used for mundane tasks, from building construction to fashion design. The 1995 anthology *100 Wicked Little Witch Stories* contains several of these works that treat a similar subject, including "1-900-Witches" by Nancy and Wayne Holder.

Use of African-American magic in American literature and film is usually stereotyped and racist, such as the movie *The Believers* (1987) with its sorcerer who runs a malevolent voodoo cult. Three major exceptions are the writings of Nalo Hopkinson, including her character Mami Gros-Jeanne in *Brown Girl in the Ring* (1995) and the short stories in an anthology she edited, *Mojo: Conjure Stories* (2003), and the character Mama Day in Gloria Naylor's 1988 novel of the same name.

Bernadette Lynn Bosky

References and Suggested Reading

Bosky, Bernadette Lynn. "The Witch." In *Icons of Horror and the Supernatural*, vol. 2, edited by S.T. Joshi, 689–722. Westport, CT: Greenwood Press, 2007.

Mathews, Chris. *Modern Satanism: Anatomy of a Radical Subculture*. Santa Barbara, CA: Praeger, 2009.

Matthews, John. *Wizards: The Quest for the Wizard from Merlin to Harry Potter*. New York: Barrons Educational Series, 2003.

Savage, Candace. *Witch: The Wild Ride from Wicked to Wicca*. Toronto: Greystone, 2003.

Witches and Wizards in Spanish and Latin American Literature and Film

Spain and Latin America share a turbulent history, seen in the development of the witch character in literature produced after the Spanish Conquest. Yet witches and wizards are complicated terms that were applied to a broad range of practitioners that the Spanish *conquistadores* discovered when they arrived in the New World (Castro-Kláren 204). In Catholic Spain, the Inquisition generated numerous documents about witches that eventually found their way into both peninsular (mainland Spain) and Latin American literature and film reaching into the twenty-first century. Terms such as *brujalo*, *hechicderalo*, *yergateralo*, *herbolario/a*, *celestine*, and *curandera/o* can loosely be translated as witch, sorceress, herbal-healer, herbalist, and healer, and are all included under the larger heading of witches and wizards, sorcerers and sorceresses, prevalent through the literature and film of Spain and Latin America (Castro-Kláren 204).

Although the witch figure is seen more often in the literature of Protestant countries than Catholic ones, the emergence of the *celestine* figure in Spain at the end of the fifteenth century marked a transition from the medieval era to the early modern Renaissance, during which Spanish stories of all types began to be published and a more pronounced use of the witch figure became visible in stories. Texts featuring this seductive figure include Fernando de Rojas's play, *La Celestina* (1491), which set the tone for many stories that followed, including Cervantes's short story "El licenciado vidriera" ("The Lawyer of Glass," 1613) from his collection *Novelas ejemplares* (*Exemplary Novels*).

As early as in the Dominican Friar Diego Duran's *Historia de la Indias de la Nueva España e islas de Tierra Firme* (*History of the Indies of New Spain*, 1581), witches and wizards have shown up in the literature of the New World. In Chapter XXVII of Duran's history, he tells the story of how Motecuzoma used witches and wizards to search for the truth of their ancestors. This was followed by colonial writer Juan Rodríguez Freile's book *El carnero* (*The Ram*), a book of short stories written between 1636 and 1638 about several witch-like characters living in the urban centers of the Spanish and Creole world of Colombia (Castro-Kláren 146). In Spain, plays were also popular in the seventeenth and eighteenth centuries and a number focused on the witch character. These include the Spanish *Entremés famoso de las brujas* (*Famous Interlude of the Witches*, 1675) by Agustín Moreto, and *Entremés de las brujas* (*Interlude of the Witches*, 1742) by Francisco de Castro. A small number of late nineteenth-century Spanish writers carried forward this tradition in their work, most notably Ramón María del Valle-Inclán whose main character in his novel *Sonata de otoño* (*Sonata of Autumn*, 1902) is the seductress Cándida, who is accused of witch-like behavior. This story was rewritten by Spanish author Marina Mayoral in *Candida, otra vez* (*Candida, Once Again*, 1979) in which she casts the witch-like protagonist from a feminist point of view, rather than through a nineteenth-century male voice.

In the twentieth and now twenty-first centuries, Latin American authors have made extensive use of witch and wizard characters, often in the service of political commentary or satire. Setting the stage was Guatemalan author Miguel Ángel Asturias's chilling novel *El Señor Presidente* (*Mr President*, 1946), written to protest social injustice in Guatemala and painting the main dictator character as a shadowy figure that has omniscient power over his people.

Asturias's books created a template for similar approaches to the strong man (and woman) figure whose powers are enhanced by magic. This includes magical realist novels of the 1960s and 1970s that are filled with various witch and wizard characters. Of particular note here are the works of Colombian author Gabriel García Márquez such as *Cien años de la soledad* (*One Hundred Years of Solitude*, 1967) and *La increíble y triste historia de la cándida Eréndira y de su abuela desalmada* (*The Incredible and Sad Tale of Innocent Eréndira and her Soulless Grandmother*, 1972).

Chilean author Isabel Allende in her novel *La casa de los espíritus* (*The House of the Spirits*, 1982), and Argentine author Luisa Valenzuela in *La cola de lagartija* (*The Lizard's Tail*, 1983) both employ witch and wizard figures in the service of political satire. Valenzuela's work, which takes place in some of the darker years of Argentina's history in the mid 1970s, is a fictional rendition of the evil doings of Juan Péron's Minister of Social Welfare, José López Rega (1916–89), who was in reality nicknamed the "Sorcerer of Argentina." Valenzuela also includes characters such as the "old Machi," whose name connects her to the shamanic women of the Mapuche people who inhabit southern Chile. More recent is Tomás Eloy Martínez's novel *Santa Evita* (*Saint Evita*, 1995) that depicts the evil doings of a thinly veiled warlock-like character who believes that Evita's finger from her dead body has magical powers that he can use to gain influence.

There are many Spanish and Latin American films with witch-like characters, including *El Espejo de la Bruja* (*The Witch's Mirror*; Mexico; Chano Urueto, 1962) in which a husband (Armando Calvo) who murders his wife (Dina de Marco) must then face the revenge of his wife's godmother, the conjuror (Isabela Corona). *La Noche de los Brujos* (*The Night of the Witches*) is a 1973 horror film written and directed by Amando de Ossorio, the premise for which is that a group of African explorers run afoul of a native cult that performs magic. It is the grandmother (Irene Papas) who seems to possess the power in the 1983 Mexican art film *Eréndira*, directed by Ruy Guerra and adapted from Carlos Fuente's novella. *Akellare* is a 1984 film by Spanish filmmaker Pedro Olea about the Logroño trial conducted by the Spanish Inquisition against the Zugarramurdi witches. The 1992 Mexican film *Como agua para chocolate* (*Like Water for Chocolate*), directed by Alfonso Arau, comes from Laura Esquivel's novel of the same name and features a good witch character named Tita (Lumi Cavazos) who seduces and curses with her magical food, fighting the bad witch character Mamá Elena (Regina Torné) who tries to curse Tita's life. In the more recent film *Biutiful* (Mexico; Alejandro González Iñárritu, 2010), Uxbal, played by Javier Bardem, has the ability to communicate with the dead. More recent and on the lighter side is the Nickolodean telenovela called *Grachi*, about Graciela "Grachi" Alonso (Isabella Castillo), a teenage witch who moves to a new school called the "Escolarium" and fights against another witch rival for the attention of Daniel (Andrés Mercado; premiered 2 May 2011).

Stephenie Young

References and Suggested Reading

Castro-Kláren, Sara, ed. *A Companion to Latin American Literature and Culture*. Malden, MA: Blackwell, 2008.

Johnson, Roberta. "Marina Mayoral's *Candida otra vez:* Invitation to a Retroactive Reading of *Sonata del otoño*." In *Ramón María Del Valle-Inclán: Questions of Gender*, edited by Carol Maier and Roberta L. Salper, 239–54. Cranbury, NJ: Associated University Presses, 1994.

McKee, Sally, ed. *Crossing Boundaries: Issues of Cultural and Individual Identity in the Middle Ages and the Renaissance.* Turnhout, Belgium: Brepols, 1999.

Swanson, Philip, ed. *A Companion to Latin American Studies.* London: Arnold, 2003.

African and Caribbean Witches and Wizards

Able to levy and to lift curses, to torture and to comfort, to make medicine for bruises and battles, witches are integral to everyday life across Africa and the Caribbean. Witches in the many cultures of Africa and the Caribbean differ from one another, and most cultures include several different types of witches. Local terms persist, from the Zulu *thakatha* and *inyanga* to the Creole *soucouyant*, designating particular kinds of witches; but with colonial languages serving as official and common languages throughout Africa and the Caribbean, the term witch (and its French, Spanish, Portuguese, and Dutch equivalents) is more common than any single local word. This issue of terminology offers the reminder that the identification of witches in Africa and the Caribbean necessarily involves questions of colonization and cultural misunderstanding. Maryse Condé's novel *I, Tituba, Black Witch of Salem* (Guadeloupe, 1986) explores the clash between Western and Afro-Caribbean conceptions of witchcraft as Tituba, well respected for her healing powers in Barbados, stands accused in the Salem witch trials. Patrick Chamoiseau's play *Maman Dlo Against the Carabosse Fairy* (Martinique, 1981) presents the witch as a figure of Christianity and colonialism unable to understand Afro-Caribbean sorceresses-goddesses like Maman Dlo, or animist and voodoo traditions where magic is a tool and where divine forces work to maintain a balance between good, evil, and chance.

African and Caribbean witches combine qualities and perform offices that in the West are divided between witches and wizards; the wizard as such is virtually non-existent in Africa and the Caribbean. A majority of African and Caribbean witches are referred to as female, but both men and women can be witches, and witches often fall outside of the gender binary or are androgynous. In addition to witches, both witch doctors and any number of regular people practice witchcraft.

Although they are common, African and Caribbean witches occupy a marginal position both in the human order and in the communities they inhabit. Witches look like people, but their ability to transform—into animals, insects, or magical creatures—often leaves a physical mark on their human form: Miranda in Helen Oyeyemi's novel *White is for Witching* (Nigeria/England, 2008) eats chalk; Célanire in Maryse Condé's novel *Who Slashed Célanire's Throat*? (Guadeloupe, 2004) has a jagged scar across her neck. And while villagers know how to find them, most often, like Ma Cia in Simone Schwartz-Bart's *The Bridge of Beyond* (Guadeloupe, 1972), witches live in outlying woods, bogs or hills. African and Caribbean witches can be evil or benevolent but are most often forces of both, similar to the trickster but drawing primarily on otherworldly, rather than worldly, knowledge. The Nine Witches of Darkness in *The Epic of Son Jara* (Mali, thirteenth century), for example, first threaten to kill the hero, then, when he makes them a worthwhile offer, lend him their support. In Southern Africa, witches are more regularly evil than in West Africa and the Caribbean, but Southern African literature often focuses on the double edge of witchcraft: in Hilda Kuper's play *A Witch in My Heart* (Swaziland, 1970), the protagonist's co-wives accuse her of being a witch—whether she is or not—in order to gain social power; in Zoë Wicomb's novel *David's Story* (South Africa, 2000), Bronwyn the Brown Witch uses her powers to help her friends, but in the process may upset the order of things.

While witches constitute a distinct category of beings, witch doctors are people trained in witchcraft who exercise it as a calling or vocation. Witch doctors communicate with the dead and call on a variety of spiritual and otherworldly beings, know the medicinal properties of plants and animals, understand community dynamics, and can often remedy bad witchcraft; they are more closely related to traditional healers than to Euro-American witches. The title story of Amos Tutuola's collection *The Village Witch Doctor and Other Stories* (Nigeria, 1990) describes the integral role of the witch doctor in many Afro-Caribbean communities. Often initiated members of local religions, witch doctors regularly serve as or work with priests and imams, as in Chinua Achebe's novels *Things Fall Apart* (Nigeria, 1958) and *Arrow of God* (Nigeria, 1964). Independent witch doctors can become dangerous because their services are rendered indiscriminately, as in the film *Dingaka* (South Africa; Jamie Uys, 1965) in which the witch doctor assists both a murderer and the father of the murdered girl. Like all doctors and spiritual healers, witch doctors cannot cure all ailments and encounter particular problems at times of massive cultural change. In *Xala*, Sembène Ousmane's novel (Senegal, 1973) and film (Ousmane Sembène, 1975), the protagonist visits many witch doctors who fail to cure an impotence that turns out to be the curse of the new African bourgeoisie. At the same time, the witch doctor is often an important figure in anti-colonial struggle: representing African and Caribbean tradition, as in Joseph Zobel's novel *Black Shack Ally* (Martinique, 1950—made into the film *Sugar Cane Alley* by Euzhene Palcy [1983]); training and curing rebels like Mackandal and Ti Noel in Alejo Carpentier's *The Kingdom of this World* (Cuba, 1949); and, like Jamaica's Nanny of the Maroons, immortalized in countless myths and in the poetry of Grace Nichols (1950–) and Lorna Goodison (1947–), serving directly as a maroon leader.

Even as the general category of witch demonstrates how colonial conceptions of evil and magic determine the understanding of key figures across Africa and the Caribbean, the stories of witches that populate African and Caribbean literature and film show how traditional conceptions survive and resist on their own, often creolized, terms. African and Caribbean witches represent occult forces, but also the difficulty in distinguishing between worldly and otherworldly, good and bad, curse and cure, witch and non-witch.

Keja Valens

References and Suggested Reading

Bongmba, Elias Kifon. *African Witchcraft and Otherness: A Philosophical and Theological Critique of Intersubjective Relations*. Albany: SUNY Press, 2000.

Dorsey, Lilith. *Voodoo and Afro-Caribbean Paganism*. Secaucus, NJ: Citadel, 2005.

Hurston, Zora Neale. *Tell My Horse* [1938]. Reprint, New York: Harper Perennial, 2009.

Moore, Henrietta, and Todd Sanders, eds. *Magical Interpretations, Material Realities: Modernity, Witchcraft, and the Occult in Postcolonial Africa*. New York: Routledge, 2002.

WOLAND—*see* Demon

WOMEN, MONSTROUS

Female monstrosity—the female as monster—has long been a part of patriarchal culture, chiefly resulting from

Fig. 39 ***Squid Lady*** **by Anki King**

anxieties concerning femininity. While world literature and film is overflowing with manipulative "evil" women who tempt men from the straight and narrow path and drive them to acts of desperation, this entry will concentrate on representations of women such as **witches**, **sirens**, and **succubi** who possess supernatural powers because they are another order of being, or who become another order of being by virtue of their excessive and threatening power. For the sake of succinctness, one can divide the monstrous representation of women into four at times overlapping categories: the virgin, the seductress, the repellent, and the threatening maternal. Each of these four forms is "archetypal" insofar as it is a recurring image of women going back to Western culture's earliest oral traditions and mythologies. The link between them is the shared reflection of patriarchal fear of sexual difference; in addition, each archetype marks a contested site of male fascination. Societies and cultures have defined accepted and acceptable roles for women based on the need to control women's sexual and intellectual expression (one need only refer to psychoanalytic musings on the *vagina dentata*, which are the organizing premise of Mitchell Lichtenstein's 2007 horror film *Teeth*, to see how these themes are given shape). Those women who step out of prescribed roles, and especially those who strategically deploy their sexuality as a form of control, become monstrous in the patriarchal imaginary.

Pure, Young, Untouched: The Virgin

The female virgin, while on the one hand glorified, is, on the other hand, a monstrous archetype because of the ways in which she denies male participation in the development of her sexually assigned role. Since the ancient Greeks, the virgin can be seen as a provocation and a refusal: the virgin goddess Artemis punishes Actaeon for having seen her naked by changing him into a stag (one that is then torn apart by Actaeon's own hunting dogs). Virginity in the *parthenos* (unwed girl) was seen as potentially dangerous because it had an innate power that, if not properly channeled, could lead to bedlam. Therefore, as early as the ancient Greeks one sees the need to penetrate the virgin and usher her into womanhood through a heterosexual sexual initiation. It is interesting to note that the Romans had sacred vestal virgins as protectors of the moral health of the state. If the vestal virgin lost her virginity, she was sacrificed by being sealed within a cave; during times of religious or political crisis, the vestal virgin could be sacrificed by the community as the scapegoat. As a scapegoat, the Roman vestal virgin was held responsible for the evils that occurred within the community, such as miscarriages, sterility of women, and diseases among cattle—all similar to common witchcraft charges. From the fourteenth century comes the image of St Wilgefortis who was said to have taken a vow of chastity and prayed that she would appear repulsive to men, so as to avoid an arranged marriage.

In her 1994 novel, *The Miracle Worker*, the Mexican novelist Carmen Boullosa tells the story of a young virgin who has been told that her supernatural powers are dependent on her virginal status. Upon losing her virginity, she learns that her new-found sexual identity actually introduces other supernatural powers to her (comparable to the initiation of Carrie's telekinetic powers with her first menstruation in Stephen King's *Carrie* [1974], and its cinematic adaptation by Brian de Palma in 1976). Similarly, Stephenie Meyer's *Twilight* saga (2003–2008) and the various adaptations (film, graphic novels, and a reported television series) amplifies the discussion of female virginity and monstrosity in its portrayal of Bella Swan as a virginal bride who gives birth to a **vampire**-human hybrid child and who is later transformed into a vampire after childbirth so as to "save" her life. The monstrous virgin is perhaps taken to its extreme in the television series *True Blood*, based on the Sookie Stackhouse novels (2001–11) by Charlaine Harris. Jessica (Deborah Ann Woll), a vampire virgin, remains a virgin forever because vampire wounds always heal; in other words, Jessica is afforded a perpetual hymen, which always heals itself.

Monstrous Female Sexuality

The provocation of the virgin finds its inverted reflection in anxieties about sexually experienced women, variously figured as succubi, vampires, **mermaids**, and sirens. One of the sources for the female vampire figure dates back to ancient Greek mythology in the person of **Lamia**, a mother who witnessed all but one of her children killed by the jealous goddess Hera. Lamia went insane and was said to then steal and eat other people's children. In Indonesia, the *langsuyar* is the **ghost** of a woman who died in childbirth that preys upon pregnant women and sucks their blood. The succubus is a female **demon** that drains life from her victims through intercourse (the corresponding male version is the **incubus**).

In contemporary culture, representations of monstrously sexual women include the succubus in the Canadian supernatural crime drama *Lost Girl* (2010–11) who learns to control her sexual abilities. Drawing inspiration from Bram Stoker's 1897 novel ***Dracula*** and the eponymous Count's three vampire brides, Stephen Sommer's 2004 film *Van Helsing* depicts female vampires in Dracula's harem as sexually powerful, seductive, and able to mesmerize their victims. The infamous **Countess Bathory**, too, must be numbered among the depictions of the seductive female vampire. The Countess is famous for having allegedly murdered hundreds of virgins and bathed in their blood. The extensive body of cinema that fixates on the Countess, including *Bathory* (Juraj Jakubisko, 2008), *The Countess* (Julie Delpy, 2009), *Countess Dracula* (Peter Sasdy, 1971), *Vampire Lovers* (Roy Ward Baker, 1970), *Eternal* (Wilhelm Liebenberg, 2004), and *Night Fangs* (Ricardo Islas, 2005), emphasize her sexuality, frequently with a lesbian twist—especially notable here is *Daughters of Darkness* (Harry Kümel, 1971), which contrasts the Countess's (Delphine Seyrig) dazzling and absorptive sexuality against the crude, masculine violence of patriarchal heterosexuality as embodied in the character Stefan (John Karlen).

Female monstrosity has been associated not just with sexual self-expression, but also with verbal eloquence; both mermaids and sirens seduce through their voices as well as their bodies. The Greek sirens were beautiful half-fish, half-women whose voices enticed men to jump from their ships and swim with them. Parodying this is an episode of *The Simpsons* in which Patty and Selma appear as sirens ("She of Little Faith," season 6, episode 13; 16 December 2001; Steven Dean Moore). Mermaids, similar to sirens, also enchant men with their beauty and voices. Seduction in familiar narratives tends to be inverted, however, as the mermaid in Hans Christian Andersen's *The Little Mermaid* (1837) and the mermaids in J.M Barrie's *Peter Pan* (1911), for example, pine for a human prince and Peter Pan respectively.

The Repellent Female

The cult of female beauty finds its antithesis in the figure of the crone or witch, an older (and often wiser) sexually experienced woman. **Circe** in Greek mythology was a goddess of magic who was sometimes also depicted as a nymph, witch, enchantress, or sorceress—all roles incorporating a knowledge of magical potions and herbs. Historically, there are examples of midwives being equated with witch figures because of their intimate knowledge of the female reproductive system. During the Salem Witch Trials (1692–93), for instance, many midwives were tried as witches. In early folklore and fairytales, these women are often threatened by the prospect of being replaced by a younger and more beautiful female. One need only think of the infamous line, "Mirror, mirror on the wall, who is the fairest of them all?" from the Walt Disney version of *Snow White and the Seven Dwarfs* (David Hand et al., 1937). But witches and crones (as is the case for most of the archetypes) are not just found in children's literature; Shakespeare's *Macbeth* (c. 1603–1607), for example, famously opens with three witches chanting. The narrator in Roald Dahl's controversial *The Witches* (1983), produced as a film in 1990 (Nicolas Roeg) featuring Angelica Huston as the Grand High Witch—a beautiful and yet grotesque witch—asserts that all women are witches, though some of them may be lovely.

The Threatening Maternal

The fourth archetype, and perhaps the most problematic, fuses each of the preceding three categories in the figures of the mother and the wife. The mother figure is monstrous precisely because she combines many of these archetypes all at once: she transforms from virgin to sexually empowered woman/wife to pregnant to mother. Rosi Braidotti has written that the mother's body "is therefore capable of defeating the notion of fixed *bodily form*, of visible, recognizable, clear, and distinct shapes as that which marks the contour of the body. She is morphologically dubious" (64). The mother's body literally transforms during pregnancy and thus she has an immense power over life and death. The Oedipal conventions at play, of course, are noticeable as well, and it may be that it is this confusion between the mother and the wife that lends itself so well to monstrosity. Because of deep-seated anxieties about the capabilities of mothers to turn against their offspring, the monstrous mother is frequently displaced by the stepmother in many fairytales, as seen in various iterations of *Cinderella* and *Snow White*.

In any event, the figure of the mother is arguably the female monster par excellence. Echidna in Greek mythology gives birth to six monsters. Medea commits filicide because of Jason's betrayal; throughout the New World, **La Llorona** kills her children out of jealousy and rage. One of the most fascinating manifestations of the mother as monstrous is the figure of La Malinche, one of the most complex figures in the history of the New World. La Malinche is the "mother" of the first "mestizo" (mixed raced child) and becomes quite literally, in the words of Octavio Paz, "the mother of the nation" (75). In Ira Levin's 1972 novel *The Stepford Wives*, as well as its cinematic adaptations, the frighteningly submissive wives turn out to be **robots**, suggesting that from the patriarchal perspective, the "perfect woman" is really a machine.

Reclaiming Monstrous Women

Despite—or, indeed, because of—each of these well-developed archetypes of female monstrosity, in recent years there has been an active attempt to recast or rehabilitate these forms in ways that empower women. The witch/crone, for instance, in the made-for-television *Snow White: The Fairest of them All* (Caroline Thompson, 2001) is presented as a victim of the societal valuation that renders beauty as limited to youth. These recent reappropriations of the witch figure have shed light on different aspects of these monstrous women: the witch is able to become beautiful, younger, and sexual. The television series *The Secret Circle* (2011), the character of Bonnie (Kat Graham) in *The Vampire Diaries* (2009–present), *Charmed* (1998–2006), and the character of Willow (Alyson Hannigan) in *Buffy the Vampire Slayer* (1997–2003) each revise to varying extents conventional representations of witches—as do Samantha (Elizabeth Montgomery) in *Bewitched* (1964–72), and Sabrina (Melissa Joan Hart) in *Sabrina, the Teenage Witch* (1996–2003), who use their supernatural powers to comedic and family-friendly ends. The reclamation of "monstrous women" enables the rewriting of monstrous archetypes so as to render them more human, less monstrous. The paradox of monstrosity is, of course, that it is always a matter of perception: one person's monster is another person's idol.

Cristina Santos and Jonathan A. Allan

References and Suggested Reading

Almond, Barbara. *The Monster Within: The Hidden Side of Motherhood.* Berkeley: University of California Press, 2010.

Auerbach, Nina. *Woman and the Demon: The Life of a Victorian Myth*. Cambridge: Harvard University Press, 1982.

Braidotti, Rosi. "Mothers, Monsters, and Machines." In *Writing on the Body: Female Embodiment and Feminist Theory*, edited by Kate Conboy, Nadia Medina, and Sarah Stanbury, 59–79. New York: Columbia University Press, 1997.

Creed, Barbara. *The Monstrous-Feminine: Film, Feminism, Psychoanalysis*. London: Routledge, 1993.

Dinnerstein, Dorothy. *The Mermaid and the Minotaur*. New York: Harper & Row, 1976.

Paz, Octavio. *The Labyrinth of Solitude and Other Writings*. Translated by Lysander Kemp, Yaro Millos, and Rachel Phillips Belash. New York: Grove Press, 1985.

Walker, Barbara G. *The Crone: Woman of Age, Wisdom, and Power*. New York: HarperCollins Publishers, 1988.

Warner, Marina. *Monsters of Our Own Making: The Peculiar Pleasures of Fear*. Lexington: University of Kentucky Press, 1998.

WRAITH

The wraith is a supernatural creature of Scottish origin that appears in literature and cinema in three different forms. It is first and foremost the **ghost** of a person. Secondarily, it is the immaterial or spectral projection of a living person—a "fetch" or spiritual being that is connected to an individual's soul. This second denotation frequently portends death and appears as a warning to that individual or those close to him or her. The third and least common understanding of the wraith is as an anonymous spectral figure that haunts water or the sea and often speaks or calls to those who are fated to die. The etymology of "wraith" is obscure, but Tom Shippey traces the word back through its Scottish origin and connects it to the Old English verb "wriðan" (to writhe) (149), an etymological connection that links wraith with "wreath" (something twisted or bent) and "wrath" (a twisted emotion and expression of anger).

Scottish folklorist James Napier (1810–84) explains the origin of the wraith in the ancient Persian and Jewish belief that each person has an invisible spirit or guardian **angel**, which can separate itself and appear in that person's form. He cites the Acts of the Apostles 12:15 in which Peter journeys to visit the disciples, but they believe him to be imprisoned and maintain that his "angelus" (angel) or wraith has come to see them. Napier describes the Scottish folk belief that if a wraith is seen in the morning, the person whose wraith is seen will recover from illness, but a wraith seen in the afternoon or evening "betokened evil or approaching death, and the time within which death would occur was considered to be within a year" (58–9). Scottish minister Robert Kirk, in *The Secret Commonwealth of Elves, Fauns, and Fairies* (1691), further explains that the wraith is a spirit formed by the exhaled breath of someone on the verge of death, although some believe that it is a more corporeal spirit.

The literary wraith first appeared in 1513 in Middle Scots poet Gavin Douglas's *Eneados*, a translation of Virgil's Latin *Aeneid* (c. 20 BCE). Douglas uses both primary senses of wraith in his epic poem—it refers to the spirit or ghost of those slain in battle, but it also describes a phantom creature in the likeness of Aeneas. The goddess Juno fashions this specter out of the air, and it is without real substance but it can still speak and fight like Aeneas. Douglas compares this shadowy figure to the wraiths of the dead who walk from place to place and the illusions of dreams (330). The wraith is also used by the court poets Alexander Montgomerie and Sir Patrick Hume of Polwarth in the poem "The Flyting Betwixt Montgomerie and Polwart" (c. 1583), in which Polwarth insults his rival for writing about **witches**, warlocks, wraiths, and other supernatural creatures. In Lady Anne Lindsay's poem "Auld Robin Gray" (1771), the speaker of the poem loses her lover at sea and is forced to marry Auld Robin because of family destitution, and when her lover miraculously returns, she hopes that he is merely a wraith because she must now remain true to her new husband. The ghostly wraith also appears in a fragment poem from Robert Burns's *Poems, Chiefly in the Scottish Dialect* (1787) and in Sir Walter Scott's narrative poem "Marmion: A Tale of Flodden Field" (1808).

Wraiths as death messengers and water spirits also have their origins in Scottish literature and folk belief. King James VI, in *Daemonologie* (1597), created a dialogue on witchcraft, demonic possession (see **Demon**), and supernatural creatures, and he states that wraiths prophesying death are a creation of the **Devil** and that only the ignorant believe that the dead can return and appear to the living. The poet Robert Fergusson, in his poem "An Eclogue, To the Memory of Dr Wilkie" (1773), includes a character named Geordie who sees a wraith in a dream and awakes to a cold night certain that this specter foretells of approaching woe. The representation of the wraith as death messenger continued into the nineteenth century, including in the Scotsman George Allan's poem "Is Your War-pipe Asleep?" (1802); the English novel *Shirley* (1849) by Charlotte Brontë; and Alfred Lord Tennyson's poetic elegy

"In Memoriam" (1850). The water wraith is first mentioned in Scottish bishop Robert Forbes's "A Journal from London to Portsmouth" (1755) and his poem "Ajax his Speech to the Grecian Knabbs" (1755), but is usually connected with the Scottish countryside. For example, English novelist M.G. Lewis's poem "Bothwell's Bonny Jane" (1801) describes Bothwell Castle and the mournful cries of the wraiths that can be heard from the River Clyde far below.

The wraith experienced a renaissance in the mid twentieth century in the writing of the Inklings, professors at Oxford University in England who met every week to discuss literature, theology, and their own in-progress fantasy writing. This literary circle, including J.R.R. Tolkien (1892–1973; see **Tolkien, Monsters In**), C.S. Lewis (1898–1963), and Charles Williams (1886–1945), discussed, among other topics, the linguistic history and literary character of the wraith. One of the main characters in Williams's novel *All Hallows Eve* (1944) dies at the beginning of the novel and must then walk the streets of London as a wraith. In Lewis's novel *That Hideous Strength* (1945), the deputy director of an evil scientific organization lives his day-to-day life using only a quarter of his mind, so that although his body is present, his spirit or wraith is detached and free to pursue its own endeavors. Tolkien's *The Lord of the Rings* trilogy (first published 1954–55) includes haunting characters called Ringwraiths that retain a linguistic and etymological connection to the early Scottish wraiths. These creatures were once humans with a lust for power and everlasting life, but the forces of evil twisted and corrupted them into undead wraiths, and as shadowy riders in black they instill fear, despair, and madness with their fierce cries. During the climactic battle in Tolkien's epic, the Lord of the Ringwraiths is described as "a great black shape against the fires beyond [and] a vast menace of despair" (811), and as "a shape, black-mantled, huge and threatening ... A crown of steel he bore, but between rim and robe naught was there to see, save only a deadly gleam of eyes" (822). The Ringwraiths are defined by their shape but have no actual substance; as Tom Shippey notes, "under their hoods and cloaks there is nothing, or at least nothing visible, but just the same they can wield weapons, ride horses, be pierced by blades or swept away by flood" (148). The Ringwraiths exist between life and death and embody the duality of the wraith as both living spirits and ghostly apparitions.

The resonance of Tolkien's writing has at least partially inspired later twentieth-century cinema and fiction. The Ringwraiths are fantastically visualized in director Peter Jackson's film trilogy *The Fellowship of the Ring* (2001), *The Two Towers* (2002), and *The Return of the King* (2003). Wraiths also appear in the adventure film *The Wraith* (Mike Marvin, 1986), in which a young man returns from death as a vengeful spirit in a futuristic black sports car, and in the Japanese horror film *Shadow of the Wraith* (Toshiharu Ikeda, 2001). Wraiths also appear in recent literature, including the snake-like shapeshifting wraiths of T.A. Barron's "The Lost Years of Merlin" series (1996–2000), and the monstrous but intelligent mortiwraiths of Wayne Thomas Batson's "The Door Within" trilogy (2005–2006). Janny Wurts's "War of Light and Shadow" series (1993–2011) includes the Mistwraith, a swarming mass of individual specters that block the sun and cast the world of Athera into a perpetual gloom. And Stephen R. Donaldson alters the traditional shadowy wraith character in his "The Chronicles of Thomas Covenant" series (2004–10); in these works, his Wraiths of Andelain are flame-like creatures of light that represent beauty and song, and they perform the Dance of the

Wraiths at the Spring celebration. Wraiths and wraith-like beings can also be found in the pages of comic books, such as the vigilante crime fighter with the power of mind control Wraith, and the sinister alien species the Dire Wraiths, who hearken back to early Scottish folk belief because they can change their appearance to mimic other living beings.

Justin T. Noetzel

References and Suggested Reading

Douglas, Gavin. *The Poetical Works of Gavin Douglas, Bishop of Dunkeld*, vol. III, edited by John Small. Edinburgh: William Paterson, 1874.

Montgomerie, Alexander. *The Poems of Alexander Montgomerie*. Edited by James Cranstoun. Edinburgh: Scottish Text Society, 1887.

Napier, James. *Folk Lore: Superstitious Beliefs in the West of Scotland within this Century*. Paisley: Alexander Gardner, 1879.

Shippey, Tom. *The Road to Middle-Earth: How J.R.R. Tolkien Created a New Mythology*. New York: Houghton Mifflin, 2003.

Tolkien, J.R.R. *The Lord of the Rings* [1954–55]. Reprint, New York: Houghton Mifflin, 1994.

WUCHANG—*see* Demon

WUTONG—*see* Demon

YAHOO—*see* Swift, Jonathan, Monsters In (*Gulliver*)

YAKSA—*see* Demon

YAM—*see* Bible, Monsters In The

YAMA—*see* Demon

YAMANBA—*see* Demon

YAMATA NO OROCHI—*see* Demon

YAMAUBA—*see* Demon

YASHA—*see* Demon

YETI—*see* Bigfoot; Cryptid

YOMOTSU-SHIKOME—*see* Demon

YOWIE

Fig. 40 ***Yowie* by Robyn O'Neil**

The yowie, like the **bunyip**, originates in the mythology of Aboriginal Australians and was incorporated into colonial folklore. The yowie may also be referred to as the indigenous ape, the Hairy Man, or yahoo, and is distinguished from other native monsters by its humanoid form. It inhabits wooded or bush locales. Yowies are typically described as giant men (see **Giant**; **Bigfoot**), excessively hairy, with large feet, a talent for climbing, and a taste for eating humans—especially women. They have also been described as possessing backwards feet and red faces, although these traits are not uniform.

Tracing the history of yowie appearances by name alone is quite challenging, due to the diversity of Aboriginal linguistic and cultural groups and the difficulties colonizers experienced in communicating with the populations they encountered. White colonizers adopted the terms yowie and bunyip, but during the nineteenth century often used the terms interchangeably for any bush monster (Holden 47–8).

Prior to the twentieth century, most references to yowies or yahoos are in newspaper or magazines articles, rather than in fiction. These references include sightings, such as reported in the *Australian Town and Country Journal* on 4 November 1876 and 18 November 1876, and the *Australian and New Zealand Monthly Magazine*, which ran an article "Superstitions of the Australian Aborigines: The Yahoo" in February 1842.

Judging from the relatively few examples in Australian fiction and film, the yowie did not achieve the same dissemination within colonial folklore that its compatriot the bunyip did. There are, however, some stand-out examples. May Gibbs's villainous Banksia Men in *Snugglepot and Cuddlepie* (1918) are good examples of the abduction narrative common to folk stories about yowies. Inclusion in poetry has not been significant, but the yowie appears in such poems as Norman Smith's "Yowie" (1983) and Lynnette McKenzie's "The Yowie" (1982). The beast has featured in children's picture books by Ann Ferns including *The Yowie Finds a Home* (1981), *The Yowie Is Very Brave* (1981), and *The Adventures of the Yowie* (1983). Geoff Barlow's 1995 mystery novel *The Yarra Yowie* also made use of the creature.

In 1997, Cadbury launched a range of Yowie chocolates, which were accompanied by an advertising campaign showing each colored yowie in a different Australian ecosystem and encouraging children to take care of their native flora and fauna. The original concept for these yowies came from Geoff Pike, who authored a series of children's picture books on the same themes, also published in 1997. *The Midnight Monster* by Edel Wignell, published in 1998, features a young girl being stalked by a "wow-ee" (a variant spelling of yowie) during the night. *Nor of Human: An Anthology of Fantastic Creatures* (2001), edited by Geoffrey Maloney, features two yowie stories. In 2010, a short film titled *The Yowie*, directed by Jens Hertzum, explored the difficulties of small town life, as a father (Alan Dearth) and son (Samuel Faull) manufacture yowie sightings in their local area in a bid to increase tourism.

The yowie, although less popular in Australian fiction and film than other mythic creatures, remains an important element within Australia's folklore and indigenous oral histories.

A.C. Blackmore

References and Suggested Reading

Australian Town and Country Journal. 4 November 1876, 729.

Australian Town and Country Journal. 18 November 1876, 811.

Barrett, Charles. *The Bunyip and Other Mythical Monsters and Legends*. Melbourne: Reed & Harris, 1946.

Holden, Robert. *Bunyips: Australia's Folklore of Fear*. Canberra: National Library of Australia, 2001.

Kennedy, Eva, Michael Friday, and Tom Derbyshire, eds. *Tulpi: A Collection of*

Literature by Aboriginal/Islander Children in the Townsville Catholic Diocese. Townsville: Catholic Education Office, 1982.

"Superstitions of the Australian Aborigines: The Yahoo." *Australian and New Zealand Monthly Magazine* 1, no. 2 (February 1842): 92.

Wignell, Edel. *A Boggle of Bunyips*. Sydney: Hodder & Stoughton, 1989.

YSBADDADEN—*see* Giant

YUKI-ONNA—*see* Demon

ZAMZUMMIN—*see* Giant

ZIZ

In rabbinic typology, four exemplary creatures serve as archetypes and rulers in the natural world—the lion over the wild beasts, the ox over the domestic beasts, the eagle over the beasts of the air, and the human being, who is *sui generis*. However, there are also three entirely mythical beasts that are imagined as being of extraordinary size and strength: the **Leviathan**, the great **sea monster**; the **Behemoth**, the largest and most powerful of wild beasts, sometimes called the *Shor HaBar* (the wild ox); and the Ziz, which is a bird of epic proportions. It seems that the four archetypical but real creatures were chosen because of their abstract qualities—leonine gravitas, aquiline transcendence, bovine perseverance, and human intellection—whereas the mythical beasts were chosen to represent the abstract qualities of the strata of the universe that they represented: the unfathomable depths of the sea, the ruggedness and impenetrability of the terrain of Earth, and the endless breadth and seemingly endless span of the sky. In this sense, the Leviathan, the Behemoth, and the Ziz are more primal, more demi-god-like, more threatening to the sovereignty of the One God who created the universe, and more in need of suppression and vanquishing at the moment of the eschaton than the beasts of the natural world.

The Ziz is a kosher bird of incredible proportions, with the ability to spread itself over an astonishingly wide area and some creative power of its own (according to one legend, it created worlds and would have continued to do so had Adam not eaten it!). Its name may be related to the root "zz—to move," reflecting its mobility. Its body spans the heavens (when it flies, it occludes the sun's disk) and like Azrael, the **angel** of death in Islamic lore, it connects Earth with Heaven. Like the (much smaller) *rukh* (see **Birds, Giant**) of the tales of the *Thousand and One Nights* (see **Arabian Nights, Monsters In The**), the Ziz is glimpsed by a famed traveler, Rabbah Bar Hanna, whose tall tales, like Sindbad's, beggar the imagination. Once, on board a ship, Rabbah and his companions saw a bird that seemed to stand ankle-deep in apparently shallow water. This caused them to misjudge the depth of the water until a heavenly voice warned them that a carpenter's axe dropped into the water seven years previously had not yet reached the bottom. The bird—whose feet in fact rested on the very bottom of the ocean—was the Ziz (*Babylonian Talmud Bava Batra* 73b). In some accounts, the head of the Ziz reaches the Divine Throne in Heaven. The entire Talmudic tale is interpreted allegorically in the nineteenth century by the Hassidic master Rabbi Nachman of Bratslav, who includes the account in *Likutei Moharon*, his collected teachings (1865).

The Ziz is conflated with other monstrous birds mentioned in rabbinic sources, its name used interchangeably with theirs. One of its guises is that of the Bar Yokhni—the "son of the nest," so-called because its fledglings do not need to be hatched by the mother bird; rather, they seem to emerge directly from the nest. A Ziz/Bar Yokhni is alleged to have once cast an egg away from the nest because it was rotten. The egg cracked and its contents were so voluminous that they swamped 16 cities and uprooted 300 cedar trees (*Babylonian Talmud Bekhorot* 59b). Another name/aspect of the Ziz is "Renanin," the celestial singer that draws the Chariot of the Sun. Finally, it is also called "Sekvi," the one who sees, due to the proximity of its head to the divine realm.

Along with the Behemoth and the Leviathan, the Ziz will be served at the Feast of the Righteous when the Messiah appears, in order to compensate the pious for refraining from the consumption of non-kosher birds prohibited by the Torah. Like the manna in the wilderness, which tasted of whatever the eater wished it to taste of, the flesh of the Ziz contains all possible tastes, "like this (*zeh*) and that (*zeh*)." ("Ziz" is an acronym for "*zeh*" and "*zeh*." *VaYikrah Rabbah, Ahare Mot* 22:10).

The Ziz, along with its fellow mythical creatures the Leviathan and the Behemoth (or *Shor HaBar*), are popular subjects in medieval Jewish manuscript illumination. In the North French Miscellany, made in Northern France, c. 1278–98, it appears as an ostrich-like bird (London, British Library Add. MS 11639, folio 517v). The Ambrosian Bible, from early thirteenth-century southern Germany, depicts it as a **griffin** (Milan, Biblioteca Ambrosiana, MS B. 32, folio 136r). The Ziz is a minor figure in works of Jewish folklore, where it serves as a messenger from God. It has more recently appeared as a lead character in a series of Jewish children's books by Jacqueline Jules and Katherine Janus Kahn (*Noah and the Ziz*, 2005; *The Ziz and the Hanukkah Miracle*, 2006; *The Princess and the Ziz*, 2008).

Marc Michael Epstein

References and Suggested Reading

Drewer, Lois. "Leviathan, Behemoth and Ziz: A Christian Adaptation." *Journal of the Warburg and Courtauld Institutes* 44 (1981): 148–56.

Guttman, Alexander. "Leviathan, Behemoth and Ziz: Jewish Messianic Symbols in Art." *Hebrew Union College Annual* 39 (1968): 219–30.

Schwartz, Howard. *Tree of Souls: The Mythology of Judaism*. New York: Oxford University Press, 2004.

ZOMBIE

The zombie is a figure that transcends any one medium, pervading literature, film, popular culture, and philosophy. The *Oxford English Dictionary* first recorded the term "zombie" in 1819, tracing its etymology to the Creole word "*zonbi*," a person who is believed to have died and been reanimated devoid of free will. The zombie emerged from Afro-Caribbean voodoo culture and entered American and then European popular culture in the late 1920s, at the height of the United States' geopolitical interest in Haiti. It has since made its way into comic books, video games, television series, and a myriad of literary and philosophical texts.

Zombies first migrated to American culture from Haitian folklore. In 1887, amateur anthropologist Lafcadio Hearn traveled to the island of Martinique to study the local customs and folklore. While there, Hearn encountered the legend of the *corps cadavers*, or "walking dead." The zombie then made its initial appearance in the English-speaking world in 1890 in Hearn's account of his travels, *Two Years in the French West Indies*.

The United States occupied Haiti in 1915, and so developed an interest in Haiti's voodoo legends and their accompanying allegations of cannibalism that assisted in justifying the occupation on ethical grounds. As the monster whose existence could be cited as proof of Haitian savagery, the zombie made its way into American popular culture. In 1928, William Buehler Seabrook (1884–1945), an explorer and journalist from Westminster, Maryland, arrived in Haiti to research superstitions in voodoo culture. He wrote about the zombie as a powerful symbol of fear and an integral part of Haitian religious beliefs. In 1929, he published *The Magic Island*, a travelogue detailing his explorations in Haiti. An entire chapter of the text explores the image of the zombie and the voodoo tradition in Haiti. The book's popularity spawned a stage play, *Zombie*. Seabrook's travelogue was moreover very influential in the making of the first American zombie film, *White Zombie* (Victor Halperin, 1932).

Universal Pictures had produced both *Dracula* (Tod Browning, 1931, starring Bela Lugosi) and *Frankenstein* (James Whale, 1931, starring Boris Karloff) by the time Seabrook's book widely entered American distribution. And in 1932, brothers Victor and Edward Halperin produced and directed *White Zombie*, an independently made horror movie that first introduced voodoo zombies to American cinema-goers. *White Zombie* was made in the pre-code era of Hollywood: a roughly five-year period, beginning with the widespread adoption of sound in 1929 and ending in 1934 with the adoption of a policy of rigid censorship enacted by the Production Code Administration. Set in Haiti, *White Zombie* depicts zombies as reanimated slaves forced to work in a sugar mill by a voodoo sorcerer. Written by Garnett Weston, the script features a young couple, Neil Parker (John Harron) and Madeline Short (Madge Bellamy), who have been invited by a casual acquaintance, Charles Beaumont (Robert Frazer), to be married on his Haitian plantation. Beaumont, who is secretly in love with Madeline, approaches the local voodoo master "Murder" Legendre (Bela Lugosi) to temporarily turn Madeline into a zombie and revive her in order to woo her anew. *White Zombie* inspired a B-movie explosion throughout the 1930s, 1940s, 1950s, and 1960s, including RKO Pictures' *I Walked with a Zombie* (Val Lewton, 1943), and Hammer Horror Film's *Plague of the Zombies* (John Gilling, 1966).

The evolution of the modern, post-voodoo zombie began with Richard Matheson's 1954 novel *I Am Legend*, which spawned several film versions including *The Last Man on Earth* (Ubaldo Ragona and Sidney Salkow, 1964), *The Omega Man* (Boris Sagal, 1971), and *I Am Legend* (Francis Lawrence, 2007). Although Matheson's creatures are **vampires**, they are reduced by a vicious plague to a violent population, and are widely considered to have influenced the zombie genre. The zombie only fully emerged in film form in 1968 with George A. Romero's *Night of the Living Dead*. Romero adapted the voodoo zombie and turned zombie-ism into a cannibalistic plague. The Afro-Caribbean otherness of the voodoo zombie was transformed into a domestic political allegory. In an eerie post-apocalyptic set-up, Romero created what is still considered a subversive critique of Vietnam-era United States, although throughout his film Romero demanded that his creatures be referred to as "**ghouls**," insisting that the word "zombie" carried with it voodoo connotations. Romero then went on to make *Dawn of the Dead* (1978), *Day of the Dead* (1985), *Land of the Dead* (2005), *Diary of the Dead* (2007), and *Survival of the Dead* (2009), each of which sets its protagonists in slightly different locations (a shopping mall, an army base, an island), and expands on the repercussions of the zombie plague.

Romero's films, moreover, inspired a wave of zombie movies in Italy in the 1970s and 1980s. In 1979, Italian director Lucio Fulci released *Zombi 2* as an unofficial sequel to Romero's *Dawn of the Dead*, which was distributed throughout Europe under the title *Zombi*. By the 1980s, the Italian film industry had developed a reputation for shamelessly and cheaply remaking other countries' films. Italian zombie movies followed a simplistic formula: a man-made disaster in a Third World locale causes a violent and bloody zombie revolution and the threat of a global apocalypse. Fulci's *Zombi 2* triggered a tremendous outpouring of Italian zombie movies in this period, including two 1980 films: Umberto Lenzi's *Nightmare City* (*Incubo sulla cittá contaminata*), and Andrea Binach's *Zombie Creeping Flesh* (*Virus, Apocalipsis cannibal*).

In 1985, cinematic zombies were transformed from tottering, moaning ghouls to speaking creatures with an insatiable craving for brains. Dan O'Bannon's *The Return of the Living Dead* (1985) was an early zombie comedy ("zom com"), which follows a group of teenage punks fleeing a horde of brain-hungry zombies. *The Return of the Living Dead* was followed by several sequels. An important year in the zombie film calendar, 1985 also marked the opening of Stuart Gordon's *Re-Animator*, a science fiction horror comedy based on the H.P. Lovecraft story "Herbert West – Reanimator" (1922; see **Lovecraft, Monsters In**).

In the early 2000s, zombies experienced a cinematic resurgence brought on by Paul W.S. Anderson's 2002 film version of *Resident Evil*. Originally a survival horror video game also known as *Biohazard*, *Resident Evil* was first released in 1996 by Capcom for the Playstation (see **Video Games, Monsters In**). Borrowing elements from the video game, Anderson created a film that follows amnesiac heroine Alice and a group of commandos attempting to contain the outbreak of the "T-Virus" at a secret underground facility. Clearly influenced by Romero's take on zombies as "infectious," *Resident Evil*, which has since been followed by three sequels (*Resident Evil: Apocalypse* [Alexander Witt, 2004], *Resident Evil: Extinction* [Russell Mulcahy, 2007], and *Resident Evil: Afterlife* [Paul W.S. Anderson, 2010]), literalizes the trope of infection and transmission (see **Virus**). This concretization of Romero's figurative conceit continued with Danny Boyle's 2002 British zombie film *28 Days Later*, in which the breakdown of society is precipitated by the accidental release of the "rage" virus, and the zombie is updated as fast-moving and more physically threatening than merely uncanny. Boyle refers to his creatures as "the infected," and insists they are the products of a virus and not part of the illustrious zombie lineage. Zack Snyder's 2004 remake of Romero's *Dawn of the Dead* then solidified the place of the fast-moving zombie in horror cinema.

The 2000s also saw a resurgence of zombie comic books, including *The Walking Dead*, a monthly black-and-white American comic book series published by Image Comics beginning in 2003. Created by Robert Kirkman and Tony Moore, *The Walking Dead* follows a group of people attempting to survive in a post-apocalyptic zombie universe. In 2010, director Frank Darabont adapted the comic book for television, and AMC Network began to air episodes of *The Walking Dead*. The pilot garnered 5.3 million viewers, and the show became the most watched basic cable series in its demographic.

Although zombies are most commonly known for their cinematic appearances, they also have a notable literary and philosophical history. Within the field of the philosophy of the mind, zombies are far from the rotting corpses present in popular culture. Rather, the philosophical zombie is physically indistinguishable from a living person, but lacks consciousness. Philosopher David Chalmers argues that the ability to conceive of a philosophical zombie confirms that consciousness is not a mere brain substrate, while critics like Daniel Dennett denounce Chalmers's concept and insist on a biological perspective.

In addition to their centrality in philosophical treatises, zombies have a prodigious fictional history, including works by Richard Matheson and Stephen King. In 2007, Max Brooks, son of director Mel Brooks, published *World War Z: An Oral History of the Zombie War*, a faux oral history told by several survivors of an imagined zombie apocalypse. Brooks prefaced *World War Z* with *The Zombie Survival Guide* (2003), which makes an attempt to think through the many contingencies attendant in an actual zombie plague. In 2009, Seth Grahame-Smith expanded the zombie fiction genre by writing *Pride and Prejudice and Zombies*, a novel that incorporates the entirety of Jane Austen's *Pride and Prejudice* with elements of modern zombie fiction. Grahame-Smith's zombie mash-up laid the groundwork for a series of such fictional combinations, including his follow-up work, *Abraham Lincoln, Vampire Hunter* (2010), which was made into a film, released in 2012, directed by Timur Bekmambetov.

The figure of the zombie has become a popular literary, filmic, cultural, and even philosophic device. Whether in its original voodoo context, Romero's cannibalistic context, or its contemporary combination with classic fiction, the zombie perpetually straddles the border between the living and the dead. As an interstitial figure, the zombie functions both literally and allegorically, calling into question the boundary of the human, of the living, and of the conscious.

Sara Simcha Cohen

References and Suggested Reading

Brooks, Max. *World War Z*. New York: Three Rivers Press, 2007.

——. *The Zombie Survival Guide*. New York: Three Rivers Press, 2003.

Chalmers, David. *The Conscious Mind: In Search of a Fundamental Theory*. New York and Oxford: Oxford University Press, 1996.

Dennett, Daniel. "The Unimagined Preposterousness of Zombies." *Journal of Consciousness Studies* 2, no. 4 (1995): 322–6.

Gagne, Paul R. *The Zombies that Ate Pittsburgh: The Films of George A. Romero*. New York: Dodd, Mead & Company, 1987.

Grahame-Smith, Seth, and Jane Austen. *Pride and Prejudice and Zombies*. Philadelphia: Quirk Books, 2009.

Hearn, Lafcadio. *Two Years in the French West Indies*. Oxford: Signal Books, 1890.

Matheson, Richard. *I Am Legend*. New York: Tom Doherty Associates, 1995.

Russell, Jamie. *Book of the Dead: The Complete History of Zombie Cinema*. Surrey: FAB Press, 2005.

Seabrook, W.B. *The Magic Island*. New York: Harcourt, Brace and Company, 1929.